MORNING OF THE RISING SUN

The Heroic Story of the Battles for Guadalcanal

By Kenneth I. Friedman, Ph.D

ISBN: 1-4196-8096-X

ISBN-13: 978-1419680960

Library of Congress Control Number: TXu1-365-095

Visit *www.booksurge.com* or *www.battlesforguadalcanal.com* to order additional copies.

Dedication

To my dear departed wife and life partner,
Lydia Barbara Joyce Friedman

(October 3, 1945 - December 9, 2006)

Table of Contents

List of Figures ... 8

List of Tables ... 9

Glossary ... 10

Preface ... 18

Prelude A Murder of Nature ... 20

Part 1: Getting Ready

Chapter 1 A Depressing Sight ... 26

Chapter 2 The Best Laid Plans ... 30

Chapter 3 The Japanese Conquests Continue ... 34

Chapter 4 A New South Pacific Commander ... 39

Chapter 5 A Tiger in the Fold ... 45

Part 2: Invasion

Chapter 6 Fijian Rendezvous ... 55

Chapter 7 Controversy and Rehearsal ... 63

Chapter 8 The Trek ... 74

Chapter 9 Progress and Setbacks ... 76

Chapter 10 At Last, Going on the Offensive ... 85

Chapter 11 Attack! ... 92

Chapter 12 The Japanese Strike by Air! ... 97

Chapter 13 Encore! ... 110

Chapter 14 Taking the Prize! ... 116

Part 3: Savo Island: A Disaster Waiting to Happen

Chapter 15 Anatomy of an Allied Tragedy 119

Chapter 16 A Stinging, Savage Defeat 132

Chapter 17 All Alone 148

Part 4: Battle of the Eastern Solomons

Chapter 18 Look to the East 158

Chapter 19 Let the Shooting Begin 169

Chapter 20 Japanese Retaliation 179

Chapter 21 Counterattack! 193

Chapter 22 Trouble Ahead 199

Part 5: Holding the Line

Chapter 23 Defending Henderson Field 205

Chapter 24 A Stand for the Ages 211

Chapter 25 Assessment 230

Part 6: The Battle of Cape Esperance

Chapter 26 The Tokyo Express Begins Again 242

Chapter 27 Crossing the "T" 257

Chapter 28 Japanese Heavy Guns Arrive 270

Part 7: The Americans Take a Checkpoint

Chapter 29 A Much Needed Change of Command 288

Chapter 30 Recapturing Henderson Field? 297

Part 8: The Battle of the Santa Cruz Islands

Chapter 31 Prepare for Another Carrier Battle ... 319

Chapter 32 The Japanese Feel the Heat ... 328

Chapter 33 The Embattled Hornet ... 348

Chapter 34 Attacking the "Big E" ... 361

Chapter 35 Winners & Losers at Santa Cruz ... 376

Part 9: The Naval Battle of Guadalcanal - Day 1

Chapter 36 Reaching a Turning Point ... 392

Chapter 37 Moving into Position ... 403

Chapter 38 Barroom Brawl with the Lights Out ... 415

Chapter 39 Taking on All Comers ... 434

Chapter 40 Picking up the Pieces ... 443

Chapter 41 Some Fateful Decisions to Make ... 447

Chapter 42 Bringing Back the Cripples ... 453

Chapter 43 Surveying the Carnage ... 458

Chapter 44 Command Decisions ... 464

Chapter 45 Sink the Hiei ... 467

Part 10: The Naval Battle of Guadalcanal - Day 2

Chapter 46 Chess Movements and Air Attacks ... 476

Chapter 47 Moving into Combat ... 494

Chapter 48 Clash of Giants ... 499

Chapter 49 A Failure to Deliver ... 512

Part 11: The Battle of Tassafaronga

Chapter 50 Plans and Ship Movements 522

Chapter 51 Night of the Long Lances 533

Chapter 52 So Who Won? 552

Part 12: Nearing the End

Chapter 53 Still a Question of Supplies 567

Chapter 54 Building for Going on the Offensive 576

Chapter 55 Capturing Mount Austen 585

Chapter 56 A Major American Offensive Begins 597

Chapter 57 Sealing the Southern Flank 615

Chapter 58 Moving Northwest 627

Chapter 59 Planning for Operation "KE" 636

Chapter 60 The Japanese Finally Leave 642

Part 13: The End of the Beginning

Chapter 61 Casualties and Losses 661

Chapter 62 Epilogue 668

Bibliography 685

Notes 686

Index 694

Other Books by Kenneth I. Friedman

Afternoon of the Rising Sun: The Battle of Leyte Gulf

List of Figures

Battles for Guadalcanal - Theater of Operations 16

Western Front—World War I 20

War Plan Rainbow Five 33

Japanese Empire - 1942 35

Guadalcanal Invasion Fleet Rendezvous 55

Turner's Task Force Moves into Position to invade 88

Guadalcanal Landing Beaches 93

Tulagi-Gavutu Invasion 95

Japanese Naval Air Bases 97

Mikawa's Course to Savo Island 121

Allied Ships at the Battle of Savo Island 133

Allied Ships Battle the Japanese 135

The Japanese Ships Battle the Allied Ships at Savo Island 136

The Japanese Return to their Bases after Savo Island Victory 145

Seki's Bombers Attack Task Force 16 186

Edson Prepares as the Japanese Approach 214

Edson's Defensive Positions 219

Kawanishi "Emily" Flying Boat 242

Task Force 64.2's Formation 249

Scott's Countermarch Maneuver 254

Admiral Goto's Formation 256

The Battle of Cape Esperance 259

Japanese Attack Plans to Retake Henderson Field 299

Air Group 10's Formation 334

Hornet's First Wave 340

Japanese First Strike 250

Callaghan's B-1 Battle Formation 413

The Two Forces Approach Each Other 416

Callaghan Opens Fire 419

Japanese Ship Movements after Firing Began. 422

Damaged Ships Left off Guadalcanal after the First Day 458

Mikawa's and Tanaka's Voyages to Guadalcanal 477

Kondo's and Lee's Approach 496

Lee Circles Around Savo Island 499

Naval Battle of Guadalcanal—November 14—11:17 p.m.—11:30 p.m. 501

The American Battleships Enter the Fray—November 14-15 506

The Washington versus the Kirishima 509

The Japanese Put Their Transports on the Beach 513

Tanaka's and Wright's Routes to Guadalcanal 529

Getting into Position for Battle 533

The Battle of Tassafaronga 537

Locations of American Airfields on Guadalcanal 581

The American December Offensive Begins 585

American Assault to Capture Hill 27 - December 31 - January 2 591

American Ground Forces on Guadalcanal - January 1943 598

The American 25th Division's Attack Plans 601

Capturing Hills 53 and 57—January 12-13 610

Attacking the Sea Horse 616

American and Japanese Positions around the Gifu 620

Breaking down the Gifu 624

Shattering the Gifu's Defenses 625

The American XIV Corps' Begin Their Attack 629

Capturing Kokumbona and Moving to the Poha River 634

Chasing the Japanese off Guadalcanal 645

P-38 675

List of Tables

Distances to Guadalcanal 16

Battles for Guadalcanal—Timeline 17

Turner's Invasion Fleet, August 7, 1942 56

Warships at the WATCHTOWER Rendezvous 64

The Japanese Long Lance vs. the American Mark 15 83

First Marine Units to Land on at Guadalcanal 116

Japanese Naval Forces—Battle of the Eastern Solomons 159

Task Force 61—Battle of the Eastern Solomons 161

Japanese Strike Group Losses 196

Task Force 64.2 245

American Casualties (Recapture of Henderson Field and Fighter One) 315

Ships at the Battle of the Santa Cruz Islands 319

Carrier-Based Planes at the Battle of the Santa Cruz Islands 319

Land-Based Planes at the Battle of the Santa Cruz Islands 319

Aircraft Losses—the Battle of the Santa Cruz Islands—October 26, 1942 387

Air Crew losses—The Battle of the Santa Cruz Islands—October 26, 1942 387

Japanese Naval Forces at Truk - November 1942 395

Imperial Japanese Navy's Mid-November Plan 396

American Warships - Naval Battle of Guadalcana 401

Result of the First Six Attacks on the Hiei

Vadm. Mikawa's Eighth Fleet 471

Composition of Forces—Admirals Kondo and Lee—November 14-15 476

Relative American and Japanese Firepower 497

American XIV Corps on Guadalcanal—January 7, 1943 580

Reinforcement (First Evacuation) Unit 650

Reinforcement (Second Evacuation) Unit 654

Ship Losses from the Naval Battles of Guadalcanal 661

Naval Aircraft and Air Crew Losses at Guadalcanal's Carrier Battles 662

Japanese Aircraft Losses - August 1 - November 15, 1942 664

Approximate Japanese Aircraft Losses November 16, 1942 - February 9, 1943 664

Allied Aircraft Losses - August 1 - November 15, 1942 665

Allied Aircraft Losses - November 16, 1942 - February 9, 1943 665

American Aircrew Losses by Service 665

American Ground Casualties on Guadalcanal 666

Estimated Number Killed at Guadalcanal 667

Glossary of Terms

1/27	A notation used by armies to denote the battalion number and regiment number. For instance, this notation reflects the 1st Battalion of the 27th Infantry Regiment.
A.A.F.	United States Army Air Force
AA	Antiaircraft (also given the slang expression "ack-ack")
Ace	A combat pilot who had shot down at least five enemy aircraft.
Angels 10	Directions given by flight directors to indicate planes flying at 10,000 feet (or any altitude in multiples of 1,000 feet.)
ANZAC	Australia-New Zealand Area Command
APD	Destroyer Transport
AK	Cargo ship
Arresting Gear	An aircraft carrier's mechanism that decelerates a landing plane's forward speed
ATIS	Allied Translator and Interpreter Section, Gen. MacArthur's command
BAR	Browning Automatic Rifle
Barbette	Large steel cylinder that supports a ship's gun turret
BB	Battleship (such as BB-56, USS *Washington*)
Beam	Ship's side
Black Gang	Part of a ship's crew stationed in the engine room.
Black Shoe Navy	Expression used in the U. S. Navy to designate sailors who served on surface ships and a term of disdain used by naval aviators. (See also Brown Shoe Navy)
Blip	A bright dot displayed on a radar scope.
Bogey	Term used by the Americans to indicate a radar contact of unknown origin.
BOLERO	Allied code name given in 1942 to the operation of building up forces for a subsequent cross-English channel invasion.
Brown Shoe Navy	Expression used in the U. S. Navy to designate naval aviators. (See also Black Shoe Navy)
BUDOCKS	Abbreviation for U. S. Navy's Bureau of Yards and Docks
BUORD	Abbreviation the U. S. Navy's Bureau of Ordnance located at the main Navy Building on Constitution Avenue in Washington, D.C. and responsible for all armaments aboard all American ships and naval aircraft.
BUSHIPS	Bureau of Ships
BUTTON	Code name for the American Air Base at Espiritu Santo
Buster	Fighter director term, to proceed at best sustained speed
CA	Heavy Cruiser (such as CA-26, USS *Northampton*)
CACTUS	Code name for Allied air forces on Guadalcanal
CAG	Carrier Air Group. Also used to designate the commander of a carrier's Air Group.
CAP	Combat Air Patrol
Cardiv	Carrier Division
C. in C.	Commander in Chief
Charthouse	Room on board a ship where maps and navigational charts are stored
Check fire	A command used by gun crews to stop firing their guns.
Chutai	Japanese word for a group of six to nine aircraft
C.I.C	Combat Information Center – a place onboard a ship in which all information concerning a tactical situation is collected, analyzed, and disseminated to naval commanders to aid them in making decisions. This center was developed in the latter stages of World War II as naval battles became more complex and fast-moving.

CINCLANT	Commander in Chief, United States Atlantic Fleet
CINCPAC	Commander in Chief, United States Pacific Fleet (sometimes abbreviated as CincPac.)
CINCPOA	Commander in Chief, Pacific Ocean Areas
CINCSWPA	Commander in chief, Southwest Pacific Area
CINCUS	Commander in Chief, United States Fleet (sometimes abbreviated as CinCUS)
CL	Light Cruiser (such as CL-47, USS *Boise*)
C.N.O.	Chief of Naval Operations
C.O.	Commanding Officer
COM	as prefix means Commander. **Examples:** **COMAIRSOPAC** – Commander Aircraft South Pacific **COMCRUDIV** – Commander Cruiser Division **COMINCH** – Commander in Chief United States Fleet **COMSOPAC** – Commander South Pacific Force and Area **COMAIRPAC** - Commander Air Forces, South Pacific
Conn	Term used to refer to commanding the steering and speed of a ship
CTF	Commander Task Force
CTG	Commander Task Group
CV	Fleet Carrier (such as CV-6, USS *Enterprise*)
CVL	Light Carrier (such as CVL-22 (USS *Independence*)
CVE	Escort Carrier (such as CVE-55 (USS *Casablanca*)
CXAM	Type of radar developed and installed on U.S. warships in 1940 that was in wide use on American naval vessels during World War II
DD	Destroyer (such as DD-448, USS *La Vallette*)
DMS	Destroyer-Minesweeper (such as DMS-29, USS *Butler* [formerly DD-636])
DESDIV	Destroyer Division
DESRON	Destroyer Squadron
DOVETAIL	Code name for the Allied rehearsal conducted in the Fiji Islands for the Guadalcanal invasion
DSM	Distinguished Service Medal
DUKW	Pronounced "Duck" were amphibious trucks that could be loaded while on a ship and then driven through the water onto the shore
ETO	European Theater of Operations
FAB	Field Artillery Battalion
FDO	Fighter Director Officer (Directs aircraft to ground and air targets)
FC Radar	A generic term use to designate Fire Control radar used to direct the fire of the ship's guns.
FD Radar	Fire Direction Radar – used by warships to detect potential targets and direct a ship's gunfire
Fighter One	Additional fighter landing strip at CACTUS
Fighter Two	Second fighter landing strip at CACTUS
Fish	The term used to refer to torpedoes.
Forecastle	The forward area of a ship from the bow to the bridge.
FRUPac	Fleet Radio Unit - Pacific

G	A generic label the American Army used for staff positions in large units such as at the division or higher levels. These designations had sublevels: **G-1** Personnel **G-2** Intelligence **G-3** Operations **G-4** Supply and evacuation The staff designations below the division level carried the prefix S
General Quarters	Alarm sounded that orders a ship's crew to their battle stations
GMT	Greenwich Mean Time.
H.M.A.S.	His Majesty's Australian Ship
H.M.N.Z.S.	His Majesty's New Zealand Ship
Hara-Kiri	Japanese word for a ritual of committing suicide.
IAP	Inner Air Patrol
ICPOA	Intelligence Center, Pacific Ocean Area
IGHQ	Imperial General Headquarters (Japanese)
IFF	Identification, Friend or Foe (an American radio device or radar identification system)
JANAC	Joint Army-Navy Assessment Committee
JCS	Joint Chiefs of Staff
JICPOA	Joint Intelligence Center, Pacific Ocean Center
JNAF	Japanese Naval Air Force
Kido Butai	Japanese name for the Japanese carrier fleet
LCT	Landing craft tank (such as *LCT-1* through *LCT-500*)
LIFO	Last in, first out
Long ton	Equivalent to 1.12 2000-pound tons or 2,240 pounds
LST	Landing Ship Tank (such as LST 722, USS *Dodge County*)
LSO	Landing Signal Officer - person in charge of landing carrier-based aircraft on the ship's flight deck.
Mae West	The name given to the life jacket worked by US personnel.
MAG	Marine Air Group
MAW	Marine Air Wing. The First MAW commanded the American land based airpower on Guadalcanal. The 2nd MAW relieved them on December 26.
MIA	Missing in Action (a designation used to list combat casualties when the fate of the person in question could not be confirmed. Sometimes a person listed MIA returned; when they did not return, they were presumed and later listed as dead.)
MTB	Motor torpedo boat (such as *PT-109*) – see also PT
Knots	1.15 miles per hour
OOD	Officer of the Deck – Officer placed in temporary command and responsible for a ship's maneuvers when the ship's captain is not on deck.
O.N.I.	Office of Naval Intelligence
Op	Operation
OTC	Officer in Tactical Command – a practice used by navies that gives the most senior officer in command when more than one force joins another.
Pestilence	Code name for the entire American offensive operation in the South Pacific.
PO	Petty Officer
Port	Nautical term for the left side of a ship
POW	Prisoner of war

PPI	Plan Position Indicator, the display commonly associated with radar today, in which a number of circles set at certain ranges with the radar-carrying ship in the center gave the radar observer a clear view of the area around him. The PPI made navigation, position-holding, and threat evaluation much easier.
PT	Motor torpedo boat (see also MTB)
R4D	Navy version of the famous two-engine Douglas C-47 (DC-3) transport aircraft
R.A.A.F.	Royal Australian Air Force
Radar	**RA**dio **D**etection **A**nd **R**anging
RAN	Royal Australian Navy
RANVR	Royal Australian Navy Volunteer Reserve
RBA	Rescue Breathing Apparatus – used by US Navy damage control parties when air that cannot be breathed safely may be present
RCT	Regimental Combat Team
Reciprical Course	A ship's course that is 180° opposite to another ship's course
RN	Royal Navy
RNZAF	Royal New Zealand Air Force
SC Radar	Type of radar installed on American naval vessels to detect approaching aircraft
SCAP	Screen Combat Air Patrol
SCR Radar	Latest radar installed on Guadalcanal in early 1943
SEABEES	American Naval Construction Battalions
SG Radar	Another more advanced type of radar installed on American naval vessels to detect approaching ships
Shoestring	Nickname for Guadalcanal invasion (see Watchtower)
Shotai	The Japanese word for a collection of two to four planes – usually three
SNLF	Special Naval Landing Force (Japanese)
Sonar	(**SO**und **N**avigation **A**nd **R**anging) Echo-ranging sound gear
SOPAC	South Pacific
Starboard	Nautical term for the right side of a ship
Station Hypo	Code breaking operation reporting to CINCPAC at Pearl Harbor
STO	Call letters for Australian coastwatcher Paul Mason
TBS	Talk Between Ships (Voice radio)
TF	Task Force
TG	Task Group
TOT	Time on Target – a term used by artillery
True	A bearing based on the actual compass direction relative to the North Pole rather than a heading based on a magnetic compass direction.
ULTRA	American/British code-breaking activities
USA	United States Army
U.S.A.	United States of America
USAAF	United States Army Air Force
USMC	United States Marine Corps
USMCR	United States Marine Corps Reserve
USN	United States Navy
USSBS	United States Strategic Bombing Survey
VB	American naval bombing plane or squadron
VF	American naval fighter plane or squadron

Very gun	A gun that shoots flares
VMF	U. S. Marine fighter squadron
VMSB	U.S. Marine scout or dive-bombing squadron
VP	Patrol plane or squadron
VS, VSB	Scout plane, Scout plane-bomber or squadron
VT, VTB	Torpedo-bomber or squadron
Watchtower	Code name of the operation for the invasion of Guadalcanal and Tulagi
WDC	Washington Document Center
YP	Yard Patrol Boat (such as Y- 676)

Aircraft designations
(numerals in parentheses indicate number of engines).

United States

B-17 Flying Fortress, Army (4 engines) heavy bomber, land-based

B-26 Marauder, Army (2 engines) medium bomber, land-based

F4F Wildcat, Navy (1 engine) fighter, land- or carrier-based

Hudson Two-engine, single wing patrol bomber

J2F A naval amphibious single-engine biplane (Duck)

OS2U Kingfisher, Navy (1 engine) scout-observation seaplane

P-38 Lightning, Army (2 engines) pursuit (fighter) plane, land-based

P-39, P-40 Army (1 engine) pursuit (fighter) planes, land-based

PBY Catalina, Navy (2 engines) patrol seaplane;

SB2 U-3 Vindicator, Navy (1 engine) scout bomber, land- or carrier-based

SBD Dauntless, Navy (1 engine) scout or dive-bomber, land- or carrier-based

SOC Curtiss Scout Plane - Seagull (1-engine) Biplane

TBD Devastator, Navy (1 engine) torpedo-bomber, carrier-based

TBF Avenger, Navy (1 engine) torpedo-bombers, carrier-based

Japanese *(Names in quotes are American designations)*

"Alf" Kawanishi E7K2 Type 94 reconnaissance seaplane

"Betty" Mitsubishi G4M1 Type 1 (2 engines) medium bomber

"Claude" Mitsubishi A5M4 Type 96 carrier fighter

"Dave" Nakajima E8N1 Type 95 reconnaissance seaplane

"Dinah" Mitsubishi Ki-46 Type 100 command reconnaissance plane

"Emily" Kawanishi H8K1 Type 2 (4 engines) bomber (flying boat)

"Hamp" Mitsubishi A6M6 Type 0, Model 32 carrier fighter (1 engine)

"Irving" Nakajima J1N1-C Type 2 land reconnaissance plane

"Jake" Aichi E13A1 Type 0 reconnaissance seaplane

"Judy" Yokosuka D4Y1-C Type 2 carrier reconnaissance plane

"Kate" Nakajima B5N2 Type 97 (1 engine) high-level or torpedo-bomber

"Lily" Kawasaki Ki-48 Light bomber (2 engines)

"Mavis" Kawanishi H6K4 Type 97 (4 engines) patrol bomber (flying boat)

"Oscar" Army version of the Zero

"Pete" Mitsubishi F1M2 Type 0 observation plane (Two-wing Biplane)

"Rufe" Nakajima A6M2-N Type 2 fighter

"Val" Aichi D3A1 Type 99 (1 engine) dive-bomber

"Zeke" Mitsubishi A6M6 Type 0, Model 21 carrier fighter (1 engine)

"Zero" See "Zeke"

Military Ranks *(Commissioned)*

U. S. Navy and Imperial Japanese Navy	Army, USAAF and USMC
Admiral (Adm.)	General (Gen.)
Vice Admiral (Vadm.)	Lieutenant General (Lt. Gen.)
Rear Admiral (Radm.)	Major General (Maj. Gen.)
Commodore (Comdr.)	Brigadier General (Brig.Gen.)
Captain (Capt.)	Colonel (Col.)
Commander (Cmdr.)	Lieutenant Colonel (LTC)
Lieutenant Commander. (Lt. Cmdr.)	Major (Maj.)
Lieutenant (Lt.)	Captain (Capt.)
Lieutenant (junior grade or jg) (Lt. (jg))	First Lieutenant (1st Lt.)
Ensign (Ens.)	Second Lieutenant (2nd Lt.)
Warrant Officer (WO)	

Military Ranks *(Enlisted)*

Gunner Marine Gunner (USMC only)
Mach. Machinist
Priv. Private
Rad. Elec. Radio Electrician

PFC Private First Class
Sgt. Sergeant
Cpl. Corporal

Petty Officers

Chief (AOM). AOM lc, AOM2c, AOM3c)	Aviation Ordnance Mate
Chief (ACMM), AMMlc, AMM2c, AMM3c)	Aviation Machinist's Mate
Chief (CAP), AP1c, AP2c)	Aviation Pilot
Chief (ACRM), ARM lc, ARM2c, ARM3c)	Aviation Radioman
Chief (BM), BM lc, BM2c, BM3c)	Boatswain Mate
Chief (CRM), RM lc, RM2c. RM3c)	Radioman
Chief (EM), EM lc, EM2c, EM3c)	Electrician's Mate
Chief (QM), QM lc, QM2c, QM3c)	Quartermaster's Mate

Other naval enlisted ranks *(USN)*

Sea1c Seaman, 1st Class
Sea2c Seaman, 2nd Class
Sea3c Seaman, 3rd Class

Imperial Japanese naval enlisted ranks *(Aviation Branch)*

CPO (after 1 November 1942)	Flight Chief Petty Officer
PO1c	Flight Petty Officer, 1st Class
PO2c	Flight Petty Officer, 2nd Class
PO3c (to 1 November 1942)	Flight Petty Officer, 3rd Class
LdgSea (after 1 November 1942)	Flight Leading Seaman
SupSea (after 1 November 1942)	Flight Superior Seaman
Sea1c	Flight Seaman, 1st Class
Sea2c	Flight Seaman, 2nd Class

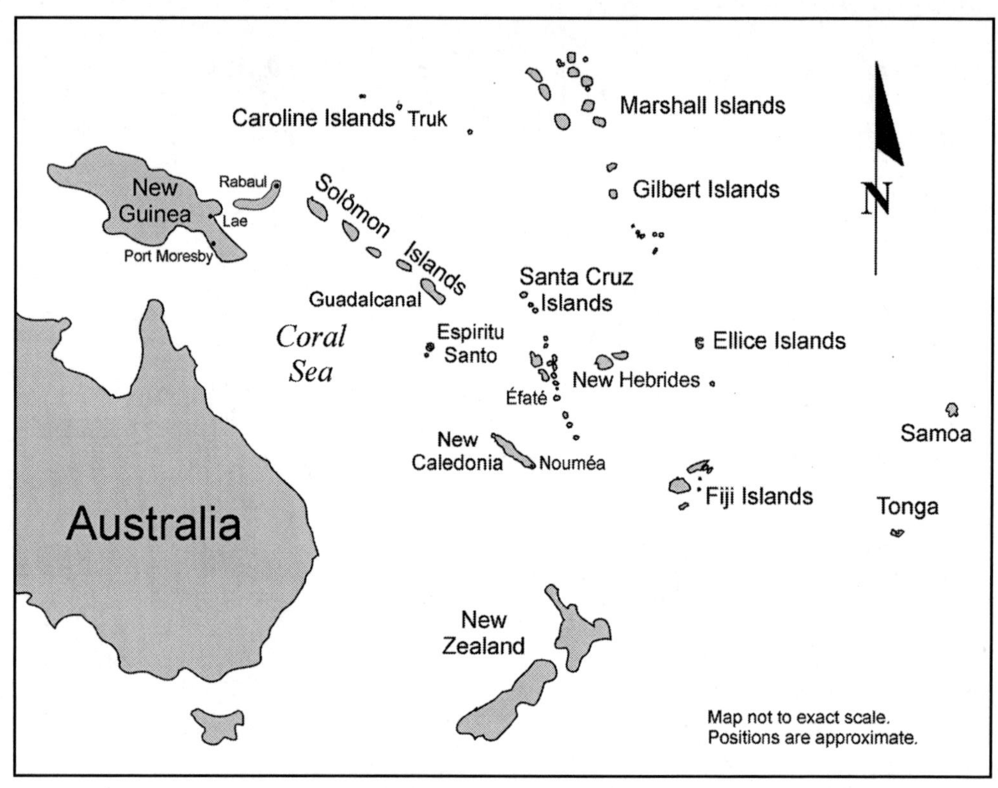

Battles for Guadalcanal - Theater of Operations

Distances to Guadalcanal *(Nautical miles)**

American Bases	Mileage	Japanese Bases	Mileage
Honolulu, HA	3,150	Tokyo	2,939
San Diego, CA	5,348	Truk	1,130
San Francisco, CA	5,163	Lae	809
Samoa	1,700	Rabaul	565
Tonga	1,576	Buna	553
Fiji Islands	1,177		
Efaté	850		
Espiritu Santo	580		
Nouméa	869		
Port Moresby	755		
**1 Nautical Mile = 1.151 Miles (statute) or 1.852 Kilometers*			

Battles for Guadalcanal—Timeline

Date & Event

1-2 May 1942 Australians evacuate Tulagi when Japanese occupy the island

28 May-July 8 Japanese occupy Guadalcanal and begin construction of airbase

4 July American B-17 flies over Guadalcanal and confirms presence of Japanese building an airstrip

6 July Allied headquarters in Australia receive confirmation of Japanese construction of an airfield from coastwatchers

10 July Nimitz orders Ghormley to invade and capture Guadalcanal and Tulagi

7 Aug. Americans land 10,000 Marines on Guadalcanal against a 2,200 Japanese defending force

8 Aug. Japanese airfield captured and Americans name it "Henderson Field" after a Marine pilot who died during the Battle of Midway

9 Aug. Battle of Savo Island. Heavy cruisers *Canberra, Astoria, Quincy, & Vincennes* sunk

10 Aug. US submarine *S-44* sinks Japanese heavy cruiser *Kako* off New Ireland

21 Aug. Battle of the Tenaru (Ilu) River

24 Aug. Battle of the Eastern Solomons. Japanese light carrier *Ryujo* sunk, American carrier *Enterprise* damaged

31 Aug. American carrier *Saratoga* torpedoed near San Cristobal

12-14 Sept. Battle of Edson's (Bloody) Ridge

15 Sept. American carrier *Wasp* sunk, battleship *North Carolina* torpedoed

11-12 Oct. Battle of Cape Esperance. Japanese heavy cruisers *Furutaka* and *Fubuki* and one destroyer sunk. Americans lose one destroyer

13 Oct. Japanese battleships *Kongo* and *Haruna* shell Marine positions

14 Oct. Japanese heavy cruisers *Chokai* and *Kinugasa* bombard Marines

18 Oct. Halsey takes command, relieving Ghormley

24-25 Oct. Battle for Henderson Field

26 Oct. Battle of the Santa Cruz Islands, American carrier *Hornet* sunk

12-15 Nov. Naval Battle of Guadalcanal. Japanese lose battleships *Hiei, Kirishima,* heavy cruiser *Kinugasa,* three destroyers, and seven transports.
Americans lose heavy cruisers *Atlanta, San Francisco,* light cruiser *Juneau,* and seven destroyers

13 Nov. Japanese heavy cruisers *Suzuya* and *Maya* bombard Henderson Field

30 Nov. Battle of Tassafaronga. Japanese lose one destroyer. Americans lose heavy cruiser *Northampton*

9 Dec. Army Gen. Alexander M. Patch relieves Marine Gen. Vandegrift. U.S. Army takes command of major ground offensive operations

12 Dec. American PT boats sink Japanese destroyer *Teruzuki* at Cape Esperance

15 Dec. - 7 Feb. American ground offensive to evict Japanese 17th Army from Guadalcanal begins

29-30 Jan. 1943 Battle of Rennell Island. American heavy cruiser *Chicago* sunk

1-7 Feb. Japanese evacuate Guadalcanal

9 Feb. Guadalcanal campaign ends. Americans take full control

Preface

When I decided to write this book, I had just published my first one. I had always wanted to write a series of books about World War II naval warfare in the Pacific. The only choice for me was to pick the part of the Pacific War about which to write. Without much procrastination, I decide to write about Guadalcanal. Much had already been published about it. Nonetheless, I wanted to write about that great struggle.

When I began my research, I had no idea what a huge project this would be. The battle lasted more than six months from beginning to end and involved several major sea, air, and ground battles. It took me six years to finish the first draft. As in any creative endeavor, there were times when my writing seemed to have no end. I also had occasional bouts of writer's block when I had to step away from the work and think carefully how to approach a topic and how to structure my writing so the reader could easily follow the narrative.

I decided on the title *Morning of the Rising Sun* because this episode in the Pacific War represented Japan's continuing power ascendancy after Pearl Harbor. Despite the Doolittle Raid's success and their stinging defeat at the Battle of Midway, Japan was still a formidable naval power still surpassing anything the Americans could throw at them. When they occupied Tulagi and began building the airstrip on Guadalcanal, their territory was still expanding, and they were on the offensive to extend their control in the Pacific. The six-month-long struggle at Guadalcanal would represent a major turn of events for both sides.

Guadalcanal is an island in the Solomon Islands chain and has many characteristics typical of the islands that make up that region of the South Pacific called Melanesia. It has a massive collection of dense, impenetrable vegetation, fiercely hot, humid weather that challenged any humans who dared trying to stay there to survive, and it is infested with every imaginable tropical disease, insect, plant, and animal that nature could create in the Earth's tropical climes. Not many people have ever lived there. Even the natives that did would often move to other islands with less inclement climates. Nevertheless, the island took on a far more strategic position in World War II. It sat in the direct path between the U.S. and Australia. The Japanese occupied it first. The Americans arrived on August 7, 1942, to evict them. What followed was the first massive ground, sea, and air conflict in the most destructive war the world had ever seen.

I wish express my deep appreciation to my editor, James C. Wright. He has been a great help to me, making this book the best it can be. The editors at my publisher, BookSurge, also deserved much praise as well. I also express my appreciation for the professionals at BookSurge, LLC—the publisher I hired to actually do the hard work of extensive editing and turning my manuscript into book form.

There are several authors I wish to thank for their contributions to this book. The first is Samuel L. Morison for his mighty work, *History of United States Naval Operations in World War II, Volumes IV and V*; Richard B. Frank for his work, *Guadalcanal*; John B. Lundstrom for his massive history of naval air operations, *The First Team and the Guadalcanal Campaign: Naval Fighter Combat from August to November 1942*; James W. Grace in his work *Naval Battle of Guadalcanal: Night Action 13, November 1942*; and Russell Crenshaw in his book *The Battle of Tassafaronga*. I also show many other books, articles, and recollections in my bibliography, without which this book would have been impossible to write. The first three gentlemen are primary in my mind when I think of their outstanding works. I have attempted to portray the events of all the momentous struggles both sides endured in the most personal way I knew by telling a story.

The mighty struggle for Guadalcanal had many facets and subtleties, particularly in how many of the men responsible for giving orders reacted and believed what they thought truly guided their actions. As in all human endeavors, errors in judgment occurred. And these mistakes were indeed plentiful. But, despite these errors, the men who decided the fates of their fellow sailors, soldiers, marines, and airmen did the best they could under the circumstances they faced: inadequate training and preparation, lack of actual battle experience, and, for the Americans, paying the price for the neglect of their nation's military readiness in those years leading up to Pearl Harbor. For the Japanese, their commanders suffered from unshakable beliefs that their nation had a destiny to conquer Asia for their nation's economic and political power. Each side grossly underestimated its opponent's ability to fight a "modern" war and paid the price with many men's lives. In the end, the Americans developed a healthy respect for the Japanese fighting man. And the same could be said for the Japanese for the Americans.

Guadalcanal solidified those developed opinions, and the Pacific War would continue for another three horrible years that included some of the bloodiest and most hotly contested battles in military history. One nation would emerge victorious and become the predominant world power of its age. The other would be laid in ruins and then rise like a phoenix to become the world's second greatest economic power.

It is my intent to tell the story of Guadalcanal from the perspective of a lay historian and a lover of the study of history. I hope that you agree that this tale of bravery and sacrifice is a most compelling narrative that deserves the attention of even the most casual reader of history.

Kenneth I. Friedman

Prelude: A Murder of Nature

About 26 years before the struggle for Guadalcanal, another confrontation occurred that was similar to it in many ways, the Battle of Verdun. I contend that for one to gain some understanding of what Guadalcanal was like for the men who fought there and what was at stake on that South Pacific island, an appreciation of Verdun and what it meant for those who fought and died there is important.

Stalemate on the Western Front

The Meuse River meanders north through the eastern French countryside and drains into the Rhine River in the Netherlands. Thick forests of trees, pastures, and farmland cover the gently rolling hills on its banks. At a place about 140 miles east of Paris, it passes Verdun, a town where Germany and France fought the greatest battle of World War I. In February 1916, it was a quiet part of the Western Front after the fast wheeling movements of the German Army failed to defeat France at the Battle of the Marne in 1914. The war had become a deadly struggle in which the French and the British, known as the Allies, and the Germans were at a stalemate. On the Eastern Front, the Central Powers, which included Germany, Austria, and Turkey, had a string of successes against the huge Russian Army. A string of trenches sprang up in France from the Swiss border in the south to the North Sea in the north. The war then degenerated into a series of deadly battles in which each side attacked the other with gains and losses of, at most, a few hundred yards in either direction. Both sides desperately needed to change this situation; to continue that way would have bled both sides dry with no end in sight. The Germans put a plan together to permanently alter these circumstances.

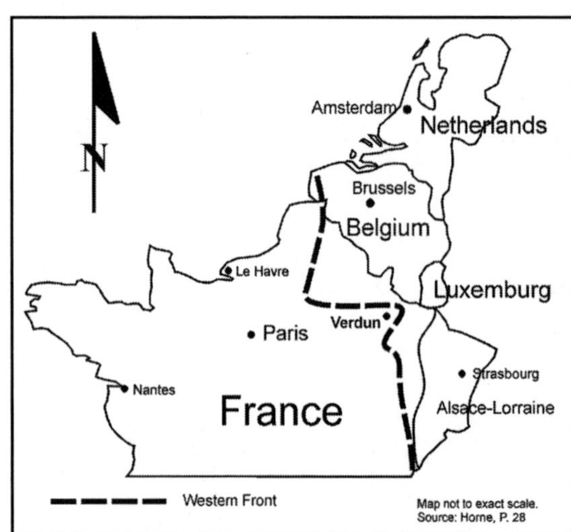

Western Front—World War I

The year 1915 had brought considerable success to the German Army. At no other time in the war did victory seem so close. The British and French suffered disastrous losses on the Western Front. The Turks had inflicted a disastrous defeat on the British and French as they evicted them from the Gallipoli peninsula in the Dardanelles. The German High Seas fleet had fought the British Grand Fleet to a tactical standstill at Jutland. By September, Gen. Paul von Hindenburg and his Chief of Staff, Gen. Erich von Ludendorf, led the German Army to a series of victories on the Eastern Front that captured 750,000 prisoners. The Allies' fortunes had reached its nadir.[1]

In December 1915, German Commander-in-Chief Gen. Erich von Falkenhayn had an idea that he firmly believed could bring victory to his country. He had a reputation for ruthlessness, which had spread throughout the German Army. Falkenhayn had strongly promoted dueling by German officers as necessary to uphold the "honor of the army." The main failing of his ruthless attitudes was that he lacked the tenaciousness of Gen. Erich von Ludendorf; this would lead to disastrous results for the Germans in the Battle of Verdun.

A Controversial Letter

Nevertheless, he demonstrated just how ruthless a fellow he was when he wrote a long memorandum to the Kaiser Wilhelm II that began with Falkenhayn's view of the status of the war:

> "France has been weakened almost to the limits of endurance...The Russian armies have not been overthrown, but their offensive powers have been so shattered that she can never revive anything like her old strength."[2]

He further stated that the British were keeping the Allies together and, therefore, should be considered the greater threat. "The history of the English wars against the Netherlands, Spain, France, and Napoleon is being repeated. Germany can expect no mercy."

The memorandum further contended that Germany could not remain on the defensive against the British:

> "Our enemies, thanks to the superiority in men and material, are increasing their resources much more than we are. If that process continues, a moment must come when the balance of numbers itself will deprive Germany of all remaining hope."[3]

Falkenhayn further argued that the British were using the Russians, French, and Italians as surrogates so that they would not suffer as many casualties as if they were fighting the Germans alone. After writing more rambling passages about the state of the war and his contempt for the Italians, Falkenhayn argued that the British must be forced to realize that they could not win the war without their Allies. At the end of his memorandum, he finally made his proposal:

> "There remains only France...If we succeeded in opening the eyes of her people to the fact that in a military sense they have nothing more to hope for, that breaking point would be reached and England's best sword knocked out of her hand. To achieve that objective the uncertain method of a mass breakthrough, in any case beyond our means, is unnecessary. We can probably do enough for our purposes with limited resources. Within our reach behind the French sector of the Western front there are objectives for the retention of which

> the French General Staff would be compelled to throw in every man they have. If they do so the forces of France will bleed to death[4]—as there can be no question of a voluntary withdrawal—whether we reach our goal or not. If they do not do so, and we reach our objectives, the moral effect on France will be enormous. For an operation limited to a narrow front, Germany will not be compelled to spend herself so completely...
>
> "The objectives of which I am speaking now are Belfort and Verdun. The considerations urged above apply to both, yet the preference must be given to Verdun."[5]

Thus, Falkenhayn convinced the Kaiser and German High Command to launch a massive offensive against Verdun. And, as he predicted in his letter, France would send the cream of her young men to the killing machine that Verdun became.

The Battle

After much planning by the Germans and movements of large numbers of troops and large caliber guns, the Germans set the attack's date for February 12, 1916. However, excessive snowfall and heavy fog caused several postponements. The Germans were determined to win this upcoming battle by the overpowering use of their enormous superiority in heavy artillery. They planned to use their giant "Big Bertha" 420-mm mortars. These had been used with great success in destroying the seemingly impenetrable Belgian forts when they invaded that country in 1914. Thus, the Germans took advantage of the delay to bring up more heavy artillery such as their 280 mm howitzers, along with millions of shells.

The French lacked equivalently heavy guns due to unexplainable decisions to keep their artillery light to foster "rapid movement." Of course this policy had been rendered moot because of the stalemate along the Western Front. Many months would pass at the Verdun front before the French realized this ridiculous strategy was a dismal failure and started using heavier artillery at Verdun.[6]

On February 21, 1916, the weather cleared. Therefore, at 4:00 a.m., the German guns started one of the most devastating artillery barrages in World War I. At 4:45 a.m., the German infantry attacked the French positions north, east, and west of Verdun, beginning the massive, vicious, and extremely ravaging battle.

For the next ten months, Verdun was the scene of one of the most costly battles of World War I and in military history. The Germans introduced new and more deadly technological advancements in ways to slaughter human beings: the flamethrower, use of aircraft to strafe troops on the ground, and deadly phosgene gas.

The soldiers were subjected to unimaginable horrors in the trenches and of death wherever they were. Some of the participants described the terrible privations in their own ways. An American pilot, James McConnell, while flying for the Lafayette Escadrille[7], wrote this description after seeing the shell-hole pocked battlefield from the air as he passed:

> "...red-roofed Verdun...[had] spots in it where no red shows and you know what has happened there ...[abruptly]...there is only that sinister brown belt, a strip of *murdered nature* [my em-

> phasis]. It seems to belong to another world. Every sign of humanity has been swept away. The woods and roads have vanished like chalk from a blackboard; of the villages nothing remains but gray smears... During heavy bombardments and attacks I have seen shells falling like rain. Countless towers of smoke remind one of Gustave Doré's picture of the fiery tombs of the arch-heretics in Dante's 'Hell'...Now and then monster projectiles hurtling through the air close by leave one's plane rocking violently in their wake. Airplanes have been cut in two by them."[8]

The overwhelming odor of decomposing bodies attacked the soldiers' senses whenever they were at the front. As the battle raged for more than ten months, parts of bodies would be exhumed as the men dug new trenches over the old ones. The shell holes were so numerous that when more shells exploded in the dirt, bodies and parts of bodies that previous bombardments had buried were thrown into the air. Once a soldier fought at Verdun, he never could get the odor of the place off his body, out of his uniform, or from his memory.

Bringing in food, clothing, ammunition, and medical supplies was particularly troublesome to the French. German artillery had destroyed the only railroad from Paris to Verdun early in the battle. Therefore, the only way to get supplies to the front was over a narrow two lane road the French called the "*Voie Sacrée*" or Sacred Way.[9]

The Germans had an easier time getting supplies to their forces by using their highly efficient railroad system built for and upgraded after the 1871 Franco-Prussian War; they brought vast amounts of food, ammunition, and medical materiel, thus keeping their troops relatively well supplied. However, as the Battle of Verdun raged on, the effects of the British naval blockade began to be felt by the Germans since it became increasingly difficult for the German home front to produce what was needed. Conditions at home worsened for German civilians as agricultural production was diverted almost exclusively to feed the army. Meanwhile, the entry of the Americans into the war and the British attack at the Somme River in July 1916 helped improve the French supply problem. By December 1916, the French supply system was able to reach the French soldiers at the front. This critical event caused the Germans to give up trying to take Verdun. The French artillery finally got the upper hand with the introduction of large caliber guns. The French also had obtained air superiority over the Verdun front so that it could more effectively act as spotters for the artillery and to attack German positions.

The tide at Verdun turned when the French recaptured Fort Douaumont and Fort Vaux. These were initially captured by the Germans in the early phases of the battle. These forts became a symbol of French bravery and sacrifice. The names of these embattlements have been continuously burned into the French national conscious. The Battle of Verdun turned the tide of World War I in favor of the Allies. Less than two years later, the war ended with an Allied victory when the Germans agreed to an armistice and, later, capitulation.[10]

The End of a Disaster

On December 19, 1916, the eastern French countryside resembled a moonscape rather than the green forests and fields that were there before February 21 that same year. Putrid odors of decaying flesh, the pungent aroma of burnt cordite from exploded artillery shells and the overwhelming presence of death permeated the air. There had not been such a scene of utter destruction since the American Civil War. Many years would pass before nature restored the trees and fields. Today, there are still places where no crops can be planted; skeletons and remnants of artillery shells, helmets, and pieces of uniforms are still being excavated by souvenir hunters and farmers.

This horrible battle was the longest and costliest fought during World War I. The loss of life was cataclysmic for both sides: 328,500 Germans and 348,000 French.

Verdun versus Guadalcanal

There would be no other battle fought like Verdun until the Battle for Guadalcanal 26 years later. The similarities of Guadalcanal to Verdun are striking. Both sides accepted that each battle was a vital element for realizing victory; they poured in everything they could spare in terms of men, material, and command attention with appalling losses. Both battles took months to reach a conclusion. Vital struggles for such places like Edson's (Bloody) Ridge, the Gifu, the Naval Battle of Guadalcanal, and Tassafaronga would remind both French and German World War I veterans of Fort Douaumont and Fort Vaux. Like the French trying to bring supplies via the Sacred Way, the Americans also faced almost impossible odds trying to keep their forces supplied while the Japanese Navy continued running their Tokyo Express down the Solomon Islands' Slot to supply their troops. French air power made its presence felt at Verdun. When the Americans gained air supremacy over the South Pacific by creating the "land-based" aircraft carrier on Guadalcanal, they sealed their victory over the Japanese. However, Verdun ended in a tactical stalemate but a strategic defeat for the Germans. World War I would go on its inexorable path to further death and destruction until the Germans, exhausted at home and at the front, sued for an armistice. Guadalcanal would end in a tactical and strategic defeat for the Japanese. After Guadalcanal, the Americans, backed by the overwhelmingly powerful American economy, relentlessly went on the offensive until the Pacific War's end more than two years later.

Nevertheless, before the Americans could launch their first offensive action by invading Guadalcanal, they had to learn how to fight a new kind of war in the vast Pacific Ocean. All of their battleships, which were to have been the main offensive naval weapon in taking the fight to the Japanese, now lay in the mud of Pearl Harbor. The Philippines were under attack by the Japanese. Pleas for help flowed in from those beleaguered islands and from other American possessions such Guam and Wake. The Americans had to adjust to this war in the Pacific Ocean while also stopping the very real threat from Nazi Germany. This was where the fundamental importance of war planning would make its presence felt.

Part 1: Getting Ready

CHAPTER 1
A Depressing Sight

The smoke and stench of death and defeat hung over Pearl Harbor like a funereal pall. The once mighty Pacific Fleet of the U.S. Navy lay in ruins. Vadm. William F. Halsey, silent and gloomy on the bridge of the aircraft carrier *Enterprise*, observed the full nature and extent of the carnage. It was the most depressing sight he had witnessed in his entire naval career.

As Halsey's task force passed through the narrow mouth of Pearl Harbor on December 8, 1941, every man in every ship remaining afloat in the harbor stood at his post in hushed silence. Exhausted soldiers kept vigil next to antiaircraft guns along the shore near Hickam Field. A thick layer of smoke lay over everything, and a black oil slick covered the water's surface like an unearthly, lethal ink.

The heavily damaged battleship *Nevada* was beached off Waipio Point. When the bombs fell, she had tried to escape, but couldn't make it out to sea. Her captain put her on the shore to avoid blocking the main channel to the harbor.

The *Enterprise* approached Ford Island in the gathering dusk. As the acrid odor of burnt flesh filled the air, it nauseated the ship's company. Men on deck gaped at the line of wrecks strung out along Battleship Row.

The *California*'s superstructure broke just above the water line.

The capsized *Oklahoma* lay on her side like a beached whale. Only her hull bottom was visible above the water.

The *West Virginia* was a scorched hulk.

The *Arizona*'s mast was barely discernable above the water's rim as thick, black smoke billowed over the waves where she had once floated majestically in the warm Hawaiian sun. The *Arizona*'s water-covered hull had trapped and entombed more than 1,000 souls below deck when she sank, while wracked by explosions.

Observers on the *Enterprise* gazed, too, at the charred skeletons that had once been the airplane hangars on Ford Island. As the big carrier swung past this devastation, they saw the capsized battleship *Utah* in the berth where the big "E" normally docked. Halsey's face darkened, consumed with a smoldering anger as he surveyed the dismal scene. Dismay filled his voice as he growled, "Before we are through with them, the Japanese language will be spoken in Hell."

This excitable and volatile admiral became known for venting his hatred for the Japanese throughout the war. The idea of destroying the entire Japanese nation filled his days and nights. His habit of expressing these strongly-held feelings in a public way prompted the press to give him the nickname "Bull" Halsey.[1]

☆ ☆ ☆

After receiving repeated intelligence reports about possible Japanese naval activities in the Pacific, America's Pacific Fleet Commander-in-Chief, Adm. Husband E. Kimmel, had ordered a conference in Pearl Harbor on November 27, 1941. Halsey was invited. Much of the discussion at the meeting was about which airplanes should be sent to defend Wake Island and Midway. One of the fruits of this meeting was to send the *Enterprise* and her escorts to deliver these planes to Wake. The intent was to bolster that island's defenses.[2]

A message arrived from Washington later that afternoon issuing a war warning to the commanders at Pearl Harbor. This message greatly concerned Halsey. Later, as his task force approached Wake Island, it would come within flying range of the Japanese naval installations in the Marshall and Gilbert Islands. These installations contained a large number of aircraft. Wake Island was the American possession closest to Japan.[3] The close proximity of Wake to Japan's naval power was a reminder to Halsey that he soon would be in the middle of a fight.

Before departing on his mission, Halsey spoke with his superior, Adm. Kimmel, who asked whether Halsey wanted to take the battleships with him. In a reply quite typical of Halsey's style, he retorted, "Hell, no! If I have to run, I don't want anything interfering with my running."[4]

Kimmel understood this because the battleships had a top speed of only 20 knots. This was at least 10 knots slower than that of the carriers, cruisers, and destroyers. At 6:00 p.m., as Halsey rose to leave, he asked Kimmel, "How far do you want me to go?"[5]

Kimmel replied, "Use your common sense."[6] Halsey smiled. Later, he would recall, "That was the finest order a subordinate could ever receive."[7] The *Enterprise* task force left Pearl Harbor on November 28.[8]

☆ ☆ ☆

As radio reports began pouring in on the morning of December 7, Halsey's returning force was 200 miles out to sea. On hearing them, he ordered his task force to make a speedy return to Pearl Harbor. However, heavy seas prevented their arrival until the next day.[9]

Halsey thanked a beneficent providence for seeing that his task force had not been caught like sitting ducks in "a landlocked duck pond." Some semblance of a naval fighting force remained in the American arsenal as a result. This nucleus could and later would be used to take the fight to the Japanese.

The *Enterprise* anchored and waited to take on fuel from a Navy oiler. At midnight, December 8, 1941, the *Enterprise* filled her fuel tanks and prepared to leave the debris-strewn harbor by 5:00 a.m. Her mission was to hunt down enemy submarines believed to be in the Hawaiian area. Halsey could not help but wonder why his force had been placed at a maximum risk to chase after such elusive targets. He was utterly determined to get in, refuel, replenish his supplies, and get out as quickly as possible. The threat of yet another Japanese attack and invasion was still hanging in the air like a Sword of Damocles over Hawaii. The American mainland faced the very same danger.

The suddenness and savagery of Japan's attack led every American Navy expert to expect a long, bloody, barbaric struggle. No longer could the Pacific be regarded as an American lake. It now belonged to the Japanese. This war was going to set records for the destruction of ships and men.

Many men on the *Enterprise* had never before experienced war, but now they felt its looming presence. It was palpable and very much something one could see and feel. Some of the inexperienced officers and men allowed their imaginations to run wild. They imagined there were snipers and oncoming bomber squadrons lurking everywhere. The aviators' nerves were frayed, too, by dwelling too long and hard on the empty seats of comrades who had been lost over Oahu. Halsey sensed the nervousness of the flyers. In a visit to the *Enterprise* ward room before lunch on December 10, he gave a pep talk. While the words he spoke were never recorded, the *Enterprise* Fighter Squadron's diary noted, "The Japs had better look out for that man!"[10]

William Frederick Halsey, Jr., was born on October 30, 1882, in Elizabeth, New Jersey, and came from a long line of seafaring men. One of these men was Capt. John Halsey, who had commanded a privateer that had attacked French shipping under a Massachusetts governor's commission during Queen Anne's War (1702-1713). Another Halsey ancestor was Capt. Eliphalet Halsey. He was one of the first to sail a Long Island whaler around Cape Horn and into the South Pacific. Many Halseys succeeded him as whaling masters and followed the same course.

Halsey's father attended the U.S. Naval Academy, graduating in 1873. He then served in the South Pacific where his forebears had hunted whales. His son, in his time, would see glory in the Pacific.[11]

Halsey's interest in naval aviation was stimulated when the Naval Academy received its first naval air detachment. During that time, he commanded the seaplane tender, *Reina*, at Annapolis. He became convinced the airplane would replace the battleship as the primary weapon of modern navies.

His enthusiasm for naval aviation grew as he flew with pilots under his command. In 1930, he was invited to Pensacola, Florida, for a flight training course. Later, he received his wings, but never became a full-time naval aviator because his eyesight was substandard for a pilot. Yet, he remained intensely involved in naval aviation throughout his career.[12]

Halsey became a firm believer in the aircraft carrier as the primary offensive naval weapon system. When he testified at Adm. Kimmel's hearing after the Pearl Harbor debacle, he stated that the Americans had to "get to the other fellow with everything you have as fast as you can and to dump it on him."[13] Halsey testified he would never hesitate to use the carrier as an offensive weapon. Its original role as the protector of battleships and heavy cruisers was obsolete in his view. Now, the battleships, along with the cruisers and destroyers, would protect the carriers. This became the primary naval strategy for the U.S. Navy in the Pacific. The Japanese had shown that the carrier was indeed a powerful offensive naval weapon, and the Americans would soon use that new knowledge to great effect against their enemy.[14]

"Bull" Halsey achieved great fame during the early days of World War II by leading the early raids on the Japanese-held islands. He commanded the task force transporting Lt. Col. James H. Doolittle's B-25 bombers to their departure point 824 miles west of Tokyo. Doolittle's bombers took off April 18, 1942, from the carrier *Hornet* for their historic raid to bomb Tokyo, Yokohama, Nagoya, Osaka, and Kobe on the Japanese home island of Honshu.[15]

Halsey would have been the one to command the aircraft carriers that lay in wait for the Japanese at Midway. However, he contracted a serious skin disease, forcing him to stay ashore. Some naval historians, critics of Halsey, are of the opinion that his absence from the Midway ambush was one of the major reasons the Americans emerged victorious. Winston Churchill called this action the turning point in the Pacific War.

Halsey's hospital stay ended with a new assignment. On October 18, 1942, he would assume command of the South Pacific area, COMSOPAC, which was where the Americans and their allies were engaged in a life and death struggle for control of the Solomon Islands. It was to be in the Solomons where his leadership skills would be tested to their limits. The operation there was run on a shoestring because of losses in ships and men at the battles of both Coral Sea and Midway. Nevertheless, his ability to motivate the men under his command would shine. He would emerge from the fight for Guadalcanal an American naval hero.

CHAPTER 2
The Best Laid Plans

The Pearl Harbor attack meant that the U.S. Navy would undergo significant command changes at the highest levels. The acerbic and laconic Adm. Ernest J. King replaced Adm. Harold R. Stark as Chief of Naval Operations (CNO). The highly respected Adm. Chester W. Nimitz took command as commander-in-chief—Pacific Fleet (CINCPAC) from the beleaguered and starstruck Adm. Husband Kimmel. Pearl Harbor changed many naval commanders' minds about the viability of the battleship as the primary naval offensive weapon. Much of the planning done before the Americans' entry into World War II might have seemed destined for the dust heap. But the opposite was true. The then-current plans for fighting a war against the Japanese in the Pacific needed to be changed to reflect the new realities. However, pre-World War II planning that began around the beginning of 20th century had evolved from the original thinking about the possibilities of war with Japan. Planning that occurred during those 40-plus years resulted in a series of plan iterations known as War Plan Orange. As it turned out, pre-World War II planning set the stage for many of the battles that ultimately did occur within the Pacific Theater during the war.

A Plan by Any Other Color

In 1898, America's isolation from the world stage ended after they defeated the Spanish in the Spanish-American War. That victory was the first time the U.S. had defeated a European power (although Spain's influence over world events had been waning for several years) in a global conflict. In the late 18th and early 19th centuries, the U.S. fought two wars with Great Britain that essentially settled the question of whether the U.S. would exist as an independent nation. Although the U.S. had significant interactions with European powers after that time, the Americans kept to themselves in a military sense. An example of such interactions include when they successfully aided the Mexicans to expel the French in the 1860s while still recovering from the Civil War fought between the North and South.

The Americans had beaten the Spanish through the use of overwhelming naval power by winning big naval confrontations in Manila Bay in the Philippines and at Santiago off the Cuban coast. During the period between the mid-19th century and the turn of the 20th, Japan became more of a power in the western Pacific as she embraced western economic methods under the influence of the Emperor Meiji. When the 20th century began, both countries became viable commercial and military powers on the world stage.

The Japanese took on the Russians in 1905 and thoroughly defeated the hapless Czarist power on land and particularly at sea at the Battle of Tsushima Straits (eastern Channel of the Korea Straits separating Korea and Japan). As a result of both of these wins over European powers, the spheres of influence of both nations expanded. The Japanese occupied the Korean peninsula and the Americans took possession of the Philippines and Guam in the Marshall Islands (western Pacific Ocean). From that time, the probability that both nations' interests would clash in the Pacific increased markedly.

✲ ✲ ✲

In 1905, President Theodore Roosevelt had a vision to expand the American presence throughout the world. He oversaw an expansion of the American fleet to such an extent that it became the third largest fleet in the world (after Great Britain and Germany). He sent American battleships on an around-the-world tour so other countries could see the growing power of the U.S. The "Great White Fleet" toured the world from December 16, 1907, through February 22, 1909.

Consequently, the U.S. Navy started to formalize its planning operations, resulting in the plan called War Plan Orange. The colors used reflected the country the plan was about. There were other war plans as well with colors in their name. Orange stood for Japan, red for Great Britain, blue for the U.S., and black for Germany.

War Plan Orange's geographical premise was that war would break out between the two nations in spite of the then-current friendly relationship between them. The basic reason for the conflict would be Japan's striving for national greatness to dominate the Pacific Basin's land, people, and resources. That desire could be in conflict with American commercial, diplomatic, and military interests in that part of the world. The Japanese would realize their objective by attempting to forcibly remove American strength from their eastern Pacific flank. The anticipated theater would encompass 5,000 miles of the Pacific Ocean from the Aleutians Island chain (Alaska) in the North, southward to Hawaii, and then westward to the Asian coast.

War Plan Orange was divided into three phases because of the vast distances in the Pacific Ocean Basin.

Phase I anticipated that Japan would capture lightly defended bases to assure a free flow of resources between the Japanese home islands and rich resources of the East Indies. The U.S. Navy, concentrated in its home ports, would be unable to defend their remote Pacific outposts. American soldiers in the Philippines would be isolated from any help and ultimately be forced to surrender. Japanese power would reach its peak in about six months after hostilities began.

Phase II addressed having the American armed forces responding to the Japanese aggression by sending its navy and army to the west. The two sides would fight several small-scaled, fierce battles in the central Pacific so as to capture vitally important Japanese-held islands for the Americans to use as forward bases and to secure lines of supply. These bases would be steppingstones for advancing across the Pacific toward the Japanese home islands. The U.S. would defeat the Japanese forces primarily by attrition because of the vastly more potent American industrial base. The anticipated time for the successful completion of Phase II could be as long as two to three years.

After capturing these advanced bases, the fight would be taken to the Japanese home islands in Phase III. American military and naval might would destroy Japanese cities through naval and air bombardment by taking advantage of Japan's isolation from the rest of the world. Phase III could take as long as one year.[1]

A Plan's Evolution

As the American between-war planning continued, War Plan Orange evolved to reflect the politics of inter-service rivalries and, more importantly, the changing world situation. The U.S. signed several naval treaties that placed limits on the ratios of battleships the signatories (U.S., Japan, United Kingdom, and Italy) could build. Also, the American government wanted to maintain friendly relations with Japan. Therefore, the war planning efforts and any action the American government would have to take to get the bases needed to implement it were not acted upon.

By the time World War II broke out in Europe in 1939, American war planners derived a set of plans that bore the name of Rainbow. Five iterations of this base plan reflected the various potential scenarios that might occur. "Rainbow" meant that the plans were not just focused on one country, such as "Orange" meaning Japan. The Rainbow plans evolved as the world situation changed with the rise of Nazi Germany, events including Germany's occupation of the Rhineland in 1936, annexing Austria in 1938, marching into the Sudetanland after the British and French appeasement at Munich in 1938, and invading Poland in 1939 that started World War II. Also, the plans showed the Americans' attempt to develop worldwide strategies to fight a two-front war.

Rainbow plans one through four covered various contingencies that turned out to be unrealistic based on the availability of forces in existence. The Americans also realistically implemented a Europe-first strategy that recognized Nazi Germany as the greater threat. Rainbow Five incorporated much of what War Plan Orange was, but set the timetable back for taking the fight to the Japanese to reflect the Europe-first strategy. When the U.S. entered the war after the Pearl Harbor attack, the Navy followed Rainbow Five's war plan, particularly in the central Pacific. Nevertheless, all the Rainbow iterations had War Plan Orange as their foundation. The next map shows how Rainbow Five, which was the result of many iterations of War Plan Orange with the emphasis on Europe, and the actual Pacific campaigns compared.

As shown on this map, the offensives in the South Pacific and Southwest Pacific did not have any precedent based on either the iterations of War Plan Orange or the Rainbow plans. What plans formed the basis for the offensives particularly in the Solomon Islands? We shall now examine what planning activities, if any, played any role whatsoever in the Solomons' offensive actions, particularly Guadalcanal.[2]

Lack of Prewar Planning for Guadalcanal

The obvious missing element in the pre-World War II planning for war in the Pacific was any struggle for the islands in the South Pacific. One of the most influential men to address this issue was Adm. Ernest J. King, the CNO. King took over naval operations as a result of the removal of Adm. Harold Stark as part of the house cleaning done to the American military after the disaster at Pearl Harbor.

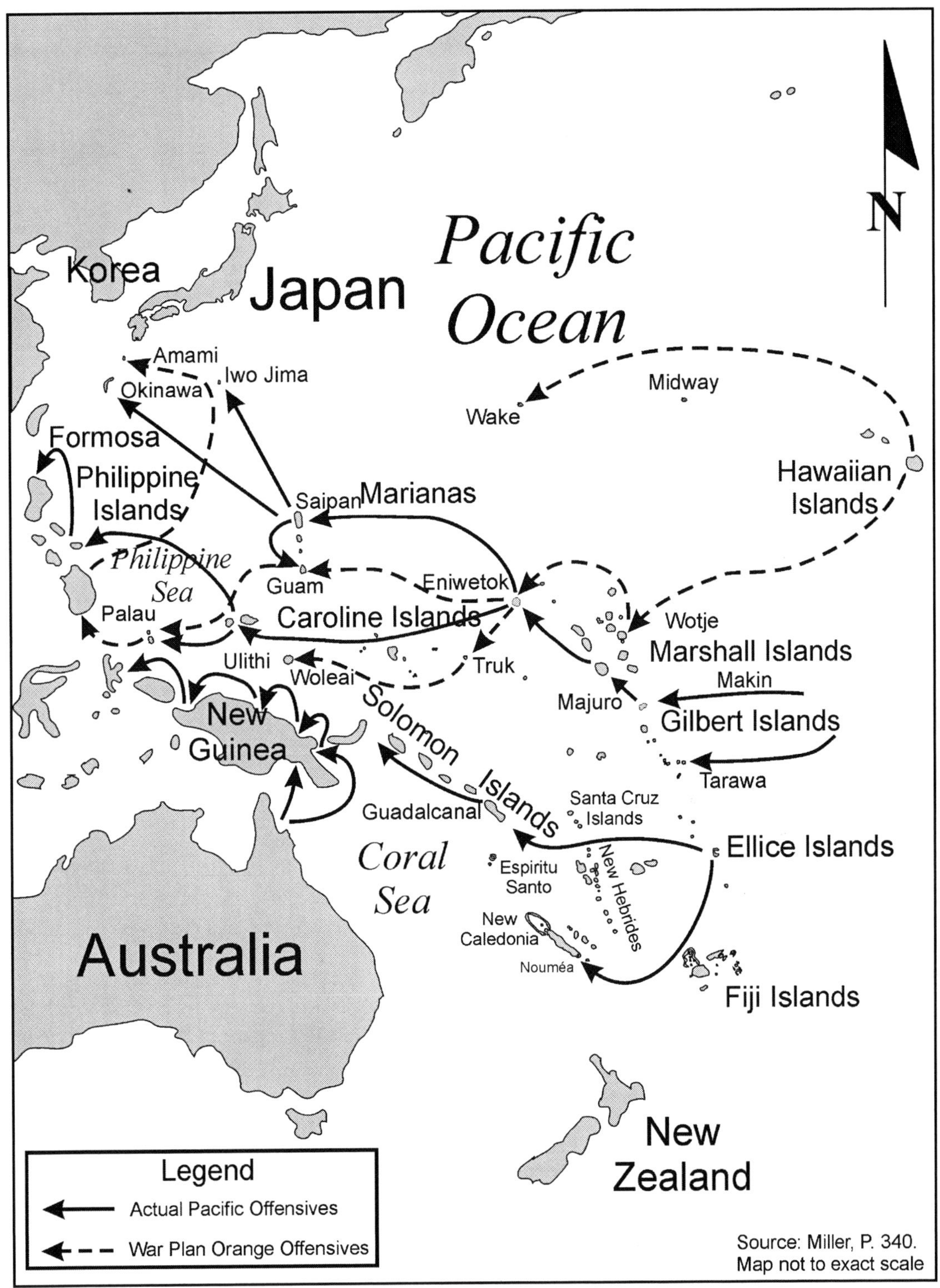

War Plan Rainbow Five

CHAPTER 3
The Japanese Conquests Continue

The Dirge Plays On

A litany of Allied defeats continued during the early months of 1942. The beleaguered American and Filipino troops on the Bataan Peninsula succumbed to the Japanese on April 8, 1942. Corregidor fell on May 5; with that loss, the U.S. lost its last base in the Far East. The infamous Bataan Death March followed in which between 7,000 and 10,000 Americans and Filipinos perished from disease, beatings, and executions.[1]

Other events favorable to the Japanese occurred elsewhere. In December 1941, Japanese airplanes sank the British battleship, *Prince of Wales*, and the battlecruiser, *Repulse*. On February 15, 1942, the British bastion of Singapore surrendered to a Japanese army that had daringly traveled hundreds of miles through supposedly impenetrable Malaysian jungle to attack the British fortress from the rear.

In 1941, Singapore had more than half a million people and was the crown of British presence in Asia. British forces in Singapore outnumbered the Japanese by more than two to one, so the loss of this British bastion was a stunning defeat. Singapore was then absorbed into Japan's Greater East Asia Co-Prosperity Sphere.

Meanwhile, the huge naval guns that had guarded the Straits of Malacca between the Malaya Peninsula and the Island of Sumatra were also rendered helpless. The Japanese drove the British up the Malayan Peninsula into Burma and on to the Indian subcontinent. For more than 100 years, the sun had never set on the Union Jack, but this was now no longer true.[2]

In a rapid succession of victories, the Japanese captured the remaining Dutch and British possessions. During March 1942 alone, the Japanese sank the Allied fleet's last remnants in the Battle of the Java Sea (March 1); they captured the Netherlands East Indies and Rangoon, Burma (March 8); they occupied Andaman and Nicobar Islands (March 23); and they overran the entire island of Sumatra (March 28). By means of these assaults, they evicted all the European presence from the Far East. The Greater East Asia Co-Prosperity Sphere became a reality. Japan's primary objective in taking control of Southeast Asia's vast and strategic resources had been achieved.[3]

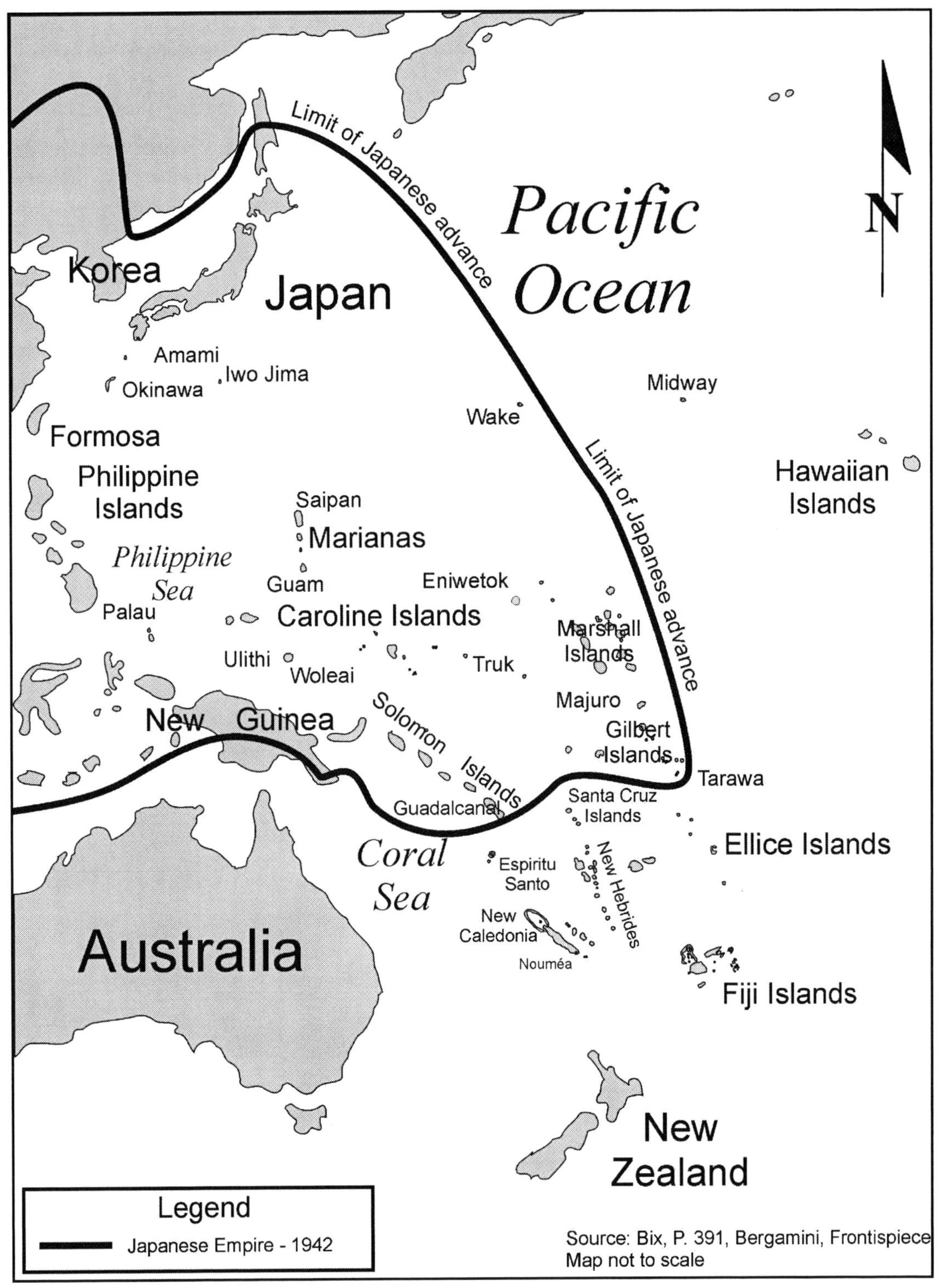

Japanese Empire - 1942

A Major Strategic Defeat

Alone in the waters of the vast Pacific, Ens. George Gay held his black floating cushion over his head, staring at the incredible scene unfolding before him. Only a few minutes had passed since his torpedo bomber crashed into the sea, shot down and full of holes from intense Japanese AA gunfire. His squadron, Torpedo 8, from the American aircraft carrier, *Hornet*, had attacked a Japanese carrier without the benefit of fighter cover. The Japanese had shot down every plane in his squadron. Gay was the sole survivor.

This and other incredible acts of sacrifice by American naval aviators and their crews would be duplicated many times before the end of the Battle of Midway on June 4, 1942. Nonetheless, Gay occupied a great sideline seat to see the destruction of the Imperial Japanese Fleet's four fleet carriers.

✲ ✲ ✲

Gay held onto his floating cushion and witnessed probably the most one-sided slaughter in the Pacific thus far. Bombers from the *Enterprise*, *Hornet*, and *Yorktown* caught the Japanese carriers just turning into the wind trying to launch aircraft to attack Midway Island again. With the carriers' decks loaded with fully fueled aircraft and bombs all over the place, American dive-bombers repeatedly sent their own bombs onto the decks. Explosion after explosion sent huge blossoms of fire and smoke into the air.

Gay cheered like an enthusiastic sports fan, but this was far more serious than seeing an athletic event. This was war's most brutal and lethal face. By the time a PBY picked Gay out of the water and took him to safety, the Imperial Japanese Navy had suffered a devastating and crushing defeat, one that would alter the course of the Pacific War and be called by many a turning point of the war in the Pacific. With this tremendous and exhilarating American victory, any Japanese invasion threat to the Hawaiian Islands and west coast of the continental U.S. vanished.[4]

Closing the Defensive Ring

Nonetheless, Japanese planning did not anticipate Gen. Douglas MacArthur's escape to Australia, where he would establish the basis for the retaking of the Philippines. Nor did they anticipate the ultimate defeat of the Japanese Empire. When MacArthur arrived in Australia, the existing forces at his disposal were paltry and almost invisible. Therefore, he vowed to build them up so he could go on the offensive. His arrival and this intent to go on the offensive against the Japanese made the U.S. and Australian forces there a threat to Japanese defenses in the South Pacific.

Therefore, the Japanese began an offensive to occupy the Papuan Peninsula on the jungle-infested island of New Guinea. They used their captured base at Rabaul on New Britain Island with its excellent harbor to hold major units of the Imperial Japanese Fleet and naval aircraft. Also, the Japanese made plans to capture Port Moresby, a port on New Guinea's southern coast which is just 350 miles from Cape York, Australia's northernmost point and only 1,125 miles from Darwin, Australia's northernmost city. The major Japanese objective was to threaten American supply lines between Australia, New Zealand, and North America.

To protect its left flank while attempting to capture New Guinea, the Japanese planned an offensive to take the Solomon Islands and build fighter airfields on Tulagi and Guadalcanal. The operation in the Solomons had lower priority than in New Guinea; therefore, it did not receive the same intensive attention and planning.

As part of their attempt to capture Port Moresby, the Japanese launched an invasion fleet accompanied by a large naval task force of three carriers, nine cruisers, and 14 destroyers in May 1942. The Americans sent the carriers *Yorktown* and *Lexington* with eight cruisers and 13 destroyers to stop the Japanese. The result was the Battle of the Coral Sea, the first naval battle in history where opposing ships never saw each other. Naval aircraft decided the confrontation's outcome. In the battle, the Americans lost the *Lexington* while the *Yorktown* suffered heavy damage, causing the Americans to suffer a tactical defeat at Coral Sea. The Japanese lost a light carrier and suffered heavy damage to a heavy carrier. More importantly, the Americans stopped the Japanese invasion of Port Moresby and the threat to Australia. Like many of the battles fought in the early months in the Pacific against the Americans, the Japanese continued to suffer strategic retreats. The tide of Japanese advances was ebbing and started to favor the Americans.[5]

Circumstances now forced both sides to turn their attention toward the southern Solomons. A strong-willed American CNO forced the Americans on the offensive for the first time in the Pacific, and the Japanese had no choice but to respond. What many have called the turning point on the ground and some have called the real turning point in the Pacific War was about to begin. What followed was a long, bitter struggle for a jungle-infested island that would soon grab the world's attention—Guadalcanal. At stake were the fortunes of the Japanese Empire and the American ability to take the war to the Japanese for the first time.

Confirmation

On July 4, the roar of a heavy aircraft engines rumbled over the oppressively hot, humid, and calm air of Guadalcanal. It had been a backwater for the nearly four centuries since Don Alvaro Mendaña of Spain discovered it on February 7, 1568. Guadalcanal, about 90 miles long and 30 miles wide, is part of the Solomon Islands, an island chain that stretches for about 600 miles from northwest near the island of New Britain to the southeast astride the equator. The climate in this part of the world is almost uninhabitable to human life. Consequently, not many Europeans ever lived there.

The few Australian coastwatchers and natives present wondered from where the sound came. An American B-17 roared overhead. This had occurred many times in the recent months since the Japanese had occupied the island to build an airstrip. Allied planes also appeared to bomb the Japanese seaplane base on Tulagi, just a few miles across the water. Apparent to those on Guadalcanal, this plane was there to do what its predecessors had done before.

But that was not why this B-17 was there. The pilot had been ordered to reconnoiter Guadalcanal to find out if the coastwatchers' report that the Japanese were building an airfield on Guadalcanal was true. The big plane flew over Lunga Point. Below them, the jungle had been cleared, and the unmistakable look of long, straight, hardened airstrips was present. Aircraft could be operated from there. Pressing his intercom button, the pilot ordered his radio operator to send a message to the headquarters of Robert L. Ghormley in New Zealand that the Japanese *were* attempting to make Guadalcanal a direct threat to sever the critical supply lines between the U.S. and Australia. The plans for the Allies to invade Tulagi and Guadalcanal could now proceed in earnest.

Australian coastwatchers confirmed the plane's report on July 6 to Allied headquarters in Australia. Indeed, the Japanese were building an airstrip there. If the Americans needed any more reasons to invade Guadalcanal, they now had plenty of justification. If the Japanese placed aircraft on Guadalcanal, the long, tenuous supply lines between Hawaii, the continental U.S., Australia, and New Zealand would become much longer, more tenuous or even cut.

The first American offensive of the war was about to begin. They gathered whatever forces they could spare, given the demands for troops, ships, and planes in the European Theater. They cobbled together a somewhat rag-tag collection of naval units to act as escort for the troop ships and transports and to provide a shore bombardment. The force, given the sarcastic name of "Operation Shoestring," moved toward the steamy Solomons. Exactly eight months after the devastating defeat at Pearl Harbor and two months after their dramatic victory at Midway, the Americans were about to take the war to the Japanese. Most expected a relatively quick victory, but it is safe to say no one thought the Battle for Guadalcanal would become the longest and one of the bloodiest confrontations in the Pacific War.

CHAPTER 4
A New South Pacific Commander

The streets of Wellington, New Zealand, showed puddles from a recent rainfall as newly appointed Vadm. Robert L. Ghormley's plane circled for its final approach to the airport. The wind sock at the end of the runway hung almost limp, indicating a light wind blew. It was May 21, 1942, and New Zealand, being in the Southern Hemisphere, was just about to start its winter months. This part of New Zealand has a climate somewhat similar to the northern California coastal region. May's temperatures are in the 40s-50s Fahrenheit. Rainfall averages more than three inches annually, and the winds average about 11 miles per hour. Except for no rainfall with light winds that day, May 21 was a typical day, but not for Ghormley. After his aircraft landed, he began the difficult job of commanding the first American offensive in the war.[1]

Born on October 15, 1883, in Portland, Oregon, to the Reverend David Owen Ghormley and Alice Minerva Irwin, Robert Ghormley demonstrated a superior intellect at the University of Idaho and graduated with a Phi Beta Kappa key in 1902. He graduated from Annapolis in 1906 with a ranking of twelfth as a Passed Midshipman (in those days, graduates of the U.S. Naval Academy did not immediately receive the rank of ensign). He immediately began what seemed to be a promising naval career. There were a number of assignments serving in the U.S. Fleet such as flag lieutenant and aide to the commander of the Pacific Fleet 1911-1913, onboard the battleship *Nevada* during World War I. He was promoted to the rank of commander in July 1921. After serving as an aide to the Assistant Secretary of the Navy in 1923-1925, he became executive officer on the battleship *Oklahoma* for the next two years. When promoted to the exalted rank of captain in the 1930s, Ghormley continued building his political connections with his appointment as chief of staff to the commanders in the Battle Force and U.S. Fleet. After a stint in the office of the CNO, he achieved what was and still is the dream of any naval officer—the command of a capital ship. His new command was the battleship *Nevada.* After completing a senior course at the Naval War College in 1938, he achieved flag rank and served as the director of the war plans division and was assistant chief of naval operations.

In August 1940, as the alliance between the British and Americans began taking shape, Ghormley received orders to go to London with two senior officers. Their task was to assess whether the British could last after Hitler's blitz. While there, he displayed his formidable diplomatic and administrative skills and earned the respect of his superiors and his British colleagues.[2]

Nevertheless, dramatic historical events occurred and the U.S. was suddenly at war with the Axis powers. The Americans asked Churchill and the New Zealand government for permission to land Marines in New Zealand in preparation for offensive operations in the Pacific. Rewarding Ghormley for his service in Britain, Adm. King (CNO) appointed Ghormley as Commander, South Pacific Area (COMSOPAC) and promoted him to the lofty rank of vice admiral on April 17, 1942. Adm. Ghormley was a highly respected, widely experienced naval officer with fine diplomatic skills and in possession of an outstanding intellect. During his meeting with King, Ghormley spoke about his new assignment and what was expected of him. King was not the most sanguine about what Ghormley was about to face:

> "You have a large area and a most difficult task, I do not have the tools to give you to carry out the task as it should be, you will establish your headquarters in Auckland, New Zealand, with an advance base at Tongatabu.[3] In time, possibly this fall, 1942, we hope to start an offensive in the South Pacific, you will then probably find it necessary to shift your advance base as the situation demands and move your own headquarters to meet special situations. I would like you to leave Washington in one week."

When he assumed command, Ghormley found that what King had said to him understated the difficulties of this new assignment. In Ghormley's written recollections of his career in the Navy, he says:

> "There was an utter lack of intelligence information available as to the Area or the Japanese forces which might be encountered. My Combat Intelligence Officer, Lt. Cmdr. (Marion O. 'Mike') Cheek, USNR, did a wonderful job in collecting information but had to start from scratch to get the information and train his assistants in their duties. 'Mike' Cheek had been through the beginning of the war at Manila as District Intelligence Officer, and had gotten away from Corregidor on board one of our subs shortly before the fall of Bataan."[4]

At this time of the war, the Americans had little knowledge or intelligence about Japan's capabilities in advanced optics and expert levels of training that enabled the Imperial Japanese Navy to fight at night. The Japanese Navy had perfected tactics for fighting nighttime naval battles, which were far superior to the abilities of any other navy in the world. In a more deadly development, the Japanese had perfected a potent, dependable, high-speed torpedo that could be fired at much longer ranges than any torpedoes the Americans had. In the earlier naval battles with the Japanese, Allied naval officers reported that their torpedoes seemed to be fired from such great distances that they thought them launched from submarines.

Perhaps one question that any inquisitive reader may ask is: Why did King pick Ghormley for the assignment? One requirement for the job was to have impressive diplomatic skills to coordinate the actions of the forces under his command. Also, Ghormley would have to work effectively with the Free French government at their possession of New Caledonia. The Americans needed to establish a base in Nouméa because of its fine harbor and close proximity to the Solomon Islands. Dealing with the French at this time of the war when their homeland had been occupied by the Nazis would be, to say the least, quite tricky and fraught with perilous traps. Nonetheless, Ghormley had demonstrated impressive political skills while working with the British during his assignment in England.

Despite having a superior intellect, Ghormley had never commanded a joint force. In this job, he would have to be aggressive in portraying a positive attitude to the people under his command as well as being assertive for getting what his command needed from the French and from Washington. He had a fine analytical mind, but perhaps this would work against him.

He had not been in the job long before he started to receive letters from his Navy colleagues that could not have helped enforce any optimism in his thought. They "...warned that it was a situation which would prove as difficult as any military situation could be, in view of the fact that the Japanese offensive was well underway and rolling fast, they had gained objectives in the west and Southwest Pacific, while our Naval and Military forces were negligible at that time. This was accented by our shortage of aircraft and shipping facilities to maintain a long line of supply. Some of these officers also knew of our commitments to the European Theater and to our Allies. What Adm. King said was true, but I believe it was much more deadly true than he realized."[5]

✲ ✲ ✲

Ghormley arrived in San Francisco on May 5th and spent three days scrutinizing the logistical and support facilities currently in the South Pacific. He flew to Pearl Harbor on May 8th accompanied by some of his staff he had met in San Francisco. They were Capt. Daniel J. Callaghan, the chief of staff; Col. De Witt Peck, USMC, assistant chief of staff; and Lt. Cmdr. L. Hardy, communications officer. After examining the situation in the South Pacific with Nimitz and his staff, Ghormley left Pearl Harbor on May 11. He had originally planned to visit all the American bases in the South Pacific, but received orders two days after leaving Pearl Harbor to go directly to New Zealand. Nevertheless, he visited Canton Island (Phoenix group, Gilbert Islands), Palmyra atoll, and inspected the 11,000 New Zealand troops on Fiji. While he surveyed the situation on Fiji, the Joint Chiefs of Staff in Washington decided those troops on Fiji were needed to defend their homeland from Japanese invasion, and so they were ordered home.

Nouméa, New Caledonia, was Ghormley's next stop On May 17. Major Gen. Alexander M. Patch, commander of the U.S. Army Americal Division stationed there, met the admiral. After reviewing the circumstances with the general, Ghormley concluded that the conditions ashore were highly unsatisfactory.

Nimitz then ordered Ghormley to orchestrate the occupation of Wallis Island (Uvea)[6] to be used as an advance base for supporting the Americans there.

Recently, Gen. Charles DeGaulle's Free French representative, Contre-Admiral Georges D'Argenlieu, had overthrown the popular Vichy governor of New Caledonia. Gen. Patch had to declare martial law as a result of the populace's displeasure with this takeover. D'Argenlieu possessed a fine record while serving in the French Navy during World War I and felt he deserved some respect. He bristled that the British or Americans never consulted him regarding their plans for French territory in the South Pacific. Consequently, he gave Gen. Patch a tough time. Using his considerable diplomatic skills, Ghormley smoothed the situation over and, according to Nimitz's orders, the Free French force occupied Wallis Island on May 26. The U.S. Marines, under the command of Major Gen. Charles F. B. Price, also moved in as planned.

New Caledonia had rich nickel mines (estimated to have about 30% of the world's reserves). This made that island a highly valued strategic location. Japanese mining companies owned the rights to exploit this valuable mineral and had become an integral part of the island's economic life. They had a high degree of reliance on that island for their nickel needs, and this resource was no longer available to Japanese industry because of the Americans moving in.

The island's strategic value was not lost on the Americans, either. They knew about the intense Japanese interest in the island and desperately wanted to prevent Japanese occupation of that valuable resource. Located about 1,400 miles east of Brisbane, Australia, and 900 miles north of Wellington, New Zealand, New Caledonia possessed a fine harbor able to accommodate large fleets. The establishment of an American base in Nouméa thus became a critical need as plans for South Pacific military operations accelerated.

Making one of his better decisions while in command of the South Pacific Theater, Ghormley picked Radm. John S. McCain as Commander Aircraft, South Pacific (COMAIRSOPAC). McCain was an avid promoter of naval aviation, and one of the highest ranking officers from the "brown shoe" navy. He would control all aircraft forces except for aircraft from New Zealand and would play an important part in the upcoming conquest of Guadalcanal. McCain set up systems to take advantage of coast-watcher reports by New Zealanders and Australians. These reports would play a vital role in defending Allied forces in the Solomons.

Ghormley and McCain wanted to build a base and airfield in the New Hebrides, an island group about 530 miles north of New Caledonia and 610 miles southwest of Guadalcanal. Ghormley also wanted to construct another similar facility in the Ellice Islands, located about 650 miles north of the Fijis. Ghormley argued that the critical locations of these islands made ideal places to set up to protect his supply lines. He submitted his request to Washington, and it was rejected. There were barely enough resources to set up a base in Nouméa, let alone for the construction of more bases at other locations. After the First Marine Division, under the command of Gen. Alexander A. Vandegrift, arrived on June 14, Ghormley took formal command of the South Pacific Theater five days later.

Less than a month after taking command, Ghormley was responsible for the first American offensive in the Pacific when he received orders to invade Guadalcanal and Tulagi. Upon arriving in Wellington, New Zealand, Ghormley noted:

> "After this long trip, from Pearl Harbor through the South Pacific Area, my first reactions were, the tremendous size of the South Pacific; the great distance between bases; and with existing shortage of aircraft for overseas search and patrol, the ease with which enemy raiders could slip through our poorly defended lines and strike at our line of communications to New Zealand and Australia; the large size of many of the islands, and the high mountain ranges of most of the islands in the Western part of the South Pacific area; the primitive state of native civilization, the total lack of harbor facilities or any other facilities at the various

> bases; the lack of communications by cable or radio; the long distance from our base of supplies, either Hawaii or the Mainland; the lack of a Naval striking force and naval escort vessels; the shortage of aircraft of all types. I feel that these facts were not appreciated by our planners in Washington, in drawing up their plans for setting up the necessary lines of communication and making provision for transport, or for base and airfield construction. *An outstanding fact was the failure to take proper cognizance of the time element in providing material for the construction, of bases and airfields, and for allowing the actual time for accomplishing construction work, under various and adverse conditions."* (Ghormley's emphasis).

With a planned invasion date of August 1, Ghormley continued his dialog with Washington and tried to convince his superiors that he did not have the resources he thought he needed to be successful. But there were no more resources to be had. Therefore, he reconciled himself to make do with what he had been given. Nimitz sent an operation order on July 10 for Ghormley to assume strategic command of the Guadalcanal-Tulagi invasion and move his headquarters to New Caledonia-New Hebrides. On August 1, he moved his headquarters from Wellington to Nouméa and took up residence on the submarine tender *Argonne*, built in 1920 and not the most efficient place for an admiral to have as his flag ship. At this time, he made no requests of the local French government for permission to set up his headquarters ashore, where his staff and he would be in far more comfortable surroundings.

It was now clear that Ghormley's skepticism over the upcoming operation was growing in intensity. After conferring with MacArthur when they met on July 10, the two men shared an almost equal level of misgivings about the upcoming Guadalcanal-Tulagi invasion. They had one conviction—without further resources and higher priority for the invasion, its chances for success were dubious at best. The admiral's finely-tuned analytical mind now saw many difficulties: (1) maintaining tenuous supply lines in what he perceived to be overly long distances, (2) the lack of the needed forward bases to keep the supplies flowing and the means to build those bases, (3) a scarcity of trained troops to carry out the invasion to capture Guadalcanal and Tulagi, and (4) the high risk of rushing forward with the operation before he thought everything would be ready. An objective observer of Ghormley's behavior at this time indicates he was having problems by seeing the glass as half-empty. The number and seriousness of the problems he thought he faced overwhelmed any thinking directed at seeing how the operation could succeed.

Ghormley repeatedly requested more resources from Washington; they went unheeded. He undoubtedly felt Washington did not fully appreciate his needs despite what he thought of the higher priority requirements for the European Theater. Under the circumstances, he must not have been in the most positive mood as he faced his new and difficult mission.[7]

✲ ✲ ✲

Meanwhile, political warfare between the American Armed Forces senior commanders raged trying to decide where they should strike next. On June 29, Adm. King proposed that the U.S. Navy should lead an offensive in the southern Solomon Islands. The next day, Gen. Marshall and King reached the compromise that started the planning for an invasion of Guadalcanal and Tulagi, known as Operation Watchtower.

After meeting with MacArthur, both commanders had expressed their reservations about the lack of troops, ships, aircraft, and materiel to invade both the Solomons and New Guinea. Nevertheless, one day later, King and Marshall ordered Ghormley and MacArthur to go ahead with the planning of their respective offensives. Later, after thinking over Ghormley's objections and realizing Ghormley probably only had enough forces to get ashore but not enough resources to sustain them in that remote part of the Pacific, King moved Watchtower's date back six days from August 1, 1942 (Saturday), to August 7 (Friday) to allow more time to gather additional resources.

CHAPTER 5
A Tiger in the Fold

Another admiral entered the stage of this upcoming operation who would have a dramatic effect on the battles to come. Richmond Kelly Turner acquired the nickname "Terrible" Turner during his career in the Navy. He would play an important part in the Guadalcanal invasion, and his decisions would also become the subject of many debates by naval historians for years to come.

Turner was born the seventh of eight children to Enoch Turner and Laura Francis Kelly in East Portland, Oregon, on May 27, 1885. His father was the sixth son and eleventh of John Turner's 12 offspring. Photographs of Turner's predecessors on his father's side show that they were a tall and upright-standing clan with straight black or brown hair and dark eyes; some displayed a hooked nose. They were physically sturdy and lived long lives. One ancestor who had come to America from England in the 17th century lived to be 104 and died in 1760. Turner's grandfather lived to a ripe old age of 91 and a great uncle lived to 102.[1]

Turner's first name, Richmond, was his mother's brother's name, Richmond Kelly. A family legend said that the name came from the Duke of Richmond[2], who sympathized with the American colonists fighting for independence from the British and for Irish independence. Thus, the name Richmond was carried forward in the Kelly family for years as a symbol of honor. His mother firmly supported the causes of Irish independence during her life. His sisters and brothers called him Rich or Kelly. The name Kelly stuck, so that was what nearly everyone called him for the rest of his life.[3]

The Turner family moved to California when Kelly was a small boy, and he received his primary and secondary education mainly in Stockton, California. He was a bright and studious youth who impressed his teachers. His family never accumulated much wealth, so when he chose how to further his education after high school, Kelly applied to the Naval Academy in Annapolis. He knew he could get a fine education there while not requiring his family to spend any significant funds for him. He entered the academy in the 1904 academic year and became a midshipman on June 13, 1904. By this time, Turner had grown to a man resembling his ancestors: erect, tall and slim-built—six-feet-one-and-three-quarters inches tall, weighing 150 pounds—with black hair and a handsome, sober countenance.[4]

While at Annapolis, Turner received instruction from some of the most qualified instructors ever to teach at the academy. To demonstrate the outstanding quality of these men, four became CNOs, and 23 became flag officers. The naval victories in World War I, World War II, and the Korean Conflict are directly attributable to the high quality of instruction the naval officers who served in these conflicts received while attending the academy.[5]

Turner graduated as a passed midshipman in the Class of 1908 with an overall class rank of fifth. After two years, he attained the rank of Ensign. When Turner achieved the rank of senior lieutenant in 1910, he ranked first for the class of 1908 and would remain ranked first for the next 25 listings in the *Naval Register*.[6]

While attending Annapolis, he had his first interaction with Lt. Ernest J. King, the future CNO and Turner's future boss. This happened during Turner's summer cruise between his second class (junior) and first class (senior) years on the cruiser *Olympia*. King had served as an ordnance and gunnery instructor at the academy and had been temporarily assigned to the *Olympia* for the summer cruise. The young naval officer earned Turner's respect for his intelligence, professionalism, and rigorous emphasis on discipline. Turner's naval career was obviously influenced by his encounter with King, particularly when one examines the reputation Kelly Turner would acquire in his future naval career.

After reaching the rank of lieutenant commander, he commanded the destroyer *Mervine*. While commanding this vessel, he started to accumulate a reputation as being tough-minded, hard-working, highly respected, brilliant, and a by-the-book officer. Some of the comments by some of his subordinates confirm the veracity of that observation:

- "brilliant, forceful, theoretical mind"
- "a personal hard worker"
- "refuses to delegate authority"
- "impatience and intolerance with other points of view"
- "a detail artist"
- "a driver not a leader"
- "In my opinion he had no weakness, unless you would call his driving urgency one."

When Adm. George Dyer conducted his research writing his biography of Turner, *The Amphibians Came to Conquer*, he asked the officers then alive who had served under Turner's command on the *Mervine* to offer observations of their then-commander. Some of those comments include that their ship was not a "happy ship," while another said Turner was "rank poison" to me. When asked to rank Turner by the scale of (1) tops, (2) quite all right, (3) so, so, and (4) nuts, two officers, who had served with him the longest, placed in the first category, and two put him in the fourth.[7]

While second-in-command to Turner on the collier turned tender, the *Jason*, in the Asiatic Fleet, one of Turner's executive officers offered the following comments:

> "Kelly Turner had a strong mind and lots of drive. He was up at dawn and still going strong at ten that night. If he had an objective in mind, he would seek to reach it, exploring any and all ways. He would accept no half-way job of any kind from an officer subordinate. He drove, and would not listen to excuses, and certainly not always to reason. You either met his standards or got to hell out of the *way.*
>
> His primary weakness was his lack of consideration and cooperation down the ladder to the wardroom.

> He was a bold seaman and an excellent ship handler. The *Jason* was a big old tub with inadequate power. Turner took her into holes on the East Coast of Luzon, which required a very high degree of skill. The *Jason* had no sonic depth finder, and the charts were old and inadequate, but he dodged coral heads adeptly and frequently.
>
> The *Jason* had good discipline. The men got a fair shake at mast, but Kelly Turner was no molly-coddler.
>
> He was about as far from a beach hound as one could get. He played golf with me and with Russ (Russell H.) Ihrig (Skipper of the *Heron)* on week-ends. He was a long iron hitter. With a number 7 iron, he could drive nearly 200 yards."

One of the other executive officers who served under Turner for the longest time on the *Jason* offered the following:

> "Before I reported for duty on the *Jason,* the advice to me was to watch out for Commander Turner. He was a Son-of-a-bitch.
>
> Kelly Turner turned out to be a close approximation to what I consider an officer and gentleman should be. One who could lead in any direction. He had no weak points, but instead a variety of strong ones which would only come in focus as occasion required...
>
> To the enlisted personnel, he had for them the aura of the master about him...For the officers, he was the gentleman's gentleman...Hence, he never once lost the respect of any of the personnel he came in contact with, officers or men."

Turner's commanding officer, Adm. Mark Bristol, took a less critical view in his annual fitness reports. While recognizing his weaknesses, on which he gave average ratings for patience and self-control, Bristol gave Turner high marks in most other qualities and penned these remarks:

- "Active mind and desire to be doing something is very gratifying."
- "A very good mind which he keeps working with a very desirable imagination. He never hesitates to undertake anything."

This ambivalence about Turner would continue throughout his career. Nonetheless, he continued up the Navy's promotional ladder, receiving high marks from his superiors.[8]

On October 1, 1933, and befitting the future of naval officers who would be flag officers in World War II, Cmdr. Turner became the executive officer of the carrier *Saratoga*, then one-half of the total carrier strength the United States Navy. The other carrier was the *Lexington*. Another carrier existed; the collier turned into carrier *Langley,* but was not considered to be capable of combat operations. Here, Turner would get the required exposure to naval aviation.

His term as the carrier's second-in-command was noteworthy because of Capt. Rufus F. Zogbaum's, the *Saratoga*'s skipper and Turner's commanding officer, who wrote about Turner in his last fitness report before Turner became a captain:

> "No Commanding Officer could ask for a better Executive...Recently selected for captain and should go far in the Naval Service."

Now, Cmdr. Turner was ready to move in the rarefied circles of those on their way to flag rank.[9]

✲ ✲ ✲

Appointed to captain in 1936 at the age of 51 with 29 years of his naval career behind him, Turner's next assignments included the needed work to achieve flag rank. The officer who relieved him wrote:

> "I went to the Naval War College as a student in June 1937. Turner was Head of the Strategy Section of the College Staff. I felt that I learned a great deal from him during the year ending May 1938.
>
> I remained on the War College Staff until late May 1940, serving the last year as Head of the Strategy Section.
>
> This experience was invaluable to me in the commands I held in World War II and later. I observed convincing evidence during my tour at the College of the outstanding contributions Adm. Turner had made to the course of instruction."[10]

Two new carriers, the *Wasp* and the *Ranger*, were about to be commissioned, and Turner was being considered to command one of these ships. Although he firmly believed that naval aviation would be the way future naval wars would be fought, his thoughts about remaining in the aviation branch of the Navy turned serious when he considered the fastest path to achieving flag rank. While serving on the *Saratoga* and on the staff of the Aircraft Battle Force, his acerbic command style stepped on many toes and caused some animosity among fellow officers who had decided naval aviation was in their future. He never was inclined to win a popularity contest. That was not his style. So he knew he was moving back into the "black shoe" navy where guns, not airplanes, were the primary weapons. When he was offered the command of one of the two new carriers, he turned it down. However, whether he would stay in naval aviation or not was rendered moot when the results of his physical examination said he could only fly when accompanied by another pilot. Thus he was given the command of a heavy cruiser, the 10,000-ton *Astoria*.[11]

Like his other assignments, the opinions of others who served under his command varied but were consistent. The remarks by the *Astoria*'s department heads include "thoroughness," "brilliant mind," "long hours," and "hard work." One officer said he was "very strict, very impatient, intolerant of any mistakes, sharp tongued" but "fair." Another officer stated Turner was "easily understood, and when his requirements were definitely understood, easily followed." Still another officer said Turner was "exceptionally smart, but by the same token he expected everyone else to be in the same category."[12]

✲ ✲ ✲

After Capt. Preston B. Haines relieved him of the *Astoria*'s command, Turner moved to Washington to enter the rarefied atmosphere of the Navy's center of power. This assignment, as the Director of War Plans, almost guaranteed him a promotion to flag rank. Ample precedent supported this assumption. Other men who served in the post he was about to take over such as William R. Shoemaker, William H. Standley, Frank H. Schofield, Montgomery Meigs Taylor, William S. Pye, and Royal E. Ingersoll all achieved flag rank. After Turner became the newest Director of War Plans on October 19, 1940, the December 1940 Selection Board chose him to be promoted to rear admiral. On January 8, 1941, a special presidential fiat made it official, although he was an admiral in name only with the salary of a captain.

When Turner arrived in Washington, names that were to become well-known in future events occupied powerful posts in the Navy: Secretary of the Navy Frank Knox and Adm. Harold R. Stark as CNO. The largest part of the U.S. Fleet was in Pearl Harbor under the command of Adm. James O. Richardson who would be replaced by Husband E. Kimmel. Rapidly moving events during 1941 would vastly change the Atlantic Squadron, now relegated to a patrol function close to America's eastern and Gulf Coast shorelines. The Germans occupied France and threatened Western civilization like no force since Attila the Hun.[13] Turner was right in the middle of all that would transpire.

Turner's reputation for tough-minded decision making stood him well in the hurly-burly infighting of the Washington military. As the Germans became more powerful and invaded the Soviet Union in June 1941, the Nazi threat was more real than ever before. The British pleaded for American help, and political leaders, led by President Franklin D. Roosevelt, tried their best to do what they could. Congress passed the Two Ocean Navy Act in July 1940 and the Selective Service Act became law on September 16, 1940. America was getting ready to go to war, and the Navy, by necessity, had to follow.[14]

When Turner reported to CNO Stark, five major war plans existed known as Rainbow One through Five.

> *Rainbow One*'s objective was to guard the Western Hemisphere, to stop any violation of the Monroe Doctrine, and protect the vital interests of the U.S., its possessions, and its sea trade, wherever these might be.
>
> *Rainbow Two* included *Rainbow One* plus overcoming any enemy forces in the Pacific, support the interests of Pacific Democratic Powers (primarily Australia and New Zealand), while avoiding any significant involvement in Continental Europe.
>
> *Rainbow Three* again included the objectives of *Rainbow One* and added protection and secure control of vital interests of the U.S. in the western Pacific.
>
> *Rainbow Four* also included *Rainbow One* with no help of either allies or neutrals. Allied areas in the Western Hemisphere would be occupied, and the Western Hemisphere would be defended no farther south than the Brazilian bulge. If circumstances warranted such action, fall back to Hawaii in the Pacific.
>
> *Rainbow Five* initially projected U.S. Armed Forces to the eastern Atlantic and for decisively defeating Germany or Italy or both by invading either or both of the African or

European continents as rapidly as possible, consistent with the mission of *Rainbow One*. Subsequent drafts emphasized that winning the war in Europe was the primary objective.[15]

After much debate involving all the American military services, Rainbow Five eventually became the plan guiding initial planning after Pearl Harbor. And Kelly Turner was right in the middle of those arguments, many of which were quite heated. Kelly's personality fit in quite well.

By the time Turner had fully ensconced himself in his new job, the Battle of the Atlantic raged with the British hanging on with their last breath. Nazi U-boats sank hundreds of thousands of tons of shipping that tried to keep the beleaguered island people in the war. Although Hitler had abandoned Operation Sea Lion, to invade the British Isles after suffering defeat in the Battle of Britain, his war against the British continued unabated.

Turner played an important role in establishing the U.S. Navy's role in the Atlantic. He advised Stark, on January 17, 1941, that the U.S. Navy would be able to escort convoys from the east coast to Scotland by the first of April. Turner drafted a memorandum that Secretary of the Navy Frank Knox signed on March 20, 1941. This was 22 months after the European war began. If senior naval command made the decision to send naval forces into the Atlantic, the duties of American escorts were to confront the Nazis. The memo ended with the words:

> "Our Navy is ready to undertake it [convoying] as soon as directed, but could do it more effectively were we to have six to eight weeks for special training."

Not much time transpired before a German submarine sank an American merchant ship, the *Robin Moore*, on May 21, 1941. It took about two months before CINCLANT issued the orders to begin escorting convoys between the U.S. East Coast and Iceland. Without a declaration of war, the American Atlantic Fleet was in a shooting war by September 16. Later, Turner stated that if the Germans had torpedoed [a ship] in the Pacific, the Americans would have been better prepared for the Japanese attack on Pearl Harbor on December 7.[16]

Turner's participation in the mainstream changes in the Navy leading up to World War II continued when he was a member of the American party on board the British battleship *Prince of Wales*. From August 10 through August 15, 1941, the American and British met to discuss strategy and the needs of Britain, so that nation could stay in the war. At this historical meeting between Prime Minister Churchill and President Roosevelt, they signed the *Atlantic Charter* thus sealing the constantly escalating cooperation between the two democracies.[17]

✲ ✲ ✲

Turner was among those with the foresight to realize that this next war would be the largest and most complex conflict ever fought. The current command structure that had won past wars was no longer relevant. A new way to run the war was clearly needed. On January 28, 1942, the high command gave to Turner and his counterpart in the Department of the Army and a name soon to be thrust into the limelight, Brig. Gen. Dwight D. Eisenhower, the politically hot issue of recommending what the new command structure should look like.

Eisenhower recommended establishing a 15-member joint general staff reporting directly to the

President and to be chaired by a chief of staff responsible only to the President. The general staff's duties included coordination of operations and logistics, responsibility for strategy, and deployment of forces. Command of forces would be under Theater Commanders.

Turner proposed a Joint Chiefs of Staff committee that included the Chief of Naval Operations, Army Chief of Staff, U.S. Fleet Commander-in-Chief, and the Commanding Gen. of the Army Field Forces. He also recommended a joint training system for both the Army and Navy. He saw this as an important ingredient to prepare commanders from both services to command joint operations that would later become the standard *modus operandi* in future battles. The third part of Turner's proposal was that command responsibility should be assigned in each campaign area to a commanding officer of the service that had the primary expertise and relevance to expected complications.

The Joint Board accepted neither proposal when they presented them to the President on March 16, 1942. Perhaps circumspect of Eisenhower's proposal (which also reflected Marshall's thinking) and perhaps believing that it might weaken his own rights as commander-in-chief to direct the war's conduct, Roosevelt agreed in due course with Turner's proposal. As the war progressed, all three parts of Turner's plan became a reality. Nevertheless, Roosevelt also accepted part of Eisenhower's proposal by appointing Adm. William D. Leahy as chief of staff to the President in July 1942 with neither command authority nor staff. Turner thus became the "father" of what later became the Joint Chiefs of Staff.[18]

✲ ✲ ✲

The actual war in the Pacific meshed with prewar planning done by the Americans for fighting in this vast expanse of water. The Pacific Ocean is speckled by tiny island groups, which made amphibious warfare an indispensable part of naval strategy. The U.S. Marines had practiced amphibious landings in the domestic U.S. and in the Caribbean Sea during the years following World War I. Also, the French-British debacle at Gallipoli (Turkey 1915) became the subject of intense study at the Navy War College at Newport, Rhode Island. The lessons learned from that unfortunate part of military history were:

1. Provide clear command channels to all forces of all Services and arms involved. A single *forceful* (my emphasis) overall commander is mandatory.

2. Highly detailed orders must be issued and sent to all levels in the command to make certain everyone clearly understands and believes in the mission's objectives, who does what when, and the location of the coordinating levels of command.

3. Attack with sufficient forces and only when you are ready.

4. Make sure supplies and equipment are stowed aboard ship close to the order they will be used or needed ashore. This became known as combat loading (L.I.F.O. or Last In, First Out).

One can assume that Turner learned these principles while a student during three years at the Naval War College. The potential that what happened at Gallipoli could happen at the upcoming Guadalcanal invasion undoubtedly disturbed him. Both Nimitz in 1923 and King in 1932 had attended the War College and most likely took the lessons to heart when both applied what they had learned and implemented the clear command channels and forceful commanders provisions throughout the war.

As far as Turner was concerned, two more lessons needed to be put into place:

1. Secure lines of communication to the combat area.
2. Command of the sea and air surrounding the combat zone.

After attaining these prerequisites, the following becomes absolutely essential:

1. Pick landing areas favorable to the Navy and topography favorable to the Marines and/or Army.
2. Mislead the enemy about the intended landing area for the maximum possible time.
3. Prepare the landing area with air bombing and naval gunfire so the troops landing on the hostile beach can do so with confidence.
4. Once the troops have landed and taken the beachhead, make sure artillery is rapidly placed ashore and takes to the high ground to allow a rapid build up of materiel.
5. After accomplishing these objectives, the attacker can anticipate a shift from amphibious warfare to ground conflict.

A Navy publication, *Fleet Tactical Publication No. 167*, later contained all these provisions and much more. It became the bible for amphibious warfare during World War II with much of what it contained being applied to similar operations today. Although it was published in 1941, much of what was written there would be severely tested at Guadalcanal.[19]

✲ ✲ ✲

Turner was in the middle of the work to initiate amphibious operations against the Japanese and following the prewar planning designed to fight the Japanese based on *War Plan Orange* and its ultimate successor, *Rainbow Five*. The Navy began gathering whatever ships could be used to transport the needed troops and materiel for invading the islands in the South Pacific. But landing craft—the ships and boats needed to deposit troops and materiel on the beaches—were in severely short supply. The likelihood of having suitable docking facilities in any potentially hostile landing area was essentially nonexistent. With the pressure on for a landing either on Continental Europe or North Africa, arguments intensified over where these scarce craft should be sent.

Anyone who drew a straight line on a Mercator projection of the Pacific Ocean between the continental U.S., Hawaii, and northern Australia could observe that the line goes right through Guadalcanal. King argued that the Japanese could also read maps and came to the conclusion that

Guadalcanal was the critical place to control the 7,000 mile American supply line to that continent. Therefore, Guadalcanal was where the Americans would launch their first offensive action against the Japanese. Turner was a powerful advocate for the required landing craft, and he ultimately outlasted his counterparts. The American-British debate about where to begin the war in the European Theater also helped. The British wanted to invade North Africa while the Americans wanted to invade Continental Europe. While that squabbling continued, King and the Navy, with Turner's effective debating, won the day. Operation Watchtower (Guadalcanal) would get the landing craft and transports it needed to invade Guadalcanal in August 1942.[20]

All that was needed was to assemble the Watchtower invasion force and get it to the Solomon Islands. Adm. Richmond Kelly Turner was just the man for the job. He was the only man with flag rank who clearly understood the problems and intricacies of amphibious warfare. King made Turner available to CINCPAC for a new assignment on May 20, 1942. On July 18, 1942, Turner took command of the South Pacific Amphibious Force and began gathering forces scattered all over the South Pacific and on the West Coast and routing them to Guadalcanal. It would take all Turner had in him to organize and assure the operation's success.[21]

Part 2: Invasion

CHAPTER 6
Fijian Rendezvous

Admirals Fletcher and Turner and their staffs met on July 5 through 9 to set the strategies needed for Watchtower. This was the largest invasion force America had ever assembled up to that time. It had to be brought together from locations including San Diego, Pearl Harbor, and New Zealand. The best location for the invasion fleet to gather seemed to be the Fiji Islands. The advantages of that island group were: (1) It was a British possession that was not threatened by a Japanese invasion. (2) It was out of Japanese bomber range. (3) The slower ships in Turner's fleet had the shortest distance to travel from Wellington, New Zealand (about 1,600 miles vs. 3,000 miles from Pearl Harbor or 5,000 miles from San Diego). Therefore, all ships could rendezvous at the same time. (4) There were sheltered harbors and seas large and deep enough to accommodate the naval warships. The staffs also decided that, since these varied commands had never worked together before and the Americans had never attempted an amphibious landing on such a large scale, a necessary rehearsal for the landings would be held in the Koro Sea (Fiji).

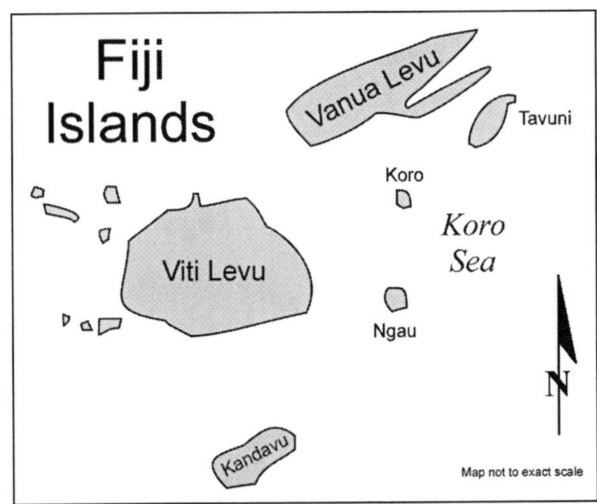

Guadalcanal Invasion Fleet Rendezvous

The memory of the trip from Pearl Harbor to Auckland weighed heavily on Turner's mind. He was impatient to take command of his combat assignment as an admiral. His plane left Pearl Harbor in normally fine Hawaiian weather, thus enforcing his optimism that he would soon be in New Zealand. But his enthusiasm waned when bad weather further fed the impatience that was so much a part of him. He was forced to spend an extra day on Canton Island and another day on Tongatabu in the Tonga Islands. Naturally driven to not waste any time, he reviewed the status of construction projects currently underway near Wellington and concluded, in a thorough four-page report he sent to Adm. Raymond Spruance, Nimitz's chief of staff, that "most of the work can be done within the next four months." After suffering another delay because of bad weather that forced him to take a roundabout way from Fiji, his plane finally landed in Auckland on July 15. It had taken him one week to get there from Pearl Harbor on a trip that should have taken just three days.

At long last, he met with Ghormley and told his commander that his force could pull off the ticklish operation. Ghormley told him the invasion date was to be August 7, 1942. Turner flew south to Wellington and formally took command aboard his flagship, the transport *McCawley*.[1]

Turner's command was the first balanced amphibious force the U.S. Navy had ever assembled. The pillars of the force's strength were the First Marine Division, commanded by Maj. Gen. Vandegrift, 13 transports, and five cargo vessels.[2] The fleet under Turner's command included:[3]

Turner's Invasion Fleet, August 7, 1942

Ship Type	**Ship's Name**
Heavy Cruisers	*Australia, Canberra, Chicago, Vincennes, Quincy, Astoria*
Light Cruisers	*Hobart, San Juan*
Destroyers	*Selfridge, Patterson, Ralph Talbot, Mugford, Jarvis, Blue, Helm, Henley, Bagley, Hull, Dewey, Ellet, Wilson, Monssen, Buchanan*
Minesweepers	*Hopkins, Trever, Zane, Southard, Hovey*
Transports	*Zeilin, Crescent City, President Hayes, President Adams, President Jackson, Neville, Hunter Liggett, American Legion, Barnett, McCawley*, George F. Elliott*
Destroyer-Transports:	*Little, McKean, Gregory, Colhoun*
Cargo Ships	*Alhena, Betelgeuse, Bellatrix, Formahaut, Libra*

**—McCawley—Turner's flagship*

Turner's task force was a large one—the largest thus far in the war—but it could not be expected to do the job on its own. Before describing the force that had to provide air support, another commander, an Englishman, became part of the action at Guadalcanal.

Radm. Victor A.C. Crutchley of the Royal Navy commanded the warships escorting transports and cargo ships. These included the cruisers *Australia*, *Canberra*, *Chicago*, and *Hobart*, the destroyers *Selfridge*, *Patterson*, *Ralph Talbot*, *Mugford*, *Jarvis*, *Blue*, *Helm*, *Henley*, and *Bagley*. He had been awarded the Victoria Cross in 1918 for his courage at the Battle of Ostend during World War I. He also possessed the Distinguished Service Cross for bravery commanding the British battlecruiser *Warspite* during the abortive British attempt to invade Norway at Narvik (April 8, 1940).

The Royal Australian Navy (RAN) had come into existence about 30 years earlier and did not have any officers with enough sea experience to have admirals of its own. The Royal Navy agreed to loan Crutchley to the RAN, which appointed him as the commander of the Australian squadron.

His appointment was a source of some controversy in that the British were not the primary naval fighting force in the Pacific. Adm. King was never in favor of having the Royal Navy command any American naval force but had to give way to some political realities. The Americans needed the British to carry the war to the Nazis in the European Theater. The one price they had to pay was to give some token recognition that the British were an ally in the Pacific as well. The Royal Australian Navy contributed heavy cruisers *Australia* and *Canberra*, and light cruiser *Hobart*. The Americans needed them all. Turner also wanted Crutchley to be his second-in-command, which Crutchley reluctantly accepted.[4,5] Crutchley would become a controversial figure for some of his command decisions in the upcoming debacle off Savo Island.

✲ ✲ ✲

One of the tenets that Turner developed while the Navy's Director of War Plans and for a successful amphibious invasion was the need for air support. None of the Army Air Force planes currently in the South Pacific had the range to provide it. Besides, King would never allow the Army or MacArthur any control over what was strictly a navy show. So it was up to the Navy to bring air power to Guadalcanal. The losses of the *Lexington* at Coral Sea and the *Yorktown* at Midway meant that Navy carrier strength had been whittled down to only three operational carriers in the Pacific—the *Saratoga, Wasp*, and *Enterprise*. The *Hornet* was at Pearl Harbor for repairs and not yet available. Thus, the three operational carriers and their crews answered the call to duty under the command of Adm. Jack Fletcher. The newly constructed battleship *North Carolina* joined Fletcher's task force to provide more powerful AA support and to combat Japanese battleships known to be at Rabaul (500 miles to the northeast) and Truk (about 1,400 miles north-northeast of Guadalcanal) that might come out to destroy the Guadalcanal landings.

From the beginnings of Fletcher's command, controversy became the natural order of things. He was the same rank as Leigh Noyes, commander of the Task Group that had the carrier *Wasp*, but Noyes had seniority over Fletcher. In an attempt to resolve this situation, Nimitz requested Fletcher be promoted to vice admiral on May 10 and again on June 21, 1942. Fletcher had the most combat experience of any American admiral in the Pacific, and Nimitz continued to push for Fletcher's promotion when he sent the promotion request to King for the third time on June 28, 1942. Finally, Fletcher received his third star on July 15 and named commander of the expeditionary force with Noyes reporting to Fletcher as Commander Carrier Aircraft of the Expeditionary Force.[6]

✲ ✲ ✲

The brilliantly bright Hawaiian morning sun and stunningly clear blue sky flooded Fletcher's senses as the *Saratoga* left her moorings in Pearl Harbor and slowly and majestically made her way down the narrow channel toward the open sea. After guiding the U.S. Navy's fortunes in the two most significant naval battles thus far fought in the Pacific, Fletcher was a weary man but refused to let his commander (Nimitz) know this. Nimitz needed him again, and Halsey was still in the hospital recovering from a severe case of dermatitis. On July 7, Adm. Fletcher was going to war again, although many thought the *Saratoga* was on her way to another training mission.

The big carrier along with the four heavy cruisers *Astoria, Vincennes, Minneapolis*, and *New Orleans*, seven destroyers, three oilers, and four old former four-stack destroyers converted into fast transports, headed out to sea under secret orders on a southward course. About 80 miles out of Pearl Harbor, the *Saratoga*'s Air Group found their home ship that afternoon. The air group was a formidable contingent with 37 SBDs, 16 TBFs, and 37 F4Fs for a total of 90 planes.

The next morning, the four cruisers fired their eight-inch and five-inch guns at Cape Kahae on the southern tip of the big island of Hawaii to practice what they would be doing when they reached

Guadalcanal. Some of the aircraft flew as observers for the cruisers' fire. The practice exercises ended later that afternoon.

To the surprise of many, the task force changed course to a southwesterly heading of 210° and began the trip to Guadalcanal instead of turning back to Pearl Harbor. The new destination became the subject of endless rumors as usually happens aboard a ship whenever it changes directions. After three days of sailing, Palmyra Island appeared on the horizon. The equator was near, and the crew prepared for the ancient ceremony for all those who would cross the equator for the first time. As always, a good time was had by all as the "Pollywogs" joined thousands of their predecessors to be crowned by King Neptune as "shellbacks."

It was there that the *Saratoga*'s air crew first learned of their upcoming mission. They and their comrades on the *Wasp* would attack ground targets to support the invasion troops as they went ashore on Guadalcanal and Tulagi as well as fly Combat Air Patrol (CAP).

At about 12 p.m. on July 12, Fletcher's task force crossed northeast of Canton Island. Thus far, the weather stayed normal for that part of the Pacific Ocean. The sizzling heat and oppressive humidity prompted numerous squalls and rough seas. On July 15, Fletcher marked time as he waited for Noyes and the *Wasp* task force to catch up south of the Tongan island of Tongatabu. A gale battered the carrier, and the men who had not served on her before learned that she was not the easiest ship on which to ride out a storm.

Ghormley released his operations plan for the Guadalcanal-Tulagi invasion on July 16 and surprised Fletcher by naming him tactical commander of the expeditionary force (Task Force 61). The flabbergasted Fletcher had no idea what Turner—commander of the SOPAC Amphibious Force (Task Force 61.1)—planned for landing the troops ashore or what was needed to prepare the landing areas with shore and air bombardment. He could not participate in any planning since he rode out the continuous mid-Pacific storms while Turner prepared his landing force in New Zealand. He also could not meet with Noyes while he and the *Wasp* struggled to make their way to Fiji. Fletcher hoped that at least he would be able to meet with both men at Fiji and work out the details there.[7]

During their journey from Pearl Harbor to Fiji, a nearly continuous stream of unfortunate mishaps plagued the *Saratoga*'s air crew. Not only did the pilots have to overcome a pitching deck when taking off or landing, mechanical failures and other calamities continued to beleaguer their aircraft. An example of these maladies was the death of Machinist Mate, 2nd Class John I. Brunnell when the *Saratoga*'s rolling caused him to be thrown into a spinning propeller. He died of massive head injuries, and the crew of the *Saratoga* buried him at sea with full military honors.[8]

As it would turn out, these incidents were common to Fletcher's task force. Since the Pearl Harbor attack, American pilots and aircraft were subjected to wartime conditions for the first time. Therefore, the time that onboard mechanics had to maintain the aircraft in maximum flying efficiency was significantly reduced. Aircrews had to practice carrier air operations in far less time than was available during peacetime. War games that senior officers planned at the convenience of the available forces were one thing; real wartime conditions never offered such a luxury. During the first months of the war, American naval aviation had to learn how to make sure planes kept flying and pilots performed their wartime assignments. The Japanese had more time to iron out the kinks before Pearl Harbor. It was "on the job" training for the Americans as the pressure to defeat an implacable enemy rapidly grew.

During his command at Coral Sea and Midway, Fletcher observed that American pilots lacked proper training under actual combat conditions to coordinate their attacks among the various groups—fighters, dive-bombers, and torpedo planes—not only from the same carrier, but between groups from different carriers. Because of the vehement arguments between the battleship admirals and the carrier admirals before the war, the carrier was not regarded as the dominant capital ship that would carry the fight to the enemy. Pearl Harbor changed that balance in favor of the carrier forever. Nevertheless, the struggle between the two factions in the U.S. Navy continued and tactics for fighting a naval aviation war had not yet coalesced. The Japanese had already developed these tactics, and thus they had more time to perfect them than the Americans.

After observing American naval aviators perform their duties under actual combat conditions and the uneven results they achieved, Fletcher believed that the American naval aviators were still not ready to confront and dominate the Japanese at sea. When his carriers would encounter the Japanese in the upcoming struggles around the waters of the Solomon Islands, these impressions and opinion would dictate his decisions and thus provoke more controversy about his fitness to command carrier fleets in future battles.[9]

The Wasp *and* Enterprise *Join Task Force 61*

The low-lying hills surrounding the sheltered and highly valued San Diego Harbor silently looked down on the great carrier *Wasp* as she slowly steamed toward the harbor mouth and the open Pacific. Radm. Leigh Noyes, who had served with Kelly Turner as Director of Communication in 1940, had little or no senior-level combat command proficiency like many admirals in the U.S. Navy. Twenty years of peacetime was the primary reason. Despite being just three numbers higher than Jack Fletcher in the Navy's seniority list and Fletcher's classmate at Annapolis, Noyes lacked Fletcher's combat experience. Thus, he was Fletcher's subordinate in the upcoming Guadalcanal invasion. His mission was to escort five transports and join Fletcher's *Saratoga* group southeast of Christmas Island.

Adm. Noyes' orders to sail on July 1 arrived on June 27; the *Wasp* left San Diego on June 30. Noyes commanded one of the three carrier groups in the Guadalcanal invasion, and it had all the ships the Navy could spare in those resource sparse days. On the evening of July 1, the *Wasp* met the heavy cruiser *Quincy*, the light antiaircraft cruiser *San Juan*, seven destroyers, and the five transports off San Diego. Noyes assembled his ships and ordered his task force on a course of 230° at a speed of 13 knots. The carrier took her place to the rear of the ships formation to make it easier to conduct flight operations. Some destroyers were used to recover pilots who might be forced to ditch their planes in the ocean. The *Wasp*'s captain, Capt. Forrest P. Sherman, kept his pilots busy patrolling the surrounding seas and on practice exercises.

The following days of mild weather and calm seas proceeded monotonously. After finding out on July 3 that his anticipated meeting day with Fletcher would not happen as planned, it was rescheduled for July 19. Noyes' task force continued on its southward course. One day seemed to be like the next, which always happens on long ocean voyages. As the force steamed southward, the days grew hotter.

The *Wasp* task force crossed the equator on July 10—the first time for the carrier. As is the practice at sea for centuries, ceremonies broke out all over the ship with first-timers crossing the equator being the subject of numerous embarrassing hazing practices and taking on weird dress. It was a fine party and enjoyed by all aboard. But the uneventful voyage took an unfortunate turn.

Approaching Samoa from the northeast on July 13, piercing, rasping sounds from the *Wasp*'s starboard high-pressure steam turbine spread throughout the ship. The ship's engineers had no choice but to shut down the starboard propulsion system and continue steaming using only the port-side engine. Rapidly losing speed down to 15 knots, the big carrier fell farther behind the rest of the task force. Noyes immediately sent a message to CINCPAC and Ghormley telling them of the mishap and his plans to repair the turbine while north of Tongatabu Island. Working feverishly day and night, the *Wasp*'s engineers found that damaged turbine blades were the cause of the calamity. They worked nonstop on the enormous task of rebuilding all of the turbine's rotor blades. As the crippled *Wasp* lumbered to the south toward Tongatabu, the engineers completed their work and made ready for high speed trials on July 21.

Capt. Sherman took the big ship through her paces and pronounced her ready to resume her position as the force's leader since she was again able to steam at 25 knots. Nevertheless, her engineers strongly recommended that the whole starboard turbine blade assembly be replaced at Pearl Harbor. On July 24, the *Wasp* finally rendezvoused with the *Saratoga* just south of Tongatabu.[10]

The third and last carrier task force that would become part of Fletcher's Task Force 61 left Pearl Harbor on July 15. Based on sheer firepower, Radm. Thomas C. Kinkaid's force was a sight to behold, and Kinkaid was in awe of it himself. Following what was to Kinkaid a familiar course, he stood on the flag bridge high on the *Enterprise*'s *(Big E)* island and observed the largest force he was privileged to command thus far in the war.

Ten powerful surface ships surrounded the great carrier. Bracketing the *Enterprise*'s bow were the heavy cruiser *Portland* and the new antiaircraft cruiser *Atlanta* where Radm. Mahlon Tisdale flew his flag. To the *Big E*'s stern, the new, fast battleship *North Carolina* followed in the carrier's wake. The battleship, newly commissioned in the spring of 1941 after finishing her sea trials on the East Coast, had arrived in Pearl Harbor just in time to join Kinkaid's force. Sporting 25-inch guns plus an awesome collection of smaller automatic weapons, she would add a formidable AA gun platform to defend against Japanese aircraft attacks. If the Japanese Navy should send out some of her heavier ships to confront the Americans, her nine powerful 16-inch guns would give quite a battle as well. Seven destroyers under the command of Capt. Edward P. Sauer—*Balch*, *Benham*, *Ellet*, *Grayson*, *Gwin*, *Maury*, and *Monssen*—formed a protective circle around the carrier, battleship, and two cruisers. Except for the *North Carolina* and the *Grayson*, all the ships in Kinkaid's force were battle hardened veterans after fighting with him at Coral Sea and Midway.

The *North Carolina* was the first of the modern battleships. She took her place in the new U.S. Navy, but not as a main offensive weapon like her predecessors had been. Therefore, the placement of this vessel was different than for the cruisers. If she had been put where a cruiser would normally be, that is 45° relative to a carrier's bow or stern, she could not keep up during battle conditions because she was slower than the carrier and the cruisers. Her size, 35,000 tons, caused her to slide in a slipping movement under a high speed turn and she would fall back from the fleet. Thus, she was placed directly in the wake of the *Enterprise*. However, Kinkaid would later learn that she could not maintain her station during flank speed turning movements under actual battle conditions and would fall away from the carrier. This decreased the battleship's ability to protect the carrier. After she served in combat at Guadalcanal, the *North Carolina* became a learning tool about how to build future fast battleships of the *Iowa* class. Despite her shortcomings, she still was a formidable weapon, and Kinkaid was glad to have her in his task force.[11]

Kinkaid's schedule called for his force to rendezvous with Fletcher and the rest of Task Force 61 on July 26 at 2:00 p.m. at 23° 15'S latitude, 180° longitude or about 430 miles south of Koro Island. However, after several delays caused by the necessity to fuel his destroyers, guarding against submarine attacks, and conducting air operations that forced the *Enterprise* to alter her course by turning into the wind, Kinkaid realized that he was falling behind schedule. If he steamed at 17 knots, which was a comfortable cruising speed for the ships of his task force, they would not make it to the assembly point on time. So he ordered his ships to increase their speed to 25 knots on July 22 and close the distance to the Fijis.

He was one day's steaming from reaching Tongatabu on July 23 when Kinkaid ordered two torpedo planes to that island to arrange for his task force to refuel at the port of Nukualofa. Acting as Kinkaid's representative, his chief of staff Lt. Cmdr. Sherman E. Burroughs flew in one of the planes. The fleet anchored in the port's harbor early the next morning and began refueling operations by taking on oil from two tankers. Burroughs returned onboard the *Enterprise* and stunned Kinkaid by telling him that because of confusion caused by crossing the international dateline it was July 25 not the 24th. They had lost a day's steaming time. Kinkaid immediately ordered his ships to weigh anchor and leave the harbor as soon as possible. His task force left Nukualofa Harbor with haste at 3:30 p.m.[12]

Adm. Turner's Ships Arrive

The last part of the naval force needed to invade Guadalcanal and Tulagi was under the command of Radm. Richmond Kelly Turner. It was fully loaded with Marines and supplies and left Wellington Harbor on July 22 at 8:00 a.m. Proceeding on a southeasterly course of 140° at a speed of 14 knots, Turner wanted to avoid or render any enemy sightings irrelevant as to their true heading. Later that afternoon, Turner changed his course to the northeast and headed straight toward the Fijis. His force had the shortest distance to travel, but the slower speed of his ships dictated the timing of their departure from New Zealand.

The weather was nearly perfect on the first day out, but that changed on July 24 when the seas became rough. High winds whipped the sea surface from glassy smooth to high waves and countless whitecaps. The crews on the heavily loaded transports experienced seasickness. Many a ships' captain reported gale force winds and Task Force 62's log stated the weather was "heavy." Visibility degraded as Turner ordered the fleet to slow its speed to 11 knots.

In spite of the weather, the ships had a relatively easy trip with the exception of the constant communications from Adm. King. This caused many typewriters and mimeograph machines to work overtime handling the deluge of paper. Nevertheless, Turner's amphibious force arrived on schedule south of Koro Island and was ready to proceed with the task ahead.

Ghormley ordered that the invasion force conduct a rehearsal since the various commanders, along with the ships and men they commanded, had never worked together. Fletcher thought this was a good idea and ordered the senior commanders to meet, discuss the rehearsal, and decide how to conduct the coming invasion. It was at that meeting that the controversy that would surround the conduct of the Guadalcanal operation began.[13]

CHAPTER 7
Controversy and Rehearsal

Aboard the transport *Crescent City,* Richard Tregaskis, the author of *Guadalcanal Diary,* spent a pleasant Sunday now that the ship stood anchored off the Fiji Islands and no longer rolled, pitched, and yawed. After spending the morning talking with the Marines, he came on deck to take in this restful, lazy day that everyone on board relished. No one except for the most senior commanders knew where they were going, but everyone knew that would soon change. The now familiar shapes of the ships that accompanied them from New Zealand surrounded him.

He went down to the ship's lounge and found Maj. Cornelius P. Van Ness, the 2nd Marine Regiment's planning officer, unfolding an envelope that a naval lieutenant had just handed to him. Tregaskis asked, "Something to do with our destination?"

Lifting his head and smiling, Van Ness said, "No, but I wish it were. I'd like to know, too."

Lunchtime soon came; Tregaskis went below and had a quiet meal. Returning to his stateroom for a nap, he started chatting with his bunk mates, Albert Campbell, a Red Cross worker, and Father Francis W. Kelly of Philadelphia when his fourth roommate, Dr. John Garrison, a husky dentist from Los Angeles and now a naval medical officer, came into the room and fell into his bunk.

"A lot of ships just came up," Garrison said, "A whole navy. Better go look at 'em."

They ran onto the deck and saw many more ships on the horizon. Surrounding the transport in a semicircle formation were more transports, freighters, destroyers, and cruisers. Farther away on the distant horizon were the unmistakably long, high, boxlike shapes that could only be aircraft carriers.

The talk now became louder and more energetic as officers, sailors, and Marines counted the new additions and what ship types they were. Conscious that this was the largest and strongest American force ever gathered, all knew that the battle to come was to be the most important yet in this war.[1]

A Fateful Meeting

On Sunday, July 26 at 2:00 p.m., almost the entire Watchtower naval invasion force stood arrayed in the waters 350 miles south of the Fijian island of Suva. Only four of the original 76 ships were not present. The remaining ships—the transports *Betelgeuse* and *Zeilin* escorted by the destroyers *Dewey* and *Mugford*—finally joined the invasion force on August 3.

As Radm. Thomas Kinkaid sat in the bosun's chair to move from the destroyer *Balch* high above the choppy sea to the *Saratoga,* his thoughts turned to the impending meeting of the senior commanders to discuss the rehearsal. This had been assigned the codename, DOVETAIL. The intent of the rehearsal was to attack Koro Island between July 28 and 31 and attempt to simulate the conditions as far as possible to what the ships, planes, and men would encounter on Guadalcanal and Tulagi. Kinkaid hoped that the strategy to be used in the WATCHTOWER operation would also be an important discussion topic on the agenda.

Kinkaid knew that this type of operation had never been attempted by the AmericanU.S. Navy on such a large scale. Because of shortages of all kinds of materiel in the early months of the war and the priorities being placed on the European war, there was not much that could be sent as backup for the American forces if the invasion should run into trouble or if losses of ships and men became so serious that defeat became imminent. Nevertheless, the force that Kinkaid observed as the *Enterprise* entered the area was a powerful one—certainly larger than the one assembled to stop the Japanese at Coral Sea and Midway. A total of 39 warships spanned the horizon in all directions with many transports, oilers, and other ships filling the seas.

Warships at the WATCHTOWER Rendezvous[2]

Commander	Carriers	Battleships	Heavy Cruisers	Light Cruisers	Destroyers
Fletcher	1	0	2	0	5
Kinkaid	1	1	1	1	5
Noyes	1	0	2	0	6
Turner	0	0	3	1	9
TOTALS	3	1	8	2	25

Later in the Pacific War, the U.S. Navy would assemble far larger and more powerful forces for the invasions of the Marianas and the Philippines in 1944. But this was 1942. The ships assembled in this part of the South Pacific were all that the Americans could spare at that time and would have to handle any situation that could occur. Ghormley's small planning staff warrants credit for making sure all the disparate forces from widely dispersed departure locations arrived on time in Fijian waters. This was a pyrrhic triumph for Ghormley.

It had been a long journey for Fletcher, Kinkaid and Noyes to make it to this point in the middle of the South Pacific. Both the Fletcher and Kinkaid forces made the 3,100-mile trip from Pearl Harbor. Noyes' ships traveled the great circle route for 5,500 miles from San Diego. Turner's ships made the shortest voyage—1,000 miles—from Wellington. They were finally together.

Noyes had arrived by airplane from the *Wasp*. Turner, along with Radm. McCain, commander, Aircraft, South Pacific (COMAIRSOPAC) and Maj. Gen. Vandegrift, commander of the First Marine Division arrived aboard the *Saratoga* in the destroyer *Hull*'s whaleboat. By the time Turner and his party arrived, the seas were calmer. But this did not stop McCain from having a rather undignified entrance. As he grabbed the ladder trailing down the big carrier's side, the big ship rolled under a large wave and dunked the admiral into the water. He was soaked to the skin up to his waist. Vandegrift recalled later in a wry moment that the "mad little admiral" had been appropriately christened.

✲ ✲ ✲

Kinkaid, the last senior commander to arrive and escorted by a junior officer, walked up the several ladders and entered Fletcher's crowded ward room. Noyes, Turner, and McCain were already there and had just arrived themselves. Vandegrift and all the senior officers of the 1st Marine Division filled the room. Kinkaid looked for Ghormley. After all, he expected the overall commander of the South Pacific Theater's first major war operation to be present to preside over this meeting. Several important strategic and tactical operations needed to be discussed and decided upon. But Ghormley was conspicuous in his absence. He sent his chief of staff, Radm. Daniel J. Callaghan, in his place.

It can only be guessed what feelings of foreboding Kinkaid and others in the room that day must have had. This was not a good start for the first major American offensive in World War II with the overall theater commander missing. And the meeting's tone would only get worse.[3]

Fletcher: Now that we are all here, it is time to convene this meeting. I want to welcome all who traveled long distances to be here. I congratulate those of you who overcame some serious technical problems encountered during your journey to this spot.

We have much to cover and time is short.

After we rehearse the landings on Koro Island, our force will head for the Solomons. The planned invasion date is August 7. We do know that the Japanese are building an airbase on Guadalcanal and have placed bombers there. There are no intelligence reports that the Japanese know we are coming. I believe we might catch them by surprise.

One item I want to mention is that I plan to keep the carriers close enough to provide air support and fighter cover until D+2. At that time, the carriers will withdraw to a safe distance to be out of range of possible retaliation by Japanese land based aircraft.

A stunned silence in the room fell upon everyone like dark, dense, looming storm clouds. Turner and Vandegrift looked at each other, too flabbergasted to speak. Turner's famous temper started to boil to the surface, but he controlled himself sufficiently to respond calmly to Fletcher.

Turner: Sir, if I understand what you just said, the carriers and the air support will be withdrawn two days after we begin the invasion. Is that correct?

Fletcher: Yes.

Turner: I do not believe that is enough time for the unloading of necessary supplies and troops to assure the operation's success. We need four days to offload the transports; *you are giving us only two!* While we are off-loading in the waters off Guadalcanal, our ships are the most vulnerable to an enemy attack because they cannot maneuver in the restricted spaces.

After you withdraw your forces, we will be at the total mercy of land-based Japanese aircraft that are sure to get the word that we are invading Guadalcanal and Tulagi and attacking their bases there. We can expect the Japanese Navy will send their ships to sink our transports. They have a large base at Rabaul and have aircraft bases in eastern New Guinea and on New Britain. One thing I'm sure of—they will not allow us to take the airbase on Guadalcanal away from them and will fight with everything they have to stop us from doing it.

Fletcher: I know that, Kelly. It is for those same reasons that I cannot keep the carriers close enough to give you constant air support and combat air patrol. The three carriers we have comprise three-fourths of the carriers we have in the Pacific. As you already know, the *Hornet* is still in Pearl Harbor undergoing a much needed overhaul. She will not be available for several weeks.

The waters off Cape Esperance are quite shallow and narrow. The channel off Cape Esperance is only 7½ miles wide and navigable water less than that. The charts we have are old and probably outdated and inaccurate. So, we cannot be sure that these distances are accurate and might be less than that. If we should get caught by Japanese aircraft or if the Japanese Navy should send some heavy cruisers or battleships down from Rabaul to attack us, we would have little or no room to maneuver.

Fletcher noticed Adm. Callaghan trying to get his attention and directed him to speak:

Fletcher: Dan, do you have something to say?

Callaghan: This operation has not been called Operation SHOESTRING for nothing. Adm. Ghormley has protested to Washington that we do not have enough resources for this operation to succeed. Our supply chain is stretched to the breaking point. We have to transport supplies over vast distances that can take many days. The Japanese supply lines are much shorter because they have heavily fortified and well supplied bases at Rabaul and Truk.

However, withdrawing the carrier air support too soon could make the supply situation worse. If there is no air support after Day 2, the likelihood of a Japanese counterattack increases and thus prolongs the length of time we have to stay there. This will increase the demand for more materiel of which we are in short supply. The air support must be there for a longer time.

Any land-based bombers in the South Pacific do not have range to reach Guadalcanal and cannot help. There are no more ships that anyone can send to help us. We are on our own.

Fletcher: What can Gen. MacArthur do to help us?

Callaghan: He has nothing to spare and faces the same supply shortages we do. Adm. Ghormley went to see MacArthur. They sent a joint letter to Washington complaining that Watchtower was a high risk operation and should be postponed until we have sufficient forces and supplies for it to be successful. The war in Europe has the priority for supplies and troops; we are a second class operation. We were able to postpone "D-Day" by seven days. This operation must go on. Nothing will stop it now.

Now everyone realized that Ghormley's absence was making its impact on the way the invasion would happen. Callaghan did not have the authority to change Fletcher's mind because he was junior to Fletcher, who outranked him. If Ghormley had been there, he would have perhaps reversed Fletcher's single-mindedness on this issue. However, if one judged Ghormley's behavior up to that time, his natural lack of aggressiveness and cautious demeanor would most likely have acquiesced to Fletcher's arguments.

Turner: I understand the supply line problems and that we are on our own. Nevertheless, withdrawing the carriers in just two days places my ships off shore and the Marines on Guadalcanal and Tulagi in great peril. We must have the equivalent of one fighter and three bomber squadrons to give us the air support we need. In addition, we require one added squadron for the initial two hours of D-Day. About half this force would stay as combat air patrol to protect the transports. I also urged that a FDO be placed on the cruiser-destroyer screening group's flagship.

As each officer spoke, the tone of the interchange became increasingly strained. The escalating tension filled the cramped room like a thick cloud. It now became obvious to Fletcher that no one was going to give in to the other's point-of-view. The debate needed to end if the rehearsal was to proceed on schedule. The ships had to leave soon so that each ship would be in place in time to begin the invasion on August 7.

Fletcher: Kelly, I do understand your strong opinions about my decision. However, as overall commander of this operation, I need to consider many factors to ensure this invasion is a success while balancing the need to preserve the meager naval forces we have in the Pacific. Ever since this operation began,I have had my doubts about it. Arguing that position serves no useful purpose,so let's get on with it.

We have to rehearse the landings on Koro Island. You are responsible for that operation, and I know that you have planned that part of our activities very well like I know you can. Now is the time to look to the future of this invasion and do everything we can to be victorious. We must get on with it.

There are many details about the rehearsal and the invasion that we must discuss. So let's proceed with that.

The meeting then turned to the various levels of details needed to bring off the upcoming operation. Each commander presented their plans and Fletcher resolved any conflicts and differences as they occurred. At about one and a half hours after the conference began, there was nothing left to discuss. Nevertheless, the pall of Fletcher's stunning decision hung over the entire proceedings.

Turner, Vandegrift, and Callaghan still seethed as Fletcher proclaimed, "This meeting is adjourned."

With that, Turner and Vandegrift left the room; Turner went to the *McCawley* and Vandegrift to the *Hunter Liggett*. The others followed to their assignments. Some recollections of what happened at that meeting have been recorded and demonstrate that all did not go well in that vital conference.

Callaghan apparently did not show much sympathy with Fletcher's decision when he wrote:

> "Task Force must withdraw to South from objective area (i.e. general advanced position) within two days after D day!"[4]

Callaghan's exclamation point undoubtedly came from his unhappiness after Ghormley sent a message to Fletcher a few days later suggesting that the carrier fighters could be equipped with belly tanks to increase their range while Fletcher's carriers lay some 300 miles south of Guadalcanal. Fletcher did not agree with the proposal so it was dropped.

Capt. Thomas G. Peyton, Turner's chief of staff and also present, recalled how the meeting transpired:

> "The conference was one long bitter argument between Vadm. Fletcher and my new boss [Turner]. Fletcher questioned the whole upcoming operation. Since he kept implying that it was largely Turner's brainchild, and mentioning that those who planned it had no real fighting experience, he seemed to be doubting the competence of its parent.
>
> Fletcher's main point of view was the operation was too hurriedly and therefore not thoroughly planned, the Task Force not trained together; and the logistic support inadequate.
>
> My boss kept saying 'the decision has been made. It's up to us to make it a success.'
>
> I was amazed and disturbed by the way these two admirals talked to each other. I had never heard anything like it.
>
> In my opinion too much of the conference was devoted to 'fighting the problem,' as we used to say at the [Naval] War College, and too little time to trying to solve the problem."[5]

Kinkaid remembered the meeting during an interview after the war:

> "I would call the mood of the conference animated rather than stormy. Turner asked for a lot of things, much of which he didn't get, because they were not in the realm of the possible.
>
> The sharpest divergence of opinion was in regard to the length of time the carriers should be held in an area where they could support the landings. Fletcher insisted that two days was all that could be risked because of both the submarine danger and the risk of Japanese shore based air attack.
>
> Other divergences of opinion related to air search and logistics.
>
> After the conference was over, I overheard Turner ask Vandegrift 'How did I do? Vandegrift's answer was 'all right.' That also was my personal assessment."[6]

Turner did nothing to change the situation when he did not go over Fletcher's head and appeal his controversial decision. Twenty years later, when asked why he did not do so, he replied, "Whom to, and who was I to do so? Fletcher was my old boss, and at that moment the most battle experienced commander in our Navy. It was his judgment, and it was my job to live with it."[7]

Fletcher recalled that:

> "Kelly and I spent most of our time picking on Dan Callaghan because of the poor logistics situation...Fuel was my main consideration. Kelly was no shrinking violet, and always spoke his piece in conferences.
>
> But there was no bitterness in the discussion. Plenty of opinions vigorously expressed as to what might or could be done.
>
> One thing I remember particularly well and have been telling it ever since the Battle of Savo Island. I said: `Now Kelly, you are making plans to take that island from the Japs and the Japs may turn on you and wallop the hell out of you. What are you going to do then?' Kelly said: `I am just going to stay there and take my licking.'
>
> Kelly was tough, a brain, and a son-of-a-bitch, and that's just what he did."[8]

That, as someone once said, proved to be an understatement. But a rehearsal was in the wings, and it, like the invasion it preceded, would not be an easy nut to crack.[9]

An Event Full of Portent

Turner knew that the best way to not think about his anger at Fletcher was to get on with the tasks before him. There was an invasion rehearsal to do so his ships and the Marines would be ready to do their duty once they arrived in the waters off Guadalcanal. Ordering his task force to the north and nearer to Koro Island, he now reviewed what had to be done to make sure this practice exercise was a success.

He had recommended the Fiji Islands as the site for the exercise. They were now becoming a rear area in the Pacific War and far enough from prying Japanese eyes—about 1,100 miles from Guadalcanal—so that the presence of such a large force of American ships could not be reported. These islands were in a central location so all the required forces could gather there, making it the most practical place to get together. Koro Island, in the reef-locked Koro Sea, was the site of the rehearsal to take place from July 28 through 31.

CINCPAC staff had reviewed and suggested that Koro Island should *not* be one of the islands used for the rehearsal. It would become clear when the rehearsal began that perhaps their judgment had some validity.

As the preparations for the rehearsal developed, Turner began having problems organizing the effort. Not only were the participants new to war and unaccustomed to such large-scale operations, the answer as to which ships and who would be the squadron commanders became more complicated than originally anticipated.

As of July 24, Radm. Crutchley's force of the heavy cruisers *Australia*, *Canberra*, and *Chicago*, the light cruiser *Hobart*, and nine destroyers had not yet arrived at the gathering point. Turner had not had the opportunity to discuss the details of the upcoming rehearsal with Crutchley, who had been designated as Turner's second-in command. Also, Turner did not know whether he would have any minesweepers to participate in the exercise. The cargo ship *Betelgeuse* and the transport *Zeilin* carrying the 3rd Marine Defensive Battalion units were still on their way with an estimated arrival date of July 30, well near the end of the rehearsal.

With all these ambiguities looming over the rehearsal, Turner had no choice but to take direct command of the operation, which deprived Crutchley of any chance of facing the responsibilities he would accept off Guadalcanal or experience gained from the rehearsal. Since the British admiral was a distinguished naval officer, it was a difficult decision for Turner to make, but he had no choice. Kelly Turner had and would receive many criticisms during his naval career, but avoiding the tough decisions was not among them.

In a July 24 letter to Crutchley, he wrote:

> "The thing which most concerns me at the moment is the prompt organization of the Attack Force, once we meet the other elements of the Pacific Fleet.
>
> I regret deeply that lack of time and ability to consult you require that I myself make the assignment of vessels to stations in Squadrons X-RAY and YOLK. [Which Adm. Crutchley's Screening Force was to protect from air and submarine attack, as well as from enemy surface force attack.] However, I believe this is necessary if we are to obtain a prompt organization of the squadrons on the 26th and 27th."[10]

In a letter to Radm. Norman Scott, Turner's doubts about the rehearsal become even more readily apparent:

> "I foresee considerable difficulty, particularly in the rehearsal, in keeping the transports in the same locality all day long while loading and unloading. The water is too deep to anchor, of course, and I hope we don't have a lot of collisions. However, there will be more important difficulties in the combat operations, so we can't worry about these.
>
> The rehearsal, from 28 through 31 July, was less than full blown. The original plan had been to conduct landing exercises on 28 July, re-embark the Marines on 29 July, and then conduct further landing exercises on the 30th, with accompanying air bombings and ship gunfire support fire, and again re-embark the troops on the 31st."[11]

Turner undoubtedly had several reservations about the rehearsal. Nevertheless, dedicated to the task at hand, he made sure the rehearsal proceeded as planned. But, right from the start, all did not go well.

✲ ✲ ✲

As early as July 28 at 9:00 a.m., in spite of smooth seas, the beach conditions on Koro Island were less than optimal. Turner's orders specifically mentioned safeguarding the boats, since there were none to spare if any of them should be damaged during the rehearsal. However, conditions on Koro Island proved to be inadequate to safely conduct landings on Beach Red. Landings went more smoothly on beaches Blue and Green. An entry in the COMPHIBFORSOPAC's (Commander, Amphibious Forces, South Pacific) War Diary more than adequately shows what it was like for those landing craft attempting to disembark troops on Koro Island's beaches:

> "Beach condition proved hazardous and endangered future employment of ship's boats and tank lighters. Troops not ashore were recalled. Boats were hoisted in and troops not landed were re-embarked."[12]

The second day of the rehearsal went more smoothly. While there was still worry over the landing boats, troops on Blue and Green beaches successfully re-embarked. On the rehearsal's last two days, troops went down the nets into their boats, rode around for awhile in them, and then climbed back up the nets. No more men landed on Koro Island. But this was not the end of the troubles for Turner.

Three Marines from the *American Legion* were stragglers on Koro. A graver situation occurred when the critically needed fleet tanker *Kaskaskia* still had not rendezvoused with Turner's ships by August 1. Apparently, the tanker's captain, Cmdr. Walter L. Taylor, in the same convoy as the *Betelgeuse* and *Zeilin*, had not received orders he could read concerning the rehearsal or the rendezvous. The coded message containing those instructions had been garbled and was undecipherable due to an error setting up the coding equipment used in encoding the message.[13]

Despite that slightly more than one-third of the Marines were able to get any value from the rehearsal, the lessons learned from that exercise proved to be indispensable. The gunfire support ships and invasion air support aircraft successfully carried out their assignments according to Turner's plan. The amphibious ships obtained considerable benefit that became the basis for future successes. Cmdr. Charles B. Hunt, the commanding officer of the cargo transport *Alhena,* wrote:

> "We had hoisted our wooden-hulled Higgins boats [before leaving San Diego] in and out for so long that we thought that we knew all there was to know; but always in harbor and never in any sort of landing exercise. Off Onslow Beach in the early days I had acted as a spare parts supply ship, doling out engines and propellers as they were burned or beaten up. How well the others had been trained I do not know, but we all certainly heard from U-NO-HOO after the first rehearsal in the Fijis. Kelly sounded off in no uncertain terms and no one was spared. We hoisted the boats in and did it again. Times were cut about fifty percent but still it was not good enough. The third time we all thought that we did a real bang up job, but not so, according to the Boss. And he was right. After a conference aboard his ship that night we went out to sea, came in and did it again in about one third the time of our first try and with ten times the precision. Here again Kelly was the perfectionist—not the sundowner and his driving was certainly needed and paid off."[14]

Later in the war, Vandegrift wrote that despite the landing problems on Koro Island's beaches, the lessons learned, "...proved invaluable...in providing an opportunity for familiarization with debarking procedure, ascertaining debarkation intervals and the conduct and timing of large scale boat movements..." He also stated that, "It also permitted the necessary exchange of staff visits and conferences...during which further details of execution of the attack were agreed upon and minor changes carried into effect. In the light of this experience an effective and workable boat pool was established..."[15]

After the war, Vandegrift apparently changed his view of the rehearsal when he said to the Marine Corps History Group in a March 12, 1948, speech that the rehearsal was "a complete bust." Turner took exception to Vandegrift's assessment stating that while the partial rehearsal off Koro Island was "unsatisfactory," it was not "a complete bust." Vandegrift, reflecting some second thoughts, wrote in 1964:

> "Although I later described the rehearsal as 'a complete bust,' in retrospect it probably was not that bad. At the very least, it got the boats off the transports, and the men down the nets and away. It uncovered deficiencies such as defective boat engines in time to have them repaired and gave both Turner and me a chance to take important corrective measures in other spheres."[16]

This reaffirmed what he had said in March 1943:

> "The unusually successful landings' reflected the benefits to be obtained from a period of rehearsals of the precise operation immediately prior to its execution."[17]

✲ ✲ ✲

Watchtower faced many obstacles as Fletcher's carriers and Turner's amphibious invasion force sailed from the Fiji Islands to the Southern Solomons. One of those was the lack of air support from both carrier-based and land-based aircraft. The primary drawback was the South Pacific's vastness and equally daunting distances between possible air bases and Guadalcanal. The technology of combat aircraft in mid-1942 limited particularly fighter aircraft from flying the long distances to Guadalcanal and then returning to any bases close enough to be remotely viable. Guadalcanal-Tulagi lay far beyond the range of American aircraft based on Espiritu Santo, New Hebrides—more than 600 miles from possible air bases on Éfaté and 550 miles from Tontouta Field on New Caledonia. To add to these problems, all of these bases were well within bombing range of Japanese aircraft on Rabaul.

The Americans tried to overcome this severe problem by shifting whatever aircraft they had nearer to Guadalcanal. King ordered Nimitz to provide two Marine fighter squadrons and two Marine scouting squadrons. These were to augment the Marine photo reconnaissance squadron already in the South Pacific. Obeying his superior's orders, Nimitz designated Col. William J. Wallace's newly organized Air Group stationed at Ewa Field on Oahu. They had the Marine fighter and scouting squadrons King had asked for. However, there was one problem—there were not enough pilots who had the experience in carrier operations to take them there.

The closest air bases to Guadalcanal were at Éfaté in the New Hebrides, Tontouta field in New Caledonia, and Espiritu Santo. At Éfaté, Maj. Harold W. Baker commanded 18 F4F-3A fighters. Lt. Col. John N. Hart led 16 F4F-3P fighters and Capt. Dale D. Brannon commanded 38 Army P-400 fighters at Tontouta Field. Hart awaited the completion of the new field on Espiritu Santo—planned for early August, but finished on July 30. Radm. John S. McCain, commander of all aircraft in the South Pacific Theater, called this early completion a miraculous achievement by the Navy's Construction Battalions

(CBs or SEABEES). This was not the last miracle the SEABEES would accomplish in the Pacific. They would make more history by accomplishing the impossible and becoming absolutely essential to the American victory.

Turner sent a letter to CINCPAC on July 21 that outlined a plan to transfer the 18 F4F-3As at Éfaté and 16 F4F-3P fighters at Tontouta by flying them to Espiritu Santo, refuel, and then fly them to Guadalcanal after the Americans captured the airfield there. He also wished to send, without delay, two of Wallace's scouting squadrons to Guadalcanal and place one fighter squadron on Espiritu Santo and the other on Éfaté. There was one problem with this approach. The planes on Espiritu Santo could not fly to Guadalcanal because of their limited range. None of these aircraft had the belly tanks that could extend their range.

McCain made the point on July 22 that the planes could not be ferried on the *Saratoga* since only a few of the Marine pilots were qualified for carrier takeoffs and landings. According to McCain, the best approach would be to leave these squadrons where they were and only move them when there was a way to get them to Guadalcanal.

CINCPAC responded that same day that one fighter squadron and one scouting squadron would leave Pearl Harbor on or about August 1 on the auxiliary carrier *Long Island.* The remaining fighter and scouting squadrons would leave on August 15.

After all these machinations, it was clear that the number of land-based aircraft available to cover the August invasion would be zero. Operation "Shoestring" would again live up to its nickname. The carriers had to be the only source of air support, and those would be over the invasion area only for the first two days of the invasion.[18]

✲ ✲ ✲

Fletcher also viewed the rehearsal as unsuccessful and expressed concerns of the limited fuel supplies. His carriers stayed away from the rehearsal's location, simulating the conditions they would encounter during the actual invasion.

During that time, Fletcher still stewed over the problems facing his command. The limited fuel supplies, due to tanker shortages and the lack of fueling capabilities during tough sea conditions, did nothing to allay his worries. Ghormley had already expressed concerns that the great distances in the South Pacific made the supply conditions tenuous. The ability to top off the tanks on the ships before starting the invasion also concerned him. Fletcher's normally cautious nature and what he considered his duty to protect the carriers under his command darkened his thoughts as Task Force 61 reassembled south of Koro Island and began the trek to an uncertain destiny.[19]

CHAPTER 8
The Trek

An Uncertain Journey

The journey of Fletcher's carrier and Turner's amphibious task forces followed an almost identical course from the Fiji Islands to Guadalcanal. In spite of being refueled and resupplied, concerns about fuel, ammunition, and other supply constraints continued to haunt both commanders as their ships steamed westward. Their path took them near Éfaté with the hope that some of the refueling problems would be alleviated. Unfortunately, the Éfaté shore facilities had no refueling capabilities.

Ghormley planned to have the chartered tanker SS *Esso Little Rock* in Éfaté's harbor when the invasion force arrived to satisfy their thirst, but, alas, this was not meant to be. On August 2 at 2:00 a.m., Lt. Cmdr. Walter H. Price, the commanding officer of the destroyer *Wilson*, which was steaming on Turner's Task Force 61.2's northern flank, diverted the tanker to make a one and a half hour trip around the task force's formation to keep the tanker from interfering with it. This unfortunate order issued by an inexperienced junior officer caused the tanker to miss her planned rendezvous with Capt. Cornelius W. Flynn's destroyer squadron. This mishap, along with a dearth of fueling facilities at Éfaté, threw any plans for an intermediate refueling stop for both Turner's and Fletcher's task forces into disarray.

On August 4 and with no other fuel available, all 24 of Turner's destroyers, destroyer-types, and the short-ranged Australian light cruiser H.M.A.S. *Hobart* had to take fuel from the transports and cargo ships. Meanwhile, three destroyers emptied the oiler *Cimarron*'s tanks after the tanker finished fueling Fletcher's force.

Turner stopped his task force on August 5 to transfer 17 newly commissioned ensigns from the transport *Zeilin* to their assigned ships using the ships' boats. He could have ordered the transfer using bosun's chairs and kept his force moving toward Guadalcanal. But he chose otherwise.

Aboard the *Saratoga*, Fletcher, in spite of not steaming with Turner's invasion force and being worried about the possible presence of Japanese submarines, observed that Turner had stopped and sent an order for Turner to get moving again. Later in the war, he remembered the incident:

> "I just figured that Kelly was punch drunk and my short dispatch would snap him out of it. When I next saw him, which was in Nouméa, we laughed together about the incident, and he admitted he might not have been very bright. But he still said there were no Jap submarines anywhere around."[1]

Later that day, both Fletcher's carrier force and Turner's invasion force changed their courses and headed northward toward Guadalcanal. The invasion was two days away.

✲ ✲ ✲

Haze loomed over the sea on August 6, 1942, adding to the prevailing pessimism. Visibility was down to four miles. The forecast called for worse conditions. Excerpts from Turner's Staff Log best depicts the deteriorating weather:

"No navigational sights possible..."

"At 0800 reported positions [from ships of the force] differed by 27 miles in latitude and 15 miles in longitude..."

"At 1200 dispatched COMDESRON Four in *Selfridge* (DD-357) to Bellona Island, about 60 miles to the northeast, with orders to fix navigational position, and rejoin disposition by 1800..."

"Haze closed down, with some rain...Still not zigzagging in order not to complicate navigational data."[2]

There was no turning back. America's first offensive in World War II was less than 24 hours away.[3]

CHAPTER 9
Progress and Setbacks

What to do next?

A gloom descended over the *Yamato*'s wardroom as the catastrophic news continued to arrive. Three of the Imperial Japanese Navy's first line carriers, *Akagi*, *Kaga*, and *Soryu*, had been rendered burning hulks by American naval aircraft in the ocean northwest of Midway Island. The Americans had inflicted a devastating defeat on the cream of the Imperial Japanese Navy. Vadm. Isoroku Yamamoto's plans of inflicting a fatal blow on the U.S. Navy had gone up in flames. Then the news arrived that the last of the Japanese first line carriers, the *Hiryu*, was out of action and also turned into a burning wreck. It was June 5, 1942, a date that would later be called the day when the Japanese Empire's fortunes turned for the worse.

The latest news stunned Yamamoto and forced him to think hard of the consequences of what he had just digested. He knew he had no other alternative but to cancel the Midway operation and withdraw the fleet to Japan. However, excitement among his subordinates was too intense for anyone to agree. In spite of the depressing revelations, others in the room reverted to their natural instinct to strike back.

Capt. Yasuji Watanabe, administrative staff officer, argued, "If we used the guns of the *Yamato* and our other ships to put the Midway airfield out of action, then sent the troops ashore, we could still occupy the island. Let's try!"

Yamamoto's showed his fading patience when he replied, "You ought to know that of all naval tactics, firing one's guns at an island is considered the most stupid. You've been playing too much *shogi*!"

Tears filling his eyes, Radm. Kameto Kuroshima, senior staff officer reporting to Yamamoto, said, "The *Akagi's* still afloat, sir. Supposing it was towed to America and put on show? We can't sink it with our own torpedoes!" Realizing the political explosiveness of the moment and their ingrained reverence to the emperor, others wondered out loud how to apologize to him. In a characteristic display of integrity, he realized that it was his responsibility when he said, "I'll apologize to the emperor myself."

The bad news poured in like an avalanche. The *Kaga* slipped beneath the waves at 4:25 p.m. The *Soryu* followed her under just five minutes later. The *Akagi* and the *Hiryu* were still afloat but reduced to pyres of flame and smoke. Making a painful decision affecting the ship with which he had a long association, Yamamoto ordered a destroyer to fire its first torpedo against a warship to sink one of its own—the *Akagi*. Finally, at 11:55 p.m., he ordered the fleet to turn westward and retreat to Japan.

With the astounding successes the Imperial Japanese Navy had when war began against the U.S., the crushing defeat at Midway absolutely stunned everyone at the highest levels of the Japanese Navy. Yamamoto had fought hard with the General Staff to gain approval for his Operation MI (Midway). According to unconfirmed reports, he threatened to resign if he did not get his way. How could such an obviously superior naval force be obliterated by such an inferior fleet? Even in spite of the American intelligence successes, it seemed incredible that such a fate should fall upon the Empire when destiny was clearly on their side. They were absolutely incredulous that such a setback could ever happen.

Nevertheless, as the American press reported its naval victory and joy spread throughout that nation, a Japanese diplomat, one of those who was about to be exchanged for their American counterparts still in Japan, was about to board a ship when he read about the American victory at Midway in an American newspaper and saw the a picture of the *Akagi*'s burning hulk. The news of the debacle sank in. When the remaining Japanese ships arrived back at their bases, the Navy ordered the surviving crew members to be dispersed around Kyushu and confined to their quarters lest the news of the defeat leak to the public.

Safely back in Japanese waters, the Imperial Japanese Navy saw little in the way of new threats from the Americans. Setting up a defensive perimeter in the South Pacific from the Bismarck Islands to New Guinea, they advanced farther south from Bougainville and Rabaul to attack Tulagi, established a seaplane base there, and built an airfield on Guadalcanal to protect their eastern flank as they attempted to retake Port Moresby by moving their Army over the 7,000-foot high passes of the Owen Stanley Mountains. This was part of their strategy to neutralize Australia and New Zealand as bases for the Americans. On August 6, all seemed to be proceeding according to their plans. But that was about to change...[1]

✲ ✲ ✲

From the beginning, when his country moved inexorably to war with the rest of the world, Emperor Hirohito shared the same faulty strategic misconceptions held by his admirals and generals and their muddled thinking about who they would fight. The Japanese Army had an almost Lorelei-like fixation on the Soviet Union since they believed it was the chief opposition to their designs in China. They continued feeding off their victory over the Russian Fleet at Tsushima in May 1905. That victory had shocked the Western World and gained Japan worldwide respect and recognition as a rising world power. If the Imperial Japanese Navy could win a final, climatic winner-take-all naval battle against the U.S., Japan would be victorious over the decadent Americans and finally win for the Japanese Empire its predestined place as a major world power and turn the Pacific Ocean into a Japanese lake.

But the battles of the Coral Sea and Midway and the fact that the Soviet Union was currently neutral vis-à-vis Japan proved how wrong the Japanese Army and the Imperial Japanese Navy were. As victory after victory rolled in during the first days of the Pacific War, Japanese euphoria ran high. Trying to force Great Britain out of the Pacific War and reduce the U.S. willingness to continue the fight, the Japanese moved to the south. This included setting up bases in Rabaul on New Britain and Lae and Salamaua on New Guinea. Nevertheless, the Japanese Army kept tens of thousands of troops in Korea, Manchuria, and China that could not be released to face the then unknown American threat in the South Pacific.

The Japanese believed Coral Sea was a tactical victory because they sank more American ships than they themselves lost. However, they failed to comprehend the strategic loss they had suffered. The Americans had stopped Japanese plans to occupy Port Moresby and thwarted any immediate threat to Australia. Even after their crushing defeat at Midway, Hirohito seemed clueless about its impact on the war. Koichi Kido, a member of the Emperor's court, had a conversation with Hirohito concerning Midway on June 8 and later wrote about that meeting:

> "I had presumed the news of the terrible losses sustained by the naval air force would have caused him untold anxiety, yet when I saw him he was as calm as usual and his countenance showed not the least chance. He said he told the navy chief of staff that the loss was regrettable but to take care that the navy not lose its fighting spirit. He ordered him to ensure that future operations continue bold and aggressive. When I witness the courage and wisdom of the emperor, I am very thankful that our imperial country Japan is blessed with such a sovereign."[2]

Their South Pacific operations continued in spite of the losses of their naval aircraft and pilots at Midway. At Combined Fleet headquarters on Rabaul, 5,000 miles from Tokyo, planning continued for the construction of naval facilities and an airstrip on Guadalcanal. By August 6, Gen. Hajime Sugiyama briefed the Emperor about the New Guinea campaign's progress.

As he continued to discuss the New Guinea operation, Hirohito interrupted him with a question that caught the general off guard. "I am not so sure the navy air [force] can count on effective enough army support in the landing operations in New Guinea. Don't we need to send in the army air too?" The Emperor's question undoubtedly reflected his concerns about the losses of skilled pilots at Midway. Sugiyama replied that the Army had no plans to support the Navy's New Guinea operations thus clearly demonstrating the poor communications and the total lack of coordination that existed between the Army and Navy. What Sugiyama did not mention to the Emperor was that their almost total fixation on China caused them to withdraw their air forces from New Guinea and send them to the Chinese Theater so they could begin their assault on Chungking. Supporting the New Guinea campaign was clearly not the Army's highest priority.[3]

Vadm. Matome Ugaki, Yamamoto's chief of staff, wilted in the August heat as the *Yamato* returned to Hashira Jima after finishing training exercises on August 1. Two days later, Capt. Kaoru Arima, the new battleship *Musashi* commander, came into Ugaki's office on the battleship *Nagato*. The Japanese now had two super battleships—the *Yamato* and the *Musashi*—and much hope rode on their success. The *Musashi* was to be commissioned on August 5 and would return to Hashira Jima on the 10th.

The record breaking heat wave had continued for the last 32 days. On August 4, the overpowering heat particularly bothered Ugaki as he received another briefing from Cmdr. Masahiko Asada, a staff officer from the 11th Air Fleet, who had been aboard the *Nagato* for a day. Japanese troops had advanced as far south as Kokoda in their attempt to cross the Owen Stanley Mountains and capture Port Moresby. According to Asada, the Army had reinforced their air forces in the area. (Apparently he had not heard they were already withdrawing forces to China.) Nevertheless, Ugaki remained optimistic that their small losses would not seriously affect their progress.

Ugaki's concern over the lack of a follow-up plan did not abate while he listened to Asada—no such plan existed. Increasing concerns over the destruction of British sea power in the area gained more prominence in Japanese naval strategic thinking. Ugaki agreed that this was a problem but still fretted because of the lack of a coherent plan. He sent two staff officers to Tokyo by float plane to press for a plan.

August 5 and 6 passed uneventfully. Discussions about naval officers' classification in the Imperial Japanese Navy came up but Ugaki was rather uninterested in this topic. He had been aboard the *Nagato* for one year.[4]

✡ ✡ ✡

While the Japanese seemed apparently oblivious regarding future American moves in the South Pacific, this did not mean they were unprepared. During the years after the end of World War I and the beginning of the Second World War, the Treaty of Versailles gave the Japanese Empire the authority to administer what were called the Mandated Islands. The Japanese seized the Marianas, Marshalls, and Caroline Islands when World War I began in 1914. The Versailles Treaty gave the control of these islands to the Japanese. During the inter-war years, Japan built bases on Truk, Palau, and Ponape in the Carolines and used these bases to attack the Netherlands, East Indies, and the Philippines when their war with the Americans began. After those victories, they built bases at Rabaul on New Britain with its excellent harbor and established an airbase at Lae in eastern New Guinea.[5]

The forces the Japanese had were considerable but not overpowering when one considered the American task forces headed their way. The forces Vadm. Gunichi Mikawa, Commander of the Japanese 8th Fleet, had at his disposal included no capital ships but a powerful array of heavy and light cruisers.

The heavy cruisers included his flagship, the *Takao*-class *Chokai*, which displaced over 11,000 tons and carried ten eight-inch and eight five-inch guns. She, like others in her class, had undergone extensive modifications before the Pacific War began that included replacing older small caliber guns with improved AA guns. Driven by four turbine engines and 12 boilers, she had a top speed of almost 35 knots. She was built for speed and inflicting devastating destruction on any potential foes. The three other heavy cruisers were no exception to that rule. They included the older heavy cruisers *Aoba* and *Kinugasa*, *Kako*, and *Furutaka*, each carrying six eight-inch guns, displacing 10,000+ tons and also capable of almost 35 knots.

The light cruiser *Yubari*, launched in 1923 and displacing over 6,000 tons, carried six five and a half-inch guns. The much older *Tenryu*, launched in 1918, was considered to be a second-class cruiser because she only displaced about 3,900 tons, about the same size and carrying similar armament as the destroyers of that day.

He also had eight destroyers: the *Oite*, *Yunagi*, *Yuzuki*, *Asakaze*, *Mutsuki*, *Uzuki*, *Yayoi*, and *Mochizuki*. To help him scout the waters around the Solomons and provide an undersea threat, he had the submarine tender *Jingai* and ten submarines: the *I-11*, *I-121*, *I-122*, *I-123*, *I-171*, *I-169*, *I-174*, *I-176*, *I-179*, *RO-33*, and *RO-34*. None of the Japanese submarines had the cruising range of the American fleet submarines, but that was not a disadvantage since their base was much closer to their intended cruising area than the American fleet submarines were to where the Japanese merchant fleet plied their trade.

The Japanese also had 112 aircraft at Rabaul and Tulagi within range of Guadalcanal. Just as was demonstrated at Pearl Harbor, air power would become the deciding factor in the confrontation that was coming. World War II was the air war, and Guadalcanal was to be no exception to that fact.[6]

Meanwhile, Mikawa kept his force ready to sail at a moment's notice. He knew his ships and the planes at Rabaul were then the only force of any size that could protect the Japanese left flank for their New Guinea campaign. His sailors were at a training peak and ready to fight. That was the commander he was, and he was not about change his ways now that his country was in a desperate struggle with the formidable Americans. He did not underestimate the Americans and their resolve. The stinging defeat at Midway was a readily apparent reminder of the kind of enemy he would face.

An Air Warrior

In August 1942, Ens. Saburo Sakai thought about how much his life had changed since he left the nearly impossible and extreme training regimen at the Imperial Japanese Navy's flying school at 19. He had flown combat missions in the skies of China, the Philippines, and New Guinea. After demonstrating phenomenal flying skills, fearless courage, and a relentless killer instinct, he had become one of Japan's greatest flying aces. After the war ended in 1945, Sakai summarized his strong beliefs about his service in the Japanese armed forces:

> "In the Imperial Japanese Navy I learned only one trade—how to man a fighter plane and how to kill enemies of my country. This I did for nearly five years, in China and across the Pacific. I knew of no other life; I was a warrior of the air."[7]

After enlisting as a 16-year-old seaman recruit at the Sasebo Naval Base in 1933, he began the severe life of a Japanese naval trainee that proved far worse than he had ever dreamed. The harsh treatment meted out by petty officers during Sakai's upward rise in rank and responsibilities never abated. After serving at sea for several years and suffering continued harassment, he passed the highly competitive Naval Gunners School's entrance examinations in 1935. Several months later, he attained the rank of petty officer, third class.

Before going to war against the Americans, the highly selective nomination process and even more rigidly competitive training program at the Naval Fliers School at Tsuchiura yielded few qualified pilots. Nevertheless, the trainees who successfully graduated from there were the best pilots the Japanese Navy had to send into combat. Sakai was among those. After the war began against the Unites States, the more relaxed graduation criteria yielded more but less qualified graduates; Sakai said, "At best questionable" pilots.

When Sakai applied for the school in 1937, it accepted only 70 non-commissioned officers out of a list of more than 1,500.[8] Only 25 non-commissioned officers graduated near the end of 1937. Sakai received an award of an Emperor's silver watch. He was the outstanding student pilot of his class. He had shown how good he was and how good he would become.

Sakai began his flying service with several training squadrons and finally went to war when he received orders in May 1938 to report to Kiukiang in southeastern China. Sakai was promoted to naval aviation pilot, second class, an achievement that he proudly sported. The Zero fighter plane had not yet entered service at that time, so Sakai flew the Mitsubishi Type 96 fighter plane, called the "Claude" by Allied intelligence. These aircraft had nonretractable landing gear and thus was at a disadvantage relative to the planes they flew against. Nonetheless, the greater skills of Sakai and his fellow pilots yielded victory after victory over their enemies.[9]

After over a year of combat in China, Sakai returned to Japan, utterly depressed over the death of a young woman with whom he had fallen in love. However, his combat record in China had made him a hero among his superiors, colleagues, and upcoming pilot trainees.[10]

After enjoying a restful service and more leave with a newly-discovered love, the sister of his previous love, he saw the Mitsubishi Zero. This new, sleek, streamlined fighter plane would dominate the air in the early years of the Pacific and Asian struggles. It had twice the speed, twice the range, and was more powerfully armed than the fighter he had flown before. He was one of the first pilots to take the new fighter into combat when he returned to the China Theater later in the fall of 1940.[11]

From that time until August 1942, Sakai fought vicious battles against American pilots in the skies over the Philippines and New Guinea while his base of operations changed from China to Rabaul and then to a primitive airstrip in Lae, New Guinea. By this time, he was an ace many times over with 60 victories. He found that his opposition was far more formidable once he faced more highly trained American pilots. He achieved the commissioned officer rank of ensign after rising up from the Imperial Japanese Navy's enlisted ranks—not an entirely common phenomenon in Japanese society. Nonetheless, he did this with his extraordinary ability as a natural born combat fighter pilot and his dedication to fight for what he believed. The Japanese Empire had to triumph over its enemies, in the way of the *bushido* warrior.[12]

On August 3, the naval command at Rabaul recalled most of the fighters from its Lae base. Although they had left their personal possessions at Lae and hoped to return there, Sakai and his comrades relished returning from the "hell hole" that was Lae to the relative comforts of Rabaul. Realizing they would now avoid the nightly attacks from American bombers and the dangerous daily patrols over Buna, they hoped for a more relaxed atmosphere. It did not take long before all those hopes proved wrong. Daily patrols filled the next four days. To Sakai and his fellow pilots, it seemed that a new routine was ahead for them. But that also was not to be. For the first time in his military career, he would face an extremely personal crisis.[13]

A Powerful, Deadly Weapon

After World War I, the navies of the victorious Allied powers underwent significant changes in both how their respective nations viewed their role and in naval strategies and tactics. Caught up in the sweeping pacifist movements that almost always follow catastrophic wars, the U.S., Great Britain, and

Japan signed two major naval disarmament treaties. These limited the size of their navies relative to each other and the composition of those navies. The Five Power Washington Naval Treaty of 1922 set the relative tonnage of the navies of the U.S., Great Britain, Japan, Italy, and France to a 5:5:3:1.7:1.7 ratio. That placed the Japanese at a strategic disadvantage to their potential naval rivals. The London Conference of 1931 raised the ratio in favor of the Japanese to 5:3.5. In 1936, the Japanese withdrew from the Five Power pact and accelerated a full fledged naval building program.

Realizing they had to find ways to overcome this disparity, the Japanese Navy turned their attention to build upon their past naval victories over the Russians in the Russo-Japanese War and exploit their superiority in night tactics and using torpedoes. Ever since the days of sail, the primary naval weapon was the high-powered, large-caliber, long-range gun. Technological improvement extended the gun's range, caliber, and accuracy through World War I. The torpedo also changed from a weapon placed at the end of a spar and rammed against a ship's side to one that propelled itself through the water toward its intended target.

However, the disadvantage to the Japanese brought about by the 1922 treaty in terms of tonnage and, consequently, gunfire range and power, forced them to overcome that weakness and improve their chances in naval battle against larger and more powerful ships. Thus, they changed their naval construction priority toward building faster, more powerful, and lighter ships such as cruisers and destroyers. But they had to compensate for the shorter range of the smaller guns carried by cruisers and destroyers compared to that of their rivals' capital ships by extending their torpedoes' range and increasing their explosive power. If they were successful in this endeavor, the Imperial Japanese Navy could engage a superior naval force from greater distances and partially, if not completely, nullifying a foe's superiority because of their guns' greater firepower

By the late 1930s, the primary means of propelling a torpedo was a steam engine powered by a mixture of compressed air, fuel, and water (turned into steam created in a combustion chamber). The Imperial Japanese Navy discovered and became convinced that oxygen was a viable propulsion alternative. Oxygen had the advantage of reducing the torpedo's weight so a larger warhead could be carried and would increase the missile's range. The results of oxygen's burning were carbon dioxide, carbon monoxide, and water thus making the oxygen torpedo wakeless and rendering it less likely to be seen by enemy lookouts. The gases produced by the torpedo steam engine left a distinctive trail in the water that could be easily sighted.

This information was well known among the world's naval powers, but most of them, including the U.S. and Great Britain, rejected the oxygen torpedo because of its shortcomings. Pure oxygen chemically reacts quickly and violently with many of the metals and lubricants in the torpedo, which can result in a violent explosion. Carrying pure oxygen on a ship was a dangerous operation because of its potential to also react with the high explosives carried onboard. Nevertheless, the Japanese believed they could overcome these deficiencies with more effective design and manufacture. The Japanese experimented with oxygen torpedoes in 1924, but these attempts proved to be unsuccessful. In 1927, they visited the Whitehead Torpedo Works in Weymouth, England, and found information that the Royal Navy was indeed experimenting with oxygen torpedoes. This ultimately proved to be untrue but did not deter the Japanese from pursuing their own research. By the end of 1928, a concentrated research project began. In 1932, at the Kure Naval Arsenal, Capt. Kishimoto Kaneharu took command of the research. As expected, the project suffered many disappointments and later successes until the Japanese had the weapon they wanted—the Type 93 or, as it became known by the Western navies, the "Long Lance" torpedo. Formal trials carried out on the heavy cruiser *Chokai* proved the weapon's success.

A comparison of the Type 93 with the then current American torpedo, the Mark 15, shows the Long Lance torpedo's clear superiority.

The Japanese Long Lance vs. the American Mark 15[14]

Japanese Long Lance		**American Mark 15**	
Speed (knots)	Range (yards)	Speed (knots)	Range (yards)
37	44,000	26	15,000
41	25,000	33.5	10,000
49	22,000	45	6,000

The Japanese approved the Type 93 torpedo as its standard for surface ships in November 1935 and installed an upgraded version on its most advanced cruisers in 1938. They built an aerial version, the Type 94, and a version for submarines, the Type 95, in 1935. Because the Long Lance was the most advanced torpedo in the world, the Japanese kept its existence a closely held military secret. Judging by torpedo development then proceeding in the U.S., the Japanese were quite successful in keeping it that way until 1942.

Meanwhile, the U.S. Navy continued developing their own torpedo in the quiet waters off Rhode Island, totally oblivious to its weaknesses. The Japanese, now armed with a remarkable weapon, developed a new torpedo tactic that they called *enkyori ommitsu hassha* or long-distance concealed firing. They designed these new maneuvers so that they could out-range any enemy force and deal it a death blow from far greater distance than ever used before.

Japanese advanced units, most likely cruisers, would stay in contact with the enemy ships in daylight before they could get ready for battle. Firing a massive barrage of 120 to 200 torpedoes from long ranges of about 20,000 yards to overcome the inherent inaccuracy of firing from such a great distance, the enemy ships could be severely damaged before they knew from where the attack came. Although the Japanese estimated that only about ten percent of the torpedoes fired could find a target, some 12 to 20 torpedoes could inflict great damage. The enemy would think the attack came out of nowhere and it would result in a dramatic morale drop off. Like they always did, the Japanese repetitively practiced their new tactic. They merged this tactic into a new two-phase surface battle strategy. The long-distance concealed firing tactic would be the first phase. The second phase would be a large-scale torpedo destroyer attack firing torpedoes from close range. Such tactics required greater coordination among various fleet units. Therefore, the Japanese Navy stepped up torpedo training in all cruiser and destroyer units in the mid-1930s. They eagerly, intensively, and repetitively practiced both daylight and nighttime attacks and expanded their maneuvers to include ever larger fleet units.

By the time war broke out in the Pacific, the Japanese enjoyed a clear tactical superiority over the Americans in cruiser versus cruiser tactics.

The Americans remained blissfully ignorant that their surface battle tactics suffered such a great disparity in both tactics and weaponry. After all, American ships were being equipped with ship-borne radar that they thought would overcome any advantage the Japanese might have in fighting at night. According to the Americans, the Japanese Navy had not faced the U.S. Navy's full power and force and, when they did, would suffer one bitter defeat after another. The events of the Guadalcanal invasion's first nights would prove how wrong they were![15]

CHAPTER 10
At Last, Going on the Offensive

A Prevailing Sense of Defeat

On August 6, Coastwatcher Martin Clemens was in a gloomy mood after a series of severe thunderstorms blanketed Guadalcanal. The storms passed and left the streams only a few inches above their normal depth. The Japanese now had a firm hold on the island, and Clemens and his colleagues had to proceed cautiously as they tried to get as much intelligence as they could about what the Japanese were up to.

The day went too slowly for Clemens and only added to his sense of depression. The weather started to clear as he heard the constant rumble of sound that could only come from some kind of combat operations at the Japanese airfield at Lunga. Sounds of heavy AA fire punctuated the almost constant din. In spite of seeing a B-17 bomber zoom over the island and the sight of some Japanese aircraft falling from the air, he concluded that he would never see his native Australia again. He felt cut off from the rest of the world. After finishing a meal of potatoes for lunch and not eating an evening meal, Clemens lay down in his bed and drifted off to sleep listening to the roar of the river near his hovel.

In spite of his despair, he slept soundly through the night. The light of an early dawn did not awaken him until frequent and heavy explosive sounds shook him fully alert. There was no doubt what those sounds were. Suddenly, whatever mood of depression he had the night before now vanished from his mind. It was still hard to grasp that the help he had yearned for had arrived; he knew it had finally come.

An out-of-breath native scout quickly ran up to Martin's cabin and said that the whole Japanese fleet was now anchored between Guadalcanal and Tulagi. This could not be true; it seemed that his heart stopped beating. Overcoming his immediate feelings of pessimism, he sat down in front of his radio and tried to listen to any radio traffic the ships and planes might be transmitting. The language being spoken over radio was definitely not Japanese; it was English and mostly sounded like American. The days for the Japanese on Guadalcanal were now numbered.[1]

A Great Armada Approaches

Approaching the big island of Guadalcanal from the south as the western sky darkened on August 6, Radm. Kelly Turner knew that the moment he had worked so hard to see become reality was an imminent event. Feeling the historical import of the moment, he sat down at his desk and started to write a message to his command to prepare his men for what was about to happen to them.

Turner was a man with a serious mind and of few words. He did not believe in rah-rah language or delivering pep-talks. Of all the messages he would write prior to operations he would command in the future, the one he wrote on this night of portent was the only one he thought highly enough of to keep for the historical record:

PUBLISH TO ALL HANDS

> On August seventh, this Force will recapture Tulagi and Guadalcanal Islands, which are now in the hands of the enemy.
>
> In this first step forward toward clearing the Japanese out of conquered territory, we have strong support from the Pacific Fleet, and from the air, surface and submarine forces in the South Pacific and Australia.
>
> It is significant of victory that we see here shoulder to shoulder, the U. S. Navy, Marines and Army, and the Australian and New Zealand Air, Naval and Army Services.
>
> I have confidence that all elements of this armada will, in skill and courage, show themselves fit comrades of those brave men who already have dealt the enemy mighty blows for our great cause.
>
> God bless you all.
> R. K. TURNER
> Rear Admiral
> U. S. Navy, Commanding[2]

After Turner's Task Force 62 turned northward at noon on August 6, it proceeded toward the gap between the Russell Islands and Guadalcanal at a reduced speed of 13 knots. The weather turned hazy with intermittent rain squalls further reducing visibility. While the distance between the two land masses showed as 12 miles on the maps, the maps the U.S. Navy had did not show accurately the shoals located there. Pilots and information obtained from New Zealand sources indicated the real distance between Guadalcanal and the Russells was much less than seven miles. Since Turner planned to approach Guadalcanal in the dark in time to start the invasion in the early dawn hours of August 7, the actual safe gap was much less than that, between two to seven miles. Another navigational hazard not shown on the maps was that the currents in the gap were hazardous and unpredictable. The few surface radars available at this stage of the war in Turner's Task Force could not yet detect the outlines of Guadalcanal. Nevertheless, Turner and his 51 ships made it safely through the gap and turned eastward to go between Savo and Guadalcanal Islands with some careful navigating through the potentially treacherous waters. Further reconnaissance uncovered two narrow passages just east of the landing areas, Sealark and Lengo Channels, that would play a role later.

Another hazard Turner wanted to avoid was to be sighted by a Japanese sentry so as to sound an early alarm. He kept the formation's outlying ships as far as possible away from land on either side of the narrow channel. His Task Force avoided this added danger by splitting the narrow passage with highly precise navigation. Turner's Staff Log for August 6 indicated the difficulty of navigation faced by his ships' navigators:

> Last [good] sight about 1400, August 5, 1942...
>
> During forenoon obtained various sun lines of doubtful value... [No] zigzagging in order not to complicate navigational data...
>
> At 1730 *Selfridge* [DD-357, Lt. Cmdr. Carroll D. Reynolds after sighting Bellona Island] rejoined disposition reporting position of *San Juan* [CL-54], Capt. James E. Maher] at 1655 as Latitude 10-58 South, Longitude 159-01 East [115 miles due south of Russell Islands].[3]

The rain squalls and hazy skies were a blessing to the approaching Americans. Since Japanese aircraft in 1942 did not have radar aboard, the only way they could discover the Americans as they approached Guadalcanal was by eyesight. No Japanese aircraft had been seen. Whether they were aloft or not, the weather was definitely in the Americans' favor. Thus far, the Japanese had no idea the Americans were there.[4]

✲ ✲ ✲

By midnight on the 6th, the invasion force was about three miles from its planned position. The flagship *McCawley*'s crew still observed the poor visibility with overcast skies. At 1:33 a.m. on the 7th, the destroyer *Henley*'s lookouts sighted a looming dark land mass with only about 50 minutes left of complete darkness before the moon in its last quarter would try to shine its light through the murky haze. At 50 minutes past midnight, the visibility improved markedly so that men on the flagship could see some nearby ships. However, fortune continued to favor the Americans as the overcast was still there and the temperature held at 80° F.

When the task force was just north of Cape Esperance, it split into two groups. The first, Landing Force X-ray, turned south toward Guadalcanal. The second, designated as Landing Force Yolk, proceeded to the east-northeast toward Florida Island and would later land troops on Tulagi and Gavutu Islands.[5]

✲ ✲ ✲

Fletcher's Task Force 61 of 26 ships separated from Turner's force to position itself to provide air support for the Guadalcanal-Tulagi invasion. Japanese search aircraft constantly patrolled near the carriers, but fortunately for Fletcher, a heavy fog moved in over the ships and hid them from view. Fletcher and his fleet commanders anticipated fighting through Japanese air attacks to reach Guadalcanal, but they need not have worried. The final stages of preparing for invasion day were almost finished.

Three Japanese flying boats left Tulagi in the early morning hours of August 6 and separated to assume their normal patrol zones. Each was to fly south for 400 miles and turn on a 60-mile course as part of a wedge-shaped patrol segment. At about 8:00 a.m., one plane, flying its outbound leg, came very close to Task Force 61, but the cloudy overcast kept the ships from being sighted. Another aircraft flying its outbound leg in the westernmost wedge had to return to its base due to bad weather.

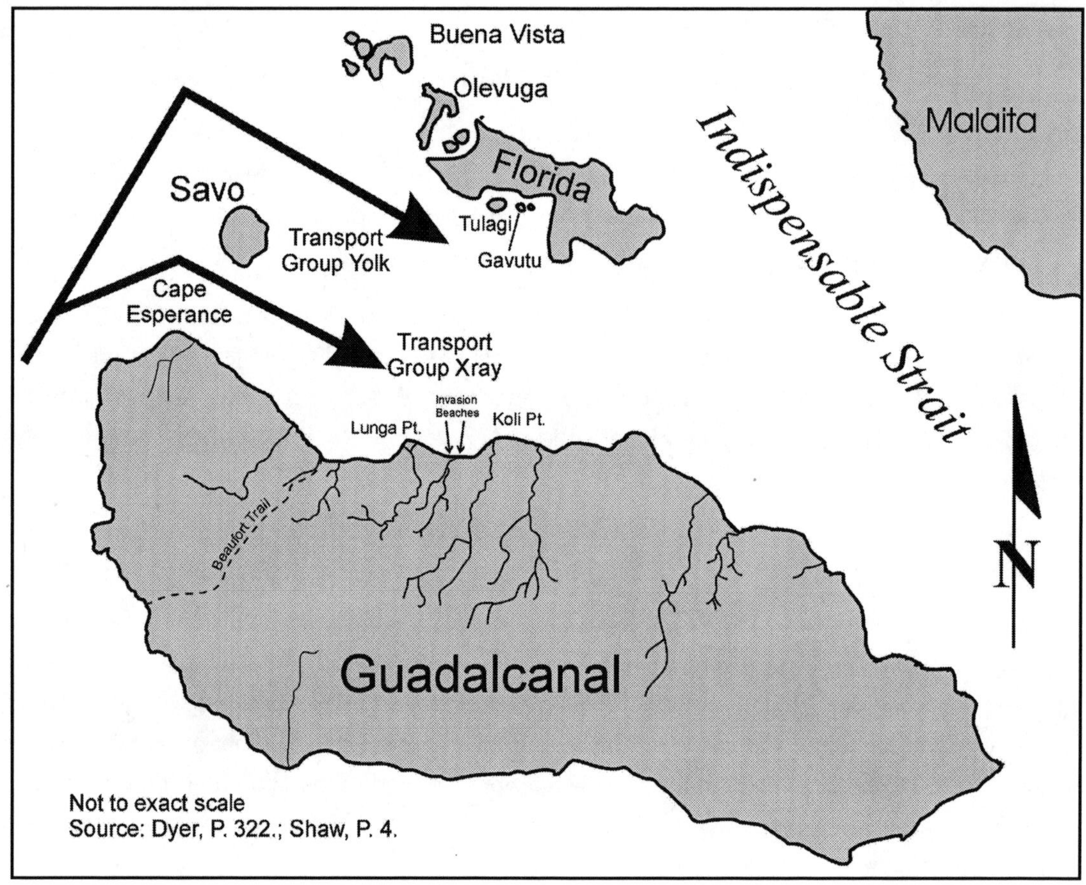

Turner's Task Force Moves into Position to Invade

Radm. Leigh Noyes took tactical command of flight operations at 8:00 a.m. on August 6. He planned to launch planes the next day, but decided not to launch any search aircraft to keep the Japanese from detecting them.

By sunset, the large land mass of Guadalcanal's southern coast appeared on the distant northern horizon just 85 miles away. After the sun went down, the deck crews began their well-organized ritual of moving aircraft that would be part of the first-wave into their launching positions. The crew cleared the decks below for action by piling all bedding on deck in the compartments' center and putting dangerous flammable material in steel cabinets and lockers. Nervous naval aviators tried to get some sleep before being awakened the next morning. All three carriers, *Wasp*, *Enterprise*, and *Saratoga*, had 234 aircraft—98 fighters, 96 dive-bombers, and 40 torpedo bombers—ready to begin the first American offensive of the war.[6]

Is It Fear or Nerves?

Two days before the invasion, the officers and men onboard the attack transport *American Legion* sat down to dinner. A mimeographed message appeared under the plates. Richard Tregaskis, the author of *Guadalcanal Diary* and narrator of the Marines' experiences during this important time in American history, picked up the paper under his plate and read:

> "The American Legion has been singularly honored to be entrusted with getting ashore the first assault wave of the first U. S. ground force offensive action in the present war. Our ship has a good name. I expect it to have an honored and revered name after this coming action."
>
> [signed] Thomas D. Warner
> Captain (USN)
> Commanding Officer"

Adding to the tension of what was to come, an additional note on the sheet stated, "We may expect sudden attack from submarines or bombers at any time from now on."[7]

The men in Turner's invasion force became increasingly edgy and nervous as their moment of truth approached. Many of them had never been in combat before, so it was a natural reaction.

After finishing dinner, Tregaskis went back to his cabin and found his roommate, Marine Capt. William Hawkins, who was to be one of the first to "hit the beach," oiling his submachine gun and cartridges. Tregaskis, somewhat prompted by the ship's captain's note, started talking about the upcoming struggle; the conversation turned to how Hawkins felt about his being one of the assault's leaders. Coming from his background as a seller of wholesale groceries in Boston, he said, "I don't feel funny about it. I don't feel any more nervous than if I were being sent out to do a tough job in civilian life—you know, like trying to sell a big order, when there's a lot of sales resistance."[8]

Was he scared or just nervous? His words said he was nervous. Ask any combat veteran whether he was frightened while waiting to go into combat. Interviews with war veterans have shown that, while they spoke of being somewhat nervous, they were really frightened by the knowledge that they might be killed in the next few hours. It was a rare person who felt nothing in these circumstances. These men overcame their fear by concentrating on their jobs in a very single-minded way.

On August 6, that was exactly what the men on the *American Legion* did. Sailors on deck prepared the booms that would lower the landing boats into the water once they anchored off Guadalcanal. Marines received canned rations—enough to sustain them for two to three days until the field kitchens could be brought ashore—containing concentrated coffee, biscuits, meat and beans, vegetable stew, and chocolate bars. In the ship's armory, crowds of men checked their weapons for any needed last-minute adjustments and cleaning.

More nervousness surfaced at lunch when Lt. Patrick Jones of Kansas City reminded all who could hear him that this ship carried the battalion's ammunition and gasoline reserves and hoped that a Japanese bomb would not find them.

Fortunately, the weather favored the Americans with a dense overcast and hazy visibility. Any Japanese airplane would have to get very close before they could see any target. Nevertheless, many wondered if all this quiet was a Japanese ruse to lure the task force into a trap.

Trying to break the sense of gloom and foreboding, Dr. Malcolm Pratt, the senior medical officer on the *American Legion*, recited a funny encounter he had the night before. "I went below to look around in the hold last night, expecting to find the kids praying, and instead I found 'em doing a native war dance. One of them had a towel for a loin cloth and a blackened face, and he was doing a cancan while another beat a tom-tom. In one corner of the room, there were about four or five boys wrestling around, but no one paid any attention to them."[9]

The afternoon passed as Marines completed the stocking of their packs by neatly tying rolled blankets to them. Men scurried up and down the passageways with their arms full of black hand grenades. Sailors on deck opened up cases of medium caliber artillery ammunition in preparation for the next day.

More nervousness surfaced at dinner later that night in the officers' mess. One man thought he had heard AA fire. Another officer confirmed he had heard it too. But this was not the case. The rolling of heavy drums on the deck was the cause of the rumbling sounds. Later that night, a ship's announcement said that breakfast would be served at 4:30 a.m. the next morning. The history of warfare would soon be forever changed with the launch of the largest amphibious operation ever undertaken. The time for war was near.[10]

Launch Aircraft!

Jack Fletcher's carrier Task Force 61 moved northward at midnight on August 7 toward Guadalcanal to get into position for the launch of its aircraft to support the landings scheduled to begin that morning. The *Saratoga* steamed due north at 15 knots with all its lights off to avoid being detected by Japanese submarines that might be nearby.

Radm. Noyes was now in tactical command as the other two carriers, the *Enterprise* and *Wasp,* also began preparations to launch their aircraft. 30 minutes past midnight, the *Saratoga* turned east to course 090° and began zigzagging three hours later according to standing orders to prevent submarine attacks.

At 4:30 a.m., flight operations began on the *Saratoga* with General Quarters to be sounded 45 minutes later. Stopping zigzagging at 5:26 a.m., the *Saratoga* turned into the wind by changing its course to 125°. The first F4F aircraft left the carrier's flight deck and lifted into the darkness. Although the pilots of Task Force 61 had practiced takeoffs and landings at night before, they had never launched their planes in such a large operation. Again, trying to prevent sightings by the Japanese, Noyes allowed only the planes' taillights to be lit for the first five miles after takeoff. The plan was to turn the planes' running lights on after that to allow other aircraft to rendezvous away from the carriers. Nevertheless, the lights from the launching planes' exhausts could be seen for miles, thus making Noyes' order somewhat superfluous and potentially dangerous. Taking off in the darkness resulted in the carrier squadrons being intermixed and caused much confusion among the aircrews. Planes joined the wrong air groups while others formed up in small groups. Blaming others for the chaos, the flight crews muddled through and followed their orders to attack their targets.

Lt. Cmdr. Wallace M. Beakley of the *Wasp*, flying the only torpedo bomber on the mission (a TBF), led the strike group to attack Tulagi accompanied by 16 F4F fighters and 15 SBD dive-bombers from his ship and 9 dive-bombers from the *Enterprise* led by Lt. Turner F. Caldwell. The *Saratoga*'s Cmdr.

Harry D. Felt, flying a SBD dive-bomber, led the Guadalcanal strike group with 12 F4F fighters and 23 SBD dive-bombers from the *Saratoga*. Lt. Louis H. Bauer led a group of eight F4F fighters from the *Enterprise* as additional support for the Guadalcanal strike. Eighty-five American aircraft—36 American naval fighters, 48 SBD dive-bombers, and one torpedo bomber—headed northward to begin the aerial bombardment of Guadalcanal and Tulagi islands.[11]

Firing the First Shot

The ships of Turner's Task Force 62 slowed as they slipped quietly through the waters of what would be later named Iron Bottom Sound. Their speed slowed as the water hissed beneath their hulls. The sky had cleared and the dawn's light began illuminating the hills of Guadalcanal and Florida islands. Led to believe by the literature of that day that Guadalcanal was a pesthole of decay, vermin, and rotten vegetation, the sailors on deck stood awestruck by the seemingly breathtaking beauty of the two islands on either side of their ships.

One Marine war correspondent vividly described what all the others saw that day:

> "...Guadalcanal is an island of striking beauty. Blue-green mountains, towering into a brilliant tropical sky or crowned with cloud masses, dominate the island. The dark green of jungle growth blends into the softer greens and browns of coconut groves and grassy plains and ridges."

The unfolding sight also moved the normally taciturn Turner to recall: "A truly beautiful sight that morning."

Turner's plan was to open fire at 6:15 a.m. Two minutes before that, Capt. Samuel N. Moore of the heavy cruiser *Quincy* ordered his nine eight-inch guns to begin the invasion. The muzzles of the nine great guns lit up the dawn sky by belching fire and smoke. Nine eight-inch shells screamed for the Guadalcanal shore to wreak their havoc. The rest of the fleet followed immediately and joined in the bombardment. The invasion of Guadalcanal had begun.[12]

CHAPTER 11
Attack!

Hitting the Beach

Knowing they were going to war that morning, no Marine had any problem getting up at four in the morning. They had been training for this day for a long time and were anxious to get going and get the job done.

The quiet tone at the officers' and enlisted men's mess belied the tension that filled the room. Today, for some of them, would be their last day. Everyone understood these feelings, but they were ready. All ate heartedly and some comical banter passed between them. It seemed that it was the most normal thing to do to climb down into small boats, head for an unknown island, and engage an unknown enemy.

The *American Legion*'s starboard rail faced the Guadalcanal shore, and the Marines lined it to observe the bombardment the navy had begun just a few minutes after 6 a.m. The water was glassy-smooth as many of the men pointed their binoculars towards Guadalcanal's still dark shore and coolly observed the effects of the now cacophonous barrage on the beaches. There was an almost delusional aura that what was happening in front of them was not actually occurring at all. They were thousands of miles from home at a place they only knew by name; an almost surreal aura hung in the air.

The mood among the ship's officers on the bridge was less calm. Just before the cruisers opened fire, one officer exclaimed, "I can't believe it. I wonder if the Japs can be that dumb. Either they're very dumb, or it's a trick." The building suspicion that the Americans had caught the Japanese completely by surprise was now confirmed.

The bombardment continued its intense fury along the murky outline of Tulagi and the other islands in the Florida group now alight from the guns' flashes. To the south of the *American Legion*, the jagged, looming mass of Guadalcanal became more distinct. No return fire came from the shore.

The *American Legion* and other attack transports changed their course so their bows pointed at the Guadalcanal shore. The sound of the clinking davits foretold the lowering of boats. Muffled engine sounds surrounded the ships as very young boys, soon to become men, dressed in dark green uniforms clambered to the rails preparing to get into their boats. With all the firing and tremendous noise engulfing them, they carried out their duties according to their training with a calm that belied the seeming chaos going on around them. Concussions from the naval guns engulfed the men on the decks as hot breezes from the gunfire moved over the decks in spite of their distance from the naval guns. The signal went out to start loading the boats. The naval bombardment stopped. The moment of combat for the Marines was soon to be upon them.

The cruisers again opened fire. Repeated salvoes arched their way to the darkened beaches, leaving traces of red in their wake. Suddenly, a large column of black, dense smoke rose from the shore. The men in the boats knew that a Japanese gasoline dump had been struck. A few moments later, searing flames violently rose from where the smoke was.

American aircraft strafed and bombed the beaches with seemingly devastating effect. The men on deck were quiet, deep in their own thoughts about what was ahead for them. One Marine could be heard saying, "Well, this is it."

Now it was time to get into the boats. The cruisers continued firing. The first men in line clambered over the rails and started down the rope net ladders. In spite of calm waters, the boats and ships bobbed in the water. Getting down a pitching rope ladder into a bobbing landing craft was not an easy thing to do; the tensions of anticipating combat and death did not make it any easier. Nevertheless, their intense training took over and the Marines made the climb down the nets to the landing craft with little trouble. As boats left the ship's side, others immediately took their place. After following Col. Hunt and his staff down the rope nets into the bobbing landing boat, Richard

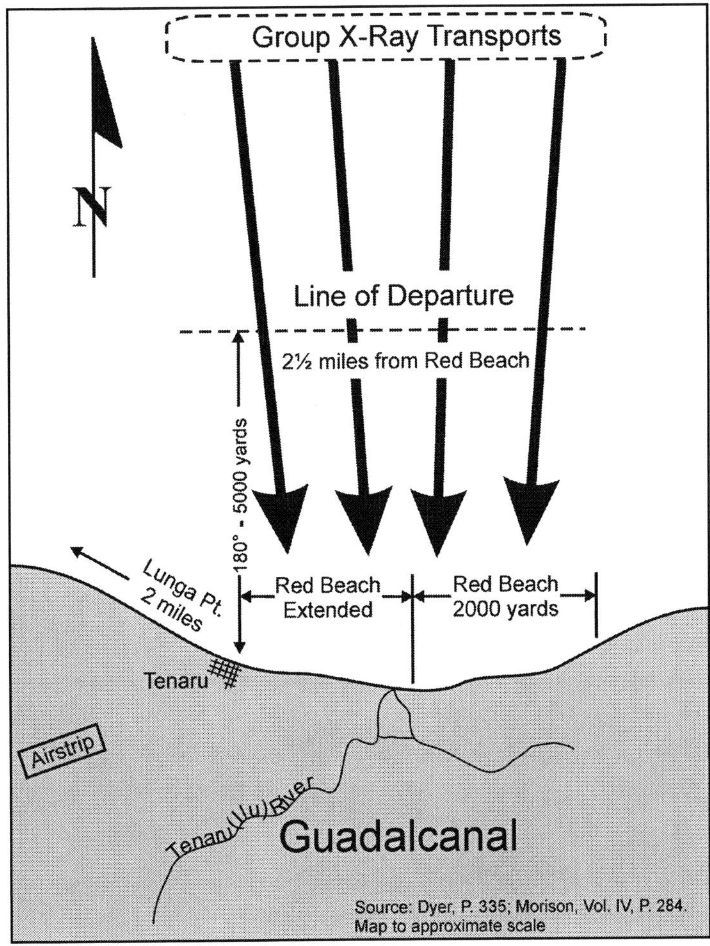

Guadalcanal Landing Beaches

Tregaskis crouched near the gunwale of his landing boat and slowly raised his head to peer over the parapet. The warships had by now moved closer to the shore to increase the accuracy of their gunfire. Suddenly, they ceased firing although Tregaskis could still hear the distant loud, heavy, and deep throated rumbles of naval gunfire near the Tulagi landing zones.

The landing boat's motor increased its sound as its coxswain pushed the throttle to its maximum. The boat surged forward and passed some cruisers and destroyers. Suddenly, the eardrum-crushing sound of large caliber naval gunfire explosively engulfed everyone in the boat as the ships once again opened fire on the beaches. Yellow sheets of flame surged from the gun muzzles followed by ominous black and blue geysers shooting up on the rapidly approaching Guadalcanal beaches. Three minutes after the firing started, it stopped again. Tregaskis' boat headed for a huge looming column of black smoke that obviously had resulted from the withering gunfire.

White spots of foam from the first wave of landing boats moved onto the beaches as black spots. These were the landing boats themselves, moving onto the shore. Tregaskis' boat was not far behind. Although they could not actually see the leading boats touch the shore, the first troops to reach land waved signal flags. Col. Hunt, commander of the 5th Marine Regiment, First Marine Division, turned to everyone with a big smile. No words were necessary. The first American amphibious landing on a hostile shore in World War II and the largest since the Spanish-American War was a great success.

A signalman relayed the good news to the mother ship. The acknowledgment came back just as quickly.

Everyone knew that a successful landing did not mean, by itself, that there was no opposition waiting for the Marines of the First Marine Division. Just to be safe, all in Tregaskis' boat kept their heads low behind the gunwales. Soon, they passed the first wave boats returning from shore and heading back to their respective ships for more troops. Their boat continued its unstoppable course toward the shore.

By 9:40 a.m., the palm trees came into view, which meant Tregaskis and his compatriots in the landing boat were now close to the oncoming shore. The boat's noisy motor prevented anyone who wanted to talk from hearing each other. It was clear that the excitement of the moment overcame any attempt to talk. Each man in the boat looked at each other with a silent recognition that fear was the prime emotion each was trying to conquer.

In the next seven minutes, their boat drew nearer to the shore where they could see a long line of boats up on the shore. Troops crowded onto the shore and moved inland. Some mingled among a group of thatched huts adjacent to the beach. It was obvious that no Japanese troops were anywhere near the beach. The fear held by those in Tregaskis' boat dissipated somewhat as they poked their heads over the gunwale to get a better look at what was ahead for them.

Three minutes later, their boat crunched on the sand and everyone scrambled over the boat's sides and bow onto land. Expecting to hear the deadly rattle of Japanese machine guns, they heard no opposing gunfire whatsoever. Red Beach bristled with activity: vehicles moving up and down the beach, working parties setting up communications, more troops landing and larger barges moving onshore and disgorging machinery, vehicles and supplies.

The Marines had landed, and they meant to stay! The Americans had successfully launched the first major American ground offensive of the war.[1]

Protecting the Flank

The islands of Tulagi and Gavutu had the only significant Japanese military presence in the southern Solomon Islands, and that threat had to be removed. If it had not been eliminated, there would be a danger to the larger landings on Guadalcanal. Transport Group "YOLK" had split from the main body off the northwest Guadalcanal coast about 3:00 a.m. on August 7, rounded the northern side of Savo Island, and steamed off the southern coast of Tulagi and Gavutu Islands and their much larger neighbor to the north, Florida Island. The invasion force was much smaller than the one off Guadalcanal's northern coast. It had only four transports (*Neville*, *Heywood*, *President Jackson*, and *Zeilin*) and four destroyer-transports (*Little*, *McKean*, *Gregory*, and *Colhoun*). This reflected an assumption that the effort to take Tulagi would not require as much effort as that thought needed to capture Guadalcanal. Only four Marine battalions under the command of Brig. Gen. William B. Rupertus made up the invasion force to be dropped off on the small island beach. One of the Marine battalions in the invasion force was the 1st Raider Battalion. The man who commanded this unit would become one of most famous Marine officers to emerge from World War II combat, Lt. Col. Merritt Edson. His name would be part of Marine folklore and the place where one of the most gallant defense named after him would be fought on Guadalcanal.

Tulagi was a small island only 4,000 yards long and 18 miles north of the Guadalcanal landing beach. Tulagi's southern third had been turned into the Solomon Island Protectorate by the Australians with the development of the customary governor's residence atop a hill, golf course, cricket field, courthouse, jail, wharves, and merchant shops.

Tulagi's harbor is on the island's northeast side with the small, high island of Gavutu about 3,500 yards across the harbor's mouth. The much smaller island of Tanambogo lay to the north with a causeway connecting the two tiny islands. Before the war, Lever Soap had constructed offices, warehouses, and wharves on the harbor's shores.

In May 1941, the Japanese arrived in an almost bloodless fashion and set up a seaplane base. About 500 Japanese troops on Tulagi and 1,000 more on the two smaller islands dug in and prepared to be attacked, although that did not happen right away.

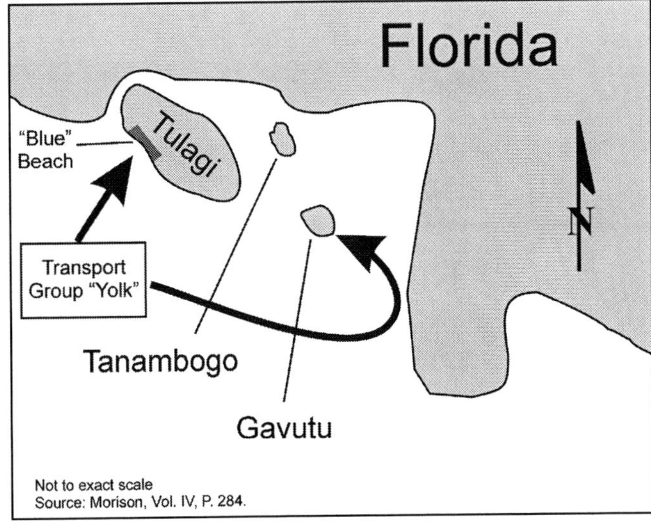

Tulagi-Gavutu Invasion

The Tulagi and Gavutu terrain dictated a complicated landing plan that both Adm. Turner and Gen. Vandegrift had put together to the last level of detail. The landing took place on "Blue" Beach on the Tulagi's southwestern side, which was thought to be thinly defended, if defended at all. On August 6, the Japanese propagandist, Tokyo Rose, listened to by almost every American soldier, sailor, Marine, or coast guardsman in the Pacific Theater, broadcast an indication of how clueless the Japanese were about American intentions in the South Pacific, "Where are the U.S. Marines hiding?...No one has seen them yet!"[2]

At 8:00 a.m., the first wave of Marine raiders waded ashore on "Blue" beach. No one was there to greet them. However, the surprise did not last long. The Japanese had seen the boats moving off shore and sent out the warning message, "Enemy has commenced landing," 45 minutes earlier. Those who hoped the landings would be unopposed would soon see this wish dashed. The Marines immediately moved inland, crossed a ridge that divided the island, and soon were on Tulagi's eastern shore.

The second wave landed a few minutes later, moved along the island's crest, and along the western shore. Another battalion immediately followed. The Japanese's Tulagi radio station sent off another message, "Enemy strength is overwhelming" at 8:00 a.m. The cruiser *San Juan* snuffed out the transmitter with a salvo shortly after that. A too-brief naval bombardment—not unusual at this time in the war with amphibious warfare still new in the minds of American planners—did little to pave the way for the American troops. It only forced the Japanese defenders underground instead of killing them.

Resistance on Tulagi, Tanambogo, and Gavutu soon stiffened, and the Marines realized they were in for a fight. The fight for Gavutu and Tanambogo proved to be even tougher than for Tulagi, but the Japanese eventually succumbed to overwhelming force at 10:00 p.m. on August 8. The relatively easy struggle for Guadalcanal would soon become much more difficult. The Japanese knew the Americans had arrived.[3]

CHAPTER 12
The Japanese Strike by Air!

Radm. Sadayashi Yamada, the commander of the 5th Air Attack Force at the ever burgeoning Japanese base at Rabaul, awoke after a fitful sleep early on August 7. The Japanese Navy held him in high esteem. A naval aviator since 1919 and probably the most senior naval pilot to hold a combat command, Yamada had much cause to be pessimistic about the conduct of Japanese campaigns in the South Pacific.

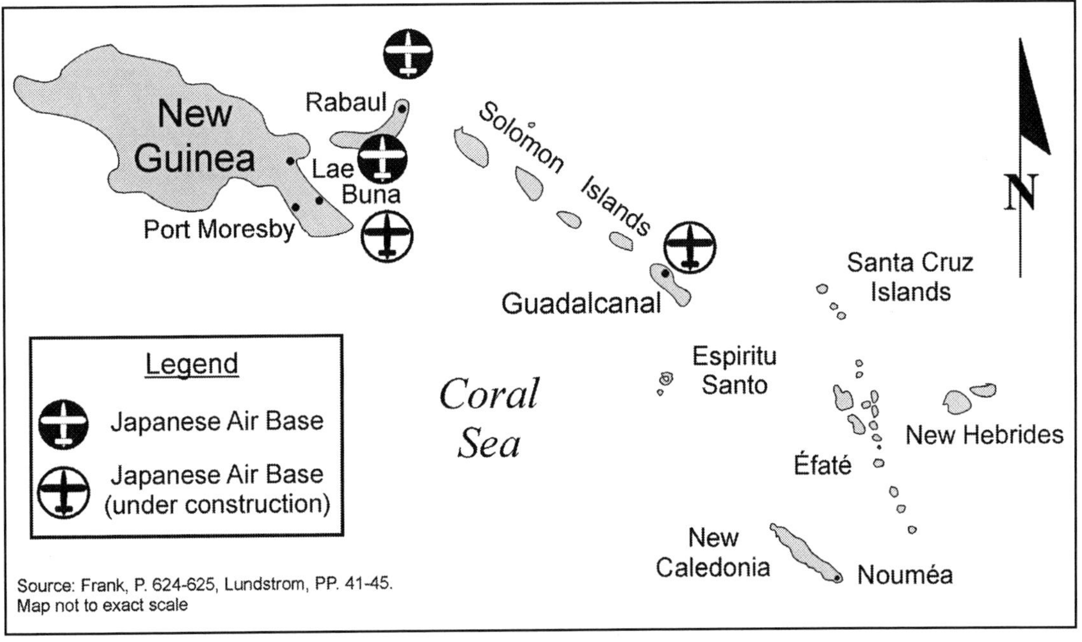

Japanese Naval Air Bases

Air attacks against the Americans and Australians from Japanese bases on Rabaul and at Lae on New Guinea continued, but with mixed results. Japanese construction units on Guadalcanal and at Buna on Papua were making fine progress building new airfields. Since the Japanese attempt to capture Port Moresby on the New Guinea south coast had failed with the Imperial Japanese Navy's withdrawal after being confronted by Fletcher's task force in the Coral Sea, the Allies had grown in strength so that losses of Japanese aircraft and pilots had increased. Yamada's command was being stretched beyond the limits of available resources.

The Japanese Army's campaign to traverse the formidable Owen Stanley Mountains and take Port Moresby by land moved too slowly for Yamada's liking. Australian and American troops had met the Japanese, and the results of that fighting could be optimistically described as a stalemate. Japanese intelligence had no information where the Americans would strike next. The information vacuum on American intentions was a troubling matter indeed.

His primary mission was to support the New Guinea operations. However, Japanese ambitions in the South Pacific were much broader than that. Among the objectives for Japanese armed forces were the occupations of the Fiji Islands, New Caledonia, and Samoa. The latter was an even more ambitious target because of the long distances from Japanese supply bases, thus stretching supply lines even more than they already were.[1]

✲ ✲ ✲

When the American ships appeared in the early daylight hours at 6:00 a.m., the first message from the Japanese commander at the air base on Tulagi arrived in Rabaul. Yamada received the message at 6:52 a.m. and said, "Enemy force sighted."

That missive startled Yamada and members of his staff. He waited until he had more details before alerting his command. He did not have to wait long. Another message arrived at Rabaul that provided scant but more information 13 minutes later: "Enemy task force of twenty ships attacking Tulagi, undergoing severe bombings, landing preparations underway; help requested."

At 7:15, the following message confirmed what Yamada knew to be true: "Enemy has commenced landing."[2]

✲ ✲ ✲

Before the war, the Allies estimated that the 5th Air Attack Force had 60 fighters, 60 bombers, and 30 flying boats for a total of 150 planes. Yamada knew his force was weaker than the Americans had estimated. His unit reported to the 11th Air Fleet, which was the Japanese Navy's main land-based air command in the South Pacific, commanded by of Vadm. Nishizo Tsukahara. When the Americans landed on Tulagi and Guadalcanal, Yamada had 39 fighters, 32 medium bombers, 16 dive-bombers, six pontoon fighters located at his Rabaul and Lae bases, and the 11 flying boats located on Tulagi, a total of 104 combat aircraft. Despite Yamada's misgivings, the 5th Air Attack Force was a powerful force.[3]

Japanese Air Counterattack

On August 3, Yamada's scout planes found a small airstrip being built by the Allies at Rabi on Milne Bay at New Guinea's easternmost point. If his enemy could place aircraft there, his airfields at Buna and Lae could be attacked with very little warning. Ordering the return of all his Zero fighters, he started the planning for an overwhelmingly destructive attack on the airstrip for August 7.

As he sat at his desk with his officers planning for the Rabi mission, another note arrived. It was the last message transmitted from the air commander on Tulagi before the Americans destroyed his radio transmitter. It reported that one battleship, one carrier, three cruisers, 15 destroyers, and many transports were in the channel off Guadalcanal and in the surrounding seas.

Realizing the new combat situation had become critical, Yamada immediately cancelled the Rabi mission and issued orders to attack American naval, shipping, and land forces in and around Guadalcanal.[4]

The fighter pilots of the Tainan Group stood around the headquarters building to hear their orders for the day. Yamada's newest order to cancel the Rabi mission and mount an attack on the Americans at Guadalcanal caused chaos to run rampant throughout the Command Post. Lt. Cmdr. Tadashi Nakajima, the Tainan Group's commander, stormed out of Yamada's office and angrily said, "Today's mission has been called off. We're going somewhere else." Looking around the room, he shouted, "Where the hell is that orderly?" Pointing to an astonished messenger, "You, get me a chart, quick!" Ignoring the pilots as he looked at the map spread out covering the table before him, he intently looked at the situation facing him. Lt. (jg) Junichi Sasai tried to ask his superior what was going on, but Nakajima brusquely brushed his query aside and went back to see Yamada.

It was not a surprise to learn their scheduled attack on Rabi had been cancelled. But then Nakajima told them:

> "At 0520 hours this morning a powerful enemy amphibious force began an invasion at Lunga, on the southern end of Guadalcanal Island. Our first reports indicate that the Americans are throwing a tremendous amount of men and equipment onto the island. They also have struck in simultaneous attacks at Tulagi on Florida Island. Our entire flying-boat flotilla has been destroyed. As soon as the commander has worked out our new routes, we will take off at once for Guadalcanal to attack the enemy forces on the beaches."[5]

The flyers gasped in shock and amazement. No one in the Japanese Navy ever expected the Americans to execute such a daring operation. The pilots immediately pored over the charts of the attack area. Guadalcanal was 560 nautical miles to the southeast, the longest mission they would ever attempt. The room was in full turmoil. Nakajima asked for quiet and clearly warned them of the difficulties they were about to face:

> "You are going to fly the longest fighter operation in history," he warned us. "Don't take any unnecessary chances today. Stick to your orders, and, above all, don't fly recklessly and waste your fuel. Any pilot who runs short of fuel on the return from Guadalcanal is to make a forced landing at Buka Island. Our troops there have been instructed to be on the lookout for our planes.
>
> Now, to fly to Guadalcanal and return to Buka means covering roughly the same distance as we flew from Tainan to Clark Field in the Philippines, and return. I am positive that we can fly that distance without trouble. Returning to Rabaul is another matter. You should be able to make it, but there may be trouble. So I repeat my warning: don't waste fuel."[6]

To put this in perspective, the American and British bombers flying missions over Nazi Germany from their bases in eastern England to Berlin had to travel 460 nautical miles—about 20 percent shorter than the distance the Japanese pilots would have to fly. The new mission would surely test the endurance of both pilots and aircraft.

The Tainan Air Group had some of the best pilots ever to fly for Japan. Many of them were already aces (five or more victories), and some of them had already gained heroic stature in the Navy and with the people in the homeland. Formed in October 1941 from mostly veterans of the air war over China, the group dominated skies over the Dutch East Indies and the Philippines. They carried out their missions from Rabaul and Lae and fought tough air battles against American and Australian pilots who proved to be a far more formidable enemy than the vastly under trained pilots in China. Their commanding officer had been Capt. Masahisa Saito, a veteran fighter pilot with years of flying experience. The leader of the group chosen to fly this operation this day was Nakajima, one of the oldest fighter pilots still flying combat missions for the Japanese Navy.

The appearance of the Imperial Japanese Navy's new Mitsubishi A6M2 Type 0 carrier fighter, Model 21 (later Zeke to the Allies) or, as it became known throughout the world, the Zero, in the Pacific War completely stunned the Americans and their Allies. Using racist stereotyping somewhat prevalent at that time, it seemed impossible that "Oriental" people could ever produce anything superior to what the Western Powers could build. But after aerial combat against the well-trained and experienced Japanese pilots, the Allies realized how wrong that assessment was. The sleek and light aircraft, called the *Reisen* by the Japanese, was the clearly superior combat fighter aircraft at that time of the war.[7] In spite of a lack of any armor plate or self-sealing fuel tanks, the Zero's superlative maneuverability, climbing speed, acceleration, strong armament, and superior range made this plane the scourge of the sky. The Zero lost that claim when the P-51 Mustang entered combat in 1943.[8]

Fully armed with their wing tanks and an extra fuel tank with all the gas they could hold, 18 Type 21 Zeroes took off from Lakunai at 9:50 a.m. under Nakajima's command. The formation made a long climb to conserve fuel and joined 27 Bettys from Vunakanau as escorts. The bombers formed three nine-plane Vee-of-Vees formations while the Zeroes moved into their escort positions. Divided into three flights (*Chutai*s), Nakajima led the 1st *Chutai* to its place at the bombers' rear and to the right. Sasai, considered as a rising star combat pilot in the Imperial Japanese Navy, moved his 3rd *Chutai* also to the bombers' rear but to their right. Lt. Shiro Kawai's 2nd *Chutai* flew above the formation to protect it from high attacks.

Each *Chutai* had three sections (*Shotai*s). Kawai's 2nd *Shotai*'s group leader was the Imperial Japanese Navy's leading ace, PO1c Saburo Sakai. He had 46 victories up to that time and was a celebrity in the Navy and at home.[9]

✡ ✡ ✡

Sakai was not happy that the bombers carried bombs instead of torpedoes. He had already witnessed that trying to hit ships with bombs from high altitudes was a hopeless task. He had seen that even the dauntingly precise American B-17 wasted many bombs, thus scoring very few hits against Japanese ships near Buna. The "Betty" was not nearly as accurate as that.

The formation slowly climbed to an altitude of 13,000 feet and flew eastward toward Buka Island. About 60 miles south of Rabaul, Sakai glanced out the bubble canopy of his Zero. A strikingly beautiful green-forested, horseshoe-shaped island on the deep blue water appeared below him. Glancing at his map, he noticed it was aptly called Green Island. Although he did not realize it at the time, this place would be vital in saving his life.

Sakai and the rest of the pilots turned their planes southward from there and proceeded along Bougainville's west coast toward Guadalcanal. The sun's rays flooded his compartment making it uncomfortably warm. He wanted to drink some cool liquid to satisfy his thirst. Knowing there was still plenty of time before he reached where the Americans were, he reached down into his lunch box and took out a can of soda. Forgetting that his plane was at a high altitude, he used his pocket knife to make a slit in the tin can's top. Much to his shock, the soda water squirted violently out of the can, covering his flight suit and goggles. Drying fast in the rarefied altitude, the liquid soon evaporated and left a film on his goggle lenses. This soon became an impenetrable fog of dried sugar. Sakai disgustedly tried to wipe them clean, but only succeeded in making them foggier and harder to see through them.

The next 40 minutes filled Sakai's time as he tried to clean up the soda spill from the windscreen and his plane's controls. The rest of the pilots in his formation must have thought he was sick as his plane veered out of its place and drifted as if it was being piloted by a drunkard. Sakai's irritation with himself increased as he frantically wiped all around his compartment. He finally succeeded getting it clean enough to see the island of Vella Lavella below him—about half way to Guadalcanal from Rabaul.

The formation flew higher over New Georgia Island and reached 20,000 feet as it passed over the Russell Islands. A huge mound of land appeared ahead in the ocean. Guadalcanal was now in sight, a mere 50 miles away. Despite the bright sun and blue sky, Sakai could see yellow flashes of gunfire. It was obvious that battles between other Zero fighters from Rabaul and his enemy's planes had already begun. It was not long before he flew near Guadalcanal's northern coastline and saw the wakes of hundreds of ships making white foam in the ocean below. He had never seen so many warships and transports in one place before.

Sakai was awestruck by the size and apparent power of the amphibious landing proceeding before his very eyes. He observed at least 70 ships relentlessly pushing toward the beaches in the waters between Florida and Guadalcanal islands. More ships loomed over the horizon, but they were too far away for him to identify or number.

The Japanese bombers moved toward their intended targets to wreak maximum damage on the Allied transports and warships. The Japanese had come to beat back this encroachment on their empire.[10] The Americans knew they were on their way.

✲ ✲ ✲

Three messages turned the routine of Adm. Noyes' pilots, currently performing normal Combat Air Patrol (CAP) duties protecting the precious American carriers, into chaos. The first of two messages from CINCPAC arrived at about 11:30 a.m. in Fletcher's communications center on the *Saratoga*. After being decrypted by ULTRA, the first message said 18 bombers and 17 Zeros had left Rabaul for Guadalcanal. With the American carrier force within 60 miles of Guadalcanal, Fletcher became more apprehensive about where these planes were heading. Arriving nine minutes later, the second message (also decrypted by ULTRA) said that Japanese submarines were on their way to Tulagi.

The most definitive message that disturbed everyone was the third, which came from an Australian coastwatcher with the call sign (STO) that identified him as PO Paul E. Mason, RANVR. Perched on a mountain side at Malabita Hill in southern Bougainville, he saw approaching Japanese planes. His chilling and ominous message reported, "From STO, 24 bombers headed yours."[11] Mason's message was the first giving direct, precise information about Japanese ships and aircraft movements after the Allied ships arrived off Guadalcanal and Tulagi. He was part of the network of coastwatchers established by the Australian Navy throughout the South Pacific. And his message would certainly not be the last.

Now, Fletcher, already nervous about the potential fate of his carriers, was caught in a difficult quandary. Already within a short flying distance from the invasion area and with a limited number of fighters to fly CAP, the need to provide support for the Marines on the ground and protect against Japanese air attacks over the invasion beaches, he had to choose which mission was the most important. Again exhibiting his usually cautious nature and ever mindful of his earlier decision to withdraw the carriers after two days of the invasion's start, he decided that protection of the carriers was the most important. With 24 F4Fs flying CAP over the carriers and 24 more fighters waiting on carrier decks to relieve them, Fletcher decided these planes would not fly to Guadalcanal but stay near the carriers to protect them.

Meanwhile, the situation over the invasion area became more tense. Fourteen F4Fs had been providing SCAP over the invasion area for about an hour and a half. But they started to run out of fuel and had to return to their carriers. Only eight F4Fs remained for the next 90 minutes. Reinforcing the carriers' ground support mission strained their capabilities to land, refuel, rearm, and launch aircraft beyond the maximum. As the Japanese had learned at Midway, the intricate and arduous nature of carrier launching and landing operations made it impossible to do this on demand. It took the planes 30 minutes to fly from their bases to reach their assigned combat stations over the invasion area. This forced them to consume even more fuel and thus reduce their time over the combat areas.

The *Saratoga* had been scheduled to launch eight F4Fs for CAP under the command of Lt. Richard E. Harmer and Lt. Herbert S. Brown Jr.'s four fighters for SCAP at 12:03 p.m. The carrier's captain ordered Lt. James J. (Pug) Southerland's division plus four F4Fs to take off 75 minutes early and give help to the American fighters.

Southerland and his fellow pilots relaxed in the wardroom relishing a badly needed breather after undergoing two stressful CAP assignments. Knowing this quiet time would not last long, they ate a quick lunch. But that respite ended quickly when a messenger came into the room. The *Saratoga*'s skipper Capt. DeWitt W. Ramsey finally realized that the eight F4Fs over the invasion area was dangerously insufficient after 12 F4Fs launched to take over CAP. Southerland read the paper handed to him by the messenger and bolted from his chair. He ran up to the ready room to warn his men that the stress of the day would not end soon. They, along with four additional F4Fs, would be launching and heading for the Guadalcanal invasion to fly SCAP.

The pilots sprinted up to the flight deck where the plane captains had equipped their 16 fighters with belly tanks that would give more flying time over target area. Soon, the first of them, with engines run up to full throttle, accelerated down the *Saratoga*'s deck and lifted into the air at 12:03 p.m. After all 16 were airborne, they turned northward on a flight path toward Guadalcanal.

The situation over the Guadalcanal invasion area was about to become even more confused. Lt. Louis H. Bauer left the *Enterprise* with his six F4Fs to fly to the invasion area. Two of these were designated to replace the two F4Fs that were protecting Lt. Cmdr. Maxwell F. (Max) Leslie, the strike director over Lunga. Lt. Hawley ("Monk") Russell's four fighters, the remaining F4Fs over Guadalcanal, had no direct assignment and therefore flew an ad hoc form of CAP.

Bauer's division reached their place over the invasion area at 12:30 p.m. Soon, the *Chicago*'s radar picked up a large formation of planes heading for Guadalcanal from the northwest. Lt. Robert M. Bruning, acting as FDO, ordered Bauer's fighters to the northwest on a 310° heading and an altitude of 8,000 feet. However, Bauer, still east of Savo Island, received an order about 30 minutes later to head *south-southeast* over western Guadalcanal—almost in the opposite direction. That course which would take his formation toward the carriers now about 25 miles away. Bauer asked for a confirmation of these orders and received a positive acknowledgment that his new course was indeed south-southwest, away from Guadalcanal.

But the confusion did not end there. Bauer overheard orders that four fighters currently providing CAP over the carriers should head north toward Guadalcanal. Not understanding why his planes were ordered south, his confusion and bewilderment increased. Nevertheless, he dutifully obeyed his new orders and soon orbited over the carriers. If his planes had orbited over Savo Island as originally planned, they would have been in the direct path of the approaching Japanese bombers.

The *Enterprise* and *Wasp* continued launching CAP fighters, increasing the CAP over the carriers to nearly 40 planes. No Japanese planes appeared overhead. Realizing that a dreadful mistake had been made after once fearing that the oncoming Japanese planes might turn southward and head for the carriers, Lt. Henry A. Rowe, acting FDO onboard the *Enterprise* responsible for CAP, finally directed Lt. Carl W. Rooney's eight F4Fs toward Tulagi. But they would get there too late to be of any help.

The American fighter defenses had just eight fighters protecting the invasion force.[12]

Above 13,000 feet, the bottoms of thick, cumulus clouds covered the waters around Guadalcanal, Savo, and Florida Islands. The bright blue ocean surrounded the huge mound of land that was Guadalcanal and Savo Island, its smaller companion. Flying at 16,000 feet, the Japanese bombers moved closer to their intended targets and maneuvered into three nine-plane v-like formations. Lt. Renpei Egawa, the leader of the bomber force, asked the pilot of the rear plane of his formation, PO2c Shoji Sekine, if he could see any of the escorting fighters. Sekine replied that he also saw nothing. The location of American carriers was still unknown. Undaunted, Egawa ordered his bombers into a shallow dive. The aiming point was toward the American ships along the northern Guadalcanal coast.

There were so many of them; Egawa counted more than 50. He did not think the Americans had that many. Still, these ships were targets that could not be ignored. He had his orders and was determined to obey them.

And no one could see any American fighters. That situation would soon change in a dramatic way.[13]

At 1:15 p.m., Sakai saw the bombers bank slowly into their shallow dive as small clouds moved in between them at 13,000 feet. A blinding sun blazed above and to the right, a perfect place from which to attack. Striking without warning and echoing his thoughts, six fighters dove through the Zeroes out of the sun and headed for the bombers. Seeing the fighters out of the corner of his right eye, he noticed the stubby bodies of Grumman F4Fs. Sakai had not seen them before but knew about them by their reputation for being tough to shoot down. The F4Fs had a coat of green paint with their undersides painted white to camouflage them from being seen from below. He did not know that meant they were American naval pilots; the same kinds of pilots who had demonstrated their incredible bravery and fighting spirit at Coral Sea and Midway.[14]

Southerland's formation flew just over Savo Island when an order came over the radio to turn left 10º. Just as he completed his turn, he glanced to his left and saw the Japanese bombers clear the cloud cover with the nearest three-bomber formation about 500 yards away. Counting 27 bombers just above him, he picked up his radio microphone, pressed the send button, and radioed:

> "Horizontal bombers, three divisions, nine planes each, over Savo, headed for transports. Angels 12 (12,000 feet). This division from Pug: drop belly tanks, put gun switches and sight lamps on. Let's go get 'em boys!"[15]

The bombers came so close to his left wing that he could not climb to turn and attack them in the usual way. He glanced up and saw the bombers' bomb bays open like giant crocodiles; they were getting ready to attack the ships below. He dropped his tanks and fired short bursts as the bombers came into his sights.[16]

✲ ✲ ✲

The bomber crews did not see the American fighters attack them because they came out of the blinding sun. The Americans left the Zeroes completely alone to focus their deadly intentions on the attacking bombers. Sakai thought that this was not the right way to attack ships since they had already started to zigzag. Bombing ships from this high up was fruitless. The American fighters' gunfire did not score many hits; Sakai guessed they were trying to make the bombers change their attack. Nevertheless, the bombers pressed their attacks and started to release their bombs.[17]

✲ ✲ ✲

As Southerland moved in to attack the bombers, his three wing mates did not fare well when five Zeroes led by Lt. Shiro Kawai cut them off. The Zeroes dove steeply at the F4Fs and inflicted heavy damage. The daring attack startled Ens. Donald A. Innis. In recovering from the surprise, he pulled back hard on the stick and immediately took his plane into a hard climb. While exchanging shots with the Zeroes, he looked to his rear and saw a Zero on his tail. The Japanese Zeroes' gunfire tore 49 holes into his plane's fuselage while ripping the fabric of the left elevator to tatters. In spite of the heavy damage inflicted on his aircraft, Innis returned to his carrier alive. Unfortunately, his two comrades did not experience the same fortune. Lt. (jg) Charles A. Tabberer and Ens. Robert I. Price never returned and were listed as MIA.[18]

An Ace Earns a Hard-won Victory

After getting over his frustration about the futility of bombing moving ships from a high altitude, Sakai saw that the bombers had banked left and sped up. He and his 17 wing mates were now ready to take on the American F4Fs. In a *déjà vu*-like moment, the Grummans again dove out of the glaring sun, unseen by anyone. Sakai was the first and only pilot in his formation to see the Americans, who this time assaulted the fighters. He pulled his plane into a steep climb with his mates following him. Seeing the Zeroes attacking, the American formation separated and headed down in different directions.

Sakai again turned around to see where his wingmen were. They were nowhere to be seen! Although thinking that the Americans were not ready to fight, this idea proved to be false. Glancing about 1,500 feet below, an unbelievable sight spread before him. One F4F Wildcat was in a chaotic, rolling, turning dogfight with four Zeroes. The American desperately fired at his four enemies while the Zeroes flew tight spirals trying to engage the lone American. Outnumbering the American 4:1, the Zeroes held an overwhelming advantage but could not shoot him down. Sakai had never seen the Americans fly in this expert, frantic way. Every time a Zero got on his tail, the F4F pilot flew out of danger by suddenly and gracefully rolling over.

Sakai signaled to the Zeroes below and tried to engage the American, who was on a Zero's tail and inflicting severe damage as his plane's guns ripped huge holes into the Japanese plane's wings and tail. Sakai got behind the American, but the American rolled again and soon was heading directly for Sakai. He tried to get away from the American, who hung on like a bulldog. Sakai could not shake him off.

Sakai reduced his speed and his Zero shook, almost stalling. He pushed the throttle forward hard and rolled to the left. He put the Zero into a roll, dropped in a spin, and exited in left vertical spiral. He repeated this maneuver two more times. The American matched his maneuvers each time. Sakai realized this American was no ordinary pilot but one that could match his skills in spite of the Zero's supposedly superior maneuverability and Sakai's extensive combat skills.

Powerful G forces pummeled both pilots' bodies as their planes continued to spiral. Human physiology started to catch up to Sakai as a film glossed over his eyes, his heart pounded against his ribs, and his head seemed like it weighed a ton. He was convinced the American was having the same problems, but he was determined he could take the abuse as long as the American could. The first one who succumbed or made even the smallest mistake would lose this battle.

Just when it seemed the stalemate in the air would not end soon, the American pilot made a critical mistake. During the fifth spiral, the F4F slipped sideways. Sakai thought, "I have him now." The American pilot dove, increased his speed, and got control of his plane once again. Sakai's respect for this formidable opponent grew even more.

But the American did not fly into a sixth spiral, thus making another critical and now potentially fatal mistake. Running out of attitude, he went into a loop and, in a fraction of a second, Sakai used his Zero's first-class maneuverability to get inside the Wildcat's loop. He was now on the American's tail. Knowing that he was now at a severe disadvantage, the American responded by flying increasingly smaller loops, but Sakai matched his every move by keeping the diameter of his loop less than his opponent's. No plane in the world at this time could defeat the Zero in this maneuver.

Sakai was now just a mere 50 yards away when the American stopped looping and flew in a straight line. Sakai could not believe his fortune. At the range, cannons were not needed; machine guns could do the job. He pulled the trigger to his machine guns and sent 200 rounds smashing into the F4F.[19]

✲ ✲ ✲

Southerland's plane shuddered as he heard the 7.7-mm bullets hammering into the aircraft's body. But the Wildcat's armored plate absorbed the shock. He could still fly his plane and try to shake off his pursuer. The Zero came alongside; he was taking pictures; how bizarre!

Nevertheless, the F4F now flew sluggishly, and Southerland knew he was in trouble. There was no choice but to prepare to bail out. Using the discipline he learned from his extensive flight training, there was no panic in his mind as he went through the checklist: disconnect the radio cord, undo the safety belts, and open the canopy. He looked outside and checked the condition of his tough aircraft.

Later, he recalled, "My plane was in bad shape but still performing nicely in low blower, full throttle, and full low pitch. Flaps and radio had been put out of commission...The after part of my fuselage was like a sieve. She was still smoking from incendiary but not on fire. All of the ammunition box covers on my left wing were gone and 20 mm explosives had torn some gaping holes in its upper surface...My instrument panel was badly shot up, goggles on my forehead had been shattered, my rear view mirror was broken, my Plexiglas windshield was riddled. The leak proof tanks had been punctured apparently many times as some fuel had leaked down into the bottom of the cockpit even though there was no steady leakage. My oil tank had been punctured and oil was pouring down my right leg."[20]

Southerland's time in the air would soon end.

✲ ✲ ✲

After taking so much punishment, the Wildcat's sturdiness astonished Sakai. If a Zero had 200 machine gun bullets pumped into it, it would not be flying. But the Wildcat was in bad shape. Countless bullet holes pierced the fuselage and both wings; the rudder's skin was in tatters, its metal ribs exposed. The two planes flew next to each other, and the American's canopy was open. Sakai saw the American pilot was older than he expected, a big man with a round face. A dark stain appeared on the American's right shoulder and moved down his chest.

Strange feelings came into Sakai's mind. He had never seen anything like this episode in combat. Never had he faced such a formidable aircraft and a man with such incredibly honed flying skills. He did not want to kill this man. He was a sitting duck. But this American was the enemy of the Japanese Empire, and Sakai's mission was to kill his nation's enemies.

He wanted to destroy the plane, not kill the pilot. Dropping back behind the Wildcat and moving on its tail, he moved in for the victory. Suddenly, the American increased his speed and flew into a loop. All misgivings about mercy for this American instantly vanished; Sakai aimed for the engine and squeezed off a few rounds from his cannon; flames and smoke erupted from the F4F's engine.[21]

Southerland later recalled, "At this time a Zero making a run from the port quarter put a burst in just under the left wing root and good old 5-F-12 finally exploded. I think the explosion occurred from gasoline vapor. The flash was below and forward of my left foot. I was ready for it...Consequently I dove over the right side just aft of the starboard wing root, head first. My .45 holster caught on the hood track, but I got rid of it immediately, though I don't remember how."[22]

He did not have altitude when he bailed out of his plane. Somehow, he managed to get his parachute open and drifted toward some trees. Easily reaching the ground and not wanting to get caught on open ground by a strafing Japanese plane, he took off the parachute and ran for cover. He recalled later, "My first grateful thought was to thank God that I was alive. I can guarantee that this was a wholly unexpected outcome of the battle." He estimated he was about ten miles east of Cape Esperance and four miles from the beach. It was a downhill walk toward the American positions on the coast. Wanting to walk on the high ground, he now knew he would have to go through the jungle. Eventually, Southerland made it back to friendly lines.[23]

✲ ✲ ✲

Sakai saw the American's parachute canopy blossom near the Guadalcanal coast. The pilot's body hung limp in the chute's shrouds. The chute drifted towards the beach and disappeared from sight.

Three Zeroes formed on his wings. Climbing to look for more American aircraft, explosions of black smoke from American flak appeared all around him. This only could have come from American ground fire. The Americans had been on shore for less than a day and could already fire at Japanese planes. Whenever the Japanese landed, it would take them almost three days to set up AA defenses. The fact that the Americans could perform the same task in just one-third the time deeply disturbed him. This did not bode well for Japanese chances to hold that strategically important island.[24]

Trying to Save the Day

The initial Japanese high altitude bomber attacks on August 7 had lofty expectations that proved largely unrealized. There was no damage to Turner's invasion fleet, and this attack did not convince Turner to withdraw the fleet before he had originally planned. All bombs dropped by the Japanese in that first wave exploded harmlessly in the water, only succeeding in making large splashes.

After a brief respite from attacks from the high level bombers, another wave of Japanese planes came over to try to wreak more havoc. Desperately trying to salvage something that might be called a victory for this day's action, Radm. Sadayoshi Yamada ordered Lt. Fumito Inoue's nine "Val" carrier bombers to attack the American invasion fleet.

The Vals were older and slower planes that did well in the Pearl Harbor attacks. Nonetheless, because of their slow speed and short range, they had to land in the water off Shortland Island south of Bougainville where a seaplane tender and a flying boat would rescue the pilots.

They took off from Rabaul at 10:40 a.m. and leisurely climbed to 9,840 feet and flew along the northern coastlines of the Solomons toward Guadalcanal. This course hid them from detection by coastwatchers and the American ship radar. In two and three-quarters of an hour, they passed over Tulagi and turned south over Florida Island. Although clouds hid the ships off Tulagi, the American ships off Guadalcanal appeared a bit farther away.

Four widely scattered flights of F4Fs flew CAP over the fleet as the Vals approached from the north. Inoue sent three bombers commanded by WO Gengo Ota to attack the ships to the west while taking the remaining six to attack the transports off Guadalcanal's Red Beach.

Ota steered his plane and his wingman, PO2c Koji Takahashi, toward a destroyer positioned at the westernmost edge of the transports. The way the ship moved seemed like it was on antisubmarine patrol.

Three minutes before 3:00 p.m., the American destroyer *Mugford*'s lookout turned his binoculars at the planes he had heard approaching and looked at the nearing danger. He saw two planes diving at his ship. He screamed into the voice pipe that led to the bridge, "Planes! They've got wheels." The destroyer's captain, Lt. Cdr. Edward W. Young, ordered a hard right turn to starboard; the destroyer leaned hard to port trying to avoid being hit.

Ota dropped two 60 kg bombs while Takahashi dropped one. Ota's two missiles landed into the water, but Takahashi's struck the ship's superstructure just forward of the rear five-inch gun.[25]

Radarman Third Class Howard A. Selz served on the heavy cruiser *Quincy* on that day. The cruiser was part of the invasion fleet that had entered the waters off Guadalcanal and bombarded the Japanese, who had offered no resistance. He was at his assigned station in "Sky Forward," which was the fire director and located in a small steel enclosure just forward of the ship's mainmast. Its purpose was to direct the firing of the cruiser's eight-inch main battery and starboard five-inch guns. His seat gave him a superior view of the action, up high with no restrictions to what he could see. The *Quincy* cruised back and forth parallel to Guadalcanal's northern shore while the Marines landed ashore.

The ship's squawk box blared out that Japanese planes were heading for the American fleet. Selz looked up and saw bombers diving toward them. They dropped some bombs, but the bombs fell harmlessly into the water. They only left tall splashes of water. Nonetheless, one bomb did hit a destroyer steaming nearby in the stern. That hit seemingly knocked out two gun positions.

The American ships could not fire at the attacking bombers because American fighters were attacking them. A fighter plane flew over his ship while dive-bombers blasted Japanese targets on Guadalcanal. Selz, Electrician's Mate Third Class Albert L. Stires and the rest of their shipmates were grateful that they had escaped damage. But, later that evening, this would no longer be the case.[26]

The Japanese lost far fewer planes than the American pilots claimed they had destroyed. Similarly, the Americans did not lose a single ship to the day's bombing, despite claims by Japanese pilots. The Japanese damaged only one American ship that day—the destroyer *Mugford*.

Nonetheless, American losses of pilots and planes were still quite substantial. In spite of Southerland's heroic battle with Sakai, the Zero's superior flying characteristics had proven its supremacy in the air. The American naval fighter squadrons suffered the greatest losses: 15 out of 99 F4Fs did not return. In one battle, the Americans lost half of their fighters. The inexperienced American pilots had fought the best naval fighter pilots the Japanese had.[27]

But the ruthless struggle for Guadalcanal in the air, on the ground, and at sea had only begun. Like the struggle between the Germans and French at Verdun on that battlefield near the Meuse in the last great war, Guadalcanal would match it in brutality and savageness. And, like Verdun, it would not end soon.

CHAPTER 13
Encore!

Yielding to the Inevitable

Although their air attacks on August 7 yielded what could be charitably called "limited successes," the Japanese were not about to stop attacking the American invasion fleet on August 8. Adm. Ugaki still received news that the Japanese garrisons on Tulagi and Guadalcanal were fighting the invaders. Reports about the attacks on "two enemy heavy cruisers" said they were "not so effective."[1]

Yamada concluded that, in spite of a lack of success the day before, he had to order another attack and immediately began to prepare his plan. His forces had lost 16 seaplanes at Tulagi, four land attack planes, six carrier bombers, and two Zeroes. Two land attack planes and three carrier bombers had crashed into the ocean or crashed trying to land. After analyzing what planes he had at his disposal, there were 30 operative planes to attack the American fleet.

American B-17s had attacked the Rabaul airfields on August 7. Maj. Gen. George C. Kenney, MacArthur's newly-arrived air commander, sent in the big bombers without the benefit of fighter cover because fighters did not have the range to escort bombers to Rabaul and back. Thirteen B-17s, led by Lt. Col. Richard H. Carmichael, bravely attacked the runways and revetments at Vunakanau Field. As was the usual case, the American flyers claimed to have destroyed more than they did: the destruction of the facilities and shooting down seven Zeroes. However, they lost one B-17. Yamada's repair crews restored the runways almost immediately after the B-17s left and well before Egawa's return.

Kenney later claimed to MacArthur that his B-17s had destroyed 75 of the 150 planes parked "wing-to-wing" at Vunakanau Field. However, there were not anywhere near that many planes on the ground when the American bombers attacked because they were performing their duties elsewhere. This was not the first time Kenney or many other USAAF officers would claim to have destroyed more than American bombers had actually done, and it certainly would not be the last.[2]

✲ ✲ ✲

After his returning pilots debriefed him that they had been attacked by American naval aircraft, Yamada knew at least two or maybe three American carriers steamed near Guadalcanal. Frustrated by the lack of success of the previous day's attacks, he put a plan together to search the entire Solomons area for the carriers and to attack them with land-based torpedo bombers. Vadm. Tsukahara approved Yamada's plan while reminding his subordinate that since American naval fighters had a limited range, the American carriers were most likely within 150 miles of Tulagi. The territory that Yamada's search would have to cover became considerably smaller.

Three land attack planes (Bettys) and two flying boats left Rabaul at 6:20 a.m. to look for the American carriers. Led by Lt. Shigeru Kotani, 26 land attack planes left Vunakanau Field an hour later. Kotani's formation had three flights commanded by Kotani, Lt. Bakuro Fujita, and Lt. Hiromi Ikeda respectively. Providing escort protection were 15 Zeroes from the Tainan group led by Lt. Kikuichi Inano. The formation lifted off at 8:10 a.m. with two of the fighters' pilots, PO1c Sadao Yamashita and PO2c Enji Kakimoto, who had been part of the attack the day before.[3]

One of the group's best pilots, Saburo Sakai, who had been part of the prior day's attack, was not with the Zeroes that took off that day. While engaging American planes in the skies over Guadalcanal the day before, he ran into a formation of eight American Avenger TBFs, planes he had never seen before. These planes, which could drop either bombs or torpedoes, were more heavily armed than earlier American bombers. Sakai thought the Avenger looked like a Wildcat from the rear, but when he approached more closely, he saw the big plane had a deadly machine gun in a rear-firing rotating turret and another one in its belly. This plane was clearly a new threat to be reckoned with.

He got caught in a formation of eight of them and was trapped among the eight planes with four on one side and four on his other side. Having no other choice, he pressed the button to fire his cannons, then all hell broke lose. Every Avenger opened fire with every machine gun they could bring to bear on Sakai's plane. He saw two bombers' engines explode with fire. Suddenly, a violent explosion racked his body. He could only see red and became blind.

It seemed just a few seconds before he woke up. Wind whipped around his face as his shattered windshield no longer blocked any air. Unable to control his senses, he kept blacking out and waking up. Sleep now tried to sweep over him as he realized he was severely wounded. It was like being in a dream world, with impending death now a pleasant possibility. Suddenly, the image of his mother's face flooded his vision screaming, "Shame! Shame! Wake up, Saburo, wake up! You are acting like a sissy. You are no coward! Wake up!"[4]

Struggling to regain consciousness, his plane was in a steep dive. Instinctively reverting to his disciplined training, he reached for the Zero's stick and gently pulled it back. He could feel the plane return to what he felt was level flight.

He had a long way to go to return to Rabaul. The journey was fraught with danger from American aircraft or drowning if his plane should land in the ocean. Nevertheless, he bravely struggled to stay alive and flew his plane for more than 500 miles until landing at his home field on Rabaul. Sakai's heroic story was one of an unstoppable will to live and a dedication to fight again. The two Avengers he had hit with his cannons plunged to earth; they were his 61st and 62nd victories. He survived his wounds and would continue to fly until the end of the war.[5]

The Japanese planes flew low following the Solomon Islands chain toward Guadalcanal. Kotani planned to find the American carriers. If he could not, he would then attack American ships near Tulagi. But his formation would soon be detected.

Lt. W. J. (Jack) Read (RANVR), one of the several coastwatchers placed along the Solomon Islands by the Australians when war broke out, was perched on a hillside on the northernmost point of Bougainville. He scanned the skies for any approaching ships or planes. It was 9:42 a.m. when he saw a low-flying formation of planes approaching his position from the northwest and moving southeast. They were apparently flying along Bougainville's coast. After identifying the planes as Japanese, he estimated there were about 40 of them. He sent a message some 15 minutes later that 42 two-engine bombers were heading from the northwest to the southeast. Another coastwatcher picked up his message and forwarded it, reaching the Australian heavy cruiser *Australia* about 45 minutes after Read's first sighting.

Positioning his fleet so it could maneuver from the anticipated air attack, Turner prepared to meet the new menace. The transports moved to the center of a stretch of water between Guadalcanal and Florida Islands escorted by Turner's cruisers and destroyers. The message center on the cruiser *Chicago* logged the message at 10:46 a.m., and Lt. Robert M. Bruning, Fletcher's FDO onboard the cruiser, estimated the Japanese planes would be overhead in about 30 minutes.

Fletcher received Read's message five minutes after the *Chicago* logged it. The American response to the impending threat was confused and chaotic. At this stage of the war, carrier air warfare was still a primitive doctrine with poor communications between each carrier unit a contributory factor. Little or no coordination existed between the carriers as to when to launch aircraft and where they should fly once aloft. Although Midway was a great American victory, it was by luck when American dive-bombers arrived over Vadm. Chuichi Nagumo's carriers with his decks loaded with armed and fueled aircraft. Each squadron operated independently and attacked when they arrived over their targets. The situation at Guadalcanal was no different. Fletcher and his subordinates responded the best they could, but were hampered by lack of any disciplined approach to carrier warfare. That improvement would come later in the war after some bitter experiences.

The *Enterprise* was the first to launch 13 F4Fs aircraft at 11:01 a.m. to fly CAP. Noyes, onboard the *Saratoga*, realized at last that there were no Japanese carriers nearby that could threaten Task Force 61 and ordered Lt. Cmdr. Leroy C. Simpler's 27 fighters to leave the *Saratoga* four minutes later. Unfortunately, it would not be until 11:35 a.m. that his approval reached the flyers—a vitally critical and deadly half-hour delay.

Bruning sent 21 fighters to 17,000 feet so they would be above the approaching Japanese bombers when they arrived. While they orbited above the fleet, the American fighters burned precious fuel waiting for the Japanese, who had not yet arrived as originally thought. The *Wasp* had no choice but to order its 15 planes to return to refuel—leaving just three fighters to protect the fleet. Trying to fill the gap, the *Wasp* launched nine fighters that took 30 minutes to arrive over the invasion area. Still fearing submarine attacks, the *Wasp* ordered 13 SBDs to protect against torpedo attacks. With no clear indication whether the Japanese would attack Turner's ships or Fletcher's carriers, Fletcher's and Noyes' confusion continued unabated.

Meanwhile, *Saratoga*'s 27 fighters did not take off until 30 minutes later. Radio frequencies on the American planes needed to be set to a given channel depending on the planes' current mission. Aircraft were landing, refueling, and taking off to proceed on CAP, SCAP, screening Turner's fleet, looking for phantom Japanese carriers, and protecting against torpedo attacks by submarines. As their mission changed, the radio frequencies had to be adjusted to accommodate their missions. The hangar deck crews became so confused that it was common that some planes could not communicate with each other and, therefore, could not get directions from their respective FDOs. With all of the carriers' planes returning, taking off on missions that had no bearing on protecting Turner's fleet, mistakes in estimating when the Japanese planes would arrive, seemingly inexcusable communications delays, and being unsure of the true targets the Japanese intended to attack, it is not surprising that Fletcher seemed incapable of taking command of the situation and establish order. The result was that CAP over Guadalcanal and Tulagi would be overwhelmed when the Japanese planes arrived.

Kotani did not receive any messages concerning the whereabouts of the American carriers, although a Japanese flying boat had passed within sighting distance of Fletcher's Task Force 61 at 10:50 a.m. but did not find it. Kotani stayed north of the Solomons hoping to find the American carriers somewhere northeast of Tulagi. Although not his intent, his flight path behind the hills of Santa Isabel and Florida Islands hid his approach from the American radars. He now had 23 planes since three "Betty"s had returned to Rabaul because of mechanical problems.

By this time, Turner's ships had moved into more maneuverable waters. At five minutes before noon, his lookouts saw a large formation of Japanese bombers approaching at high speed from the east over Florida Island's eastern tip at the low altitude of 2,000 feet.

✲ ✲ ✲

The Japanese planes headed eastward for the ships off Tulagi and dove toward them for the attack. Kotani's plane led the center group of seven planes while seven bombers were on his right and nine planes on his left. The American ships unleashed a concentrated fusillade of AA fire as the Japanese planes came in at between 10 and 150 feet above the water. To the southwest, the *McCawley*, Turner's flagship, steered into two 30° turns with the rest of the Guadalcanal-positioned ships following in its wake. The American AA barrage of tracers trailing red fire and dense black puffs of smoke from exploding shells unsettled the attacking bombers. Eyewitnesses remembered, "The fire of all these ships was so extensive and of such volume that the Japanese pilots showed utter confusion and state of mind and reacted accordingly."[6]

The intensity of the American AA fire forced Kotani to turn all 23 planes southward and head for the American ships off Guadalcanal. Kotani saw the water rapidly pass beneath his plane as the shapes of the American ships grew ever closer. The three plane formations separated to attack individual ships. Again the Americans opened up with every gun they could bring to bear on the approaching Japanese planes. Eight-inch shells from the American cruisers knocked down one bomber. Several planes crashed in flames while not many others fired their torpedoes. The Japanese pilots flew straight and level and did not disperse into individual attack patterns. They continued to fly in parallel, predictable courses, increasing their risk of being shot down.

One flaming Betty barely missed the *Vincennes'* stern while another flew through the *Barnett*'s rigging and splashed into the water just a few yards away. But the American ships did not escape without getting hit. A torpedo plowed into and exploded just to the rear of the *George F. Elliott*'s smokestack. Huge flames soared to the sky, and a roaring fire engulfed the transport. Only one Japanese torpedo found its mark when it struck the *Jarvis* just forward of her beam on the ill-fated destroyer's starboard side.

Meanwhile, American SBDs had just finished their assigned ground support bombing mission when its leader, the *Wasp*'s Lt. Cmdr. John Eldridge, saw what he thought were five SBDs from the *Enterprise* about 3,000 feet above him. But he realized these were not friendly planes but Japanese Zeroes. The Japanese flight leader did not see the American planes below, but two of his wing mates did. They attacked the SBDs; after making several passes without doing much damage, they were forced to keep their distance because of the accurate machine gun from three SBDs.[7]

The whompf, whompf of gunfire at about noon caused Richard Tregaskis to turn his head toward the sound. Black blotches of smoke covered the entire sky over Tulagi. He saw flashes of gunfire coming from an Australian cruiser just off Guadalcanal's northern shore. Soon, the other ships joined the chorus. Sounds surrounded him, joining together to seem like a single sound while still distinctive. Meanwhile, dark smoke covered the sky above him. Tregaskis remembered that it was "one of the most awe-inspiring spectacles I have ever witnessed."[8]

Smaller guns added their "rata-tat-tat" staccato sounds to the rising cacophony. The big guns thundered; the sounds now engulfed him. A Japanese aircraft, described by Tregaskis as a "long, flat-shaped plane" and "like some preying shark," entered his sight as it moved in the midst of the American transports just above the water's surface while just clearing the ships' masts. The thought flashed through his mind, "Torpedo plane."[9]

Other Japanese planes, just like the first one, flew between the ships, looking for targets. Black water spouts appeared in the water as the planes dropped their missiles of death and destruction. Tregaskis thought that the planes dropped either bombs or torpedoes. The ships started to move to avoid their attackers, seemingly trying to reach the open sea. Nevertheless, the splashes became more frequent and were getting closer.

But the answer to the Japanese attack appeared as American fighters dove into the fracas from on high. One got on a Japanese plane's tail and shot it down in a plume of black smoke that soon turned into flames. Looking through his binoculars, he saw the transports and immediately saw a pyre of flames and smoke rising into the sky, correctly guessing that the Japanese had hit one of them.

More smoke and fire rose into the sky. More ships must have taken hits, Tregaskis supposed. A wounded transport continued to burn with the volume of smoke and fire spreading over its decks. Suddenly, an explosion wracked the doomed transport. Just as suddenly, there were no Japanese planes to be seen. Looking at his watch, Tregaskis observed the battle had lasted only ten minutes. But it seemed to have taken longer.

The transports continued to move about and back toward the beach where they could disgorge their cargoes. But the stricken ship continued to burn fiercely—its fires clearly beyond anyone's ability to control them.[10]

The American fighters and the AA fire from Turner's ships had much greater success than the Japanese did. Just two American ships had been hit and badly damaged. Meanwhile, the attacking Japanese lost 17 bombers and their crews. The surviving six bombers headed back on a westward course toward Rabaul. One bomber went down on the way because of severe damage. More importantly, 125 Japanese flyers lost their lives or were listed as missing, the worst loss for Japanese land-based attack bombers in the Guadalcanal campaign.

Naturally, the survivors reported inflicting incredible losses on the Americans, sinking four heavy cruisers, three light cruisers, two destroyers, three transports, and severely damaging a heavy cruiser, one destroyer, and six transports. Knowing the wild exaggerations of the returnees, Yamada changed those claims to one heavy cruiser, one destroyer, nine transports sunk, and three light cruisers, two ships of unknown type badly damaged. Of course, history shows that Yamada's claims were just as optimistic.

The Japanese Zero pilots claimed shooting down four of ten American fighters. Actually, they shot down three SBDs and one unconfirmed F4F while losing two Zeroes with one returning badly damaged.

At the site of the battle, American destroyers moved amid the wreckage of downed Japanese bombers. The *Bagley*'s crew saw men sitting on the wing of a tailless Betty. The Japanese fired their pistols on the approaching ship and then shot themselves. Most of the Japanese survivors had sustained such serious wounds that they thought it was better to surrender and be given medical treatment rather than shoot themselves. The *Blue* plucked four flyers from the sea; the *Selfridge* and *Mugford* picked up two each while the destroyer-minesweeper *Trever* picked up one.[11]

✲ ✲ ✲

The Japanese had launched two air attacks in the first two days with limited success. So far, their responses to the American incursion against Guadalcanal and Tulagi had poor results. Meanwhile, on the ground on steamy Guadalcanal, the misfortunes of the totally surprised Japanese continued.

CHAPTER 14
Taking the Prize!

The primary strategic objective of the invasion of Guadalcanal and Tulagi was to prevent the Japanese from establishing an airfield near Lunga Point on Guadalcanal so that they could cut the supply lines between the U.S., Australia, and New Zealand. Now that the Marines were on Guadalcanal and Tulagi, the Americans had the opportunity to turn the tables against the Japanese and establish their own airbase. Any look at the map of the South Pacific yields the conclusion that whoever controlled Guadalcanal and its valuable airbase controlled the air over the southern Solomon Islands. And whoever controlled the air, controlled the sea around these islands.

It was always part of the American strategy that a march up the Solomon Islands would lead to the conquest or, at least the isolation of, the powerful Japanese naval base at Rabaul. If that occurred, then Gen. MacArthur's march up New Guinea's coast toward the Philippine Islands could happen with almost no interference from Japanese air or naval forces.

As laudable as these objectives were, none of them would ever become real unless Guadalcanal could be taken and held. And this would never happen unless the Americans captured the almost completed Japanese airfield and turned it into what could be a land-based aircraft carrier. Then Guadalcanal could become the base the Americans desperately needed to capture the rest of the Solomon Islands.

The landings on Red Beach by the American First Marine Division came off without any appreciable Japanese opposition. The following Marine units were the first to occupy the beachhead:[1]

First Marine Units to Land on at Guadalcanal

Regiment	Battalion	Commanding Officer
1st	—	Col. Clifton B. Cates
1st	1st	Lt. Col. Lenard B. Cresswell
1st	2nd	Lt. Col. Edwin A. Pollock
1st	3rd	Lt. Col. William J. McKelvy, Jr.
5th	—	Col. Roy B. Hunt
5th	1st	Lt. Col. William E. Maxwell
5th	3rd	Lt. Col. Frederick C. Biebush

Confused by the suddenness and power of the American invasion, the Japanese opposition, made up of mostly labor and construction troops, retreated to the west of Lunga Point in the village of Kukum. While some of the Marines consolidated and created a defensive position on the beach so the landings of troops and material could continue unabated, Gen. Vandegrift sent Maxwell's battalion along the northern coast to destroy the Japanese known to be there. He also ordered Cates' 1st Regiment to move southwesterly and take the high ground at a place called Mt. Austen.

By August 8, Vandegrift received reports from his troops that they had not found any Japanese. What Japanese they did see all ran off into the jungle, apparently reluctant to fight. Therefore, Vandegrift cancelled Cates' advance toward Mount Austen and ordered Hunt to capture Kukum. Hunt did run into some Japanese resistance, light rifle and machine gun fire, and took Kukum at 3:00 p.m. on the 8th.

Cates' sent his 1st Battalion on a somewhat parallel path to Hunt's but to the south toward the Japanese airfield. He also ordered his 2nd and 3rd Battalions to the west to comb the jungle for the Japanese.

Cates rapidly overcame a small Japanese patrol and entered a clearing. The Japanese airfield lay before him with its 2,600-foot runway still unfinished. The original plan was to bring their own equipment ashore, but that became impossible. However, the Japanese equipment would prove to be quite sufficient. Construction began to lengthen the runway to 3,778 feet—more than enough to accommodate even large B-17 bombers. On August 10, Vandegrift later named the airstrip Henderson Field after Maj. Lofton R. Henderson, the first Marine aviator to die during the Battle of Midway.[2]

✲ ✲ ✲

August 7 and 8 had not gone well for the Japanese. Being caught completely by surprise, their attempts to stop the invasion with air attacks over two days proved fruitless. Their trained infantry on Tulagi, Gavutu and Tanambogo had put up a good fight. But the Americans landed with overwhelming force and soon those islands were in American hands. With no significant opposition on Guadalcanal, the Americans' main strategic objective, the airfield that started the entire Guadalcanal operation, was soon secured. By all standards, the Japanese should have been utterly dispirited and ready to surrender Guadalcanal without much of a fight.

But the Japanese were not ready give up yet. The U.S. Navy was in for one of the most trying nights of its long, illustrious history. It would all happen near a small island just off the northwestern coast of Guadalcanal and sear the heart of American naval consciousness with just one word—Savo.

Part 3:
Savo Island: A Disaster Waiting to Happen

CHAPTER 15
Anatomy of an Allied Tragedy

Planning for Battle

The changing fortunes of war during the early morning hours of August 7 jolted the Japanese commanders in Rabaul out of their complacency. Urgent messages from Cmdr. Masaaki Suzuki, the Japanese commander on Tulagi, poured into Vadm. Gunichi Mikawa's[1]headquarters, and the news from Tulagi was not good. The first message on his desk read, "0630. Tulagi being heavily bombarded from air and sea. Enemy carrier task force sighted."[2]

The Japanese garrison's dimming fortunes continued as another message arrived: "One battleship...two carriers...three cruisers...fifteen destroyers...and thirty to forty transports." Mikawa now knew that this was not a mere raid by the Americans. They had come in force and in overwhelming numbers. What the planners in Tokyo thought unthinkable was now reality. The Americans had launched their first full-scale offensive in the Pacific and in Japanese Empire territory. Another message from the doomed garrison arrived soon after the previous one, "...encountered American landing forces and are retreating into the jungle hills." At 0800, the last dispatch tried to show a brave ardor, but belied its inner meaning of hopelessness; "The enemy force is overwhelming. We will defend our positions to the death. We pray for enduring fortunes of war to the last man"[3]

Mikawa knew the threat from the Americans was real; he had to respond with all the resources his command could bring. The 25th Air Flotilla planned to launch an air attack that morning, but it was Mikawa's turn to act.

A naval surface force needed to steam from Rabaul to Guadalcanal and attack the transports now disgorging troops and materiel onto Guadalcanal's beaches. The Americans had come to stay and capture the now valuable airstrip there.

Reinforcements for the garrison on Guadalcanal had to be moved and landed to evict the American Marines. Dangerously underestimating the American strength on Guadalcanal, the 17th Army staff believed the Americans could be easily removed from Guadalcanal. But the 17th Army could not make that decision themselves; that honor belonged to a higher authority. With time being a premium, Mikawa made a decision himself. Under the command of a Lt. Endo, a small detachment of 410 troops quickly boarded the 5,600-ton *Miyo Maru* and sailed to Guadalcanal escorted by the minelayer *Tsugaru* and the supply ship *Soya*.

While steaming on August 8 at midnight about 14 miles west of Cape St. George, the American submarine *S-38*, under the command of Lt. Cmdr. Henry G. Munson, sighted the ships. Munson submerged his boat, used sound tracking instead of his periscope, maneuvered to within 1,000 yards, and fired two torpedoes. They both struck the *Miyo Maru* and sank it. 14 officers and 328 men went down with her. The *S-38* escaped the depth charge counterattack by the escort and returned to Brisbane on August 22. With the loss of its largest transport, the Japanese convoy commander had no choice but to turn around and head back to Rabaul. The first Japanese attempt to reinforce the Guadalcanal garrison had ended in failure.[4] However, *S-38* was not finished with Mikawa's plans to respond to the Guadalcanal invasion.

Mikawa ordered the five submarines under his command to cluster around Guadalcanal, attack the American ships, and keep him informed of all American ship movements and locations. He also made a major decision to order all the cruisers in his command to prepare for battle. He sent the heavy cruisers *Chokai, Aoba, Kinugasa, Kako,* and *Furutaka* in Kavieng to Rabaul to join the light cruisers *Tenryu, Yubari,* and the destroyer *Yunagi*. The assembled powerful force of fast ships could wreak havoc on the American fleet off Guadalcanal.

The American carriers, which Japanese intelligence thought numbered at least two, possibly three, were operating near Guadalcanal. These warships posed a special problem to the planning of the upcoming operation. Any Japanese ship moving near the American invasion would be in the range of attacking carrier aircraft. As the Japanese had learned thus far, no ship sailed without peril when near enemy aircraft. The best answer to this threat would be if the 25th Air Flotilla could find and attack the American carriers—the key word was *find*. But the location of the American carriers had not yet been confirmed. The location of the invasion fleet off Guadalcanal was known, so the attacking Japanese aircraft flew there. Destruction of the carriers was clearly not a sure thing. But the Japanese did have one advantage the Americans did not. If Mikawa's force could escape attacks by American carrier aircraft, their training in night surface battle tactics lent credence to what would prove a reason to be optimistic.[5]

Thirteen American B-17s flying at over 20,000 feet appeared over Rabaul at 10:30 a.m. to raid the airfield at Vunakanau and caused much havoc to the thinking going on by Mikawa and his staff. But the raid forced the Japanese to focus even more to the matter at hand, the destruction of the American invasion fleet off Guadalcanal. One major difficulty in planning the operation was that the ships in the task force had never sailed together, much less in combat. Only the *Aoba, Kinugasa, Kako,* and *Furutaka* had trained together at sea. The speed differences among the ships had to be accounted for to allow for smooth maneuvering as the force made changes in speed while conducting battle maneuvers at night. But Capt. Toshikazu Ohmae[6], Mikawa's chief of staff, knew this would not present any significant problem because each ship's commander was a skilled veteran.

Mikawa was particularly worried about the unknown waters around the Solomons since they knew the charts of these waters were inaccurate. Ohmae remembers Mikawa telling him that the admiral was confident that his mission would result in a victory only after his command passed through the poorly charted waters in safety. The 8th Base Force staff recommended that Mikawa should steam to the south through a passage between the Solomon Islands known as the Slot to minimize any chance his ships would run aground.

Noon arrived much too quickly as Mikawa's plan came together. Mikawa forwarded his plan to the Imperial Japanese Navy headquarters for approval. Capt. Sadamu Sanagi, one of the Naval

General Staff's chief planners, later told Ohmae that the General Staff reaction was not what one would consider to be positive. Adm. Osami Nagano, the Emperor's chief naval advisor[7], considered Mikawa's plan as high risk and fraught with potential for disaster. Nevertheless, after thinking for a while and discussing the plan with his staff, Nagano decided to defer to the local commander and approved the plan.

Unleashing a Sea Tiger

The *Chokai* and the *Yunagi* left the other ships that had steamed from Kavieng and sailed into Rabaul's Simpson Harbor at 2:00 p.m. (local time) to await Mikawa's orders. Mikawa now knew had to proceed with his plan to attack the Americans.

He boarded his flagship, the *Chokai*, with his staff, and, with the light cruisers *Tenryu* and *Yubari* and the destroyer *Yunagi*, left Simpson Harbor to join the other heavy cruisers waiting for him about three hours sailing time away. The sun shimmered on a glass-smooth sea as the newly constituted task force proceeded. It was a powerful one that had seven cruisers and one destroyer, built for speed and expertly trained for night fighting at sea, and tailor-made to inflict maximum damage on the merchant ships and other forces that might oppose it. Confidence for success was high on the bridges of all the ships in the force. Mikawa ordered his fleet to "Alert cruising disposition." The fleet was about 15 miles west of Cape St. George.

The looming darkness made the land mass of Cape St. George on New Ireland's most southern

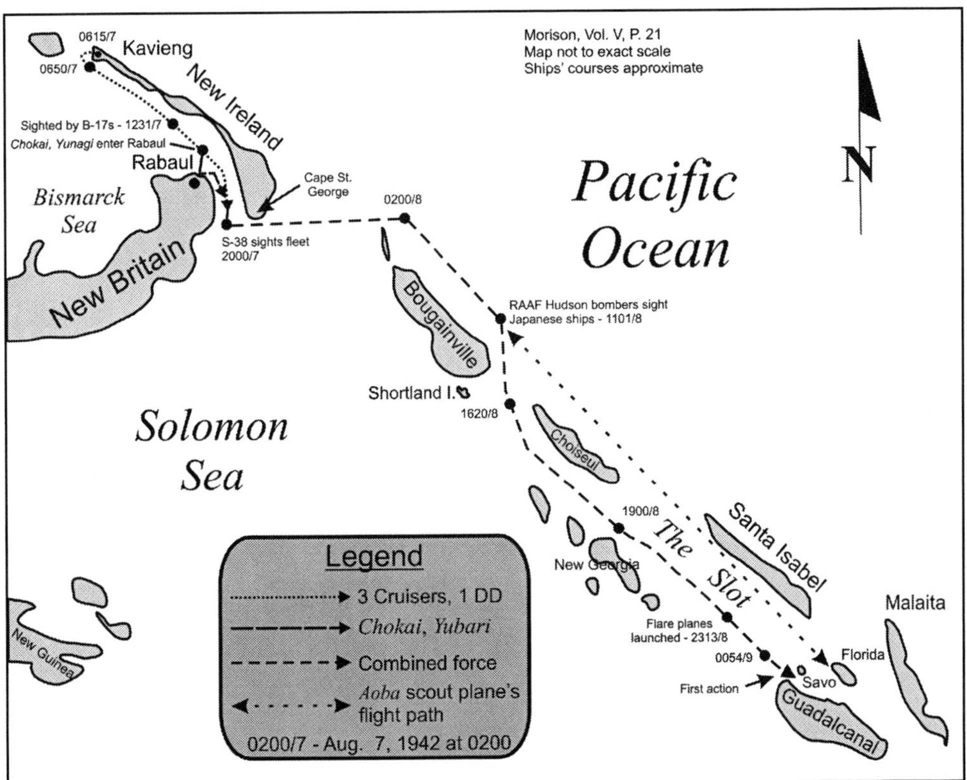

Mikawa's Course to Savo Island

point appear almost black. Mikawa did not want to be discovered by American reconnaissance aircraft, submarines, or Australian coastwatchers for fear of being attacked during daylight hours by American carrier aircraft he knew were within their range. He planned to steam on the northeastern side of Bougainville to keep his force out of range of any aircraft that may be looking for him. But his plan to avoid detection would "come a cropper."[8]

The S-38 *Does Its Job*

Before he stopped the first Japanese attempt to reinforce the Guadalcanal garrison, Munson was on station south of the St. George Channel's southern entrance. At about 10:00 p.m., he stared into the eyepiece of the periscope when he saw them. Several large cruisers and what seemed to be at least one destroyer moved menacingly on a southerly course. They were so close to him that the wash from their wakes prevented him from attacking them with torpedoes. The *S-38* rocked in the turbulent water.

But that did not stop him from reporting their position course and speed. He immediately sent a message that said "two destroyers and three larger ships of unknown type" moving southeasterly at "high speed." This confirmed an earlier sighting by B-17s under MacArthur's command that the general forwarded at 11:19 p.m. that said, "Six unidentified ships sighted by Forts in St. George Channel, Course SE." Mikawa's plan had been discovered. The *S-38*'s crew had earned their pay that day.[9]

Continuing the Journey

Mikawa knew the American submarine was there and tried to avoid it, but he did not know that the Americans had already reported his force's position, course, and speed. He changed his course eastward to head for Bougainville's northeastern coast. At 2:00 a.m. on August 8, Mikawa headed southeasterly having reached Bougainville, confidently believing he was safe and secure of the success of his mission.

Wanting to know more about what was ahead of him near Guadalcanal, he ordered five seaplanes launched from his cruisers at 6:00 a.m. to find out what was there. Six hours later, the *Aoba*'s plane reported sighting one battleship, four cruisers, and seven destroyers north of Guadalcanal. It also spotted two Allied heavy cruisers, 12 destroyers, and three transports near Tulagi.

It became clear the earlier claims by the 25th Air Flotilla's earlier air attacks of having sunk numerous American ships were overly exaggerated. Mikawa and his staff realized that the American invasion fleet was essentially untouched and were a far more powerful force than earlier believed. The returning pilots said they did not see any American carriers nearby. If the American carriers were not near Guadalcanal, then his ships would not be in any danger of being attacked by their aircraft. But Mikawa was not complacent about this menace. He sent a message to Rabaul asking if they had any more information of the carriers' whereabouts. He received no reply until much later that said that the carriers were not nearby.

Mikawa had to wait for his search planes to return before resuming his planned course. This waiting kept his force about 55 miles northeast of Kieta on Bougainville and made it easier to be discovered. He prized the secrecy of his movements. If he should be discovered by Allied air reconnaissance, he could be attacked by American carrier-based aircraft and caught in the open sea without any fighter cover. Ever since his experience at Midway, he knew what could happen to warships under air attack, and he did not want that fate to befall his ships. But wanting something did not always mean you got what you wanted. Upon returning from its mission, the *Aoba*'s plane and later *Chokai*'s search craft also sighted an unknown aircraft.[10]

☆ ☆ ☆

Bougainville's massive green expanse of jungle plains and tree covered mountains gave way to the blue seas on the island's northern coast. R.A.A.F. pilot Sergeant William J. Stutt's Hudson bomber slowly cleared the coast near the town of Kieta. Visibility was good and the sea calm, ideal for aerial searches.

Each member of the bomber's crew—Stutt, Sergeant Wilbur Courtis, the navigator, Sergeant Eric Geddes, the radio operator, and Sergeant John Bell, the gunner—were new to searching for ships over the sea. They had flown together for only 30 hours and had been on their first mission together on August 4 when they photographed the area near Yule Island.

The Australian squadron of Hudson patrol bombers had moved from Port Moresby to the Fall River advanced airbase near Milne Bay the next day to carry out an air reconnaissance over Buka Island near Bougainville. Their briefing for that mission, which was to become a typical experience in the days to come, did not include reliable maps, accurate weather forecasts, or specific reasons for the mission. They had no idea why they had been moved to the remote base with its infestation of malaria-carrying mosquitoes and a 5,000 feet long, 80 feet wide, mud-caked, steel-matting covered runway, quite different than what they had experienced at their Port Moresby base!

After their first mission from the Fall River field had been cancelled because of bad weather, their next mission promised better weather. There was a need to search the waters between New Georgia and New Britain Islands. Flight Lt. Lloyd Milne, Stutt's commanding officer, conducted the briefing on August 7 and warned his flight crews to watch out for American naval activity that might be operating in the area where they were going. No one mentioned that Operation Watchtower existed. During the briefing, Stutt and the rest of the men thought their mission was about defending Port Moresby. After receiving their destinations' coordinates, the flight crews left the briefing room and walked to their planes.

Stutt and crew climbed aboard their Hudson the morning of August 8. It was nearing 7:00 a.m. Two other planes from Stutt's squadron were also going on a search for Japanese ships.

Stutt taxied his plane to the end of the runway. He reached for the two throttle handles with his right hand and pushed them forward. The two 1,200 horsepower Wright engines roared as the squat, round-bellied plane accelerated down the muddy runway with the wheels bumping on the steel matting. Soon the craft lifted off, and Stutt turned to a northeasterly course toward Kieta.

This time the weather was good and the visibility clear. It was 10:25 a.m. when the Hudson was about 37 miles northeast of Kieta. Stutt looked at the sea and saw eight ships straight ahead. Mindful of the previous warning that the U.S. Navy might be operating in these waters, some of the crew thought these ships might be friendly. Nonetheless, Stutt flew four miles closer and removed all doubt from his mind—the ships were Japanese.

Stutt saw a Japanese float plane that he thought was a Japanese fighter. Meanwhile, the rest of his crew peered through binoculars at the ships below. Due to a lack of training in ship recognition, the crew could not accurately decide what types of ships these were and a discussion among them ensued. Sergeant Courtis thought the ships were cruisers and destroyers. However, there were two ships that could not be readily identified because they had an unfamiliar shape. Courtis argued that the sighting of the float plane could only come from some sort of "backup" vessel designed to carry planes. After much discussion and wanting to indicate they were not sure about the types of these two ships, the crew decided to send a report that was forwarded through a communications labyrinth[11] to MacArthur's headquarters in Townsville, Australia, and received on Turner's flagship *McCawley* at 6:45 p.m., more than eight hours after Stutt had spotted Mikawa's force:

> "Aircraft reports at 2325Z/7Z 3 cruisers 3 destroyers 2 *seaplane tenders or gunboats* [my emphasis]. 05—19 S 156-07 E course 120 true speed 15 knots. At 0027/8Z 2 subs 07—35 S 154-07 E course 150 true."[12]

This strange, obviously erroneous, observation would later have disastrous consequences!

With the benefit of hindsight, the report that they saw seaplane tenders with cruisers and destroyers was not as strange as it now seems. The Japanese had built four seaplane tenders with flush decks fast enough to keep up with faster warships such as cruisers and destroyers. When seen from a great distance, their superstructure could be easily confused with being a light cruiser. Nevertheless, the report did say that two tenders or gunboats were there, an impossibility according to the naval doctrine prevalent at that time.

Not wanting to be attacked by the Japanese airplane, Stutt turned his aircraft on a northwesterly course to head home. He knew this was an important observation and wanted to get back to Fall River to debrief his superiors what he and his crew had seen. Their message had not been acknowledged by any Allied radio station. Another Hudson also spotted Mikawa's ships and reported their presence. But their report would not have as much impact and cause as much controversy as Stutt's[13]

✲ ✲ ✲

It was 10:35 a.m. when Mikawa and others watched the Stutt's Hudson bomber fly toward Bougainville. He still had to wait to recover all his aircraft. Having done so and assuming that the Allies knew of his presence, he did not want to be caught by attacking aircraft. Therefore, he changed his plan to arrive slightly later than planned.

Mikawa was now ready to move forward with his plan. The Japanese understanding of the current situation was about as complete as it could be. In spite of being spotted by the Allied planes and receiving no reports of the American carriers' location, there was not enough information that would cause Mikawa to change his mission. He issued orders to move southward through the Bougainville Strait, a passage between Bougainville and Choiseul Islands. The plan was now to attack the American forces near Guadalcanal after midnight on August 9.

It was now time to make sure all his ships knew what he intended to do. Flushed with the confidence that they would be victorious, Ohmae drafted Mikawa's order to all ships:

"We will penetrate south of Savo Island and torpedo the enemy main force at Guadalcanal. Thence we will move toward the forward area at Tulagi and strike with torpedoes and gunfire, after which we will withdraw to the north of Savo Island."[14]

A temporarily tense moment occurred at 1:30 p.m. when the lookouts spotted a mast on their starboard bow about 33,000 yards away. Was it a friendly or an enemy ship? To their great relief, it was the seaplane tender *Akitsushima*, which was on its way to Gizo Island to set up a seaplane base.

Their radios picked up considerable chatter on Allied frequencies about carrier air operations and multiple references to "Green Base" and "Red Base." They felt lucky that these intercepts meant that there would be no immediate air attacks on their force. It was also clear they could expect air attacks during the daylight hours of August 9. The concern over air attacks was still very much in Mikawa's mind and would greatly affect his future tactical decisions.

The radio chatter stopped and darkness descended over the Bougainville Strait's waters. Twenty minutes after hearing the American carriers' radio transmissions, Mikawa turned his force southeasterly and began moving down the Slot. The sun set on the western horizon. In a moment that echoed the British Royal Navy's influence on the Imperial Japanese Navy, Ohmae wrote a Nelsonian-like message for Mikawa that he transmitted to all his ships:

"Let us attack with certain victory in the traditional night attack of the Imperial Navy. May each one calmly do his utmost!"[15]

To minimize any tactical problems and in keeping with Japanese night fighting naval tactics before the night's darkness fully engulfed them, the menacing force changed their formation to the battle formation that would be used that night. Spaced 1,300 yards apart, Mikawa's flagship, the *Chokai*, led the way, followed by the *Aoba*, *Kako*, *Kinugasa*, *Furutaka*, *Tenryu*, *Yubari*, and *Yunagi*. Seaplanes catapulted aloft to provide tactical reconnaissance and light the target area, again following Japanese night naval doctrine.

About one half-hour before midnight on August 8, intermittent rain squalls passed over the Japanese formation but did not slow their advance. Signal flags flew up into each ship's halyards to identify them to every other ship. Eighteen minutes before midnight, the formation's speed increased to 26 knots. The seaplanes aloft reported sighting three Allied cruisers at Savo Island's eastern entrance to Iron Bottom Sound, just south of Savo Island.

Mikawa ordered all crews to "Battle Stations" and increased the ships' speed to 28 knots. It was important that they tightly held their formation because of the narrow waters surrounding Savo Island and the need to keep to their battle plan. They were ready to fight.[16]

Unprepared and Unaware

After almost two days of combat activities, Adm. Ghormley sent a naively confident message to all the Allied commands from his safe base on the tender *Argonne* many miles from the front that stated, "... results so far achieved make every officer and man in the South Pacific area proud of the task forces."[17] In his autobiography, Ghormley recaps the two days' action in an optimistic tone:

"On the 8th of August, enemy resistance in the Tulagi Area was cleared up so that landing on the Tulagi and neighboring islands went ahead. One attack by enemy heavy bombers

> and one attack by enemy dive-bombers was made on our transports. Also an attack by forty enemy torpedo planes. Fortunately, we received warning of the torpedo attack from a 'coast-watcher' stationed on Bougainville, so that the transports were underway and maneuvered clear when the attack was delivered. Minor damage was received."[18]

Events that would transpire later that evening would prove his optimism to be overly exaggerated. The Japanese were on their way to inflict the worst defeat ever experienced by the U.S. Navy.

✲ ✲ ✲

Adm. Turner read the tardy message from Stutt's plane and was a confused man. The mention of "two seaplane tenders" meant to Turner that he could expect a seaplane attack, not a surface attack by fast cruisers and destroyers. This only could mean the Japanese most likely were going to establish a seaplane base at Rekata's well-sheltered harbor on Santa Isabel Island's northwestern coast—only 155 miles from Savo Island and well within flying range of the Guadalcanal landing area. MacArthur's command at Townsville, Australia, came to the same conclusion.

One major problem in Turner's mind was Adm. Fletcher's decision to withdraw his carriers out of air-support range about eight hours before Fletcher said he would in their July 26 meeting off the Fiji Islands. In that meeting, Fletcher had said he would withdraw his carrier after two days. Turner protested that decision at that time, saying that two days was not enough time to unload his transports and have the supplies available for the Marines on Guadalcanal and Tulagi. But other unplanned factors now caused Fletcher to rethink and revise his decision.

Fletcher saw the results of the Japanese air attacks of the last two days and decided a grave danger existed that these aircraft could return and attack his carriers. The three carriers under his command comprised three-quarters of the entire American carrier strength with the *Hornet* still unavailable. He reasoned that his carriers were all the Americans had that stood between the possibility of strategic success or defeat. The loss of the *Yorktown* at Midway and the *Lexington* at Coral Sea still seared in his memory.

The American Navy had to have the time to add more carriers to the Pacific fleet. The *Essex*-class carriers were already being built in America's shipyards and would soon be rolling down the quays, but these were nine months away from making their presence felt. Until that happened, the American Navy would have to fight the Pacific War with the four carriers they had. Nonetheless, these factors were in play when Fletcher said he would withdraw his carriers after two days. Why did he decide to move up his planned withdrawal to the waning daylight hours of August 8?

One possible reason is that he did get agreement from Noyes, the tactical commander of air operations. He sent the following message to Noyes at 3:25 p.m.:

> "In view of the possibility of torpedo plane attack and reduction of our fighter strength I intend to recommend immediate withdrawal of carriers. Do you agree? In case we continue present operation I believe same area should be used tomorrow. What do you think?"

Noyes wasted little time when he replied in the affirmative.[19]

Another possible reason may be concluded by looking at the message Fletcher sent to Ghormley at 6:07 p.m.:

> Fighter-plane strength reduced from 99 to 78. In view of the large number of enemy torpedo planes and bombers in this area, I recommend the immediate withdrawal of my carriers. Request tankers sent forward immediately as fuel running low.[20]

Japanese fighter planes had shown they were clearly superior to the American Grumman Wildcat fighters, although the American pilots had acquitted themselves with valor and skill. But the Japanese pilots flying the Zero fighters were combat-hardened veterans who were formidable, dedicated warriors and showed no hesitation to close and make a kill. Fletcher's losses of fighter planes were the majority of the casualties after two days of aerial combat.

In a now developing and all too familiar pattern of a "bunker" mentality, Ghormley approved Fletcher's decision by deferring to who he called "the man on the spot." Now that there would be no air support for Turner's ships; the SOPAC commander ordered Turner to withdraw his transports, even though the equipment needed to complete the upgrades to Henderson Field had not been off-loaded. The Marines would now be on their own.

He moved his carriers away from the combat area thus putting Turner's ships in greater danger than if his carriers had stayed for the two days to which he had committed at that July 26 meeting. Turner was now in a bind. He would have to withdraw his transports the next day, August 9.[21]

✲ ✲ ✲

The Allies conducted additional air searches, but with inclusive results. Three separate groups had the responsibility to search the waters in and around the Solomons. The first were the B-17s under MacArthur's command, the only planes that had the range to search from Rabaul to Guadalcanal and return to their bases. They sighted Mikawa's ships at 10:25 a.m. on August 8 and reported seeing one destroyer; another sighting reported seeing one cruiser, one destroyer, and two merchant ships; and the third sighting reported seeing one corvette and one merchant ship. The carrier *Enterprise* sent five planes that searched the waters in a 90º pattern from east to north of Guadalcanal. Only one plane flew over the Slot but reached its maximum search range at 3:50 p.m. on August 8, too early to see Mikawa's ships, which began moving down the Slot after 4:00 p.m.[22]

Adm. John S. McCain had the responsibility for all the aircraft under COMSOPAC's command. On August 8, PBYs searched the waters between Truk and Guadalcanal. The lack of any searches of the Slot greatly concerned Turner; he asked McCain to look for approaching ships over that only viable approach for any Japanese ships between Rabaul and Guadalcanal. B-17s based on Espiritu Santo flew over the waters east of Choiseul, not where Mikawa was to steam, and again too early to spot Mikawa. Thus, the only sighting that had definitely seen the approaching Japanese was Stutt's—again the report arrived very late and contained highly dubious observations, particularly with the references to seaplane tenders.

✲ ✲ ✲

Being almost in the dark, Turner ordered the protecting warships to guard against any Japanese incursion from the Slot. Commanding the cruisers and destroyers, Adm. Crutchley divided the waters between Guadalcanal and Florida into three patrol areas, each covered by a Northern, Southern, and an Eastern force.

Crutchley decided to take command of the Southern Force, which had the Australian heavy cruisers *Canberra* and *Australia*, the American heavy cruiser *Chicago*, and the American destroyers *Patterson* and *Bagley*. They would steam between Cape Esperance and Savo Island. The Northern Force, which had the heavy cruisers *Vincennes*, *Astoria*, and *Quincy* and the destroyers *Wilson* and *Helm*, would patrol the entrance between Savo and Florida Islands and commanded by the *Vincennes*' skipper, Capt. Frederick L. Riefkohl. The Eastern Force, under Rear Adm. Norman Scott's command, having the light cruisers *San Juan* and HMAS *Hobart* and the destroyers *Monssen* and *Buchanan*, would patrol just south of Florida Island. To provide an early warning screen to detect any Japanese ships entering the area, Crutchley placed the destroyer *Blue* west of Savo and the destroyer *Ralph Talbot* to Savo's north.

The major power of Crutchley's force steamed in two formations. He had therefore split his forces. This tactic had the main advantage that both northern passages into the sound between Guadalcanal and Florida were now covered. However, the major disadvantage was that he split their firepower. If the Japanese approached in a single line with enough force, they could take on each Allied force separately and destroy it in detail by simply out gunning them. The placement of the lightly armored *San Juan*, with Radm. Norman Scott on board, outside the range of naval gunfire seemed to be a wise precaution. However, the most advanced radar was on that light cruiser and could not be used to detect a northerly approach by any Japanese force.[23]

Technology and Tactics

Many military historians agree that radar was the most significant scientific discovery to have come out of World War II. Invented by the British in the years before World War II, it played a vital role when the British stopped the German Luftwaffe in the Battle of Britain and in the sinking of the German battleship *Bismarck*. British Prime Minister Winston Churchill acknowledged that winning the Battle of Britain would not have happened without radar.

The Americans began experimenting with placing radar systems on warships during the 1930s. The research at the Naval Research Laboratories in Washington, D.C., resulted in the first operational radars being placed on several warships including the battleships *New York* and *Texas* in 1939. After experimentation under simulated battle conditions, American naval radar evolved. The predecessor to the radars that would have a major impact at the Battle of Savo Island was the CXAM radar. However, the U.S. Navy only had this radar on a few capital ships. Further research at Bell Telephone Laboratories in New Jersey improved the CXAM into further generations of radars, notably the SC and SG radars.

Two types of radar were the SC version, used for detection approaching aircraft, and the SG version, which was meant for the detection of approaching ships. The U.S. Navy started placing both versions of radar on their ships. The SG radar was state of the art when it appeared in 1942. The years of radar research concluded that short wavelength was needed for radars that would be used for low altitudes, but no energy source was available with enough power to produce such high frequencies. Nonetheless, the British solved this problem by achieving an engineering breakthrough with the invention of the magnetron. As part of the trading of scientific information between the two countries, the British gave the invention to the Americans.

The Americans placed an early SG radar prototype on the destroyer *Semmes* in June 1941. Beginning in June 1942, the U.S. Navy rapidly installed SG radars on ships as small as a destroyer.[24] However, SG radars were not as pervasive on the American ships in Task Force 62.

On Guard or Not

The only ship at Guadalcanal that had the latest SG radar was the *San Juan*, and it was out of place for detecting any approach by Japanese ships near Savo Island. The two radar picket destroyers, *Blue* and *Ralph Talbot*, which were patrolling the eastern and western approaches from the Slot, had the less advanced SC radar. Therefore, they were at a severe disadvantage in detecting the approach of any ship at night. Another problem with the American use of radar under actual surface battle conditions was that it had never even been tested. While there might have been training exercises using even the older radar version on the screening destroyers, the cruiser force under Crutchley's command had never conducted training exercises that simulated a night surface battle. One reason for this circumstance was that there was little or no time available to conduct such exercises between the meeting off Koro and the August 7 invasion date.

When setting up his force after the meeting aboard the *McCawley* off Koro Island on July 26, Crutchley reasoned that if the Japanese were to launch a surface attack against the invasion force it would be during daylight hours. If they should try it, they would be attacked and destroyed by Fletcher's carrier-borne aircraft in the confining waters between Guadalcanal and Florida Islands.

The Australian admiral also faced other problems. The three Australian ships, *Australia*, *Canberra*, and *Hobart*, had been part of the Australian squadron under Crutchley's command for some time and trained together in night surface battle tactics over the past three months. The other American ships had not. If the American crews had been trained in night fighting tactics, Crutchley did not know or attempt to find out. The signaling methods between the two nations' ships also had some subtle differences. The Australians used low-powered signal lamps. The Americans had some problems trying to use the Australian method, and Crutchley did not have the time to train the Americans to use his ships' signaling system. Thus, he decided to use voice TBS radio as the primary communications technique.

After he decided to split his cruisers to protect against an incursion of Japanese ships from either side of Savo Island, he had also placed two destroyers, the *Blue* and *Ralph Talbot*, for picket duty to provide an early warning. Crutchley had to assign the rest of his destroyers to screen his cruisers and transports against submarine attacks. He chose these two destroyers after conferring with Capt. Cornelius W. Flynn, the commander of DESRON 4. Flynn told him that these two destroyers had achieved the best results using their search radar.[25]

In spite of this careful placement of ships, Crutchley issued no detailed battle plan. It is not clear what his intentions were, other than hoping that if the Japanese should appear, each ship's captain would react with valor and skill.

With the withdrawal of Fletcher's carriers and the need to offload supplies onboard his transports as rapidly as possible, Turner urgently ordered Crutchley and Vandegrift at 8:32 p.m. to the *McCawley* for a commander's conference. Turner wanted to know from Vandegrift what the supply situation was like on Guadalcanal for the Marines and whether Crutchley's ships could hold their own without air support from Fletcher's carriers. Fletcher's decision to withdraw his carriers now imperiled the Marines ashore with the possibility of short supplies of food and ammunition and the ships in danger of air attacks from what Turner believed to be a Japanese air base at Rekata Bay on Santa Isabel Island.

Crutchley delegated his command duties to the *Chicago*'s commander, Capt. Howard D. Bode, and directed his flagship, the *Australia*, to rendezvous with the *McCawley*, now lying north of Lunga Point. Turner welcomed Crutchley at 10:30 p.m. onboard the *McCawley*. Vandegrift arrived 45 minutes later because he was not in his command post on Guadalcanal when Turner's message arrived.

The three days of combat and almost unbearable tension had taken a toll on all three senior commanders. Their exhaustion was plain to all who saw them that night. Vandegrift later admitted that he was "pretty tired, but as for those other two, I thought they were both ready to pass out."

In his normal straight-talking manner, Turner said that he had to withdraw his transports. Vandegrift was not happy with the decision and the likelihood that his 18,000 Marines would be left to fend for themselves without food and ammunition. Turner said he would try to unload the most-needed items off the transports throughout the night before the transports left.

Now that he was face-to-face with his superior, Crutchley asked Turner what he thought about the report that there was a Japanese force of cruisers, destroyers, and "seaplane tenders or gunboats." Turner replied that he thought the reported force would anchor at Rekata Bay from where they would launch torpedo air attacks. After all, why would the Japanese bring down two seaplane tenders? Surely they would never bring them into a surface battle. Turner felt that, if the Japanese should come down the Slot and try to enter the waters around Guadalcanal, his forces could handle whatever the Japanese might throw at them.

Exhausted men were not confined to the senior commanders on the *McCawley*. While Turner's conference went on, the cruisers and destroyers guarding the waters around Savo Island routinely continued at their assigned stations. The earlier Japanese air attacks and the tension leading up to and being part of the invasion had also affected these sailors. The commanders of each ship had been on constant duty for almost 48 hours and needed rest, so each ship received orders to rest half their crew.

The need for rest pressed like a heavy, wet blanket on everyone in the waters that night. The night was heavy with heat and extreme humidity, laying a pall of "doom and destiny" on every sailor. For those who were on duty, it was very difficult to stay vigilant.

The mood of those weary Allied sailors turned even gloomier as a heavy rain squall started on Savo Island's mountain slopes at 11:30 p.m. and moved slowly between the two cruiser formations. The heavy blanket of water blocked each formation's view of the other and added pessimism to the moment. As the crews prepared to hand over their watch to the next watch, reports of three airplane sightings broke the sailors' nadir and instantly brought them to a heightened sense of anxiety. The *Ralph Talbot* saw one of the two seaplanes Mikawa had launched to survey the seas ahead of his ship formation. Recognizing it as one that came from a cruiser, they transmitted an alarming message, "Warning—Warning: Plane over Savo headed east."[26] Fifteen minutes later, repetitive transmissions of this alert had failed to reach Turner's flagship, just 20 miles away.

The *Blue*, in the direct path of the approaching Japanese ships and steaming back and forth on its assigned station, heard the *Ralph Talbot*'s message and also detected a plane on her SC radar, just what the radar was designed to do. Only a few Allied ships picked up the alarm, but seemingly ignored the planes that flew right over them. For various reasons, several ships either ignored or treated the message as unimportant, viewed the planes as friendly because they had their running lights on, or assumed that, if the planes belonged to the Japanese, Turner would have sent out an alarm and put his ships on alert. Of course, the statement that assumptions are the nexus of all "screw-ups" was becoming true. The *Blue*'s radar detected nothing, and its lookouts saw nothing of the approaching ships because she steamed with her stern toward them and her lookouts only looked forward, a common mistake made by tired lookouts.

An exhausted Crutchley returned to the *Australia* five minutes before midnight and could not see anything in the rainy murkiness. Just a zephyr of wind moved across the water and barely moved the now sprouting rain squalls. Savo was hidden behind thick rain peppering the seas. To the east, faint lightning flashes barely illuminated the transports off Guadalcanal. The flickering glow of the still burning *George F. Elliott* lit the northeastern sky and proved to be a guiding beacon for the approaching Japanese. Rather than rendezvousing with the *Canberra* and the *Chicago* less than an hour away, he decided to keep the cruiser patrolling between Savo and the transports. Trying to explain his decision, later he wrote:

> "I decided not to rejoin my night patrol group for the short time that remained before 0500 when units would resume screening stations round the transports, and accordingly I ordered *Australia* to patrol in the vicinity of Squadron 'X.'"[27]

Only one hour after he met with Turner on the *McCawley*, Crutchley agreed with Turner that the probability of a Japanese attack that night was quite low, but *possible*. No record exists that he ever told Turner that he was not returning the *Australia* to form up with the other two cruisers. To the contrary, Turner recalled in 1946 that Crutchley sent a message, received at 1:30 a.m., saying that the *Australia* would stay near and guard the transports. Nevertheless, Crutchley's decision not to return to the patrol with the *Chicago* and *Canberra* reduced that formation's cruiser strength by one-third. One possible explanation for this competent naval officer making such a fateful decision might be that he was too tired to make rational decisions.

The gloomy silence did little to increase the Allied sailors' alertness. It was about to be shattered with the momentous opening shot to the Battle of Savo Island just minutes away.[28]

CHAPTER 16
A Stinging, Savage Defeat

Destiny Approaches

The well-known shape of Savo Island was 20 degrees off the *Chokai*'s starboard bow as Mikawa's formation neared their intended battle area. Every Japanese sailor was ready for whatever fate awaited them. Their tension increased at three minutes past midnight on August 9 when one of *Chokai*'s lookouts exclaimed, "Ship approaching, 30 degrees starboard!"[1] The Americans were at hand.

The sighted ship approximately 10,000 meters away was the American destroyer *Blue* and crossing Mikawa's bows from right to left. Mikawa ordered, "Stand by for action!" Some indecision was apparent on the *Chokai*'s bridge. A critical decision was about to be made whether to attack this destroyer or not. If they fired on the American ship, their position would be revealed to the American invasion ships, and the opportunity for surprise would be lost. Mikawa thought that the element for shocking the Americans into chaos far outweighed the almost reflexive reaction to immediately open fire on an imminent enemy. He ordered, "Left rudder. Slow to 22 knots."

The tension temporarily lessened as they watched the American destroyer proceed on her way almost nonchalantly, obviously unaware of their presence. The Japanese aimed every gun at her. Just as Mikawa and the rest of his men thought she must see them, she reversed her course in a starboard turn without reducing her speed. The Japanese had not been seen.

Counting themselves as a group of very lucky ships, another lookout dashed their confidence when he shouted, "Ship sighted, 20 degrees port." The ship was the destroyer *Ralph Talbot*. What was she doing there? Answering that question, the destroyer moved away from them. Mikawa did not hesitate to withhold his fire as he commanded, "Right rudder. Steer course 150 degrees."

They had avoided being discovered by the American picket ships. All that training for night sea battle and nighttime lookout preparation was about to yield a bonus beyond their most optimistic expectations. The lighting conditions were also in their favor. The transport *George F. Elliott*, one of the two casualties of the previous two days' air attacks, still burned ferociously in the distance and provided ideal backlighting that would silhouette any ships to the south. The Japanese remained in darkness as they moved toward the American transport ships' anchorage. Mikawa knew that the lighting and surprise advantage he now had would not last long as his ships moved into their attack plan.

Recalling that his search planes had seen three Allied cruisers steaming south of Savo Island, Mikawa ordered at 1:30 a.m. for his ships to attack the Allied warships. He instructed the destroyer *Yunagi* to leave the line of ships and attack the destroyers now at the formation's rear. Mikawa also wanted to secure his line of departure after he left the Savo area if the American ships should counterattack from his formation's rear.

Capt. Ohmae stood beside Mikawa as they looked at the chart and into the omnipresent darkness that engulfed them. Suddenly, a lookout's voice pierced the tense quiet: "Cruiser, seven degrees port!" They immediately turned their binoculars in the sighting's direction. The ship in the distance appeared tiny. It could not be a cruiser but a destroyer. Another sighting report swiftly came: "Three cruisers, nine degrees starboard, moving to the right!" The light from a parachute flare suddenly pierced the gloomy night and changed the moonless darkness into almost daylight. There they were, three cruisers just 8,000 meters away.

Well-trained and ready to go into immediate action, the *Chokai*'s captain, Mikio Hayakawa, overwhelmed the silence with a loud and commanding voice: "Torpedoes fire to starboard—Fire!" At 1:37 a.m., deadly "Long Lance" torpedoes whooshed one at a time out of their tubes and hit the water with resounding slaps. A radio report said that the cruisers to the rear of the *Chokai* had fired their guns and launched torpedoes.

The Battle of Savo Island had begun.

The torpedoes did not take long to reach their targets. Blazing explosions filled the night as the torpedoes found their marks. Mikawa's ships now turned on a northeasterly course.[2]

✡ ✡ ✡

At 1:43 a.m., the lookouts on the destroyer *Patterson*, the only Allied ship that seemed to be awake, suddenly saw a large, looming ship only 5,000 yards away—it was the *Chokai*. The destroyer sent a radio alarm:

WARNING—WARNING: STRANGE SHIPS ENTERING HARBOR!

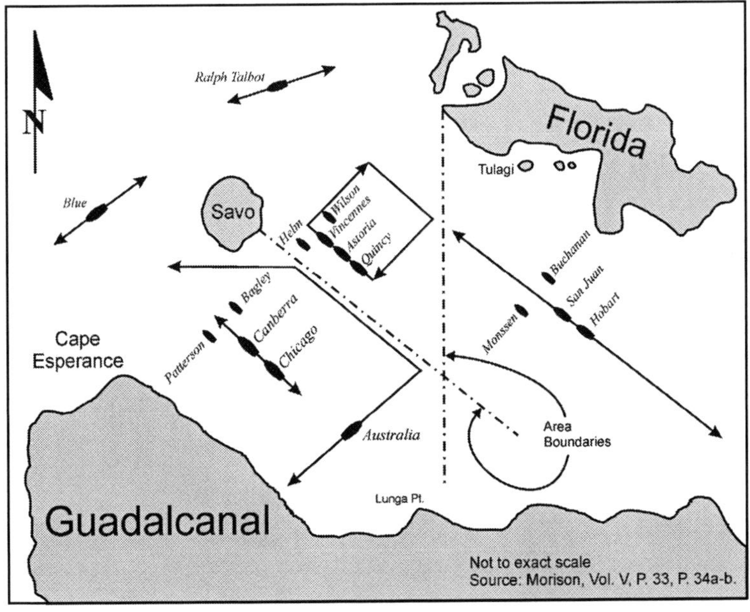

Allied Ships at the Battle of Savo Island

But the warning arrived too late to be of any help. The night was now as bright as day from the floating flares dropped by Japanese search planes. Torpedoes and shells from the guns of the *Chokai*, *Aoba*, and *Furutaka* were already on their way.

Meanwhile, an eagle-eyed lookout on the Australian heavy cruiser *Canberra* tried to show his officer-of-the-deck an unfamiliar ship straight ahead. The two men tried to see what this ship was. But it was to no avail. At the same time the *Patterson* issued its warning, two torpedoes slammed into the cruiser's sides and exploded. Almost instantaneously, 24 eight-inch and 4.7-inch shells smacked into the cruiser's deck and hull just as the sounds of General Alarm[3] flooded the ship. The cruiser's captain, Capt. Frank E. Getting, received mortal wounds while his gunnery officer lay dead. His ship did launch two torpedoes and fire a few secondary battery four-inch shells. Her main eight-inch guns never fired a shot. Fire spread fatally over her main deck, and she began to list ten degrees to starboard. It was only a matter of time before the *Canberra* began sinking.

The *Patterson* made a hard left turn so she could fire broadsides from her main four-inch guns. Fighting back in a Lilliputian-way, her skipper, Cmdr. Frank R. Walker, shouted, "Fire Torpedoes!" and ordered her 4-inch guns to open fire. He put his ship on a zigzag course and engaged the approaching Japanese. But the incoming fire from the Japanese ships soon overwhelmed her. One shell smashed and exploded near her No. 4 turret, setting powder on deck afire and knocking out two guns. She turned 180º and was on a parallel course with the Japanese ships trying to catch up with them. Her executive officer, rudely awakened by the sounds of battle, came on deck, and directed fire control parties to put out deck fires.

The destroyer *Bagley* saw the Japanese cruisers just a few minutes after the *Patterson* did. Protecting the Australian cruiser *Canberra* off its starboard bow, the *Bagley* turned hard to starboard so that it could fire its torpedoes. The turn was so quick that its torpedomen did not have enough time to arm the torpedoes. Realizing that time was short, Lt. Cmdr. George A. Sinclair, the ship's captain, abruptly turned his ship to port and fired his port torpedo tubes at the oncoming Japanese. The delay cost the destroyer its opportunity to inflict any damage. The Japanese ships moved off and disappeared in the night. They were too far away and moving too fast for any torpedoes the *Bagley* had fired to catch up with them.

The heavy cruiser *Chicago* had seen three signs the Japanese were coming. Orange flashes from gunfire lit the horizon at 1:42 a.m. A flare dropped by a Japanese plane suddenly flooded the transports with an eerie light. Just ahead of the *Chicago* in the formation, the *Canberra* made a sudden, hard right turn. The *Chicago*'s General Quarters gong rudely woke up its captain, Capt. Howard D. Bode, who then ordered his five-inch guns to light up the night with illuminated star shells. But a torpedo sighted by one of the cruiser's lookouts abruptly turned these orders to counterattack into chaos. Bode tried to move his ship so the torpedo would miss by "combing its wake" but to no avail. The Japanese "Long Lance" slammed into the *Chicago*'s bow at 1:46 a.m. and detonated with a deafening blast. A huge column of water rose up and flooded the cruiser from the bow to the No. 1 stack.

After overcoming the shock of the explosion, the ship's gunners, trained to react to adverse circumstances, fired more five-inch star shells to find the Japanese ships, but all failed to light up. One shell from a Japanese cruiser hit on her foremast and caused limited damage. The cruiser did not turn away as the destroyers had done. Bode changed his course westward and pursued what seemed to be two targets about two minutes out of gun range with a course change westward.

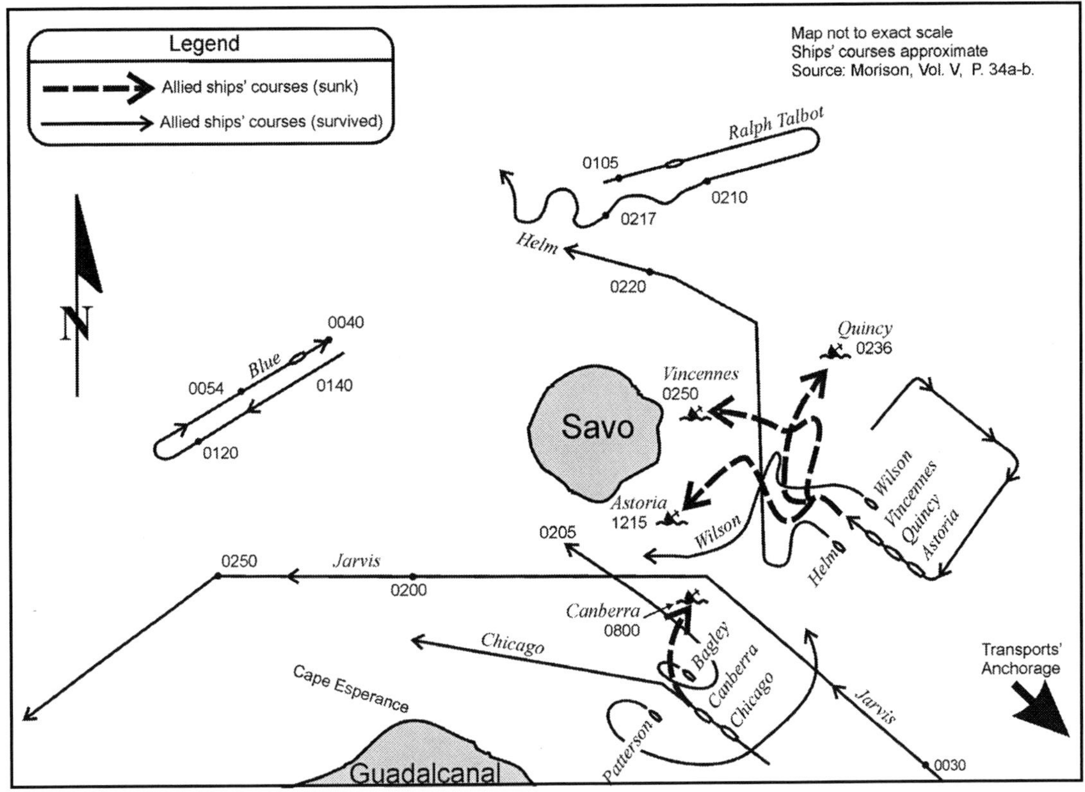

Allied Ships Battle the Japanese

One target the *Chicago*'s lookouts saw was the Japanese destroyer *Yunagi*'s searchlight. The cruiser fired 25 rounds at the destroyer. The destroyer's searchlight extinguished at 1:51 a.m., which caused the *Chicago* to light up hers, pointing the lamp to port. Nothing! By this time, the *Chicago* steamed westward, taking her farther away from the Japanese, who were moving to the northeast. To make matters worse, Bode failed to warn the *Vincennes'* cruiser formation. Hell was on its way![4]

✲ ✲ ✲

The Japanese changed their course to the northeast as they prepared to round Savo Island and return home. Mikawa knew there were more American ships ahead of him. The *Chokai* fired more torpedoes. Another explosion rocked the night with more following one after another. Ten minutes later, a cacophony of violent blasts pierced the darkness with a light show of destruction flared into the night. Ohmae believed that every torpedo and gun shell the Japanese fired hit everything at which they were aimed.

Mikawa's lookouts spied more ships 30º to port while the *Chokai*'s searchlights revealed more targets. The cruiser opened fire at 1:53 a.m. on an American cruiser with its searchlights seeking out more ships and acting as a guide for the rest of the Japanese ships. Ohmae recalled later that it was as if the cruiser was saying to its compatriots, "Here is the *Chokai*! Fire on *that* target!...Now *that* target!... This is *Chokai*! Hit *that* target!"[5]

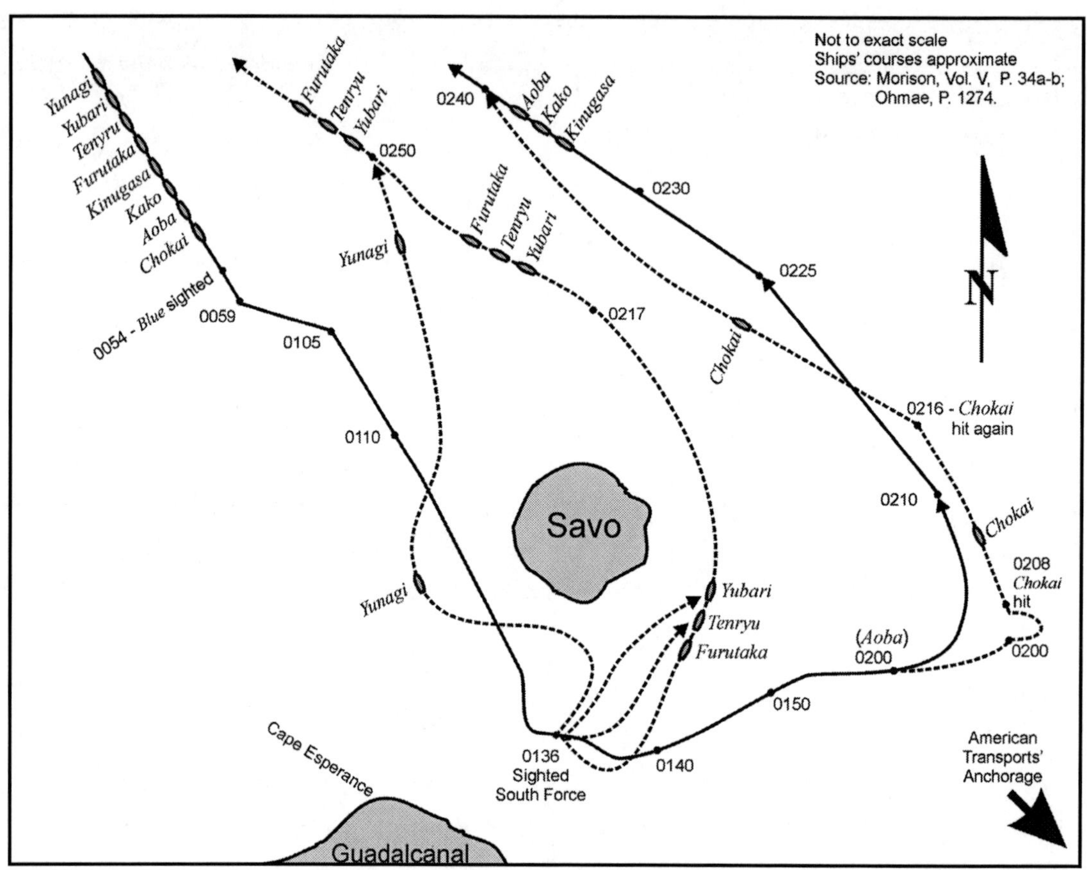

The Japanese Ships Battle the Allied Ships at Savo Island

Incredibly, the American ships' gun turrets had not yet rotated to fire on the onrushing Japanese. It was as if they did not know the Japanese were even there. The only guns firing at the Japanese ships were machine guns. Tracer bullets from both sides made light tracks across the water. While they made a colorful spectacle, they had little effect on their intended targets. Rapidly closing the distance to the American ships to about 4,300 yards, Mikawa and others on his flagship could see the outline of their adversaries.

One ship,[6] manned by a brave crew from a group of three, turned toward the Japanese with the apparent intent of ramming whatever ship should to come in its path. The Japanese aimed every gun they could spare at the oncoming American ship. Several shells hit the ship and flames covered her upper deck. She started to list but belligerently fired an eight-inch shell from a short distance that hit the *Chokai*'s operations room and knocked out her front-most turret. Mikawa and the others on the bridge felt the shock, and it temporarily threw them off balance. But the hit on the *Chokai* and the American ships firing back did not stop Japanese ships from inflicting crippling blows on their targets. The American returning gunfire lessened. Ohmae remembered thinking that they had won the battle.

An American cruiser burned brightly behind the departing Japanese ships as the crew of the *Chokai* assessed the damage of the eight-inch shell hit. If it had hit about five yards closer to the bridge, it would have killed all who were there. Mikawa and his staff examined the battle situation and began to inspect it in great detail—they were so deeply analyzing that gunfire to their port surprised them. They had been turning more northward. The cruisers *Furutaka*, *Tenryu*, and *Yubari* had turned more to the left when the Japanese had first fired their torpedoes and were on a parallel course with the *Chokai*. The three ships turned northward around the northwest coast of Savo Island when their lookouts saw more American ships. They opened fire at the new targets. Mikawa ordered a message sent via signal lamp for the others to avoid firing at the *Chokai*.

With that potential danger nipped in the bud, Mikawa's staff now tried to decide their next move. They examined several factors while trying to reach a decision:

1. By 2:30 a.m., the Japanese ships were a divided force with several groups of ships each pursuing independent courses. If Mikawa wanted to bring them together in the cloudless darkness, all ships would have to slow down and reassemble—that would take half-an-hour. It would take another half hour to increase speed for battle. They would have to turn around and head back to where the transports were—taking another half hour. Mikawa estimated that if he made these moves, his ships would not arrive where the American ships were until 5:00 a.m.—one hour before daylight.

2. Mikawa had received radio intelligence the night before that indicated there were American carriers within 100 miles of his present position. The battle would prompt the carriers to move closer to Guadalcanal and launch air attacks at first light.

3. If the Japanese withdrew without delay, the American carrier-based aircraft would most surely go after and strike at them. The sooner they left the battle scene, the lower the probability that aircraft could find them. In any case, the American aircraft would come within range of Japanese land-based aircraft and be attacked themselves.

They had achieved a great naval victory. The Imperial Japanese Navy would need these ships to continue what was thought to be a long, hard-fought war. The Japanese Army's report that they could drive the American Marines into the sea and hold onto Guadalcanal also influenced this analysis. The staff reported their recommendations to their superior, and he made his decision. The order issued at 2:23 a.m. read, "All forces withdraw." Unquestionably, the *Chokai* bridge's signal lamp blinked. "Force in line ahead, course 320 degrees, speed 30 knots."[7]

The *Chokai* showed a speed signal light as the bridge's occupants saw the *Furutaka*'s identification lamp. The cruiser's radio sent a message to Rabaul projecting where they would be at dawn and warned them to be on alert for American carrier-based aircraft that may be following them.[8]

✲ ✲ ✲

By 1:49 a.m., the Allied ships guarding the waters between Guadalcanal and Savo Islands were finished as an effective fighting force. The Australian cruiser *Canberra* was sinking and would slip beneath the waves in just a few hours. The *Chicago* was out of the fight and steaming away from the battle. The destroyer *Bagley*, its fires now under control, headed to the northwest and also left the area. The *Patterson* could not engage the Japanese alone because they were now moving to the northeast to take on the American ships in the waters between Savo and Florida Islands.

Just six minutes earlier—the same time the *Patterson* broadcast her "WARNING—WARNING: STRANGE SHIPS ENTERING HARBOR!" message, blinding bright, long-burning parachute flares dropped by Japanese float planes lit the sky above the transports' anchorage and were seen by the cruisers *Vincennes*, *Quincy*, and *Astoria* accompanied by the destroyers *Helm* and *Wilson*. Capt. Riefkohl, now in tactical command, heard the warning message and observed the flares. For some unexplained reason, he thought these were "friendly" in spite of the fact these planes droned overhead. He issued no orders to prepare for battle as his force was turning in its box course from southwest to northwest.

In keeping with the mood of fatigue permeating the *Vincennes* ships' group, Capt. William G. Greenman, skipper of the cruiser *Astoria* and worn out from the air attacks of the past two days, lay in his emergency quarter's bunk, fully clothed and in a deep sleep. The *Astoria*'s officer of the deck paid close attention to the change in his ship's course as Quartermaster A. Radke dutifully and routinely entered the change of course into the ship's log. Lt. Cmdr. James R. Topper, the damage control officer and acting supervisor of the bridge watch, saw gunfire flashes on Florida Island and remarked to others on the bridge that the Marines must be in the middle of a fight. Lt. Cmdr. William H. Truesdell, the gunnery officer, had been having trouble with the fire control radar and ordered it to be tested. The technician fixed the radar's problem, and the radar became fully operational again. The sound of "three bells" clanged; the "graveyard watch" had two and one-half hours to go. The attitude of "business as usual" would be rudely shaken. Torpedoes launched from the *Chokai* slid through the water past the *Chicago*'s group of ships toward the soon-doomed American cruiser.

As the *Astoria*'s blissfully ignorant officers paid little attention to the flares to the south and the warning from the *Patterson*, a slight tremor shook the *Astoria* at 1:45 a.m. Topper thought depth charges dropped by destroyers were the cause since they had reports of submarines in the area. Had the crew been alert and aware, they would have realized that several Japanese torpedoes had struck their ship and inflicted heavy damage. Picking up the ship's phone, Topper called damage control and asked if they too had felt the slight blow. The answer was affirmative, and they were now fully alerted.

The loud noises made by the ship's boilers drowned out the sound of an airplane flying overhead. Someone on the port bridge wing shouted, "Star shell on the port quarter!" Topper ran to the ship's port side. A strand of flares lit up the sky and clouds to the south. Truesdell, also noticing the light from the flares, urged the bridge to go to General Quarters. More than four minutes had passed since torpedoes had struck the *Astoria*. A few seconds later, at 1:50 a.m., searchlights pierced the darkness. Japanese shells now splatted on the water surrounding the cruiser. Finally, the main battery spotter proclaimed that Japanese cruisers were off the port quarter. Not willing the wait for any formalities like notifying the captain, Truesdell ordered the main batteries to open fire. Thirty seconds after 1:52 a.m., six eight-inch guns roared, belching fire and smoke; six deadly missiles were on their way to the *Chokai*.

Confusion reigned on the bridge. Radke pulled the cord that sounded General Quarters. Trying to wipe the sleep from his eyes, Capt. Greenman arrived on the bridge just before the *Astoria*'s second deafening salvo. He did not know whose ships now attacked his command or why. Taking command of the situation, although not sure what the battle situation was, he shouted a series of harried questions and commands:—"Who sounded the general alarm? Who gave the order to commence firing? Topper, I think we are firing on our own ships; let's not get excited and act too hasty. Cease firing!"[9]

By this time, the *Chokai* had fired four salvoes, but miraculously no shells hit the *Astoria*. The American cruiser's brief span of good luck would not last. As the *Astoria*'s bridge crew argued among themselves, another salvo of eight-inch shells finally found the range. They hit amidships and turned the deck into an inferno. The raging fires gave the Japanese an ideal aiming point. Moving in close for the kill, the Japanese cruisers deluged the American cruiser with shells. Their accuracy increased as they closed the distance from 6,000 to 5,300 yards. Blast after blast erupted on the doomed cruiser. Greenman vainly tried to turn his ship slightly to port and increase the ship's speed to bring what was left of the guns in his main battery to bear while watching out for the *Quincy* just ahead. The effect of so many hits, the resulting fires and smoke, loss of communication, the death of so many men and ammunition exploding everywhere, left the *Astoria* a fighting ship in name only. She had fired 11 salvoes at her tormentors, but could fire no longer. Greenman tried to steer a zigzag course as an incessant stream of lethal shells fell like rain. The forward two turrets were destroyed, the cruiser's spotter airplane was on fire amidships, and his navigator and quartermaster were both dead.

But the Japanese did not escape damage. One of *Quincy*'s shells struck the *Chokai*. The two flaming American cruisers made an ideal beacon for both the damaged American cruisers to stay on station, but, more disastrously, lit up the battle scene. A shell blasted the *Astoria*'s starboard side at 2:02 a.m. as Greenman tried to get his ship out of the firing line between the Japanese and the *Quincy*. The explosion killed the signal officer, helmsman, and a boatswain's mate. The ship steamed without a helmsman for about 30 seconds when a badly injured Boatswain's Mate J. Young untangled himself from a pile of bodies, took the wheel, and steered the ship in a northwesterly direction. The heat and smoke below decks forced the black gang[10] to head toward the decks above and abandon their assigned stations. The *Astoria*'s speed slowed noticeably. Although her propellers churned in the water, her top speed was a crippling and pathetic seven knots. Fires covered her entire topside deck. The ship that Adm. Turner had commanded in 1939 to take the ashes of Hiroshi Saito to Japan was now a funeral pyre. The proud *Astoria* would go down fighting. Communications Officer Lt. Cmdr. Walter B. Davidson climbed into the undamaged turret No. 2 and aimed the guns toward an onrushing Japanese cruiser. A shell from the *Astoria*'s twelfth and last salvo hit on the *Chokai*'s forward turret. The *Astoria*'s crew fought to keep her afloat, but the gallant ship inevitably slipped beneath the waves later that day at 12:15 p.m.[11]

✲ ✲ ✲

The devastating damage to the *Astoria*'s now blazing hulk had been bad enough. Unbelievably, the damage to the *Quincy*, steaming ahead of the *Astoria* in the formation, would be worse than that. The cruiser's bridge crew also heard the planes flying overhead. However, when a junior officer suggested they might be Japanese, the more senior officers' reaction was almost comically incredulous. Therefore, the captain never received these reports. But the sighting of Japanese flares finally woke the bridge crew to the fact that the planes were indeed Japanese. Then they heard the *Patterson*'s warning message, and, unlike the reaction of the *Astoria*'s bridge personnel, the ship immediately sounded General Quarters. The *Quincy*'s gunnery control officer, Lt. Cmdr. John D. Andrew, now knew the source of the flares when the alarm brought him back from his uncertainty. Capt. Samuel N. Moore, the *Quincy*'s commander, answered the bridge's call and came to the bridge from his cabin. For some unexplainable reason, no message ever went out to the gunners to prepare for action.

The Japanese cruiser *Aoba* closed its range to the *Quincy* by coming up on the American cruiser's stern. She opened her searchlight's shutters. The *Quincy* was in clear sight for the *Aoba*'s gunners; she was a sitting duck. Being bathed in such a clear, bright light horrified the *Quincy*'s crew. Japanese shells raised water columns all around the ill-fated cruiser. The *Quincy*'s nine eight-inch guns answered with two fast salvoes of her own from a distance of 8,000 yards. Their totally befuddled captain, thinking that his ship had fired on friendly ships, ordered his recognition lights turned on. Junior officers tried to argue with him to cancel the order. Fearing they would collide with the *Vincennes* ahead of them in the formation, the officer of the deck ordered a turn to the right. In doing so, his own forward batteries could not fire since the cruiser's stern faced the Japanese. But the turn had not yet been finished; a Japanese shell crashed into the cruiser's search plane and exploded, flooding the deck with flames. Searchlights were no longer needed. The fire made an excellent aiming point.

Shell after shell pummeled the American cruiser again, again, and again. Trying to fight back and show his defiance in a doomed situation, the captain picked up the telephone to the gunners and yelled, "We're going down between them—give them hell!" Just as he spoke those words, a shell exploded in the pilothouse, killing everyone there and mortally wounding Moore. A torpedo exploded on the port side and caved in the wall in the No. 4 fireroom. Speaking his last words, the engineering officer, Lt. Cmdr. Eugene E. Elmore, sent a messenger to tell the captain that the ship must stop.

Thus far, the engine rooms had not been damaged, but the crew had no way to reach the bridge because all connections to the outside world had been cut. Thoroughly sealed, the engine rooms became the tomb for all trapped there. Sailors in mess compartments, repair stations, and bunk rooms vainly tried to get on deck, but fires and explosions stopped them. Scattered body parts of men who served in the AA batteries were everywhere.

Lt. Cmdr. Harry B. Heneberger wrote in the ship's action report that a Japanese shell had set fire to shells in the No. 4 five-inch batteries and caused "them to burn like a Roman candle killing all hands on the left side of the gun." There was no doubt now. The *Quincy* was finished. Trying to reach the bridge to get them to announce an "Abandon Ship" order, Heneberger sent his assistant, Lt. Cmdr. John D. Andrew, to that almost inaccessible objective. Andrew later recalled:

> "When I reached the bridge level, I found it a shambles of dead bodies with only three or four people still standing. In the pilothouse itself the only person standing was the signalman at the wheel, who was vainly endeavoring to check the ship's swing to starboard and to bring her to port. On questioning him I found out that the Captain, who was at that time lying near the wheel, had instructed him to beach the ship and he was trying to head the ship for Savo Island, distant some four miles on the port quarter. I stepped to the port

side of the pilothouse, looked out to find the island, and noted that the ship was heeling rapidly to port, sinking by the bow. At that instant the Captain straightened up and fell back, apparently dead, without having uttered any sound other than a moan."[12]

As the last surviving senior officer, Heneberger ordered to "Abandon Ship" after Andrew reported the captain was dead. Water flooded the forecastle as the crew threw the life rafts and anything else that could float overboard and jumped into the water. She had put up quite a fight against overwhelming odds. In the end, she had to give way to the power of the Imperial Japanese Navy. The *Quincy* turned turtle to port, her stern twisting in the air and, in her last agony, slipped beneath the waves at 2:35 a.m., thus being the first American ship to give the waters north of Guadalcanal the name of Iron Bottom Sound.[13]

✲ ✲ ✲

The torment for the Americans was not over yet. The cruiser *Vincennes*, affectionately called the "Vinny Maru" by her crew and leading the column of cruisers steaming to protect against any incursion from the north side of Savo Island, was the next cruiser to be destroyed. She was a sister ship of the *Astoria* and *Quincy* and belonged to the *New Orleans*-class of heavy cruisers built by the U.S. in the 1930s.

Her captain, Capt. Frederick L. Riefkohl, given the nickname "Fearless Freddie" by his colleagues, was 51 years old and had risen up the ranks to his command of the *Vincennes* since graduating from the Naval Academy. He had received a Navy Cross during World War I in a sea action against a German U-boat. In his early career, he had shown a preference to serve in destroyers and served on the destroyers *Smith*, *Thompson*, and *Corry*. His reputation was he never ran away from a fight; and his conduct during the Battle of Savo Island did nothing to contradict that assessment.

At 12:50 a.m., Riefkohl turned the command of the cruiser over to his executive officer, Cmdr. William E. A. Mullan, and went to his cabin to get some badly needed rest. He had been awake for 21 hours defending against Japanese air attacks. As he left the bridge, he told Mullan to "wake me if anything unusual happens." Lt. Cmdr. Cleaveland D. Miller was the OOD and Lt. Cmdr. Robert. R. Craighill was the watch's gunnery officer. Mullan and Craighill knew that the *Ralph Talbot* had sent a message at 11:45 p.m. reporting sighting a Japanese plane. Riefkohl had notified them to be on high alert. Miller ordered a course change at 1:20 a.m. with the *Quincy* following 600 yards behind and *Astoria*, 1,200 yards to the rear.

Like her sister ship *Quincy*, she was not aware of any danger until flares appeared off her port quarter. The *Vincennes* was at what is called Condition II, a step below full alert, with all main guns manned and loaded. Craighill was at his station in the gun aiming platform when a lookout exclaimed, "Object broad on the port bow!" Craighill swept the horizon with his binoculars from the port beam and found nothing. A rain squall drenched Savo Island. Craighill peered again through his glasses and looked in a 360º arc — again seeing nothing. Twenty-three uneventful minutes passed. The lookouts on the bridge's port wing intently looked at the corner of Savo Island where the rain squall was. It was 1:43 a.m.

Craighill checked the southern horizon again. A flash of light appeared that might have come from gunfire. Four other pairs of eyes also peered through their glasses. The light disappeared. Suddenly, four flares flashed about eight miles away. Craighill had seen enough. He picked up the telephone and reported to the bridge, "Four star shells on the port quarter!"

Miller, the OOD, turned to the messenger and said, "Call the captain."

A bright display now fully lit the southeastern sky, completely flooding the Allied cruiser force to the south in a bath of light. The *Vincennes'* bridge crew could now see the ships' silhouettes. Still fighting to shake off the effects of his nap, Riefkohl arrived on the bridge. Mullan briefed him of the situation. Riefkohl immediately acted by sounding the general alarm.

The sounds of the crew rushing to their battle stations filled the ship as Riefkohl turned to look at another star shell burst to the southeast. Lt. Cmdr. Robert L. Adams, Craighill's immediate superior and the ship's gunnery officer, had been getting some rest in the sky gun control tower. Instantly awakened by a bright light, he saw strings of star shells falling over Lunga Point. Initially thinking these lights came from ships firing on shore installations, he changed his mind when he saw flashes that confirmed that ships were exchanging gunfire.

Adams ordered "Action Report!" to the AA batteries, ran into the gun control station, and ordered the main guns to be ready to fire. The captain ordered Craighill to fire star shells. Craighill then ran to his battle station in sky control.

Meanwhile, Riefkohl and Mullan discussed what this firing to the southeast meant. Riefkohl even speculated that it was a ploy to lure the *Vincennes* and the rest of the cruisers following it away from their present location while the Japanese escaped. He wrote in his notes, "If enemy fire had been sighted, I expected *Australia* group would illuminate and engage them." He ordered a speed increase to 15 knots but stayed on his present course. Two underwater explosions rumbled through his ship. Riefkohl obliviously did not react.

Mullan left the bridge to go to his battle station in Battery No. 2, leaving Riefkohl alone to mull over the confusing situation. His mystification lasted until 1:50 a.m. when three searchlights appeared off the port stern quarter. As perplexed as ever, Riefkohl thought these lights came from the Allied southern cruisers and, in what seems to be a completely fantastic moment of unreality, sent an order over the TBS to turn off the searchlights. Reality arrived with a vengeance when a salvo from the Japanese cruiser *Kako* screamed into the air and fell 500 yards short. The *Vincennes'* star shells illuminated the Japanese cruisers, immediately followed by a mighty nine-gun eight-inch salvo of its own from a range of 8,250 yards. Just as the Japanese's second salvo was on it way, the *Vincennes* second bellowed out in the night and smashed onto the *Kinugasa*. But the reverie of hitting the Japanese was short-lived.

A five-inch salvo hit the cruiser's well deck and engulfed it in flames. Fully fueled aircraft erupted in explosive balls of fire. Like her sister ships, the fires that now inundated her decks were the beacon the Japanese could use as an aiming point as they closed in for the kill.

As Mullan tried to reach his battle station, one salvo hit the movie booth while another struck on the well deck. He arrived on deck and saw an eight-inch shell hit the hangar, go through it, and fall on the other side of the ship. Turning his attention to try to save his ship, he began organizing firefighting parties and tried to get the pumps going. The crews made some headway against the fires when another shell exploded and destroyed the water pressure outlets. Water pressure so sorely needed to fight the fires dropped precipitously. Flames now covered the *Vincennes*, dooming her to a fiery end.

Riefkohl decided to take the initiative away from the Japanese by moving closer to their cruisers. In his notes, he wrote, "Speed was increased to 20 knots and a turn made to left with a view of closing with the enemy and continuing around on a reverse course if he stood in toward the transport area. Attempts to signal an increase in speed failed due to loss of inter-ship communications facilities (TBS) after the bridge was hit...One five-inch shell struck the port side of the bridge, killing the communications officer. Fragments entered the pilot house, killing or seriously wounding several men."[14] In spite of these difficulties, the *Vincennes* still turned; the *Quincy* and the *Astoria* dutifully followed. But the undeterred Japanese bored in to administer killing blows. Shell after shell smashed the ship's superstructure, demolished gun emplacements, destroyed communications, and started blistering hot fires that bubbled paint and engulfed men in flames. The bodies of the wounded and dead silently lay intertwined.

Any attempt to return any eight-inch fire was hopeless. The turrets could not turn because there was no power to move them. The ship could no longer be steered from the bridge. Riefkohl moved to the wheel house to direct the ship from there. The No. 2 fireroom was now clouded with heavy smoke and overheated debris was everywhere. The men in the after engine room watched helplessly as steam pressure dropped. All calls to the bridge failed. A torpedo from the light cruiser *Yubari* penetrated the hull at 2:03 a.m. and exploded in the No. 1 fireroom killing all men in the compartment. The radar failed because it could no longer transmit or receive, and all communications within the ship ceased to work.

Riefkohl wrote in his notes, "*Quincy* was observed on fire aft, on our port hand. *Astoria* was not seen. *Helm* and *Wilson* were ahead on the starboard hand when we turned right. One destroyer was then crossing starboard to port. The one crossing from port to starboard may have been an enemy. But as the two vessels barely missed colliding and did not fire at one another it is believed that they were both friendly. One DD (destroyer) on our starboard hand, probably *Wilson,* fired star shells and what appeared to be heavy AA machine-gun fire."[15] He ordered a desperate hard right turn to avoid more damage, but to no avail. Three *Chokai* torpedoes struck the No. 4 fireroom and destroyed everything there. The *Vincennes* was now a burning hulk.

All Riefkohl could see was chaos as he witnessed the complete disintegration of his command. The heat from the blazing fires melted the ladders. Men trapped in the fire and smoke below decks tried to get to the main deck, but could not. No relief could be sent below. They were already dead men. Others tried to get whomever they could to the upper decks. One of the badly wounded was Cmdr. Mullan, whose broken leg rendered him nearly an invalid. Everyone who could help tried to get everyone they could into the rafts since it was clear the ship was going down. The men in the radio and coding rooms threw all decoding machines overboard while bridge personnel locked classified documents in the ship's 400-pound safe, which would sink with the ship. Riefkohl, his Marine orderly, Corporal James L. Patrick, and Chief Yeoman Leonard E. Stucker abandoned the bridge.

The ship's surgeon, Dr. Samuel A. Isquith, remembered:

> "When I had taken care of the last man, I opened the dressing station door and called out topside asking if the order to abandon ship had been given. There was no answer. Dead

silence. The deck, I noticed, was now listing about a 25-degree angle. I ordered my detail and casualties topside.

A fierce fire was raging amidships. I could see that the *Vincennes* had only a few minutes' floating time left in her. The whole superstructure was rapidly rolling over on her port side. Her deck guns were awash. We got the wounded into the life jackets and, one by one, helped them down the side into the water on the port side. By this time the blazing superstructure bad begun to crumble. Flaming beams toppled to the deck, cutting off my own escape on the port side. At the same time, shells began exploding in the ready boxes.

I hurried across the deck to the starboard rail and poised for a dive. I felt something sear into my right knee. I plunged into the dark water some 20 feet below, narrowly missing the after starboard propeller blade. When I came up, I tasted oil. Far off to my left I could see our sister ship, the Astoria, flaming amidships, silhouetted in the sky..."[16]

Riefkohl and his orderly had reached the main deck. The ship was going to sink at any minute, forcing Patrick and Stucker to head for the nearest place to escape into the water. The *Vincennes* had a steep port list as water washed over their legs. Bending to the inevitable, Riefkohl ordered the abandon ship, and the three men climbed over the rail and jumped into the water. They swam as hard as they could so they would not be sucked under when the ship went down.

It was 2:50 a.m., the cruiser rolled over, showed her keel, twisted with her bow deep in the water, and disappeared in clouds of loudly hissing steam. Three hundred officers and men went down to a watery grave in a gallant ship.[17]

The Victorious Japanese Leave

Mikawa's ships had achieved a great tactical victory by catching the Americans totally unprepared and clueless to their approach. Ohmae received overly optimistic reports of damage inflicted on the American ships that later were toned down to what really happened. They had sunk one Australian and three American cruisers. Now their main concern was avoiding being caught by American carrier aircraft Mikawa knew were not far away in the narrow waters of the Slot. So they turned back to where that had come.

Mindful of the ferocity of an earlier Allied air attack on Rabaul, Mikawa believed it was too dangerous to keep all his cruisers at Rabaul. When just south of Bougainville at 8:00 a.m., he ordered the cruisers *Aoba, Kako, Kinugasa,* and *Furutaka* to steam for Kavieng while the rest of his force headed for Rabaul.[18]

But the trip to Kavieng was anything but uneventful. On August 10, the 17-year-old American submarine *S-44* commanded by Lt. Cmdr. John R. Moore rudely changed the overly optimistic Japanese mood. Just south of Simbari Island and a short 70 miles away from the safety of Kavieng Harbor, she lay in wait. The Japanese cruisers approached the submerged submarine in an approximately rectangular formation, leisurely moving at 16 knots. Moore peered though his periscope just before

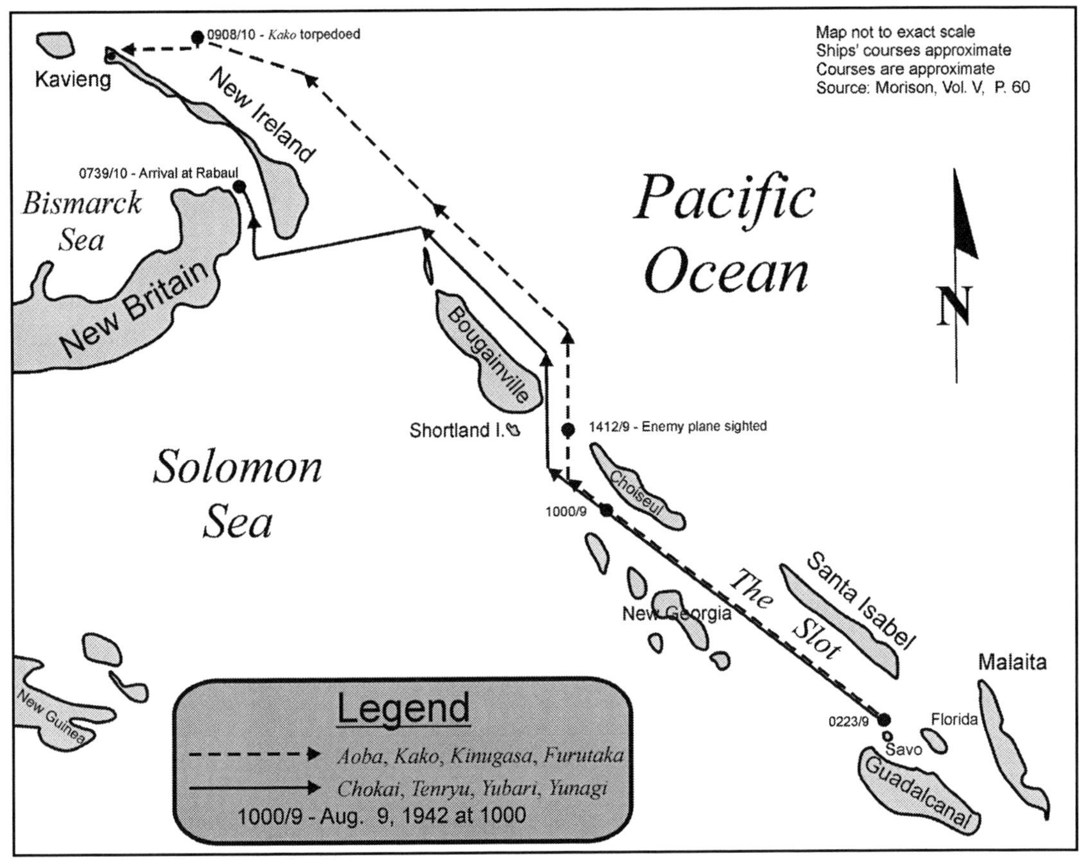

The Japanese Return to their Bases after Savo Island Victory

9:00 a.m. and saw the tempting targets approaching his position. He moved his submarine closer to within 700 yards and fired four torpedoes.

The *Kako*'s captain saw the missiles' wakes and tried get out of their way, but it was too late. All four torpedoes smacked into her sides. She sank in six minutes. Although it was a blow, not on the scale of the Allied defeat at Savo Island, it was a moment of revenge against the force that had inflicted such a rout.[19]

What Went Wrong and Who Is to Blame

Savo Island was a stinging defeat for the U.S. Navy. A combination of factors all contributed to this debacle. Among these were communications failures that led to the Allied force being caught unprepared for the Japanese attack. Although the Australian pilot's message that warned about Mikawa's ships moving toward Guadalcanal finally reached Turner, it was many hours after being reported to the pilot's superiors. It also mislead Turner about the composition of the Japanese force. In this case, the delays caused by having to forward the message through many commands still did not change what was in the message in the first place. The Australian pilot's message indicated that there were two seaplane tenders with the Japanese ships he sighted.

Another factor that contributed to the Savo debacle was that the commanders in the waters surrounding Guadalcanal did not seem to be ready for battle. When Crutchley left his command to meet with Turner in the evening hours of August 8, the officer left in charge had no idea what to do if the Japanese should attack. There was no battle plan other than to react to any Japanese initiative.

Turner did not believe the Japanese would attack because he thought they were setting up a seaplane base rather than coming down the Slot. What seemed to make matters worse was that Crutchley did not take his flagship, the *Australia*, back to the southern group of Allied cruisers, thus removing one-third of his major firepower from the scene of the upcoming battle. The *Vincennes'* captain also seemed completely unprepared as to what to do when Mikawa's cruisers attacked his northern force of cruisers. Although Riefkohl was the senior office present at that scene, he certainly did not act like he was in charge.

One common problem seemed to be the Allied commanders' inability to distinguish between friend and foe. Perhaps this was caused by the lack of any combined training exercises between the cruisers and destroyers before the Guadalcanal invasion. This might be attributed to the rapid assembly of the force due to pressure from Washington to invade Guadalcanal. Regardless, the reactions by Allied ship commanders proved they were completely unprepared to fight a serious surface sea battle.

The defeat at Savo Island caused earthquake-like repercussions within the U.S. Navy. The U.S. Navy had never suffered such a devastating setback at sea. The Secretary of the Navy launched an investigation in December 1942 and chaired by Adm. Arthur J. Hepburn. After holding extensive hearings by traveling all over the South Pacific and interviewing those involved, Hepburn issued a report. It stated that being caught by surprise was the primary cause of the defeat. The reasons for this surprise were, according to Hepburn's report, in order of their importance:

1. The ships were not ready to meet a sudden night attack.
2. Repeated failures to acknowledge that the planes sighted were Japanese.
3. Too much optimism about radar's capabilities to fight a night surface battle.
4. Failure in receiving timely information about Japanese' intentions.
5. Failure in communication and that there was no effective reconnaissance above the battle area. This led commanders to believe the northern approaches to the invasion area were being watched.

The report added another remark that the early withdrawal of the carriers contributed to the defeat but was not a direct contributing factor. Both Nimitz and King agreed with the report's conclusion, but did not assign blame to any particular officer. They concluded that there was plenty of blame to go around.

The tone of Hepburn's report reinforced the prevalent attitude among senior officers for their perception of the inferiority of the Japanese. It was not until mid-1943 when Adm. King's office actually received the report. King's flag secretary, Capt. George L. Russell, initially analyzed the report and wisely wrote, "It does not necessarily follow that we took a beating somebody must be the goat." King agreed with that opinion.

The Allied losses were substantial. The toll was 1,073 killed or died of wounds and 709 wounded. Four heavy cruisers, the *Canberra, Astoria, Quincy*, and *Vincennes*, sank, and the *Chicago* suffered heavy damage.[20] In stark contrast, Mikawa's force lost 129 men killed and 85 wounded.[21]

The brilliance of the plan and its execution by Mikawa's cruisers was the primary cause of the Allied defeat at Savo. Their training for night surface battle without having to rely on radar and the long range torpedoes they possessed completely overcame any advantages the Allies had in their favor, whatever they were. But Mikawa did not achieve his objectives. His ships failed to attack the transports, which still unloaded their cargoes while the battle happened. Although loading stopped temporarily at 1:45 a.m. when Turner saw the flares, it resumed five minutes later.[22] Thus, the Marines on Guadalcanal would have more of what they needed to stand against onslaughts by the Japanese Army, which were about to begin.

Another outcome of the Battle of Savo Island was a change in how the American Navy viewed the competence of the Japanese to wage a war against a Western power. Before the war, the Americans believed the Japanese to be an inferior foe. Adm. Turner perhaps offers the best perspective on the attitudes of senior American naval officers of the Japanese before Savo changed them:

> "...The Navy was still obsessed with a strong feeling of technical and mental superiority over the enemy. In spite of ample evidence as to enemy capabilities, most of our officers and men despised the enemy and felt themselves sure victors in all encounters under any circumstances.
>
> ...The net result of all this was a fatal lethargy of mind which induced a confidence without readiness, and a routine acceptance of outworn peacetime standards of conduct. I believe that this psychological factor as a cause of our defeat, was even more important than the element of surprise."[23]

In his work *Guadalcanal*, Richard B. Frank states:

> "This lethargy of mind would not be completely shaken off without some more hard blows to Navy pride around Guadalcanal, but after Savo the United States Navy picked itself up off the deck and prepared for the most savage combat in its history."[24]

CHAPTER 17
All Alone

Preparing to Leave

Turner knew his transports needed to continue unloading supplies if Vandegrift and his Marines were to have any chance to fight, but he also knew that his transports could not stay anchored in the narrow waters between Florida and Guadalcanal Islands and be exposed to more Japanese air attacks. Although his landing force had escaped major damage from the two air attacks of August 7 and August 8, he knew the airplanes would be back and his transports would not be as lucky when they did. Fletcher was already withdrawing his carriers, thus removing any air cover Turner might have to fight more Japanese air attacks. Because he had not heard from Vandegrift, Turner did not know how the unloading progress for supplies was proceeding on Tulagi. He had no word of what had happened yet at Savo Island. Being between the proverbial "rock and a hard place," he made the courageous decision to stay one more day and keep the unloading operation going.

As the sun rose on the morning of August 9, Turner learned more of what had happened to his cruiser and destroyer screening force, but the information that dribbled in left him more in the dark about what had happened at Savo Island. When a coastwatcher report arrived at 8:40 a.m. saying that Japanese planes were heading south, he ordered all unloading to stop. To his and others' bewilderment, hours went by without any air attacks. The unloading again resumed.

As the day wore on, Turner received more information about how bad the Savo Island losses were. Essentially, the Japanese had wiped out his screening force. With no air support and now with no ships to protect against another Japanese surface attack on his transports, he had no choice but to take the transports to a safe place.

As the sun set in the western sky over the waters near Guadalcanal, Maj. Gen. Alexander A. Vandegrift[1], USMC, stood near his headquarters and looked with a heavy heart through his binoculars at Turner's ships slowly steaming westward through the passage between Savo Island and Guadalcanal. Turner had stayed as long as he could and wanted to stay longer, but the sinking of four heavy cruisers off Savo Island forced his hand.

Intellectually, he knew that Turner's decision was for sound military reasons. With the defeat at Savo and the withdrawal of Fletcher's carriers, there was no effective defense against Japanese surface or air raids. If Turner stayed to unload all cargoes meant to supply the Marines, he could lose the entire transport fleet in the next Japanese attack. Although the admiral did not promise when he would return, Vandegrift knew Turner would do everything to try to send as many supplies, ships, troops, and aircraft as he could. Could his Marines hold out for that long? His emotions roiled inside him when he realized that this command was now on its own. But being the professional he was, his mind turned to the military realities facing his command.

The Marines on Guadalcanal had three problems facing them. If Vandegrift's men failed to solve any one of them, their mission would end in disaster. First, they had to fight off the anticipated Japanese counterattacks they knew would be coming. The Japanese were now desperate to drive the Americans off the island while bringing in supplies for their own troops. Vandegrift established a five-mile-long defensive line from the Ilu (Tenaru) River to Kukum. There was not enough time to unload any coastal artillery. The only guns of any caliber large enough to defend against a landing of Japanese troops were 75-mm guns mounted on half-tracks, 37-mm field artillery, and one captured Japanese three-inch gun. He set up skirmish lines inland and to the south to defend against any nighttime Japanese infiltration. The Marines on Tulagi would wipe out the Japanese garrison there, and then reinforce Guadalcanal.

The threat of Japanese air attacks and bombardment by the Japanese Navy from the sea hung over his command like a shroud of death. Since there were no American aircraft at Henderson Field, the only defense he could mount was to wait until the Japanese planes showed up and use the few 90-mm AA guns he had to fight back. When the planes came over, the 90-mm guns could keep the planes at the relatively high altitude of 27,000 feet. Nonetheless, the Japanese bomber crews proved to be quite accurate, even though they did not have the vaunted Norden bombsight. The lone three-inch gun did keep the Japanese submarines from getting too close since they stayed outside the gun's limited range. The converted minesweeper, the *Gamble*, sank a Japanese submarine, the *I-123*, when it mistakenly ventured too close.

The second major problem Vandegrift had was keeping the flow of ammunition, food, and medical supplies moving. When Turner's ships stopped unloading, the coastal guns, heavy construction equipment needed to complete Henderson Field, and half the ammunition did not make it ashore. What food they had could, along with whatever Japanese rice they could purloin, only feed the Marines twice a day. Even if American aircraft could land at Henderson Field, there were not enough supplies to keep them flying, including vitally needed high-octane aviation fuel. With no protection from the air, the scarce and defenseless transports the Americans had in the South Pacific could not be risked. Therefore, the only way available to the Americans was to use warships to bring in supplies.

The third and most important problem was to rebuild Henderson Field into a powerful, indestructible air base. After all, the primary reason for attacking Guadalcanal and Florida islands was to prevent the Japanese from using the airfield and turn the tables on the Americans. The 1st Marine Engineer Battalion landed with the mission of getting Henderson Field into flying shape. The Japanese had not made much progress in preparing the field. When the Marines landed on August 7, they had only cleared and leveled the land for the airstrip. It was unpaved and definitely not in any condition to allow planes to either take off and land. Vandegrift wanted to add 1,000 feet to the runway's length.

✲ ✲ ✲

It seemed that the war gods conspired against the Marines who worked to get the airstrip ready to accept aircraft. Kunai grass surrounded much of the airstrip and proved to be as tough a foe to expanding the field as the Japanese were. Natively growing throughout Melanesia, it had long blade-like leaves with saw tooth edges that could cut open a man's skin by just brushing up against them. It was also impervious to being burned, making the task of clearing it away very difficult. Bulldozers were not available because there had not been enough time to unload them before Turner's ships left, so the grass had to be cut away with bayonet blades. This was a slow process. A large hole in the middle of the runway had to be filled using the Japanese truck that had to be loaded by hand. Constant, heavy rain showers turned the dirt into a dark, viscous muck that would suck a man's boots off his feet if he should step into it and make a truck's wheels sink to the axle.

Despite all these obstacles, August 12 was a red letter day for the Americans at Henderson Field. The 150-foot wide runway had been lengthened to 2,660 feet and was on an east-west axis. Commander Aircraft South Pacific (COMAIRSOPAC) Radm. John S. McCain arrived in his PBY Catalina patrol bomber with his aide, Lt. W. S. Simpson, at the controls. The field had fortunately dried in the hot tropical sun, but still was a mixture of compressed dirt and gravel with no metal matting. For the time being, Henderson Field could only be used in dry weather. Nevertheless, the marines had constructed aircraft shelters, set up an operations center in the Japanese-built control tower nick-named the "Pagoda," put the finishing touches on the refueling details, and organized an air warning scheme. However, there were no barracks, mess halls, or fuel tanks. By any standard measure, the conditions at Henderson Field were embarrassingly primitive. Nevertheless, Simpson examined the field, and pronounced it ready for air operations.[2]

The first attempt to supply the marines on Guadalcanal happened on August 15 when the destroyer-transports *Colhoun*, *Gregory*, *Little*, and *McKean* sailed into Iron Bottom Sound. They brought in aviation gasoline, bombs, and ammunition, thus demonstrating that at least the most vital supplies the Marines could not scavenge for could be delivered. More important than the supplies was the arrival of USMC Maj. Charles H. Hayes, Henderson Field's first operations officer, Ens. George W. Polk, and 120 men who were the cadre that would keep the planes flying from Henderson Field, if and when those machines arrived.

Five days later, the *Colhoun*, *Gregory*, and *Little* returned with 120 tons, enough food to last three and a half days. After unloading their precious cargoes, they left and returned safely to Nouméa. Meanwhile, the China river boat *Lakatoi*, trying to repeat what the destroyer-transports had done, met with an unfortunate end while trying to deliver 400 tons of rations and ammunition. After being at sea from Nouméa for three days, she turned over and sank. Her more fortunate crew survived and reached land after spending two weeks in rubber rafts and a lifeboat.

The Ground Battle Begins

The Japanese Army, having been given the responsibility for recapturing Guadalcanal, began planning ground operations. Lt. Gen. Harukichi Hyakutake, commander of the 17th Army on Rabaul, and his staff assessed the situation and determined they needed 6,000 troops to defeat the Marines. But there were not nearly that many soldiers available for duty; therefore, they had to get by with less than the 1,000 troops they did have. They estimated there were about 2,000 Americans on Guadalcanal. Strongly believing that the inexperienced Americans could never match the quality of battle-hardened Japanese veterans, Hyakutake gave command of the 916 men to Col. Kiyoano Ichiki who departed Truk in six destroyers on August 18.

Hoping to catch the Marines by surprise, they hoped to land near Taivu Point, move westward along the north coast, and kick the Marines off the island. Nonetheless, a Marine patrol commanded by Capt. Charles Brush ambushed a Japanese patrol under Ichiki's command on August 19 and killed 31 of the 34 soldiers. After examining the bodies, Brush and his men saw these were not the starved and unprepared troops they had encountered when the Americans landed on August 7. They were well fed and equipped. Clearly, these soldiers had just arrived and were only there to counterattack.

The Battle of the Tenaru River[3] began on August 21. It did not last long.

Still oblivious of being discovered, Ichiki's detachment fought several bloody but short clashes with the Marines that all resulted in the same outcome. The 2,000 troops the Japanese thought the Americans had on Guadalcanal were closer to 17,000. By charging the entrenched, well-armed, and prepared Marine positions with suicidal bayonet assaults, the Americans slaughtered the Japanese and destroyed Ichiki's command. He and his staff officer committed *Hara-kiri.*

The Marines met the much hyped toughness and courage of the Japanese soldiers with a new set of guts the Japanese never thought they would ever see. It seemed that the Marines were not only the equals to the Japanese soldier, but his better and even unconquerable. As a model for the combat that would come in the next six months, the scenario showed Japanese soldiers vainly trying to overwhelm American well-defended positions only to meet the same deadly fate.[4]

Building a Land-Based Aircraft Carrier

Once ashore, recognition of the supply problems at Guadalcanal finally started sinking in for the Marine senior officers. After Turner's ships departed with most of the supplies that should have been offloaded still in the ships' hulls, the only way that a constant flow of supplies could continue was for the Americans to gain control of the air. With Fletcher's carriers too far away to be of any help, Henderson Field had to become like an aircraft carrier, but on land. Only when there was a powerful air presence on Guadalcanal could the Japanese attempts to reinforce their troops on that island be stopped, or at least slowed. And the only way for the Americans to gain air superiority or, if they were lucky, gain air supremacy was to build Henderson Field into a formidable air base.

Since the field became ready to land planes, the first task was to get the planes there. At the time, there were not enough planes the Marines could send to meet every need. Fletcher was not ready to lend any of his planes from his carriers because he needed them for his mission. Ghormley had 49 Wildcats, the only fighter planes in the U.S. Navy's arsenal that could protect transports as they made their way from widely dispersed locations to Guadalcanal. However, he would not release them to fly CAP because he believed he needed them to protect his bases at Nouméa and Éfaté. On July 21, Turner recommended that Ghormley release two fighter squadrons to immediately fly to Guadalcanal. However, the Wildcats did not have the range to make the flight.

Nimitz had the third and last source of aircraft in a unit called Marine Air Group 23 (MAG-23) that could meet this need, but he was highly reluctant to let them go. As it turned out, he had a good reason for this before August 1 because the air crews badly needed training. MAG-23 began on May 1 at Ewa Field on Oahu with two fighter squadrons (VMF-223 and VMF-224) and two bomber squadrons (VMSB-231 and VMSB-232). MAG-23 originally had obsolete Brewster Buffalo F2A-3 fighters and Douglas Dauntless SBD-2's. Orders notifying MAG-23's squadron leaders to prepare for a new mission resulted in a major upgrade to the latest World War II aircraft when the Grumman F4F-4 and SBD-3 replaced the outmoded Buffaloes and SBD-2s. Not only did MAG-23 get the latest aircraft the Navy had, but a new infusion of pilots arrived from the flight schools as well as survivors from the Battle of Midway. VMSB-232 also welcomed new pilots. But these new aviators were poorly prepared for actual combat. Knowing that combat was coming, the squadron commanders, Capt. John L. Smith of VMF-223 and Maj. Richard C. Mangrum of VMSB-232, squeezed in as much gunnery and bombing practice as they could to get their pilots ready.[5] But one problem raised its serious countenance—it was too far to fly from Oahu to Guadalcanal, even in stages, much less nonstop. Another solution had to be found, and American ingenuity came through.

Completed in May 1940, the American motor ship *Mormacmail* had a dull existence by engaging in profitable trade filling her hull with cargo and livestock and making repeated voyages between North and South America. But the approach of war changed that when the U.S. Navy bought her. Aircraft carriers were in such short supply and the requirement to transport aircraft too important to wait to build new ones. It would just take too long. So the Navy put a flat deck on her, added a few guns, and renamed her the *Long Island.* Commissioned on June 2, 1941, and given the hull number CVE-1, she was the Navy's first escort carrier and would be the model for many ships like her. Displacing 15,000 tons when fully loaded, powered by a diesel engine, armed with one four-inch gun, two three-inch guns, and four half-inch AA guns, and having a top speed of 16.5 knots, she sailed for Hawaii and arrived to load VMF-223's 19 Wildcats and VMSB-232's 12 Dauntless dive-bombers on her deck. On August 2, 1942, her captain, Cmdr. James D. Barner, took her out of Pearl Harbor to begin her historic voyage from Hawaii to Guadalcanal. She arrived at Fiji Island on August 13 for fueling and replenishment. Naval warfare entered a new era.[6]

As the *Long Island* refueled at Fiji, Barner sent a message to Ghormley that VMF-223's pilots had not been trained to take off from the deck of a carrier. Ghormley forwarded the note to McCain who suggested that Barner exchange the green fighter pilots for more combat-hardened veterans from Lt. Col. Harold W. Bauer's VMF-212 at Éfaté. Barner changed his original itinerary by diverting to Éfaté and arrived there on August 17.

After meeting with Noyes on the *Saratoga* on August 17, Fletcher's highest priority was to meet the *Long Island* and escort it to a location where her planes could be launched to land at Henderson Field. At 2:11 p.m., the *Enterprise* sighted the *Long Island* 12 miles away at a bearing of 134º and relayed the sighting to Fletcher on the *Saratoga*. The *Saratoga* saw the little carrier at 3:39 p.m. directly to the south. With the *Long Island* under his task force's welcome protection, Fletcher headed northward toward Guadalcanal. Less than 22 hours later, San Cristobal Island was 46 miles away directly to the west. Vandegrift wanted to land the planes at Henderson Field after the noontime air raid. At 1:05 p.m., Task Force 61 turned into the wind to launch aircraft.

Since the *Long Island*'s deck was too short and the winds not fast enough to launch her aircraft by just using the aircraft's power alone, she used catapults. For some of MAG-23's pilots, this was the first time they used a catapult to take off from the deck of a carrier. Nevertheless, all 31 of her aircraft safely lifted off her deck and headed for Guadalcanal. Lt. Col. Charles L. Fike, MAG-23's executive officer, piloted the last plane off the carrier, an F4F, joined the other planes, and led the formation to its first combat assignment. In the first operation using an escort carrier, she had performed her mission well and began the glorious history these small ships would make until the end of the war.[7]

The end of the daily Japanese bombing at about noon brought quiet to the men at Henderson Field. The hot sun baked the dirt runway and turned it into a hard, almost unyielding surface. The heat did not make it any easier for the Marine engineers to repair the limited damage. In spite of the almost routine appearance by Japanese bombers, their attacks had shown that air power had its limits. The Marines were dug in well, and the few aircraft the Japanese did send inflicted little damage or casualties. They just did not send enough aircraft to seriously damage the entrenched Marines at Henderson Field. Nonetheless, whenever the Japanese aircraft did appear over Guadalcanal to bomb and strafe Henderson Field, they definitely disrupted the Marines' routine and negatively affected their morale.

Repairs continued into the afternoon when the Marines heard welcome sounds. The drone of American aircraft grew louder so that the men looked to the sky. Some looked through their binoculars and saw a magnificent sight. The unmistakable stubby bodies of F4Fs and the graceful silhouettes of Dauntless SBD's flew in trim formations and started to make their approaches to the field's runway. As the planes made their first low runs over the field, the sight of the white stars on their fuselages and wings brought cheers from all who saw them. Mangrum banked his SBD and touched down in a cloud of dust. As more planes landed, the wild cheers and the sight of helmets being thrown into the air caught the flight crews by surprise. Vandegrift looked over the happy scene and noticed that many Marines' eyes filled with tears of joy. In a moment of weakness, his eyes moistened too. After being bombed, strafed, and sniped at for the last 11 days, the arrival of these planes was the answer to a hopeful prayer. They no longer had to just take it; they could now take the battle to the Japanese.

More planes arrived to add to the force collecting at Henderson Field. Although several of MAG-23's planes became inoperable for one of several reasons, help came. A part of the U.S. Army's 67th Fighter Squadron landed on August 22 with several P-400s, a modified version of the P-39. These planes could not climb high enough and were too slow to be used as fighter aircraft. But they had a 37-mm cannon in their noses and six machine guns in their wings. That armament made an ideal weapon for close ground support for strafing Japanese troops.

Naval planes also added to the air forces with the arrival of SBDs from the *Enterprise* on August 24. Henderson Field became the home to a hodgepodge of combat aircraft of all shapes, types, and sizes. That did not matter to the Marines. As long as there were planes that could protect them from air raids, prevent the Japanese from bringing in reinforcements, and attack Japanese ships trying to shell them, that was all right with them.

By August 31, Col. William J. Wallace, in command of 19 Wildcats and 12 SBDs, arrived to take over for Fike. But the man who would make an indelible mark on all those who served at Henderson Field also arrived. He was Maj. Gen. Roy S. Geiger.[8] You could not miss him; he had a commanding countenance that might have been attributed to his huge chest and majestic bearing. Assuming command for all Navy, Army, and Marine Corps aviation activity on Guadalcanal, he never let formality stand in the way of getting things done. Fliers from all three services flew missions together and forgot their inter-service rivalries.

Although the attack by Japanese troops in the Battle of the Tenaru River put a damper on their enthusiasm, the Marines at Henderson Field could now turn that airfield into a burgeoning fortress of American air power, but they would need help. That help came in a new way during World War II; the Seabees were on their way.[9]

Here Come the Seabees

Before Pearl Harbor, the Americans used civilian workers to build what was required to meet their military needs. The dangers of building military bases in combat zones made that impractical. International law prohibited civilians from fighting in war zones. If they were caught, they could be executed as guerilla fighters.

Recognizing the need for a militarized construction capability, Chief of the U.S. Navy's Bureau of Yards and Docks (BUDOCKS) Radm. Ben Moreell, began lobbying for construction units under the Navy's command. A regulation at that time required that only line naval officers could command naval personnel. Moreell wanted the officers of the Civil Engineer Corps to command the men of the naval construction units. He argued that these officers had the necessary technical and management skills to achieve the unit's goals. Considerable opposition came from the entrenched naval bureaucracy. Moreell wanted the new unit to be called Naval Construction Regiment. It would have several Naval Construction Battalions or CBs, hence, the name Seabees. Their motto was "*Construimus, Batuimus*"—"We Build, We Fight."

Secretary of the Navy Frank Knox resolved the controversy by agreeing with Moreell's position on March 19, 1942, and the Seabees became a reality. Many men flocked to join the newly formed unit; many of those who worked on building Boulder Dam (later known as Hoover Dam) were among them. By the end of World War II, 325,000 enlisted men from more than 60 skilled trades served in the Seabees, along with 7,960 officers.

All recruits went to three weeks of boot training at Camp Allen (Norfolk, VA) and later to Camp Peary (York County, VA). Here, they received military training since it was certain they would be facing Japanese, German, or Italian troops in combat. While the usual procedure after completing training was to go to an Advance Base Depot at Davisville, RI, or Port Hueneme, CA, the urgent need to build bases overseas in those early war years required sending a construction battalion directly into a combat zone.[10]

With an average age of 31 years, these volunteers left their high-paying civilian jobs to serve their country and brought such diverse skills as carpentry, plumbing, surveying, and road building with them. And, when needed, they immediately dropped their tools and took up weapons to fight. As the war wore on, their reputation grew as skilled workers who accomplished so much with so little, which delighted their friends, and they could fight like seasoned combat veterans, which unsettled their enemies.

September 1, 1942, was the day the first Seabees of the 6th Seabee Battalion under the command of Lt. Cmdr. John P. Blundon arrived on Guadalcanal. Bringing two bulldozers and other sorely needed equipment with them, they took over the construction responsibilities from the Marine Corps engineers for the maintenance and development of Henderson Field. The Seabees immediately went to work expanding the runway, building hangars and revetments to protect parked aircraft, and building up the refueling facilities. But they did not stop with just that. They also added wharves, roads, bridges, power generation plants, camps for the men, and air raid shelters. This was the beginning of turning Guadalcanal into the vital base needed to take the battle to the Japanese in the Solomons.

Nevertheless, what the Seabees did was not easy. In addition to having to fight the Japanese, they faced other formidable obstacles. When it rained, which occurred almost daily, the water would collect in giant pools that severely taxed drainage facilities the Seabees tried to build and maintain. Constant Japanese air raids and bombardment by the Imperial Japanese Navy forced them to constantly repair shell holes on the runway. The equipment they needed took a long time to arrive but they made do with what they had.

Despite all these difficulties, Henderson Field's runway soon had a crown down its middle to aid drainage. Its surface was no longer just a dirt strip, but had a base of gravel, coral, and clay. They increased the runway's length by blasting away coconut trees with Japanese explosives. The addition of a steel Marston matting to Henderson Field turned it into a field that could operate in almost all kinds of weather. Perhaps Blundon's own words best describe what the Seabees faced:

> "We found that 100 Seabees could repair the damage of a 500-pound bomb hit on an airstrip in forty minutes, including the replacing of the Marston mat. In other words, forty minutes after that bomb exploded, you couldn't tell that the airstrip had ever been hit. But we needed all of this speed and more. In twenty-four hours on October 13 and 14, fifty-three bombs and shells hit the Henderson airstrip! During one hour on the lath we filled thirteen bomb craters while our planes circled around overhead waiting to land. We got no food during that period because our cooks were all busy passing up the steel plank. There were not enough shovels to go around, so some of our men used their helmets to scoop up earth and carry it to the bomb craters. In the period from September 1 to November 18, we had 140 Jap raids in which the strip was hit at least once.
>
> Our worst moments were when the Jap bomb or shell failed to explode when it hit. It still tore up our mat, and it had to come out. When you see men choke down their fear and dive in after an unexploded bomb so that our planes can land safely, a lump comes in your throat and you know why America wins wars.
>
> Shell craters are more dangerous to work on than bomb craters. You have a feeling that no two bombs ever hit in the same place; but this isn't true of shells. A Jap five-inch gun lobs a shell over on your airstrip and blasts a helluva hole. What are you going to do? You know, just as that Jap artilleryman knows, that if he leaves his gun in the same position and fires

> another shell, the second shell will hit in almost the same spot as the first one. So a good old Jap trick was to give us just enough time to start repairing the hole and then fire a second shell. All you can do is depend on hearing that second shell coming and hope you can scramble far enough away before it explodes. But this is a gamble which is frowned upon by life insurance companies."[11]

As time passed, Guadalcanal became a formidable bastion that the Japanese continually tried to eliminate. They soon realized that if the Americans succeeded in building up a powerful base of operations on Guadalcanal, their hold on the Solomon Islands would become tenuous and their key base at Rabaul would be vulnerable to American air and naval attacks and rendered inoperable. If Rabaul fell, their hold on New Guinea would become impossible to keep, and they would have to do the unthinkable: withdraw from the South Pacific. With that, their dreams of an empire where they could be guaranteed a source of the critical resources needed to keep their war machine going would evaporate. Clearly, the Japanese could not let the Americans on Guadalcanal succeed. And they would try every tactic they could to force the Americans to abandon that embattled island.

Part 4: Battle of the Eastern Solomons

CHAPTER 18
Look to the East

Continuing the Counterattack

In spite of Adm. Mikawa's stunning victory over the Allies at the Battle of Savo Island, the news coming in from Guadalcanal was not good. On August 20, reports arrived that indicated the Americans had landed fighters at the island's airfield. Adm. Isoroku Yamamoto wondered what happened to the Ichiki Detachment attempting to remove the Americans. The only reports he possessed were that they had landed and attacked. The Japanese Army estimated that only 2,000 Americans had landed and most of them were engineers to repair the airfield. The Japanese Army believed that Ichiki should have removed the Americans by now or, at least, inflicted sufficient casualties to force the American to leave.

The Japanese Army held American ground troops in contempt. An episode witnessed by Keisuke Matsunaga, while stationed at Rabaul and who was once Yamamoto's aide when the admiral was Vice Minister of the Navy, indicated how pervasive these opinions were within the Army's officer ranks. An Army staff officer asked Matsunaga what his assessment was of the American Marines on Guadalcanal. He started to tell what he thought. When he stopped, the Army officer responded by saying, "I see, a kind of naval land unit, eh?"[1] Apparently confirming his prejudices, he seemed satisfied to need no further information. Although Ichiki had only 900 soldiers with him, these troops were hardened combat veterans who had fought in China, the Philippines, and New Guinea. After all, 900 of the Japanese Empire's best should have been more than a match for the Americans on Guadalcanal.

But the Japanese view of the American presence on Guadalcanal changed with the arrival of a devastatingly disappointing radio message. The Ichiki detachment had been annihilated, with only 20 survivors. They sent the message. The situation demanded action, and Yamamoto responded. It was obvious that Ichiki's mission had failed, or, if they were still battling the Americans, they needed to be reinforced.

With light rain falling at the Japanese naval base at Hashira Jima, most of the Imperial Japanese Navy's Combined Fleet left for Truk on August 17. Yamamoto and his staff put a new plan together called Operation "KA." Its most important part was to land 1,500 troops from the Second Echelon of Ichiki's 5th Special Landing Force on Guadalcanal. Radm. Raizo Tanaka would lead the invasion force in the four-funneled light cruiser *Jintsu* with eight destroyers and three transports carrying the soldiers who would retake Guadalcanal for the Japanese. To protect Tanaka's force, Yamamoto assembled the most powerful fleet since Midway. As had become the pattern, Yamamoto's plan was a complex one with divided forces as he had done at Midway. The ships under his command included:[2]

Japanese Naval Forces—Battle of the Eastern Solomons

Force Designation	Commander	Ship type	Ships
Carrier Strike Force	Nagumo	Fleet carriers	*Shokaku, Zuikaku with 51 Zeroes, 54 Vals, 36 Kates*
		Destroyers	*Kazegumo, Yugumo, Makigumo, Akigumo, Hatsukaze, Akizuki*
Vanguard Force	Abe	Battleships	*Hiei, Kirishima*
		Heavy cruisers	*Kumano, Suzuya, Chikuma*
		Light cruiser	*Nagara*
Advanced Force	Kondo	Heavy cruisers	*Atago, Maya, Takao, Myoko, Haguro*
		Light Cruiser	*Yura*
		Destroyers	*Kuroshio, Oyashio, Minegumo, Hayashio, Natsugumo, Asagumo*
Detached Carrier Strike Force	Hara	Light carrier	*Ryujo with 24 Zeroes, nine Kates*
		Heavy Cruiser	*Tone*
Main Body (at Truk)	Yamamoto	Battleship	*Yamato*
		Escort Carrier	*Taiyo*
		Destroyers	*Akebono, Ushio*
Convoy Escort Force	Tanaka	Light Cruiser	*Jintsu*
		Destroyers	*Kagero, Mutsuki, Yayoi, Isokaze, Kawakaze, Suzukaze, Umikaze, Uzuki*

This rapidly mustered collection of 35 ships with two fleet carriers, one light carrier, two battleships, nine heavy cruisers, two light cruisers, and 19 destroyers was to go from Truk for the waters about 250 miles north of Guadalcanal. All were ready to go on August 21 while Yamamoto was still at sea aboard the super battleship *Yamato*. Meanwhile, Tanaka's force headed down the Slot toward Guadalcanal.

Yamamoto's plan was that Nagumo's Carrier Strike Force would advance southward and try to engage the American carriers known to be somewhere south of Guadalcanal. After Nagumo's carrier planes had either sunk or severely damaged the American carriers and their aircraft, Kondo's Advanced force followed by Radm. Hiraoki Abe's Vanguard Force would steam at high speed to sink and destroy the American ships or sink any cripples. Hara's Detached Striking Force aircraft from the *Ryujo* would attack the American airbase on Guadalcanal and destroy their aircraft on the ground. If the plan succeeded, all American naval power and air power in the Solomons would be destroyed. The Marines on Guadalcanal would then be at the complete mercy of Japanese sea and air power. It would only be a matter of time before the Americans would be forced to negotiate a settlement with all their naval power gone from the Pacific. Again, the theme of Japanese naval strategy for a final sea battle still dominated their thinking since Adm. Togo defeated the Russians at Tsushima in 1905. And it would continue to control their naval strategy until after the Battle of Leyte Gulf, when Japan would no longer be a naval power.[3]

How Much Did the Americans Know?

Unfortunately for the Americans, the Japanese changed their naval code so that their messages could no longer be read as before Coral Sea and Midway. Just before the Guadalcanal-Tulagi invasion, Cmdr. Edwin T. Layton, CINCPAC's fleet intelligence officer, issued a fleet intelligence estimate on August 6 that definitively stated the *Kidô Butai*[4] was in Japanese home waters. However, Layton also indicated in that report that the fleet could sortie at any time. If they did, their likely target would be in the Malayan Peninsula-Indian Ocean area. Another report issued on August 12 stated that Japanese carriers were still in home waters. On August 15, the carriers were still in home waters, but an imminent departure for other waters was not far off. A report the next day stated that several Japanese light carriers might have sailed and the *Kidô Butai* also might have sailed south. Nagumo and the fleet carriers *Shokaku* and *Zuikaku* sailed that same day.

Nevertheless, CINCPAC's intelligence reported the Japanese carriers would remain in home waters for the next five days. In its summary for August 21, Layton's group stated that, "...unless ORANGE (Japanese) radio deception is remarkably efficient, this force remains in the homeland still."[5] However, Layton dramatically altered that judgment when his unit reported that the *Shokaku* was either at or near Truk. After some confusion between CINCPAC's and the 14th Naval District's intelligence units as to the whereabouts of the light carrier *Ryujo*, CINCPAC's unit definitely reported the *Shokaku, Zuikaku* and *Ryujo* were around Truk.

The CINCPAC war diary entry for August 16 was far more definite about what was to come. It also noted that there were sufficient signs a major Japanese operation to recapture Guadalcanal was imminent. The Japanese carriers could not be ready for that operation until August 25. Based on that observation, it appeared that the Americans were right on target about what the Japanese would do next. The August 17 entry states, "It is not at all certain that the Jap [carriers] are still in home waters." But adding to the confusion, the next day's entry reversed that observation by stating that there was "...no evidence of the carriers' departure."[6]

Despite the confusing intelligence, Ghormley prepared for an attack by the *Kidô Butai* that he estimated would happen between August 20 and 23. His command believed that Japanese surface ships were on their way to attack shipping in the Guadalcanal area. He issued more warnings on August 18 that said, "No positive info as to presence of carriers with hostile force however such presence considered highly likely." By the 22nd, Ghormley sent as firm a message as he had ever sent to Fletcher during his command in the South Pacific that said the situation was as threatening as the passage in his dispatch could say:

> "Indications point strongly to enemy attack in force on cactus area 23-26 August. From available intelligence...presence of carriers possible but not confirmed...Important fueling be conducted soonest possible and if practicable one carrier task force at a time retiring for that purpose."[7]

If there was unambiguous evidence the Japanese were up to no good, this was it. Now Fletcher had to get his force ready for the onslaught.[8]

Making a Fateful Decision

Ever since Fletcher took command of the American carrier forces, the fueling status of the ships under his command became an obsession with him. There were good reasons for this belief. Despite the U.S. Navy's prewar planning, America was not prepared for a full-fledged naval war in the Pacific. There was an acute shortage of fueling tankers in the U.S. Navy. These ships were what stood in the way of a viable fighting force and a fleet dead in the water with no way to keep going. Ships of that day used copious amounts of fuel oil, particularly the battleships and carriers. Smaller ships like the destroyers could not carry anywhere near the fuel the larger ships could so they had to be refueled by taking on fuel from the larger ships.

Although the U.S. Navy did not have the naval power the Japanese had before the Battle of the Eastern Solomons, the ships the Americans did have made a powerful force in its own right. Here is a table of those ships in Task Force 61 with Vadm. Jack Fletcher in overall command:[9]

Task Force 61—Battle of the Eastern Solomons

Task Force	Commander	Ship Type	Ships
11	Fletcher	Carrier	*Saratoga*
		Heavy cruisers	*Minneapolis, New Orleans*
		Destroyers	*Phelps, Farragut, Worden, MacDonough, Dale*
16	Kinkaid	Carrier	*Enterprise*
		Battleship	*North Carolina*
		Heavy cruiser	*Portland*
		Light cruiser	*Atlanta*
		Destroyers	*Balch, Benham, Maury, Ellet, Grayson, Monssen*
18	Noyes	Carrier	*Wasp*
		Heavy cruisers	*San Francisco, Salt Lake City*
		Light cruiser	*San Juan*
		Destroyers	*Farenholt, Aaron Ward, Buchanan, Lang, Stack, Sterett, Selfridge*

Fletcher's carriers (*Saratoga*, *Enterprise*, *Wasp*) and their support ships left on August 22 with San Cristobal Island to their sterns as they proceeded toward a position south of Guadalcanal. Adm. Noyes, in command of air operations for Fletcher's Task Force 61, ordered the *Saratoga* to launch air searches, the *Enterprise* to relieve the *Saratoga*'s CAP duties, and the *Wasp* to standby in reserve. The *Saratoga* launched 14 SBDs at 6:00 a.m. from a position about 50 miles south of Guadalcanal. As Task Force 16 reversed its course and turned northward toward Malaita at 7:30 p.m., Fletcher reviewed the latest intelligence estimate of the Japanese intentions. The picture was not as clear as he wanted it to be. While intelligence dispatches indicated that Japanese ships were heading toward him, any specific information on Japanese carrier whereabouts was conspicuous in its absence. His fixation on making sure his force had enough fuel to conduct combat operations raised itself like an overriding specter. With no Japanese carriers reported nearby, Fletcher rationalized that his force would not soon be in a combat situation and sent a message to Ghormley that he wanted to refuel his force on August 25. Ghormley, believing that Japanese carriers could be present, but thus far their proximity to Fletcher had not yet been confirmed, responded with his assessment:

> "Important fueling be conducted soonest possible and if practical one CV [fleet carrier] TASK FORCE at a time retiring for that purpose your 211120 [21 August]. Am sending *Platte* [AO-24] and *Cimarron* [AO-22] from ROSES [Éfaté] daylight tomorrow."[10]

In the darkened hours of August 22 and 23, Fletcher moved on a northward course parallel to Malaita Island's east coast. He wanted to continue that course and then turn southward to conduct air searches and effectively defend Guadalcanal. His fears concerning the fuel situation prompted him to send a message to Noyes that said if there were no contacts with Japanese ships reported during August 23, Noyes should take Task Force 18 south to meet the tankers Ghormley was sending and refuel. The reader should take note of the proviso in Fletcher's instructions. The decision to send Noyes south had not yet been made.

Meanwhile, one of McCain's PBYs reported seeing Tanaka's force at 9:42 a.m. about 300 miles to Fletcher's northwest moving on a course of 190° at a speed of 17 knots. The sighting indicated there were two heavy cruisers, three destroyers, and four transports. Fearing that Japanese carriers could not be far away and that Japanese troops were about to invade Guadalcanal, Fletcher wanted to move Task Force 61 toward Guadalcanal. Nevertheless, Task Force 61 continued moving southeastward, away from Guadalcanal. He planned to hold his current course until the sun went down and then prepare to attack any Japanese carriers if they should appear.

Thirty-one SBDs and eight TBFs were on *Saratoga*'s flight deck loaded with bombs and torpedoes waiting to take off to attack Tanaka's ships. Waiting in their ready rooms, the pilots spoiled for a fight. Upon hearing that Japanese ships were heading their way, the pilots wanted to take off immediately. Cmdr. Harry D. Felt announced what to do next, "Let's go boys! No carriers have been found. We will attack the cruisers."[11] However, Fletcher could not give the SBDs any fighter cover. So, he ordered them to land at Henderson Field before dark, spend the night with the Marines, and return to the *Saratoga* the next morning. With the weather worsening, the command came: "Pilots! Man your planes." Rushing to the flight deck amid the increased anticipation among the carrier's crew, the planes lifted off at 2:40 p.m.

As darkness fell east of Malaita, Task Force 61 turned around and headed to the southeast. The time to make a decision about whether to refuel Noyes' task force had come. In his normally deliberative mode, Fletcher looked at what faced him. If he was to order the refueling of each carrier group one at a time as Ghormley had ordered, the command had to be given within the next few minutes. No Japanese carriers had been sighted by any American search plane. CINCPAC's latest intelligence report placed the *Shokaku* and *Zuikaku* steaming from Japan to Truk with carriers *Hiyo, Junyo, Zuiho,* and *Ryujo* still in Japanese home waters.

In Fletcher's mind, all information available to him indicated that there were no Japanese carriers south of Truk, out of attack range of his task force and thus not immediately threatening his ships or the Marines on Guadalcanal. He made his bed and would have to lie in it. At 6:23 p.m., he ordered Noyes to take Task force 18 southward to meet the tankers Ghormley had sent out just north of Espiritu Santo. Without delay, Task Force 61 reversed its course and headed north. As the *Wasp* increased its distance between herself and Task Force 61, 26 fighters, 26 dive-bombers, and 11 torpedo bombers went with her. Task Force 61's effective aerial fighting force had been reduced by almost one-third. Task Force 18's AA guns also disappeared as its ships vanished over the southern horizon.

Did Fletcher make the right decision? All the information available to him indicated the Japanese carriers were not an immediate threat. Ever since he had been at sea, the overriding factor in his decision making was to keep Task Force 61 fueled and ready to engage the Japanese. He felt there was enough time to top Task Force 18's tanks since even the latest CINCPAC intelligence report issued at 11:23 a.m. on August 24 showed the *Zuikaku* and *Shokaku* at Truk and the rest of Japanese carriers except the CVE *Kasuga Maru* in Japanese home waters. Some naval historians, such as Morison, severely criticized Fletcher for being too cautious. Others, such as Lundstrom, say he made the right decision with the now known to be faulty information he had. Either way, he made the decision to reduce his force's fighting strength. The decision would directly affect the upcoming battle.[12]

The Japanese Main Mission Begins

Radm. Raizo Tanaka also felt the urgency that surrounded the Imperial Japanese Navy when the Americans landed on Guadalcanal. After Mikawa had pummeled the U.S. Navy in the Battle of Savo Island, attempts to land Japanese reinforcements on Guadalcanal still did not happen. Then Yamamoto put together Operation "KA" in another attempt to get more troops on Guadalcanal. As part of this plan, Tanaka received orders to immediately take his still small force that included his flagship, the light cruiser *Jintsu*, and four destroyers, the *Kagero*, *Umikaze*, *Kawakaze*, and *Suzukaze* to Truk.

Tanaka's ships left the Yokosuka Naval Base on August 11 with just his flagship and the destroyer *Kagero*. The other destroyers that were part of his command had been called away to Hiroshima to expand the escorts for Kondo's Advance Force. As his now even smaller force made its way to Truk, orders arrived that Tanaka would be part of Mikawa's 8th Fleet and be made commander of the Guadalcanal Reinforcement Force. The Imperial Japanese Navy high command had chosen well when it selected Tanaka for this vital assignment. He was the Imperial Japanese Navy's most experienced destroyer commander. A veteran of the battles at Coral Sea and Midway, he now directly commanded the naval force assigned to land more troops on Guadalcanal that hopefully would stem the rising tide of American power in the southern Solomons.

After arriving at Truk, supplies started to be loaded on his ships and the work continued unabated. On August 15, Tanaka received new orders that had four important provisions:

1. His force was now considerably larger with the addition of five destroyers and four converted patrol boats.
2. The 900-man Ichiki detachment would embark in six destroyers and land at Taivu Point

on Guadalcanal on August 18.

3. The *Jintsu* and two patrol boats would escort the slow transports *Boston Maru* and *Daifuku Maru*, which had a maximum speed of nine knots and carried the invasion force's service units.

4. Two other patrol boats would escort the faster 13-knot transport *Kinryu Maru* carrying the Yokosuka 5th Special Landing Force. It would also land at Taivu Point on August 23 to reinforce the Ichiki Detachment.

Tanaka did not like the plan since he knew it was a difficult scheme to execute successfully. It would be the hardest assignment he had ever been ordered to do because no rehearsals would be held, and no serious planning had been done how these troops could defeat a force of unknown size and strength. There was no plan to neutralize the invasion area by bombarding the Americans. Realizing that the current situation on the southern Solomons had become desperate and that such emergency conditions demanded a rapid response, he knew the order was absolutely irrational and could never succeed. Nevertheless, he had his orders and, despite the apparent confusion at 8th Fleet headquarters, the plan was now in inexorable motion. He would carry out his orders with the best he had within him.

There was no time to waste as the workmen rapidly finished loading supplies. Troops came aboard their designated ships. Tanaka's staff finished all operational orders so his force could leave early in the morning. The six destroyers, with the 900-man Ichiki Detachment aboard, left Truk on August 16 at 5:00 a.m. under the command of Capt. Yasuo Sato. The transports *Boston Maru* and *Daifuku Maru* escorted by two patrol boats left next. Later that morning, Tanaka left in his flagship *Jintsu* to command the whole operation.

The six destroyers ran into no submarines as it steamed southward at 22 knots. Again to avoid being attacked by submarines, the rest of Tanaka's force trailed on a zigzag course at eight and a half knots.

A message arrived the next day that said the heavy cruisers and recent victors from the Battle of Savo Island, *Kinugasa*, *Aoba*, and *Furutaka*, would provide additional escorts. The destroyers *Umikaze*, *Kawakaze*, and *Suzukaze* would rejoin Tanaka's command. These ships overtook the slower moving convoy at noon.

On August 18 at 8:00 p.m., the six destroyers landed the Ichiki detachment on schedule at Taivu Point, and all 900 troops reached the Guadalcanal shore before midnight. Three destroyers turned around and headed back to Rabaul while three destroyers remained behind. One of them, the *Hagikaze*, sustained heavy damage during early morning hours of August 19 by bombs from a B-17 bomber.

No Japanese aircraft conducted any reconnaissance near Guadalcanal, so it was only inevitable that Tanaka's force would be in further jeopardy. In the early morning hours of August 20, American carrier planes attacked the destroyer *Kagero*. No bombs hit her, but it was abundantly clear that an American carrier task force was not far away. A Kawanishi flying boat from Shortland Island confirmed that a carrier task force was indeed nearby. The plane's pilot reported the force had one carrier, two cruisers, and nine destroyers about 250 miles to the southeast of Guadalcanal.

As mentioned earlier, the Ichiki detachment encountered powerful opposition from the Marines on Guadalcanal and ceased to exist. Tanaka had the utmost respect for Col. Kiyonao Ichiki and knew him to be a brave and outstanding leader. It was a sad moment when he found out Ichiki had burned his unit's regimental colors and committed suicide. But Tanaka knew this debacle was coming. There was no way a small force only armed with rifles, no matter how much *élan* they had, could charge recklessly into entrenched positions of well-armed riflemen supported by mortars and artillery and survive. To Tanaka, this was another example of the fallacy of the Japanese Guadalcanal strategy that he knew could only end disastrously.

The definite presence of an American carrier task force nearby so alarmed Vadm. Nishizo Tsukahara that he immediately ordered Tanaka to head north. Confusion rampaged throughout the Japanese higher command levels when Mikawa sent a contradictory order to Tanaka. It instructed the perplexed Tanaka to change his course to 250°, not north but *20° south of west* [my emphasis]. Tanaka was now uncertain what to do. Nonetheless, he changed his course to 320° thus somewhat striking a balance between the two conflicting orders. After all, he was heading back toward Truk in any case.

More bad news arrived on the *Jintsu* when Tanaka found out that American planes had landed at the Guadalcanal airfield. In just less than two weeks, the Americans had landed on Guadalcanal and upgraded a barely started airfield into a full-fledged airbase. If anyone thought it would be hard to land troops on the island, that mission's risk of failure had dramatically increased. The news for Tanaka's force improved when he received information that Nagumo's carrier force and Kondo's cruiser force would steam to the east of the Solomon Islands and support his mission to land his troops on Guadalcanal by August 23. Now, the Japanese had the forces to attack and destroy the American carrier task force. But the powerful Japanese naval forces would not be in place in time to keep the original invasion date; so the invasion date was moved back to the 23rd. The Japanese soldiers would land the next night.

With Tanaka's spirits uplifted again, he turned his invasion force around and headed southward. Because of the changes in course, he had to send four patrol boats to refuel at Shortland Island. Japanese planes sighted the American carriers again; they were still in the same position as before. Another Japanese aircraft sighted two transports and a light cruiser 160 miles south of Guadalcanal. He ordered the destroyers *Kawakaze* and *Yunagi* to look for these ships but the trip was in vain. On the 22nd, the *Kawakaze* returned to north of Lunga Point where she attacked the American destroyer *Blue* and sank her with torpedoes.

Moving at the pace of his slowest transports, Tanaka arrived at a position 200 miles north of Guadalcanal on August 23, but he did not get there alone. Two American PBY patrol planes continuously tailed his convoy despite being shrouded in nearly constant rain squalls. They undoubtedly reported his position to American commanders. Undaunted and following his orders with the dedication for which he was well known, his force unrelentingly moved toward the point from where they would launch their invasion. There was no doubt in Tanaka's mind that American carrier planes would appear on the horizon the next day and attack his ships.

Yet another message arrived from Mikawa at 8:30 a.m. ordering Tanaka to turn his ships around *again* and head north to take his ships away from any possibility of being attacked by American carrier aircraft. He obeyed that order at once knowing that he could not land the troops until August 25. Six hours later, another even more bewildering order arrived from the commander of the 11th Air Fleet that said, "The convoy will carry out the landing on the 24th." With his frustration at the constant barrage of conflicting orders from different sources bubbling to the surface, he replied that this was an impossible order to obey. If they had to retreat from Guadalcanal to avoid being attacked by carrier planes, his ships would be too far away to land any troops on the 24th. That atmospheric interference disrupting his radio communication did little to perk up his enthusiasm for his assignment.

PBYs continued to follow his progress as long it was daytime. Soon the likely fruit of their work came to pass. A radio message arrived at 8:00 a.m. that warned that 36 American planes had taken off from Guadalcanal and were likely heading his way. His command continued to head north with the ominous specter of a massive air attack hanging over their heads.

As his force headed to the northeast, Tanaka turned his force around again to head for Guadalcanal when he heard that Nagumo's planes had attacked the American carriers and left two of them burning. Still having doubts that his mission would succeed, he pressed on once more to the south. He now felt that the next day would be a fateful one for his force. It would indeed be one of those days.[13]

A Major Japanese Loss in the Making

After the *Ryujo*, *Tone*, and the destroyers *Tokitsukaze* and *Amatsukaze* carried out their mission to bombard Henderson Field, Nagumo's carriers turned at 6:00 a.m. on the 24th to a 150° heading at a speed of 15 knots. Kondo's Advanced Force, 150 miles to the southeast, also did the same to protect Nagumo's eastern flank. Both men believed the American carriers, if they were nearby, would likely be steaming farther to the south. Fifteen minutes later, Nagumo wanted more information. He ordered the *Shokaku* and *Zuikaku* to send 19 Vals to search to the south. Kondo augmented the search by sending seven seaplanes southward. While the search was underway, Nagumo ordered three waves of aircraft to get ready to attack the American carriers as soon as the search planes found them. The first two waves had 54 dive-bombers and 24 fighters while the third wave, if needed, would have 36 torpedo bombers and 12 fighters. After the lessons of Coral Sea and Midway, Nagumo changed his tactics to hold back his slower and less maneuverable torpedo bombers until the targets had been properly softened up by the dive and high level bombers.

The Japanese land-based Base Air Force also began longer range air searches by sending four flying boats on a 700-mile radius search to the east and southeast. Another group of land attack planes would search on an 800-mile radius from Rabaul in an adjacent sector.

The Americans had their own search planes aloft. While *Enterprise*'s planes found only a Japanese submarine, which they bombed, McCain organized a comprehensive air search pattern using six PBYs that would each fly a seven-degree sector, 650 miles long from Ndeni (Santa Cruz Island). One PBY, piloted by Ens. Gale C. Burkey, found one carrier, two cruisers, and four destroyers steaming due south at latitude 4°40'S, longitude 161°15'E. The Americans had found Radm. Chuichi Hara's Detached Carrier Strike Force with the light carrier *Ryujo*. Burkey immediately transmitted a message that reported his findings. The *Enterprise*'s radio room copied Burkey's message. Kinkaid asked Fletcher at 9:45 a.m. over the TBS radio whether he had also received the message. Fletcher replied that he had not. Kinkaid then sent it to him. For the first time, Fletcher had a positive sighting of a Japanese carrier. Fletcher ordered Kinkaid at 10:12 a.m. to get ready to launch planes and attack the Japanese carrier about 281 miles away.

A second sighting from Burkey's PBY found the *Ryujo* on the same course and speed but now 36 miles closer. Hara launched Zeroes to attack Burkey's PBY, but he showed nimble flying skills by using cloud cover and dodging the attacking Japanese fighters. They finally got his slow plane in their cross-hairs but could only shoot a few holes into her. The aircraft returned to Ndeni safely with no casualties to her flight crew.

The opportunity to strike could not be any better. Like a race horse chafing at the bit to run a race, Kinkaid asked Fletcher at 11:29 a.m. for permission to attack:

> "Fighter and attack group ready, 20 VF, 25 SBD with 1,000 pound bombs, 8 VTB with two 500 pound bombs each, 1 VTB group commander with belly tank. Plan to use 8 VTB and 12 VSB for afternoon search. Recommend sector 290—090 radius 250 miles."[14]

But Fletcher was not yet ready to launch any of his aircraft until he knew where the other Japanese carriers were. Later, he recalled why he made the decision to delay Kinkaid's attack:

> "In order to verify these [search] reports and guard against a repetition of the attack made under similar circumstances on the 23rd which never found its objective, I reluctantly ordered Commander Task Force SIXTEEN to immediately launch a search covering the arc 290º–090º to a distance of 250 miles."[15]

Another reason Fletcher delayed ordering the attack on the Japanese light carrier was the *déjà vu*-like circumstance in which he now found himself. He still regretted having launched what now seemed to be a premature attack on the light carrier *Shoho* at Coral Sea only to lose the *Lexington* to a Japanese counter air attack from Japanese fleet carriers. Wanting to make sure he knew where the Japanese carriers were, he ordered Kinkaid at 11:40 a.m. to immediately launch the air search.

After the *Saratoga*'s CAP splashed an "Emily" flying boat, Fletcher turned his attention to going on the offensive. He asked Kinkaid what planes he would have to send on the attack. Kinkaid said at 12:34 a.m. he would have 20 fighters, 12 dive-bombers armed with 1,000-pound bombs, and six torpedo bombers ready by 1:30 p.m. Fletcher became decisive when he told Kinkaid, "Will hold your attack group in reserve for possible second carrier. Do not launch attack group until I direct you."[16]

The *Enterprise* launched 23 planes for its search and 22 planes to reinforce Task Force 61's CAP between 12:35 and 12:47 p.m. Meanwhile, the CAP splashed another Japanese search plane. Now Fletcher's certainty about the Japanese knowing where he was could be confirmed.[17] The Japanese were on their way to counterattack and retake Guadalcanal. All Fletcher knew was that Japanese transports were on their way to Guadalcanal, and a force including one light carrier had been sighted. Now knowing the Japanese carrier's location, he rightly reasoned that the Japanese would never mount what had to be a major counteroffensive with just one carrier. There had to be more carriers to his north despite what seemed to him the overly optimistic ULTRA-based assessments indicating these ships were nowhere near him. And his search planes had not yet sighted any more carriers either. As he organized his plan for battle, the *Enterprise*'s responsibilities were:

1. Maintain CAP, IAP, and direct fighters.
2. Have planes ready to attack a second Japanese carrier when it is found.
3. Provide service for and direct 12 of the *Saratoga*'s fighters.

The *Saratoga*'s responsibilities were:

1. Keep her planes ready to strike the Japanese carriers.
2. Get ready to service fighters as they returned from their assigned missions.
3. Arm those TBFs not part of its strike group with torpedoes to make them ready to join with the *Enterprise*'s strike group.

He would now wait to hear from his search planes before ordering his powerful air strike force into action.[18]

The opposing forces were now in motion that would participate in the third carrier battle of the Pacific War. The Imperial Japanese Navy occupied 60 miles of ocean to Guadalcanal's northwest knowing that American carriers were to their south. The American carrier search planes were flying and looking for the rest of the Japanese force. Many planes crowded their home ship flight and hangar decks waiting for the order to launch and attack their opposing naval forces. The Battle of the Eastern Solomons was about to begin.

CHAPTER 19
Let the Shooting Begin

The Japanese Attack Henderson Field

The noon sun was at its zenith when Radm. Chuichi Hara's Detached Strike Force reached its planned launch position 200 miles north of Guadalcanal. The *Ryujo* turned into the wind, her decks crowded with a powerful air attack force ready to take off. Lt. Binichi Murakami, commanding officer of the ship's Carrier Attack Squadron, sat in his Val bomber waiting for the signal from the carrier's bridge to take off. He was the first wave's strike leader for six Val bombers each carrying six 60-kg high-explosive bombs. Six Zeroes led by Warrant Officer Katsuma Shigemi would escort them to the target. Nine Zeroes commanded by Lt. Kenjiro Notomi would follow Shigemi's group. Their primary assignment was to strafe Henderson Field after the bombers had done their work.

The *Ryujo*'s captain, Capt. Tadao Kato, had the ship's four radio masts on either side of the flight deck lowered to allow room for the planes to take off. The bridge signaled to launch all aircraft at 12:20 p.m., and Murakami's six bombers and Shigemi's six fighters lifted off into the sky followed by Notomi's nine Zeroes. Twenty-eight minutes later, the flight deck had cleared so the *Ryujo* could recover her CAP. There were nine Zeroes and three Vals left on board.

Hara turned northward, but did not go far so he could recover the strike group when it returned.

✲ ✲ ✲

Meanwhile, Lt. Joseph M. Kellam's PBY was on the return leg of its search pattern when he sighted Hara's force at 2:05 p.m. He radioed his report that he had seen one carrier, two cruisers, and two destroyers at latitude 5°40′ S, longitude 162°20′ E on a course of 140°. A few minutes later, Fletcher saw Kellam's report but with the PBY's call sign pointing to a different PBY, the most likely cause being either sent incorrectly or garbled while being decoded. Again, Fletcher was uncertain as to whether this was the carrier sighted earlier by Burkey or a new sighting.

The debate was rendered almost moot since Fletcher had already sent out all the planes he could spare looking for Hara's force. He also had sent up 12 F4Fs for CAP. With such a shortage of fighters needed for other duties, Cmdr. Harry D. Felt's group of 30 SBDs and eight TBFs[1] had no fighter escort. Felt's planes flew on a heading of 320° and 216 miles away for the place of Burkey's original sighting of one carrier, two heavy cruisers and four destroyers. However, the latest PBY sighting indicated the ships were 60 miles to the northeast from the place reported by the first sighting. *Saratoga*'s radio unsuccessfully tried to reach Felt to redirect him. Felt was heading for the wrong place.

From an altitude of almost 10,000 feet, Malaita Island appeared ahead as the *Ryujo*'s strike force neared Guadalcanal. Murakami peered through the Plexiglas of his plane's cockpit and could see Florida and Guadalcanal Islands straight ahead. He ordered his wingman at 2:15 p.m., WO Shinkichi Takehira, to lead his planes in a Vee formation to bomb from a high altitude. Takehira was the *Ryujo*'s most experienced bombardier and Murakami had confidence in his ability. Shigemi's Zeroes were about 500 meters to the bombers' right. The bomber pilots pushed their planes into a shallow dive. Notomi's nine Zeroes followed.

✲ ✲ ✲

CACTUS had no radar to give an early warning for any approaching aircraft. So, the only way to detect the approach of Japanese aircraft was to have a CAP aloft during the daylight hours. At the same time Murakami prepared his command to bomb Henderson Field, four F4Fs flying CAP circled at 12,000 feet above Sealark Channel. Twelve more F4Fs and a few Bell P-400s waited at high alert on the ground.

Marine Capt. Marion Carl, flying one of the CAP F4Fs, looked northward, and there they were, Japanese aircraft coming toward Guadalcanal about 2,000 feet below him. He picked up his radio microphone and alerted CACTUS that the Japanese were on their way. Henderson Field's air raid siren wailed. A black flag flew up its mast to warn everyone that an air attack was not far off. It was Condition Red.

The sound of the incoming Japanese airplanes increased as the American pilots ran to their planes. With their planes' engines already running, they climbed onto the wing and into the cockpit. Ground crews assisted them locking their safety harnesses. The pilots pushed their engine throttles forward, and the planes quickly bounded along the rough-hewn taxiways to line up for takeoff. Ten F4Fs took off with two P-400s following close behind.

Meanwhile, Carl and his three wing mates saw what seemed to be Japanese bombers with no fighter escort below them. At 2:23 p.m., Carl and Tech. Sergeant John D. Lindley banked into a steep dive and attacked a group of six planes that trailed to the right of the other planes. Although Carl claimed he shot down one of them, Lindley and he had attacked a group of Zeroes, not the Japanese bombers as they originally thought. The plane Carl actually shot down was one of Shigemi's six fighters flown by PO1c Jinsaku Nojima.

Marine Gunner Henry B. Hamilton engaged in an intensive gunfight with Shigemi's Zeroes. While three planes of the four-plane American CAP engaged the fighters, 2nd Lt. Fred E. Gutt went after Murakami's bombers just before they were about to drop their bombs. Not much time passed before the missiles headed for the ground.

Meanwhile, spotters on the ground saw the Japanese bombers diving from a bearing of 315° at an altitude of 8,200 feet five minutes after Carl had seen them. Four 90-mm guns pointed toward the rapidly approaching planes and opened fire. At 2:30 p.m., all 36 60-kg bombs dropped from the planes. Explosions rocked the gun emplacements in a tight pattern, making great craters in the dark, damp earth. The 90-mm guns were not touched.

As the bombs exploded, Notomi's nine Zeroes swooped in from three directions and strafed the airfield. Just as 2nd Lt. Robert R. Read's F4F had lifted off and reached 500 feet, one of the nine Zeroes filled his plane with cannon fire. He looked around just as the Japanese shells struck his plane; blood flowed from wounds in his head and right shoulder. Struggling mightily to keep his plane in the air, he landed in the water two miles from Florida Island. Forced to be in the water for a day, a native boat finally rescued him and took him to Tulagi.

Both American and Japanese planes ran into each other with varied results. A Japanese pilot claimed shooting down a P-400 while one of those American plane's pilots claimed a Zero. American AA fire hit PO1c Hiroshi Kurihara's Zero, but his plane could still fly. One of his wingmen, PO2c Chiune Yotsumoto, escaped damage to his Zero as he tried to stay away from an exploding fuel dump.

Now free of their payload, Murakami's Vals made a sweeping 180° turn and headed to the north. But they did not escape Carl's busy and scattered CAP. Carl and his mates pounced on the slow-moving bombers and mercilessly battered them. Six more Marine aircraft that had taken off after the air-raid alarm sounded joined the slaughter. Carl shot down his second Japanese plane at 2:33 p.m. on the bomber formations right side, while 2nd Lt. Kenneth D. Frazier blasted another bomber from the sky on the left. One minute later, a Val exploded in flames and headed down, a burning arrow.

Seven Zeroes tried to come to the bombers' rescue and exacted some revenge. Gutt's plane took cannon fire, some of which wounded him in the left arm and leg. He escaped further damage by going into a steep dive. After dividing a kill with 2nd Lt. Cloyd R. Jeans, 2nd Lt. Lawrence C. Taylor's F4F fell in flames. Meanwhile, 2nd Lt. John H. King found one bomber, fired one machine gun burst into it, and it exploded in a ball of fire.

The Zeroes failed to protect Murakami's charges. The Marines had knocked one-half of the attacking Japanese bombers from the sky. One heavily-damaged bomber limped away as the remaining two bombers and seven Zeroes headed back to the *Ryujo*. Three Zeroes no longer flew.

The Americans did not escape casualties. Three F4Fs had been lost with two pilots killed. The already bomber-short *Ryujo* had lost three bombers while three of its fighters never returned along with their now increasingly scarce veteran air crews.

The Japanese strike on Henderson Field, still fully operational, can only be judged as a dismal failure. In historical perspective, it now seems obvious that sending just six bombers against an established airbase with a substantial fighter defense was inadequate to put the airfield out of business. Perhaps the Japanese had again underestimated the power the Americans had already built up.

But the effect on the *Ryujo*'s air strength would prove to be even more disastrous. The carrier lost six planes, one-half of its bomber complement and one-eighth of its fighter strength. There were now only 20 fighters left to be sent against air attacks. The *Ryujo*'s situation was desperate. And it would soon become more so.[2]

The Japanese Lose a Carrier

The news about Hara's strike force's bombing at Henderson Field was not good. Despite claiming exaggerated losses on the Americans by his pilots (as all pilots do), the truth was that Henderson Field was still operational, and the American losses were, to say the least, modest. He lost three Vals and three Zeroes. It was a cause for concern and consternation. But Hara's difficulties were only beginning and about to get worse.

Three groups of American planes from the *Enterprise* were over his force and sending messages to Task Force 61 that his ships had been found. These were not just search planes; they had bombs attached to their bellies and torpedoes inside them. Their intent could only be modestly described as malicious.

The first group was two TBFs flown by Lt. Cmdr. Charles M. Jett and Ens. Robert J. Bye. Jett and Bye both saw Hara's ships at 2:40 p.m. Jett forwarded his sighting report about one carrier and three destroyers on the horizon directly ahead of him and two cruisers two miles from the carrier's starboard beam. As he sent his report, the two TBFs executed a spiral climb to the north to get into position to carry out a horizontal bombing attack.

Almost simultaneous with Jett's discovery, two SBDs flown by Lt. Stockton B. Strong and Ens. Gerald S. Richey flew closer to the Japanese ships. Strong flew five miles closer, sent his report, and then flew away.

The third group of planes included one TBF piloted by Ens. Harold L. Bingaman and a SBD flown by Ens. John H. Jorgenson. Approaching from the southwest, they saw the same four ships and reported them as a carrier and three destroyers. When they got too close, the Japanese CAP chased them away.

Jett and Bye had climbed to 12,000 feet at 2:55 p.m. when the Japanese finally spotted them. Mistakenly identifying the two planes as B-17s, the destroyer *Amatsukaze* opened fire with 12.7-cm AA fire. The cruiser *Tone* and destroyer *Tokitsukaze* joined the party. The *Ryujo* turned into the wind to launch three Vals and one Zero to defend against submarines. The reasons why Hara decided to launch aircraft at this particularly vulnerable moment when American planes had been seen in its vicinity can only be left to speculation. It almost led to a catastrophe. Jett and Bye released their four 500-pound bombs just as the *Ryujo* turned sharply to starboard. They fell in a nice tight group and exploded in the carrier's wake.

Jett's report was in Fletcher's hands at 3:00 p.m. Despite another report that arrived ten minutes later, which said there were no planes left on the *Ryujo*'s flight deck, the new information did little to change Fletcher's mind to keep the *Enterprise*'s planes on board to be ready in case his search planes found the other Japanese carriers. Thinking that Jett's report was the same as Burkey's message, the new sighting report confused him in that it indicated the Japanese carrier was 260 miles farther away.

The *Enterprise* had a strike force of 11 SBDs and seven TBFs with an escort of 15 F4Fs ready to go to attack the *Ryujo*. Kinkaid asked Fletcher for permission to send the planes to the northwest to reduce the return flight's distance. Fletcher denied Kinkaid's request because he wanted to keep the option to head to the east to intercept the other Japanese carriers. The *Enterprise*'s flight crews' frustration continued.

Frustration was not just an exclusively American emotion. Cmdr. Tameichi Hara, the destroyer *Amatsukaze*'s skipper, emotionally revealed his feelings about the effectiveness, or rather the lack of it, when he sent a message to Cmdr. Hisakichi Kishi, the *Ryujo*'s executive officer: "Fully realizing my impertinence, am forced to advise you my impression. Your flight operations are far short of expectations. What is the matter?" Kishi's response reflects the traditionally Japanese way of handling conflict: "Deeply appreciate your admonition. We shall do better and count on your cooperation." Apparently reacting to Hara's criticism, the *Ryujo* launched two Zeroes, thus intensifying Japanese awareness of imminent danger.

After fruitlessly searching for the *Ryujo*, Cmdr. Harry D. Felt had monitored Jett's report and adjusted his path to fly farther north to where Jett had said the Japanese ships were. He had a powerful force of 36 aircraft that included his own plane, 15 SBDs commanded by Lt. Cmdr. Louis J. Kirn, 13 under the command of Lt. Cmdr. Dewitt W. Shumway, and Lt. Bruce L. Harwood's seven TBFs. After leaving the *Saratoga* and reaching cruising attitude, the SBDs flew at 15,000 feet with the TBFs 3,000 feet below. His *Saratoga* strike group finally reached their objective at 3:56 p.m. when they saw the Japanese ships to their northwest, their white wakes on the blue water making white arrows pointing to their location. Deciding to attack from the northeast, Felt ordered Kirn's 15 and seven of Shumway's SBDs with six of Harwood's TBFs to attack the carrier. The other six SBDs and one TBF would attack the *Tone*.

The lack of radar again placed Japanese ships in great jeopardy. The *Ryujo*'s lookouts scanned the skies for the American planes they knew were on their way to attack. Soon, the unmistakable shapes of American carrier aircraft appeared in their lenses. The urgency of their sighting can be heard in the frantically terse tone of their report: "Many enemy planes approaching." Hara knew his task group was in grave danger when he ordered the *Ryujo* to turn into the wind and launch two more Zeroes to reinforce his CAP. Two Vals sat on the flight deck. The rest of Hara's ships scattered so they could easily maneuver in less cramped waters and defend themselves against the oncoming American onslaught; however, they were now too far away to give any AA defense for the light carrier. Capt. Tadao Kato started to maneuver his ship to make it harder to hit with dive-bomber attacks. It was every ship for herself.

Kirn's SBDs were at 14,000 feet when they rolled over at 3:30 p.m. and went into their diving attack. No Japanese fighters had yet appeared. In each SBD cockpit, the wind screamed past the plane as it plummeted to earth. Every single plane shook as the airspeed indicator turned toward the absolute maximum speed. Each pilot knew when his plane was about to reach the time to drop his bomb. Peering onto his glass sight, he adjusted his plane's direction so the cross hairs covered the ever-enlarging carrier. When the planes reached that point, each released their 1,000-pound bomb.

The carrier circled to the starboard as the SBDs' bombs smacked the water and exploded. The splashes bracketed the carrier. With no Zeroes interfering with their bomb run, Shumway's seven SBDs followed their comrades with the same result. No hits!

By now, four Zeroes caught up with the SBDs near the water and pulling out of their dives. Ens. William A. Behr's SBD took the brunt of their attacks as cannon fire punctured his plane.

Felt still cruised at 14,000 feet and watched the bombs miss their target. He was not a happy man. Ordering the rest of the planes to attack the carrier, he waited until all the other planes were in their dives and dove his plane at the *Ryujo*. As he looked into his bomb sight and his plane plunged toward the ship, he could see that the carrier's flight deck was still intact. Not a single bomb had hit it. He released his bomb and confidently thought he had hit the carrier. His bomb actually hit the water just near the ship and was a near miss.

Attacking the heavy cruiser *Tone*, Lt. Harold S. Bottomley also saw that the SBDs' bombs were not hitting the carrier. He ordered his six SBDs to stop attacking the cruiser and turn their attentions toward the carrier. Four Zeroes now attacked his planes, but his attack continued. Six bombs fell, and scored three hits. One bomb hit the edge of the starboard deck forward; another hit aft. The third 1,000-pounder exploded far abaft also on the starboard side.

The SBDs were not the only American planes assaulting the *Ryujo*. The seven TBFs went into long shallow dives from 12,000 feet. Five split to simultaneously approach from opposite sides in an anvil attack. The other two attacked the *Tone*. Two Zeroes tried to stop the attacking TBFs. Smoke poured from the carrier. The Zeroes claimed that they scored one hit and probably two others on the attacking American bombers.

One torpedo crashed into the carrier's aft starboard side, exploded, disabled the carrier's fire and engine rooms, and knocked out her steering gear. Two of the TBFs' torpedoes missed the carrier near her port bow. Nevertheless, the *Ryujo* was finished.

The *Saratoga*'s planes had destroyed one Japanese carrier as they turned southward to head home. Claiming to have shot down two Japanese aircraft and scoring a hit on a cruiser, they were a self-assured bunch as they flew away from the battle. That confidence proved to be exaggerated as the cruiser *Tone* escaped unscathed and all Japanese aircraft remained undamaged.

Hara ordered his ships to retreat to the north at 4:08 p.m. and leave the hopelessly crippled *Ryujo* to her fate. Felt wanted to stay behind and watch the carrier sink. He circled his plane until turning for home at 4:20. As he left the scene, he sent his observations: "Carrier continued to run in circles to the right pouring forth black smoke which would die down and belch forth in great volume again."[3]

✡ ✡ ✡

Fires spread all over her as the *Ryujo* suffered from the effects of the two bomb hits on her flight deck starboard side. One torpedo punched a huge hole in her hull's starboard side. Water poured into her starboard engine room. The carrier listed at 23° and finally stopped dead in the water. Kato ordered the planes still aboard to take off and head for the Japanese airbase at Buka. The planes that had attacked Henderson Field soon arrived to the horrible site of their home base in flames and sinking.

Flames and thick, black smoke poured from the *Ryujo*. These planes did not have enough fuel to go to a safe base and had to ditch in the water, their crews facing an uncertain fate.

The gallant *Ryujo* slipped beneath the waves at 8:00 p.m., taking 121 men, two Zeroes, and two Vals with her. The Japanese had lost yet another aircraft carrier.

However, the Americans were destined to suffer a similar fate. The aircraft from the powerful fleet carriers *Shokaku* and *Zuikaku* had their own business to perform on the American carriers to the south.[4]

Finding the American Carriers

While the *Saratoga*'s aircraft searched for the still illusive light carrier, the Japanese kept looking for the American carriers. Nagumo not only had carrier aircraft to do this search, but he also had planes on his heavy cruisers to perform that duty as well. One of those was an Aichi E13A1 Type 0 ("Jake") reconnaissance seaplane from the *Chikuma*, which was part of Radm. Hiroaki Abe's Vanguard Force in support of Nagumo's carriers.

Ens. Kazutoshi Fukuyama sat in the pilot's seat with two of his fellow crewmen on the *Chikuma*'s catapult waiting for the sudden, bone-jarring surge of compressed air to hurl his plane into the air. His plane was the seventh added at the last minute to an original six-plane search team that had orders to find the American carriers.

As circumstances turned out, Nagumo made a most fortuitous decision. The admiral did not have the same problem Fletcher had, too many conflicting sightings of Japanese ships. In fact,his search planes had not yet seen a single American ship. But he had to know where to send his air strike force. His thoughts went back to those horrible days off Midway when poor intelligence forced him to make decisions that put his four-carrier task force in extreme jeopardy. He vowed that would never happen to him again. This time he would know for certain where the American carrier (still believing there was just one) was and would do everything in his power to wreak revenge on them for what happened during those dark days more than four months before. It was 11:00 a.m. on August 24 when he ordered the launch of search aircraft.

Fukuyama's plane shot from the catapult; the acceleration forces violently pushed his head back against his head rest. His plane easily gained altitude as the combination of the speed of the cruiser and that added by the catapult gave him more than enough airspeed to get aloft. He turned southward and headed for Stewart Island—the last known location of the American ships. Almost three hours later at 1:55 p.m. and flying at about 3,000 feet, he neared Stewart Island. His assigned sector was from 160º to 165º relative to the Vanguard Force, the westernmost sector of the Japanese search plan.

✲ ✲ ✲

The eight F4Fs from the *Enterprise* commanded by Lt. Cmdr. Louis H. Bauer flew CAP at 15,000 feet that morning and early afternoon. Lt. Henry A. Rowe, Ens. Douglas M. Johnson, Gunner Charles E. Brewer, and Machinist Doyle C. Barnes flew four of these fighters with him near Stewart Island. At 1:45 p.m. Rowe saw what seemed to be a Japanese plane and warned Bauer, "Bogey close in back of you."

Three minutes later, Bauer ordered his F4Fs to go after the trespasser. For the next few minutes, he skillfully maneuvered his fighters into a position to surround and cut off the Japanese plane's retreat. The targeted plane was alone and could only be Japanese.

Bauer could not see the plane. At 1:55 p.m., Johnson had better luck. There he was, flying at 3,000 feet over the island. He radioed Bauer his sighting; one minute later, Barnes picked up his radio's microphone and sent his report, "Bogey is bandit, apparently a slow seaplane type."

Fukuyama looked up at the approaching American fighter and used every flying skill he knew to evade it. He rolled his plane over and slipped into some cloud cover. Thinking he was lucky to escape, he knew that this was a false confidence in how his mission would end. Nonetheless, he remembered why he was there and radioed the *Chikuma* what he had seen, "Spotted large enemy force. Being pursued by enemy fighters, 1200." [local time 2:00 p.m.]. His luck was about run out.

✲ ✲ ✲

About 28 miles from Task Force 61, Brewer saw the seaplane emerge from the cloud cover and almost had it in his gun sight for the second time. He squeezed the trigger on the stick and dozens of .50-cal. machine bullets riddled the haplessly slow seaplane. It immediately burst into flames at 2:00 p.m. and headed in a fireball to the sea below. He confirmed his victory by transmitting, "Tally ho, bomber in water, Bingo! Got him Chuck, landed in the water. RED 2, 1 bogey down."

✲ ✲ ✲

The *Chikuma* received Fukuyama's last message and relayed it to the *Shokaku*. Nagumo read it 25 minutes later. The message did not have the American task force's location but the admiral's staff analyzed the flying time and search schedule and ascertained that the American carriers were at a bearing of 153° about 260 miles away. The Japanese at last knew where the Americans were.

Not wanting to get caught with his flight decks full of fully fueled and armed planes should the Americans arrive with attacking planes as had happened at Midway, Nagumo did not hesitate. The *Shokaku* had every plane it could spare—26 Zeroes, 27 Vals, and 18 Kates—ready to go after the American carriers. Lt. Cmdr. Mamoru Seki, the *Shokaku*'s bomber group commander, had 18 planes fully fueled and armed along with Lt. Yasuhiro Shigematsu's nine Zeroes. The *Zuikaku* was just as ready with 25 Zeroes, 27 Vals and 18 Kates. She added nine more Vals led by Coral Sea veteran Lt. Reijiro Otsuka and six Zeroes commanded by Lt. Saneyasu Hidaka to Seki's strike force.

Seki's planes left the *Shokaku*'s flight deck at 2:50 p.m. and the *Zuikaku*'s aircraft took off ten minutes later. They turned to a course of 153° and climbed to a high cruising altitude. During that time, the two carriers brought the second wave of planes on deck while keeping a reserve onboard for a follow-up torpedo attack. The American carrier had to be softened up first before Nagumo would risk the slower, more vulnerable torpedo bombers. Nevertheless, Nagumo's carriers were not invincible to American carrier plane attacks.

Japanese Carriers under Attack

Two *Enterprise* SBDs, piloted by Lt. Ray Davis and Ens. Robert C. Shaw, were on a mission to search for the Japanese carriers that Fletcher felt were out there. Heading northward at 2:45 p.m., Davis and Shaw noticed a large group of ships to the northwest. In this part of the sea, they could only be Japanese. As they turned to attack what they thought was a light cruiser, Davis observed a large Japanese carrier farther away with many planes on its flight deck. The two planes flew between Nagumo's Main Body and Abe's Vanguard Force 40 miles ahead. Davis pressed the attack on the nearest carrier when he climbed to 14,000 feet while staying away from the Japanese CAP. They were in position to start the diving attack.

As Seki's strike force left, the *Shokaku*'s lookouts saw the two American carrier bombers just ready to go into their steep dives. The carrier's crew was caught completely off guard. However, the report of seeing the American planes did not reach Nagumo so he could give orders to react. The carrier's radar[5] also saw the approaching American planes but did not call the Japanese CAP. The only Japanese fighters to see the SBDs were the nine Zeroes escorting the Japanese air strike force on its way to attack Task Force 61. The Japanese pilots were in a quandary. Should they continue on their mission or intercept the American planes to defend the *Shokaku*? The answer was to send five Zeroes to stop the American planes, thus reducing the strike force's escort to only four fighters.

* * *

Davis and Shaw reached 14,000 feet at 3:15 p.m. and pushed their sticks forward to put their dive-bombers into the classic American-styled steep dive. As Davis' and Shaw's planes plummeted toward the water and just before reaching the point to drop their 500-pound bombs, the Japanese carrier turned sharply starboard. One bomb smacked the water, making a huge white splash just ten meters on the *Shokaku*'s starboard side, killing six of her crew. The second bomb hit the water ten meters beyond the first one. The Japanese CAP never saw the attacking Americans. Some of the escort Zeroes got close, but the two American pilots managed to escape undamaged.

Davis sent a sighting message to Task Force 61 that he had seen two fleet carriers loaded with planes along with their position, course, and speed. Only part of Davis' message reached the *Enterprise* and the *Saratoga* because of extremely poor radio reception. While the information about the Japanese carriers' presence was incomplete, Fletcher now surely knew they were out there. However, Fletcher still did not know the position, course, and speed. He still did not know enough to his satisfaction to send out an attacking airborne force to add to Davis' and Shaw's attack.

* * *

Thankfully, Nagumo realized the two bombs did not damage his flagship. But the attack had taken his command completely by surprise. However, he immediately acted:

1. Between 3:20 and 3:30 p.m., the *Shokaku* sent up 11 Zeroes, every fighter she had, while the *Zuikaku* ordered four more Zeroes aloft to bring the CAP strength to 29.
2. At 3:30 p.m. Abe's Vanguard Force headed south to destroy any American ship that should be still afloat after the Japanese air strike force had finished their work.
3. Under Lt. Sadamu Takahashi's overall command, the air strike's second wave with 27 Vals commanded by Lt. Shohei Yamada and nine Zeroes led by Lt. Ayao Shirane left the two carriers between 3:50 and 4:00 p.m.

The search plane pilot flying in the adjacent sector to Fukuyama sent an important report to Nagumo. The American carrier had been definitely sighted at latitude 9°30′ S, longitude 163°20′ E, course 130°, speed 20 knots. Takahashi formed up his second wave and headed on a course of 150°, expecting to find the American ships at 6:00 p.m. just when sun would set. Nagumo turned to port from 150° to a new course of 100°, set his speed at 24 knots and waited to hear the results of his strike.[6]

CHAPTER 20
Japanese Retaliation

Offense to Defense

As Nagumo's planes winged their way toward Task Force 61, Fletcher still had no idea that his force was about to be attacked. The location of the Japanese fleet carriers remained a mystery to him. Therefore, he kept his planes in reserve waiting to go on the offensive should their presence become known to him. A strike force commanded by Lt. Cmdr. Maxwell F. Leslie was now ready on the *Enterprise*'s flight deck while 16 F4Fs landed at 4:50 p.m. on the *Saratoga* for refueling. By this time of the war, air operations had become more coordinated, so serving one carrier's planes by another carrier was more commonplace.

Almost two hours before at 3:05 p.m., an unknown aircraft approached Task Force 61 that confused the American air defense. After several reports from the CAP about what this contact was, Lt. Albert O. Vorse Jr., an F4F pilot, confirmed the plane was a friendly PBY. Lt. Joseph M. Kellam flew that plane and was returning from his search with something of significance to report. Kellam was not sure his original report had been received; so he wanted to make certain it was. A signal lamp from his PBY blinked out the signal, "Small enemy carrier bearing 320 True distance 195 miles," as well as its course and speed. Again demonstrating his caution, Fletcher later confirmed with COMAIRPAC that the PBY was definitely American. There had been reports of Japanese stealing PBYs and using them to mislead American commanders.

Fletcher and Kinkaid tried to comprehend the total effect of Jett's sighting and what kind and size of force to send to attack. Jett's sighting convinced Kinkaid that he should send what he could to attack it while Fletcher still equivocated when he sent the message at 3:36 p.m. to Kinkaid, "If you consider contact good send your boys in."[1] Kellam's report persuaded Kinkaid beyond any doubt. The *Enterprise* was now ready to launch her strike. By 4:00 p.m., Task Force 61's CAP had 24 F4Fs in the air and 29 on deck.

The *Saratoga* turned into the wind at 4:00 p.m. to the southeast and added Bauer's 16 F4Fs to the CAP. Meanwhile, Cmdr. Edgar A. Cruise, the carrier's air operations officer, ordered the air crews of five TBFs and two SBDs to taxi their aircraft forward as soon as the fighters had taken off. The *Enterprise* flight deck crews moved Leslie's group of 11 SBDs, eight TBFs, and seven F4Fs into the ready position. Two minutes later, the tactical circumstances changed drastically.

An *Enterprise* CXAM radar operator was at his station at 4:02 p.m. when a large return signal appeared. It was on a bearing of 320° and 88 miles away. The *Saratoga*'s radar picked up the same signal, but at a distance of 103 miles. Just as quickly as it appeared, it vanished. Lt. Cmdr. Oscar Pederson,

Task Force 61's air operations officer, also had no doubt. But Task Force 61 was now ready to launch many aircraft, and Pederson later recalled how Fletcher and his staff reacted to the latest news:

> "To say the least we were in a bad predicament—all of our attack planes were committed on missions with the main enemy force still unlocated and his planes coming in to attack us. The best we could do was to get ready for an air attack and hope for the best."[2]

The *Enterprise*'s FDO, Lt. Henry A. Rowe, asked that the *Saratoga* to send every fighter it had to intercept the contact. He directed 10 F4Fs to fly on a 320° bearing.

☆ ☆ ☆

Indeed these approaching bogeys were real. They were Seki's first strike force of 27 bombers and ten fighters. Responding to a new sighting by the battleship *Hiei*'s observation seaplane, Seki now turned from 153° to 160° at 4:00 p.m. and continued to look to the distant horizon for his targets.

☆ ☆ ☆

A second radar return at 4:04 p.m. introduced even more defensive problems for Task Force 61. It was not as large as the first report. However, it forced Fletcher to divide and therefore weaken his CAP. The *Saratoga*'s 10 fighters that had been launched were directed to check out the new contact, and Rowe warned Vorse's four F4Fs to be ready to intercept the sighting. At 4:08 p.m., the bogey was 30 miles away. While reinforcing the CAP to make up for the fighter depletion, Rowe also ordered the *Saratoga* to launch eight more F4Fs and directed them to fly northwest toward the bogey's latest reported position.

Fletcher ordered Task Force 16 to reduce its distance to Task Force 11 and also ordered Kinkaid to finally launch his attack. The fighters directed after the second contact now closed the range to them. As his planes got close enough to see what type of plane it was, Vorse saw that it was a friendly TBF returning from a search. Its pilot had disabled the plane's IFF so it could not be identified, a waste of valuable CAP strength diverted to go after one plane!

The *Enterprise*'s radar again picked up the large return signal at 4:18 p.m. It was only 44 miles away, estimated to be flying at 12,000 feet and rapidly reducing its distance to Task Force 61. As it turned out, the altitude estimate turned out to be too low because of the relative lack of sophistication of radar target analysis at this stage of the war. Rowe immediately decided and reacted to this serious threat. He signaled, "Many bogeys ahead," and ordered two *Enterprise*'s F4Fs, led by Lt. (jg) Harold E. Rutherford, to "Get up high." He then ordered the remaining 16 fighters being held in reserve for CAP duty to fly on a new heading of 300° (northwest) at 12,000 feet toward the large group of unidentified planes that could only be Japanese. But only 12 planes turned to the new course. Four of them had to return to the *Saratoga* to refuel. There was now no CAP over Task Force 16; they were all out either chasing falsely reported bogeys or on search missions.

Rowe positioned the remaining Task Force 61 CAP of 11 F4Fs in an outer ring 40 or more miles away with 15 more fighters returning from previously assigned missions. Assuming these fighters returned in time and 26 fighters still being held reserve on the *Saratoga* and *Enterprise* flight decks could be launched soon enough to intercept the approaching Japanese aircraft, Task Force 61 could put up a CAP of 53 F4Fs, hopefully sufficient to deter the attack everyone knew was on its way.

The sky around where this carrier battle would take place was a wondrous sight even for these tropical latitudes. Tall, billowy, roiling white cumulus clouds rose like giant towers from some medieval castle from the blue, white-capped, two mile deep sea. The clear sky between the huge cloudy columns meant that there would be unlimited visibility on this day.

Seki had been leading his group of carrier bombers for some time now without sighting anything that he could attack. Normally a patient man, he became increasingly concerned that he had made a navigational mistake and would never find the American carriers.

Seki's doubts about ever seeing the American carriers soon vanished when he looked to port at 4:20 p.m., and there was one of them, 40 miles away and in an AA defensive ring formation. Turning east so he could attack from the north, he then saw a second carrier to the southeast and farther from the first one. Now there were two carriers to attack. His radio operator, Ens. Jiro Nakasada, sent the signal for all planes to assume attack formation. Following the prearranged attack plan, Lt. Yasuhiro Shigematsu's four Zeroes flew ahead to repel any F4Fs that might intercept them. If an American fighter got through Shigematsu's fighters, Lt. Saneyasu Hidaka's remaining six Zeroes were all that stood between the closing F4Fs and Seki's 27 bombers.

✲ ✲ ✲

Fletcher knew that Japanese planes were on their way because the *Enterprise*'s radar had picked up Seki's turn to 160°. As four *Saratoga* F4Fs landed at 4:25 p.m. to refuel, pilots immediately jumped out as their planes came to a stop on the carrier's flight deck. They knew they would be needed immediately for CAP as they helped the planes' handlers push the fighters so they could immediately be refueled. The *Enterprise* launched seven F4Fs to augment the CAP. The Japanese aircraft were only 27 miles away.

To clear the *Enterprise*'s flight deck, Kinkaid launched Max Leslie's strike group that had seven TBFs led by Lt. Rubin H. Konig and 11 SBDs led by Lt. Turner F. Caldwell. He wanted to send them to attack. Jett's 2:40 p.m. contact reported to have one fleet carrier, one light cruiser and two destroyers. Leslie's plane was the last to lift off at 4:38 p.m.

Tom Barnes' flight of four F4Fs flew westward and was still climbing at 4:29 p.m. when he saw the approaching Japanese planes 25 miles to the northwest. On their right, they saw a trailing group of what appeared to be Japanese dive-bombers flying eastward.

✲ ✲ ✲

Lt. Reijiro Otsuka's nine bombers headed to the east at 16,400 feet to attack the carrier closest to them. On Otsuka's command, all nine pilots pushed their sticks forward into a shallow dive. Much to their surprise, they passed extremely close to a group of American F4Fs moving westward below them.

Brewer looked up and saw the Japanese bombers. He immediately let everyone else know they were there with a quick, succinct radio transmission:

> "At 1 o'clock above this is RED 2, Tally ho! There are about 1 or 2...9 bogeys unidentified about 12,000 feet, 300...Many ahead of those...bogey bears 350, 20 [miles] Angels 12. They're dive-bombers. [signed] Chuck."[3]

He quickly pulled back on his stick, pushed his throttle as far forward as it could go, and put his F4F into a climb. He tried to reach the Japanese bombers but the F4F was not the fastest climbing fighter in the world.

As soon as Brewer's message arrived, Rowe radioed Bauer at 4:30 p.m. to go after the Japanese planes. But Barnes looked around and saw only empty sky. Nevertheless, he turned to intercept the oncoming Japanese.

✲ ✲ ✲

Seki's formation approached the *Enterprise* while still in a shallow dive. Not a single American fighter had yet attacked his formation.

✲ ✲ ✲

Brewer maintained contact with the Japanese planes, but was too far away to attack them; however, he was able to send more information at 4:31 p.m.:

> "Some at one o'clock — some directly above us 8 o'clock. They look like Zeros. RED BASE from Chuck, astern about 20 miles, Angels 13. They disappeared. Keep a good lookout."[4]

✲ ✲ ✲

Shigematsu's fighters flew air cover for Seki's bombers as they passed near some American fighters. Seeing the Americans out of the corner of his eye, he went after them.

✲ ✲ ✲

Vorse's four fighters had finished looking over the wayward TBF and had reached 8,000 feet. Not knowing that some Japanese zeroes were hunting them, he saw Japanese planes directly ahead to the north. He and the other pilots in his flight discussed the situation on their radios:

"About 36 bombers, course 120."

"Any fighters? Are they ours?"

"Hey, Scoop, on our right."

"Get in back of them. Let's go get them."

"Get up there."[5]

✲ ✲ ✲

"Scoop" Vorse placed his two most inexperienced pilots, Lt. (jg) Richards L. Loesch, Jr. and Lt. (jg) Francis R. Register, between himself and veteran Machinist Howell M. Sumrall. He moved in to attack the Japanese bombers. One minute after Brewer's second report, Sumrall looked overhead and saw danger approaching, "Zero right above us, Scoop."[6]

✲ ✲ ✲

After being too aggressive at Midway when he abandoned the bombers he was supposed to escort and to attack some American SBDs, Shigematsu did not want to attack right away and placed his three Zeroes between the attacking American fighters and Seki's bombers. He was 4,000 feet from the American F4Fs.

But one of his pilots had an itch to attack the Americans. Sea1c Shigeru Hayashi had waited for a minute or two when he decided he could wait no longer. He repeatedly placed his Zero on its back so he could keep tabs on the Americans.

✲ ✲ ✲

Sumrall looked up and saw the Zero rolling over several times and trailing behind the other two Japanese fighters. Later, Sumrall recalled, "I knew he was looking for a straggler so I straggled." Vorse's F4Fs now passed through 10,000 feet.

✲ ✲ ✲

Hayashi rocked his wings several times and rolled over into a steep dive. He was now ready to get a victory as he closed on the nearest F4F.

✲ ✲ ✲

Using his finely tuned flying skills, Sumrall turned in an opposite direction and prevented the Zero from firing his guns. The Zero zoomed past him and Sumrall abruptly reversed his turn by going to the right and firing a short machine gun burst. The Zero was in a steep dive. He was now behind the Zero and had him in his gun sight. He moved closer and loosed a burst into the Zero's fuselage and into the place where the wing met the Zero's body.

✲ ✲ ✲

Surprised by the American pilot's skills, Hayashi felt his plane tremble as machine gun bullets smashed into its belly and wing. Flames streamed from the Zero's external fuel tank as his plane streaked for the water below. Just when he thought the Americans were through with him, another F4F moved in for the kill.

✲ ✲ ✲

Flying on Sumrall's wing, Register thought the Zero that went after Sumrall actually was after him. Putting his F4F into a steep snap wing-over, he closed on the Zero and fired a burst just as the Japanese plane burst into flames. What he had done entirely violated the rules of engagement, which stated that he should stay with his assigned formation. Sumrall screamed into his radio for Register to rejoin him on his wing. Register was close to the Zero when he saw the pilot open his canopy, jump off the wing at 6,000 feet, and saw an opening parachute gently descend toward the sea. Sumrall saw the now empty Zero in a shallow downward dive. Trailing flames behind it, its nose lifted, and the plane finally met its end at 4:40 p.m. in a roaring conflagration on the sea. Hayashi survived his adventure.

✲ ✲ ✲

Dogfights continued between the American CAP and covering Zeroes for several more minutes with neither side gaining any perceptible advantage. The accompanying Zeroes, while losing three more fighters to the American F4Fs, succeeded in protecting the bombers and allowing Seki to continue his attack. Undeterred by all the actions going on around him, Seki and his bombers continued their dive toward the *Enterprise*.

Still flying to the southeast, Seki ordered his bombers to divide and attack the first American carrier just 15 miles away and the second carrier 25 miles in the distance. Nakasada sent the message, "*to-to-to*," the abbreviation for "*zengun totsugeki seyo*" or "all forces attack." Seki's 18 carrier bombers from the *Shokaku* turned abruptly to the south to attack the *Enterprise*, and Otsuka's nine *Zuikaku* bombers flew southeast to go after the *Saratoga*. Both bomber formations spread out and headed toward the points where they would begin their diving attacks from about 3,500 meters or 11,480 feet. Two waves of attacking bombers approached Task Force 61 with malicious intent.[7]

Task Force 16 in Peril

Seki's bombers had escaped unscathed from the American fighter's futile attempts to stop them.[8] Since dividing his bombers at 4:38 p.m. to attack the two American carrier groups, the 18 Vals turned to the right and rapidly closed the distance to the nearest American carrier. The Japanese aircraft flew in two nine-plane groups. Preparing to begin the attack, Seki ordered the two groups to form one long column with a distance of about 100 meters between each plane. This was the air crews' first chance to avenge the embarrassing defeat at Midway. But they knew that, despite not suffering damage by American F4Fs, the American fighters were in hot pursuit while the rest of the American CAP waited for them. At 4:40 p.m., the attacking planes pushed into a steeper dive.

Lt. Richard E. Harmer's four F4Fs pushed their throttles to the maximum trying to climb from 5,000 to 14,000 feet and reach the oncoming Japanese planes before they began dropping their bombs. Now five miles behind Task Force 61, Harmer's pilots were just below the attacking bombers as they went into shallow dives. The first bomber had just gone into its steep dive when Harmer caught up to the first group of Japanese planes.

Kinkaid had Task Force 16 cruising at 4:40 p.m. on a heading of 80° and then changed course to 170° one minute later. Radar warnings of approaching Japanese planes had the ships in a state of readiness to repel an air attack. Task Force 16 was now in a circular antiaircraft defense formation with the *Enterprise* in its center. The heavy cruiser *Portland* was off the carrier's port quarter while the cruiser *Atlanta* was to its starboard quarter and the battleship *North Carolina* to its stern. Kinkaid then ordered the formation to increase speed to 27 knots, the *North Carolina*'s maximum speed. American fighters flying CAP along with three SBDs flying IAP filled the skies above Task Force 16. More aircraft were returning, and the flight deck crew worked arduously to clear the carrier's decks for action when the Japanese planes arrived. With all the protection covering Task Force 16, it would seem that the Japanese could never breach such a seemingly impregnable defense. But that source of confidence would prove to be illusory.

Even after more than nine months of the Pacific War, poor radio discipline among American naval air crews was still a severe problem and proved to be a hindrance in organizing an air defense. The *Enterprise's* regular FDO, Lt. Cmdr. Leonard J. Dow, was not a happy man as he tried in vain to defend against the oncoming Japanese attack. The messages between aircraft of the CAP were too long and that prevented the FDO's orders being heard because of the jammed frequencies. More misfortune would befall the *Enterprise* this day.

The carrier's fire control radar then stopped working. Her gunners had to rely on their own senses or eye sightings by fire control personnel. The lookouts had to look into a setting sun for the Japanese planes and could not see them. A destroyer's lookout saw the sun's reflection off a Japanese plane's wing. First Sergeant Joseph R. Schinka, commanding a 20-mm battery on the *Enterprise*'s port side, saw a puff of smoke at 4:40 p.m. and a Japanese bomber heading for the carrier. He shouted for his battery to open fire and tracer bullets pierced the sky. The carrier's five-inch guns added to the din of fire and smoke. The *Atlanta*'s five-inchers fired a massive salvo; the cacophony was now approaching a fever pitch. The battleship *North Carolina* also opened up with continuous fire so that Lt. (jg) Frederick Mears remembered, "The battleship accompanying our carrier lit up like a Christmas tree. Black and white puffs of smoke covered the late afternoon sky."[9]

One minute later, Seki's leading plane was beginning its dive when an impulsive Ens. John B. McDonald broke from his formation and went after it. With AA shells exploding around his fighter, McDonald was on the bomber's tail as both planes passed through 8,000 feet. With the American fighter close behind, Seki released his 250-kilogram bomb at 1,500 feet just as the *Enterprise* turned to starboard. That maneuver temporarily spared the carrier from any damage as the Japanese bomb splashed and exploded in the sea on the port beam. McDonald claimed he had shot down a Japanese plane, but that proved to be a false assertion. Seki escaped undamaged, but was still aware that American fighters were attacking his bombers in the vain attempt to shoot them down.

Piloted by PO1c Tetsu Imada, the second bomber behind Seki's plane ran into a problem with Harmer. The American pilot also followed Imada down in a steep dive firing his machine guns. The lone gunner in the Japanese plane fired back with his single Lewis 7.7-mm machine gun. Harmer later thought he had killed the gunner and shot down the bomber. But as was the case with Seki, Imada dropped his bomb and missed the carrier; he then escaped while following Seki as both planes headed home just above the water's surface.

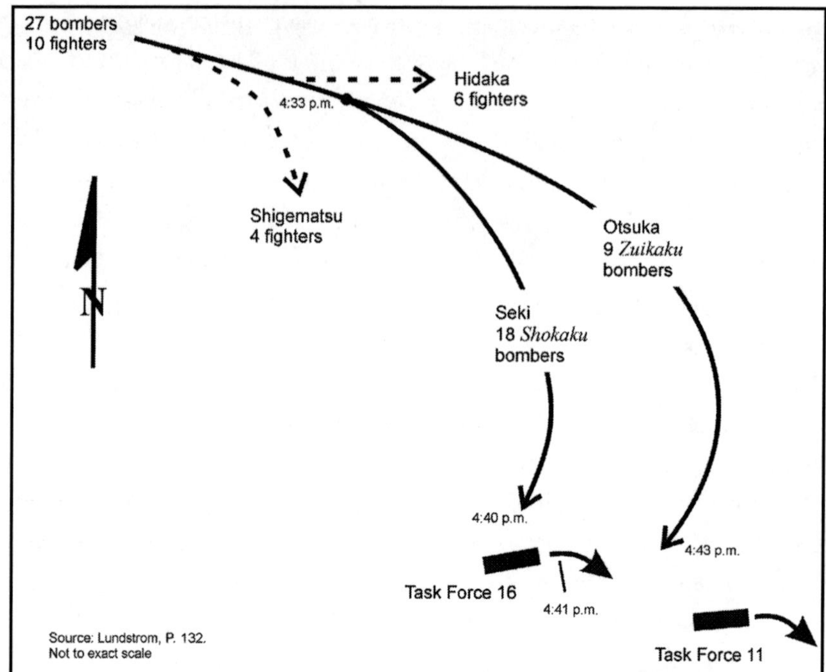

Seki's Bombers Attack Task Force 16

PO1c Mitsuo Sasaki's plane unfortunately did not share the same luck as his two colleagues. Lt. Howard W. Crews followed Sasaki's plane as it dove toward the *Enterprise* and fired a burst into the Japanese plane. He watched the bullets rip through the plane's fuselage and wings. Crews fired another two-second fusillade. The bullets blasted into the Japanese bomber's engine and cowling. Antiaircraft fire swarmed all around the two planes. Sasaki released his bomb and, like his predecessors, missed the carrier by hitting the water with a giant splash 200 yards off the carrier's port quarter. The Japanese plane was now spinning in flames and smacked the water 600 yards from the *Enterprise*'s port beam.

Nevertheless, the American fighters had affected the Japanese bombing attack led by the first three planes in Seki's formation. Four Vals, flown by Lt. Kazuo Yoshimoto, PO1c Fumio Someno, PO3c Hirokichi Tanaka, and Ens. Chiaki Saito, started their diving attack at 4:42 p.m. toward the *Enterprise*'s port beam and quarter. No American fighters interfered with their attack as the four Japanese planes dove toward their target. Again, their bombs missed and made "dirty, brown circles" in the water. But they did inflict some damage to Task Force 16. As they flew along the water's surface, their path took them over the destroyer *Grayson* as they fired machine gun bullets into the ship.

While Seki's leading bombers were diving and the *Enterprise* underwent their ordeal, four F4Fs intercepted nine Japanese dive-bombers led by Lt. Keiichi Arima that trailed the first nine Vals. Each bomber seemed to be taking turns in their attacks. "OK, let's go give them hell," broadcasted over the American fighters' radios at 4:40 p.m., and the four American fighters divided their attacks. Barnes and Ens. Robert A.M. Dibb moved to the back of the first group of three bombers. Now flying at 14,000 feet, Dibb fired his guns into one bomber. It exploded in flames and plummeted downward. Unfortunately, Barnes' plane took a five-inch shell hit on his own plane. It exploded and killed the American pilot. Some of the destroyer *Balch*'s crew saw a plane, missing its tail and wings, hit the water 2,000 yards from the destroyer's port quarter.

Two Vals, commanded by PO1c Nobuyoshi Yasuda and PO2c Kenze Kitamura, began their dives almost at the same time. Intense AA fire from the ships below ripped into Yasuda's plane and turned it into a burning mass. Brewer's F4F was on the two planes' tails. The destruction of Yasuda's plane forced its pilot, PO2c Goro Shirai, to prematurely release his bomb. It hit the water in a giant column near the *Enterprise*'s starboard bow. Yasuda's flaming plane crashed into the sea 1,000 yards farther away. By now, Brewer was in a position to shoot at Kitamura's plane when its pilot, PO2c Isamu Miki, tried to turn his plane so its gunner could get a good shot at the F4F. Brewer let loose a burst of .50-cal. machine gun fire and filled the Japanese plane with holes. However, he had to pull out of his dive at 4,000 feet because the fire from the ships below was too intense to stay with the diving Japanese plane. Miki, his plane now fatally damaged, still guided it to 2,000 feet and dropped his bomb. It exploded in the water very close to the *Enterprise*'s starboard beam. Miki wanted to crash his plane on the carrier's flight deck, but he could not control it. He zoomed past the carrier's sky control and crashed into the sea on the *Enterprise*'s port side just as the ship was in a sharp starboard turn. Thus far, the Japanese bombers had not touched the big carrier, but that was about to change.

✲ ✲ ✲

After seeing several of his fellow flight crews die trying to hit the carrier, Arima decided to attack as his plane began its dive. His pilot, PO1c Kiyoto Furuta, could hear his commander scream out the altitudes as their plane plummeted toward the big carrier. Furuta increased his plane's dive brakes to slow the plane for a good drop. Remembering his combat experience in China, Arima had never seen such intense AA fire. Shrapnel clattered all over his plane's body at 4:44 p.m., but that did not deter Furuta from releasing his bomb. His aim proved true as the missile was the first to hit the *Enterprise*. The 250-kg semi-armor-piercing bomb punched a hole in the carrier's No. 3 aft elevator on its starboard forward corner. The bomb penetrated to the third deck, exploded in the chief's quarters, and inflicted heavy damage and death.

Following close behind Arima's plane, PO1c Hiroshi Koitabashi's bomber, flown by PO1c Tamotsu Akimoto, a highly experienced and competent flyer, dove through the American antiaircraft fusillade. Koitabashi released his 242-kg high explosive bomb with contact fuses. Thirty seconds after the first bomb hit the carrier, the projectile also hit the No. 3 elevator 11 feet from the starboard edge of the deck. Exploding in a ball of flame and surrounding the starboard aft five-inch gun platform in a giant fire ball, the bomb set fire to the five-inch shells on deck, killed 38 crewmen, and started a fire that endangered the powder magazines below. Exacting some revenge for the damage it had just suffered, the *Enterprise*'s 20-mm gunners set fire to PO2c Yoshihiro Iida's bomber and exploded its bomb. The mortally ravaged plane dove and disintegrated in a ball of flame.

Lt. (jg) Hiroyuki Motoyama's, PO2c Ryoroku Tsuchiya's, and PO2c Kazumi Horie's three planes followed with another attack. A bomb, released by either Motoyama or Tsuchiya, hit the water, exploded close to the carrier's island, and drenched it in sea water. But Horie would have more success. With AA fire repeatedly smacking into his plane, he dropped his 242-kg high explosive bomb; it exploded at 4:46 p.m. on the *Enterprise*'s amidships and tore a 10-foot hole in the flight deck. Now filled with too many holes to stay airborne, Horie's plane and its brave crew crashed into the sea off the carrier's starboard bow.

The *Enterprise* was not the only ship under attack. The *North Carolina* also drew attention from the attacking planes. Warrant Officer Masaki Aragane's three plane group got through the concentrated American AA fire and F4Fs and began attacking the battleship. She had dropped back in Task Force 16's formation because she could not keep up with the *Enterprise*'s rapid turns and frequent speed changes. Her lookouts saw the approaching Japanese bombers at 4:43 p.m. diving at her off the ship's starboard bow. With the two other planes in his formation, commanded by PO3c Shingi Murakami and PO3c Toyojiro Aoki, Aragane moved in closer one minute later. Ens. Douglas M. Johnson's F4F followed the three bombers. All the Vals dropped their bombs; all missed. Hit by either AA fire or shot down by Johnson, one smoking Japanese bomber hit the water 1,500 yards off her starboard quarter. An AA shell hit a second bomber, and it crashed near the *Enterprise*. The third bomber escaped, but was shot down later by the American CAP. Johnson's F4F also took AA hits, but he later landed safely.

Fifteen of the 18 Japanese bombers had attacked the *Enterprise* and three assaulted the *North Carolina*. The senior LSO aboard the *Enterprise*, Lt. Robin M. Lindsey, watched and expressed his admiration for the skill and courage of the Japanese aviators:

> "These Jap planes launched about the most beautiful awe-inspiring attack I have ever seen. It was almost suicidal in fact, they came so low. They used a roll-over approach, a rather shallow dive...about 60 to 55 degrees...came down and released at about a thousand feet and were pulling out at 200 feet."[10]

Seven Japanese bombers and their crews had been destroyed. Although they claimed six hits, only three bombs had hit and heavily damaged the *Enterprise*. The remaining 11 Japanese Vals had a tough time getting away from the now swarming CAP.

The first Japanese attack wave had finished its work but the *Enterprise*'s ordeal had by no means ended. More hell was on the way.[11]

The Trial by Fire Continues

Lt. Otsuka's nine *Zuikaku* bombers pressed their attack at 4:38 p.m. on the *Saratoga* and the rest of Task Force 11. He changed his formation from a nine-plane Vee to three Vees of Vees. American F4Fs diverted his Hidaka-led fighter escort's attention. Otsuka now had no fighter protection but went in for the attack as he started his dive from 16,400 feet. Unlike Seki who had almost no initial opposition, the American CAP took advantage of the situation and swarmed all over the Japanese bombers.

About 10 miles northeast of Task Force 16, three F4Fs moved into position to attack Otsuka's formation. Lt. Hayden M. Jensen saw the Japanese bombers at 4:32 p.m. from 10,000 feet and climbed rapidly to gain altitude so he could attack the oncoming Japanese from above. His group included two F4Fs flown by Ensigns Carlton B. Starkes[12] and John M. Kleinman. As Japanese planes changed their formation from three Vee of Vees to a long, loosely formed column. Jensen attacked one of the wingmen to the lead Japanese plane and shot it down in flames. Using Sergeant Alvin C. York's technique of picking off the last in a flight of turkeys,[13] Jensen then went after the last plane in the line and blasted that unfortunate flight crew from the sky. The Japanese formation began to separate; so Jensen exploited a lone plane and destroyed the next bomber in line. Starkes registered two kills as two Japanese bombers now headed to the sea in flames. Kleinman got two more. Jensen's flight shot down seven planes in all.

The American CAP had more work to do. Four *Saratoga* F4Fs led by Machinist Donald E. Runyon flew with wide-open throttles trying to intercept the Japanese fighters before they could attack the American ships. As Otsuka continued his attack, Runyon's higher speed allowed him to get nearer to the Japanese bomber. Runyon fired his guns thus causing Otsuka to realize that the American fighter defense was far more intense than he had thought, and that he could not reach Task Force 11 as he had originally intended. So he turned sharply to the northeast so he could concentrate his attack on the nearer Task Force 16.

About one minute after Jensen's group attacked, Runyon turned abruptly and dove out of the sun from 20,000 feet, found Otsuka, and sent him down in flames. As he passed Otsuka, Runyon climbed toward the sun, saw another bomber, and scored one more victory. Two Japanese bombers, their crews now believing in the hopelessness of their attack, turned tail and headed north.

After being involved with F4Fs to the north, four Zeroes entered the fray by attacking Jensen's fighters, which by now were strewn all over the sky. Jensen had to skillfully execute a tricky maneuver. A Zero was on his tail, but Starkes claimed a victory believing he flamed the fighter trying to shoot Jensen down. Another Zero was on Kleinman's tail, and he dove to escape from it. A Zero from the *Zuikaku* also was on Runyon's tail as he climbed for a third attack on the Vals. Somehow the Zero leveled off below Runyon; he dove, pressed the stick's trigger, and the Zero disintegrated in a ball of fire. He touched off a third bomber as he descended. A Zero interfered with his firing but got in his guns' sights. It was like shooting fish in a barrel. A short burst from Runyon's guns sent the fighter down in flames and smoke. In just a few minutes of dramatic and hair-raising air-to-air combat, Jensen had destroyed three Vals and one fighter. Quite a haul!

The torment on Otsuka's attack persisted as more F4Fs joined the fracas. One Japanese bomber stubbornly kept flying as three F4Fs attacked it. Lt. Frank O. Green saw this happening, so he seized the opportunity and fired his guns at the recalcitrant bomber; it exploded in flames and smoke and plunged to the sea. The other three F4Fs' pilots claimed it as a victory too.

Despite the furious opposition by the American F4Fs, some of the Vals got close enough to drop their bombs on Task Force 16. The *North Carolina* lookouts spotted six carrier bombers approaching from the battleship's stern. The big ship was now falling farther behind the task force and became more isolated from their protection. But that did not leave it as vulnerable to aircraft attack as some would have thought. She had five-inch guns that could reach farther out than the predominant 20-mm armament on the other ships. Unfortunately, those bigger guns were being aimed forward to try to protect the *Enterprise* and not at the oncoming Japanese planes. The only guns that could defend from the air attack were mostly 20-mm guns with limited range. Thus, four Japanese planes attacked at 4:46 p.m. one after another and dropped four bombs at the battleship. Columns of white water surrounded the battleship—no damage at all. The planes tried to escape, but met their deaths from the American CAP.

Meanwhile, Ens. Dibb was the only F4F left in the CAP with the rest of his mates locked into battle with Zeroes and attacking Vals. He flew high above the *Enterprise* at 12,000 feet while deftly trying to avoid the black puffs from exploding shells being fired by the ships below him. Suddenly, a Zero passed overhead, and he moved onto its tail. He pressed the fighter's trigger and fired a short burst at the Japanese fighter, but missed. The Vals now had a clear path toward their target.

PO2c Goichi Koretsune, flying one of three Vals but separated from the rest of his section, at 4:46 p.m. dove at what he saw as the "rear carrier," dropped his bomb, but missed the target. Two Vals that had accompanied the now dead Otsuka flew in a two-plane formation. They were flown by PO1c Sakuo Igata and Sea1c Okawa Toyonobu and commanded by PO1c Kota Shirakura and PO2c Hiroshi Maeno respectively. These two planes might have been the two Vals that Runyon had forced to break away earlier. They moved southwest past Task Force 16 and then turned around and headed straight for the *Enterprise*'s starboard quarter. As if they heard each other's thoughts, the two planes started their attacking dive at 4:47 p.m. while the carrier started a hard port turn. Ens. Charles E. Eichenberger got onto Shirakura's tail at 12,000 feet and followed him all the way down to 4,000 but failed to stop his bombing run. Shirakura reached the point for launching his bomb and released it. Later, Eichenberger saw his plane crash in the water.

Lt. Lindsey watched from the Landing Signal Platform next to the *Enterprise*'s flight deck and remembered what the sight of that 250-kg bomb meant to him:

> "It is really horrifying to watch the Jap dive-bombers come down, because you felt rather helpless, especially about the next to the last plane [that] came down, and I would just see my name written on the nose of that bomb. It looked like it was coming to light right in my lap...It fell a little short of my Landing Signal Platform, just missed the ramp by about a foot and went into the water underneath the Landing Signal Platform and caved in the side of the ship...Although it did not puncture the hull [it] sent up a column of water so hard it blew up the deck about two feet."[14]

Maeno's attack was not as successful because his bomb exploded in the water 300 yards to the carrier's port side.

With a Zero still on his F4F's tail, Dibb saw Shirakura's Val fly clear of the *Enterprise* and jumped at the chance to wreak some revenge. The Japanese plane was now flying toward the *Grayson* when Dibb loosed a fusillade of machine gun fire. Shirakura's Val suddenly trailed a streak of black smoke and crashed into the water. Dibb turned and pursued another Val, but that plane executed a tight turn and got away. He had exhausted his ammunition and had a damaged gun mount. Running out of options, he left the area and got out of harm's way.

Maeno also saw Shirakura's plane hit the water and, with his bomb gone, also flew away. He would later claim hits on a carrier. But the attack on Task Force 16 was a costly one for the Japanese flyers. Twenty-seven Vals had entered the fray; seven attacked the *North Carolina*; 18 assaulted the *Enterprise*; and two had been lost before the attack began. They had lost 10 Vals up to this time while losing two Zeroes. As they tried to escape to their home carriers, their losses mounted when the American CAP retaliated.[15]

✲ ✲ ✲

Now that their attack on Task Force 16 had ended, the surviving 17 Vals and eight Zeroes tried to get home; however, powerful formations of F4Fs and SBDs blocked their way.

It was not an easy journey for the Japanese air crews. By the time the planes reached their home carriers, seven more Vals and two more Zeroes went down. Out of the original 27 carrier bombers and 10 Zeroes that took off from the *Shokaku* and *Zuikaku*, only nine Vals and four Zeroes survived the assault on Task Force 61. Seki, the strike leader, also survived, but Otsuka, the leader of the second wave, did not. All nine Zeroes sent out in the second wave returned safely, but five Vals did not.[16]

Their mission had ended in failure. While they had inflicted heavy damage on the *Enterprise*, Task Force 61's carriers continued flight operations and operated in the waters off Guadalcanal. Nevertheless, the *Enterprise* had some problems of its own.[17]

Fighting for Survival

Lt. Cmdr. Frederick J. Bell, aboard the destroyer *Grayson*, sarcastically stated that "a lull in the action—is what every respectable battle is supposed to have."[18] The Japanese attack on Task Force 16 had ended, but that was no consolation to the crew of the *Enterprise*. She had been hit hard. Fires now roiled on deck and below decks as well. The U.S. Navy's damage control parties had previously shown how good they were at Midway on the *Yorktown* and at Pearl Harbor when they prevented several battleships from being destroyed. The skills of the *Enterprise*'s damage control parties under the command of Lt. Cmdr. Herschel A. Smith would be severely tested to save her.

In just minutes after the last Japanese plane had left the battle, carpenters, ship fitters, electricians, and ordinary seamen rushed from below decks to quench the fires on the flight deck. Their skill stopped the fires and patched holes on the flight deck. *Enterprise* could now resume flight operations.

The rapid response of the Navy corpsmen caring for the 99 wounded saved all but four of them. They also recovered the remains of the 71 men who had given their last full measure of devotion. The devastating damage on deck particularly at the five-inch gun platform destroyed by a Japanese bomb left an indelible impression on an *Enterprise* pilot:

> "Sailors' bodies were still in the gun gallery. Most of the men died from the concussion and then were roasted. The majority of the bodies were in one piece. They were blackened but not burned or withered, and they looked like iron statues of men, their limbs smooth and whole, their heads rounded with no hair. The faces were indistinguishable, but in almost every case the lips were drawn back in a wizened grin giving them the expression of rodents.
>
> The postures seemed either strangely normal or frankly grotesque. One gun pointer was still in his seat leaning on his sight with one arm. He looked as though a sculptor had created him. His body was nicely proportioned, the buttocks were rounded, and there was no hair anywhere. Other iron men were lying outstretched, face up or down. Two or three lying face up were shielding themselves with their arms bent at the elbows and their hands before their faces. One, who was not burned so badly, had his chest thrown out, his head way back, and his hands clenched.

> The blackened bodies did not appear as shocking as those only partially roasted. They looked more human in their distortion."[19]

By 5:46 p.m., just one hour after the last Japanese bomb had hit her, the *Enterprise*'s flight operations resumed. With fuel critically short, her planes that had been flying CAP and those returning from their attack missions needed to be recovered. That retrieval immediately commenced.

But the carrier's problems continued at 6:21 p.m. when the effects from the continuous bomb hits caused her steering to cease functioning. The carrier had two electrical motors that controlled her steering installed in a compartment below decks occupied by the seven men who operated them. One was a primary motor; the other was its backup. After bombs had exploded nearby, the men in the compartment closed off all ventilation to prevent fire and smoke from entering the room. However, the room's temperature rapidly rose to more than 170° F. A remotely controlled ventilation control accidentally opened a ceiling vent to the room. Water flooded the compartment and shorted out the motor that controlled the ship's rudder. All seven men immediately lost consciousness before they could switch the steering control to the backup motor. With her rudder jammed hard to starboard, she now uncontrollably steamed in a circle, endangering the rest of Task Force 16's formation and almost hitting the destroyer *Balch*. Trying to bring the big ship under control, Capt. Arthur C. Davis ordered the ship's speed reduced to 10 knots.

It was time for someone to take charge, and one man did. Chief Machinist William A. Smith commanded the detail responsible for the ship's steering gear. By this time, the steering gear compartment's temperature had reached oven-hot levels. He put on a specially modified breathing device, attached a safety line, and stepped into the cauldron. The blast furnace-like heat overcame him two times, and he had to be extracted each time. The third time was the charm. He reentered the compartment and switched the control to the backup motor. The *Enterprise* was again cruising under full control at two minutes before seven o'clock.

But the *Enterprise* was not out of danger yet. The ship's radar screen picked up a blip showing several bogeys coming in on a 265° bearing just 50 miles distant. These were Lt. Takahashi's second wave of 27 Vals and nine Zeroes expecting to find the American carriers at about 6:00 p.m., and he was early when the radar found his planes at 4:51 p.m. Despite the *Chikuma*'s search plane reporting seeing the American carriers, Takahashi never received the sighting report and did not find Task Force 61. By 5:43 p.m., he reached the place where he expected to find the carriers, but by this time they were 83 miles to his north.

One can just imagine what would have happened if these planes had appeared over the damaged *Enterprise* with her damage control crews fighting to save the ship and the American CAP in nearly complete disarray. The *Enterprise* again proved that she was a lucky ship, and she would again show what that meant to its adversaries.[20]

CHAPTER 21
Counterattack!

When the Japanese attacked Task Force 61, three American air strikes left to attack Nagumo's carriers. The first group from the *Saratoga* included five TBFs led by Lt. Harold H. Larsen and two SBDs commanded by Lt. (jg) Robert M. Elder. Larsen's and Elder's planes departed at different times and rendezvoused at 5:10 p.m. Elder led the combined force as his fighter climbed to 9,000 feet while Larson's bombers flew 2,000 feet below. Fifteen minutes later, they arrived over where they were led to believe the Japanese carriers ought to be. Peering from the cockpit of his plane, Larsen saw nothing. It did not help that heavy clouds severely inhibited visibility. Larsen fortunately ordered his planes to search northward. Twenty-five minutes after they joined up, Vadm. Kondo's Advance Force spread out below them: four heavy cruisers, six light cruisers, and eight destroyers moved at about 15 to 20 knots through the water on a course of 150º. Small tails of white water from the wakes trailed behind each ship. Larsen ordered an immediate attack.

The lookouts on the seaplane carrier *Chitose* saw the American planes, and an alarm immediately sounded on the seaplane carrier. Her skipper, Capt. Seigo Sasaki, ordered three Petes to force what seemed to be two American SBDs to leave.

Larsen's TBFs lined up at 5:40 p.m. for a torpedo attack on the heavy cruisers' port side and dropped their torpedoes. The American pilots believed they scored one hit; like most other overly optimistic combat reports from aviators, they exaggerated their accomplishments. All four of Kondo's heavy cruisers escaped without a scratch.

Elder and Ens. Robert M. Gordon flew their SBDs at 12,500 feet above the clouds, which made it difficult to see Kondo's ships. But they did spy what they originally thought was a battleship. It was actually the *Chitose*. The two dive-bombers dove at high speed toward the ship and dropped their bombs. The two missiles exploded in the water near the carrier's port side. Although the bombs did not directly hit the carrier, the explosions in the water were close enough to severely damage the carrier and destroy three Petes. Sasaki had no choice but to leave for repairs at Truk.

Hoping to justify again their usefulness as high level bombers against naval vessels moving in the water, four B-17 bombers from Col. LaVerne G. Sanders' 11th Bombing Group commanded by Maj. J. Allan Sewart left Espiritu Santo at 1:05 p.m. and headed for where they believed the Japanese fleet was. Four hours and 45 minutes later, they saw Kondo's force, which was now about 30 miles south of Nagumo's carriers. They dropped some of their bombs, missed the destroyer *Maikaze* and continued northward. It was not long when they saw the Japanese carriers and started their bombing runs. But waiting for them were three Zeroes from the *Shokaku* flown by PO1c Tsuguo Ogihara,

PO2c Masao Sasakibara, and PO1c Masao Taniguchi. The Zeroes attacked the bombers, but failed to inflict any damage while only receiving a few minor hits. Sewart claimed hits on a carrier, but that too proved solely to be in his imagination.

✲ ✲ ✲

Flying westward and looking for the *Ryujo* where Jett had earlier reported her position, Caldwell's 11 SBDs did not meet up with Konig's six TBFs[1]. Leslie, the strike leader, was still the "tail-end Charlie." By the time they arrived over the burning Japanese light carrier, it was clear that their mission was superfluous, so the American planes turned around and headed home.

Konig's TBFs were now 275 miles from the *Enterprise* when they saw what appeared to be ships' wakes. Closer examination showed the "wakes" to be actually coming from the Roncador Reef's islets north of Santa Isabel. He ordered his planes to release their torpedoes and fly for home, but not to Henderson Field. He had never received any orders to fly there, so he ordered his planes to return to the *Enterprise*. Frustrated by finding nothing, Caldwell did not waver about flying to the safety of Henderson Field. When they arrived there, they were indeed a welcome addition to CACTUS. Leslie headed back to the *Enterprise*.[2]

✲ ✲ ✲

The carrier battles had ended, and it was time for each side to recover aircraft returning from their missions. The heavily damaged *Enterprise* headed south at 7:19 p.m. at a speed of 25 knots. Meanwhile, the unscathed *Saratoga* continued heading into the wind on a southeasterly course. Larsen's three TBFs and Elder's two SBDs arrived at 7:30 p.m., and their flight crews soon were comfortably aboard the *Saratoga*.

The *Enterprise*'s surprised crew sighted Konig's six TBFs above her at 9:28 p.m. These planes should have been heading for Henderson Field but here they were. The planes had lost their way in the dark but the navigational skills of ARM2c David H. Lane, Konig's radioman, found the carrier's homing beacon. It was now pitch black, so Kinkaid ordered the carrier's truck lights illuminated to help the pilots find their way. One TBF landed safely. Another flown by Ens. Edward B. Holley was not as fortunate. It smashed into a crane to the rear of the island. The plane's crew got out safely but its debris now was all over the flight deck, rendering it unusable until the wreckage could be removed. Thus, the remaining four TBFs had to land on the *Saratoga*. Max Leslie landed safely at 11:03 p.m. on the *Saratoga*. With all flight operations completed, Task Force 11 followed Task Force 16 south.

Fletcher still had the nagging reminder that the Japanese carriers were still to the north of Task Force 61, but his weakened force was not capable of going after them. The *Enterprise* had to get to a safe port for repairs. Task Force 16 and the rest of Task Force 11 had to refuel before joining Noyes' Task Force 18 with the carrier *Wasp*. Although the Japanese carriers had to recover their aircraft, Fletcher did not know where they were and would have to launch another search to find them. But it was now dark, and such a search could not be launched until daylight. He had no choice but to withdraw and reassemble his force.

Like their American counterparts, Japanese naval aviators also had to cope with the dangers of landing in the dark. The *Shokaku* began recovering her aircraft at 6:35 p.m., and ten CAP Zeroes made safe landings by 6:50 p.m. on the carrier. Unfortunately, PO3c Yoshihide Ishizawa's Zero ran out fuel before he could land on the carrier, and he had to ditch his plane in the water.

Ten minutes later, planes from Seki's strike force began appearing over the *Shokaku* and *Zuikaku*. Because the carriers had moved from their last reported position, the planes had severe problems locating them. One Val and one Zero had to land near Abe's Vanguard Force, located 60 miles from Nagumo's carriers. Fortunately, the cruiser *Chikuma* picked the crews out of the water. At the same time, the *Shokaku* recovered eight bombers, two of Shigematsu's fighters, four CAP fighters, and two *Zuikaku* Zeroes. Arima's damaged Zero landed and taxied to a stop just as its fuel tanks drained dry.

PO3c Sadamu Komachi tried in vain to find the *Shokaku*, but his Zero exhausted its fuel tanks. His spirits lifted when he saw two destroyers nearby. He felt he could make a water landing and have a good chance of being picked up, but the destroyer skippers did not have time to recover just one pilot and vanished over the horizon. Now alone in the water, he drifted for eight hours wearing just his life jacket. When a group of destroyers mercifully appeared, one ship saw him by shining a searchlight on the water as he desperately tried hailing it by waving his arms. That ship picked him up and saved his life.

PO2c Goichi Koretsune had problems with his Val's radio and never tried to reach his homebase on the *Zuikaku*. So his pilot, PO2c Yukio Hikiune, found the nearest island, Malaita, and gently landed the out-of-fuel plane in the water. Rescued by some Japanese coastwatchers, Koretsune and Hikiune lived until the U S. Marines destroyed that small group of Japanese on November 5. The Marines found Koretsune's diary describing his and his pilot's ordeal.

The *Shokaku* retrieved its last three CAP Zeroes at 8:00 p.m. while four more Zeroes orbited the *Zuikaku* in the dark. Nagumo radioed Yamamoto and Kondo that he was taking his carriers northward after he finished recovering his aircraft. Disagreeing with Nagumo's order, Masafumi Arima, the *Shokaku*'s captain, argued for another strike, but that squabble proved to be moot when Kondo radioed orders five minutes later reasoning that another attack was out of the question. The American carriers had withdrawn 25 miles southward and were too far away to try a night surface battle. Nagumo had interviewed Seki and learned that one American carrier had been hit three times and another hit two times. So Kondo's Advanced Force and Abe's Vanguard Force would head south and try to find the supposedly crippled American carriers only until midnight. If they were not found by then, they would turn around and head northward to refuel.

Meanwhile, the unsuccessful second strike flew over the Japanese carriers, trying to find a place to land. At 8:15 p.m., 16 of Takahashi's Vals, six of Lt. Ayao Shirane's Zeroes, and the *Zuikaku*'s remaining four CAP Zeroes landed on the carrier. PO2c Hisao Matsushita's Val never returned while the destroyer *Amatsukaze* plucked another crew from the water. The *Shokaku* recovered her second strike's three Zeroes and three Vals. Six other Vals also did not return. At 10:15 p.m., Nagumo turned on his search lights so he could land three more Vals while another three Vals failed to come back. Thus, the second strike lost four Vals, three never returning and one ditched in the water. The Japanese strike groups that Nagumo sent out to attack Task Force 61 lost the following aircraft:[3]

Japanese Strike Group Losses

Strike/Wave	Bombers	Fighters	Total
First	19	6	25
Second	11	0	11
Totals	30	6	36

Kondo's ships never found any American ships by the midnight deadline, so he turned his force around as planned. Both the American and Japanese fleets left the combat area to fight another day. But the Battle of the Eastern Solomons was not over. The Japanese's original objective had not yet been decided. Adm. Tanaka's Invasion Force still had its own mission to carry out.

CACTUS Strikes Back

With the early morning hours of August 25 approaching, the destroyers *Mutsuki, Yayoi, Kagero, Kawakaze,* and *Isokaze* from Tanaka's force arrived off Lunga Point to inflict havoc on the Marines. The Americans on Guadalcanal did not have a good night's sleep while Tanaka's soldiers rested well on their ships. The destroyers' bombardment did little damage, but certainly did not endear them to the Marines by keeping them awake that night. Bombs from the *Chokai, Kinugasa,* and *Yura* float planes added to the Americans' lack of sleep when they dropped daisy-cutter bombs on the angry men. The Marines' moment of revenge would soon come.

Tanaka's Transport force had escaped any attacks while his compatriots in the *Kido Butai* were not as fortunate. He personally had seen a huge column of smoke to the southeast that he later found out to be the death knell of the light carrier *Ryujo*. The five destroyers had rejoined his force by 6:00 a.m., so he was again at full strength. He was 150 miles from Guadalcanal. But about two hours later, his thus-far peaceful albeit erratic journey suddenly worsened when American aircraft suddenly appeared in the skies above. He and his men were not prepared for what was to come.

The night of August 24/25 was also a busy one for the air and ground crews at Henderson Field. After the Japanese finished shelling the Marines, the flyers at Henderson Field decided to let the Japanese know they would not let them get away with their harassment of them. A bright moon let eight SBDs take off at 3:00 a.m. without any artificial light. They were over the Japanese destroyers almost right away when they dropped their bombs. They hit nothing and returned to Henderson Field to refuel and rearm for the morning's missions.

They were ready to go at 6:00 a.m. when Lt. Col. Mangrum led five Marine and three Navy SBDs with an escort of ten F4Fs led by Maj. Smith lifted off. The fighters did not have their belly tanks so they could not stay with the SBDs for long. They flew toward the *Ryujo* group's last reported position about 180 miles north of Guadalcanal, but the Japanese ships were nowhere to be found since the *Ryujo* had sunk, and her escorts had left that location. Smith's fighters had to return to Henderson Field because of low fuel supplies. Mangrum's SBDs were on their own.

When Mangrum's bombers flew north of Malaita, they ran into WO Tomosaburo Fujiwara's Kawanishi Type 97 ("Mavis") flying boat on the 107° line from Shortland. Capt. Rivers J. Morrell and 2nd Lt. Cloyd R. Jeans jumped the big seaplane, riddled it with many machine-gun holes, and both claimed a victory. Fujiwara successfully landed the well-holed aircraft and ran it aground. It sank from the damage inflicted by the two American pilots, and one of his crewmen died of wounds. The pilots' claims proved to be valid this time.

Mangrum's SBDs turned to the west and flew 50 miles when they finally found Tanaka's convoy. First Lt. Lawrence Baldinus dove his plane at 8:05 a.m. and dropped his 1,000-pound bomb on the *Jintsu*. It hit on the hapless light cruiser's forward section with a terrible explosion. Other bombs hit the water and huge water columns surrounded the ship. Another bomb detonated between the two forward six-inch turrets in a ball of fire and a hail of metal splinters, heavily damaging and wreaking chaos on the bridge. The explosions knocked Tanaka unconscious, but he amazingly woke up uninjured. For some unknown reason, the heavily damaged cruiser did not list. The ship's damage control crew brought order by flooding the forward magazine, putting out the many fires spreading all over her, and saved the cruiser from sinking. The engines were still operational, and she could still steer. However, she could not run at high speed because of the heavy damage and could no longer operate as Tanaka's flagship. But the American air attacks did not confine their attack to just the warships.

Carrying 1,000 troops, the transport *Kinryu Maru* got the undivided attention of Ens. Christian Fink at 8:07 a.m. when he dropped his bomb. It exploded and set the ship afire. The fire spread to the cargo hold and caused the ammunition supplies stored there to explode. She stopped in the water and was about to go under. Seeing this happening to one of his charges, Tanaka ordered three destroyers and two patrol boats to rescue whatever soldiers could get off. He also ordered the rest of his ships to turn around and head north at their fastest possible speed.

He transferred his flag to the destroyer *Kagero* and sent the *Jintsu* to Truk for repairs. The cruiser was able to steam at 12 knots, but his force's torment was not yet over. Capt. Walter E. Chambers' three B-17s suddenly came into view and unloaded their entire bomb loads. The destroyer *Mutsuki* was alongside the burning *Kinryu Maru* trying to get the troops off the doomed ship. Several bombs exploded on the hapless destroyer, and she sank like a stone. The *Yayoi* rescued her crew while the two patrol boats continued rescuing men from the troopship, which soon sank.

As his planes turned to head back to Henderson Field, Mangrum learned that his bomb had not yet been released. He did not want it to go to waste, so he turned his SBD around to make it count. He saw the *Boston Maru* and dove to attack it. He dropped his bomb; it landed near the transport's stern and did no damage—so much for the divergence between wanting and getting.

Tanaka was never optimistic about his mission's prospects, and now saw his most pessimistic expectations come to fruition. His mission was a failure. The 300 Japanese soldiers would do no good on Guadalcanal even if he could get them there. He had lost one destroyer and one troop transport. His flagship was a wreck heading back to its base for substantial repairs. He headed northward to Shortland Island.

Whatever Japanese soldiers remained on Guadalcanal were at the total mercy of the American Marines, which appeared to be getting stronger as time passed. The Japanese carrier and battle fleets were also in retreat. From now on, the only way the Japanese could reinforce their garrison on Guadalcanal would be to send them aboard warships and drop them off at night. The nightly runs by the Japanese trying to supply their Guadalcanal garrison and land reinforcements was about to begin. The Tokyo Express was born.[4]

CHAPTER 22
Trouble Ahead

The Battle of the Eastern Solomons, the third carrier battle of the World War II Pacific War, had the same result as its predecessors at Coral Sea and Midway: an American strategic victory and a defeat for the Japanese. Despite the power of the Imperial Japanese Navy, it failed to achieve its primary mission: landing supplies and reinforcements for the Japanese garrison on Guadalcanal. After its defeat, the high command of the Imperial Japanese Navy began to reassess their prospects in the Solomon Islands. It was not positive.

Japanese Thoughts after the Battle

Adm. Ugaki, Yamamoto's chief of staff, was aboard the battleship *Yamato* with his superior during the battle. He reflected upon the loss of light carrier *Ryujo* in his diary and offers his reasons for the ship's loss:

1. The Americans knew the *Ryujo* and the Landing Force were on the way to Guadalcanal the day before the Americans attacked them.
2. When the Japanese knew the location of Task Force 61, Ugaki renewed his optimism that his long-cherished objective of an all-out, winner-take-all battle with the American carriers was still possible.[1]
3. The Imperial Japanese Navy should have defeated the U.S. Navy but it did not. Based on my [Ugaki's] observation, it seems the Japanese objectives were not properly synchronized. What were they? Land reinforcements on Guadalcanal or defeat the American Navy with the long-cherished dream of having that climactic sea battle? It seems to me that these objectives did not complement each other very well.
4. The causes for failure to achieve victory were:
    a. They depended too much on flying boats so that the American carriers had not been found by the morning of the 24th.
    b. When the search planes found the American carriers, that message did not reach Nagumo in a timely manner.

c. While the two attack waves left quickly, only the first wave found the Americans because of the faulty reconnaissance.

d. Japanese search planes did not stay with the American carriers. Therefore, Kondo's force could not find the Americans in time to engage in a night surface battle.

e. American aircraft concentrated on the *Ryujo* while the Japanese aircraft attacked Henderson Field.

Therefore, there was no CAP to protect the light carrier.

Tanaka's failure to land supplies and reinforcements demonstrated that landing troops using slow transports showed that these ships were highly vulnerable to air attacks. The Japanese changed their tactics toward using fast destroyers to carry out that mission. These operations could be conducted at night, rendering them less vulnerable to air attacks.

It was also clear the Japanese vastly underestimated the strength of the American aircraft on Guadalcanal. So the Japanese's priorities shifted to launching attacks on Henderson Field to destroy the American control of the air over the waters surrounding Guadalcanal. This shift in tactics forced the Japanese to recognize that the struggle to recapture Guadalcanal could not end quickly and had become a prolonged battle of attrition. The Japanese were now at a serious tactical disadvantage since they were not prepared for a long battle. The strategy of their armed forces had been configured to win quick victories and not to engage the Americans over a long period. Japanese morale sank to a new low.[2]

The substantial Japanese losses included the light carrier *Ryujo*, the destroyer *Mutsuki*, and the transport *Kinryu Maru*. The light cruiser *Jintsu* sustained heavy damage and had to steam to Truk for repairs. No accurate count exists for losses of Japanese sailors, but it can be assumed that those were most likely greater than for the Americans. The aircraft losses totaled 75, which included 33 Zeroes, 23 Vals, eight Kates, seven float planes, two Emilys, one Betty, and one Mavis. But the losses of valuable air crews were even more serious. Twenty-one Zero pilots survived, but the Japanese only recovered the crews of one Val, three Kates, and several men from the Mavis.

Yamamoto turned his attention on the New Guinea and the Bismarck Archipelago campaigns and left Nagumo and Kondo to their own devices. The strategy for what the Japanese called the Second Battle of the Solomons was, at best, loosely conceived and, at worst, lacked any significant coordination with Tanaka's mission. It seemed that there were two separate campaigns: Nagumo pursuing the American carriers and Tanaka landing supplies and troops on Guadalcanal. This lack of detailed, contingency planning began after Pearl Harbor and worsened starting with Coral Sea. It was almost like, "Let's send up our planes, find the American carriers and, if we're lucky, sink them. And, by the way, Tanaka, land those troops, but don't expect much help from our carriers." Perhaps, Yamamoto was not as formidable as he had seemed after Pearl Harbor.[3]

The Americans Have Their Own Catharsis

Adm. King was never happy with Fletcher's performance during his tour of duty commanding the American carriers. When Nimitz wanted to promote Fletcher to vice admiral, King initially resisted, but relented when he realized that Fletcher needed to be promoted to be able to command such a powerful force. Nimitz had been one of Fletcher's strongest supporters, and his opinion of Fletcher remained high.

The *Wasp* with Noyes in command refueled and rejoined Task Force 61 on August 25. Nimitz sent Rear Adm. George D. Murray's Task Force 17 with the *Hornet* to join the *Wasp*. Murray arrived on scene four days later.

But fortune would not shine on the U.S. Navy in the near future. Cmdr. Minoru Yokota's *I-26* got within ten yards of the destroyer *MacDonough* on August 31 at 7:41 a.m., dodged her depth charge attack, fired a torpedo at the *Saratoga*, and hit her. The missile hit the carrier just to the rear of the carrier island on the starboard side and wounded 12 sailors. Fletcher was one of those. Lt. Howard W. Crews remembered that he was playing cards in the ready room, as he wrote in his remembrances: "Our game terminated with a dull thud and the ship heaved a couple of times like some old antiquated street car lurching along an equally old track." Lt. Frank O. Green recalled that the carrier "went into a fit and fairly lifted itself out of the water and then shook itself good." The *Saratoga* was now dead in the water. She developed a four-degree starboard list as seawater rushed into two fire rooms. Nevertheless, she resumed flight operations by 8:36 a.m. when she turned into the wind and her engines stopped again. The heavy cruiser *Minneapolis* sent over a tow line and the carrier was again underway four hours later. Her crew restored power by 4:37 p.m., but she was no longer combat-ready.

Just like the *Enterprise*, the *Saratoga* also had to head back to Pearl Harbor for repairs. Fletcher sustained slight wounds so, after receiving the rare order from Ghormley asserting his command to proceed to Pearl Harbor, he arrived there with the *Saratoga* for rest and rehabilitation. Fletcher's record cannot be considered as stellar since the Japanese had sunk two carriers under his command, the *Lexington* at Coral Sea and the *Yorktown* at Midway and damaged two others. American carrier strength in the Pacific was down to just two going into the month of September 1942.

Some argued Fletcher's combat record had a stretch of bad luck while others in the U.S. Navy began to question Fletcher's fitness to command carrier forces. Nimitz was still not one of those. After relieving Fletcher of his command, Nimitz sent Fletcher back to Washington for temporary duty to give King a chance to further evaluate him.

Nimitz looked at his fleet's condition in the Solomons and concluded that the two remaining carriers could not be risked for the second and third stages of the campaign to take Rabaul. He recorded in his diary, "There are too many other tasks ahead for our all-too-few carriers to allow them to be subjected to almost certain damage and destruction in an effort to accomplish a task which can be accomplished by other means."[4]

After Fletcher arrived in Pearl Harbor, he prepared a report, dated September 24, 1942, outlining the lessons learned from his command in the first three carrier battles of the war. Of all the American senior naval commanders, Fletcher had the most combat experience in this new form of naval warfare up to that time, despite not being a naval aviator. He had commanded the attempt to relieve Wake Island and was the senior commander at Coral Sea, Midway, and the Eastern Solomons. Therefore, his perspective offered unique observations.

Nimitz forwarded Fletcher's letter to Halsey who generally agreed with Fletcher's conclusions. However, two of Fletcher's opinions added new controversies to the discussions. The first source of disagreement was with Fletcher's tactics when he advocated carriers should turn away from oncoming air attacks. Halsey disagreed with this ploy by asserting that no carrier had the speed to get away from any air attack.

Fletcher's second recommendation that carrier task forces should operate in tandem and close to each other so that they could organize a more effective air defense raised even greater, intense arguments. The Navy's carrier experts immediately reacted negatively to that suggestion. Capt. Arthur C. Davis, the *Enterprise* skipper, wrote in his report about his ship's operation in the Battle of the Eastern Solomons that coordinating two carrier groups' combat movements was dangerously, if not inconveniently, cumbersome. He argued that the groups should be kept 15 to 20 miles apart and reinforced that claim by stating the *Saratoga* escaped damage from attacking Japanese aircraft because he could maneuver independently from the rest of Task Force 61. Adm. Kinkaid, the commander of the *Enterprise*'s Task Force 16, agreed with Davis' arguments. Fletcher countered these contentions with the argument that Task Force 61's CAP kept Japanese aircraft from attacking the *Saratoga* and not the distance between the task forces.

Fletcher was right in that regard. Powerful, concentrated air power was the best protection against air attacks instead of the separation of task forces. In that regard, Fletcher showed greater insight since future carrier battles would be decided by the amount of air power a carrier task force could put into the air.

Halsey stated that Fletcher's idea of concentrating carriers in a small area was dangerous. He wanted to scatter carriers over a wide area while having carrier task forces tactically coordinated until enemy forces detected the task forces' presence. Halsey argued that the distance between carriers should be twice the visible range so that attacking aircraft could only see one carrier at a time. One factor Halsey did not mention was the difficulty of coordinating air defenses while being under radio silence or when there were problems with poor communications, either by failing equipment or bad atmospheric conditions.

As it turned out, neither admiral's arguments would prove to be valid in the next carrier battle in the Solomons on October 26, the Battle of the Santa Cruz Islands. In that battle, the American carriers would be about ten miles apart. The debate over carrier battle tactics would continue into 1943 as the Americans began launching the new *Essex*-class carriers.

When Fletcher arrived in Washington and reported to King, he received a rather chilly reception from his superior and soon would be relegated to backwater command assignments. King was particularly upset at Fletcher's caution at Coral Sea and the Battle of the Eastern Solomons and his apparent obsession with keeping his ships' fuel tanks near full even to the detriment of attacking and sinking the Japanese carriers. Many naval historians have not been kind to Fletcher's record as a carrier commander, and he would never see a carrier command again. It was not too long before another admiral, Radm. Leigh Noyes, took command of Task Force 61 on September 3.[5]

A Case of Misplaced Priorities

Noyes visited Ghormley, his classmate at Annapolis, the evening of September 3 on the *Argonne* anchored in Nouméa Harbor. Ghormley had not met his carrier task force commanders before this time being seemingly content commanding his forces from his flagship almost 1,000 miles from Guadalcanal.

During that meeting, Ghormley seemed preoccupied with what he believed to be the greater threat of a Japanese invasion somewhere on the Espiritu Santo-Fiji-Samoa line. Despite the Japanese capture of Nauru and Ocean Islands[6], there was no concrete intelligence to support his concern. Believing his desires reflected sound strategic thinking, Ghormley wanted to move Task Force 61 eastward toward the Santa Cruz Islands, thus taking carrier air support farther away from Guadalcanal. He was willing to accept the risk without asking or telling his commanders on the scene.

Noyes moved Task Force 18 from Nouméa on September 9, rounded the southern end of New Caledonia, and headed northeast toward Espiritu Santo. While she was in Nouméa, the *Wasp* reinforced her aircraft with four F4Fs from Éfaté and six SBDs from the *Enterprise*. These planes replaced two inoperable F4Fs and three SBDs. The *Wasp* now had 32 F4Fs, 28 SBDs, and 10 TBFs.

While Task Force 18 escorted Turner's flagship *McCawley*, Turner sent a draft operations plan to Noyes that would bring Marine reinforcements to Guadalcanal. Turner said he needed two more land-based fighter squadrons and two more bomber squadrons to be sent to Henderson Field and, if McCain could not furnish them, perhaps the carriers could. Noyes denied Turner's request. This decision further heightened tensions among Ghormley's senior commanders that had begun before Fletcher's departure. It would soon become apparent to Nimitz and King that all was not going well in the Solomons.[7]

Part 5: Holding the Line

CHAPTER 23
Defending Henderson Field

A Matter of Logistics

By the time the Battle of the Eastern Solomons ended, idleness was not among the problems the Marines faced on Guadalcanal. During the battle, they took the brunt of the shelling by Japanese destroyers, air attacks by Japanese aircraft from the carrier *Ryujo*, and incessant attempts by the Japanese to reinforce their forces. They were also annihilating the Kawanishi detachment, and fighting land crabs, poisonous snakes, jungle rot, malaria, and other maladies that came from living in the "tropical paradise" that was Guadalcanal. The effects of foraging for every food morsel, every bullet, and the medical supplies they could find took its toll. After Turner left the waters off Guadalcanal three days after the invasion, the problem of keeping the Marines supplied so they could hold Guadalcanal became even more pressing and critical.

The Japanese had their own problems. First, the American invasion of Guadalcanal caught them completely by surprise. They had placed prime importance on the New Guinea campaign and found it difficult diverting their emphasis to Guadalcanal. After several attempts to land reinforcements and supplies culminating in the abortive try during the Battle of the Eastern Solomons, they resorted to a more inventive tactic. They would load troops and materiel on faster destroyer-transports and make high-speed runs down the Slot. Thus, the Tokyo Express began.

Henderson Field was the focal point of both sides' efforts. After the Americans invaded that island and captured the field, the Japanese realized the Americans were turning it into a land-based aircraft carrier that could be the source of a Japanese defeat. If that happened, a powerful American presence would be only several hundred miles from their bases at Rabaul and Kavieng. If they lost these bases, their New Guinea Campaign would be placed in jeopardy along with their foothold in the South Pacific. So they concentrated their attacks on recapturing or neutralizing Henderson Field. To sustain this strategy, the Tokyo Express became the centerpiece for recapturing Guadalcanal and annihilating the Americans fighting mightily to hold it.

✲ ✲ ✲

Logistics is defined as "organization of troop movements: the planning and organization of the movement of troops, their equipment, and supplies."[1] Another definition is "the detailed coordination of a large and complex operation—meaning 'movement and supply of troops and equipment.'"[2] For both sides, the logistical battle was by no means less difficult or critical than the actual warfare being conducted by each. And no man knew how important the role logistics would play in the battle for Guadalcanal than Adm. Kelly Turner.

✲ ✲ ✲

When Adm. King decided to attack Guadalcanal, the U.S. Navy was totally unprepared to wage such a conflict on a foreign shore thousands of miles from the continental U.S. The logistical planning for an undertaking that senior officers, such as Adm. Turner, advocated never existed. There were several reasons for this lack of forethought in the Navy. First, the Navy never had conducted such a sustained effort so far from home. The line officers' corps never had any experience in serious logistical planning and viewed such work as secondary to conducting naval operations.

The second reason was that line officers thought that logistics should be sparsely funded when compared to operations. After Pearl Harbor, these naval officers in the Navy Department were not prepared to fight World War II and the complexities of the logistics of military operations fought across the vast distances in the Pacific.

The officers that populated the intelligence and logistics section in the Navy Department primarily came from civilian life when the war began and were not viewed by line naval officers as an integral part of operational success. The logicians would therefore be under the command of officers who thought that these underlings were not essential and given what could only be called secondary status and not worthy of their own lofty attentions.

Turner was an exception to that rule. During the early months of the war, he was an active supporter of bringing logistics to the forefront of naval strategy. He believed that:

1. Naval understanding of logistical concepts vastly expanded during the early months of World War II.

2. As amphibious operations became the mainstay of American naval strategy in the Pacific, logistics began to dominate in commanding officers' considerations.

The funding shortages for logistical support so prevalent before war, plus the sheer underappreciated problems associated supporting sustained operation in the vast Pacific, led to some serious shortfalls that affected the Guadalcanal invasion. When the Marines landed on August 7, there were no LSTs, LCTs, and only a few DUKWs available. Whatever supplies were used during the early days of Watchtower had to be lifted from the cavernous holds of cargo ships, placed into barges waiting alongside, taken ashore, and offloaded by hand to be placed on the beach. They then had to reload the materials on whatever trucks or other vehicles were available and delivered to the Marines. Combat-trained Marines were used to do the lifting where they could be better used fighting with their comrades inland.

Turner observed that:

> "Eighty percent of my time was given to logistics during the first four months of the WATCHTOWER operation [because] we were living from one logistic crisis to another."[3]

✲ ✲ ✲

Another problem transport ship captains complained about was that they had to unload their cargo—stored to make maximum use of cargo space—in Auckland and reload it to satisfy combat cargo needs—in the order those supplies would be needed in the combat zone. In those circumstances, cargo space utilization was never as good as the way supplies were loaded for initial shipment. Despite the best efforts by logistical planners in the U.S., the space utilization could never be completely satisfactory to meet combat conditions. Consequently, the result was an inherent inefficiency when the time came to actually deliver the goods to the people who needed them the most.[4]

From the time Turner landed the Marines and their supplies on August 7. American attempts to resupply the Marines proceeded poorly. The primary reasons for this were some dubious decisions made by senior naval officers that ignored the distances in the South Pacific and a lack of understanding of the unique logistical problems in that war theater.

Early requests for supplies bypassed CINCPAC at Pearl Harbor since that location did not have the resources to satisfy their needs. Loading Army supplies took place in San Francisco, 5,680 miles from Auckland, the designated offloading point for all supplies meant for SOPAC. In what seemed to be a good decision at the time, the Navy directed that it would handle all supply requests for all services in SOPAC. In what were confusing and contradictory instructions, the Navy said:

> "The various joint plans [for the establishment of defense and logistic support of island bases] did not, however, constitute a general supply procedure, nor did they stipulate in any detail the channels through which supply would be furnished."[5]

The Army countered:

> "In general, the Army will furnish and transport its own logistic support, plus rations for Navy personnel, and the Navy its own, plus fuel, diesel and aviation gasoline."[6]

Thus, there were no *unified* (my italics) supply procedures for the South Pacific. Each service was going its own way. Ghormley added to the uncertainty in July 1942 by designating that Auckland would be the disembarkation point for all supplies meant for his SOPAC command. In February 1942, King had declared that Tongatabu in the Tonga Islands would be that point. Ghormley's decision had some rational basis in that Auckland was far enough away from any Japanese attacks and already had a Joint Purchasing Board. However, Auckland was 1,100 more miles from San Francisco than Tongatabu. It was also 1,250 miles from Guadalcanal and 250 miles farther from Guadalcanal that the Tonga Islands.

Following Ghormley's orders, Capt. Mark C. Bowman established his headquarters in Auckland as the center for all SOPAC supply activities. All supply requests from islands to the north and northeast of Auckland came through Bowman's command and, because of the great distances involved, had to be sent primarily by air mail to fulfill their needs in a timely way. Until October 1942, actual shipments had to be sent by ship plying their way at a 10-12 knot pace all the way from San Francisco to Auckland, unloaded and reloaded, and sent back in the direction they came, 1,000 miles to the north and northeast for an overall trip of almost 7,000 miles.

But some relief was on its way when the Army and Navy agreed in mid-July to a "Joint Logistic

Plan for the Support of U.S. Bases in the South Pacific Area" that determined which service would meet both services' supply needs. But SOPAC threw a monkey wrench into that mix by stating that Watchtower's logistical requirements had to be met by its SOPAC supply bases. All requests had to go through Auckland, thus increasing request's response time. Adding to these difficulties was the logistical planning for the operations coming after Watchtower.

Nonetheless, Turner's intellect was up to the task of handling the logistical complexities while also managing his other command responsibilities. He would need all he had to tackle the supply problems that followed the American invasion of Guadalcanal. When he took the cargo ships away from Guadalcanal on August 9, he worried both about the sailors on those ships and the Marines left to fight the Japanese while not being able keep these brave men fully supplied.

Before leaving on August 9, the ships and their crews worked as hard as they could to unload all the supplies they had and send them ashore. After witnessing the logistical problems encountered getting these supplies to the Marines, Turner became convinced that logistical problems would become the dominant consideration during the battle to take and hold Guadalcanal and its most valuable asset, Henderson Field. After his force arrived in Nouméa, the Task Force 62 staff report had the following entry dated August 14:

> "Commenced preparation for the hospitalization of wounded, transferring and equipping of survivors, and logistics plans for supply of forces in the CACTUS-RINGBOLT [Guadalcanal-Tulagi] Area. Transports and AKs [Cargo ships] proceeding with unloading and rearrangement of cargo in order that essential supplies may be forwarded to CACTUS [Guadalcanal] for quick unloading."[7]

Six days after Task Force 62 arrived in Nouméa on August 13, a senior lieutenant, trained in the discipline of logistics, reported for duty as the only supply-logistics officer. Not having a trained logistical officer on Turner's staff contributed to the initial supply problems in the early days of the Guadalcanal invasion. In his first post invasion report dated August 12, Vandegrift reiterated that his troops needed supplies and reinforcements if they were to hold the island. And the situation would become increasingly more difficult.[8]

The Navy's supply situation in and around Guadalcanal stressed every sinew in its logistics network. Even Turner realized that this formidable problem placed enormous pressure on even his considerable intellect. He could not solve those problems by himself. That realization even reached the hallowed halls of the Navy Department when Adm. King purportedly told the Joint Chiefs of Staff on September 16 that "the Navy is in a bad way at this particular moment."[9] When Chief of the U.S. Army Air Corps Lt. Gen. Henry H. Arnold toured the Pacific Theater in late September, he concluded that:

1. "...The Navy was hard-pressed at Guadalcanal. They needed a 'shot in the arm' — and needed it badly; but I was not sure that the way to give it to them was by sending airplanes that might better be used against the Germans from England.

2. It was obvious to me that the Naval Officers in this area were under a terrific strain. It was also obvious that they had chips on their shoulders.

3. ...Ghormley and other Naval officers in that area — Admiral John ('Slew') McCain and Admiral Daniel Callaghan — were very worried about the situation there.

4. It was obvious the Navy could not hold Guadalcanal if they could not get supplies in, and they could not get supplies in if the Japanese bombers continued to arrive and bomb the ships unloading supplies.

5. ...Gen. Patch [Commanding Gen. of the Army's Americal Division at Nouméa] was very insistent that the Navy had no plan of logistics; that the Marines and the Navy would both have been in one hell of a fix had he not dug into his reserve stock and furnished them with supplies.

6. My estimate, upon leaving Admiral Ghormley's headquarters, was this: So far, the Navy had taken one hell of a beating and at that time was hanging on by a shoestring. They did not have a logistic setup efficient enough to insure success."

Arnold never doubted the Navy's determination to achieve a victory at Guadalcanal when he wrote:

"As I traveled through the Southwest Pacific, it was impossible not to get the impression that the Navy was determined to carry on the campaign in that theater, and determined to do it with as little help from the Army as possible.

It was their fight, the Navy's fight; it was their war against the Japanese; and they were going to clean it up if they could."[10]

When Arnold returned to Washington, he briefed many high level military and civilian officials including President Roosevelt. The outcome of that meeting was a "For Your Eyes Only" letter to the Joint Chiefs in October. The president wrote:

"My anxiety about the Southwest Pacific is to make sure that every possible weapon gets into the area to hold Guadalcanal, and that having held in this crisis, munitions, planes and crews are on the way to take advantage of our success."[11]

That memo gave a badly needed impetus to change the logistical situation in the South Pacific.

Changes had to be made in the logistics situation and soon. The most important was to establish more supply bases near Guadalcanal, but the world "near" was a relative term given the distance between land masses in that part of the world. To his credit, Ghormley realized that modern warfare needed to integrate the needs of operations and logistics before Washington did when he wrote:

"Our supply set up is not right under present conditions. For operations such as this, logistics and operations must go hand in hand."[12]

Only three weeks transpired when all levels of his command recognized the situation needed change and things began to happen. The recognition surfaced that advanced bases need to be substantially and significantly expanded.

The first of these was the base at Éfaté, 285 miles northeast of Nouméa but still 700 miles from Guadalcanal. That island began building supply facilities in May 1942. By the time of the Guadalcanal invasion, it was still a small operation although its airfield was in use almost immediately after being established. Construction crews rapidly finished underground tanks for storing aviation gasoline. However, Éfaté was too small to meet the needs of the Marines on Guadalcanal all by itself.

Espiritu Santo was the closest land mass to Guadalcanal, "only" 500 miles away, and soon rapidly expanded. It began rather modestly when 30 B-17 bombers operated from its first airstrip on July 30. But the situation there substantially changed when Ghormley and Turner ordered that a branch of supply be set up for the 1st Marine Division. However, that location really could not be called a major supply base until February 1943, well after Guadalcanal had been pacified.

Major changes began in mid-August at Nouméa, 840 miles from Guadalcanal. The Navy began building a major naval base there in November that soon became the main supply point for all naval operations in the South Pacific. Nonetheless, Guadalcanal kept receiving supplies from four sources:

1. A still being built but not fully stocked base at Auckland, New Zealand—1,825 miles away.
2. A small but not fully supported base at Éfaté in the New Hebrides—700 miles southeast of Guadalcanal.
3. A larger base in its early construction stages at Espiritu Santo—560 miles southeast from Guadalcanal.
4. Direct shipments from the continental U.S.—about 5,000 miles away.

Early estimates stated it would be three months before the Marines could be fully supplied, but because of the efforts of many, the Marines were fully supplied by September 18, just one-half the original time estimate. But all was still not that rosy.

By mid-September, the battle for Guadalcanal reached another critical point. While the Americans still held Henderson Field, the Tokyo Express had been delivering vitally needed supplies and Japanese troops to continue resisting the American occupation of the island. Refreshed and supplied, they tried to inflict a devastating defeat on the Marines at a place that would burn a lasting legacy in the lore of the U.S. Marine Corps. After the battle ended, that place would be named Edson's Ridge, after the commander of the Marines who defended that location.

CHAPTER 24
A Stand for the Ages

A Japanese Warrior

He had a rugged, ferocious countenance about him as he strode into Radm. Raizo Tanaka's office on his flagship, the *Kinugasa*, anchored in the harbor of Shortland Island—a man who had seen much of war. Almost a throwback to a time when Japan was a feudal kingdom, his dark brushy mustache and close-cropped black hair gave him the appearance of the typical Samurai warrior of that bygone era. Maj. Gen. Kiyotake Kawaguchi, commander of the 35th Infantry Brigade, had a long career in the Imperial Japanese Army. It began in 1914 when he received his commission as a 2nd lieutenant. He rose in the ranks and achieved his current rank in 1940 when he took command of his brigade. He had the look of a man in total command and exuded an aura of self-assurance. And he had much upon which to base that confidence. His brigade had accumulated considerable success in the capture of Singapore, taking the Philippines, and fighting in Borneo's rugged terrain and dense jungle. Now he was under the command of Lt. Gen. Harukichi Hyakutake, commander of the 17th Army, and at 49 years old, had a new assignment for his newly reinforced command that now stood at more than 5,200 men.

After the Americans slaughtered the Ichiki Detachment and following abortive attempts to reinforce the Japanese ground forces on Guadalcanal during the Battle of the Eastern Solomons, the Japanese high command decided that there were more Americans on that island than they originally thought. They needed a more powerful and experienced force to recapture Guadalcanal, and the 35th Brigade seemed to be just the outfit for the job.

But they had to get to Guadalcanal, and that is why Kawaguchi now met with Tanaka. The brigade had arrived in the transport *Sado Maru* on August 29. Tanaka had orders from Mikawa that any attempts to land reinforcements must now be done with fast destroyers to minimize their vulnerability to American air attacks. But Kawaguchi had other ideas. He insisted that his troops had to be landed by landing barges after the *Sado Maru* sailed about 100 miles to the southeast and into the harbor on Gizo Island. The soldiers would be transferred to barges. The navy would then tow the barges more than 250 miles to land them on Guadalcanal. After all, those were his orders.

So an impasse resulted. Tanaka did not want to disobey his orders but also did not want to use landing barges for the reinforcements. They were vulnerable to air and sea attacks because they could not be towed at the higher speeds of his destroyers. Using transports had proven to be totally disastrous for the same reasons. As far as he was concerned, he would not move another soldier and subject them to being strafed by American aircraft and doomed to a merciless death by drowning in the sea. There had been too much of that kind of disaster occurring, and he wanted to do everything in his power to prevent it from happening again.

Kawaguchi was equally adamant. He did not see what the Imperial Japanese Navy's problem was. He had brought his brigade to Borneo in barges over more than 500 miles of open sea and successfully landed them on that island's shores. But he was new to the Solomons' Theater and did not realize how effective the pilots of the U.S. Navy and the pilots at Henderson Field were. But he also had his orders and was resolved to obey them.

Not knowing the actual wording of Kawaguchi's orders, Tanaka asked his superiors to confirm them. His conference with the headstrong general ended with a mutual agreement to hold more meetings about how to fulfill their respective assignments.

But an unfortunate situation developed with one of Tanaka's subordinates that would have serious personal repercussions for the admiral. Capt. Yonosuke Murakami, commander of four destroyers, landed soldiers at Cape Taivu on the night of August 29. Meanwhile, Adm. Mikawa received a radio message from Guadalcanal that an American force of one cruiser, two destroyers, and two transports were off Lunga Point that day. Mikawa directly ordered Murakami to attack these ships after he finished landing the Japanese troops. For some unknown reason and to Tanaka's amazement, Murakami ignored Mikawa's direct order by not launching the attack, reversed his course, and returned to Shortland.

Tanaka immediately called Murakami before him and demanded an explanation. The captain said that there was a full moon and clear skies that night, and he had seen many American planes in the air. This was a clear case of either cowardice at worst or dereliction of duty at best. But the blame fell on Tanaka. He had to bear the responsibility for his subordinate's actions and would pay for Murakami's transgression.

Tanaka met again with Kawaguchi in an attempt to break the stalemate. The general's insistence on transporting his brigade by landing barges continued unabated. Any orders from the Army had not yet arrived allowing him to change his mind. Tanaka was just as adamant for landing the reinforcements with no further delay. Time was on the Americans' side. Every day they would get stronger while they landed more troops and their industrial might would continue to build more ships, planes, guns, and other supplies. It would not be long before they would bring huge fleets of ships to the Solomons and seal the fate of the Japanese on Guadalcanal.

Tanaka immediately ordered eight destroyers under his command to prepare to take the 13th Brigade to Guadalcanal the next morning. Finally, a message arrived from Eighth Fleet headquarters at 8:00 p.m. that settled the matter to Tanaka's satisfaction:

> "Under our agreement with Commander Seventeenth Army, the bulk of the Kawaguchi Detachment will be transported to Guadalcanal by destroyers, the remainder by large landing barges."[1]

Tanaka did not let a moment slip by in again resuming discussions with Kawaguchi. The general still stubbornly refused to accept what the orders said. But the time pressures forced Kawaguchi to finally agree with Tanaka.

On August 31, 1942, at noon, Tanaka's eight destroyers left Shortland with 1,000 men of Kawaguchi's brigade on board. Twelve hours later, they landed on Guadalcanal with no opposition.

But before that happened, Tanaka received surprising orders on August 30:

"COMDESRON 3 will depart Rabaul for Shortland early in the morning of the 30th. Upon the arrival of COMDESRON 3, COMDESRON 2 will relinquish his command and proceed to Truk on board Yugiri."[2]

He was losing his command because of several mishaps for which he was responsible. The three major reasons were:

1. Loss of several ships in his command.
2. Murakami's refusal to attack the American force after he landed reinforcements and thus disobeying Mikawa's direct order.
3. Delays in launching the landing of Kawaguchi's brigade on Guadalcanal.

Thus, Japan lost a valued senior naval commander. But Kawaguchi was on Guadalcanal and ready to begin his campaign as soon as the rest of his soldiers landed. And land they did.[3]

The Beginning of an American Legend

The jungle plain stretched from Lunga Point to the south toward the mountains that loom over Guadalcanal. Jungle vegetation covered almost all of it, with two exceptions: Henderson Field and a slight rise covered only by Kunai grass (because of a lack of top soil) about a mile to the southeast. If the jungle growth had covered it, the little hill, which was actually a pile of coral, would not have been noticed. The hill had two prominent rises on it, one about 120 feet high at its northern end and another about 100 feet high at the southern end. To anyone who studied military tactics, that hill also provided a ready-made path to attack Henderson Field from the south while not forcing assaulting troops to hack their way through the thick surrounding jungle.

The Americans had a tenuous hold on the vitally important airfield. If the Japanese took Henderson Field, there would be no reason for the Americans to stay in the Solomons; their mission to prevent the Japanese from cutting off the American supply lines to Australia and New Zealand would fail.

A Marine officer also saw this as he walked over the hill on September 12. He did not look like a commander. His short stature—five feet, seven inches tall—belied the strength of his character and abilities to be in firm command while under extreme stress. Looking younger than he was, Lt. Col. Merritt Austin Edson's close-cropped, now-receding red hair still stood out from under the too-large helmet perched on his small head. Born on April 25, 1897, he was 45 years old and, as one of his men once mentioned, looked like the antithesis of a fighting man. He was a quiet-spoken, mild-mannered, and reserved man who caused those who met him to underestimate his abilities. But one look into the pale blue eyes of this unimposing individual uncovered a totally different impression. They stared at you with the hard, cold determination of a man that clearly showed him to be a relentless individual in total command. Marines quickly realized that this was a man to be feared and respected. Anyone who witnessed Edson in the incredible intensity of combat saw a man miraculously stay in total control of his temper and mind and capable of making incredibly sound military decisions.

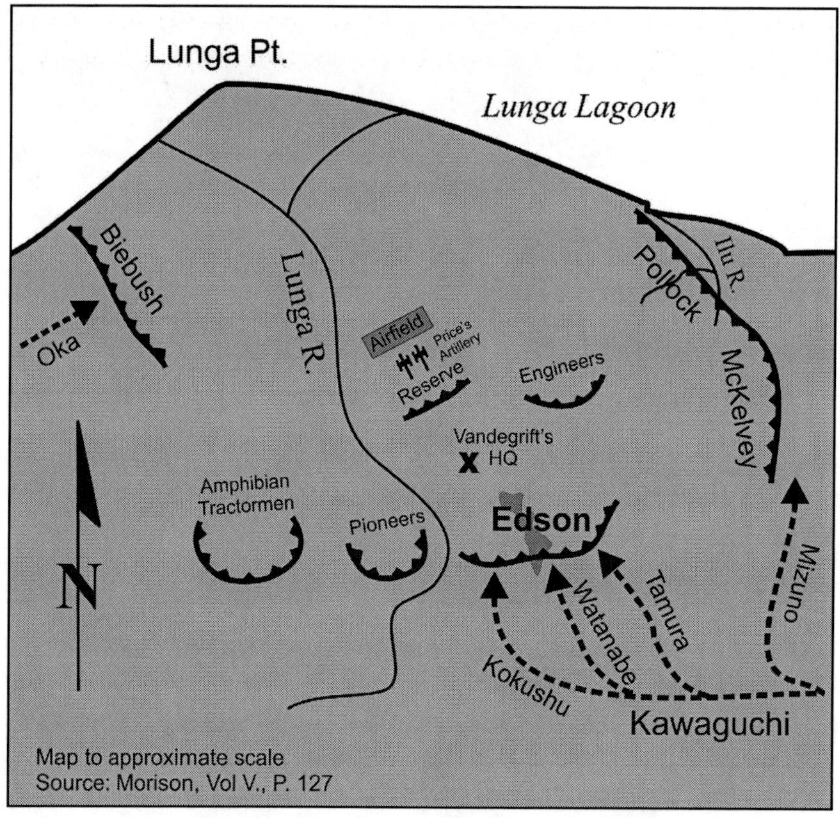

Edson Prepares as the Japanese Approach

Edson had seen intelligence reports that stated the Japanese had landed about 3,000 men who now moved through the jungle toward this hill. As commander of the 1st Marine Raider Battalion, 5th Marine Regiment, he had the mission to defend this hill and prevent the Japanese from taking Henderson Field. Meanwhile, Gen. Vandegrift moved his headquarters between Henderson Field and the hill to be closer to the coming battle.

Edson's Raiders had already been bloodied by fighting a tougher-than-anticipated battle with Japanese troops on Tulagi. There, his men found out that the Japanese were tough jungle fighters not to be taken lightly. After the Japanese reinforcements landed, Edson's 800-man battalion boarded the APDs *McKean* and *Manley* and the patrol boats *YP-298* and *YP-346*. Landing at three spots around Taivu Point on September 8, the Marines completely caught the Japanese off-guard, took the village of Tasimboko, and captured abandoned Japanese supplies. The purloined rations would be sorely needed later since food was in short supply. Edson also learned that the troops the Japanese landed were first line soldiers, not just garrison troops the Marines encountered when the invasion began. Captured Japanese documents also revealed Kawaguchi's battle plans, so the Marines knew where and when the Japanese would attack. The Japanese incursion was not just a small effort; the Japanese had landed at least a brigade.

The time had come for Edson's Raiders to prepare for the battle of their lives. He positioned his companies in strategic positions and dug holes. And the Japanese drew near.

Edson was not alone to defend against Kawaguchi's advance. After reinforcing Edson's battalion with the 1st Parachute Battalion, Gen. Vandegrift deployed LTC William N. McKelvy's 3rd Battalion and LTC Edwin A. Pollock's 2nd Battalion of the 1st Regiment to his eastern flank along the Ilu (Tenaru) River. LTC Frederick C. Biebush's 3rd Battalion, 5th Marine Regiment was on the western flank. When Martin Clemens' native scouts reported the Japanese were moving south out of Tasimboko through the jungle and westward toward Henderson Field, Vandegrift ordered Col. Pedro del Valle, commanding the Marines' 11th Artillery Regiment, to place his 5th Battalion's 105-mm howitzers, commanded by LTC E. H. Price, just south of the airfield so that these guns could fire on the approaching Japanese. Vandegrift flanked the Raider's position on the ridge with the 1st Pioneer Battalion, the 1st Amphibian Tractor Battalion on Edson's left rear, and the 1st Engineer Battalion to Edson's right rear.

The 1st Marine Division did not have enough men to fully encircle Henderson Field with a defensive perimeter. Vandegrift relied on the dense jungle to plug some of the holes and hoped that the Japanese would attack in the places where his defenses were. In most cases, he would be proven correct in that assumption.[4]

✲ ✲ ✲

Kawaguchi began moving his brigade toward Henderson Field with a typical overly complex plan that split his forces into five salients. His main attack would use three battalions (1st Battalion, 124 Infantry Regiment [I/124] under the command of Maj. Yukichi Kokusho, 3rd Battalion, 124th Infantry [III/124] commanded by LTC Kusukichi Watanabe, and the 2nd Battalion, 4th Infantry (II/4) commanded by Maj. Masuro Tamura) to come from the south and move over the small hill south of Henderson Field. Maj. Eishi Mizuno's Kuma Battalion, 28th Infantry Regiment would break off from the main force and attack Col. Edwin A. Pollock's and LTC William J. McKelvy's positions on Vandegrift's eastern flank. Col. Akinosuka Oka, commander of the 124th Regiment with his headquarters battalion plus two battalions (II/124 and III/4) would attack the Marines' western flank.

Not fully comprehending the difficulty moving along Guadalcanal's difficult terrain and through its dense jungle, Kawaguchi quickly lost contact with his now widely separated forces. He could no longer maintain command and control of his brigade. As in other Japanese attack plans, the success of his attack relied heavily on a precise timetable that proved impossible to keep. Thus his attack would prove to be haphazard and give the hill's defenders a fighting chance to stop him. His artillery had heavy 75-mm guns more suited for battles on open land. His soldiers had to break these down into three pieces to move them. Each piece weighed more than four men could carry. After trying mightily to move these guns through the jungle, his men had no choice but to leave them behind. Consequently, he had no heavy artillery to launch his attack. However, he did have the Imperial Japanese Navy and the bomber attacks that he hoped would be an effective substitute for heavy bombardment of the Americans' positions.[5]

Gearing Up for the Onslaught

When Edson's battalion dug in, they placed barbed wire on the ridge. On September 10, any hope vanished that the Marines would get any rest after their raid on Tasimboko. The coral soil's hardness and the Kunai grass' tough leaves made digging holes especially hard in the hot Guadalcanal sun. The

Marines had no tool with which to dig other than the folding trenching tools (called an e-tool) that were better suited for the soft soils of Europe. They could have used sledge hammers, spades or picks, but these were not the kinds of tools issued to a raider battalion that had to travel light and remain mobile. Some Marines, such as 2nd Lt. John "Tiger" Erskine, lacking an e-tool, used his helmet to dig his hole. PFC Henry Neal remembered his frustration trying to make a hole for himself. "I announced I wasn't digging any more. Just then Sgt. Tom (Thomas D.) Pollard came by, reached down, jerked me about a foot off the deck, said one word—'DIG!' I dug."[6]

Although they did not know what all this preparation was all about, they all knew that something big was heading their way. On September 11, they saw Col. del Valle, commander of the 11th Marine Artillery Regiment, and his men carefully walking over and around the ridge, mapping the ground. The 105-mm howitzers under his command, fully covered by camouflage nets to hide them from prying Japanese eyes, would soon have every square yard carefully plotted and zeroed-in when Edson would call for artillery fire during the next four days.

The daily Japanese air raid came over nearly on schedule at noon, bypassed Henderson Field, and dropped shrapnel and 500-pound bombs right on the ridge. Having not been subjected to such a bombing attack before, fear filled Edson's men. PFC Ben Quintana recalled, "It wasn't like the 'boom' of a distant bomb. This was 'CRACK!'—like lightning coming right down your spine."[7] The raid killed two men and wounded nine.

Although Edson had ordered reconnaissance patrols earlier in the day just after his Raiders and the parachutists arrived on the ridge, he ordered Capt. John W. Anthony Antonelli to send out another patrol to gather more intelligence about what the Japanese were doing. After being assigned to lead the patrol, Platoon Sergeant Joseph S. Buntin and Sergeant Frank Guidone's squads moved into the jungle below the ridge's southern slopes. Just as the Japanese bombers began dropping their bombs, a Japanese patrol appeared in front of the Marines. Some of the bombs fell into the jungle and threatened both patrols. The two groups separated and avoided further contact.

But the Marine patrol made one fact become crystal-clear. After learning what the patrol discovered, Edson's men now knew what their leader had known all along—a big, powerful Japanese force was on its way and would soon arrive.[8]

An American High Command Meeting

Admirals Kelly Turner and John McCain landed at Henderson Field in the afternoon of September 11 from Espiritu Santo. It had been about one month since Turner had set foot on Guadalcanal and McCain had never been there. The Marines made their presence felt now that the aircraft at Henderson Field regularly intercepted the daily Japanese bombing attacks and also attacked Japanese ships. However, the situation on the ground was still a tenuous one with the Marines desperately holding onto a small thinly defended perimeter around the airfield. The nickname "Operation Shoestring" originally applied to Operation Watchtower had lived up to its implied reputation.

Turner and McCain walked into Gen. Vandegrift's crudely assembled headquarters and quickly exchanged the military formalities. Turner carried a handwritten note from Adm. Ghormley in his pocket. With a stony countenance on his face, he handed the document to Vandegrift with a heavy heart. The general noticed Turner's bearing and immediately became concerned as he opened the note and began reading it. The color drained from his face as the letter's impact fell upon him.

Passing the note to his operations officer, LTC Gerald Thomas, Vandegrift stood coldly silent. Thomas looked at the note and a depressing feeling came over him. Ghormley, still the absent commander who had not yet ventured off the *Argonne* at anchor in Nouméa's harbor, offered an extremely pessimistic assessment of his command.

According to Ghormley, the Japanese, gathering powerful land, sea, and air forces at Rabaul and Truk, were about to attack the American forces on Guadalcanal and the surrounding islands and would attempt to repossess the island. The attack would come in the next three weeks or perhaps in the next ten days. The gloomy litany continued.

Ghormley said his command could not resist the Japanese efforts because of shortages in carriers, cruisers, destroyers, and transports. Thus, he could not send any reinforcements or supplies to the Marines on Guadalcanal. Although we do not know if he wanted to send the shocking note to Nimitz and his superiors in Washington, the effect on the officers in Vandegrift's headquarters was just as if they had been subjected to a tsunami.

Turner had essentially resigned himself that the Marines were in severe jeopardy, but had agreed to send the 7th Marine Regiment to improve the balance of Vandegrift's command against what the Japanese would throw at him.

That was the primary reason for Turner's visit. But he did not share his immediate superior's dark assessment of the Solomons' invasion. To break the gloomy atmosphere, he took out a bottle of Scotch from his kit bag, offered a drink to all, and said to Vandegrift, "Vandegrift, I'm not inclined to take so pessimistic a view of the situation as Ghormley does. He doesn't believe I can get the 7th Marine Regiment here, but I believe I have a scheme that will fool the Japs."[9]

Vandegrift later described Turner's plan as "quaint." Turner wanted the general to disperse the men of the 7th all over the island at every possible landing spot where the Japanese might deposit their troops. As far as Vandegrift was concerned, this was an idiotic idea. He was spread so thin now that his ability to defend against the ever increasing number of Japanese troops was dubious at best. All the Japanese had to do was to find where the Marine reinforcements were, surround them, and annihilate them. He wanted the 7th Marines to be put ashore at Lunga Point to defend the primary target of the Japanese, Henderson Field. With such a wide gap between the two men, the meeting ended with no decision made. An unhappy Turner with McCain in tow returned to Espiritu Santo the next day. Despite Ghormley's pessimistic outlook, Vandegrift's determination remained undaunted. If the Japanese captured Henderson Field, he would take what troops he had left, head for Guadalcanal's mountains, and fight a guerilla war from there.[10]

The First Attack

Action on the next day, September 12, returned to what had happened in past days. Around 11:50 a.m., the daily bombing by Japanese Betty bombers began again. They unloaded their deadly cargo; the bombs decimated the radio station, blew up some gasoline and destroyed three SBDs. Thirty-two Wildcats took off, engaged the bombers, destroyed five of them along with one Zero.

Kawaguchi's day began well. He learned from a captured American pilot that his planned path through the jungle would not be opposed by the Americans. Apparently, the Marines had placed their defensive lines to the east and spread along the coast. Kawaguchi's planned approach path also could not be seen from the air because of the cover of dense jungle overgrowth. The Kuma Battalion was in position to attack by 12:25 p.m. So far, so good! But all was not rosy for the Japanese general. Col. Oka reported that he had only two companies to launch his attack, NOT the two battalions he should have had at his disposal. He would not have the two battalions until September 13. In spite of this and buoyed by the good news from the American flyer, Kawaguchi decided to begin attacking the ridge south of the airfield that night, just as he planned all along.

The evening of September 12 began innocently enough. The Marines dug in as best as they could and, thoroughly exhausted, waited for the onslaught they knew would come. A Japanese float plane flew over Henderson Field at 9:30 p.m. It was not the first time this unwelcome visitor had flown over Guadalcanal. He had become such a familiar presence that the Marine and Navy personnel on the island tagged the plane "Louie the Louse."

Of course, there was no way to know whether the plane or its pilot was the same every time it flew over Henderson Field. Keeping with the name the Americans had bestowed on it, the plane's approach was not comical. The aircraft's deadly purpose was to drop parachute flares to flood the area around Henderson Field with bright light and call the fall of shot that the ships of the Tokyo Express would soon deliver. That night, the light cruiser *Sendai* and destroyers *Shikinami*, *Fubuki*, and *Suzukaze* opened fire with a withering, albeit a short, barrage of six- and five-inch shells. Fortunately, most of the shells did not hit Edson's position, but fell farther to the east, killing three pilots.

The ships' bombardment ended about 20 minutes after it began. The Japanese then attacked. They found the Americans' most vulnerable defensive spot on Edson's right flank. There, the Marines had dug in between the east bank of the Lunga River and the ridge while trying to defend an 800-yard line. Dense jungle growth surrounded and engulfed them on fairly flat ground. Any advantages the Marines had in terms of concentrating fire was somewhat negated since it was more difficult to see the Japanese approach. The jungle did not allow the Marines to set up continuous lines of defense; they could only set platoon-sized clusters while the Japanese could slip by them through gaps in the Marine defensive lines.

The jungle hid Japanese movements so that most of the Marine firepower could not be brought to bear on them. Edson later remembered that the Japanese began chattering and shouting insults. The Marines, veterans of jungle warfare, stayed silent, not wanting to give away their locations and wanting the Japanese to come to them.

Suddenly, the Japanese opened with sporadic and weak machine gun and mortar fire as small uncoordinated groups began moving toward the Marines. The guns of the 11th Artillery Regiment thundered in the darkness and the Marines opened fire with machine guns and rifles. The Raider's

Company C, on the extreme right flank, took the full force of the Japanese attack, and soon the Japanese surrounded them. The shortest path to the ridge was just a log that substituted for a bridge over a lagoon to their left. Lacking the shelter of the jungle, crossing that log exposed any who dared that feat to Japanese fire. The other route to withdraw to the better defensive positions on the ridge itself was a narrow path between the Lunga River and the Lagoon itself. BAR-man Joseph M. Rushton later recalled, "As the long night was drawing to a close it became apparent to even the dim-witted that we were in for big trouble. If our positions became untenable, we were then to withdraw back across the log, or that not being possible to fight our way out as best we could...We were expendable."[11]

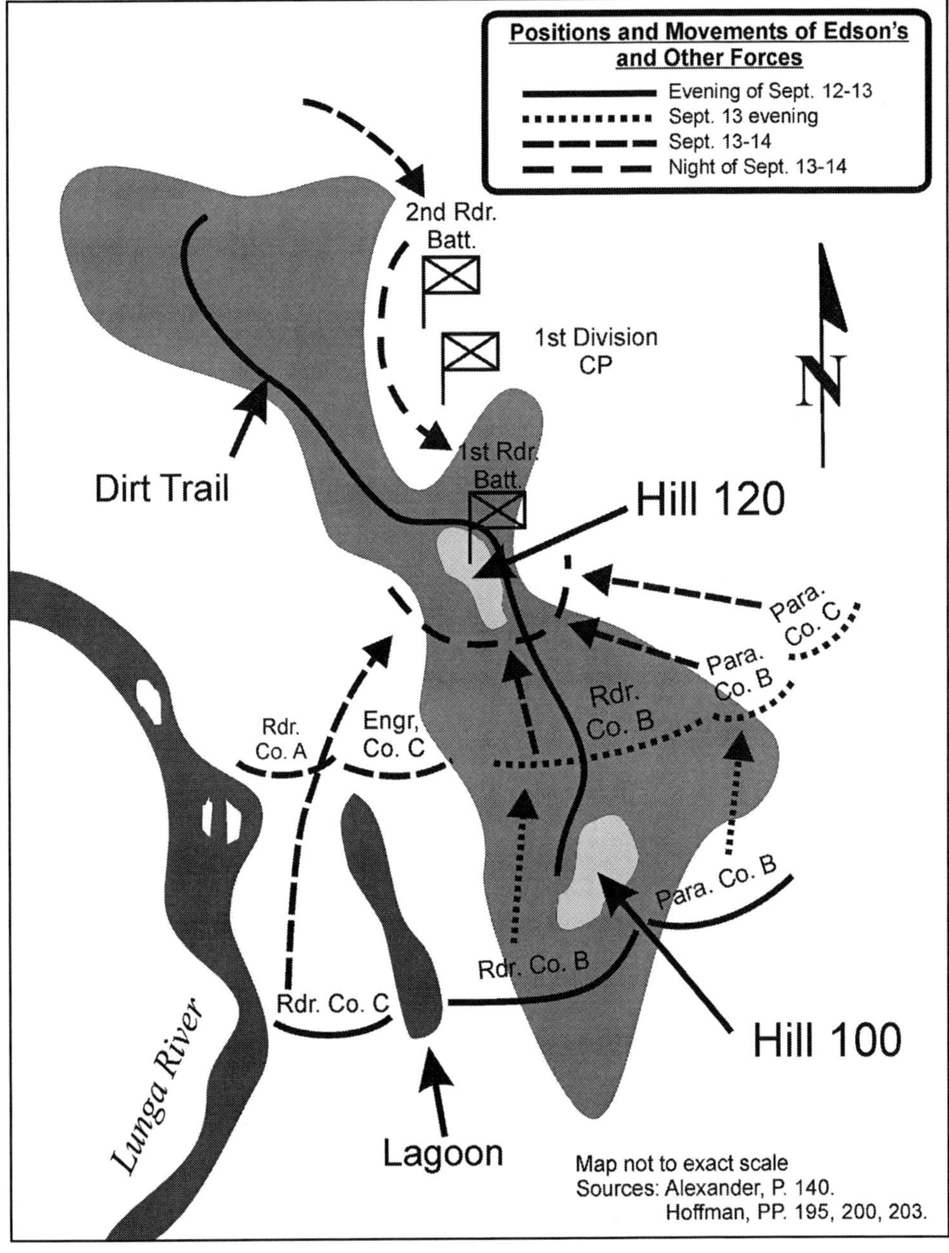

Edson's Defensive Positions

The Japanese aimed the strength of their attack at a place between Companies B and C on the lagoon's east bank and severed any possible communication between them. Company B had to turn its right flank inward to hold their line. The whereabouts of seven Marines became unknown but Company B safely withdrew up the ridge. One Japanese thrust menaced one of Company C's isolated platoons on the lagoon's western edge while another salient tried to turn Company C's right flank. Adding to the peril was another 45-minute Japanese naval bombardment that began just after midnight. But this time, those salvoes did not go unchallenged when the 3rd Defense Battalion's Batteries B and C fired their American five-inch coastal guns in retaliation.[12]

✲ ✲ ✲

The Japanese attacks were fierce and brave. Nevertheless, the results could only be judged as spotty. Kawaguchi wanted to begin his attack at 8:00 p.m. before the naval fusillade began. But the three battalions anointed to begin the attack arrived late. Thus, they could only start two to three hours behind schedule. Their rush to attack resulted in their losing track where they were and caused them to miss the ridge. But serendipity led them to assault the Marines at their most vulnerable point. However, the thick jungle forced the attack to be piecemeal and scattered. Kawaguchi and his officers lost contact with their troops as their attack became a jumble of captains, lieutenants, sergeants, and privates going up against a few concentrated Marine groups in the dense jungle undergrowth.

One battalion, the I/124, waded in the Lunga River's chest-high, swirling waters and thus became mixed up with the III/124 battalion's men. The first battalion's commander, Maj. Yukichi Kokusho, extracted his men by continuing along the river's west bank. Having lost all control over his attack, Kawaguchi tried to redirect his troops out of the river's muck and toward the ridge but to no avail.

The Americans seemed to have escaped serious losses; so, in frustration, Kawaguchi ordered his troops to gather again for another attack the next night of September 13.[13]

The Crucible of Battle

Kawaguchi's superiors in Rabaul had no word on the evening of September 12 of what happened on Guadalcanal. The only information they did get was from American radio intercepts, and these officers remained optimistic. When one Japanese plane reported sighting what was a prearranged sign of success, two fires about 50 meters apart, their optimism soared from what they had heard. After sending an officer in one of two reconnaissance planes escorted by nine Zeroes, their positive attitude continued as Japanese scouts still sent optimistic messages that Kawaguchi had taken and now held the airfield despite the fact that 28 American fighters continued to harass and shoot at the scout planes. One can only guess whether they had confused their hopes with military reality.

The previous night's battle had been intense, but Edson's Raiders had previously battled tough Japanese troops on Tulagi. The early dawn hours of September 13 found the Marines in a dangerous situation. Although the Japanese had not been successful driving the Americans off the ridge, the surrounding jungle now teemed with Kawaguchi's brigade. Two Japanese battalions, in position to attack as soon as it turned dark, rested, ate their meals, and sent out patrols to assess the Marines' defenses.

Based on what had happened the night before, Kawaguchi should have been as optimistic as his superiors in Rabaul. Later he described the first evening's action as a "tragedy...a miserable failure. On the morning of the 13th to the officers of each battalion I sent the order. 'The Brigade will again execute a night attack tonight. The duty of each battalion is same as before.'"[14]

In stark contrast, Edson took the earlier attack in stride in his normal, unemotional way. His executive officer, Lt. Col. Samuel B. Griffith, remembered him saying, "They were testing. They'll be back. But maybe not as many of them." He was silent for just a moment as if thinking about what he had said. "Or maybe more. I want all positions improved, all wire lines paralleled, a hot meal for the men. Today, dig, wire up tight, get some sleep. We'll all need it. The Nip will be back. I want to surprise him."[15]

Everyone knew that what "Red Mike" wanted meant that some of them would get no rest that day. Edson did not know how many Japanese opposed him, and he wanted to find out precisely (or as close to as he could) the answer to that question. He ordered Platoon Sergeant Peter Pettus to lead a small patrol to go where Company C once was to gather that intelligence. Also, he wanted retake the ground lost to the right of now-exposed Company B. Lt. John Antonelli had that unenviable assignment.

As the sun rose, the heat on the treeless ridge became unbearable. There was no breeze. Company B's Irvin Reynolds, laying low in the tall grass, recalled, "We spent much of the next day pinned down in the tall grass, and it was boiling hot with no wind stirring. The sun looked like a red ball, directly overhead."[16] The heat forced Company B's newly appointed commander, Capt. Louis Monville, into incoherency. Edson replaced him with Company B's third commander in a day, Capt. John Sweeney.

The daily bombing attack by Rabaul's Betty bombers appeared at noon, right on their usual schedule. Owing to faulty intelligence, and not knowing Kawaguchi's precise location, the 26 pilots aimed their bombs to avoid the hill and hit the suspected Marine bridgehead at Tasimboko instead. Martin Clemens' scouts watched as the missiles tore into Kawaguchi's rear guard with feelings of revenge. At least Edson's Marines had finally caught a short-lived break.

The oppressive heat affected the planned small unit forays. But that did not deter Sergeant Pettus from taking four men with him into the jungle to look for the Japanese. They crossed the log over the lagoon and moved into the holes formerly occupied by Company C's 2nd Platoon. Suddenly, small arms fire poured out of the jungle, forcing the five man patrol to dive for cover. The fire sounded like it came from .30-caliber machine-guns and made Pettus think they had run into remnants of Company C. When he screamed today and yesterday's code words, the response was more fire. The Japanese had captured two BARs and were now using them against the Marines. Bullets splatted against the trunks of the banyan trees and cut into the Kunai grass.

Pettus' only rational response was to leave quickly and get back to Edson to report what he had found. His patrol double-timed up the ridge. The Japanese were in firm control of the Company's right flank and in overwhelming numbers

Lt. Antonelli slowly and deliberately led his platoon into the jungle looking for the Japanese. He knew they were there after seeing Pettus' patrol coming out of the undergrowth with fire following them. He suspected that there would be survivors of Company C's previous night's ordeal since some of the bodies had been neither seen nor recovered. The low hanging mist over the jungle plain gave a group of 11 men a spectral appearance as they stumbled toward his platoon. They were the exhausted and wounded Marine survivors from Sergeant Lawrence Harrison's platoon of the night's attack on Company C. Two of them died right there. Antonelli could not spare the time to tend to their needs, so he ordered a small squad to bury the dead and accompany the rest of the injured men back to the aid station. His mission was to engage the Japanese; the rest of his platoon moved forward at a faster pace into the dense vegetation that stood in front of them like a green, impenetrable wall. The Japanese, having just finished with Pettus' patrol, lay waiting in the jungle with their weapons ready to fire.

The Marines moved close enough to throw grenades when massive gunfire came at them. They had no choice but to stop where they were. Antonelli soon realized that he did not have enough men to overcome what was in front of him and retake the lost ground. The Marines traded fire with the Japanese for about an hour when Antonelli ordered a departure. One Marine, PFC Donald J. Coffey, lost his life in the firefight. PFC Thomas D. Smith's recollection offers the best summary what happened that day:

> "Patrolled up the river a short ways and were hit from the sides and front. The Japs had broken through by the river and the evidence of battle was all around. Returned down river firing and moving."[17]

Antonelli's report to Edson confirmed what Pettus had earlier told the colonel. The Japanese solidly occupied much of the ground given up by Company C the night before. They had enough strength to threaten and potentially collapse Company B's right flank as soon as darkness fell. After discussing the situation with his officers and concluding that he could not hold the ground where Company B presently was, Edson decided to withdraw Company B from the overgrown jungle plain to a position on the ridge about halfway closer to his command post.

Edson replaced the battered Company C with a fresh Company A on his extreme right flank but north of the lagoon. Right next to them were the men of a relatively combat inexperienced Engineering Company C. Reflecting positively on his superior's military acumen, Griffith wrote in his book, *The Battle for Guadalcanal*:

> "This move greatly improved fields of fire for automatic weapons and imposed upon the attacker a trip of about 100 yards from the jungle's edge before he could physically contact the battle position. In traversing this open space he could be brought under killing grazing fire."[18]

The Marines were as ready as they could be. They only had to wait for the Japanese attack to fall upon them.

✲ ✲ ✲

The sun went down and, as is normal in the tropical latitudes, darkness descended quickly. Louie the Louse made another appearance at 9:00 p.m. and dropped his usual parachute flares. The Marines knew what this meant. Seven Japanese destroyers immediately opened up with a one-hour barrage that hit Henderson Field and, unlike the previous evening, avoided the ridge.

While Edson repositioned his troops to anticipate the next Japanese attack he knew would come, several of Kawaguchi's officers carefully and thoroughly watched the Marine movements. An eagle-eyed Maj. Masuro Tamura, commander of the 2nd Battalion, 4th Infantry Regiment observed the Marines' changing their positions in the late afternoon. He then moved his command to better positions to begin his attack later that night. Located on Kawaguchi's western flank, the 1st Battalion, 124th Infantry Regiment and its leader, Maj. Yukichi Kokusho, moved his men along the lagoon to be ready to attack when he got the order.

Repeating his lack of command and control in the attacks the previous night, Kawaguchi expected Lt. Col. Kusukichi Watanabe's 3rd Battalion, 124th Infantry Regiment to attack on his left flank. But this would prove untrue. The long march through the dense jungle and earlier wounds suffered in other battles had taken their toll on Watanabe's men. They would still be trudging through the jungle and only fragments of his battalion would be part of the battle about to begin.

As soon as darkness descended upon Guadalcanal, the Japanese did not wait for the destroyers' 9:00 p.m. barrage to end when they attacked. Platoons from Maj. Kokusho's battalion clandestinely and carefully moved along the lagoon trying to find gaps in the American lines. Edson, knowing that he did not have enough men to completely seal off his right flank along the lagoon, placed skirmishing groups in small conclaves to detect Japanese movements and send warnings of their approach.

Edson expected that the first attack would hit B Company, and his prediction proved correct. The attack struck Gunnery Sergeant Robert J. Anielski's platoon first. Private Russell Whittlesey, waiting in a hurriedly-dug foxhole, alertly listened and searched for any evidence of Japanese movements. Not far from Whittlesey, PFC Edward Shepherd, hunkered down in his shallow hole, recalled in a 1943 letter what he saw and heard: "All was quiet except for the movement of small animals. Then we could hear the Japs cautiously advancing. They reached the far edge of the lagoon. The word was passed to hold our fire until they started crossing."[19]

Just to the north, Corporal Joseph Sweeda of Gunnery Sergeant Clinton F. Haines' 2nd Platoon, tried to hear and decipher the sounds that engulfed him. He had been on Guadalcanal long enough to recognize the "normal" nightly sounds that the jungle emitted. New sounds now surrounded him. He later recalled, "It seemed like only minutes between when darkness fell and the jungle seemed to come alive in front of us. We could hear jabbering, then movement in the brush."[20]

Private James Mallamas cradled his BAR in his arms while sharing a hole with Sergeant John Morrell on the outer edge of Haines' skirmish line. Mallamas knew his platoon's assignment was to spot any Japanese encroachment and immediately request pre-spotted artillery fire and then move back up the ridge. Just after the war's end, he recalled, "I heard a twig snap, then another, and more. We were quiet, hardly breathing. The Japs were crawling directly towards us."[21]

✲ ✲ ✲

The first Japanese attack by Kokusho's battalion struck Anielski's platoon directly at Shepherd and Whittlesey's positions on the lagoon's eastern bank. Shepherd heard the Japanese move across the lagoon and immediately threw a grenade. He heard it splash in the water but did not explode. He later remembered, "Then, all hell broke loose, the jungle was lit up like a stage, battle cries broke out from both sides." He raised his rifle, but did not get the chance to shoot. Bullets from a Japanese light machine struck him in the chest, left arm, and right shoulder. The searing pain forced him to cry out for Whittlesey. A sudden numbness in his arms forced him to drop his rifle, and it slid down into the lagoon. Whittlesey pulled Shepherd out of danger and looked for a way to get up the ridge to relative, albeit temporary, safety.

The battle now escalated chaotically with men from both sides running through the jungle and shouting to each other. "Maline, you die," and "Gas attack!" were the cries from the Japanese with the Americans replying, "You'll eat shit first, you bastards!" The American lines gave way under the weight of the vicious Japanese assaults. Japanese soldiers and American marines were so close to each other that each lobbed hand grenades at the other. Irvin Reynolds later recalled, "All hell broke loose. The Japs were crashing through the brush throwing grenades in front of them. They got the last two or three men at the end of our line."[22] Soon, the Japanese overran Company B's lines. The combat was hand-to-hand with fists, knives, teeth, and knees. It was time to call for help.

The 105-mm shells from the 11th Marine Artillery Regiment fell like rain on Japanese and Americans alike. Both Mallamas and Morrell heard the deep-throated boom of a gun firing in the distance followed by the high-pitched scream of the shell as it came toward them. It landed and exploded nearby, throwing Mallamas and Morrell into the air. But it also took its toll among the Japanese as its shards tore into flesh and bone. Now almost unconscious and bleeding from the nose and ears, Morrell lost contact with Mallamas and headed toward Edson's headquarters on top of the ridge. Mallamas wandered aimlessly in the jungle, hid in wild pig dens, tried to avoid Japanese patrols, and finally reached safety with the Company C Engineers. The men of Company B sustained many casualties but more than achieved their mission's objective. They reported the Japanese movements and their attacks to their battalion while forcing the Japanese into the preplanned killing zones set up by Edson.

Nonetheless, the action was not just isolated at Company B's position. Company A's lines lay farther north and nearer to the Lunga River. Small clusters of Japanese brushed past the Marine's lines but did not attack. Capt. Antonelli's men heard loud, raucous battle sounds to their left rear. Edson's battalion headquarters seemed to be under attack. Several marines sporadically fired their rifles into the dark and threw a few hand grenades. The 11th Marine's Artillery barrage loudly and forcefully penetrated every Marine's senses causing their ears to ring. PFC Thomas D. Smith wrote in his diary, "The dirty work is now on. We notice that the center of our [battalion] lines are breaking. Small Jap units may be heard within our lines. The shells, grenades, and machine-gun fire made a rifleman feel quite impotent. I kept eyes peeled to the front and threw an occasional grenade."[23]

The close quarters where the soldiers and Marines now fought each other made the bayonet a better weapon with which to fight than the rifle to which it was attached. The shells from the Marine 105-mm guns would kill more Japanese but, for the man in the dark jungle undergrowth, the only weapon that could kill their enemy was that deadly weapon. Hand grenades and machine guns that sprayed lethal shrapnel and bullets into the surrounding growth took a terrible toll on human flesh. With all the grenades being thrown by the Marines, they soon became an extremely precious commodity. Shouts of "More grenades!" now sprang out as those who had them would likely live and those who did not would likely perish. Edson responded by yelling to his supply officer, Capt. Ira J. Irwin, "More grenades, more machine-gun belts!" Irwin and his men worked tirelessly to get as many grenades as possible to the struggling Marines, but it proved to be inadequate. Several men at the division's HQ took the initiative and volunteered to deliver what the Marines, now fighting to the death, desperately needed. Maj. Kenneth D. Bailey, Corporal Walter Burak, Sergeant-Maj. James Childs, and Sergeant Peter Pettus joined the ad hoc group. Capt. Clarence R. Schwenke, Col. Merrill B. Twining's[24] assistant operations officer, found a truck, gathered all volunteers, loaded the truck with cases of grenades and all the machine gun ammunition they could find, and drove to the sounds of battle.

Capt. Houston Stiff, commanding E Company's mortars, also pitched in. He got lost trying to deliver grenades as the Japanese severed his escape route back to his battalion's HQ, and he was wounded twice. But these brave men were not the only ones who were busy. Navy corpsmen tended to the many critically wounded marines who staggered into a crude aid station in a small tent near the battalion HQ. Two Navy doctors, Edward McLarney and Robert W. Skinner III, along with the corpsmen, worked tirelessly tending to the men's wounds. The tent was just a few steps from Edson's HQ toward which the battle approached.

The Japanese destroyers' barrage straddled the ridge and ended with a magnesium flare bathing the ground with glaring light. Maj. Kokusho drew his sword, shouted "Banzai!" and "Death to Roosevelt!" as his 1st Battalion poured from the jungle onto the open ground. The flare's light was behind the lowly crouching Marines and poured over the approaching Japanese. They climbed up the ridge's long slope in the Kunai grass and had to gather in small groups at the barbed wire. The Americans opened with a deadly fusillade of rifle and machine gun fire and a barrage of hand grenades. The Japanese fell like weeds being cut down by a razor-sharp scythe. The Japanese did not stop. The disciplined, well-trained Marines continued to pour their fire into them by carefully firing their rifles at one man and slipping a bayonet into a second. Grenades exploded in the Japanese rear ranks. The attackers pulled back as Japanese mortar fire landed continuously on the Marine's positions.

The Japanese had not yet finished their assault. More of them poured from the jungle. Not having time to draw a single breath, the Marines' entire defensive line came under attack. Maj. Tamura, knowing that the American artillery would take a terrible toll, did not wait for Kawaguchi's order. He ordered his men of the *Sendai* battalion to climb the ridge's rise and attack the Marines. Kokusho's battalion, now battered, bloodied, and angry veterans of Borneo's jungle war, also reformed their forces and attacked with a renewed fury. They threw smoke grenades and smudge pots to hide their advance. The combination of the foul-smelling smoke and cries of "*Tsu-geki!*" [Charge!] let the Marines know they were under a gas attack. The memories of some Marine veterans of World War I introduced an old fear. World War II had yet to witness the use of poisonous gas. As far as these Marines were concerned, that meant it might start right here. Their fears proved groundless, but that still did little to allay their fear. Some panic-stricken Marines began to flee their holes. But 1st Sergeant Brice Maddox and Capt. William J. McKennan dragged and cajoled those scared souls back to their foxholes.

The Marine artillery fire continued almost unabated. When the Japanese destroyers opened fire again, some of their shells landed on the ridge's spine, taking their toll on the Marines. Tragically, more shells landed on Kawaguchi's new command post. He had relocated it to the jungle's edge just south of the ridge's southern edge. It seemed that whatever he tried did not seem to work the way he wanted. He wanted to atone for the previous night's debacle with this night's attacks. Nevertheless, the news from the ridge was not good. Reports began to filter in that portrayed this night's outcome to be worse than on the prior evening. His memoirs recorded the catastrophe that unfolded that night: "This battalion commander killed. That battalion completely annihilated. Whereabouts of [the other] battalion commander not known." Maj. Watanabe was missing. The charge by Maj. Kokusho's command killed the battalion commander as he charged up the ridge's slope. The withering fire from the Marines and their 105-mm artillery barrage cut him down. Kawaguchi wrote that Kokusho "took the lead with a drawn sword in his hand, fought like a demon in fury, killed several enemy soldiers, [and] occupied an important enemy position."[25]

Kawaguchi planned to have Oka's Battalion attack the Marine western flank along the Matanikau River while the Kuma Battalion attacked to the east near Alligator Creek. Neither attack succeeded since they became disorganized when the Marines stopped them cold. Meanwhile, on the ridge itself, the remnants of Kokusho's battalion under the command of a subaltern resumed their attacks but with little effect. However, the other two battalions that had attacked the southern front did so with increased intensity. The relentless Japanese assaults had shrunk the Marine defensive perimeter around Edson's command post on Hill 120 to a rough horseshoe-shaped line.

A deadly struggle between the 5th and 7th companies from Tamura's battalion and the Marines defending the southern "nose" of their perimeter reached a fevered pitch. Edson asked for and received intensified artillery fire that crept ever more and dangerously nearer to his lines. An English-speaking Japanese soldier tried to interfere with the instructions to the artillery battery. Edson outwitted them by recognizing the voices of his own men. The Japanese subterfuge failed.

Despite the Japanese soldiers' battle experience, they had never encountered artillery as deadly and effective as what the 11th Marines poured into them. The Japanese officers later thought the American artillery was so accurate that it seemed to be "automatic." They thought that the Americans had laid "sound detectors and automatic communications equipment" on the ridge. Marines who watched the battle from afar stared in wonder at what happened on the ridge. Bursts of light and the boom from artillery being fired rose in a steady crescendo immediately followed by brilliant flashes and the "crump" of the exploding shells on the ridge. Machine gun tracers sent lines of light that could only mean death to the men at which it was aimed. The Japanese now experienced the hell of an artillery barrage that matched the intensity of a previous war's deadly fire.

While the Japanese took heavy casualties, all was not rosy for the Marines either. Edson needed more men to replace those who had fallen in battle. He diverted the communicators to fight alongside the other riflemen. But this was not enough. His center could not hold. He tried to consolidate his position by allowing the withdrawal of some units while withering Japanese mortar, machine gun, and rifle fire poured into the Americans, a dangerous and chaotic operation under any circumstances, but more so at night.

Watanabe's attack on Edson's left flank put tremendous pressure on the Parachute Companies B and C. If they were to withdraw, they had the farthest distance to go up the ridge's slope to reach the Raider's command post. So they dug in where they were and held their lines with a spirited defense against the intense, vicious Japanese attack. Capt. William J. McKennan, the commander of Company B, 1st Parachute Battalion, which was one of two Parachute companies that held Edson's extreme left flank, wrote in 1943: "The [Japanese] attack was almost constant, like a rain that subsides for a moment and then pours the harder...When one wave was mowed down—and I mean mowed down—another followed it into death...Some of the Jap rushes were now carrying them into our positions and there was ugly hand-to-hand fighting."[26]

A Desperate Situation Getting Worse

With all the fire, smoke, and bright light flashes going on around him, Edson remained cool under the pressure. Bullets nicked his clothing and some of his command post equipment. His cold blue eyes looked at the Japanese moving up the slope, getting ever closer to where he stood. With an unemotional detachment, he picked up the telephone and called in increasing artillery fire that followed the Japanese advancement. After putting down the phone, he walked away. Seconds later, a mortar round arrived in a blinding explosion on the same spot he had just left and destroyed the phone equipment. Mortar shells landed all over Hill 120. Edson knew that the Marines defending his right flank near the lagoon were cut off by a Japanese salient from the command post. The Parachute companies on his right were in a fight for their very lives. At 4:00 a.m., an exploding mortar round cut the telephone wires to del Valle's artillery.

At about the same time, Edson and Bailey yelled for Lt. Col. William J. Whaling's 2nd Battalion, 5th Marines, which held a position a few hundred yards northwest of the command post, for help. If they did not come up soon, Edson would have to retreat and allow the Japanese to overrun the ridge and perhaps capture Henderson Field. The first appeals for help seemed to go unheeded. Despite the deafening sounds of combat, Whaling heard someone shout his name, but did not know why someone would do this.

As Edson's desperation reached an almost excruciatingly severe level, he sent Corporal Burak to run down the hill and tell the 11th Marines that his phone was out and to keep firing their batteries. After delivering his message, Burak acted independently by grabbing a reel of communication wire and dragging it up the hill as Japanese bullets whizzed around him. When he arrived to where the battalion's switchboard was, he restored the vital connection by attaching the wire to it. As soon as the telephone became ready to use, Edson picked up the receiver and called LTC Gerald C. Thomas, Vandegrift's operations officer. In his memoirs, Thomas recalled what Edson said in a tone of voice that revealed how serious the combat situation had become. In his characteristically unemotional manner, but with a rasping voice, Edson told Thomas, "I've been hit hard and I need more men. Unless you do something for yourselves, the Japs will come through you like shit through a tin horn."[27] Thomas knew Edson was not one to overly exaggerate how bad things were. Thomas collected his emotions and coolly analyzed what needed to be done. He picked up the radio microphone and contacted Whaling, who by this time was understandably inquisitive why someone had called his name. Thomas ordered Whaling to reinforce Edson. Finally knowing how serious everything was, Whaling ordered his own battalion up the ridge toward Edson's command post.

Not wanting to repeat a Pickett's-charge-like debacle,[28] he sent three rifle companies to move independently up the hill. By this time, the Japanese occupied positions from where they tried to stop Whaling's men as they climbed to Edson's aid. But the 2nd Battalion would not be denied. They arrived just in time because Edson's men were almost out of ammunition. After he and Bailey counted noses, there were only about 300 men left to fight the Japanese. But a fresh battalion was now on the scene. The tide of battle turned in favor of the Americans as the strength of Kawaguchi's attacks passed its zenith. The Marines' 105-mm howitzers, withering rifle and machine gun fire, and hand grenade barrages had mowed them down in waves. Nevertheless, the night's darkness hid the extent of the Japanese defeat.

✲ ✲ ✲

As dawn's light poured over the ridge, the battlefield's gruesome carnage yielded a scene that would have invoked stark memories from many World War I veterans. Wounded and dead bodies covered the hillside. Marine stretcher bearers became sick to their stomachs as they overloaded a three-ton truck with the wounded to carry them back to Henderson Field for air evacuation. Skirmishes continued and became so serious that Edson called for air support. The P-400s from Henderson Field immediately answered with devastating accuracy as they raked Japanese positions with .30-caliber machine gun fire. Commanding the Army aircraft with sharks' teeth painted under their nose, Capt. John A. Thompson led his three planes in a high-speed dive from 1,000 feet toward the ridge. Later, he recalled, "I saw the Marines on the ridge as I came in over the trees and below the ridge in a clearing were hundreds of enemy troops crowded together, caught by surprise."[29]

Kawaguchi had sustained the first defeat of his career, and he knew it. Daylight exposed his command to American air superiority. He had no choice but to withdraw his men back under the jungle's protective cover and away from the ridge. His plan to retake Henderson Field was a miserable failure. He estimated his casualties at 41 officers and 1,092 men killed or wounded or 1,133 casualties. This blight on his record sent his career into a downward spiral from which he never recovered.

Although victory belonged to the Marines, they were not exactly in a mood to celebrate. As the men came down the ridge, they had the look of men who had fought an exhausting struggle: gaunt, starved, dehydrated, circles around their eyes, pale gray skin, and seeming barely alive. They did not know how many they had lost. Many of them, dead and wounded, lay in the jungle and hidden by the high Kunai grass on the ridge's slopes. The author of Edson's official biography, Jon T. Hoffman, estimated that the Raiders' losses at 41 killed and 129 wounded—a total of 163 casualties and almost one-fourth of Edson's command. This was just as one-sided a victory as another small unit battle, the British defense of the 1876 Rorke's Drift Mission Station in South Africa's Natal Province where about 139 British infantry soldiers defeated a Zulu army of more than 4,000 warriors.[30]

Vandegrift nominated both Edson[31] and Bailey (posthumous)[32] for the Congressional Medal of Honor. The American nation awarded the medal to both officers.

It is usual that everyone who earned these honors did not actually receive them. Many Marines conducted themselves with bravery and sacrifice those two nights of September 12 and 13, 1942, and still were not awarded any recognition. Nonetheless, 14 men received the Navy Cross for their actions in this battle.[33]

What Did "Bloody Ridge" All Mean?

Kawaguchi's failure to capture Henderson Field meant that the "permanent land-based aircraft carrier" the Americans now possessed would remain so, not only for that time but for the rest of the Guadalcanal campaign. The Japanese would attempt to land more troops in the future and still Henderson Field would hold, despite repeated Japanese tries to change that fact. With the Americans continuing to pour in aircraft, men, and supplies, the strategic situation for the Japanese could only worsen, and it did. However, there were more battles to fight and more changes to come. The Americans had solidified their foothold on Guadalcanal although their strategic situation would, in their eyes, remain uncertain.[34]

The struggle for Guadalcanal reached a turning point on land. More battles at sea would have to be fought to decide if the Americans would assume a dominant position there or not. The Japanese still believed they could retake Henderson Field, and soon attempted another landing. The result would be another sea battle near Guadalcanal's northwest corner off Cape Esperance. Nevertheless, the strategic situation remained fluid and would be tested repeatedly as long the Japanese believed they could win. There were more battles to fight, and, as has been certain in warfare throughout the ages, many more men would die.

CHAPTER 25
Assessment

An Important Visitor from Washington

The fight in Washington over the aircraft availability for Operation Torch, the invasion of North Africa, and the Navy's operation in the Solomon Islands reached a crisis. Adm. King raged at a meeting of the Joint Chiefs on September 16, "There should be a reconsideration of allocation every time there is a new critical situation; the Navy is in a bad way at this particular moment." Gen. Arnold, the senior officer who had responsibility for meeting America's needs for aircraft, told King that Marshall and he agreed to send 15 P-38s to the South Pacific. But Arnold made the point that he did not have enough aircraft to "saturate" that theater: "What is the saturation point? Certainly, not several hundred planes sitting on airdromes so far in the rear that they cannot be used. They will not do us any good, and may do us some harm." Arnold mentioned that Gen. Marshall had asked him to go to the South Pacific to check out the situation for himself. King seemed to be placated, but one could never know what King really thought at any moment.

Maj. Gen. Millard F. Harmon commanded American Army Forces in the Southwest Pacific. He had two subordinates, Maj. Gen. Alexander M. ("Sandy") Patch and Brig. Gen. Nathan F. Twining. Patch commanded the ground forces, and Twining led the Army air forces. Arnold knew him well and had great confidence in Harmon's ability. He had served as Arnold's chief of staff before being promoted to his current assignment. Harmon had been in the Air Force for more than 17 years and intimately knew airplanes and their capabilities. Arnold knew he would get the straight story from Harmon when he visited him during his trip.

Arnold met with Marshall on September 18 to ask his superior's advice. Marshall told him to listen to what everyone had to say, keep his temper, and keep an open mind. Two days later, Arnold, along with members of his staff, Brig. Gen. St. Claire Streett, Col. Charles P. Cabell, and Col. Emmett McCabe, flew to Hamilton Field in California and on to Hawaii. When they arrived in Honolulu, Lt. Gen. Delos C. Emmons, commander of all Hawaiian Army air units, and Maj. Gen. Willis Hale, commander of the 7th Air Force met Arnold.

Emmons had just returned from a trip to the Southwest Pacific where he met with Ghormley, Harmon, and MacArthur. His report to Arnold of these meetings did little to raise Arnold's optimism. MacArthur seemed to be ill and complained that the Air Force commanders neglected their duty when aircraft were caught on the ground when the Japanese invaded the Philippines in 1941.

Arnold's meeting with Nimitz and the admiral's staff revealed the Navy had an optimistic view of the situation in the Southwest Pacific. Emmons did not share that optimism. He felt that the Japanese would recapture Guadalcanal because it could not be held. Nimitz disagreed. The admiral argued that the Japanese could not continue to suffer their heavy shipping losses and keep their troops on Guadalcanal supplied with enough materiel to sustain their effort to keep Guadalcanal. According to Nimitz, Japanese worries were on the rise. Showing a firmer and broader grasp of the strategic situation, he backed his assessment with the following arguments:

1. The Japanese would continue to hold New Guinea's north coast, try to capture Port Moresby, and throw the Marines off Guadalcanal. Their resources were being stretched to their limits.
2. They only had one-half the men the Americans had in the Southern Solomons.
3. The Navy could meet and defeat every Japanese move.
4. Henderson Field would be ready to use in a few days.
5. The Japanese would move through Ellice Island.
6. The Japanese lost 650 planes at the Battle of Midway and from air battles over and around Guadalcanal New Guinea.
7. The Japanese had lost two carriers and all the aircraft aboard them.
8. Japanese planes and pilots were inferior to their American counterparts.
9. Bombing Germany would yield limited results.
10. His command's first priority for their air forces was to protect shipping to Australia.
11. Alaska did not need any more aircraft.
12. The Japanese had no desire to invade Alaska.
13. They would not reinforce Kiska with either planes or ships.
14. Japanese priorities were to move everything they had to the Southeast—particularly the Philippines, the Celebes, Sumatra, and Borneo.

Arnold listened carefully to Nimitz's claims and said he would meet with the admiral again after he returned form the Southwest Pacific. He flew to New Caledonia, with stops at Christmas Island, Vite Levu (Fiji), and Tongatabu. As soon as his plane landed at Tongatabu, Twining met him and they flew 120 miles in a B-17 to an airport 30 miles from Nouméa that had a runway long enough to accommodate the bomber. Gen. Patch met them, and they drove to Nouméa. Harmon could not meet Arnold because he was at Guadalcanal. All rested at Patch's quarters and later went to see Ghormley on the *Argonne*.

It became abundantly clear the naval officers were under considerable strain and, as Arnold said in his book, *Global Mission*, "had chips on their shoulders." Ghormley said he was too busy to leave his ship for almost a month. Arnold tried to persuade him that the opposite should be true when he emphasized that a commander had to be out in his command to better appreciate the problems his men faced.

It did not take long for Arnold to realize that something had to change here and the sooner, the better. Ghormley jealously guarded his prerogatives by saying this was his command and no one could tell him how to run it. As Arnold tried to calm the admiral by stating that all he wanted was information, the general knew the naval officers—Ghormley, McCain, and Callaghan—were very worried about the outcome in that theater.

Ghormley's concerns almost exclusively focused on logistics, which seemed ludicrous because he had more than 80 ships loaded with supplies waiting to be unloaded. He also worried about potential, albeit unconfirmed, Japanese southeastern movements. Guadalcanal's supply situation was especially critical with desperate shortages in gasoline and supplies. Sending ships to Guadalcanal was particularly difficult because of Ghormley's fears of Japanese naval and air attacks.

Ghormley's obsession with problems rather than solutions left Arnold aghast. It seemed ludicrous that all those ships were in that harbor because the naval officers did not know what was on them. They had to send them to New Zealand to unload and reload just to know what was on aboard. When Arnold realized the shortages Operation Torch faced and that here were supplies languishing on these ships, he understood why supplies for that operation were so short.

McCain was an aviation expert and knew the power of American heavy bombers, but he wanted to use Army bombers for reconnaissance just as the Navy used their PBYs. McCain wanted Army fighters to defend Henderson Field from Japanese bombing attacks. As he sat and listened, Arnold became incensed. Unless Guadalcanal could be supplied and soon, the Marines' position there was precarious. Guadalcanal could not be held unless the Japanese air attacks could be stopped so ships could be sent there and supplies unloaded unimpeded.

Arnold left Ghormley and met with Patch, who said the Navy had no clue about how to manage the logistics for Guadalcanal. Patch did everything he could for the Marines and the Navy by sending them 20,000 pairs of shoes and other supplies. The Navy had not established priority for gasoline and ammunition for the planes at Henderson Field, resulting in critical shortages of those vital items. The planes at Henderson Field had no gasoline reserves at all.

Arnold revisited Ghormley and his senior commanders the next day. McCain criticized the European air war by saying that while the bombers were effective in bombing European targets, it was a waste of valuable fighter resources to use them there. They would be far more effective being used in the Southwest Pacific. Arnold then thought of several key questions: "Where is this war to be won? What is our plan for winning the war—if we have a plan? Is this a local affair, and should it be treated as such?"[1] As far as Arnold was concerned, the American military had agreed to a joint Allied strategy: the war's priority was to defeat the Nazis in Europe and everyone, including the Navy in the Pacific, should get on board and add their unrestrained support for that plan.

He concluded that Marines were in a bad way on Guadalcanal, and the nickname given to the campaign, "Operation Shoestring," was apt. The men on Guadalcanal were tired and on the verge of collapse unless the Navy solved their logistics problem. His visit convinced him that there had to be a unified command in the entire Pacific Theater. Nonetheless, he obviously did not understand MacArthur's political clout and the Navy's adamant opposition to allowing MacArthur command of any American naval force.

☆ ☆ ☆

Arnold flew to Brisbane on September 25 to see MacArthur. MacArthur and his chief of staff, Maj. Gen. Richard K. Sutherland, met Arnold at the airport. MacArthur's assessment of the Pacific Theater was that while they had effectively fought the Japanese Army in New Guinea, they could not be defeated with the troops he currently had. He was satisfied with his Air Force commanders since they had successfully transported an entire brigade of Australian soldiers to New Guinea to stop the Japanese from taking Port Moresby.

After visiting New Guinea and meeting with various American and Australian generals, Arnold strongly felt that the Allies had to go on the offensive soon or they could lose New Guinea and Australia with it. His meetings with MacArthur and his generals convinced him that this part of the Pacific War had a good chance to deliver a victory. However, he could not say the same for the Guadalcanal operation because of the pessimism of the Southwest Pacific's top commander. The people actually doing the fighting believed they could defeat the Japanese if they got the men and materiel they badly needed.

☆ ☆ ☆

After stopping at Espiritu Santo, he flew to Nouméa to meet Radm. Aubrey W. Fitch. During that meeting, Fitch did not make any more demands on the Army Air Force resources. Fitch was not too concerned about Guadalcanal and had deep convictions the Americans would be victorious.

Arnold then met with Admirals Nimitz, Ghormley, Callaghan, and Turner and Generals Sutherland, Harmon, Kenney, and Streett. The meetings strengthened Arnold's ever stronger belief that the command of this theater had to be unified. The advance of Ghormley's forces up the Solomon chain would eventually meet MacArthur's advance in New Guinea. When this happened, both commands' troops, ships, and aircraft would be operating in the same place and time, which would lead to a ridiculously confusing and dangerous circumstances.

However, Arnold hoped the arrival of the B-29 long range bomber would force a solution. They could directly attack the Japanese homeland and thus operate far beyond the geographical boundaries of either command. He knew he had to retain control of this new weapon in the Pacific. He could not give them to MacArthur because they would operate ahead of Nimitz's command. He also could not give them to Nimitz because they would operate ahead of MacArthur's command. In spite of his strong opinions on a unified Pacific command, he could not find anyone who wanted that job unless that man was made supreme commander. The Navy's determination to carry on with the Guadalcanal campaign meant that there was no way on God's green earth that they would allow an Army general, particularly Douglas MacArthur, to gain that exalted title.

Return to Hawaii

The trip seemed long when Arnold's plane finally landed at Hickam Field. The warm tropical air with its refreshing trade wind breezes greeted Arnold and his party as they descended to the tarmac. Gen. Emmons greeted them and reported that he had developed a satisfactory and rewarding working relationship with Nimitz. Arnold was undoubtedly relieved to hear this news after being subjected to the Southwest Pacific naval officers' ridiculously defensive attitudes. Emmons thought Nimitz was one of the most brilliant naval officers with whom he had ever had contact. Since Arnold had many dealings with other naval officers, this news pleasantly surprised him.

Arnold needed to take advantage of that positive assessment as he prepared his thoughts for his report to Marshall and other senior officials in Washington. The Navy would command Army troops, but never have their own forces commanded by an Army officer. They did not understand massed ground operations and the use of massive air power the way the Army Air Force—and the way the Germans tried to during the Battle of Britain—applied it to destroy an enemy's air force. The Navy dispersed their air forces over several bases on distant islands rather than concentrating them. This prevented the Japanese air forces from destroying them all on the ground. Their logistics system seemed unsuited for supplying ground troops engaged in a long, difficult ground war. Arnold thought this was a waste of valuable air crews and scarce supplies. But the most important shortcoming was, in Arnold's mind, the lack of a unified command structure under a single commanding officer.

Reporting to Washington

The trip by Arnold and his staff to the South Pacific lasted for 12 days. It was an exhausted group that finally landed in Washington on October 2. But the trip was a highly educational and fruitful journey that would have a direct impact on the Navy's efforts in the Pacific. Although tired, Arnold presented his findings to Secretary of War Henry L. Stimson and Gen. Marshall who found his findings equally valuable. Stimson suggested that Arnold present his findings to Secretary of the Navy Frank Knox and Adm. King. Arnold's briefing to Under Secretary of the Navy James V. Forrestal, Adm. King, and King's staff officers went quite well. They seemed genuinely interested in what Arnold had to say and took copious notes. Forrestal asked many questions and seemed to want to learn as many facts as he could. But Knox's reception of Arnold's report met with quite a different results.

Knox asked Arnold to present his findings, and the general immediately went over to see the Secretary. After exchanging the normally courteous pleasantries, Arnold began talking.[2]

Arnold: Mr. Secretary, I completed my trip to the South Pacific Theater and enjoyed meeting with the naval officers there. There is a very difficult campaign going on down there, and the Navy really has its hands full. The gallantry of the marines on Guadalcanal cannot be exaggerated. The Navy's efforts to prevent the Japanese from supplying their troops on that island have been brave but with grave loses.

Nevertheless, I want to tell you my findings with the hope that positive changes can come from them. There are a number of concerns I have about that I want to...

Knox: I don't want to hear about your concerns. How dare you criticize the Navy who, as you say, are in a tough fight? All the Army wants is to give MacArthur control. That will never happen on my watch. And I know the President shares that opinion too.

If Knox would not listen, that was all right with Arnold. All the general wanted to do was to present the facts as he saw them and let the Secretary take any action he saw fit. The meeting ended abruptly, and Arnold left the Secretary's office wondering how the U.S. would ever win the war with the parochial attitudes and jealousy of prerogatives that existed at that time. Nonetheless, Nimitz was about to begin his own investigation.[3]

Nimitz's Fact Finding

After meeting with Arnold, Nimitz's thoughts of the reasons for the Army Air Force most senior officer's trip led him to decide to observe the Guadalcanal scene for himself. Although his optimism that the Marines would hold onto Guadalcanal was still with him, he was not entirely satisfied that all that needed to be done to ensure success there was being done. He had to know how serious the state of affairs was in the Southwest Pacific before Arnold reported his findings to the Joint Chiefs and the Navy in Washington. He knew that after Arnold presented his trip's findings he would be bombarded with "helpful suggestions" from King. Being proactive, he left Pearl Harbor and flew to Nouméa on September 25 in a Coronado flying boat. Col. Omar T. Pfeiffer, his senior Marine staff office, Capt. John R. Redman, his communicator; Cmdr. Ralph Ofstie, his air officer; Cmdr. William M. Callaghan, his petroleum and tanker expert; and Lt. H. Arthur Lamar, his aide joined him on the plane.

Nimitz sent a telegram to MacArthur asking the general to join him at Nouméa. MacArthur answered that while he could not leave his command at this time, he would send some of his senior officers to represent him.

A burned-out bearing on one of the plane's engines forced the party to land on Canton Island where they had to wait for a replacement aircraft to be flown in from Pearl Harbor. Knowing he would be delayed on Canton until his planes arrived from Pearl, he arranged to meet with Adm. McCain there. McCain had just begun a new job in Washington and was on his way there when he landed and met his old comrade. Nimitz and McCain knew each other from the time McCain served with Nimitz aboard the gunboat *Panay*. Nimitz wanted to hear McCain's opinion about the Guadalcanal situation and looked forward to seeing him. McCain was only one year older than Nimitz; his thin, skeleton-like body, hooked nose, and sunken cheeks made him look older by more than just that one year.

The two men went to the posh Pan American Hotel that had been completed just before war broke out. They moved into two separate bedrooms that shared an adjacent bathroom. At last, they sat down together, and McCain began to talk. McCain said that the Americans could hold Guadalcanal only if they could have enough fighter planes with trained pilots to shoot down enough Japanese bombers that had by now been delivering almost daily bombing attacks on Henderson Field. As if to punctuate the point, an air raid alert that night forced everyone on Canton to head for the nearest shelter.

Nimitz's replacement plane arrived from Hawaii the next morning. He immediately flew to Nouméa and arrived there on September 28. As the plane circled to land in the harbor, Nimitz looked through the windows and saw a harbor crowded with more than 80 transport ships. Apparently, Arnold's report was accurate after all, although Nimitz had no reason to believe otherwise. The rationale given for the ships remaining unloaded was that they originated in the U.S. and had not been loaded for combat operations. For instance, artillery guns and the ammunition needed for their operation were on separate vessels. Nouméa's harbor did not have the necessary docks, trucks, workers, and railroad facilities to unload the ships' cargoes and reload them to be ready for delivery in the forward area. Therefore, they had to be sent to New Zealand where such capabilities existed and returned to the combat areas. The logical question was: Why were the Americans not engaged in an aggressive effort to get such facilities expeditiously built? We do not know what Nimitz thought about when he saw the chaotic scene. But if he did, he got his answer when he met with Ghormley.

A depressing sight greeted Nimitz as he walked aboard the *Argonne* and saw a weary and worried Ghormley sitting at his desk. The cramped cabin had no air conditioning and the oppressive, humid, stale air suffocated all there like a damp blanket. Ghormley had a haggard look like a beaten man, and seemed to be glued to his chair. He hardly ever left the cramped cabin. Nimitz knew that as the senior American representative in Nouméa, Ghormley deserved more comfortable quarters. But it never occurred to Ghormley's narrowly inflexible, bureaucratic, and administrative mind to ask the French officials in New Caledonia for the facilities to which he was entitled.

Nimitz convened the conference for which he traveled to New Caledonia in the first place. It began at 4:30 p.m. aboard the *Argonne.* The attendees were an imposing group of officers that represented every possible American service branch that had an interest in the Southwest Pacific. Besides Nimitz and Ghormley and their staffs, the following senior officers were there:

1. Gen. Arnold and his assistant, Gen. Streett; on their way back to Washington
2. MacArthur's chief of staff, Maj. Gen. Richard K. Sutherland, and his air commander, Lt. Gen. George C. Kenney;
3. Adm. Turner;
4. Maj. Gen. Millard F. Harmon, SOPAC Army commander;
5. Marine Corps Colonels De Witt Peck and Omar T. Pfeiffer.

As each man settled into their chairs, Nimitz opened the meeting, "The purpose of my visit is to inform myself and members of my staff with conditions in the SOPAC area, and to inform myself on the problems of Adm. Ghormley and Gen. MacArthur. We will begin the conference by having Ghormley or Harmon outline the situation in this area."[4] Ghormley presented the situation as he saw it in his command. Turner gave his opinion on the overall American strategy in the Southwest Pacific.

Arnold portrayed the overall global strategy by talking about the various campaigns being planned in the various theaters. He emphasized that the mounting demands for ships, planes, and tanks placed particular stresses on the supply systems to meet the needs of each theater's commander. His criticisms of Ghormley's practice of holding fighter aircraft in reserve at the Southwest Pacific's various bases while the need for these planes on Guadalcanal continued to grow hit particularly hard. He indicated that while there were aircraft available in the Southwest Pacific, there would be no more planes sent until Ghormley sent the planes he had to where they were needed.

After the meeting's transition from presentation to discussion, Nimitz asked some tough questions. With doubts rising about the Marines' ability to hold Guadalcanal, why were Army troops being held in reserve on New Caledonia? Did Ghormley investigate whether any aircraft could be brought in from New Zealand? Why had additional naval resources not been deployed to stop the Tokyo Express? As the questions mounted that seemed to point to Ghormley's inadequacies as a theater commander, a staff officer twice brought him newly-arrived priority radio dispatches. Seeming to be totally befuddled by the mounting pressures of command, he reacted to these messages by mumbling under his breath, "My God, what are we going to do about this?"[5] It never seemed to occur to him to excuse himself from the meeting to address the situation or at least issue orders to act upon what the messages said. We do not know Nimitz's or any of the other senior officers' thoughts of this behavior, but their thoughts could not have been positive. After three and a half hours, the meeting disbanded.

✲ ✲ ✲

In a more relaxed atmosphere, Nimitz awarded the Navy Cross to Turner the next day. Accompanied by Maj. Gen. Alexander Patch, commander of the ground forces on New Caledonia, he then inspected Nouméa's defenses. After lunch, he boarded his seaplane and flew to Espiritu Santo. There he presented several decorations including a Distinguished Service medal to Adm. Fitch.

On September 30, Nimitz and his party flew to Guadalcanal in a B-17 because there was no safe place for his seaplane to land. The plane's pilot had no charts showing the course to get there, but he pointed the plane in the correct direction. It was raining hard when the B-17 flew over Guadalcanal. Poor visibility increased the danger as the pilot could not find Henderson Field. Fortunately, Lt. Lamar had brought a *National Geographic* with him. This proved to be a life saver when Lamar went up to the cockpit and guided the pilot to the airstrip.

Rain poured as Nimitz stepped off the plane. Gen. Vandegrift greeted him with a crisp military salute. Not letting the rain stop him from his reasons for coming to Guadalcanal, Nimitz carefully scrutinized the airfield, Bloody Ridge (Edson's Ridge), and the Marine defensive positions. He asked to see a temporary hospital and then talked to the wounded being housed there and those with more serious injuries waiting to be transported to Nouméa and Espiritu Santo.

Nimitz and the other officers had dinner and met afterward for a short time. Vandegrift and he met alone and had a fruitful exchange. Vandegrift minced no words expressing his opinions:[6]

Vandegrift: Sir, Admiral Turner wants me to go on the offensive and attack Japanese positions along the northern coast. In my opinion, my division's resources are too limited to do anything but stay on the defensive to protect Henderson Field. This airstrip is what the Japanese want more than anything else. After all, establishing that field was the original reason they came to this place. If we can hold Henderson Field, we can hold Guadalcanal. If I dispersed my forces to do what Admiral Turner wants, my perimeter defense would become too thin to prevent the Japanese from taking Henderson Field.

My men have only been reinforced with the 7th Regiment thus far, and there is no immediate prospect of getting more men or being relieved as was originally planned. We do not get enough replacement planes to backfill for those that are lost or heavily damaged. We need more men and planes.

Nimitz: Alex, thank you for your straight talk. I have been impressed with what you and your men have done with the limited resources you have. I have much to think over. One thing I can say at this time, something will be done although I cannot say at this time what that will be. Now, let's relax over a drink before I have to leave tomorrow.

As the two men relaxed over that drink later, Nimitz said, "You know, Vandegrift, when this war is over we are going to write a new set of *Navy Regulations.* So just keep it in the back of your mind because I will want to know some of the things you think ought to be changed." Vandegrift replied in his normally frank manner, "I know one right now. Leave out all reference that he who runs his ship aground will face a fate worse than death. Out here too many commanders have been far too leery about risking their ships." As the general said these critical words, a smile came over Nimitz's face as he recalled the only blight on his own record was when he ran the *Decatur*, his first command, aground and received a gentle reprimand.

Nimitz awarded decorations to some men the next morning before boarding a B-17 to return to Espiritu Santo. Since Henderson Field's runway was too short for the takeoff of loaded heavy bombers, Nimitz split his staff among two B-17s to lighten their loads. Before he left, he promised Vandegrift he would get all the support that he could to the general.

It was vital that the admiral's plane depart soon since Espiritu Santo's airfield had no landing lights. Therefore, they could only land in daylight. Henderson Field's airstrip was still muddy from the heavy rains. After one abortive attempt to takeoff, Nimitz's plane left on the second try with the second B-17 leaving 20 minutes later. Just as sunset descended on Espiritu Santo, his plane landed in the partial light. The second B-17 arrived in the dark after Nimitz ordered that a searchlight point to the sky and that oil drums be placed along the runway and lit to bring the second plane safely home.

Nimitz flew on to Nouméa and met with Ghormley on October 2 for a final time before returning to Pearl Harbor. We do not know what the conversation between the two men was, but the two main topics undoubtedly were reinforcing Guadalcanal and stopping the Tokyo Express. Perhaps the two admirals had a talk something like this:

Nimitz: Bob, I have just returned from meetings with Vandegrift, McCain, Turner and other officers under your command. The Marines and sailors are giving everything they've got, but they, particularly the Marines on Guadalcanal, are tired and need relief. You have troops and planes on other islands that are not fighting anyone. Why have you not transferred some of them to help out the Marines?

Ghormley: Sir, I have intelligence the Japanese are planning to invade Ndeni and other outlying islands to the south and east of Guadalcanal. I have to keep them in reserve in case they launch an attack.

Nimitz: The Japanese are too busy trying to hold on to Buna and kick the Marines off Guadalcanal. MacArthur is giving them a bad time in New Guinea. They have no time, men or planes for any other offensives. Guadalcanal must be reinforced and Vandegrift's division relieved immediately. We also need more planes sent to reinforce those at Henderson Field.

Ghormley: I already have sent the 7th Marine regiment to add more men to Guadalcanal. But I do not have the supplies and ships to transfer such a large force to relieve Vandegrift. The supply situation here is so tough that I do not know how we can win here. All the priorities are being given to Eisenhower for Operation Torch, and we just get the dregs.

Nimitz: Yes, I saw over 80 ships in the harbor when I landed here the first time. Hap Arnold told me that he could not understand why so many ships were sitting idle in that harbor out there and with no supplies being unloaded. The supplies on those ships must get to where they are needed the most—to the front lines.

I know the nearest facilities to get them unloaded and their cargoes redistributed to meet combat requirements are in New Zealand. We must start constructing what we need at Espiritu Santo and here in Nouméa. You cannot continue to avoid meeting with the French officials to gain their agreement to get this done. I am sure that if you insist that construction be started immediately, the French would not stand in your way.

The Marines are fighting for their lives on Guadalcanal. If they lose Guadalcanal, we lose the island to the Japanese and any dream of stopping them from cutting our supply lines to New Zealand and Australia. Guadalcanal needs the supplies on those ships, more men, more planes to replace battle losses and to add to their numbers, and build up Henderson Field to stop the Tokyo Express.

I know you have supply problems with this theater because you are not getting the same high priority Torch has. Every theater commander in this war has the same problems you have. And they have learned to adjust to their predicament. You must be more aggressive. Those Marines are desperate for reinforcements, planes, and supplies. Orders must be issued immediately by you to transfer those men and planes and start building this port into a full-fledged supply base.

The previously recalcitrant Ghormley finally issued orders to send an Army regiment on New Caledonia. The planes all stayed where they were. Nimitz left Nouméa and headed back to Pearl Harbor. As he took the long flight home, he knew something had to change. He was concerned about Ghormley's health and how that must be affecting his ability to command. But he was not yet sure what needed to be done. He would think about it and meet with his staff at Pearl Harbor as soon as he returned home.

Ghormley's orders began a sequence of events that would have a considerable effect of the course of the battle for Guadalcanal. The Americal Division's 164th Infantry Regiment, a former National Guard unit from North and South Dakota, left New Caledonia for Nouméa. They boarded the transports *Zeilin* and *McCawley* and sailed for Lunga Point on October 8. A large naval force covered their journey that included battle groups led by the carrier *Hornet* and the battleship *Washington*. Task Force 64, commanded by Radm. Norman Scott with four cruisers and five destroyers was supplying close tactical support for the Regiment's landings.[7] The next major naval battle of Guadalcanal was about to be fought.

Part 6: The Battle of Cape Esperance

CHAPTER 26
The Tokyo Express Begins Again

A New Japanese Approach

The giant Kawanishi Flying Boat[1] had been on an 800-mile northward course for almost seven hours across the western Pacific Ocean. It carried in it the Japanese dream to recapture the airfield on Guadalcanal and evict the American invaders. Aboard were two Imperial Japanese Navy and two Imperial Army officers. They were Capt. Yasuji Watanabe, the Combined Fleet's planning officer; Cmdr. Toshikazu Ohmae, 11th Air Fleet staff; Col. Masanobu Tsuji, chief of the Operations Section, Army Gen. Staff; and Maj. Tadahiko Hayashi of the 17th Army. The big plane banked and landed smoothly in the Truk lagoon. A boat met the plane and took the four officers ashore to meet with a man who had by now become a legend in Japanese military lore.

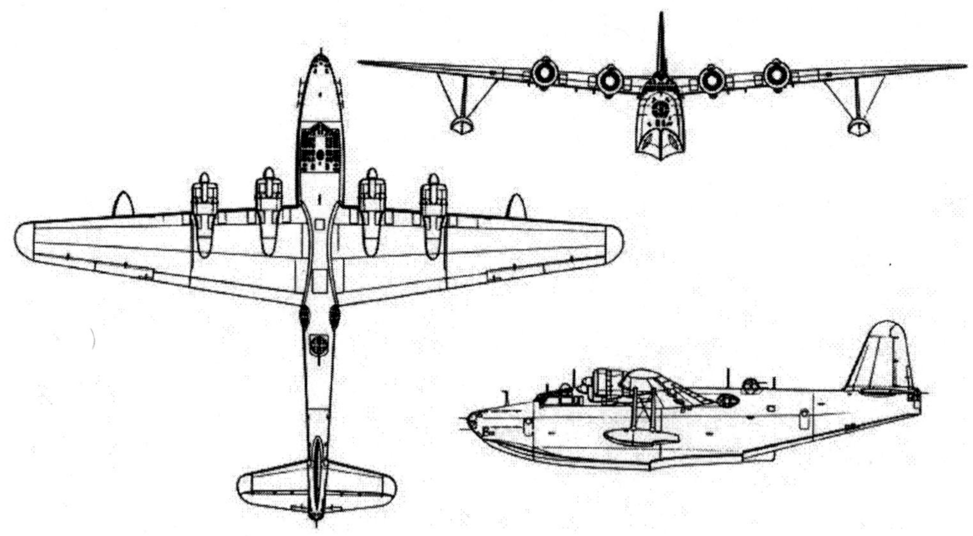

Kawanishi "Emily" Flying Boat

The purpose of this trip was to meet with Adm. Yamamoto and persuade him to provide help from the Imperial Japanese Navy in a planned joint operation. The Japanese had grand plans to retake the airfield on Guadalcanal ever since the Marines arrived on August 7. The Japanese Army's three attempts to achieve that goal had thus far ended in failure: (1) The Ichiki Detachment's attack, (2) Kawaguchi Brigade's failure at Bloody Ridge, and (3) Kawaguchi's second attempt at the Matanikau

River. They had grossly underestimated American strength on the island. These repeated failures forced the Japanese to increase their estimates by September 19. They concluded there were 7,500 American ground troops on Guadalcanal. They still could not believe that the Americans could ever land that many troops, much less any more. But the reality was something else again. By the end of September, American ground forces numbered 19,000. By October 13, it would increase to more than 23,000.

The Japanese judged that the next attack on the Americans had to have much more power than before. So they decided to send down an entire division along with more heavy guns to counter the apparent American artillery advantage that was one of the major causes of their humiliating defeat at Bloody Ridge. Despite losing all the ground battles to date, the victory at Savo Island buoyed their confidence. Since they estimated that only 7,500 American troops were on Guadalcanal, the landing of an entire division should seal their victory on Guadalcanal.

However, sending an entire division required a much greater naval and transport effort than anything the Japanese attempted thus far. So, this required a much more coordinated operation than previous attempts to reinforce Guadalcanal. Yamamoto's approval of the plan became essential for the plan's success. Col. Tsuji presented the plan to the admiral and described the Japanese soldiers' problems on Guadalcanal as they were "thinner than [Mahatma] Gandhi himself." Clearly moved by Tsuji's plea, Yamamoto responded, "If Army men have been starving through lack of supplies, then the Navy should be ashamed of itself." He approved the use of five transports, now in critically short supply, to carry the troops. He also took advantage of the situation to finalize a plan that had been in the detailed discussion stage among his staff officers to begin using his battleships to bombard Henderson Field and further cripple the CACTUS Air Force. The invasion of Guadalcanal by a large Army force and the heavy shelling of Guadalcanal's airfield became the two pillars of the Navy's role in retaking Guadalcanal.

Tsuji returned to Rabaul and told a now happy Lt. Gen. Harukichi Hyakutake, commander of the 17th Army headquartered on Rabaul, that the Navy would back the Army general's plan. Hyakutake set the tentative date for the invasion for October 21. Hyakutake's plan expressed the optimism of the Japanese with the grandiose expression: "The operation to surround and recapture Guadalcanal will truly decide the fate of the control of the entire Pacific area..."[2]

Realizing that the American Solomons' operation now had to be taken seriously as well as the need to capture Port Moresby on New Guinea, the Imperial Gen. Headquarters ordered the Japanese Army to take troops from operations in China, the East Indies, the Philippines, and Truk, send them to Rabaul, and place them under Hyakutake's command. The combined force was a powerful one that consisted of two divisions, one brigade, and one reinforced battalion. This force did not lack the support needed to launch a full-fledged infantry attack. The 4th Heavy Field Artillery Regiment along with its powerful 150-mm field guns arrived at Rabaul in September 1942.

The disparate units, although consisting of veterans of warfare in other parts of the Japanese Empire, had never fought as a single force and had never been challenged by a larger, well-trained force such as the 1st Marine Division now ensconced on Guadalcanal.

The seriousness of the Japanese purpose was quite clear. They wanted to end this American intrusion into their grand plan for the Solomon Islands, and nothing would stop them.

Hyakutake collected the following Army units at Rabaul with Hyakutake himself in command:

- Maruyama's 2nd Division,
- Lt. Gen. Masao Maruyama commanding two battalions from the 38th Division,
- one regiment and three batteries of heavy field artillery,
- three battalions and one battery of field antiaircraft artillery plus extra batteries,
- one battalion and one battery of independent mountain artillery,
- one trench mortar battalion,
- one tank company,
- three rapid-fire gun battalions
- engineering, transport, and medical troops,
- and a few Special Naval Landing Force troops.

The Navy assembled the Reinforcement Group, with Radm. Takaji Joshima in command, that had the capacity to carry such a large force in the following ships:

Light Carriers: *Chitose, Nisshin*

Destroyers: *Akizuki, Asagumo, Natsugumo, Yamagumo, Murakumo, Shirayuki*

The *Chitose* and *Nisshin* carried 280 Army personnel, two field guns, four 150-mm howitzers with vehicles that could tow them, four tractors, one AA gun, ammunition, miscellaneous equipment, medical supplies, and six landing craft. The rest of the Army personnel loaded aboard five of the six destroyers.

To prepare for landing the troops, the Bombardment Group commanded by Radm. Aritomo Goto would arrive after the Army and clobber Henderson Field with high explosive shells intended to devastate Henderson Field's effectiveness as a "land-based aircraft carrier." It had the heavy cruisers *Aoba*, commanded by Capt. Yonejiro Hisamune, *Furutaka*, led by Capt. Araki Tsutau, and *Kinugasa*, commanded by Capt. Masao Sawa, and the destroyers *Hatsuyuki*, and *Fubuki*. Normally, heavy ship bombardments preceded amphibious operations to suppress defenses on land before troops touched the shore. The Japanese confidence in their superiority in fighting a night surface battle justified in their minds this departure from military doctrine. Adm. Mikawa, commander of the 8th Fleet, assigned the relatively junior Goto to command the cruiser force—again reinforcing their belief that no American naval force could defeat the Imperial Japanese Navy in a night surface battle.

The Reinforcement Group sailed from Rabaul on October 3. The Bombardment Group left the Shortlands eight days later.[3]

The American Plans

An American fleet also approached Guadalcanal for the same reason the Japanese Bombardment Group steamed nearer. The Marines badly needed reinforcements. This fact forced Ghormley to send the Army's 146th Infantry Regiment to add to the Marines' numbers. Three powerful American naval forces moved nearer to the Solomons. The first and second forces were the *Hornet* (Task Force 17) and *Washington* (Task Group 17.8) to defend against any possible interference from Japanese air forces.

Task Force 17, under the command of Radm. George D. Murray, moved to a position about 180 miles away to the southwest of Guadalcanal. The *Washington*'s task group, commanded by Radm. Willis A. Lee, moved to about 50 miles east of Malaita.

The third was Radm. Norman Scott's Task Force 64.2. This was the strongest surface force the Americans had sent to the waters near Guadalcanal since the Battle of Savo Island and included two heavy cruisers, the *San Francisco* and *Salt Lake City*, two light cruisers, the *Helena* and *Boise*, and five destroyers, the *Farenholt*, *Buchanan*, *Laffey*, *Duncan*, and *McCalla*. Scott would have normally had two more cruisers and more destroyers under his command. But these vitally needed warships were in short supply in the U.S. Navy. The shortage was due to two factors: Only ten months had transpired since Pearl Harbor and the higher priority needs for the upcoming invasion of North Africa. Consequently Task Force 64 carried the designation of Task Force 64.2 to accurately portray Scott's actual strength in radio communications. Task Force 64.2's command structure was as follows:

Task Force 64.2

Ship Type	**Ship**	**Commander**
Cruisers	---------------	Radm. Norman Scott
	San Francisco	Capt. Charles H. McMorris
	Boise	Capt. Edward G. Moran
	Salt Lake City	Capt. Ernest G. Small
	Helena	Capt. Gilbert C. Hoover
Destroyers	-------------	Capt. Robert G. Tobin
	Farenholt	Lt. Cmdr. Eugene T. Seaward
	Duncan	Lt. Cmdr. Edmund B. Taylor
	Laffey	Lt. Cmdr. William E. Hank
	Buchanan	Cmdr. Ralph E. Wilson
	McCalla	Lt. Cmdr. William G. Cooper

Radm. Norman Scott - Commanding

Introducing Norman Scott

Scott had already had a fine naval career. Born in Indianapolis, Indiana on August 10, 1889, he received his appointment to the U.S. Naval Academy in 1907, graduated four years later, and received his commission as an ensign in March 1912. His first assignment after graduation from the Naval Academy was to serve aboard the battleship *Idaho* followed by assignments in destroyers and other duties meant to develop junior officers. After the U.S. entered World War I, Scott was the executive office on the destroyer *Jacob Jones*. After a German submarine sank his ship in December 1917, Scott received a commendation for his actions during that incident. He transferred to the Navy Department and was a naval aide to President Woodrow Wilson for the rest of that war. Promoted to the temporary rank of lieutenant commander in 1919, he led a division of Eagle Boats[4] and got his first command experience as the captain of the *USS Eagle* #2 and #3.

Scott served aboard destroyers, the battleship *New York*, and had shore jobs in Hawaii in the early 1920s. He was on the staff of the Commander, Battle Fleet, and had the prestigious appointment as a Naval Academy instructor from 1924-1930. With the permanent rank of lieutenant commander, he commanded the destroyers *MacLeish* and *Paul Jones* in the early 1930s followed by a staff assignment at the Navy Department and as a student at the Naval War College Senior Course. After serving as the executive officer on the light cruiser *Cincinnati*, Cmdr. Scott was a member of the U.S. Naval Mission to Brazil in 1937-1939. After promotion to the rank of captain, he became the captain of the heavy cruiser *Pensacola* until just before America entered World War II. Adm. King tapped Scott to serve on his staff in the CNO's office in early 1942. He achieved flag rank in May 1942 and was sent to the South Pacific.[5]

Preparing for Battle

Scott decided to make the *San Francisco* his flagship—an act that became the subject of controversy among naval historians. All of the ships in Task Force 64.2 did not have the latest radar installed on them. The ships with the most firepower, the heavy cruisers *San Francisco* and *Salt Lake City*, had the older longer-wavelength SC radars. These were only good for sighting objects at higher altitudes such as approaching aircraft. The latest SG radars were only on Scott's light cruisers, the *Helena* and *Boise*. The destroyers had no radar at all. The SG radars could spot an intruder at lower altitudes such as ships coming in for an attack. Another weakness with the SC radars was that the Japanese had equipment that could detect the SC radar's frequencies and measure the precise position of any ship carrying this radar capability.[6]

Therefore, Scott ordered his SC radars turned off as his force approached the waters around Guadalcanal. He did not have much experience using radar in combat since that technology was very new to many senior American naval officers in 1942. Therefore, he did not have detailed knowledge of how to use this innovative technology in naval warfare. Scott did not believe his order to turn the SC radars off was a critical decision at the time he made it.

The ships in Scott's force had never worked together before in combat, so he ordered three weeks of training exercises to get them ready. Because America had only been at war for ten months, few American naval officers had any experience meeting the Imperial Japanese Navy in combat. Nevertheless, Scott was the first American naval commander about to enter a battle with a definite battle plan. His ships would steam in a column with the destroyers leading and trailing the cruisers. The destroyers would use their searchlights to illuminate possible targets, and the cruisers would fire at any spotted Japanese ship without waiting for orders from him. The cruisers would launch their planes to search for the Japanese, locate them, and light them up with flares when spotted. Since the Japanese had already shown their superior destroyer and torpedo tactics in prior battles, Scott would divide his force if the Japanese should deploy superior destroyer forces. This would lessen the effectiveness of Japanese torpedoes as had been more than amply demonstrated at the Battle of Savo Island. Scott hoped his brief training of Task Force 64.2 would help to overcome part of the Japanese edge.

✲ ✲ ✲

Perhaps it would be useful to provide more information about the differences between the American "heavy" and "light" cruisers that existed when this battle occurred. Both ship types had almost the same displacement. For instance, the heavy cruiser *San Francisco* displaced 12,400 tons fully loaded while the year-older *Salt Lake City* displaced 11,500 tons. The light cruisers and sister ships *Boise* and *Helena* similarly displaced 12,200 tons.

The main difference between the two ship-types was the size of the guns they carried. The *San Francisco* carried nine eight-inch guns mounted in three turrets, two forward and one aft. She also had eight five-inch guns singly-mounted along her perimeter. The *Salt Lake City* carried ten eight-inch guns mounted in four turrets, two turrets mounting three guns and two turrets mounting two guns. Two turrets, one three-gun turret and one two-gun turret, were forward and the other two were aft with the three-gun turret mounted ahead of the two-gun turret. She also had four five-inch guns, but singly mounted. Both ships carried smaller-caliber AA guns.

The *Boise* and the *Helena* each had 15 six-inch guns mounted in five three-gun turrets. Three turrets were forward and two aft. They also had eight five-inch guns with the *Helena* carrying these guns in four two-gunned turrets and the *Boise* carrying these guns on single mounts. Like their "heavier" counterparts, these ships carried a complement of smaller-bored AA guns.

Of course, the heavy cruisers' larger guns could deliver a bigger blast, but the light cruisers could fire more shells because they carried more guns. As we will see when we read about the battle to come, the light cruisers would deliver more than their share of damage on their adversaries.

Each cruiser carried as many as four seaplanes that were used for scouting and spotting the fall of shot. They would also play a significant role in the upcoming battle.[7]

Preliminaries

While the *Hornet* and *Washington* steamed south of Guadalcanal, Task Force 64.2 moved nearer to Guadalcanal twice on October 9 and 10, but turned around when the seaplanes could not find any Japanese ships. Thus, Scott's ships lingered out of range of Japanese air attack from Rabaul until an air reconnaissance report found something that entirely changed the situation on October 11.

An Army Air Force B-17 from Col. LaVerne G. Saunders' 11th Bombardment Group left Espiritu Santo that morning to search the waters in the northern Solomon Islands. At 10:30 a.m., the big plane flew about 800 miles northwest from its home base and approached Bougainville's east coast. The crew had constantly scoured the sea below when they spotted eight ships, apparently two cruisers and six destroyers. Their wakes made white Vees in the blue water and steamed down the Slot at an estimated 25 knots. They were about 260 miles from Guadalcanal. The pilot ordered the plane's radio operator to report the sighting to Henderson Field. Task Force 64 also heard the relay of the B-17's radio report.

Henderson Field's radar also picked up a contact during the noon hour that showed two groups of unidentified planes 138 miles southeast of their Rabaul base. For some unknown reason, the coast-watchers had not seen the planes. Pilots scrambled to their planes, and 52 of them took off in a hodgepodge of 39 F4Fs, nine P-39s and three P-400s.

The two groups of Japanese planes were from the Rabaul-based Base Air Force. The first group that left Rabaul at 9:10 a.m. had 18 Zeroes along with nine Betty bombers under the command of

Lt. Cmdr. Tadashi Nakajima. They flew as far as the Russell Islands where two fighters aborted their missions. The second group left 45 minutes later and had 45 Betty bombers with Lt. Cmdr. Tomoyuki Uchida in command. It was the strongest bomber force ever sent to attack Guadalcanal. Lt. Toshitaka Ito commanded the second strike's fighter escort that had 29 Zeroes. Ninety Japanese planes aimed their noses toward Henderson Field with nothing but malicious intent.

The American F4Fs climbed to their higher patrol altitudes because they could while the P-39s leveled out a bit lower and the P-400s flew at still a lower attitude. The Henderson Field command sounded "CONDITION RED" at 12:54 p.m. It was not long before Nakajima's 16 Zeroes dove down on Lunga Point where eight F4Fs intercepted them. PO1c Hiroyoshi Nishizawa, one of Japan's greatest aces, damaged 2nd Lt. Arthur N. Nehf's plane, Nehf had to ditch his plane in the water off Guadalcanal. All 16 Zeroes returned to their base while claiming two victories, one more than actually happened.

Uchida's second wave of bombers and 29 Zeroes appeared overhead at 1:45 p.m. but cloud cover blocked their view of Henderson Field. While 27 bombers turned around, Lt. Cmdr. Kazuo Nishioka led his 18 bombers over Henderson Field and dropped 180 60-kg bombs that fell harmlessly in the jungle south of the airfield.

About 12 F4Fs commanded by Maj. Robert E. Galer were on their approach to land when Maj. Joseph N. Renner reported that 20 bombers and four Zeroes were approaching Henderson Field. Galer's fighters' fuel tanks were almost empty so they could only make one attack on the Japanese planes. That pass proved to be a fruitful one as the Americans crippled one bomber and badly damaged three more. The escorting Japanese fighters claimed three F4Fs with no losses.

The air battles before Task Force 64.2 arrived delivered inconclusive results. Henderson Field was still fully operational. The largest Japanese air raid since the Americans landed on August 7 was a bust, but Henderson Field was not out of danger.[8]

Meeting the Japanese Threat

Meanwhile, another American plane confirmed the B-17's prior report at 2:45 p.m. when its crew sighted a Japanese eight-ship formation 210 miles from Guadalcanal, passing between Kolombangara and Choiseul Islands. Six destroyers steamed in an oval around two larger ships. A flight of Zeroes flew protective cover. CACTUS sent a flash message to all commands:

> "6 DDs 2 cruisers bearing 305 distance 210 from Guadalcanal course 120."

This contact was the Japanese Reinforcement Force that had the Japanese troops to reinforce their comrades on Guadalcanal. The Americans had not yet found Goto's force. Maj. Gen. Roy S. Geiger, commanding all air forces on Guadalcanal, wondered if this was another Tokyo Express run. Knowing that U.S. warships were on their way, he did not want to risk his critically short air resources trying to stop what now seemed another Japanese attempt to land more troops. He continued to send up reconnaissance planes. At sundown, the Japanese Reinforcement Force was 110 miles from Guadalcanal.

If everything went according to plan, Scott knew that the 146th Regiment would arrive on October 13, and his force would be in place to protect that landing force when the Japanese arrived. A submarine might see him first, but he had kept Japanese aircraft from spotting his ships.

Having already received the B-17's sighting report and the latest sighting on October 11, Scott now had a reason move his force into position to stop the next Japanese attempt to run the Tokyo Express. His task force steamed at 29 knots and, hoping to reach Guadalcanal before midnight, headed for the waters to the east of Savo Island. He sent a message of intentions to his task force:

"We are going in. Jap force believed to be two cruisers and six DDs."

At sunset, Scott ordered his ships to go to battle stations. One hour later, the night turned so dark that the men felt like they were in an unlit closed room. Not wanting to repeat the mistake made by the American ship commanders at the Battle of Savo Island, Scott's orders left no doubt in his ship captains' minds. As soon they spotted the Japanese, their guns would fire as soon as they came within range.

Task Force 64.2's ships steamed in line and moved into the waters south of Guadalcanal, heading toward a spot to the west of Savo Island. The destroyers *Farenholt*, *Duncan*, and *Laffey* led the way followed by heavy cruiser and flagship *San Francisco*, the light cruiser *Boise*, the heavy cruiser *Salt Lake City*, and the light cruiser *Helena* with the destroyers *Buchanan* and *McCalla* bringing up the rear.

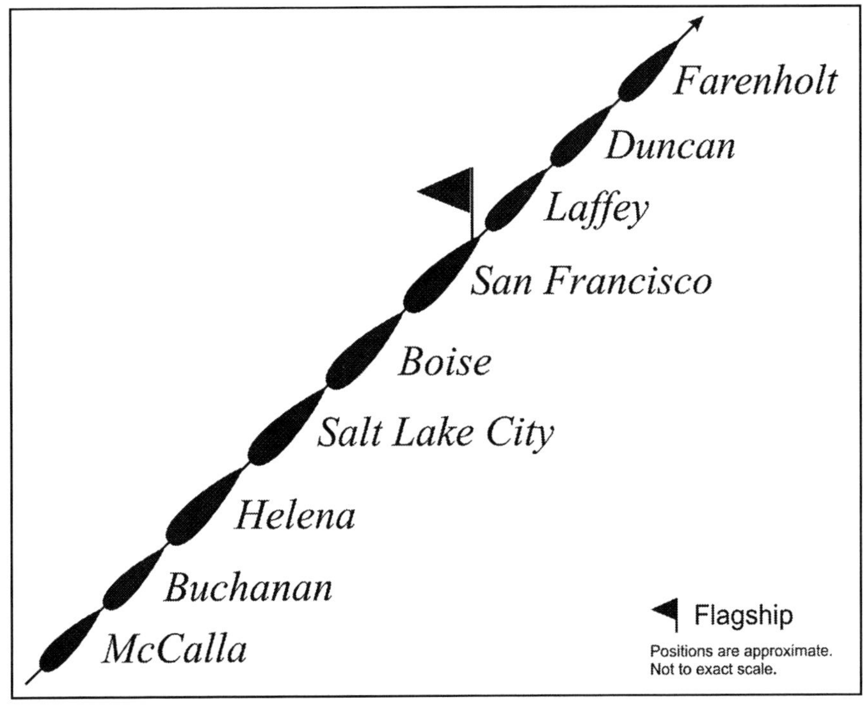

Task Force 64.2's Formation

Only the *Helena* had been damaged previously because she was at Pearl Harbor on December 7. A torpedo tore a hole in the forward engine room's bilge that was 40 feet long and tall enough for a man to pass through at its middle. The missile's blast ripped the No. 1 main engine's reduction gear from its mounting and tossed it on its side. That extensive damage plus what was inflicted on the propeller and turbine shafts would have forced any ship away from the war for some time. American shipbuilders returned her to service in just six months. Now she was here, ready to fight again.

Scott's ships were off Guadalcanal's southwestern corner at 8:30 p.m., an escarpment of land called Cape Hunter, where the island's coast turned northwesterly. The latest charts showed coral reefs along the next stretch of coast and mountain peaks up to 2,800 feet high. Task Force 64.2 was still some distance from the island with its features just beginning to appear on the SG radar scopes. Scott changed his course northward with West Cape, Guadalcanal's most western point, ahead to starboard. The coast, now ten miles to starboard, turned to the north after this land feature, and Scott wanted to steam parallel to it. The northernmost point on Guadalcanal, Cape Esperance, was where he planned to enter the area where the Japanese would most likely land their reinforcements.

He reasoned that his course would cross the Japanese ships' path about 25 miles away. The Japanese would likely move closer to the beach east of Cape Esperance and begin to unload troops from their destroyers. The cruisers would stay farther offshore to be ready to intercept any American attempts to stop their landings, then move eastward to shell Henderson Field. However, Scott did not want to rush in to attack the Japanese landing force and get caught in the narrow waters between Guadalcanal and Florida Islands by another Japanese naval force that may have followed their invasion force. So he proceeded cautiously and ordered his search planes to be launched, as he originally planned. In that way, they could get a better view of what was happening near Guadalcanal. Meanwhile, he kept his force farther offshore to keep his options open to react if any Japanese force should appear from the Slot. The situation was rife for the possibility of unpredictable events. Radar scope operators hovered intently over their displays and lookouts strained their eyes through their binoculars for any evidence of a Japanese ship.

Scott's search planes by now flew over Cape Esperance. The pitch-black night was as intense as before. At 9:45 p.m., his force was just 13 miles from the position where his ships would be west of Cape Esperance.

✲ ✲ ✲

The command, "Launch Aircraft," echoed throughout Task Force 64.2's cruisers. Lt. William F. Tate, Jr. sat in the cockpit of his Curtis SOC Seagull as it perched atop the *Salt Lake City*'s catapult and waited for the Catapult Officer's launch order. The Catapult officer signaled to rev up the biplane's engine. Tate pushed the throttle forward as far as could go. The plane shook from the vibration as the catapult's clamps kept it from leaping into the air. Tate kept one hand on the stick, the other hand on the throttle, both feet on the rudder pedals, and his head firmly against the seat's back. The plane's observer, ARM1c Claude M. Morgan, prepared for the jolting lurch that was to come by lowering his head, extending his arms against the cockpit front, and firmly placing his back against the rear bulkhead.

Waiting for the cruiser to roll up so that the plane's nose elevated, the launch officer tried to gauge when that would happen. If the plane's launch happened during daylight, he would wait for the horizon to be at its lowest point before he gave the order. But it was so dark he could not see more than several feet from the ship's rail. He had to wait until the pressure on his feet felt that the ship was on the high roll. When he thought the ship's roll was right, he fired the catapult's launching charge.

The immediate jolt as the catapult's charge fired placed the greatest impact on the plane's crew.

As the plane flew, the pressure immediately dissipated. This time, all was not as it should be. Morgan felt and then saw a hot, fiery glow at his feet. Extra magnesium flares on the cockpit's floor had not been properly stowed away and were now filling the space with an acrid, blinding smoke. The heat and sparks from the glowing flares burned Morgan's feet. Wanting to tell Tate, Morgan could not because the fire was too hot.

He had not fastened his harness as was the practice when launching catapult planes. Desperately wanting get out of the plane, he tried to escape after releasing his seat belt but the cord from his flight helmet to his radio stopped him. He did not have much time to waste. The plane's tail was on fire as the craft careened toward the water. Morgan climbed out his seat and crawled over the canopy past Tate. The wind from the plane's slipstream almost blew him into the water. Frantically trying to grasp for any nearby handhold, he found a handle on the upper wing and stood upright on the lower wing next to the fuselage and screamed at Tate, "Land! Land!"

The plane's gleaming fire pierced the darkness and shocked the men on the *Salt Lake City* as it splashed into the water about 500 yards from the cruiser column off the starboard beam. The fire was now on the water as the plane continued to burn brightly. It did not last long. In two minutes, the fire died out.

The horrific accident had an immediate effect on Scott's task force. The fire's glow had undoubtedly been seen for miles from every shore facing the waters near where the American ships steamed. Whatever advantages the Americans had that surprise brings were gone. Nonetheless, Scott continued as before, his orders unchanged.[9]

Fulfilling Their Mission

The Japanese Reinforcement Group's 250-mile voyage from Rabaul down the Slot to the waters northwest of Guadalcanal became known to the Americans when the B-17 sighted them at 10:30 that morning. Nonetheless, they steamed down the Slot despite being sighted. The Japanese knew that any ships steaming during daylight hours had a high probability of being spotted by American reconnaissance planes.

Six Zero fighters took up CAP stations at noon. Once the ships moved within 200 miles from Guadalcanal at 3:00 p.m., the likelihood of an air attack increased. American submarine attacks became less likely as they closed the distance to Guadalcanal. So, they stopped zigzagging and increased their speed. Bright skies and a smooth sea greeted them, and it seemed like this voyage would be a routine supply mission. No American planes had challenged their progress.

As sunset loomed over the ships, the Zeroes had to ditch in the water because they were too far away to reach any Japanese bases before they ran out of fuel. The Japanese had made a conscious decision to sacrifice these planes and make sure the ships fulfilled their mission. Each pilot landed his plane in the water with his wheels up and did not have to wait long before a friendly destroyer plucked them from the sea. Nonetheless, one plane flipped over attempting the hazardous water landing, killing the pilot.

Darkness descended over the ships, and they increased their speed. Battle stations sounded at 7:40 p.m., and the men prepared to meet any threat that might come their way. Two hours and five minutes later, the Reinforcement Group passed between Savo Island and Cape Esperance. The ships scattered to their appointed places off Guadalcanal's northern shore. No one had seen the glow from the *Salt Lake City* seaplane's fire at 10:00 p.m. As soon as the ships reached their assigned spots, they dropped anchor and began unloading supplies.

They had completed their mission and reached their destination with no interference from the Americans. Although the earlier Japanese air attacks did not do much damage to Henderson Field and the CACTUS air force, they forced the American planes to defend their base and prevented them from attacking the Reinforcement Group. Confidence grew among the Japanese that all would proceed as planned. Adm. Goto's Bombardment Group was on its way and would defend the landings from any American threat from the sea.[10]

Prelude to a Sea Battle

Task Force 64.2 continued on its northerly course as it passed to the west of Cape Esperance. Scott then ordered a course change to starboard at 10:25 p.m. toward Savo Island where the ships would be considerably closer to Guadalcanal's shore. Knowing that this is where any Japanese ships would likely be, he sent the codeword to all ships in his command, "Doubleheader!" — move into battle formation. Thus, all ships moved into the classic battle line as originally planned.

Since the days of sailing warships, the purpose of this formation was to direct maximum firepower toward ships approaching on its flank. It allowed the ships to cross the opponent's "T" and impose withering fire on them while the approaching opponent could only fire forward. In theory, this tactic should work most of the time. But, if there was poor visibility or, in this case, darkness, the ships in line could not see their own ships, and the line could begin to disintegrate. In these conditions, ships had to maintain contact with the other ships in the formation by following the ship in front of it. Also, if the opposing ships should sever the battle line, then the attackers would in turn cross the battle line's "T" as Nelson did at Trafalgar in 1805.

Naval tactics of that time used destroyers to attack an approaching enemy with torpedoes. The battle line Scott had ordered made using this tactic difficult to execute since the approaching ships' bows headed straight for the line and presented a poor target for torpedo attacks. Scott's task force had not had much time to practice more complicated maneuvers such as destroyer torpedo attacks; therefore, Scott's formation was the best he could arrange within the limitations he faced. If he intended to use torpedoes, he had not yet issued any such orders. The guns he had in Task Force 64.2 would have to suffice. And there was more than enough firepower to handle any Japanese force he might encounter.

Task Force 64.2's line was three miles long with the destroyer *Farenholt* leading the way and the destroyer *McCalla* bringing up the rear. Scott's flagship, the cruiser *San Francisco*, was in the middle. It was too dark for him to see more than the ship forward or aft of the flagship. With a breeze blowing from the southeast, the damp, suffocating, and heavy odor from Guadalcanal's rotting jungle vegetation wafted over his ships. *Farenholt*'s lookouts peered with strained eyes into the moonless night, looking for any sight of anything. Its radar was not working and turned off.

The destroyer's lookouts saw a shape to starboard at 10:45 p.m. with its path closely lined up within six miles from Guadalcanal's northern shore. A dark background stood behind the contact. They could not see the beach. Japanese ships could be there. Blue lights suddenly lit up forward and to starboard. Just as unexpectedly as they showed, they disappeared. The *Farenholt* did not report the sighting, hoping the flagship had seen them. But the *San Francisco* missed them.

There was a tense mood aboard the flagship. Scott stood on the flag bridge, just below the ship's bridge, and waited for events to unfold. His small staff of commissioned officers waited with him. The signalmen kept out of Scott's way and to themselves, muttering in low voices so their superiors could not hear them. They had been at their assigned stations for almost four and one-half hours. The barely visible skyline to their right remained indiscernible and mysterious.

The mystery disappeared at 10:50 p.m. with a message from Lt. John A. Thomas, the *San Francisco* search plane's pilot, "One large, two small vessels, one six miles from Savo off northern beach Guadalcanal. Will investigate closer." He had seen the Japanese Reinforcement Group.

Nevertheless, Thomas' message fostered more questions to Scott and his staff than it answered. Were the ships Japanese? Was there one ship six miles from Savo or three ships 16 miles from that island? If there was one ship six miles from Savo, where were the other two ships? Eight ships had been previously sighted. Where were the remaining five? If Thomas had spotted a cruiser and three destroyers, the whereabouts of one cruiser and four destroyers remained unknown. If they were Japanese, his force stood between them and any approaching force. Whatever they were, they could be handled later. Task Force 64.2 stayed on its present course, looking for other "fish to fry."

A white light flashed to starboard at 11:05 p.m. from one of the mountaintops. While the light's sighting caused considerable conversation among Scott's staff officers, no one could answer the fundamental questions: What was that light? And who lit it? *Farenholt*'s starboard quarter moved abreast of Savo Island five minutes later and nine miles away. Scott changed course to the northeast to pass Savo Island to starboard.

More reports arrived on the flag bridge from Scott's search planes. The *San Francisco*'s aircraft clarified its earlier sighting by reporting the three ships it had seen before by saying they were 16 miles east of Savo Island and one mile from Guadalcanal's northern shore. The *Boise*'s plane radioed that it had to land in the water because of engine problems. This latest news lent a pessimistic mood among the American ships because that meant the *San Francisco*'s plane was the only one still aloft.

Scott wanted to position his task force so that they could still steam across the channel between Savo and Guadalcanal Islands. But his ships were too far north. Therefore, he wanted to turn his force 180° so they could head back from where they had come. Again, the lack of training among the ships would play to their disadvantage as they executed the maneuver.

There were two ways the course reversal movement could be made. The simplest way was for each ship to turn around while still keeping its place in the line. In this case, the *McCalla* would become the lead ship with the *Farenholt* trailing. The second way was for the entire line to turn around like a line of soldiers would when executing a countermarch on a parade ground. This maneuver theoretically would result with the destroyer *Farenholt* still in the lead but had the important disadvantage of being more complex. Proper execution normally required considerable practice among any group of ships. Another need to successfully carry it off was to have perfect communications between the flagship with the other ships in the formation and among all those ships. An advantage was that only one ship turned at a time, and the formation remained intact.

At 11:33 p.m., Scott issued the order, "Left to Course 230 degrees!"[11]

The *Farenholt*'s captain, Lt. Cmdr. Eugene T. Seaward, turned his ship to port as soon as he received the execution order. While turning and reaching a point where the destroyer's course was perpendicular to task force's formation, the *Duncan*, the ship immediately behind the *Farenholt*, began her turn. Capt. Robert G. Tobin, aboard the *Farenholt* and commanding all the task force's destroyers, and Seaward turned toward the rest of the ships' formation and looked through their binoculars. What they saw was a reason to be uneasy.

While the *Duncan* and *Laffey* followed the *Farenholt* in its path, the *San Francisco*'s looming image was abreast of the three destroyers. It appeared the cruiser had begun her turn just as the *Farenholt* turned. Tobin worried that he might have not fully understood Scott's countermarch order or that the cruiser's steering gear had sustained some unknown damage. He ordered the three destroyers to reduce their speed and warned the *Duncan* and *Laffey* to be ready to follow the *Farenholt*'s path without any further maneuvering orders. Now, Tobin could wait to see what the other two destroyers would do. Would they follow the admiral's flagship or turn to follow his destroyers? If they moved ahead of the cruisers, he would move the three destroyers behind the other cruisers. If they continued to follow the cruisers in their original position, he would need to increase the three destroyers' speed to move them back into their leading position.

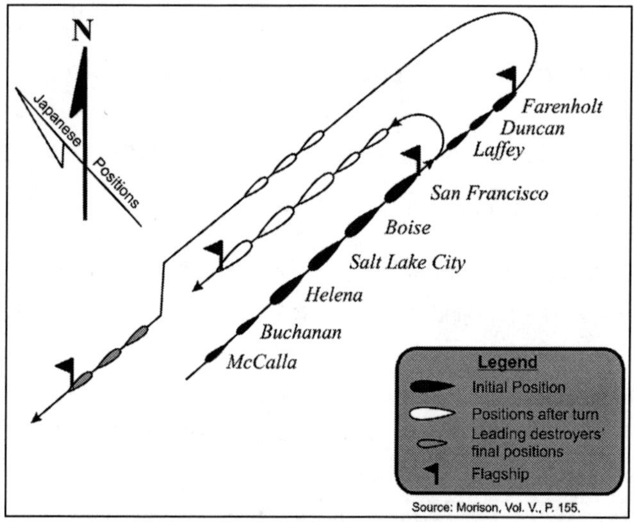

Scott's Countermarch Maneuver

Tobin got his answer when he saw the *Boise* turn and follow in the *San Francisco*'s wake. The other two cruisers turned in the *Boise*'s wake with the *Buchanan* and *McCalla* bringing up the rear. Seaward ordered full speed while the rest of the task force steamed at about 20 knots. Believing the Japanese ships were now to his port and would soon make contact with the Americans, Tobin ordered Seaward on the *Farenholt* to move up the task force starboard side so that its guns would have a clear line of fire to port.

✲ ✲ ✲

Clearly, something went wrong after Scott issued his maneuvering order. The lack of sufficient electronic communications equipment aboard his flagship was the primary culprit. While the *San Francisco* had been at port on the American West Coast, the shipyard installed an additional speaker ("squawk box") on the bridge so that any order issued from the flag bridge could be heard above on the ship's bridge. Therefore, the ship's captain could hear the admiral's orders and immediately react to them. Unfortunately, the squawk box only fed TBS communications and therefore any other radio messages shared the same channel as the admiral's orders. While Scott's order was to turn in column, Capt. Charles H. McMorris, the flagship's commander, believed the order was to execute a simultaneous turn. So when the order came and the *Farenholt* began her turn, so did the *San Francisco*.

Her maneuver confused the *Boise*'s captain, Capt. Edward J. Moran. He had not heard that anything was wrong with the flagship nor did he believe he misinterpreted Scott's order, so he turned and followed the *San Francisco*'s wake. The rest of the task force followed him. The formation had now lost its original formation; this mishap would have consequences in the minutes to come.

Believing his plan would give his task force the best chance for success in battle, Scott had chosen to form the line of battle when he believed he would meet the Imperial Japanese Navy. As in all warfare, all plans do not proceed as originally thought. The situation was about to abruptly change.[12]

✲ ✲ ✲

Cmdr. Minoru Yokota had his *I-26* submarine on the water's surface off Kamimbo Bay near the northwest tip of Guadalcanal. One of the sub's lookouts reported at 9:22 p.m. seeing a ship that looked like an American cruiser moving at a high speed on a northward course. Yokota, hungry to make a score on an American warship, ordered his boat to submerge and go after it before he reported the sighting. After spending more than two hours trying to reach the American cruiser, he surfaced to send his sighting report; it was too late.

Scott had not gone undetected as he had thought. The Japanese knew about his ships, but that knowledge spread no further than the confines of the *I-26*.

✲ ✲ ✲

Adm. Goto's Bombardment Group weighed anchor on October 11 at 2:00p.m., left the safety of the Shortland Islands, and began steaming down the Slot on a southeasterly course. The 8th Fleet at Rabaul planned Goto's movements to arrive off Guadalcanal's north shore two hours after the Reinforcement Group. Clearly, the Japanese command did not expect any opposition. Goto's force could be quite effective bombarding the Guadalcanal beaches but not particularly powerful enough to stand up to any opposing American surface forces, particularly the ones awaiting them.

Their trek down the Slot was not entirely uneventful. From the time they left the Shortland anchorage, heavy rain squalls and poor visibility plagued their journey. The poor weather had one advantage: American search aircraft could not find them. If they could not be seen, then no American planes could attack them.

At about the same time Scott had ordered his course change to the northeast, the Bombardment

Group sped down the Slot at 30 knots. The *Nisshin* reported to him at 10:20 p.m. that it had not seen any signs of any significant American naval presence. Despite the Reinforcement Group's sailors spotting Scott's search planes, Goto never knew any naval force stood in his way.

His ships had no radar as they approached the waters northwest of Savo Island. So Goto had to rely on his lookouts to see if any ships steamed ahead of them. He had his ships in a formation suitable for firing on shore targets. His cruisers, led by his flagship, the heavy cruisers *Aoba*, the *Kinugasa*, and the *Furutaka*, were now on a 120° course. The destroyer *Fubuki* was on the flagship's starboard bow and the destroyer *Hatsuyuki* on the port bow.[13]

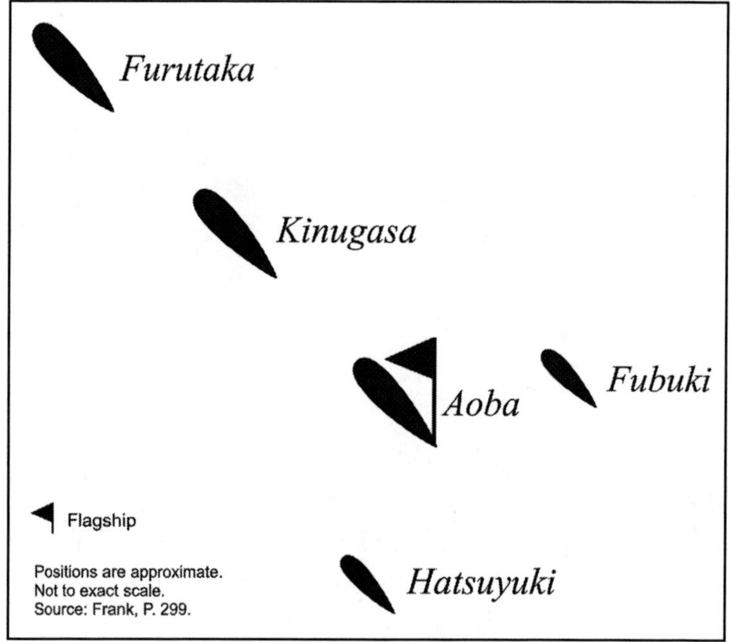

Admiral Goto's Formation

Goto's behavior indicates that he confidently approached his mission to deliver fatal blows to Henderson Field to support the Reinforcement Group's landings and supply deliveries at Lunga. After all, he had not received any reports that opposition awaited him. His superior, Adm. Mikawa, believed this mission was to be a relatively easy one. Any evidence to the contrary was conspicuous by its absence. But any belief in his future success would soon be shattered by explosive events to come.

CHAPTER 27
Crossing the "T"

Task Force 64.2 finally finished its jumbled and stumbling course reversal at 11:42 p.m. on a course of 230°. But Scott did not know that three of his cruisers earlier had detected radar contacts of ships coming down the Slot.

The *Helena*'s chart house was the navigator's place to work. The SC and SG radars had taken over much of the small compartment's space, which had been designed for other purposes before the devices' invention. An operator stared at the SG radar scope where a line symbolizing the beam radiating from the circling antenna atop the ship's mainmast and revolved around the display. The ship was always at the scope's center.

Guadalcanal's coast appeared to the southeast and southwest. Cape Esperance was directly southward, and Savo Island was only six miles to the east. The ships of Task Force 64.2 displayed as a northeast-southwest line of six blips forward and two aft. The *Helena* showed at the scope's center.

A slight blinking dot suddenly showed to the northwest and startled the operator. Not wanting to report a false sighting, he waited for the beam to circle a few more times to make sure it was genuine. The dot did not go away.

The ship's radar officer, Ens. Gash,[1] also saw the persistent dot as he peered over the operator's shoulder. Believing the image represented a real sighting, Gash wasted no time when he called the bridge at 11:30 p.m. and reported the contact on a 315° bearing and 29,000 yards or 16½ miles away. The still new SG radar had shown false reports before. Gash wanted to watch the contact for a few minutes more. Two minutes later, the dot had become three separate ships and moving at 35 knots on a course of 120° and a distance of 24,000 yards.

Just then Task Force 64.2 began its countermarch maneuver. The cruiser's officers assumed that the flagship also saw the formation, and so did not report it to Scott. The *Helena*'s forward five-inch gunnery radar also picked up the contact.

Despite Scott's standing order about not using the SC radar, the *Salt Lake City*'s older SC radar "saw" the Japanese ships at 11:31 p.m. Her captain, Capt. Ernest G. Small, although turning his guns in that direction, did not have much faith in the radar's accuracy, and so did not report his sighting.

The *Helena*'s forward six-inch gunnery radar then picked up the contact at 11:35 p.m. at a range of 18,500 yards. Gash then reported the contact had five ships moving in a "T" formation. By now, there was no question these ships belonged to the Imperial Japanese Navy.

The cruiser began her turn one minute later. She turned her gun directors to point at the contact. As she finished her turn, her gun turrets pointed at the oncoming ships. Hoover did not have a scope on the bridge with which to see what the men in the chart house saw. But reports continued coming over the ship's telephone. He was also convinced the contact was genuine. However, the flagship's silence worried him. Gunnery Officer Lt. Cmdr. Rodman D. Smith said, "What are we waiting for?" over the telephone. Reports about the five approaching Japanese ships poured in.

As the *Boise* began her countermarching maneuver at 11:42 p.m., her SG radar picked up the approaching ships just as the *Helena* had. The officers on this cruiser made the same assumption as the *Helena*'s officers had, and so also did not report the contact to the flagship. The *Helena* finally confirmed Goto's approach at 11:42 p.m. with another radar contact showing ships in a "T" formation bearing 298º at a distance of 12,000 yards or almost seven miles away, well within the range of her five-inch guns. This time, Capt. Hoover, not wanting to wait to hear from the flagship, radioed the sighting to the flagship. He prepared his ship to fight when he issued the order. "Load all turrets!"

The *San Francisco*'s TBS squawk box rattled with the sighting report. She aimed her fire control radar in that direction but detected nothing. *Helena*'s reported sightings were in the opposite direction of the previous sighting by the search planes. The contact must be one of the American destroyers that steamed off the flagship's starboard beam, or so Scott and his staff must have thought. Scott still did not act.

Two minutes later, the *Boise* reported a radar contact of five bogies, the typical report for sighting unidentified aircraft, on a 65º bearing. Adding to Scott's confusion, this bearing revealed another group of ships to port. The *Boise* cleared up this error by saying the bearing was relative to the ship's course and not a true bearing. Scott attempted to get a better picture of what was going on at 11:45 p.m. when he asked Tobin on the TBS, "Are you taking station ahead?" Tobin, now more puzzled than before and wanting to line up with his task force commander's intentions, replied, "Affirmative, coming up on your starboard side," and assumed that the *Duncan* and the *Laffey* would do as the *Farenholt* did. But this assumption, like many other assumptions made in battle, would prove to be wrong. The time, 11:45 p.m., proved a fateful moment for Scott and his men.

The Battle of Cape Esperance was about to begin. The time for guns had arrived.

Before she turned for her countermarch maneuver, the *Duncan*'s gunnery radar had been tracking Goto's ships. As she turned, the contact was unmistakable. Lt. Cmdr. Edmund B. Taylor, the *Duncan*'s captain, quickly decided that a Japanese attack on the turning American column was about to happen, and Tobin's movements meant that the destroyers were about to attack. She now left her assigned station and headed for the Japanese ships to the northwest. Taylor increased his destroyer's speed to 30 knots. With her wake now roiling white foam, the destroyer's stern dug deeply into the water. The *Laffey*'s skipper, Lt. Cmdr. William E. Hank, decided to follow the *Farenholt* in her turn. The *Duncan* launched her attack alone.

Scott was more confused than ever. Did *Helena*'s sighting really mean that there were ships to the west? What were these ships—friendly or hostile? *Boise*'s report of ships bearing 65º meant that there were more ships to the *south*. If both reports were accurate, then that meant he could be between two hostile forces—a position in which no naval commander ever wanted to be caught. His gut told him that he should not act too impulsively because of the two conflicting sighting reports.

The *San Francisco*'s gunnery radar now had a definite, unidentified contact a short 5,000 yards to starboard. There was no doubt on the *Helena* where and what the contact rapidly getting closer from the northwest was. A report reached the bridge, "Ships visible to the naked eye," and an exasperated Ens. Gash asked Lt. Cmdr. Charles L. Carpenter, the cruiser's navigator, "What are we going to do, board them?" Although Hoover had orders that he could open fire if he felt justified doing so, he got on the TBS and called the flagship.

The flagship's TBS now squawked from the *Helena*, "Interrogatory Roger," the prearranged code for asking for permission to open fire. An immediate "Roger" response came back. The *Helena* asked again with the same instantaneous answer. We do not know whether Scott actually heard the *Helena*'s messages. Only the *Boise* and *Helena* had actually reported spotting the approaching ships. He still did not definitely know whether there were Japanese ships out there. Not wanting to fire on his own ships, he began to shape a reply to his task force.

The *Helena*'s gun crews anxiously waited for the order they hoped would come from their captain. Each of her 15 six-inch guns had a powder bag behind their six-inch shell in its chamber—loaded and ready to fire. The ammunition trains had a steady flow of shells and powder bags to make sure the guns could keep up continuous fire. Their fire directors had a firm lock on the Japanese ships bearing down on the task force.

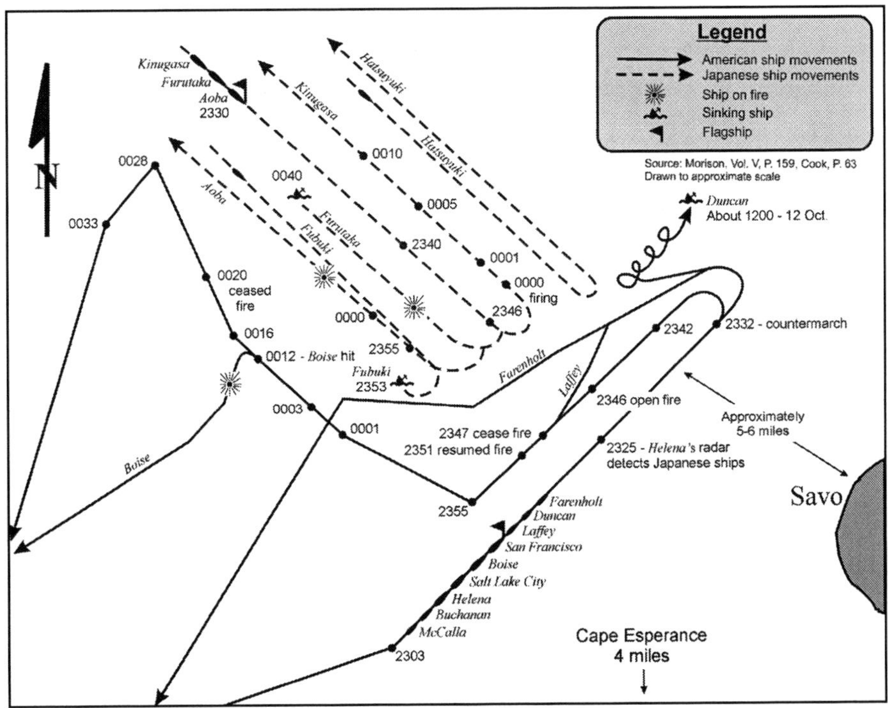

The Battle of Cape Esperance

Hoover was no stranger to the workings of the new SG radar on his cruiser. He had served in the Navy's Bureau of Ordnance where he learned the latest classified data of the new, remarkable invention. His assignment before taking command of the *Helena* was as the commander of a destroyer squadron where he had plenty of practice and gained valuable experience in how to use this new technology in naval warfare. Now it was his chance to apply what he had learned under actual combat conditions. And radar would be the tool to initiate the action.

Hoover never doubted what a confirmed "roger" meant. Hoover exclaimed, "Commence firing!" Smith repeated the order. At 11:46 p.m., with the Japanese ships a short 3,600 yards away, the *Helena*'s 15 six-inch guns exploded with fire and smoke and lit the night's darkness.

The gunfire's flashes from his formation's starboard side shook away Scott's indecisive thoughts. Now more flashes of light and loud explosions of guns firing in twos and threes filled the darkness. A sudden light blinded Scott as the *San Francisco*'s eight-inch guns opened fire. He lost his hearing from the overwhelming explosions.

He might have also felt that he had lost command and control of his task force. But he had ordered his ships' captains to open fire and not wait for any such instructions from him when they had seen the Japanese ships. Captains in every first-class navy in the world have similar orders. Hoover showed the same initiative Nelson did at the Battle of Cape Saint Vincent on February 14, 1797, when he left his formation to stop the Spanish ships from escaping, thus guaranteeing Adm. Sir John Jervis' (later Earl St. Vincent) a far-reaching victory.

✲ ✲ ✲

Three minutes before the *Helena* opened fire, Goto's force slowed to 26 knots. The *Aoba*'s lookout reported seeing three warships 10,000 meters just off the port bow. Thinking these ships were from the Reinforcement Group and believing there were no American ships nearby, Goto sent the customary recognition signal. His range to the sighted ships reduced to about 4,300 yards when his lookouts screamed the shapes of the ships were American. Capt. Yonejiro Hisamune, skipper of the *Aoba*, ordered his ship to go to Gen. Quarters. Goto still stayed with his conviction that those ships his lookouts had seen could not be American. He ordered a course change of 10° to port and sent another recognition signal. Goto blithely sailed his ships into a deadly maelstrom.

As the ship was in her turn, the first American salvo blasted into her superstructure. Heavy shells smashed the flag bridge. Goto lay on the flag bridge deck, mortally wounded with many men around him already dead. The salvo's blast interrupted ship communications, destroyed two eight-inch turrets, and the main battery director.

✲ ✲ ✲

The *Boise* was the likely source of the first fusillade. The American cruiser sent a continuous avalanche of six-inch shell salvoes at the *Aoba*. Fire from the *Salt Lake City* and *San Francisco*'s eight-inch and the destroyer *Farenholt*'s five-inch guns pummeled the already crippled cruiser in a deluge of shells. The luckless *Laffey* got caught in the shells' path. Lt. Cmdr. Hank removed her from danger by executing an emergency reversal of her engines. She just missed colliding with the *McCalla*.

Then, Scott ordered a cease fire just five minutes after the firing began. He did not know where his ships were and was concerned about American shells striking his destroyers then moving to his starboard. Wanting to get a closer view of what was happening in his command, he went to the flag bridge to see how his ships were carrying out his orders. The firing continued albeit with less intensity—clearly not all of his commanders had heard his order. But he did want to know if Task Force 64.2's firing put his destroyers in danger.

Scott and Tobin had a short exchange over the TBS:

Scott: "How are you?"

Tobin: "OK. We are going up ahead on your starboard side."

Scott: "Were we shooting at Twelve?"[2]

Tobin: "I do not know who you were shooting at."

What an extraordinary exchange that was! One can only guess how a battle can generate such confusion and apparent chaos. Scott, not realizing the Japanese also used lights to identify their ships at night, ordered Tobin's destroyers to flash their recognition lights. Task Force 64.2's prearranged light combination was three vertically aligned lights, green over green over white.

When her captain received the cease fire order, the *San Francisco*'s now-silent guns still pointed at the ship at which she fired. McMorris, Gunnery Officer Lt. Cmdr. William W. Wilbourne, and all the gunners kept wary eyes on their intended victim. The ship did not flash the green-green-white signal; she aimed a dim beam down at the water. The men on the American cruiser did not know if this was a recognition signal or not.

As if to answer the questions in their minds, the ship showed a vertical display of flashing red and white lights. A sudden message came from of the cruiser's spotting stations, "For God's sake, shoot!"—this ship definitely was Japanese! Fearing that his ship could be hit by torpedoes and having no orders to open fire, Wilbourne aimed a searchlight at the suspect ship. The light illuminated a superstructure that no American sailors recognized. The ship was clearly a destroyer that had two white bands on her forward stack. No American ship had markings like that. And she moved in a tight turn away from the cruiser.

McMorris wasted no time. "Commence firing!" The flagship's eight-inch guns roared before he could finish speaking his order.

☆ ☆ ☆

The lights from the big cruiser surprised the *Fubuki*'s captain. His ship was in deep trouble now, and he had to find a way to escape. Flashing recognition lights availed him nothing. When the American cruiser pointed its searchlight at his ship, he knew it would not take very long for his ship to be recognized as Japanese. As he ordered his ship to turn away from the big warship, the cruiser's main battery opened up in a fiery barrage. The destroyer began to turn just as two eight-inch shells splashed near the ship's port and starboard beams. The shells straddled her, a position no warship commander ever wants to be caught in. More shells smacked the water forward and aft of the now doomed destroyer. Her existence was about to end.

Another shell exploded at the after smokestack base. Several missiles hit her again; the explosions broke her into two pieces. Her bow quickly sank. Her stern turned vertical to the water, her propellers and rudder were lit up by the cruiser's searchlight, and she quickly sank without firing a shot.

✲ ✲ ✲

Seeing the Japanese destroyer with his own eyes at last convinced Scott that all those sightings were definitely Japanese ships. At 11:51 p.m., he ordered Task Force 64.2 to again fire at the Japanese. He wrote later in his action report, "It took some time to stop our fire. In fact, it never did completely stop." Now, the sounds of battle increased their crescendo.

✲ ✲ ✲

The *Aoba* had already taken considerable punishment. She turned around to escape the carnage now being inflicted on her. Her foremast lay on her deck and only one turret still worked. With her bow facing west, her captain put the ship into a zigzag course to dodge the shells surrounding and hitting her. Thick, black, and acrid smoke poured from her smokestacks at 11:50 p.m. to hide her from prying American spotters' eyes. The Americans believed they had sunk her. However, by the time she headed to the northwest, her tactics allowed her to escape further damage.

Nevertheless, damage to the Japanese cruisers did not end there. Following the *Aoba* was her companion, the cruiser *Furutaka*. American shellfire caught Capt. Araki Tsutau, her skipper, totally by surprise. He quickly recovered his wits when he realized the Americans had crossed Goto's "T." He ordered a turn to port. But when he saw how heavily damaged the flagship was, Tsutau changed his mind and turned right to follow the *Aoba*. One minute before the flagship made smoke, several shells had hit the *Furutaka*. At the same time the *Aoba* began to make smoke, many shells raked the hapless *Furutaka* that struck her torpedo tubes, resulting in a large fire breaking out on her main deck. While smoke enshrouded the *Aoba*, the light from the *Furutaka*'s fire became an ideal aiming point for the American guns. Tsutau fearlessly tried to come to the flagship's aid. That act placed her in deadly jeopardy.

The *Furutaka* was now a doomed ship. At 12:40 a.m. on October 12, she disappeared beneath the waves after an unsuccessful attempt to return home.

The *Kinugasa*'s captain, Capt. Masao Sawa, seeing the punishment the cruisers ahead of him had taken, exercised discretion over valor when he ordered a reverse turn to port to save his ship from annihilation. Clearly outgunned and outmaneuvered, there was no point in directly confronting the superior firepower of the American ships to the southeast. His cruiser would be sorely needed in later battles with the Americans. The least he could do was to leave the battle scene and head to the northwest for safe anchorage at Shortland Island, well outside the range of American aircraft and under the safety umbrella of the Japanese planes on Rabaul.[3]

✲ ✲ ✲

The Americans did not escape damage. One ship, the destroyer *Duncan*, would have its own trial by fire. The *Boise*'s tribulations would be to a lesser extent but, nevertheless, would have an impact on its crew. Let's look what happened to the *Boise* first.

Ordeal and Survival

Scott, seeing the Japanese ships trying to escape up the Slot, ordered Task Force 64.2 to chase after them. However, his command was in disarray. He had to regain control over his command because the melee of battle resulted in several of his ships being out of position. The flagship's recognition lights flashed to the American ships to reform to its original formation if at all possible. The SG radars on the *Boise* and *Helena* should have noticed the Japanese leaving. But the randomness of battle caused radarmen not able to distinguish friends from foes. Its operators' inexperience did not help matters either. A blown fuse on the *Boise* disabled its SG radar for five minutes. When it came back online, the pips on its scope showed no difference between American and Japanese ships.

At five minutes before midnight, the American task force turned to the northwest to finish off Goto's ships. Now the Americans would be under the Japanese guns just as the Japanese were when Scott crossed their "T."

Capt. Edward J. Moran, the *Boise*'s commander, did not receive Scott's cease fire order. His guns still fired away at the Japanese. The cruiser's shells had their effect as lookouts reported seeing many fires in the distance. Finally, its radar operator reported that the pip in the direction of the fires had disappeared. Having no more targets to fire at, Moran ordered, "Cease Firing!" He saw the flagship's flashing lights and took a position astern of her.

The *Boise* had absorbed some damage thus far. A shell, one of two that earlier had knocked out two five-inch guns, caused a fire to break out in the captain's cabin. Damage control parties fought to keep the fire from spreading. Another shell hit near amidships that caused little damage. But her plight soon changed for the worse.

Six minutes after midnight, Moran, his eyes still recovering from the blinding light of the gunfire, saw a thin trail of phosphorescent bubbles head for his ship. This could only mean one thing: a torpedo was about to strike his cruiser. It made no sound, understating its treacherous intent. Moran shouted, "Hard right rudder!" The ship leaned hard to the left as she swung to starboard. The warning "Torpedo Approaching!" reached every station. As the ship turned, the wake passed under her turning bow and soon paralleled her course on her port side, a brief reprieve.

But another shouted warning reported another wake that paralleled the previous one and somewhat to its right approached along the cruiser's starboard beam. These missiles came from the remaining operational Japanese cruiser, the *Kinugasa*. They passed within 30 yards of the ship's swinging stern as Moran reversed his rudder to port. Breathing a sigh of relief, he maneuvered his ship to take his station behind the flagship.

Moran's luck ran out when the *Kinugasa* showed that, while her sister cruisers no longer had any effect on the course of this sea battle, she was still a fighting ship in the finest tradition of the Imperial Japanese Navy. The *Boise* and the *Salt Lake City* lit up their searchlights to help their gunners find their next targets. The guns of both ships erupted, adding more light that pinpointed where they were. But the law of unintended consequences raised its specter when these same lights gave the *Kinugasa*'s gunners a prime aiming point.

As the *Boise* fired its guns, the Japanese cruiser fired an eight-inch barrage with the accuracy for which the Japanese Navy had become famous. The first salvo straddled the *San Francisco*'s wake. The next series of barrages found the *Boise* and surrounded her. The *Kinugasa*'s gunners, having found a most tempting target, kept firing and drew Moran's admiration for their ability to send one salvo after another with outstanding accuracy and rapidity.

One eight-inch shell smashed into the *Boise*'s No. 1 turret's barbette at 12:11 a.m., jammed the turret, and prevented it from turning. Smoke filled the turret, and the turret officer ordered the men inside to abandon it. As the 11 men came out of the turret's lower hatch and moved onto the main deck, a second eight-inch shell smacked into the deck, penetrated to the main ammunition magazine below located between the cruiser's No. 1 and No. 2 turrets, and exploded. The magazine's shells and powder bags ignited and loosed a deluge of deadly inflammable gases into all the forward magazines, ammunition handling rooms, and gun rooms. Almost 100 men died where they stood as the conflagration consumed them. Turret No. 3's room escaped any damage. Searing yellow flames shot from every opening on turrets one and two. Flames inundated the forecastle; the fire even burned the men who had evacuated Turret No. 1.

Scott, looking at the tragedy unfolding before his very eyes, believed the fires on the *Boise* would finish her. Moran shared this pessimism and, taking measures that would save his ship almost inevitable destruction, ordered the flooding of the forward magazines. Unfortunately, the men who would carry out that order were now dead, killed by the lethal flames. But two factors prevented the loss of the *Boise*. The first was the dedication to duty by the men who died as they hid many of the powder bags in a safer place to keep them from exploding. The holes in the cruiser's hull caused by Japanese shells allowed the sea to pour into the magazines and quench the raging fires.

Moran ordered a hard left turn and increased her speed to 30 knots to take her away from the deadly Japanese gunfire. The *Kinugasa*'s salvoes fell astern but still dangerously close at 50 to 100 yards. The *Boise*'s still undamaged after turrets kept firing at her tormenter and stopped two minutes later.

The *Salt Lake City*'s captain heroically tried to move his ship between the embattled light cruiser and the Japanese heavy cruiser and opened fire at the Japanese ship. The *San Francisco* continued to pummel the *Aoba*. An exchange of gunfire between the two heavy cruisers yielded indecisive results. The *Kinugasa* took some shell hits from the *Salt Lake City* during this battle. Two Japanese eight-inch shells hit the *Salt Lake City*. The first did little damage. But the second lost its thrust as it penetrated the ship's frame, rolled on the boiler room's deck, exploded, killed one man, and punctured a steam line. A torrent of steam filled the compartment and caused the American cruiser to slow to 22 knots.

After chasing the Japanese for about 20 minutes, Scott decided to change Task Force 64.2's course to 330º. All firing stopped at 20 minutes past midnight. The battle was over. So Scott decided to break off the action. The *Aoba*, *Kinugasa* and *Hatsuyuki* steamed up the Slot to comparative safety. Both sides had taken considerable losses in ships and men, although no one yet knew who had won.[4] But that is another discussion that will follow.

The Duncan*'s Last Hours*

When the *Duncan* separated herself from the rest of Task Force 64.2 as Scott ordered his countermarch maneuver, she attacked the Japanese with no help from any other ship. Her isolation would doom her. Before making the turn, her gunnery radar picked up a pip to the west on its scope. Taylor skeptically disbelieved that the contact was genuine. Nevertheless, if it was real, it was definitely unfriendly. The contact had nothing but malevolent intentions for Task Force 64.2.

After discussing the contact's viability with the *Farenholt*, the contact still showed on the *Duncan*'s radar, moving closer to the American ship formation. Soon, the *Farenholt* would be well within the range of the Japanese guns and torpedoes.

Although we do not know precisely what Taylor's thoughts were, the sloppiness of the countermarch maneuver and lack of instructions from the flagship to keep the formation intact undoubtedly added to any uncertainty in his mind. By this time, the *Duncan* was on its own course and separated from the rest of the American ships. The contact was closing fast; he had to act and could not wait for orders. The ship's quartermaster recorded in his notebook, "@ 2341 CS to 30kts, CC to 225T."[5] The contact moved left, and Taylor adjusted his ship's course to keep heading for it.

The range to the contact continued to diminish to 5,000 yards, well within sighting distance, when a lookout saw a formless blob 30° off the starboard bow. As the destroyer closed the distance to the now sighted contact, its shape sharpened. A long shadow, formerly indefinite and low in the water, turned into a superstructure. More outlines appeared with a sharper appearing bow and stern. It moved from right to left. Her shape was now clear to see. Its distinctive outline—two dramatically raked stacks with the larger stack forward, a curved stem, and a sloping deck near her stern—did not belong to any ship in the U.S. Navy. This ship was a Japanese cruiser, no doubt about it.

She obviously was not ready for battle. Her guns pointed forward and her decks showed no one on them. Two light flashes hit her bridge. Naval gunfire exploded in the night. Task Force 64.2 had opened fire!

Seeing the lights on the Japanese cruiser's bridge and hearing the gunfire, Taylor wanted to get out of the way of the shells roaring overhead by turning his destroyer's rudder hard right. The *Duncan*'s stern swung left as the cruiser crossed the destroyer's bow. All events began to move at a much faster pace, a frequent occurrence in battle. Taylor continued to look at the target. He wanted to pursue the cruiser by returning to his original direction when his executive officer, Lt. Cmdr. Louis J. Bryan, yelled for him to come over the other side of the bridge. Another cruiser was on his ship's starboard bow, its shape like the first, with guns pointing forward. The *Duncan* kept turning right; Taylor decided to attack the second cruiser. He wanted to attack her with torpedoes, followed by gunfire.

But the timing of events accelerated too fast for Taylor to execute his plan. Another ship appeared to port headed on the same course as his ship and also turning right. She headed straight toward the *Duncan*. Taylor reasoned she could be the *Laffey* and could run into his ship if she stayed on her course. He had no other alternative but to keep turning and miss a nearly picture-perfect opportunity to fire his torpedoes at the second cruiser. But all was not lost.

Knowing he had an excellent chance to attack the first sighted cruiser, he ordered, "Hard left rudder." The quartermaster spun the ship's wheel left, and the nimble destroyer characteristically responded like a hunting dog pursuing a rabbit. The Japanese cruiser was in plain sight as the destroyer continued turning. He straightened his ship's course; the cruiser was now on the *Duncan*'s starboard bow.

The setup for a torpedo attack was not the best it could be; opportunities to attack a cruiser did not happen too often. The torpedomen took the best advantage of the situation. The cruiser was closer than they wanted it to be and heading away from them. Nonetheless, when the order to fire from Torpedo Officer Ens. R. A. Fowler squawked over the ship's telephone, a torpedo leapt from a tube with a loud hiss of escaping gas and hit the water with a splat. The *Duncan*'s five-inch guns fired not long after that.

As the torpedo ran "hot, straight, and normal" and the five-inch guns fired at the nearby cruiser, a shell smashed at the base of the *Duncan*'s forward stack and knocked it over like a felled tree. The sounds of battle drowned out the sound of the shell hitting the destroyer so no one noticed. The shell exploded and killed many men in a repair party working near the toppled stack. But the men of the *Duncan* had much to cheer about as her torpedo hit its intended target in a massive explosion. The big cruiser shuddered. As the cruiser aimed its guns at another ship on its starboard side, the *Duncan* kept firing its own five-inchers. Suddenly, two shells smashed simultaneously into the destroyer. One missile penetrated the destroyer's thin armor into the ammunition handling room under Turret No. 2 and exploded in a deadly inferno, wounding and killing men at their stations there. The second shell struck the superstructure above the pilothouse, wounding Fowler and several other men and wiping out gunnery and torpedo control equipment.

The situation only got worse when the forward fire room informed the forward engine room that the shell that collapsed the forward stack had knocked out the boilers. Acting under standing orders, the boiler room crew turned off the boilers and abandoned their stations, but they stayed long enough to extinguish a small fire and would leave when "everything is straightened out."

The downed stack endangered the torpedo mount's crew and forced them to leave for their safety. Chief Torpedoman D. H. Boyd had returned to the torpedo mount just before the stack collapsed. Not leaving his post when some of his shipmates had, he looked to starboard at the big cruiser. Noticing that the torpedo mount had somehow escaped damage and despite not having any telephone connection to the bridge, he manually aimed the mount toward the cruiser and fired another torpedo. A trail of bubbles showed its intended deadly purpose as it headed toward the big warship. The torpedo smacked into the cruiser's side and exploded with a towering column of water putting a large hole in her.

Although the destroyer's Turret No. 2 could no longer fire, the other three could. Their continuous firing sent salvo after salvo into the cruiser. But the smoke became too thick to see their target, and they had to stop. Other ships fired at her too as shell splashes surrounded her. The continuous punishment thrown at her was too much to continue her existence. She fell apart into two pieces, rolled over, and quickly sank. Based on the descriptions supplied, one can confidently conclude she was the *Furutaka*.

The danger to the *Duncan* only worsened. Seeing the danger of being caught too near the sinking cruiser, Taylor ordered a hard left rudder to get away. Realizing his ship had been the victim of friendly fire, he turned on his recognition lights. He felt his ship slowing and could no longer talk to his guns. A raging fire burned in front of the bridge. He knew several men had been killed or wounded, but did not know how many. The ship continued its left turn when a devastating blast jolted the bridge, killing a man standing next to Taylor, plus three more. The fire consumed the chart house, burning five men to cinders. With the steering gear and ship's telegraph rendered useless and recognition lights permanently extinguished, he had lost any ability to continue commanding his ship. No electric power came into the bridge. All communications to the rest of the ship had been cut. Heat from the fire made it impossible to send or receive any messages using messenger.

No one could escape forward because of the fire in the handling room. Leaking steam from holes caused by the explosion's blast filled the pilothouse, the destroyer continued at 15 knots in a hard left turn. Fires fore and aft of the bridge totally isolated Taylor and those still alive from the rest of the ship. Some of the 20-mm ammunition exploded when the fire reached it.

Taylor finally realized that no one could survive on the burning ship. Only the sea surrounding his ship offered any sanctuary from death. He ordered Bryan to begin evacuating men still at their stations above the bridge. They would be lowered and prepared for entering the water. The intense heat from the fire prevented anyone from leaving the ship from its port side. One by one, the able-bodied lowered the wounded into the water on the starboard side, checking to assure their life-jackets were secured to their bodies.

The ship still moved in a left turn, scattering the men in the water. With the remaining wounded now in the water, the able-bodied men shinnied down the ropes into the water. After an hour passed, Taylor and Bryan believed they were the only living beings still aboard. The fire's heat made it impossible to leave from the bridge's port side. Adding to the danger, the 20-mm shells kept exploding. Escape was not possible directly from the bridge. Bryan and Taylor looked at each other with an unspoken understanding. Shaking hands with his captain, Bryan leapt into the water. Believing he was the only living person on the ship, Taylor also leapt into the water.

After surfacing from his jump into the pleasantly warm water, he saw the *Duncan* go past him and saw her hull number, 485, painted on her bow. She moved in a curved turn away, the flames lighting her progress. Seeing his command disappear into the distance, Taylor could not take his eyes off her.

But some men were still aboard the valiant destroyer and fought to keep their ship afloat and fighting. Men in the after turrets still fired their guns at an invisible enemy. After leaving his station for the after conning station, Ens. Frank A. Andrews conferred with Lt. Herbert R. Kabat, who was the most senior officer still aboard. Working with Chief Torpedoman D. H. Boyd, Andrews tried to take the crippled destroyer onto the beach on Savo Island. But the damage control parties still aboard had made some headway bringing the raging fires under control. With the possibility of still saving the ship, Andrews abandoned that plan.

Valiantly trying to save their ship, success was within their reach but for the fires below decks that burned entirely out of control. This forced them to seek safety in the forward engine room. The *Duncan*'s situation became more precarious when the after boiler room could not get any water needed to generate the steam to make headway. The steam pressure dropped so that no energy could flow to the engines. All power ceased. The pumps ceased their critical function of evacuating sea water. Lt. (jg) Wade H. Coley and Chief Watertender A.H. Holt tried to run the boiler with cold sea water but to no avail. Ferocious fires amidships surrounded one group of men who had no choice but to jump into the sea or be burned alive. The ship slowed to a stop.

Their heroic effort to keep the ship afloat now hopeless, the remaining men abandoned her at 2:00 a.m. to save themselves. Her crew, swimming with anything that could keep them from drowning, saw explosions and fires consuming their ship. She was a burning hulk and being annihilated by continuous explosions of ammunition that fed rampaging fires above and below her main deck.

Dispatched by Adm. Scott, the destroyer *McCalla* arrived on a scene to render any help it could. Her captain, Lt. Cmdr. William G. Cooper, realizing the potential hazards of getting too close to the blazing wreck, made a highly cautious approach. He waited for some time before lowering a boat at 3:00 p.m. and was guardedly optimistic they could save the burning warship. The plan was to put a salvage crew commanded by the *McCalla*'s executive officer aboard her. But the sea would begin to claim its due.

Swarms of sharks infested the waters near Savo Island. Light reflections off the aluminum buoys being used as floatation devices attracted them to where the *Duncan*'s men swam. The men had no chance against these vicious predators as the sharks fed voraciously. The *McCalla* unsuccessfully tried to drive the beasts away with rifle fire. Blood-red stains spread over the water. However, the *McCalla* did manage to save 196 men while 48 of the *Duncan*'s crew perished in the sea.

All attempts to save the doomed destroyer ended with failure. Sea water rushed into her innards. Only her main deck was visible. Just before noon on October 12, the salvage party left the gallant ship to her destiny with the sea. She sank within minutes six miles north of Savo Island. The waters around Guadalcanal claimed another victim. She was not the first ship to sink in Iron Bottom Sound and would definitely not be the last.[6]

Keeping Score

Besides the *Duncan*, the cruiser *Boise* sustained the most damage in this battle. After losing her forward turrets and turning to the southwest, she left the task force formation at 30 knots to escape from the gunfire that had inflicted so much damage to her. The after turret gunners saw the last Japanese shells fall short at a place where their ship would have been had not Moran ordered the hard left turn. They knew the danger from that quarter had temporarily disappeared. Many men still onboard feared that the fires raging in the forward sections of the ship would spread to the powder and shell magazines and cause massive explosions that would surely destroy her.

That is when her superbly trained damage control parties got to work to save their ship. The *Boise*'s bow was down in the water, and the ship listed slightly to starboard. Moran ordered a slowing to 20 knots to put less pressure on the bow and give his damage control people a better chance to keep her afloat. With the fires on the cruiser's deck lighting the night sky, the damage control men fought a tough, successful battle. Beaten but not bowed, she rejoined Scott's formation in the morning hours of October 12.[7]

The destroyers *Buchanan* and *Laffey* kept in formation throughout the battle while the *Farenholt*, damaged in the first minutes, separated from Task Force 64.2 during the abortive countermarch maneuver. Her damage control parties patched shell holes in her hull after pumping oil and water from one side of the ship to the other to clear the holes from the water. Listing nine degrees to starboard, she got help from the newly arrived destroyer *Aaron Ward*. She escorted the damaged *Farenholt* to the main formation later on October 12. The *McCalla* saved all she could of the *Duncan*'s survivors from the cruel waters off Savo Island.

Task Force 64.2 had a successful struggle against a strong Japanese naval force. Scott lost the *Duncan*, and the *Boise* would be out of the war for some time to come, but the Japanese forces had lost one heavy cruiser, the *Furutaka*, one destroyer, the *Fubuki*, and its commander. Goto's flagship, the *Aoba*, sustained heavy damage. Of the five ships that had comprised the Bombardment Group, two lay on the sea bottom. They never got close to achieving their mission of approaching the Guadalcanal beaches and pummeling the Americans ashore.

An American Pyrrhic Victory

While the Battle of Cape Esperance raged north of Guadalcanal and Adm. Goto lay dying on the bridge of the *Aoba*, Radm. Takaji Joshima, commander of the Reinforcement Group, achieved his mission by successfully landing troops, 150-mm guns, and supplies on the beach near Kokumbona. His ships had reached Guadalcanal unmolested and would escape with little or no interference from the Americans. The much needed Japanese reinforcements had landed with enough heavy artillery to make the Marine's job of holding Guadalcanal more difficult.

The Battle of Cape Esperance made Adm. Scott an American hero for avenging the humbling and disastrous American defeat at Savo Island. At 2:00 a.m. on October 14, the *New York Times* proudly displayed the banner headline: "6 ENEMY SHIPS SUNK IN SOLOMONS BATTLE; LANDING IS BALKED,"[8] thus satisfying the American public's thirst for some positive war news. Not mentioned were the American casualties: 163 killed and 125 wounded[9]—most of them occurred on the *Boise* and included seven Marines.

At Savo Island in August, the Japanese had a great tactical victory, but failed their strategic mission by not being able to land their troops. The reverse argument was true at the Battle of Cape Esperance. The Americans achieved a tactical victory by inflicting a major naval defeat on the Japanese, but suffered a strategic defeat by failing to stop the Japanese from landing their reinforcements.

Scott revenged Savo Island's stinging defeat at Cape Esperance. Thus, another episode passed in the saga for the struggle for Guadalcanal. And the life for the Americans on that embattled island would not get any easier as the Imperial Japanese Navy sent some big guns and larger numbers of reinforcements. Henderson Field, as it had been since the Americans landed on August 7, was still the major target.

CHAPTER 28
Japanese Heavy Guns Arrive

The U.S. Army's First Reinforcements Come Ashore

After long discussions with Gen. Harmon and much pressure from Nimitz, Ghormley finally relented and diverted the Americal Division's 164th Infantry Regiment from their "vacation" spot on New Caledonia to add to the Marine force on Guadalcanal. Adm. Turner looked out from the *McCawley*'s bridge to see more of the desperately needed reinforcements leave their transports and make their way to Lunga Point's beaches. They had been at sea since boarding the ships on October 9 in Nouméa's harbor and arrived four days later without any interference from the Japanese. The boats made repeated trips to the beaches and back again delivering the 2,850 men of the 164th, 210 men for Henderson Field, 85 Marine replacements, and badly needed supplies, food, and vehicles.

The Japanese had planned to stop any possible landings with Goto's Bombardment Group. Turner could thank Adm. Scott's Task Force 64.2 for stopping that attempt in its tracks. The tenacious Japanese were in no way about to give up their quest to kick the Americans off Guadalcanal.

The soldiers landing on Guadalcanal were National Guard volunteers from North Dakota. Unlike other National Guard units that existed in the U.S. early in the war, the 164th lacked the problems others faced—lack of discipline, amateur competence levels among the officers, and other incapacitating attributes. The primary reason for this could be placed at the feet of its commanding officer, Lt. Col. Bryant E. Moore. He was a thoroughly professional West Point graduate who Col. Gerald Thomas said ran his outfit "like a czar." While training his regiment, he noticed that one of his companies was not operating to the level of excellence he expected of all his soldiers. Not waiting to conduct any reviews of the situation, he immediately acted and instantly promoted the company sergeant to company commander and demoted the commander to sergeant.

Nonetheless, the Japanese had plans of their own. Unchastened by the Bombardment Group's defeat but heartened by their successful landing the previous day, they wanted to add still more troops to those already ashore.

✲ ✲ ✲

Previous Japanese strategies used the tactic of keeping their approaching convoys out of the range of American aircraft and had the 11th Air Fleet or Army artillery bombard Henderson Field. But the defeats of the Imperial Japanese Army during the land battle along the Matanikau River as recent as

October 10 cost them any position from which their artillery could shoot at the airfield. The Imperial Japanese Navy could not rely on the Army to disable Henderson Field and therefore took matters into their own hands. The situation on Guadalcanal had become even more desperate, so the Navy abandoned the idea of neutralizing Henderson Field before attempting to land any additional reinforcements.

They did, however, continue to use faster ships to minimize the risk of being discovered by American scout planes. The soldiers they had landed after the Battle of Cape Esperance needed to increase their numbers. So they decided to send a large force of soldiers and back that effort up with more force than they had tried before. The core of that plan was to deliver the troops to the Guadalcanal beaches. The second part was to attack Henderson Field with planes from the Base Air Force. The last part was to deliver overwhelming naval force that would hopefully bombard the airfield with sufficient firepower to pummel it into submission.

They began the initial part of their plan by sending what the called the "High Speed Convoy" at high speed from the Shortlands down the Slot on October 13, the same day that the Americans landed their Army reinforcements. The convoy had 4,500 soldiers from the 17th Army aboard six transports: the *Sasago Maru*, *Sakido Maru*, *Kyushu Maru*, *Azumasan Maru*, *Nankai Maru*, and *Sado Maru*. Each of them carried six to eight landing craft along with one company of powerful artillery batteries that included two batteries each having 100-mm and 150-mm guns, the 1st Tank Independent Company, large inventories of ammunition and food, and the equivalent of six battalions distributed among them. These units were the 16th Infantry Regiment, two battalions of the 230th Infantry Regiment, and 824 men of the 4th Maizuru Special Naval Landing Force. Escorting the fleet were the eight destroyers *Samidare*, *Harusame*, *Yudachi*, *Murasame*, *Ariake*, *Shiratsuyu*, *Shigure*, and the antiaircraft destroyer *Akizuki*, the flagship of the screen's commander and Midway veteran, Radm. Tamotsu Takama.

Before the convoy arrived, Japanese aircraft from the Base Air Force came over the Lunga Beaches and Henderson Field. Their new commanding officer, Vadm. Jinichi Kusaka, who replaced the ailing Vadm. Nishizo Tsukahara on October 8, had planned the attack in two waves. The first group, led by Lt. Shigeji Makino, had 24 bombers escorted by 18 Zeroes led by Lt. Takahide Aioi. The second wave, trailing the first by two hours, had Lt. Cmdr. Kazuo Nishioka's 14 bombers escorted by Lt. Shiro Kawai's 18 Zeroes.

Kusaka optimistically hoped his planes would fly all the way to Guadalcanal undetected. But his hopes, like many of those held by senior Japanese officers, proved fruitless. Australian coastwatcher Maj. Donald Kennedy saw the first wave at 11:15 a.m. from his vantage point at the Segi Plantation on New Georgia's southern end and radioed the warning to Henderson Field. CACTUS' radar picked up the Japanese first wave 15 minutes later thus triggering the takeoff of 42 F4Fs, seven P-39s, and six P-400s. The Japanese aircraft arrived faster than expected when they appeared over Lunga Point at 12:02 p.m. and flew right over Turner's transports. Facing no opposition at just less than 25,000 feet, Makino led his bombers over Henderson Field where they dropped their loads that reportedly destroyed 20 aircraft on the ground. The actual damage was one destroyed B-17 while only slightly damaging 12 other planes. Perhaps the reason for the optimistic Japanese damage assessment was that some of their bombs hit a 5,000-gallon aviation gasoline dump that exploded in a fiery blast. The American Seabees quickly abandoned their shelters to fill in the craters left by the bombs and replace damaged metal matting. Some of them were forced to use their helmets for digging because they did not have enough shovels. Still not facing any American aircraft, the first wave's bombers turned toward their home base.

Just four F4Fs commanded by Maj. Leonard K. Davis reached the first wave more than 30 minutes after they dropped their bombs. Davis dove at a formation of Japanese bombers but some Zeroes forced him to abort his attack. One F4F flown by 2nd Lt. William B. Freeman shot at and took a nick out of PO2c Genji Negishi's bomber. Second Lt. Joseph L. Narr took on the entire Japanese Zero escort and pumped several .50-cal. machine-gun bullets into Sea1c Manri Ito's Zero. Narr did not escape unscathed as his plane took several hits and had to land in the water near Lunga Point. Fortunately, he was unhurt and able fly once more. Ito was not as lucky. He lost his life making a water landing at Rekata Bay. Negishi survived and was barely able to land his plane at Rabaul.

CACTUS' radar detected the approach of Nishioka's second wave at 1:35 p.m. Twelve F4Fs, flying above the Japanese formation, dove on the 14 Japanese bombers. Kawai's Zeroes effectively countered the American attack thus allowing the bombers to reach their intended targets. Flying at 8,000 meters (or 26,240 feet), all 14 planes dropped their entire bomb loads and believed they either damaged or destroyed 30 American aircraft. The Marine Air Wing claimed the Japanese bombs "slightly" damaged just a few planes.

The second wave's escorting Zeroes got into dogfights with the American F4Fs and claimed to have shot down five of ten American fighters. The only recorded American plane shot down was Capt. Joseph J. Foss' F4F, which landed with bouncing thumps at Lunga near the Ilu River.

The results of Japanese air attacks could only be described, at best, as mixed. Kusaka heard the reports from his pilots that pleased him. As far he was concerned, these latest air assaults clearly showed an opening in the Americans' ability to continue defending the Guadalcanal airfields. Nonetheless, after landing their planes, the American pilots took advantage of a rare treat of ice-cold Coca Colas that considerably lifted their spirits. The Japanese had again not significantly affected air operations on Guadalcanal after so many nearly continuous daily attacks.

But the Japanese had other ideas. An SBD spotted three transports and three destroyers of the High Speed Convoy steaming at 15 knots just 200 miles northwest of Guadalcanal.

The Japanese Bring on the Heavy Guns

It all began after 6:00 p.m. with one obviously large-caliber artillery shell screeching over the jungle and exploding into the ground near Henderson Field's western edge. The missile came from one of the Japanese 4th Artillery Regiment's two 15-cm guns that had been brought ashore just two days previous. Well camouflaged in the dense jungle's undergrowth west of the Matanikau River about two and a half miles southwest of Kokumbona, these big guns, the biggest the Japanese had ever landed thus far, were well beyond the range of any artillery the Americans had on Guadalcanal. The shells kept coming, churning huge holes on Henderson Field's western edge and forcing American air operations to move to the airfield's eastern side. The accuracy of the Japanese gunners improved as they continued firing. One huge shell splashed and exploded in the water just 25 yards from Turner's flagship *McCawley*. The guns of the destroyers *Nicholas*, *Gwin*, and *Sterett* retaliated against Japanese troops at Point Cruz but never came near the two Japanese guns.

The arrival of the big shells caught the American aviators completely by surprise. Men frantically dove for any nearby shelter. Lt. Cmdr. Leroy C. Simpler, commander of the Navy's VF-5 sent to Guadalcanal to reinforce Maj. Gen. Roy S. Geiger's First Marine Air Wing (MAW-1), had been talking to the general when the first shell exploded. Extricating himself from the pile of men seeking shelter, Simpler looked around for Geiger. Seeing the general standing with his fingers in his ears, trying to protect his hearing from the exploding shells, Simpler told him, "General, you know that you should seek shelter as fast as possible in such a danger." Geiger replied, "Yes, I know, but I am not going to let a goddamn Jap cause me to get my last clean uniform dirty."[1] From this moment on, the men on Guadalcanal had several new names for these massive bombardments, among them were, "Millimeter Mike," "Pistol Pete," or "Mountain Joe." As is so characteristic of Americans, they tried to introduce dark humor to relieve the incredible stresses associated with tense combat situations. No nicknames would be sufficient to allay what was to come.

The shelling worried Vandegrift. The Japanese had not done anything like this before. He ordered a general alert, confidently believing this was only the beginning. As darkness descended upon the beleaguered island, events would make Vandegrift more right than he ever wanted to be.[2]

One of the basic tenets of amphibious warfare is that the landing force must have control of the air over the landing beaches for a successful operation. Thus far, the Japanese could only have that during nighttime hours as long as CACTUS continued to operate. They had tried to capture the airfields by ground attacks, shelling by field artillery, destroyers, and light cruisers, or bombing from the air. Nevertheless, American air operations on Guadalcanal continued. So they decided to use the big guns of their battleships again and at night to destroy the American aircraft on the ground.

Their base at Rabaul received a new naval bombardment shell from Japan, carrying the designation Type Zero, that exploded like a powerful firecracker and spread 470 incendiary missiles in all directions when they detonated. Intended initially to be fired at attacking aircraft, they could fit into the 36-cm (14-inch) guns on the two *Kongo*-class battleships they had at Rabaul, the *Kongo* and *Haruna*.[3]

The Japanese planned to send both battleships in a task force commanded by Vadm. Takeo Kurita. The force would also include the light cruiser *Isuzu*, the flagship of the escort's commander, Radm. Raizo Tanaka, and the nine destroyers: *Oyashio*, *Kuroshio*, *Hayashio*, *Umikaze*, *Kawakaze*, *Suzukaze*, *Takanami*, *Makinami*, and *Naganami*. An earlier plan would have added the super-battleship *Yamato* with her nine massive 18.1-inch guns and four heavy cruisers. However, the Advanced Force's commander, Adm. Kondo, cancelled that plan because of the narrowness of the waters around Guadalcanal and Savo Islands that lacked sufficient maneuvering room. Kurita, reflecting in his normally cautious and conservative naval attitude, protested to Yamamoto that the plan he was to command was too risky in that it placed the Japanese ships too near American attacking aircraft. Yamamoto overruled him, and like the loyal officer he was, Kurita boarded the *Kongo* and left Rabaul on October 12. Nonetheless, Kurita's force was the largest and most powerful naval force the Japanese would send to the waters near Guadalcanal since the American invasion. They headed down the Slot at 25 knots with a planned arrival off the Guadalcanal beaches on the 14th between midnight and 1:00 a.m.

As they approached a point west of Savo Island just before midnight, Kurita slowed his force to 18 knots. Luckily, they had escaped detection by American ships or planes. Kurita launched three observation planes that would drop flares over the airfield's runways: red over the western edge, white over the runway's center, and green over the field's eastern side. His plan was to saturate a 2,200 square meter area with a crippling barrage. The *Kongo*'s gun crews loaded eight of the new shells into the 14-inch guns as the ships' turned to 77°. The *Haruna*'s gun crews placed eight high-explosive shells in its big guns. Both big ships turned their turrets to aim at the American airfields. Gunnery officers pointed their range finders toward the darkened island's mass to get the best range estimates they could. Lt. Cmdr. Kenji Mitsui, a gunnery officer assigned to spot the fall of shot and recently transferred from the *Yamato*, crouched atop Mount Austen and peered down at the airfields. He had a radio at the ready so he could call the fall of shot back to the ships offshore.

The Americans were about to feel the effect of a massive ship barrage the likes of which they had never experienced before. The Japanese wanted to give the Americans the business. And that's what the Americans would emphatically receive.

Many aircraft being heard overhead caused earsplitting alarms to be sounded all over the American positions as the sky darkened into night. A more ominous chugging sound, described by Capt. Joseph J. Foss as sounding like a popcorn machine, of a Japanese observation plane meant that something deadly was about to happen. At 1:30 a.m., Louie the Louse began dropping flares.

Three and a half minutes later, the *Kongo*'s guns filled the night with massive bursts of sound and light. Eight huge 14-inch shells arched into the night sky. The *Haruna* opened fire at 1:35 a.m., eight more 14-inch shells were on their way to do their worst.

☆ ☆ ☆

Coastwatcher Martin Clemens had just returned from an exhausting trek into the jungle on another mission. He plopped down onto his cot and dropped into an overdue, deep sleep. Suddenly, a bright flare lit up the sky with a blinding light that turned the night into day. The flare burned for almost one-half minutes when a salvo of what seemed to be high caliber shells exploded on the ridge just behind Clemens' tent. Since being on Guadalcanal, Clemens had never undergone such a heavy shelling. The explosions threw blinding dust and acrid-smelling smoke everywhere. It seemed like a huge earthquake had struck the island as more shells struck.[4]

The Japanese first rounds hit west of the Henderson Field runway. More shells "marched" from west to east as they struck aircraft parking areas and the American pilots' living quarters in the coconut groves north of the runway. Destruction rained down on aircraft, gasoline dumps, and ammunition storage areas. Plane after plane erupted in blinding explosions as the great shells found their marks. When the special shells struck and exploded, a fiery trail followed their destructive path and "spewed forth hundreds of tiny cylinders, open at both ends and spitting fire."[5]

In just the few minutes since the shelling had begun, many fires burned with an intensity fueled by great amounts of combustible materials. Their emitted light made the darkness seem like a day in hell. The battleships steamed in line with impunity 16 miles away and untouchable by the relatively puny American five-inch shore batteries. The light cruiser *Isuzu*, moved closer to the Lunga beaches and fired its six-inch guns at the American shore artillery emplacements.

The Japanese sailors impulsively cheered as they saw a giant fireworks display just like the ones they once saw at home as children. More optimism filled the atmosphere aboard the Japanese ships as they listened to frantic American messages that said, for example, "Intensive bombardment by enemy ships. Damage tremendous." Just to make sure of the awful work they began, the battleships kept firing salvo after salvo that covered a 14 square mile zone but confined the greatest devastation to about one-third of that area.

Other Americans who were there recalled how horrible the shelling was. One veteran of the Army Air Force's 67th Fighter Squadron recalled:

> "They had hardly hit the foxholes before the air was filled with a bedlam of sound: the screaming of shells. The dull roar of cannonading offshore, the whine of shrapnel, the thud of palm trees as they were severed and hit the ground, and in the lulls from the big noises, the ceaseless sifting of dirt into the foxhole."[6]

Capt. Joe Foss, a man never known to mince words, remembered, "It seemed as if all the props had been kicked from under the sky and we were crushed beneath."[7] One shell exploded near Gen. Vandegrift and sent him to the floor of his tent in a most undignified, fetal-like position. Later, he recalled:

> "A man comes close to himself at such times...and until someone has experienced naval or artillery shelling or aerial bombardment, he cannot easily grasp a sensation compounded of frustration, helplessness, fear and, in the case of close hits, shock..."[8]

Lt. Cmdr. Louis J. Kirn later related what it was like to experience the agony of that night, "You feel so utterly helpless...feel, rather than hear, salvos being walked right over your position."

When the battleships were on an eastward course at 2:13 a.m. and out of range, they turned back toward Guadalcanal. Kurita realized he had no more special shells and had to begin using far less destructive armor piercing shells. Knowing this was a waste of ammunition that could only be effectively used against heavily armored warships and after firing 973 shells at the American airfield, he ordered a cease fire at 2:56 a.m. and retired up the Slot.

While the Japanese battleships switched to armor piercing shells, their guns temporarily stopped firing. The scene at Henderson Field was totally chaotic. Lt. Frederick Mears and about 70 others jumped into a truck to drive to the beach and escape the slaughter. He remembered, "Men were yelling, even crying and trying to hide behind one another or force their way to the bottom of the truck."

The bombardment was obviously the result of an excellent firing strategy designed to cripple American aviation on Guadalcanal. And the results were better than the Japanese hoped. Almost all of the American aviation gasoline had gone up in flames. Most of the planes either had been burned to their skeletons while others had many shrapnel holes in their metal skins. Just seven of the 39 SBDs could fly. All the TBFs had been destroyed. Only four P-400s and two P-39s were combat-ready. Eight B-17s had landed the previous night after a difficult mission. Hoping for a respite, that likelihood disappeared when the first Japanese shells hit Henderson Field. Two B-17s were a wreck with another heavily damaged. Four F4Fs were a shambles and only eight could still fly.

The pilots' living quarters were in total disarray as the coconut grove where they were located received many shell bursts that hit the tree tops. Fallen trees and broken coconuts spread debris everywhere and fell on those trying to clean up the palm fronds, pieces of tents, and personal belongings. Fortunately, the shelling injured only one pilot in the fighter squadron. The other squadrons were not as fortunate. Five pilots were fatal casualties.

The Japanese had gambled that the battleships would deliver a knockout blow to CACTUS. They sure did not hold back on the ammunition they threw at Henderson Field and the fighter strip.

The Japanese had fired a total of 973 large caliber shells at the airfields with devastating effect. The Americans suffered heavy losses in aircraft, vehicles, and provisions. Henderson Field staggered from the shattering destruction to planes, men, and supplies. They should have been totally out of action. But they were not.

The Ants Attack the Elephant

To add an insult to injury, Adm. Mikawa appeared on his flagship, the heavy cruiser *Chokai*, along with the cruiser *Kinugasa*, the fortunate survivor of the Battle of Cape Esperance, and began to lob more eight-inch shells at Henderson Field. As if there were not enough big craters on the airfield's runway, the Japanese cruisers added more of them by pummeling the airfield with 752 shells. But the cruisers were not unopposed.

Several PT boats on Tulagi commanded by Lt. Cmdr. Allen R. Montgomery had just arrived on October 12. Wanting to keep the presence of his boats secret until they could attack targets Montgomery considered important, he kept his four PTs at anchor. During the night of the Japanese battleships' shelling of Guadalcanal, the dull thumping of gunfire woke him. He thought that this was the chance for his PTs to do something meaningful. He called the skippers of the four boats who were all naval reserve officers carrying the rank of Lt. Junior Grade: Henry S. Taylor of the *PT-46,* Robert C. Wark of the *PT-48*, and two brothers, John M. Searles of the *PT-60* and Robert L. Searles of the *PT-38.* Their orders: "Go get 'em!"

Montgomery rode on the *PT-60* as it and the three other boats left Tulagi's harbor and moved into the darkness-shrouded water toward the flashes of the guns. Based on the loud sounds of the gunfire, there were targets worthy of his small flotilla's attention. The four PTs soon separated and proceeded independently.

The *PT-38* got close enough to what its crew thought was a light cruiser and loosed four torpedoes at the murky target. The boat passed within 100 yards of its target. Its crew felt the heat from several explosions and believed these were from their torpedoes exploding as they hit the ship, but the heat was from the muzzles of the big guns firing at the beach.

The *PT-60* fired two torpedoes and claimed they hit a warship. Again, the explosions were not from detonating torpedoes; they were from gunfire. The Japanese destroyer *Naganami* spotted the *PT-60* and gave chase. The boat put up a smoke screen and escaped without being damaged.

Montgomery's PTs put on a great show, but the torpedoes they launched streamed harmlessly past the Japanese ships. With no damage inflicted, Montgomery's boats retired to Tulagi's harbor. Henderson Field had taken another beating.

Down, but Not Out

Later that morning at 5:00 a.m., the Japanese trumpeted their glee by proclaiming that CACTUS had been destroyed. Now filled with more confidence since his humiliating defeat at Midway, Yamamoto sent the carriers of the Third Fleet and the cruisers of the Second Fleet to finish off what was left of any American naval forces in the southern Solomons.

Lt. Cmdr. Mitsui, perched on his vantage point on Mount Austen, probably had a less optimistic perspective of Henderson Field's troubles than Yamamoto's when he peered though his binoculars 40 minutes later. He saw some SBDs takeoff for their normal morning search mission. Two F4Fs took off for the morning patrol. Punctuating their present domination, the 17th Army's two 150-mm howitzers, now nicknamed "Millimeter Mike" by the Americans on Guadalcanal, lobbed several shells at the airfield's western edge. Attempts by four P-400 fighters to disable these pesky guns proved to be in vain as they could not find the well-camouflaged weapons.

The damage to Henderson Field was so extensive that many aircraft had to be asked to leave. Col. Saunders wanted to get his five operational B-17s to safety at Espiritu Santo. However, only 1,800 feet of runway was clear enough to allow planes to takeoff. There were several large craters pocketing the airstrip. Nevertheless, he ordered his air crews to get ready to leave and begin warming up their planes' engines. At 5:00 p.m., as the B-17s stood with their engines running, seven F4F pilots received orders to leave immediately. Since their fighters were either too damaged to fly or laying as burning hulks, the pilots had to hitch rides on the departing bombers because there were no transport planes on Guadalcanal. As soon as they got onboard, the bombers took off, dodging the many craters strewn all over the runway. All but one of the F4F pilots made the trip to Espiritu Santo on the B-17s. The remaining pilot escaped on Gen. Geiger's PBY-5a. One B-17 took off later on three engines, but the two left at Henderson Field stayed there, never to fly again. The Marines siphoned valuable aviation gasoline from their tanks and salvaged all the spare parts they could.

The SBDs spotted the "High Speed Convoy" just 140 miles to the northwest proceeding down the Slot with six transports and eight destroyers. Such a large number of transports meant only one thing. With deadly serious intent, the Japanese had several thousand soldiers on their way with the sole purpose of destroying the American presence on Guadalcanal. Vandegrift sent a desperate message to Ghormley: "Urgently necessary this force receive maximum support of air and surface units. Absolutely essential aviation gas be flown here continuously."[9] Trying to make it harder for further bombardment to have aiming points, he ordered the control tower, nicknamed "The Pagoda" that had been at Henderson Field since the marines landed, torn down. With Scott's task force licking its wounds and replenishing itself and the carrier *Hornet* still refueling, there was no large naval force nearby to challenge the power of the Combined Fleet. Geiger barely had enough aircraft to conduct search missions much less perform any combat assignments. CINCPAC's daily situation report for October 14 tautly stated, "Our position is not favorable to prevent a major enemy landing"—a classic understatement of Guadalcanal's situation.

Adm. Fitch, now in command of all air power in the Southwest Pacific, was one American senior officer who did not stand by and wring his hands. He immediately ordered all 17 available SBDs and 20 F4Fs currently wasting time on Espiritu Santo to fly immediately to Guadalcanal. But they needed fuel. Fitch ordered Marine and Army Douglas R4D/C47 transports to fly fuel to CACTUS. Each transport plane carried ten 55-gallon drums; each drum could keep one F4F in the air for one hour. As someone once said, "Desperate times require desperate measures." This was clearly one of these times, and Fitch stepped up to the challenge.

Lt. Col. John C. "Toby" Munn, one of Geiger's staff officers visited the 67th Fighter Squadron's pilots and soberly spoke as Japanese 150-mm shells exploded around the gathered pilots:

> "I want you to pass the word along that the situation is desperate. We don't know whether we'll be able to hold the field or not. There's a Japanese task force of destroyers, cruisers, and troop transports headed this way. We have enough gasoline left for one mission against them. Load your airplanes with bombs and go out with the dive-bombers and hit them. After the gas is gone we'll have to let the ground troops take over. Then your officers and men will attach themselves to some infantry outfit. Good luck and goodbye."[10]

✲ ✲ ✲

Another Japanese air raid arrived over Guadalcanal later that morning. Coastwatcher Donald Kennedy sent a warning message as the Japanese planes passed New Georgia Island. CACTUS raised an alert at 9:45 a.m. followed by a "Condition RED" 18 minutes later. Henderson Field sent 25 F4Fs aloft. The only operational radar station, which functioned erratically, picked up no contacts. Maj. Renner declared an "all clear" and the aircraft landed.

When the Japanese planes did come over Henderson Field, they caught the American planes on the ground. Using the previous tactic of attacking in two waves, the first wave of 45 planes had 27 bombers escorted by 18 Zeroes left Rabaul at 8:10 a.m. One bomber had to abort and return to Rabaul. The second wave left about an hour later and had 12 bombers and 15 Zeroes.

After sighting the approaching Japanese first wave without the advantage of an early radar warning, the Americans sent up 24 F4Fs at 11:57 a.m. just before the first wave's leading planes were over the airfield. Before the American fighters could gain enough altitude to stop them, the 27 Japanese bombers loomed over the field at 24,600 feet (7,500 meters) from the west-southwest and dropped their loads.

After their return to Rabaul, the bomber crews reported the airfield had many large craters with about 50 parked planes that were mostly wrecks. The American antiaircraft artillery also claimed to have shot down one bomber with four probables.

The first wave's pilots had to fight off eight American carrier bombers and fighters. The Zeroes returned to Buka to refuel. All of the first wave planes that bombed Guadalcanal that day returned safely. The Americans also lost no planes.

When the second wave arrived, they flew over Lunga and reduced their altitude to 8,000 meters (26,400 feet) at almost full speed. Some F4Fs, cruising higher, waited for them. Nine of them attacked the Japanese bombers and claimed five bombers and two Zeroes. One damaged Zero had to leave its formation. The other Zeroes could not stop the F4F attack.

The Japanese bombers split into two formations to bomb CACTUS. Five bombers dropped their bombs on what they saw as three large planes. Three other bombers attacked ten smaller planes. Four of the F4Fs were not finished with their work. Diving from a high altitude, they claimed to have shot down five bombers. Actually, the American fighters heavily damaged two Japanese bombers that eventually crash-landed before reaching Rabaul.

The American pilots claimed 14 victories: 11 bombers and three Zeroes with one bomber and one Zero as probable wins. The 3rd Defense Battalion changed its victories during the first wave to four confirmed bomber kills and one probable. One American pilot, 2nd Lt. Koller C. Brandon, lost his life. All the Zeroes safely returned to Rabaul and, their confidence deflated, claimed no victories. The actual Japanese losses were three shot down or missing, one ditched in the water at Rekata, one force-landed at Buka, and three heavily damaged.

CACTUS had been bloodied but showed itself and the world that it could defend itself. And now it would attack.

Adm. Takama swelled with confidence as his High Speed Convoy steamed down the Slot toward his objective. His ships carried the hope of his superiors on Rabaul that the soldiers and the supplies to go with them would return Guadalcanal and its strategically vital airfield to Japanese control. The only aircraft he could see were float planes and Zeroes flying protective cover. He and his lookouts had seen the American SBDs earlier, but this did not concern him too much since, based on the destruction he knew Kurita's battleships could do to ground targets, the American planes on the island posed no real danger.

Meanwhile, four SBDs, four P-39s, three p-400s, and 17 F4Fs flew toward the approaching Japanese ships. It was a paltry force when compared to prior air attacks launched from CACTUS before the Japanese battleships had done their worst. But the air crews in those planes had not lost the determination to destroy any attackers. Arriving over the Japanese ships at 3:45 p.m., the Americans dove on them, loosed their bombs, and hit nothing. After returning to refuel by using the gasoline drained from the crippled B-17s, Kirn led a modest formation of seven P-39s and nine SBDs with an escort flight of eight F4Fs that found the Japanese ships at 6:05 p.m. Seven Japanese float planes tried in vain to stop the Americans. While the SBD crews claimed to have scored several hits or near-misses, the attack inflicted only light damage on the destroyer *Samidare*. The Japanese Zeroes shot down one P-39 and claimed victories of one F4F and one P-39. The Americans had tried their best, but clearly did not have enough air power to make a difference this time.

As far as he was concerned, Maj. Gen. Shuicho Miyazaki, the 17th Army's chief of staff, had good reasons to feel convinced of his nation's ultimate victory at Guadalcanal. The "High Speed Convoy" seemed impervious to any chance the Americans could or would stop it. Feeling this movement would decide Guadalcanal's fate, he wrote in his diary, "The arrow has already left the bow."[11] The ferocious tiger that once was American air power on Guadalcanal had been rendered toothless.

A Turning Point for the Japanese?

Midnight on October 15 brought the Tokyo Express with its full power to the shores of Guadalcanal. Takama's confidence in his success seemed more than well founded when his convoy arrived safely and began to offload its deadly cargoes. No American planes could be found in the skies above. The Japanese could not know that Geiger had ordered no nighttime sorties.

As if the High Speed Convoy was not enough, the light cruisers *Sendai* and *Yura*, the seaplane carrier *Nisshin*, and the destroyers *Asagumo*, *Akatsuki*, and *Ikazuchi* appeared off Cape Esperance and deposited 1,100 soldiers and all the ammunition they could carry on the beach. The destroyer *Shirayuki* sent supplies ashore that were the beginnings of a midget submarine base.

Martin Clemens and his compatriots survived the battleship and cruiser shelling during the night. When daylight arrived on October 15, he walked down to Kukum and found Dwight H. Dexter who had been forced to quickly evacuate his base. Clemens noticed Dexter's pallid facial expression. Dexter could not speak. All he could do was point to the ocean past the Matanikau River. Clemens looked through his binoculars and saw a spectacle that could only be seen as a bad omen.

Dozens of ships superstructures and masts filled the horizon off the beach between the Tassafaronga and Mamara plantations just a few miles from where Dexter and he stood. Six transports, their bows pushed nearly on the shore, disgorged streams of soldiers and supplies. Thousands of soldiers ran down the transports' gangways and congregated in groups on the beach. He saw Japanese destroyers patrolling the water back and forth less than 5,000 yards from the shoreline between Lunga Point and Tulagi. Clemens felt helpless about what he could do and about what was unfolding in front of him.

The American marines and soldiers saw what Clemens saw but from a much closer distance. Japanese Zeroes and float planes flew above the ships. Wanting to show that CACTUS could still fight back, Maj. Davis led a flight of six F4Fs that lifted off at about 8:00 a.m. to strafe the transports. Two F4Fs, flown by Lt. Carl W. Rooney and Lt. (jg) Elisha T. "Smokey" Stover, came in at below mast-high level and loosed their machine guns. They shot at the transports, damaged a landing barge, banked to the right, and headed for Cape Esperance.

Stover climbed to 7,000 feet and headed for Lunga. He looked up and saw the observation plane from the *Sanuki Maru*, a biplane piloted by PO1c Kiichi Sakuma with Sea1c Shigeru Yoshimitsu aboard as the plane's observer, diving at him. Stover pushed his throttle lever forward, yanked the stick, and climbed in a tight turn. As he reached 8,000 feet, he now faced his pursuer. Both planes headed toward each other on a headlong collision course. Sakuma was the first to fire his 7.7-mm guns. His errant aim caused the tracers from his gun to veer to the right. With just 500 yards between the two planes, Stover fired all four .50-cal. guns, but the bullets hit nothing. Seemingly in a trance, both pilots still headed for each other. It is not clear whether either pilot tried to avoid a collision. Nevertheless, Stover's right wing cut one of Sakuma's fabric-covered wings and ripped away the wing strut. Stover stayed in control of his F4F and turned to get another crack at the Japanese biplane. He pressed the trigger button on his stick but only one of his four guns fired. Not knowing he had hit the Japanese plane, he saw Sakuma's plane go into a spin and head for the water. Rooney saw the plane crash.

Stover landed his plane. As he taxed his plane, the right wing hung down as the wing flap dropped off onto the runway. He climbed out of the cockpit and looked at the wing. There was a foot-long tear in the leading edge with a "yard square strip of black fabric containing part of a blood-red Rising Sun, edged with a gray circle," that came from Sakuma's plane. His aircraft also had four holes from 25-mm AA fire.

✲ ✲ ✲

The mechanics commanded by Lt. William Woodruff struggled to repair the planes as fast as they could. They worked all night on the 14th, but Mikawa's guns had done their worst by leaving only three SBDs that could fly. One plummeted into a crater while taxiing on the fighter strip—Henderson Field's runways were out of commission. Another SBD tried to take off, but ground looped as the bomber hit another crater. First Lt. Robert M. Patterson tried to take the last SBD aloft, got into the air, and found he had no hydraulic controls. He still claimed a hit on a transport despite having no flaps and his landing gear still in the down position.

Woodruff's men worked hard and eventually repaired one plane at a time. As each plane could fly, its pilot took off. Not only was there a shortage of planes, but there was an equally short supply of aviation gasoline. By this time, there was no more gasoline to be foraged from any of the crippled planes. Fortunately, one of Geiger's staff officers remembered that Col. Louis E. Woods had buried a backup cache of gasoline. An immediate search over the airfield turned up 465 barrels. Now they had enough gasoline to keep CACTUS flying for two days. The gasoline flown in by R4Ds from VMJ-253 and C47s from the USAAF made their modest contribution to alleviate the fuel shortage crisis. YP boats from Tulagi ferried 200 drums across the channel, but the seriousness of the crisis had not abated; a more permanent solution had to be found quickly, or CACTUS would cease to exist as a fighting force.

Gen. Geiger wanted to stop the single, impromptu attacks that had been occurring since the Japanese battleships had attacked. He ordered the assembly of 12 SBDs, two P-39s—each carrying a 500-pound bomb; four P-400s—each carrying a 100-pound bombs; and five F4Fs for an organized attack on the Japanese transports. Obeying the instructions from CACTUS control, Maj. Jack R. Cram and Geiger's pilot, had tried to land the general's personal plane, a PBY-5A, onto the fighter strip the previous afternoon. Fearing the runway was not long enough to land the big amphibious plane, he landed on Henderson Field's pockmarked runway. After Cram landed, the ground crews hung a torpedo under each of the plane's wings. There was no other operational plane that could carry a torpedo. All TBFs lay crippled—strewn like so many corpses all over Henderson Field. No one had ever tried a torpedo attack with the Catalina bomber, and Cram had also never tried a torpedo attack, period.

Nonetheless, the big PBY and the other 21 planes took off at 10:15 a.m. and headed southwest. The unlikely formation made a big turn to attack from the north. Cram's plane turned inside the other planes to fly southeast and leveled off at 6,000 feet.

Lt. (jg) Takeyoshi Ono, leading a flight of nine Zeroes from Buka flying CAP over the Japanese transports, ordered his command to stop the attacking American planes. The SBDs dropped into their attacking dives from 10,000 feet. Cram jammed the throttles to the wall and dove his plane into the characteristic shallow dive for a torpedo attack. Flying at 234 knots, the ungainly PBY strained its structure beyond its manufacturer's recommended speed. The torpedoes on his wings caused his plane to be unbalanced to the right, so he kicked the right rudder pedal and pointed the plane's nose to a new target. Successfully penetrating the Japanese destroyer screen, he loosed both torpedoes at a big transport and thought the missiles had hit it. The transport *Sasago Maru* burst into an enormous and fatal column of flames. Other SBDs pummeled the *Kyushu Maru*. She later had to be run aground on the beach at Bunina Point near Kokumbona—a total loss.

One P-39 pilot, Capt. William C. Sharpsteen, claimed a victory of one Zero. The attacking SBD pilots claimed two Zeroes but lost three of their own flown by Second Lieutenants Anthony J. Turtora, Dante Benedetti, and Robert C. Le Blanc. Meanwhile, Cram's ungainly PBY flew agonizingly slow when three Zeroes flown by PO1c Toshio Ota, PO2c Chuji Sakurai, and Sea1c Yozo Sugawara attacked. Ota fired his guns at the sluggish American flying boat and thought he had shot it down. As his Zero flew past the American, his two compatriots pressed their attacks. Sakurai was on the PBY's tail as Cram came in low over Henderson Field with dense AA fire flying all around him. Second Lt. Roger A. Haberman, trying to land his badly smoking F4F with his wheels down and banking his plane on his final approach to land, saw Sakurai's Zero and kept turning. The Zero quickly lined up in his gunsight, and Haberman opened fire with his four .50-cal. machine guns. He missed the first time, came around, and fired his guns again. The Zero exploded in a fireball and smashed into the ground near Fighter One; Haberman had his first verified victory. As Sugawara continued his pass and strafed Henderson Field, Cram landed the PBY on Fighter One to a hero's welcome with Haberman leading the celebration.

Although CACTUS could not deliver heavy blows on the Japanese landing force, Maj. Ernest R. Maniere's B-17s, nicknamed the "Gray Geese," at Espiritu Santo had some power to bring. Fifteen minutes after the transport *Nankai Maru* successfully offloaded its entire cargo and began steaming away from Guadalcanal at 11:45 a.m., the "Gray Geese" arrived overhead to the enthusiastic cheers from CACTUS' embattled men. The big bombers dropped their loads on the transports below as the buzzing Zeroes ferociously attacked. Some of the bombs smashed onto the *Azumasan Maru* and turned the transport into a smashed, burning hulk. The B-17 crews claimed three or four Zeroes while the Japanese claimed two B-17s. Neither claim had any validity. However, one Zero crash-landed at Buin (Bougainville) and three other Zero pilots ditched their planes in the ocean and were rescued.

Since the noon hour had arrived, it was time for the daily Japanese bombing attack from Rabaul. The Japanese did not disappoint the men on Guadalcanal. Lt. Makino returned in command of 23 Betty bombers accompanied by an escort of eight Zeroes led by Lt. (jg) Masayoshi Baba. Approaching at 24,600 feet, Makino's bombers this time made a good bomb run and dropped their loads on both Henderson Field and Fighter One. There was not enough warning for the Americans to get any opposition into the air. American written reports, in the absence of any other information, indicated that this bombing raid damaged runways and planes.

When the American planes got into the air, Baba's Zeroes pounced on seven F4Fs. Lt. David C. Richardson and Lt. (jg) Wildon M. Rouse climbed their fighters to 20,000 feet east of Lunga when three Zeroes flown by PO2c Tadahiro Sakai, PO3c Giichi Ohara, and PO3c Tatsuo Morioka appeared suddenly from above and jumped them. Rouse's F4F took a hit in his engine that cut his oil line. Protected by two other F4Fs, he dove immediately to get away. His engine froze up and had to ditch in the water near the mouth of the Tenaru River. He spent an almost life-ending time in the water, but was rescued and survived. Richardson and another F4F pilot, 1st Lt. William M. Watkins, Jr. each claimed one Zero. Baba's formation claimed to have shot down five of the seven F4Fs they attacked and escaped back to Rabaul with no losses. The actual American fighter losses were two shot down with both pilots being rescued and one fighter destroyed on the ground. There were now only four F4Fs remaining that could still fly.

Faced with the loss of three of the six precious transports caused by CACTUS' relentless attacks, Adm. Takama had no choice but to take what was left of his fleet out of danger and head to safety off Savo Island despite the Zeroes flying overhead providing CAP. He wanted to return after dark, but Gen. Ito (17th Army) warned him not to return. Nonetheless, Takama did achieve his major objective of landing most of the reinforcements—about 4,500 soldiers and more than two-thirds of the supplies—under his charge. The Japanese did lose three transports, five Zeroes, one "Pete" float plane, and one Betty bomber.

American aviation on Guadalcanal, while seriously affected by the previous night's bombardment, had shown it could still fight—definitely broken but not bowed. Takama's fleet had sustained serious losses. The landing of reinforcements during daylight hours was still a risky operation. It now becomes clear, at least to those of us who examine these events from the advantage of historical hindsight, that no matter what the Japanese tried, the Americans meant to hold onto Guadalcanal—no matter what the cost.

Nevertheless, if the Japanese could have had spies around to hear what the American commanders thought of their situation on Guadalcanal, their spirits would have been somewhat more optimistic. The American losses from the air combat on October 15 amounted to four SBDs with three of their crews, two P-39s and one pilot, three F4Fs and one pilot. In patrol operation at sea that day, Japanese carrier pilots shot down two PBYs while losing one "Mavis" to American F4Fs. CACTUS' fuel situation was still at the critical stage.

The withdrawal of American fighter pilots, with no planes to fly, continued. Prominent among the units whose personnel withdrew were those from VF-5 or Fighting 5. Pilots Lt. Cmdr. Walter E. Clarke, Lt. Frank O. Green, "Smokey" Stover, Lt. (jg) Howard L. Grimmell, Jr., Lt. (jg) Mortimer C. Kleinman, Jr., Will Rouse, and AP1c Robert H. Nesbitt boarded an R4D transport along with four enlisted men, AMM1c Edward E. Popovich, AMM2c Carl J. Duracher, AMM3c Philip F. Belger, and ARM3c John H. Lynch, joining them. The two-engine plane took off and headed to Espiritu Santo. About one hour after leaving CACTUS, four American destroyers mistakenly identified the plane as Japanese and fired at the Douglas transport. All shells missed the plane. The gunfire shook the plane and prompted the men, thinking that Japanese aircraft had attacked them, to pick up submachine guns. Clarke thought it would have been ironic that, after all the combat he and the others aboard had seen fighting the Japanese, they would lose their lives to "friendly" fire.

Lt. Cmdr. Simpler, VF-5's commander, and six other pilots[12], Lt. William S. Robb, and 36 enlisted men stayed behind. VF-5 had been in continuous combat but now its end as a combat air unit seemed near. Working with his friend and Geiger's air Intelligence Officer, Lt. Col. John C. "Toby" Munn, Simpler visited the general. The conversation was short and sweet. "The Striking Eagles," could no longer fly. It had no pilots, planes, or equipment with which to fight. Showing a sense of humor, he told Geiger that he only had his binoculars left. He then lifted the strap over his head and handed them to the general.

The Marine squadrons at CACTUS had lost three F4Fs, three SBDs, and one P-39 during the air battles of October 15. Despite losing VF-5, Geiger's 1st Marine Air Wing (MAW-1) could still fight. Geiger, Vandegrift, and Cmdr. Michael H. Kernodle, the commanding officer of Guadalcanal's naval air base, met to discuss the situation they all faced. The Japanese had gained control of the seas and air such that they could run the Tokyo Express whenever they wished. CACTUS no longer had enough planes, fuel, ammunition, pilots, and other needed supplies to stop them. If the Imperial Japanese Navy sent their battleships for another mission like the one that had just occurred, Henderson Field would cease to exist. The only offensive air operations the Americans could execute were from Espiritu Santo. Kernodle sent these credible albeit pessimistic conclusions to Adm. Fitch.

Still a Matter of Logistics

The Americans never gave up trying to bring critically needed gasoline to Guadalcanal. Ghormley ordered the cargo ships *Alchiba* and *Bellatrix* along the motor torpedo boat tender *Jamestown* to each tow a barge filled with aviation gasoline. The destroyers *Nicholas* and *Meredith* and the tugboat *Vireo* acted as escorts. Kurita's battleships had not yet arrived off Guadalcanal when the fueling supply convoy was at sea. Early in the afternoon of October 15, a Japanese reconnaissance seaplane found what its crew reported as a "convoy" cruising southeast of San Cristobal. The *Shokaku* and *Zuikaku* sent some of their planes to attack the small supply expedition.

At 6:08 a.m. on the 16th, Ghormley ordered all ships except the *Meredith*, the *Vireo*, and one fuel barge being towed by the tug to return to Espiritu Santo. They continued to steam toward Guadalcanal when two Japanese aircraft attacked. Lt. Cmdr. Harry Hubbard, the *Meredith*'s skipper, also received intelligence that there were two Japanese ships nearby. Clearly recognizing how dangerous the situation was, he ordered his ship and the *Vireo* to turn around and head back home. Because of the *Vireo*'s slow maximum 14-knot speed and the need to escape as fast as possible, he ordered the tug be abandoned—a move that drew vociferous criticisms from staff officers at Pearl Harbor.

Hubbard's decision was not as foolish as some thought. The two planes that found his little flotilla were from Yamamoto's Carrier Division 1 that had been looking for Task Force 17 and its most valuable prize and the sole operational carrier the Americans had in the South Pacific, the *Hornet*. From a position east of the Stewart Islands, the Japanese launched 22 Vals, nine Kates, and eight

Zeroes, a total of 38 planes, at 11:37 a.m. to find the *Hornet*. As they flew near to the waters between San Cristobal and Guadalcanal, Hubbard's ships appeared below.

Hubbard was in the midst of transferring the *Vireo*'s crew before he sank the tug when the 38 Japanese planes arrived overhead. The two American ships did not stand a chance of survival. Using their normally efficient attack methods, the bombers surrounded the *Meredith* with accurately placed bombs and put three torpedoes into the doomed destroyer. She sank in ten minutes after putting up a most valiant defense and shooting down one Val and two Kates. One Japanese destroyer picked up one "Val" crew and the *Grayson* picked up another. A second group of Vals found the transports *Bellatrix* and *Alchiba* and the destroyer *Nicholas*. They did little damage after several of their bombs barely missed the *Bellatrix*.

Hubbard and his men spent several horrible days in the water that began by being strafed by Japanese planes. Sharks attacked the men in the water, and drinkable water became a scarce commodity. The blistering sun unmercifully burned the men's flesh and salt water raised pus-filled blisters. Hubbard and most of the other injured men expired. When the destroyers *Grayson* and *Gwin* finally arrived at the scene three days later to rescue the survivors, they only found 87 men alive—187 had died. The *Vireo* and the barge she towed were still afloat.[13]

The refueling attempt to keep CACTUS flying had failed. But some emergency relief came when Adm. Fitch ordered Lt. Cmdr. John C. Alderman, the destroyer-seaplane tender *McFarland*'s skipper, to take his ship and two more like her, the *Southard* and *Hovey*, to Lunga with 40,000 precious gallons. The three ships arrived off Guadalcanal on October 16 and disgorged the gasoline, 12 torpedoes, and more ammunition for the beleaguered CACTUS.

Meanwhile, the 11th Air Fleet had sent several planes to find the *Hornet* and sink her. One group of nine Vals from Buin found a less glamorous target when it flew over Guadalcanal. A barge containing the fuel and boats with supplies that went from the ship to shore and returned with evacuating air and ground crews. The Japanese bombers dove at the *McFarland* at 5:50 p.m. Alderman cut the barge loose and fired her AA guns as he tried to take his ship away from the threat. One bomb hit the barge and blew it up in a ball of flames and smoke. Another bomb hit the *McFarland*'s depth charges. The explosion blew off her stern. Her crew tried save their ship as a small group of the evacuees panicked and blocked the crew's work. Nevertheless, they successfully used the barely working port screw to get the severely crippled ship to move at an agonizingly slow five knots to Tulagi, but the Japanese attackers would not escape unscathed.

Just as the Japanese air attack began, Lt. Col. Harold F. Bauer's 19 F4Fs and seven SBDs arrived. They were almost out of fuel, but that did not stop Bauer from seeing the *McFarland* in trouble and doing something about it. He dove his fighter at the vulnerable Vals and took just a few seconds to splash three of them. At least CACTUS had a brief respite from its supply problems.

Vandegrift reported to his superiors that the Japanese troop landings increased their troop strength to 15,000 men. Stating that although more Americans were on Guadalcanal than that, one-half of them were in no condition as fighting men and had to be relieved. He urgently asked for two steps: (1) take back control of the sea around Guadalcanal and (2) send a division of fresh troops to replace those who had been on Guadalcanal since August 7. Until something happened and soon, the Americans were in dire straits, and the situation could only get worse.[14]

Fitting It All Into the Grand Scheme

The Japanese had achieved their major objective of landing badly needed reinforcements for the 17th Army on Guadalcanal. They had inflicted crippling damage on Henderson Field and Fighter One. But, despite losses in aircraft and valuable gasoline, the Americans had hit the High Speed Convoy with crippling losses that made the Japanese think twice about running the Tokyo Express during daylight hours. Nevertheless, Japanese warships continued to arrive during darkness to pummel Henderson Field. CACTUS continued to fight and resist its destruction. The Marines' plight continued to be precarious, but they were not going to give up.

Ignorant senior American naval and civilian officials had a different view. The situation had reached a critical stage after the massive Japanese clobbering on the evening of October 14-15 and the landing of a mass of Japanese troops. To them, Guadalcanal should be written off and surrendered to the Japanese, but Marshall had another view. He ordered that 50 Army Air Force fighters be sent to the South Pacific along with a fresh division of Army troops to come to the aid of the Marines on Guadalcanal. That would turn out to be the 25th Division.

The Southwest Pacific command situation needed immediate attention, and that responsibility fell directly on the shoulders of Adm. Nimitz.

Part 7: The Americans Take a Checkpoint

CHAPTER 29
A Much Needed Change of Command

A Rising Pessimistic Tide

Chester Nimitz stepped off his Coronado flying boat at Pearl Harbor after the long flight from Nouméa. He was a tired man after reviewing the serious situation at Guadalcanal and the rest of the Southwest Pacific command. The Marines, sailors, and soldiers on that beleaguered island and its strategically vital airfields had been subjected to air attacks, naval bombardment by the Imperial Japanese Navy, and fought several tough battles against fanatical Japanese soldiers. Henderson Field and its smaller field, Fighter One, could still defend themselves and subject Japanese ships and attacking aircraft to some crushing defeats. But getting supplies, troops, and aircraft to replace losses and to increase air power had reached a critical state. His assessment was that the commanders actually doing the fighting had the confidence they could hold Guadalcanal, but the senior officers in the rear were of a far more pessimistic view. His own experience taught him that the closer you got to where the fighting actually occurred, the better appreciation you had of the local commanders' ability to succeed.

There were many pessimistic indications concerning the American ability to hold Guadalcanal. The first was an October 16 editorial in the *New York Herald Tribune* that stated, "The shadows of a great conflict lie heavily over the Solomons—all that can be perceived is the magnitude of the stakes at issue." On the same day, the *New York Times* echoed a similar sentiment, "...Guadalcanal. The name will not die out of the memories of this generation. It will endure in honor." The *Times'* words sounded very close to a death knell to the Guadalcanal campaign. These opinions found their way to radio broadcasts from the U.S. heard by the soldiers, sailors, and Marines in the South Pacific and rose to a doom-laden cacophony predicting an impending disaster. These statements by the American media certainly caused a deterioration of morale among some of these servicemen.

Nonetheless, the lion's share of their opinions remained confident and optimistic. Marine Col. Clifton B. Cates defiantly expressed his certainty that the Marines would eventually be victorious and emerge from the struggle for Guadalcanal when he said the situation there was "no pink tea," and the "weak-kneed reports by some officials about our precarious situation." During the week of October 16, the home front pessimism reached a crescendo when a reporter uncompromisingly asked Secretary of the Navy Frank Knox: "Do you think we can hold Guadalcanal?" Knox's answer was not a ringing endorsement of the Navy's ability to deliver a victory:

"I certainly hope so and expect so...I will not make any predictions, but every man will give a good account of himself. What I am trying to say is that there is a good stiff fight going on. Everybody hopes we can hold on."[1]

However, Ghormley reflected an acceptance that all was lost when his October 15 message to Nimitz stated, "My forces [are] totally inadequate to meet [the] situation." The Navy had done all it could to help Ghormley. King and Nimitz sent the 25th Infantry Division from Oahu to Guadalcanal to reinforce the Marines. The Navy yard at Pearl Harbor expedited repairs to the battleship *South Dakota*, which had run aground on a rock pinnacle, and the carrier *Enterprise*. Both ships were returning to the South Pacific. King's and Nimitz's orders sent every plane in the South Pacific that could fly to Henderson Field.

Even Nimitz's staff saw the situation for what it was in its very own command summary:

"It now appears that we are unable to control the sea in the Guadalcanal area. Thus our supply of the positions will only be done at great expense to us. The situation is not hopeless, but it is certainly critical."

The crisis in the Southwest Pacific had reached monumental proportions. Nimitz had to move quickly before he lost all control of the situation.

Reaching a Command Decision

Not wanting to come to a conclusion alone, Nimitz called a staff meeting the evening of October 15. The staff officers noticed that the admiral's normally pleasant countenance had vanished. His usually sparkling blue eyes now had an icy gray stare, familiar to those who knew him, that clearly showed how serious Nimitz was about the topic. He looked into each man's eyes and said, "I don't want to hear, or see, such pessimism. Remember, the enemy is hurt too." He then delivered his personal assessment of what was happening at Guadalcanal. It was obvious the Japanese were going to land substantial reinforcements. Now was the time to look at the American command structure in that theater. After praising Adm. Ghormley's virtues as a bright and dedicated officer, Nimitz wanted to hear his staff's personal opinions about what was happening there.

Each officer voiced his view that the theater commander lacked effective leadership qualities, and this led to an unendurable environment in Nouméa. When one officer tried to disparage Ghormley's persona, Nimitz nipped that train of discussion in the bud by calling such discussion "mutiny."

After hearing all he wanted to hear, he said, "All right, I am going to poll you." He pointed his finger at each officer and asked, "Is it time for me to relieve Admiral Ghormley?"

It was unanimous. Ghormley had to go.

Obviously, with that decision reached, Nimitz had to know the answer to the question, "Who should replace him?" Turner's name came up, but his reputation for being known as "Terrible Turner" would be a severe inhibitor to being an effective theater commander. Turner's problematic relationship with Vandegrift would only make matters worse

Someone mentioned Halsey's name. He was popular with the men who had served under him and had a high enough senior rank to command. He was not much of an administrator but had excelled as a carrier commander. Nimitz listened carefully and, without stating any opinion, left the meeting to think it over.

After dinner, Nimitz changed into his pajamas and dressing gown. His orderly came into his bedroom saying that there was a telephone call for him. A group of his staff officers who did not attend the staff meeting wanted to come over to the admiral's quarters to discuss informally what had been discussed at that meeting. They arrived just a few minutes later. Nimitz came out to meet them. The group's spokesman began to talk:[2]

Spokesman: Admiral, we know that you have the utmost respect for Admiral Ghormley and, as a brother officer, can sympathize with the pressures he faces. We all feel that Admiral Halsey should go to Nouméa and immediately replace Admiral Ghormley.

Nimitz: Gentlemen, thank you for your thoughts. I'll give them the serious considerations they deserve. Now, if you will please leave so I can get some rest.

Actually, Nimitz had already made up his mind. After the group left, he drafted a dispatch that ordered Halsey to cancel his trip to Guadalcanal and change his plane's direction as it flew south of Canton Island and proceed to Nouméa. He then went to sleep.

The next morning, he sent a message that asked Adm. King for authorization to replace Ghormley with Halsey. King immediately answered with a one word: "Affirmative." Nimitz then sat down with a heavy heart and carefully created a message to the about-to-be-replaced Southwest Pacific commander.

> "After carefully weighing all factors, have decided that talents and previous experience of Halsey can best be applied to the situation by having him take over duties of COMSOPAC as soon as practicable after his arrival Nouméa 18th your date. I greatly appreciate your loyal and devoted efforts toward the accomplishment of a most difficult task. I shall order you to report to Halsey for the time being, as I believe he will need your thorough knowledge of situation and your loyal help. COMINCH has approved this change. Orders will follow shortly."[3]

The best way to portray Nimitz's feelings is to show a portion of a letter he wrote to his wife:

> "Today I have replaced Ghormley with Halsey. It was a sore mental struggle and the decision was not reached until after hours of anguished consideration. Reason (private): Ghormley was too immersed in detail and not sufficiently bold and aggressive at the right times. I feel better now that it has been done. I am very fond of G. [Ghormley] and hope I have not made a life enemy. I believe not. The interests of the nation transcend private interests."[4]

After he sent Ghormley's message, he sent his orders to Halsey with instructions they should be opened when he arrived in Nouméa. Events now dictated the days ahead.[5]

Returning to Duty

Adm. William F. "Bull" Halsey had endured a stay in the Johnston-Willis Hospital in Richmond, Virginia, during the summer of 1942. He had contracted a serious case of dermatitis just after he returned from his highly successful mission bombing Japanese possessions just after the war's outbreak. He already knew that Nimitz's plan to defend Midway from the Imperial Japanese Navy's attack was in advanced stages. But Halsey's illness prevented him from leading the *Enterprise* and *Hornet* out to meet them for what became arguably the Pacific War's turning point. As his stay in Pearl Harbor's naval hospital lengthened, his disease worsened until he could not even wear pajamas. By mutual decision, Halsey secretly moved to the hospital in Richmond, Virginia.

Contrary to what has been portrayed by Hollywood in the movie *Midway*, Halsey was a considerate patient and treated the attending doctors and nurses with respect and kindness. The admiral was a popular patient and had many visitors. It became impossible to keep his presence in the hospital a secret. Nonetheless, his treatment by Dr. Warren T. Vaughan hastened his recovery from the debilitating disease so he could leave the hospital on August 5. He went to Washington to see what his next assignment would be.

During those early days of the war, the Navy Department was a hectic place. The lights never went out as the people worked 24 hours a day. The Battle of the Atlantic and the upcoming invasion in North Africa had taken on the highest priority. Despite the clamor that pervaded the Navy Department, Halsey managed to get his orders: Take one month's leave. Proceed to Pearl Harbor and report for duty to Adm. Nimitz.

After ending his vacation with his family on August 31, Halsey greeted Capt. Miles Browning, his former chief of staff, who had flown in from Pearl Harbor, and his aide, Lt. Cmdr. William H. Ashford. They met all day to discuss their next assignment and drove to Annapolis to deliver a speech to the Naval Academy entitled "Missing the Battle of Midway." Never one to hold back what he really believed and speaking in tones that are considered today as "politically incorrect," he uttered some words that became his trademarked way of expressing his thoughts about the Japanese. He said that missing that milestone in American naval history, "...has been the greatest disappointment of my life, but I am going back to the Pacific where I intend personally to have a crack at those yellow-bellied sons of bitches and their carriers."[6] Reflecting the fervent patriotism of the day, the audience spontaneously rose to a standing ovation and loud cheers.

On September 1, the admiral, his chief of staff, and flag lieutenant flew to the West Coast to inspect naval aviation bases there. Nimitz, who had flown from Pearl Harbor with his staff for another periodic meeting with Adm. King, met Halsey at the St. Francis Hotel in San Francisco on September 7. Nimitz took Halsey to the opening meeting. The greetings for Halsey overwhelmed him. The attendees met him with vigorous handshakes and slaps on the back. He sat in on the meetings for the next three days. Since he had been absent from the war for too many months, he did not participate in the gatherings but listened carefully to the discussions. It was like a rapid training exercise as he enthusiastically absorbed what he heard and quickly got an appreciation of where the war was and for the situation in the Pacific Theater.

After the conference ended, Halsey, Browning, and Ashford flew to Pearl Harbor. When he arrived, Nimitz gave Halsey the temporary assignment of Commander of the Naval Air Force Pacific Fleet and placed him in an office in the recently completed CINCPAC building. Perched on high ground overlooking Pearl Harbor, it was a bombproof concrete three-story edifice with two stories above ground and one below. It must have seemed to Halsey as *déjà vu* because he had held a similar job to this one as Commander Aircraft Battle Force. Essentially, Halsey's new job was a desk job that managed aviation personnel, ships, and equipment. The plan was for Halsey to hold this post after Fitch left to take command of all air forces under Ghormley and until Fitch's replacement, Vadm. John H. Towers, finished his current job as chief of the Bureau of Aeronautics.

Undergoing repairs from combat damage in the Pearl Harbor shipyards, the *Enterprise* was still part of Task Force 16 under the command of Adm. Kinkaid, who had replaced Adm. Spruance when he had become Nimitz's chief of staff. When the shipyard finished the repairs on the carrier and made her ready for combat, Halsey was to take command of Task Force 16. Normally, the command of a task force was given to a rear admiral and would have resulted in Halsey being reduced in rank, but the Navy would never embarrass the man the press believed was America's greatest naval hero by taking him down a single notch. By keeping his present rank of vice admiral, he could readily assume total command of any combination of task forces as the senior officer. The way events had gone in the South Pacific, it was apparent to anyone that Halsey would soon be in a sea battle.

On September 22, the day after the damaged *Saratoga* arrived in Pearl Harbor for repairs and was in its drydock, Nimitz and Halsey were on her flight deck with her entire crew lined up at attention. Only a few of the officers and men most likely identified the other admiral with Nimitz. Halsey had been out of the public eye since his illness forced him into hospitalization. Nimitz wanted to use this particular moment on the flight deck of Halsey's former flagship to make a startling announcement. He stepped to the microphone and waved his hand for Halsey to step up next to him. "Boys, I've got a surprise for you. Bill Halsey's back!" With his words barely dying down in the disciplined air on that deck, the men abandoned their military stiffness. A loud cheer erupted over the ship. Reflecting his emotional nature and appreciating the power of that moment, tears brimmed in Halsey's eyes.

Now part of CINCPAC's command structure, Halsey participated in the daily briefings conducted by Nimitz's staff and began to know how serious the problems were in MacArthur and Ghormley's commands. Realizing that he needed to get a closeup look at what was going on in the Southwest Pacific, Nimitz sent Spruance and Radm. William L. Calhoun, his service force commander, to the Southwest Pacific. Their mission was to meet with the commanders, inspect bases, and assess problems and needs. Halsey also wanted to go, and Nimitz agreed.

Halsey wanted to take Browning and Maj. Julian Brown, his intelligence officer, with him. Ashford, now a lieutenant commander, had been his flag lieutenant long enough. So Halsey assigned him as Kinkaid's tactical officer. Halsey's old staff stayed behind on board the *Enterprise*. Kinkaid kept temporary command of Task Force 16 and would turn it over to Halsey when it went back into combat in the Southwest Pacific.

Halsey, Spruance, Calhoun, Browning, and Brown boarded a Coronado seaplane and left Pearl Harbor on October 14. They flew 800 miles to Johnston Island and inspected the island's facilities that afternoon. After spending the night there, they flew to Canton Island to stay another night.

Meanwhile, Nimitz had made his decision to relieve Ghormley and replace him with Halsey.

Halsey planned to go to Guadalcanal after visiting Nouméa. As his plane landed at Canton Island, he received a message from Ghormley suggesting that he not go to Guadalcanal because of the volatile tactical situation there. Halsey answered Ghormley that unless ordered otherwise by CINCPAC he would go to Guadalcanal as planned. Halsey sent copies of Ghormley's message and his reply to Nimitz. At 2:00 a.m., an aide woke Halsey and handed him a note from Nimitz. It ordered him to fly with all dispatch to Nouméa with an intervening stop at Fiji.[7]

Halsey Takes Command

Adm. Halsey's Coronado flying boat landed in Nouméa's harbor at 3:15 p.m. on October 18. Ghormley's flagship, the *Argonne*, was nearby. The plane's four engines had just been shut down with their propellers still spinning when a whaleboat eased alongside the plane. As Halsey stepped into the boat, Adm. Ghormley's flag lieutenant was waiting for him, snapped a salute, and handed a sealed envelope to the admiral. Realizing that he would soon be on the *Argonne*, the envelope obviously contained a very important message. Opening the envelope, there was another envelope inside it with a stamp in large letters that said, "SECRET." He anxiously opened the second envelope, took the message out to read it.

As he read it once and reread it again, Halsey's exclaimed, "Jesus Christ and General Jackson! This is the hottest potato they ever handed me!"[8] The message left no doubt why the normally excitable admiral was so animated.

> "Immediately upon your arrival at Nouméa, you will relieve Vice Admiral Robert L. Ghormley of the duties of Commander South Pacific and South Pacific Force."[9]

Later, he described his reaction to Nimitz's order as being astonished, filled with regret, and apprehensive about the meaning of this order. Taking command of such a vital campaign meant he would do things he had never done before in his career. His new responsibilities covered a huge geographical area stretching from New Zealand to Nouméa and also involved commanding U.S. Army soldiers. He had been sitting in on the daily CINCPAC briefings and had heard how both MacArthur and Ghormley had described the South Pacific's military situation as hopeless. Halsey had been a close friend with Ghormley for more than 40 years. They began as classmates and football teammates at the Naval Academy. Relieving his good friend was a task he did not welcome. Halsey knew this new assignment was not going to be any picnic in the country.

While there might have been some regret that he would not command a carrier task force in a sea battle and be more of an administrator than a commander, he had his orders and he would do everything in his power to carry them out. While Spruance and Calhoun went to see Turner on the *McCawley*, the whaleboat with Halsey, Browning, and Brown aboard headed for the *Argonne*.

Halsey stepped off the boat and walked up the *Argonne*'s gangway. He looked up and saw Ghormley waiting for him at the top. Their long-standing friendship allowed this meeting to be an amiable one, but the drama of that moment increased the tension between the two men. Ghormley broke the uneasiness by saying, "This is a tough job they've given you, Bill." Knowing that with all that was in his soul, Halsey replied, "I damn well know it."

He followed his friend to his cabin to complete the formalities of turning over a command. Ghormley informed Halsey of the current situation and critical challenges in the Southwest Pacific command. Following a Navy custom, Ghormley called the ship's company to quarters and read the orders announcing the turnover of command.

Halsey's first act as the new Southwest Pacific commander was to radio a message to MacArthur and all of Halsey's senior naval officers and commanding generals:

> "Vice Admiral William F. Halsey has this date relieved Vice Admiral Robert L. Ghormley as Commander South Pacific Force and South Pacific Area."[10]

The news spread like wildfire throughout the South Pacific. Not many men knew the new commander on a personal level, but everyone knew his name. Nearly all the men ecstatically greeted the news. One air combat intelligence officer later summed up his feelings upon hearing the news: "I'll never forget it! One minute we were too limp with malaria to crawl out of our foxholes; the next we were running around whooping like kids."[11]

Nimitz's orders to Ghormley were to temporarily report to Halsey and remain at Nouméa to help the transition to the new command. Remembering the humiliation that Adm. Husband E. Kimmel faced when being forced to stay behind after being relieved of command of the Pacific Fleet after the Pearl Harbor debacle, Halsey cleanly broke the chain of command by releasing Ghormley after a few days had passed so he could return home and get out of the limelight.

Halsey wasted no time taking over what had been a chaotic and confused command. He immediately had to decide whether to order a new airfield to be built on Ndeni Island in the Santa Cruz Islands. Up to this time, Henderson Field was the sole advanced American airbase and thus was the prime Japanese target. The Japanese could temporarily knock out the field. The Americans had virtually no defense against runs of the Tokyo Express. The nearest American airfield was 600 miles away at Espiritu Santo. The new field on Ndeni would bring American air power 200 miles closer to Guadalcanal.

The American Army engineers had landed on Ndeni to make surveys, and soldiers were on their way from Tongatabu to occupy the island. Ghormley and Turner advocated building this field while Vandegrift opposed it. The general wanted any spare aircraft to be sent to Guadalcanal. Both admirals believed that Ndeni was sorely needed as a backup to Henderson Field, and its aircraft could be used for reconnaissance and to protect supply convoys headed for Guadalcanal. Ghormley also argued that he had to build the Ndeni Airfield since he had orders from the Joint Chiefs, CINCPOA, and Adm. King to do it.

Not getting much help from Ghormley's staff, Halsey wished had he could have gone to Guadalcanal before assuming command. Facing many tough problems needing solutions, he took over a difficult command situation forcing him to stay in Nouméa. He sent a radio message to Vandegrift to fly to Nouméa as soon as he could and meet with the general's new superior.

Vandegrift and Lt. Gen. Thomas Holcomb, Commandant of the Marine Corps, arrived by air at Nouméa on October 23. Holcomb had been meeting with Vandegrift on Guadalcanal when Halsey's request for Vandegrift to come to Nouméa arrived and wanted to come along. Halsey convened a meeting after dinner. All senior Southwest Pacific commanders sat around the table, including Harmon, the Army commander, just returned from Guadalcanal; Maj. Gen. Patch, commander of ground forces on New Caledonia; and Radm. Turner, Commander, Amphibious Forces.

Not wanting to waste precious time, Halsey asked Vandegrift to review the situation on Guadalcanal. The general was brutally to the point.

1. The Japanese continue their air attacks by day and shell CACTUS' airfields with battleships and cruisers at night.

2. The Tokyo Express has increased its power by landing more troops and supplies than it ever had. He estimated there were more than 22,000 fresh Japanese soldiers on the island while the American ground troops, suffering from malaria, less than needed food intake, and lack of sleep, were battle fatigued and sorely in need of reinforcements and relief.

3. There was no question that he needed immediate air and ground reinforcements. Harmon and Holcomb enthusiastically agreed with everything Vandegrift said.

Halsey could not wait to ask the question that got to the heart of the matter, "Can you hold?" Vandegrift unhesitatingly answered, "Yes, I can hold, but I have to have more active support than I've been getting."

Turner bristled at what seemed to be a slap at his command's ability to do its duty. He vehemently insisted the Navy was doing everything in its power to get Vandegrift what he needed. He had lost more cargo ships and transports than could be replaced. There were not enough warships to protect them. Although he did not want to be that way, it became apparent that Turner's remarks became defensive. Halsey had heard enough when he looked at the Marine general and said, "You go on back there, Vandegrift. I promise you everything I've got."

Halsey then made up his mind what to do on the Santa Cruz Islands. On the morning of the 14th, he did not wait to consult anyone and, countermanding Ghormley's standing orders from the JCS, ordered the troop convoy headed for Ndeni to immediately change its course and head for Guadalcanal. The Santa Cruz operation was now only a memory.

However, there were more disagreements between Turner and Vandegrift that had to be settled. One of these was the manner in how Turner had intervened with the general's defense of Henderson Field. While briefing Holcomb before going to Nouméa, Vandegrift asked the commandant to arrange for Turner to stop his continuous interference in what was clearly the ground commander's business. Happy to help in any way he could, Holcomb drafted a dispatch to King and brought it with him to Nouméa to show Halsey. The admiral endorsed the message. Holcomb then flew to Pearl Harbor. Nimitz also endorsed the message and transmitted it to Adm. King. After arriving in Washington, Holcomb met with King, who showed him the message and asked for his opinion. Holcomb said there should be a new policy regarding the span of command between ground and landing force commanders to avoid conflicts such as this one. King agreed and forwarded the note with his recommendation to the Joint Chiefs. They put a new policy in place for future Pacific operations.

Buoyed with a new sense of purpose, Vandegrift arrived back at Guadalcanal only to find the vestiges of Ghormley's regime still present. Acting on his own and without consulting Vandegrift, Fitch had sent his Espiritu Santo land-based aircraft to look for a Japanese carrier fleet reported to be operating in the waters north of the Solomons. Not only were these planes wasting precious fuel, but Vandegrift angrily grumbled these planes could be better used on Guadalcanal to defend against the daily daytime Japanese air attacks and the nightly runs of the Tokyo Express. He was guardedly optimistic about Halsey's ability to make the changes needed to deliver victory.

If Vandegrift could have been in Nouméa, he would see that changes were indeed being made. One of these was a need for Halsey to bring a staff onboard with which he could implement the changes he knew had to be done. Task Force 16 left Pearl Harbor two days after Halsey did. It now had the repaired carrier *Enterprise* and the new battleship *South Dakota*. They rendezvoused with Task Force 17 and its carrier, the *Hornet*, east of Espiritu Santo on October 24 and began refueling. Halsey sent a radio message to Kinkaid to take command of the two task forces with the designation of Task Force 61. He also wanted Kinkaid to transfer some of his staff from the *Enterprise*: Commanders Bromfield B. Nichol and Leonard J. Dow, Lt. Commanders H. Douglass Moulton and William H. Ashford Jr., and several key enlisted men to Nouméa to join Halsey's staff. They boarded a tanker heading for Espiritu Santo. When it arrived, a waiting plane took them to Nouméa.

Halsey's order was not arbitrary. Kinkaid did not want to lose these men as they had proven to be valuable. But there were too many staff officers in the combined task forces who had overlapping duties. For example, the *Enterprise* had three different staff groups. The first was the *Enterprise*'s captain's, Capt. Osbourne B. Hardison, who had been on the staff of the carrier's former skipper, Capt. George Murray, recently promoted to rear admiral and now commanding Task Force 17. Next was Kinkaid's staff from his command of Task Force 16. The last were Halsey's combined staffs from the *Enterprise-Hornet* of Task Force 61 that Halsey had turned over to Kinkaid. Halsey took some of those men who had served with him before Midway and with Adm. Spruance during and after that epic battle.

After arriving at Nouméa, the four officers went to Halsey's cabin on the *Argonne*. The admiral was alone at his desk and reading dispatches. When he saw the men walking in, he looked up and, in his characteristically direct manner, said, "It's a goddamn mess!" Guadalcanal's situation teetered on the brink of disaster. If the Japanese captured Henderson Field, Kinkaid would have to ensure they could never use the field again. Knowing the men were likely hungry, Halsey ordered a steward to bring some food. As the men began walking out, Halsey pulled no punches when he said, "Look around and see what's to be done, and do it."

The main reason for replacing Ghormley's staff was, as Ashford recalled, "Admiral Ghormley's staff members aboard the *Argonne,* were so exhausted from lack of sleep, overwork, and the strain being placed on their shoulders that they were in a kind of a daze. I felt they had just about reached the limit of human endurance." Halsey wanted dependable staff officers around him.

And he would soon need them more than ever. A large, powerful Japanese carrier force lurked somewhere north of the Santa Cruz Islands. Kinkaid's Task Force 61 was the only one powerful enough to meet that threat. Another carrier battle was about to begin. It would become known as the Battle of the Santa Cruz Islands.[12]

CHAPTER 30
Recapturing Henderson Field?

A Critical Time for the Japanese

The Americans had taken a beating during the massive bombardment of Henderson Field, but aircraft still took off and attacked Japanese naval and ground forces. As always, the American tenacious defense of that airfield remained a thorn in the Japanese attempts to retake Guadalcanal. Until that happened, the southeastern left flank of their Empire was in terrible jeopardy of being exposed.

Adm. Yamamoto, again wanting that "climactic" naval battle against the U.S. Navy, ordered the Combined Fleet to sail from Truk on October 11, steam for an area north of the Solomon Islands, and engage and destroy any American capital ship formations it could find. The Imperial General Headquarters had been preparing a massive joint operation involving an all-out attack to capture Henderson Field, the successful landing of 4,500 soldiers on October 15, continuing the daily air attacks on the airfield, and nightly trips of the Tokyo Express to bombard the airstrip. The Japanese completed a new fighter base at Buin on New Guinea followed by flying 30 of the planned 100 Zeroes to the field. However, this did not happen until October 25.

During mid-September, the Japanese Army and Navy reached a joint agreement for overall operations in the South Pacific. Because of lack of progress in the Solomons, Guadalcanal received the highest priority with operations on New Guinea taking a back seat. The first paragraph of the agreement describes what the Japanese wanted to accomplish on Guadalcanal:

> "After reinforcement of Army forces has been completed, Army and Navy forces will combine and in one action attack and retake Guadalcanal Island airfield. During this operation the Navy will take all necessary action to halt the efforts of the enemy to augment his forces in the Solomons Area."[1]

The Army's plan was to occupy Henderson Field on October 22 while the Combined Fleet steamed north of Guadalcanal with the intention to "apprehend and annihilate any powerful forces in the Solomons area, as well as any reinforcements."[2] This strategy seemed to fly in the face of Mahan's doctrine[3] to project naval power to force land power on an enemy. The Japanese wanted to wait for the results of their army's attack *before* bringing naval power to bear to destroy the U.S. Navy. Also, there seemed to be a lack of a clear, precise strategy of how the Army and the Navy would coordinate their tactics. Without sounding too judgmental, the Japanese strategy seemed to be to let events on the ground and at sea unfold independently and hope for the best. The best evaluation of the Japanese plan is to describe it as muddled.

Nevertheless, all senior commanders realized the plan had to succeed despite problems that might arise. But these had to be overcome. The Japanese had everything riding on this plan to finally evict the Americans from Guadalcanal and solidify their southeastern flank.

✲ ✲ ✲

It would seem the Japanese Army learned their lessons from their defeat on Bloody (Edson's) Ridge in September. Also, they continued to greatly underestimate the number of American ground troops on Guadalcanal. The Army Section of the Imperial Gen. Headquarters estimated on October 8 that there was one Marine division of 10,000 men on Guadalcanal. However, their analysis warned that the Americans could land an additional Army division to add to these numbers. The actual number of marines and soldiers on Guadalcanal on that date was 23,088 with an additional 4,639 on Tulagi, which brought the total number of American troops to 27,727.

The Japanese Attack Plan

Gen. Hyakutake had another disturbing surprise when he arrived on Guadalcanal on October 10. Due to combat casualties and disease, the five 600-man battalions that comprised Ichiki's and Kawaguchi's combat units had been whittled down to the equivalent of just barely one battalion. What were previously counted as artillery batteries were now counted as just the number of guns: two field and two mountain 75-mm guns with four 150-mm howitzers. One day later, Hyakutake ordered the 38th Division's headquarters and the 228th Infantry Regiment less one battalion to reinforce Guadalcanal.

These added troops still left the Japanese with a severe artillery firepower disadvantage versus the Americans despite the use of the more inaccurate Japanese naval guns. Without an ability to concentrate artillery at the point of attack at the Matanikau River for instance, a headlong infantry attack would only result in the needless slaughter of many Japanese soldiers by American artillery and small-arms firepower. To make matters worse, the Japanese did not have ammunition to sustain an artillery barrage long enough to take out the American defensive positions and guns. An additional division would be needed to effect the recapture of Henderson Field.

✲ ✲ ✲

In an attempt to gain more intelligence, the 2nd Division's—(also known as the Sendai Division)—chief of staff, Col. Tamaoki[4], and its operations officer, Col. Hiroshi Matsumoto, climbed Mount Austen to get a better look at the American positions. The two officers peered southward through their binoculars at the Field and noticed small clearings in the dense jungle undergrowth. Believing that their troops now had a clearer path to Henderson Field and did not have to hack their way through the thick vegetation as had to be done before the Battle of Bloody Ridge[5], they returned to their headquarters to make their report to Hyakutake. Matsumoto also opined that there were no Americans defending the southern approach to the airfield. After this was confirmed by a 17th Army Japanese staff officer, Hyakutake changed his plans to add an attack from the south at Henderson Field.

The Japanese Move into Position

As with all Japanese plans, whether they came from the Army or Navy, this one was as complex as it was risky. Maj. Gen. Tadashi Sumiyoshi, commanding the 17th Army's artillery, briefed a group of sweating officers as the soldiers from the High Speed Convoy walked ashore. Sumiyoshi would fire a barrage to distract the Americans' attention from the main southern assault. He would command the initial attack on the Americans western flank on the Matanikau River's western bank with three regiments or nine battalions on X-day, originally set for October 22. Lt. Gen. Masao Maruyama, commander of the 2nd Division, would lead the southern attack with a two-prong assault near where the Battle of Bloody Ridge had been fought. Commanding the western prong was Maj. Gen. Yumio Nasu, who would lead troops from the 29th Regiment. Maj. Gen. Kiyotake Kawaguchi would lead the III/230 Battalion with most of the soldiers coming from the III/124. Maruyama would have direct command of the 16th Regiment, which would be held in reserve. Nasu would begin his command's march through the jungle on October 16 with Kawaguchi, the division headquarters, and the 16th Infantry following in order.

Maruyama's intelligence officer reported that the Americans had placed outposts in front of their main defensive positions so that any Japanese movements would be detected before they reached the American lines. He also issued a cautionary comment that the Americans would rely on superior firepower to hold their ground. Secrecy had to be the watchword, with no cooking fires allowed. Any food the soldiers consumed had to be eaten cold.

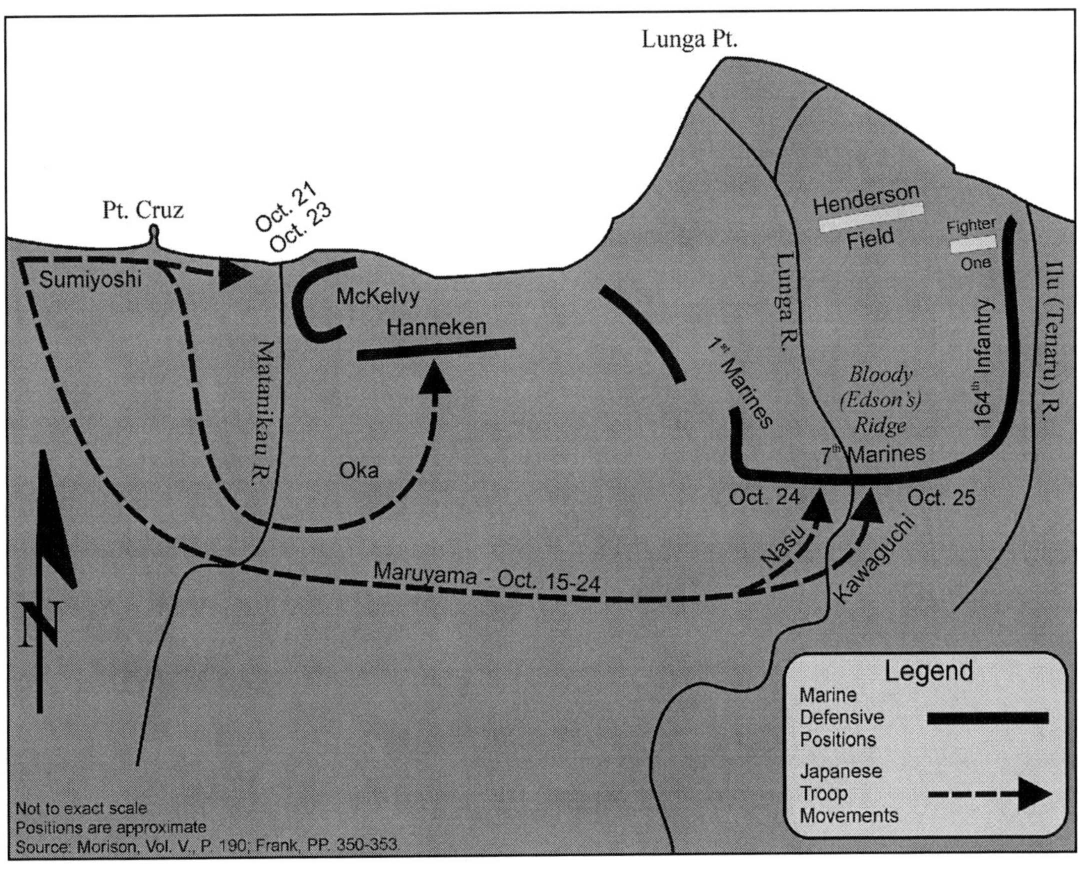

Japanese Attack Plans to Retake Henderson Field

Kawaguchi, in his characteristically eccentric style, issued a flyer entitled "Spirit of the Right Wing" to his soldiers. It said that while the Americans had superior firepower, the Japanese soldier's bayonet would carry the day, a disturbingly familiar technique used by the French during World War I extolling the spirit of *élan* that would conquer superior German artillery. Despite shortages of food and ammunition, the Japanese soldier was made of better stuff and would overcome such trivial deficiencies.

Hyakutake named the trail that Maruyama's force would follow after its leader—the Maruyama Road. The name was only a grandiose designation for a dirt path embedded in the dense jungle undergrowth. It was between 20 and 24 inches in width. The rain forest's canopy of trees over the path made it seem the soldiers moved inside a dark, shady tunnel. Wanting to be nearer to the battles that were about to begin, he set up another headquarters about halfway between the jumping-off point and where these men would attack Henderson Field.

From the very beginning of the Army's planning, the original "X-Day," the capture of Henderson Field, of October 22 was never firmly set but would be determined by how long Maruyama's slog through the dense jungle would take before his men reached their intended attacking positions. To meet that deadline, Gen. Nasu began his march on October 16 with each soldier burdened by extra ammunition, one artillery shell, and 12 days' rations (although later information indicated each man only carried about five days' rations.) The only maps of the jungle the Japanese possessed were grossly inaccurate and had not been updated with the benefit of any advanced reconnaissance. The only navigational aids they possessed were compasses that failed to reveal in advance any huge boulders or the dangerously steep slopes the Japanese troops encountered during the tortuous journey to their objective. The march proceeded so slowly that the first men would began their day's march in the morning while those men in the trailing units did not begin their trek until late in the afternoon. Trying to manhandle their guns through the dense undergrowth, the artillerymen fell farther behind the rest of their comrades every day.

The last elements of Maruyama's men started their march on October 18, two days later than the first units. The line of march stretched for 18 miles when the leaders reached the Lunga River's western bank. After searching upstream and downstream, the officers in the lead picked a 50-meter-wide fording point in chest-deep water. Not wanting to be seen by American aircraft, they delayed crossing the river until sunset.

Col. Masanobu Tsuji telephoned 17th Army headquarters that the Americans had not yet discovered the movements and guessed that it would take four days to complete the march. The day the Japanese would attack the American's southern flank was calculated to be October 22. This meant that if Henderson Field's capture had happened on X-Day, the attacking soldiers would have accomplished that feat in one day.

Hyakutake sent a melancholic request to Rabaul for more air support and reported the destruction of about one-third of his supplies brought ashore from the High Speed Convoy. Reflecting its persistent optimistic outlook of how they believed the battle would end, the 17th Army transmitted, "The victory is already in our hands. Please rest your minds."[6]

Two exultant reports on October 19 inflated the 17th Army command's exuberance. First, Maruyama's intelligence officer informed the general that he heard that the Americans were reinforcing their western flank near the Matanikau River and saw this as evidence that Sumiyoshi's deception was accomplishing its objective. Second, the Imperial Japanese Navy also sent dispatches that the American radio broadcasts reported extremely pessimistic news about their prospects of hanging onto Guadalcanal. After looking at its problems, the 17th Army now viewed that they were not as bad off as the Americans. By the evening of the 19th, Maruyama's men estimated they were four miles from the place where they would cross the Lunga River.

The next day was an eventful one for the Japanese. Hyakutake's division command headquarters reached a place early that morning that Maruyama called "Clear Water Valley," which he believed to be about one mile from the place where he would launch his attack, about four miles south of the airfield. "Clear Water Valley" actually was two miles from the Lunga fording location and eight miles from Henderson Field. Based on this assessment, Maruyama ordered the attack on the American southern flank for 6:00 p.m. on October 22.

The Japanese Attack Begins

Sumiyoshi's 150-mm guns fired again on Henderson Field on October 18 as Col. Nakaguma's 4th Infantry Regiment made their best effort near the northern coast west of the Matanikau River to convince the Americans that they were the main Japanese attack. Oka's force crossed the Matanikau River the next day in the evening and turned north over rugged rocks, crags, and dense growth. The Americans reacted with such ferocious artillery fire that Nakaguma sadly responded, "One shot from us brings one hundred in retaliation."[7] On October 20, one of his platoons tried to penetrate the Marine's defenses with three light tanks near the mouth of the Matanikau River. The Americans returned fire that killed the Japanese platoon commander and damaged one tank. The Japanese feint seemed like a drop in the bucket rather than the deluge they wanted the Americans to believe.

Sumiyoshi's men moved out on October 20 along the northern coast to create the "diversion" that had become so much an integral part in Japanese military and naval planning. Dividing his artillery into two groups, one that aimed his 15 150-mm howitzers at Henderson Field and the other 17 guns, ten 75-mm guns and seven 100-mm guns, to support the infantry's attack. He still did not have enough ammunition to carry out either assignment. He also sent Col. Akinosuku Oka's 124th Infantry Regiment, less its own 3rd Battalion, but including the 3rd Battalion, 4th Infantry Regiment, to circle to the south and attack the Marines at what he hoped to be the American southern defensive position on the Matanikau River. The two other battalions from the 4th Regiment moved along the coast to attack the Marines' defensive lines along the Matanikau's eastern bank.

The Americans Get Ready

The Americans had only experienced the Japanese attacks near the Matanikau and started to believe this attack was serious. They had limited albeit soft intelligence about the details of the impending assault but confidently believed that there would be one. Ground patrols to the south of Henderson Field reported seeing "bands of dispirited, half starved, poorly armed stragglers and deserters." Air reconnaissance saw nothing. But a captured Japanese map revealed the plan for an attack at three points from the east, west, and south. Not wanting to be caught unawares, Vandegrift modified his main defensive perimeter.

The newly arrived Army 164th Infantry Regiment allowed the general to strengthen his defenses as it took up a position on the easternmost side of the perimeter, the least likely place to receive a Japanese attack. The Marine 7th Infantry Regiment occupied the perimeter's southern line on both sides of the Lunga River. The 1st Marine Regiment, and later the 5th Marine Infantry Regiment, defended the perimeter's western flank. Vandegrift kept the 2nd Infantry Regiment as a mobile reserve to be moved by trucks as required. The 1st Tank Battalion had several light tanks that would pitch in where needed when the Japanese attack should come. Each infantry regiment kept one battalion in reserve that the general would later use for special assignments.

To protect his western flank, Vandegrift kept two battalions—the 3rd Battalion, 1st Marine Infantry Regiment and the 3rd Battalion, 7th Marine Infantry Regiment—at the mouth of the Matanikau River on its eastern bank. This deployment admittedly weakened his defenses by inserting a huge gap between the Matanikau River and the defensive line around Henderson Field and blocked the route by which trucks, artillery, and tanks could drive westward along the coast. Vandegrift believed the situation was a calculated risk that prevented the Japanese from using this same road to attack from the west. These Marines, known as the "McKelvy Group"—named for the 3rd Battalion, 1st Marine Regiment's commander—constructed a horseshoe defensive perimeter and dug in, ready for what was to come.

Nine Japanese bombers supported by 26 Zeroes paid one of their regular visits to Guadalcanal in two waves on October 21 and tried to bomb Henderson Field. Fifteen F4Fs rose to meet them and engaged the Japanese planes in a dogfight that resulted in one Zero and two F4Fs being shot down. Meanwhile, Maruyama's force was in their sixth day and struggling mightily to struggle through the dense Guadalcanal jungle to reach their objective. The thick vegetation forced the Japanese to waver off their path. As darkness descended over Guadalcanal, the Japanese command had to face up to the possibility that the timetable for their attack on the Americans for October 22 might have been too optimistic. Maruyama postponed the attack by one day to October 23. Hyakutake sent an apologetic note to Rabaul notifying them of the postponement stating the reason for the delay was "due to the topography in front of the enemy position."[8]

The naval command began to lose their belief in the Army's ability to achieve their objective. Yamamoto's chief of staff, Adm. Ugaki, realized the Navy could do nothing about the delay but expressed his frustrations in an entry in his diary: "How unreliable they are!" He tried to explain in vain that "one or two days' delay would not mean much in land warfare, but it has a great effect on naval operational forces coordinating over vast areas." Trying to keep a balanced perspective, Ugaki's last entry for October 21 stated, "It might be our fault that we did not dispatch a naval liaison officer of senior rank on the spot."[9]

Resuming the Attack

Sumiyoshi attacked McKelvy's group on the evening of October 22. His troops crossed the Matanikau River and took some high ground. Japanese artillery continued to bombard Henderson Field. As the shells fell, Gen. Thomas Holcomb, Commandant of the Marine Corps, had recently arrived on Guadalcanal to review the combat situation with Vandegrift. He toured the combat areas amid occasional artillery shell explosions. As he climbed the rise to the top of Edson's Ridge, Vandegrift asked Holcomb to notice that the firing lane he was looking down was a "machine-gunner's dream."

Meanwhile, Japanese engineers had just finished carving the tunnel through the jungle to allow the first of Maruyama's force making up the left side of his planned attack to reach the place from where they would attack. The rest of the Japanese general's troops were still fighting their way through the rain-drenched vegetation along many miles of the track. Some of Maruyama's subordinates wondered if the rest of the force including the artillery and reserves could reach to attack positions in time. Doubts began to emerge whether they could attack on October 23. Maruyama refused to even consider another delay. Long into the night's darkness, the Japanese soldiers continued to lurch along the twisting trail.

Hyakutake remained optimistic that Maruyama would attack on October 23. Receiving Hyakutake's order to attack on the 23rd, Sumiyoshi ordered Oka to attack from the south and Nakaguma from the west in a two-pronged assault designed to surround and isolate the Marines on the American main defensive perimeter.

When Vandegrift went with Holcomb to Nouméa on October 23 to meet with Halsey, Geiger assumed command. As usual, another Japanese air raid led by 12 Zeroes followed by 16 bombers escorted by another 17 Zeroes arrived overhead. Lt. Col. Harold Bauer, commander of the CACTUS Air Force's fighters, sent up every fighter plane he could spare—24 F4Fs and four P-39s—to intercept and destroy every Japanese plane they could. By this time American air tactics had been refined to take advantage of the perceptible deterioration of the Zero pilots' skill. Based on claims of American victories—21 Zeroes and two bombers were shot down with slight damage to just seven F4Fs—that adjustment seemed justified. However, as is usual in this case, American claims were overly optimistic; actual Japanese losses were six fighters and one bomber.

In the early morning hours of October 23, Japanese soldiers lightened the load on their backs by getting rid of their backpacks and moved northward to the American perimeter. Several soldiers went ahead to scout the terrain. Many did not come back. Those that did reported they lost their way through the thick jungle. The jungle surrounded them like a dense, green shroud. The jungle's heat and humidity drained the men's strength. Their once-shining bayonets began to rust. They moved like automatons without any drive or enthusiasm. An officer in Nasu's left attack prong wrote in his diary:

> "I cannot any longer think of anything, the enemy, food, home or even myself... [I am] only a spirit drifting toward an undefined, unknowable world."[10]

Lacking any intelligence of what was ahead of them, Maruyama and his ragtag bunch staggered through the undergrowth, having no idea where they were and in what direction they were heading. Nevertheless, they got a break when some air reconnaissance photographs taken on October 13 and 14 reached them that showed American supply depots existed just south of Bloody Ridge. Originally received with what could be called calloused apathy by the 17th Army, the lower echelons viewed them with considerable interest. Gen. Kawaguchi, however, took these observations seriously and used his own initiative to reposition his men.

Not much has been documented about the relationships among the Japanese Army senior commanders on the ground during this attempt to recapture Henderson Field. Based on what we do know of what happened before Maruyama's force tried to attack the Marine southern defensive line, we can possibly deduce what these men's personalities were based on what they did.

Col. Tsuji reported to the 17th Army's Headquarters at noon on October 23 that much stronger American defenses faced Nasu's left point of the attack than would be facing Kawaguchi's men. Consequently, Maruyama reassigned the 16th Infantry Regiment to Kawaguchi's command. There is no way to know whether Tsuji's conclusions had any validity or not. Kawaguchi's men still struggled through the dense jungle and had no way of knowing whether they would end up where they needed to go. Kawaguchi sent Maruyama a message at 2:45 p.m. that his men were still mired in the jungle but indicated they had just reached some level land that allowed easier progress. Maruyama did not receive that message until one hour and 15 minutes later.

Kawaguchi's reconnaissance units had been scouting ahead for over a day and had not reported anything to him. Two of Kawaguchi's battalions from Col. Shoji's 230th Infantry Regiment were still hard-pressed trying to move through the jungle and strung out along the trail. Kawaguchi had only one battalion (the III/124) with him to make the planned attack that night. Kawaguchi sent another message to Maruyama saying that he planned to attack farther to the east than originally planned. Maruyama vehemently disagreed with his subordinate's stand because that maneuver would delay the planned attack to the next day.

Maruyama's chief of staff, Col. Tamaoki, got on the field telephone and ordered Kawaguchi not to change the plan in midstream. Kawaguchi's angry reply illustrates his frustration, "I cannot take responsibility for a frontal attack as a unit commander." After asking Tamaoki to discuss the matter with Maruyama, Kawaguchi received his answer 30 minutes later. Maruyama had relieved him of his command and appointed Col. Shoji, the next most senior officer, to replace him. Shoji, not feeling too well himself, replied that to replace a commander before a battle was about to begin was contrary to Samurai tradition. As he tried to talk over the telephone, only shouts came back at him, "Orders! Orders!"

Meanwhile, Nasu's men had reached a position between two to two and a half miles south of Edson's Ridge but continued to believe they were much closer to the American lines than that. Another blow to 17th Army plans happened when it learned that Kawaguchi would not be able to attack that evening. Maruyama still held firm in his determination to stay on schedule. But the facts soon sank in when he learned that his men still struggled along his "road." Another officer on the 17th Army's headquarters staff, Col. Norio Konuma, knew that any delay would further anger the already displeased Navy and result in abandonment of Combined Fleet support. He also knew that only a coordinated massive attack could possibly succeed. If Kawaguchi attacked piecemeal, each attack would be torn to pieces by the tough Marine defenses. The only possible chance to succeed was to allow enough time for Maruyama's right wing to get in place and then for both wings to attack simultaneously. Hyakutake had no choice but to agree to postpone Maruyama's attack until 7:00 p.m. on October 24.

Yamamoto received the news and told his units already at sea that X-day was now October 24. But he and Ugaki were not happy about the change in the schedule. Ugaki wrote an angry entry in his diary that while he understood that American opposition was a justifiable reason for delays and attributable to the fortunes of war, the current postponement could only be blamed on inadequate preparation by the Army. He wondered if future joint plans should be more flexible and allow for unexpected events.

Nonetheless, success favored Sumiyoshi's force to the west on October 23. The Americans thus far believed that his attack was the only action and had no idea of Maruyama's movements to the south. No blame should be placed on poor American intelligence because Maruyama's march was too far south and under the protection of dense jungle growth to be seen by aerial reconnaissance. Not one of Clemens' scouts had seen hide or hair of any Japanese so far in Guadalcanal's thick jungle. American patrols sent out to look for the Japanese returned having sighted nothing.

The Americans accordingly adjusted to the new conditions by moving some artillery guns so that nine batteries pointed to the west. Wanting to consolidate the command structure at the Matanikau River, Geiger also replaced McKelvy's battalion from the 1st Marine Infantry Regiment with the 2nd Battalion, 7th Marine Infantry Regiment along with the 7th Marines' headquarters company. Thus, only Lt. Col. Lewis B. "Chesty" Puller's 1st Battalion, 7th Marine Infantry Regiment now guarded the whole 2,500 yard-long line south of Henderson Field. Only one battalion held a position that should have been held by two. The Japanese deception had thus far been wildly successful. Four Japanese battalions were on their way to do their intended worst.

But all was not going as well as Sumiyoshi had originally planned. He wanted to attack in force on October 23 to coordinate his assaults with Maruyama's. However, Col. Oka's force had been encountering the same tough conditions as Maruyama's men had. After swinging northward on October 19, he arrived just northwest of Mt. Austen two days later. It took him all day on October 22 to move just slightly more than one-half mile across a deep ravine filled with thick vegetation. His report of October 23 said that he did not know where two of his three rifle battalions were but believed they had marched eastward to capture some high ground between the Marine defenses on the Matanikau River and those near the Lunga. Nonetheless, he confirmed his intention to attack at 3:00 p.m. on the 23rd.

Col. Nakaguma planned that his 2nd Battalion, 4th Infantry Regiment (II/4) and the 1st Independent Tank Company with the 1st Battalion, 4th Infantry Regiment (I/4) would immediately assault the Americans. Sumiyoshi ordered him at 1:20 p.m. to delay his attack until 3:00 p.m. to coordinate with Oka's planned attack. Nakaguma ordered the II/4 to get ready, but more of the now-all-too-familiar delays occurred. Sporadic Japanese artillery fire covered the 1st Tank Company's noisy movements as it drew nearer to the American lines. But they had to wait for the II/4, as that battalion could not begin moving until 5:00 p.m. Meanwhile, news of the main attack's postponement reached Sumiyoshi so that he ordered his men at 5:20 p.m. to delay until the next day. However, some of his units did not receive his order because of his radios' inability to communicate across the rugged terrain. Nakaguma's battalions raggedly attacked the Marines anyway.

At sunset, the Japanese artillery barrage rose to a deafening crescendo on the Marines' horseshoe perimeter. The screeching sound of the Japanese 15-ton tank tracks could be heard as they neared the Matanikau's western bank. An American 37-mm antitank shell exploded on one of the steel beasts and stopped it dead. Another tank suddenly burst from the jungle, its tracks throwing up sand behind it as it crossed a sandbar, crossed over a flimsy barbed wire barricade like it was not there, overran a machine-gun nest, squashing its occupants like insects. It came near the foxhole occupied by Private Joseph D. R. Champagne. He placed a hand grenade on the tank's side that exploded and tore the track into pieces. As the vehicle veered onto the beach's sand, an American half-track with a 75-mm gun mounted on it chased the tank, fired one shell that hit the tank and turned it into a burning coffin for its crew. Flares then lit up the night and brought a volley of American antitank fire. The last two 7.5-ton tanks became burning, smoking hulks. A second wave of tanks met the same fate as the volleys of fire cremated them. Only 17 of the 44 men in the 1st Independent Tank company lived through this brief struggle with seven of those wounded.

The Marines more than equaled the Japanese artillery barrage with devastating fusillades of their own. Forty howitzers of the 2nd, 3rd, and 5th Battalion, 11th Marine Regiment and I Battery, 10th Marine Regiment poured shell after shell into the attacking Japanese blanketing preplanned target areas located 500 yards east and west of Pt. Cruz. A bomb from an SBD smashed into the base of Pt. Cruz. McKelvy asked for more air support as the Japanese infantry advanced across the river. American artillery shells exploded on top of the Japanese and the Marines heard death-rattling moans of the dying across from them. The Japanese infantry attack never even got started. More than 6,000 American howitzer shells landed on the Japanese forces and stopped it dead. The battlefield became quiet as a graveyard after a short exchange of fire. While McKelvy's battalion sustained losses of two killed and 11 wounded, Japanese casualty figures are unknown. Undoubtedly, the most serious losses were among the riflemen who tried to cross that river in that abortive attack.

Maruyama's Attack Finally Comes

When the sun rose on October 24, the Marines near the Matanikau looked to the south and saw one of Oka's battalions moving toward the American left rear in a long line through a heavily wooded ravine's deep crevice. Despite air attacks and artillery shelling, these Japanese soldiers threatened the American Matanikau rear defensive flank. Lt. Col. Hanneken's 2nd Battalion, 7th Marine Infantry Regiment, originally ordered to replace McKelvy's battalion, moved to a high south-facing ridge that extended the Matanikau River defensive line southward. However, gaps remained between McKelvy's left flank and Hanneken's right flank and between Hannekan and Puller's main defensive line.

Puller's battalion was all that stood between Henderson Field and Maruyama's force. His defensive line spread for more than 2,500 yards, a line that normally required a regiment to defend. It ran east-to-west along a grassy plain southeast of Henderson Field facing a wall of thick jungle and then westward over the still bloody ground of Edson's Ridge. After considering spreading his battalion over the whole 2,500 yard line and consulting with his executive officer, Capt. Charles W. Kelly Jr., he took one platoon from each company and moved them with their machine-guns along Edson's Ridge where Hannekan's battalion had been. As he inspected every one of his emplacements of men and guns, Puller had no illusions about the trouble facing his battalion despite their higher command's apparent unawareness of what was facing his unit.

Nonetheless, American ignorance ended when two enticing informational tidbits came into their possession on October 24. One man from a 7th Marines' patrol had somehow separated from his unit and saw a Japanese officer peering at Edson's Ridge through his binoculars. A scout-sniper saw the smoke from many rice fires several miles upriver along the Lunga. But there was no more time left to change American placements. They would have to take the initial brunt of the Japanese assault to come with what they had.

Nasu's and Shoji's soldiers moved to a place at 2:00 p.m. that their leaders believed to be just more than one mile south of Henderson Field. Their superior, Maruyama, ordered the attack to begin five hours later. Each group started to cut four trails through the jungle. However, their progress slowed measurably at 4:00 p.m. as the rain became a drenching downpour. The ground along the trails turned treacherous as the mud each soldier waded through reached their waists. The sun set and heavy, moisture-laden clouds covered the moon. Navigation through the dense undergrowth was now impossible. The men could only see what was just a few feet in front of them. Seven o'clock, the planned time of attack, came and went, and still the Japanese had not come within sight of the American lines. The rain finally stopped at 9:00 p.m. The oppressive jungle, rain, and darkness had taken their toll on Maruyama's men. Confusion was now rampant among them. Each wing of the Japanese attack, consisting of three battalions that were supposed to be about the same size as Puller's unit, had been chopping trails side-by-side with their comrades. A reserve force of three battalions trailed behind them. The situation got out-of-control as Shoji's wing moved too far to the east and followed a track that would totally miss the American lines. One of the leading battalions in Nasu's wing passed within hearing of Sergeant Briggs' position about 9:30 p.m. that resulted in Puller ordering him to a different place farther to the east, near to the area being defended by the 164th Infantry.

No one truly knows how confusing the situation was with Shoji's men leading up to their battle with Puller's Marines. The most likely turn of events was that, at 10:00 p.m., Shoji's 1st Battalion, 230th Infantry almost literally tripped over the Marines. Puller waited for his advanced outposts to retreat to his main line before giving the order to open fire. At the same time, the 17th Army received a report that the right wing had swamped the Marines' defenses and was advancing through the clear area south of Henderson Field. The euphoria reached an irrational level when the malarial-addled mind of Col. Matsumoto, the 2nd Division's operations officer, called the 17th Army to say that Henderson Field had been captured and was in the hands of the Japanese. It is unknown what possessed Japanese Army commanders that night, but it became ridiculous when the 17th Army sent a message at 12:50 a.m. stating, "2300 Banzai—a little before 2300 the Right Wing captured the airfield." Wonders of wonders! Miracles of miracles! The long-desired goal of kicking the Americans off Guadalcanal had come at last. Or so everyone in the Japanese Army mistakenly thought! Shoji was not even in the battle yet!

Nevertheless, Nasu's left wing was fighting. After arranging his three battalions in columnar formation, his leading 1st Battalion, 29th Infantry (I/29) aggressively marched to where the Marines were, but some of its men from the 3rd Company lost their way. Finally, Capt. Kihei Nakajima, the battalion's commander, discovered that another company from the 3rd Battalion commingled with his battalion. He created an ad hoc reorganization of his command that made him the leader of the "right front line unit" and the III/29 leader of the "left front line unit."

Five scouts, Capt. Jiro Katsumata's 11th Company, and the battalion headquarters were among the first troops to reach the American positions. The scouts found the American barbed wire defensive line on October 25 at 12:30 a.m. in a flat plain of jungle undergrowth. Rifle fire unceremoniously greeted them. Katsumata walked into a clearing covered with barbed wire about 60 feet from the jungle's edge. Machine gun fire came at him from his right and left as his executive and engineering officers met him in the clearing. The three men quickly decided to move their company forward before the deadly American artillery fire came. He ordered one platoon to decoy the machine guns and moved the rest of the company through the gap between the machine gun nests.

Katsumata's engineers began cutting openings in the wire as the rest of his company crawled on their bellies through the less-than-one-foot-tall grass. The soldiers' fatigue from their tortuous march through the jungle got the best of them. Some of them stood up without any orders from their superiors; one of them shouted a war whoop; several more followed, and charged against the Americans. Katsumata watched in dismay and disbelief as a barrage of machine gun and mortar fire descended on the charging men. Now tangled up in the barbed wire, the bullets, blasts from exploding mortar shells, and shrapnel slaughtered the soldiers in front of Puller's men. It was 1:00 a.m.

The 9th Company moved west, let out a shout to get up their courage, and charged at 1:15 a.m. straight into Puller's Company C machine guns positioned to fire into prearranged firing lanes. Five minutes later, all of the 9th Company lay dead. Most of the dead were the result of the bravery and dedication to duty by Sergeant John Basilone's machine section. He received the Congressional Medal of Honor for his work that October night.

Ten minutes later, American artillery fire fell directly into the left wing's path. Exploding shells cut down Japanese soldiers who made the fatal mistake of standing up. Those who survived escaped into the jungle and became lost.

If he did not know it before, Puller now realized that these latest Japanese attacks were part of a major assault. He needed to reinforce his positions and called three platoons from the 3rd Battalion, 164th Infantry to fill in the gaps in his line. But he knew this was not enough when he asked for even more help. It came when the rest of Lt. Col. Robert Hall's 3/164 received orders at 2:00 a.m. to come to Puller's aid. These green National Guard troops had never experienced the tribulations of trying to march through jungles as thick and impenetrable as those on Guadalcanal. They now had to march through heavy rain and viscous mud and did not reach Puller's position until 1¾ hours later.

As the American artillery salvoes fell like a wall of steel, Col. Furimiya, the 29th Regiment's commander, pierced the American lines with his headquarters and 7th Company just before dawn. His lost company suddenly appeared out of the jungle; now he had a force with which to attack. He ordered the commander of the III/29 to charge the American lines with bayonets bared.

As the Japanese shouted and ran toward their target, an American machine gun company opened up with four guns furiously blazing death. The withering fire cut down soldier after soldier so that only 200 Japanese reached the American positions. By this time, the American machine guns had exhausted their ammunition, and the men had to take the brunt of the Japanese charge with bayonets, knives, and bare knuckles. Furimiya led his men as the 7th Company tried to attack to the east, but they met the same fate as their other comrades. Japanese dead littered the ground in front of the barbed wire.

Before his personal assault, Furimiya ordered the II/29 to reinforce his assault. However, the battalion could not reach the place of that attack until 4:00 a.m. just as the eastern sky began to brighten. Two companies attacked at sunrise, but again with the same result: they never got past the jungle's edge. Nasu assessed his attack's lack of success and, at 7:30 a.m., decided to retreat and get ready for another attack that night.

The superiority of American firepower had taken a terrible toll. As daylight covered the scene, the results of the night's assaults became clear. One group of Japanese had penetrated into Puller's lines and created a wedge 150 yards wide and 100 yards deep. But Puller's battalion turned them back and eliminated the bulge with deadly effect. The Marines also took back two of their own machine guns and captured three Japanese machine guns amidst 37 dead Japanese troops. Those Japanese soldiers who had gotten through the American lines were so scattered that Furimiya only commanded ten men. Marine patrols had killed 67 of the dispersed Japanese to add to the slaughter. The Japanese dead numbered a minimum of 300 men; American artillery had killed more than that in the jungle outside the perimeter.

The initial Japanese ground assault to capture Henderson Field had ended as a dismal, deadly failure, but the Imperial Japanese Army had not yet given up their objective of capturing Henderson Field. They would attack again with their remaining soldiers.

✲ ✲ ✲

Ugaki received the "2300 Banzai" telegram at 11:35 p.m. on October 24th and recorded his reaction in his diary that this message "meant the capture of the airfield. This settled everything. March, all forces, to enlarge the result gained! Hesitation or indecision at this moment would leave a regret forever."[11]

Ugaki went to bed at 2:00 a.m. with a sense of relief that all was going according to plan.

As more became known, his attitude would change. Another message arrived more than two hours later that said the airfield had not been captured. Ugaki's understandable confusion remained until another longer telegram arrived around lunchtime:

> "Control of the units was difficult due to the complicated terrain. Only an enemy position protruding from the south end of the airfield was taken, but the airfield has not been penetrated. Under regrouping since this morning. The force on the right bank of Lunga River pressed the enemy and reached to a point five kilometers south-southwest of Cape Lunga. Four enemy planes took off and two of them landed soon afterward."[12]

Another signal arrived later that day saying the Army would attack that night and avenge their previous losses. It was time for the Imperial Japanese Navy to pitch in and help secure a successful conclusion to the mission.

Another Visit from the Tokyo Express

The Imperial Japanese Army wanted to know the progress being made in their campaign to recapture Henderson Field. A 76th Independent Air Squadron's Dinah reconnaissance plane piloted by Capt. Hideo Kirita with an escort of eight Zeros left Rabaul to take a look. With the American fighter support grounded because of muddy runways caused by the night's heavy rains, a wall of AA fire rose from Henderson Field to greet the small formation as it flew over Guadalcanal at 8:00 a.m. The reconnaissance plane's pilot bravely and foolishly dove to get a better look. His reckless decision caused the pilot and his crew to die in a funereal bonfire as their craft crashed and exploded near the airfield.

Buoyed by the confident message from the 17th Army's headquarters, Adm. Mikawa gathered ships from the 8th Fleet to give the Army a helpful push. He ordered his units at 12:37 a.m. to move toward Guadalcanal and carry out their assigned tasks. After receiving the message that said Henderson Field had not been captured, he ordered his units to reverse their courses. But he soon countered that order and sent his units to the southeast again.

Japanese actions did not stop there. The Base Air Force decided to augment their usual bombing run by adding 28 Zeroes to fly over Guadalcanal in four waves and patrol over the island. Their assignment was to circle the airfield for two hours and land after they saw that Japanese troops had actually captured it.

Coastwatchers spied the first wave of nine Zeroes led by Lt. (jg) Sadao Yamaguchi and warned Guadalcanal of their coming. Despite the muddy conditions of Henderson Field's runways, Capt. Joseph J. Foss managed to lead five F4Fs aloft to meet Yamaguchi's flight. The American fighters reached 1,500 feet when the Zeroes arrived. It was not until the fighters reached 6,000 feet that they began aerial combat. Foss shot down two Zeroes flown by PO1c Rokuzo Iwamoto and PO2c Naoichi Maeda while a Zero sent 2nd Lt. Oscar M. Bate's F4F down in flames. Bate fortunately was able to parachute to safety and later walked back to Henderson Field. The other seven Zeroes fought with the other seven F4Fs with all 14 planes safely escaping serious damage.

✲ ✲ ✲

Earlier that morning, SBDs searching up the Slot discovered Mikawa's attempts at 7:00 a.m. to help his Army brethren. Three Japanese destroyers were just 35 miles away and steaming toward Guadalcanal. Coastwatchers also radioed reports of sighting more Japanese planes heading southeast. SBDs found more Japanese ships two hours later 105 miles northwest of Guadalcanal heading in the same direction. Mikawa was about to pay another call on the Americans.

His five task groups included the following forces:

1. Reinforcement Unit A with the light cruiser *Tatsuta*, the minelayer *Tsugaru*, and two destroyers transporting additional Japanese troops from the Koli Detachment.
2. Reinforcement Unit B with three destroyers to provide fuel and supplies to Japanese troops after they (hopefully) captured Henderson Field.
3. The light cruiser *Sendai* and more destroyers patrolled to the west.
4. Destroyer Division 6 with the three destroyers *Akatsuki, Ikazuchi,* and *Shiratsuyu* sighted by the American SBDs earlier in the day and commanded by Cmdr. Yusuke Yamada had the designation of First Assault Unit with the mission of stopping American reinforcements at Lunga and Koli Points. Answering a call from the Army for support by a ship bombardment, the First Assault Unit moved closer to Lunga Point to shell American positions.
5. The Second Assault Unit had the light cruiser *Yura* and five destroyers commanded by Radm. Tamotsu Takama, whose flag flew aboard the antiaircraft destroyer *Akizuki*

Meanwhile, the American destroyer-minesweepers *Trever* and *Zane*, their decks piled high with torpedoes, ammunition, and gasoline for the PT boats on Tulagi and towing two new PT boats, successfully delivered their cargoes to the PT crews. Waiting for new orders, their commanders anticipated that their two ships would soon move across the water nearer to Guadalcanal and bombard Japanese troop positions. Suddenly, three Japanese destroyers appeared at 10:00 a.m. with the American lookouts sighting them 14 minutes later. Lt. Cmdr. D. M. Agnew, the senior skipper of the two ships, knew the two ancient converted minesweepers with their three three-inch guns could not possibly match up with the far more modern Japanese destroyers and decided to take the two ships out of harm's way. He ordered the two ships to make maximum steam and leave through Sealark Channel at their best speed, 29 knots under the best of circumstances.

But the Japanese destroyers quickly caught up with the hapless American ships at 10:27 a.m. and opened fire from the nearly point-blank range of five miles. Five-inch shells soon landed within feet of the *Trever*'s decks. Agnew ordered a zigzag pattern but to no avail. One five-inch shell blasted into the *Zane* at 10:38 a.m., destroying one three-inch gun and killing three crewmen. Realizing he could not stand and trade broadsides with overpowering Japanese, he made a daring move. He turned both ships directly into the dangerous waters of the Nagella Channel. Yamada decided to leave the two American ships for Takama's ships to destroy and to proceed with his mission to shell the Americans on Guadalcanal.

Yamada moved toward the beaches and found the tug *Seminole* and the converted fishing boat *YP-284*, which had just finished delivering an artillery battery and their customary cargoes of gasoline and ammunition. Several Japanese shells exploded on *YP-284*, killed three Marines, and ignited the gasoline she carried. Before long, destructive flames engulfed her, and she sank in a fiery, smoky cloud. The *Seminole* did not fare much better. Shells pierced her thin hull while not exploding and she sank taking one man with her. Flush with easy victories, the destroyers fired on the Americans near the Lunga River. They paid for their overconfidence when the American 3rd Defense Battalion's five-inch shore guns fired back. At 10:53 a.m., one shell put a hole in one of the *Akatsuki*'s gun mounts, starting a fire. Realizing that they possibly had over committed themselves, the three warships belched a smoke screen and began to withdraw.

But the planes of the CACTUS Air Force would have their say in the fate of those three destroyers. The American pilots' day had already been a busy one defending Henderson Field from continuous waves of Japanese Zeroes. After two of the six F4Fs, led by 1st Lt. Robert F. Stout, could not take off because of engine trouble and being stuck in the mud, the remaining four fighters lifted off at 10:30 a.m. and soon found the three Japanese destroyers exchanging fire with the shore batteries. The fighters dove down on the ships and began a series of intensive strafing attacks. Soon, the three ships retired at high speed. Stout's group had to return for fuel and ammunition when they found a new set of adversaries.

Three of the eight Zeroes led by Lt. (jg) Tokitane Futagami had been busy strafing the Americans along the beach when they began clashing with Stout's four F4Fs. First Lt. Jack E. Conger got on the tail of the last of the three Zeroes and sent it plummeting to the ground in flames. He fired at another Zero, but did not see what happened to it; he learned later that people on the ground saw the Japanese fighter crash in a ball of flame. Conger had emptied his guns when he rammed the leading Zero head-on at an altitude of 1,500 feet. He safely parachuted into the water having destroyed all three strafing Zeroes with their valuable pilots—Futagami, PO3c Toyoo Morita, and Sea1c Naoshi Ubukata.

☆ ☆ ☆

After Yamada left the battle scene, Takama's force of the light cruiser *Yura* and five destroyers moved into Indispensable Strait to do their worst. Led by Lt. Cmdr. John Eldridge, five SBDs attacked the Japanese ships at 1:00 p.m. Eldridge dropped his 1,000-pound bomb that exploded in the water near the cruiser's aft engine room. A 500-pound bomb exploded on her deck near the same place. One bomb smacked the water near the destroyer *Akizuki*, Takama's flagship, flooding her after engine room and disabling her starboard screw. As in other instances when American aircraft aggressively attacked surface ships, Mikawa terminated Yamada's bombardment mission and ordered his ships to withdraw.

Three P-39s attacked Takama's force at 2:15 p.m. and four SBDs assaulted the Japanese ships at 3:30 p.m., but inflicted no damage. Nevertheless, the *Yura*'s and Takama's problems only worsened.

Her stern began to sink as her crew could not control the aft engine room flooding. She slowed measurably as her crew tried to beach her at 5:00 p.m. By this time, Eldridge had landed to refuel and rearm his group and returned with his four SBDs, four bomb-laden P39s, and three F4Fs. After they attacked and unloaded everything they carried, six B-17s dropped their bomb loads near the struggling cruiser. One bomb hit the cruiser and restarted fires on her deck. Bomb fragments made Swiss cheese of the destroyer *Samidare*'s starboard side and knocked out the destroyer *Akizuki*'s boiler. Flames engulfed the hapless cruiser; she was finished. Takama ordered her torpedoed by the destroyers *Harusame* and *Yudachi*. She sank at 9:00 p.m., another loss for the cream of the Imperial Japanese Navy.

The Japanese Navy had tried to help out the 17th Army, but that effort came up short. Again, the Japanese underestimated CACTUS' air power and resolution and paid the price. But the Army had not finished what they had started. The Marines would still feel the full force of another devastating ground attack that night.

Once More into the Breech

While the Americans and Japanese bashed each other in the air and at sea, the Imperial Japanese Army planned to restart their attacks on the Marine defenses protecting the airfields. The Americans did the same, ever mindful of how intense the prior night and early morning Japanese attacks were. They meant to be prepared for another one.

The 5th Marine Infantry Regiment moved into the gap between the position on the horseshoe-shaped line held by Hanneken's 2/7 left flank east of the Matanikau River and the Marine's perimeter protecting the airfields. Lt. Col. William J. Whaling, the 5th Marine's executive officer, knew a large, regimental-size Japanese force, Oka's men, was out there and wanted to place his men so they could move from one position to another without having to wade through knee-high mud.

Puller also knew the Japanese force that had attacked his battalion the previous night, although badly hurt, was not yet destroyed and would likely attack again. After being combined because of the prior night's blistering action, his Marine and the Army battalions separated with the Marines occupying the 1,400 yard part of the western defensive line and the Army moved to the 1,100 yard eastern part of the American defenses. The last reserve the 1st Marine Division had, the 3rd Battalion, 2nd Marines, took their place behind the lines between the Marine and Army troops so they could help out wherever needed.

Intelligence reached Marine divisional headquarters from interceptions of Japanese radio transmissions that indicated the Japanese Army had received orders to "expedite" their planned takeover of the airfields. Another landing could also happen. Lt. Merillat reflected the Marine's nervousness when he wrote a diary entry that night, "Attempted landing tonight? Looks like this is the night."[13]

✲ ✲ ✲

The Sendai Division officers at their jungle command post realized that many brave Japanese soldiers now lay dead or seriously wounded in front the Marine lines. But they believed that Furimiya's apparent success could be the lynchpin for a successful attack later that night and wanted to send reinforcements to him. Maruyama sent a message to his command at 1:00 p.m. that the "Left Wing" had penetrated the American defenses and ordered an attack be made as soon it got dark. He gave control of his reserves, the 16th Infantry Regiment and 2nd Engineer Battalion, to Nasu. The 17th Army's headquarters now focused on the details to resupply the troops and to bring the Koli Detachment, due to come ashore the morning of October 26, into the battle. One battalion from the 38th Infantry group had to be moved to Tassafaronga. The 228th Infantry Regiment (less one battalion) also had to be sent to Koli Point as soon as possible. Requests for more supplies went back to Rabaul to replace seriously diminished ammunition stocks.

The Japanese attack began at about 8:00 p.m. when the remaining Japanese artillery fired upon Puller's and Hall's positions. The barrage was a poor imitation of what they had thrown at the Americans the night before. The sporadic barrage continued for about an hour and dwindled to nothing. A series of attacks occurred for the next four hours with most of them directed at Hall's 3/164. The American defenders observed that the Japanese assaults came in groups of 30 to 200 men under machine gun covering fire. Accompanied by heavy infantry weapons fire, the Japanese 16th Infantry Regiment launched a massed attack just after midnight on October 26 directly at Hall's center and left with some troops attacking the 2/164. The brunt of attack came at the boundary between the 2/164 and 3/164. But two American 37-mm guns from the Weapons Company of the 7th Marines blasted the oncoming Japanese with canister shot and slaughtered more than 250 men. Some Japanese soldiers penetrated small parts of the American defensive lines. Marines from the 3rd Battalion, 2nd Marines and soldiers of the 164th stopped the leaks and killed the attackers where they could find them.

The American fire fatally wounded Nasu, Col. Hiroyasu, commander of the 16th Infantry Regiment, and most of his officers. The "Left Wing" attack dissipated to a mere shadow of its former self. The "Right Wing" aimlessly wandered in the jungle and still could not find the American lines. Shoji received reports of the Americans circling around his right flank. He ordered two battalions to stop the apparent movement. However, like most of the Japanese intelligence estimates, these proved to be false. Shoji faced no such threat.

Oka, not an active participant so far in the Japanese attack, at long last decided to move. He wanted to attack an east-west ridge line and located just southeast of the Matanikau River mouth. Hanneken's 2nd Battalion, 7th Marines defended this area along a tightly packed line. Company F held the battalion's far east flank on the ridge's highest ground. Two other companies extended to the west with one platoon formerly attached to Company F on the far right flank. That platoon had to stop any Japanese infiltration through a gap between Hannekan and the 3rd Battalion. At 5:35 p.m. and for the next 40 minutes thereafter, the Japanese artillery bombarded Hanneken's lines. The Marines heard a Japanese column cutting their way through the jungle in front of them.

Oka launched his main attack at 3:00 a.m. with the major force directed at Company F. It was clear the Japanese wanted to take the high ground with all they had. Japanese rifle fire poured from the jungle tree line on the Marines. Platoon Sergeant Mitchell Paige returned machine gun fire, killing and wounding many Japanese. But the Japanese fire finally took its toll on his men; Paige began firing the machine guns himself. When Japanese fire destroyed one of his guns, Paige ran through withering fire to get a replacement. Despite Paige's valor that garnered him the Congressional Medal of Honor and the 2/7's powerful mortar fire, the Japanese finally forced Company F's survivors from the ridge.

Nevertheless, the Japanese occupation of the ridge line proved to be a brief stay. Maj. Odell M. Conoley, the 2/7's executive officer, led a counterattack at 5:40 a.m. comprising approximately 17 men including communications specialists, cooks, a bandsman, and a few riflemen. Men from Company G, two platoons from Company C, 5th Marines, and Paige joined Conoley's assault, and totally surprised the Japanese. As the Japanese tried to set up a defense for their newly won positions, the Americans deluged the Japanese with hand grenades, charged up the ridge and evicted the Japanese from their too briefly held prize. Twenty minutes later, it was all over. The Marines counted 98 Japanese bodies on the ridge with 200 more Japanese dead on the ridge's slope. Trails of blood ran into the surrounding jungle. Marine patrols found small groups of Japanese soldiers throughout the American perimeter and destroyed them where they stood. A few Japanese managed to escape into the jungle. The second Japanese attempt to capture Henderson Field and Fighter One in as many days had ended in the slaughter of finely trained Japanese soldiers.

After finally hearing from their "Left Wing" just before sunrise, a Sendai division staff officer concluded that the second assault had also failed. All of Maruyama's reserves had been spent. He sent a message to 17th Army Headquarters that he no longer could hope to penetrate the American lines with his divisions in tatters. Hyakutake stopped the attack at 8:00 a.m. The Americans had completely stopped the Japanese assaults while inflicting heavy casualties on the attackers. The same happened on the night of October 26-27. The Japanese tried to retrieve their units' colors to save their honor as American patrols continued to eliminate any Japanese soldiers found in their perimeter.

Assessing the Carnage

While there can never be an accurate count of both sides' casualties, an examination of what was reported sheds some light on how severe the Japanese defeat was. One Marine report stated that the American losses for October 21-26 were 86 killed and 192 wounded. Included in these were:[14]

American Casualties (Recapture of Henderson Field and Fighter One)

Unit	Killed or Missing	Wounded	Total Casualties
Marine 1/7 (Puller)	26	33	59
Army 164th Regiment	19	About 50	69
Marine 2/7 (Hanneken)	14	32	46
Marine 3/1 (McKelvy)	2	11	13
Totals	61	126	187

The Japanese estimates of their losses show them to be far greater than for the Americans. However, there is not as precise an estimate of the number of Japanese soldiers killed or wounded as there is for the American losses. The 1st Marine Division estimated that two-day battle to retake Henderson Field and Fighter One caused the death of more than 2,200 Japanese soldiers.[15]

The 17th Army's failure to recapture the American-held airfields caused a massive depression among its officers. The losses severely crippled their ability to carry on any further ground operations on Guadalcanal. As it sometimes happens in failed efforts, the Army staff placed the blame for the debacle on factors outside their control. As far as they were concerned, the lack of air cover prevented the landing of reinforcements and critically needed supplies. The Imperial Japanese Navy's pressure to attack so they could carry on their anticipated carrier battle with the U.S. Navy, and an Imperial General Staff promise to the emperor that the airfields would be captured by a certain date were reasons the 17th Army failed to capture their objectives.

Nonetheless, other members of the Japanese military offered their own reasons. When Adm. Ugaki learned of the Army's failure, he made the following entry in his diary:

> "At about 0340 we received a report from our liaison staff on Guadalcanal stating that the army commenced the attack at 2200 last night but could not break through into the airfield by 0200. It was just as I thought...They should have prepared for both regular and surprise attacks and displayed the skill to use them properly."

Ugaki pointed out in his diary that this failure had been repeated three times. "It was not a failure of the army alone and I was extremely sorry."[16] It almost seems the Japanese Navy had already reconciled itself to a preordained Army defeat. Apparently, the Navy already knew the Army's battle was flawed from its inception.

Cmdr. Toshikazu Ohmae contended the Army completely disregarded the potentially terrible problems its soldiers would have trying to cut their way through the dense Guadalcanal jungle undergrowth thus delaying the time when they could begin their attacks. These delays allowed the Americans to prepare their defenses since they detected Japanese movements through the jungle. Faulty local intelligence that solely relied on aerial reconnaissance missed detecting how the Americans had set up their defensive perimeter and how strong that defense was. Crowning the list of Ohmae's criticisms were the failures of proper command of the battlefield as evidenced by the following events:

1. Dissension among the various command levels.
2. Maruyama's neuralgia.
3. Kawaguchi's insubordination.
4. Oka's disobedience of standing orders
5. Nasu's incompetence as demonstrated by his charging into an unknown defensive position.

Col. Furimiya, after aimlessly drifting through the jungle to preserve his regiment's honor, observed in his diary found on his body, "we must not overlook firepower." He wrote a message for Maruyama, "I am going to return my borrowed life today with little interest."[17]

Had the 17th Army's attacks succeeded, criticisms could have been leveled at the American command. Vandegrift's cordoned defense, spreading his men too thinly, and isolating two battalions would have been in a litany of complaints against the general and other officers in his command. But there is an adage spoken by Count Galeazzo Ciano, Benito Mussolini's Minister of Propaganda, close confidant, and son-in-law: "As always, victory finds a hundred fathers, but defeat is an orphan." The victorious defense of the critical airfield saved Vandegrift's command from all such condemnations. In the light of historical perspective, the Marines and soldiers on Guadalcanal covered themselves with glory when they inflicted a potentially crippling blow on the Japanese Army's attempts to recapture Guadalcanal.

Between September 26 through October 26, the Japanese had thrown in every resource they could to recapture the airfields only to be met with repeated failures. The CACTUS Air Force claimed it destroyed 228 Japanese aircraft. In comparison, its aircraft losses were 118 planes.

The Japanese 11th Air Fleet lost a total 103 planes. Losses of Japanese aircraft carrier planes were 12 aircraft. As usual, claims of planes destroyed always outdistanced actual losses.

When the actual losses were added up, the total aircraft losses during that period were: American: 118; Japanese: 115. This observation seems to be slightly in favor of the Japanese, but American industrial power increased during the war, so more American aircraft would be manufactured more quickly than the Japanese could match. Therefore, the Americans could readily replace their losses while the Japanese could not. Also, more American pilots were undergoing training than for the Japanese; therefore, those losses could also be more easily sustained. Thus, the Japanese aircraft losses caused the death of irreplaceable, inexperienced pilots and aircrews that would be much more difficult for the Japanese to replace.[18]

The valiant Japanese attacks on the Marine defenses resulted in a severe defeat. The Americans still had Henderson Field and Fighter One. The "unsinkable" aircraft carrier still could send aircraft against any Japanese attempts to evict the Americans. But the Japanese had another card to play. The Combined Fleet had been looking for the American carriers and would soon find them. When that happened, the fourth carrier battle of the Pacific War would be fought, the Battle of the Santa Cruz Islands.

Part 8: The Battle of the Santa Cruz Islands

CHAPTER 31
Prepare for Another Carrier Battle

Comparing Forces

While the Japanese Army fought desperately to retake the American-held airfields on Guadalcanal, the Imperial Japanese Navy anxiously searched for the American carriers. Despite the loss of ships and men at Coral Sea, Midway, and the Battle of Eastern Solomons, Adm. Yamamoto still had a powerful fleet at his disposal—far more so than what the Americans had.

The most useful way to compare the forces is with the following tables.

Ships at the Battle of the Santa Cruz Islands

	Fleet Carriers	Light Carriers	Battle-ships	Heavy Cruisers	Light Cruisers	Destroyers	Subs	Total
American[1]	2	0	1	2	4	14	0	23
Japanese[2]	2	2	4	8	3	30	12	61

Carrier-Based Planes at the Battle of the Santa Cruz Islands

	Fighters	Dive-bombers	Torpedo Planes	Total
Americans	70	72	87	171
Japanese	87	67	57	211

Land-Based Planes at the Battle of the Santa Cruz Islands

	Fighters	Bombers	Army Fighter Planes	Dive bombers	Torpedo Bombers	Heavy, medium, patrol Bombers	Other	Total
American	122	20	2	39	51	37	0	271
Japanese	0	0	0	0	0	0	220	220

A first look at the overall totals shows an approximate balance between the American and Japanese forces. However, when one examines the vital resources that would affect the outcome of the battle, the disparity between the American and Japanese (two American carriers versus four Japanese carriers and 171 American carrier-based planes versus 211 Japanese carrier-based planes)—the resources each side could *directly* bring to bear during the heat of battle—becomes quite clear.[3] Advantage Japan!

The Japanese Get Ready

When Adm. Ugaki awoke from his night's sleep that began after he absorbed the bad news of the Army's failure to capture Henderson Field, the fears he expressed about potential American warship movements came to fruition. The Imperial Japanese Navy still did not know the whereabouts of the American carriers. Ugaki and others anticipated that the U.S. Navy was about to move their ships closer to Guadalcanal and urged that the Combined Fleet take precautionary measures. He knew that another big sea battle was about to happen in an area east of the Solomon Islands and north of the Santa Cruz Islands.

Everything was now in the Japanese Navy's favor for such a conflict. They had powerful carrier and surface ship forces at their disposal. After their carrier air forces destroyed the American carrier air forces, their powerful battleships and heavy cruisers could move in and destroy the last remaining American naval forces using their superior numbers and firepower. In an optimistic mood, they relished the possibility of a night surface battle—where the Japanese believed they still excelled. A golden opportunity to overcome the Army's debacle on Guadalcanal clearly was in the offing.

The confirmation the Japanese desperately needed occurred when the first report of sighting American ships arrived on October 25 at 5:00 a.m.. An American B-17 had attacked the Japanese fleet three and a half hours earlier. This assault resulted in the launching of a search plane that spied one American carrier and 15 other ships 140 miles to the northeast of Ndeni Island.[4]

Another sighting report arrived about the same time spotting what seemed to be three battleships, one cruiser and ten destroyers. Its position was 30 miles west of the Rennell Islands on a 150º course. Ugaki wanted Japanese land-based planes to deal with this force.[5] All this lined up just the way the Japanese wanted. Optimism increased within Yamamoto's Combined Fleet.[6]

The Battle of the Santa Cruz Islands was about to begin, and the Americans were prepared.

The Americans Brace Themselves for Battle

For a few months before Halsey took command, the three groups of cryptoanalysts located at Pearl Harbor (HYPO), Washington (NEGAT), and Brisbane (BELCONNECT) could not discover any information about future Japanese intentions and warship movements near the Solomons. The Japanese carriers that supposedly threatened Nouméa and dominated Ghormley's fears turned out to be mere specters. But after Halsey met with Vandegrift and Turner, he became concerned the Navy was not doing all it could to support the men on Guadalcanal. CACTUS was still in jeopardy and the key to holding onto the strategically important island.

Prepare for Another Carrier Battle

The carrier *Enterprise* was about to return to full combat readiness. The battleship *Washington* had returned from duty supporting the Royal Navy in their struggles in the Mediterranean Sea and Indian Ocean. The carrier *Hornet* and battleship *South Dakota* were now near Guadalcanal. American naval power had enough strength, at least in Halsey's mind, to challenge any thrust by the Imperial Japanese Navy in the Solomons. He gathered his staff in several meetings to look at ways this newfound naval power could be projected around Guadalcanal. He ordered Kinkaid to take the *Enterprise* and the rest of Task Force 16 to depart Pearl Harbor on October 16 and join Radm. Murray's Task Force 17 steaming at sea near Nouméa. Halsey sent a radio message to Kinkaid that he was to assume overall command of both task forces after rendezvousing with Murray. The new combination carried the designation of Task Force 61, which became a reality when the two carriers met on October 24 near the New Hebrides Islands. While Task Force 16 moved southward, Radm. Lee's Task Force 64 had to return to Espiritu Santo after the heavy cruiser *Chester* sustained severe damage on October 20 from a Japanese submarine's torpedoes. Lee refueled and sailed on October 23.

Halsey devised a plan that significantly departed from his predecessor's defensive posture. He went on the offensive with an audacious plan that ordered Task Force 61 to steam into the waters north of the Santa Cruz Islands, aggressively search for Japanese carriers in an area that could not be covered by land-based air searches from Espiritu Santo, and then turn southwesterly toward San Cristobal. Lee's task force would steam southeast of Guadalcanal to meet any Japanese battleship and/or heavy cruiser runs of the Tokyo Express. Their mission was to protect Guadalcanal's western flank and be on any Japanese fleet's left flank should they threaten that island or if they should move from Truk and advance to the southeast. In a way, Halsey's plan was to be a repeat of the American strategy at Midway where American carriers lay in wait to spring a trap on the Japanese. Although he did not say so in his orders to Kinkaid, Halsey had intended that the "sweep" would stop the Japanese carriers should they appear. Lee, Kinkaid and Murray learned of Halsey's plan on October 22 and immediately proceeded to obey his orders.

✲ ✲ ✲

That same day, Halsey's command learned from naval intelligence of a Japanese plan to move once again on Guadalcanal. After assembling several tidbits of information, the cryptoanalysts learned of a Japanese codeword called "Y-Day." But they unfortunately could not tell when "Y-Day" would occur and what would happen on that day. To add more confusion, Halsey told Vandegrift that there were no imminent threats against Guadalcanal. Nevertheless, more information came from intelligence the next morning that said that at least eight Japanese submarines would line up near the Solomons. Clearly, the Japanese expected that American naval forces would be moving nearby. Intelligence clarified that estimate of Japanese submarine strength by stating there would be at least ten of them ready to spy any major American ship movements. That report also implied a major Japanese offensive against Guadalcanal in two or three days.

The current American naval intelligence estimate reported the definite whereabouts of the Japanese fleet carriers *Shokaku* and *Zuikaku* but did not know where the other combat-ready Japanese carriers were. It was believed that the "*Hitaka*" (*Hiyo*) and "*Hayataka*" (*Junyo*) were still in Japanese home waters. In fact, they were at Truk along with the other two carriers. There was no information of the *Zuiho*'s location. Naval intelligence in Washington estimated that four Japanese carriers with 72 fighters and 132 dive-bombers and torpedo planes probably were in the Solomons' area. Knowing these facts, Halsey did not cancel Kinkaid's "sweep" orders.

The Americans learned more definitive facts about Japanese naval activity on October 23. Adm. Fitch's PBYs were aloft looking for the Japanese ships. One of them spotted a Japanese carrier in the morning about 650 miles north of Espiritu Santo and sent out an alert. Later that evening, a night flying PBY flown by Lt. (jg) Donald L. Jackson reported seeing one heavy cruiser, one light cruiser, and two destroyers steaming ten miles ahead of another group of ships that included one carrier.

The Americans no longer doubted that there was at least one Japanese carrier in the waters north of the Santa Cruz Islands. It was now vital that Task Force 61 form up and go after this fleet.

Radm. Thomas Kinkaid's Task Force 16 had a humdrum voyage from Pearl Harbor. The oiler *Sabine* arrived on October 23 to refuel Kinkaid's ship. Task Force 16 then proceeded to rendezvous with Task Force 17. They joined up the next day at 12:45 p.m. about 250 miles northeast of Espiritu Santo to become Task Force 61 with Kinkaid as Officer in Tactical Command (OTC). As had been the U.S. Navy's practice in circumstances like this, the *Enterprise* and *Hornet* exchanged the responsibility for conducting air searches and patrols that would hunt for the Japanese. Kinkaid ordered Task Force 61 to increase speed to 23 knots and, obeying Halsey's orders while desiring to avoid Japanese submarines, headed for the waters north of the Santa Cruz Islands.

The reader might interpret that all was smooth as glass with Task Force 61 while reading this narrative. Nonetheless, some disturbing problems still existed with communications in Halsey's command. While Kinkaid refueled Task Force 16 on October 23, Cmdr. Leonard Dow, the *Enterprise*'s FDO and Halsey's communications officer when the admiral commanded the carrier, left for Nouméa to help Halsey fix some of these problems. Cmdr. John H. Griffin, after he replaced Dow, had won high esteem while running the Fighter Director School at Oahu and as a member of Kinkaid's staff aboard the *Enterprise,* but did not have experience at actually directing fighters under combat conditions. The replacement for Lt. John Baumeister, Jr., also a highly experienced radar officer who left the carrier before it left Pearl Harboron October 16, lacked actual combat experience commanding the carrier's radars. The transfer of other important radar personnel showed that both Kinkaid and Murray lacked a comprehensive appreciation of their ships' radar capabilities. These problems would become more evident in the fight to come.

✲ ✲ ✲

Yamamoto's frustration with the Army's failure to take Henderson Field extended to wondering what Kondo, Nagumo, and Kinkaid were doing in the meantime. An American PBY attack on the *Zuikaku* in the early morning of October 25 set off alarms in Yamamoto's mind. The Americans had spotted his battle fleet. It was only a matter of time before the American carrier aircraft would find and attack his carriers. It must have seemed to him that this might be Midway—Part II. An important exception to that situation was that he already knew the American carriers were out there.

Actually Kondo had moved his Advance Force during the night of October 24/25 to try to capitalize on the Army's expected taking of Henderson Field. His force was about 120 miles southwest of Nagumo's Striking Force. This force's three carriers—the *Zuikaku*, *Shokaku*, and *Zuiho*—prepared to launch as many planes as they could spare to search for the American carriers to the south and east of the Solomons. Two and one-half hours after they received the ecstatic message reporting Henderson Field's capture, Kondo and Nagumo knew this report was prematurely optimistic and not at all true. The power of the American aircraft on Guadalcanal still existed and was more invincible than ever. There was no way the Navy would risk severe damage to its precious Combined Fleet again by trying to help their Army comrades. The only option open to them was to finish what they had planned all along—find and destroy the American carriers. Kondo's Advance Force immediately reversed its course to the north to move out of range of Henderson Field's aircraft. Both Nagumo's and Kondo's search planes would have to find the American carriers. Nonetheless, the American search craft were also quite busy.

Ten PBY's and six B-17s left Espiritu Santo in the early dawn hours of October 25 to look for the Japanese. Their search patterns covered 650- to 800-mile-long sectors to the northwest. The seaplane tender *Ballard* steamed to Vanikoro Island, the southernmost of the Santa Cruz Islands, to become an advanced base for refueling and rearming the PBYs. Fitch's search soon produced results.

Flying on a 325° bearing and 525 miles from Espiritu Santo at 9:30 a.m., 1st Lt. Mario Sesso's B-17 spotted Kondo's Advance Force. But the B-17 ran into trouble with Zeros from the carrier *Junyo*. PO1c Sawada Mankichi's three Zeroes attacked the outgunned B-17 and killed Sesso's bombardier, Sergeant Eldon M. Elliot. Nevertheless, Sesso made contact with Espiritu Santo at 9:48 a.m. and reported seeing Kondo's ships. Fitch immediately sent 12 B-17s to attack the Japanese.

Ten minutes after Sesso's message, a PBY flown by Lt. (jg) Warren B. Matthew searched in a 332° to 338° sector found Abe's Vanguard Force, eight ships at 7° S., 163° E, steaming south of Nagumo's carriers. As the PBY tried to escape through the clouds, two of the battleship *Kirishima*'s seaplanes pursued and attacked the American plane. Fortunately, Matthew eluded the two fighters and escaped undamaged. Nevertheless, he maintained contact with the Japanese ships and continued to radio any Japanese course changes. SOPAC and Task Force 61 regrettably never heard Matthew's reports. When the PBY returned to Espiritu Santo, the crew counted 76 new holes and damage to the port engine.

At about the same time that Matthew radioed his report, Lt. (jg) Robert T. Lampshire's PBY sent a report to Halsey's headquarters at 10:00 a.m. that really got the admiral's attention. Lampshire had flown in a 338-344° sector next to where Matthew was and reported seeing "unidentified task forces." Another of Lampshire's messages forwarded by the *Ballard* to Nouméa reported two battleships, two light cruisers, and four destroyers steaming at 8°05′ S., 164° E. Lampshire then reported seeing one carrier, the *Zuiho*, launching fighters. He then radioed at 11:03 a.m. that he spotted two additional carriers steaming at 145° at 25 knots. The Americans had found Nagumo's Striking Force, the power of the Japanese fleet. A gloomy mood must have descended on Nagumo's bridge that morning.
Task Force 61's humdrum morning changed when the sighting reports of the Japanese fleet began

arriving. Kinkaid, still obeying Halsey's orders by steaming on a northwesterly course toward the Santa Cruz Islands, observed the *Enterprise*'s launch of search planes as the *Hornet* prepared an air strike. Kinkaid heard a relay of Sesso's 9:48 a.m. sighting of two battleships, two heavy cruisers, two light cruisers, and four destroyers about 150 miles northeast of Guadalcanal 25 minutes after it had been sent. Task Force 61 was still out of range, 375 miles away. He could do nothing at this stage and soon expected to hear sightings of the Japanese carriers.

After landing the *Enterprise*'s three extra SBDs and two F4Fs, the *Hornet*'s aircraft complement now stood at 85 planes: 38 F4Fs, 31 SBDs, and 16 TBFs. However, her deck could only hold 33 F4Fs, 24 SBDs, and 16 TBFs and still conduct air operations. The remaining 12 planes—five F4Fs and seven SBDs—stayed on the hangar deck. The *Enterprise* had a similar situation with its 90 aircraft—36 F4Fs, 41 SBDs, and 13 TBFs. For the same reason the *Hornet* had, only 69 aircraft—29 F4Fs, 27 SBDs, and 13 TBFs—that could be on-deck with the other 21 planes—seven F4Fs and 4 SBDs—stored below in the hangar deck. Of course, the air crews for the stored planes' were inactive as well. Halsey's October 24 order that no spare carrier planes could be sent to reinforce a land airbase further restricted Kinkaid's freedom of action.

Another mishap occurred that showed one reason this policy was not a good one when one of the *Enterprise*'s F4Fs flying CAP had a mechanical failure. The stressed pilot forgot to drop his landing gear when he tried to land, crashed into the planes parked on the carrier's landing deck, and damaged five planes. The damage control parties immediately went to work to clear the wreckage. While they worked as fast as they could, the *Enterprise* could not conduct any air operations. Kinkaid's worries increased because of the Japanese ships he already knew about steamed to his task force's west.

Adding fuel to his apprehension, the *Enterprise* received one of Lampshire's messages at 11:50 a.m. forwarded from Espiritu Santo. Two carriers and supporting ships were now steaming—speed: 25 knots, course: 145º—about 130 miles northwest of Sesso's first sighting and heading straight for Task Force 61. Kinkaid's staff calculated the Japanese carriers' location to be 355 miles away on a bearing of 287º. The Japanese carriers were also 250 miles northeast of Guadalcanal and well within striking distance of Henderson Field. When Halsey learned of the presence of the Japanese carriers, he did not hesitate to issue an order that became enshrined in history: "Strike, Repeat, Strike." There was more to that message that specifically stated what Halsey wanted to have done: "COMSOPAC sends Action CTF61 and 64."[7]

✲ ✲ ✲

The two forces rapidly closed the range with each other. An afternoon air strike *by both sides* was soon to be a realistic possibility. Nevertheless, Task Force 61 had to turn 180º into the southeasterly wind before launching its planes. This course change increased the closing distance to the Japanese and forced Kinkaid to delay his launch until he was well within range before turning into the wind. He ordered an increase in speed to 27 knots to get closer.

The *Enterprise*'s Air Group 10 lacked the combat experience the *Hornet*'s air group had. Whether Kinkaid knew that fact or not, he wanted to send Air Group 10 instead of *Hornet*'s aircraft, now ready for launch on-deck, to attack the Japanese. Perhaps it was the larger wing tanks on the *Enterprise* F4Fs that gave them a longer range than *Hornet*'s fighters that entered his thoughts as he made that decision. Of course, we will never know what prompted him to decide that way. Nonetheless, the decision would have a definite effect during the upcoming battle.

Meanwhile, Nagumo turned northward to take his ships out of striking range. He sent out four *Zuikaku* Kates and followed Abe when he also turned to the north at 1:00 p.m.

The Base Air Force found what they reported as two battleships, four heavy cruisers, one light cruiser, and at least 12 destroyers about 30 miles east of Rennell Island, Lee's Task Force 64, at 2:15 p.m. Lee steamed northward from Espiritu Santo and intended to stop any more runs of the Tokyo Express. Kondo wanted to attack Lee, now 340 miles away, but Nagumo balked. Nagumo did not believe there would be any combat that day. But he did not think for the Americans.

Kinkaid sent out 12 SBDs at 1:36 p.m. led by Lt. Cmdr. James R. Lee to search a 280°-010° sector ahead of the task force. Their mission was to locate the Japanese ships for a planned 35-plane (16 F4Fs, 12 SBDs, and eight TBFs) strike force that would leave one hour later with Air Group 10's CAG, Cmdr. Richard K. Gaines, going along to evaluate the attack in accordance with standing COMSOPAC policy put into place in July. Lt. Cmdr. James Thomas flew his SBD into the lead and, as senior squadron commander, took command of the strike. But the plan began to unravel when the strike group took off at 2:08 p.m. with just 11 F4Fs equipped with wing tanks. Three F4Fs flown by Ensigns M. Philip Long, Donald Gordon, and Lynn E. Slagle missed the rendezvous point and had to return to the carrier. The fighter escort dwindled to just eight planes. Only five SBDs instead of 12 and six out of seven TBFs carrying torpedoes made it into the air. Gaines followed in the rear carrying no torpedoes. Kinkaid's intended range limit of 150 miles while authorizing a 200-mile search became a source of confusion.

After the last plane left the *Enterprise* at 2:25 p.m., Thomas quickly formed the strike group, comprising just 22 instead of the planned 35 planes. The planes climbed toward the sun. The clear blue sky offered excellent visibility and good flying weather. After the fighters reached 17,000 feet with the dive-bombers and torpedo planes flying at a lower altitude, Thomas turned the group on a 287° bearing, which was near the search sector's western edge instead of on a bearing of about 325°, which was the sector's mid-bearing. One possible explanation of this decision might have been Thomas thinking that the Japanese ships still were closing on Task Force 61 at high speed. If this was the case, their best chance was to take the shortest path to the anticipated spot where the Japanese would likely be, at the sector's southernmost edge. Blissfully ignorant of other events occurring around them, Air Group 10 continued on its way to an uncertain outcome.

Meanwhile, 1st Lt. John H. Buie's second flight of B-17s caught up with Abe's Vanguard Force at 2:30 p.m. steaming northward at 25 knots. At ten minutes past three o'clock, the B-17s came over Abe's ships and dropped their loads on the battleship *Kirishima* from 15,000 feet. Just like other attempts to drops bombs from a high altitude on moving ships attempted earlier in the war, the bombs hit nothing but water as the ships moved out of the way of the dropping missiles. Three Zeroes attacked the bombers and claimed one B-17. But all bombers returned safely to Espiritu Santo after reporting that the Japanese were not heading south, but moving in the opposite direction. After receiving this information from Nouméa, Kinkaid realized that his strike group had no chance at all to catch up with the Japanese. He was unhappy about not receiving the message soon enough to prevent sending the strike group out in the first place. He assumed that Thomas would remember to limit his search to 150 miles and return to base if he did not see any Japanese ships, but Kinkaid did not want to break radio silence to recall the planes.

Thomas' group continued to fly on the same bearing and, when reaching Kinkaid's assumed search limit of 150 miles from the *Enterprise* and finding no Japanese ships, decided to continue searching and continue to look for the Japanese until he reached the original 200-mile limit. He turned northward for 80 miles and again saw nothing. Realizing his planes continued to burning precious fuel with no results, he finally turned to the southeast toward Task Force 61. But the darkening sky and dwindling fuel supplies now greatly concerned both Thomas and Gaines. The *Enterprise* believed the planes would return at 5:35 p.m. at sunset. But they would not make that schedule.

The planes tried to follow the carrier's homing beacon as darkness descended upon the ocean below. An experienced ex-SBD pilot now flying an F4F, Lt. Frederick (Fritz) L. Faulkner, knew the homing beacon was less accurate as the planes got closer to the carrier. He tried leading the fighters on the corrected course toward the *Enterprise*. But he lost the other fighters in the dark and eventually landed safely. The rest of the fighters flew in the black night by following the glowing exhausts of their comrades' planes. Forty miles to the northwest of Task Force 61's position, Lt. Frank Don Miller's F4F engine quit and, waving farewell to Ens. Maurice N. Wickendoll, Miller bailed out into the dark sea below and disappeared. He was never found.

As the SBDs descended to a lower altitude, their pilots dropped their 1,000-pound bombs with one of them exploding in the water. The flash revealed an oil slick to an alert Lt. Stanley W. Vejtasa, who remembered that the *Enterprise* leaking a small amount of oil when he took off earlier that afternoon. Correctly reasoning that following the oil trail would get his fellow pilots home, the planes arrived over Task Force 61 at 6:30 p.m. They had to land at night, a feat that many of the pilots had never previously done.

Despite the *Enterprise* displaying lighted wands and sending a blinker lamp message that the fuel-thirsty fighters should land first, chaos reigned as pilots cut in front of each other trying to land. LSO Lt. Robin M. Lindsey guided the fighters onboard but the process took a long time because of many wave-offs. Vejtasa almost collided with another F4F that tried to land at the same time. One SBD pilot ran out of fuel and had to ditch at 7:05 p.m. Another SBD flown by Ens. Jefferson H. Carroum ignored Lindsey's wave-off signals, landed too high, and crashed into the carrier's island in a ball of flame, and smashed the tail of Ens. Robert D. Gibson's SBD. Both dive-bombers were totally disabled from any further combat. The other planes that still circled had to wait to clear the deck while burning scarce fuel. One TBF landed short of the flight deck and crashed into the carrier's wake. Still in the landing pattern, the last two TBFs exhausted their fuel at 7:27 p.m. and crashed into the water. Two more SBDs and three more TBFs also ran out of fuel and had to ditch. Destroyers rescued all the air crews except for one aircrewman, Sea1c Arthur M. Browning.

The calamitous *Enterprise* first strike resulted in two deaths and the loss of one F4F, four SBDs, and three TBFs. The confusion between the aircrews and Task Force 61's staff over the whereabouts of the Japanese ships repeated the same mistakes that happened at the Battle of Midway. Lt. Cmdr. James H. Flatley, the *Enterprise* fighter squadron's commanding officer, believed that Task Force 61 should have closed the range before launching the air strike. However, Kinkaid never talked to the air commanders, which was the standard operating procedure aboard American carriers at that time because these men did not report to the admiral but to the carrier commanding officer.

A time of quiet descended onto the waters north of Santa Cruz. Now commanders of both sides got ready for the next day's battle.

✲ ✲ ✲

Nagumo and Kondo separately planned for dawn searches on October 26. They turned south again, Kondo at 7:00 p.m. and Nagumo at 8:00 p.m. Abe moved his Vanguard Force to position his ships 60 miles ahead of Nagumo. The Striking Force carriers moved their planes on deck to be ready to takeoff for their search and first strike. The *Shokaku*'s and *Zuikaku*'s hangar decks bristled with frenzied activity as the crews armed and fueled more planes for their second strike.

Fitch, fearing an air strike, ordered all available F4Fs on Éfaté to fly to Espiritu Santo. With four fighter pilots on their way to Hawaii, only eight F4Fs could respond to that order. He wanted to send some of the fighters to CACTUS the next day. He sent a PBY "Black Cat" and five PBYs armed with bombs and torpedoes to search in a 325°-350° sector out to 500 miles. Fitch also ordered ten PBYs and six B-17s to take off at 3:30 a.m. to search at sunrise.

Task Force 61's first strike debacle left Kinkaid's air strength in disarray. Air Group 10 had lost 12 aircraft—two F4Fs, seven SBDs, and three TBFs—with three SBD and two TBF crews stranded on the *Hornet*. Kinkaid placed four spare F4Fs into operation thus raising the *Enterprise*'s effective fighter strength to 31. The dive-bomber and torpedo plane squadrons now only had 23 bombers and ten torpedo planes. Cmdr. John G. Crommelin, the *Enterprise*'s air commander, called a meeting of all pilots and gave them an outstanding pep talk. One of the pilots reflected his fellow pilots' heightened morale when he said, "If you get back to the ship and into the groove, we'll get you aboard!"

As the full moon rose over the water, Kinkaid ordered the *Hornet*'s air group to be ready for a night strike if Fitch's search found the Japanese. He ordered a course change to the northwest on a bearing of 305° degrees at a speed of 22 knots. The *Hornet*'s pilots greeted the orders with some apprehension but were relieved when later orders cancelled the night mission.

✲ ✲ ✲

Both sides girded themselves for the next day's battle. Halsey knew he was risking two-thirds of the American carrier strength but felt he had no choice but to defend the American ground troops on Guadalcanal at all costs. The Japanese, as they had at Midway, had superior strength in carriers and carrier aircraft. It would be four carriers against two with mixed results.[8]

CHAPTER 32
The Japanese Feel the Heat

Finding Each Other's Forces

Lt. (jg) George S. Clute flew his radar-equipped PBY in the nearly cloudless sky over the ocean on the night of October 25-26. The full, bright moon reflected off the sea below and shimmered on the water. It was a perfect night to search for ships. He and the other PBY pilots had been aloft that evening to look for Japanese ships the American senior naval officers knew were not far away from Kinkaid's Task Force 61. The number one question was: Were they near enough to attack with carrier aircraft?

Clute and his crew had binoculars nearly glued to their eyes as they scanned the ocean ahead, to the left, and right. His radar operator peered into the display tube while looking for telltale blips on the screen that could mean that the radar's beam had reflected off the hulls of ships on the ocean beneath them. Around midnight, the echoes of the radar beam showed as blips on the scope. After flying a few minutes more, Clute confirmed the sighting and ordered his radio operator to report the sighting to Espiritu Santo. Task Force 61 received a message at 12:01 a.m. on October 26 that reported sighting "the enemy" about 300 miles northwest of Kinkaid's position, well beyond American carrier plane striking distance.

Just 24 minutes later, Clute sent another report saying he had attacked heavy cruisers with his torpedoes producing uncertain results. Actually the ship Clute tried to torpedo was the destroyer *Isokaze*, which was part of the screening escort for Adm. Abe's Vanguard Force that steamed 20 miles south of Nagumo's Striking Force. The PBY's attack somewhat unnerved Nagumo, who wondered if the Americans had sighted his carriers. He should not have wasted time thinking about it. The Americans had found his carriers, and Nagumo finally came to that realization at 2:50 a.m. when another PBY piloted by Lt. Glen E. Hoffman attacked the *Zuikaku*. Four 500-pound bombs fell from the patrol plane and one of them exploded in the water just 300 meters away. Trying to blind the Japanese antiaircraft crews by dropping a bright-red flare, Hoffman escaped unscathed.

Adm. Nagumo must have felt it was history about to repeat itself when he ran out of the flag plot room at 3:30 a.m. to order his task force to turn around 180°. He sent his strike planes below to the *Zuikaku*'s and *Shokaku*'s hangar decks to disarm them and drain their fuel tanks. Any second strike that he wanted to send to attack the American carriers would be delayed. His new plan was to continue steaming north, order a search for the American carriers before sunrise, find them, and attack them.

The Japanese Feel the Heat

Meanwhile, Abe's Vanguard Force arrived at a point 250 miles northeast of Guadalcanal. He sent seven reconnaissance planes from the cruisers *Tone* and *Chikuma* to look for the American battleship force believed to be located south of Guadalcanal.

Nagumo's three carriers then went into action. Men swarmed over the flight decks. Some of them worked on the hangar decks and moved planes onto the elevators to bring the machines up to the flight deck. More had red-colored flashlights in their hands to guide planes on the flight deck into takeoff positions. Others directed planes into the departure queue.

The admiral ordered all planes to get ready to search in an eastward 050°-230° on 300-mile-long sectors. Thirteen planes including four Vals from the *Shokaku*, four more from the *Zuikaku*, and five more from the *Zuiho* took off at 4:45 a.m., about one hour before sunrise. After the decks cleared of the search planes, 22 Zeroes to fly CAP and 70 attack planes, a powerful force of 92 aircraft, filled the three carriers' flight decks for the first strike. Nagumo, now displaying his normal indecisiveness, paced on the *Shokaku*'s flag bridge wearing his snow-white gloves. Finally, the *Zuiho* launched its first three-plane CAP at 5:20 a.m. and led by Lt. Masao Sato, a former officer from the sunken *Kaga*.

Task Force 61 steamed on a northwesterly course in a gently rolling sea. Scattered low clouds dotted the skies, a common occurrence for a fair day in South Pacific seas. A southeasterly eight-knot breeze wafted over the ships' upper decks and raised ripples on the sea that changed its surface texture to smooth sandpaper. The 5:23 a.m. sunrise changed the sea color from black to gray to blue. The weather was perfect for what would fall upon the American and Japanese navies that day, intense dive-bomber attacks.

While the *Hornet* stood by as Task Force 61's secondary naval air attack carrier, Kinkaid had ordered the *Enterprise* to turn into the wind a little past 5:00 a.m. to launch his CAP. Twelve minutes later, seven F4Fs lifted off in the darkness. Sixteen SBDs took off and flew in pairs to search the western sector from 235° to 000° out to 200 miles. In the event any of them found a Japanese ship, each dive-bomber carried one 500-pound bomb. The last four SBDs flew antisubmarine patrol around the task force perimeter. As the sun rose at 5:51 a.m., the *Hornet* added eight F4Fs to the CAP.

Kinkaid received Hoffman's 3:10 a.m. sighting report at 5:12 a.m., a delay of more than two hours. that said, "One large carrier, six other vessels on a southerly course, speed 10."[1] The intolerably late arrival of this critical sighting of the Japanese was the first indication of severe communications problems that would be encountered during this battle. After the battle, Halsey remarked that this was an example of a "serious communications delinquency."[2] Kinkaid also stated later that if he had learned of Hoffman's sighting report earlier, he would have reduced the number of planes he sent out and saved these critical bombers for the attack on the Japanese carriers. He did not believe the Japanese knew of Task Force 61's whereabouts.

Cautiously mindful that he had two-thirds of the remaining American carrier strength under his command and of the earlier losses of the *Lexington* at Coral Sea, the *Yorktown* at Midway, and the *Wasp* to a Japanese submarine's torpedo attack, Kinkaid kept *Hornet*'s planes at a ready status and did not send them out with *Enterprise*'s planes despite the urging of Capt. Edward P. ("Country") Moore, his chief of staff, and other staff members. Thus, the circumspect Kinkaid gave up the chance that

Spruance had at Midway, to attack the Japanese carriers with their decks loaded with fully armed and fueled planes.

Two of *Enterprise*'s SBD search planes piloted by Lt. Vivien W. Welch, and Lt. (jg) Bruce A. McGraw flew on a westward course in a 266º-282º sector when they sighted a Kate approaching them, obviously doing what they were doing. The Japanese bomber was from the *Shokaku* and flying on a 125º bearing from the Japanese carriers. Welch and McGraw ignored the Japanese plane and continued on their mission, flying west. At 6:17 a.m., they saw a large and obviously powerful group of ships that they reported to be two battleships, one heavy cruiser, and seven destroyers steaming on a 275º bearing, 170 miles from Task Force 61 and moving at a speed of 20 knots on a northward course. When Kinkaid received their message at 6:39 a.m., he knew the Japanese ships were nearby. The SBD pilots flew the rest of their mission and began their return leg. They passed the Japanese plane they had seen earlier that was also was on its return leg.

Upon seeing the American planes and realizing that the Americans had found his ships, Abe increased his force's speed to 30 knots and turned left to 300º to move away from any planes that should follow the ones he had seen. Lt.s (jg) Howard R. Burnett and Kenneth R. Miller, flying at 14,000 feet in 282º-298º sector next to where Welch and McGraw were, spotted Abe at 6:45 a.m. and banked their planes into a turning dive. Each dropped their 500-pound bomb. Both missed the cruiser *Tone,* but Burnett's SBD took minor hits.

Lt. Cmdr. James R. (Bucky) Lee and Lt. (jg) William E. Johnson flew at 6:45 a.m. in the 298º-314º sector north of Burnett and McGraw when they saw Nagumo's Striking Force. They circled while Lee radioed Task Force 61 at 6:50 a.m. that they had seen one carrier steaming on a 330º course at a speed of 15 knots. After circling for another 15 minutes, Lee reported seeing two more carriers. For some strange, unknown reason, neither pilot received any acknowledgment that Task Force 61 had heard their reports. Nonetheless, the Americans had found all three of Nagumo's carriers.

The Americans Launch Their Attack

Since their current northward course caused Kinkaid's task force to open the range to the Japanese ships, he ordered a course change to 330º and launched a strike from the *Enterprise* and *Hornet*. Task Force 61 turned at 7:08 a.m.; three minutes later the cruiser *Northampton* sent a message using its flags that its radar had spotted an unknown contact 28 miles away on a 200º bearing. The contact moved to within 20 miles. The *South Dakota* broke radio silence at 7:37 a.m. and used the TBS to report its radio operators had heard Japanese voices over the airways. Again, none of these reports ever reached Kinkaid.

The *Hornet*'s eight F4Fs, 15 SBDs, and six TBFs originally planned for a midnight strike still stood on the carrier's flight deck with eight F4Fs, nine SBDs, and ten TBFs languishing below in her hangar deck. The squadrons' teletype machines broke the silence at 7:14 a.m. reporting that a Japanese carrier task force just 196 miles away on a 302º bearing. The messages on the machines ended with the words, "Pilots man planes — Good luck." The pilots, their plotting boards in their hands, clambered out of their ready rooms and ran to their planes parked on the flight deck. Action at last!

Task Force 17 turned into the wind and, at 7:32 a.m., began launching *Hornet*'s planes. Eleven minutes later, the last of the 29 planes on the flight deck lifted off. Lt. Cmdr. William J. Widhelm led the 15 SBDs while Lt. Cmdr. Henry G. Sanchez commanded the four F4Fs that made up the group's escort. Both men were veterans of carrier air warfare and had seen plenty of action while serving on the now-defunct *Wasp*. Lt. John C. Bower's four F4Fs escorted Lt. Edwin B. Parker's six TBFs. All F4Fs carried a large 42-gallon belly tank so that they could escort their charges to the target and back home. Meanwhile, pilots climbed into the second strike's planes and started their engines below in the carrier's hangar deck.

Murray returned Task Force 17 to its original course of 330º as the *Hornet*'s deck crew brought the planes onto the flight deck. The specter of an impending Japanese air attack forced Murray to separate the two groups of planes. Thus, Widhelm directed the first strike on a 210-mile leg at a 300º course. If everything went according to plan, he and his charges would return to the *Hornet* by 11:00 a.m.

Soon afterward, the *Enterprise* also turned into the wind at 7:47 a.m. and launched an additional CAP of 11 F4Fs. Since the "Big E" had the responsibility for CAP and searches, the carrier could only contribute 21 planes to Task Force 61's strike force with the major striking power coming from Lt. Cmdr. John A. Collett's nine torpedo planes. So to provide even a modicum of dive-bombing power, Capt. Osborne B. Hardison, the *Enterprise* commanding officer, assigned three SBDs led by Lt. (jg) George Glen Estes to the carrier's contribution. Jim Flatley, not one to let a broken foot stop him from flying, gingerly climbed into his F4F to lead an eight-fighter escort with each F4F carrying a 58-gallon external fuel tank.

The *Enterprise* launched Flatley's eight F4Fs first at about 7:50 a.m. followed by Collett's eight TBFs and Estes' three SBDs. The carrier's CAG, Cmdr. Richard K. Gaines, led the force in his unarmed TBF. As each pilot taxied their plane to the takeoff point on the flight deck, two signs greeted them, one saying "Proceed without Hornet" and the other stating the Japanese ships' speed at 7:30 a.m. was 25 knots. The message on the first card directly contradicted Kinkaid's verbal orders that Task Force 61's aircraft would work together. As the *Enterprise*'s planes finished rendezvousing after leaving their carrier's flight deck after 8:00 a.m., Flatley saw Widhelm's first strike pass them and thought that it was a bad idea not combining planes from the two carriers into one coordinated strike.

Ten minutes after launching its first strike, the *Hornet* circled into the wind to launch its second strike. The first plane revved up its engine and began to move down the flight deck in less than two minutes. The strike's power was to come from Lt. John J. Lynch's nine SBDs, each carrying one 1,000-pound bomb. Nine TBFs led by Lt. Ward F. Powell joined the striking group with each carrying four 500-pound bombs instead of their normal load of one more powerful torpedo. Seven F4Fs carried belly-mounted fuel tanks. There was not enough time for the *Hornet* to launch another strike so only seven fighters could escort the formation. Cmdr. Walter F. Rodee, the *Hornet*'s CAG, was in overall command of this strike in his unarmed TBF. His planned return was one-half hour later than Widhelm's. The uncoordinated, haphazardly organized Task Force 61 air strike was on its way to hit the Japanese carriers.

The Japanese Air Attack Begins

Warrant Officer Tadaaki Ukita flew his aircraft at 6:10 a.m. through low clouds on a 110° heading from the *Shokaku* when he looked below him. Several ships, which could only be American in this part of the ocean, appeared on the horizon in the early dawn's light. The poor visibility made an accurate identification of the number and types of ships difficult. The ships were on a northerly heading so he turned on a parallel course to follow them. He did not know that the *Northampton*'s radar had detected him. He quickly radioed that there was one *Saratoga*-class carrier and 15 other ships on a 125° heading and 210 miles from Nagumo's carriers. The admiral received the message at 6:58 a.m. and grateful for at least one American carrier to attack. Ukita sent an incorrect identification but, nonetheless, Nagumo immediately acted. He ordered his three carriers to launch their first strike. He also wanted to make sure of the sighting by sending a *Shokaku*-based search plane to fly a 140° course, confirm Ukita's sighting, and maybe finding more American ships.

The First Carrier Division pilots received a short briefing before scrambling to the planes. The carrier crews cheered lustily as the planes moved down the fight decks and lifted into the air, a repeat of the sendoffs the pilots received when they took off for Pearl Harbor and Midway. The *Shokaku*'s search plane was the first to leave at 7:10 a.m. Lt. Hisayoshi Miyajima's four escort Zeroes and Lt. Cmdr. Shigeharu Murata's 20 torpedo-carrying Kate bombers followed immediately with Murata commanding the strike. Five minutes later, the *Zuiho* launched five CAP Zeroes, Lt. Saneyasu Hidaka's nine escorting Zeroes, and one unarmed Kate to act as a radio relay. The *Zuikaku* contributed Lt. Ayao Shirane's eight escort Zeroes, Lt. Sadamu Takahashi's 21 Val dive-bombers, with one Kate to act as a tracker.

Murata's planes and Hidaka's fighters left at 7:30 a.m., giving them a 25-minute head start over Task Force 61's air strikes. Takahashi's *Zuikaku*-based group left ten minutes later and soon rendezvoused with Murata. Nagumo's Striking Force had 64 planes aloft: 21 fighters, 21 dive-bombers, and 22 torpedo planes.

Now that all of the flight decks were empty, the *Zuikaku*'s deck crew began bringing their second strike planes up from the hangar deck. Despite the fact that Nagumo had 21 fighters flying CAP and the *Shokaku*'s radar operators staring intently into their monitors, there was no warning when two of the *Enterprise*'s SBDs flown by Lt. Stockton Birney Strong and Ens. Charles B. Irvine attacked. The two pilots had been cruising for about 80 miles on the southwesterly leg of their assigned 330°-345° sector search when they spied a Japanese carrier and climbed to 14,000 feet to hide behind some intermittent clouds.

Strong and Irvine followed the carrier until the two bombers were in a position to begin their attack. The two fliers rolled their bombers over at 7:40 a.m. and dove toward what they believed to be a *Shokaku*-class carrier. As their airspeed increased, the sound roared past their windshields. Both pilots lined up the carrier's flight deck in their sights. As the deck loomed so large that it nearly took the whole view in their sights, they pulled their planes' bomb release levers. Two 500-pound bombs precipitously dropped at a nearly vertical trajectory toward the ship.

One bomb smacked into the *Zuiho*'s flight deck and exploded in a ball of fire and smoke. A cavernous 15-meter-wide hole suddenly appeared. A huge fire ignited that blew up three Zeroes parked on the flight deck and destroyed the carrier's arresting gear. All landing operations on the *Zuiho* ceased. Her planes would have to either land on another carrier or splash down in the water. Nagumo really did have another reason to be worried.

After releasing their bombs, the two SBDs pulled out of their dives near the water's surface. Eager to avenge the attack on the *Zuiho,* three *Zuikaku* Zeroes led by Lt. (jg) Hiroshi Yoshimura jumped on the American dive-bombers. The three fighters stayed on the SBDs' tails for about 45 miles, but could not get their pound of flesh. Both of the bombers' radiomen, ARM1c Clarence H. Garlow in Strong's plane and ARM3c Elgie P. Williams in Irvine's plane, fired their machine guns during the tormenting chase and claimed shooting down two Zeroes. One of them flown by Sea1c Koichi Nakagami did not return to the *Zuikaku.* During the pursuit and more importantly, Garlow sent a report to the *Enterprise* that the two SBDs had hit a Japanese carrier. Again demonstrating the communications failure that would plague the Americans in this and other battles to come, only a few American ships ever heard the message.

The *Zuikaku*'s and the *Shokaku*'s deck crews immediately stopped fueling aircraft and labored to push at their refueling carts over the side. Then the *Shokaku*'s deck crew feverishly prepared the carrier's second strike for takeoff. The force included Abe's three Zeroes flying CAP, five Zeroes led by the carrier's fighter squadron commander, Lt. Hideki Shingo, and Lt. Cmdr. Mamoru Seki's 20 Val dive-bombers. Meanwhile, the *Zuikaku*'s air officer delayed that carrier strike force takeoff because he ordered his 14 Kates rearmed with torpedoes instead of bombs. While the crews desperately wrestled with the heavy torpedoes, the *Zuikaku* landed her four-plane Kate search group with two of them being saved for the upcoming strike.

Nagumo decided to launch the *Shokaku*'s strike with the *Zuikaku*'s planes following later when they became ready. The first *Shokaku* plane took off at 8:10 a.m. Eight minutes later, the formation formed while one "Val" had to abort because of mechanical problems. Seki now had only 19 bombers in his strike group.

Japanese activity was not solely isolated to Nagumo's Striking Force. Kondo's Advance Force and Abe's Vanguard Force cruised far to the south of the Striking Force. Kondo's force steamed farther to the south of Abe's while closing the distance toward the American carriers. His lone carrier, the *Junyo,* would soon be within long range striking distance. Kondo ordered Abe at 7:40 a.m. to attack the American ships at the location reported by the *Shokaku*'s search planes. Abe changed his course at 9:25 a.m. to due east. The Vanguard Force separated into two groups with Abe commanding the battleships *Kirishima* and *Hiei,* heavy cruiser *Suzuya,* light cruiser *Nagara,* and destroyers *Akigumo, Makikumo, Yugumo, Kazegumo.* Radm. Chuichi Hara steamed to Abe's southeast commanding the heavy cruisers *Tone* and *Chikuma* and destroyers *Tanikaze* and *Urakaze.* Once their carrier planes sank the American carriers, these battleships, cruisers, and destroyers would move in for the kill and destroy what remained of the American Fleet.

Baptism to Aerial Combat

Task Force 61's three divided flights totaling 75 aircraft flew their inexorable path toward Nagumo's carriers. Widhelm's 15 SBDs and Sanchez's four F4Fs from the *Hornet* were in front as they slowly climbed to 12,000 feet. The rest of that carrier's ten planes—Parker's six TBFs and Bower's escorting four F4Fs—disappeared behind scattered clouds so that their comrades could not see them. Bower's fighters flew a few thousand feet above Parker whose TBFs skimmed the water's surface.

Ens. Phillip E. Souza's F4F brought up the Widhelm formation's rear as lookout for Japanese planes. Before long, he performed that task quite well. At about 8:30 a.m. and approximately 75 miles northwest of Task Force 17, he looked to his right and observed several planes flying toward the *Hornet*. With a combined closing speed of about 400 miles-per-hour, the approaching planes almost passed without being seen by the SBDs. Souza immediately recognized the planes unmistakable silhouettes—they were definitely Japanese. He just as quickly picked up his radio microphone and called Sanchez and his section leader, Lt. Thomas Johnson. Sanchez unhesitatingly alerted Task Force 61, "24 dive-bombers RED BASE. Approach. Standby for bombing attack."[3] He never knew whether anyone received his message since no one acknowledged it. The Japanese planes flew a few thousand feet above the Americans from the southeast and were part of Murata's 20 *Shokaku*-based bombers escorted by 13 Zeroes. Murata also saw the American planes and radioed a warning to Nagumo that 15 American planes were on their way to attack the admiral's ships. Takahashi's bombers and Shirane's fighters flew too high to see the American planes.

The 20-plane *Enterprise* strike group (Air Group 10) was on a course a few miles east and nearly parallel to but five minutes behind Widhelm's strike force. Leading the way were Estes' three SBDs in a slight climb. Two divisions of four TBFs each flew behind Estes with the first led by Collett and the second led by Lt. MacDonald Thompson flying behind and just to the left of Estes' formation. Optimizing the firepower of their two rearward firing and two forward facing guns, each division's formation was in the newly adopted "box-step down formation" with three TBFs flying in a "Vee" while the fourth flew to the rear and below the other three. Flatley's four F4Fs flew cover on the formation's right and Lt. (jg) John A. Leppla's four fighters on the group's left. Gaines' unarmed TBF flew just above and followed Collett's TBFs as the strike group's commander. Because the SBDs were the slowest planes, the TBFs and F4Fs flew in wide S-turns to reduce their effective forward air speed to 120 knots.

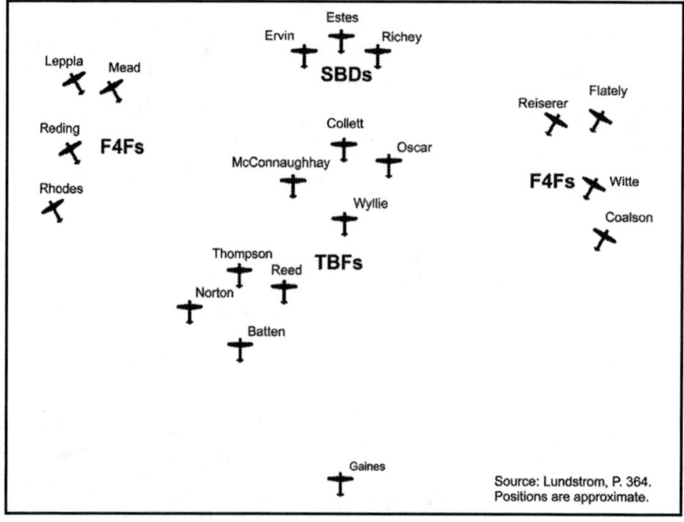

Air Group 10's Formation

They had flown 60 miles since leaving the *Enterprise* when the SBDs and Collett's TBFs climbed past 6,000 feet and were now higher than the still S-turning F4Fs. Gaines rose to 9,000 feet so that he could see all of his command in front of him. With their radios still silent, no one heard Sanchez's warning.

Hidaka's formation from the *Zuiho* was at 14,000 feet when he saw American planes coming directly toward him on an almost head-on collision course. After missing the chance to attack Widhelm's formation, the approaching target presented an irresistible opportunity to inflict considerable damage. Assuming the risk of leaving his assignment escorting Murata's planes and because he believed his attack would not take too much time, he ordered his nine Zeroes into a single line. He already had the advantage of a higher altitude and had much to feel optimistic about since his attack came out of the sun. Hidaka turned his Zeroes in a wide 180° turn to get on the American planes' rear.

The Zeroes rolled into a steep turn as Hidaka lined his gunsight on the leading TBF. The American plane was in his gunsight cross-hairs when he squeezed the trigger. Red tracers and cannon shells darted toward the TBF.

Taken off guard, Collett suddenly felt and heard a fusillade of shells pummel his plane. Flames erupted in his cockpit and from the plane's engine as the craft shook itself apart. With the wind whipping past his canopy, he forced it open and climbed out on the right wing. Making sure he was clear of the flames, he jumped off toward the water below. His radioman, ARM1c Thomas C. Nelson, Jr., was at his assigned station below the turret when he felt the TBF tremble and looked out of the port-side glass port and noticing Collett's wingman, Ens. Robert E. Oscar, looking at the stricken plane with a facial expression of "sheer horror."[4] The doomed TBF rolled to the right and began a deadly downward spiral. Nelson knew he was in severe danger as he rapidly put on his chute and desperately kicked the side door open. He dropped into the air and opened his parachute as soon as he was clear. A Zero tried to shoot at him but he managed to safely land in the water. AM1c Stephen Nadison, Jr., the plane's radioman, did not escape and listed later as missing in action, presumed dead.

Most of the Americans never saw the attacking Japanese fighters but some managed to fight back. Some of the TBF turret gunners lined up their sights at PO3c Shizuta Takagi's Zero and blasted away with their .50-cal. guns. As Takagi dove at the American torpedo planes from the starboard quarter, tracers poured into his Zero. The engine exploded in flames, and the plane abruptly swerved to the left. Despite falling in a fatal dive, Takagi could still fire his cannons at Lt. Marvin D. ("Doc") Norton's TBF and punch several holes in its right wing. Norton's turret gunner, AMM3c Robert W. Gruebel, fired back. He saw the Zero "pull up about 50 or 75 feet above the flight and explode in a fireball"[5]above Lt. (jg) Richard K. Batten's TBF. Pieces from the demolished Zero tore holes into one of Batten's elevators.

Collett's squadron credited the kill to AM2c Rexford B. Holmgrin, who was Batten's turret gunner.

ARM3c Murray Glasser, a crewman on Ens. John M. Reed's TBF, turned his gun toward the attacking Zeroes as he heard and saw pieces of his plane's canopy zip past his turret. Reed yelled into the intercom to bail out. Realizing the deadly threat to his life, Glasser climbed below into the radio compartment, threw a parachute to radioman ARM3c Morse Grant Harrison, took another chute for himself, and clambered into it. He "opened the hatch, backed out, pulled the ripcord, and floated on down."[6] As he fell, he saw his plane explode in a ball of flame. Neither Harrison nor Reed escaped. ARM3c Charles E. Shinneman, the lower compartment's gunner on Thompson's TBF, saw the engine from Reed's ill-fated plane zip by his plane's wingtip—its propeller still spinning. Just before Glasser hit the water, a Zero hit the surface just below his feet.

Three Zeroes flown by WO Masaaki Kawahara, PO1c Masaichi Kondo, and Sea2c Yasuhiro Nakamura attacked. Batten's plane, the nearest target to the attacking Zeroes, bore the brunt of the assault. Shinneman had a front row seat to what happened next. Japanese gunfire raked Batten's TBF. Shinneman saw holes tear inboard of its port wing "like live coals in a piece of paper." A fire from burning hydraulic fluid spread over the wing as its elevator abruptly stood up straight. Holmgrin yelled into the intercom, "Mr. Batten, our wing is on fire!" Batten unhesitatingly spoke into the plane's radio, "Get ready to jump, I'll put her in the water. V-11[7] landing in the water. I am on fire."[8] The critically damaged TBF dropped out of formation but miraculously remained airborne as its crippled elevator separated itself from the wing. The plane's bomb bay doors sprung open as its hydraulic system failed and did not allow Batten to rid his plane of its torpedo. He headed toward Task Force 61.

Some time passed before the F4F pilots realized the Japanese had attacked their charges. Leppla saw the last of Hidaka's fighters attacking the TBFs and maneuvered his flight to get on the Zeroes' tails as they finished their attacks. Ordering his F4Fs to drop their wing tanks, he banked his plane in a hard right turn toward the beleaguered TBFs. Ensigns Willis B. Reding and Raleigh E. "Dusty" Rhodes had mechanical problems releasing their wing tanks that caused their planes to rapidly lose altitude and they soon ended up at the same level as the torpedo planes. Ens. Albert E. Mead, Leppla's wingman, saw his dropping wing tank almost hit one F4F and then another. Leppla's intention to begin a mass attack fell apart. Mead and he managed to coordinate their movements by trying to attack the Zeroes tormenting the TBFs but to no avail. Hidaka and PO1c Jiro Mitsumoto caught the two F4Fs in their sights and opened fire. Reding and Rhodes were having too many problems to even think of joining in. Leppla's F4Fs had to fight for their very lives.

Meanwhile, Flatley's F4Fs were to the right side of Air Group 10's formation and had just finished their port side S-turn when they saw the unfolding debacle. Flatley looked in shock as he saw Collett, his classmate at Annapolis, plummet in flames while the Zeroes slaughtered Leppla's formation. PO3c Zenpei Matsumoto had just finished his attack when he turned to attack the leading American torpedo planes. Flatley ordered his flight to drop their wing tanks and rolled over to stop Matsumoto. He and the other three pilots, Lt. (jg) Russell L. Reiserer, Ens. Roland R. "Cliff" Witte, and Ens. Edward Coalson, fired their guns at the Zero. Matsumoto pulled his plane into a steep, twisting climb, but Flatley anticipated the Japanese pilot's maneuver. He and the rest of his F4Fs climbed above the Zero and attacked it from its rear topside. All four F4Fs fired their guns from long range. The Zero began to trail smoke as it leveled off, flying in a straight line. What an inviting target! Flatley and his charges continued to fire at the doomed Zero. Soon it dove toward the sea, trailing flames and smoke.

Lt. (jg) Shuichi Utsumi and PO1c Masao Kawasaki flew in Matsumoto's three-plane flight, suffered an uncertain short-term future this day. One of them decided to attack the TBFs a second time. "Doc" Norton examined the damage to his plane and what he saw was not good. Bullet holes riddled his right wing, and the hydraulic system was on the verge of failing. He notified Thompson that he was returning to the *Enterprise*. Dropping out of the formation, he was now alone and vulnerable. It did not take long for him to comprehend his defenselessness when Thompson radioed, "Zero coming up underneath us!" The Zero climbed toward the TBFs and loosed a barrage of tracer fire. The bullets missed as he impetuously closed to Norton's plane. Seeing a target of opportunity, Shinneman fired his machine gun at the Zero and later recalled:

> "At that time [the Zero] was underneath and behind us and was a sitting duck as he drifted away. I put about a half canister of .30s into his cockpit. He drifted away and fell off on a wing below us out of sight."[9]

Flatley soon realized that the mission was more important than dogfighting the Japanese Zeroes. He could not help Leppla anymore. Making one of most difficult decisions of his naval career, he ordered the remaining F4Fs to proceed as originally planned. Thompson acted in the same way when he reformed his TBFs behind the SBDs. The *Enterprise* strike groups still had five TBFs remaining aloft including Gaines' plane, three SBDs and four F4Fs.

Meanwhile, Mead and Leppla continued to battle the Zeroes. The Americans' situation became desperate. Leppla tested his guns and discovered he had only one working machine gun. Mead stayed with his leader, who may have been wounded, as he related later that Leppla, "seemed to fly straight ahead and I don't believe fired a shot. I shot for both of us and believe I got three." He actually shot down one Zero. But the two fighters' battle continued as 7.7-mm cannon fire that Mead remembered sounding like "popcorn popping" continued to hammer the planes. The cannon shells smacked into the extra thick armor plate behind his seat as they ripped his tail assembly. It did not take long before his cockpit's canopy and instruments shattered into shards of glass and metal cut into his ankle.

One Zero finally finished Mead's career as a naval combat pilot when it headed directly for his F4F, firing its cannons and rapidly closed the range. Mead's engine stopped working, and his plane headed for the water. Meanwhile, Leppla fought a losing battle trying to keep his plane flying straight and level. Rhodes saw one Zero move close to the doomed F4F while another came head on. No one saw Leppla bail out; he must have died in his plane. Mead, flying with a dead engine, landed in the water, scrambled out of his cockpit, and inflated his life raft as his plane sank. He climbed into it in comparative safety. A deafening silence surrounded him as he floated on the sea—a stark contrast from the scene he had just experienced.

Three Zeroes flown by Kawahara, Kondo, and Nakamura moved toward Reding and Rhodes for the kill. The two American pilots teamed up and put on a clinic on how to fly the "Thach Weave[10]," a fighter tactic developed by Lt. Cmdr. John S. Thach in 1942. But it was a hopelessly one-sided fight since they could not fire their guns. But their maneuvers confused the Japanese attackers when they chased one F4F only to be confronted by the other coming straight at them. The two American fighters continued to weave and lose altitude to 2,500 feet. Smoke came out of Rhodes' engine while his plane kept losing altitude. Realizing that it was fruitless to stay with his plane and remembering what he had learned in flying school to never bail out lower than 500 feet, he made the only decision he could. He later remembered what he did that day:

> "I had thought about that statement and what to do if one had to bail out at such a low altitude. I pushed the remains of the canopy aft, unsnapped the seat belt then stood up, kicked the stick and pulled the ripcord simultaneously. I was catapulted clear of the aircraft, and the parachute opened almost immediately, snapping my shoes off. At the bottom of the first swing I hit the water."[11]

After he was safely in the water, he inflated his life raft, and climbed into it, then finally realized he had a leg wound.

Reding saw Rhodes land in the water and was now alone with three viciously attacking Zeroes surrounding him with ill intent. He pushed the stick forward and put his plane into a steep dive. One Zero followed him down but gave up the chase when Reding leveled off at 100 feet. He pancaked the fatally damaged F4F in the water, climbed out on its wing, inflated the life raft, got into it, and joined Nelson, Glasser, and Mead floating in the ocean. Any chance of being rescued was miles from where they were. Reding also noted how quiet everything was. He heard only the water lapping on the bottom of his raft.

✲ ✲ ✲

The toll from this air battle shows that both sides sustained significant losses. The Americans truly had a baptism to aerial combat against some of the best Japanese carrier fighter pilots. But their casualties—three F4Fs and two TBFs shot down, two TBFs and one F4F forced to turn back, five men killed and four now floating in the sea, not knowing if they would ever live—left a brutal legacy brought about by inexperienced senior leadership and lack of coordination. The *Enterprise* strike force was now a severely depleted group that continued on to its targets.

The Japanese did not by any measure escape paying a terrible price: two pilots killed, two more missing, one Zero heavily damaged. Hidaka, commanding a crippled fighter group, had no choice but to cease escorting Murata's strike group. He turned his fighters around and staggered back to his home base.

The *Hornet*'s strike force, flying behind and to the left of the stricken *Enterprise* pilots, saw what happened to their comrades. While being tempted to intervene, they continued on their mission. Cmdr. Rodee, their leader, kept his charges focused on flying toward their target. His TBF led the SBDs and TBFs as their escort of F4Fs flew above and on both sides. They saw Murata's striking force approaching from dead ahead. But both sides had a mission to perform, and they both had a firm dedication to carry it out.

"Do You See Carriers?"

The *Shokaku* had already received Murata's warning of the *Hornet*'s first strike approach. If there was any doubt, the carrier's radar, operating uncharacteristically well, also found the American planes at 8:40 a.m. approaching on a 135° bearing from a distance of 145 km. Meanwhile, 19 Zeroes flew CAP overhead. Again taking advantage of the hard-learned lessons of Midway, the fleet FDO ordered the CAP to fly at different altitudes to defend against both dive bombing and torpedo attacks. Likely because of the poor performance of their planes' radios, Nagumo's staff wanted to be able to see the CAP. Nevertheless, Warrant Officer Shigeru Okamoto, with three Zeroes, headed toward Abe's Vanguard Force to try to intercept the American search planes in that area.

Just as the radar contact occurred, the *Zuikaku* at last finished preparing its second wave and launched 17 Vals led by Lt. Shigeichiro Imajuku and four Zeroes commanded by Warrant Officer Katsuma Shigemi. The carrier and two destroyers turned into the wind. Imajuku took off at 9:00 a.m.

Two American PBYs came near Nagumo's Striking Force from opposite directions just as the Japanese carrier planes took off. Lt. (jg) Enos L. Jones' plane flew from the southeast, and he saw a "large cargo vessel"—it was the *Zuikaku*. He radioed the sighting report to the *Curtiss* that for some unexplainable reason never received it. Three Japanese CAP Zeroes chased the PBY out of sighting range.

Flying from the southwest, the PBY piloted by Lt. (jg) George F. Poulos came within sighting range. Looking below out of his port side canopy's window, he saw many white feathers in the blue water that could only be caused by large ships. He ordered his radioman to send a report that he had seen one carrier, three heavy cruisers, and four destroyers on a 50° course at a speed of 18 knots. The radio operator had problems sending the message that were caused by either the Japanese jamming his radio frequencies or poor atmospheric conditions. He had to resend the message many times before the *Curtiss* received it at 9:25 a.m. Experiencing the same transmission difficulties, the tender repeatedly resent the report to Task Force 61, which did not receive it until mid-afternoon.

But Poulos' problems only worsened when he turned to the north. Four of the *Zuikaku*'s Zeroes attacked his plane. He radioed a perfunctory message, "Enemy CV aircraft." Convinced they had destroyed the American search plane, the fighters rejoined their strike force and headed for Task Force 61. The PBY escaped just slightly damaged.

Twenty minutes after flying past Radm. Hara's strike force, Widhelm looked straight ahead and saw four ships' wakes belonging to the heavy cruisers *Tone* and *Chikuma* and the destroyers *Tanikaze* and *Urakaze*. Abe's Vanguard Force had been steaming toward Task Force 61 at high speed on a due east course at 26 knots. But, at 8:50 a.m., the fast maneuvering caused Hara to lose sight of the main force. When Widhelm saw Hara's ships, they were 150 miles northwest of Task Force 61. Meanwhile, concerned by the repeated American sightings, Nagumo's ships steamed northward to increase his range from the American carriers.

Widhelm radioed, "Gus to Mike: Do you see carriers?" Sanchez replied, "Mike to Gus: No carriers in sight out here. Let's return."[12] After giving Sanchez's reply some thought, he did not want to turn back. Convinced of the Japanese carriers' close proximity, he left Hara's ships to the rear and led the strike force on 300° course. After flying for another 20 miles, he looked into the haze to his left. More ship wakes appeared. Based on prior sightings, these ships must be Japanese carriers. There were too many telltale wakes to be anything else. Picking up his radio microphone at 9:50 a.m., he wanted fighter cover for his attack and asked Sanchez, "Gus to Mike: I'm going up. Help me dive-bomb." As he closed the distance to the ships, he could see what seemed to be an assorted assembly of two battleships along with some cruisers and destroyers. The *Hornet* strike force had actually found the main body of Abe's Vanguard Force: the battleships *Hiei* and *Kirishima*, heavy cruiser *Suzuya*, light cruiser *Nagara*, and four destroyers *Makigumo, Akigumo, Yugumo,* and *Isokaze.* It did not take too long before the *Isokaze* reported seeing the American aircraft at 9:10 a.m. and informed the other ships.

Casually flying at 120 knots, the *Hornet*'s first wave cruised with the Japanese ships in their sights. Sanchez's TBFs were at 12,000 feet, slightly above a trailing group of 15 SBDs led by Widhelm. As they passed east of the Japanese battleships and cruisers, one of the SBD pilots radioed at 9:10 a.m., "Tally ho dead ahead; Tally ho down below two Zeros." Warrant Officer Okamoto and his two wingmen, PO1c Kazuo Seki and Sea1c Masanao Maki were in those Zeroes when they saw the American formation above them and pulled back on their sticks. Their nimble planes responded in the normally quick way beginning a fast, steep climb. They maneuvered above the American planes and crossed over their adversaries from left to right. Having gained a tactical advantage, Okamoto rolled his plane into an elevated run to attack the F4Fs first so that their destruction would render the slower and less maneuverable SBDs highly vulnerable. Despite some SBD crews spotting the attacking Zeroes, the Japanese attack completely surprised Sanchez's four F4Fs.

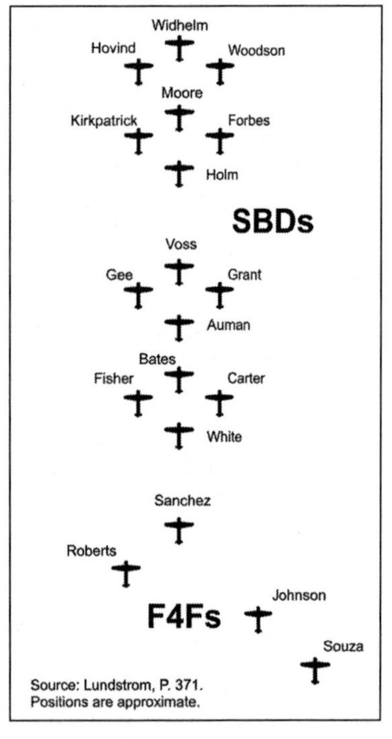

Hornet's First Wave

Souza was the first of the F4F pilots to feel the brunt of the assault. Demonstrating their clearly superior combat experience, the Zeroes attacked skillfully. While Souza watched with awe, he also grasped the desperate situation facing him and took what measures he could. After unsuccessfully trying to drop his 42-gallon wing tank, he went into a hard climbing turn, but his slower and less agile plane could not respond in time. Okamoto continued his diving turn and fired his cannons at the American fighter. Souza heard and felt the disastrously accurate cannon shells explode and tear holes in his right wing. The F4F reacted to the shells' impact by going into a hard snap roll to the right. Fortunately, the plane's reaction took Souza away from immediate harm. Okamoto passed in front of Sanchez who fired his guns. The Japanese pilot had no choice but to continue diving.

Seki lined up his sights on the tail of Johnson's F4F, which for some unknown reason kept flying in a straight, level line. The

Zero's cannons spit deadly fire that put many holes into the tough, sturdy F4F. The plane seemed to shake them off like a cat fluffing its fur.

Souza, rolling his plane after his encounter with Okamoto, saw Seki's Zero appear in his gunsight cross hairs and squeezed off a burst of his six .50-cal. guns. The Zero disintegrated in a ball of flame. But Johnson's F4F was in more trouble than the pilot originally thought as the damaged plane glided down to the water. Souza noticed that his right aileron tab was in a permanent upright position. It took all his flying skills to keep the F4F in level flight.

Lt. (jg) William V. Roberts, Sanchez's wingman, soon experienced the sting of aerial battle. Maki got on Roberts' tail and fired his cannons. Souza saw the F4F's tail separate and flames break out. The doomed plane headed down trailing black smoke. After only one attack on the American fighters and losing Seki, the Japanese Zeroes departed.

Nonetheless, their legacy of destruction lingered. They had killed Johnson and severely wounded Roberts. Souza flew alongside Roberts' nearly crippled F4F and saw blood covering the wounded pilot's canopy as blood poured from Roberts' left shoulder. Realizing that his remaining charges had to fly to safety, he radioed at 9:15 a.m., "Let's get out of here." The only way home he knew was to fly in the opposite direction of his original bearing. He searched in vain for the rest of the *Hornet*'s first strike.

Okamoto and Maki had not yet finished inflicting crippling damage on the Americans. They found Bower's F4Fs flying 2,000 feet above Parker's TBFs and set their sights on Bower. They got on his tail, fired their guns, and sent the fighter down to the water. However, three of Bower's compatriots—Lt. (jg) Robert H. Jennings, Lt. (jg) Robert E. Sorensen, and Ens. Roy B. Dalton—would make one Japanese pilot pay for Bower's demise. Sorensen and Jennings engaged the two Zeroes, destroyed Okamoto's plane, and killed the Warrant Officer. The attacking Zeroes never reached Parker's torpedo planes but took a severe toll on the American pilots, destroying two F4Fs along with their pilots, ravaging two others and severely wounding one American pilot. Although the *Hornet*'s attack force approached the Japanese carriers with their dive-bombers and torpedo planes intact, no *Hornet*-based F4Fs went past Abe's Vanguard Force. Thus, the Americans went in for the attack on Nagumo's carriers with severely depleted fighter escorts.

Maki, the sole survivor from Okamoto's flight, safely landed on the *Junyo* with eight holes in his plane. He and his two comrades were the only Japanese CAP pilots to meet the Americans and make their mark. They had acquitted themselves well but with the loss of two-thirds of their force.

It was time for Nagumo to witness what might have felt like another *déjà vu* experience. American aircraft now drew maliciously near.

Striking the Shokaku

Widhelm wanted to avoid the *Hornet* escorts' problems and turned his formation of SBDs to the right. There were clouds to the north that offered at least a temporary respite from the danger of attacking Zeroes that had inflicted such crippling damage on the fighters. Nonetheless, Parker did not see Widhelm's turn and remained on his original course of 300°, taking him past Abe's Vanguard Force. The TBFs and SBDs would not see each other again until they returned to Task Force 61.

Widhelm's turn became the most important decision of the entire Battle of the Santa Cruz Islands. Just five minutes later, when Widhelm's formation came out of the clouds, Widhelm saw the unmistakable wakes and smoke from ships off to his left and 25 miles away. He sent an immediate radio message, "Contact bearing 345." As his planes drew closer, he could spy one fleet carrier and another smaller ship with smoke billowing from it. These were the *Shokaku* and the burning *Zuiho*, which had been damaged by Strong's earlier bombing attack. Distant clouds hid the *Zuikaku*. He repeatedly tried to reach the *Hornet*'s second strike which was about 60 miles back. Rodee never heard him. However, the *Enterprise* strike leaders did. Widhelm radioed the electrifying message that every American combat pilot wanted to hear, "I have one in sight and am going after them." However, the Japanese CAP would soon confront the Americans.

As the SBDs cleared the clouds' northern edge, four *Shokaku* Zeros flown by PO1c Shigetaka Omori, PO1c Yoshinao Kodaira, PO3c Sadamu Komachi, and Sea1c Tomitaro Ito appeared. Having felt the sting of American carrier bomber guns at Midway, Omori knew better than to attack them either from the rear or directly head-on. The Americans flew in a new, diamond-shaped, stacked formation that maximized their guns' power, and Omori wanted to divide that structure. He rolled his Zero into a steep vertical frontal dive that would take him through the middle of the American planes. The other Zeroes attacked on the formation's side, overhead, and rear. In just less than two minutes later, two more Zeroes flown by PO1c Akira Yamamoto and PO1c Tasuke Mukai joined the fray. Widhelm's rear gunner, ARM1c George D. Stokely, saw many fighters fly toward the plane's tail and warned his pilot of where the Zeroes were. Widhelm tried to maneuver to frustrate Japanese attempts to shoot him down. The other SBDs' pilots tried similar movements. As they did so, their formation's integrity eventually fell apart—it was now every man for himself.

Omori flew his Zero head-on toward Widhelm's SBD. But the American now had a golden opportunity to make the Japanese pilot regret that move. The Zero flew directly into his gunsight cross hairs, and he fired a burst from his two forward-facing .50-cal. guns from just 100 yards away. The bullets struck Omori's engine, which exploded in a ball of flame. Omori pushed the stick forward to ram the SBD but Widhelm ducked under the fatally crippled Zero as it disintegrated. The heroic Japanese pilot posthumously received a double promotion to special duty ensign.

The SBDs approached the *Shokaku*'s stern, but not without more interference from five Japanese Zeroes flown by Lt. Shigeru Araki, PO1c Tomio Kamei, PO1c Junjiro Ito, PO3c Takashi Takayama, and Sea1c Yoshitake Egawa. The Japanese had learned from their CAP mistakes at Midway. Twelve CAP Zeroes had thus attacked the SBDs while five Zeroes still flew at low altitudes to defend against torpedo attacks while two fighters flew over the *Zuikaku*. The destroyer *Amatsukaze* was fishing the pilot of a malfunctioning search plane from the sea when its lookouts saw the approaching American bombers.

More aerial combat continued when Lt. (jg) Kenneth B. White saw a Zero that seemed to be "stalking us." Widhelm also saw but did not pay much attention to it since he was busy fighting his own battles. The Zero attacked Widhelm as Lt. (jg) Clayton Evan Fisher noticed what appeared to be "sickly blue flashes" flickering from its 20-mm cannons. It was a classic fast, rolling overhead attack that had disastrous effects. The cannon shells ripped into Widhelm's left wing, tail, and engine. Its engine's oil pressure dropped, and his plane was now doomed with only minutes left in its life. White also had to prematurely head for home after a Zero destroyed his left aileron and its fire wounded him in the left arm.

Widhelm's engine froze at 9:25 a.m., and its propeller stopped spinning. He and his fellow pilots were still several miles from the point where they would begin their diving attacks. His wingman, Lt. (jg) Ralph B. Hovind, noticed Widhelm was an angry man because he now could not lead the attack. He vented these sentiments over his radio that Sanchez's F4Fs were not as effective protecting the SBDs as they should have been. Before ditching in the water below, he delegated his command to Lt. James E. Vose. After gently setting his spent aircraft down in the sea, Stokely and he sought refuge in their raft to later witness the American attack on the big Japanese carrier. Thomas Lea, an artist aboard the *Hornet*, described Widhelm's character and integrity:

> "He was born to fly; he was born to lead men; he was born to fight. He was the stuff of which heroic tradition was made. In all things he stuck his square chin out and dared the world to take a poke at it."[13]

Vose now led a scattered formation but brought some organization to the impending attack by lining them up abreast. As the bombers closed the range to the *Shokaku*, Zeroes continued to inflict more damage on the SBDs. One Zero ripped 20-mm holes into Lt. (jg) Clayton Evan Fisher's bomber. With the plane's hydraulic system no longer working, his gunner, ARM3c George E. Ferguson, effectively kept the marauding fighter from inflicting more serious damage with careful considerably accurate fire from his machine gun. The formation was near the diving point when Lt. Fred L. Bates saw Lt. (jg) Philip F. Grant's plane drop out of formation, its fuselage full of holes. The dive bomber disappeared from sight. Grant and his radioman, ARM2c Floyd D. Kilmer, were never seen again. Four SBDs were now gone—Widhelm and Grant shot down; White and Fisher dropping out. Finally, the time had come for the diving attack.

Five SBDs, flying on the left side of the formation, at last reached their pushover point at 9:27 a.m. with the *Shokaku* desperately zigzagging below. Vose's five bombers came in from the south. Ten American carrier dive-bombers, each loaded with powerful 1,000-pound bombs, went into their steep dives with nothing but malice toward the Japanese carrier. To those sailors on the *Shokaku* who had served at Coral Sea, the upcoming attack would seem like history repeating itself. The Japanese ships opened up with a withering AA barrage. Capt. Masafumi Arima, the carrier's commanding officer, saw the first three or four 1,000-pound bombs fall and tried to avoid them. Nonetheless, several bombs hit the carrier and exploded. The ship's wooden deck shattered into splinters. Another bomb destroyed AA gun positions. After being hit in his cockpit by flying wooden splinters from the carrier's flight deck, Bates put his bomb onto the flight deck in the exact center. A firestorm of flames roared upward. The carrier flight deck was now incapable of sustaining flight operations. Although there were no armed bombs and torpedoes carelessly left on deck as they were at Midway, two parked planes exploded in the fiery inferno. The fire crippled the ship's center elevator and most of the hangar deck. She now trailed fire and smoke but could still steam at 31 knots.

✲ ✲ ✲

The SBDs were not out of danger yet. Two Zeroes flown by PO1c Gonji Moriyama and PO3c Hajime Tochi pounced on three SBDs piloted by Lt. Ben Moore, Lt. (jg) Donald Kirkpatrick, and Roy Gee as they tried to leave the battle scene. One 20-mm shell put a hole in the armor behind Moore's seat and scraped his neck. Blood splattered on his canopy and windscreen. The bullet hit Moore's radioman, ACRM Ralph Phillips, in the arm. Kirkpatrick's gunner, ARM2c Richard T. Woodson, also received wounds from the Zero attack. But the Americans struck back at the marauding Zeroes. Lt. (jg) Stanley R. Holm had just finished his bombing run on the destroyer *Teruzuki*—his bomb missed—when he strafed the cruiser *Kumano*. The sole American radioman to shoot down a Zero flew in Holm's plane and was ARM3c James Black, Jr.

Two-thirds of Nagumo's carriers could no longer conduct battle operations. He did not want to endanger the *Zuikaku*, the only operational carrier he had left. There was a high risk that more American planes from the *Hornet* and *Enterprise* were on their way toward his force. His dark memories from Midway must have been haunting his fears.

✲ ✲ ✲

Meanwhile, the severe American communications problems continued. Parker never heard Widhelm's sighting reports. He led his planes on a 300° course for 210 miles and never found any carriers and flew too far to the south and west to ever find Nagumo's ships. His fuel reserves had reached the critical stage. He had no choice but to begin heading for home. Turning west and then north for another 50 miles, he decided he would attack the battleships and cruisers he had passed earlier.

Attacking the Vanguard Force

After enduring crippling attacks, the *Enterprise* strike force lost four F4Fs and four TBFs. The carrier had just four F4Fs, five TBFs, and three SBDs remaining to continue its mission. All hoped they could still find the Japanese carriers. The fighters and torpedo planes climbed to 10,000 feet, but Gaines took his SBD higher. Estes, leading his three SBDs and flying at 9,000 feet, lost sight of the *Hornet* strike force as it disappeared through the many scattered cumulus clouds that dotted the sky. Bringing up the rear and leading his F4Fs, Flatley spotted the *Hornet*'s second strike force and tried to convince Gaines or Thompson, who led the TBFs, to join up with them and enjoy the added security they provided. But his urging was to no avail.

Flatley and Thompson overheard Widhelm's report on the sighting of a Japanese carrier between 9:15 a.m. and 9:20 a.m. Thompson saw Hara's ships in the distance but also noticed Abe's ships nearer and to the west. After radioing, "There is another group of ships 270 way over there. Let's go." He banked westward toward them. Flatley, relieved that they were finally doing what they had been sent to do, and Gaines followed Thompson's lead. Meanwhile, Estes' three SBDs inexplicably did not follow their comrades, but continued flying on a northwest course while entering a large mass of cumulus clouds.

While Widhelm's SBDs attacked the *Shokaku*, Thompson did not have long to wait before spotting a huge group of juicy targets: the battleships *Hiei* and *Kirishima*, the heavy cruisers *Nagara* and *Suzuya*, and four destroyers but without any carriers in sight. He kept flying past the Vanguard Force to search the water beyond a bank of towering, white cumulus clouds. Not a ship in sight! Thompson asked Flatley if his fighters could continue flying for another 90 miles. Flatley impatiently balked because his fighters had dropped their wing tanks almost an hour earlier and did not have enough fuel to go farther.

Just as Widhelm's SBDs attacked the *Shokaku*, Thompson turned around at 9:30 a.m. and attacked the nearest ship, a heavy cruiser—it was the *Suzuya*—steaming on the western side of Abe's flagship. As Gaines circled overhead to photograph the upcoming attack, Thompson's four TBFs went into a shallow, high-speed dive. The planes rapidly closed the distance to the cruiser and dropped their torpedoes. Two of the four torpedoes did not drop while the other two trailed their telltale wakes behind and missed their target. The cruiser's captain had more than enough time to evade the torpedoes after his sharp-eyed lookouts saw their wakes and gave ample warning to the ship's bridge of their coming. Nonetheless, Lt. (jg) Raymond G. Wyllie turned around to attack the *Suzuya* again. He dropped his torpedo and saw its wake head for the ship. Again, the cruiser avoided the incoming missile as it passed harmlessly off the starboard bow. Flatley's fighters tried in vain to inflict damage by strafing the cruiser. As the American aircraft turned to the southwest at 9:38 a.m., the *Suzuya* stopped firing its AA guns.

✲ ✲ ✲

Hara worried about the repeated American air attacks and steered his 8th Cruiser Division away from the American carriers in a northwesterly direction. But the Americans would soon find him again.

Estes' three SBDs finally found a target at 9:15 a.m. when they saw four ships steaming below at high speed and to the northwest. The ships were the heavy cruisers *Tone* and *Chikuma* and the destroyers *Tanikaze* and *Urakaze*. Five minutes later, Rodee's seven F4Fs, nine SBDs, and ten TBFs—the *Hornet*'s second strike that had been looking for targets and had miraculously escaped damage from the Japanese CAP—came on the scene. Hara's ships opened fire with their AA guns.

The continuing American communication glitches prevented Rodee and Lynch from knowing what had happened to Widhelm and his strike force. Lynch radioed that since he had no other target to assault, he would lead his nine SBDs and Lt. Warren Ford's three F4Fs to attack one of the two Japanese cruisers—the *Chikuma*. Rodee, along with his escorting F4Fs flown by Lt. (jg) David B. Freeman and Lt. (jg) Alfred E. Dietrich, followed Lynch in his TBF and broke away from the strike formation. Meanwhile, Lt. Ward F. Powell's nine TBFs armed with bombs and two F4Fs flown by Lt. John F. Sutherland and Lt. (jg) Henry A. Carey stayed on their northwesterly course and that took them out of the action. Again, the American lack of a coordinated carrier-based air attack strategy had decimated their formation integrity.

While their *Hornet*'s first wave comrades clobbered the *Shokaku* between 9:26 a.m. and 9:31 a.m. 50 miles north, Lynch's dive-bombers reached the point to begin their dives at the *Chikuma*. Meanwhile, Rodee circled above to record the attack on film as Ford's F4Fs flew air cover. Six diving SBDs attacked first followed by Lt. Edgar E. Stebbins' three dive-bombers. The cruiser, like her sister ship, the *Tone*, had all four of her eight-inch gun turrets located forward of her bridge. The diving pilots saw that this unusual configuration left a large open rear deck that allowed space for float planes. But that did not stop the attacking dive-bombers from placing their bombs where they would *not* do the most damage.

One 1,000-pound bomb hit at 9:26 a.m., exploded on the bridge's port side, and disabled the cruiser's main-battery fire directors. Another bomb hit five minutes later and heavily damaged the superstructure starboard side. Two bombs destroyed the bridge, wounded Capt. Keizo Kimura, killed the executive officer, and wounded several unlucky crew members who were on the bridge at the time. Seeing the results of his assault, Lynch turned his bombers and flew away at surface level. He believed that he had inflicted crippling damage on the cruiser, but missed an opportunity to sink her by not directing his bombers' aim at its open, relatively lightly armored rear deck. More importantly, he failed to attack a far more important target—a Japanese fleet carrier.

Estes saw nothing as he flew to the northwest, so he turned around toward Hara's small force. He led his three dive-bombers at 9:39 a.m. to attack what the *Enterprise* air intelligence later believed was the battleship *Kongo*. But the ship was the harassed *Chikuma*. One bomb tore a large hole in the ship's starboard side. Water poured into her starboard fireroom, and she slowed down.

The Japanese CAP was not yet finished with the American interlopers. Finding no new target, Powell's three TBFs and its two F4F escorts continued to fly to the northwest at 10,000 feet. Some Japanese CAP Zeroes arrived nearby but only two of their pilots from the *Zuikaku*, PO1c Junjiro Ito and Sea1c Takashi Takayama, saw the American planes. Ito tried a head-on attack through the American formation and forced it to separate. He flew away and later claimed shooting down one TBF.

Takayama attacked from the opposite direction and flew over the American torpedo planes. He made a wide turn, climbed to attack from above, and crossed in front of Sutherland and Carey's F4Fs, which were flying 4,000 feet beneath and behind the TBFs. Sutherland wasted no time in bringing the Zero in his sights and fired his six .50-cal. guns. The Zero was 400 yards away as the F4F's fire blasted into the doomed fighter. His F4F was only 100 yards away when the Zero exploded in a ball of flame. Only Sutherland's deft flying skills prevented the Zero's debris from severely damaging his own plane.

Meanwhile, Parker and Powell's torpedo plane divisions moved toward the *Tone* and struggling *Chikuma*. Parker's journey had thus far been unsuccessful. He and the other pilots of his division had not seen any carriers. At last, targets at which he could vent his natural frustration presented themselves. His six TBFs directed their attack at the fully-operational *Tone*, which responded to approaching torpedo-plane attack by making violent turns to avoid the deadly torpedo wakes. Although Parker's pilots claimed to have scored three hits, all six torpedoes, like many of their predecessors, missed the cruiser. Their attack took their planes northward, and, as they gained altitude, they saw a pyre of smoke belching from the crippled *Shokaku* in the distance. But they had no more torpedoes so had to head back to the *Hornet*.

Powell's bomb-armed TBF picked on the burning *Chikuma* when he put his plane into a gliding bombing attack. When he got close to the cruiser, he loosed a 500-pound bomb that smashed into an aft torpedo mount and exploded. The conflagration set a reconnaissance plane afire while it perched on the starboard catapult. The *Chikuma* was covered in flames with 192 of its crew dead and 95 wounded, but could still steam at 23 knots. Widhelm saw the cruiser burn from his raft and thought that all of its rear turrets had disappeared. Of course, he did not know the ship never had any aft turrets—all its eight-inch turrets were forward. She would survive to fight more battles before being lost in the Battle of Samar on October 25, 1944.

✲ ✲ ✲

The American planes had finished their work—such as it was—and began their return journey by 10:00 a.m. Task Force 61 had sent 75 planes—all it could spare—with mixed results. Abe's Vanguard Force had taken the brunt of the American attacks. If Widhelm and Strong had not executed their assaults, Nagumo's carriers would have escaped unscathed. The American fighter escorts could not protect their charges.

Despite Kinkaid's orders to coordinate their attacks, the American attacks were disjointed and fragmentary. Much of this could be blamed on extremely poor communications. The Americans lost five F4Fs, two SBDs, and two TBFs over the battle area. More planes ditched later. The carriers *Shokaku* and *Zuiho* and the heavy cruiser *Chikuma* had taken heavy damage. Nine CAP Zeroes never returned and may have ditched in the ocean.

But the Battle of Santa Cruz had not yet ended. Task Force 61 would feel the sting of Japanese carrier aircraft. Hell was on the wing![14]

CHAPTER 33
The Embattled Hornet

"Stand by for Dive-bombing Attack"

Kinkaid did not hesitate to move Task Force 61 from offense to defense while still steaming to the northwest toward the Japanese carriers. But he had to make sure that he had many fighters aloft with enough fuel so the CAP planes could stay at their patrol altitudes for as long as possible. Task Force 16's new FDO, Cmdr. John H. Griffin, had assigned Lt. Albert David Pollock and Thomas E. Edwards Jr.'s seven F4Fs to fly overhead at 10,000 feet and Lt. Cmdr. William R. Kane's four F4Fs to patrol to the south between Task Force 16 and Task Force 17. Griffin wanted to conserve fuel so he only allowed the F4Fs to fly no higher than 10,000 feet. After all, he had the newest radar that would give more than adequate warning if Japanese planes should appear on the distant horizon. Again, Griffin never knew that Kinkaid had sent a blinker light message to Task Force 61 at 8:11 a.m. that said the Japanese had found the American carriers.

Task Force 61's CAP had been aloft for more than three hours. It was time for them to land and refuel. Since the *Enterprise* had already launched her strike, she could immediately begin landing the fighters on her now-idle fight deck. Ens. Millard W. Axelrod's ailing F4F was the first to touch down followed by Lt. Stanley E. Ruehlow and Lt. MacGregor Kilpatrick's seven F4Fs. After refueling, these fighters joined four other planes and took off at 8:30 a.m., climbed to 10,000 feet, and began circling over Task Force 16.

The *Hornet* landed Lt. (jg) Robert S. Merritt's F4F, nearly dry of oil and just returning from its strike. Eight F4Fs led by Lieutenants Edward W. Hessel and Robert W. Rynd took off at 8:22 a.m. and, acting under the orders of Lt. Allan F. Fleming, the *Hornet*'s FDO, also climbed to 10,000 feet. The carrier then landed seven CAP fighters that had been aloft. One plane's landing gear collapsed while landing. After replacing the damaged plane and while these planes refueled, Fleming reassigned the planes to different divisions. Seven F4F pilots waited for the launch order. Meanwhile, Merritt's plane and the other crippled F4F descended on a deck elevator to the hangar deck for repairs.

Meanwhile, Sanchez's 8:30 a.m. warning, "Stand by for dive-bombing," loudly and clearly spread throughout Task Force 61. Before any planes launched, Kinkaid, realizing his task force would soon be facing a Japanese onslaught, broke radio silence at 8:37 a.m. and ordered the *Hornet* over the TBS, "Launch all planes immediately. Jap planes coming in." As snippets of radio transmissions showing the plight of the *Hornet*'s strike force filtered into many ship radio rooms, it became clear that a deadly battle was happening 60 miles to the northwest.

Task Force 16 now had 22 planes flying CAP with half of those still climbing to their assigned altitude of 10,000 feet. Eight more Task Force 17 CAP fighters approached 10,000 feet as well. Turning into the wind, the *Hornet* readied the seven fighters waiting on its flight deck for takeoff. After launching the seven F4Fs, she returned to her 330° course. Kinkaid now had 37 fighters aloft to wait for the Japanese aircraft to appear.

The carrier radar operators intently stared at their scopes for any returns that would show the Japanese aircraft getting closer. The radar detection range was 75 miles and, with the Japanese planes flying ever nearer, the ship radars should have detected their approach. Again, for some unknown reason, the scopes showed nothing! Griffin overheard a report from a dubious source that spotted an approaching formation to the south. It was actually the *Enterprise* strike force on its return leg. Again, there was nothing on the radar scope, but Griffin decided to warn the rest of Task Force 61 when he broke radio silence on the fighter direction frequency, "Look for Hawks [dive-bombers] on port bow and port quarter. Angels [altitude] probably high. Look south of REAPER [*Enterprise*] BASE." He did not send a more precise bearing because this was the only useful information he knew.

Murray had intercepted the *Hornet* strike force's transmissions that said the Japanese were approaching from a different direction. He warned Task Force 61 over the TBS at 8:43 a.m. that Japanese planes were approaching from a 275° bearing. Believing that the oncoming Japanese strike would soon be within interception range, Kinkaid told Murray that the *Enterprise* would direct all CAP fighters.

The lack of any specific knowledge of the approaching Japanese air strike coming from the west concerned Griffin. But neither the *Enterprise* nor the *Hornet* radars showed any indication whatsoever that there were Japanese aircraft within range. Making sure he had not forgotten any precaution he could make in these circumstances, he sent a message at 8:47 a.m. to Kane, whose four F4Fs patrolled between the two carrier groups, to watch for approaching planes from the southwest. Less than a minute later with still no radar contacts on which to base any meaningful knowledge, Griffin warned the CAP flying over the *Hornet* to "protect BLUE BASE." Fleming also became uneasy over the clear radar scopes and warned Hessel and Rynd to continue to circle the *Enterprise*.

If the Japanese were on their way, why did the carrier radars not detect them? The simple answer is that these instruments were not working properly. The cruiser *Northampton*'s radar was, and its scopes detected the planes at 8:41 a.m. approaching on a 295° course, 70 miles out, and closing at high speed. Radm. Howard H. Good, on board the cruiser, which was also his flagship, assumed the carriers had also seen the contacts, so he forwarded the sighting report by signal flag instead of using the TBS. A considerable amount of time passed before Griffin knew of the *Northampton* contact. Fleming never knew the contact ever existed.

✲ ✲ ✲

Murata's *Shokaku* strike group had been patiently flying for some time. Every eye stared at the blue water ahead to look for white wakes that could only be from the American ships. Their patience was soon rewarded when they saw the trailing white wakes of large ships to their left. As they closed the range to the sighting, the shapes of the ships became clear—one carrier (the *Hornet*), two cruisers, and four destroyers (Task Force 17). They could not see Task Force 16 (the *Enterprise*) to the east because clouds obscured their vision. Twenty Kates flew at 14,000 feet with two more unarmed Kates from the *Zuikaku* and *Zuiho* that would act as observers and lookouts for more American targets. Lt. Miyajima's four Zeroes were the bombers' only escorts since Hidaka's Zeroes could not join up earlier. Flying 3,000 feet higher were Takahashi's 21 Vals from the *Zuikaku*. Shirane's eight Zeroes flew above and behind at 21,000 feet looking for any American CAP.

It was time to attack. Murata ordered his radioman, PO1c Tokunobu Mizuki to send, "*To-tsu-re* [Assume attack formation]." In a sense this was a moment repeating history. Mizuki was Cmdr. Mitsuo Fuchida's radioman when he had sent the famous message, "*Tora, Tora, Tora* [Tiger, Tiger, Tiger]," that announced the Japanese had completely surprised the Americans before the attack on Pearl Harbor.

Fleming at last had a radar sighting of approaching "Bogeys" two minutes after Murata had seen Task Force 17. At 8:55 a.m., he ordered Hessel and Rynd to fly west to intercept "a fairly large bogey"—bearing 260º, distance 35 miles. The *Enterprise* radar also picked up the Japanese planes on a 255º bearing at a distance of 45 miles. Griffin ordered Pollock and Edwards' seven F4Fs to fly 15 miles west and climb to 20,000 feet and added the new information he had, "Large Group now 20 miles from base."

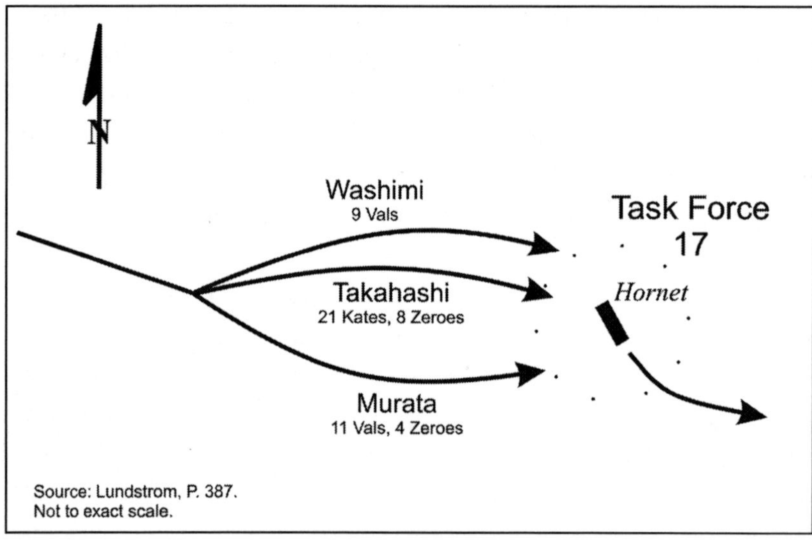

Japanese First Strike

As Hessel led eight F4Fs at high speed to the west, he realized the reality of the situation he and his fellow pilots were about to encounter. He remembered the radio chatter as the *Hornet* air strike broadcast its struggles against the Japanese Zeroes. Contradicting his orders to patrol at 10,000 feet, he climbed to a higher altitude. As the F4Fs climbed, his wingman, Lt. (jg) Thomas J. Gallagher, saw the Japanese aircraft, picked up his radio's microphone and broadcast at 8:59 a.m., "BLUE 14 Tally ho, dead ahead Angels 17." Fleming immediately got on the radio and wanted to know more, "What have you got? To Red from Al what is composition of Tally ho?" Gallagher wasted no time in responding, "I think they are Hawks, Angels 17."

Based on this description, these sighted planes were most likely Takahashi's 21 Vals. The sighting expanded to include the entire Japanese strike group. More information arrived, and Fleming then knew there were 55 Japanese planes—fighters, dive-bombers, and torpedo planes—in a "compact, formidable looking column." Hessel's eight fighters were clearly outnumbered and desperately needed help. Fleming ordered Lt. Alberto C. Emerson's and Lt. Louis K. Bliss' seven F4Fs, now flying on a 250º (magnetic) from Task Force 17, toward the Japanese planes 20 miles away. The *Hornet* had sent every CAP aircraft it had. Griffin exhorted Lt. Stanley W. Vejtasa's five F4Fs and Lt. Frederick L. Faulkner's six fighters to, "Climb, climb!"

The time at long last had arrived for the Japanese to use their training and attack the American carriers in the same coordinated manner they had used at Coral Sea. Cloud cover prevented Murata from seeing the *Hornet* until 8:58 a.m. Suddenly, the cloud cover slipped past his plane, and there was the American carrier, trailing a curved wake as it tried to turn away from his approaching aircraft. He ordered Mizuki to send the message every Japanese sailor had been waiting to hear, "*To-to-to* [All forces attack]." He split the strike force into three groups so he could attack the carrier simultaneously with torpedoes from both sides at the bow. Noticing the eight F4Fs heading directly for him, he and his 11 dive-bombers with four Zeroes went into a high-speed, shallow dive directly aimed at the carrier. Lt. Goro Washimi took nine torpedo planes to the north. Takahashi led 21 "Kates" and eight Zeroes directly on the *Hornet*'s starboard beam. The plan was to place the carrier in a vise from which there was no escape.

Resuming Aerial Combat

Takahashi's 21 carrier bombers maintained their shallow dive from 17,000 feet and planned to go into their final steep dive from 12,000 feet. They flew in three seven-plane formations with Takahashi leading the first group, Lt. Toshio Tsuda leading the second, and Lt. Yutaka Ishimaru the third. Shirane's eight escorting Zeroes were above and behind the bombers and not in an advantageous position to intercept the approaching American fighters.

As Hessel closed on the Japanese planes, he decided to attack the nearest three planes flying in the commonly-used Vee formation when he could confirm they were actually green-painted Japanese carrier aircraft. He fixed his attention on the leading plane (Takahashi) to force the formation to break up and thus leave each plane more vulnerable. With Gallagher's F4F on his right wing, Hessel banked hard left for a level attack approach at 15,000 feet and went for the leading bomber. Gallagher lined up his sights on the left outside plane flown by PO2c Toshio Nishimori and opened fire. Bullet holes riddled Nishimori's plane, but he kept flying albeit now separated from the attacking formation. Hessel fired his guns and severely damaged Takahashi's rudder. The Japanese leader never made the diving attack on the *Hornet* and was forced to harmlessly jettison his bomb into the ocean.

Two F4Fs flown by Lt. Claude R. Phillips, Jr. and Lt. (jg) John R. Franklin followed Hessel and Gallagher in a broad turn to starboard and attacked the Japanese formation's left side. Phillips' gunfire punched several holes into PO2c Yoshiaki Tsuchiya's bomber, which was the "tail-end Charlie" in the middle Vee. The plane abruptly dove out of sight. The Americans circled back for a second attack, and struck one plane in Special Duty Ens. Hajime Murai's Vee formation with withering gunfire. By this time, Phillip's second pass had taken him beyond the Japanese bombers. Suddenly, his plane violently shook as 20-mm shells raked his rear fuselage. Choking smoke filled his cockpit. As more Zeroes joined the fray, Phillips pushed back his canopy preparing to bail out. But the wind cleared his cockpit of all smoke. While he might have breathed a sigh of relief that he did not have to abandon his aircraft, he looked with terror to see Franklin's F4F being viciously attacked. He tried to aid his wingman by rolling his plane and make a head-on movement to tempt the attacking Zero to quit attacking Gallagher. But it was too late. Franklin's F4F, full of holes and its rudder completely disabled, went into a steep, unrecoverable dive. Phillips saw Franklin abandon his plane and parachute toward the water. Franklin's body was never found, and he was later listed as missing-in-action. With his plane too heavily damaged to continue any combat, Phillips descended to a low altitude and nursed the crippled plane toward home.

Trailing Hessel's fighters, Rynd's four F4Fs attacked Ishimaru's bomber formation by coming at the Japanese planes from a shallow, side angle. Rynd lined one bomber in his gunsight, but its pilot escaped by rolling his plane away. The American pilot soon had problems of his own. Warrant Officer Suekichi Osanai's flight of Zeroes jumped Rynd. One Zero flew right past him. Wanting to destroy the intruder, he pulled back his stick, and the F4F's nose rose. His wingman, Ens. George L. Wrenn, tried to climb as well, but his plane stalled and nosed downward. Now diving, the F4F picked up speed but a Zero soon got on his tail. Wrenn had to stay in the dive to escape. But all was not lost since his diving fighter put him in a highly advantageous position to threaten the Japanese torpedo planes flying below. Meanwhile, Rynd later claimed two bombers and one probable.

Two F4Fs from Rynd's formation flown by Lt. (jg) Kenneth C. Kiekhoefer and Lt. (jg) Paul Landry had just begun its attack on Ishimaru's Zeroes when PO1c Mitsutomi Noda and PO1c Yoshikazu Nagahama's two Zeroes maneuvered behind the F4Fs. The American fighters' guns spouted fire at one Japanese bomber that burst into flame. After the two American fighters separated, a Zero moved right into Kiekhoefer's sight. He fired a volley at the fighter. Smoke trailed behind the stricken plane as it rolled over and headed for the water. Nagahama got onto Landry's tail and fired his cannons. The doomed American plane went into a straight dive and was never seen again. Kiekhoefer escaped into some clouds.

But the *Zuikaku* carrier bomber formation broke apart as Takahashi's irregular maneuvers forced his flight to follow him northward. Tsuda's six bombers filled the space in the formation. As PO2c Tsuchiya's plane tried to follow Tsuda, Phillips raked his bomber. Fortunately for Tsuda, his formation managed to get away without damage. But Lt. Ishimaru's formation was not so lucky. Two bombers took heavy gunfire and had to fall away. His flight, like Takahashi's, fell apart.

Despite the Zeroes inflicting crippling damage on the other American fighters, Hessel and Gallagher put deadly gunfire into a lone Japanese bomber as they flew the classic scissor maneuver. Despite almost running into each other, the two American pilots saw the bomber go into a steep dive and never pull up as he crashed into the water. By this time, Hessel had exhausted his ammunition and headed back to the *Hornet* to rearm and refuel. Gallagher was not yet finished and tangled with a revengeful carrier bomber. The Japanese plane put several holes into his F4F. He had no choice but to land his plane in the water, break out his life raft before the fighter sank, and await a rescue. Both American pilots received credit for one kill each and two probables.

The eight CAP F4Fs claimed to have shot down four dive-bombers, one fighter, and seven probable dive-bomber kills, but they paid a heavy price. Three F4Fs, flown by Franklin, Landry, and Gallagher, did not return, and the five remaining CAP F4Fs were now scattered all over the sky.

Tsuda's flight ran into the second CAP as the American radar showed the Japanese planes moving to the south of Task Force 17. Fleming tried to direct Alberto C. Emerson and Bliss' seven F4Fs at 9:04 a.m. to fly a 225º bearing. Lt. (jg) Richard Z. Hughes trailed the formation and saw a few dark-green-colored bombers flying northward about 1,000 feet below, but they passed before he could tell Bliss about them. Four F4F pilots saw the Japanese bombers and turned to intercept them. Emerson never heard Hughes' message. Bliss overtook Tsuchiya's crippled bomber that flew behind the other six Vals and moved in for his attack run with the other F4Fs following him. Willing to sacrifice himself for the good of his mission, Tsuchiya put his plane into a steep dive and headed for Task Force 17. PO3c Motomu Kato, piloting Tsuchiya's plane, demonstrated outstanding flying skills by luring the four American fighters away from the other carrier bombers, leaving them unopposed to attack the American carrier.

Hughes was not happy as he also realized the seriousness of the situation. Nevertheless, he was now committed to shooting down the Japanese bomber. His wingman, Lt. (jg) Robert E. Holland, and he fired their guns at the plummeting plane and set it afire. Both pilots saw thick, black smoke trailing behind the seemingly doomed bomber. The rest of Tsuda's Vals and Murata's Kates now had a clear path to inflict their worst on the *Hornet*, whose only remaining defenses were its AA guns.

As the *Hornet*'s crew braced themselves for the attack about to befall them, both the *Enterprise* and *Hornet* FDOs struggled to organize their CAP defenses. Fleming tried to call Emerson to redirect his group of fighters to stop the attack. After finally reaching Emerson at 9:05 a.m. with a "Hey, Rube" message, which meant to return to the *Hornet* if there were no Japanese planes. Five minutes later, Emerson answered that he made no contact despite Bliss' gloating message, "Have shot down one hawk, don't see any more around."

Griffin also saw the planes approaching the *Hornet* on the *Enterprise*'s radar and attempted to help Task Force 17. But he also had the responsibility for defending the *Enterprise* and the rest of Task Force 16 from any air attack. After asking Fleming if there were more than one group of Japanese planes nearing Task Force 17, he received a reply from the *Hornet*'s FDO that there was only widely dispersed groups of approaching planes.

It now became clear the Japanese were only going after the *Hornet*. Griffin wanted to help Task Force 17 if he could. He ordered seven F4Fs to circle on a 10-mile radius from Task Force 16 with the hope these fighters could give the *Hornet* some help. He kept the other 15 F4Fs nearer to Task Force 16 to defend against any attack that might come its way. Meanwhile, Fleming answered Griffin's question about the approaching Japanese planes' altitude with "Angels 7" (7,000 feet). The *Enterprise*'s FDO then warned his CAP to look to the south for any approaching planes. Foreseeing a possible torpedo-plane attack, he told Kane, Vejtasa, and Faulkner's F4Fs, "Look for fish." Nevertheless, by this time, Griffin had no control over his CAP. Twenty-one of 22 F4Fs were now flying to the aid of Task Force 17. Neither carrier had any effective CAP to protect them.

The Hornet*'s Nightmare*

As soon as Murray knew of the approaching Japanese planes, he ordered Task Force 17 into a circular formation around the *Hornet* designed to deliver maximum antiaircraft protection. The screen of two heavy cruisers, two light AA cruisers, and six destroyers maneuvered into a 4,000-yard-diameter circle. The lookouts anxiously peered into the cloud-studded albeit clear skies. They had not yet seen the aircraft they all knew were on their way. Because Task Force 17 led Kinkaid's Task Force 61, he ordered the *Hornet* at 9:02 a.m. to reduce its distance to the *Enterprise*, which trailed 12 miles to the northeast. Murray immediately complied by swinging Task Force 17 to a northern bearing of 40º.

Three minutes later, the *Hornet*'s lookouts finally spotted Tsuda's Vals in a long line approaching from the west. There were seven of them, but one soon disappeared because of Bliss downing Tsuchiya's plane. Clouds obscured the fire director's aim. Not long afterward, the *Hornet*'s five-inch guns began firing at 9:09 a.m. from a range of 10,500 yards. The carrier lacked the modern AA guns the *Enterprise* had; so Capt. Charles P. Mason had to use evasive maneuvers to minimize potential damage. The big ship began wildly swinging 28-knot turns to avoid the falling bombs and oncoming torpedoes. But the Japanese were experts at delivering combined torpedo and dive-bombing attacks, and the *Hornet* soon became the victim of that well-earned reputation.

Tsuda's six dive-bombers met no further resistance from American fighters and only encountered light AA fire. They began a slow descent at 9:10 a.m. through some clouds and came out in the clear at a 5,000-foot altitude. Tsuda and his two wingmen, PO2c Katsuhi Miyakashi and PO2c Ichiro Kitamura, pushed over into steep dives directly at the *Hornet*'s stern as the other three bombers continued in their 45º shallow dives. Tsuda lined up the carrier in his bomb sight and released his bomb. It hit and exploded in the water off the ship's starboard bow. Miyakashi had more success as his 250-kg semi-armor-piercing bomb penetrated the center of the carrier's flight deck near the island and descended on its harmful path through three decks. It exploded in a deadly ball of flame in the mess deck and severely wounded many members of the repair party. Kitamura, his bomb still on his plane, met a deadly end as AA fire sent his aircraft splashing into the water just 30 feet from the ship's starboard bow.

Lt. (jg) Yozo Shimada successfully led his four-plane formation that also included PO2c Yoshiaki Tsuchiya, PO3c Akitatsu Hirayama, and PO3c Shoichi Yano in the dive-bombing attack. Piloting Shimada's plane, PO1c Asataro Taka accurately dropped his 242-kg bomb onto the carrier's flight deck and put an 11-foot hole just 20 feet from the deck's starboard edge. A towering chute of flame roared from the fissure that killed 30 men next to the aft starboard gun gallery. Shimada's plane drew the ire of the carrier's 20-mm gunners as shells pierced the plane's skin. Dense smoke trailed behind the stricken craft. Taka managed to gain enough height for Shimada to bail out, but he could not get out. Shimada's plane slowly fell to the sea and landed in the water near the cruiser *Pensacola*. The destroyer *Isokaze* rescued him later.

Another semi-armor-piercing bomb, dropped by either Hirayama or Yano, smashed near the second hit, passed through four decks, exploded in the CPO's dining area, and ended many men's lives. Meanwhile, Tsuchiya's crippled bomber tried to attack by dropping its bomb. But the missile and the plane crashed in the water and inflicted no damage.

All in all, the Japanese dive-bombing assault successfully achieved its mission despite losing two of its planes. Tsuda, Miyakashi, Hirayama, and Yano fled the battle scene by flying close to the water surface. Meanwhile, the heavily damaged *Hornet*'s struggle had not yet run its course.

Lt. Cmdr. Shigeharu Murata was a highly respected naval aviator and considered as one of the best that ever served during World War II. He was in illustrious company when the famous Cmdr. Minoru Genda showered him with high praise:

> "(Murata) was the torpedo ace of the Japanese Navy. He would fly his bomber anywhere at any time. Murata knew no fear, he was calm and cold as a rock in zero weather, was never nervous, and under the worst of circumstances always smiling."[1]

His 11 Kates flew a curved course from the south of Task Force 17 as he also organized Washimi's attack to coincide with his. Washimi led seven torpedo planes approaching Task Force 17 from the north. Murray's earlier maneuver that turned Task Force 17 northeastward unfortunately forced Murata to overtake the American ships from their sterns. His four formations became more unorganized as he moved to the *Hornet*'s starboard beam and into their attacking positions. Losing the advantage of concentrating their assaults, they pivoted off Murata's three-plane formation, which was to the left of them. After Murata, Lt. (jg) Takeo Suzuki's three torpedo planes swooped to the right followed by Warrant Officer Masanobu Shibata's three aircraft and, behind and far to the right, WO Taneichi Nakai's two-plane group. All went into their long, shallow dives and increased speed to move ahead of the carrier's bow.

Murata, Warrant Officer Tadashi Matsushima, and PO1c Zensaku Kawamura flew between the cruiser *Northampton* and destroyer *Anderson*, dropped down to 300 feet above the water, and closed the distance to the carrier's starboard quarter. Harassed by dense and withering AA fire, one pilot dropped his torpedo from 1,500 yards away but took several hits from the American five-inch guns. The plane exploded in flames and dove into the water. The other two got to within 1,000 yards, dropped their torpedoes, and banked right to fly parallel to the carrier. The second Kate took a shell hit in its left wing tank, burst into flames, rolled to port, and trailed flames and smoke as it crashed in the water. Gray smoke trailed behind the third plane but it escaped. Murata's and Matsushima's crews lost their lives while only Kawamura survived.

But Murata and his comrades had successfully fulfilled their mission. One torpedo hit and exploded at 9:14 a.m. on the *Hornet*'s starboard side amidships below the 1.1-inch AA guns to the rear of the carrier's island. Another torpedo exploded in the engineering compartments aft on the starboard side. The third missile barely missed striking the carrier's bow. The two torpedoes that blew up did extensive damage. Water rushed into the forward engine room and two fire rooms. All electrical power and communications failed. Any hope of directing the *Hornet*'s CAP disappeared. The stricken ship's lights went out, and she began to list to starboard at a 10.5º angle. The *Hornet* lost headway and slowed to a dead stop. She was now dead in the water.

Murata's second three-plane group (Suzuki, PO1c Yukio Okazaki, and PO1c Kokichi Kurita) followed him one minute later when they turned toward the carrier while passing the *Anderson*'s stern. Several 20-mm shells struck Okazaki's plane forcing him to release his torpedo just 75 yards past the *Anderson*'s and then turn sharply left. His bomber was on fire as it smacked into the water and disintegrated near the *Northampton*'s port bow. Chasing the *Hornet* from its stern and unable to get a good firing angle on the carrier, Suzuki and Kurita fired their torpedoes anyway. Both missed badly. Their attempts and those of the remaining five Kates to launch torpedoes while chasing the target at its stern doomed the rest of these planes' attacks. Any torpedoes they could release had no chance of reaching the carrier.

The last group under Murata's leadership, led by Warrant Officer Taneichi Nakai along with PO2c Yoshihiko Kobayashi, separated. Nakai flew inside the screening ships and passed the *Pensacola*'s port quarter. By this time, Nakai gave up trying to attack the *Hornet* and decided to go after the cruiser. He skirted the water's surface, aimed for the *Pensacola*'s port beam, and released his torpedo as soon as he could. Kobayashi also went into his attack position. The cruiser was between him and the carrier. The *Pensacola* presented itself as the only possible target, so he fired his torpedo at that ship, too. Capt. Frank L. Lowe, the cruiser's commander, saw the two wakes heading for his ship and ordered a hard right turn to swing the ship's bow into the approaching torpedoes' wakes. Withering AA gunfire came from the cruiser and struck Kobayashi's plane. He tried to send his doomed aircraft crashing into the *Pensacola* but it burst into flames and crashed into the sea just 100 feet off the cruiser's port bow. Seeing the splash near the ship's bow, Nakai assumed his torpedo had hit it. But both torpedoes missed their target thanks to the Lowe's quick reactions.

While scoring two torpedo hits among the eight launched forced the *Hornet* to stop dead in the water, Murata's torpedo plane formation lost five of 11 Kates: Murata, Matsushima, Okazaki, Kodama, and Kobayashi. With heavy smoke pouring from the American carrier, Nagumo received a brief moment of euphoria with a 9:15 a.m. radio message from one Japanese radioman, "Enemy Saratoga large fire." A few moments later, four bombs from Widhelm's SBDs decimated the *Shokaku*.

✲ ✲ ✲

About one minute before Tsuda's dive-bombing attack and Murata's torpedo assault, Lt. (jg) Nobuo Yoneda's five Vals dove from 12,000 feet to attack on the *Hornet*'s port beam. Four of these planes dove at the carrier and dropped their bombs. Not one of them hit the ship. So the Vals flew away just above the water's surface. The fifth bomber, with flames flowing from its underside and flown by

Warrant Officer Shigeyuki Sato with PO1c Kojiro Yasuda as his observer, flew high above the *Hornet*. Clearly struggling to control his plane, Sato flew straight at the carrier with his bomb still attached. The plane's starboard wing ripped away the ship's starboard halyard and tore a hole in its stack. The fuselage bounced off the island and disintegrated in a ball of flames. Burning gasoline from the aircraft's fuel tank spread over the bridge. The remnants of the decimated plane blasted a hole in the flight deck and dropped into one of the ready rooms below. Several aircrews were in the room when the flames began consuming the room and barely escaped with their lives.

Luckily, Sato's 250-kg bomb failed to explode and rolled along the corridor outside the burning ready room. Continuing to burn for more than two hours, the fires alone were more than enough to kill or cripple many men. The fires on the bridge killed seven signalmen while consuming all the ships flags. In what seemed to be a prelude to tactics the increasingly desperate Imperial Japanese Navy would use later in the war, Sato's last minutes inflicted more cruel damage on an already crippled carrier.

At the same time Murata's attack happened, Lt. Goro Washimi's nine Kates closed the distance to Task Force 17 from the northwest. Unlike Murata, these torpedo planes had no fighter escort and had clashed with the doggedly determined American fighters. Washimi and his wingmates, PO2c Hiroshi Akiyama and PO2c Toshiaki Nakamura, led the other two three-plane formations. Flying to the left were Lt. (jg) Akira Chosokabe and his two compatriots, PO1c Yoshio Mitsumori and PO2c Hiroshi Ikeda. Special Duty Ens. Rokuro Iwagami and two other planes commanded by PO1c Gonari Sano and Katsu Suzuki trailed behind Chosokabe and farther to the left. The nine aircraft were ahead of the *Hornet*'s port side and therefore had a much better firing angle for their torpedo attacks.

Two F4Fs flown by Ensigns Donald Gordon and Gerald V. Davis flew at 15,000 feet and southwest of Task Force 17. With the signal to attack, "Tally Ho," ringing in their headphones, they saw five Japanese torpedo planes below their right wings passing though 7,000 feet. They were Washimi's and Chosokabe's formations turning toward the *Hornet*. The F4F pilots pushed their noses down and turned around 180° to go after the Washimi's leading plane, which was now diving and about to level-off for his torpedo attack. Gordon, now in a high-speed dive, fired his guns. His tracers caught Washimi off-guard; he made a tight right turn to get away from the F4F. Just then, the torpedo plane came into Davis' sights. Firing his guns at the Japanese plane's tail, smoke soon trailed behind the Kate as it turned away from the ships.

Meanwhile, Lt. Macgregor "Mac" Kilpatrick moved in to attack Akiyama's plane. The Japanese plane jerked and lurched in a way to avoid presenting an inviting target. Kilpatrick tried to get the bomber in his sights. He squeezed off several bursts that wounded Akiyama's gunner, Sea2c Kazuo Oguri. His 7.7-mm machine's barrel pointed harmlessly skyward. Akiyama moved down to just 50 feet off the water. Gordon and Davis also joined Kilpatrick. Davis moved in for the kill and fired his guns at the Kate's unguarded tail. Flames burst from the slowly descending Japanese plane, now flying a mere 10 feet above the waves. None of the American pilots saw the plane crash because the intense AA fire from the ships forced them to flee for their own sake. Akiyama did crash into the sea. He and his crew lost their lives.

George Wrenn was a fortunate man to successfully escape his scrape with Shirane's Zeroes. He found himself in an advantageous position to attack Iwagami's and Chosokabe's six torpedo planes, which were in their attacking dives toward Task Force 17. He went into a high-speed shallow dive and soon had Suzuki's plane in his sights. Rolling over into an inverted position, he fired his guns. The plane's rear gunner stopped firing, leaving his plane defenseless. More bursts blasted the plane until Wrenn saw smoke belch from his target as it headed for the water. He next brought Sano's plane into his sights. The plane's side made an ideal target. Wrenn's guns set the Kate ablaze. However, the intense AA fire from the ships below forced him to give up pursuing the torpedo planes. Suzuki, his aircraft badly damaged, had to head back to the *Zuikaku*. Sano, wanting to make the most of the moments he had left in his life, tried to crash into the cruiser *Juneau,* but missed her as her port-side AA battery blew his plane from the sky.

The destroyer *Morris*, steaming off the *Hornet*'s port bow, soon contributed to the air battle. Five torpedo planes, flying about 200 to 300 feet above the water, turned left at 9:14 a.m. toward the carrier. Nakamura led the assault with Chosokabe, Mitsumori, and Ikeda right behind him and passed behind the destroyer's stern. Sailors on the *Morris* saw the four green-colored planes fly past their ship as murderous AA fire sent Mitsumori into the sea. The other four dodged the destroyer's gunfire and launched their torpedoes at the *Hornet*'s port bow. All four missed. Three torpedoes continued roiling southward. The *Northampton*'s captain saw them approaching and turned to port to comb their wakes. The missiles just missed the cruiser's stern. So far, three of Iwagami's planes had crashed into the sea.

With four of his seven original dive-bombers still flying, Ishimaru made a wide turn to the south of Task Force 17 and began his attack on the *Hornet*. Meanwhile, Pollock plus his three F4Fs, flying at 22,000 feet and 10 miles past the *Hornet*, looked back at 9:12 a.m. and saw AA bursts, black smoke, and fires from falling planes. He did not want to give up the superior altitude advantage, but there were no Japanese planes nearby. Nonetheless, he also noticed what seemed to be three Japanese dive-bombers flying 6,000 feet below him and trying to attack the *Hornet*. He issued the "Tally Ho!" command over his radio, and his planes dove at the Japanese dive-bombers.

Ishimaru was in his dive when the American F4Fs appeared above his planes. Pollock lined up the second plane in his sights and fired his guns. The rear gunner stopped returning fire. By this time, Pollock had a point-blank clear shot and opened up again with his six .50-cal. Browning machine guns. Flames erupted from the Japanese aircraft at 13,000 feet and it fell. Ensigns Steve Kona and Lyman J. Fulton attacked the third dive-bomber at 12,000 feet and kept firing all the way down to 5,000 feet. As tracer bullets flew all around them, the American pilots finally broke off the attack.

The remaining three dive-bombers continued their attack, dropped their bombs and hit nothing. As they tried to leave, Kona and Fulton tried to intercept them to no avail. But more F4Fs came in to finish them off. Vejtasa destroyed one bomber at a lower altitude. Ruehlow joined the party by splashing one more bomber. Ens. William H. Leder claimed the third bomber, but Ishimaru managed to get away.

Two heavily damaged Japanese planes arrived later to again threaten the *Hornet*. A Val with smoke streaming behind it and in a shallow dive approached the carrier's stern at 9:17 a.m. The ship's guns fired a withering barrage at the newest menace. The plane shook as it turned into a flaming missile heading toward the ship's port quarter. Whether the pilot was in full control of the airplane or not is unknown. Nonetheless, the plane continued its deadly last moments of flight. The crippled carrier had by this time slowed to a complete stop. After dropping his bomb 50 yards short of the carrier, the pilot pulled up over the carrier's starboard bow, headed for the *Northampton*, turned around, and headed back toward the carrier. By now, every gun in Task Force 17 desperately tried to protect their most valuable asset. They opened up on the bomber with an almost impenetrable wall of gunfire. But the Japanese plane penetrated that barrier, flew toward the *Hornet*'s bow, crashed into the hull just ahead of the port side gun gallery, and exploded in a flaming ball. Burning gasoline spread into the forward elevator pit and ignited a lethal fire.

About a minute later, a torpedo plane, most likely with Washimi at its controls, flew west of the task force and dropped its torpedo to reduce its weight and stay in the air. Approaching from the northwest, it headed right for the *Hornet* stopped. But it could not stay aloft and crashed into the water within just a few yards of the carrier.

After losing one more torpedo bomber to American fighters, the surviving Japanese planes headed for home. Five torpedo planes flew northward while another five torpedo planes to the task force's south, circled around the American ships and then headed in the same direction. As they left the combat area, one Kate crew saw another American carrier task force to the northeast and radioed its sighting at 10:20 a.m. to Nagumo. They reported the other carrier was on a 20° bearing, about 15 miles from the first carrier, and steaming on a course of 000° at a speed of 24 knots. However, the message did not arrive the way it was sent. Apparently garbled during transmission, one Japanese ship picked up the message that said the second American carrier task force on a bearing of 45° about 40 miles from the first carrier. This error would obviously play a dramatic role later. Nevertheless, this new sighting had the undivided attention of the Japanese.

Results of the First Japanese Carrier Strike

Not counting two reconnaissance aircraft, the Japanese sent 53 carrier planes—12 Zeroes, 21 Vals, and 20 Kates—to strike Task Force 17. After the survivors returned, they claimed to have sunk one carrier, one heavy cruiser, one destroyer, causing heavy damage to one destroyer, and to have shot down 20 American fighters. This attack was the Imperial Japanese Navy's last and best coordinated air strike. But the price Japan paid was not cheap. They lost 38 planes—five Zeroes, 17 Vals and 16 Kates—or about 72% of the original numbers of planes.

The actual American air losses were six F4Fs. Nonetheless, the *Hornet* was now a floating wreck and had no power to move the ship. Obviously, she could not conduct air operations. Eight F4Fs were unable to leave, and seven inoperable SBDs lay helplessly aboard. She listed at an 8° tilt to starboard as fires spread from the signal bridge to the fourth deck and from the forward elevator to the after hangar deck. Since she had no power, there was no water in the main pipes to fight the fires. Water flooded into her forward engine room and two fire rooms. Her list continued to worsen, but briefly abated through the use of counter flooding. While still salvageable, her life now depended upon how much help she would get from Task Force 16's aircraft.

✲ ✲ ✲

Meanwhile, Warrant Officer Shigenobu Tanaka's Kates stayed behind over Task Force 17 to keep an eye on the crippled *Hornet*. He had no torpedo, but, as he noticed the operations commence to tow the *Hornet*, he wanted to delay the carrier's possible journey to safety. He went into a shallow dive at 10:07 a.m. and either dropped a marker buoy or navigational aid that came very close to hitting the destroyer *Morris* and the carrier. Concerned their ships were in danger, the captains of the *Northampton* and the surrounding destroyers moved their ships away from the carrier. Tanaka had succeeded delaying the towing of the *Hornet*. She was still a sitting duck for another air assault or a submarine attack.[2]

CHAPTER 34
Attacking the "Big E"

The Japanese Second Wave Arrives

Adm. Kinkaid stood on the *Enterprise* bridge with his binoculars looking to the southwestern horizon. Task Force 16 was about 12 miles from where the *Hornet* was being attacked. He saw smoke rising high in the sky. Falling Japanese aircraft looked like "fireflies" that would burst with light and disappear. Although he did not know the precise condition of the *Hornet*, radio reports confirmed the smoke came from the crippled carrier, and he did not want the same fate to befall the *Enterprise*. He ordered Task Force 16 to turn to the southeast at 28 knots. There were clouds from rain squalls in that direction that would provide a hiding place from the Japanese aircraft he knew were on their way. The 20 SBDs that had gone on the search for Japanese appeared over the *Enterprise* at 9:30 a.m. and were low on fuel. The seven CAP F4Fs also needed to be refueled. Five of the aircraft had combat damage that spelled some possible problems when they attempted to land.

Lt. James G. Daniels, III, the *Enterprise*'s LSO, began to direct the SBDs aboard the carrier at 9:31 a.m. but not without difficulty. Meanwhile, the F4Fs joined the SBDs in the landing pattern. Edwards landed his F4F, but its propeller pitch was locked in a high angle. Kilpatrick's engine overheated, but he landed safely. Kona, Hessel, Rynd, and Kiekhoefer followed with their damaged planes. The LSO waved off Claude Phillips' first try to land because the pilot did not have his flaps in landing position. He landed safely on his second attempt. By 9:48 a.m., Daniels had brought all 20 SBDs and seven F4Fs aboard. Twelve more aircraft—ten F4Fs and two damaged TBFs—were still in the landing pattern when the carrier had to remove all the planes from her flight deck.

Meanwhile, Kinkaid radioed Radm. Howard H. Good, Task Force 17's cruiser commander, at 9:41 a.m. to ask if the *Enterprise* needed to land any *Hornet* aircraft still aloft. Good replied, "Affirmative"—that answer gave Kinkaid the bad news he did not want to hear. Good wanted to put a tow line on the *Hornet* and have the *Northampton* tow her to safety. He wanted to keep the remaining F4Fs for CAP, but the planes needed to fill up but had to fly to the *Enterprise* to refuel. The *Enterprise* only had 11 F4Fs in her CAP; it could not send any help to the *Hornet*.

Kinkaid sent a cryptic message to Halsey at 9:49 a.m. that said, "*Hornet* hurt." COMSOPAC, desperately wanting to be in the middle of the battle, directed his commanders, "Operate from and in positions from which you can strike quickly and effectively. We must use everything we have to the limit."[1] Whether Task Force 61's limit would be enough was the key question to be answered.

Not only did the *Enterprise* have to land the aircraft already in its landing pattern, it also had to bring home the rest of the *Hornet*'s wayward birds. After returning from their search mission, Welch and McGraw told Capt. Hardison they had spotted the Vanguard Force. Hardison then went to Kinkaid and recommended the *Enterprise* launch a ten-plane dive-bomber strike at about 10:00 a.m. without a fighter escort, attack the Vanguard Force, and then land at Henderson Field. But the carrier first had to land the waiting planes. Task Force 16 turned right to 200° to not open too much distance to the returning American strike planes. After being lined up again to land planes, the hangar deck's rearming crews reloaded bombs, ammunition, and fuel onto the SBDs. After the strike launched, Hardison wanted to land some of the *Enterprise*'s CAP to refuel, send the already fueled fighters aloft to take their place, and later launch the refueled fighters to increase the CAP. Griffin ordered Faulkner's three F4Fs to land. Task Force 16 only had 8 CAP F4Fs aloft as of 10:00 a.m.: Vejtasa's four and Kane's four F4Fs. The task force was highly vulnerable and nearly defenseless.

Seki's 19 Vals now flew at 16,140 feet escorted by Lt. Shingo's five Zeroes. Imajuku's 17 Kates and Shigemi's four escorting Zeroes straggled 45 minutes behind the dive-bombers.

Before Nagumo and his officers listened to their first strike radio talk, they made up their minds that there was another carrier near the one already spotted by their aircrews. Their radio technicians had been listening to the radio transmission of the American FDOs. So Nagumo sent an alert at 9:27 a.m. to all his ships, "There appear to be two carriers, one as yet unknown, estimated south of Saratoga's position, 8-35 S, 166-45 E." One minute later, Radm. Kakuji Kakuta on the *Junyo* sent a message that added to Nagumo's, "Enemy force is in two groups of at least 10 ships centering around large carriers." Flying the contact plane in the approaching torpedo plane formation, Lt. (jg) Tsugimi Sakumuki confirmed his leaders' messages at 9:27 a.m., "Another large enemy force, one carrier, one light cruiser, six destroyers, speed 20 knots, position 8-37 S, 166-37 E, 0730 [Z-9]."[2] Seki had all the information he needed to begin his attack.

✲ ✲ ✲

The *Northampton*'s radar spotted the approaching Japanese planes, and Good relayed the sighting to Kinkaid at about 9:30 a.m. that they were approaching on a bearing of 315°, 76 miles away. Seven minutes later, he sent Kinkaid another report that the Japanese planes were approaching from at 290°, 35 miles. The *South Dakota*'s radar picked up many planes at 9:45 a.m. bearing 325°, 55 miles. Eight minutes later, the *Enterprise*'s shorter range radar spotted the planes—bearing 340°, distance 45 miles.

✲ ✲ ✲

Seki looked to his right and saw Task Force 17's screen surrounding the *Hornet* and knew that Murata had done his job. A radio report spotted the second carrier about 15 miles north of the first one. But he could not see the second task force as it had apparently moved to the southeast. So he decided to keep flying on his original course. That decision soon proved to be fruitful as he saw Task Force 16 and sent a message at 10:00 a.m. that reported a new carrier task force on a bearing of 90° about 20 miles from the *Hornet*.

The *South Dakota* radar reported spotting multiple bogeys 25 miles away; the *Enterprise* radar picked up the planes circling to the east of Task Force 16. The radio intercepting unit on the *Enterprise* picked up snippets of the Japanese inter-plane transmissions and gave the translated versions to Kinkaid. As Seki's formation moved closer, the pilots discerned an *Enterprise*-class carrier with 20 planes on her deck. They also saw a *South Dakota*-class battleship they had not seen before. At 11:08 a.m., Seki issued the order: "All Forces attack." The time to attack had arrived.

Jack Griffin, the *Enterprise*'s FDO, tried mightily to straighten out the confusion over the precise way to organize the fighter defense against the impending Japanese air attack. Many Japanese aircraft had been detected in the last hour. But the defense was still in disarray and the disposition of the approaching planes unclear. Actually, there were 21 F4Fs circling Task Force 16, eight directly over the task force at about 10,000 feet and 13 at a lower altitude. Griffin knew the Japanese planes approached from the north and wanted to get some planes up to intercept them. He sent Kane northward to look for the Japanese. Kane flew for five minutes and began circling. Griffin warned all fighters to look for approaching planes from the north. He then ordered Kane to come back at 10:06 a.m. and told him to "look behind you to east and northeast."[3]

Meanwhile, three damaged American planes, two TBFs and one F4F, were returning from their attack on Nagumo's ships. Batten's TBF was on fire. He doused the fire, but he could not drop his torpedo. He turned into the *Enterprise*'s landing pattern at 9:59 a.m., but the ship waved him off. Running out of fuel, he splashed down two minutes later off the carrier's port quarter and 1,500 yards ahead of the destroyer *Porter*. Being the nearest to the downed pilot, the destroyer moved toward the pancaked plane to rescue its aircrew. The plane had nosed over when it hit the water, and the crew climbed out of the plane and into their life raft. The *Porter* slowed and moved near the raft to retrieve the aircrew. What should have been a routine pickup soon became anything but normal.

One of the *Porter*'s lookouts shouted, "Torpedo on the port bow!" Lt. Albert D. Pollock and Ens. James H. Dowden saw a porpoising torpedo turning in a circle ahead of the destroyer. They tried to stop it by strafing it with their machine guns to explode its warhead. They made two runs from 300 feet above the water but the only impact they made was to scare the crews of the ships around them, which began firing at the missile with their AA guns. Despite the withering wall of fire, the wayward torpedo kept curving toward the destroyer. It struck her amidships between her No. 1 and No. 2 fireroom and exploded. Clouds of white smoke rose into the air from her boilers, and she quickly became a hopeless derelict. Everyone thought the torpedo had come from a Japanese submarine. It had separated from Batten's downed TBF as the plane hit the water. Kinkaid ordered the destroyer *Shaw* to stay behind and rescue the doomed *Porter*'s crew. Task Force 16 continued on her present course and speed. Obeying Kinkaid's further orders, the *Shaw* finally sank her stricken companion at 12:08 p.m.

Now fully aware of the impending Japanese air attack, Kinkaid changed Task Force 16's course with a starboard turn to 235° and ordered the destroyer *Conyngham* to fill the gap made by the now missing *Porter* and *Shaw*. The screen surrounding the carrier had the battleship *South Dakota* 2,500 yards astern, the heavy cruiser *Portland* 2,500 yards on the carrier's port bow, the AA cruiser *San Juan* in the same relative slot off the *Enterprise*'s starboard bow, and the rest of the destroyers in an approximate circle 1,500 yards from the carrier. Still getting ready to launch its planned strike against the Japanese ships, one SBD was on the aft end of the flight deck. Other dive-bombers were parked forward on the flight deck. Some of them had a full load of fuel and an armed 500-pound bomb attached to their bellies. Hangar deck crews continued to arm and fuel several more SBDs. Reflecting a sense of irony, the carrier was in the same precarious condition Nagumo's carriers were in at Midway when American planes moved in for the kill.

Griffin warned all fighters at 10:07 a.m., "Look out for bogeys approaching from north and northeast, angels probably low." Four minutes later, he told them to circle three to five miles northeast of the *Enterprise* and ordered Kane to the southeast to place himself between the approaching Japanese planes and the carrier. Realizing that this mission would accomplish little, he recalled Kane to return to the *Enterprise* and "Look for bogeys northeast. They are astern of BB [*South Dakota*]."

Griffin's effort to set up an effective defense went awry when he did not order the fighters to climb. The Japanese were now closer to Task Force 16. The American pilots could not discern whether they faced dive-bombers or torpedo planes. He relied upon the sightings of the aloft fighters to find the Japanese; unfortunately, they saw nothing. The Japanese planes had an unobstructed path to the carrier.

Seki Moves in for the Attack

Seki wanted to approach the American carrier's starboard side from out of the sun. Seven Vals commanded by Seki approached in three groups:

First Group:	Seki, PO1c Tetsu Imada, PO2c Yoshimi Itaya
Second Group:	Lt. Kazuo Yoshimoto, PO1c Fumio Someno
Third Group:	Ens. Chiaki Saito, Sea1c Goichi Hiroso

Shingo's five escorting Zeroes led the attack. Seven more dive-bombers led by Lt. Keiichi Arima were in three groups:

First Group:	Arima, PO1c Hiroshi Koitabashi, PO2c Yoshimaru Honda
Second Group:	Lt. (jg) Toshiji Saito, PO2c Ryoroku Tsuchiya
Third Group:	WO Yoshiharu Tanaka, PO2c Masanari Sugano

Trailing behind, another formation of five Vals in three groups was led by Lt. Shohei Yamada accompanied by Arima's planes:

First Group:	Yamada, PO3c Isaku Mochizuki
Second Group:	Lt. (jg) Haruo Miyauchi
Third Group:	Warrant Officer Tsukushi Shimuzu, PO2c Kazuhito Sueyasu.

The F4Fs were still orbiting below the approaching Japanese planes. Pollock was the nearest but flew at 12,000 feet and did not see the approaching bogeys. The Japanese dive-bombers continued their seemingly unstoppable path toward the *Enterprise*.

Ensigns Maurice N. Wickendoll and Frederick L. Feightner finally saw the Japanese dive-bombers flying toward the carrier and moved into an attacking position. Wickendoll unsuccessfully attacked the formation four times, but he had problems keeping his plane properly pointed at his intended target. Only one left outboard gun could fire that caused the plane to veer left. Feightner lined up one Val in his sights, fired his guns, and sent it into a flaming dive toward the water. It hit the water 4,000 feet from the *Portland*'s bow.

After Seki had pushed his plane into his attacking dive at 10:15 a.m., the *Enterprise* spotters finally saw the planes plummeting toward the carrier. No American fighters were near enough to stop them. The Japanese bombers disappeared into a cloud bank and emerged unscathed. The destroyer *Maury* began firing its five-inch guns at the attacking planes. The carrier, sporting 16 new Bofors 40-mm guns, let loose a barrage. Responding to the lookouts' warnings, Griffin alerted the CAP, "REAPERS look for planes in dives. REAPERS from base: Look for bogeys diving on port bow." The *South Dakota* significantly added to the barrage at 10:15 a.m. with a fusillade of its own. The dive-bombers were in their high, steep dives and approaching from the carriers' stern toward its starboard side.

Although Task Force 16 did not receive much advance warning, its AA fire was nearing maximum intensity. Lt. Cmdr. Elias B. Mott, the *Enterprise* assistant gunnery and antiaircraft officer and who was at his post on the top observer station, described the Japanese diving attack from his own perspective, "As each plane came down, a veritable cone of tracer shells enveloped it. You could see it being hit and bounced by exploding shells."[4]

Kazuo Yoshimoto's dive-bomber was in the group just behind Seki's as all planes plummeted toward the American carrier. He saw the lead plane absorb many hits from blistering AA fire rising to meet them from the ships below. Seki's doomed plane then rolled on its back, went into a flaming dive, and broke into pieces as it headed for the water. Its separated bomb hit the water and exploded alongside the amidships of the carrier just as the ship turned hard left.

Not one of the six planes in the first two three-plane groups hit anything because of the withering AA fire. They tried to escape by flying low as a deluge of machine-gun fire whizzed past them. Bullets riddled Itaya's, Someno's, and Hiroso's planes and destroyed them. The escorting Zeros tried to protect the dive-bombers by flying alongside them at near wave top levels.

The *Enterprise* was now in a fast turn as Arima's seven plane formation attacked the carrier about two minutes after Seki's attack. The intensity of the American AA fire surprised Arima as it was much more brutal than at the Battle of the Eastern Solomons in August. Mott saw Arima's bomber come out of a cloud at 8,000 feet and head for his ship's starboard quarter. Despite Mott's efforts to alert the AA guns to the danger of the approaching aircraft and the barrage of fire now piercing the sky, Arima's pilot, PO1c Kiyoto Furuta, released his 250-kg bomb at his dive's lowest point right at the center of the carrier's flight deck. It put a hole 20 feet from the deck's forward edge, plummeted past the forecastle, and exploded in the air near the port bow. The blast knocked an SBD off the deck and killed its rear machine-gunner, AMM1c Sam D. Presley. Another SBD's gasoline tank sprung a leak and several fires erupted. The damage control crews immediately responded to the emergency and quickly extinguished the fires. Ens. Marshall Field, commanding a recently-installed 1.1-inch AA gun battery, sustained wounds, although they were not serious. The bomb did only minor damage.

The rest of Arima's flight followed with Yamada's five-plane formation right behind them. By now, the American carrier was in a turn that moved away from the approaching planes. Thus they could not go into their normal steep dives and had to attack the carrier at a shallower diving angle. The withering American AA fire intensity had not lessened. The Japanese pilots did their best to dodge it and had some success. One minute after Arima's bomb hit the carrier, another 250-kg semi-armor-piercing bomb smacked into the center of the ship's flight deck 10 feet to the rear of the No. 1 elevator, pierced the deck, detonated, and caused two explosions to erupt inside the ship. The first conflagration spread through the hangar deck, killing and wounding many men, setting three SBDs afire, and endangering five nearby fully armed and fueled dive-bombers. The hangar crews fearlessly pushed the burning planes overboard along with three more in mortal danger of catching afire. The second explosion spread through the second deck just below the hangar deck, killed all in a repair party, destroyed several officers' sleeping quarters, and started a fire in the No. 1 elevator pit.

The Japanese planes kept coming and continued to drop their bombs at the carrier. One of their last bombs smacked into the sea at 10:20 a.m. It exploded just ten feet from the carrier's starboard quarter, and caused leaks under the ship's waterline. Airplanes on the forward flight deck jumped up from the deck, and Kona's F4F, closest to the explosion, wobbled over the side and fell into the sea. An SBD bounded sideways and ended up perilously astride a 20-mm battery.

Griffin finally called his CAP at 10:17 a.m. to the carrier's defense, "Hey Rube—Looks like hawks—Close in quick!" It appears that the CAP shot down three attacking bombers and the antiaircraft got ten more. The Japanese believed they hit the carrier with six bombs. One of the surviving crews sent a radio message at 10:30 a.m. that one carrier was left burning. Arima reported that he and his comrades had accomplished their mission with a cryptic message, "Good health to two enemy carriers."

Just as he did on August 24, Seki had led the attack, but this one cost him his life. The *Enterprise* had taken two hits with another near miss that resulted in the loss of 44 lives and many more wounded. Her No. 1 elevator was frozen in the up position with its future ability to operate in doubt. Nine SBDs of the 31 onboard went over the side along with one F4F. Nevertheless, she was not in any danger of sinking.

The war diary of one of the *Enterprise* bombing squadrons has an entry depicting what it was like to be on board the carrier that day with the Japanese dive-bombers attacking.

> "The squadron ready room was piled in some cases two and three deep...It was a grim time. The ship rocked with its own firing, the near misses and direct hits from the enemy and its violent maneuvering. In the ready room the squadron heard the attack, felt it, and waited anxiously for the next portentous announcement from the public address system...ventilation and air conditioning turned off in the ready room—steel helmets, sweat, life preservers, and anxiety sitting heavily on the squadron squeezed together on the deck, awaiting the next explosion, the next violent shudder of the ship.[5]"

The situation was the same for the carrier's fighter squadron ready room. Kilpatrick later related that an "acrid dust cloud" permeated the room as the bomb that hit amidships did its deadly work.

But the persistent Japanese had one more card to play. Imajuku's torpedo planes from the *Zuikaku* were nearing the carrier. The *Enterprise*'s destiny still had to be decided.

Torpedo Attack

The Japanese dive-bombers had finished their work by 10:30 a.m. Kinkaid had to land some of his CAP for rearming and refueling. But he had a message from Adm. Good that put more demands in his hands for fighter projection, "JOE [*Hornet*] stopped burning. Request fighter coverage." But Kinkaid had no fighters to spare for Task Force 17 since he worried about more Japanese aircraft that might be on their way to sink the *Enterprise*. Griffin, also equally concerned, ordered the CAP to climb back to its patrol altitude. Fourteen F4Fs answered his request while another equal number of fighters still flew low. Kane (2 F4Fs) and Pollock (F4Fs) responded. Vejtasa (4 F4Fs) and Faulkner (3 F4Fs) never heard Griffin's order. Meanwhile, a squall line began to build to the west.

The carrier radar detected an aerial contact at 10:35 a.m. that became a large formation of Japanese planes on a 330° bearing five minutes later. Griffin ordered Kane to investigate the contact and ordered Pollock to look to the northwest. Meanwhile, acting on his own initiative and not wanting to be left out of the fight that was to come, Vejtasa directed his four F4Fs toward the target. Faulkner took his formation that included Long and Barnes westward to search for torpedo planes. Barnes soon dropped out of sight. Obviously, Griffin's attempts to coordinate the CAP accomplished little. It seemed as if it was every man for himself.

Imajuku's 17 Kates left the *Zuikaku* 50 minutes before Seki's Vals and included one unarmed observation craft flown by Warrant Officer Naoichiro Suzuki. Escorted by Shigemi's four Zeroes, they now flew at 4,000 meters (13,123 feet) when Imajuku saw a smoking carrier (*Hornet*) at 10:35 a.m. with the telltale wakes of several ships trying to help her. Just beyond the rain clouds, he and his compatriots saw more ship wakes two minutes later and to the southeast that they later identified as an *Enterprise*-class carrier, a *South Dakota*-class battleship, two cruisers and eight destroyers. Those ships were Task Force 16 now steaming to the southwest on a 235° course. The Japanese flight leader saw a real target to attack and continued to fly toward it.

Barnes' missing F4F suddenly appeared striking the *South Dakota*'s starboard bow. The captain of the destroyer *Maury*, Lt. Cmdr. Gelzer L. Sims, ordered his ship to break formation and rescue the downed pilot. Barnes had exited his aircraft and was seen bobbing in the water to the destroyer's stern. Sims believed that the pickup would become a routine one.

Griffin noticed the approaching planes initially flying at a higher altitude but he soon changed his assessment. Now believing these planes could be torpedo bombers, he sent a 10:44 a.m. warning message to his CAP of approaching Japanese planes, "Look out for fish [torpedo planes]. Look out for fish. Fish bear about 330 degrees from base." The American CAP was in the right position between the Japanese planes and Task Force 16.

As his force proceeded with their shallow dives, Imajuku ordered them to split into two groups to attack the carrier simultaneously from both sides. He would lead eight Kates to his right toward the carrier's port bow while Lt. Masayuki Yusuhara would take the other torpedo bombers toward the carrier's port stern. Shigemi's Zeroes would go with Yusuhara's aircraft. When the two groups parted, Imajuku waved goodbye. But these movements did not go unnoticed by the American CAP. Ens. William H. Leder, flying in his F4F with Vejtasa's formation at 13,000 feet, looked down and saw Japanese planes flying below him. He picked up his radio microphone and spoke into it, "Tally ho nine o'clock down." His section leader, Lt. Stanley E. Ruehlow, and he went into a steep dive toward two Zeroes.

About one minute later, Vejtasa and Lt. Leroy E. ("Tex") Harris saw what seemed to be 11 Japanese torpedo bombers flying in a column and diving toward the rain clouds at a speed of more than 250 knots. These planes were Yusuhara's eight Kates and some Zeroes in the attacking dives. Vejtasa's and Harris' F4Fs had reached 350 knots when both pilots fired their guns and set two torpedo planes afire. On their next pass, they blasted PO1c Kenichiro Toshida's plane from the sky.

Pollock and Holland saw several torpedo bombers about 8,000 yards to their right and diving 1,000 feet below. Pollock made an overhead pass and moved onto the tail of what looked like one Kate. Holland warned his wing mate this was a Zero. Wanting to defend his ship against planes that could actually damage it, he stopped his attack and went after the other torpedo planes.

The Japanese torpedo planes disappeared into the storm clouds and rapidly descended toward Task Force 16. Vejtasa saw Pollock get on one bomber's tail and fire his guns from point-blank range. Smoke belched from the stricken plane, flown by PO3c Yasuo Kikuchi, as it also vanished into the storm clouds. Vejtasa followed three Kates and got on the tail of PO1c Heiji Tamura's plane. After firing two brief machine gun bursts, he turned his attention to the leader of the three-plane group, Special Duty Ens. Kazumasa Kanada, and kept firing bursts. Vejtasa saw pieces of the plane's tail split away. Then he went after the third plane, flown by PO1c Kazuo Yamauchi, and thought he damaged it as well. Nevertheless, all three planes continued flying toward their intended target.

As Pollock's plane came out of the clouds, he thought he saw one burning Japanese plane smack into the water. Other shipboard people also saw a fiery ball hit the water about five miles astern of the task force. While still inside the storm clouds, Vejtasa saw one torpedo plane, likely the one hit by Pollock's gunfire, and moved under it for another attack. However, he missed the plane and then got on its tail as it dove steeply for the water. He could not get off another shot, but the American CAP had apparently shot down one torpedo bomber (Toshida), damaged another (Kikuchi), forced one to abandon its attack, while putting bullet holes into the other five planes from Yusuhara's eight-plane formation. Together, Yusuhara's group had fared none too well from their encounters with the American CAP. They would yet make their mark later.

Meanwhile, Imajuku's group continued its course toward the *Enterprise*'s port bow and went down to wave-top level to defend themselves against the fighter that had been harassing Yusuhara. But they still had some distance to go before they could launch their torpedoes at the carrier if it stayed on its 235° course. The eight torpedo bombers fanned out to put themselves in position to attack Task Force 16 from the west and southwest. Imajuku and the two planes in his formation commanded by PO1c Tadayoshi Kawada and PO1c Oyoshi Kawabata stayed in the lead. Lt. (jg) Tetsu Ito's plane, others commanded by PO1c Masayoshi Nagashima and PO1c Masatoshi Sato, and Special Duty Ens. Nakakura Suzuki led the third group including PO1c Nagao Yukawa's plane followed behind.

Wrenn and Dowden's F4Fs were among other fighters flying at 500 feet that were waiting to land for refueling and rearming when Imajuku's formation flew past just 10 feet above the water. Wrenn forgot about waiting to land, dove onto Imajuku's tail, and fired his guns. The Japanese pilot's troubles multiplied as he looked ahead and saw the shape of an American destroyer (*Maury*) loom in his windshield. The destroyer opened up with her 20-mm guns as she was attempting to pick up a downed American pilot (Barnes). Sims, her captain, saw six Japanese torpedo planes heading straight for his ship. Potentially sacrificing the pilot's fate to meet the greater threat, Sims steered his ship to bring all his firepower to bear on the approaching planes.

The combination of Wrenn's gunfire and the destroyer's cannon fire caused the Japanese plane's port wing to break away. The plane rolled to starboard, and its right wingtip hit the water.

The *Maury* did not go back to find Barnes, who was never recovered. Sims later recommended that ships throw life rafts to downed pilots; CINCPAC agreed and Sims' proposal became standard procedure for the rest of the war.

Their leader's demise did not deter the remaining seven torpedo planes from continuing their assault despite the American ships' withering AA fire. At 10:46 a.m., Kawada flew past the *Maury*'s port beam, lined up his sights at the carrier's starboard bow, fired his torpedo, and banked away to escape. The torpedo missed its target. Kawabata zipped past the destroyer on a parallel course to the American task force to get a better firing angle.

Ito's three-plane group stayed in attack formation, moved toward the carrier's port bow, and dropped their three missiles. Acting on the advice of his highly respected navigator, Cmdr. Richard W. Ruble, Hardison turned the *Enterprise* to starboard to comb the oncoming torpedo wakes. All three bubbled harmlessly past her. The three planes flew past the carrier's port side and escaped through the hail of gunfire from the *South Dakota*.

Suzuki and Yukawa could not get a good firing position on the carrier, so they turned their attention on the battleship. Yukawa fired his torpedo at the *South Dakota*'s starboard side and turned away toward the northwest. Suzuki showed more determination and flew nearer to the battleship. At 10:48 a.m., he launched his torpedo into the air like a bomb. The unconventional attack caused the torpedo to fly over the ship's stern from starboard to port and plop into the water about 20 yards away. Suzuki's plane by now was hopelessly damaged by the ship's AA fire and splatted into the water 200 yards past the point from where it had launched its weird attack. Lookouts on the destroyer *Preston* saw Yukawa's torpedo burble passed the battleship's port quarter. Nonetheless, Yukawa left the battle highly confident he had inflicted a fatal blow on the *South Dakota*.

Hardison swung the *Enterprise*'s rudder to port to avoid the damaged (explained later) destroyer *Smith* approaching her on the port quarter. He then ordered a leftward course change to 135°. By this time, Kawabata had maneuvered his plane into the firing position he wanted and lined up the big carrier in his sights. She was dead ahead of him. He would never have a better opportunity. Pulling the torpedo launch handle, he felt the torpedo release from its mount and turned away. The carrier's lookouts did not see the missile's wake until it was only 800 yards away. Hardison ordered a hard right rudder. As the big ship's stern swung left, the torpedo passed harmlessly just 100 yards from her starboard side. Recovering from the bombing attack's damage rear 1.1-inch AA battery opened fire and hit Kawabata's plane just as the pilot dropped his torpedo. The shells pummeled the doomed plane; it splashed into the sea. The crew survived the crash, but ship gunfire killed them as they climbed onto the wreckage.

Six Kates had attacked the *Enterprise* while two others assaulted the *South Dakota*. Three planes crashed into the sea and the other five escaped to the northwest.

✲ ✲ ✲

Meanwhile, after running the American fighter defensive gauntlet, six Kates from Yusuhara's group came out of the storm clouds in a loose formation. The background of dark clouds camouflaged the emerging dark-green planes as they approached Task Force 16 from the rear.

Vejtasa still was on a torpedo bomber's tail and firing his guns. He judged that this Japanese plane was not a true threat to the task force and broke off his pursuit when intense AA fire rose toward it. The Kate began trailing flames behind.

Sea1c Kiyomi Takei soon understood he could not get his flaming plane near enough to the carrier to launch his torpedo. He turned his plane toward a nearby destroyer at 10:47 a.m. (*Smith*) and smashed into its No. 1 gun mount's shield. The plane's fuselage rolled into the water but its unexploded torpedo rolled toward the destroyer's forecastle. The missile exploded six minutes later in a horrific blast right under the No. 1 gun. Gasoline poured from its split-open tanks and started a serious conflagration. The heavily damaged destroyer pulled to its starboard so that the *Enterprise* had to change its own direction to avoid hitting her.

The other five torpedo planes kept coming at the carrier's stern, trying to gain an advantageous firing position off its starboard bow. Hardison expertly maneuvered the big ship so that he kept the stern toward the attacking planes. As AA fire continued pouring at the planes, one of them flown by Sea1c Rinzo Oba impatiently increased his speed to pass the carrier. There were six SBDs parked on the flight deck near the stern that had been moved there to avoid the fires in the ship's forward sections. Two LSOs, Lieutenants Robin M. Lindsey and James G. Daniels, III, saw the torpedo plane approaching their ship's stern and decided to take matters into their own hands. Each leapt into the rear gun position of an SBD nearest the stern and fired the twin 30-cal. guns at the oncoming plane. Oba felt several bullets hit his plane but managed to launch his torpedo and pulled away. But his plane was now on fire; it gracelessly rolled into the water and exploded in flames. The rest of the four Kates managed to get on the carrier's port quarter and drop their torpedoes. The carrier combed one missile's wake while the other three missed their target. The four planes continued flying southward ten feet above the waves and drew out of range. The torpedo attack ended at 10:57 a.m., and Task Force 16 ceased firing its AA guns.

But the wave-hopping torpedo planes were not yet out of danger. Vejtasa, Feightner, and Gordon noticed two Japanese planes coming toward them. Feightner attacked the one closest to him, and Vejtasa joined the fracas and emptied his guns into it. The Japanese plane, with not much maneuvering room at such a low height, tried to slip away in a horizontal turn, but to no avail. Flames burst from the plane. It flew another five miles before crashing into the water.

Gordon moved in for a head-on attack on the second Kate. The Japanese pilot suddenly saw the approaching F4F coming straight at him and quickly banked left to get out of the way. But he was too low; his left wing's tip hit the water. His plane spun in a cartwheel and broke into several pieces.

The Japanese lost one-half of the 16 torpedo planes as well as the squadron leader. Despite Japanese claims to have put two torpedoes into the carrier, the *Enterprise* sustained no hits. The CAP's effectiveness and the withering AA barrage put up by Task Force 16 took a heavy toll on the attacking aircraft. If any of the torpedoes had hit the carrier, the second American carrier could have been rendered a crippled wreck like its sister ship. But it did not happen.

The Americans generously praised the Japanese torpedo attack as one executed with "obvious skill and great determination." The brave Japanese flight crews did their best but could not overcome the aggressive American CAP and antiaircraft defense.

The *Enterprise* was still operational, but she had one more ordeal to endure. Another Japanese air strike would soon attack her and inflict more damage.

The Japanese Strike Task Force 16 Again

As Nagumo's Striking Force licked its wounds and retreated to the northwest, Kondo's Advance Force along with Kakuta's light carrier *Junyo* headed northeast toward Nagumo's position. With a full complement of planes and crews not yet bloodied in this battle and Task Force 16 about 250 miles away, Kakuta ordered his first strike to launch at 9:05 a.m. Lt. Yoshio Shiga led 17 Vals, with Lt. Masao Yamaguchi, and 12 Zeroes commanded by Lt. Yoshio Shiga added their numbers to the total of 138 aircraft that the Japanese launched against the Americans, almost twice the number of aircraft Kinkaid sent against Japanese ships.

As four CAP Zeroes took off, the carrier deck crews readied the second strike of seven Kates with Lt. Yoshiaki Irikiin in command. Meanwhile, Kondo received messages that Nagumo's first strike had inflicted heavy damage on the American ships. He turned his force to the southeast to go after what seemed like an ideal target for his surface ships and sent Kakuta with two destroyers at 10:18 a.m. to join Nagumo. Just as Kakuta was about to leave, the battleship *Haruna*'s lookouts thought they saw ten large American airplanes. The Junyo sent four Zeroes to intercept and ordered Irikiin's "Kates" aloft to clear the fight deck. The sighting turned out to be false; Irikiin's planes landed again to continue preparation to strike the Americans. Kakuta steamed to join Nagumo.

✲ ✲ ✲

The *Enterprise* seemed to be out of danger, at least for the moment. Her CAP had run out of fuel and ammunition. To add to Kinkaid's concern, the radar also stopped working at 10:58 a.m. because its antenna could not turn. Lt. Dwight M. B. Williams, the carrier's radar officer, came up to Mott's sky control carrying his toolbox. The stalled antenna was just above sky control on a platform exposed to the elements and the highest part of the ship one could climb. Mott and Williams conferred and believed the antenna had been jammed due to some sort of battle damage. Williams did not want to go up there, but he had no choice. The antenna had to be fixed, and he was the only man available to do it. Mustering his courage, he climbed the treacherous ladder to where the antenna was and discovered it was not properly aligned. Williams eventually fixed it, albeit after a harrowing experience of having to be strapped to the structure because someone mistakenly started its rotor motors while being exposed to the Japanese air attack.[6]

While the carrier was blinded with no operational radar, Griffin told the almost helpless 18-fighter CAP, "Remain close to base; no definite bogeys now," as they continued to circle in the landing pattern with their fuel supplies approaching a critical state. Vejtasa desperately radioed for permission to land. The only CAP section that had enough fuel and ammunition to fight was the two-plane formation piloted by Kane and Lt. John C. Eckhardt. Coming in from the west, the *Hornet*'s planes arrived in small groups to join ever more crowded skies over Task Force 16. By 11:20 a.m., ten F4Fs, ten SBDs, and 16 TBFs circled the carrier. All eagerly wanted to land.

John Crommelin's flight deck crew moved some SBDs below at 11:00 a.m. to clear landing space for the circling planes. The No. 1 elevator was too heavily damaged to use for this job; so the crew began using the other two elevators to the rear of the runup and landing areas. No. 2 elevator jammed in the dangerous down position, but shortly became operational again. By 11:15 a.m., the carrier could begin landing aircraft. Daniels waved in some F4Fs (Sanchez, Emerson, and Ens. James O. Weimer) and probably some others (Sorensen, Jennings, Dalton, and Dowden). Souza thought his disabled right aileron would prevent him from landing, but Daniels guided him in as well. After he landed, the flabbergasted deck crew saw a wrecked plane with its right wing full of 20-mm holes. As the deck crew moved his plane to the elevator to be placed below, Japanese dive-bombers attacked with no advanced warning.

Shiga had been flying for almost two hours as he searched for an American task force that had not been previously attacked. His group had seen the crippled *Hornet* 20 minutes earlier with the *Northampton* taking the carrier in tow. He wanted to attack ships where his planes could do the most damage. Heavy cloud cover blocked his vision as he thought about turning around and attacking the "battleship" when he received an enlightening message at 11:00 a.m. Nagumo radioed that a second American task force had been spotted on a bearing of 300° and 30 miles from the first force. Shiga did not believe the message, but he knew the other American ships had to be close.

The temporarily disabled radar on the *Enterprise* caused unintended consequences to Task Force 16's ability to decipher whether approaching aircraft were friend or foe. The *South Dakota*'s radar detected planes approaching from 285° and 45 miles away. Griffin never received the sighting report. The *Portland* sent an alert at 11:10 a.m. that reported many planes 25 miles to the west. But Kinkaid, thinking these planes were returning American strike groups, dismissed the warning stating that the approaching planes were friendly. The *South Dakota* fired on some of the *Hornet*'s returning planes in error.

Nonetheless, the *Enterprise* radar came back on line at 11:15 a.m. and detected a large group of planes just 20 miles away. That was no warning at all. Griffin relayed the sighting to the CAP stating, "They may not be friendly," and ordered, "All planes in air prepare to repel attack" with a warning not to get too close to Task Force 16's nervous gunners. Four minutes later, the *South Dakota* loosed a barrage at what its crew thought were Japanese. An anonymous report occurred about sighting Japanese planes, and Griffin broadcast to the CAP, "Bandits reported above clouds. All planes in air standby to repel attack approaching from north. Above clouds. Above clouds."[7] Two minutes later, the Japanese dive-bombers suddenly burst from the clouds and dove toward the *Enterprise* with Williams still strapped to the radar antenna.

Lt. Yamaguchi saw the American task force screen through a break in the clouds and led his nine dive-bombers through the clouds. Yamaguchi's sudden maneuver surprised Shiga, and his Zeroes followed the dive-bombers into the clouds. Lt. Naohiko Miura tried to lead his eight Vals, but lost sight of them in the murky clouds. Shiga respotted the American ships through a break in the clouds, signaled his Zeroes by rocking his wings to drop their wing tanks and follow him. Miura also readied for an attack.

With the ceiling as low as 500 feet, the thick clouds hid the American ships from Miura's bombers as they continued their shallow 45° dives toward the carrier's stern. Their speed became very slow forcing them into a stall so that the pilots had to activate their dive brakes. Shiga had to fly his Zero in a loop to stay with the dive-bombers and almost hit a destroyer smoke stack. The bomber's shallow dives increased their danger from American AA fire mainly from the lethal 40-mm Bofors. The ships' gunfire set Miura's Val afire and shot the tail off PO1c Katsuyoshi Yabuki's bomber, which followed just behind. Their two bombs hit the water near each other just astern of the carrier. Flying the third plane in Miura's formation, PO2c Yoshiharu Kataoka dropped his bomb. Despite not showing any apparent damage, his plane hit the water.

Warrant Officer Masataka Honmura, following behind Miura's three-plane group, dropped his 250-kg bomb, which deflected off the carrier's bow near the waterline and detonated underwater. The explosion's concussion split open hull plates, opened holes to the sea, and water gushed in to flood the area where the No. 1 elevator's operating mechanism was and permanently disabled it. The bombs dropped by Honmura's wingmen and the two planes in Warrant Officer Masahiko Nakako's formation exploded harmlessly in the water.

With the loss of three of his five planes and believing all their bombs had hit their mark, Honmura led his five survivors supposedly out of danger by flying low over the water. But his temporary euphoria disappeared as this group ran into a buzz saw of American planes in the *Enterprise* landing pattern. Kinkaid humorously expressed his concern to the *South Dakota* because of its firing on American planes, "You are reported firing on friendly planes." Griffin was far more serious about it when he sent a warning to the circling American planes, "Friendly planes, turn to your right. Hawks reported diving astern."[8]

Wrenn, his fuel tank now dangerously approaching empty, worried that the *Enterprise* might wave him off the first time he tried to land. If this happened, he might not have enough gas to make another turn and thus be forced to ditch his plane. As he was on his approach, the carrier suddenly changed its course to avoid the bombs coming from the attacking Japanese bomber. Now, Wrenn really had something to worry about. Nonetheless, the LSO waved him to land. More bombs began to fall on Task Force 16's other ships.

Yamaguchi's reduced force of nine Vals groped through the clouds and at last spotted Task Force 16 at 11:29 a.m. But they did not see the *Enterprise*. Miura's attack had forced Task Force 16's ships to scatter and lose defensive formation integrity. Visibility was quite obscured so that the Japanese attack became fragmented and disorganized. The low cloud ceiling at 1,000 to 1,500 feet prevented the oncoming bomber crews from effectively identifying the ships they wanted to attack. The murk also prevented the American antiaircraft gunners from accurately aiming at the planes. It did not help that matters became even more confused when Kinkaid's warning message came over the TBS, "Do not fire at chickens [U.S. planes]. Bogeys coming in now, also friendly aircraft."

Yamaguchi and three of his compatriots individually burst from the dark rain clouds about 1,000 feet over the *South Dakota*'s port bow and dropped all four of their 250-kg bombs. The first three missed the battleship by hitting the water on the ship's port and starboard sides. But the fourth bomb had better luck when it directly smacked into and exploded on one of the 16-inch gun turrets. Bomb splinters pelted the catwalk forward of the armored conning tower and wounded Capt. Thomas L. Gatch. The bomb inflicted little damage but temporarily forced the battleship to lose control of its steering, hazardously run pell-mell through the task force formation, and forced the *Enterprise* to swing wildly to avoid her. When no more Japanese bombers came into view, the battleship stopped firing.

The *San Juan* was the next ship to bear the brunt of the dive-bomber assault when Lt. (jg) Shunko Kato's five Vals went after the cruiser. Each plane riskily attacked against what would normally be the cruiser's formidable antiaircraft defenses. But the planes came on the cruiser so quickly that the ship fire control systems could not respond to the attack before the bombs began falling. Shellfire from the five-inch guns harmlessly exploded well behind the attacking planes. The normally deadly 20-mm gunfire had no effect whatsoever. One 250-kg semi-armor piercing bomb exploded in the water near the cruiser's port side and caused her hull to begin leaking. The fifth and last of the Japanese bombs went through the ship's starboard side, pierced the ship's thin armor, and exploded underneath her. Several compartments began taking water. The explosion's concussion wedged the rudder into a hard right position. The ship began to run in circles, but the damaged control parties managed to set the rudder free at 11:41 a.m., and she could again steer normally.

✲ ✲ ✲

Based on the information known today, the number of planes destroyed when the *Junyo*'s dive-bombers attacked Task Force 16 can only be estimated. While the American CAP could not engage the Japanese planes because of their low fuel and exhausted ammunition reserves, the F4Fs attempting to land had a field day against the first wave of attacking "Vals" and destroyed several dive-bombers. About 14 dive-bombers from both the first and second waves managed to survive and claimed to have damaged the American ships. Nevertheless, the damage by *Junyo* planes was minimal and did not affect Task Force 16's operations to the same extent the earlier Japanese assaults did. Unlike the *Hornet*, the *Enterprise* was still operational along with the damaged *South Dakota* and *San Juan*. But the *Hornet*'s struggle for survival continued with her future in doubt.[9]

CHAPTER 35
Winners & Losers at Santa Cruz

Gathering Forces to Attack Again

Nagumo watched the *Hornet*'s bombers leave the scene of the latest attacks and surveyed what they had done to his command. Flames and smoke towered above the *Shokaku*'s buckled flight deck. Smoke continued to pour from the *Zuiho*'s stern. Red flags flew from the damaged carriers' masts indicating they could neither land nor launch aircraft. As 17 Zeroes orbited above as the CAP, the *Zuikaku* still could conduct air operations and did so when it landed some of these fighters at 10:00 a.m. and launched six Zeroes to replace the landing planes. The carrier continued to land some CAP planes. But one of them ran into hard luck. While trying to land, Sea2c Katsuo Sugano's plane flipped over, hit the water, sank like a stone, and killed the pilot.

Radm. Abe's Vanguard Force was still 50 miles astern steaming to the northwest. But Kondo recalled him to go after the American ships. Before Abe reversed his course, he ordered the heavily damaged *Chikuma* returned to Truk with two destroyers acting as an escort.

After hearing the triumphant news that the *Junyo*'s dive-bombers had inflicted heavy damage on another American carrier, the cheerful Nagumo wanted to attack the Americans again. After analyzing the numerous combat reports from their air crews, his staff decided there were three American carriers out there: one meandering aimlessly with no power, one ship to the east of the cripple, and another carrier to the northeast. To reconsolidate his forces for his next attack, Nagumo issued the following order at 11:25 a.m.: "Cancel assumption that there is an enemy carrier south of the first carrier."[1]

That message gave Task Force 16 the reprieve it so sorely needed. The Japanese would now search to the east of the *Hornet* and not to the southeast where Task Force 16 steamed. Nagumo firmly believed that since one American carrier was out of action, there were two others to attack.

But he did not have sufficient planes to attack two carriers with only 33 planes (ten dive-bombers, nine torpedo planes, and 14 fighters) returning. Some of them had been damaged. Five torpedo planes from the *Zuiho* and one *Shokaku* dive-bomber wanted to land. The *Shokaku*'s inoperable radio could not inform the *Zuiho* that no planes could land on her. The aircraft fruitlessly searched for the heavily damaged carrier and unfortunately continued to use their precious fuel. The *Zuikaku* resumed landing aircraft at 11:40 a.m. and radioed those planes still aloft to find the *Junyo* and land there.

Forty minutes later, the carrier had landed ten fighters, eight Kates, and one Val. The *Junyo* brought in six of her own CAP Zeroes, two *Zuikaku* fighters, four *Zuikaku* dive-bombers, and one

Shokaku torpedo plane. Thirteen planes from the first wave—two Zeroes, five Vals, and six Kates—landed in the ocean. The strike leaders, Lt.s Takahashi and Ishimaru, died later on the ships that pulled them from the water. As the *Junyo* finished landing her charges, Nagumo ordered the *Zuikaku* and five destroyers to join the light carrier for the planned attack. The captain of the damaged *Shokaku*, Capt. Masafumi Arima, pleaded with Nagumo to have his ship join the attacking force. But Nagumo had made up his mind. The damaged ship would return to Truk for repairs with Nagumo still on board. The *Zuikaku* and *Junyo* would go after the "two" American carriers.

Kinkaid Decides to Withdraw

Kinkaid realized that if he kept Task Force 16 in the vicinity of any Japanese warships he would place the sole remaining and operational American carrier in the Pacific further at risk. He had no fighters to spare to help Murray's Task Force 17. Nevertheless, he had to land those planes still aloft so he could take the *Enterprise* to safer waters. His fear became moreover justified later when Lt. (jg) George F. Poulos' PBY, which had been keeping track of Nagumo's force, reported to be following a carrier force at a bearing of 90º. Being the deliberate commander he was, Kinkaid weighed his alternatives and decided to withdraw all the forces he could spare as soon as he recovered his planes. His message to Murray and COMSOPAC sent at 11:35 a.m. was, "I am proceeding southeastward toward ROSES [Éfaté]. When ready proceed in the same direction."[2]

Adm. Good sent a message to COMSOPAC some minutes later that Task Force 16 also overheard:

> "*Hornet* attacked by ORANGE carrier planes at 0911L...Several bomb hits one or more torpedo hits. Now dead in the water and burning somewhat. *Northampton* preparing take in tow. Have lost touch with Kinkaid."[3]

The *Northampton* at last got a towline on the disabled *Hornet*. Not long after that, the towline broke apart at 11:08 a.m. Meanwhile, Murray transferred his flag to the *Pensacola*. Kinkaid sent his final message to Good, "If Murray safe direct him to take charge salvaging operations. Have been under continuous air attack. Otherwise you take charge."[4]

As Kinkaid communicated his decisions and intentions to the rest of his command, the *Enterprise* began recovering the rest of Task Force 61's aircraft as her deck crews removed planes still on her flight deck. There were aircraft from both carriers low on fuel—28 F4Fs, 24 SBDs and 21 TBFs—still waiting in the air to land as of 11:40 a.m. These planes and their valuable crews had to be recovered. To do less would be a disaster that would directly affect the outcome of future battles.

The carrier's damaged forward elevator meant that the aircraft already parked on her forward flight deck could not be moved in time to the hangar deck below for the other planes to land. As the planes landed, they added to the congestion on the flight deck. Some of the older SBDs did not have folding wings, which added to the crowding. After landing, the planes moved toward the forward barriers, the landing space shrank, which increased the danger. Robin Lindsey and Jim Daniels, the carrier LSOs, had a tough task ahead of them.

Hardison turned the carrier southeast into the wind at 11:39 a.m. She could now begin landing the planes still circling and burning fuel. Daniels started landing planes but too slowly for the pilots still aloft who watched their fuel gauges dangerously indicate draining fuel tanks. Lt. (jg) Kenneth

B. White, flying an orbiting SBD, remembered that landing pattern. It seemed it was so large as to stretch "from Maine to Florida," so that the pilots were, "eager to get in before their engines sputtered from lack of fuel and they went into the drink."[5] Some irritated and impatient pilots began to crowd ahead of their compatriots in the landing pattern. Daniels wanted to first land the F4Fs and SBDs with injured crews. The others would have to wait for their turn. So he had to wave off several aircraft, some of them already flying on vapors.

The first planes to come aboard were the CAP F4Fs with some of them running out of fuel. F4F pilot Lt. (jg) James D. Billo had to ditch after twice not being allowed to land. Fortunately, the destroyer *Preston*, commanded by Cmdr. Max C. Stormes, plucked him from the water while risking being torpedoed by any Japanese submarine that might be lurking in the area. Despite that danger, the destroyer rescued 11 pilots that day.

Cmdr. Kane, Lt. Eckhardt, and Lt. (jg) Merl P. Long also had to land in the water. The destroyer *Maury* pulled Kane from the sea, and the *Cushing* rescued the other two. The *Mahan* saved Lt. Bliss who was forced to splash down with inoperable flaps. The recovery operation continued despite the dangers of some planes landing with the No. 2 (amidships) elevator open to lower planes to the hangar deck. In a period of 43 minutes, Daniels and Lindsey continued guiding the American planes aboard and landed all the F4Fs and SBDs except for five F4Fs that had to ditch.

However, her flight deck was now full of planes with 21 TBFs still circling. There was no more room left to land them until enough space on the flight deck could be cleared. Since the carrier could not launch any F4Fs for CAP, Griffin asked the TBFs to volunteer as CAP. Six TBFs responded as a report of Japanese planes approaching Task Force 16 on a bearing of 30º, distance 25 miles. The contact turned out to be a damaged PBY, flown by Lt. (jg) Norman S. Haber. He had fought off seven Zeroes. With his rudder or elevator controls shot out, Haber landed the partially crippled patrol bomber at Espiritu Santo with 144 bullet holes in it.

The clearing of the flight deck continued as fast the crews could separate the fighter and dive-bombers and send them below. Meanwhile, the TBFs continued circling and running short of fuel. Cmdr. Rodee, the *Hornet*'s CAG and flying his own TBF, decided he had enough fuel to go to Espiritu Santo and landed there about 3:00 p.m. Nonetheless, Lt. (jg) Humphrey L. Tallman was not as lucky. With no fuel left on his heavily damaged TBF, he landed safely in the water, and the busy *Preston* picked him up. Still concerned about TBFs still flying, the carrier tried to reassure Cmdr. Gaines, the *Enterprise*'s CAG, flying in one those planes still circling, "Hang on 20 to 25 minutes, and we will take you on." Gaines answered that he only had that much flying time remaining.

As her deck crews freed up space, the *Enterprise* could launch the first planes since 8:25 a.m. Twenty-five CAP F4Fs in six divisions led by Sanchez, Emerson, Hessel, Phillips, Pollock and Edwards took to the air between 12:51 p.m. and 1:05 p.m. The deck crews feverishly labored to clear enough space so the TBFs could come onboard. The LSOs resumed landing operations at 1:18 p.m. Nine TBFs landed safely. Gaines' plane landed four minutes later. Meanwhile, eight torpedo planes ditched near the cruiser *Juneau*, which joined Task Force 16 at 12:28 p.m. The destroyers plucked the pilots from the sea. Of the 73 aircraft orbiting almost one hour before, 57 landed safely despite all the problems the carrier deck crews confronted while making room. It was quite a feat of dedicated hard work by these men under the most demanding conditions.

By 3:40 p.m., Kinkaid alerted Halsey that damages to the *Enterprise* were worse than he had originally stated. He asked for an oiler to rendevous with Task Force 16 as soon as possible somewhere northeast of Espiritu Santo. As Kinkaid's message crossed the ether, a message from Halsey arrived ordering all SOPAC task forces to "retire to southward."[6] While Kinkaid had begun to extricate Task Force 16 from any further danger by Japanese attacks, Murray's Task Force 17 was still trying to bring the crippled *Hornet* home. Would Murray escape as well?[7]

One More Japanese Air Attack?

The attitude from Combined Fleet Headquarters at Truk had now turned to one of impatience and concern. Adm. Ugaki assessed the situation and came to the conclusion that despite Nagumo's withdrawal and taking the *Shokaku* and *Zuiho* with him, the Japanese had the *Zuikaku* and the *Junyo*, still operational, while the Americans only had one remaining carrier. But these other carriers also followed Nagumo's retreat. If they stayed on that course, they would soon be out of aircraft attacking range. There was some hesitance from Yamamoto's staff to launch another attack. One staff officer argued that movements to the northeast would bring an advantage to the Japanese since they would be "outranging" the Americans. Ugaki wanted to scream at this officer that his attitude would surely prevent the Imperial Japanese Navy from realizing their long-sought dream of an all-out, winner-take-all naval battle. Ugaki then ordered most of the fleet's submarines to attack any American ships north of the Santa Cruz Islands and south of the Rennell Islands.

As usual, the Japanese action reports presented a situation indicating the Japanese air attacks had sunk as many as four carriers. For instance, the summary action report from the captain of *Zuikaku*, Capt. Tameteru Nomoto, stated, "Summing up the reports of the returned attack planes up to First CV Division's second wave, two carriers heavily damaged and an unidentified vessel exploded, the remnant of which is still seen." A pilot flying a plane from the *Zuiho* reported, "The enemy strength: one carrier, one battleship, two cruisers, and four destroyers. The carrier was drifting without fighter screen overhead. No damage on our side."[8] Ugaki concluded the American task force had been so severely crippled that now was the time to close in for the kill and annihilate all American ships still out there.

Radm. Kakuta sent another message that Ugaki received, "At 1315 [Truk time] we torpedoed an enemy carrier of the *Yorktown* type, hitting with three torpedoes. Its sinking almost certain. One torpedo hit a cruiser, setting a big fire. They were among the group consisting of two battleships, three cruisers, and five destroyers."

However, any attempt to attack the Americans had to be tempered by the knowledge that the Japanese land-based air forces were not ready to launch an attack. By the time any surface attack could be tried, it would be too dark unless any Japanese search planes could stay in contact with the Americans. Nevertheless, Yamamoto ordered all Japanese carrier ships to close to within launching distance and attack the American carriers still north of Santa Cruz. All other ships must move at maximum speed to clean up the remnants of any air attacks in a surface battle.[9]

☆ ☆ ☆

Upon receiving the order from Truk at 1:00 p.m., Kakuta on the *Junyo* and Nomoto on the *Zuikaku* prepared to launch more air strikes. Meanwhile, the battleships, cruisers, and destroyers in Kondo's Advance Force and Abe's Vanguard Force steamed at high speed to the southeast.

The *Junyo* launched a second strike at 1:13 p.m. commanded by Lt. Yoshiaki Irikiin. Eight Zeroes led by Lt. Ayao Shirane and seven Kates took off. Irikiin's torpedo-less plane's assignment was to coordinate any attacks. After forming up, the planes turned to a 120º heading and began searching for the American ships up to a distance of 260 miles. The *Zuikaku* simultaneously launched another wave of planes that included five Zeroes led by Lt. (jg) Hohei Kobayashi, two Vals led by PO1c Kenzo Hori, seven Kates—six of them carried 800-kg bombs—commanded by Lt. (jg) Ichiro Tanaka, who was the strike's leader and carried no bomb. The fact that such inexperienced pilots led both strikes showed the crippling losses of veteran combat pilots the Japanese had sustained.

The two carriers began landing their planes still aloft now that they had room on their flight decks. Many of the returning planes had been heavily damaged and struggled to land safely. The *Zuikaku* landed five Zeroes that included Lt. Shigematsu's plane along with Lt. Arima's seven Vals, Lt. Yusuhara's six Kates, and one additional Kate that had been searching for the Americans between 1:20 p.m. and 2:00 p.m. The *Junyo* landed Lt. Shiga with eight Zeroes and Lt. (jg) Kato's six Vals during the same time. Not all the Japanese planes returned safely. Two Zeroes, four Vals, and one Kate had to ditch in the sea.

Adm. Kakuta's air staff officer, Lt. Cmdr. Masatake Okumiya, later recalled the return of the *Junyo*'s first wave:

> "We searched the sky with apprehension. There were only a few planes in the air in comparison with the numbers launched several hours before...The planes lurched and staggered onto the deck, every single fighter and bomber bullet holed.
>
> As the pilots climbed wearily from their cramped cockpits, they told of unbelievable opposition, of skies choked with antiaircraft shell bursts and tracers. Lt. (jg) Kato, the *Junyo*'s sole surviving dive-bomber leader, reported to Captain Tametsugu Okada, the carrier's skipper, and appeared to be so disturbed that his report approached incoherency."[10]

Nomoto decided not to launch another attack after recovering the rest of the planes trying to land on the *Zuikaku*. But Kakuta was not yet ready to give up his determination to deliver a crushing blow on the Americans. He ordered Shiga to gather as many planes that could still fly and lead another attack. Okumiya went down to the *Junyo*'s wardroom to repeat those orders only to be confronted by an apparently combat-fatigued Shunko Kato, "Again? Am I to fly again today?" But Shiga leapt to his feet and shouted, "Ton-chan [Kato's shipboard nickname]; this is war! There can be no rest in our fight against the enemy...We cannot afford to give them a chance when their ships are crippled...We have no choice...We go!" Gathering himself and what courage he had in him, Kato relented and said, "I will go."[11] A third wave of six fighters and four dive-bombers left the *Junyo*'s flight deck at 3:35 p.m.

Dooming the Hornet

Task Force 16 along with its fighters headed toward Espiritu Santo and away from the approaching Japanese. Task Force 17 had to fend for itself. Nonetheless, the prospect of towing the *Hornet* to safety improved some time after noon. The *Northampton* managed to send another tow rope over to the carrier two hours after the first one parted. With the line firmly attached to the *Hornet*, the cruiser took up the slack and began to get the big ship to move. Soon the two ships' speed was three knots as the engineers in the carrier engine rooms managed to start some boilers and add more speed. Murray wanted to tow the ship eastward to Tongatabu to not risk an attack from Japanese submarines known to be to the south. The carrier's wounded sailors and its air crews transferred to the destroyers *Russell* and *Hughes*. The *Northampton* and its charge moved along at six knots. But trouble was on the wing as several Japanese search planes watched their painfully slow progress, and there were no fighters to shoot them down. Not realizing the damage endured by the *Enterprise*, anger spread among many Task Force 17 sailors, infuriated by the lack of a CAP.

When Murray thought he might be lucky enough to escape further attacks, the *Northampton*'s radar detected a large number of planes at 1:45 p.m. There were Irikiin's eight Zeroes and seven Kates on a 310º bearing and 103 miles away. While radar crews observed that the planes seemed to be milling about, the aircraft actually searched for more than one American carrier. Fifteen minutes later, the American radars picked up Tanaka's strike group, also circling while searching for two American carriers, on a 310º bearing and 110 miles from the American ships.

The *Russell* left the other ships at 2:40 p.m. to take the personnel aboard out of danger. By this time, Irikiin ceased his search and headed straight toward Task Force 17, whose radars showed the Japanese planes closing fast. Irikiin looked from his plane's cockpit window at 3:13 p.m. and saw the crippled carrier struggling to get away. It was now too dangerous to continue towing the *Hornet*. Murray ordered the cruiser to cease her towing and join an antiaircraft circle around the carrier.

Irikiin's Kates began their attack dives from 6,000 feet and headed for the *Hornet*'s starboard side. All of the ships' guns let loose a huge barrage desperately trying to upset the air attacks. Irikiin flew over the *Russell*, lined up his sights on the carrier's starboard beam and pulled the torpedo's release. The missile hit the water and, with the bubbles from it leaving a telltale path, struck the ship's aft side and exploded in a huge water column. The *Horne*t's power was now totally disabled. Nevertheless, the Japanese flyer tried to pull up, but could not escape his fate as many shells pierced his plane's body. It turned sharply to the right and smacked in the water just ahead of *Northampton*'s bow. The *Hornet*'s list was now 14º. The other five Japanese bombers' torpedoes all missed and two aircraft hit the water. The Japanese pilots claimed to have scored three hits on the carrier and one on a cruiser. Two Zeroes flown by PO1c Kiyonobu Suzuki and Sea2c Kiyoshi Nakamoto disappeared and were never seen again. The Japanese air attack had cost them two Kates and two Zeroes. Three more Zeroes had to ditch later. But the carrier's agony continued.

By now, Murray knew the *Hornet*'s fate was beyond his control after he asked for fighter support from Kinkaid, who refused to send any more assistance. Mason, worried about the drastic increase in his ship's list, ordered his crew to get ready to abandon the ship.

The *Zuikaku*'s strike was now near Task Force 17 and split into separate groups. PO1c Hori was the first to see the listing carrier and led his collection of dive-bombers at her at 1:41 p.m. One bomb exploded so close to the carrier that she rocked in the water from the blast.

The *Hornet* now listed at between 18° to 20°. Two minutes after Hori's attack, Mason ordered "Abandon Ship."

Fourteen minutes after Hori's assault, Tanaka's six Vals flew at 8,000 feet off the carrier's port quarter and dove at her from that height. All six planes simultaneously dropped their 800-kg bombs. One of them hit the carrier and exploded on the flight deck aft, but, to everyone's amazement, caused little damage. The rest of the missiles hit and exploded in the water with a monstrous splash to the carrier's rear.

Tanaka was convinced the carrier that his planes attacked was not the same carrier other Japanese pilots reported damaging, but another ship. As far as he was concerned, this was a third American carrier.

As soon Tanaka's attack ended, Mason accelerated the ship's evacuation of personnel. The last man left the ship at 4:27 p.m. Task Force 17's other ships began rescuing the survivors as Shiga's formation of four Vals and six Zeroes arrived overhead. Kato's three bombers began their dives at 5:10 p.m. and released their bombs. One 250-kg bomb pierced the carrier's flight deck, exploded in the hangar deck in front of the island, and starting a brief but large fire. After claiming striking the carrier with four hits, Kato and Shiga's planes landed safely on the *Junyo* after sunset.

The *Hornet* was finished. After receiving reports translated from decrypted Japanese messages from COMSOPAC that had come through Nimitz about what the Japanese intended for Task Force 17, Murray needed no more incentives to act. He ordered the destroyer *Mustin* at 5:40 p.m. to sink the hapless wreck with torpedoes and withdrew the rest of Task Force 17 to the east at 27 knots. With three Japanese float planes from the cruisers *Maya*, *Isuzu*, and *Nagara* circling overhead and witnessing the heartbreaking drama below, the destroyer's torpedo tubes hissed and sent eight missiles at the carrier 23 minutes later. All eight hit her side, but only four exploded. The gallant carrier defiantly stayed afloat. Murray then ordered the destroyer *Anderson* to end her life. This destroyer also fired eight torpedoes and only six detonated. The *Hornet* was still afloat. The two destroyers turned their five-inch guns on the carrier and fired 430 shells at her. As they left the wreck at 8:30 p.m. with the three Japanese float planes following nearby, flames engulfed her entire length, but she refused to sink. Murray did not want to leave the brave vessel to such a fate. However, he had little choice but to let her continue to burn and take what remained of his task force to safety.

Kondo and Kakuta received confusing and contradictory reports from the returning air crews. Were there two or three American carriers nearby? What had happened to them? Their best guess that three American carriers still prowled the waters to the south. But the *Zuikaku*'s Nomoto talked to several aircrews as well and was not as optimistic as his superiors. He sent a message to Kondo at

4:28 p.m. stating that no air crews ever saw three carriers together. No one had seen any carriers other than one burning ship. Nonetheless, Kakuta surmised two hours later that the Japanese aircraft had either sunk or heavily damaged three carriers.

Kondo desperately wanted to send his surface ships to mop up any stragglers they could find. He unhesitatingly ordered his Support Force ships at 7:04 p.m. to look for any American ships on a course from the east to southeast and attack them in a night surface battle if necessary. He also directed Kakuta to steam northward to search for and attack any ships his planes could find.

Japanese naval aviation had lost at least 106 planes with only 97 left to carry the fight to the Americans. The *Junyo* had just 30 planes (12 fighters, 12 dive-bombers, and six torpedo planes) while the *Zuikaku* had 47 planes (18 fighters, 10 dive-bombers, and 19 torpedo planes) with which to launch their attack. More importantly, they had lost many combat-experienced Officers, including two group and four squadron commanders believed to be dead.

Yamamoto later expressed the opinion that four American carriers had been in the battle. After all, the returning air crews had reported sinking one carrier and inflicting heavy damage on three others. Nagumo agreed with that assessment. Yamamoto believed the Americans were in a desperate, chaotic retreat and ordered Kondo to continue pursuing the Americans until he was positive they could not be caught.

Kondo obeyed his superior's orders and pressed forward to destroy the American ships with his ships' guns. His ships arrived at 9:00 p.m., and Kakuta noted with some satisfaction seeing the American carrier covered with fire. The destroyers *Akigumo* and *Makikumo* moved in to do with their Long-Lance torpedoes the work the defective American torpedoes could not accomplish earlier. After noticing the numeral "8" on her island confirming her identity, each destroyer sent two of the deadly effective torpedoes into her. All four of them hit their target.

After seeing there was no American ship with which to do battle, Kondo's force left the area at midnight by turning north then west. The defiantly gallant *Hornet*'s agony ended at 1:35 a.m. on October 27 as she disappeared beneath the waves while spewing billowing clouds of steam and smoke.[12]

✲ ✲ ✲

Kondo's ships did not proceed toward Truk without some American interference. Three "Black Cat" PBYs from Adm. Fitch's COMAIRSOPAC left Espiritu Santo on the evening of October 26 to avenge the *Hornet*'s sinking. At about midnight on the 26th, one of the PBY pilots, Lt. (jg) Donald L. Jackson, spotted one carrier, one battleship, and three cruisers and destroyers. These ships were Kakuta's *Junyo* task groups heading to meet up with the *Zuikaku*. Lt. Melvin K. Atwell's PBY bombed what was thought to be a heavy cruiser at 1:00 a.m., which was actually the destroyer *Teruzuki* screening the big fleet carrier. One of Atwell's 500-pound bombs exploded in the water near the destroyer's starboard beam and killed or wounded about 50 of her crew. Thirty minutes later, Jackson's plane launched a torpedo at the *Junyo*, and Jackson later claimed to have hit the carrier.

Meanwhile, Kinkaid and Lee's ships followed Halsey's orders and steamed at their best speed to either Espiritu Santo or Nouméa but not without incident. The Japanese submarines *I-21*, *I-24*, and *I-5* lay in wait right in the path of the approaching ships. All three submarines sent reports of the American ships moving away from Truk. The Americans were indeed leaving the battle area. The *I-21* and *I-24* harmlessly fired torpedoes at the *Washington* at 3:20 a.m. and 5:30 a.m. on October 27.

The destroyer *Mahan* and battleship *South Dakota* ran into each other. The smaller destroyer took the brunt of the damage and had to steam to a dockyard for repairs.

The Battle of the Santa Cruz Islands was over at last.

Separation of Forces

The once euphoric mood at the Combined Fleet Headquarters on Truk turned increasingly somber. A telegram arrived from the 17th Army's chief of staff stating that the battle to take Henderson Field had ended badly and, despite praising the assistance the Army had already received from the Imperial Japanese Navy, asked the Navy for more help. The Fleet's staff sent a polite reply that said while the Navy empathized with the Army's difficulties, the Navy would continue to cooperate with the Army and expressed the hope that the Army would eventually emerge victorious. In other words, the Army would get no more help from the Navy.

The Combined Fleet later issued a Summary Action report that said what the Navy planned to do next:

> "The Combined Fleet, operating in the seas near the Solomons, engaged the enemy fleet, which consisted of more than 20 ships, including four carriers, four battleships, and cruisers and destroyers in the sea north of Santa Cruz in the early morning of the 26th. All of the enemy carriers were destroyed by 2000 [8:00 p.m.], driving the enemy into confusion. We are now chasing the remnant with the whole strength of our night assault force."
>
> Summary of the battle result up to 10:00 p.m. is:
>
> 1. Sunk: one Saratoga type carrier, one Yorktown type carrier, two new type carriers, one battleship, and one type unidentified.
> 2. Damaged: one battleship, three cruisers, and one destroyer.
> 3. Our losses: Shokaku and Zuiho incapable of continuing carrier operations, though both are able to make full power running. Chikuma hit with bombs and sailing at 23 knots. Telegram follows for our damage to planes."[13]

Apparently, the Imperial Japanese Navy had a problem deciding how many carriers its planes sank or damaged. The destroyer *Kazegumo* pulled Ens. Mead from the water while the *Makigumo* also rescued aircrewman Murray ("Mick") Glasser. After being aggressively interrogated, each man either admitted or was found to carry items identified to have come from the *Enterprise*. The Japanese also found out the force they had attacked had the carriers *Hornet* and *Enterprise*, the battleship *South Dakota*, one cruiser each of the *Pensacola-*, *Portland-*, and *Indianapolis*-class, and ten destroyers that had left Hawaii on October 16. They also discovered the system the Americans used to serially number their carriers. These were, in numerical order: *Langley, Lexington, Saratoga, Ranger, Yorktown, Enterprise, Wasp, Hornet, Essex, Bonhomme Richard*. The carrier the Japanese had sunk with four torpedoes had the number "8" painted on it—clearly it was the *Hornet*. Therefore the only carrier they could confirm to have sunk was the one with an "8" painted on it despite the contradictory and optimistic reports from their aircrews. Ugaki made an entry in his diary that partially explains why the Japanese claimed to have sunk the same American carrier more than once:

> "The enemy builds and christens second and third generations of carriers, as many as we destroy. No wonder they do not need to change the names and numbers, but at present most of them are considered to be the missing numbers."[14]

Nagumo boarded the *Zuikaku* on October 27 to lead the Japanese carriers back to Truk. Abe's Vanguard Force rendezvoused with them the next day. Meanwhile, the heavily damaged *Shokaku* and *Zuiho* limped into Truk's harbor. No longer a proud member of the fleet carrier force, the visible damage on the *Shokaku* displayed a badly mutilated flight deck, seared burn marks from the fire, and a solitary Kate parked aft.

The carrier captains came aboard the *Yamato* and met with Ugaki. He congratulated them for bringing their cripples safely home. But the two captains did not express any satisfaction with their accomplishment. After listening to Ugaki's complementary remarks, they asked him if it was better to bring home a heavily damaged carrier as long as it does not sink. Ugaki replied with conviction in a way to lift their depression, "That's right, because we cannot alone remain unscathed while the enemy is destroyed."[15]

Meanwhile, congratulatory telegrams arrived from the Emperor, Navy Minister, the chief of the Naval General Staff, and Gen. Hisaichi Terauchi, commander of the Japanese Southern Army. Ugaki knew this operation was not as successful as everyone had hoped. Kondo's Support force arrived on October 30 and dropped anchor in Truk's harbor. All the Japanese ships that could had returned.

Task Force 16 arrived off Espiritu Santo's northeast coast at dawn on October 27 with Task Force 17 following close behind. As soon as he saw Murray's cruisers and destroyers over the horizon later that morning, Kinkaid kept steaming toward Nouméa. Meanwhile, Halsey informed New Caledonia's Marine Air Group to expect the arrival of 80 airplanes at Tontouta airfield 40 miles northwest of Nouméa along with their pilots and crews and make accommodations for them. Four F4Fs commanded by Sanchez and an SBD flown by Welch landed at Tontouta the next day followed by most of the *Enterprise*'s air group that included one TBF, 32 F4Fs, and 18 SBDs. Task Force 16 dropped anchor in Nouméa harbor the same day.

Adm. Murray came aboard the *Enterprise* to meet with Kinkaid. It was not a happy occasion as witnessed by Lt. Claude Phillips, an F4F pilot still on board the carrier:

> "Riding in the stern alone was Rear Admiral Murray, a dejected looking figure in rumpled khakis apparently on his way to Rear Admiral Kinkaid. I knew it was a sad day in his life and it was a sight that I still recall with too great clarity and sadness."[16]

Although there is no record of the men's conversation, the sadness of losing the *Hornet* must have hung over Kinkaid's quarters like a shroud.

Keeping Score

After the naval commanders examined what happened at the Battle of the Santa Cruz Islands[17], the Americans had suffered a tactical defeat primarily because they lost half of their operational carrier strength in the Pacific. They forestalled a total and catastrophic debacle by recovering almost all the *Enterprise*'s and most of the *Hornet*'s aircraft and aircrews as well as saving the *Enterprise* to fight another day. But, as had happened in prior battles for Guadalcanal, the Japanese suffered a strategic defeat because of the 17th Army's failure to capture Henderson Field and destroy the American air command still ensconced there. CACTUS would remain the same thorn in the Japanese side it had always been and become stronger. In spite of the loss of the *Hornet*, the Americans had taken a terrible toll on Japanese naval aircraft and crews.

Japanese ships critical to the Imperial Japanese Navy's ability to continue the struggle to recapture Guadalcanal also sustained heavy damage. Damages to the carriers *Shokaku* and *Zuiho* and to the heavy cruiser *Chikuma* were so severe that these ships had to return to Japan for repairs. They would not reenter the war for many months. But the Japanese losses of aircraft and aircrews hurt the most.

The Combined Fleet acted to replace the air losses by sending the undamaged *Zuikaku*, which could have remained at Truk to conduct further air operations, back to home waters to train new pilots. The immobilized carrier *Hiyo* had to stay at Truk leaving the *Junyo* the sole operational Japanese carrier in the waters near Guadalcanal. It was not Yamamoto's intention to force another carrier action because the Japanese still believed they had sunk all American carriers in the Pacific. A parity in carrier strength now existed between the two combatants.

Adm. Nagumo's star began to wan after this third great carrier battle of the war. He had led the greatest carrier force the world had ever seen and achieved the Japanese Empire's greatest naval victory at Pearl Harbor. But defeats at Midway and disastrous aircrew losses at the Battle of Santa Cruz tainted his fortunes. He was an exhausted man as he sailed aboard the *Zuikaku* making its way to home waters. He would no longer command any ships at sea after becoming commander of the Sasebo Naval District.

Like the Japanese, the Americans believed that, while they did not sink any carriers, they still had problems determining how many Japanese carriers they had fought in this battle. Kinkaid believed they did not have as many carriers as they encountered. American naval intelligence correctly estimated that Kinkaid had fought the fleet carriers *Zuikaku* and *Shokaku*, but could not precisely determine if Kinkaid's aviators had fought any more Japanese carriers. Over time, they decided the *Zuiho* was in the battle. The destroyer *Smith* captured evidence from a Japanese aircrewman's notebook that subsequently confirmed the *Junyo* was there as well. So it took some time for the Americans to realize they did indeed face four carriers with two carriers of their own. After losing the *Hornet* and the destroyer *Porter* along with several damaged ships limping back to New Caledonia, the Americans now needed time to repair their battle damage and replace the lost aircrews and airplanes.

But, unlike Yamamoto, Halsey decided to keep the *Enterprise* and the rest of Task Force 61's ships with him. He said what he wanted to do with the *Enterprise* and the rest of Task Force 61 in a correspondence to Nimitz on October 31:

> "We are in need of everything we can get, planes, ships, escort vessels, so on ad nauseam. You are well aware of our needs and this is not offered in complaint or as an excuse, but just to keep the pot boiling. We are not in the least downhearted or upset by our difficulties, but obsessed with one idea only, to kill the yellow bastards and we shall do it."[18]

Halsey would fight with what he had and not send any ship back to Pearl Harbor unless there was no other choice. In that same letter, Halsey again demonstrated the same fighting spirit that endeared him to the men under his command and earned his superiors' respect. He told Nimitz he was determined to "patch up what we have and go with them" and that "half a loaf is better than none."

✲ ✲ ✲

When looking at the effect of the Battle of the Santa Cruz Islands, the comparison of American and Japanese air losses hammers home the conflict's full impact. The number of aircraft shot down, ditched and destroyed on board the home bases from bomb damage shows comparable losses. Let's look at the following table to compare the beating the two sides took:

Aircraft Losses—the Battle of the Santa Cruz Islands—October 26, 1942

	American			**Japanese**		
	Beginning	***Losses***	***Remaining***	***Beginning***	***Losses***	***Remaining***
Fighters	74	33	41	82	27	55
Dive-bombers	72	28	44	63	41	22
Torpedo Planes	29	19	10	58	31	27
Totals	175	80	95	203	99	104

The Japanese had a slight advantage in total number of aircraft when the action commenced on October 26 and lost about the same percentage of total planes as the Americans—49% for the Japanese versus 46% for the Americans. But looking at comparative aircrews' losses between the two sides yields quite a different perspective:

Air Crew losses—The Battle of the Santa Cruz Islands—October 26, 1942

	American	**Japanese**
Pilots	18	**68**
Observers/Air Crew	8	**77**
Totals	26	**145**
Section Leaders and above	5	**23**

Now a better picture emerges how ruinous the Japanese aircrew losses were compared to American losses. The loss of experienced Japanese leaders was particularly devastating. No wonder Yamamoto sent the *Zuikaku* home to train new aircrews to replace the ones no longer there. The fact that one of his key offensive weapons had to be taken away from a combat theater to train new naval aviation crews and pilots demonstrates how stressed the Imperial Japanese Navy's aircrew training program truly was.

At the same time, American training of naval flight crews and pilots geared up to levels never seen before at Naval Air Stations all over the U.S. The American shipyards bustled with frenzied building activity as a new kind of carrier was about to emerge into the Pacific War—the fast, powerful *Essex*-class. And American industry would create the most powerful naval presence the world had ever seen. About one year later, the U.S. Navy would send these vast armadas to take the war to the Japanese.

Admonitions for the Future

While the Japanese basked in what seemed to be a victory, the Americans, prompted by the sinking of one half of their operational Pacific carrier strength, recognized the seriousness of their tactical defeat at the Battle of the Santa Cruz Islands. Criticisms, recriminations, and finger-pointing flowed profusely from the various combat action reports sent by the naval commanders. It became clear this battle taught the Americans many lessons that required a complete re-examination of American carrier battle tactics with the primary emphasis on how to deploy these vital ships.

When Task Force 16 and 17 joined to become Task Force 61, Kinkaid used the standard carrier deployment tactics the U.S. Navy had used after Midway before the battle began because he did not think of any other way. Each carrier had its own battle formation circled by its screen and stayed about five miles apart so they could readily use visual signals. When the Japanese planes approached, the ship formations did not change as Kinkaid remained consistent with then current American tactical doctrine. The optimum use of the task force aircraft was for one FDO, usually aboard the commanding admiral's flagship, to direct and coordinate both carriers' planes for both offensive and defensive operations. Kinkaid kept the two carriers in separate formations to allow each carrier admiral maximum flexibility. We shall probably never know why he did not combine the strength of the two forces and perhaps gain some synergistic increase in antiaircraft defense.

Murray did not agree with Kinkaid's tactics even though his opinions were not in step with current doctrine and said so in his combat action report. Just like Kinkaid, no one knew what Murray's thoughts were before the battle began. He never did discuss battle tactics with Kinkaid either before or during the battle. Murray did agree that the two carriers should separate to a distance of at least 25 to 50 miles once the Japanese aircraft attacked. However, Murray advocated that once the carrier groups separated, overall command should be transferred to a senior commander located ashore, since that officer did not need to maintain radio silence. He disagreed with Kinkaid that the direction of fighters and CAP should be under the control of each carrier's FDO.

The officers on the *Enterprise* and at Halsey's headquarters agreed with Murray. Halsey was a strong proponent of separating the carriers once an attack became "imminent" although there was no precise definition what "imminent" meant. However, Halsey's doctrine assumed there would be a land-based air presence to provide a defensive umbrella and longer range search aircraft. Some of the action reports gave the Japanese high marks for their use of advanced surface forces that could detect and defend against the approach of attacking airplanes. Similarly, Lt. Cmdr. Flatley argued for the use of a ring of destroyers to act as radar pickets to give advanced warning of approaching "bogeys," a tactic implemented later by the U.S. Navy. Nonetheless, the debate over how to employ multiple carrier task forces vigorously continued. Lt. Cmdr. H. A. I. Luard, who acted as an observer from the British Royal Navy during the battle, sardonically noted that Task Force 61's carrier organization seemed to "retain all the disadvantages of concentration with none of its advantages."

✲ ✲ ✲

Another contentious issue was the way the FDOs directed fighter defenses. Flatley called it "inadequate"; Sanchez said they were "ineffective"; Hardison called them "disappointing"; and the worst criticism came from Halsey who said they were "confused and disorganized." Even the fighter pilots piled on. While they felt they had enough planes to defend the two carriers, they wasted too much time being directed to places where they could do no good.

As stated earlier in this book, Count Galeazzo Ciano's quotation had said, "As always, victory finds a hundred fathers, but defeat is an orphan."[19] And that saying came home in full force in the irrational blame-game that occurred during the American post-mortem. When Cmdr. Griffin wrote his frank report on his actions and tried to get them incorporated into the *Enterprise*'s battle report, he was told that his comments were not needed. Kinkaid did recapitulate a few of Griffin's observations and recommendations, but essentially discounted them.

The American post-battle reports categorized the concerns over fighter support in three areas for improvement:

1. Lack of enough reliable warning time about approaching Japanese planes and getting the CAP planes in an advantageous position to intercept them.
2. The fighters were not at the proper altitude to intercept the attacking Japanese aircraft.
3. Griffin's use of directional terms relative to the Enterprise's current course to identify the location of the Japanese planes that changed whenever the carrier's course changed.

The short warning time forced American fighters to intercept the Japanese too close to the American ships. The *Hornet*'s pilots gave their FDO (Fleming) higher marks than those directed at Griffin. In defense of both Griffin (*Enterprise*) and Fleming (*Hornet*), the primary reason was that they could not give the fighters an earlier warning due to the carrier CXAM radar having a short sighting range of 45 miles that did not vary for higher altitudes. Another contributing factor was poor radio communications, which garbled many received messages.

Because he did not know when or from where the Japanese planes would arrive, Griffin kept the fighters at 10,000 feet to conserve precious fuel and oxygen supplies. The F4F was a heavy airplane designed before the war and not equipped to stay aloft for a long time and at a high altitude. The new F4U Corsair, which was so equipped, was not yet ready for combat. Again, the ship CXAM radar could not detect any approaching planes at altitude, thus forcing Griffin to wait until he received other reports that set the altitude of Japanese planes. The most prevalent recommendation was for the fighters to patrol at 20,000 feet, which reduced the time to intercept.

The solution of the third point of concern was to provide absolute compass bearings instead of the relative positions as given by Griffin. That became an easy change when the radars improved. Nonetheless, the criticisms of Griffin continued despite technical shortcomings with the radar and radio technology that existed at that time.

The acrimonious lessons of this battle stayed with both Fleming and Griffin as they continued their naval aviation careers. But the Americans had learned much from the battle's outcome and made the necessary changes. This included adoption of the "Thach Weave" into fighter tactics after much lobbying by James Flatley. He also argued for placing fighter escorts farther ahead and above strike aircraft by deploying four-plane, line-abreast formations with one two-plane section slightly below the other. The Thach Weave was an even more effective tactic. When the American carrier task forces went into battle in 1943 and further into the war, the dive- and torpedo-bomber losses decreased measurably while the fighters destroyed more Japanese aircraft.[20]

Adm. Nimitz wrote his official reaction to what had happened at Santa Cruz in his action drafted several weeks after the battle's end:

> "This battle cost us the lives of many gallant men, many planes and two ships that could ill be spared. Despite the loss of about three carrier air groups and damage to a number of ships, the enemy retired with all his ships. We nevertheless turned back the Japanese again in their offensive to regain Guadalcanal and shattered their carrier air strength on the eve of the critical days of mid-November."[21]

✲ ✲ ✲

Neither side had the capacity, and more importantly, the desire to engage again in the near future. But the fortunes of war do not always necessarily coincide with each side's ability and determination to fight. Destiny would soon take another turn. Robert Southwell, a 16th century English poet once wrote:

"Times go by turns,
and chances change by course,
From foul to fair,
from better hap to worse."[22]

Times certainly would not get better for the protagonists in this deadly struggle. More battles were on the horizon of time and needed to be fought before settling who would permanently occupy Guadalcanal. The next naval battle would be one for the ages and would change the battle fortunes for both sides.

Part 9: The Naval Battle of Guadalcanal - Day 1

CHAPTER 36
Reaching a Turning Point

Testing Japanese Resolve

The American tactical defeat at the Battle of the Santa Cruz Islands convinced the Imperial Japanese Navy that their adversary had no carrier air power left in the South Pacific. After all, returning Japanese air crews reporting the sinking of at least two American *Yorktown*-class carriers, and the Japanese just knew the American carriers were now gone. However, their previous efforts to land reinforcements on Guadalcanal had been stymied partly due to American control of the air in and around the waters of Guadalcanal. The Americans also happened to bring in their carrier aircraft at the same times the Imperial Japanese Navy tried to support landing their troops and would engage in knockdown air battles against the Japanese Navy. However, the one constant factor to that control of the air was the aircrews and planes on the Henderson Field and Fighter One airstrips on that island.

Nonetheless, the struggle on the ground between units of the Japanese 17th Army and the American Marines and soldiers had thus far produced what could charitably be called a stalemate. The Japanese had thus far failed to take Henderson Field. But the American ground forces did not yet have sufficient strength to totally defeat the Japanese. If the Japanese wanted to kick the Americans off that island, resume building their airfield, and achieve their original objective of interdicting American supply lines to and from Australia, they had to do two things: (1) maintain a continuous train of troops, ammunition, and supplies to add to and replace their ground losses; and (2) neutralize and, if possible, destroy the U.S. Navy and Army air forces presence on Guadalcanal.

The past three Army failures to recapture the airfields on Guadalcanal led to increasing frustrations within the Navy, which did not know what the Army's intentions were. Nevertheless, the Navy knew that another convoy had to be sent to Guadalcanal. According to the Army, the Japanese soldiers did not have enough supplies to maintain a high state of combat readiness. In addition, the Navy knew that these men's morale had sunk to a new low despite the Navy's perceived victory at the Battle of the Santa Cruz Islands. Some of the answers as to what the Army planned to do would be decided after the return of two Japanese naval staff officers from Guadalcanal.

✲ ✲ ✲

Capt. Yasuji Watanabe and Cmdr. Toshikazu Ohmae arrived on November 8 from Guadalcanal and made their report to the senior naval officers one hour after their arrival. According to their assessment, after visiting the battle scene on the island, the reasons for the Army's failures could be summarized as:

1. The island's rough terrain made the movement of equipment and men to launch their offensive much harder than anticipated.
2. The soldiers had enough men and supplies because 80% of the materiel sent via the Tokyo Express had been successfully off-loaded despite the losses of ships and men from American air and destroyer attacks.
3. The Army's leadership was poor for the following reasons:
    a. The Army's chief of staff had never visited the combat zone. This resulted in poor command and control by the staff.
    b. Although the 17th Army had placed the 2nd Division's command with Lt. Gen. Maruyama, it constantly infringed on his command decisions.
    c. The officers on the Army General staff constantly argued among themselves resulting in confusing orders and policies.
    d. Maruyama suffered from severe neuralgia, and the division's staff officers were incompetent.
    e. There was poor intelligence of the American movements and positions due to poor reconnaissance.
    f. The Kawaguchi Detachment commander relinquished his command when he protested that he did not have sufficient troops to attack in the area he was assigned. The 17th Army replaced him with a relatively inexperienced officer.
    g. The Oka force did not follow its orders when it ignored the order to advance along the west coast.
4. There was not enough strength because of:
    a. Disproportionate fear of American aircraft.
    b. The 16th Regiment's advance was disorganized.
    c. The 2nd Division lacked combat experience against first-rate American troops since the only battle it had fought previously achieved an easy victory against inferior soldiers. It tried to compensate for this deficiency with disastrous suicidal bayonet charges.
    d. By the time troops had moved into the place to launch their assaults, many of them experienced severe fatigue.
    e. Illness had affected one-third of the officers.
    f. The amount of food available lessened as the soldiers neared the front.

But the Army was not ready to give up. They had established their future plans:

1. The 2nd Division would retreat to the west. Four mountain guns would remain south of the airfield and kept supplied with ammunition.

2. The two battalions, 100 ragtag fragments of the Ichiki Detachment, and 400 recently disembarked soldiers would conduct guerilla warfare until they consumed all their food.

3. A front from which to launch further attacks had to be opened to recapture the Matanikau River's eastern bank.

4. The 38th Division would be sent immediately in a new convoy along with enough materiel for 60 days. The 51st Division and another brigade would arrive in late December.

5. The arrival of the December reinforcement would enable the launching of a major offensive.

Some of the officers at the briefing seemed to be impressed about the Army's plans, but Ugaki was not so easily moved. He wanted to be more aggressive and plan for more attempts to send reinforcements and supplies than the Army wanted. Despite assurances from Maj. Gen. Kesao Kijima, the 38th Division commander, that his division plus a brigade consisting of troops from various regiments could successively fulfill his mission, the Navy did not have any confidence in anything the Army said. Ugaki urged the naval staff to carefully examine the Army's plan and immediately forward its recommendations to the Naval General Staff. Anticipating the approval of the Army's plan, the Combined Fleet issued an order to assemble a large enough convoy to take Kijima's force to Guadalcanal.

Yamamoto wasted no time in putting his plan in place to get as many soldiers as the Combined Fleet could carry to Guadalcanal as fast as his ships could get them there. There were two objectives to the orders that Yamamoto issued on November 8. The first was to land a large ground force to reinforce the beleaguered soldiers on Guadalcanal. Therefore, every fully loaded transport that could be spared would be sent down the Slot. The second was to neutralize the American airfield by bombarding it with battleship and cruiser gunfire. If they could disable the American airfield long enough for the Japanese to gain even temporary air superiority, the Army could capture the island without constant interference from American land-based aircraft. Then they could turn the tables on the Americans, establish air superiority over the southern Solomons, and achieve their original objective to block supply routes to Australia. Meanwhile, the carrier *Junyo* with the battleships *Kongo* and *Haruna*, the heavy cruiser *Tone*, and supporting destroyers would lie to the north of Guadalcanal to supply air support as needed.

The Imperial Japanese Navy still had a powerful naval presence despite the withdrawal of the carriers *Shokaku*, *Zuikaku*, and *Zuiho*. The following table shows the ships and senior commanders at Truk with Adm. Yamamoto in overall command:[1]

Japanese Naval Forces - November 1942

Advanced Force (Kondo)	
Raiding Group (Abe)	
Battleships	*Hiei, Kirishima*
Light Cruisers	*Nagara*
Destroyers	*Amatsukaze, Yukikaze, Akatsuki, Ikazuchi, Inazuma, Teruzuki, Asagumo, Murasame, Samidare, Yudachi, Harusame, Shigure, Shiratsuyu, Yugure*
Main Body (Kondo)[2]	
Battleship	*Kirishima*
Heavy cruisers	*Atago, Takao*
Light cruiser	*Sendai*
Destroyers	*Teruzuki, Inazuma, Shirayuki, Hatsuyuki, Asagumo, Uranami, Shikinami, Ayanami, Oyashio, Kagero*
Carrier Support (Kurita)	
Light Carrier	*Junyo*
Battleships	*Kongo, Haruna*
Heavy cruisers	*Tone*
Destroyers	*Hatsuyuki, Shirayuki, Uranami, Shikinami*[3]
Outer South Seas Force (Mikawa)	
Support Group (Mikawa)	
Heavy cruisers	*Chokai, Kinugasa, Suzuya, Maya*
Light cruisers	*Isuzu, Tenryu*
Destroyers	*Makigumo, Yugumo, Kazagumo, Michishio*
Reinforcement Group (Tanaka)	
Destroyers	*Hayashio, Oyashio, Kagero, Umikaze, Kawakaze, Suzukaze, Takanami, Makinami, Naganami, Amagiri, Mochizuki*
Transports	*Arizona Maru, Kumagawa Maru, Sado Maru, Nagara Maru, Nako Maru, Canberra Maru, Brisbane Maru, Kinugawa Maru, Hirokawa Maru, Yamaura Maru, Yamatsuki Maru*

As usual, the Japanese plan was complex requiring many activities to occur as planned for the scheme to be a success. If any part of the plan failed for any reason, the entire enterprise could also fail.

On November 9, Yamamoto's instructions began to be implemented. The Japanese Advanced Force including the carrier *Junyo* with Adm. Kondo in command sortied from Truk around midday. It was a powerful force, although not as large as the ships that sailed to do battle in October. This time, the Japanese decided not to commit its only carrier into the main battle area, but sent two of its four *Kongo*-class battleships to be part of the planned bombardment of the American airfields. These ships were not really battleships but built as battlecruisers before World War I. Carrying eight 14-inch main guns and 14 six-inch secondary guns, these two ships, the *Kirishima* and *Hiei,* displaced about 32,000 tons and 36,400 tons respectively but, like the other battlecruisers built in that era, had thinner armor plate than the modern American battleships that had recently been introduced in the beginning years of World War II. This disparity would influence the outcome of future battles.[4]

The operation's timetable set a day for the actual landings as Z-Day, November 13, 1942. The plan's precise Japanese timetable was:[5]

Imperial Japanese Navy's Mid-November Plan

Day	Actions
Z-3	Land-based aircraft bomb American airfields.
Z-2	Battleships and cruisers shell Henderson Field.
Z-1	Japanese carrier aircraft bomb American airfields.
Z-0	Japanese troops and supplies land in force on Guadalcanal.

The latest intelligence gleaned from search aircraft showed an American convoy heading west from Hawaii and another heading east from Auckland, New Zealand. If some of Kondo's force arrived on time, it might have a chance to intercept them and inflict a crippling blow.

Meanwhile, a report by Col. Taksuhiro Hattori of the Army General Staff brought some discouraging news about the conditions at the Guadalcanal front. He passed through Truk on his way from Rabaul to Japan and reported what he observed to Ugaki and the rest of the Combined Fleet staff. The circumstances that the Japanese soldiers faced were far worse than anyone previously believed. The number of soldiers ready to effectively take the fight to the Americans was now one-third to one-fourth of the original numbers of troops landed on the island. Unless American air forces could be destroyed, matters could only get worse. His best estimate when an effective offensive could be launched was now January 1943! That fact shocked the senior naval commanders and reinforced their mistrust of and contempt for the Army's ability to emerge victorious on Guadalcanal. After more discussions, the best estimate for another offensive moved back to the end of 1942.

The next day, November 10, brought news of a sighting of one American heavy cruiser, several destroyers, and three transports heading northwest about 150 miles from Guadalcanal. Everyone at Combined Fleet headquarters hoped that Kondo's sortie would find and destroy them. Something big was about to happen, and the Japanese were ready to engage the Americans in yet another severe battle.[6]

Crunch Time on Guadalcanal

After the Battle of the Santa Cruz Islands and the loss of the *Hornet*, the Americans in Washington came to the realization just how dire the conditions were on Guadalcanal. The war had by now reached a critical stage where the U.S. was about to embark on a real two-front war. American ground forces would not only fight in the Pacific on Guadalcanal and New Guinea, but would engage the Germans and Italians in major ground operations in the European Theater for the first time. Operation Torch, the Allied landings on the shore of North Africa, was scheduled to begin on November 7.

Their allies, the Soviet Union and the United Kingdom, were about to engage in critical battles against the Germans. The Russians had battled Hitler's minions to a standstill at Stalingrad and were holding them on other fronts. Gen. Bernard Montgomery was about to launch his assault on October 23 against Gen. Erwin Rommel's renowned Afrika Corps at El Alamein. The Battle of the Atlantic had reached a peak in October as the Nazis sent more than 600,000 tons of Allied merchant shipping to the bottom of the Atlantic. American and British shipping, already overextended well beyond its limits, struggled mightily to get supplies to the Russians over the treacherous run to Murmansk past German-held Norway and around the Cape of Good Hope to the British in Egypt. Also, a plan for the invasion of Continental Europe to take place in 1943 was in full swing.

Despite the risk of offending his Allied partners, Roosevelt went against the conventional wisdom of a Europe-first strategy and defensive posture in the Pacific strategy when he sent a memorandum to all the Joint Chiefs of Staff on October 24 that stressed the importance of the war in the Pacific and the desperate need for a victory on Guadalcanal. In that note he wrote:

> "My anxiety about the Southwest Pacific is to make sure that every possible weapon gets into that area to hold Guadalcanal. And that having held it in this crisis that munitions and planes and crews are on the way to take advantage of our success. We will soon find ourselves engaged in two active fronts and we must have adequate air support in both places even tho it means delay in our other commitments, particularly to England. Our long range plans could be set back for months if we fail to throw our full strength in our immediate and impending conflicts.
>
> I wish therefore you would canvass over the week end every possible temporary division of munitions which you will require for our active fronts and let me know what they are. Please also review the number and use of all combat planes now in the continental U.S.."[7]

Clearly, Roosevelt worried about whether the Americans would be victorious on Guadalcanal or not. Nonetheless, he still did not want to fully embrace the "Europe first" doctrine at the expense of the soldiers, sailors, and marines fighting for their lives on and around Guadalcanal.[8]

✲ ✲ ✲

Halsey knew the situation on Guadalcanal was coming to a head. Despite the Japanese stopping their major operations to land reinforcements, less ambitious runs of the Tokyo Express continued to bring in troops and supplies. They successively landed 65 destroyer loads and two cruiser loads of reinforcements and materiel between November 2 and November 9. Those new troops immediately joined their comrades in the front lines. The American air forces at Henderson Field had been stretched to the breaking point in October, but still managed to keep the Imperial Japanese Navy at bay. Halsey had never visited the front and decided now was the time to do so.

He also needed every ship he had. Without consulting the French authorities on New Caledonia, Halsey confiscated more comfortable quarters to gain more space for his growing operation and freed up the *Argonne* for a more worthwhile use. When the French officials wanted to know what the Americans would provide in return, Col. Julian Brown, Halsey's appointee to find the space the admiral desperately needed, quickly settled the matter by succinctly telling the French, "We will continue to protect you as we have always done."[9]

Recognizing the need to see the combat situation first-hand, he took his war plans officer, Marine Brig. Gen. Dewitt Peck, and his new flag lieutenant, Lt. William D. Kitchell, with him and boarded a B-17 to head for Guadalcanal. The bomber landed at Henderson Field on November 8. Vandegrift was a happy man and met Halsey when he arrived. He expressed his delight with Halsey's visit by saying the admiral's arrival was "like a wonderful breath of fresh air." Halsey only had one afternoon to spend on the island and thus wanted to make the most of the time he had. He clambered into a jeep with Vandegrift and his two staff officers to examine the Marine defenses.

Wanting to get first-hand knowledge of what the American troops actually faced, he ordered the jeep's driver to stop so he could directly talk to the Marines. Their bony skeletal appearance due to pervasive malarial infections showed the strain these brave men confronted in their everyday struggle for survival. But seeing their theater commander talking to them and asking how they were doing buoyed their morale. Halsey still had that charisma to inspire men to fight beyond what they believed they could do.

He did not have much time to stop at many places; so most of the men only saw glimpses of him. He dressed in khakis, and his three stars were difficult to see. Peck and Kitchell wanted Halsey to visit more than he did but the admiral thought it would be too ostentatious when he said, "It smells of exhibitionism. The hell with it." He held a brief press conference and again was in his element. The press loved the outspoken leader; he did not disappoint them. One reporter asked Halsey what his plans were to win the war. He answered bluntly, "Kill Japs, kill Japs, and keep on killing Japs." Another reporter asked when the Japanese would give up. In another one of his characteristically short, direct replies, Halsey said, "How long do you think they can take it?"[10]

After seeing the brutal conditions his men faced on Guadalcanal, Halsey had a far more pleasant experience when he joined Vandegrift and some of the general's staff officers for a superb meal. Vandegrift had one of his officers find the best food he could to give the admiral a fine send-off before returning to Nouméa. Halsey was so amazed at the quality of the food that he asked to talk to the cook who had prepared such a sumptuous feast under such impossible conditions. After Vandegrift tried to dissuade Halsey by saying it was not necessary for the admiral to complement the chef, he found his cook, Sergeant "Butch" Morgan, and asked the man to speak to Halsey.

The cook walked into the dining tent wearing khaki pants and a skivvy shirt and spunkily displaying a bushy red mustache. He snapped to a crisp salute and stood stiffly at attention in front of the admiral. Halsey profusely praised the cook for his fine work preparing such a fine meal and said effort like his played an important role in the eventual American victory. The man's face turned beet red with embarrassment at all this effusive praise. As he nervously pulled on his shirt, he caused everyone to break out into uproarious laughter. Morgan said, "Aw, horseshit, Admiral. 'Twarn't nothin.'"[11]

Halsey experienced the power of the Tokyo Express as he spent the night in Vandegrift's ramshackle quarters. Just as both men got into bed and began to fall asleep, a Japanese ship arrived in Iron Bottom Sound and began shelling the airfield and Marine quarters surrounding the field. The American and Japanese guns ashore joined the cacophony. The admiral could not sleep and, like all honest men who have ever been in combat, admitted that it was his fear that kept him awake and not the noise.

Early the next morning he pinned medals on some officers, drove to the airfield and boarded his plane for his return trip home. As he climbed onto the plane, he looked into Vandegrift's eyes and said jokingly, "Vandegrift, don't you do a thing to that cook."

Wanting to see how the naval medical staff attended to the needs of the wounded, he stopped at Éfaté and visited the base hospital. As he walked the wards, he talked to some of the wounded and was impressed by their positive morale despite their serious medical conditions. He left for Nouméa with the satisfaction that everything that was medically possible was being done for those suffering men. The news of his hospital visit spread throughout his command and convinced many who served there that he really cared about their welfare. He arrived in Nouméa on November 10 in the afternoon and immediately went to work to make sure these men were not suffering in vain. This was classic Halsey.[12]

✲ ✲ ✲

The Americans had again cracked a revision of the Japanese JN-25 naval code and made some startling discoveries. On November 4, Cmdr. Edwin T. Layton's CINCPAC code breakers began detecting increased radio traffic among the Imperial Japanese Navy's commanders that pointed to another large upcoming operation and more Tokyo Express runs than usual.

Successive fleet intelligence summaries supported that thesis:[13]

November 9: "New operation involving Guadalcanal either already begun or is about to begin, with Z day fixed and at least one phase of the operation concerned with the airfield on Guadalcanal fixed for Z-3 Day. Likely date appears to be November 12."

November 10: "Opord from C-in-C Combined Fleet 1830 November 8, parts unintelligible as yet, (a) Army convoy will arrive Guadalcanal on Z Day, (b) air attacks on Blue installations on Guadalcanal from Z-3, (c) escorts, air patrol and patrols of certain sectors provided for protection of convoy from Z-3, (d) air forces will be under the command of the Striking Force from Z-3, (e) Striking Force will operate against Guadalcanal from Z-1. Z-Day now November 13."

November 11: "Indications strong C-in-C 8th Fleet [Mikawa] in *Chokai* directly concerned in the command and protection of two Army convoys scheduled to arrive Guadalcanal on November 13. Convoys are large and important."

CINCPAC issued its own intelligence bulletin on November 10:[14]

> "Big Japanese offensive against Guadalcanal to begin soon. Believe enemy striking force intends to hit that place followed by attempted landings by army units from transports. At present striking force believed either at or en route to position east of Greenwich Island." [South of Malaita and east of Guadalcanal]

The November 9 prediction presented a severe and unmistakable warning that another major Japanese operation was coming. Lt. Robert E. Hudson, Layton's assistant, guessed two days later the Japanese offensive would begin either on November 12 or 13. His November 11 report also stated that JNAF aircraft crews had already landed on Guadalcanal to immediately get Henderson Field ready for air operations when the Japanese captured the airfield. The 14th Naval District's Combat Intelligence Unit's report of November 9 confirmed Hudson's assessment by including a summary of an intercepted Combined Fleet message that stated Yamamoto's operations order. This proved to be the greatest American code-breaking effort in the Pacific Theater since Midway. However, American assessment of Japanese naval strength overestimated the number of carriers they would use. American intelligence estimated their naval strength to include the fleet carriers *Shokaku* and *Zuikaku* and the light carrier *Zuiho* as being still at Truk and did not know those ships had departed for the Japanese home islands.[15]

✲ ✲ ✲

After arriving on the *Argonne* on the 10th, Miles Browning, Halsey's chief of staff, put a damper on the admiral's ebullient spirits with a shocking report on the state of his SOPAC command. The Japanese had begun a pattern by launching three successive major attacks near the ends of August, September, and October. Halsey sensed from this the Japanese were about to launch another assault. He hoped for at least one week's respite to get ready for them, but naval intelligence's latest reports signaled the Japanese would attack in the middle of November. The Japanese would bomb Guadalcanal on the 10th; the Imperial Japanese Navy would shell the Marines late that evening of the 11th; carrier aircraft would hit Guadalcanal the late evening of the 12th; and a large landing force along with a big cache of supplies would come ashore on November 13.

Before traveling to Guadalcanal, Halsey ordered Adm. Kelly Turner to take 6,000 marines and soldiers in two convoys from Espiritu Santo and Nouméa to reinforce Vandegrift's beleaguered men. While Halsey visited Guadalcanal, Turner assembled his forces for the long and dangerous voyage. This effort would take the largest number of reinforcements to Guadalcanal since the Americans invaded on August 7. The troops would come from the following units:

- 8th Regiment, 2nd Marine Division
- 1st Battalion, 147th Infantry Regiment, Americal Division
- Two companies from 2nd Marine Raider Battalion
- A detachment from the 5th Defense Battalion
- Battery K, 246th Field Artillery Battalion, Americal Division
- 3rd Battalion. 147th Infantry Regiment
- Elements of 246th Artillery Regiment

- Part of 9th Marine Defense Battalion
- Seabees
- 1st Marine Aviation Engineer Battalion;
- Marine Air Wing 1 ground personnel
- 182nd Infantry (less 3rd Battalion)
- 4th Marine Replacement Battalion
- Naval Local Defense Force

To carry all these men and the materiel to support them, Turner needed the four large, high speed transports affectionately called the "Unholy Four" by those who had previously sailed in them. These were the *McCawley*, *Crescent City*, *President Adams*, and *President Jackson*. Each ship was a former luxury liner, displaced between 9,000 and 10,000 tons, and was capable of speeds of up to about 15 knots. In addition, the attack cargo ships *Betelgeuse*, *Libra*, and *Zeilin* had to be added to deliver the men and cargo. All these intrepid vessels were by now Solomon Islands' veterans with experienced crews.

The seven transports had to have protection from Japanese air and surface attacks. Therefore, Halsey gave Turner the following warships to escort and protect the transports:[16]

American Warships - Naval Battle of Guadalcanal

Turner (Task Force 67)	
Callaghan (Task Force 67.4)	
Cruisers	*San Francisco, Pensacola, Portland, Helena, Juneau*
Destroyers	*Barton, Monssen, Cushing, Laffey, Sterett, O'Bannon, Shaw, Gwin, Preston, Buchanan*
Scott (Task Force 62.4)	
Cruiser	*Atlanta*
Destroyers	*Aaron Ward, Fletcher, Lardner, McCalla*
Halsey (Nouméa)	
Kinkaid (Task Force 16)	
Carrier	*Enterprise*
Cruisers	*Northampton, San Diego*
Destroyers	*Clark, Anderson, Hughes, Morris, Mustin, Russell*
Lee (Task Force 64)	
Battleships	*Washington, South Dakota*
Destroyers	*Walke, Benham*

Kinkaid and Lee's assignments were to position their ships to be able to come to Turner's aid if the Japanese should attack the landings. But American military power was not confined to just a naval presence. Adm. Fitch had two powerful air power contingents on Guadalcanal and at Espiritu Santo. Henderson Field had 28 F4Fs, 18 P-38s, 37 SBDs, nine TBFs and one P-400 and one P-39. Additionally, 21 F4Fs, 16 TBFs, 37 B-17s, five B-26s, two PB4Ys, five RNZAF Hudsons, 24 PBYs, and one PBY-5A were at Espiritu Santo. The aircraft, their pilots and aircrews at Henderson Field would again inflict crippling blows at Japanese attempts to land reinforcements.[17]

Both sides were now ready to face each other in the most critical battle for deciding who would eventually remain on Guadalcanal. The outcome of that confrontation would be the turning point of not only who would emerge victorious in the southern Solomon Islands but would force one side to go from the offensive to a totally defensive posture in the Pacific.

CHAPTER 37
Moving into Position

A Tale of Two Admirals

Daniel Judson Callaghan stood in his admiral's barge as it glided through the smooth waters of Espiritu Santo harbor and saw the ship loom larger as they moved closer to her. He had seen her before when he was her captain for one year from May 1941 to May 1942. The vessel was the U.S. Navy *New Orleans*-class heavy cruiser *San Francisco*. Launched on March 9, 1933, and commissioned on April 23, 1934, she displaced 12,463 tons fully loaded and carried nine powerful eight-inch guns.[1] Sleek and built for speeds of more than 30 knots, she was a tiger of the sea and ready to do her worst against her nation's enemies. As all sailors who fall in love with the ships on which they serve, Callaghan's Irish poetic nature could not help but be moved as his barge pulled near her side. He was at the zenith of his career and eager to prove his worth.

Born in San Francisco, California, on July 26, 1892, to a piously Catholic, highly respected family of merchants and named for his Cork, Ireland-born grandfather, Callaghan attained his education with the Dominicans at St. Elizabeth's in Oakland and completed high school with the Jesuits at the College of St. Ignatius. He qualified for the US Naval Academy in 1907 and graduated 38th in a class of 193 in 1911. His first assignment was in the armored cruiser *California*, where he commanded an eight-inch gun turret. He later transferred to the destroyer *Truxtun* as an engineering officer and later became that ship's commander.

He came aboard the cruiser *New Orleans* in 1916 as its engineering officer. When the U.S. entered World War I in April 1917, his ship moved to the Atlantic where it served as an escort for convoys to and from the Mediterranean. His time on the cruiser ended along with the war in November 1918, and he entered the tough life of the peacetime, postwar Navy. After suffering the indignities of serving in a drastically reduced service, he eventually received an assignment as the fire control officer in the new battleship *Idaho* and advanced from one assignment to another until he became the gunnery officer on the staff of Adm. Richard H. Leigh, who was then commander-in-chief of the U.S. Fleet, 1932-1933.

His next assignment in 1936, while routine for an advancing naval officer, was as the executive officer of the cruiser *Portland* and the preferred path to attaining the rarefied rank of captain, changed the course of his career. Ross McIntire, who had served with Callaghan on the *New Orleans*, was President Roosevelt's personal physician and had maintained contact with Callaghan over the years. He recommended Callaghan to become a naval aide to the President. The President also remembered the young naval officer after meeting him at the Bureau of Navigation in 1919. Callaghan wanted very much to get his fourth stripe, but this was not to be. Although he did not really want the advantageous and highly political job, he could not refuse his commander-in-chief. Being the dedicated naval officer he was, Callaghan enthusiastically executed his shore-based assignments and made a significant contribution to placing the 40-mm Bofors AA guns on American ships. Later, political connections he established within the highest echelons of Washington would serve him well and gave him some extra advantage over his peers.[2]

He desperately wanted to return to sea duty, and Roosevelt finally gave him his wish with a fourth stripe and the command of the *San Francisco* in the spring of 1941. After Pearl Harbor and the appointment of Vadm. Ghormley as the new commander of the South Pacific, Callaghan achieved the dream of every career naval officer—flag rank. He became a rear admiral and Ghormley's chief-of-staff in the spring of 1942. His new assignment was to prepare for the next offensive operations the Americans would undertake in the South Pacific. That preparation later provided the foundation for the Guadalcanal invasion.

As he built his career and reputation in the Navy, he became known as a serious-minded, self-effacing, religiously-devout, get-it-done, meticulous man who had earned the highest level of respect of his peers and the love of the men who served under his command. Called "Uncle Dan" by his men, he still had a certain aloofness about him as his thoughts ran to an esoteric level. He was a lover of stories of medieval chivalry and the warriors of those bygone days.[3]

After Halsey replaced Ghormley on October 18, the new commander returned Callaghan to the *San Francisco* on October 30 to replace Radm. Howard H. Good who was ill. This time he had the command of a task group with the cruiser as his flagship under the tactical command of Adm. Turner. His ships would be part of an escort of the seven transports carrying the newest reinforcements for Guadalcanal.

As he climbed the ship's ladder up the cruiser's side and the bosun's pipe blared the admiral's beeps, he felt he had at last come home and back to sea where he belonged. With the Imperial Japanese Navy still active in the Solomons, there was a good chance he would also see combat—a sailor's call to duty.[4]

✡ ✡ ✡

There was another admiral in the harbor at Espiritu Santo—Radm. Norman E. Scott—and Callaghan's Annapolis classmate. He had already experienced naval combat as well as the fury and terror of a night surface battle in the Battle of Cape Esperance. Scott also commanded a task group and was Callaghan's peer in Turner's Task Force 67. Unlike Callaghan, Scott had already been bloodied in combat and was more knowledgeable of the Imperial Japanese Navy's tactics. It would be a matter of time to see if that experience would bring any advantage to the Americans in the actions yet to come.

Anchors Aweigh

Three groups of ships had to leave their destinations so they could meet on November 12 in time to land their men and cargoes. The first to sail were Turner's ships, which included the transports *Presi-*

dent Jackson, President Adams, Crescent City, and *McCawley*, Turner's flagship. The escorts for the transports were the cruisers *Portland* and *Juneau* and the destroyers *Barton, Monssen*, and *O'Bannon*.

By this time, Turner was no stranger to bringing desperately needed men and materiel to Guadalcanal. It had been the sole reason his command existed. With the Japanese running the Tokyo Express nearly every day, bringing supplies and men for their efforts to recapture Guadalcanal, he wished he could have done more. But with the American supply trains stretched to their limits trying to meet its military obligations all over the world, he had made some peace in his own mind he had done his best.

On November 8 at 3:30 p.m., the bosuns' pipes blew their signals for the ships to get under way, leave Nouméa's harbor, and steam to their November 11 rendezvous with the Adm. Scott and Callaghan task groups. Chains squealed as the ships' winches pulled their anchors from the water with high pressure water hoses cleaning the harbor mud from them. Smoke began to pour from the ship smokestacks as their boilers increased steam pressure to begin turning their propellers. Task Force 67 was on its way.

✲ ✲ ✲

Radm. Scott with Task Force 62.4, the second group of ships, got under way from Espiritu Santo on November 9 because he was one day's steaming time closer to Guadalcanal. His flagship, the cruiser *Atlanta*, along with the destroyers *Aaron Ward, Fletcher, Lardner*, and *McCalla* were to escort the *Zeilin, Betelgeuse*, and *Libra* to Guadalcanal. Scott's added duties were to provide gun support for the Marines on that island.

An area of ocean in the Coral Sea had become known as "Torpedo Junction" because of the many Japanese submarines that had been previously detected there. Scott wanted to avoid this part of ocean. He, therefore, took his ships north of San Cristobal Island and away from these waters to minimize the chances of being found by Japanese search planes and submarines. Nevertheless, the Japanese had the *I-7* off the Santa Cruz Islands and *I-9, I-21*, and *I-31* near San Cristobal, Nouméa, and Suva. Some of these submarines had seaplanes stowed aboard them. One of the seaplanes found Scott's convoy and reported his position to the Imperial Japanese Navy on November 10.

Adm. Callaghan's third group of faster warships left Espiritu Santo at 7:30 a.m. on November 10. His command carried the designation of Task Force 67.4 and included his flagship, the cruiser *San Francisco*, the cruiser *Helena*, and the destroyers *Buchanan, Cushing, Gwin, Laffey, Preston*, and *Sterett*. Fully provisioned and ready for combat like the other warships in Turner's Task Force, the last ships of the American resupply convoy sailed for southeast of San Cristobal Island where they would join up with Turner and Scott.

✲ ✲ ✲

The final task force within Halsey's naval forces was Kinkaid's Task Force 16, containing the carrier *Enterprise*, the cruisers *Northampton* and *San Diego*, and the destroyers *Morris* and *Benham*. The battleships *South Dakota* and newly-arrived *Washington* under the command of Radm. Willis A. "Ching" Lee added more firepower and were ready for any Japanese battleships that might be in their way.

The *Enterprise* and the *South Dakota* arrived in Nouméa after taking heavy damage in the Battle of the Santa Cruz Islands. The carrier's forward No. 1 elevator was locked in the upward position but still flush with the flight deck. The damage to the No. 1 elevator allowed the single carrier Halsey had to only carry 38 F4Fs, 31 SBDs, and nine TBFs. But she could still conduct flight operations and steam at her top speed. The *South Dakota*'s forward turret could not operate at all but she still could fire her remaining six 16-inch guns in the other two turrets.

Halsey gave Kinkaid only two hours notice to get Task Force 16 underway on November 11. Nonetheless, the ships left Nouméa's harbor at noon and the *Enterprise* air group landed one hour later. His orders from Halsey were to reach a position near 14°S and 161° 30'E by 8:00 a.m.[5] on the 13th and to "be prepared to strike targets CACTUS area."[6] Unlike his previous combat assignments, Kinkaid's ships would have to wait for more orders from Halsey. The *Enterprise* was in no shape to enter into any battle situations because she was the only operational carrier Halsey had. However, Lee and his battleships were ready to do battle with the Imperial Japanese Navy, and that time would soon come.

At 5:00 a.m. on November 11, the radar on the *San Francisco* picked up Turner's convoy approaching from the southeast. Both task groups rendezvoused to the southeast of San Cristobal Island—right on schedule. A Japanese plane flew near the American ships and circled for about one-half hour after sunrise and then departed. The *San Francisco* launched its seaplane and sent it to Tulagi. The *Portland* and the *Helena* sent their seaplanes back to Espiritu Santo.

Turner had originally planned to follow Scott's course and take his convoy north of San Cristobal Island. But he changed his mind when he found out the Japanese were now aware of his ships moving toward Guadalcanal. He changed his course to pass south of San Cristobal.

Scott's ships arrived off Lunga Point at 5:30 a.m. that same morning. He immediately ordered his warships to go to General Quarters because he expected a Japanese air attack. Meanwhile, the *Zeilin*, *Libra*, and *Betelgeuse* dropped anchor and began to disgorge cargo. But unloading the Marines and their supplies became more than an uneventful exercise when Japanese carrier bombers and fighters, now based at the new airfield at Buin on Bougainville, arrived to do their worst.

Australian coastwatchers had been observing the Japanese building their new airfield at Buin from the time the tractors, trucks, and equipment of every type arrived. Commanded by Cmdr. Eric A. Feldt, RAN, the coastwatchers Lt. W. J. (Jack) Read, RANVR, and Lt. Paul E. Mason, RANVR, saw the buildup and reported its progress almost every day. Using natives because they could easily blend with the labor being used by the Japanese and sometimes serve as laborers themselves, Mason sent a message with a definitive status of the airfield's construction:

> "Our scouts being employed Kahili aerodrome state aerodrome is expected to be completed in a week's time. Many hundreds of natives being forced to work on aerodrome. 27 lorries, 6 motor cars, 10 horses, 6 motorcycles, 4 tractors and aerodrome working equipment

> at Kahili. Stores and fuel under tarpaulins spread along foreshore from mouth of Ugumo River to mouth of Moliko River. Two antiaircraft guns near mouth of Ugumo River in fuel and ammunition dump and one antiaircraft gun on northwestern boundary of aerodrome. Wireless station on beach in front of aerodrome also eight new iron buildings. Priests and nuns interned in iron buildings on beach. Enemy troops in green uniforms with anchor badge on arm and on white hat. Scouts state about 440 enemy troops but coolies. Too numerous to count. Weather too hazy to observe ships today."[7]

Read also reported the passing of ships into and out of Buin's harbor:

> "A ship, which may be cruiser, and probably another entered Kessa 1 P.M. believe from north. Heavy destroyer and light cruiser, derrick on stem, just entered Buka Passage. Unusual air activity today; nine fighters landed [aero]drome. Believe about twenty fighters and bombers now here. First mentioned ship now leaving Kessa believe may come this way."[8]

Reports such as these kept pouring into MacArthur, Halsey, and Vandegrift's headquarters so that the Americans almost had more current information than the Japanese. MacArthur's planes constantly harassed the Shortlands and Buin with disruptive bombing raids.

The coup that the coastwatchers contributed to the Naval Battle of Guadalcanal was when Mason sighted the ships being sent by the Japanese to reinforce Guadalcanal from his vantage point near Barougo in southern Bougainville. He sent the following report on November 10:

> "At least 61 ships this area viz: 2 Nati, 1 Aoba, 1 Mogami, 1 Kiso, 1 Tatuta, [all cruisers] 2 sloops, 33 destroyers, 17 cargo, 2 tankers, 1 passenger liner of 8,000 tons."[9]

Although the accuracy of the types of ships was not as good as it could have been, Mason confirmed the intelligence intercepts Halsey already had in his possession. Something big was indeed about to happen.

✲ ✲ ✲

Tadashi Kaneko, newly-promoted to lieutenant commander, led 18 Zeroes that escorted nine Vals under the command of Lt. Zenji Abe. But the CACTUS Air Force radar detected the Japanese planes at 9:05 a.m. and scrambled 21 F4Fs to meet them. As the Marine pilots climbed to their patrol altitudes, thick clouds hid the Japanese planes from being immediately intercepted.

But the cruiser *Atlanta* saw them and opened fire. The bombers dropped their bombs and scored three near-misses on the *Zeilin*. The explosions in the water sprung a leak in the transport's hold and slightly damaged the *Betelgeuse* and *Libra*. Five carrier bombers went down with most of the damage caused by the withering American AA fire. Some Zeroes surprised six F4Fs as they emerged from the heavy clouds and killed four American pilots while losing two of their own.

No coastwatcher warnings came that told of the coming of 25 Bettys from Rabaul and commanded by Lt. Kazuo Watanabe with Lt. Toshitaka Ito leading their 26 Zero escorts. The bombers came in at a high altitude at 11:27 a.m. and dropped their bombs on Fighter One and some coconut palms but missed Henderson Field. Seventeen F4Fs jumped the bombers and shot down four of them. The heavy cloud cover prevented the Zeroes from engaging American fighters in aerial battle.

However, two F4Fs collided and Master Technical Sergeant Joseph J. Palko lost his life from this unfortunate incident.

The increasing intensity of the Japanese air attacks forced Scott to interrupt the unloading. When the assault ended, he ordered the unloading to resume. After finishing delivery of his cargoes, he moved his ships east of Indispensable Strait to meet Callaghan's force approaching from the east.

Turner's ships were about 45 miles away as Scott's ships defended against the Japanese air attacks. Scott and Callaghan's lookouts spotted Turner's convoy about an hour before sunset on November 11. The ships steamed 13 miles south of San Cristobal while constant reports indicated that Japanese submarines and aircraft were nearby. Turner ordered "General Quarters" at 6:15 p.m.

After traversing the treacherous waters between Guadalcanal and the Florida islands, all three task groups met at 10:12 p.m. The cruisers and destroyers began searching for any Japanese opposition. After detecting a submarine in the early morning hours of November 12, the destroyer *Buchanan* attacked it with guns and depth charges. Meanwhile, men on the ships saw flashes of gunfire as a cool breeze wafted the sweet smell of Guadalcanal's jungle flowers over them. The Tokyo Express was nowhere to be found.

Nonetheless, Turner knew the Japanese had not yet finished attacking his Task Force and that they would soon return. His highest priority was to unload the men and cargoes as fast as possible and remove the vulnerable transports to safety. The transports moved to 600 yards offshore at 5:40 a.m. and dropped their anchors just deep enough so they could quickly weigh anchor when and if the Japanese should appear.

The transport cranes lifted the landing boats from their decks and into the water. The cargo nets went over the ships' sides, and the troops immediately scrambled down them and into the boats. They were all ashore in just 40 minutes. Working feverishly in the holds, about 200 men moved the cargo onto nets, cranes lifted the brimming nets into waiting boats in the water, and the boats moved at their best speed to deposit the supplies on shore. Meanwhile, sweat poured from the men's bodies below decks as they worked rapidly to empty all cargo from the transports' holds.

An alarm sounded at 10:08 a.m. when the lookouts spotted several planes, and the ships opened fire. Fortunately, the gunfire never hit any of the planes since they were the first American Army P-38s to make their appearance over Guadalcanal. These fighters would soon make their presence felt.

As the transports offloaded their cargoes, the warships moved into an antiaircraft defensive formation surrounding the transports. And that move came none too soon. At 1:20 p.m. a "Condition Red" alert sounded.[10]

✲ ✲ ✲

Vadm. Jinichi Kusaka, commander of the newly-reorganized Base Air Force in Rabaul, immediately ordered another attack after receiving the message that there were American transports and a powerful fleet of warships off Lunga unloading a large force of ground reinforcements and cargoes. Lt. Cmdr. Tomoo Nakamura took off from Rabaul leading 16 Betty aircraft with torpedoes in their bomb bays. A 30-Zero escort commanded by Lt. Masaji Suganami accompanied them. It was an eerily familiar reprise of the attack the Japanese launched immediately after the American landings on August 7.

☼ ☼ ☼

Paul Mason again came through with a warning message of a large group of Japanese aircraft flying southeasterly toward Guadalcanal. Turner received Mason's message at 1:17 p.m. and sent the alert by radio and flags, "Stand by to repel air attack." All unloading ceased immediately as Turner gathered all his ships again into an antiaircraft defense and moved his ships farther off Guadalcanal's northern shore to the center of Sealark Channel. CACTUS' radar, under the leadership of Lt. Lewis C. Mattison, picked up the intruders 109 miles away and sent continuous reports of the planes' approach. Nonetheless, Nakamura cleverly hid his planes from being seen by maneuvering them behind thick clouds over Florida Island to the northeast of Lunga Point.

Two groups of fighters scrambled from CACTUS' airfields. The first, led by Capt. Foss, had eight F4Fs and eight Army P-39 Airacobras that flew to 29,000 feet and circled to wait for the Japanese planes. Maj. Paul Fontana commanded the second group of eight newly-arrived F4Fs that climbed to 5,500 feet. The American CAP was ready for the attacking planes to show up.

Sixteen Japanese bombers and 30 Zeroes burst from the clouds over Florida Island at 500 feet in a steep, fast dive. Foss saw them, picked up his microphone, and said, "Let's go gang!" His fighters dove steeply to the east toward the Japanese. Second Lt. Frank Clark became totally disoriented as his P-39's windshield fogged over in moisture while in its high-speed dive and splashed into the sea.

Noticing the attacking planes had split into two formations, Turner turned his ships to present their broadsides to maximize the first formation's firepower and direct the ship sterns to the planes carrying torpedoes. Fontana's fighters attacked the higher flights of Japanese bombers. Foss' F4Fs and the Army P-39s attacked the Japanese just 50 feet above the water and came right into the middle of a mêlée of twisting planes and exploding AA shells.

The result was as one-sided as the massacre of August 7 because only a few bombers launched their torpedoes. Eleven Japanese bombers either went down in flames or crashed into the sea. Those five planes lucky to survive the debacle sustained such heavy damage that they were no longer usable. Only two of these five bombers ever reached Rabaul with the other three missing. One Zero flown by PO2c Isao Ito did not return.

The American ships, while not receiving the damage the Japanese wanted to inflict on them, did receive some. The destroyers *Aaron Ward* and *Sterett* did take some friendly fire but the damage to the *Buchanan* was more severe as a five-inch shell hit her at the destroyer's aft funnel base and killing 15 of her crew. A 20-mm gun on the *Helena* hit the cruiser's smoke generator as it kept firing at a passing Japanese plane. Several men on the *Betelgeuse*, *Hovey*, *Buchanan*, and *Shaw* were wounded.

A Japanese plane passed near the *McCawley* as the *Laffey*'s guns poured fire into it. The aircraft burst into flames with the pilot losing control, its left wing dipping toward the water at a 45° angle. The gunners on the *Helena's* four aft 20-mm gun mounts continued to fire at it. With many of the ship's crew not realizing what was happening, the plane glanced off the cruiser's aft machine gun platform and fell into the sea near the ship's port side. But the plane's exploding fuel tanks leaked aviation fuel causing flames to erupt and cover the aft superstructure.

The Japanese again failed to inflict losses on the Americans commensurate with their own losses. Again, they lost not only hard-to-find planes, but also too many of their now-becoming irreplaceable crews.[11]

✲ ✲ ✲

Reinforcements and replacements meant for the CACTUS Air Force arrived on the escort carrier *Nassau* at Espiritu Santo on November 11. Marine flyers and pilots from the *Hornet* flew 20 SBDs, 12 TBFs, and six F4Fs ashore. In exchange, Maj. Robert Richard's ten SBDs, six TBFs led by Lt. Col. Paul ("Pat") Moret, and six F4Fs commanded by Maj. Elmer E. Brackett, Jr. arrived on the 12th.

But more powerful fighter support arrived when Army Maj. Dale D. Brannon brought eight of the highly-regarded twin-engine P-38s to Guadalcanal. These powerful planes were superior interceptors when compared to F4Fs by sporting one 20-mm cannon and four .50-cal. machine guns mounted in the nose. They could climb to 20,000 feet in a then unheard-of 8.8 seconds and reach a speed of 395 miles-per-hour at 25,000 feet. If the Japanese pilots thought the F4F was a tough plane to fight, the new P-38 would prove even more so.

✲ ✲ ✲

USAAF Capt. Frank J. Puerta flew his B-17 about 270 miles north of Santa Isabella Island or 335 miles north of Guadalcanal. He had orders to look for Japanese ships and his search soon found fruition. His crew spotted two battleships or heavy cruisers, one cruiser and six destroyers steaming due south. He sent a second report stating the formation of ships moved at a speed of 25 knots. A second B-17 reported another group of five destroyers most likely heading for the first ship group 110 miles north of Santa Isabel. The Americans had found Adm. Abe's Raiding Group.

Upon receiving these sighting reports of the approach of the Imperial Japanese Navy, Turner executed his previous order for Task Force 67's transports, escorted by the *Shaw*, *McCalla,* the damaged destroyer *Buchanan*, the minesweepers *Southard* and *Hovey,* to move through Indispensable Strait out of harm's way toward Espiritu Santo. Thirteen warships under Callaghan's command escorted Turner's ships out of Indispensable Strait and then returned to Iron Bottom Sound. Despite Scott's prior battle experience, Turner followed U.S. naval tradition when he picked Callaghan to command the warships over Scott because Callaghan was the senior officer. Turner would later receive some criticism for this action, but Halsey defended Turner's decision.

Meanwhile, Kinkaid's Task Force 16 stayed south of Rennell Island and was too far away to help in Task Force 67's defense against Japanese air attacks. The cruiser *Pensacola* and two destroyers left Espiritu Santo on November 13 to meet up with Kinkaid. He later received a report from CACTUS that two Japanese carriers north of Guadalcanal were 575 miles away—too far away to attack. Kinkaid did not agree with Turner's assessment that they had little value but his hands were tied. Nonetheless, another more critical factor existed for the outcome of the upcoming battle; Lee's two battleships were out of range to be of any help to Callaghan. Halsey realized this, but could do nothing since he did not know the full Japanese intentions until two days before—on November 10.[12]

The Imperial Japanese Navy Sails

Mikawa had called Raizo Tanaka into his office and ordered Tanaka to command a group of destroyers to escort six Army transports to Guadalcanal on November 7. Tanaka later called his captains in for a conference where he informed the officers of his plans. However, he received orders that changed the plan. The soldiers would be placed aboard the destroyers instead of the transports. He planned to command the expedition to take 1,300 soldiers to Guadalcanal but, after being ordered to stay at Shortland, he delegated that assignment to Capt. Torajiro Sato. He would take the soldiers on 11 destroyers. They left on schedule and, despite being attacked by American planes from Guadalcanal, they arrived untouched off Tassafaronga and successfully landed the troops without any interference. All 11 destroyers returned safely to Shortland in the midmorning of November 8.

The Japanese had more ambitious plans for the transports. The new plan was to use these ships to land the Army's 38th Division on Guadalcanal on November 13. The division arrived later on the 8th from Rabaul. 600 of them, under the command of Lt. Gen. Tadayoshi Sano, immediately boarded the destroyers *Makinami*, *Suzukaze*, and three other destroyers and left on another voyage down the Slot the same day. After being attacked by American aircraft and torpedo boats, the destroyers escaped undamaged, Sano and men landed safely on Guadalcanal and, like the earlier mission, the boats returned safely to Shortland on November 11. The Tokyo Express had landed 1,900 more Japanese soldiers on Guadalcanal without so much as a scratch.

A Japanese search plane sighted an American carrier task force south-southeast of Tulagi at a distance of 130 miles from that island. Several American bombers attacked the ships in Shortland's harbor, but inflicted no damage. The Japanese now knew the Americans had discovered their plan and would use everything they had to stop it. Any Japanese optimism that they might have had about landing the remainder of the 38th Division without American interference evaporated—it would not be as easy an operation as originally thought. Nonetheless, Tanaka in his flagship, the destroyer *Hayashio*, and 11 Army transports departed Shortland at 6:00 p.m. with 11 other destroyers escorting them.[13]

Adm. Abe took the two battleships *Hiei* and *Kirishima*, the light cruiser *Nagara*, and the destroyers *Amatsukaze, Yukikaze, Akatsuki, Ikazuchi, Inazuma, Teruzuki, Asagumo, Murasame, Samidare, Yudachi*, and *Harusame* southward toward Iron Bottom Sound. Abe[14] had orders to move near Guadalcanal's northern shore and shell the American positions just as the battleships *Kongo* and *Haruna* had done to Henderson Field on October 14. His objectives were part of the Japanese plan to disable the CACTUS Air Force from interfering with Japanese runs of the Tokyo Express. He had no intention or any plan to engage American naval forces in a sea battle, but had made preparations to meet such a threat if necessary.

The losses of Japanese aircraft at the Battle of the Santa Cruz Islands meant that Abe would only have two Zeroes providing CAP. When the Solomon Islands loomed on the southern horizon at 3:30 p.m. on November 12, Abe ordered his ships moved into an antisubmarine defensive formation. The two battleships and the *Nagara* moved into a column with six destroyers flanking these ships on both sides and five destroyers steaming in an arc in front to sweep the path ahead of any lurking American submarines. After a half hour passed, the formation at last was in place. After sunset and as darkness descended on the waters, Abe slowed his ship speed to 18 knots.

His planned course was to pass west of Savo Island and then turn to steam parallel to the Guadalcanal northern shore. To make matters worse for the Americans, the battleships carried new 14-inch Type 3 high-explosive shells designed to inflict the maximum amount of damage as well as flashless powder to make it harder for any American guns to locate the ships in the night's darkness. After the battleships and cruiser finished their bombardment, the troops now steaming in Tanaka's transports would land along with their desperately needed supplies. Z-day would be a time of glory for the Japanese.

He knew the Americans had spotted his ships. But he also knew that American transports with nine cruisers and seven destroyers had been seen between Lunga and Tulagi unloading troops and supplies. He had launched the *Hiei*'s seaplane to reconnoiter over Guadalcanal at 4:00 p. m. Its pilot reported, "More than a dozen enemy warships seen off Lunga."[15] The message caused discussions among Abe's staff of the possibility that the Americans may be ready to surprise his ships as they sailed into the waters near Guadalcanal.

The weather turned for the worse an hour later when a violent squall fell on the Japanese ships. It became almost impossible to see the other ships in the formation. Abe's initial reaction to the storm was positive since it would be even more difficult for the Americans to see his ships approaching. But he changed his mind when he realized the poor visibility would affect his ability to coordinate ship actions if any American ships should appear. A later report at 10:00 p.m. from the Army ashore said the weather was not good. The *Hiei*'s search plane had to fly back to Bougainville because the weather made it impossible for the pilot to find his home ship.

By this time, Abe knew the poor visibility would make the accurate spotting of the fall of shot by observers impossible. It also threw his plan into a cocked hat when he found at 12:30 a.m. on November 13 that his ships had unknowingly passed Cape Esperance. He had to turn his ships around by breaking radio silence and, as his ships reversed their courses, his formation fell apart. Ship speed slowed to 12 knots and, fortunately for him, no ships collided with each other. The weather cleared over his ships at 1:10 a.m., and Abe ordered them to turn again towards Guadalcanal. He now planned to begin shelling the American shore positions 20 minutes later.

As his ships moved into position, Abe reorganized them into a formation better suited to bombarding shore installations while still protecting against submarine attacks. The light cruiser *Nagara* led the battleships *Hiei* and *Kirishima* flanked by six destroyers with the *Teruzuki, Amatsukaze*, and *Yukikaze* to port and the *Akatsuki, Inazuma,* and *Ikazuchi* on the starboard side. Five destroyers, the *Asagumo, Samidare, Murasame, Yudachi*, and *Harusame*, led the way with the *Asagumo* in the point position.

Abe was confident in his ability to successfully execute his mission and make his command's effort become the turning point for which the Japanese had hoped. All hands were at their battle stations, and the lookouts scanned the sea around them for any appearance of American ships. Abe had heard the Americans had some of their newer battleships in the South Pacific. However, the latest intelligence reports stated the ships had been so severely damaged in previous battles that they were not capable of being in combat and were not in the immediate Guadalcanal area. Abe still took no chances and did not want to be surprised the way Goto had been in the Battle of Cape Esperance. General Quarters immediately sounded throughout his command.

Nevertheless, some dissent arose between two of Abe's staff officers about whether to proceed with the bombardment or cancel it. Capt. Masakane Suzuki, Abe's chief of staff, argued to cancel the shelling because the storm had delayed its scheduled start by one hour. Lt. Cmdr. Masataka Chihaya, the admiral's operations officer, asserted that further delay would affect the mission, and the mission should proceed as planned. Abe settled the argument by agreeing with Chihaya and ordered the staff officer to issue the essential orders.

The lookouts on the *Yudachi* and *Harusame* reported seeing lights at 1:15 a.m. at Tassafaronga Point. The storm had moved off and the visibility improved somewhat despite a mist still lurking near the water's surface. Savo Island passed to port and Guadalcanal's mass soon appeared ahead and to starboard. On the destroyer *Akatsuki*, Lt. Michiharu Shinya aimed his torpedo battery to starboard. Cmdr. Tameichi Hara, skipper of the destroyer *Amatsukaze*, ordered his crew to look to starboard for any possibility of action to come. Meanwhile, the battleships' huge 14-inch high explosive shells clattered into the hoists and moved up to the main turrets. The gun crews loaded shells into the guns and made them ready to fire. All in the ships' crews grew tense in anticipation of fulfilling their mission.

Callaghan Gets Ready

Now in command to the Americans' chances to defend against any Japanese action that he knew would come, Callaghan realized he was on his own. His ships steamed westward towards Savo Is-

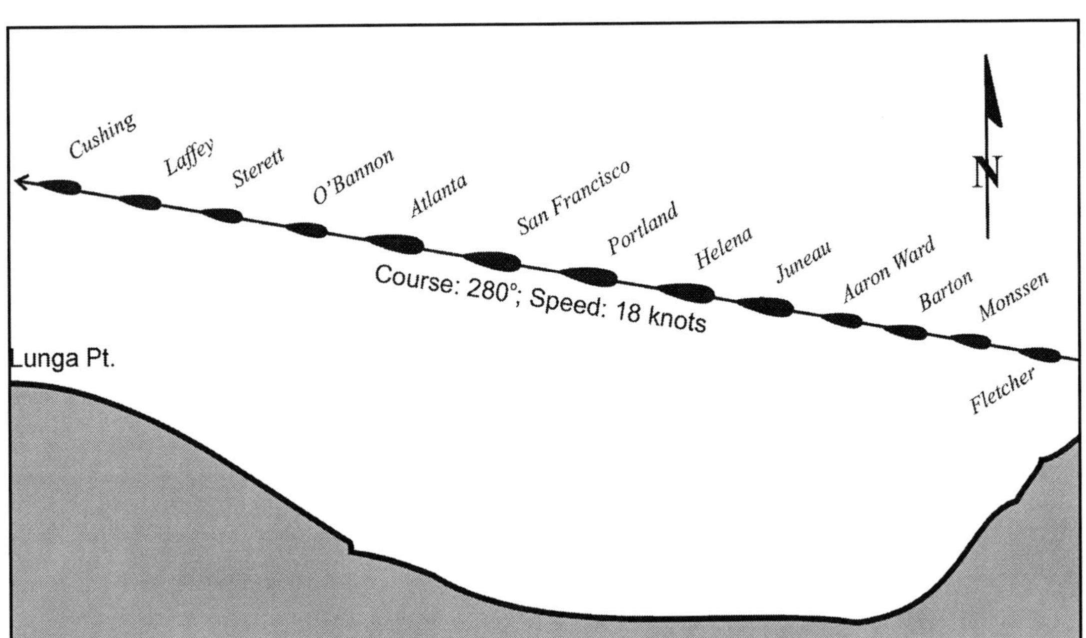

Callaghan's B-1 Battle Formation

land. Scott must have had some feeling of *déjà vu* as Savo appeared ahead. Concerned about safely navigating the narrow water and anticipating his force would soon be in combat, Callaghan ordered his ships into what he called the B-1 formation. The ships formed a single line-of-battle, much like Scott had done in the Battle of Cape Esperance and familiar to students of naval warfare who studied battles of sailing warships of bygone days.

The destroyer *Cushing* led in the van with the remaining ships behind it—the destroyers *Laffey, Sterett, O'Bannon*—followed by the cruisers *Atlanta, San Francisco, Portland, Helena*, and *Juneau*. The destroyers *Aaron Ward, Barton, Monssen*, and *Fletcher* trailed behind. Nonetheless, the sequence of ships demonstrated Callaghan's lack of knowledge of how to use the greatest advantage the Americans had at this stage of the war, radar, a capability so sorely needed to overcome the Japanese superiority in optical sighting systems and training of their lookouts as well as in fighting a night surface battle. The ships that had the latest radar installed on them were the cruisers *Helena* and *Portland*, and the destroyers *O'Bannon* and *Fletcher*, which were in the fourth, seventh, eighth, and thirteenth respective position in the formation. Callaghan's flagship, the cruiser *San Francisco*, also Scott's flagship at Cape Esperance, had the facilities to act as an admiral's flagship but lacked the latest SG Radar. Scott's flagship, the *Atlanta*, also suffered from the same deficiency. The positioning of the destroyers in a line-of-battle also prevented them from concentrating their greatest firepower asset, their torpedoes, on the oncoming Japanese ships.

The Americans had already demonstrated how poor their TBS radio communications were in prior battles, a critical need when flag communication is useless at night and signal lights had proved and would prove to be extremely dangerous for those ships that flashed them. That had not changed and would again prove to be disastrous for the Americans in the upcoming battle. The Japanese battleships also outgunned the American cruisers in terms of range and ability to inflict damage. Fortunately for the Americans, the Japanese did not come prepared for a sea battle since their mission was the bombardment of the Guadalcanal airfields for which they brought high explosive ammunition—now loaded in their guns.

As Callaghan's formation steamed through the Lengo Channel, a slight nine-knot breeze made small ripples on the water and stars shone brightly above in the moonless sky. As it is always happening in the tropics, distant lightning flashes over the islands lit up the sky. The men on deck peered into the darkness hoping to see something of their intended quarry. Others crouched over their stations in plotting rooms while some perspired heavily below in the ships' engineering and boiler rooms deep in each ship's bowels. None of these ships had spent any significant time practicing battle maneuvers with each other. Neither side's commander had sent out any battle orders since neither side knew of the other's presence. But that would soon change. So the two sides approached each other with a determination to fight one of the most desperate and bloody naval battles of the Pacific War. And that confrontation would go down in the annals of naval warfare with the name, the Naval Battle of Guadalcanal.[16]

CHAPTER 38
Barroom Brawl with the Lights Out

"It's got to be a battleship!"

Friday the 13th arrived with all the ominous portents that day presents. Abe's ships now bore down on a course parallel to Guadalcanal's northern shore off Lunga Point with lookouts straining their eyes into the night's darkness. Callaghan's Task Force was almost on a collision course with its radars searching for the Japanese. Since the flagship's radar was not as advanced as that on the *Helena,* Callaghan could not get first-hand information of any Japanese contacts that might be out there in the darkness. He did not have to wait too long before their presence became known.

His men had been at General Quarters for nearly half the time since they had left Espiritu Santoand began to suffer from fatigue. The *Helena*'s radar operator hovered over his scope as the SG radar dish rotated, sending its beam into the night. He rubbed his eyes and strained to look for any blips. Suddenly, at 1:23 a.m., he saw what he had been looking for. He spoke into the microphone on the headset he wore while on duty, "Large unidentified targets bearing three hundred twenty degrees, range thirty-two thousand yards. It's got to be a battleship!"[1] Lt. Russell W. Gash, the duty officer in the radar plotting room, notified Capt. Hoover, the cruiser's commanding officer, of the sighting report. Three minutes later, Hoover sent a TBS message to the flagship, "Jen [*Helena*] to Todd [*San Francisco*], two contacts bearing 310 degrees, distance 31,900 yards."[2]

After digesting the information he had just received, Callaghan ordered a course change at 1:27 a.m. to 310° to intercept the Japanese ships. Three minutes later, the *Helena*'s radar picked up another blip and reported three contacts bearing 312°, distance 26,000 yards followed by another report stating the Japanese course as 105° at a speed of about 23 knots. CACTUS' radar also detected the approaching ships and sent an alert for all ground personnel to prepare for another bombardment.

Callaghan and his staff examined the contact reports and plotting of the reported Japanese ship positions. Their initial analysis concluded there were two groups of ships with one of them being the Bombardment Group and the other the screen. There was not enough information at this time to decide which group was which. With the reports of sighting Japanese ships now spreading throughout the American vessels over the next ten minutes, one could cut the rising tension with a knife. For many of the sailors, this was to be their first sea battle with the veterans doing all they could to calm the fear they all felt inside them. But the lack of SG radar on the flagship left Callaghan much to guess about. The range between the two adversaries closed rapidly at a rate of about 40 knots. Decisions had to be made soon with men's and ships' lives depending upon what those decisions would be. The Americans had detected the Japanese, but not the other way around. Callaghan had the advantage and decided to act.

He ordered a course change to 000º so he could possibly cross the Japanese "T" and bring his firepower to bear for maximum effect. In this way, his more lightly armored and under gunned ships had a fighting chance against the more powerful Japanese battleships. The fire control radars followed the paths of the approaching Japanese warships and sent instructions for each gun to adjust its elevation to lower levels as the range closed.

Aboard the *Helena*, for instance, the ship's Turret IV commander, Lt. (jg) Earl Luehman, noticed that elevation of his six-inch guns had dropped from their maximum angles for long range gunfire. As the range closed to 10,000 yards, the crew began loading 108-pound armor piercing shells into the gun breaches. The shell went in first with a brass powder cartridge right behind it. In all the practices and training exercises the gun crews had done before the war, the assumption was that a sea battle would be fought at long ranges. No one had ever believed this upcoming battle would be fought at much shorter distances. The fire control directors continued to send ranges and directions to the guns as the turrets automatically turned to their commands. All that had to be done was to fire the guns when the order came from the bridge.

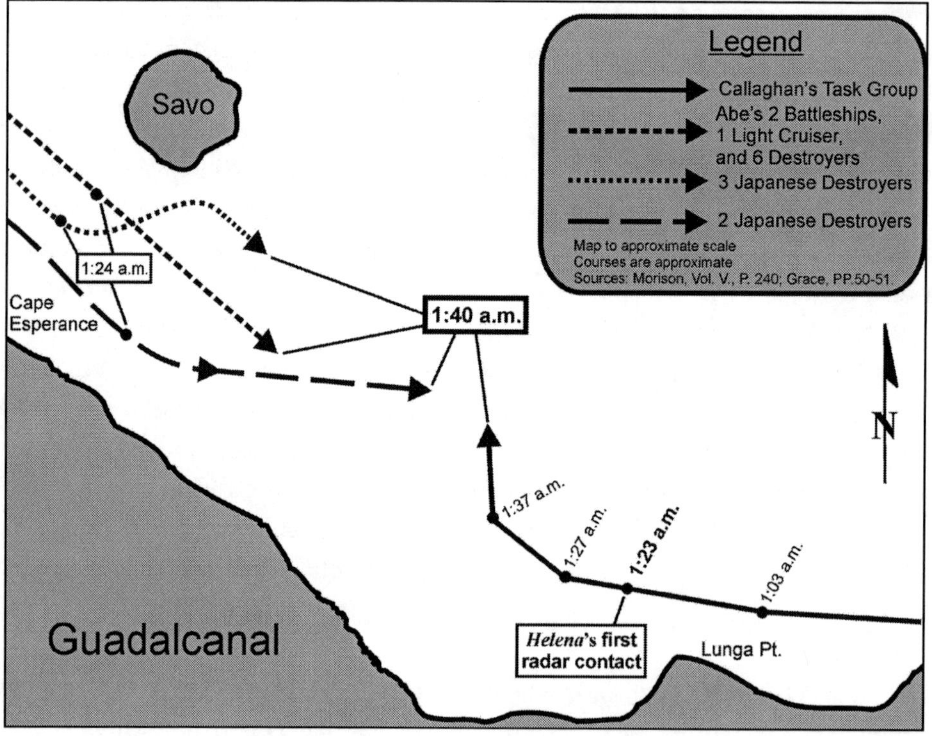

The Two Forces Approach Each Other

By this time, the Japanese ship formation had lost some of its rigid organization and began to spread out and become more ragged. Maybe the mist near the water's surface hampered lookouts' vision, or they all were looking toward the shore. But Abe did not receive any reports about the American ships. Of course, the lack of any radar capability obviously was a hindrance too. We will never know why the Japanese never saw the Americans until they were practically on top of each other. Abe had no idea the Americans were out ahead of him, and so proceeded with the confidence of beginning to fulfill his mission. It was 1:37 a.m. when the situation dramatically changed.

"Ships Ahead on the Port Bow"

The destroyer *O'Bannon*'s SG radar picked up the Japanese ships at 1:37 a.m. just 7,000 yards away. This surprised everyone in the American ships that the distance to the Japanese had closed so rapidly. The *Helena*, one of the other ships with SG radar, reported the range two minutes later to the Japanese of only 3,400 yards. The close proximity to the approaching Japanese astonished Callaghan and he asked for confirmation.

And he got it at 1:40 a.m. when the *Cushing*'s navigator, Lt. Cmdr. W. Bernard, briefly looked over the starboard bow and saw what appeared to be Japanese destroyers. Lt. (jg) Severn N. Nottingham, at his station in the gun director high above the destroyer's main deck, confirmed the ships were two or three destroyers at the nearly point-blank range of 3,000 yards moving from port to starboard on a course directly across the *Cushing*'s bow. Cmdr. Thomas M. Stokes, the destroyers' division commander, sent a TBS message, "To Todd from Seventy-Six [*Cushing*], ships ahead on port bow."[3]

Callaghan and his staff began to get a picture in their minds what the Japanese were doing. Reports of distances, courses, and speeds of the Japanese ships now poured in from many ships over the TBS. Those reports began to saturate this vital but single channel for spoken communications. The Japanese seemed to be steaming in three groups: a main force in the center where their battleships were, with two formations of smaller screening vessels on both sides of the battleships.

The *Cushing* turned at 1:41 p.m. to port to present its beam toward the Japanese ships so it could fire torpedoes. The destroyer's turn from its former northward course to the west baffled the ships following it. Each ship turned not to follow the *Cushing*'s wake but turned simultaneously to port to avoid ramming into each other. Without a specific plan from Callaghan and no time to practice together, pandemonium reigned supreme on each American ship's bridge—orders barked, telegraph bells cacophonously clanged, and reports from the lookouts overwhelmed each ship's telephone circuits. Nonetheless, each ship got ready for battle by loading their guns and training their torpedo tubes toward their targets in response from their fire control stations.

Callaghan had no clue what his ships were doing until the *Atlanta*, the ship immediately ahead of the *San Francisco*, began its port turn. He barked over the TBS, "From Todd to Rip [*Atlanta*]: What are you doing?" Capt. Samuel P. Jenkins, the *Atlanta*'s skipper, answered, "To Todd from Rip: Avoiding our own destroyers!"[4]

Lt. Cmdr. Bruce McCandless, the *San Francisco*'s OOD, having not received any notice about what to do, asked Callaghan over the TBS, "The *Atlanta*'s turning left. Shall I follow her?" After a short delay, the admiral responded, "Follow the *Atlanta*!" The finely-organized American line of battle now came apart as each ship turned to avoid hitting others. The leading destroyers nearly rammed their bows into the stern of the ship in front of them.

The TBS traffic sounded like a jumble of noise with everyone talking at once. Callaghan managed to ask the *Cushing* what it saw the situation was. The *Helena* answered that it had detected at least ten targets ahead of them. Confusion piled atop chaos as each ship did not know if the reported bearings of the Japanese ships were true or relative ones. No orders had yet been given to each American ship as to which ship it should aim its armament at much less to open fire.

The four leading American destroyers were now in a position to fire their torpedoes. The *Cushing*'s Stokes asked Callaghan, "Shall I let them have a couple of fish?" He received permission to fire at 1:43 a.m., but it was too late—the Japanese destroyers had vanished into the darkness. When this report arrived on the flagship, Callaghan ordered at 1:45 a.m. to his ships, "From Todd to Todd's boys: Stand by to open fire!"

At 1:47 a.m., Callaghan ordered the *Cushing* to return to its original course of 000º; the other following ships turned into the destroyer's wake. While turning, the *Cushing* sighted two large ships to port on a course of 105º. The *O'Bannon* and the *Atlanta* also saw the big ships. The *Juneau* reported seeing two ships on its starboard side.[5]

The Japanese formation had also become disorganized. Nevertheless, the Japanese destroyer *Yudachi* reported seeing American ships just as the *Cushing* had seen it and its companion destroyer, the *Harusame*. Seeing the American ships caught the *Yudachi*'s captain, Cmdr. Kiyoshi Kikkawa, totally by surprise. However, the Japanese knew at 1:42 a.m. that the Americans were out there.

As far as the Japanese were concerned, this was truly a worst case scenario. The Americans had ambushed them and a repeat of their defeat and the loss of Adm. Goto at the Battle of Cape Esperance was about to happen to them again. Abe desperately pleaded for course and speed information about the Americans. A flabbergasted Chihaya saw the American ships as one of the flagship's lookouts spoke into the ship's phone, "Enemy ships starboard ahead! Close!"[6] More information began to clarify the situation. There were four ships 8,000 meters away and five degrees off the starboard bow. The constantly lengthening and shortening shapes appeared as dark shadows with no clear target to shoot at.

The distance to the American ships was now reported as 9,000 meters. The light cruiser *Nagara* reported seeing the outlines of eight ships. The *Yudachi* and the *Harusame* began to move independently and no longer in tandem. Aboard the destroyer *Ikazuchi*, one of its lookouts came on the ship's telephone and exclaimed, "A few enemy cruisers thirty degrees to port!"[7] Lt. Cmdr. Saneo Maeda, the destroyer's captain, anxiously demanded an answer. "What enemy cruisers? Destroyer Squadron Four must be in that direction. Check it carefully!" Maeda received his confirmation when gunfire directed at the *Hiei* came from one of the ships the *Yudachi* had spotted.

Abe now knew he faced a surface battle he not planned for and realized that he did not have the ammunition he needed to fight warships. However, there were five salvoes of high explosive shells in the battleship hoists. He had to get armor-piercing shells into his guns as soon as possible. So he ordered loading of armor-piercing ammunition into the ships' guns as soon as they fired the five salvoes of high explosive ammunition already queued in their ammunition train. Not wanting to waste any more time, he told Chihaya to send out the order for the battleships to open fire, "The Eleventh Battleship Division change the firing target. New target is enemy ships starboard ahead. Start firing with searchlights on!"[8]

Lt. (jg) Michio Kobayashi stood on the *Kirishima*'s bridge with the assignment to record the action to come. Knowing the ship's big guns were about to open fire, he put plugs into his ears to protect from the anticipated deafening concussion from firing the 14-inch guns. The order to open fire arrived over the ship's phones as he turned to look at Guadalcanal's looming shape. Capt. Toru Iwabuchi wisely avoided turning on his searchlights but ordered his gunnery officer, who had not yet received any targeting information from the ship's fire control, to open fire. With no targets at which to shoot, he questioned the captain, "Isn't the target the air base?" Iwabuchi angrily answered, "No! The target is ahead to starboard! Enemy ships! Fire! Fire!"[9]

The *Hiei* had six searchlights with three on each side of its bridge. When Chihaya's order to open fire arrived, the beam of all six lights suddenly pierced the darkness. At 1:50 a.m., one set of beams lit up the cruiser *Nagara* while the other set sprayed bright light on the port side of the *Atlanta*'s bridge.

The *Atlanta*'s captain, Capt. Jenkins, immediately ordered, "Counter illuminate!" The cruiser's gunnery officer talked into the ship's telephone, "Counter illuminate, hell! Fire!" All 16 five-inch guns roared to life as the light from the gun fire deluged the darkness. Sound and fury descended upon the waters north of Guadalcanal. The Naval Battle of Guadalcanal was on![10]

The Mêlée Begins

Martin Clemens knew a great naval battle was about to happen that night of November 12. Impatient to see what was coming and for the battle to begin, he and his scouts waited as midnight passed and November 13 began. One hour passed and still nothing happened. Where would the Japanese come from? Were they heading for Aola? It was a clear night with no rain falling. He moved to a place where he would have an unobstructed view of any battle that might come.

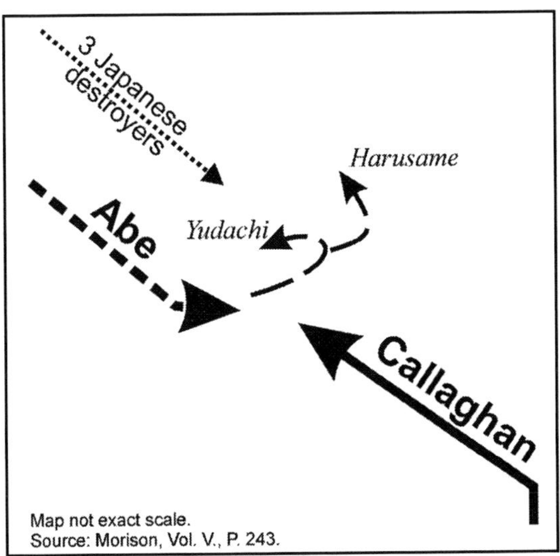

Callaghan Opens Fire

He could not see his watch but remembered it was about 1:30 a.m. when a blinding flash lit up the northwestern sky. The sounds of naval guns firing arrived a split second later. He had seen the other naval battles that happened at night off Guadalcanal, but he had never seen so much gunfire before. This was going to be the largest night naval battle yet.[11]

Callaghan had issued a confusing order over the TBS radio just two minutes before the *Atlanta* fired its guns that directed "Odd ships [to] commence fire to starboard, even ships to port!" Some ships had been tracking ships that were not on the side to where Callaghan had ordered them to fire. So, these ships had to turn their guns and/or torpedo tubes to the opposite side before firing. And this was only the beginning of the chaos to come.

The range to the *Hiei* was only 1,600 yards when the *Atlanta*'s five-inch guns fired. The shells could never be expected to do too much damage to the more heavily-armored Japanese battleship's power plants but could knock out the battleship's fire control systems and communications. After the cruiser's first salvo, Lt. G. L. McEntee directed the forward mount to fire on a destroyer that steamed last in a line and had crossed through one of the searchlight beams. Twenty five-inch shells from a second salvo blasted into what was believed to be an *Asashio*-class destroyer. An orange ball suddenly grew in the distance and the ship "broke into flames, settled, and sank."[12]

Meanwhile, Lt. (jg) Edward D. Corboy's after mounts continued firing at the *Hiei*. The first salvo hit the water and was short of the target. After adjusting the guns to increase their range by 400 yards, Corboy sent another volley that hit the big ship. The gunfire put out the battleship's searchlights but other Japanese ships now knew where the *Atlanta* was, and she began to absorb their revenge as her gun flashes further fixed her position in the Japanese gun sights.

The *Cushing* looked for a new target because her fire director team had lost contact with the *Yudachi* and *Harusame*. Her FD radar located a new target 2,000 yards away to starboard. The American destroyer opened fire at the *Amatsukaze* and her skipper believed his guns had hit her. Actually, the American destroyer missed the Japanese warship when both ships approached and passed each other going in opposite directions.

The *Laffey* was one of those ships that had to shift its aim from the one it already had on several Japanese targets because of Callaghan's chaos-creating "even-odd" order. Lt. William K. Ratliff, the destroyer's gunnery officer, picked a new target that had illuminated its searchlight, identified the destroyer *Akatsuki* as a light cruiser, and ordered his guns to fire at it. Both ships exchanged fire with 100 rounds being sent over the near point-blank range of between 800 and 1,000 yards. The Japanese ship searchlights came on, went out, came on again, and did not come on again. Flushed with the euphoria of success, the *Laffey* looked for more targets.

The *Sterett* was third ship in the American line that had a target to port but, like the *Laffey*, had to change to look for a target to starboard. She found one about 4,000 yards away but had trouble getting its range because of the difficult firing angle for her torpedoes and the blinding lights from Japanese searchlights. But her FD radar found a target and her four five-inch guns sent a salvo into the darkness followed by a second one. As she continued to fire her guns, the crew believed it had hit a light cruiser. But their confidence would soon be shaken to its roots. Suddenly, several shells hit the aft port side and set some five-inch powder afire. Her steering stopped working, and she fell out of the formation. More hits on her bridge knocked out her emergency identification lights, radar, and TBS radio antenna. But her guns kept firing.

As the *Atlanta*, *Cushing* and *Sterett* fought for their very existence, the *Helena* and the *Fletcher* fired at a destroyer but could not confirm hitting her because of the rampant confusion caused by the smoke and flames.

With the *Atlanta* fully illuminated and continuously firing its guns, the *San Francisco* fired at two destroyers off its starboard bow. At a range of 3,700 yards, the *San Francisco*'s eight-inch guns clobbered the *Akatsuki*. American five-inch starshells hovered over her thus making her totally visible to the *Atlanta*'s now accurate heavy gunfire. Fusillades of eight-inch shells pummeled the hapless Japanese destroyer, engulfing her in flames. She drifted aimlessly, and more shells relentlessly slammed into her. Flames poured high from her into the sky as explosions rocked the doomed ship.

The *Ikazuchi* was to have been the cruiser's next target but luckily reversed her course behind the *Akatsuki* and escaped unscathed. Both destroyers fired six torpedoes with one of them hitting the *Atlanta*. The *San Francisco* redirected her fire at another ship identified as a small "cruiser or large destroyer"—an apt description of the *Atlanta*. Two salvoes of "friendly" eight-inch gunfire raked the *Atlanta* by mistake and caused fires to break out from her bow to stern. Realizing the error, Callaghan ordered at 1:53 a.m., "Cease firing own ships!" The other American ship captains heard the admiral's directive that now introduced even more confusion among them. The order had come over the already crowded TBS radio circuit for all to hear.

Tracking the Japanese ships on her radar since 1:42 a.m., the *Portland*'s main and secondary battery directors picked up multiple targets. Despite a malfunctioning radar system, the cruiser's optical sighting systems found plenty of ships at which to shoot. Capt. Laurence T. DuBose, the cruiser's commander, ordered, "Action starboard," followed by an order to open fire. Lt. Cmdr. Elliot W. Shanklin, the ship's gunnery officer, already had a candidate. The target had her searchlight turned on, a great aiming point. Executing a port turn to a 270° bearing, only the *Portland*'s two forward turrets had a clear shot. Her five-inch star shells shot into the air bathed the sea in light, and six eight-inch guns belched fire. With his ship in combat, DuBose took control from the OOD. A second salvo caused the target to explode in a ball of flame.

The cruiser continued turning but her rear turret could not fire because the target had vanished. Returning fire scored one hit that opened a large hole in the starboard hangar, knocked out the starboard searchlights, disabling two five-inch gun mounts, and wounding 12 men including Cmdr. Theodore R. Wirth, the ship's executive officer. A second shell exploded on the side above the armor belt and caused some minor leaks.

The *Helena*'s gunnery officer, Lt. Cmdr. Rodman D. Smith, who had built a reputation for accurate gunfire at the Battle of Cape Esperance, obeyed Capt. Hoover's order to open fire. All of her 15 six-inch guns roared a salvo to port into the darkness at a ship 4,200 yards away that had shone its searchlight on her. The shells arched toward the target and struck it in a devastating set of explosions. Believing it had hit a cruiser, the *Helena* continued to pummel it for two minutes and claimed to have sunk it. Since the Japanese did not lose a cruiser that night, the doomed ship might have been the destroyer *Akatsuki*. As the *Helena* narrowly passed a capsized wreck, she reported seeing a Japanese transport sinking as well.

Three hits from her first target's returning fire struck the *Helena*. The first pierced the forward smokestack; the second exploded on the searchlight platform's rear legs and wounded three men and killed one, and the third damaged the aircraft crane on the fantail. As the cruiser changed course to 270°, a salvo landed in her wake. Below decks, the explosions sounded like gravel being sprayed against the ship's hull.

The next-in-line, the *Juneau*, fired her five-inch guns at a large ship that shone a searchlight on her. When the firing began, the searchlight that pointed at the *Juneau* turned toward another ship.

Thus, the cruiser aimed her guns at a Japanese destroyer. The *Yudachi* fired some torpedoes at the *Juneau* but all missed. She then fired her five-inch guns. The shells sailed over the *Juneau*'s superstructure. The cruiser continued firing her five-inch guns, but had to stop when their fire seemed to be aimed at the American destroyer *Aaron Ward* and other destroyers behind it. The cruiser then tried to find another target.

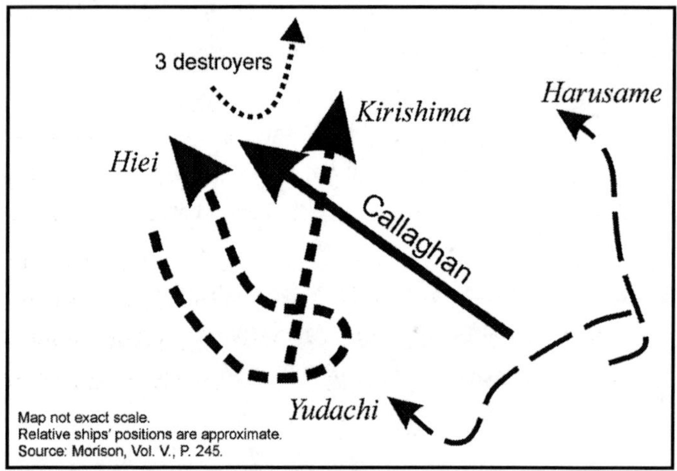

Japanese Ship Movements after Firing Began

Maintaining its northern course, the *Aaron Ward* had been the first ship of the rear destroyer group when its radar detected a target at 1:29 a.m. about 12,000 yards away. When Callaghan ordered his ships to open fire, the destroyer fired at the target off her port bow now 5,000 yards closer. Ten salvoes of five-inch fire poured into the target until American cruisers got in the way. Cmdr. Orville F. Gregor, the ship captain, believed his fire had hit the Japanese battleship *Hiei,* but he could not confirm that observation. The *Hiei* put three 14-inch shells into the destroyer that heavily damaged the area near the forecastle.

Gregor saw the cruisers directly ahead of his left turn, and then saw the Japanese destroyer *Harusame* dart directly from left to right across the American formation. With the range to the Japanese destroyer at just 1,200 yards, he stopped his engines and then reversed them so as to not collide with the Japanese warship. Then his torpedo crews reported seeing two torpedoes pass under the *Aaron Ward*'s keel with the whirring sound of their propellers heard below decks.

Like all the ships in Callaghan's force, the *Barton* fired its five five-inch guns when the order arrived. She fired 60 rounds from her forward mounts, but only ten rounds could be fired from her aft mounts because the target was too far forward before these guns could be brought to bear. The ship captain, Lt. Cmdr. Douglas H. Fox, ordered a left turn so his torpedo tubes could fire at the leading Japanese ship. No one could confirm if any of the torpedoes hit anything.

Aboard the *Barton*, Lt. (jg) Wilbur E. Quint ordered the automatic guns under his command to fire at what seemed to be a battleship. But the big ship's turrets turned toward the destroyer, and a warning came over the ship's intercom that Japanese torpedoes were heading toward the destroyer. Then, the ship in front of them, the *Aaron Ward*, suddenly slowed. The *Barton* also decreased her speed and turned to avoid hitting the *Aaron Ward*. A torpedo then hit the *Barton* and exploded in the forward fireroom. Another one then exploded in the forward engine room causing a sheet of flame to burst from the rear stack. Part of the ship suddenly disappeared beneath the water. Quint freed a life raft with the rest of the ship sinking beneath his feet. The *Barton* exploded and sank in just ten seconds after being hit. Most of her 250-man crew were never found including her captain. She was the first American ship to sink in this battle. Forty of her crew, including Quint, were now in the water with many of them badly burned.

The *Monssen*'s radar stopped working in the previous afternoon's air battle. So her crew could not see any targets other than sighting them themselves. Its crew spotted an apparently motionless Japanese battleship 4,000 yards of the starboard bow. With such an inviting target so near, the destroyer's No. 2 torpedo mount fired a two-degree spread of five torpedoes with the depth set at ten feet. The crew thought they had scored two or three hits but none of the torpedoes hit anything. Five more torpedoes hissed from the No. 1 mount—all but one missed. The destroyer's five five-inch guns along with its 20-mm guns fired at another ship off the port bow. The target had been swapping gunfire with another American ship; but the *Monssen*'s salvoes silenced the target's guns.

Carrying the advanced SG radar, the *Fletcher* was the last ship in the American line of battle. The modern radar and her position in the formation allowed her captain and subordinate officers to get the most complete picture of the battle scene. The ship's executive officer, Lt. Cmdr. Joseph C. Wylie, was with the ship's radar operator tracking every ships' course and speed, listening to the TBS, and presenting the results to Cmdr. William R. Cole, the destroyer's commander. Cole could then make the most informed decisions of any commander present. This was the forerunner of the Combat Information Center or CIC. Halsey consequently recommended that this setup be placed on all American warships. It would be adopted later in the war.

The *Fletcher* fired on the ship 5,500 yards away that had illuminated the *Atlanta* with its searchlights. Cole redirected his ship's fire to a new target when he saw the first one had already been fired upon by many ships. The new target, which everyone thought was a light cruiser, caught fire.[13]

The Atlanta*'s Troubles*

After the *Atlanta* opened fire, it immediately began to receive return fire from the battleship *Hiei*. Shells from the big ship's 14-inch guns smashed into and exploded on the lightly armored cruiser's hull, superstructure, and gun mounts. Since the *Hiei*'s gunfire shot high-explosive rather than armor-piercing ammunition, the 13-shell fusillade inflicted devastating damage on the *Atlanta*'s superstructure, set off the cruiser's ammunition, and covered her superstructure in a pyre of flames.

One 14-inch shell burst on the bridge and killed Adm. Scott and all of his staff except Lt. H. S. Moredock and an Australian naval officer. Fortunately, Capt. Jenkins had just walked off the flag bridge when another 14-inch shell smashed into one of her torpedo directors and killed its torpedo officer. The explosion threw Jenkins against a watertight door.

With bodies strewn all over her decks and compartments, the Japanese shellfire continued to pound the *Atlanta*. The dying ship's navigator, Lt. Cmdr. J. S. Smith, Jr., argued that Jenkins should take control of the ship at the secondary conning station, known as Battle II. Moredock tried to climb over a railing but fell on a cushion of dead bodies. The cruiser's torment had not yet ended.

A torpedo slammed into her port side. Its 1,100-pound warhead exploding with dreadful results. The blast lifted the cruiser out of the water and opened a huge hole in the hull. Water poured into the cruiser's innards as her entire hull began to crack. Her forward engine room filled with seawater, and she listed to port at a 10° angle. All power, lighting, and phones stopped operating below decks thus hindering the damage control parties' efforts. EM3c William B. McKinney pounded his fist on a watertight door but heard no replies. Unknown metallic sounds and the sounds of men coughing and choking came from behind the door. The lantern he had hung over the door still tilted at the same angle as before. At least the ship's list had stabilized.

The dense smoke forced McKinney and his companion, Sea2c Daniel J. Curtin, to put on RBAs. It filled the compartment so that they could only see a few feet ahead of them. McKinney climbed some stairs, entered the officer's wardroom, and moved onto the main deck just as his RBA oxygen was exhausted.

Flames engulfed the forward gun director. Control of the guns transferred to the rear director so that it could control the firing of both forward and aft guns. But this proved to be moot since the Japanese shells had wiped out the forward mounts. The ship's rudder was jammed so that the cruiser turned to port in a circular path. Another ship's shells hit her from a distance of 3,500 yards. The shelling was from eight-inch guns and uncannily accurate as if being directed by radar. Since only American ships in the battle carried eight-inch guns, the shelling must have come from another American heavy cruiser, namely the *San Francisco*. Nineteen eight-inch shells smacked into the *Atlanta* with seven of them belting the superstructure, killing several wounded men, and destroying the third five-inch gun turret. Two eight-inch shells from a second salvo hit the first rear five-inch gun turret, and the resulting explosion took off its roof and killed all save one of its 13-man crew.

Executive Officer Cmdr. Campbell D. Emory was in Battle II and wondered how anyone could have lived through the destruction at the forward part of the ship. His mouth nearly fell open as Capt. Jenkins staggered into Battle II. Nonetheless, Emory could only talk to the steering room since all communications to the rest of the ship were lost.

The *Atlanta* had only two of its six five-inch main armament turrets in operation. One mount only had manual power while the other had power but could not talk to the gun director or the plot. Just four 1.1-inch and two 20-mm guns in the fantail could fire. The cruiser was essentially harmless. Her torpedoes had never been fired because the first salvo had destroyed the directors and their crews. The mounts could be trained by hand, too slow to accurately fire at fast-moving ships.

She was in deep trouble, slowing, and out of the battle.[14]

Getting the Priorities Straight

Just after being lit up by a searchlight, the *San Francisco* turned its attention to the *Hiei* after Callaghan exclaimed, "We want the big ones! Get the big ones first!"[15] The heavy cruiser turned to the left so that all three eight-inch turrets could fire all nine guns. The Japanese battleship also turned left with the range rapidly closing. When the distance between the two ships was 2,500 yards, the *San Francisco*'s warning buzzer sounded. Next came the deafening sound and blinding flash of nine eight-inch guns simultaneously firing a deadly barrage. The guns' recoil made the cruiser shift sideways in the water as the turrets' crews worked quickly to reload the guns. A cloud of pungent smoke covered the bridge. The range was now 2,200 yards.

Lt. Cmdr. William W. Wilbourne, the ship's gunnery officer, changed the range to the target and saw all nine ready lights change to green. The nine guns once again belched fire and smoke sending the second salvo on its way just 15 seconds after the first. By the time the guns had been loaded for the third salvo, the range to the Japanese battleship was so close the guns had to be lowered. All three turrets' crews knew that their target was a battleship and began to focus on what they had been trained to do: load, fire, and reload as fast as they could.

The eight-inch salvoes from the American cruiser blasted pieces of the *Hiei*'s armor plates into the air. Several five-inch salvos also smashed into the battleship as some of their star shells provided a well-lit target. Flames erupted around the battleship's mainmast with the light from these fires illuminating a nearby American destroyer. The *Hiei* had been firing at the *Atlanta* and had been tardy in returning the *San Francisco*'s gunfire. But she soon did so by firing her forward turret's 14-inch guns along with some six-inch gunfire. Nevertheless, the shells splashed in the water short of their intended target.

The *Hiei* turned her searchlights on the heavy cruiser to help her gunners' aim. The battleship's third salvo hit the *San Francisco*'s forward starboard side. One of the 1,400-pound 14-inch shells hit the pilothouse, killing almost everyone there and fatally wounding Capt. Cassin Young. Two more 14-inchers smashed near Turret II. They pierced the deck armor, went through the captain's cabin, bounced off the barbette under the turret, made a hole in the deck, passed through the wardroom, blew up in the armory, and ignited a fire. Despite the cracks in the turret's rear third, the men inside the enclosure were unharmed, and the guns still worked. Another shell hit forward of the previous one, obliterated the captain's cabin, and started another fire. A fourth shell missed everything.

One of the cruiser's 1.1-inch machine guns fired at the battleship's searchlight. The men on the light platform fell from the gunfire, and the lights went out.

One 14-inch salvo harmlessly sailed over the cruiser's fantail, but another from the *Kirishima* did its worst. Three 14-inch shells blasted into the fantail with one shell directly hitting and destroying the No. 4 1.1-inch mount and killing several men.

Both the *Hiei* and *Kirishima* now fired at the *San Francisco*. Three of the *Kirishima*'s 14-inch high explosive shells exploded near the cruiser's armor belt just above the water. Minor leaks allowed water to enter the hull while a fire began in the ship's laundry. If these had been armor-piercing shells and impacted a little below the water line, they would have penetrated the cruiser's hull into the engineering spaces, exploded inside the ship, and caused enough seawater to enter the hull to maybe sink the ship.

From his perch in the fire director pod high atop the light cruiser's *Nagara*'s tripod foremast, Lt. Cmdr. Kazutoshi Kuhara aimed his ship's guns that put what he identified as an American *Portland*-class heavy cruiser in a crossfire. The Japanese light cruiser fired its guns over her starboard quarter from a range of 3,000 yards at the American ship's stern starboard side. A salvo of star shells filled the night with light falling on the American cruiser. This time the *Nagara* had armor-piercing shells loaded into the breeches of its five-and-a-half-inch guns. It fired its next salvo and hit the cruiser. Eight more salvos rapidly poured into the American ship and hit it four more times.

The shells started fires in the *San Francisco*'s paint locker and seaplane hangar in the stern and killed navigator Cmdr. Rae E. Arison. The *Nagara*'s captain, Capt. Katsukiyo Shinoda, could not use his ship's torpedoes since both cruisers steamed toward each other on a near collision course. He thought his ship and the destroyer *Amatsukaze* had inflicted enough damage on the American cruiser to claim they had sunk her. The battle within a battle had only lasted six minutes since the *Nagara* first sighted the *San Francisco.*

✲ ✲ ✲

The night north of Guadalcanal was a pandemonium of light and ear-splitting sounds. The booms of 14-inch guns, the loud thumps of eight-inch salvoes, the sharper and deafening din of five-inch gunfire, and the "crump" from firing 1.1-inch and 20-mm guns attacked everyone's eardrums with a roar of sounds that threatened to render all deaf as a tree stump. Greenish magnesium star shells filled the sky with an eerie ghost-like light with red and white tracers flying across the sky like some unruly fireworks display. Reddish-orange and white explosions blossomed on the sea that could only mean that men and ships were being hit and dying.

It's the San Francisco*'s Turn*

The *Hiei* and the *San Francisco* had been trading gunfire for about two minutes when Callaghan ordered a cease-fire, despite not knowing the *San Francisco* had stopped firing at the *Atlanta.* He wanted to cross the *Hiei*'s "T" to fire at its stern. Turning to a northern course, the cruiser moved up on the battleship's stern. Then a six-inch shell hit just below the navigation bridge and detonated with a deafening blast. The explosion's concussion expanded downward to the signal bridge, killing Callaghan and three of his four-man staff who were on the bridge's starboard wing.

The battle had cut the flagship's TBS antenna into pieces, thus preventing any voice communications with the other American ships. All command and control cohesion vanished. Every American ship was on its own.

The *Hiei* moved away from the *San Francisco,* still firing 14-inch salvoes at the rate of about two per minute. But the American cruiser, despite all the punishment she had absorbed, still defiantly fired it guns until the battleship could no longer be seen. Sparks and flashes from the cruiser's hits broke over the big ship's massive shape as the cruiser's shells continued to hit the fleeing Japanese ship. At one point in the exchange, a sparkling white cloud appeared over the battleship that the Americans thought was some sort of distress signal.

The only Americans still alive on the cruiser's bridge were Lt. Cmdr. Bruce McCandless and QM2c Harry S. Higdon. Water poured over the deck and moved the dead bodies into a pile in a corner. Steel splinters had pierced McCandless' life jacket and blood poured from his wounds. Higdon rose from the deck and announced that he could no longer steer the ship. The cruiser slowed to 17 knots and began veering left. Only one phone to the central station of the damage control center still worked.

Cmdr. Joseph C. Hubbard, the executive officer, assumed command but could not talk to the bridge. After ordering Lt. Cmdr. Herbert E. Schonland to shift the ship's control to Battle II, one of the *Kirishima*'s 14-inch shells smashed into Battle II, exploded, and killed Hubbard along with all men there with him. Another shell explosion rendered the aft five-inch fire director useless. The blast sent many steel splinters against the more thickly armored aft main gun director, and knocked out all communications to the aft eight-inch turret. The turret could only operate independently under its own control.

Schonland moved the ship's control to the conning tower where backup helmsman, QM3c Floyd A. Rogers, called McCandless to say he could control the ship's course and speed. McCandless and Rogers moved down one deck to the more heavily armored conning tower. McCandless ordered a new course toward the waters between Savo Island and Guadalcanal in an attempt to restore the line of battle, but the cruiser's rudder did not respond to the wheel, and the ship kept turning to the left.

McCandless told Schonland that all the senior officers were either badly wounded or killed and could no longer command the ship and that Schonland should assume command. As acting first lieutenant, Schonland ordered McCandless to return to the navigation bridge and direct the ship there. Schonland would command the damage control parties to try to keep the cruiser afloat and extinguish or control the many fires now raging everywhere.

McCandless returned to the bridge just as the destroyer *Amatsukaze* approached the cruiser on its port side and shone its searchlight on the burning ship. The cruiser's five-inch gun director's crew asked for permission to open fire. There was some hesitation because the attacking destroyer may be American. All doubt dissipated when the destroyer fired its five-inch guns. The *San Francisco* fired back and hit the Japanese destroyer several times. One shell exploded on the destroyer's fantail and detonated depth charges. The Japanese ship exploded and apparently sank. But if she did sink, her crew managed to hit the cruiser six times, with fours of shells hitting its superstructure.

The *Hiei* and *San Francisco* resumed exchanging fire at about 2:00 a.m. with the battleship hitting the cruiser with 15 six-inch shells. Some of these clobbered the beleaguered cruiser's superstructure and probably were among those that killed Callaghan. Three of the battleship's AA guns also scored hits on the superstructure. The *Hiei* then stopped firing at the *San Francisco.* After sighting gunfire and a searchlight to the north, one of the cruiser's five-inch gun mounts fired at the target. McCandless and Wilbourne discussed whether to keep firing at the distant ship and jointly decided for all guns to cease their fire. Meanwhile, the distant *Hiei* exchanged fire with another ship as the *San Francisco* moved away from the action. But danger still lurked in the darkness from the other Japanese battleship.

☆ ☆ ☆

The *Kirishima* unexpectedly appeared about 2,500 yards away on the cruiser's starboard side. Both ships fired at each other, but scored no hits. The Japanese battleship had thus far not been as hard-hit as her companion. She was second in line with the American fire aimed primarily at the *Hiei*, first in line and, to the Americans, most likely the Japanese flagship. Capt. Sanji Iwabuchi, the *Kirishima*'s commander, did not turn on her searchlights and thus become a lightning rod for American gunfire. So he could advantageously pick his target among those firing at the flagship because the other Japanese ship searchlights had already illuminated the American warships.

The *Kirishima* lookouts spotted two American cruisers, and Iwabuchi ordered his 14-inch guns to fire at them. He later claimed to have sunk one and hit the other four times. Her actual results were seven hits on the *San Francisco* and maybe hitting the *Helena* once. Her guns also damaged the *Laffey*, the *Monssen*, and likely the *Aaron Ward.* She had only been hit once by one eight-inch shell despite the Americans directing heavy fire toward her. Her assistant gunnery officer, Lt. Cmdr. Hiroshi Tokuno, later said, "Many salvos landed around both battleships."[16]

The *Portland*'s Capt. DuBose skeptically viewed Callaghan's order to cease fire. When he asked Callaghan to confirm the order, he received an affirmative response. The admiral also ordered his ships to form up behind the flagship in a line of battle and head north. DuBose dutifully followed Callaghan's orders.

A Japanese destroyer, most likely the *Ikazuchi*, had been firing on the *Atlanta* and moved to within 7,000 yards of the *Portland*. The cruiser's nine eight-inch guns fired two salvoes that started several fires on the destroyer. Meanwhile, another Japanese destroyer, tentatively identified as the *Yudachi*, fired at the cruiser's starboard side.

The *Portland*, affectionately nicknamed "Sweet Pea" by its sailors, had been struck by three torpedoes at the Battle of Santa Cruz—all luckily turned out to be duds. But at 1:58 a.m., her fortunes dramatically changed when she would feel the uncanny accuracy and power of the Japanese Long Lance torpedo. After one of his lookouts sighted the American cruiser, Cmdr. Kikkawa ordered the *Yudachi* to fire a spread of eight torpedoes at her.

The missiles headed for their target. One torpedo hit below the cruiser's water line on its port side and blasted a hole in the hull. The explosion blew a piece of armor plate and parts of the main and second decks in an upward direction. The armor plate and deck pieces became deadly missiles and struck Turret III's gun barrels, forcing them into their fully raised position and destroying the gears that aided raising and lowering the guns. Ammunition, loaded and ready to shoot, was in the guns and could ignite to cause further damage to the ship while endangering the men in the turret. All the men in Turret III had to evacuate to avoid being killed.

A 40-feet section of the hull from Turret III to almost the ship's stern was now warped from the force of the explosion. The rudder locked in a right-turn position that forced the *Portland* into a skidding, uncontrollable starboard turn. Although steering control was in the Steering Aft control station, there was no way to talk to it. Ens. John C. Haynie unsuccessfully tried to reach it from the forward engine room and then correctly surmised the reason no one answered was that no one could.

With no wind, a pall of smoke from ship guns and burning ships spread over the water's surface. The cruiser's guns that could fire did so as the ships' gunners drew a bead on a Japanese battleship. After receiving Callaghan's response to a question about where the battleship was and completing a full-circle turn, the two forward turret six eight-inch guns loosed a salvo from a close range of 4,200 yards. The glow from the floating star shells and burning ships bathed the water in a harsh green-yellow light. The *Hiei* was now a target that could not be missed. After firing four salvos and claiming to have hit the Japanese ship ten to 14 times, the *Portland*'s crew could no longer see the battleship. She disappeared in the night. All of the *Hiei*'s 14-inch returning fire passed harmlessly overhead.

With no target to shoot at and seeing the hulks of nine burning ships, the *Portland* steamed in a circle past the burning *San Francisco* as the *Helena* moved quickly up the starboard side. Some of the other burning ships included the *Atlanta* and what seemed to be two burning Japanese cruisers. With no ability to correctly determine the ships' identity, DuBose decided to not fire his guns at targets of dubious value and directed his crew's attention to repairing his badly damaged command.

✲ ✲ ✲

Still undamaged and spoiling for a fight, the *Helena* meanwhile had to nimbly avoid colliding with the burning hulks scattered all over the water. After making a hard right turn to miss the crippled *Atlanta*, her SG radar picked up targets just a short time after 1:52 a.m. and opened fire at the *Nagara* just 3,000 yards away. Capt. Hoover ordered his 40-mm guns to spray fire on the Japanese light cruiser. The main battery plot had to quickly change its calculations because the Japanese ship moved too quickly to get a firing solution. The *Helena* stopped firing since she no longer had a target.

The chaotic scene of star shells descending, burning ships, and smoke from ship guns made visual sighting impossible, so Hoover used his SG radar to find new opportunities. Ens. Ray J. Casten looked at the radar scope and saw so many pips displayed that it was not possible to discern what targets were American or what were Japanese. One target was a ship exchanging fire with the *San Francisco*. Hoover asked Callaghan for permission to open fire and received a reply to fire at the Japanese battleships. Using her radar to find a target believed to be a battleship, the *Helena* fired ten salvoes in two minutes at the ship. The cruiser steamed behind the battleship *Kirishima*, and the cruiser's gunnery officer asked Hoover for permission to fire at it. The captain's response was direct and to the point: "Hell, no, not with six-inch guns! Let's get away and then you can shoot!"[17]

Returning fire from the Japanese twice hit the cruiser. The first was a 14-inch shell that hit the deck's edge and sprayed shell fragments on Turret I but damaged nothing. More big shells arched over the cruiser and raised big geysers of water all around her. A second shell clanged under Turret IV's center gun and disabled it. From then on, only that turret's right and left guns could be fired after that hit.

Meanwhile, the *Helena*'s five-inch battery found a destroyer to shoot at and continued firing at the ship until the *San Francisco* got in the way. Warrant Officer William Dupay diffused a potentially dangerous situation after being ordered to one of the five-inch gun mounts. The mount's crew had ceased firing too soon and mistakenly placed an armed five-inch shell back into the shell hoist directly on top of a base fuse. All froze in place awaiting the blast that would come if the ship was shaken. Cooly, Dupay picked up the shell and fuse, extinguished the mount's firing lights, and threw the two missiles overboard. The mount could then resume firing.

The rapid firing of the cruiser's guns illuminated her for other ships to see her in the dark. Only one torpedo came at her, but Hoover's ability to maneuver his ship avoided any damage from torpedoes. The Japanese destroyers could not get a bead on her. They might have fired more torpedoes but the crew did not see any more wakes coming at her.[18]

The American Destroyers Get Their Chance

The beleaguered *Hiei* had been carrying on a firefight with the American cruisers when American destroyers moved in for a piece of the action. The *Cushing*, *Laffey*, *O'Bannon*, *Sterett*, and *Monssen* engaged the big battleship in a David versus Goliath conflict. The survivors would remember this one for the rest of their lives.

✲ ✲ ✲

The destroyer *Cushing*, the leading ship in the American single-file formation, had been concentrating her fire to starboard when one of her lookouts spotted the *Hiei* on the port beam coming right at her. Recognizing the approaching ship was indeed a battleship but not sure to what class she belonged, Lt. Cmdr. Edward N. Parker, her captain, immediately ordered his 20-mm guns to fire at the ship's superstructure. The *Hiei*'s lookouts also saw the American destroyer. Since his ship's 14-inch guns still fired on the American cruisers, the battleship's captain ordered his five-inch and six-inch guns to begin firing at the destroyer. The guns' tracers completely bracketed the destroyer in a mesh of fire.

The overall commander of the American destroyers, Cmdr. Thomas M. Stokes, knew his ships' five-inch guns were no match for the big battleship. The only chance the destroyers had to sink or seriously damage it was to attack with the deadliest weapon almost all the world's destroyers had, the torpedo. The four destroyers leading the American ships had a total of 35 torpedoes onboard and could fire one broadside of 27 of them. Firing a broadside assumed the destroyers stayed in their line of battle, but the line had disintegrated because of the raging, chaotic battle. The *Cushing*'s malfunctioning communications also made coordinated torpedo attack even more problematic.

The battleship narrowed the distance to the destroyer so quickly that the crews had no time to set up the torpedoes for a proper assault. The *Cushing*'s Numbers 1 and 2 torpedo mounts pointed to port and were ready to fire with their gyro and depth settings loaded into the torpedoes. But the battleship was just 1,000 yards away when the "open fire" order arrived, too close for the torpedoes to arm before they would hit the big ship. A Japanese shell exploded nearby that wounded several of the mounts' crew so that No. 2 mount could only fire one torpedo. Another shell hit the No. 3 five-inch gun mount, killed its crew, and ignited a fire. The *Cushing*'s lone torpedo missed the battleship.

Now a Japanese destroyer fired at the *Cushing* as the American destroyer increased the distance between herself and the *Hiei*. Both Japanese ships poured in more shells from both sides of the *Cushing*. One shell pierced the hull, exploded in the engine room, destroyed the pump feeding fuel to the engines, and killed several men. Another missile hit the forward fire room and exploded. Pieces of shrapnel from the blast punctured holes in the boiler, causing a loss of steam pressure. The ship began to lose speed and power. By this time, the *Laffey* closed near the battleship, and it was her turn to confront the *Hiei*.

✲ ✲ ✲

The *Laffey*'s torpedo battery pointed to starboard when the order came from the bridge to turn the tubes to port. There was a battleship just 1,000 yards away, and what an inviting target she was! As the tubes turned, the distance between the two ships rapidly shrank. It seemed a lifetime had passed before the tubes hissed and sent three torpedoes on their way. They had a 3° spread with a depth setting of ten feet.

The battleship's lookout saw the torpedo wakes heading toward their ship and frantically reported them to the bridge. Capt. Masao Nishida deftly maneuvered the big ship to avoid one torpedo, but could not avoid the other two from striking his command. Like the *Cushing*'s torpedoes, these missiles did not have enough time to arm themselves because the range was too short. A safety mechanism built into the torpedoes prevents them from prematurely exploding too close to the launching ship. The two torpedoes that clanged against the battleship were duds.

But that did not stop the destroyer's main battery of five five-inch guns from firing at its big target. The ship's gunnery officer, Lt. William K. Ratliff, ordered all five guns to fire at their quarry. A searchlight's beam temporarily blinded one man on the No. 2 gun mount, but did not stop him from seeing the huge pagoda superstructure looming near that could only belong to a Japanese battleship.

Lt. Cmdr. Chihaya was on the starboard wing of the battleship's bridge looking through his binoculars at the battling American destroyer so close-by. He wondered what his ship could do if they only had a battering ram like ships built long ago. But a barrage of 1.1-inch and 20-mm cannon fire sprayed everywhere over his ship's superstructure with exploding shells lighting up its compartments so clearly that the destroyer's crew could see inside them. Three shells smashed into the bridge that shattered glass and scattered steel fragments that cut men down like a razor-sharp scythe slicing wheat. A piece of shrapnel tore into Chihaya's hand while another fragment cut Adm. Abe's face. Nishida screamed for a corpsman to help the admiral who now also had a profusely bleeding gash in his left calf.

The *Laffey*'s crew thought the battleship was going to ram them. The bridge sounded the collision alarm and ordered a hard left turn to prevent the *Hiei* from striking them. The two ships passed each other by a scant ten yards. The destroyer never stopped firing its withering barrage as the range between the two combatants increased. As the destroyer moved away, Ratliff observed the battleship no longer fired its big guns, and only sporadic fire came from its five- and six-inch guns. But machine-gun fire still hit the destroyer that wounded some of the torpedo crew. The range was then 2,000 yards when Lt. Cmdr. William E. Hank, the *Laffey*'s skipper, ordered Ratliff to cease firing.

The *Hiei*'s ordeal continued when the *O'Bannon*, commanded by Cmdr. Edwin R. Wilkinson, sprinted past the crippled *Sterett*. The destroyer moved to within 1,800 yards of the battleship when the amazing "Cease Fire" came over the TBS. The destroyer was the newest of the *Fletcher*-class destroyers that had five five-inch guns—two forward, three aft—along with ten 21-inch torpedo tubes in two five-tube mounts and the newest SG radar the American Navy had at that time.[19]

✲ ✲ ✲

Wilkinson obeyed the order by commanding that all his ship's guns stop firing. He could not see the *Laffey* or the *Cushing* and realized his ship now led the American line of battle. Noticing gunfire to starboard at what appeared to be a *Tenryu*-class cruiser about 3,000 yards away. He ordered his guns to fire at the newly identified target. Pleased that his guns had started fires on the distant ship, he changed his mind when he saw the *Hiei* just 1,200 yards to port. The battleship's less intensive fire passed overhead. Like the other American destroyers that preceded his ship, his torpedo mounts had been aimed to starboard. Wilkinson frantically ordered his torpedo officer, Ens. John P. Tazewell, to aim the torpedo mount to port.

The short range to the battleship helped Tazewell decide to not fire a spread of torpedoes but shoot each one independently. The battleship seemed to stop moving. The setup was an ideal one. He ordered the torpedo directors to aim at the middle of the big ship. One man set the depth and gyro angles and waited for the order to fire. After confirming the torpedoes were ready, Tazewell pressed the firing button that fired two torpedoes by electrical signal. Despite the noise of battle that masked the hissing sound of the torpedoes being fired, he confirmed the missiles were on the way.

Thinking the range was greater than before, Tazewell ordered the next torpedoes to be aimed at the *Hiei*'s bow. Just after pressing the firing button, the third torpedo leapt from the tube as a monstrous blast came from the battleship. Wilkinson remembered that the "battleship was enveloped from bow to stern in a great sheet of fire. Burning particles fell on this vessel's forecastle."[20] After learning from Tazewell that three torpedoes had been fired, Wilkinson ordered a cease fire at 1:59 a.m. The captain firmly believed the battleship was a goner and steered the ship to a new course of due east.

A searchlight found her as more shells passed overhead. The shells landed in the water, and huge geysers mushroomed all around her with some shrapnel fragments hitting the destroyer, but causing no damage. Wilkinson and the rest of the bridge crew saw burning ships on all sides. At 2:01 a.m., she passed a burning hulk. Believed to be the *Laffey* by seeing a hull number "459", the sinking ship's hull number was instead "599" or the *Barton*. The *O'Bannon*'s crew threw life jackets to some survivors in the water. The ship tried to clear as much distance from the men in the water as possible but could not avoid running some down. Some torpedo wakes then came at the *O'Bannon* but missed their target.

A thunderous explosion—likely from the blast that struck the *Portland*—lifted the *O'Bannon*'s stern out of the water, but she was not damaged. The destroyer's engine room reported that her port reduction now vibrated; the captain ordered her speed to be reduced by one-third. All power and lights temporarily went out, but came on again after resetting her switches.

✲ ✲ ✲

Conning his heavily damaged destroyer *Sterett* through a labyrinth of burning ships, survivors in the water and splashes of the shells being fired by both sides, Cmdr. Jesse G. Coward had to use the engines to direct the ship's course because of its disabled steering system. After telling other American ships of his problems and asking for recognition signals over the TBS, the *Laffey* turned on her lights. Unfortunately, the *Sterett* could not respond since subsequent battle damage momentarily disabled her communications system.

Coward changed his attack at 2:05 a.m. when a searchlight beam shone on the *Hiei*. Torpedo officer Lt. (jg) Thomas O. McWhorter, like the other odd-numbered American destroyers, had his torpedo mounts aimed to starboard. After trying to unsuccessfully see the target though the director's sighting system, he did see a "cruiser" through his binoculars. The *Sterett*'s guns now fired at the ship and scored hits on it. The *O'Bannon* then got in the way, forcing the *Sterett* to stop firing.

Lt. Cmdr. Frank G. Gould, the *Sterett*'s executive officer, abruptly came on from the pilothouse and shouted, "Battleship close aboard on the port side dead in the water!"[21] McWhorter ran over to the port torpedo director with its operator and telephone talker right behind him. Coward ordered

McWhorter to fire as soon as he was ready. Compressed air whooshed from all the director's tubes sending four torpedoes on their way. The *Sterett* later claimed two hits.

The destroyer's gunnery officer, Lt. Walter Calhoun, then ordered his ship's guns to fire at the *Hiei*'s superstructure and aim for the battleship's pagoda. The intense training the gun crews had received demonstrated its worth as the destroyer sent a fusillade of five-inch shells every four seconds. Forty shells hit the big ship, and the destroyer's crew could see them explode with bright flashpoints of light.

Nonetheless, the *Sterett* received returning 14-inch shellfire. Three of them ignited fires in the No. 3 gun mount ready room. Another shell exploded on the mount and killed its crew. Undaunted, the destroyer's crew continued searching for more targets.

The *Cushing* confronted the *Hiei* again on its starboard quarter and fired six torpedoes from 1,200 yards. Gunfire from several American ships congregated on the embattled battleship. The destroyer's crew drew some pleasure when they heard three explosions hit the Japanese ship and saw a huge geyser of water sprout at her side. But the *Cushing*'s situation had worsened.

Her battles with the Japanese had disabled all her five-inch guns with the main battery director hit. Many of her crew had been either killed or wounded. The ship's doctor, Lt. (jg) James E. Cashman, tirelessly labored trying to attend to the wounded and comfort the dying. He was too busy to notice that some shrapnel had wounded him in his left arm.

By this time, the *Hiei* had distanced itself from the American destroyers. It had faced and brawled with the *Cushing* two times, and the *Laffey, Sterett, O'Bannon, Monssen,* and possibly the *Barton* at least once. Only the *Aaron Ward* and the *Fletcher* had not confronted her. She could no longer steam as fast as she once did. The battleship fortunately did not receive any damage from the American torpedoes. All 24 fired at her had hit, but not with the results the American believed they had achieved. What the American destroyer crews thought were explosions from torpedoes hitting the battleship actually came from the missiles' detonators exploding. Their depths might have been set too deep. No matter what the causes, American torpedoes suffered from the deadly disadvantage of inferiority during the early war years in the Pacific.

Nevertheless, those destroyers did have a tremendous impact on the course of the battle. The intensity of their attacks forced Adm. Abe to abandon his mission to bombard the Guadalcanal airfields at least for one more day. The *Hiei* limped northward with the *Kirishima* following in her wake.[22]

But there were to be more battles between American and Japanese ships, and much of that would be between destroyers.

CHAPTER 39
Taking on All Comers

The *Aaron Ward*, leading the rear group of American destroyers, returned to battle speed after nearly colliding with the *Yudachi* at 1:59 a.m. Obeying the flagship's orders received over the TBS, she turned north and found a new target for her torpedoes. But she could not open fire because the *San Francisco* was too close to her. Her torpedo director officer, Lt. (jg) John G. Drew continued in vain to find new targets for ten more minutes. He spotted the *Sterett* moving rapidly up on his port side. Simultaneously, the *Sterett*'s Lt. Calhoun identified the nearby ship as the *Aaron Ward*. Cmdr. Gregor sent an order to the engine room to increase speed to flank and turned the *Aaron Ward* to avoid hitting the *Sterett*.

A ship showing its Japanese recognition signal (white over red over green) came into view over the starboard bow. Identifying the new target as a possible *Katori*-class light cruiser, Gregor wasted no time and ordered his ship guns and torpedo batteries to open fire. She then shifted her fire to another Japanese ship, possibly the *Yudachi* or the *Murasame*. The Japanese returned gunfire that sent two shots through the main battery director and forced Lt. (jg) William T. LeBaron to locally control the guns.

Another shell cut the top foremast and destroyed the radar antenna. The toppled mast landed over the ship's whistle line. The whistle now continuously sounded with the noise piercing everyone's ears. Lt. Drew took his .45-cal. pistol from its holster, carefully aimed at the whistle line, and pulled the trigger. The bullet cut the line, the mast crashed on the main deck, and the whistle noise stopped.

The *Aaron Ward* absorbed tremendous punishment from Japanese shellfire. A Japanese five-inch shell pierced the weather screen, the director's base, a signal light on the director's other side, and exploded. Another shell exploded and blew off a piece from the back of the main battery director. Still another hit obliterated a four-gun 1.1-inch mount, setting its ammunition on fire, and blowing up two depth charges. Three 14-inch shells exploded and either damaged or destroyed a stateroom, the galley, and the laundry. The explosions put holes in several compartments, the bridge deck, ignited fires, and severed cables to the main battery director, torpedo director, steering control, and some telephone lines.

As members of the crew tried to administer first-aid to the wounded and dying, the destroyer valiantly kept firing its guns. With only two five-inch mounts still operating, these guns extinguished a searchlight as another one shined its beam on her. Star shells made the destroyer stand out more. The Japanese guns continued to pummel her.

The totally chaotic battle scene also forced the Japanese destroyer captains to be on their own and fight smaller, isolated battles with the Americans. Several of them protected their ships from being seen by firing their torpedoes before firing their guns. The gun flashes would have made them visible to the prying eyes of the American lookouts.

Steaming off the flagship starboard bow, the Japanese destroyers *Akatsuki*, *Inazuma*, and *Ikazuchi*, with the *Akatsuki* leading the way, moved in single file when one of the *Akatsuki*'s lookouts spotted another destroyer to starboard. The contact seemed to be a single-stack destroyer. It was likely the *Cushing* turning toward the leading destroyer to get its torpedo director into firing position. Capt. Yusuke Yamada, commanding the three-ship division, consulted with Cmdr. Osamu Takasuka, his flag lieutenant, as Lt. Michiharu Shinya, the *Akatsuki*'s torpedo officer, wanted to get a good shooting solution for his own torpedo director. Yamada could not decide whether the distant ship was friendly or not, but Shinya had no such doubts when he exclaimed, "It's an enemy one—no mistake, sir!"[1] He noticed more ships when Yamada ordered his three destroyers to fire at them. Lt. Tatsuo Yamagata, in charge of the *Akatsuki*'s guns, issued orders to point his guns at the American ships when a searchlight beam exposed one of them in the darkness.

When the *Akatsuki* shone its searchlight on the *Atlanta*, that sealed the Japanese destroyer's doom. The American ships immediately fired at the three destroyers with deadly results. Three cruisers—the *Atlanta*, *San Francisco*, and *Helena* and four destroyers—the *Laffey*, *O'Bannon*, *Aaron Ward*, and *Fletcher*—fired at the ship with the lit searchlight. In what seemed to be an instant later, a thunderous explosion decimated the destroyer.

Knocked flat from the blast, Shinya felt blood dribbling from his right eye and a shard of shrapnel sticking out of his shoulder. Hearing Yamada ordering a turn to port, Shinya looked over to the wheel and saw a dead helmsman. He grasped the wheel, but it would not turn. The bridge was a scene of carnage with blood covering the now slippery deck. He tried to get on his feet but his head buzzed from the explosion's deafening sound. Takasuka tried to call the gunnery officer. There was no answer.

The smell of exploded powder flooded the bridge. As the acrid smoke cleared, Shinya could see the still-alive Yamada, Takasuka, the ship's navigator, and his assistant. The dead bodies of the division doctor and paymaster, the helmsman, talkers, lookouts, and Shinya's torpedo director crew littered the deck. All possibilities of steering the ship from the bridge were gone. Shinya chose to move to the emergency steering room located aft. Moving a dead body out of his way, he saw nothing but dead bodies as he passed the communications room. Wounded men crowded into the wardroom to get medical treatment. He had his head bandaged and went back to the bridge.

By this time, the destroyer's forward momentum had stopped. Shinya tried to contact the engine rooms and received no responses. The ship's list to port increased, and her stern settled in the water. He could not see Yamada or the assistant navigator. Takasuka, the navigator, and he were the only ones left on the bridge. The stern was under water. Seeing that all hope to salvage the destroyer was gone, the three officers jumped into the water. The *Akatsuki* sank with all her guns and torpedo tubes remaining silent.

The *Inazuma* and *Ikazuchi* moved within 1,093 yards of the American ships, fired their guns, and each sent six torpedoes toward the Americans. The *Ikazuchi* claimed three hits; one of its torpedoes probably hit the *Atlanta*. It fired one salvo every eight seconds as its captain, Cmdr. Saneo Maeda, maneuvered his ship around the sinking *Akatsuki* to get a more favorable torpedo firing position.

Several shells then smashed behind the bridge, on the superstructure's base, and gun mount No. 1. Dense gas clouds penetrated into the gunnery telephone room as the men inside scrambled to put on their gas masks. The lights went out, but soon returned. No one could talk to the other sections in the ship. Two men left the bridge area to check the other gun mounts as one man tried to talk to them through the voice pipe. One man called the bridge from the gun director and asked for permission to leave his station. It was granted since all the men up there were undoubtedly dead.

The messenger sent aft to check on the aft gun mounts reached that location and saw a disabled No. 2 mount and a still-functioning but damaged No. 3 mount. He called the bridge to report their status. The No. 3 mount commander asked for firing orders and set the gun to operate under local control. Nevertheless, damage to the destroyer put her out of commission and flames engulfed her.

The *Inazuma* was far more fortunate. It escaped any damage and meanwhile fired six torpedoes and 54 five-inch salvoes. The returning American gunfire forced her to retreat northward, leaving the burning *Ikazuchi* and sinking *Akatsuki* in her wake.

While the *Akatsuki* sank, the *Amatsukaze* attacked American ships all by herself. Cmdr. Tameichi Hara, her captain, increased her speed when the firing began to get away from the *Cushing*'s gunfire. Hara's destroyer went by the *Nagara* and moved across the American ships' path. The *Amatsukaze* was now on the Americans' starboard bow and in a highly advantageous position to attack them. As star shells illuminated the Americans, Hara saw five or six ships on his starboard bow. He ordered his gunnery officer to fire three of the destroyer's guns and four torpedoes. Both the guns and torpedo tubes opened fire. The destroyer was moving at near top speed through the turbulent waters as spray drenched the bridge including the captain. He watched the battle unfolding before him and ordered his ship to reduce its speed so his torpedo crew could reload their tubes. More star shells fell and flooded the scene with their eery green light. All of a sudden, an explosion in the distance got his attention. A huge ball of flame and smoke appeared on the horizon—the American destroyer *Barton* had disappeared in a cataclysmic blast of fire and smoke.

Flushed with confidence and a sense of accomplishment but not hanging around to increase the risk of being hit by the Americans, he headed for the now-burning *Hiei*. More star shell light covered the water and helped Hara see a battle between the American cruiser *Juneau* and the Japanese destroyer *Yudachi*. At 1:59 a.m., he ordered torpedoes fired at the cruiser and saw red flames burst from her more than three minutes later. Claiming the damage as a hit, he moved his ship northwest despite appeals from Lt. Kazue Shimizu, his gunnery officer, to continue firing their guns. He spotted the *San Francisco* and fired torpedoes at her from close range. Like the mistakes committed by American destroyers, his torpedoes did not have time to arm and harmlessly hit the cruiser.

Shimizu finally got his wish when Hara ordered him to fire his five-inch guns at the cruiser. Unable to see the *San Francisco* because she had no radar, the destroyer turned on its searchlight and shone it on the cruiser. The *Helena*'s Lt. Warren Boles, from his vantage point in the main battery fire director, immediately saw the light as an inviting target. The cruiser's six-inch guns blasted the hapless destroyer with deadly fusillades. One minute of six-inch shellfire deluged the destroyer from her waterline to her bridge. The *Amatsukaze*'s fortunes had run out. Flames covered her from bow to stern.

The hits on the destroyer caused her to move sideways to starboard. Her steering gear no longer worked. Its fire director had been hit, and fires burned in her radio room under the bridge. Her guns could not fire because all hydraulic power to them had been cut. Forty-three dead bodies either covered the decks or were in the water. Shimizu and many men on the bridge were now dead. Hara had to direct his efforts away from combat and toward saving his ship.

The *Monssen* had been lucky thus far, but her luck was also about to end. After seeing star shell bursts to the north while searching for new target opportunities, Lt. Cmdr. McCombs changed his direction to a 40° northeasterly course. Soon he saw a Japanese destroyer identifiable by the two white bands on its funnels. About 500-1,000 yards in the distance, it neared the *Monssen* in a south-southeasterly direction. McCombs ordered his forward five-inch gun and 20-mm guns to open fire. Now, the Japanese destroyer was to his ship's stern. The range rapidly opened, so McCombs took his ship around Florida Island's northern end to look for Japanese transports.

The green light from more star shells flooded the early morning sky. Believing the light came from friendly ships, he turned on some recognition lights. But he guessed wrong. The Japanese light cruiser *Nagara* and the destroyers *Yukikaze* and *Teruzuki* waited to pounce on the unsuspecting American destroyer.

Two searchlight beams now covered the *Monssen*, and Lt. (jg) H.W. Wager ordered his guns to snuff out the lights. This attempt at defense failed as a shell hit the No. 2 five-inch gun mount and killed its entire crew. Two more shells smacked into the No. 2 five-inch mount and started a fire in its ammunition handling room. One more shell pierced the mount's armor shield but did not explode. More shells smashed into the fire director and knocked out automatic control for the rear guns. After Wager left the director, he lost his life trying to get to his last two operational guns.

Two torpedo wakes headed for the American destroyer but McCombs maneuvered the ship to avoid them. Another torpedo missed just five yards away. One more pierced the hull, smashed into the aft fire room, stuck in the hole it made, but did not detonate. Water sprayed into the room to douse any fires.

As McCombs ordered a change of course to 50° and flank speed, another shell hit the forward fire room and burst a steam line. Still another projectile hit the after engine room's throttle manifold and broke it open. And the hits kept coming.

An avalanche of ten more missiles hit the hull below the superstructure. The heaviest damage was on the starboard side. Nonetheless, the port side was not spared punishment either. Approximately 37 shells pounded the ship that included two large-caliber shells that penetrated the light armor but did not detonate. Four hits immersed the forward engine room in blackness, and only five men in the room escaped death. Just four men in the aft engine room lived. The damage was so severe in the engine rooms that the ship's power was gone. The rudder was in a jammed right turn position, and the ship steamed in a starboard circle.

The damage control parties, led by Lt. (jg) George S. Hamm, waged a hopeless fight against the overwhelming number of fires engulfing her. Despite help from BM2c C. C. Storey and Chief Ralph Womack, Hamm realized they could do nothing to stem the conflagration and knew that if they did not immediately leave the ship, they would be caught aboard and killed when the ship's magazines exploded. The destroyer's life neared its end.

When the battle began, a deluge of shell splashes hid the *Yudachi* from a lookout on the *Harusame*. The chaotic scene confused Cmdr. Masao Kamiyama, the *Harusame*'s captain, since all he could see were American ships. Nevertheless, he knew Japanese ships were nearby, maybe on the other side of the Americans, so he had to be cautious before firing his guns. He headed his ship to the north and turned westward when he saw what appeared to be a heavy cruiser. The sighted ship seemed to be battling another ship and did not see his vessel. With the range to the "heavy cruiser" of about 2000 meters, Kamiyama ordered his torpedo director to fire a torpedo spread. They seemed to have hit the ship, and Kamiyama claimed his missiles had hit and sunk her. He also claimed that his guns had hit another *Portland*-class cruiser's bridge.

Another threesome of Japanese destroyers—the *Asagumo*, *Murasame*, and *Samidare*—under the command of Radm. Tamotsu Takama steamed in a haggard line far off the port side and to battleships' rear. Takama had to wait for the many other ships to move out the way before he could order his own ships to fire and not hit other Japanese ships. The *Asagumo* was in the lead steaming on a northwesterly course when one of her lookouts sighted a potential target on a northward course. She got close enough at 2:00 a.m. for her captain, Cmdr. Toru Iwahashi, to see she was a cruiser, the *Helena*. His five-inch guns fired as he also launched a torpedo salvo from 4,374 yards away. He later claimed his barrage started a huge fire on the American ship and apparently sank her.

As his ship sped through the water at 34 knots, Senior Lt. Homare Kayama, the *Murasame*'s gunnery officer, was at his station in the director when he spied a target. He reasoned it was definitely not Japanese and knew the order to fire would soon come from the bridge. So he readied his guns by aiming them at the American ship now 30° to starboard.

Meanwhile, the *Murasame*'s skipper, Cmdr. Naoji Suenaga, ordered his torpedo officer, Senior Lt. Sakae Ishizuka, to quickly get a firing solution on the target. Kayama turned on one of the ship's searchlights at 2:01 a.m. so he could see the target and fired his five-inch guns at what seemed to be a *Mahan*-class destroyer—it was actually the cruiser *Juneau*. The beam of light and the shells seemed to simultaneously hit the American ship's bridge area. Ishizuka fired a full eight-torpedo salvo one minute later.

A shell from the American ship then hit the forward fireroom. Suenaga put his destroyer into a hard left turn so his guns and torpedoes could fire over the port side and ordered the searchlight turned off. The forward five-inch turret ammunition hoist temporarily jammed but soon became operational again. A shell hit the No. 3 mount, put a hole in its door, but neither damaged anything nor hurt anyone.

With his ship still turning, Kayama ordered, "Check fire," as smoke made it harder for him see anything. The destroyer finished circling as Suenaga felt her slowing. Engineering officer Senior Lt.

Genkichi Matsumo reported a shell had hit the forward fireroom and disabled the boiler. The ship's top speed was now just 27.5 knots.

☆ ☆ ☆

By this time, the mêlée on the sea north of Guadalcanal had reached the highest level of pandemonium. Shadows and silhouettes of ships passed and overtook each other like specters on an imaginary Halloween night. Searchlight beams moved across the water like visible radar beams from bats hunting insects. The pale green light from falling starshells cast a funereal pall over everything. Smoke from gunfire and burning ships permeated the air and its acrid odor attacked the senses of all who were there. Sounds from explosions and firing guns boomed over the water. Fires blossomed on the horizons and surrounded the watery battlefield. To any sailor who could see and smell what was happening around them, the illusion must have seemed as close to the underworld as it could be.

☆ ☆ ☆

Caught in the middle of it all was Cmdr. Noboru Nakamura, the *Samidare*'s captain. Neither he nor any man trying to locate targets could tell whether the ships nearby were friend or foe. When one target silhouette appeared, he ordered his torpedo battery to ready their tubes for firing. His machine guns began firing when one of his lookouts shouted, "That's *Hiei*, Captain! That's *Hiei*!" Nakamura reached for his telescope, looked into it, and immediately ordered his ship to stop firing. One of the *Hiei*'s five-inch shells rumbled overhead. After Nakamura turned on his red recognition light, the battleship stopped its firing, too.

His destroyer division commander, Capt. Masao Tachibana in the *Murasame*, meanwhile sent Nakamura an order to fire his guns. But with no targets, the destroyer captain had no idea what he should shoot at. After his searchlight beam lit the American stars and stripes flying from the *Juneau*'s mast, he finally had a target to shoot at and did not waste the opportunity to inflict some damage. His five-inch main battery loosed a full 5-gun salvo, and his torpedo crews sighted their mounts on her. Nakamura looked through his telescope and saw the ship apparently sinking. Rather than squander his precious torpedoes on a doomed ship, he ordered the torpedo crews not to fire.

Aboard the *Murasame*, some confusion arose concerning their target's identity. A concerned Suenaga thought the ship was Japanese. Tachibana, Kayama, and Ishizuka firmly believed the ship they attacked was an American warship. Later, the ship's navigator, Senior Lt. Teruo Hiroyama, retrieved a book the Imperial Japanese Navy used to identify the world's ships and found a picture of a *Mahan*-class destroyer. He put his finger on the picture and declared this was the target that they had attacked. Kayama supported Hiroyama's assertion.

☆ ☆ ☆

The *Juneau*'s suffering worsened when a torpedo hit the forward fireroom, exploded, and shook her to the bottom of her keel. The blast spewed devastation deep within her innards, threw many men off their feet, tossed three depth charges and the port-side whaleboat overboard, and slaughtered all the fireroom's occupants. She kept shooting at the *Yudachi*, now disappearing into the distance in a cloud of smoke. Nevertheless, the torpedo's detonation knocked out power to the forward section lights and the guns. Leaking fuel poured into the plot room and forced its crew to abandon their stations. More shells, possibly from Takama's destroyers, decimated the cruiser's bridge, searchlights near the rear smokestack, and the hull.

She began to list, causing some of the main deck aft crew to believe they should abandon ship. They cut the ropes that tied the life rafts to the ship. Soon, reason returned when the belief proved to be false, and the men returned to their stations.

Lt. Cmdr. Knowlton Williams, one of the engineering officers, tried to start the after engine room generators to restore power. But his attempt failed, so he tried starting the diesel generators. Control of the cruiser became more difficult, and Capt. Lyman K. Swenson had problems avoiding a collision with the *Helena*. The collision alarm blared. With steering control now in the aft section, the ship avoided the *Helena*. Demonstrating the effects of that night's rampant confusion, the *Juneau* fired her five-inch guns at the other cruiser but luckily hit nothing.

One of the signalmen saw searchlight beams shining on the water and noticed hundreds of men swimming in the water. The cruiser could not help but steam right through them and left them in her wake. Events like that became common that night with ships trying to survive the chaotic battle. It was a tragedy of war at sea that some men never forgot.

The *Juneau* had been so badly damaged that she could no longer fight. Swenson wanted to go to a safer place to try to fix the damage. He ordered the cruiser to steam to Malaita Island where she could leave the battle behind. With 17 corpses in her forward fire room, she staggered toward the island. Lt. Roger O'Neil, the junior medical officer, discovered the extent of the severe damage his ship had sustained as he treated the wounded. After attending to Lt. Cmdr. Thomas O. Oberrender's wounds, the engineering officer told him that the ship's keel was likely broken. Her life as a fighting ship of the U.S. Navy was definitely numbered in hours.

When Takama's destroyers finished their fight with the *Juneau* and headed northeast, they ran into the *Laffey*. The American destroyer had finished her fight with the *Hiei* when her spotters saw the *Kirishima*. When she was about 10,000 yards distant, Ratliff pointed his five-inch battery at her. Nevertheless, no order to fire came from the bridge. With all her torpedoes gone, her captain did not want to battle with the battleship but to face ships more like her own size. With an example of the old saying, "Be careful what you wish for. You may get it!", he got his wish. Two destroyers appeared on the port side ahead and about 3,000 yards away.

As the first destroyer passed across her bow, the *Laffey* pointed her guns at the second one. Not much time passed before the Japanese destroyer shined her searchlight on the American ship. All three ships' guns fired almost simultaneously, and the *Laffey* took all the punishment.

One five-inch shell hit her, exploded in the chart room, knocked out the room's lights, wounded Ens. Patrick H. McGann and sonar man John Curtis, and killed Ens. Joseph W. Finch. The blast knocked out the power to the director and forced the ship's guns to be locally controlled. Ratliff moved the gun director crew to the flying bridge. More hits smashed two of the three aft gun mounts. Only her remaining forward gun could fire at the Japanese destroyers.

Matters only worsened when the *Kirishima* fired at the *Laffey*. One 14-inch shell pierced the hull, passed through the electrical workshop located amidships, stopped in the after fireroom, but proved to be a dud. Another shell tore a hole in a steam line in the forward engine room. Scalding steam flooded the compartment and forced its occupants on deck. The battleship stopped firing at the destroyer and looked for more opportune targets as it steamed away. The light cruiser *Nagara* passed and fired its machine guns at the destroyer.

Water now copiously flowed into the *Laffey*'s engine and fire rooms. The men there got ready to stop all the engines and come up on deck when an order arrived from the bridge to increase speed. The destroyer's engineering officer, Lt. Eugene A. Barham, and Warrant Officer Lester E. Murphy surveyed the heavy damage in the forward engine room and saw a jumbled tangle of "broken pipes and smashed machinery."[2] The two men could not get to the pumps. Nonetheless, the forward fire room and after engine room could still function. The two men changed the power flow so that the ship could steam ahead using the two rooms still operational. They restarted the two forward room boilers. With something to be optimistic about, Cmdr. Hank now joyfully talked about taking his command home under the Golden Gate Bridge, but his confidence in his ship's future soon would be dramatically altered.

A tremendous explosion shook the ship down its keel and rolled the ship almost to the point of being capsized. A Long Lance torpedo had hit her near No. 4 gun mount, exploded, and almost severed the ship's fantail. Though still barely attached, it now hung gingerly at a 90° angle. The blast destroyed the propellers and shafts, tore huge gashes in her fuel tanks, and ignited an oil fire that rapidly surrounded her stern. With all power gone, she was dead in the water, and her forward momentum slowed.

✲ ✲ ✲

The destroyer *Fletcher*, the last ship in the American formation, began firing again at what seemed to be a heavy cruiser, likely the *Kirishima*, after getting the cease-fire order. As she fired her guns, she almost rammed the heavily damaged *Juneau*. But she avoided the disaster when her captain backed her engines, and her gunnery officer ordered his guns to stop firing.

At this time, the *Fletcher* moved past the destroyer *Barton*'s watery grave as her crew smelled the fumes from its destruction. Leaving the mortally damaged *Monssen* behind, now nearly dead in the water, smoke from the burning ships, gunfire, and her own funnels was sucked into her own vents. The acrid clouds moved into the lower decks and engulfed the engineering spaces. Towering splashes from missed shellfire surrounded the *Fletcher* as the fire from the *Barton*'s explosion revealed four torpedo wakes heading for her. Two of them were on the surface, and the other two passed under the ship. The men below could hear the whining sound of their propellers as they passed under her keel.

✲ ✲ ✲

Locked in a deadly battle for survival, the *Sterett* and the *Yudachi* fired their guns and torpedoes at each other. The American destroyer fired two five-inch salvoes and torpedoes. She received a reward for her attack when the shells smashed into the Japanese destroyer's bridge and after five-inch gun mounts. Two torpedoes hit the *Yudachi*, and their explosions lifted her out of the water. Lt. McWhorter ordered a cease fire thinking the ship hit by his shells could have been the *Sterett*.

The *Yudachi* had fought in the middle of this night's battle from its very beginning. She had engaged a "cruiser" at 1:56 a.m. by firing eight torpedoes and claimed to have hit the ship, the *Portland*, and one other with two or three strikes. Her captain, Cmdr. Kiyoshi Kikkawa, reported he had sunk both American ships.

Three minutes later, she fired at the *Juneau* and took a hit on her bridge's left side that killed one man and wounded several more. Kikkawa steamed between the American ships, made a hard right turn and laid down a smokescreen so no one could see his ship. It was an uneven match against the American cruiser, and Kikkawa knew it. But another more likely target appeared—the *Aaron Ward*. However, the Japanese destroyer had no more torpedoes ready to be loaded in her tubes. With the battle happening at such a high speed, there was not enough time to reload.

Kikkawa saw another "cruiser" at 2:04 a.m. 2,000 meters ahead on his starboard side. The *Yudachi*'s guns spit fire at the ship, now profusely burning. But after fighting all night, the Japanese destroyer had sustained heavy damage by hits from the *Juneau* and *Aaron Ward*. Nevertheless, the ship's gunners kept reloading and firing their guns. The captain turned the ship toward Savo Island to the north, a place where she could seek refuge. More shell fire from the *Aaron Ward* crashed into the forward fire room at 2:10 a.m. and slowed her forward progress. More shells hit the forecastle and set the paint locker uncontrollably afire. Another shell entered the captain's cabin that felled everyone on the bridge. Blood covered the compartment's white walls. The destroyer steamed in a westward circling turn as the fire spread. Her wake showed a random path that had no planned direction. Another shell from the *Sterett* hit her at 2:26 a.m. on the starboard side.

Kikkawa initially thought the attacking ship might be Japanese and turned on his recognition lights, a fatal mistake. The other ship fired at her; the gallant *Yudachi* fought back by returning fire of her own. Shell hits now poured into the doomed Japanese destroyer and exploded on her bridge, fire control director, forward engine room, and No. 3 fire room. Both engineering officers, Lt. Joji Yaeyoshi and Lt. Kiroku Sakai, lost their lives. She was fatally damaged, lost all power, and began slowing in the water.[3]

CHAPTER 40
Picking up the Pieces

The shooting essentially stopped by 2:30 a.m. in the first night of the Naval Battle of Guadalcanal. Thirty minutes earlier, the confusion reached its peak as ships tried to either survive or get their last shot at their nearest adversary. But the brawl wore out guns, crews, and ships to the extent that both sides ran out of targets to shoot at or retreated to lick their wounds. Nonetheless, the overall strategic objective of both sides had not been decided. The extent that situation would be resolved depended on events to take place over the next 36 hours.

The Battleships Move Away

The decision by the *Hiei*'s captain to turn on his searchlight exacted a terrible toll on her. She could still steam well because the under-armed American ships' shells did not have enough power to penetrate deep within the battleship's innards. Her relatively thicker armor plate protected her magazines, engineering spaces, turrets, and conning tower. Nevertheless, she had taken a severe pummeling from American five-inch, six-inch, and eight-inch shells on her superstructure, AA guns, and large parts of her hull. No less than 25 shell hits destroyed her main battery, searchlight controls, and power to the directors. They also inflicted heavy damage on wiring rooms, combat bridge, anti-aircraft command post and platform, radio rooms, and compass bridge.

With the exception of one telephone line between the bridge and the engine room, no other ship communications worked. Enfilades of machine gun fire from the *Cushing*, *Sterett*, *Laffey*, and *San Francisco* killed and wounded dozens of men on the combat bridge. The dead included Cmdr. Suzuki, Abe's chief of staff, the assistant gunnery officer, searchlight control officer, and paymaster. Adm. Abe, Capt. Nishida, the executive officer, Cmdr. Raizo Tamura, and Masataka Chihaya suffered wounds. The bodies of the dead and wounded lay strewn all over the bridge. Their blood covered the floor and was all over the walls.

The painted wood of the combat bridge, insulation, plus anything else that could burn turned the fire into a relentless inferno. Billowing, stinking smoke blinded anyone who tried to stay there. Nonetheless, anyone who could do so abandoned their stations on the bridge as smoke, scorching flames, and potentially fatal fumes poured up from the lower decks. The only means of escape was to tie ropes together through the windows and descend through the fiery gauntlet over the side. Chihaya's blistered hands forced him to wait until nearly the last moment to leave the bridge. As he slid down the ropes, he glanced up to see the fire's power increasing and creating a ready-made aiming point for the Americans.

Like her sister ship, the *Kirishima* finished its battles with the American cruisers and destroyers. She turned northward at 2:30 a.m., but did not suffer extensive damage like the *Hiei*. Only one eight-inch shell had hit her. American machine-gun fire had peppered her bridge and killed seven men. As his ship headed away from Guadalcanal's north shore, Capt. Iwabuchi knew that shelling the American airfields was impossible for this day, and he reported this assessment to his superiors. The battleship had enough ammunition to return to battle the next day since she had only fired 57 14-inch and 313 six-inch shells. Nevertheless, Iwabuchi knew that to bombard the airfields in daylight would be much more difficult since the American aircraft on the island could then attack her with near impunity. Also, targeting of his guns could not be accomplished without light signals from Japanese onshore observation posts.

Other Japanese Ships Steam to the North

More of Abe's task force also steamed northward. The carnage of the night clash had ended with the *Akatsuki* lying on the bottom of Iron Bottom Sound. The *Asagumo* and *Murasame* steamed on a northeasterly course, and the *Samidare* moved to the south to salvage the crippled and damaged *Yudachi*, which steamed erratically south of Savo Island. Also, steaming north along Savo Island's eastern shore were the *Yukikaze, Teruzuki,* and *Harusame*. As the *Inazuma* moved by herself between Florida and Savo Islands, the crippled *Amatsukaze* and *Ikazuchi* meandered northward while trying to catch up with the other Japanese ships.

The *Nagara* had sustained one hit on her forward No. 7 gun mount that killed six men and wounded seven others. She was fully ready to re-engage any American ships if that opportunity should occur. As the executive officer led the damage control parties to return their ship to a fully prepared, battle-ready state, Capt. Shinoda looked for more targets as he ordered his ship to turn westward. Now in command after Abe relinquished it upon being wounded, Adm. Kimura wanted to know why the *Hiei* had not obeyed his order and went to look for the battleship west of Savo Island. Soon he saw the beleaguered former flagship trying to steer a straight course. The *Nagara* accompanied the *Hiei* so it could render any aid the damaged ship might need.

The Americans Lick Their Wounds

Like the Japanese, one American destroyer, the *Barton*, had sunk after blowing up. Three destroyers—the *Cushing*, *Laffey*, and *Monssen*—had been seriously damaged and their crews struggled mightily to keep their ships afloat. The Japanese Long Lance torpedoes more than lived up to their much deserved reputation when they rendered the cruisers *Atlanta*, *Portland*, and *Juneau* incapable of any further surface battle combat. The deceased Adm. Callaghan's flagship, the *San Francisco*, could no longer issue any orders because battle damage had destroyed her communications capability. The *Aaron Ward* suffered the same fate as she limped to the east. The *Helena*, the only remaining combat-ready American cruiser, also headed east since she had no more targets.

The destroyer *Fletcher*, undamaged and still full of fight, looked for targets. She fired five torpedoes at 2:22 a.m. and fired five more one minute later. She reported seeing a glow on the horizon from "a large cruiser or a battleship...her general outline was somewhat comparable to our AUGUSTA class. She could have been a 'KONGO' battleship or a 'MAYA' cruiser."[1] The more likely correct identification of the ship hit by the destroyer's torpedoes was an American cruiser. With no more targets at which to shoot, the destroyer started to head east along with the other American ships.

A minimum of seven ships burned all around the *O'Bannon* as she steamed southeast. Her lookouts spotted the *San Francisco* and *Helena* at 2:15 a.m. After seeing a light coming from Guadalcanal, she changed her course to the south to look for any transports that might be landing Japanese troops. None were there. She moved eastward through the Lengo Channel while staying in the deepest water and to be as safely close to the island's northern shore to avoid running aground. There was still gunfire to the west. The Japanese seemed to be firing at each other. Actually, the gunfire was from American ships firing at other American ships.

The sounds of the shooting faded away, and a welcome silence came over the waters north of Guadalcanal. After the horrifying bedlam of sounds, lights, and fires, the lack of any activity seemed a bizarre turn of events. Only the light from burning ships penetrated the moonless night darkness. Sounds from water-bound survivors' moaning and pleas for help along with the occasional exploding of ammunition or of flames igniting flammable gasses dominated the night. But it was the smell of burning flesh, oil, high explosives, and hot steel that permanently stuck into the survivors' minds.

The *Sterett* also steamed southeast. After dodging what were thought to be torpedoes, two of her boilers stopped working at 3:00 a.m. She could talk to the *Helena* at 3:22 a.m. after repairing her communications system. Her rudder jammed five minutes later, and she almost ran aground. Forced to reduce her speed at times to stem the spreading of the fires that still burned aboard her, she could maintain steam pressure and keep moving.

At five minutes before 3:00 a.m., the *Aaron Ward* was not having an easy time of it when she lost steering control. Her captain had to use his engines to guide the ship away from the battle scene. At 3:05 a.m., she could no longer make forward progress because water streamed into the forward engine room. She managed to begin moving once again, stop, move again, and stop. All power then failed.

After firing her last shots at the *Kirishima*, the *San Francisco* slowed to a forward speed of ten knots to reduce flooding below decks. Fearing that he might have to put the cruiser on the beach, her captain maintained a course near Guadalcanal's north shore. Now in command of the crippled cruiser, Lt. Cmdr. Herbert E. Schonland went to the bridge to survey the condition of the ship he now led. What greeted his senses was a sickening scene of bodies, blood, and debris strewn all over the decks. Big holes in the windscreen caused by the shells that penetrated it made a mockery of its name. Some men administered to the needs of the wounded while others attempted to bring back military discipline. Turning the coding room into a makeshift first aid room, Lt. B. H. Bieri helped tend to the wounded as Lt. Cmdr. James I. Cone and Ens. Tazewell T. Shepard found Capt. Young and carried him to the communications room.

As Schonland came onto the bridge, the *Helena* arrived nearby. Its crew could barely recognize the former flagship. They originally thought she was a Japanese ship and prepared to open fire on her. She sent a blinker light challenge to the heavy cruiser. McCandless tried to use the codes needed to answer it. But battle damage had obliterated the chalk boards on which they were written. There was not sufficient time for McCandless to run to the signal bridge and find the codes. Signalman Victor Gibson tried to yell the correct response at the *Helena*. Finally, the desperate McCandless found a blinker light in time to send a message in plain English:

> C 50 V C 38 [*Helena* from *San Francisco*] BT ADMIRAL CALLAGHAN AND CAPTAIN YOUNG KILLED X SHIP BADLY DAMAGED X TAKE CHARGE.[2]

Now, the *San Francisco*'s crew believed the *Helena* was the only ship left and had to take command and get all ships and men to a safe haven. With both Admirals Callaghan and Scott and Capt. Young dead, the *Portland*'s Capt. DuBose was the most senior commander alive. However, DuBose's ship sustained too much damage to exercise command and therefore refused to take control. He wished to focus all his energies on bringing his crippled ship home. By default, the *Helena*'s Capt. Hoover assumed command and asked all ships:

> "ANY SHIP FROM HELENA: CAN YOU HEAR ME?"[3]

After hearing from as many ships as could receive his TBS transmission, he asked at 2:26 a.m. for all ships to rendezvous with his ship and proceed to Espiritu Santo. Nine minutes later, Hoover asked all ships to turn on their recognition lights. Meanwhile, he received the following more detailed report from the *San Francisco* that only confirmed his worst fears:

> "ADMIRAL AND ALL OF STAFF EXCEPT ONE KILLED. CAPTAIN SERIOUSLY WOUNDED HUNDREDS OF CASUALTIES. CAN USE TWO TURRETS SIX FIVE INCH AND MAKE TWENTY EIGHT KNOTS. STEERING FROM CONN. URGENTLY NEED ALL MEDICAL ASSISTANCE YOU CAN SPARE"[4]

All the American ships formed a ragtag formation and steamed to the southeast and safety. The *O'Bannon* and *Fletcher* finally joined the formation after responding to Hoover's inquiries over the TBS.

The first part of the Naval Battle of Guadalcanal was over. More problems faced the ships that fought that night. Nothing had been decided, and more carnage would follow.[5]

CHAPTER 41
Some Fateful Decisions to Make

Both the Americans and Japanese had ships that were in severe jeopardy of not returning to their home bases. These vessels had taken a terrible beating and had trouble making any headway at all. Power systems that supplied propulsion to their propellers had been alternately failing and restoring operations. Deadly fires covered their decks and spaces below. All these ships had hundreds of wounded and dead men. The damage control parties strenuously and hopefully labored to keep their ships afloat long enough to get them to a repair base. The following stories are synopses of these travails.

The Plight of Three American Destroyers

After its running battle with Adm. Takama's destroyers, the *Monssen* was in deep trouble. Her sole remaining whaleboat had been blasted into pieces, and four of her life rafts in the forward section of the ship had been blown away. The survival of many of her crew was in severe jeopardy if she should sink. Casualties increased after shells hit both dressing stations. Mount 4 and the No. 4 five-inch gun could no longer operate. Fires burned fiercely all over the ship. The devastating fires that covered the superstructure made it impossible to recover classified documents. Lt. Cmdr. McCombs had no choice but order his crew to abandon the ship.

Shell hits set the 20-mm ammunition afire. The blaze was so hot that it knocked out all ship communications and made the bridge uninhabitable. Lt. Cmdr. James L. Kemper, the executive officer, and QM1c Edward A. Dawson climbed down the bridge's aft ladder but its lower section was destroyed by a shell hit. Dawson fell to the deck below with Kemper landing on him. Another shell hit near them and killed Kemper who protected Dawson from certain death. The fires spread so much that the men still alive on the bridge had no other way to escape other than jumping to the deck below. Ens. Robert W. Lassen and another man, R. W. Kittredge, chose to jump into the water. Lassen made it safely but Kittredge hit a life boat davit and died.

McCombs surveyed his now hapless command and tugged at his binoculars to get them off before jumping overboard. After jumping over the port side, the impact of hitting the water broke both his shoulders. He still managed to jettison his .45-cal. pistol and tie himself to a piece of floating balsa wood.

The men in the aft magazines heard the "Abandon Ship" order but their ship was now dark and debris blocked the escape hatch. They moved to the ship's stern and got on deck near the No. 4

mount. Another shell exploded and killed a group of men trying to cut some life rafts free on the port side aft. Not far from that action, SM3c John A. Pease and several other men tried to free some starboard life rafts and floater nets.

✲ ✲ ✲

The *Laffey*'s power was gone and her ability to fight along with it. She was just three miles north of the *Monssen*. Her gun crews moved aft with an order to help stop the fires raging there. With the loss of power, no water flowed from the nearby hose spigot so they formed a bucket brigade to bring water to the fires. The damage control party managed to put the fire out in Mount 4 using ammunition cans, wet mattresses and life jackets. Their small gasoline-powered pump did not have pumping power to make any progress putting out the aft fires, which could set fire to and blow up the aft powder magazines. Lt. E. W. Bergman, the ship's first lieutenant, ordered their flooding and of the No. 4 ammunition handling room as well.

With the stern's deck buckled six feet upward above the aft-most gun mount, the damage control parties had a difficult time trying to get to the fires. With all communication to the bridge gone, a messenger brought a message to the executive officer, Lt. Cmdr. William T. Doyle, to take control aft and change the ship's course northward. He sent the messenger back to the bridge to report the serious damage to the ship stern. When the fires' intensity lessened, Doyle went to the bridge to meet with Cmdr. Hank.

Both men agreed to destroy all the ship's documents and wait for daylight. The good news about the stern fire vanished as it flared up again. Doyle reluctantly concluded they could never control it. Hank had no choice but to order, "Abandon ship."

After hearing the order to leave the destroyer, men began coming up from the lower spaces to join their topside shipmates on the main deck. Like they were performing a practice drill, they maintained discipline and went over the side—some into life rafts, some into whaleboats and others into the water—all awaiting rescue from some friendly ship that might come by.

The *Laffey*'s OOD and communications officer, Lt. A. H. Damon, risked his safety when he went to his room below decks to retrieve several thousand dollars of the crew pay. Supervising the movement of the wounded to the main deck, Lt. (jg) Aaron S. Michelson, the medical officer, checked the dressing station to make sure not one wounded man remained below decks. Meanwhile, three life rafts were in flames and, despite damage to the port side whaleboat, two other whaleboats were in the water. Hank and Doyle moved to the port side to get ready to leave the ship. Doyle helped release a jammed life raft into the water as Hank went forward. He walked past Ens. David S. Sterrett in the forecastle as the junior officer threw mattresses into the water to be used in the life rafts. While recovering the ship's commissioning pennant and putting the ship's mascot dog, "Chafing Gear," into the nearest whaleboat, the after powder magazine unexpectedly vanished in a tremendous blast along with Hank, Michelson, and several of the wounded still onboard.

As he stood in a whaleboat, the huge explosion knocked Doyle into the water. He finally rose to the water's surface and felt a searing pain from a severe wound. Nevertheless, he managed to organize a rescue effort to search for any survivors of the ship's last agony. The explosion's concussion drove many of the men already in the water underwater. Flaming debris rained all over them as they surfaced.

Rolling over on her starboard side, the *Laffey*'s stern rapidly sank, and she disappeared in a roiling bubble of water. The ship's cook, Tommie M. Campbell, happened to be looking at his watch and noticed the time was 2:20 a.m. as he saw his ship's life end.

Just two miles southwest of the doomed *Laffey*, the *Cushing* could no longer move. She had taken on all Japanese ships that came within the range of her guns and torpedoes and gave as good as she received. But the Japanese ships she fought had too much firepower for her. Her struggles disabled all her five-inch guns and emptied her starboard torpedo tubes. She kept firing her 20-mm guns but they proved to be grossly mismatched against the five-inch and six-inch shells that continued bashing her into a flaming wreck.

Her captain, Lt. Cmdr. Parker, observed that his ship could no longer fight back and realized his command was finished when he ordered, "Abandon Ship" between 2:30 a.m. and 2:45 a.m. He saw the ship's doctor, Lt. (jg) James E. Cashman, after leaving the bridge. The ship's doctor had seen enough butchery to last a lifetime as he tried to attend to the wounded and dying in the wardroom. Cashman wanted help to fight the fires now engulfing the ship, but Parker convinced Cashman how bleak the situation was and told Cashman he had ordered the ship to be abandoned.

The crew placed just four life rafts over her side—the rest of the life rafts and both her whaleboats had been demolished in her battle against the Japanese. There was only enough room for the wounded in the life rafts; the rest of the survivors had to fend for themselves in the water. But the destroyer's fighting spirit was still alive as the Mount 4 gun captain continued to manually fire his gun. Parker thought he could still try to salvage his ship. Nonetheless, a blazing hot fire now covered the bridge; any further attempt to save the ship was doomed to fail. But that did not mean that Parker had not personally given up hope.

EM1c E. W. Johnson helped launch the port side whaleboat, now shot full of holes, and it sank as soon as it dropped in the water. He met Parker and Stokes, who saw a ship just 600 yards away and ordered Johnson to use the *Cushing*'s battle lantern to signal it. The answer was a barrage of heavy shells.

Johnson returned to the ship from a life raft and heard voices in an area aft of the port torpedo tubes. He put some of the wounded men he found there into a life raft and again left the ship. He saw that Parker was still aboard the destroyer and once more returned to the ship. Parker and he made sure the depth charges were on a safe setting and then went their own way to look for more wounded men. Johnson's quest to rescue any more men proved fruitless after he found a dying man trapped under the port torpedo tubes and the dead engineering officer. He rejoined Parker, told the captain that an auxiliary diesel engine was still working and wanted to know if he should try restarting the pumps. Parker now had some confidence that if he could stay on board until daylight, he could flag down a friendly ship to get help. But the 20-mm ammunition began to explode, and all those blasts and the resulting fires dashed his hopes. So he reluctantly concluded that now was the time to leave the ship.

Cashman continued to administer to the wounded and look for any more casualties. He found a wounded mess attendant, treated his wounds, and convinced him to leave the ship. Cashman soon followed the man overboard. Stokes followed by executive officer Lt. Cmdr. Bernard W. Freund went overboard. Parker and Johnson were the last to leave at 3:15 a.m. for the final time and stayed afloat in the water with the aid of empty five-inch powder cans.

The men in the water now saw their flaming former home drift aimlessly away. Explosions from five-inch and 20-mm ammunition continued. Bright white flashes from the blasts combined with burning oil on the water's surface added more light to the scene. Part of her crew believed their ship had absorbed no less than 20 hits; an estimated six officers and 53 men had died with her.

The Ordeal of Survival

For the survivors of the American ships forced to abandon their ships, many of them had whale boats and life rafts to help them to stay alive. Others swam with their life jackets on and clung to any wreckage still afloat. The *Barton*'s survivors had no life rafts. All of those means to stay alive had vanished when the ship sank after a ruinous blast. Some of the crew hung onto an ammunition case. Others gathered around Lt. Quint as he found more men than he thought he would after the ship went down.

They floated in warm water in a sticky, stinking oil slick several inches thick that marked a place where a ship had sunk. Not much time passed when the oil covered the floating men in a slime that burned their eyes, throats, and noses. Many men threw up after swallowing the vile goo. Commanded by Lt. Eugene A. Barham, the *Laffey*'s surviving engineering officer, a whaleboat from that ship came to rescue any survivors that could be found and kept looking for Cmdr. Hank. Preference was given to the wounded to be taken out of the water. When the *Laffey*'s other damaged whaleboats came into view, Barham threw it a line and began to tow it. He did the same for any life rafts found with living men on them. As the swimmers tired, they traded places with healthy men in the rafts.

Many men in the water thought they saw rescue ships on the horizon. Others in the boats and on the life rafts did not know if these ships were American or Japanese. The *Monssen*'s survivors saw a ship in the distance. As the vessel drew near, they heard an unfamiliar language being spoken and, to their horror, realized that tongue was Japanese. The Americans did not want to head for Guadalcanal and risk being captured since they knew that the Japanese occupied much of the island.

Japanese Stories of Survival

Lt. Michiharu Shinya barely escaped the *Akatsuki*'s bridge before she rolled over on her port side and sank by the stern. He had no choice but to enter the water since there were no rafts or boats nearby into which he could climb. The warm water surrounded him in a false blanket of security when the ocean beneath him erupted and pulled him under the surface. He had to swallow some water because his lungs ached, and he finally surfaced. He reasoned that the sinking destroyer's depth charges had exploded underneath him. Someone obviously did not set their fuses to a safe setting before the destroyer went down. He finally found some wreckage to cling to and paddled toward an area where he heard voices. Finding about 30 to 40 survivors, he led them in swimming to Guadalcanal, where he felt confident Japanese soldiers would eventually find them. But his plan soon went awry.

The sun appeared as his ragtag group drew near Lunga Point. Some American landing craft appeared suddenly quite close to his group so that he could see faces of the men in the boats. Not wanting to be captured, he left the group to their own fates and swam away from them. He then saw what seemed to be an American cruiser that was shooting at some target. A worn American flag flew from her damaged stern. With his worse fears about to become true, he swam away from the ship.

Now dead in the water, the *Yudachi* waited for help from other Japanese ships. The destroyer's division commander, Capt. Masao Tachibana, ordered the *Samidare* at 3:10 a.m. to help the hapless destroyer. Tachibana's flagship, the *Murasame*, and the *Asagumo* were already nearby as Adm. Kimura ordered them at 3:35 a.m. to join the *Kirishima* at maximum speed. A torpedo hit in the *Murasame*'s bow and restricted her speed to 27 knots. Both destroyers put a boat overboard until the *Samidare* arrived or until the *Yudachi*'s crew could navigate the five kilometers to Cape Esperance and beach her there.

Meanwhile, the doomed destroyer's engineers that were still alive tried mightily to restore power so it could move. But their effort proved fruitless. The *Samidare* arrived 17 minutes after she received Tachibana's order. Her captain, Cmdr. Noboru Nakamura, saw a hulk beyond any help. He gingerly navigated his ship to come along the crippled ship's starboard side to rescue anyone aboard her. The *Yudachi*'s dire predicament forced Kikkawa to reject the idea of her being towed and ordered his crew to leave her. He met Nakamura on *Samidare*'s bridge and asked that his ship be scuttled. Nakamura agreed with Kikkawa and ordered his ship to move away from the dead destroyer. As soon as she was at a safe distance, Nakamura fired two torpedoes at the crippled ship but they ran too deep and passed under the *Yudachi*'s keel. He then fired his five-inch guns and fired another torpedo at her. Convinced he had done all he could to sink the destroyer, he noticed that dawn was about make its appearance. Not wanting to get caught alone in the narrow waters near Guadalcanal by American aircraft or an American ship, he ordered his destroyer to immediately steam northward and join the rest of the fleeing Japanese ships.

When Adm. Takama wrote his action report later that day, he acknowledged the gallant *Yudachi* with the following praise:

> "*Yudachi* had a great influence on the battle...first, putting the enemy into confusion and then afterward...battling boldly...The crew, beginning with the captain...fully used their... fighting power...and their merit is outstanding."[1]

But the stubborn destroyer did not yet sink. She burned so furiously that she attracted the attention of the cruiser *Portland*, which also had considerable battle damage to be worried about. Nonetheless, she still had enough power to finish off the *Yudachi*. The cruiser did not have enough maneuvering capability to be in full combat, but she was more than a match for the burning wreck. The only course the helpless cruiser could manage was to steam in a circle. So she fired six salvoes because her main director could not get a good firing solution. The first five fusillades straddled the destroyer but the sixth one found home. One shell hit the *Yudachi*'s aft magazine and wreaked revenge for its sinking of the destroyer-transports *Little* and *Gregory* off Guadalcanal in September. The *Yudachi* disappeared in a fiery, thunderous explosion.

But other crippled ships would have troubles of their own.[2]

CHAPTER 42
Bringing Back the Cripples

The Hiei

After the shooting stopped, the men's senses on the battleship's bridge picked up the sickening smell of blood and dead bodies. Since the deafening noises of the battle ended, the *Hiei's* damage control parties managed to extinguish the fires that once raged on her superstructure. Adm. Abe went below to have the ship's doctor attend to his wounds followed by Capt. Nishida because his leg wounds forced him to hobble around the main deck. When both men returned to the bridge, they surveyed the water around them and saw many fires from burning ships with parts of the sky blocked by smoke.

The battleship had not followed its fellow ships to the north and now steamed along Savo Island's western shoreline. Her steering gear did not act normally. An eight-inch shell had pierced her hull on the starboard side below her water line and jammed the rudder. While it luckily did not explode, the hole it opened caused water to enter the steering engine room. Sea water shorted out the steering engine and forced the crew to try guiding the behemoth with just their sheer muscle.

The water level rose high enough to force the men in the compartment to stand on their toes and to avoid drowning. The man in command, Petty Officer Minoru Kurabawa, had to order the compartment abandoned and then wait for the damage control parties to stem the flooding. When that happened, the crew and he could return there to resume their efforts to restore steering power. But the escape ladder was two compartments away on the middle deck. Their escape had to begin immediately before the rising water blocked their way. After managing to open the door to the middle deck, water rushed into the room. The men swam to the ladder, escaped to safety, and waited for orders to return.

Capt. Nishida began receiving damage reports from all over the ship. The news was mixed. The ship's gunnery officer, Cmdr. Kiyoshi Takeya, reported that the main battery control had taken two hits and was no longer working. Shells had blasted all four 14-inch turrets; nonetheless, all the guns could still be fired. The six-inch guns had been more seriously damaged with all directors disabled and a fire blazing in the ammunition compartments. The five-inch AA guns had taken shell hits, too. Mounts 1, 2, and 3 had been hit, and fires also raged in the Mounts 1 and 3 ammunition compartments. The 25-mm guns and crews also were hit with many of the men wounded or dead.

There were six holes near her waterline that caused flooding in several compartments and the ship to list to starboard. Power had been cut to many pumps which made it even harder to correct the list. All radio communications no longer worked as at least 24 fires burned over her superstructure. About 100 shells had smacked into her. Fortunately, many of them never exploded.

Despite all the damage inflicted on the battleship, there was no danger she would sink. Her thick armor had protected her from the ineffective American smaller caliber shells. She was still a formidable force that befitted her with the designation "battleship." Her propulsion systems still worked satisfactorily, but Nishida ordered her to slow so his crew could control the flooding. She moved northward at 5:00 a.m. at a dead slow speed when the destroyer *Amatsukaze* saw her.

The Portland

When the first reports of the battle reached Nouméa, the news was not good. The cruiser *Portland* requested a tow from Halsey at 2:31 a.m. because of damage to the steering gear and flooding caused by torpedo hits.

An explosion jammed her third eight-inch turret so that the turret could no longer turn or elevate its three guns. A huge hole in her side stretched from her main deck to the waterline. A huge section of the main deck had collapsed onto the second deck. Another blast had destroyed the second deck aft dressing station and killed all in that space. Damage control parties made progress stemming the flooding as they managed to isolate the flooded compartments and reinforce failing bulkheads. Another explosion knocked out the throttles for the No. 2 and 3 engines and disabled both of them.

Turret III's commander, Lt. William Walker, secured his disabled station and ordered his men to abandon it to help Lt. Lawrence K. Griffin's damage control parties. Another man helped others place loose eight-inch shells rolling around into a safe place and throw dangerous powder cartridges overboard.

As others attended to the wounded, the ship's inclinometer showed a 4º starboard list. However, the hard working damage control parties corrected this malady by either pumping water into the sea or counter-flooding selected compartments. Twenty-three spaces were now either hopelessly damaged or full of sea water. Timber braces and loose mattresses buttressed bulging bulkheads and stopped further flooding. About a half hour after the torpedo hit to cause her to list, she was back on an even keel.

The Atlanta

A desperate message from the *Atlanta* arrived at Nouméa at 3:01 a.m. that told of a ship in trouble: "Help needed." One Long Lance torpedo hit and blasts from almost 50 shells had turned the once "tiger of the sea" into a mangled wreck. Listing to port and bow down in the water, the cruiser's damage control parties struggled to keep her afloat. Slippery decks covered with oil, dense acrid smoke, and impenetrable darkness did not make their job any easier. All communications ceased when all the sound-powered telephones no longer worked. False orders to abandon the ship confused crew members and some of them actually did leave the ship. They got into eight life boats, drifted slowly away into the darkness, but were afraid to reach land at the risk of being captured by the Japanese while not realizing the *Atlanta* had not sunk.

As she drifted aimlessly to the southeast, the crew still aboard her also saw the distant funeral pyres from burning ships. Some of them continued to be convulsively wracked by explosions. Capt. Jenkins saw one destroyer pass his stern, fire its guns, and hit his cruiser's crow's nest. The wounded continued to move as best they could to the dressing stations to get some relief from their dire straits. Volunteers flocked in to help the overworked and overtired Pharmacist Mates. Some of them worked for more than ten straight hours with no rest or respite.

The *Atlanta* had absorbed in excess of 12 hits from 14-inch shells with ruinous effects. The cruiser's superstructure was a mass of tangled and twisted metal, dangling wires and cables, and blood-soaked decks. Exploding 1.1-inch ammunition prevented any rescue of trapped personnel or any hope of extinguishing fires either fore or aft. Despite lacking power to pump water, a bucket brigade controlled one of the worst fires.

Order at last began to be restored as the damage control parties brought some of the most serious problems under control. Lt. Cmdr. W. R. D. Nickelson, the gunnery officer, came onto the main deck and asked for help to jettison the port anchor. He wanted to shed weight on the port side to reduce her list. His hastily assembled work detail released the anchor into the water. He also arranged to empty the port side torpedo tubes by firing the missiles already in them. After setting all but three depth charges on safe, he and his work party deposited them overboard, detached the damaged whale boat and its davits, threw all the five-inch ammunition from the two rear mounts, and all deck gear that was not attached to anything into the water. All that could be done to reduce the weight on the cruiser's port side had been done. The collapsed foremast lay on the deck but could not be jettisoned because it was still attached to the ship.

After helping out with Nickelson's impromptu work party, EM3c William B. McKinney saw that the spreading flames and heat from the blazes inundating the superstructure could cause the forward magazines to explode and sink the ship. His assigned general quarters station, nicknamed "The Ritz," was directly above the magazines and forward of the engineering stations. He quickly decided that if the Ritz's fire-fighting water spigot line were used to flood the space below, an insulating "wall" would be placed between the fires and the magazines. He proposed the idea to Nicholson who bucked the request to Cmdr. Emory, the ship's executive officer. After warning McKinney the flooding could capsize the ship, he approved the idea.

McKinney returned to the Ritz and noticed with some relief the angle by which a lantern hung on the wall. The ship's list was not any worse. He had to allow three feet of water to accumulate to evenly distribute the water's weight between the magazine's port and starboard side. He opened the fire main's valve and waited until the water's depth was three feet. When it did, he closed the valve and climbed the ladder nearest to the main deck to see if any more work needed to be done. The ship had been saved, at least for the moment.

The next problem the crew had to solve was restoring engine power so the ship could move. A torpedo explosion had destroyed the forward engine room, totally filling it with water, and killing all the men there. Water also flooded the forward fireroom, but its crew managed to escape. Three feet of water covered the forward engine room and fireroom spaces, making these rooms totally inaccessible and inoperable.

The ship's only chance to restore power was to restart the engines from the aft engine room and fireroom. The flooding of the aft engine room was under control. A distinct possibility existed the same could be accomplished for the aft fireroom, but that idea proved to be impossible because as soon, as the men lifted the latches on the fireroom's hatch cover, water gushed in, indicating the fireroom had water up to its ceiling.

Another problem the men on the *Atlanta* faced was that none of the communications inside the ship worked. Repair crews worked desperately to string new wires to get the telephone working again. The crew almost panicked when they saw a large ship approaching. After some men rushed to fire its lone set of torpedo tubes, Lt. Cmdr. Lloyd T. Mustin nipped the danger in the bud by reporting the approaching ship was the *Portland*.

The San Francisco

Unlike the *Atlanta*, the *San Francisco*'s damage was from gunfire and not from torpedoes. Her hull had no holes below the water line. Two shells had hit her below the armor belt that caused some leakage from the sea. The major cause for concern was the 25 fires that fiercely burned in the superstructure, hangar, and the crew sleeping quarters. Water flooding into several deck spaces and the inadvertent flooding of a five-inch magazine raised concerns about the ship's stability. A shell had damaged the engine room blowers that dangerously raised the compartment's temperature. The crew had to take frequent breaks and the steam pressure dropped. Not one place aboard the ship had escaped battle damage.

Lt. Cmdr. Schonland was now the most senior officer alive and therefore in command. His sole goal was to keep his ship afloat and get her back to a repair yard by all possible means. He delegated responsibility for maneuvering the ship to Lt. Cmdr. McCandless, who was on the bridge, while he directed efforts below decks to fight the flooding and fires. When heat and poor ventilation made further occupation of the Central Station impossible, Schonland moved one deck up to the Marine sleeping compartment.

One major problem was the rising water in Turret II's magazine that caused an electrical short in the room's flood control panel. The sprinkling system automatically began to spray water into the magazine and ammunition handling room. Some men managed to wade through the flood and turn the sprinkler valves off so the pumps could lower the water level.

Water rose in the sick bay where Dr. Edward S. Lowe treated the wounded. After Schonland moved to his latest place, he commanded that all men leave the sick bay until the pumps could empty water from the room. Lowe moved the sick bay two decks up to the admiral's cabin. Continued flooding on lower decks caused worries the ship was sinking, but Schonland reassured everyone that the ship was not going to sink.

Meanwhile, BM1c Reinhard J. Keppler waged a one-man battle aft against the fire burning in the hangar. He had already commanded the rescue of Battle II's wounded men after the plane crashed there. Already fatally wounded, he fought the fire, ordered where any arriving help could provide assistance, and aided the wounded to leave the area. He then collapsed and died from his injuries. For his bravery under such extreme conditions, he would later be posthumously awarded the Congressional Medal of Honor.

After the shooting stopped, the *San Francisco*'s dangerous predicament was not over. Water washed around the second deck that also caused the ship to be unstable and increased difficulties of maneuvering the ship. When the ship made a sharp right turn to avoid running aground on Malaita Island, it heeled over at a 45° angle. The damage control parties continued stopping the leaks from holes in the ship's hull. A bucket brigade worked tirelessly as well. After spending many hours in the stifling heat below, the "Black Gang" at last could come up on the main deck and take welcoming breaths fresh sea air.

The *Helena*'s Capt. Hoover wanted to increase the speed of his fleet of cripples to 20 knots. Ens. Ray Casten asked for and received permission to set the speed to 15 knots so he could get an accurate radar fix. Meanwhile the *O'Bannon* detected the crippled *Juneau* on her radar and later sighted her when daylight dawned.

Three American cruisers—the *San Francisco*, *Helena*, and *Juneau*—and three destroyers—the *Fletcher*, *O'Bannon*, and *Sterett*—steamed to the southeast. The *San Francisco*'s dead included 14 officers and 69 men with 106 seriously wounded. Because of flooding in its magazines, Turret II could no longer operate. Turret I lost electrical power soon after the ship sent the previous message. Most of the men aboard did not know how serious the damage was to their ship until they saw the masses of mangled steel in daylight.[1]

CHAPTER 43
Surveying the Carnage

All battles have one thing in common: they all end. But they leave behind ample evidence of their passage. First, there is the damage from the battle itself: debris, fires, smoke, and holes in the ground caused by the massive explosions of shells. Second, there are the bodies of those who have fallen. Third, there are the smells of the decaying bodies, body parts, and smoke. Fourth, the surviving wounded men litter the field, all pleading for help and relief from their suffering.

A land battle has all of these. Nevertheless, a sea battle's aftermath is different. The sea shows no permanent evidence the conflict ever took place. The water assumes its normal appearance soon after the explosions stop with no permanent holes on its surface. But, although most of the debris has sunk, some of it remains and litters the surface along with the pungent, sticky, and multicolored floating oil slicks. Broken pieces of wood from whale boats, furniture from sunken ships, life rings, life jackets, and smoke can be found all over the scene. And then there are the survivors in boats, on life rafts, and floating in the water who wait for any ship to come near and retrieve them from an almost certain watery demise.

The waters north of Guadalcanal had all these pieces of evidence that a great sea battle had indeed occurred. Added to what one would expect to find on the water's surface, eight ships in various degrees of disrepair still were afloat: three Japanese (the battleship *Hiei* and the destroyers *Yudachi*

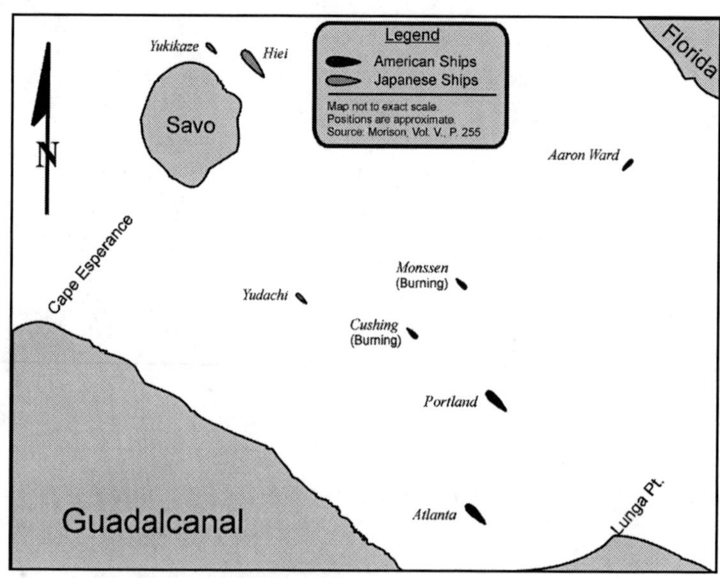

Damaged Ships Left off Guadalcanal after the First Day

and *Yukikaze*) and five American (the cruisers *Atlanta* and *Portland* and the destroyers *Aaron Ward*, *Monssen*, and *Cushing*).

The Fate of the Remaining Japanese Warships

After the *Portland* pummeled her to oblivion, the destroyer *Yudachi* blew up in a fireball and sank beneath the water's surface. With the Rising Sun flag and his own flag still flying from the *Hiei*'s mainmast, Abe surveyed the condition of his flagship and found she could not be steered. The undamaged destroyer *Yukikaze* stood by to render any assistance the crippled battleship might need.

The destroyer *Akatsuki* had sunk early in the battle and left several survivors to stay alive any way they could. Her former torpedo officer, Lt. Shinya, still tried to swim to Guadalcanal. But his oil-coated body with his eyes stinging from oil and salt water impaired his progress. After swallowing too much sea water and the oil that had become part of it, he became weak from diarrhea. He tried to close his eyes to keep them from hurting, but a ringing in his ears from a night of too many explosions made that relief more difficult to realize. With the sun rising, the air temperature rose with it and further added to his suffering. Nevertheless, his determination to avoid being captured had not diminished. However, American ships had already plucked several of his shipmates from the water. After overcoming the fear of being strafed by two nearby float planes, he heard a motor boat's engine approaching and reversing its forward motion. Two American sailors asked him if he wanted to be pulled aboard. Summoning all the strength he had, he answered in English, "No, thanks!" and struggled to swim away. Several hands reached down toward him and pulled him inside the boat. Finally, his exhaustion got the best of him, and he collapsed into a sleep brought on by sheer fatigue.

After the boat stopped next to a ship that Shinya recognized as the new antiaircraft cruiser *Atlanta*, the boat began moving again. He and 20-25 of his fellow *Akatsuki* survivors soon stood on the beach east of Lunga Point. A truck picked them up and drove them to a compound under the coconuts. They were prisoners of war and would remain so for the next three years.

More Serious Problems for the Americans

The *Portland*'s crew, buoyant from their triumph over the hapless *Yudachi*, had to return the main task at hand and save their ship. They had some success after rescuing two trapped men from the aft gyro compass room. But there were men still in the water, and Capt. DuBose put a whaleboat over the side to retrieve the struggling survivors from certain death.

The craft came back with enough men to fill two life rafts, all covered with an obnoxious film of fuel oil and many of them wounded. The ship rescued 38 men in all with 34 of them coming from the sunken *Barton*, three from the *Sterett*, and one from the crippled *Cushing*. When DuBose saw that Higgins boats had come out from Guadalcanal to continue pulling men from the water and received reports of Japanese aircraft, he ordered his whaleboat to be brought aboard.

By 7:00 a.m., DuBose gave up trying to steer his cruiser and asked for a tow from Capt. William G. Greenman, who commanded all naval activities in the Guadalcanal area. Later that day, the towboat *Bobolink* appeared and performed a heroic effort towing the crippled cruiser to Tulagi. In the meantime, daylight revealed to the ship's crew the mangled mass that was once the cruiser's stern. DuBose ordered a review of the ship's muster list. The battle had killed nine men, including the junior medical officer, Lt. Robert H. Williams, with nine others missing in battle.

✲ ✲ ✲

Just four miles from where the *Yudachi* sank, fires covered the destroyer *Cushing*. But at 5:00 p.m. on November 14, the flames got to her magazines, and she disappeared beneath the waves in a violent explosion. Many of her 56 wounded survivors died of their injuries.

The *Portland*'s crew continued to see men in the water, but, by this time, the sharks began attacking the struggling survivors. The cruiser's men tried to also rescue Japanese survivors but were rebuffed. The *Monssen*'s Jack Pease saw the predators take their toll, but some of the men frightened them away by shouting and making load splashing noises. A bleeding Cecil Howard saw a shark attack one of his shipmates. He used his knife to stab at the beast and forced it to abandon its intended meal. After spending all night in the water and trying to attend to his many wounds, a Higgins boat arrived after dawn and ended his struggle to survive by plucking him from his potentially watery grave. Fireman Clifford L. Bickel somehow managed to avoid the shark attack, but received a jellyfish sting. He drifted away from his comrades. Only one of those survived in the water.

The *Monssen* burned so fiercely that her crew abandoned her at 2:20 a.m. between Savo Island and Lunga Point. After sunrise, her crew noticed the ferocity of the sharks' attacks and chose to share the crippled destroyer with the fire, which was preferable to being eaten alive. BM2c C. C. Storey, GM2c Leo F. Sturgeon, and F1c Joseph Hughes heard Howard's thrashing battle with a shark and swam to the burning hulk a quarter-of-a-mile away. They climbed aboard by using her propeller guard. Once onboard, they heard the cries of eight wounded men and administered the best first-aid they could. Storey saw a Higgins boat nearby and sent a signal for it to come alongside and get the men off the doomed destroyer. The boat's crew took the survivors off her. Five of the eight men Storey and his compatriots found survived. The *Monssen* blew up and sank at noon that day.

✲ ✲ ✲

The PT base on Tulagi heard radioed pleas for help from the *Portland* and *Aaron Ward* at dawn. Some former tuna fishing boats near Mocambo Island, known as YPs [Yippies] by the Navy, answered the call at 5:40 a.m. and ventured out to help any damaged ships and rescue any men in the water they could find.

Meanwhile, the tugboat *Seminole*'s skipper, Lt. William Fewell, gathered his Higgins boat crews, told them to get their rifles and canteens, and prepare for a busy day of rescue. The boats began firing up their motors and moved out into the waters north of Lunga Point. By now Seaman 2nd Class Donald G. Collver was an expert in rescuing sailors from the sea since surviving the sinking of his ship, the cruiser *Astoria*, after the Battle of Savo Island in August. He then became part of the transport

President Jackson's boat pool. He headed his boat toward the nearest crippled ship, likely the *Cushing*, and, as he got within 500 yards of the stricken ship, he noticed water covering her main deck and her superstructure shot full of holes. Seeing no one alive, he turned his boat toward the next damaged American ship.

His boat drew near the devastated *Atlanta*, and the image of her fully decimated five-inch turrets shocked him. After Collver identified himself and his men as Americans coming to the cruiser crew's rescue, a Jacob's ladder dropped over the cruiser's side. Capt. Jenkins appeared and gave a status report of his command's condition. He asked for more boats and said he wanted Collver's boat to take off some of his ship's wounded. He told Jenkins that the *Atlanta* was in range of Japanese guns ashore as he left the cruiser and promised he would come back.

When he returned to the base on Guadalcanal, he briefed Fewel about the *Atlanta*'s condition. After eating, he boarded his boat. Several larger-capacity tank lighters joined him as they headed back to the cruiser. As the boats' wakes trailed behind them, their crews saw several aircraft on the northern horizon attacking the *Hiei*.

The surviving ships, boats, and their crews pulled approximately 800 men from the water. About 250 of them were seriously wounded, with some of those injuries proving to be fatal. The rescuers saw how bad a beating the American ships had taken by observing the seriousness of the wounds on the survivors and the extensive battle damage to the ships.

Halsey kept receiving updates from Guadalcanal, including the following message:

> "TEN MILES NORTH SAVO ISLAND FIVE ENEMY DDS ATTEMPTING ASSIST KONGO-CLASS BB WHICH HAS BEEN HIT BY SEVEN TORPEDOES AND ONE THOUSAND LB BOMB X AFTER PART OF SHIP BURNING FIERCELY X SHIP BELIEVED HOSTILE DD BEACHED AND SMOKING NORTH COAST OLEVUGA ISLAND X LARGE VESSEL BURNING INDISPENSABLE STRAIT X USS CUSHING BURNING FIVE MILES SE SAVO ISLAND AND USS MONSSEN DEAD IN WATER BOTH ABANDONED X SEVEN HUNDRED SURVIVORS PICKED UP TWENTY FIVE PERCENT OF THESE WOUNDED."[1]

But the news only got worse.

✲ ✲ ✲

Capt. Hoover commanded a ragtag group of ships whose condition ranged from fully operational to just barely getting by. Nonetheless, there was malicious opposition lurking beneath the surface.

Cmdr. Minoru Yokota stared through the *I-26*'s periscope and saw what every submariner sought, a crippled warship limping along at a snail's pace. His submarine had been following the escaping American fleet as it headed to the southeast through Indispensable Strait. His underwater microphone picked up the sounds of many ships at 10:30 a.m. on the 13th and its sonar detected a massive explosion. The ship he saw was the *San Francisco*, which was an ideal target for a slow-moving submerged submarine. The *I-26*'s forward torpedo tubes all had ready-to-fire missiles in them. He lined up the cruiser in the periscope's cross-hairs and got his submarine into a position from which he could fire his torpedoes. The submarine's No. 1 and No. 4 tubes hissed bursts of compressed air and sent deadly torpedoes on their way. Yokota took his boat down to a depth of 230 feet.

The *San Francisco*'s lookouts alerted the bridge that they saw two torpedo wakes heading straight for their ship. The cruiser turned to starboard and evaded the oncoming "fish" that passed quite close to the ship's port bow. She could not warn any other ship because of disabled communications. One of the torpedoes headed straight for the *Juneau*.

The now doomed cruiser could not escape its fate since its lookouts did not see the torpedoes coming in time for the bridge to steer away from the impending danger. The missile struck the *Juneau* beneath her bridge and exploded. The *San Francisco*'s bridge crew had run to the starboard wing just in time to see the *Juneau*'s life end. A huge, roaring, and fiery blast lifted the cruiser's bridge into the air and engulfed the ship in a monstrous cloud of smoke. Debris flew into the air. When the smoke cleared there was nothing. She had just disappeared as if she had never existed.

Hoover (on the *Helena*) contacted a B-17 requesting help from Nouméa. It reached Halsey or someone assigned to his staff. More than 100 of the *Juneau*'s men survived the disaster, but only had floating flotsam to cling to in the water. Of those men in the water, only 10 remained alive the next day. Three of them paddled to a small island where natives pulled them from the water and a resident European trader nursed them back to health. Later, a PBY came by and took them to Nouméa. Another Catalina pulled six men from the sea, and the converted flush-deck destroyer *Ballard* picked the one remaining man from a life raft a week later. Slightly less that 700 men perished with her, including the five Sullivan brothers.[2]

The *Juneau* was not the last American cruiser to be lost. The *Atlanta*'s predicament worsened to such a point that Capt. Jenkins knew she could not be saved. She could no longer navigate, and the fires that engulfed her consumed everything aboard the doomed warship. With the danger of more Japanese ships on the way, Jenkins did not want his command to fall into their possession. All attempts to salvage her became fruitless. A meeting with his remaining officers concluded that she had to be scuttled. He sent a message at 2:22 a.m. notifying the *Portland* of the sad news.

About 470 men who had not suffered any wounds climbed into the Higgins boats now streaming from Guadalcanal. They did not have much time to retrieve personal possessions. When Quartermaster Henry Durham arrived on the bridge to get the ship's chart that Jenkins would need to prepare his action report, he saw the dead bodies of the officers and men that he had known so well in his service aboard the cruiser. He looked inside the pilothouse for the chart he sought and could not find it. Not having much time before the ship would be sunk, he left the bridge so he could get off her. The dead would lie where they had died and go under when their ship sank.

Jenkins asked the *Portland* to sink his ship, but the crippled cruiser was being towed. The men who were still on the *Atlanta* would have to scuttle it themselves. Lt. Commanders Nickelson and Wulff placed a detonation charge in the diesel generator room, opened the hatches of all the compartments below that had no water in them, and unwound the detonation wires to the forecastle.

Jenkins nodded and the charges blew up below at 4:30 p.m. with a nearly inaudible boom. All the men left their ship.

More explosions could be heard rumbling inside the *Atlanta* as Capt. Jenkins boarded Collver's boat and stood at its gunwales as Collver maneuvered around it so Jenkins could look at his lost command for the last time. He had been her skipper since the sleek cruiser had been commissioned nearly a year before. Jenkins and the rest of the men in Collver's boat watched her turn on her side and slowly sink at 7:30 p.m. on November 13 just three miles off Lunga Point.

The U.S. Navy's lightly armored and armed light antiaircraft cruisers had just been shown to be a failure as far as sending them into a surface battle with other more heavily armed warships. Whether they would continue to be of any use in the future of the Pacific War was a matter yet to be settled.[3]

The fortunes of war now put added pressure on Yamamoto and Halsey. The quality of their decisions would decide how this part of the Guadalcanal drama would proceed.

CHAPTER 44
Command Decisions

Adm. Ugaki read the dispatches that came into his office from Guadalcanal in fits and starts. The more he read, the greater his concerns grew. He read about damage done to the Japanese ships and became quite worried about the heavy punishment the battleship *Hiei* had adsorbed. After Kimura exercised tactical command over Abe and ordered that the *Kirishima* be sent north, Kimura sent a countermanding instruction for the battleship to move south again and help the *Hiei*. The Combined Fleet still believed the *Hiei* could be salvaged. After being attacked by an American submarine with torpedoes, the *Kirishima* turned around and headed north to join Kondo's task force. But the ship's inability to steer sealed her fate.

Meanwhile, Yamamoto examined a flash message sent from the *Kirishima* at 3:00 a.m. that described a "severe mixed battle" where "both sides [suffered] considerable damage." Another *Kirishima* message reported that Kimura had cancelled the shelling of the American airfield scheduled for that day. Consequently, Yamamoto ordered a delay at 3:44 a.m. in landing the reinforcements for one more day until November 14. Tanaka, still escorting the transports that had the soldiers on board, received Yamamoto's order shortly afterward and turned around to head back to the Shortlands.[1]

Scott, Callaghan, and the American sailors' bravery had saved the day by forcing the postponement of the Japanese plans to land their reinforcements. Also, Henderson Field had escaped what would have been a devastating barrage by the *Hiei* and *Kirishima*'s big 14-inch guns at least for one more day.

✲ ✲ ✲

The bad news poured into Halsey's headquarters. Guadalcanal's radio reported at 1:30 a.m. on November 13 that the Marines had seen bright flashes to the north. Bursts of light like those could only come from naval guns. Halsey received Guadalcanal's reports, but they did not calm his nerves. He had the reputation for being a fighting admiral. The job he now held was the first that required he be totally isolated from the battle's action. He had always been at sea and exercised command from the deck of a ship. In an intellectual sense, he understood that this was the hand dealt to him, but his normally aggressive nature allowed him to think with his heart rather than his head. He was 870 nautical miles from Guadalcanal. It might as well have been 8,700 miles. Halsey restlessly paced waiting for more news to arrive. But there was one piece of news that lent him some encouragement—Guadalcanal had not been bombarded by the Imperial Japanese Navy. Then, there was nothing but silence from Guadalcanal.

For a man not known for being patient, the lack of news churned at his insides. He later remembered, "I must have drunk a gallon of coffee and smoked two packs of cigarettes." Trying to read a magazine to pass the time, his eyes blurred from the incredible tension that roiled inside him.

Morning arrived to overcast skies over Nouméa's harbor when the first authoritative news was put into the admiral's hands. It was a copy of a message from the *Portland* asking for a tow. Water flooded her steering room, and her jammed rudder prevented the cruiser from going anywhere. Thirty minutes later another abrupt message arrived from the *Atlanta* that exclaimed, "Help needed!" A message from the *Helena* arrived at 9:00 a.m. that reported the *San Francisco, Juneau,* and three destroyers steaming for Espiritu Santo. Her message ended with, "All ships are damaged, so request maximum air coverage."[2] Rather than answering what had happened in the waters north of Guadalcanal, the *Helena*'s message only begged more questions. What happened to the *Portland, Atlanta,* and the other five destroyers? But her message foretold a gloomier scenario. Since Hoover's ship sent the status message, and he heard from neither Callaghan nor Scott, Halsey had to assume that they had been seriously wounded or, even worse, killed in action. Halsey later remembered his mood that morning:

> "Bad news always comes first. There was no report of the enemy's losses. This is the hardest thing an area commander in the rear has to face. Your feeling is one of complete helplessness. You know you have put your men into a fight, and you hope you have done everything possible to make that fight successful, but you are always searching your mind for something you may have left undone. It is a great mental agony. You not only have your individual responsibility to your country and to the cause of the Allied Powers, but you have the responsibility of many lives on your shoulders, plus the material damage that may be inflicted on your forces."[3]

As the day wore on, more reports clarified what had happened that eventful night. One of the Japanese battleships now lay crippled north of Savo Island and was about to meet her fate. Boats from Guadalcanal constantly moved out to Iron Bottom Sound and returned with rescued survivors. But as the hours passed, it became clear that American losses had exceeded the Japanese casualties. The *Atlanta* and the *Juneau* had sunk, and the *San Francisco* and *Portland* had taken heavy damage. Four American destroyers were gone.

No one would ever know the actual total of the dead from both sides. But Halsey felt the loss of the men he knew the most. Scott had been one of Halsey's best friends. When Halsey took command, Callaghan was Ghormley's chief of staff and wanted to go to sea. Halsey granted his wish and gave him a sea command so he could bring Capt. Miles Browning on board as his chief of staff. Callaghan got the command he had been trained for, and that move cost him his life.

Halsey knew the Japanese would continue to strive for their objective of landing their reinforcements. They never gave up easily from such an important goal despite being turned away by Callaghan and Scott's gallant stand. They would try at least once more. Halsey still had other forces at his disposal to stop another Japanese attempt and knew he had to use them despite the losses his command had already sustained. He clearly explained his thinking with the following statement:

> "That is what a commander is for. On his judgment at this moment depends the end of the campaign. We were on the defensive at this moment. If I have any principle of war-

> fare burned within my brain, it is that the best defense is a strong offense. Lord Nelson expressed this very well: 'No captain can do very wrong if he places his ship alongside that of an enemy.'"[4]

His initial decision to place Callaghan's task force in the way of the Japanese had saved the American airfields from being destroyed by naval gunfire. The Japanese transports carrying more than 13,000 soldiers had been forced to turn back to the Shortlands for at least one more day. When a coastwatcher reported Japanese cruisers departing the Shortlands with the supposed mission to shell Henderson Field, Halsey decided to act with a powerful force he still had in his pocket—Radm. Thomas C. Kinkaid's Task Force 16 which had Radm. "Ching" Lee's modern battleships to bring to the table.[5]

The Japanese battleship *Hiei* nursed her wounds and wallowed off Savo Island's northern shore. She had inflicted terrible damage on the American ships that bloody night of November 12-13 and had also absorbed considerable destruction herself. It was the Americans' turn to finish her off.

CHAPTER 45
Sink the *Hiei*

CACTUS Strikes Back

When the American soldiers heard the naval gunfire beginning the night of November 12, they worried the Japanese would bring their big guns off Guadalcanal's northern shore and bombard the airfields. But that did not happen because Callaghan's Task Force forced the Japanese ships to withdraw. The men of the 1st Marine Air Wing (MAW), thankful for not being clobbered by the Japanese Navy the previous night, awoke before first light on the 13th to see what they could do to help. They had a formidable force of Marine and Army aircraft with which to attack any Japanese stragglers. The aircraft ready for action included 19 F4Fs, 23 SBDs, and eight TBFs flown by Marine and Navy pilots, along with 18 Army-piloted P-39s and eight new P-38s. Guadalcanal's land-based aircraft carrier would again prove its worth.

Seven SBDs took off at first light and split into three groups to search the western approaches as far as New Georgia, the northwest near Santa Isabel, and the north around Malaita. Marine Maj. Joseph Sailer, Jr., the commander of one of the Henderson Field SBD squadrons, led three bombers toward Savo Island and saw a sad sight of crippled and doomed warships spread over the water ahead. A listing *Atlanta* with its crew still onboard wallowed in fire and smoke. A circling *Portland* steamed slowly in a circle with her stern at an awkward angle to the rest of her. When his three SBDs reached a place about four miles south of Savo Island, the pilots saw the destroyer *Yudachi* disappear in an explosion and leave a watery grave of debris, bodies, and an oil slick.

Sailer and the other two pilots then saw the aimlessly circling *Hiei* moving the snail's pace of five knots. A fire burned ferociously near her bow, and her rear turrets were turned in such a lopsided position that their guns could not be fired. The destroyer *Yukikaze* was nearby, presumably to help the damaged big ship any way it could. The pilots also saw four destroyers moving closer to meet the *Hiei* with the battleship *Kirishima* and four destroyers moving southward just 20 miles away.

The *Hiei* was just 30 miles from Henderson Field and posed a severe threat to the 1st MAW. She had to be attacked immediately to protect the American airfields before the other Japanese ships got within shooting range. Brig. Gen. Louis E. Woods, newly promoted to command the 1st MAW after Halsey ordered him to replace an exhausted Maj. Gen. Geiger following Halsey's early November visit[1], wasted no time preparing the air attack. Maj. Robert H. Richard led the first six SBDs to leave Henderson Field at 6:15 a.m., and they shortly reached their attacking altitude. When Richard attempted to arm his bomb, it dropped harmlessly into the water due to a faulty electrical arming switch, a fairly common problem in American naval aircraft during the early war years.

Six TBFs commanded by Capt. George E. Dooley along with seven escorting F4Fs led by Maj. William R. Campbell lifted off several minutes later. Two of Dooley's torpedo bombers had to return to Henderson Field due to mechanical problems. When Guadalcanal's radar detected ten Japanese fighters heading for Savo Island at 6:55 a.m., Lt. Col. Bauer ordered 2nd Lt. Archie G. Donahue's three F4Fs to climb quickly to CAP altitudes and intercept them.

Richard's SBDs flew north of Savo Island and maneuvered into the most advantageous attacking position. Visibility was not the best it could be because smoke and broken clouds partially obscured sight of the Japanese ships below. It was a good thing for the men on the *Aaron Ward* the SBDs were about to attack. The *Hiei* appeared to be getting ready to bombard the destroyer when its lookouts saw the American bombers. The dive-bombers pushed over into their dives at 7:10 a.m. and headed directly for the battleship. Lining up the big ship in his bombing sight, Master Technical Sergeant Donald V. Thornbury released his 1,000-pound bomb. It fell in a shallow arc, struck the battleship's amidships on its superstructure, and exploded. Four other bombs hit the water, exploded near the struggling ship's port side, and undoubtedly caused underwater damage on her hull.

Shigematsu's eight Zeroes did not see any of the SBDs when they flew past the *Hiei* at 7:00 a.m. but did run into some of Donahue's F4Fs. After a brief, intense dogfight, 2nd Lt. Thomas H. Hughes, Jr., got on the tail of one Zero and emptied his guns at the Japanese fighter, which managed to escape to temporary safety. Donahue pursed the Japanese fighter and shot down Chief Petty Officer Tasuke Mukai's plane when the American's bullets caused the veteran Japanese flight leader's Zero to disappear in a fiery ball. Second Lt. Howard W. Bollman lined up another Zero in his sights and squeezed off some good shots. While he claimed to have destroyed the Japanese plane, his F4F returned to Henderson Field riddled with bullet holes.

As the SBDs executed their diving attack at 7:15 a.m., Dooley's four left over TBFs moved into a high-speed torpedo attack at the *Hiei*. They suddenly flew into a buzzsaw of swarming Zeroes that caught the American torpedo bomber pilots completely by surprise. Three Zeroes led by Warrant Officer Zenji Ono, who spotted the TBFs, immediately attacked the unwary bombers. One American pilot yelled, "Zeroes!" while another exclaimed, "Hell! The air is full of 'em right around me."[2] One Zero fired its 20-mm cannons and put many holes in a TBF flown by 1st Lt. Douglas Bangert while wounding one of the plane's crewmen. The Avenger's turret gun operator, Technical Sergeant John L. Dewey, fired his 50-cal. machine gun and forced the Zero to retreat, but help was on the wing.

Maj. Campbell's seven F4Fs, patrolling at 12,000 feet, dove on the seven remaining attacking Zeroes. All 14 planes headed down near the water and brawled at low altitudes. While each of the seven American pilots claimed at least one Zero, Shigematsu's group actually lost three Zeroes in the most savage fighter battle occurring that day.

Nevertheless, the attacking Zeroes did not stop Dooley's TBFs from bearing down on the battleship. The battleship sent up extremely heavy AA fire that included the experimental 14-inch incendiary-shrapnel shells that had the same effect as large shotgun pellets. These hit the water ahead of the attacking Avengers and numerous water splashes sprung up. Dooley and 1st Lt. William C. Hayter claimed hits on the battleship. Bangert's plane returned so heavily damaged that it had to be turned into a source of parts for other TBFs.

Fleet and Air Movements

The Americans and the Japanese each had a carrier task force near the southern Solomon Islands to support their side's objective. Steaming northwest of Guadalcanal, Adm. Kakuta's light carrier *Junyo*, the only operational carrier the Combined Fleet had at this time, received orders to come to Abe's aid and provide air cover for his retreating ships. Besides the fighters he had aloft to conduct searches and fly CAP, Kakuta ordered Lt. Yasuhiro Shigematsu at 5:30 a.m. to lead eight Zeroes to protect the *Hiei*. The weather had turned for the worse. So, the carrier commander, Capt. Tametsugu Okada, sent two Kates to direct the fighters to the *Hiei*'s location.

Adm. Kinkaid's Task Force 16 led by the *Enterprise* steamed 250 miles due south of San Cristobal Island and 270 miles to CACTUS' southeast. It was 5:00 a.m. on the 13th and Kinkaid's worries about the previous afternoon's sightings of Japanese carriers north of Guadalcanal persisted. He ordered ten SBDs to search the waters 200 miles ahead of Task Force 16, kept a strike group armed and fueled on deck, and maintained eight F4Fs aloft flying CAP. The receipt of sighting reports and the *Enterprise*'s inoperable forward elevator would dictate what Kinkaid would do next.

Kinkaid and Capt. Hardison did not want to do any more testing on the carrier's forward elevator since it might freeze during testing in a down position and totally disable the carrier's ability to conduct air operations. They decided to send a TBF squadron to CACTUS to reinforce the 1st MAW's power. The *Enterprise*'s Air Boss, Cmdr. John G. Crommelin, brought Lt. Albert P. Coffin into his office and gave him simple, clear orders. He was to take his squadron to conduct an "offensive sweep" on a course of 345º at a distance of 285 miles from Henderson Field. His flight could then conduct a brief search west of Guadalcanal before landing on the island. Eight of the nine TBFs would each take a torpedo while the ninth bomber would carry three 500-pound bombs in their bellies. The bombers would not go alone. Lt. Cmdr. Flatley ordered six F4Fs with extra fuel tanks tucked under their wings to escort the TBFs. The fighters included one flight led by Lt. John F. Sutherland and a section commanded by Lt. (jg) Robert E. Holland. After not hearing any word from the SBD search group by 7:00 a.m., he approved sending the Coffin strike group. Twenty-two minutes later, the nine TBFs and six F4Fs lifted off the carrier and turned to the northwest.

After more than a three hour flight, the *Enterprise* strike force was ten miles east of Savo Island when they spied what looked like one battleship along with several cruisers and destroyers slowly steaming toward Guadalcanal to shell the American positions there. Coffin's TBFs climbed to 5,000 feet and flew in and out of the clouds that dotted the sky to hide his planes' movements from the prying eyes of Japanese lookouts. As he flew at 10:20 a.m. from behind a cloud, the big Japanese battleship was right in front of him. And what a big, slow moving, and inviting target she was! Splitting his squadron into two groups to simultaneously assault the *Hiei* from both sides, he chose to attack the battleship's port side and sent Lt. Macdonald Thompson's group to attack on the ship's starboard. Meanwhile, Lt. (jg) John E. Boudreaux, flying the one TBF armed with bombs, readied for a perilous assault on the big ship.

Since there were no Zeroes within sight[3], Lt. Sutherland led his diving F4Fs to strafe the ships and attract the Japanese AA fire away from the attacking bombers. As she continued to slowly circle, the battleship threw up a withering AA barrage. Coffin's torpedo planes slid down to 200 feet above the water flying at 200 knots and launched their torpedoes. His pilots reported hitting the battleship several times with strikes on the port bow and stern. Thompson's pilots claimed a hit from an exploding torpedo on her starboard amidships. Recalling the unsuccessful record of American torpedoes thus far in the Pacific War, Lt. (jg) George D. Welles believed the water spouts that sprung from the ship's sides were due to the explosions of the torpedo detonation charges and not their warheads. His assessment of his torpedo squadron's attack on the *Hiei* was that the attack had no effect on the battleship, "Anyhow after the attack she was sailing along just as majestically as before. We must not have even damaged her paint job."[4]

Flushed with feelings of success, Coffin and his TBFs landed at 10:45 a.m. They were not expected and greeted with an enthusiastic welcome nonetheless. Surprised by the large numbers of scavenged planes scattered in the airfield's bone yard near the runway, they taxied their planes as directed by the ground crews and stopped their engines. Ground personnel wasted no time climbing onto the planes to assess their damage and decide whether each plane could remain operational. Gen. Woods and Capt. Cooley enthusiastically greeted the navy flyers. Woods said to them, "Boys, I don't know where you came from, but you look like angels dropping out of heaven to us." The journal of CACTUS' unofficial history, "History of the Buzzard Brigade" reflected his reaction to the landing of the *Enterprise* planes, "And the boys did look good, with their khakis fresh from the ship's laundry, faces smooth-shaven, and smelling faintly of hair oil and shaving lotion. By sunset perspiration, dust, and blood had altered this natty appearance considerably."[5]

CACTUS Continues Attacking

While the American planes returned to Henderson Field for refueling and rearming, the search planes from Espiritu Santo had reached their maximum search range. Finally, they saw parts of Kondo's Advanced Force near Ontong Java Atoll 225 miles north of Guadalcanal. First Lt. Robert M. Creech flew his B-17 above the Japanese ships at 7:50 a.m. and sent a sighting report of spotting one carrier (the *Junyo*), one battleship, and three destroyers. Ten minutes later, 1st Lt. Robert E. Hawes, flying a B-17 along with Creech, reported seeing three heavy cruisers and one destroyer just 27 miles south of Creech's sighting. Both ship groups steamed at high speed to the north. Radm. Fitch ordered a flight of B-17s to take off and attack the carrier force. Meanwhile, another B-17 found Tanaka's ships also moving away from Guadalcanal to the northwest. CINCPAC's estimate was that Callaghan's stand had indeed deterred the Japanese from bombarding Henderson Field and landing their reinforcements.

☼ ☼ ☼

As BUTTON (Espiritu Santo) analyzed the incoming sightings, Woods' men frantically worked at rearming and refueling their planes for another attack on the battleship and its accompanying destroyer. Four Japanese destroyers (the *Teruzuki*, *Shigure*, *Yugure*, and *Shiratsuyu*) had since joined the beleaguered battleship and therefore presented more targets of opportunity for the American pilots. Maj. Sailer led a flight of nine SBDs along with Dooley's three flyable TBFs on a second attack on the *Hiei*. Seven F4Fs led by Capt. Robert Fraser escorted the bombers. The SBDs dropped their bombs, but none hit their intended target. TBF pilot 1st Lt. William W. Dean claimed and received credit for one probable torpedo hit on the ship's port side. The F4Fs strafed the ships to divert AA fire from the attacking bombers and torpedo planes.

CACTUS' third attack on the *Hiei*, the first of the next three attacks on the battleship, took off at 11:00 a.m. with nine fully rearmed and unescorted TBFs trying again to attack the *Hiei*. Three pilots, Dooley, Bangert and 1st Lt. James E. Maguire, Jr., believed that two of their torpedoes had struck the battleship. But none of CACTUS' records ever confirmed these results much less that the mission ever happened.

The next attack of three came from B-17 bombers that had been redirected to attack the *Hiei* instead of their original mission to attack reported Japanese carrier sightings. Led by Maj. Donald E. Ridings of the 72nd Bomb Squadron based at BUTTON, they arrived in two flights at 14,000 feet and dropped 68 500-pound bombs at 11:10 a.m. while the hapless battleship aimlessly circled. Aerial photographs of that attack revealed a large oil slick trailing behind her and one bomb hit.

The last of the three assaults occurred around noon when Sailer led six SBDs and Lt. Harold H. Larsen six TBFs along with a Campbell-led escort of 12 F4Fs came back to deal out yet more punishment on the now-doomed Japanese battleship. Despite a dense barrage of AA fire, the Americans claimed three bomb hits by Sailer, Second Lt.s Charles E. Kollman, John O. Hull. Larsen, and Marin B. Roush claimed two torpedo hits.

✲ ✲ ✲

It seemed like the Americans wanted to take a break from attacking the battleship as a strangely quiet lull descended on the waters north of Savo Island. CACTUS, BUTTON, and Task Force 16 had sent six assault waves that included:

Results of the First Six Attacks on the *Hiei*

Aircraft	**Total Hits**
21 SBDs	Four bombs
26 TBFs	One bomb, eight torpedoes
14 B-17s	One bomb
35 F4Fs, P-38s	Multiple strafing machine gun hits
P-39s	Unknown number

Nevertheless, the Japanese observed that 60 American planes had attacked the battleship, acknowledged the ship took three bomb hits, many near misses, but no torpedo strikes. When the bombs exploded on the ship, they mutilated the vessel's lightly armored superstructure. The near misses did the damage that explosions like these normally do. Many leaks sprung in the ship's hull, three boilers stopped operating, and the ship began listing to port. Her crew gallantly and successfully labored repairing the damage aft trying to help her get back her steering and controlling the many fires raging all over her. Meanwhile, Japanese attempts to provide some sort of CAP failed when violent thunderstorms over the Slot prevented fighters from navigating to where the *Hiei*'s crew fought.

Nevertheless, the Americans were not yet finished attacking the battleship. The seventh and fatal strike was about to descend on her. Eight SBDs, led by 2nd Lt. John H. McEniry, and Coffin's six TBFs, escorted by 14 F4Fs took off just when there was no Japanese CAP over Savo Island. Dense, low flying clouds obscured the SBDs pilots' view of the target so that they could not make their high altitude dive bombing attacks. But the foul weather did not stop the TBFs from attacking the doomed ship and, despite heavy AA fire coming from the battleship, claiming three torpedo hits. As Foss strafed the battleship, he saw what he called a "wonderful" occurrence. A huge plume of "water, steam, fire, and debris" spouted into the air near the *Hiei* amidships.

Abe hoped the battleship's steering could be restored because of the positive progress being made pumping seawater from the steering room. But that was before the American seventh wave attacked. Based on the Japanese counts of the seventh American attack that included a strafing assault by the American fighters, Abe and his staff believed that 12 American planes had attacked his flagship and put two torpedoes into her starboard side. The explosion Foss had seen hit the battleship just below the 14-inch turret and forward of the bridge. The second torpedo exploded, put a hole into her hull, and flooded the starboard engine room. No more power could be supplied to the pumps attempting to remove water from the steering room. The sea rushed in with nothing to hold it back. The big ship's starboard list increased and continued to worsen. She was finished.

Meanwhile, the Combined Fleet's officers at Truk continued to debate whether the *Hiei* should be salvaged or not. The arguments continued for the rest of November 13 and into the 14th.

Weary from the continuous American air attacks and his flagship's worsening conditioning, Abe sadly and reluctantly ordered the *Yukikaze* at 3:30 p.m. to destroy the *Hiei*. Nonetheless, Capt. Masao Nishida and his officers still hoped to salvage their ship by restoring her power and steering.

CACTUS sent Maj. Sailer leading eight SBDs at 5:45 p.m. with two dive-bombers turning back due to mechanical malfunctions. Sailer and the remaining six bombers continued toward Savo Island. However, the weather worsened so that only Sailer dove at her and dropped his bomb. He claimed to have hit her, but also saw she no longer moved and seemed to have been abandoned. Two SBDs went down due to the severe weather.

Nonetheless, the battleship still had men aboard her as the sun set over the waters around Savo Island. But Nishida now realized that any more attempts to save his command would prove to be fruitless. The rest of the crew and he departed their ship leaving her to her fate. No one saw her sink some time during the night. The Japanese had lost their first battleship in the war.[6]

Criticisms Abound

The Americans lost the cruisers *Atlanta* and *Juneau* and four destroyers. There were some benefit-by-hindsight criticisms of Callaghan's actions during the encounter. One of those was that he had no battle plan before engaging the Japanese. Adm. William S. Pye, President of the Naval War College, caustically censured Callaghan's actions, "Orders...such as 'Give them Hell,' [and] `We want the big ones,' make better newspaper headlines than they do battle plans."[7]

The critics added one more issue concerning the use of the radar Callaghan had at his disposal.

None of the American senior commanders had the latest radars on their flagships. The ships that did have such capabilities should have been inserted in the line of battle to make the optimum use of this latest advancement in technology.

The choice of the line of battle formation also drew critics' attention. They claimed the ship formation made it easier for the loose Japanese formation to take advantage of the inflexible American formation. However, the Americans had no naval doctrine to fight Japanese naval tactics so early in the war.

Using a single TBS radio channel for all tactical communications caused a bottleneck that prevented Callaghan from effectively ordering his ships to react to Japanese actions after the *Helena* first reported the presence of Japanese warships. This was not the first time that the lack of effective tactical communications resulted in lost ships and lives.

The critics, none of whom actually fought the battle, also disapproved of Callaghan's six-minute delay between the sighting of the *Yudachi* and giving the order to open fire. But the key question is whether Callaghan did all he could tactically to seal a victory. Were his tactics so unconventional that this caused the loss of his life and ships? According to Richard Frank in his book, *Guadalcanal*, the answer is "Maybe." Frank contends that given the inferiority of American weapons in overall firepower and those faulty torpedoes, he could have used more conventional tactics, *not stopped* [emphasis intended] Abe from clobbering Henderson Field, and still would have sustained his own fearful losses.

The Japanese lost fewer ships than the Americans; one battleship and two destroyers. One of their reports listed losing 552 sailors, probably from the destroyer *Akatsuki*. That included 297 dead and 255 missing. This did not include the losses from the other destroyers, the 450 dead on the *Hiei* later reported by her officers, or any losses on the *Kirishima*.

Recent Japanese analyses stated that the presence of American warships completely surprised Abe and caused the battle to result in the mêlée it became. After the battle, Abe combined the reports from his ship commanders and his staff and claimed to have sunk five heavy cruisers, two *Atlanta*-class light cruisers, and three destroyers. His report also asserted he had damaged two cruisers, six destroyers, and one motor torpedo boat. He guessed his ships had totally decimated the American fleet.

He was more right than wrong with that claim. But he was less pessimistic reporting the damage the Americans had done to his command. While admitting the loss of the *Hiei*, *Akatsuki*, and *Yudachi*, he stated the damage to the destroyers *Amatsukaze* and *Ikazuchi* was just "slight." The *Amatsukaze*'s captain stated his command was a "floating wreck." The fact the *Ikazuchi* did not participate in the next day's conflict implies her damage was far more serious than Abe reported. His report likely either portrays an ignorance of what actually happened to his command or his being less forthright than he should have been.

The Japanese destroyer captains took maximum advantage of the cramped waters north of Guadalcanal and therefore were allowed to be audacious as they maneuvered their ships. The *Yudachi*'s captain and crew drew particular praise as the Imperial Japanese Navy awarded them a commendation for the way they conducted themselves during the battle. But such praise came to neither Abe nor Nishida. Both men immediately and involuntarily retired from the Navy.[8]

The first day of the Naval Battle of Guadalcanal had come to an end. Both sides suffered much with sunken ships and many dead. The Japanese objective to land reinforcements was turned back albeit temporarily. Nonetheless, the situation for the Japanese soldiers on Guadalcanal was still worsening and had reached a critical point. In order to win, American air power on Guadalcanal had to be defeated so that the island could be recaptured. The Imperial Japanese Navy still had powerful forces and many troops at sea. They did not retreat from what they wanted to accomplish. The Combined Fleet at Truk knew that if the Americans could not be thrown off Guadalcanal, the war in the Pacific would begin to turn in favor of the Americans.

The Japanese had expended considerable resources to bring more Japanese soldiers to help the ones already on the island. But they had more to throw into the cauldron of battle.

Reflecting the personality and attitude of their SOPAC commander, the Americans also had the determination to win at all costs. To do less was unthinkable. And the naval battle that would happen the night of November 13 and into the early morning of November 14 would be one for the ages. After that, the war in the Pacific would indeed reach a turning point.

Part 10:
The Naval Battle of Guadalcanal - Day 2

CHAPTER 46
Chess Movements and Air Attacks

The Japanese Come Back

No sooner than Tanaka's convoy reached Shortland Island, than he received orders from Truk to turn around and go back to Guadalcanal. Despite the loss of the *Hiei*, he also received orders that the invasion was only postponed until November 14, a delay of one day. However, a foretelling of doom came over him after he knew he would have to return to the waters between Guadalcanal and Savo Islands. The land-based American aircraft at Henderson Field waited there for his ships to come into their lair.

Adm. Mikawa's 8th Fleet of cruisers and destroyers with orders to bombard the Americans departed Shortland 11 hours before Tanaka's convoy left. They headed for the Guadalcanal airfields. Mikawa, the victor at the Battle of Savo Island, commanded a powerful force.

Vadm. Mikawa's Eighth Fleet

Ship Unit	**Commander**	**Heavy Cruisers**	**Light Cruisers**	**Destroyers**
Main	Mikawa	*Chokai, Kinugasa*	*Isuzu*	*Asashio, Arashio*
Bombardment	Nishimura	*Suzuya, Maya*	*Tenryu*	*Makigumo, Yugumo, Kazegumo, Michishio*

His Main Unit had two heavy cruisers, one light cruiser, and two destroyers. The Bombardment Unit, which reported to Mikawa and commanded by his subordinate, Radm. Shoji Nishimura, had two heavy cruisers, one light cruiser and four destroyers.[1] They steamed far to the north of Choiseul and Santa Isabel Islands to avoid being seen by American search aircraft or submarines. They soon appeared off Savo Island just after midnight. Nishimura's orders from Mikawa were to separate from the Main Unit and enter Iron Bottom Sound while Mikawa kept his ships to the west to stop any American interference.

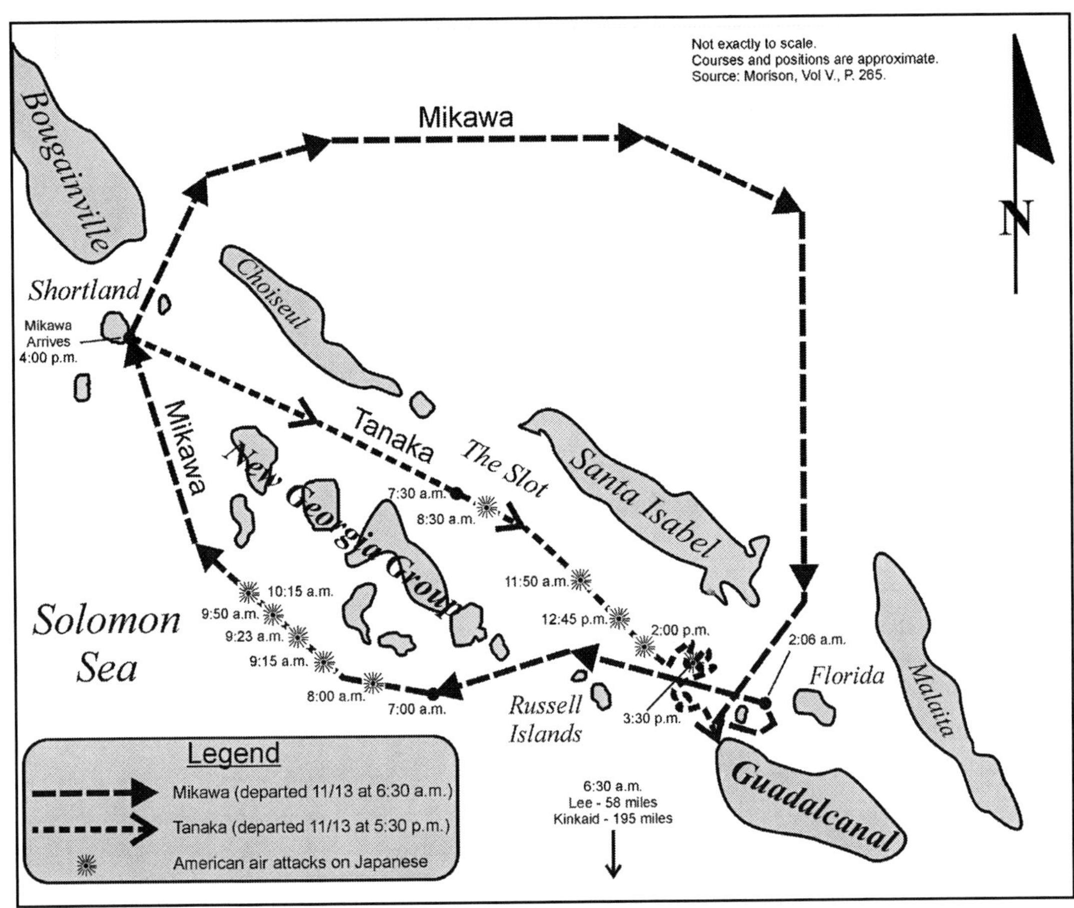

Mikawa's and Tanaka's Voyages to Guadalcanal

The cruisers launched their float planes that climbed high enough over Guadalcanal to drop two green-colored flares to light the way for the barrage to come. The *Maya* and *Suzuya*'s eight-inch guns opened fire at 1:25 a.m. on November 14. The fusillade of 989 eight-inch shells lasted 31 minutes. Nishimura observed several fires flare up and noticed some chain explosions. However, he correctly surmised his bombardment had not disabled the American airfields. The actual results were that none of his shells had hit Henderson Field and only peripherally hit the Fighter One airstrip. The shellfire destroyed just two F4Fs while putting several holes into an SBD.

The Army's aircraft took most of the punishment from the shelling. All except one salvo hit near the 347th Fighter Group's headquarters. One of the pilots remembered, "The men kneeling in their foxholes could hear trees falling, tents collapsing, shrapnel cutting through their airplanes nearby."[2] Flying shrapnel put holes into 16 previously untouched P-39s and P-400s with only one P-400 unscathed. But the damage to the aircraft was not significant enough to prevent them from being repaired. All the P-38s endured the assault undamaged. Despite two holes in Fighter One's runway, the 1st MAW was still in business. The ferocity of the shelling had some Americans believing that the battleship [*Hiei*] that been wallowing near Savo Island had been towed toward Lunga Point and shelled the airfields. Nishimura's assessment as to the effectiveness of his shelling proved to be correct.

Nishimura later rejoined Mikawa south of New Georgia at 7:50 a.m. Nonetheless, before that would happen, the Americans wasted no time avenging the assault.

✲ ✲ ✲

Forty minutes before first light on November 14, four F4Fs led by 2nd Lt. James L. Secrest avoided the potholes in Fighter One and took off at 5:00 a.m. to provide CAP. Not long after the fighters left, six SBDs lifted off to search three sectors—New Georgia, Malaita, and Santa Isabel. Their mission was to find the ships that had shelled CACTUS and lead their comrades to them.

For once, clear skies and nearly unlimited visibility greeted the fliers as they climbed to their search altitudes. Where they expected to see the Japanese battleship that had been in their minds, a large oil slick about 3,000 yards across spread on the water below them. Apparently, she had sunk and would never endanger the 1st MAW again.

Two SBDs flown by Second Lieutenants William E. Hronek and Horace C. Baum near New Georgia's southern coast found Nishimura's ships at 6:30 a.m. steaming at their best speed to catch up with Mikawa. The pilots reported sighting two light cruisers and five destroyers on a 280° bearing, 140 miles from Lunga Point, and steaming at a speed of 16 knots. The sighting report spread excitement throughout the Americans at CACTUS. They had to get quickly into the air before the ships got out of their normal attack range of 200 miles.

Maj. Sailer's six SBDs, Capt. Dooley's six TBFs, and Capt. Foss' eight F4Fs took off at about 7:00 a.m. to go after the sighted ships. For some unknown reason so common during the Pacific War's early months, the sighting of Nishimura's ships never reached either Adm. Fitch's or Adm. Kinkaid's commands.[3]

American Naval Decisions

Kinkaid took Task Force 16 northward toward San Cristobal early on the morning of the 13th after Coffin's planes lifted off. However, the need to launch aircraft for air searches and conduct other air operations slowed his force's northward progress. The *Enterprise* had to turn into a southeasterly wind to land and launch aircraft. After Coffin's strike left for his new home at Henderson Field, Radm. Tisdale added to Task Force 16's strength as he brought the heavy cruiser *Pensacola* and two destroyers into the fold. Kinkaid now had one carrier, two battleships, two heavy cruisers, one antiaircraft light cruiser, and ten destroyers. With the *Enterprise* and Lee's two battleships, the *Washington* and the *South Dakota*, the Americans now had every capital ship available to them in the South Pacific in one place.

As Halsey absorbed the impact of the American losses that occurred the previous night, Pearl Harbor sent an intelligence report that the Japanese had postponed their planned landings for one more day. CINCPAC's assessment did not definitively say when the Japanese would land their troops, but the report did estimate November 14 was the Japanese landing date. One added comment stated the "main body Combined Fleet will participate." Halsey and his staff now had something new to think about. They ordered Kinkaid at 11:10 a.m. to move toward Guadalcanal to help the remnants of the deceased Callaghan's decimated task force, now moving from Iron Bottom Sound to the southeast, in any way he could.

But Halsey ordered that Kinkaid must stay far enough to the south—60 miles south of San Cristobal and at about the same latitude as the Rennell Islands—to avoid being attacked by any Japanese aircraft that may be in the area. Kinkaid had other worries. Ten minutes before Halsey's order arrived, a Japanese flying boat came near enough to Task Force 16 for Kinkaid to send his CAP to destroy it. Four TBFs led by Lt. Vejtasa found the big plane and sent it down in flames. The Japanese plane's pilot, PO1c Tadayoshi Maemura, managed to get off a brief message, "H1," before his plane crashed. The coded message meant he had seen American planes.

Kinkaid believed the flying boat had reported his Task Force's presence. In his mind, he now had another reason to be cautious. As far as he was concerned, there was still ample proof that Imperial Japanese Navy carriers were nearby. Another Japanese flying boat did actually report Task Force 16's position at 10:00 a.m., but there is no clear evidence Kinkaid ever knew of this sighting. However, the *Enterprise* radar did detect unknown plane types on a 295º bearing just 39 miles away. He scrambled 12 F4Fs that never found any planes at the reported place.

Halsey, still undecided how to counter the Japanese next move, then reported to Kinkaid at 2:32 p.m. that the morning's air searches had not seen any Japanese carriers. CINCPAC sent another intelligence report to Halsey about 30 minutes later that said Adm. Nagumo no longer commanded the Japanese carriers and was no longer in the South Pacific. Nimitz added another prophetically critical part of the bulletin, "Expect surface attack on Guadalcanal airfield night 13/14 Nov. with landing attempt from transports early 14th."[4]

That message cleared up what the Japanese were about to do. The time for waiting ended, and Halsey acted in his characteristically decisive way. Nagumo's absence suggested that the Japanese carriers were not the threat they once were and may no longer be at Truk. Halsey expected that Kinkaid's task force was at the northernmost position. He ordered Kinkaid a little after 4:00 p.m. to get ready to separate Lee's battleships and wait for his order to send them north to stop the Japanese from bombarding Henderson Field. Halsey's order to Kinkaid to send Lee arrived one hour later.

But Kinkaid continued to head south after Halsey's order arrived and soon realized he could not obey his superior's order because Task Force 16 was now 180 miles south of San Cristobal and 360 miles south of Guadalcanal—more than 120 miles farther south than where he should have been. If Lee left immediately, his ships could never reach Guadalcanal in time. Kinkaid did not want the Japanese to detect his position by breaking radio silence. So he sent the destroyer *Mustin* 50 miles east to send the message to Halsey that Lee could not arrive before 7:00 a.m. the next morning. As he sent his missive to Halsey, Kinkaid ordered Lee to detach from Task Force 16, form Task Force 64, and head for Iron Bottom Sound. At 8:49 p.m., he took Task Force 16 on a 300º course at 23 knots to move toward his assigned position 125 miles south of Guadalcanal.[5]

✲ ✲ ✲

Kinkaid's message unexpectedly stunned Halsey and his staff at Nouméa. Although we shall never know how Halsey exactly expressed his disappointment that Lee would not arrive in time to stop the Japanese from shelling the American airfields on Guadalcanal, we do know his fiery temperament.

Halsey undoubtedly exploded and unleashed a series of epithets and "colorful" metaphors that could only be generously described as colorful.

Worrying about what a Japanese naval bombardment would do to the 1st MAW, he sent a despondent message to Vandegrift later that evening, "Sorry—Lee cannot comply—too far."[6] Like their superior, all of Halsey's senior staff worried what would happen to CACTUS when the Japanese began shelling the airfields. They knew another crucial conflict would be fought the next day or evening. What they could not know was that the men at CACTUS would handle themselves well when Nishimura's cruisers began their barrage and would take revenge on them. Kinkaid's aviators would also make their presence felt as they went after Mikawa's cruisers.[7]

Attacking Mikawa's Cruisers

Task Force 16 moved at 25 knots on a northwesterly course in the dark waters south of Guadalcanal. Halsey sent Kinkaid orders at 5:18 a.m. on November 14 to move within 100 miles off the Southern Solomons and attack any transports that may be moving toward Guadalcanal. Lee's Task Force 64 with his two battleships would take a position 50 miles from the island. Halsey's additional orders to Kinkaid were, "Supplement BUTTON and CACTUS searches by your own as necessary to locate and destroy transports."[8] Kinkaid responded by changing his ships' courses at 5:32 a.m. to 352º. Rain squalls and poor visibility greeted Task Force 16 when it reached a position 200 miles south of Guadalcanal. No news about any new sightings of Japanese carriers or what had happened at Henderson Field arrived on the *Enterprise*.

By dawn, heavy rains pelted the carrier's flight deck. Kinkaid wanted to send up SBDs to search for any Japanese ships but had to wait until the rainstorms abated. He wanted to launch his search and head south to get as far away as he could from any Japanese counterattack. The rain stopped enough at 6:08 a.m. to launch an eight-F4F CAP. Ten SBDs took off a little later to search for Japanese ships and four more SBDs went to look out for any submarines. Two independently operating planes flew a 285º-315º arc out to 200 miles as four SBD pairs searched in a 315º-015º arc 250 miles out. When the pilots completed their searches, they had orders to land at CACTUS rather than return to the *Enterprise*.

Kinkaid ordered Task Force 16 to slow to 22 knots and wait for his search plane sighting reports. He did not have to wait long when Lt. William I. Martin, leading a section of SBDs, reported at 7:17 a.m. a flight of unidentified aircraft at low altitude 140 miles north of the American task force. Task Force 16 readied itself to repel the anticipated air attack by changing into a defensive formation, but the unknown aircraft never showed up. Kinkaid still feared the Japanese would find his ships and attack them. Apparently, the memories of the Battle of the Santa Cruz Islands were still indelibly seared into his memory.

Kinkaid did not want to get caught unprepared if the Japanese should attack when he ordered an air strike to search for Japanese ships to the north-northeast near Guadalcanal. The strike began leaving the *Enterprise* at 7:37 a.m. and had 17 SBDs, commanded by Lt. Cmdr. James R. Lee, armed with 1,000-pound bombs along with a ten-plane F4F escort led by Lt. Cmdr. Flatley. Cmdr. Crommelin, the *Enterprise*'s Air Officer, ordered Lee to fly north, listen to sighting reports on the radio, find the best targets he could find and attack them. After the planes had all left, Task Force 16 changed its course to 180° at 25 knots to get out of harm's way. As far as Kinkaid was concerned, he had completed his participation in the upcoming operation.

Lee's formation climbed to its cruising altitude when, after two of Flatley's fighters had a fruitless dogfight with two Japanese float planes 60 miles north of Task Force 16, he soon picked up and identified Japanese warships on the horizon. Mikawa would again feel the powerful sting of American aircraft.[9]

Mikawa's Cruisers Take a Pounding

Just when Nishimura joined Mikawa, Sailer's group of six SBDs, six TBFs, and eight F4Fs found Mikawa's cruiser force near Rendova Island in the New Georgia Group. He immediately sent a sighting report to CACTUS that there were four heavy cruisers, and three destroyers on a bearing of 280° and 170 miles from Henderson Field. Seeing no Japanese fighter CAP in the vicinity at about 8:30 a.m., his planes began their attack on an *Atago*-class cruiser with Sailer claiming one 1,000-pound hit.

Second Lt. Robert E. Kelly's bomb precisely hit and exploded on the *Kinugasa*'s bridge while three other pilots claimed near-misses. One bomb hit the forward part of the bridge, pierced the superstructure steel, and devastatingly exploded beneath the main decks and below the waterline. The detonation tore huge holes in the hull, killed Capt. Masao Sawa and his executive officer, and forced the torpedo officer to take command. Hot shrapnel hit the gasoline tanks and started a huge 30-minute-long fire. Seawater flooded into the below decks, and the *Kinugasa* began to list at a 10° angle to port. The cruiser's existence was on borrowed time.

At the same time, Capt. Dooley's six TBFs attacked Mikawa's flagship, the *Chokai*. As it has been with pilots since the first of them launched their first attack, the TBFs' pilots optimistically claimed to have hit the cruiser. Three TBFs attacked the warship on her port side. Dooley and 2nd Lt. Ervin W. Hatfield each claimed hits. Lt. James McConnaughhay, Lt. (jg) John E. Boudreaux, and Ens. Robert E. Oscar attacked the cruiser's starboard side and believed all their torpedoes hit her. When the TBFs turned to return to CACTUS, they were certain they left two heavy cruisers in trouble. Nevertheless, the *Chokai* used her speed and firepower to deter the attacking torpedo bombers and escaped undamaged.

Two of the *Enterprise*'s searching SBDs also found Mikawa's cruisers as Sailer's planes attacked them. Lt. (jg) Robert D. Gibson and Ens. Richard M. Buchanan saw white wakes at about 7:50 a.m. in the distance to their northwest. Approaching the ships cautiously, they climbed to 17,000 feet to find cover in scattered clouds so as to avoid being seen. Gibson attempted to radio his sighting report but it became garbled. His radioman, ARM2c Clifford E. Schindele, sent a keyed report at 8:15 a.m. to all the searching planes and the *Enterprise* that stated the planes had found nine ships, one of them possibly a carrier off New Georgia and heading westward. The two planes were not close enough to see the attacking CACTUS planes. Gibson maintained contact with the ships and continued sending updates. An 8:44 a.m. report from him said, "2 BB, 2 CA, 1 CV (garble), 4 DD, course 290, 08-45, 157-10."[10]

Gibson's report of seeing a carrier stirred considerable activity in Task Force 16. The *Enterprise* asked Cmdr. Lee at 8:44 a.m. if he had seen any Japanese carriers. Lee answered that the only fact he knew was the ships' reported position. One minute later, Hardison ordered Lee to attack the ships and land at CACTUS when he finished his assault. Flatley never heard the order because his radio was not equipped to tune in the correct frequency. Lee immediately complied with the order and turned his planes on a 330º course. As the planes flew toward Mikawa's cruisers, Lee saw Task Force 64's ship wakes moving to the northwest.

Staying in the clouds, Gibson and Buchanan continued to shadow Mikawa's ships. The *Enterprise* kept acknowledging his sighting reports that implied his two plane formation could attack at anytime.

The two SBDs decreased their distance to the Japanese as Gibson spied a heavy cruiser, at 9:15 a.m. with an oil slick trailing behind it. It had separated from the rest of the ships. The ship he saw was the troubled *Kinugasa*. She had counter-flooded so that she no longer listed. Water continued to pour into her innards. The two dive-bombers pushed over into their dives, aimed their bombsight cross hairs at her stern, and claimed they had struck the cruiser with their 500-pound bombs. While they actually did not hit the ship, the bombs hit the water and exploded nearby. The concussions caused by the explosions disabled her steering and created new leaks that allowed more seawater to stream into her. Black smoke soared skyward from several fires that began to engulf her. The end of her existence became a sure thing.

The cruiser did not give up quietly as she sent intensive AA fire upward. One eight-inch shell passed through the tail of Buchanan's plane, but failed to explode. After Gibson radioed the results of his attack back to the *Enterprise*, both planes turned eastward to head for Henderson Field.

Ensigns Robert A. Hoogerwerf and Paul M. Halloran flew in their assigned 315º-330º sector and were over Mikawa's cruisers as Gibson and Buchanan attacked them. As their planes approached a position at 9:23 a.m. just south of Rendova Island, they saw the wakes of two heavy cruisers, one light cruiser, and two destroyers steaming on a northwesterly course at 25 knots. As the two SBDs began descending, the pilots saw a heavy cruiser, the *Kinugasa*, with two destroyers circling it, smoke rising from its hull, and lying low in the water. They also spotted a light cruiser and one destroyer ten miles to the west and an undamaged heavy cruiser and a destroyer five miles south of the sighted pair.

Flying at 17,500 feet, they separated so each plane could attack one of the two groups of ships. Hoogerwerf attacked the heavy cruiser, the *Suzuya* and Nishimura's flagship, and dropped his bomb while in his steep dive. The bomb missed the ship and exploded nearby in the water. The *Suzuya* did not even sustain a scratch. Hoogerwerf saw Halloran go after the thought-to-be light cruiser, which actually was the heavy cruiser *Maya*. Halloran attacked her with his one 500-pound bomb. It missed the ship but Halloran ran into trouble when his right wing hit the cruiser's mainmast. His SBD crashed into the ship's superstructure near the port 12-cm AA gun mount. Flaming gasoline poured from the doomed plane that set the ready ammunition afire and destroyed the ship's port AA mounts and searchlights. The fire spread to where it threatened the torpedo mounts. The crew had no choice but to throw 16 torpedoes overboard. The *Maya* could still fight, but the American plane crash killed 37 men and wounded 24 others.

Hoogerwerf never saw his companion again and returned to the *Enterprise*. After he landed, he received some criticism for not fulfilling his mission and reporting what he had seen. Gibson and Buchanan landed safely at Henderson Field. Later, they would be part of the assault on Tanaka's transports. The search planes from the *Enterprise* had sunk one heavy cruiser and damaged another. They did more than what was expected of them. But the *Enterprise* air strike led by Lee had yet to be heard from.

✲ ✲ ✲

After losing Flatley's entire fighter escort because of navigational errors and three SBDs due to the planes running out of fuel, Lee saw the smoking and heavily listing *Kinugasa* southwest of Rendova just before 10:00 a.m. The cruiser's shepherding destroyers had by this time left their charge to face its fate alone while they fended for itself. Not wanting to waste bombs on an obviously doomed ship, he led his strike to look for more productive targets.

Lee had not long to wait. After flying another 15 minutes and 25 miles farther he spotted the foaming wakes of what seemed to be two heavy cruisers, four light cruisers, and four destroyers steaming at high speed to the northwest. These ships were Mikawa's heavy cruisers *Maya*, *Chokai*, and *Suzuya*, the light cruisers *Isuzu* and *Tenryu*, and two destroyers. Despite their superiors' fears about the possible presence of a Japanese carrier, no such ship could be seen. CINCPAC's intelligence estimate proved correct.

As his group neared the ship, Lee ordered five SBDs led by Lt. Cmdr. James A. Thomas to attack the three heavy cruisers and Lt. Stockton Birney Strong's five SBDs to assault the two light cruisers. Lee's six SBDs continued searching for the erstwhile carrier. Thomas' SBDs attracted heavy but inaccurate AA fire from the Japanese heavy cruisers as they dove toward the water. Two 1,000-pound bombs widely missed the *Chokai*. Nevertheless, Ens. Edwin J. Stevens' bomb smacked the water and exploded just 30 feet from the cruiser's starboard side. Another 1,000-pounder from another SBD exploded a mere 10 feet off the cruiser's starboard bow. Such near misses ordinarily cause damage below the waterline. This time, that rule proved to be correct. Water flooded into some of the cruiser's compartments and temporarily disabled two of the ship's boilers. Nonetheless, the cruiser could still steam at 29 knots and reached Shortland. Meanwhile, with all its bombs used, Thomas' planes flew 200 miles southeast and landed at CACTUS.

Strong's group attacked the *Isuzu* with the last two of the five dive-bombers flown by Lieutenants (jg) Howard R. Burnett and John H. Finrow claiming direct hits. Their bombs did not directly strike the light cruiser but hit the water near enough to cause some damage. The two explosions in the water resulted in some flooding in two of the ship's fire rooms and partial damage to its steering controls. However, the damage on the ship was not serious enough to impair its escape.

After fruitlessly looking for the nonexistent carrier, Lee's six SBDs went after the *Tenryu*. His bombers dove at the light cruiser and scored four near misses. But, like her sister ships, she did not sustain any damage sufficient to prevent her returning to her base.

✲ ✲ ✲

The Japanese cruiser force, minus the doomed *Kinugasa*, steamed at high speed and reached their Shortland base to refuel and then steam out again to support the transports. As the sea rushed into the *Kinugasa*, her list increased. She rolled over and sank at 11:22 a.m. Mikawa had lost one heavy cruiser with another heavily damaged. He estimated that 60 American planes had attacked his cruiser force. Believing the earlier shelling had heavily damaged the American airfields, he assumed that all those planes must have come from nearby American carriers. Actually only 40 American planes attacked his force.

Sixteen SBDs safely landed at Henderson Field at 1:15 p.m. When Lee reported to the 1st MAW that the air attacks had sunk two cruisers, damaged one heavy cruiser and one light cruiser, and only lost one SBD, this statement confirmed the CACTUS commanders own observations.

After losing sight of the SBDs, Flatley's fighters struggled to land before they ran out of fuel. Two of them flown by Lt. Stanley E. Ruehlow and Lt. (jg) Roy M. Voris found Henderson Field and safely arrived there. Flatley led the remaining fighters on a northwesterly course so he could meet up once again with the dive-bombers. After flying within sight of the most eastern island of the New Georgia group at 10:15 a.m., he gave up looking for the carrier and turned his fighters to the southeast to look for the *Enterprise*. His radios had not been tuned into the search network and never received the orders to land at Henderson Field. Two F4F pilots, Ensigns Willis B. Reding and William H. Leder, lost contact with Flatley near Rennell Island and searched nervously and hopefully for their home base. They found the wakes of "Ching" Lee's Task Force 64's ships and, not wanting to break radio silence, dropped a note asking for Lee to point their ships in the direction of the *Enterprise*. Lee mercifully turned ships in a southerly direction. The two F4Fs flew to the south with their pilots knowing that finding their carrier would not be an easy task.

Attacking Tanaka's Convoy

Tanaka once again led his convoy of transports out from the Shortlands soon after it had arrived. The invasion date was now set for November 14. American airpower would be the instrument of his worries.

The Japanese admiral commanded 11 transports that carried the 17th Army's newest attempt to reinforce their beleaguered comrades on Guadalcanal. The 11 transports, carrying 7,000 soldiers and tons of supplies and ammunition, along with 76 large landing craft and seven small landing craft strapped on their decks, were the *Nagara Maru, Hirokawa Maru, Sado Maru, Canberra Maru, Nako Maru, Yamazuki Maru, Yamaura Maru, Kinugawa Maru, Shinanogawa Maru, Brisbane Maru*, and *Arizona Maru*. Their escort had the eight destroyers *Hayashio, Umikaze, Takanami, Amagiri, Oyashio, Kawakaze, Naganami, Mochizuki, Kagero, Suzukaze,* and *Makinami*. The Japanese invasion plan called for the first five fastest transports to deposit their cargoes at Tassafaronga with the remaining and slower six ships leaving their loads at Aruligo Point near Cape Esperance. The convoy stretched out in a straight line down the Slot and moved at a pace of 10 knots so as to not outrun its slowest ship. As soon as his ships were within range of American search aircraft, not much time passed before the Americans knew where the ships were.

☆ ☆ ☆

Second Lieutenants Hronek and Baum had just sighted Nishimura's cruisers when they had been flying for some time. They found a most significant sighting at 6:30 a.m. as their planes cruised over the Slot north of New Georgia. Hronek reported seeing one carrier, two heavy cruisers, and one battleship on a bearing of 300°, 150 miles from Lunga, course 120°, speed 15 knots. Confirmation of that sighting followed shortly at 7:15 a.m. from Second Lieutenants Walter A. Eck, also from the 1st MAW, and Andrew Jackson. When flying near New Georgia, they described seeing two battleships, one light cruiser, and 11 destroyers at a place near Hronek's sighting. Just 15 minutes later, an R.A.A.F. Hudson bomber crew reported seeing 12 transports in the Slot north of New Georgia coming behind the large group of ships already sighted. To the commanders on Guadalcanal, these ships carried the Japanese reinforcements they had been warned would be coming. CACTUS immediately broadcast the sightings to all who would be near enough to help.

Two *Enterprise* search planes also found the convoy at 8:49 a.m. Lt. (jg) Martin D. "Red" Carmody sent a report of seeing "many enemy transports, 2 CA, 3 CL, 6 DD," on a course and speed consistent with the earlier sightings. He and Lt. (jg) William E. Johnson eagerly attacked one transport and dropped both of their bombs. Both bombs missed the ship. As Carmody pulled out of his dive and strafed a destroyer, he headed for the safety of the clouds, but Japanese CAP fighters shot down Johnson as the American destroyed a Zero flown by PO2c Koichi Hoshino with him. Neither pilot was ever heard from again.

At the same time, a B-17 bomber from Espiritu Santo, nicknamed "Typhoon McGoon" and piloted by the 98th Bomber Squadron's Capt. James E. Joham, found Kondo's ships. A Japanese CAP of six Zeroes led by Lt. (jg) Manzo Iwaki saw and attacked the bomber. The B-17's gunners claimed shooting five of the six fighters as the fighters relentlessly pressed their attacks. Before being forced to land at Henderson Field with many holes in his aircraft, Joham reported seeing two carriers and 23 other ships. His later report added seeing two groups of ships. The first one had one carrier, two heavy cruisers, two light cruisers, and seven destroyers bearing 300° and 150 miles from Guadalcanal; the second group had one carrier, two battleships, two heavy cruisers, two light cruisers and ten destroyers on the same course but 10 miles nearer to Guadalcanal. After Henderson Field's ground crew repaired Joham's bomber, he took off and flew back to Espiritu Santo without further incident.

After escaping the first American air attack, Tanaka still believed more trouble was on the wing. His fears were confirmed when lookouts reported seeing many planes in the distance coming from the south. After ordering the transports to split into the two groups as he had previously planned, he sent the destroyers into an antiaircraft defensive formation. The planes he had seen were Lee's air strike heading for Mikawa's cruisers on the other side of the New Georgia island group. But the first air attack on Tanaka's convoy would come from the American airfields on Guadalcanal.

Sightings of the approaching invasion convoy energized 1st MAW's ground crews to refuel and rearm all available aircraft that had just returned from their strikes on the cruisers and to quickly get the planes aloft. The first of 38 planes took off at around 11:00 a.m. with Maj. Sailer leading ten SBDs and Maj. Robert H. Richard commanding nine dive bombers. Eight F4Fs led by Capt. Robert B. Fraser and 1st Lt. Martin's four P-39s provided escorts. Several flights flew northwest past the Russells with the SBDs climbing to 12,000 feet and the fighters 1,000 feet above them. About 100 miles from Lunga at 11:45 a.m., the strike found three four-or-five transport groups along with what they saw as two light cruisers and eight or nine destroyers escorting the transports.

After his lookouts saw the approaching CACTUS aircraft, Tanaka again reformed his transports into three columns with five ships on the right, three in the center, and the remaining three ships on the left. His 11 destroyers formed a circle around the transports.

Meanwhile, six Zeroes commanded by Lt. Masao Iizuka, flew CAP over Tanaka's ships. Upon seeing the approaching American bombers, Iizuka ordered his fighters to climb to gain the advantage of higher altitude and dove to attack the oncoming Americans. 2nd Lt. James G. Percy, one of the leaders of two F4F divisions, saw the six Zeroes heading for the bombers and notified Fraser. The Marine fighter pilots climbed to meet the threat. With all guns blazing, machine gun and cannon bullets flew around the planes. Second Lieutenants Percy, John B. Maas, Jr., Archie Donahue, Joseph F. Wagner, Jr., and John R. Stack each claimed to have shot down a Zero.

Sailer's ten SBDs dropped down from the south and attacked two 8,000-ton transports. Maj. Louis Robertshaw, 1st Lt. John S, Henderson, 2nd Lieutenants John J. McEniry, Jr., George B. Herlihy, Charles E. Kollman, and Marine Gunnery Kenneth D. Gordon all claimed hitting one transport that turned out to be the *Sado Maru*. As the SBDs dove, some Zeroes attacked them. Two American radiomen, Private 1st Class Talmadge B. Johnson, flying with Henderson, and Private Travis L. Huddleston, flying in 1st Lt. Arthur O. Hellerude's SBD, each shot down one Zero while two other Zeroes left the scene with smoke trailing behind them.

Richard's six SBDs followed Sailer's assault and attacked a big transport, reported to be larger than the American luxury ship *Lurline*, in the northern column or to Tanaka's left. They reported hitting the transport several times and seeing smoke rising from the ship as they pulled out of their dives. Leading the rearmost section, Gibson along with Ens. Leonard Robinson and Staff Sergeant Albert C. Beneke took on a large ship in the center column. Although Zeroes harassed them as they dropped their bombs, the three pilots claimed two hits and one near miss. The P-39s covered the bombers leaving the battle despite facing some minor attacks from the Zeroes.

Coffin's TBFs came over the convoy a few minutes after the SBDs did and saw the transports scatter from their formation as the dive-bombers attacked. Coffin and Lt. MacDonald Thompson's divisions divided their attacks. Each chose an undamaged transport. A Zero attacked Lt. (jg) Richard K. Batten's trailing SBD, but Fraser intervened and destroyed the intruder. Coffin's four TBFs came in using their characteristic shallow dives and launched torpedoes at a large transport. He reported his planes hit the transport twice on its port side. Thompson's division also came in on the wave tops and claimed one hit on another transport's starboard side. Only moderate AA fire met the torpedo bombers. That gun fire damaged George Welles' windshield and put several holes in Coffin's TBF.

All planes from CACTUS' first strike returned to Henderson Field safely. The Americans claimed to have either sunk or heavily damaged six transports. Tanaka and his destroyer crews reported being attacked between 12:50 p.m. and 1:02 p.m. by 41 American planes including eight B-17s—(none of these were even present), eight fighters, eight torpedo planes, and 17 carrier bombers. In a definitely solemn remark in his memoirs, he noted that despite his destroyers putting up a heavy smoke and steering dramatic zigzag courses, the torpedo bombers sank the *Canberra Maru* and *Nagara Maru* while carrier bombers crippled the *Sado Maru*. After the destroyers picked up more than 1,500 survivors, the *Sado Maru* limped back to Shortland escorted by the destroyers *Amagiri* and *Mochizuki*. Shortly after the transport dropped anchor in the harbor, she sank.

The Japanese lost three of six Zeroes: Chief Petty Officer Tsumoru Okura, PO1c Minoru Tanaka, and PO1c Meiji Hikuma. The three survivors left the battle at 1:10 p.m. PO2c Katsuhiko Kawasaki flew to Buka, but Iizuka and wingman PO3c Kenichi Abe reached the airfield at Vunakanau at 5:00 p.m. After claiming to have destroyed two F4Fs out of the 31 American fighters they saw and leaving the convoy for which they were responsible, Tanaka was without CAP for at least 90 minutes.

The sole American carrier in the South Pacific contributed 31 dive-bombers, nine torpedo planes, and 20 fighters to attack Tanaka's convoy. The same could not be said for the *Junyo*. The lone Japanese carrier was part of Adm. Kondo's Advance Force. It steamed north of the Solomon Islands and could only launch a reconnaissance mission over Tulagi. Lt. (jg) Shunko Kato took off at 9:00 a.m. with three Kates and nine Zeroes commanded by Warrant Officer Saburo Kitahara. One hour and 40 minutes later they saw the crippled *Portland* and *Aaron Ward* in Tulagi's harbor. Kato's and Kitahara's planes returned to the *Junyo* at 12:40 p.m. without firing a shot.[11]

✲ ✲ ✲

Lt. Cmdr. Kusao Emura, one of the Imperial Japanese Navy's observers on shore at Guadalcanal, could not help but be amazed at the growing power of American aviation on that island. He sent a radio message the afternoon of November 14 reporting seeing 40 fighters, 40 carrier bombers, and three large planes landing at Henderson Field and Fighter One.

The 1st MAW's ground crews never stopped refueling and rearming landing planes so the crews wasted little time on the ground. After recovering planes that had attacked Tanaka's convoy, CACTUS began launching a series of assaults at the approaching Japanese transports. The next wave of five SBDs commanded by Lt. Cmdr. Lee found Tanaka's transports at 2:30 p.m. northwest of the Russell Islands. Lee and the other four pilots scanned the skies and found that no Japanese CAP existed. Having a clear path for attack, the five planes began their dives from 10,000 feet. Lee and Lt. (jg) John F. Richey claimed hitting two transports.

The next wave of eight SBDs, led by Lt. William I. Martin and escorted by Lt. James J. Sutherland's eight F4Fs, had no problems finding the slow-moving Japanese transport convoy steaming to the southeast. Knowing the convoy would not move too fast for Martin to find them again, he took his planes to look for any carriers that might be nearby. Not finding any, he turned back at 2:50 p.m. and found the convoy again while flying at 16,000 feet. Still not sighting any Japanese CAP, his bombers went into their dives and dropped their bombs on the beleaguered convoy at the optimum time during their descent. Martin, Lt. (jg) Joseph Bloch, and Ensigns Leonard Lucier and Max D. Mohr claimed hitting two ships with four bombs. Ens. Charles Irvine, diving his plane separately from the others, hit one transport.

At 2:40 p.m., the fourth Japanese CAP finally arrived over Tanaka's ships but not in time to stop Martin's dive-bombers from dropping their bombs. Seven larger and less-agile B-17s led by Maj. Allan Sewart, the commanding officer of the 26th Bomb Squadron, from Espiritu Santo approached and made far better targets for Lt. Masaji Suganami's six Zeroes. The Zeroes attacked the heavy bombers but too late to stop them from dropping 28 500-pound bombs that hit the water and exploded all around the transports. All seven B-17s returned safely to Espiritu Santo.

As Suganami's fighters tangled with Sewart's B-17s, the fifth Japanese CAP arrived with eight Zeroes commanded by Warrant Officer Kazuo Tsunoda. Like the earlier CAPs, they had specific orders to protect the convoy from American air attacks. It was a vitally critical mission since the troops on these ships had to be landed on Guadalcanal no matter how much effort it took. The Japanese planes had to circle above the convoy for one hour at 13,123 feet. As he neared the convoy's position, Tsunoda remarked in his memoirs how much the weather had improved over the Slot and saw five transports afire. Wondering if his planes had come too late, he saw Suganami's fighters attacking the B-17s and decided to enter the fray. As his plane climbed to go after the American heavy bombers, he noticed more American planes approaching from the east. These were Sutherland's escorting F4Fs flying near the water. Suganami's upper echelon also saw the American fighters.

Sutherland also saw the Zeroes chasing the B-17s far above him. Suganami, thinking the low-flying fighters might strafe the transports, dove his Zero into the middle of the F4Fs and forced them to scatter. After a brief series of dogfights, Sutherland's fighter pilots claimed shooting down two Zeroes and returned unscathed to CACTUS. Actually, all the Zeroes still flew after the altercations.

All this activity above his convoy suddenly ended at 3:00 p.m. and brought a brief respite to Tanaka's struggle to get his ships to Guadalcanal. He estimated that for the 20 minutes beginning at 2:30 p.m. that eight American B-17s and 24 carrier bombers had attacked his ships. They bombed the *Brisbane Maru*, set it on fire, and sank it. Her crew and passengers abandoned her before she went down, and the destroyer *Kawakaze* plucked 550 survivors from the water. He now had only seven transports and eight destroyers left. He knew the attacks his ships had suffered thus far were only the beginning of what the Americans had in store for him. His convoy steamed in full daylight under clear skies with all the dangers this situation portended. Despite his apprehensions, he was more determined than ever to obey his orders and carry out his mission.

With Suganami's fighters scattered because of their dogfights against the American F4Fs and also running out of fuel, they flew to a prearranged rendezvous and began their return trip to Rabaul. After all his planes had assembled, Suganami surprised his men when he announced by signal he would return by himself to the combat area. One of his pilots twice requested to go with him, but Suganami emphatically ordered the pilot to return home. The veteran of the Pearl Harbor bombing and Midway bravely but foolishly turned his plane and flew to the southeast. His pilots sadly saw his plane disappear into the distance. He was never seen again.

After leaving their carrier's flight deck beginning at 1:05 p.m. and with Flatley in overall command, the *Enterprise*'s second strike of 20 planes came onto the scene and sighted Tanaka's convoy at about 3:00 p.m. near Santa Isabel. The 12 F4Fs cruised at 22,000 feet with Lt. (jg) Ralph H. Goddard's five SBDs and Lt. (jg) William C. Edwards three SBDs flying below them at 18,000 feet. Flatley turned westward for a longer line of attack from the ship's sterns. Counting about nine transports and five to six destroyers, he also saw three or four ships burning in the distance. He also spotted some Zeroes flying overhead but they were unwilling to attack his planes. He did not see four more Zeroes climbing to place themselves between the American planes and the ships.

The American planes finished their long turn from the west at about 3:30 p.m. and neared the ships' sterns. Flatley ordered the SBD pilots to attack specific targets. The bombers descended to 15,500 feet while the fighters stayed at 22,000 feet. Goddard's five SBDs spread apart to attack three of the five transports nearest to them. Although they claimed one hit, all three transports escaped damage. Edwards' three SBDs went into their dives just as four Zeroes jumped them. Two radiomen, ARM2c Wayne C. Colley and ARM2c Raymond E. Reames, both veterans of the Battle of the Coral Sea, claimed destroying Japanese fighters. Colley claimed two while Reames claimed one. Despite their surprise attack, the Zeroes could not stop Edwards' dive-bombers from doing their worst. Edwards "Red" Carmody, and Lt. (jg) Robert F. Edmondson each picked a transport to attack and claimed direct hits on all three. Actually, they hit the leading transport, the *Shinanogawa Maru*, and the trailing ship, the *Arizona Maru*, with devastating effects.

Flatley and one of his flight leaders, Lt. Albert D. Pollock, saw the horrible carnage the bombers had done to the transports as they led their fighters to strafe the ships. Troops packed the ships' decks and tried to escape any way they could from the flames and the prospect of drowning. The F4Fs dove from 10,000 feet down to 1,500 feet and fired their six .50-cal. guns as they passed 4,000 feet. The machine gun's bullets churned the water into a foaming mass of blood and body parts before they could get away. Fires spread by burning oil on the water's surface consumed them. For those in the water, it must have seemed like hell on earth.

As the men died in the water, a second wave of eight B-17s commanded by Maj. Donald E. Ridings and flying at 20,000 feet arrived overhead. They had a good bird's-eye view of the *Enterprise*'s attack and saw one plane's bombs hit a zigzagging transport and force it to abruptly stop in the water, burst into flames and smoke, and begin sinking. Untouched by Japanese fighters and uninterrupted by AA fire, the heavy bombers dropped 32 500-pound bombs and scored not one hit. When Halsey learned they had bombed from such a high altitude with such appallingly poor results, he lost his volatile temper and lividly informed Nimitz the bomber's performance was "worse than disappointing."[12]

The Japanese Zeroes still in the area vainly tried to attack the B-17s as the bombers began their return to Espiritu Santo. The fighter pilots claimed shooting down six American bombers. Every B-17 arrived undamaged. Flatley and the rest of the *Enterprise* second strike landed at Henderson Field with far better results than their Army brethren. They left two more transports ferociously burning and dead Japanese soldiers in the water. Tanaka ordered the two destroyers *Naganami* and *Makinami* to stand by to pick up survivors. And they did ultimately pick up 1,592 men while Tanaka's lookouts inaccurately reported the Japanese CAP had destroyed all three SBDs that had recently attacked them.

Of the 11 transports he had when he left Shortland earlier that day, Tanaka had thus far lost six of them to the continuous and devastating American air attacks. There was no way to count the losses among the Japanese soldiers at this time. But, after hearing a report that Japanese search planes had sighted American ships southeast of Guadalcanal, he temporarily changed his convoy's course to the northeast toward Santa Isabel.

The 1st MAW received a 3:00 p.m. broadcast from CINCPAC to all task force commanders, "Looks like all out attempt now underway to recapture Guadalcanal regardless losses."[13] The men at CACTUS already knew how the determined the Japanese were to land their reinforcements. The several air attacks on Tanaka's convoy launched from both Guadalcanal and the carrier *Enterprise* had inflicted heavy damage resulting in burning ships and slaughtered soldiers. Nevertheless, the Japanese admiral had not given up his determination to complete his mission. Newton's third law of motion states that a strong force can only be stopped by an equally strong but opposite force. CACTUS never wavered in their own resolution to stop Tanaka.

The ground crews worked tirelessly to rearm and refuel their planes as the aircraft continued to land after completing their missions and to take off again to attack the transport convoy. About 30 minutes after receiving CINCPAC's message, Lt. Cmdr. Thomas led seven SBDs to again attack the Japanese convoy. But these planes never reached their goal. A group of Zeroes intercepted them and shot down three SBDs and heavily damaged two more. Worst of all, they did not score a single hit on the Japanese transports.

✲ ✲ ✲

Despite the disappointing lack of results from Thomas' foray, the 1st MAW's overtired ground crews prepared for another attack on the convoy late in the afternoon of November 14. The Fighter Director Officer at Fighter One, Lt. Lewis C. Mattison, encapsulated the prevailing attitudes among the wing's senior officers of that day in his war diary. After absorbing the news of the devastating damage being done to the transports by the incessant attacks, he stated that the news "seems too good" and "Skepticism, fear, hope and optimism play tag around the hilltop."[14]

The crews armed and fueled 17 SBDs to be led by Sailer, put bombs aboard three TBFs commanded by Coffin, and loaded the machine guns and filled the tanks of 14 F4Fs commanded by Maj. Fontana and Capt. Foss. Meanwhile, after being pushed by Yamamoto's Combined Fleet, the Japanese artillery on the island began shelling Henderson Field and Fighter One with two 150-mm howitzers with some 75-mm howitzers joining the bombardment party. One of the Marine fighter squadron's war diaries reflected the indifference with which the Americans on Guadalcanal greeted these almost incidental intrusions, "In spite [sic] of this, operations proceeding normally but nerves were on edge, and no one whistled or ran."[15]

With shellfire falling around them, the pilots received their mission briefings and orders. All three groups of planes took off and headed to the northwest. The sun moved down on the western horizon. The highly angled light revealed a convoy in total chaos with burning hulks scattered up the Slot and the still operational transports heading for Guadalcanal on any course that would get them there. As Tanaka saw the next group of attacking American planes at 5:15 p.m., the final Japanese CAP of six Zeroes led by the celebrated Lt. Cmdr. Mitsugi Kofukuda arrived from Buin. Forty-five minutes earlier, Lt. (jg) Shoichi Koyanagi led seven observation seaplanes from the *Kunikawa Maru*, *Sanyo Maru*, and *Sanuki Maru*, newly arrived about 30 minutes before from Rekata. The Japanese CAP now outnumbered the American fighters.

Fontana's eight F4Fs tangled with the Japanese fighters and more than held their own. The American fighters engaged in what Fontana called "one mass dogfight" and shot down six float planes and two Zeroes while only losing one F4F with the pilot surviving the battle.

Sailer's SBDs drew the most attention from the CAP. Two radiomen flying in two of the Major's SBDs claimed shooting down some Zeroes. When they landed at Buin, the four surviving Japanese pilots from Kofukuda's group stated they had only fought against American carrier bombers. The SBD pilots claimed making five hits on two transports. Tanaka stated in his memoirs that 21 bombers—17 B-17s, four carrier bombers—attacked just before sunset. He further wrote that the only transport lost was the 7,000-ton *Nako Maru*. The hapless ship took the brunt of the American bombing attack. She burst into flames when the ammunition she carried in her cargo holds exploded. The burning transport aimlessly drifted as the destroyer *Suzukaze* pulled 1,100 survivors from her decks. She was an abandoned, drifting hulk and joined the other lost transports in the convoy's list of ships incapable of fulfilling their assigned mission.

The last assault of this long, productive day came at 5:38 p.m. from Coffin's three TBFs with a horizontal bombing run. They took aim at two stalled transports and claimed two hits. Tanaka stated that no more bombs hit his transports. The third of Coffin's pilots, Lt. (jg) Jerome A. Rapp, Jr., sharply turned his TBF left and right trying to dodge the AA fire reaching up to his plane after dropping his bomb. His turret gunner, AM3c Clarence T. Wall, screamed over the plane's intercom that a Zero was now on their tail. Wall could only fire one short burst from his .50-cal. machine gun at the oncoming Zero. Confirmed by Coffin and Rapp, his aim proved to be on target as they saw the Japanese fighter roll over on its back and dive into the sea.

Although the Americans finished bombing Tanaka's convoy as the light disappeared with the coming of night, there was still enough light for the American fighters still aloft to apply some finishing touches to the successes of the day. Three F4Fs flown by Bauer, Foss, and 2nd Lt. Thomas W. Furlow circled as they looked for any SBDs that may be in difficulty. They saw the burning *Shinanogawa Maru* and *Arizona Maru* with swarming groups men on their decks still attempting to escape. The targets were too tempting to pass up so the three pilots began strafing them. Small boats crowded around the dying ships as the men tried to climb into them. The destroyers *Naganami* and *Makinami* stood nearby. Bauer and Furlow picked one ship while Foss selected the other. Their fighters' 50-cal. guns spit fire and death as their bullets churned the water, destroyed many small boats, and struck the ships' sides and decks. The carnage can only be imagined to be horrifying among the luckless men trying to save themselves.

Bauer battled and shot down a Zero only to be shot down himself—probably by Masaji Suganami who was determined to take revenge for the losses his command had sustained. Foss thought he saw Bauer in the water. A strafing Zero probably sealed the pilot's fate since his body was never found.

Assessing the Damage

Darkness descended on the waters north of Guadalcanal. Tanaka was considerably less than satisfied as he assessed the massacre his convoy had suffered. He estimated that more than 100 American planes had assaulted his ships in six attacks that day. The bombs and torpedoes had sunk six transports and killed 400 men. He had one reason for hope because he believed that his destroyers had rescued more than 5,000 of the invasion troops.

His force had taken a clobbering. His destroyers spewed black smoke from their stacks as they laid down smoke screens to hide the transports now evasively maneuvering toward Lunga. The ship's crews were near total exhaustion. As far as he could perceive, the future course of the Japanese plan was cloudier than ever. As he thought deeply about what was to come, he could still see the American bombs falling from the sky, water spouts from their explosions, bombs exploding on the ships and sending towering walls of flame and smoke roaring upward, and the ships listing that only meant their doom was near. After each attack, the remaining ships tried to reassemble and proceed on their mission, but the time they would desperately need to land their troops and supplies ebbed away.

He now had left only four transports (the *Hirokawa Maru*, *Yamazuki Maru, Yamaura Maru,* and *Kinugawa Maru)* and five destroyers (his flagship *Hayashio*, *Oyashio*, *Kagero*, *Umikaze*, and *Takanami).* Tanaka was not sure if he should continue on his mission. With the possibility of facing an American fleet of warships, he thought of retreating northward and waiting for help from any or all of Kondo's Advance Force. But a dispatch received from Yamamoto at 5:41 p.m. made up his mind for him. The Combined Fleet commander-in-chief unequivocally ordered Tanaka to take his transports toward the beaches of Guadalcanal and land those troops, no matter what it cost.

At 6:15 p.m., they now relentlessly steamed for the beaches on Guadalcanal. Nevertheless, they would not be able to land on the 14th. The earliest Japanese soldiers could touch land was dawn on November 15. Then, a Japanese search plane spotted four American cruisers and four destroyers on their way toward his convoy. Another search plane reported seeing Lee's fleet. If they kept to their reported course and speed, either group of American ships could intercept his convoy off Cape Esperance. Mikawa's cruisers were nowhere to be seen because they had escaped to Shortland. His transports were now rendered defenseless against the soon-to-arrive American warships. The foretold doom he felt when his convoy steamed from the Shortland Islands was more confirmed in his mind than ever. The invasion would have to wait until daylight on the next day.

Normally, one would expect the 1st MAW's totally spent men to be ebullient with their successes of that day. But these combat-hardened veterans knew better. The Japanese would never be stopped until the means to carry out their missions was totally destroyed. The men of CACTUS had taken quite a bite out of the Japanese forces. Meanwhile, CACTUS salvaged many of their aircraft to fight again—24 of 39 F4Fs, 16 of 32 SBDs, 13 of 15 TBFs, all 10 P-39s, 13 of 16 P-38s, and nine of 10 B-26s. After losing 38 aircraft to combat on November 14, the 1st MAW had 85 airplanes to defend Guadalcanal.[16]

☆ ☆ ☆

As daylight disappeared on the western horizon, all these planes were now rendered powerless. But powerful naval forces were approaching the waters off Guadalcanal. They were on collision courses that would settle the issue once and for all. For the first time since the Pacific War began, the mighty battleships of the U.S. Navy and the Imperial Japanese Navy would meet in a classic night surface battle, the one that the battleship worshipers in both navies had been wanting with every fiber in their bodies. And the outcome of that would decide whether the Americans would stay on Guadalcanal or be summarily evicted. The second part of the Naval Battle of Guadalcanal was about to begin.

CHAPTER 47
Moving into Combat

A New Battleship and a Fighting Admiral

Radm. Willis Augustus Lee, Jr., felt right at home on his flagship. This was his first flag command, Task Force 64, and it steamed toward Guadalcanal waters. His Task Force had two of the most modern battleships in the world, the *Washington* and *South Dakota*. He flew his flag on the *Washington*, and she was more than worthy of that honor. Launched on June 1, 1940 and commissioned into the U.S. Navy on May 15, 1941, she was one of two *North Carolina*-class of battleships the Americans launched after the Washington Naval Treaty expired. These replaced the older, slower battleships of the types that had been bombed at Pearl Harbor. The shift in emphasis toward naval aviation as the key weapon required faster and better armed battleships similar to those being built by the British and Japanese. She carried nine 16-inch guns mounted in a trio of three-gun turrets, two forward and one aft. Her secondary armament included 20 five-inch guns mounted in ten two-gun turrets, 16 1.1-inch AA guns mounted in four quad-gun emplacements, 12 .50-cal. machine guns, and she carried three aircraft. Built to withstand 14-inch shell hits and with a top speed of 28 knots, the *Washington* and the *South Dakota* were more than a match for the Japanese battleships in the South Pacific.

Lee possessed one of the best minds in the U.S. Navy. His lined and weather-beaten facial features fit the picture of a man of the sea who was more than capable of leading the Americans into their first capital ship sea battle against the more experienced Japanese admirals.

✲ ✲ ✲

Born on May 11, 1888, in Natlee, Owen County, Kentucky, Lee graduated from the Naval Academy at Annapolis in 1908 with the reputation for being a crack-shot with a rifle. He began his first sea duty on the re-commissioned cruiser *New Orleans* from November 15, 1909, until he transferred to the gunboat *Helena*, which was part of the Asiatic Station, in May 1910. Leaving the *Helena* in January 1913, he took part in inter-service rifle shooting competitions as a member of the Navy's team. He returned to sea in July 1913 aboard the battleship *Idaho*, transferred to the battleship *New Hampshire* in December, and stayed aboard her for two years. His ship participated in the occupation of Vera Cruz, Mexico, in April 1914. While carrying the rank of ensign, he went ashore as a member of his ship's landing force.

His next assignment was as the Inspector of Ordnance at the Union Tool Company in Chicago. That billet lasted three years. After America entered World War I, Lee joined the destroyer *O'Brien* in November 1918 then on duty in Queenstown, Ireland. One month after arriving in Ireland, he transferred to the destroyer *Lea* and remained aboard her until being ordered back to the U.S. in June 1919 to participate in rifle shooting matches with the Navy's rifle team.

After finishing the matches in September 1919, he became the executive officer on submarine tender *Bushnell* serving in the Atlantic Fleet. Again, the Navy needed his shooting talent when they ordered him to become a member of the American rifle team at the 1920 Olympic Games at Antwerp, Belgium. There, his team won nine gold, two silver, and two bronze medals while Lee personally won five firsts, one second, and one third.

After commanding several destroyers, finishing the senior course at the Naval War College, serving as the Inspector of Ordnance at the Naval Ordnance Plant in Baldwin, Long Island, and as the captain of the Navy's rifle team, he served in the Division of Fleet Training, Office of the Chief of Naval Operations. For the first time, he was in the Navy's center of power and drew the notice of senior naval officers in Washington. In the spring of 1931, he became the battleship *Pennsylvania*'s navigator. Serving aboard the U.S. Fleet's flagship led to his promotion to the rank of captain and becoming the *Pennsylvania*'s captain. He returned to Washington to be head of the Gunnery Section, Division of Fleet Training from 1933-1935 and head of the division's Tactical Section from 1935-1936. He went back to sea as the captain of the light cruiser *Concord* until July 1938 when he joined the staff of Radm. Harold R. Stark, a future Chief of Naval Operations, aboard his former command, now Stark's flagship.

By June 1939, Lee became the Assistant Director of the Division of Fleet Training and was promoted to be its Director in January 1941. After being appointed to the assistant chief of staff to the Commander in Chief, U.S. Fleet in February 1942, he received his promotion to rear admiral six months later and assumed the command of Battleship Division 6 aboard the battleship *Washington* as his flagship.

While there are few sources that tell what kind of man he was, one can make some fairly intelligent guesses. Based on the published reports about how he conducted himself during combat, he seemed to have a similar personality to his commander, Adm. Halsey. He was not afraid to take chances and had a quick mind to analyze complex situations that allowed him to make fast, effective decisions. He seemed to be a decisive commander who would not hesitate to engage the enemy with all the vigor and intelligence he had. These qualities would serve him well in the sea battle to come.[1]

The Japanese Come Calling

Adm. Kondo knew that Mikawa's mission to bombard the American airfields on Guadalcanal had failed. When Tanaka tried to return to the Shortlands but was forced to continue his mission under Yamamoto's direct orders, Kondo had to bring more ships closer to Guadalcanal and disable the American air power by pulverizing the airfields under a withering naval barrage. As long as the American aircraft could attack any Japanese ship during daylight hours, the only window available to the Japanese commander was to carry out the bombardment at night.

He also knew that American warships were near Guadalcanal after receiving a sighting report at 2:55 p.m. that saw Lee's ships about 100 miles south of Guadalcanal. The report also stated that there were two "cruisers" and four destroyers. The "cruisers" were actually the battleships *Washington* and *South Dakota*. A subsequent sighting at 6:25 p.m. repeated that the fleet had two "cruisers" and four destroyers still headed for Tanaka's convoy. The latest report prompted a warning to Tanaka from the Combined Fleet Headquarters at Truk. He had already positioned what was left of his convoy so that Kondo's ships would be between the oncoming American ships and his own convoy.

Kondo ordered his Bombardment Group to move southward toward Guadalcanal. He led the battleship *Kirishima*, the heavy cruisers *Atago* and *Takao*, the light cruisers *Sendai* and *Nagara*, and eight destroyers. His flag flew on the *Atago*, and he had two admirals under his command. The first was Radm. Susumu Kimura flying his flag on the *Nagara* as commander of a screening group that included the five destroyers *Shirayuki*, *Hatsuyuki*, *Teruzuki*, *Samidare*, and *Inazuma*. The second was Radm. Shintaro Hashimoto on the *Sendai* with the three destroyers *Uranami*, *Shikinami*, and *Ayanami*.

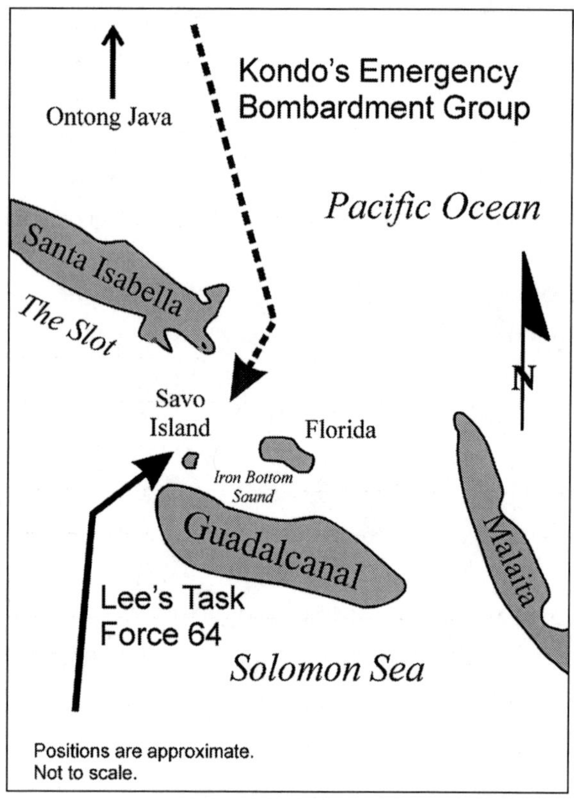

Kondo's and Lee's Approach

A disturbing development brought a new source for concern when the American submarine *Flying Fish* fired a torpedo at 4:29 p.m. that harmlessly passed under the *Asagumo*'s keel. Although the submarine caused no damage, it did radio a plain language report to the Americans of meeting the Japanese force. Japanese radio intelligence overheard the message and forwarded it to Kondo. The Americans now knew where his ships were.

By 5:35 p.m., Japanese search planes confirmed the force Kondo was about to engage had a "few" cruisers. It could be no surprise that he felt his ships could more than outgun just two cruisers and four destroyers. His confidence grew when he told Tanaka at 5:00 p.m. that he intended to clear the way for Tanaka's convoy by destroying any opposition from American naval forces. As soon as Kondo destroyed the Americans, Tanaka would move to the beaches and disgorge reinforcements and their supplies on Guadalcanal's northern shore.

He could not have been more ebullient when another sighting report arrived at 8:45 p.m. confirming that two American cruisers and four destroyers continued to approach Guadalcanal from the south at a speed of 25 knots and 16 miles west-southwest of Cape Esperance. Forty-five minutes later, a Japanese Air Force plane reported sighting two cruisers and four destroyers 50 miles west of the *Atago*. Confidence turned into bewilderment. Kondo reasoned that if this report was a valid sighting, there were *two*, not one, groups of American ships. Suddenly, the opposition had doubled in size. Therefore, he made new assumptions that his ships might confront a much larger force than originally thought.

Lee wished he knew more about the size and composition of the Japanese ships he could face as he proceeded northward. What he did know about the opposition from air search reports and the *Flying Fish*'s radio message was that there would likely be a bombardment group and a transport convoy off Guadalcanal.

Lee had no formal orders from Halsey. There had been some opposition to sending the only two American battleships into combat in the narrow waters around Guadalcanal, and Savo Island. But Halsey wanted to make sure he provided all his command had to protect the Marines on Guadalcanal and he held nothing back. He trusted Lee's ability to lead battleships into combat and gave him complete flexibility as to how to meet the Japanese naval threat. Lee decided to proceed east of Savo Island, circumnavigate it, and meet the Japanese ships coming from the north as early as possible. Lee did not send out specific orders to his captains but sent his "general intentions" by signal lamp.

A Comparison of Forces

A table showing the ships Lee and Kondo brought to this conflict shows an apparent advantage to the Japanese.

Composition of Forces—Admirals Kondo and Lee—November 14-15

Kondo	
Battleships	*Kirishima*
Heavy cruisers	*Atago, Takao*
Light cruisers	*Sendai, Nagara*
Destroyers	*Shirayuki, Hatsuyuki, Teruzuki, Samidare, Inazuma, Uranami, Shikinami, Ayanami*
Lee	
Battleships	*Washington, South Dakota*
Destroyers	*Walke, Benham, Preston, Gwin*

But, while the Japanese had more ships than the Americans, the Americans had more powerful guns. The nine 16-inch guns on each American battleship could easily penetrate any of the Japanese ships' armor including on the *Kirishima*. The *Kirishima*'s 14-inch shells could not penetrate the American battleship armor. Either American battleship's broadside sent more powerful and larger caliber shells than the *Kirishima* could fire: 24,300 pounds for the Americans versus 11,920 pounds for the *Kirishima*. The Americans had 18 16-inch guns on two battleships while the sole Japanese battleship had just eight 14-inch guns. As it had been in prior sea battles between the Americans and the Japanese, the Japanese still had two key advantages. The first was the night's darkness in the confining waters north of Guadalcanal. The second was more batteries firing their more powerful Long Lance torpedoes that could easily breach American battleship armor.

The stage was set for a confrontation between the two forces. And what a battle it would be![2]

CHAPTER 48
Clash of Giants

November 14, 10:00 p.m.—11:57 p.m.

As darkness fell over Iron Bottom Sound, some marines ashore looked out to sea and saw the glowing fires of Tanaka's transports by the time Lee's two battleships and four destroyers steamed past Cape Esperance 21 miles southwest of Savo Island. Lee then turned eastward at 9:10 p.m. and steamed on a course due east until he turned 38 minutes later to a new course of 150° at a speed of 17 knots. The magnetic compasses on the ships began to react to the steel of the sunken ships that now littered the sea bed of Iron Bottom Sound.

He looked over toward Iron Bottom Sound and saw low hanging cirrus clouds over the waters ahead. The sea was as calm and flat as a table top. Over the clouds hung a setting quarter moon whose light played over the calm waters. Darker clouds foreshadowed rain squalls around the area where the upcoming battle would happen. These small storms were a common occurrence in these waters and did not give any concern to Lee's thoughts. Another reminder his ships were in the Melanesian tropics was a sweet honeysuckle-like smell brought by a light seven knot breeze wafting over of the ships and into the crews' nostrils that belied the acrid smell of Guadalcanal's rotting jungle vegetation. The towering outlines of Guadalcanal, Florida, and Savo Islands seemed to be closing in on the ships as they continued on their east-southeasterly course at a relatively leisurely 17-knot pace. The ship radar scopes showed no indication of any nearby Japanese ships.

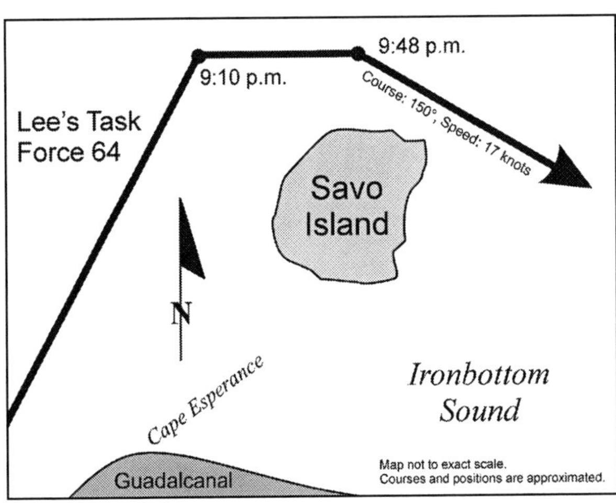

Lee Circles Around Savo Island

Apprehensive that he did not have sufficient intelligence about Japanese intentions, Lee asked the radio station on Guadalcanal what information they might have. Since his Task Force had not had the time to establish a radio call sign, Lee's first inquiry received the brusque reply from Radio Guadalcanal, "We do not recognize you." Lee used his Academy nickname that he hoped Vandegrift would remember to help convince the Americans ashore who he was, "CACTUS, this is Lee. Tell your boss 'Ching' Lee is here and wants the latest information." While he waited for Guadalcanal to answer, the *Washington*'s radio picked up a conversation from one of the captains of three PT boats patrolling northeast of Savo Island, "There go two big ones, but I don't know whose they are!" Not wanting to be mistakenly torpedoed by the American boats, Lee raised the conversation's urgency with a hastily prepared message to Guadalcanal, "Refer your big boss about Ching Lee; Chinese, catchee? Call off your boys!" A sudden flood of messages from the PT boat captains reassured Lee they now realized whose ships these were that headed into Iron Bottom Sound and who commanded them. Guadalcanal's answer did little to help Lee understand what awaited his command, "The boss has no additional information." Nevertheless, a radio message arrived a few minutes later that said Lee should expect an escorted Japanese convoy to arrive in Iron Bottom Sound's vicinity between 12:30 a.m. and 2:30 a.m. on November 15.[1]

✲ ✲ ✲

Kondo's formation steamed at 10:00 p.m. in three sections as Lee conducted his frustratingly uninformative conversation with Guadalcanal. Adm. Kimura separated his force from Kondo to be able to operate freely. He put his flagship *Nagara* leading a column of four destroyers, the *Shirayuki*, *Hatsuyuki*, *Samidare*, and *Inazuma*.

The *Shikinami*'s lookouts nearly instantly saw the outlines of American ships on a 200º bearing. The lookouts on the *Uranami* also saw the American ships that included "new-type" cruisers. The *Sendai* reported seeing "two enemy cruisers and four destroyers" north of Savo Island and heading for Iron Bottom Sound. Adm. Hashimoto sent his flagship *Sendai* and the three destroyers *Shikinami*, *Uranami*, and *Ayanami* and moved away from both Kondo and Kimura to get a better look at the American ships. Hashimoto split off the *Ayanami* ahead of his ships on a counterclockwise course around Savo Island. He wanted to make sure Kondo's battleship and cruisers would have a clear path to where they would shell the American airfields. Nonetheless, the Japanese plans would soon change.

By 10:31 p.m., Kondo began receiving disturbing reports as the *Atago* also reported seeing the Americans with more silhouettes appearing to the west. By 11:00 p.m., a flood of reports poured into the *Atago*'s radio room. A two-hour old message from a Japanese Air Force plane arrived and stated it had spotted Lee's force on its northeasterly course with two destroyers followed by two cruisers or battleships. Kondo analyzed the disparate reports and incorrectly reasoned the ships to the west were part of Tanaka's convoy while the ships to the south were the Americans.

The *Sendai* sent a signal at 11:07 p.m. that the American ships had changed their course from a southeasterly direction to due west. Kondo had wanted to take his Bombardment Group south of Savo Island. But, after reading the *Sendai*'s message, he changed his course to the northeast to avoid colliding with the American ships. Persistently believing the Americans had just two cruisers and four destroyers, he dispatched Hashimoto and Kimura's light-cruiser-led forces to attack and sink the American ships. Ten minutes later, the *Uranami* found the Americans ten miles south of Savo Island steaming on a due west course at 18 knots.

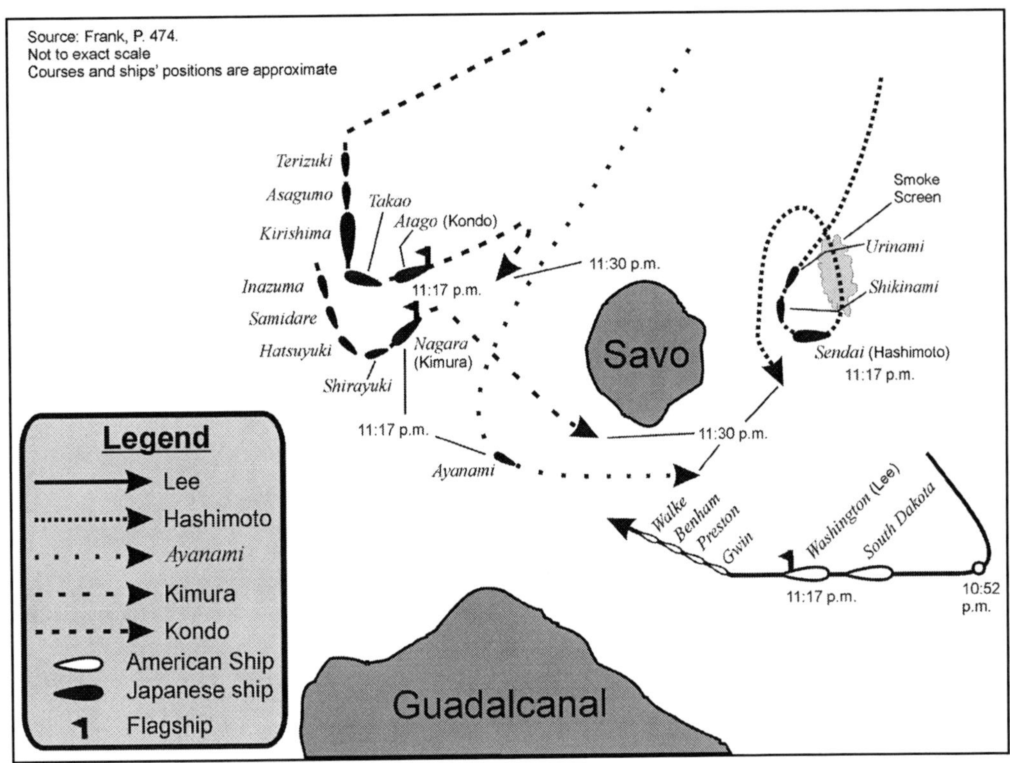

Naval Battle of Guadalcanal—November 14—11:17 p.m.—11:30 p.m.

Lee had actually turned to the west at 10:52 p.m. When the *Washington* turned into the frothy path the leading four destroyers had made, her SG radar detected Hashimoto's three ships just nine miles away to the northwest. The operators in the battleship's radar shack tracked three blips when the officer on duty in her main battery director had the Japanese ships in sight. The *South Dakota*'s fire controllers also saw the Japanese ships. Nevertheless, the American destroyers were still blind to the Japanese presence. With a confirmed sighting of Japanese ships due north under his guns, Lee ordered his captains at 11:16 p.m. to "open fire when you are ready."[2] The first battle between American and Japanese battleships was about to begin.

The *Washington*'s five-inch guns fired star shells to illuminate the ship's targets. The silence of that night shattered one minute later with an ear-drum-breaking blast and blinding light when the battleship's nine 16-inch guns fired its first broadside salvo in combat. The *South Dakota* had its guns turned northward and fired its nine big guns less than a minute later. The *Washington*'s radar operators reported seeing one pip flickering as if it had been hit and was sinking. Radio operators on the *South Dakota* heard "excited Japanese voices" all talking at once.

Hashimoto heard the distant firing to the south, saw the flashes of big guns, and observed huge water spouts blossoming all around his ships. Not one American shell hit a single Japanese ship. Probably grateful for his initial good fortune and still believing the huge spouts of water were from cruisers' eight-inch shells, he turned his ships around, laid a smoke screen, and hoped that when he emerged from the smoke, he would have a better firing solution for his own guns.

✲ ✲ ✲

When the battleships' guns blasted away in the night, the four American destroyers were two miles ahead of the flagship. They had just changed course to a 300º heading at a point south of Savo Island. The *Walke*, leading, had the only FD fire control radar, none of the four destroyers had an SG radar with which to detect the Japanese ships. The *Walke*'s radar picked up a ship on the destroyer's starboard beam on a reciprocal course with Savo Island in its background. Just as the battleships stopped firing at 11:22 p.m., the *Walke*'s five-inch guns opened fire at the intruder. The detected ship was the fearless *Ayanami*, which now headed for the American ships and ready to do battle all by itself. The next American destroyer in the column, the *Benham*, also fired away at the Japanese destroyer. Meanwhile, the sharp-eyed lookouts on the *Preston* fortunately spotted Kimura's cruiser and her escorting destroyers just ahead of its starboard bow coming around Savo Island's southwestern corner. The *Preston*'s guns blazed away at Kimura's force at 11:27 p.m. that alerted the rest of the American ships of their presence. The *Walke* pointed its guns and fired at the new threat with the *Gwin*, which had been firing star shells to light up the targets, joining the party.

✲ ✲ ✲

Believing the ships firing at his ships were three destroyers and a cruiser, Kimura's ships returned fire with the *Nagara*'s five five-inch and the *Ayanami*'s five-inch guns. Shortly thereafter, the rest of his destroyers opened fire. The Japanese flashless powder and Savo Island's outline shielded them from detection and made the American aim inaccurate. Meanwhile, the American destroyers' silhouettes were quite easy to see against the open sea. It did not take the Japanese torpedomen long to respond by firing their excellent Long Lance torpedoes. The *Ayanami* launched their missiles at 11:30 p.m. Just five minutes later, Kimura ordered a turn to port and gave permission for the rest of his ships to fire Long Lances. None of the torpedoes came close to their intended targets.

Japanese gunfire, likely from the *Nagara*, began taking its toll on the *Preston* before the torpedo wakes appeared. One shell crashed between the two fire rooms, killing all men in both compartments and piling firebrick and other rubble over the amidships' section. The shell's impact also knocked down the No. 2 stack, which fell on the starboard torpedo tubes, slashed open their warheads and set them afire. A mass of shells smashed into the engine rooms and pummeled the rear gun mounts that turned them into a blazing mass of scorching ruins. Almost every man died in the aft auxiliary conning area. The destroyer's executive officer was one of those. The forward guns jammed. The ship jerkily turned to starboard, and the stern began to sink. The ship's captain, Cmdr. Max C. Stormes, ordered the *Preston* to be abandoned at 11:36 p.m. The doomed destroyer rolled over on her starboard side, slowly settled into the water with her bow pointed straight into the air for about ten minutes, and sank less than 30 seconds later. Stormes and 117 other men went down with her.

As the men on the *Gwin* saw the *Preston* being battered, two shells hit the destroyer at 11:32 p.m. in the after engine room. The room's high pressure steam lines burst open and flooded the compartment with deadly and scalding superheated steam. The engine room and the handling room crews escaped while the explosion broke the latches that held the torpedoes in place. All of the *Gwin*'s torpedoes dangled out of their tubes; three of them slipped into the sea and luckily did not explode. Another shell hit the water and glanced into her stern. Two depth charges split open as the destroyer swung to avoid hitting the sinking *Preston*. That maneuver caused Japanese torpedoes to miss and allowed the destroyer to luckily survive the night.

Numerous shell hits clobbered the *Walke* when a Long Lance torpedo hit the destroyer just forward of her bridge. Its explosion blew up the ship's forward magazine. The entire doomed ship lifted out of the water and moved sideways to port. Her bow broke away; all power and communications shut down; several inches of oil from cracked fuel tanks covered her main deck; and flames engulfed what remained of the destroyer. Her ammunition store randomly exploded, and she began to settle in the water. Cmdr. Thomas E. Fraser, her skipper, issued the order to abandon ship. Her crew managed to get four life rafts into the water. But, as she sank, several of her depth charges exploded and killed more men who were now in the water, including her captain. Eighty men died with her as she sank at 11:42 p.m.

The *Benham* took a Long Lance torpedo in the forward-most point of her bow. While the resulting explosion caused no deaths, it opened a hole in her lower bow, shook the ship like a rag doll, and inundated her main deck with a monstrous wave of water that sent one man overboard and injured seven others. She looped to avoid more incoming shellfire and proceeded on her original course at a much slower speed of ten knots.

Kimura's command had not sustained any significant damage from the action thus far. The lone exception to that was what had happened to the *Ayanami*. She approached the American force at just less than two miles distant and paid the price. Despite using flashless powder when she fired her guns at the American ships, she gave away her position and drew the terror from the *Washington*'s big guns. No Japanese ship present that night could withstand a 16-inch barrage, and the *Ayanami* was no exception. The destroyer lost all power as the pummeling destroyed her engineering plant. She was afire from bow to stern and dead in the water.

While the *Washington* had just begun enjoying success in her first sea battle, the same could not be said for her companion, the *South Dakota*. Her crew was about to fire their guns when one of the men in the engine room accidentally tripped some circuit breakers on the switchboard at 11:30 p.m. and knocked out all electrical power throughout the ship. The search radar antennas stopped rotating and the scopes' screens immediately darkened. Capt. Thomas L. Gatch's report stated the incident's effect on the crew.

> "The psychological effect on the officers and crew was most depressing. The absence of this gear gave all hands a feeling of being blindfolded."[3]

Losing her electrical power meant her radars could not find any target for the ship's big guns. Because of Kondo's dispersal of his ships according to classic Japanese tactical tradition, all possible targets were now spread over the waters and made any visual sightings more difficult than ever. Reports came into the battleship's information center that claimed to have spotted motor torpedo boats, ships that did not exist, and gun batteries on Savo Island.

Since the *South Dakota* was the last ship in Lee's column, her lookouts had to look even harder to avoid colliding with the five ships ahead of her. The situation worsened when the American destroyers began to take shell hits, burst into flames, and fell out of their place in the formation. When the crew restored the power six minutes later, confidence surged once again among her crew. Nonetheless, the *South Dakota*'s problems did not end there.

The *Washington*'s captain maneuvered his ship such that the burning destroyers were to his starboard to hide his ship from Japanese lookouts as her crew managed to leave two life rafts for the *Walke*'s survivors. The *South Dakota*'s crew on the main deck heard shouts coming from the water and saw flashlights being shone by the *Preston*'s survivors. Alas, Gatch moved his ship so that the burning destroyers were to his port side. The *South Dakota* was now between the burning destroyers and the Japanese guns. Her silhouette made a perfect target while the ship was on the *Washington*'s starboard quarter, right in Lee's radar blind spot. The *South Dakota*'s beleaguered image on the flagship's radar appeared and vanished. The resumption of power allowed the battleship's rear 16-inch turret to open fire. The three 16-inch guns fired at 11:38 p.m., and the blast set the *South Dakota*'s three planes on fire. The next salvo extinguished the flames on one plane and blew the other two planes over the side.

With two American destroyers sinking and the other two ships unable to continue in combat, they did their job by foiling Japanese attacks on the battleships. At 11:48 p.m., Lee ordered the crippled *Gwin* and *Benham* to leave the battle area.

✲ ✲ ✲

As Hashimoto and Kimura engaged the Americans to the south and east of Savo Island, Kondo's ships languished to the west as the admiral waited for the right opportunity to bring his battleship and two cruisers within range of Henderson Field. As the fight moved toward Cape Esperance, Kondo moved his Bombardment Group to the southwest at 30 knots to put his ships between Tanaka's convoy and the approaching Americans. In order to give his two subordinates more time to finish with the Americans, he turned westward and slowed his force to 27 knots. He pointed his binoculars to the east at 11:19 p.m. and saw Hashimoto's ships generating a smokescreen. Sixteen minutes later, he looked to the south and could discern the silhouettes of three American destroyers and a "cruiser." Just as his force turned westward, his lookouts spotted ships off the starboard bow. Now more confused than ever, he ordered his force at 11:39 p.m. to remain west of Savo Island to confront the new sighting. According to Kondo, those ships' identity had not changed—they were part of Tanaka's convoy.

Kondo then ordered his force to turn northward at 11:50 p.m. Not much time passed when the *Takao* reported seeing one American battleship and three destroyers. Lee's destroyers had not departed yet. The *Atago*'s lookouts confirmed their sister ship's sighting when they believed they saw a vessel that "looked like a battleship."[4] Kondo stubbornly clung to his original information that the American forces never had any capital ships among them. After receiving a positive report at 11:50 p.m. from the *Ayanami* that the battle with the American ships was going well, he changed his course four minutes later to a 130° heading toward Lunga Point. As he did so, he also radioed his intentions to his other ship captains.

Hashimoto ordered the *Uranami* to aid the ailing *Ayanami*, followed his superior's orders, and turned the *Sendai* and *Shikinami* toward Henderson Field. But at 11:57 p.m., Kondo should have gained a newer but more dangerous perspective of what awaited his Bombardment Group when the *Nagara* reported spotting two American battleships north of Cape Esperance. He still stubbornly believed this latest sighting was not of battleships, but of cruisers.[5]

November 14-15, 11:57 p.m.—1:40 a.m.

While Kondo vacillated, Lee characteristically and aggressively turned the *Washington* to a 282° bearing as her radar detected the *Asagumo*, *Teruzuki*, *Atago*, *Takao*, and *Kirishima* and started tracking their progress. Conspicuously absent from the immediate vicinity on a meandering course, the troubled *South Dakota* was about one mile from the flagship's starboard quarter when another power failure disabled her radars at 11:55 p.m. for about five dangerous minutes. When the power came back on and her radars resumed operating, she sent a message she had spotted Japanese ships just off her starboard beam less than three miles in the distance.

☆ ☆ ☆

Kondo's lookouts saw the *South Dakota* at 11:58 p.m. Nevertheless, the admiral still insisted this was just a heavy cruiser. It took only one minute for the ship's distant silhouette details to become clearer and the Japanese lookouts insisted it was a battleship. Kondo still contended it was a cruiser. He would soon change his mind when the American 16-inch gunfire descended upon his force.

The American battleships were 11 miles west of Savo Island and just turning to clear their guns for a broadside when Kondo's force fired their deadly Long Lance torpedoes at the *South Dakota*. As the clock turned over to midnight, the beams of the *Atago*'s searchlights pierced the darkness and fell upon the American battleship. Now, Kondo could see for himself that the illuminated ship's superstructure could only belong to a battleship. At long last, the incontrovertible evidence changed his obstinate mind. More beams lit up the American battleship. The Japanese ship's guns roared almost simultaneously as shells ranging from 3.9-inches to 14-inches descended on her. Four more Long lances from the *Asagumo* hissed from their tubes at 12:02 a.m. and headed for the battleship.

Despite several of the *Atago*'s torpedoes exploding before they reached their intended target, some of the cruiser's lookouts believed they had hit the American battleship three to five times. The truth was that *none* of the torpedoes fired by any of the Japanese ships hit anything. Twenty-seven Japanese shells hit the battleship in just four minutes causing minimal damage because of the ship's superior armor. But 26 more hits impacted on the battleship's lightly-armored superstructure with some of them piercing it and not exploding. Nonetheless, one crewman remembered some of the shells exploding with "a loud crash, a rolling explosion" followed by a "the sizzling sound that metal fragments make when they crash into cables, guns, and the superstructure."[6] Neither the duds nor the ones that did detonate caused any appreciable damage but had some other effects on the ship and its crew. Lee wrote, "[to] render one of our new battleships deaf, dumb, blind, and impotent" as they disabled all the radios, left only one radar operational, killed or wounded many fire control men, and knocked out gun directors. The battleship, lacking any accurate targeting information, blindly fired four or five salvos in anger. Its four starboard five-inch guns continually fired, but had no known effect other than the Japanese reporting these guns returned "fierce" fire. While Kondo's ships gave their undivided attention to destroying the *South Dakota*, none of the Japanese noticed the *Washington* ominously near. The battleship radar and lookouts had both detected or seen the Japanese ships. Two of the *Washington*'s two-gun five-inch turrets opened fire at the cruiser *Atago*, and one five-inch turret fired star shells to cast their characteristic light over the water.

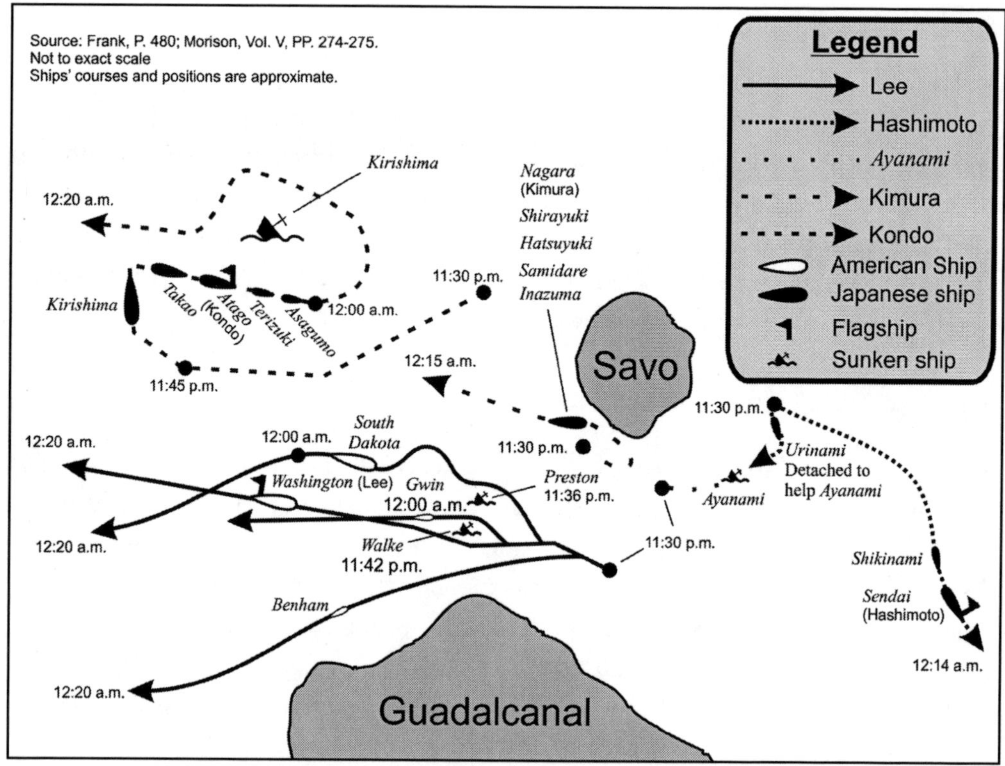

The American Battleships Enter the Fray—November 14-15

Meanwhile, all of the battleship's mighty nine 16-inch guns and 20 two-gun five-inch turrets belched fire and smoke at midnight. Their missiles of death rumbled toward the *Kirishima* from the nearly point-blank range of 8,400 yards. A deluge of water columns surrounded the Japanese battleship from nine 16-inch and more than 40 five-inch shells as some of these missiles delivered devastating blows on the ill-fated ship. And the shells kept coming and continually pummeled the hapless battleship. The barrages knocked out two 14-inch turrets, started fires deep in the ship's bowels, punched holes below the water line, and jammed the rudder. Water poured into the *Kirishima*'s starboard side below the waterline, and she began to list sharply to starboard. With her rudder jammed, she started steaming in a circle as huge clouds of thick, black, and acrid smoke poured skyward from her innards.

Kondo and his officers watched his ships deliver their blows on the *South Dakota*. She no longer answered their gunfire with fire of her own. Several fires had broken out on her superstructure. Kondo now believed his force had sunk the American battleship, but their revelry proved short-lived when star shells illuminated their positions and columns of water surrounded the flagship *Atago* and her sister ship *Takao*. Although none of the heavy cruisers received any hits from the incoming barrage, Kondo prudently ordered them to put out their searchlights. Knowing he had to increase the range to the American ships to launch their Long Lance torpedoes and escape any more American gunfire, Kondo ordered a course change to port at 12:05 a.m. Meanwhile, the *Kirishima* lost any ability to control her steering and went into spiraling turns to the west with a course resembling a drunk staggering out of a bar. Kondo changed his force's course to due west at 12:09 a.m. after he located Tanaka's convoy.

The *South Dakota* got a respite from the tormenting Japanese naval gunfire when they stopped firing their guns. Cmdr. A. E. Uehlinger and five other men were in Battle II, the ship's alternate conning location, when a shell cut the steam line to the ship's siren. Their situation seemed so perilous that they wondered what calamity would kill them first: flames, scalding steam, or choking smoke. They dutifully stayed at their posts as they fought the fires and turned off the severed steam line. Many of the ladders were so severely twisted or damaged they could no longer be used. The bodies of 39 dead or dying men and 59 wounded souls littered the decks with many of them on fire which hampered the fire fighters ability to put out or control the numerous fires. Capt. Gatch surveyed his once fine but now crippled command, decided his ship was more of a liability than an asset to Task Force 64, and asked Lee for permission to withdraw from the battle. Lee granted permission, and the battleship retreated at 12:10 a.m.

Kondo's Bombardment Unit saw a battleship about 6 miles away at 12:11 a.m. that was the *South Dakota*. He turned his ships to get a better firing angle for his torpedoes. Suddenly, his lookouts saw another American battleship ahead of the first one, the *Washington*. With a new target at which to fire his torpedoes, Kondo ordered the *Atago* and *Takao* to fire their torpedo tubes two minutes later at a range of more than 4,000 yards as he changed to a 300º course. This put his ships' broadsides facing the new threat. They thought they had hit the battleship just as the *South Dakota* turned to port and headed away from the *Washington*.

All that remained of Lee's command was the victorious, fast and powerful *Washington*. She had all her fighting capabilities intact; therefore, he was not finished inflicting damage on Kondo's ships. He altered his course to a 340º bearing at 12:20 a.m. and later observed the effect of this maneuver on the Japanese, "This move by *Washington* appeared to set the whole enemy field in motion to the north and northeast."[7] The battleship lookouts saw gun flashes off the starboard quarter. Kondo's cruisers had fired their guns and torpedo tubes. Three torpedoes and gun fire headed toward the *Washington* and missed their target.

✲ ✲ ✲

Despite no longer having the *Kirishima* with which to continue the battle, Kondo was not out of the battle yet. His heavy cruisers were potent weapons particularly with their feared Long Lance torpedoes. Poor intelligence continued to plague his efforts to determine the precise locations of the Americans. Nonetheless, he directed all his ships at 12:25 a.m. to attack two American battleships six miles north of Cape Esperance. Kimura responded by turning his ships on a pursuing course and trying to catch the fast-moving American capital ships. His ships were too far away to launch torpedoes and would catch up to the American battleships. Tanaka acted on his own by ordering the destroyers *Oyashio* and *Kagero* to attack the Americans but kept his remaining destroyers to escort the transports he had left. Hashimoto had not expected Kondo's order when it arrived and was not prepared nor capable of successfully executing it since he was off Lunga Point, like Kimura, and too far away to do any good.

When the *Washington* steered to its 340º course, it would eventually meet Kondo's ships. Kondo noticed the battleship's course change at 12:25 a.m. and ordered a speed change by slowing to 24 knots. Three minutes later, the Japanese admiral judged the American ship's course now converged with his own and was closing the range. He ordered a speed increase to 30 knots and a course change to parallel the American ships, a far superior position from which to launch his torpedoes. Japanese lookouts reported seeing torpedo hits that later proved to be false sightings. As the distance closed between the American and Japanese ships, Kondo increased his ship speed to 31 knots and made smoke.

Kimura's ships finished reloading their torpedo tubes at 12:30 a.m. and began chasing the *Washington*. Although Kimura was still too far away to inflict any damage, Lee saw the two destroyers *Oyashio* and *Kagero* generating a smoke screen to starboard and, at 12:33 a.m., that gave him something to worry about. Capt. Davis turned the battleship sharply to starboard to avoid steaming into the smoke and thus increase the danger of being torpedoed. Lee ordered the turn to continue to direct the *Washington* more to the south and leave the battle's scene. He now believed that Task Force 64 had inflicted enough damage to delay the Japanese from unloading troops and supplies until daylight when CACTUS' planes could attack the transports.

When Kondo saw the American battleship leaving the battle, he stopped the smokescreen and made the critical decision at 12:32 a.m. to cancel the bombardment of Guadalcanal. Lee continued his southward withdrawal and kept far to the west of Kondo's ships. But the *Washington* was not yet out of danger. The *Oyashio* and *Kagero* were in hot pursuit and to the starboard quarter. Kimura's light cruiser and destroyers also pursued the battleship and to the port side. While the *Kagero*'s officers had problems identifying the battleship at 12:39 a.m., the *Oyashio* fired some of its torpedoes. The *Samidare* fired a torpedo spread of its own at 12:45 a.m. Both destroyers' aim was good enough to cause their missiles to pass dangerously near the *Washington*. She zigged and zagged to evade the approaching dangers and came near enough to Lamon Island to cause some concern. Nevertheless, she managed to escape, not hit any reefs, or be struck by any torpedoes.

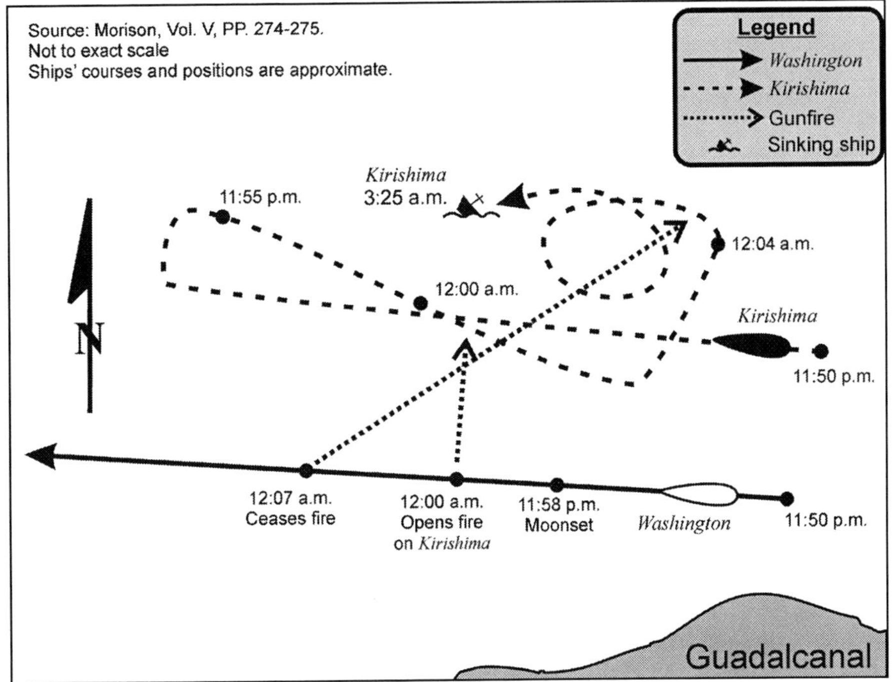

The Washington versus the Kirishima

Just when the *Samidare* fired its torpedoes at 12:45 a.m., Kondo lost all visual contact with the American battleship and took his time releasing the destroyers *Asagumo* and *Teruzuki* to go after it. He analyzed the tactical situation and concluded that Tanaka's convoy had a clear path to Guadalcanal, and he now had no requirement to protect the transports. He did not want to stay in these confining waters until daylight when his force could be attacked by carrier-based and land-based American aircraft. He reasoned that the preservation of the ships under his command was his primary duty since he had already lost two battleships. He had already canceled his planned bombardment of Guadalcanal, the only command for him to issue was to retreat. So, at 1:04 a.m., he did just that by ordering his ships northward. Not all his ships could leave right away. The cruisers *Atago* and *Takao* did not retire until nearly 30 minutes after Kondo's order.

Meanwhile, the *Kirishima*'s ordeal had not yet ended. Kondo ordered the Japanese battleship to retire at 12:45 a.m. but did not receive an acknowledgment of his instructions. The stricken ship's silence prompted him to order the destroyers *Asagumo* and *Teruzuki* and belatedly, the *Samidare*, to render any aid they could. When the *Asagumo* and *Teruzuki* arrived at 1:43 a.m. to where the battleship lay immobile five miles west of Savo Island, she was in bad shape. Sea water flowed into her hull although her boilers and engines could still operate. But the onrushing water inundated her steering machinery. With her rudder jammed at 10°, she could only move in a circle. Unlike her sister ship, the *Hiei*, the flooding below decks could no longer be controlled. Fires fiercely burned all over her hull and below deck. Despite the efforts of her hard-working damage control parties, the blazes spread and threatened the powder and ammunition magazines. Her skipper, Capt. Sanji Iwabuchi, ordered the fires below decks to be extinguished by flooding the endangered compartments, but the men in the ship's engineering compartments heard that order too late to evacuate their stations and drowned. Only one engine turned a single propeller, and she moved at an agonizingly slow speed.

The *Nagara* tried to throw a towline to the battleship but its crew refused to take it. The captain's attempt to stop her worsening list by counter-flooding now began to fail. Iwabuchi ordered the crew to the ship's bow. There, he presided over the traditional and somber Imperial Japanese Navy ceremonies taking place. To the shouts of three "Banzais" and the transfer of the Emperor's photograph to the *Asagumo*, the crew lowered the ship's ensign. The *Teruzuki* tried to come alongside, but not in time. The battleship rolled over and sank at 3:25 a.m. just 11 miles west of Savo Island, taking the captain and those participating in the ceremony with it. Another ship sank into the mud of Iron Bottom Sound.

Rescuing and Saving Lives

This was the time for each side to pull as many of their men from the water as they could. As the *Kirishima* sank, the Japanese destroyer *Uranami* plucked most of the crew of the sinking *Ayanami* from the water. The doomed ship's captain, along with 30 of the crew, stayed on board until the last possible moment before the destroyer went under and managed to get into a boat that took them to Guadalcanal. The *Ayanami*'s last moments ended with two huge explosions that sent her under at about 2:00 a.m.

✲ ✲ ✲

With much relief, Lee received messages from the *South Dakota* at 2:10 a.m. that confirmed the battleship, while damaged, could continue safely with the *Washington* to their home base. The *South Dakota* eventually joined the rest of Task Force 64 at 9:00 a.m. to return to Nouméa.

The destroyers *Benham* and *Gwin* had survived the battle with the *Benham* taking the worst of the damage. The heavily injured destroyer's hull made threatening creaks and groans as she moved through the water and her considerably shortened bow left a wider than normal wake trailing behind her. Her crew threw equipment in her bow over the side and moved as much as they could salvage to the ship's rear while attempting to repair her broken bulwarks and shoring up the ship's walls against the pressure from the sea outside. Her captain, Lt. Cmdr. John B. Taylor, moved all men from the bow to lessen the strain on her keel and the starboard side of her hull. If any of those restraints should fail, the ship was in severe danger of breaking apart.

Taylor advised Lee of his command's dire straits. The admiral ordered the two destroyers to steam to Espiritu Santo and left the decision of whether to abandon the *Benham* or not to Taylor's judgment. After the *Gwin* joined up with his ship at 3:30 a.m., Taylor gingerly conned his crippled command through calm waters until the breezes freshened and the seas became increasingly choppy.

After noon on November 15, the destroyer's predicament worsened and her chances for survival vanished. The turbulent seas prevented the *Gwin* from coming alongside. Nevertheless, she launched a boat that expertly navigated in the potentially dangerous water and managed to effectively shuttle crew members off the doomed destroyer. After rescuing all the *Benham*'s survivors, the *Gwin* tried to sink the *Benham* with four Mk-15 torpedoes that again proved to be frustratingly ineffective. As had been proven in the past, one missile exploded on the water before reaching the *Benham*, the second one missed, the third ran a course that resembled a chicken with its head cut off, and the fourth also missed the destroyer's stern. Finally, the *Gwin* fired one five-inch shell that exploded in one of the *Benham*'s magazines. The doomed destroyer finally sank at 7:35 p.m.[8]

Claims and Counterclaims

Kondo later claimed to have sunk one *South Dakota*-class battleship and another unidentified battleship as well as sending two cruisers and two destroyers "immediately to the bottom." The visual sighting capabilities of the Japanese seemed once again to prove superior to the American radar when they saw the *Washington* one hour before that ship's radar saw them. Despite poor tactics by the Japanese that took their Long Lance torpedoes out of the battle, the American torpedoes again proved to be inferior to their Japanese counterparts. The Japanese had a two-thirds advantage in torpedoes over the Americans but could only get one-third as many hits.

The American 16-inch guns outgunned the Japanese. Although the Japanese believed they had sunk the *South Dakota*, their 14-inch and eight-inch guns did not have the power to penetrate the American battleships' superior armor. Therefore, the damage on the *South Dakota*'s superstructure was the best the Japanese could do.

A debilitating lack of intelligence led Kondo to believe he faced just American cruisers and destroyers. When actual evidence to the contrary arrived in the form of huge columns of water from the *Washington*'s 16-inch guns and with actual visual confirmation, he finally realized his foe was far more powerful than he originally thought. The fact that it took Kondo so long to recognize the realities of the battle on the night of November 15 could demonstrate ineffectiveness at best or poor judgment at worst.

The loss of life between the Japanese and the American sailors could have been worse than it was: 242 American dead versus not less than 249 Japanese sailors lost. The Americans lost three destroyers—the *Preston*, *Benham*, and *Walke*—with damage to the *South Dakota* and *Gwin*. The Japanese lost the battleship *Kirishima* and destroyer *Ayanami*, one less ship than the Americans, but losing the *Kirishima* can only be viewed as a Japanese defeat.

The *South Dakota*'s struggle to return to the U.S. for repairs gained the ship much notoriety in the American press. Its captain received generous praise for himself and for his crew's courage in bringing their crippled ship safely home. Wartime censorship prevented the actual victory achieved by Lee and the *Washington* from becoming known until later in the war. Nevertheless, the *South Dakota*'s contribution to the American victory was nonexistent. For the Americans, the battle resulted in a total victory because Kondo abandoned his mission of bombarding the American airfields.

Tanaka's convoy, such as it now was, still lurked off Guadalcanal and had to land its troops and supplies. The American air power on Guadalcanal was ready and waiting to fight the next, and, as it turned out, the last part of this battle's drama.[9]

CHAPTER 49
A Failure to Deliver

Tanaka Resumes His Mission

Adm. Tanaka watched the progress of the great nighttime naval battle from his flagship, the destroyer *Hayashio*. Seeing the flashes from gunfire and explosions of the massive shells hitting ships, he became nervous about what might have happened to Kondo's force. He had much to be concerned about. Out of the 11 transports he had when he left the Shortland Islands, the sustained and devastating air attacks by American carrier and land-based aircraft had destroyed all but four and forced Tanaka to dispatch some of his destroyers to help the sinking transports. He still had his mission to deliver what he did have left onto the Guadalcanal beaches. He wanted to resume his passage toward Tassafaronga Point at high speed after resolving that he would land the troops even if it meant beaching the ships. Purposely beaching his four best transports was an unprecedented act. It concerned Tanaka, but he realized he had no other alternative. He asked Mikawa and Kondo for permission. Mikawa disapproved. Nonetheless, Kondo was in direct command of the operation and, along with Yamamoto's agreement, approved Tanaka's plan with the words, "Run aground and unload troops!"

Tanaka now gratefully headed toward Guadalcanal at 11 knots in the darkness. He arrived off Tassafaronga Point just as daylight appeared on the eastern horizon. At 4:30 a.m., he ordered the transports *Hirokawa Maru*, *Kinugawa Maru*, *Yamaura Maru*, and *Yamazuki Maru* to head for the shore and run up onto the beach. The rest of his force headed northward past Savo Island and to the north of Santa Isabel Island. This course would take him far away from danger before the American aircraft took off.

Before he left the Shortlands, he had considerable misgivings about the operation and, when he would escape northward, believed he was correct in having these concerns. The last large-scale Japanese effort to reinforce their soldiers on Guadalcanal was about to ignominiously end as American air crews awoke with the news they had another mission to fly.

A Deadly, Wrathful Rain of Fire

Obeying their admiral's orders, the Japanese transport captains headed for their assigned beach areas that ran along a line running from northwest to southeast: the *Yamazuki Maru* to Aruligo Point, the *Yamaura Maru* to Doma Cove, and the *Hirokawa Maru* and *Kinugawa Maru* near the mouth of the Bonegi River near Tassafaronga Point. Their journey had been a long and tortuous process of fits and

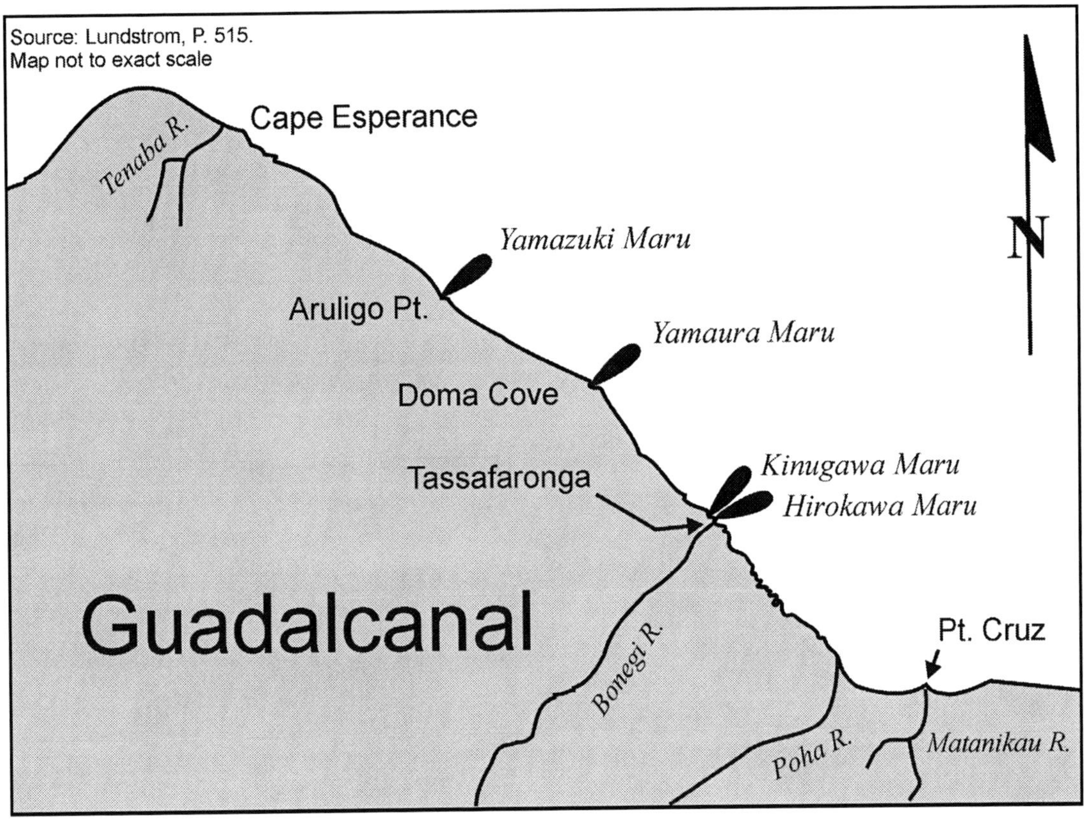

Source: Lundstrom, P. 515.
Map not to exact scale
Cape Esperance
Tenaba R.
Yamazuki Maru
Aruligo Pt.
Yamaura Maru
Doma Cove
Tassafaronga
Kinugawa Maru
Hirokawa Maru
N
Guadalcanal
Bonegi R.
Pt. Cruz
Poha R.
Matanikau R.

The Japanese Put Their Transports on the Beach

starts. The majority of their sister ships now lay on the sea bottom. They now rested on the sands of Guadalcanal and would stay there forever.

The floating survivors from the sunken American destroyers *Walke* and *Preston* witnessed the transports' passage toward the shore. Their morale received a large boost when they saw the *Kirishima*'s death throes as explosions racked her and sent her to the bottom. As daylight glowed over the waters, the water-bound sailors, still hopeful of a rescue, would observe the power of aircraft attacking the Japanese transports as they sat like beached whales on Guadalcanal's sands.

When the CACTUS aviators received the reports of the Japanese transports being beached, some confusion occurred. Those pilots had recently pummeled the *Kyushu Maru*, now a hulk on the beach between Doma Cove and Tassafaronga. As dawn rose at about 5:00 a.m., the beached transports had already begun unloading their cargoes and men while activity at the American airfields markedly increased. Maj. Renner in his Grumman J2F (Duck) amphibian and Capt. Foss with eight F4Fs were the first to leave to look for the fighter pilots Lt. Col. Bauer and Staff Sergeant Thomas C. Hurst, who had been shot down near the Russell Islands.

The Americans had just finished Fighter Two, a third airstrip on the island near the shore at Kukum and west of the Lunga River, but closer to Japanese artillery positions. The 1st MAW's commander wanted to scatter his fighters. So, several P-39s moved over there.

Just before sunrise, 1st Lt. James T. Jarman prepared a flight of P-39s for take off when shells from Japanese shore guns unexpectedly arrived. It seems that turning on the runway lights was just what the Japanese waited for to begin their shelling. The bombardment continued the rest of that day and kept the men of the 1st MAW on their toes.

Maj. Renner's F4F flight passed over the Japanese transports. Foss also saw one of them and sent a radio message that he had seen one ship with her deck full of soldiers. They flew near the Russell Islands and found no trace of Bauer. Another search of the area occurring later that afternoon yielded the same result. However, Foss managed to see one Japanese transport run aground near Aruligo Point.

The sun had by now appeared above the horizon when several American aircraft saw two transports with their keels ground hard onto the beach off Tassafaronga Point and the one near Doma Cove in the same predicament. They also saw the *Kyushu Maru*'s hulk aground. The American flyers and spotters initially believed this to be the fourth transport. The Army's Battery F, 244th Coast Artillery rolled out their two 155-mm guns near Lunga Point and began to lob shells at the closest transport about 19,500 yards away. Another 30 minutes passed when the Marines' five-inch guns began to fire salvoes of their own. Their gunfire continued as the gunners locked onto the ship with both sets of guns and were regularly hitting it. Then American aircraft joined in to add to the transports' misery.

Maj. Sailer took off with eight SBDs and attacked the two transports aground near Tassafaronga. As they dove in at 5:55 a.m., they noticed "much Japanese activity" and also saw several AA guns being offloaded onto the beach. Sailer's planes hit the transports with three bombs and returned to Henderson Field refuel and rearm.

Three SBDs led by Lt. (jg) Thomas W. Ramsay took off next along with Lt. Coffin in one TBF loaded with bombs. The SBDs climbed to their diving altitudes while Coffin attacked in his normal shallow dive. Coffin just missed a flight of eight Japanese Jake observation seaplanes led by Lt. Takeshi Horihashi—the only fighter protection the Japanese could muster for the transports. Coffin finished his attack but could only drop one of his four 500-pound bombs.

Ramsay's bombers reached their diving altitude of 12,000 feet when Horihashi's planes attacked the SBDs. But the dive-bombers pushed over into their dives anyway. Unable to continue their attacks, the Japanese planes soon left. With no opposition to stop the American planes, 16 more SBDs and 12 P-39s continuously assaulted the transports from 7:25 a.m. and 9:30 a.m. But Gen. Vandegrift had another card to play.

Lt. Cmdr. Raymond S. Lamb's destroyer, the *Meade*, was in Tulagi Harbor when Vandegrift ordered his ship at 8:30 a.m. to turn its five-inch guns on the transports. After leaving Tulagi at 9:14 a.m., the destroyer steamed across Iron Bottom Sound at 25 knots. A SOC Seagull spotter plane from the *San Francisco* and piloted by Lt. John A. Thomas, which had significantly helped end the *Hiei*'s life the night before, flew overhead and began guiding the *Meade*'s gunfire. The destroyer's five-inch guns zeroed in on all four transports and turned the *Yamazuki Maru* into a flaming wreck. She fired 600 rounds between 10:12 a.m. to 10:54 a.m. at the ships at Doma Cove and the two transports at Tassafaronga. Her shelling broke the *Yamaura Maru* at Doma Cove into a two-piece carcass. After finishing her bombardment of the doomed transport, the *Meade* then plucked the *Walke* and the *Preston* survivors from the sea. After witnessing the demise of the Japanese efforts to land their reinforcements, the water-soaked men at last received a reward for their patience with a new lease on life.

Some of the commanders became excited about the damage the destroyer had inflicted on the Japanese. Nonetheless, their enthusiasm subsided somewhat when they realized that the *Meade* could not have had the success it did if American aircraft had not put up an impenetrable fighter cover over Iron Bottom Sound.

✲ ✲ ✲

CACTUS aircraft shifted their effort to other targets after they saw the transports struggling to survive. While flying their SBDs north of Santa Isabel Island, 2nd Lieutenants John McEniry and George B. Herlihy sighted Tanaka's destroyers moving at top speed on a northwesterly course. No American planes were close enough to see Kondo's retreating ships much less attack them. Brig. Gen. Woods and Lt. Col. Albert D. Cooley knew these warships did not make ideal targets when there were other more promising ones nearby. They decided to thoroughly destroy the four abandoned transports *Brisbane Maru*, *Nako Maru*, *Arizona Maru*, and *Shinanogawa Maru* to keep the Japanese from salvaging them. The four wrecks wallowed north of the Russells and about 100 miles northwest of Lunga Point.

After receiving their orders, Lt. Larsen led four TBFs armed with torpedoes along with an escort of six F4Fs commanded by Maj. William R. Campbell. They took off at about 10:20 a.m., turned to the northwest, and leveled off at a low altitude. The results of the two days of bloody battle spread below them, and their observations tell what they saw, "...seventy miles of wreckage...along the groove: debris of ships, corpses, oil streaks, life rafts, and an occasional burning hulk."[1] As the planes were about 80 miles northwest of Savo Island, the TBF pilots could see the four Japanese transports with two of them (the *Arizona Maru* and *Shinanogawa Maru*) nearby and the other two (*Brisbane Maru* and *Nako Maru*) farther in the distance.

Lt. (jg) George D. Welles and Ens. Robert E. Oscar attacked the first two transports, which were stopped in the water and near each other. Their planes rolled into shallow dives. No Japanese fighters opposed the TBFs and no clouds blocked their vision, perfect conditions for an aerial torpedo attack. The American torpedo planes had ideal conditions for an uncontested attack. It was almost too easy.

The two pilots lined up the stationary ships in their cross-hairs, flew straight at them, and pulled their release levers. The torpedoes dropped into the water and ran hot, straight, and normal. They hit their targets and nothing happened. They were duds, now a normal occurrence with American torpedoes no matter from where they were launched.

Larsen and Lt. (jg) Lawrence S. Engel went after the other two distant transports and had at least some success. Although Larsen's torpedo missed its target, Engel's missile scored a direct hit on one transport. The two pilots circled overhead until that ship sank and then rejoined Welles and Oscar. Before their return journey to Henderson Field, they believed they saw another transport disappear beneath the waves. Now there were just two still afloat.

Espiritu Santo contributed 14 B-17s to the final demise of Tanaka's transports. Maj. Donald E. Ridings led one group of six bombers over the beaches but did not want to waste any of his bombs as they turned back to base. After one of the B-17s aborted its mission, the 98th Bomber Squadron's

Capt. Walter Y. Lucas led the remaining seven that dropped their 500-pound bombs on the beached ships. Lucas claimed one hit on one wrecked transport. Marine 2nd Lt. Robert R. Lynch flew over the waters south of Santa Isabel dropped his lone bomb on one of the two still-floating transports. Although no one saw it happen, one ship sank later that night. The sole surviving ship wandered aimlessly, probably carried by the prevailing currents, for four days before sinking.

Henderson Field's aviators had not yet completed its driving intent to mete out as much damage as possible against the beached ships. The P-39s relentlessly attacked them all day with bombing and strafing runs. Coffin's four TBFs returned at 11:45 a.m. to drop bombs and homemade incendiary bombs called "Molotov bread baskets." Lt. (jg) Gibson's three SBDs bombed the *Yamazuki Maru* at Doma Cove with Gibson's bomb scoring a near-miss. One of his wingmen, Lt. (jg) Ralph H. Goddard, looked for an AA battery at Tassafaronga but found a far better target. He dropped his bomb on a supply dump and hit it. A huge explosion resulted with a bilious, black cloud of smoke rising 2,000 feet into the sky. The fires from the blazing ships continued for 16 hours into the night and lit up the sky along the shore. CACTUS' radio sent a report that it was the "greatest sight ever seen on Guadalcanal."[2]

An anticlimactic air battle occurred two hours after the attacks on the transports ended when seven Vals with seven Zeroes escorting them arrived near Guadalcanal. Lt. Cmdr. Flatley led an intercepting seven F4Fs that forced the Japanese planes to turn back before they could damage any American installations or ships. Although Flatley claimed his group had shot down four Zeroes, only one Zero piloted by Leading Seaman Masahiro Ueno exploded in a ball of flame after Ens. Roland R. White put a deadly machine-gun burst into it. The Japanese incursion was their last air attack on Guadalcanal in 1942. Japanese planes would not return until January 25, 1943.

✲ ✲ ✲

The two-day Naval Battle of Guadalcanal was over. The results were of significant impact for both sides. The mighty struggle over which side would permanently possess the strategically important island had taken a certain turn in one direction.

Who Won and Who Lost?

The result of Tanaka's attempt to land soldiers, ammunition, and supplies on Guadalcanal fell far short of what the Japanese had originally intended. They wanted to reinforce their ground troops on Guadalcanal to such an extent that they could defeat the Americans and take control of the island. The actual outcome cost the Japanese 11 of their finest transports. The four transports that did make it to the beaches on Guadalcanal's northern coast and the destroyer *Suzukaze* managed to offload about 2,000 men, many of them infantry with the artillery and other support troops needed for a victory. Conspicuously absent were 260 boxes of ammunition and 1,500 bags of rice, about four days' rations for the starving and desperate 17th Army.

The guns had barely stopped firing before both sides claimed victory. The Imperial Japanese Navy grandiosely announced their ships had sunk eight American cruisers and four or five destroyers as well as heavily damaging two American battleships, three cruisers, and three or four destroyers. They tempered their enthusiasm by stating they had lost one battleship, one cruiser, three destroyers, 41 aircraft while admitting the Americans had damaged seven transports. The Americans counterclaimed they had sunk one Japanese battleship, five cruisers, five destroyers, and 12 transports while losing two light cruisers and six destroyers.

From the first moments when the struggle for Guadalcanal began in August and throughout October 1942, pessimism ran rampant throughout the U.S. Navy. Nevertheless, that mood changed markedly after Secretary of the Navy Frank Knox, who had led the nay-sayers, changed to an ardent optimist with statements such as, "We can lick them. I don't qualify that." When the Congress posthumously awarded the Congressional Medal of Honor to Admirals Scott and Callaghan, the Navy had two certifiable heroes to point at with pride. Lt. Commanders McCandless and Schonland also received the same honors—more American naval heroes useful for directing the public's attention toward a more positive view of the Guadalcanal struggle. The American public would not hear about the tragic death of the five Sullivan Brothers until January 1943, when the Navy finally knew that they had perished. In the meantime, euphoria ruled the day.

Closer to the action, Gen. Vandegrift, who had the advantage of seeing the suffering of the men under his command and viewing the flashes of battle in Iron Bottom Sound, had originally told Nimitz in September, "Out here too many commanders have been far too leery about risking their ships." His attitude changed when he saw that Halsey had meant what he said when he told the Marine commander he would get everything he [Halsey] had to improve the American situation on Guadalcanal. Vandegrift saw how many American sailors and their ships had been sacrificed to make sure the Marines would survive. He made his opinions known in a radioed message:

> "To them [the sailors] the men of Guadalcanal lift their battered helmets in deepest admiration."[3]

Effusive praise poured in from other quarters. Adm. Halsey, after receiving the latest news of Lee's exploits, sent a message to all ships and commanding generals in his command:

> "To the superb officers and men on land, on sea, in the air, and under the sea who have performed such magnificent deeds for our country in the past few days: You have written your names in golden letters on the pages of history and won the undying gratitude of your countrymen. No honor for you would be too great. Magnificently done! God bless each and every one of you. To the glorious dead: Hail heroes! Rest with God."[4]

After interviewing Halsey, a reporter from *Time* magazine, who wrote an article that later appeared in the magazine's November 30, 1942, issue, described the admiral's demeanor as he read combat reports:

> "The face which looked down on those reports was itself like a battlefield. Everything about it was big, broad, strong. The weather had been on it, and personal suffering behind it. The huge mouth looked like command, and above it, the nose was pugnacious. The eyes were aggressive. They and their screen of brow above the weariness below were as impressive and busy-looking as a couple of task forces?"[5]

This prompted Nimitz to express his impressions about Halsey:

> "Halsey's conduct of his present command leaves nothing to be desired. He is professionally competent and militarily aggressive without being reckless or foolhardy. He has that rare combination of intellectual capacity and military audacity, and can calculate to a cat's whisker the risk involved in operations when successful accomplishments will bring great returns. He possesses superb leadership qualities which have earned him a tremendous following of his men. His only enemies are Japs."[6]

When commendations came his way from Roosevelt, Knox, King, and Nimitz, he deflected the praise directed toward himself to his men. He said in his later writings:

> "President Roosevelt, Secretary Knox, Admiral King, Admiral Nimitz, and others sent me messages of congratulations. I had no illusions about who deserved them, so I passed them on to the men who had done the fighting."[7]

Roosevelt had been following the progress of the Naval Battle of Guadalcanal as much as he could. Adm. Callaghan had been his naval aide, and the two men had developed a friendly relationship during that time. Callaghan had achieved flag rank largely because of his job performance as the president's naval aide. When Roosevelt heard about Callaghan's death, he took the news with a deep sense of regret. Nonetheless, the good news from Iron Bottom Sound pleased the President. We can get an insight into his mood from his remarks in a speech to the *New York Herald Tribune* on November 17:

> "During the past two weeks we have had a great deal of good news and it would be seem that the turning point in this war has at last been reached. But this is no time for exultation. There is no time now for anything but fighting and working to win."[8]

✲ ✲ ✲

The Japanese assessed what had happened on November 13-15 and their conclusions, to say the least, were far more restrained. Adm. Ugaki wrote in a diary entry for November 16 what can be said to reflect not only his thinking, but the thoughts of Adm. Yamamoto as well.

> "According to a report by the Second Destroyer Squadron commander who escorted the convoy, a total of 106 enemy planes attacked them from 0555 to 1520. The enemy planes were mostly divided into two groups and were considered to be coming from carriers. One transport was rendered unable to operate, four were set on fire, and another one listed. But four other transports could reach Tassafaronga, and two thousand men, 360 cases of ammunition for field guns, and fifteen hundred bales of rice were successfully unloaded. This amount of the staple foodstuffs could not support our forces there more than several days. Even if the five thousand sick out of thirty thousand men now fighting there could be evacuated, a total of twenty-seven thousand men, including the current reinforcements, had to be supported.
>
> As we are going to have an unfavorable moonlit night for the transportation attempt, it is never an easy task to envisage a plan to meet the requirement. Incidentally, we thought of

a plan to half fill gasoline drums with rice, which could be jettisoned at sea at the destination for the receiver to pick up."[9]

A careful reading of what Ugaki wrote yields the only logical conclusion that the Japanese had given up trying to reinforce Guadalcanal by using transports. They adjusted their plans to use faster-moving destroyers with drums attached to the ships' decks with chains that would carry the supplies the Japanese soldiers would need. When the destroyers reached the Guadalcanal shore, the drums would be released from the ships' decks into the water and pulled ashore by Japanese soldiers. Whether sufficient supplies could be brought onshore to meet the Japanese needs was another question that currently had no answer. With more than 10,000 men[10] ashore, even the most optimistic logician could answer in the negative. The days remaining to the Japanese on Guadalcanal were numbered.

If the American reaction to the Naval Battle of Guadalcanal seemed to be so positive and held high hopes for the future, the Americans had good reason for such confidence. The battle was an unquestionable American victory. The reasons for this assessment are quite simple: (1) The Americans achieved their objectives; (2) The Japanese did not.

Very few Japanese troops and only a small amount of supplies came ashore. The Japanese plans to pound CACTUS into oblivion failed for two days in a row. While suffering heavy naval losses in men and ships, the Americans not only held their own but sank two Japanese battleships. The Japanese defeat forced reevaluation of their plans to reinforce ground forces on Guadalcanal.

The Japanese naval tactics, particularly with their use of torpedoes and their ability to fight a surface battle at night, proved to be superior to the Americans. The major Japanese failure was from their leadership and poor planning. They did not anticipate the movement of American carrier planes from the *Enterprise* to Guadalcanal that greatly added to the power of the American airbase. Before the battle began on November 13, CACTUS had just 31 attack planes: 23 SBDs and eight TBFs. After the *Enterprise*'s aircraft landed at Henderson Field, the total number of attack aircraft ballooned to 54 SBDs and 17 TBFs for a total of 71 attack aircraft.

American leadership, while making mistakes, proved to be superior to Japanese command abilities. Nimitz gave high priority to Turner landing reinforcements and to Turner releasing Callaghan's force to attack Abe. Halsey's decision to send Lee to Iron Bottom Sound and Lee's hard-headed determination to aggressively take on Kondo's battleship, cruisers, and destroyers and force them to retreat made a mighty contribution to the American triumph. Kondo's uncertainty about whether he faced battleships or cruisers and his timidity in attacking Lee's battleships provides a vivid contrast to the aggressiveness of the American admirals.

Yamamoto was never totally committed to the operation. He failed to unleash his land-based air power against the American ships and put tremendous pressure on CACTUS's ability to defend them. He had good reasons for deciding this way because of the high casualties suffered by these forces in previous attempts to pulverize Henderson Field. The contrast with Halsey's unflagging determination to put everything he had into the battle in a gambler's ploy did result in high American casualties but also resulted in the destruction of the Japanese transports and the failure of their mission.

Guadalcanal was now more secure than it had been since the Americans invaded on August 7.

In Richard B. Frank's book, *Guadalcanal*, the author states the Naval Battle of Guadalcanal should have been named the Air-Naval Battle of Guadalcanal because of the contributions by CACTUS pilots and air crews for the American victory. The Americans could not have won without them, and all credit should go to those who deserve it. Frank claims the American victory was as decisive to the outcome of the Pacific War as Midway. For the Japanese, their now-less-optimistic view of their prospects in the South Pacific had taken a definite turn:

> "It must be said that the success or failure in recapturing Guadalcanal Island, and the vital naval battle related to it, is the fork in the road which leads to victory for them or for us."[10]

A fork in the road toward victory had been taken as the sun went down on November 12. By November 15, the future path was decidedly in favor of the Americans.[11]

Looking to the Future

Not only had the fortunes of war turned favorably toward the Americans at Guadalcanal, the worldwide wartime situation also had decidedly given the Allies a hope for a final victory. In the Pacific Theater, Gen. MacArthur had chased the Japanese Army over the formidable Owen Stanley Mountains in eastern New Guinea and bottled them up at Buna. The Russians also had surrounded the German Sixth Army at Stalingrad and closed in for the kill. The British and Gen. Montgomery won a hard-fought victory over Rommel's Afrika Corps at El Alamein and were chasing the Germans westward back across North Africa. A combined American-British force had landed on North Africa's northwestern coast and negotiated a cease-fire with the French. The pincers closed upon Rommel's army. It was only a matter of time before the Germans would have to leave North Africa.

Nonetheless, there was more work to do at Guadalcanal. Despite their losses, the Japanese Army still survived and attacked the Americans on that island. While the Japanese Navy continued to try to reinforce them, the Japanese had to be permanently evicted to secure Guadalcanal as a base for further operations in the northern Solomon Islands. This would isolate Rabaul as a viable Japanese base. But they were yet not finished in the Solomons. When the Japanese had been seen building a new airfield at Munda on New Georgia Island—just 170 miles from Lunga point—the American assessment was divided as to whether they were going back on the offensive or just strengthening their defenses to the north of Guadalcanal.

While the Americans grew stronger, they had to cut off the Japanese supply lines to Guadalcanal once and for all. If they did not, the struggle on Guadalcanal would continue with no clear end in sight. They had to use their increasing strength against the Japanese. Nevertheless, that power would be tested once again as the new Japanese supply tactics started to be felt.[12]

PART 11: The Battle of Tassafaronga

CHAPTER 50
Plans and Ship Movements

Halsey Puts His House in Order

After the Naval Battle of Guadalcanal, Halsey held his daily briefing on November 19 as one of his officers congratulated the admiral. Halsey asked, "What for?" The officer replied, "You have just been nominated to become a full admiral." Halsey had missed the news on a broadcast of Nimitz's statement to the press, "For his successful turning back of the Jap attempt to take Guadalcanal in mid-November he has been nominated by the President for the rank of admiral, which reward he richly deserves."[1] The American Senate wasted little time when it confirmed his nomination on November 26. He became the sixth four-star admiral in the U.S. Navy. He was in eminent company, joining King, Nimitz, Leahy, Stark, and Ingersoll at the top of the heap.

Not wanting to wait for the official four-star insignia to come from the Navy, Radm. William L. Calhoun obtained four two-star pins from a Marine major general, had them welded into two four-star pins, and asked Halsey to put them on his collar. Halsey did not want to wear the stars until he received the official confirmation and had passed the required medical examination, all according to naval regulations. When his promotion became official, Miles Browning removed the three-star pins and placed the four-star insignia on Halsey's collar. He gave his former vice admiral's stars to Calhoun and said, "Send one of these to Mrs. Scott and the other to Mrs. Callaghan. Tell them it was their husbands' bravery that got me my new ones." Afterward, Halsey wrote about his promotion in his memoirs, "Naturally, I was very proud and happy but with the full realization that, although it was an individual award, it was intended for acceptance by me as a recognition of the splendid work that the South Pacific force had been continuing to do, and I was promoted as the representative of that force."[2]

The war in the Solomons was about to expand, and Halsey knew he did not have enough staff officers to get all the work done that needed to be accomplished. He also realized he had to have larger and more adequate quarters. He knew that one of the reasons Ghormley had so many problems was that his staff's offices were too cramped and extremely uncomfortable. Halsey was not like his contemporaries. With the anticipated expanded responsibilities, he wanted to delegate as much detailed work as possible so he could focus on the broader subjects such as force composition, strategy, and officer selection. He would have to conserve his energies on conferences, decisions, inspections, and ceremonial functions that only the Commander, South Pacific could do. While retaining important members from Ghormley's staff, he brought Miles Browning and Julian Brown with him and added Bromfield Nichol, Leonard Dow, Douglas Moulton, and William Ashford from the *Enterprise*. He took William Calhoun from Nimitz's staff to bring badly needed organization to the complex logistics problem and Capt. John R. Redman, CINCPAC's communications officer, to clear up the messy communications situation in the South Pacific. He used the power of his new, elevated rank to get the people he needed from the Bureau of Personnel. He added 25 new and highly proficient officers to look solely after operational problems.

The oppressively hot summer months in the southern tropics descended upon New Caledonia and made the finding of adequate facilities for his command difficult. The *Argonne* lacked enough room and air-conditioning comfort for his expanding staff. New Caledonia was a French possession and thus required a man who had experience working with them. Halsey had just that man in Marine Col. Julian Brown. The colonel had served with French forces, so he understood how to work with them. Decked out in his full dress uniform including a fourragère on his shoulder and the Croix de Guerre on his chest, both awarded to him for his service to the French armed forces, Brown went to the government building and appeared before His Excellency Monsieur Montchamps, governor of New Caledonia. After exchanging pleasantries, he stated his reason for calling on the governor: the need for adequate quarters for Halsey and his staff in Nouméa.

Thus began a series of negotiating sessions that led nowhere. In the first meeting, the governor wanted to know, "What do we get in return?" and Brown, staring coldly at the Frenchman, replied, "We will continue to protect you as we have always done." After his face shrunk into a frown, the governor said he would see what he could do. After hearing not a word from the French, Brown returned to see the governor once again only to be given promises that meant nothing. After a frustrating month passed, he strongly expressed himself to the governor, "We've got a war on our hands, and we can't continue to devote valuable time to these petty concerns. I venture to remind Your Excellency that if we Americans had not arrived here, the Japanese would have." Montchamps just shrugged, and Brown walked out in a dark mood.

After hearing Brown's exasperating accounts of his meeting with the French official, Halsey realized this man had no real power to do anything. The actual power resided with the absent Radm. Georges Thierry D'Argenlieu, the high commissioner for the French in the Pacific and now residing in London. His chief of staff was in Nouméa and commanded in the admiral's name. D'Argenlieu suspected that American intentions were not the most honorable, and these misgivings translated into a classic case of stonewalling by the French. Nonetheless, Halsey decided to act like he normally did.

Knowing he possessed the only real Allied military power in the South Pacific, he examined available locations in New Caledonia. After finding exactly what he wanted, Halsey and his staff took possession of the high commissioner's headquarters and immediately moved in. The brick building, a rare occurrence in Nouméa, had been formerly the Japanese headquarters on the island and stood on a hill with a magnificent view of the harbor. Cool breezes blew through the open windows. Halsey witnessed the Marines raising the American flag over the grounds and felt a deep satisfaction well inside him that he had just taken possession of yet another former Japanese asset.

Halsey's command was one of the first totally unified units comprising American and New Zealand ships, troops, planes, and supplies. He directly reported to CINCPAC and was only one level removed from the Navy's commander-in-chief. The future planned invasions up the Solomons' chain of islands required amphibious landings involving Army, Navy, and Marine personnel who had to cooperate by operating under a single unified command. Both Gen. Harmon, commanding all Army troops and air forces, and Gen. Vandegrift, Halsey's Marine commander, totally agreed with the Admiral's beliefs.

One way Halsey instilled unity among all his sailors and marines was to insist that they do not wear neckties. Although wearing neckties produced discomfort in the tropics, the reason Halsey issued this order was that Army personnel did not have to wear them. Perhaps the strongest expression of his views on command unity came when he called a meeting of his immediate subordinates and, as always, did not mince his words, "Gentlemen, we are the South Pacific Fighting Force. I don't want anybody even to be thinking in terms of Army, Navy, or Marines. Every man must understand this, and every man will understand it, even if I have to take off his uniform and issue coveralls with 'South Pacific Fighting Force' printed on the seat of his pants."

When any new man arrived at the door of Halsey's office, a sign now hung over the door that read:

"Complete with black tie
You do look terrific,
But take it off here:
This is the South Pacific!"[3]

✲ ✲ ✲

The destruction of Callaghan's and Scott's commands required a reorganization of the cruiser forces in the South Pacific. Feeling much empowered by the victory at the Naval Battle of Guadalcanal, King browbeat the JCS when he demanded more ships to be taken from the Atlantic Theater and sent to the Pacific. More and newer ships began arriving at Nouméa and Espiritu Santo to replace those that had been lost in battle. Two cruisers, three escort carriers, and five escorts were authorized to proceed to the Pacific and report for duty. The restored carrier *Saratoga* returned from Pearl Harbor to join the damaged *Enterprise*. The battleship *North Carolina*, her torpedo damage repaired, joined the *Washington* with the battleship *Indiana* soon to follow. With the departure of the *South Dakota* for repairs, Lee had three battleships under his command.

Halsey had ordered the *Enterprise* and the rest of Task Force 16 farther to the south and out of harm's way while Lee finished his work up north of Guadalcanal. The carrier air group left the carrier on November 14 at 8:30 a.m. and Kinkaid took Task Force 16 to Nouméa. The *Enterprise* dropped its anchor in the harbor at 2:40 p.m. the next day. Her previous battle damage had not been repaired. She had been operating at less than full combat readiness with her disabled forward elevator and was in desperate need of immediate repair. She received orders to return to Pearl Harbor for a critically needed overhaul in that base's shipyard. Kinkaid's days as a carrier task force commander had come to an end. Halsey recommended Kinkaid for his third DSM; Nimitz agreed with the nomination.

After ordering Radm. Mahlon S. Tisdale to take the cruisers *Pensacola* and *Northampton* with three destroyers to Espiritu Santo, Halsey ordered Kinkaid to take command of Task Force 67 on November 16. He was now in command of all the cruisers in the South Pacific that could still engage in combat operations with the mission to stop the Tokyo Express from landing any more troops and supplies.

Profiting by the mistakes made by American naval commanders during cruiser combat off Guadalcanal, Kinkaid decided he badly needed a new plan for fighting in the narrow waters north of Guadalcanal. On November 27, he published it with specific operational orders.[4] He split Task Force 67 into one destroyer and two cruiser groups. Each group would have one ship in the lead that had the latest SG radar. The destroyers, each equipped with radar, would search ahead for Japanese ships at a distance of 10,000 yards from the cruisers. Kinkaid believed this formation would be able to detect any approaching Japanese force and be able to launch a surprise destroyer torpedo attack. The cruisers would begin firing their guns from a range between 10,000 and 12,000 yards. The cruisers' float planes would take off for Tulagi. From there, they could scout for Japanese ships, light up the target area, and call the fall of shot. As the Americans had done in earlier nighttime naval surface battles against the Japanese near Guadalcanal, there was a singular dependence on radar to find the Japanese ships.

But he never had the chance to put his plan in operation when King ordered him to Pearl Harbor for another assignment. He arrived on December 2 and reported to Nimitz. Radm. Carleton Wright replaced him as the commander of Task Force 67. After examining his predecessor's plan, he adopted it with no changes.[5]

✲ ✲ ✲

Halsey knew that the Marines and soldiers on Guadalcanal badly needed to be relieved and his staff began the planning for that operation. But the Japanese had other ideas. They had not yet totally stopped trying to reinforce their men on Guadalcanal.[6]

Planning More Runs of the Tokyo Express

Following all the attempts to land reinforcements and supplies up to the end of November, there were still more than 10,000 Japanese troops on Guadalcanal. All the previous attempts to help them had been costly in terms of Japanese ships, planes, and men. The U.S. Navy and the aircraft from U.S. carriers and the airfields on Guadalcanal exacted a heavy toll. The needs of the men had reached a severe and desperate stage in terms of food, ammunition, and medical supplies. The latest attempt in mid-November resulted in the landing of soldiers, but produced very little aid in terms of what the soldiers already there really needed. Other means of supporting the Japanese soldiers had to be tried. Their plight worsened as time passed.

The Japanese Army bombarded Truk and Rabaul with continuous and urgent appeals for supplies. Both the Imperial Japanese Navy and the Army estimated that the men on Guadalcanal would exhaust all their supplies by the end of November. The men now ate wild animals and plants just to stay alive. Starvation became common, the lists of the sick grew, and the soldiers still healthy approached the level of total exhaustion. One of the officers in the Army's 228th Infantry Regiment told his unit's acting commander how serious the problem really was:

> "Rice. I really want rice. I want to give my men as much as they want. That is the only wish I have. Even when mortars are falling like a squall or the land is reshaped by bombs I don't worry. But I can't stand looking at my men become pale and thin."[7]

The Japanese Navy had to act soon, and the time was now. The Combined Fleet ordered on November 16 that some of the submarines previously being used to search for American shipping be assigned to supply the soldiers on Guadalcanal. The navy loaded between 20 and 30 tons of supplies on 16 submarines over the next three weeks at Rabaul for transport to Kamimbo Bay, an inlet about three and a half miles due west of Cape Esperance on the Guadalcanal's northern shore.

The Japanese first try on November 24 to bring in these supplies by submarine had to be cancelled because American PT boats and aircraft forced the expedition to turn back. Success happened the next evening when the *I-17* unloaded about 11 tons of supplies on motor boats that came from the shore. For the next night and until the end of November, Japanese submarine crews struggled mightily to move the clumsy drums from their boats' slippery and narrow decks into landing craft waiting alongside. During that time, the submarines brought in about 20 to 30 tons of supplies. Each landing brought about one day's food supply for the 17th Army. Nevertheless, the supplies had to be hand-carried through the dense Guadalcanal jungle with adverse effect on how much of the food and medicine actually reached the men who needed them the most.

The submarine crews decried these missions as a "Marutsu," the same as bringing the mail or carrying freight. When the American submarine *Seadragon* sank the *I-4* on November 20, these "freight" runs became quite hazardous as well. The submarines' comparatively slow speed, even on the surface, made them vulnerable to attacks. The navy needed these warships for what they did best, to attack and sink ships and not haul freight.

The Japanese examined using sailing craft and small motor boats to supply their soldiers to release their ever-shrinking destroyer fleet for combat duty. Dubbing the scheme with the name of "Chain Transportation," naval planners wished to set up three bases between Munda and Guadalcanal and four installations between Rabaul and Buna so these boats could make shorter runs from base to base at night in comparative safety. The selected location for the first base was at Wickham Anchorage, an inlet on the southeast coast of Vangunu, a small island in the New Georgia Island group.

Six destroyers brought 600 men of the 1st Battalion, 229th Infantry Regiment to Wickham on November 27. Two small transports, the *Kiku Maru* and *Azusa Maru*, arrived from Rabaul bearing 300 more men and the necessary cargoes of AA guns and ammunition, food, and medical supplies. However, the planners neglected to factor the growing strength of CACTUS air power into their scheme. Now enjoying full air superiority over Guadalcanal, its planes' missions grew in scope and distance from their base as they flew regular missions as far north as Munda on Bougainville. Some American search planes found the two ships anchored at Wickham. Devastating strikes by CACTUS aircraft on November 28 and 29 sank both of them before they could land any more supplies and men. Another means of attempting to appease the starvation on Guadalcanal had been rendered useless.

Plans and Ship Movements

The failures to land supplies on Guadalcanal by submarine and Chain Transportation forced the Japanese to return to what they called "Rat Transportation," using destroyers, but with a slight change. Sailors sterilized drums previously used for shipping oil and gasoline and filled them to about half their capacity with about 330 pounds of rice and barley. The drums would be tied together with ropes in clusters and about 200 to 240 drums loaded on each destroyer's main deck. After arriving off Guadalcanal, the crew would shove the drums overboard near the beach and men ashore would pull the drums to the beach. It would take 20 destroyer runs to deliver enough food for 20,000 men. The unloading method minimized how long the ships would be near the beach and lessened the danger of being attacked by the ever-growing and increasingly powerful land-based American aircraft on Guadalcanal.

Moving into Position

The Combined Fleet Headquarters scheduled five supply runs using the drum method. Adm. Tanaka drew the assignment to make the first journey down the Slot. He called a command conference with the captains of the destroyers that would go with him on November 29 and told them of his plans for the new Reinforcement Unit/Destroyer Squadron 2. The Imperial Japanese Navy gave him three newly commissioned destroyers that had joined the Navy's ranks between June and August. The new warships were *Yugumo*-class destroyers, which displaced about 2,400 tons, carried six five-inch guns in their main armament, had a rated top speed of 35 knots, and carried a crew of 228 men.[8]

Tanaka placed his flag on the *Naganami*. Another destroyer, the *Takanami*, would be in what he called the Screening Unit. Neither ship would carry any drums. The *Makinami* would be part of Capt. Torajiro Sato's 1st Transportation Unit (Desron 15) along with the destroyers *Oyashio*, *Kuroshio*, and *Kagero*. Sato's four ships would carry 240 drums each and deposit them off Tassafaronga. Capt. Giichiro Nakahara led the 2nd Transportation Unit (Desron 24) and had the destroyers *Suzukaze* and *Kawakaze* under his command. These two ships would carry 200 drums each and drop them into the water off the Umasani River's mouth. The weight of the drums the destroyers would lash to their decks determined how many torpedoes each ship would carry.

As Tanaka explained how his ships would form up for their trek to Guadalcanal, the ships' captains began to have some misgivings. The admiral explained the *Takanami* would accompany the 1st Transportation Unit by not leading the four destroyers but steaming alongside them. His flagship, the *Naganami*, would trail behind to the northwest of the 2nd Transportation Unit. The normal place for the flagship was to lead the formation, not steam behind it. Tanaka never did offer any explanation why he formed the ships the way he did, either to his officers or in his writings. In any case, it certainly was non-traditional.

Tanaka finished all preparations to get underway on November 29 and led his ships from Shortland that evening. After an uneventful passage, dawn rose over the sea north of the Solomons as Tanaka's formation of eight destroyers plied their way at a modest cruising speed. He was in no hurry since he wanted to arrive north of Guadalcanal after dark. He had planned his approach to Guadalcanal well—northward through the Bougainville Strait, turn easterly to Roncador Reef just south of Ontong Java Atoll, then move southward toward Indispensable Strait. This was a course similar to the one Mikawa followed in the days before the Naval Battle of Guadalcanal. Tanaka wanted to avoid being seen by American search aircraft. But the Gods of War would not grant his wish.

✲ ✲ ✲

Coastwatcher Paul Mason had been observing closely the movements of Japanese ships from his perch near the Shortlands' harbor in the southern end of Bougainville. The anchorage had been very busy for the past few days with ships arriving, drums being placed aboard some destroyers, and leaving. He continually radioed his observations. But on the morning of November 30, there were far fewer ship masts in the harbor. The only logical conclusion was that the destroyers had sailed. He reported what he saw to Halsey through his radio network.

About 9:30 a.m., an American search aircraft flew over Tanaka's formation and gave him cause for worry. Either the plane's crew never saw his destroyers even after flying around for about an hour or the aircraft's radio failed. We will never know what happened. It is known that the plane never sent any messages notifying anyone in the American chain of command that would have at least confirmed Mason's message.

While a decoded, intercepted message from Yamamoto to his command might have warned Halsey about Tanaka's approach, the coastwatcher sighting report was the only *known* intelligence the Americans had about this new run of the Tokyo Express. Nonetheless, it would be enough.

✲ ✲ ✲

Radm. Carlton H. "Bosco" Wright was the new commander of Task Force 67. He totally endorsed and was committed fully to Kinkaid's plan. As part of Kinkaid's staff, he had been intimately involved during its development. Born on June 2, 1892, in New Hampton, Iowa, he graduated from the U.S. Naval Academy in 1912 after demonstrating a considerable intellect sufficient for a class ranking of 16 out a class of 156. He became an acknowledged expert in naval ordnance. Before America's entry into World War II began, he was the captain of the cruiser *Augusta* and in command when she took President Roosevelt to Newfoundland to meet with Prime Minister Winston Churchill and sign the Atlantic Charter aboard the British battleship *Prince of Wales* on August 14, 1941. After Pearl Harbor, he remained the *Augusta*'s captain until he achieved the rank of rear admiral in May 1942.[9]

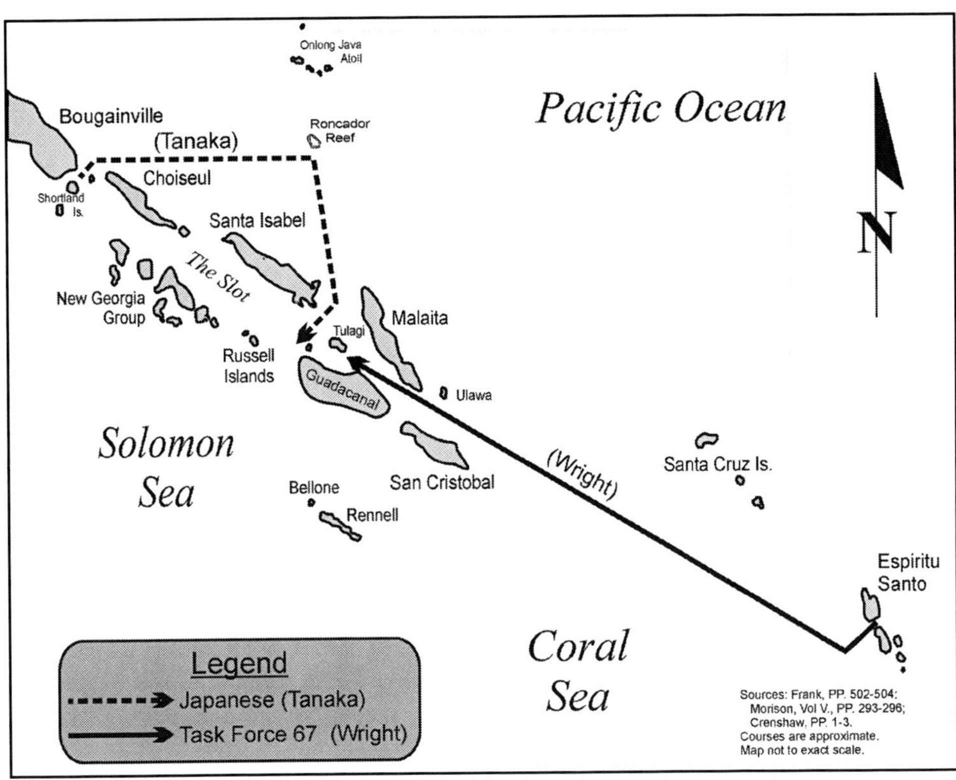

Tanaka's and Wright's Routes to Guadalcanal

By the evening of November 29, Halsey ordered Wright to make his ships ready for sea. After receiving reports that another run of Tokyo Express was about to begin, Halsey told Wright to expect that eight Japanese destroyers and six transports would appear off Guadalcanal on the evening of November 30 and ordered him to intercept them. But some time inexplicably passed before Halsey sent the order at about an hour before midnight for Wright to set sail immediately.

Wright commanded all the cruisers and destroyers Halsey could spare. COMSOPAC had made a commitment to the men on Guadalcanal that he would spare nothing to help them to victory. Task Force 67 was no exception to that rule. Adm. Wright flew his flag in the heavy cruiser *Minneapolis* that included his flagship and three other heavy cruisers, the *New Orleans*, *Pensacola*, and *Northampton*, the light cruiser *Honolulu*, and the four destroyers, *Fletcher*, *Drayton*, *Maury*, and *Perkins*. With the latest intelligence that the approaching Japanese ships only had destroyers, Wright confidently felt that his ships had more than enough firepower to handle anything that seemed to be coming their way. When comparing the relative gun power and without considering the differences in the quality of each side's torpedoes, his confidence was well placed. The following table compares their relative firepower in terms of guns and torpedoes:

Relative American and Japanese Firepower

	Guns			Torpedoes	
	8 inches	*6 inches*	*5 inches*	*21 inches*	*24 inches*
American	37	15	68	67	—
Japanese	—	—	46	—	64

Later on the afternoon of November 30, a Japanese reconnaissance plane reported seeing "twelve enemy destroyers and nine transports." Tanaka wasted no time readying his ships for combat. The destroyers carrying the cargo drums did not have enough torpedoes in reserve for a prolonged sea battle. But Tanaka was never one to fail in his missions and told his men of what awaited them: "There is great possibility of an encounter with the enemy tonight. In such an event, utmost efforts will be made to destroy the enemy without regard for the unloading of supplies."

At sunset, a heavy storm came. Darkness surrounded the eight ships, so Tanaka ordered a slower speed. But, as it always is in the tropics, the rainstorm passed, the sky cleared, and the visibility measurably improved. His ships passed Savo Island at about 11:00 p.m. He turned his formation to the southeast, and his ships moved into an attacking formation. Despite the darkness, the visibility was about seven miles.

Task Force 67 left Espiritu Santo at midnight on November 29 to begin its 580-mile journey to Guadalcanal. After carefully navigating through the treacherous American-laid minefields, its speed increased to 28 knots. Wright wanted to waste no time getting to Guadalcanal by choosing the shortest course: steam to east of San Cristobal Island by way of Indispensable Strait and through the Lengo Channel to Iron Bottom Sound. He ordered the cruisers to send their observation planes to Tulagi so they would not be a problem during combat. Tulagi was a far more advantageous base since it had refueling facilities for the planes. From there the planes could fly over the combat areas to drop flares and call the fall of shot. The task force arrived off San Cristobal Island in the late afternoon of November 30.

The heavy cruiser *Minneapolis* glided through the slate-blue waters near San Cristobal Island under partly cloudy skies. Radm. Wright sat in his relatively plush chair on the ship's flag bridge and looked forward over the two triple-eight-inch gun turrets at the horizon. The big ship rolled easily in the gentle swells that ran past her, and her wake stirred up white foam behind. The admiral's steward, steadying himself on the ship's rolling deck, expertly poured a cup of hot coffee firmly in the folds of a white linen napkin on a silver service tray. The cup and matching saucer proudly displayed the two gold stars of a rear admiral. He had been in command of Task Force 67 for just one day since assuming command with the departure of Adm. Kinkaid. He had taken his former cruiser command through the rigors of combat in the various South Pacific carrier battles since the Americans invaded Guadalcanal. However, there was not enough time to work with his new command; but he had confidence the men under his command would do their duty when the time required it.

While he had overall command of Task Force 67, he also had direct tactical command of the three heavy cruisers *Minneapolis, New Orleans*, and *Pensacola* that carried the numeric designation of Task Force 67.2.2. Radm. Mahlon S. Tisdale commanded Task Force 67.2.3 that had the heavy cruiser *Northampton* and the light cruiser *Honolulu*. The four destroyers were under the command of Cmdr. William M. Cole, who was also the captain of the destroyer *Fletcher*.

In the early morning hours of November 30, Wright sent his analysis of the situation facing his command and what he intended to do that evening. The text of his message transmitted at 6:30 a.m. said:

> "INFORMATION ENEMY FORCES ESTIMATED 8 DESTROYERS, 6 TRANSPORTS PROBABLY ATTEMPTING LAND REINFORCEMENTS TASSAFARONGA AREA 2300 TONIGHT X WILL PROCEED THROUGH LENGO CHANNEL AND DESTROY ENEMY."[10]

He then added more details in a message sent at 8:40 a.m.:

> "PRESENT INTENTION DESTROYERS CONCENTRATE TWO MILES AHEAD OF GUIDE BEFORE ENTERING LENGO CHANNEL. UPON CLEARING CHANNEL AND UNTIL CONTACT IS MADE DESTROYERS ON BEARING 300 TRUE FROM GUIDE DISTANCE TWO MILES. CRUISERS IN LINE OF BEARING 320. MANEUVER BY TURN SIGNALS TO PASS ABOUT 6 MILES FROM COAST. EXPECT TO DIRECT COMMENCE GUN FIRE AT RANGE ABOUT 12000 YARDS. SITUATION WILL PROBABLY NOT PERMIT WITHHOLDING GUNFIRE TO COMPLETE TORPEDO ATTACKS. ANY VESSEL HAVING KNOWN ENEMY WITHIN SIX THOUSAND YARDS IS AUTHORIZED TO OPEN FIRE."[11]

Reports from COMSOPAC continued to trickle into Task Force 67 communications aboard the flagship. Nonetheless, they never offered any details about the makeup of the approaching Japanese force. Rather than providing answers, they generated more questions. Were there any transports? Wright knew the Japanese sorely needed tanks, heavy artillery, and the ammunition that goes with these weapons. They would need transports to bring them to Guadalcanal.

The sky became increasingly darker as a prelude to a common occurrence in these latitudes—rain squalls. The rain arrived as sure as the running of the Tokyo Express, and it became harder to see as visibility worsened. But just as quickly as they arrived, the storm dissipated at about 4:00 p.m. Wright ordered the cruiser float planes to fly to Tulagi as planned.

Wright's ships entered Lengo Channel early that evening where they just missed colliding with three American transports and five destroyers. Wanting to give Wright all the ships that he could spare, Halsey ordered two destroyers that had escorted the transports, the *Lamson* and the *Lardner* to join Task Force 67 with Cmdr. Laurence A. Abercrombie, the most senior officer on the two destroyers and aboard the *Lamson*, commanded the two-destroyer Division 9 (Desron 9). The sudden transfer of the two ships to Wright's command did not allow time for the admiral to even send his plans to Abercrombie. All he could do is order the dazed Abercrombie to place his two destroyers to the rear of the Task Force formation since they only had the less effective SC radar aboard. Wright ordered his ships into the now classic American single-file formation with the destroyers *Fletcher, Perkins, Maury* and *Drayton* in the lead; the cruisers *Minneapolis, New Orleans, Pensacola, Honolulu* and *Northampton* following next and the destroyers *Lamson* and *Lardner* bringing up the rear. Not following the operational plan he developed with Kinkaid, he did not place any destroyer pickets ten miles ahead. The Americans would again rely solely on radar in the tight ship formation to detect any Japanese ships that should come into the area.[12]

✲ ✲ ✲

The two opposing naval forces approached. Aboard each ship, each member of its crew nervously anticipated the fire, deafening sounds and death of naval surface combat. Each man readied himself for the ordeal to come. The Battle of Tassafaronga was about to begin.

CHAPTER 51
Night of the Long Lances

Delivering the Goods

Tanaka lined his ships up at 6:45 p.m. about 650 yards apart with the non-cargo-carrying destroyer *Takanami* leading the way. The *Oyashio, Kuroshio, Kagero, Makinami, Naganami* (Tanaka's flagship and not carrying cargo), *Kawakaze*, and *Suzukaze* followed behind. As his lookouts spotted Savo Island, Tanaka's ships entered Indispensable Strait at 9:40 p.m. just as Wright's Task Force 67 entered the Lengo Channel.

Tanaka sent the *Takanami* about ten miles ahead at 10:45 p.m. to look for any American ships off Guadalcanal and to give early warning as the rest of the destroyers unloaded their cargoes. He also ordered the *Naganami* to escort the *Kawakaze* and *Suzukaze* to a point off Doma Reef where they

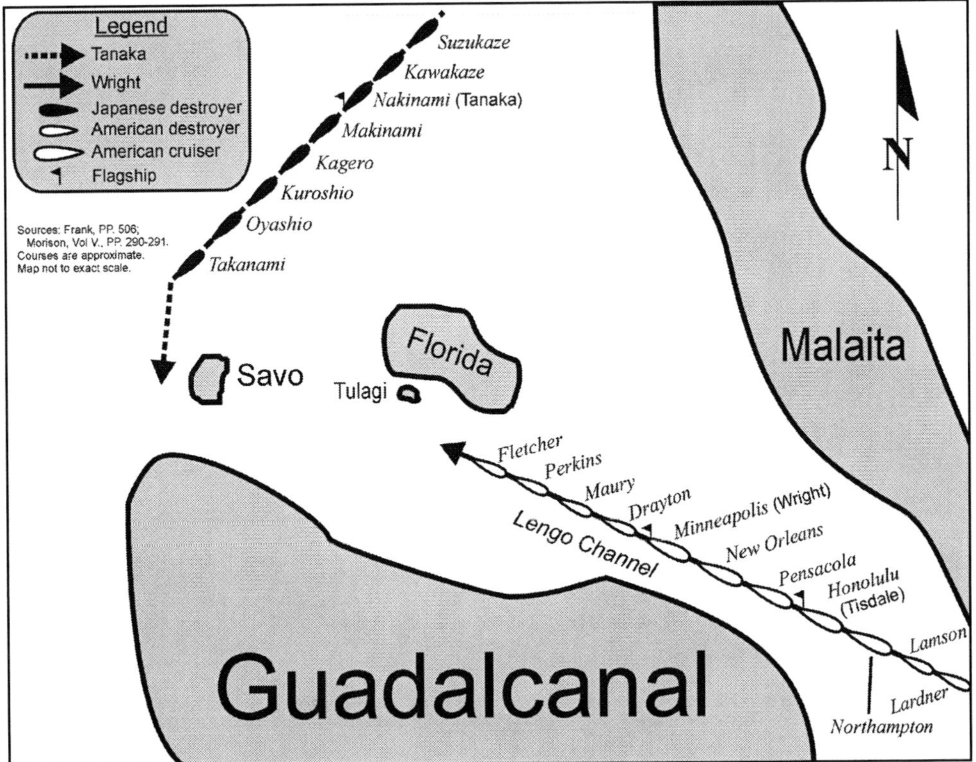

Getting into Position for Battle

would offload the drums on their decks. The *Naganami* would stay on the reef's seaward side from where it could help the *Takanami* if that ship should sight any American ships. Meanwhile, the *Oyashio, Kuroshio, Kagero*, and *Makinami* would proceed to Tassafaronga to unload their cargoes there. Tanaka planned to keep his ships in their columnar arrangement with the *Naganami* in the lead until the *Takanami* could confirm that there were no American ships nearby to interfere with his mission.

He waited until 11:00 p.m. to order his ships to separate and proceed to their assigned positions. As the *Takanami* slowed and moved on her steady course to the southeast with all her lookouts straining their eyes for any American ships, the *Naganami* made a hard right turn to lead her charges to their unloading point. The other four destroyers maintained a steady 30-knot speed toward Tassafaronga.

Just as the *Kawakaze* and *Suzukaze* appeared off Doma and reduced their speed to lower boats and begin carrying their drums ashore, Tanaka ordered the *Naganami* to leave its present location and move toward the *Takanami* so she had enough sea room to maneuver in case the *Takanami* saw anything. He began to worry about the presence of American ships when his lookouts saw three aircraft showing red and green running lights flying in a low-altitude circle off Tulagi.

He realized his worst fears when the *Takanami* sent an alarming message at 11:12 p.m., "Sighted what appear to be enemy ships, bearing 100 degrees." Tanaka looked through his binoculars and could see her in the darkness. The destroyer was about 5,000 yards ahead and farther from the shore than the rest of his ships. The horizon where he looked had more light on it than in other directions, but he saw nothing between Guadalcanal's looming shadow and the outline of Florida Island. Nonetheless, another harbinger of danger shocked him as a new message came over the radio: "Seven enemy destroyers sighted."[1]

He immediately ordered, "Stop unloading. Take battle stations." As the destroyers already began breaking away from their formations, the *Kawakaze* and *Suzukaze* were stopped in the water with men in their boats and other members of their crews manhandling the drums on their ships' decks. Despite the seemingly chaotic atmosphere, Tanaka knew his men had enough combat experience to quickly adapt to the new threats and go to their battle stations without delay.

The seconds inexorably ticked by with every eye looking for any visual evidence of the Americans. The lookouts on the *Naganami* found them, "Ship sighted. Sharp on the port bow."[2] Tanaka again looked through his binoculars, and now saw several ships silhouetted against the brighter horizon. His best guess was that these ships were destroyers.

All eight destroyers' efforts had to attend to the dangers in front of them. The unloading of the cargo drums would have to wait.

The Americans Find Their Quarry

The radar operator aboard the *Minneapolis* stared at his scope. He and his comrades knew how critical it was for them to be the first to find any hint the Japanese ships were out there. They had been warned to look for them and soon would be rewarded for their diligence. He saw two green pips that could only be Japanese ships on a bearing of 284° at 23,000 yards. He reported his sighting immediately to the bridge at 11:06 p.m. Wright ordered a TBS broadcast to report the sighting to all his ships and directed his ships to turn to a 320° course. The ship formation changed into two columns about

4,000 yards apart. The *Fletcher*, *Perkins*, and *New Orleans* radars also detected the Japanese ships. They first saw four, then six vessels.

Wright turned Task Force 67 to a 300° bearing, but kept its speed at 20 knots. After examining the charts and the plotted positions of the approaching Japanese ships, he concluded they were in a line parallel to and two miles off Guadalcanal's northeastern coastline. The range indicated on the radar scopes was about 14,600 yards and closing fast. Wright reasoned that his current speed of 20 knots allowed for ideal targeting for his guns. The radar plot reported the Japanese in a four-ship column near the shoreline on a 140° course, speed 16 knots. Two other ships were about two miles farther from the shore. He could not discern whether the ships were transports or warships or a combination of both types.

Cmdr. Cole got on the TBS at 11:16 p.m. and asked for permission to fire his destroyers' torpedoes. The range to the closest Japanese ship had not changed. Since the maximum range of the American Mk-15 torpedo at its top speed was just 6,000 yards, Wright replied, "Range to our bogey is excessive."[3] The busy TBS became much more busy when the *Northampton* reported seeing a flashing light coming from Tassafaronga.

Then the confusion between Wright and Cole increased when Wright asked Cole, "Do you have them located?" and Cole replied, "Affirmative. Range is all right for us." How could the range be OK with Cole and also be almost 10,000 yards farther than Cole's torpedoes could travel? Wright asked for a new radar plot. The returning answer indicated that the four ships were likely destroyers but the radar officer's response was full of uncertainties whether the distant Japanese ships had moved or not.

Wright correctly reasoned that no rational naval commander would send transports in front of his warships. The only logical conclusion was that these vessels were indeed destroyers and told Cole, "Suspect bogies are DDs. We now have four, " and at last gave Cole permission to fire torpedoes. Cole relayed the admiral's permission for the leading destroyers to launch torpedoes. The range was now 10,000 yards and shrinking rapidly. Knowing it was time for his Task Force to open fire, Wright picked up the TBS microphone and ordered, "Stand by to roger." He paused for just a moment and radioed, "Execute roger. And I do mean roger!"[4]

Let the Battle Begin

Meanwhile, the *Fletcher*'s SG radar had already detected the distant ships at 11:10 p.m. 14,000 yards away. Cole ordered an increase in speed to 25 knots and moved into the *Fletcher*'s radar room behind the ship's pilothouse where his executive officer, Lt. Cmdr. Joseph C. Wylie, commanded activities and had begun a plot on a small table, a new innovation aboard the newest American destroyer class. It took just two minutes to generate a clear picture of the Japanese ships' formation. There was a column of ships running parallel to and closest to the shoreline, about one and a half miles offshore, with one ship abreast of them to the formation's seaward side. Their course was 150° True, speed 15 knots. Cole ordered the *Fletcher* to a 290° course and moved to the port side of the bridge. He peered through his binoculars to see if he could see anything.

Tempered by the past failures using the one key advantage the Americans had over the Japanese, radar, he wanted to use this new technology to its maximum. He had previously conferred with the other destroyer captains and informed them he intended to use a less-than-top torpedo speed setting of 36 knots and fire his torpedoes from a range of 6,000 yards, well within the torpedoes' range at this intermediate speed. Also, the ships would be far enough away so that the Japanese lookouts could not see the attacking American destroyers.

After watching the ship's port torpedo director officer set up for firing a half-salvo of five torpedoes, the firing angle and range began to approach an ideal value when Cole sent to Wright the code for permission to open fire, "Interrogatory William." The admiral denied permission and confused Cole as the optimum time to launch the torpedoes vanished. Cole examined the radar plot—the scope now showed four pips on a 140° course, speed 15 knots. He worried about the potentially deadly delay.

Wright finally granted Cole authority to fire at 11:20 p.m., a full *five* minutes later. Cole repeated the order to his other destroyers but waited to give the order to his own torpedo officer. The range to the Japanese ships had increased to 7,300 yards, which meant the *Fletcher*'s torpedoes would have to travel 8,000 yards, too far away at the intermediate speed of 36 knots for the torpedoes to reach their targets. He ordered the speed setting reduced to 27 knots, which meant they could still reach the Japanese ships, but allowed their lookouts more time to sight their approaching wakes and evade their lookouts. Nonetheless, after giving the men on the port director time to change the speed setting, he ordered, "Fire torpedoes." The first missile hissed from its tube with a rush of compressed air and hit the water with a splat. The other four leapt from their tubes at three second intervals. Cole hoped they would at least reach their ever-more-distant targets.

Wright's order to open fire arrived just after the *Fletcher*'s five torpedoes were on their way. Cole delayed firing his guns until his second five-torpedo salvo was on its way and aimed at the second Japanese ship in the column. He then ordered his guns to begin firing at the rightmost ship in the Japanese column.

Following in *Fletcher*'s wake 500 yards behind, the *Perkins* had detected the Japanese ships almost at the same time the *Fletcher* did. Its plot showed the Japanese ships on a 125° course, speed 15 knots. The port torpedo director aimed at the Japanese ship steaming abeam of its compatriots and fired an eight-torpedo salvo just 5,000 yards off the port beam.

The *Maury* had no SG radar and could not find a target. The destroyer's captain, Lt. Cmdr. Gelzer L Sims, thus held back and waited for a more advantageous time to fire.

The *Drayton*'s SG radar was the first of the van destroyers to pick up the Japanese ships. Nevertheless, she focused on other targets 16,000 yards away and to the right of those initially detected. The ship's skipper, Lt. Cmdr. James E. Cooper, tracked the contact, but soon could not confirm what its actual composition was. When Cole ordered them to open fire, Cooper fired just two torpedoes at a range of 8,000 yards and saved the rest of his torpedoes for later in the battle.

Just after the *Fletcher* fired its first torpedo, the *Minneapolis* did not wait long to send its first nine-gun eight-inch salvo in a blinding flash of light and deafening roar of gunfire. The light from its guns lit the water around the cruiser for several hundred yards. The cruiser's port-side five-inch guns began the din just before the second eight-inch salvo blasted from the big guns.

Within one minute of the flagship's opening blast, the *New Orleans* and *Northampton*'s main guns joined in while the *Pensacola*, not equipped with SG radar and taking longer to find a target, took several more minutes to open fire. The *Honolulu*'s rapid-firing six-inch guns opened fire one minute later. Meanwhile, lacking any instructions and seeing the cruisers firing their guns, the rear destroyer *Lamson* began firing starshells in the vicinity of the shell splashes.

The *Fletcher* fired 60 shells from its five-inch guns at the trailing ship in the column when her FD radar lost contact with the ship's target, so Cole stopped firing his guns. As starshells came in from the left and filled the night with unnatural light, walls of smoke began to form over the watery battlefield and shell splashes were everywhere near the Japanese ships. As if by magic, the Japanese ships vanished in the clouds of smoke and the water columns. Cole and the other men on the bridge saw what might have been gunfire to the right of the Japanese ships.

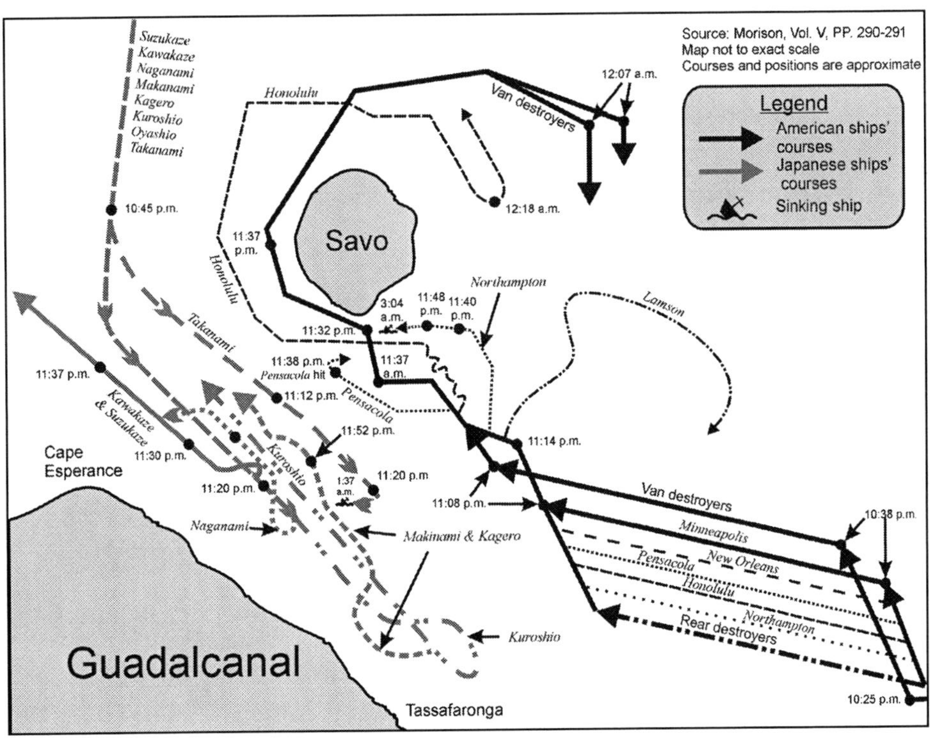

The Battle of Tassafaronga

The *Perkins* captain, Lt. Cmdr. Walter C. Reed, saw a large explosion that might have come from her torpedoes striking his ship's intended target as smoke and water columns engulfed her. Reed also saw flashes from gunfire to the left of the Japanese ships. As he turned his binoculars toward the apparent source of the fire, he saw the flashes from the cruisers firing their guns.

The *Maury*'s FD radar found a target for its guns about the same time the "Commence fire" order arrived. The firing solution was a target on a 120° course, speed 12 knots. She began firing her five-inch guns just as disaster struck. A bright flash, caused by an electrical short, exploded from her FD radar and disabled the device. Nonetheless, the destroyer continued firing as it let loose 20 salvoes from her five-inch guns using the optical range-finding equipment. Smoke enveloped her intended target as her lookouts lost sight of it. The best guess of all the ships' observer was that the target was a small transport.

With her target just 6,700 yards away and not moving, the *Drayton* fired two star-shell salvoes that were set to detonate at 12,000 yards, about 5,000 yards behind her target. She fired 100 five-inch shells that could not miss. The target disappeared in clouds of smoke. The ship's crew never saw the target or the results of their shelling.

Cole had used all his torpedoes, and his radar showed no targets to shoot at. Therefore, he maintained his westward course at 25 knots as he waited for explosions from his torpedoes hitting their targets. Five minutes had passed since he had launched his torpedoes when geysers of water from Japanese shells surrounded the *Fletcher*.

✲ ✲ ✲

The nature of Tanaka's mission was primarily defensive since the primary American opposition would most likely outnumber and out-gun his force. At it turned out, this assumption proved to be true because Task Force 67 had five cruisers with firepower that far exceeded the eight destroyers Tanaka had brought from the Shortlands.

As Tanaka looked at the distant ships through his binoculars, vividly bright flashes flared from guns on the leftmost ship. Then the next ship also fired its guns. Soon, blinding flares filled the sky between the *Takanami* and the American ships. The gunfire's flashes filled the distant horizon with an almost daylight brilliance. Huge columns of water surrounded the *Takanami* as shells smacked the water around her. Nevertheless, the harassed destroyer did not wait long before returning fire of her own. Realizing his force was now under attack and had not a minute to spare, Tanaka sent an immediate order to all his ships, "Close and Attack."[5]

Tanaka saw more flashes from the American ships as the *Naganami* answered his order and sprinted forward at full speed. Huge geysers of seawater surrounded his flagship, and it began returning fire of its own. Flashes coming from hits by his ship's gunfire now blossomed on the second and third ships in the American formation. The *Naganami* shook from the firing of its guns as falling shells from the American ships kept throwing up huge columns of water around her. As each of the destroyer's salvoes blasted away at their distant target, the smoke from the firing guns momentarily blocked his view of the battle. Nonetheless, he could still definitely feel the fire from his flagship.

Being the ship closest to the American ships, the *Takanami* began to bear the brunt of their gunfire. The shells still churned up water all around the ship, but some of them began to smack into the destroyer. As each shell hit and exploded, flames leapt from her deck, superstructure, and still-firing guns. But casualties mounted on her as the shell hits mortally wounded her captain, Cmdr. Masami Ogura, and many others of her crew. The four destroyers ahead of her also began to get the attention of the American guns. Tanaka still wondered why his flagship had not yet been hit.

The *Naganami* turned its searchlight on, and its stream of light illuminated an American cruiser that moved on an opposite course to the destroyer. Her captain ordered, "Right full rudder," to change his ship's course to parallel the cruiser's path, an ideal setup for firing torpedoes. As her stern lowered in the water and her speed surged to more than 30 knots, more shells burst in the water around the destroyer with none of them striking her. More glowing white flares floated down toward the sea, and smoke was everywhere.

Meanwhile, the *Takanami*'s torment increased as the American shells pummeled her. She shook from the relentless punishment. Fires engulfed the ship as convulsive explosions wreaked havoc from below decks. Her bridge was a shambles of bent metal and dangling cable and wires. Tanaka watched helplessly as he guessed the destroyer must be taking terrible casualties. She turned sharply to starboard and nearly stopped dead in the water while her smoke generator poured smoke into the air, only enforcing the image of a ship near the end of its life.

The *Naganami* had almost finished her hard right turn when one of her lookouts exclaimed, "Torpedo wake to starboard."[6] Tanaka turned toward the reported direction and saw an ominous sight. One wake passed ahead and another came from a torpedo that must have passed beneath the destroyer's keel. More wakes showed to the right but none of the approaching torpedoes exploded. The destroyer's luck still held. More shells fell around her as her captain kept her on a northwesterly course.

✲ ✲ ✲

The *Perkins* captain saw a torpedo cross his ship's bow followed by a deluge of shells churning the water all around his destroyer. Capt. Reed increased his speed and began making smoke as he followed in the *Fletcher*'s wake on a northward course. The *Maury* and *Drayton* also saw torpedo wakes passing nearby and columns of water from falling shells. However, none of the torpedoes or shells hit the four leading destroyers.

The four ships continued steaming to the north and passed to the west of Savo Island when their lookouts and others reported seeing large explosions along Guadalcanal's beach. Their optimism grew as many Americans on those destroyers believed their torpedoes had hit the Japanese ships.

The *Minneapolis'* second eight-inch salvo appeared to have scored a direct hit as her third and fourth barrages straddled the Japanese ships. The light from the starshells seemed to be having a positive effect so that some thought the stricken Japanese ship was either a cruiser or destroyer. The *Minneapolis'* captain and gunnery officer believed it was a transport. Since the Japanese ship had disappeared after being engulfed in fire and smoke, they pointed their guns to another target and sent four more eight-inch salvoes at that.

Another four salvoes from the *New Orleans*, trailing behind the *Minneapolis*, joined with that ship's withering gunfire and literally blew what seemed to be the second Japanese ship into two pieces. The ship vanished as its bow and stern rose out of the water. Now turning its fury to a second target, which appeared to be a cargo ship, the *New Orleans* again fired its eight-inch guns. The second salvo hit the Japanese ship and blew it apart. Flames swamped the hapless ship until it exploded and apparently sank.

Although the *Pensacola* did not have a SG radar system, the light from starshells allowed lookouts using her optical sighting system to find a target for her eight-inch guns. It was 10,000 yards away when her big guns roared. The cruiser's salvo straddled the Japanese target. She then fired some starshells from five-inch guns, and her lookouts noticed what seemed to be a target that appeared to be a heavily damaged, listing, three stack cruiser. By this time, the cruiser's FD radar found a second target at a range of 8,000 yards just to the right of the first one. With this shortened range, her guns now fired continuously as the target appeared coming out from under a smoke screen. The Japanese ship appeared to be a *Mogami*- or *Yubari*-class cruiser that disappeared in a blazing explosion as the *Pensacola*'s second salvo hit her. Now, there were no more targets to fire at, so the gun crews loaded their guns to be ready to fire again when one should appear.

With such a target rich environment, the *Honolulu*'s gunnery officer carefully sifted through the SG radar sighting reports to select one upon which she could inflict maximum damage. He selected one that had been set afire by the guns of the *Minneapolis* and *New Orleans*. The range was sufficiently close to individually and continuously fire her guns. After observing arcs of red tracers moving toward the target, her gun crews checked fire to observe how much damage, if any, her bombardment had accomplished. The blazing light from the starshells as well as the smoke and haze prevented them from seeing what they wanted to observe. Her radar continued to keep track of the target until she sent one more salvo. The distant ship stopped dead in the water.

Meanwhile, the *Northampton*'s gunners found a target to the left of the two "cruisers." When the light from starshells revealed it was a destroyer, her eight-inch guns blasted away from a range of 10,000 yards. Her lookouts observed hits on the Japanese ship and believed the cruiser's guns had sunk it.

Still not able to find any target, the *Lamson* kept firing starshells and stayed in the cruisers' wakes. The destroyer *Lardner* fired six times at a target that intermittently flashed on her radar, but then lost contact with it.

Everything seemed to be going the Americans' way. They had fired their big guns and sunk at least one ship. They had dodged some torpedoes and several Japanese shells had harmlessly splatted in the water. It must have seemed that the Japanese were hopelessly outgunned, but that situation changed dramatically.

Seven minutes had passed since the *Minneapolis* fired her first eight-inch salvo when disaster struck with the suddenness of a giant earthquake. A massive explosion in the cruiser's bow sent enormous flames and waves of oily water upward far above the ship's superstructure. The entire hull shook like an animal being torn apart in the mouth of a huge, treacherous predator. The bow disappeared as the big ship heaved over to starboard, and its bow stub nearly submerged deep into the water. The bow now dragged in the water on the ship's starboard side. Huge waves of water washed over the pilothouse, fires engulfed the forecastle, and fumes from gasoline and fuel oil wafted over the ship's stern and aft areas. The cruiser drastically slowed and could not be steered.

What the relatively puny Japanese gunfire could not do, their deadly Long Lance torpedoes did. And this was only the beginning.

✲ ✲ ✲

Tanaka's attitude changed from being worried to near elation when a dazzling column of flame erupted from the leading American destroyer followed by another huge flaming explosion and then several other equally spectacular blasts coming from the other American ships. He thought to himself that the *Takanami* had fired some of its torpedoes just before being pummeled to its destruction and inflicted its own revenge on its tormentors.

An avalanche of shells raised a forest of water geysers just off the *Naganami*'s stern. Tanaka believed the destroyer must have been moving at the blazing speed of 40 knots. Then the American cruiser passed with the flames silhouetting her against them. She was too big to be a cruiser; she must have been a *Texas*-class battleship. Her two huge forward turrets, massive superstructure, the characteristic tripod mast with the big crow's nest on top, two large smokestacks, a smaller rear tripod mast, and two more large turrets aft were now clearly visible against the light of distant flames.

Tanaka pointed at the cruiser, and the *Naganami*'s captain nodded without saying anything. He needed no more prompting for what he needed to do when he ordered his crew, "Get the big one." The destroyer closed the range to the big American ship to about 4,300 yards. With an ideal torpedo firing solution dialed into its torpedo directors, the destroyer loosed a full eight-torpedo salvo at the American ship. All eight Long Lance torpedoes leapt from their tubes in an explosive hiss of compressed air and splatted into the water. At this range, they did not miss. The captain ordered a turn to put his ship's stern toward the target and ordered even more speed from his engine room. The destroyer's engines throbbed loudly, and the ship nearly achieved a speed of 45-knots. Shells hit the water as she rushed about, but they missed, hitting behind the ship's stern. There is a saying that "fortune favors the brave" and luck was definitely on the *Naganami*'s side as *not one* of the American shells hit her. The most serious damages she sustained that night were a few holes in one of her stacks from shrapnel thrown by exploding shells as they exploded in the water near her.

The *Makinami* was 2,000 yards ahead of the burning *Takanami* when Capt. Sato wanted to reduce his speed as Tassafaronga loomed closer. However, he decided to maintain a 30-knot speed until the flashes from the American guns silhouetted their ships in the darkness. He turned his destroyer to port so that his destroyer's beam pointed toward the distant ships, an ideal position from which to fire his torpedoes. He looked behind the other ships and noticed shells bracketing the *Kuroshio*, the last ship in his formation, but not hitting it. The light from starshells showed the *Takanami* on fire and in dire straits. A barrage of large caliber shells smacked the water off his port quarter and caused huge columns of water to stand up in the air. Not more than 15 seconds passed when a salvo shot overhead and blasted the water to starboard. Massive walls of water from two more salvoes sprouted between the *Kuroshio* and *Oyashio* just behind the *Makinami*.

Now, twin columns of fire erupted from the leading American ship. It was a long way from the *Makinami* to what appeared to be battleships as Sato noticed more of them emerge from the smoke and fire. But these seemed to be moving at a slower 21-knot pace so that, as far the Japanese could reason, they could only be older American battleships. And what inviting targets they made! Despite the long range, the *Kuroshio*'s captain took the risk and fired two Long Lance torpedoes. Sato wanted to reduce the distance to the American ships and ordered his four ships to separate into two attacking groups to turn to starboard to pursue the Americans.

The *Oyashio*'s captain did not wait for Sato's orders and took the initiative to attack the American ships. He tightly turned his ship around and increased his speed to 35-knots. The American "battleship" made a perfect target against the background of fire from burning American destroyers by not changing its course. The Japanese destroyer moved past the burning *Takanami* and fired a full eight-torpedo spread at the American ship 11 minutes after the *Kuroshio* fired its two missiles. The crew on the *Oyashio* confidently anticipated that their messengers of death would hit their intended target as their ship moved westward at high speed toward Cape Esperance.

Caught totally by surprise in seeing the *Minneapolis* explode in flames, Capt. Clifford H. Roper turned the *New Orleans* hard to the right to avoid colliding with the stricken flagship. His cruiser had just begun to turn when a cataclysmic explosion rocked the *New Orleans* between Turrets One and Two. The bow with Turret One atop it broke away from the cruiser, moved past the broken ship, tore a hole in her port side, and wrenched a blade from the propeller on the shaft driven by the No. 4 engine. The ship lurched forward as the streamlined passage formerly provided by the absent bow now became a jumbled mass of bulkheads and men thrown off their feet. All power failed in the forward sections as the ship's forward progress slowed to a crawl, and her truncated bow began to sink.

Seeing flames and blazing wreckage blasted into the air about twice as high as the forward mast and water filled with the stench of fuel oil pouring into his station in the secondary conning station, convinced Cmdr. W. F. Riggs, Jr., the ship's executive officer, that his ship's ammunition magazine had exploded. Everyone in the forward sections was undoubtedly dead. No one could have survived such a disastrous conflagration. He could not make contact with the bridge over the ship's telephone, so he took command of the ship's steering and ordered a "right rudder" to turn the stern toward the Japanese to minimize the chances of being hit again by torpedoes. Riggs unsuccessfully tried to talk to anyone over TBS. With no orders coming from the bridge, he looked over the horizon to find where he was on the sea.

Meanwhile, the *Pensacola*'s Capt. Frank L. Lowe had the habit of being in his ship's top-most station atop the forward mast so he could command his ship's armament from what he felt to be a more advantageous position during an air attack. His executive officer, Cmdr. Harry Keeler, Jr., stayed in the pilothouse to direct the ship's course and speed. When the disastrous explosions clobbered the *Minneapolis* and *New Orleans*, the *Pensacola*'s gunners looked for new targets as Keeler ordered a 20° left turn to keep from colliding with the two wrecked cruisers that had been ahead of his ship. He looked over to his right and saw how badly damaged they were. Flames surged skyward with such intense heat that he could feel it from his position. The *Pensacola* drew alongside the *Minneapolis* just as she fired another broadside. The *Pensacola*'s crew felt the concussion of the eight-inch guns' blast.

When her FC radar found a new target just 6,000 yards away, the *Pensacola*'s eight-inch guns blasted a salvo toward a ship that began to display flashes from the shells' impacts. Her radar had total control over her gunfire. Her lookouts could not see their ship's fall of shot. She fired seven salvoes when their target disappeared and her gunnery officer guessed the ship had been sunk. Another blip appeared on her FC radar, this time about 12,000 yards away off her port bow. It moved at a speed of 32 knots on a 295° True heading. The cruiser fired three more eight-inch salvoes, but her spotters could not confirm they were hitting anything since the target vanished from her radar scopes.

Her lookouts saw another ship to starboard and asked the ship to identify itself. The ship fired two starshells, and turned out to be the *Honolulu*, which displayed its recognition lights. A few smaller caliber shells hit the water close to the *Pensacola*'s port bow. Lowe and the ship's gunners searched for another target to attack when a monstrous explosion came from the base of her mainmast. All steering control vanished as the cruiser markedly slowed in the water. Black oil and flames shot toward the sky and violent vibrations shook the ship. Flames engulfed the mainmast and rear stack. She began to list at a 13° angle that dipped her port scuppers nearly to the water's surface. The flames rapidly spread to the ship's forward and aft sections. The fire cut the pipes carrying water needed to fight the fires so that no water could flow through them.

The explosion devastated the engineering spaces. Miraculously, she still had one operational fireroom and engine room. The engineers wasted no time rerouting fuel oil, feed water, and steam around burst pipes and managed to restore power to one shaft and some of the generators. She was no longer able to fight and headed for Tulagi under her own limited power. The engineers redistributed the fuel oil and water to return her to an even keel. Nonetheless, the fires continued to blaze over her superstructure and main deck.

The *Honolulu*'s skipper, Capt. Robert H. Hayler, noticed the chaotic situation aboard the *Pensacola* as it made its sharp port turn and ordered "full right rudder" to avoid hitting the damaged cruiser. After his rudder had reached the amidships position, the ship's bearing passed the north heading. Wanting to bring his six-inch guns into a better firing position to look for a second target, he ordered a slight turn to port where the target showed on his SG radar's scopes. Assuming the three cruisers that had been ahead of him had been torpedoed, Hayler needed to offer a less tempting target for a Japanese torpedo attack. The stricken ships blocked his guns from taking a clear shot at the Japanese, so he checked his fire until he had a better shot. Although he felt certain his previous salvos had either sunk or severely damaged their intended targets, he waited for the optimum range and firing path to appear. Now the SG radar could not find any targets at which to fire. The best the *Honolulu* could do was fire some five-inch starshells to light any potential targets for the other ships.

Capt. Willard A. Kitts of the *Northampton* turned his cruiser to starboard and maintained his current speed when the *Honolulu* made its port turn. He did the same as the *Honolulu* when that ship slowed slightly and began steaming on a 350º True bearing. His SG radar picked up a target in the gap between the *Pensacola* and the other two burning cruisers. Kitts ordered his eight-inch guns to fire several salvoes toward the target. He turned the *Northampton* to 320º to bring his guns into a better firing angle and present the cruiser's beam to the Japanese. Fire Director One had been controlling the guns' firing and soon reported seeing several shells hit the target and sink it. With no more targets to shoot at, her guns stopped firing after eight nine-gun salvoes. Based on the reports from his spotters, Kitts confidently believed his ship's guns had sunk a light cruiser and two destroyers. As far he was concerned, the *Northampton*'s crew had earned their pay that day. But his euphoria would prove to be short-lived.

The cruiser headed toward Savo Island, just four miles ahead. Kitts turned the ship to 280º to pass to the west of the island and resume searching for more targets of opportunity. He could no longer see the *Honolulu,* but could see the burning *Pensacola* off his port beam. The *Minneapolis* and *New Orleans*, in the distance off the port quarter, still burned but their fire intensities had somewhat lessened. A fire that could only come from a Japanese ship burned off the southeastern horizon with at least two more ships on fire farther in the distance.

About 20 minutes after torpedoes smashed into the *Minneapolis* at 12 minutes before midnight, Kitts saw two torpedo wakes coming toward his ship's port bow at a sharp angle and frantically ordered. "Left full rudder." The first torpedo approached at a depth of 10-feet while the second torpedo seemed to be running on the surface.

At least one of them hit the cruiser aft of its port quarter and exploded with dreadful effects. The blast tore a huge hole in the ship's port side, which allowed the sea to rush in and flood the cruiser's aft engine room, disable three of her four propellers, and cut all communications to the rearward parts of the ship. Like the explosions on her sister cruisers, it caused massively destructive flames and huge amounts of flaming fuel oil to surge into the sky and inundate the after antiaircraft gun director. The ship violently vibrated that caused the breakdown of pumps and motors and tore critical equipment from their mountings so that these pieces now hurtled throughout the ship as deadly missiles. A fire broke out near the mainmast's port side that quickly engulfed it and the boat deck. The ship heeled over at a 10° angle and immediately slowed. Fires spread to the on deck five-inch ammunition lockers and into the hoist that led to the magazines below.

The engineers restored power to the No. 1 shaft about ten minutes later, and the ship began to move again. Kitts turned the ship to the left hoping she could make it to Tulagi. But the harbingers of her demise were heard coming from below as failing bulkheads groaned from the stress caused by her movement through the sea. Her list dangerously increased.

Commanding the destroyer *Lamson*, Lt. Cmdr. Philip H. Fitzgerald still trailed behind the cruisers when it came near the *Northampton*. The cruiser's machine gunners believed his ship was a Japanese ship and fired at the destroyer. Not wanting to wait around and plead for a cease-fire from a supposed friend, Fitzgerald ordered his outgunned ship to rapidly turn right and to the north, then headed eastward out of harm's way.

Lt. Cmdr. William M. Sweetzer, the commander of the destroyer *Lardner*, saw the ships ahead of him slow and create a traffic jam. He ordered a sharp port turn to get clear, kept in a 270° turn, then ordered a rudder amidships on a 350° True heading. His course was now parallel to the other ships. The American cruisers also fired their guns at his ship. He chose the same escape method as Fitzgerald when he turned his destroyer to the east.

The lead destroyer captains could not believe what they saw when the cruisers ahead of them turned into pyres of flame, smoke, and death. Since no orders came from anyone, Cole ordered his destroyers to increase their speed to 35 knots and head toward Savo Island. He looked back at the debacle behind him. Red tracers arched into the sky; orange flames roared skyward; smoke and haze cast the entire battle with a destructive pall.

The *Drayton*'s SG radar detected three swiftly moving targets steaming to the west. The range to the ships was 12,000 yards—within range of torpedoes on low-speed settings. Lt. Cmdr. James E. Cooper ordered his destroyer to fire a four-torpedo spread. After timing the missiles' run to their intended target, one of the torpedomen reported that the torpedoes should have reached their targets. Nevertheless, Cooper saw no evidence of any explosions and correctly reasoned the torpedoes had missed their targets.

Cole took his four destroyers around Savo Island to the north, turned to the northeast, and was about two miles from the island at 11:49 p.m. when he saw the brilliant light from an immense blast to the southeast and behind the island. He had never seen an explosion with such power before and assumed an ammunition ship must have exploded.

He searched west and north of Savo Island to make sure no Japanese ships were in the vicinity and then headed east toward Tulagi. As his ships rounded Savo Island, their radars renewed a search for targets. He separated his force into two sections about 3,000 yards from each other and turned southward in an attack formation. The *Fletcher* and *Perkins* moved to the east while the *Maury* and *Drayton* steamed westward. Contact reports began to come in, so he slowed his ships to 15 knots to have enough time to assess the reported potential targets. The lights from several fires flickered on the horizon ahead of his ships, but these might have been from friendly ships. He wanted to attack any undamaged Japanese ships that might be hidden in front of the prominent mass of Guadalcanal.

When Tanaka's order to stop unloading their cargoes off Doma arrived, the *Kawakaze* and *Suzukaze* captains pushed the drums into the water. Their boats were in the water and it would take too long to recover the boats. It took much less time to jettison the drums. As the two destroyers began moving, American shells began landing in the water around them and forced the two ship captains to order, "Emergency speed ahead." The shells surrounding them seemed to be from large caliber guns. The *Takanami* exploded in the distance. The *Suzukaze* lookouts spotted some American ships so she fired her five-inch guns at them. The *Kawakaze* then led the way in a hard port turn to reverse their courses and head for Cape Esperance.

The American ships' gun flashes indicated they were now off the two destroyers' starboard quarter. The American ships stopped firing their guns. When the two leading American ships exploded, the blasts' light gave the destroyers a ready-made aiming point. Then the silhouette of what they believed to be a battleship appeared in front of the flames and on a parallel course with them and moving at 20 knots, a torpedomen's ideal target.

Suddenly, lookouts saw the telltale bubbles coming from approaching torpedoes heading toward the *Suzukaze*. She turned sharply to port and risked running aground on the reefs close ashore. The torpedoes rapidly closed the distance, and the destroyer's crews braced for the devastating explosion that would destroy their ship. But the missiles missed the ships and exploded harmlessly on the reefs near Guadalcanal. With much of her crew understandably breathing a sigh of relief, she resumed her former course and speed and took her place behind the *Kawakaze*.

The *Kawakaze* tracked the target as six heavy caliber salvoes churned up the water all around her. But they had the American ship in their sights and fired a full spread of eight torpedoes at it. The "battleship" continued firing its main guns and stayed on its course at the same speed. About five minutes after firing torpedoes, joyous enthusiasm spread among the *Kawakaze*'s crew as flames burst into the air over the American ship's mainmast and the whole aft part of the ship disappeared in a thunderous burst of explosive power.

The *Oyashio*'s and *Kuroshio*'s crews also celebrated when the American ship exploded since enough time had passed for the *Oyashio*'s torpedoes to hit their intended targets. Clearly, the American ship had been dealt a fatal blow, so it was time to look for another target. Another large ship, either a battleship or a large cruiser, still fired its guns. The *Kuroshio* had been tracking her as the flashes from her guns betrayed her precise position, course, and speed to the destroyer's lookouts. The torpedo officer took direct aim at the ship that was now slightly to the right of Savo Island and fired the *Kuroshio*'s last four torpedoes.

Sato also saw the huge explosion coming from the "battleship" and turned the *Makinami* and the *Kagero* toward the huge cataclysmic fire to apply the *coup de grâce* to the stricken American ship.

On their way, they passed by the burning *Takanami*. They moved closer to the burning American ship, and their lookouts saw she heavily listed to port, had turned left, and was on a collision course with the Japanese destroyers. The range rapidly closed as the *Makinami*'s crew mightily struggled to get their cargo drums out of the way of the ship's torpedo tubes. Sato decided to take the destroyer farther from the burning ship to line up a better torpedo firing solution. The *Oyashio* and *Kuroshio* steamed closer to the shore and were about two miles ahead. The *Makinami* made a port turn at 11:45 p.m. to a 245° course and parallel to the two other destroyers. The *Kagero* would have to finish off the damaged American ship.

A tremendous blast surged into the night sky and turned it into day two minutes later. It was at some distance beyond the burning American ship and to the right of Savo Island. The *Kagero* purposefully stayed on her course since the latest explosion disclosed that another "battleship" was still out there. The destroyer closed the range to nearly point-blank distance, fired four torpedoes, and capped off her attack by defiantly firing her five-inch guns.

The *Naganami* steamed at high speed on a westward course as splashes from heavy caliber gunfire followed her. The American gunners had the correct range, but missed the destroyer. The shells hit the water and sent huge geysers into the air ahead and behind the Japanese ship. Watching gunfire and torpedoes score hits on just one of his destroyers, Tanaka truly believed the war gods were with the Emperor and shone their favor on his force that night!

At a point previously planned by Tanaka where his ships would rendezvous, the seven destroyers joined each other. Tanaka tried to raise the *Takanami* on the radio but received no response. The stricken destroyer's silence was an ominous sign. So, he sent the *Oyashio* and *Kuroshio* to give any aid the *Takanami* might need and rescue any survivors.

The two destroyers found the still smoldering ship at 1:15 a.m. but it had not yet sunk. Just as the *Kuroshio* was about to launch boats to begin rescuing the survivors, a group of two American cruisers and three destroyers came so close that neither side wanted to open fire. The two Japanese destroyers no longer had any torpedoes and had no choice but to leave the scene. Many of the *Takanami*'s survivors made the long journey in small boats and on rafts to Guadalcanal's shore where Japanese soldiers greeted them.

The doomed *Takanami* slipped beneath the waves one hour after her former rescuers departed. Tanaka's seven destroyers entered the harbor at Shortland at 8:30 a.m. When they inspected their ships in the daylight, no damage showed on any ship other than a few small holes in the *Naganami*'s rear stack. Tanaka radioed a message to his superiors at Rabaul and Truk that he had lost the *Takanami,* but had inflicted heavy damage on the Americans. He guessed that his destroyers had sunk one battleship, one cruiser, and one destroyer and heavily damaged one cruiser and three destroyers.

The brilliant admiral had inflicted tremendous losses on the American Navy. His men fought bravely and well. Nevertheless, he managed to get far fewer drums to the Japanese soldiers on Guadalcanal than he carried. Despite the one-sided outcome of the battle, his mission was a failure. One inescapable conclusion was that if the Japanese wanted to continue supplying their men on Guadalcanal, they would need both sea and air superiority in, around, and over Guadalcanal.

Recovery and Licking Wounds

When the *Minneapolis'* TBS and radar stopped working after her bow had been blown off, Adm. Wright lost all contact with the rest of his task force. With the *New Orleans* suffering similar damage, he could not even send visual signals that could have been relayed to Adm. Tisdale for him to take command. With the battle still raging, Wright could not shift his flag to another ship. After waiting for ten minutes and not hearing from Wright, Tisdale reported his course and speed to Wright and again received no response. The *Honolulu* moved at 30 knots to the west and passed Savo Island. With that island near his starboard beam, he ordered the cruiser to a new northwesterly 345° course. Not much time passed before the *Northampton* exploded.

After looking at the blazing *Minneapolis* and *New Orleans* and seeing the *Pensacola* being smacked by torpedoes, he tried to contact the *Pensacola* over the TBS with the question, "Can you move?" Again, no response arrived. It now became clear to him that he was the senior officer capable of assuming the command of Task Force 67 and did so immediately. He then ordered the *Honolulu* to keep circling Savo Island and to steam eastward after rounding the island.

The *Minneapolis'* TBS woke up at 12:01 a.m. with an encouraging plea for help, "We need assistance." She had continued firing her nine eight-inch guns until the power failed. Nonetheless, her damage control parties restored enough power two minutes later for her to begin moving again and for Wright to finally send a TBS message to Tisdale to take command. After 30 minutes of being without a commander, Task Force 67 was leaderless no longer.

The *Honolulu* continued on its eastward course for another ten minutes, and then turned to starboard to a course of 145° to look for American ships in Iron Bottom Sound. Tisdale ordered Cole's destroyers to join up with the *Honolulu*, but the *Fletcher* could not "see" the cruiser on its radar and queried the cruiser for her position relative to Savo Island. The *Drayton*'s still operational SG radar found the cruiser and notified Cole the *Honolulu* was northeast of Savo.

Cole moved south of Savo Island and turned eastward at 12:30 a.m. When he asked Tisdale, "Where are the other units?" Tisdale replied, "Do not know positions of other units." Believing the new flagship was north of him, Cole turned due north and increased his speed to 20 knots.

After struggling to take off from the flat calm waters of windless Tulagi Harbor, four of the cruiser seaplanes—two from the *Minneapolis* and one each from the *New Orleans* and *Honolulu*—managed to get into the air and turned to the southwest over Iron Bottom Sound. They flew over the battle area when the guns opened fire, but gave no help to Task Force 67 by spotting Japanese ships and calling the fall of shot, which was their mission in the first place. As they flew along Guadalcanal's northern coastline and between Cape Esperance and Savo Island, they gathered information that later appeared in the battle reports written long after the battle was over.

However, one from a later arriving flight of seaplanes asked Tisdale at 12:37 a.m. for permission to drop flares over some Japanese destroyers unloading cargo onto the beach. Tisdale asked for more details and broadcast a message over the TBS, "We are swinging left to fire on destroyer landing troops on Guadalcanal," and ordered Cole to help him. Cole responded by ordering his destroyers to form a column and head southwest towards Cape Esperance. The cruiser and the plane exchanged a flurry of messages as the light cruiser steamed southward at high speed west of Savo Island and Cole's destroyers came in from the east. At last, the plane dropped a flare and lit up a wrecked, beached transport. Realizing the plane was of no use, Tisdale ordered it to go back to Tulagi.

Meanwhile, the *Minneapolis'* crew fought for her very existence as her damage control parties carried out a desperate battle to keep her afloat. After that horrible explosion caused by a detonating Japanese Long Lance torpedo that had blown off her bow, she stopped moving when water rushed into three of the four fire rooms, and it became nearly impossible to pump feed water into the fourth fireroom.

But it was critical that she begin moving again. The crew had no choice but to begin using salty seawater despite the damage that would be done to her propulsion systems. Messengers had to be used to transmit orders because nearly all her telephone circuits no longer worked. The blast disabled her TBS but her radar miraculously became operational just a few minutes after the disaster. It seemed like an eternity before her engineer could respond to the engine telegraph and get the cruiser in motion at an agonizingly slow speed of three knots. Only her magnetic compass could be used since her gyro compass no longer functioned.

When Capt. Rosendahl tried to beach the cruiser at Lunga Point, the lack of ventilation in the lone operational engine room made intolerable working conditions for the men there. There was no choice but to abandon the room. The specter of losing all power and drifting onto a shore inhabited by Japanese soldiers caused Rosendahl to turn around at 2:00 a.m. and take the longer way toward Tulagi. As the ship steamed ever so slowly toward that island, she nearly ran into a piece of wreckage that was the bow of a sinking destroyer jutting up into the air.

Making her own tortured escape to the comparative safety of Tulagi Harbor, the *New Orleans* was still ten miles away from her objective when she asked for help. Tisdale sent the destroyers *Maury* and *Perkins* to assist with the *Perkins* leading the way in a column moving at 25 knots. By 1:00 a.m., a dense haze descended over the water so that it was hard for spotters to tell the sea apart from the sky. *Maury*'s lookouts sighted a target 20 minutes later in the murkiness about 5,000 yards ahead and just to starboard. Not knowing whether the ship was friend or foe, Lt. Cmdr. Gelzer L. Sims ordered his ship to ready its torpedoes and guns for a fight. He wanted to fire all 16 of his torpedoes at once and trained his guns at the target. The *Perkins* followed the *Maury*'s lead.

The range closed by another 1,000 yards when the visibility of its outline cleared enough for the lookouts to know the potential target was definitely a ship. It seemed like a ship's right-handed part closely resembled a merchantman with a shorter-than-usual bow when looking at its left part. Sims wanted to make sure the ship was a Japanese vessel before opening fire by sending a challenge signal with his ship's blinker lamp. If the ship was a friendly, the proper response should be a display of its recognition lights or by Very gun with an answer of green, white, white, in that order.

The men on the destroyer's bridge nervously waited for an answer. The torpedo director had the target dead center in its aiming mechanism with all four torpedo mounts in total synchronization and all guns fully loaded and ready to fire as soon Sims gave the order. The range was down to 2,500 yards and all the men on deck could see the ship without the aid of binoculars. The right part of the targeted ship's Very gun sent up an answer—white, green, green. Sims ordered, "Stand by to fire torpedoes," and then peered intensely into his binoculars. Then, suddenly, several Very guns from all over the target sent up the correct recognition signal: green, white, white. Relieved, Sims ordered, "Hold fire," and ordered his ship to turn left so it would not collide with the now non-target.

As the *Maury* moved close, the form of the *New Orleans* loomed ahead. She moved slowly with her bow digging deeply into the water with everything in front of her No. 2 turret gone. Sims slowed his ship to 15 knots, began circling the heavily damaged cruiser, and ordered the *Perkins* to stay on alert and continue its patrolling activities. The *Maury* slowed to match the cruiser's much slower speed and moved nearer to the *New Orleans*. He raised his bull horn, began a conversation with the cruiser's bridge crew, and learned that the crippled ship had put out her fires, controlled the flooding, and was able to move at five knots and make good progress toward Tulagi.

Sims then saw another burning ship ahead that looked like she needed more help than the *New Orleans*. Both destroyers steamed past the *New Orleans* in an eastward direction. The men on both ships soon saw a blazing ship moving at eight knots, smoky flames climbing up her mainmast, and with a drastic list to port. She was an American cruiser that used to be the third ship in Wright's original battle formation, the *Pensacola*. The *Maury* moved ahead to screen the wounded cruiser from any potential attack while the *Perkins* came alongside to help put out the fires. When the cruisers finally entered Tulagi Harbor, the *Perkins* stayed with her as the *Maury* escorted the *New Orleans* to a safe place.

The last American heavy cruiser, the *Northampton*, still had more to endure before the fortunes of war decided her fate. When the torpedo hit her after engine room, the sea rushed in. But the effect was much worse when the massive explosion cut open all her fuel and water tanks, cut a huge hole in the bulkhead to the No. 4 fireroom, and opened extremely dangerous cracks in the walls of her aft ammunition magazines. The fire from the blast roared upward to compartments on the second and main deck and inundated them with flames and oil. As every pump that still worked tried their best to pump the onrushing water back into the sea, the ship listed at 10° and never got any better. The aft part of the ship had no lighting or power. The damage control parties had to use flashlights to inspect the compartments and found them to be flooded.

Her list increased to 20° just after 1:00 a.m. Her means to supply lubricating oil failed, and her engine had to be shut down. After finally getting his TBS working once more, Kitts sent a radio message that he planned to abandon his ship. The list was 23° when he ordered all men off the bridge, secured all fire rooms and engine rooms, all hands topside, and all life rafts and floater nets into the water. His next order was for all men to leave the ship except for a few men needed for a salvage crew.

Tisdale kept the *Honolulu* about 15,000 yards off Guadalcanal's northern shore as the ship steamed eastward to look for any Japanese ships that might still be in the area. When the ship's radar detected eight ships at 1:30 a.m., he did not know whether they were friend or foe. After the *New Orleans* radioed it had seen a submarine and thinking the other cruisers had possibly had been hit by torpedoes launched from submarines, Tisdale ordered the *Honolulu* at 1:39 a.m. to move westward, leave Iron Bottom Sound, and turn south. The *Fletcher* and *Drayton* joined up and fell into positions behind the light cruiser.

When Tisdale heard that Kitts planned to abandon the *Northampton*, he ordered the *Honolulu*'s captain, Capt. Robert. W. Hayler, to pass near the stricken cruiser. Still traveling at high speed and rapidly closing the distance to the blazing *Northampton*, Hayler saw life rafts and men in the oily water straight ahead. Realizing his ship was traveling too fast and would swamp the boats and men in the water ahead, he turned his ship hard to the right, slowed his speed, and ordered the *Fletcher* and *Drayton* to pick up survivors and stay near the doomed cruiser to render any further aid she might require.

The life of the *Northampton* began to ebb at 2:00 a.m. when the damage control parties could no longer control the fires engulfing her aft and boat decks. The water pressure needed to extinguish the blazes dropped. As the cruiser's men jumped into the water, *Fletcher* and *Drayton* crews pulled them from the water as fast as they could. The cruiser's list increased to 35º. Kitts knew his command's existence was about to end and had no choice but to abandon her. After ordering the salvage crew into the water and keeping with the tradition of the sea, he was the last man alive to leave the doomed cruiser. The *Northampton* rolled over with her bow pointed to the sky at a jaunty 60º angle and slipped beneath the waves at 3:04 a.m.

After the *Lamson* and the *Lardner* steamed to the east, the commander of the two destroyer division, Capt. Laurence A. Abercrombie, received orders at 1:30 a.m. relayed through Guadalcanal to help the *Minneapolis* make her way to Lunga Point. After not being able to find her near there, he turned toward Tulagi and found her at 2:54 a.m. limping toward that island's harbor. She moved steadily, albeit slowly, and the destroyers moved alongside the cruiser.

Dawn rose over Tulagi Harbor as the *Maury* came alongside the *New Orleans*, nudged the cruiser into her place, and dropped its anchor. Sometime later that morning, the tug *Bobolink* moved the *Minneapolis* into the inner harbor. Maintenance men tied her to the coconut trees near the beach and covered her with camouflage nets. The *Maury* also acted as a tug and moved the *New Orleans* deeper into the jungle up McFarland Creek to a place alongside the PT tender *Jamestown*. Like the *Minneapolis*, men placed camouflage nets over the cruiser. The *Pensacola* dropped its anchor in the bay behind Tulagi Island. Her crew, with maintenance personnel from the rapidly growing base at Tulagi, began working to get the ship sufficiently repaired so she could go to a better equipped base to be fully repaired and returned to duty.

Daylight arrived over Iron Bottom Sound as Tisdale searched for any more Japanese and then headed for Tulagi. As soon as Wright could see the *Honolulu*, he told Tisdale to take the *Lamson* and *Lardner* with him and return to Espiritu Santo. The *Fletcher* with 646 survivors from the *Northampton* and the *Drayton* with 127 men plucked from the water were beyond Lengo Channel and moving south. The three damaged cruisers received enough repairs to move to Espiritu Santo for more repairs and eventually to the American mainland for rebuilding. They would return to the fleet before the end of the war.[7]

The fighting part of the Battle of Tassafaronga ended with a Japanese tactical victory and strategic defeat. It was time for hind-sighted criticisms and analysis.

CHAPTER 52
So Who Won?

American Commanders Report to Their Superiors

Adm. Wright supervised, ensuring that damaged ships in Task Force 67 got to Tulagi Harbor where they could lick their wounds and complete essential repairs.[1] Each ship needed to make a long trip to the continental U.S., where they would be rebuilt and returned to the fleet. After he accomplished this difficult task, he began to gather his subordinates' action reports and to develop the outline of his own report. He also relied heavily on Adm. Tisdale for information because of his command experience, such as it was. Tisdale had taken command of the task force after Wright relinquished that responsibility due to the crippling damage sustained by his flagship.

As Wright began organizing his report to Halsey, the major problem he had was confusion about what Japanese ships and ship types were actually there, what damage they had suffered, and what their movements were as they fought the Americans. The American intelligence efforts seemed to be spotty at best, or confusing at worst. An Australian coastwatcher reported seeing 12 Japanese destroyers leaving the Shortlands before noon on November 30. An American search plane sighted one carrier and one light cruiser at 8:20 a.m. on December 1 about 250 miles from Guadalcanal on a 300° course at a speed of 25 knots. Several intelligence reports from CINCPAC and SOPAC headquarters indicated that about eight destroyers were on their way to Guadalcanal. The ships in Task Force 67 that had SG radars reported at least eight ships at 11:06 p.m. A pilot of a cruiser seaplane reported seeing some large and some small ships just before the Americans opened fire. In hindsight, it appears the intelligence from Wright's superiors was right on target. For some reason, Wright chose to essentially ignore that information.

As the battle proceeded, every American ship reported hitting several Japanese ships while they actually only hit and heavily damaged just one Japanese destroyer, the *Takanami*. The Japanese *thought* they had sunk an American *Texas*-class battleship and one heavy cruiser.

✲ ✲ ✲

Wright submitted his report, along with copies of his subordinates and his ships commanding officers' action reports, to Halsey when he sent it on December 9 by courier to Nouméa. His report described how he organized his task force, what events happened before the battle began, the messages he received, his plans for fighting the battle, his orders sent to his subordinates, and how the battle unfolded on a nearly minute-by-minute basis. He also included a description of his ship movements and his assessment of the damage his force sustained.

His comments concerning the Japanese ships demonstrates the confusion he and his officers actually experienced that night. Quoting parts of his action report are indeed quite telling:[2]

"Enemy force - Composition and movements.

27. All attempts to determine with certainty the composition of the Japanese forces participating in the action, or the tactics employed by those forces, or the damage sustained by the enemy, are defeated by conditions preventing accurate observation. The night was very dark, with sky completely overcast. Surface visibility was less than 4,000 yards, and the range to enemy surface vessels was at no time less than 6,000 yards. During the approach, the firing of our torpedoes, and the opening stages of the gun action, no enemy ships were seen. Thereafter individual ships were seen, for brief intervals only, when illuminated by star shells or the loom of burning ships. In addition, no individual who did see anything could also note and record the time of the occurrence. As a result the recordings of times in all the reports are subject to suspicion.

28. In attempting to visualize the action and to comprehend the difficulties in the way of any observer's following the developments of the battle, it will be helpful to recall that the SG radars are capable of giving either a general view of objects in the vicinity of the observing ship, or an accurate bearing and distance of any single object, but that the two functions cannot be performed simultaneously. Since the SG radars were necessarily concentrated for considerable intervals on obtaining bearing and range of own ship's target, there was no continuity in the observation of the very rapidly changing situations.

29. Attempts to analyze the torpedo attack which disabled the *Minneapolis* and *New Orleans* have proven particularly baffling. The number of torpedoes involved (at least three struck the two cruisers and at least three passed through our van destroyer formation at about the same time) and the wide spread (1,000 yards apart), struck simultaneously, and other torpedo wakes crossing 3,000-4,000 yards ahead of cruiser positions) seemed to rule out the possibility of attack by a single submarine. The observed positions of the enemy surface vessels before and during the gun action makes it seem improbable that torpedoes with speed-distance characteristics similar to our own could have reached the cruisers at the time they did if launched from any of the enemy destroyers or cruisers which were observed to be present.

30. The Brief of Available Information will show how little is really known about the enemy forces participating in the action, or what their movements were, or what damage they suffered.

31. About the best we can do under the circumstances is to make those assumptions which seem most logical and which are not in conflict with such evidence as is available. Upon that basis the following opinions are ventured:

(a) That, at about 2315, Japanese surface units were under way between Cape Esperance and Tassafaronga on a southeasterly course at about 17 knots, approaching enemy-held parts of Guadalcanal Island for the purpose of landing supplies and/or troops.

(b) That Japanese submarines may have been present, stationed approximately on the line Tassafaronga - Savo Island.

(c) That the Japanese surface force was operating in at least two groups, the leading, or easternmost group, consisting of five or six destroyers and the rear group of about four cruisers and about four or five destroyers.

(d) That noncombatant Japanese ships were probably not present.

(e) That the presence of our task force was probably not known, at least until shortly before we opened fire.

(f) That at about the time we opened fire the cruisers turned to the northward, and that when two were heavily hit the others escaped to the north-westward.

(g) That most, if not all, of the destroyers stood in to make a torpedo attack on our cruisers, and that at least three survived to reach torpedo firing position.

(h) That the *Minneapolis* and *New Orleans* were disabled by torpedoes, probably fired by destroyers.

(i) That undetermined vessels to the westward of our position, perhaps cruisers trying to escape, or perhaps a submarine or submarines fortunately placed, fired long range torpedo shots which hit the *Pensacola* and *Northampton* merely through luck, since the maneuvers of those vessels in clearing our damaged ships could not have been predicted when the torpedoes were fired.

(j) That no supplies or troops were landed on the northern shore of Guadalcanal, although some personnel probably reached there by swimming.

(k) That probable Japanese losses are two light cruisers and seven destroyers."

It does not take much imagination to see that much of what Wright reported shows how confused he and his officers were about what had happened that fateful night. With the almost total reliance on radar to sight their foes, it is also understandable that any observations would be filled with uncertainties and chaotic thinking.

Wright's evaluation of how his ship captains and their crews performed during the conflict criticized the destroyer torpedo attacks as ineffective and of firing them from too far away. Of course, he could not comment on the effectiveness of the torpedoes themselves. He praised his cruisers' gunfire as "excellent," "very impressive," and inflicting "great havoc" on the Japanese ships. He expressed his doubts that any of the Japanese ships had escaped without being damaged with the possibility that two "cruisers" had left the battle on a northwesterly course. He continued:

> "A very high standard of gunnery proficiency was necessary to get results under the conditions obtaining, since it was necessary to depend largely upon radar information for ranging, pointing and spotting. Star shells appeared to function fairly well, but smoke caused great interference with vision even when star shells were advantageously placed."[3]

Wright had never commanded an American naval task force in battle. Like many of his contemporaries, he did not recognize how formidable the Imperial Japanese Navy truly was.[4]

Wright heaped lavish praise on his officers and enlisted personnel when he stated their performance under fire, "left nothing to be desired," endorsed "without reservation all the actions" of Adm. Tisdale. Wright did not blame the crews of the torpedoed cruisers and praised them for their actions in rescuing their ships so they could sail again. He severely criticized the ineffectiveness of the TBS radio, just as his predecessors had from prior battles, while praising how well the recognition lights worked. He recommended that battery backup systems be installed so that the lights could stay in continuous operation.

He commended the SG radars and recommended more repeater scopes be installed throughout critical areas onboard the ships. His remarks concerning the FC radars were far less complementary with particular attention to their failure in spotting the fall of shot. Wright recommended a new radar system be developed specifically for fighting nighttime surface battles.

Wright did not have much good to say about how the cruiser seaplanes performed when he stated, "Our planes in this case had no influence upon the course of the action." He unequivocally stated that these planes were of no use in the Pacific War. Based on Wright's observations, these planes were from a bygone era where the aircraft was supposed to be used as the "eyes" of the fleet. But with the advent of aircraft carriers, the "fleet" was the carrier and not the battleship, cruiser, or destroyer. Sea power was now projected by the airplane and not the battleship. All the seaplanes on the cruisers and battleships presented was a dangerous fire hazard in the types of surface battles then being fought.

He offered one recommendation that no other prior American task force commander had suggested up to this time. Wright contended that light cruisers were better suited than heavier warships to fight surface battles in confined waters such as in the Solomon Islands. He singled out for particular praise the *Honolulu* for its "tremendously impressive" accuracy of its six-inch guns. He states that one light cruiser such as the *Honolulu* was equal to "at least" two heavy cruisers in fighting a surface battle around Savo Island. The conclusions of Wright's report pleaded for more time for training with an emphasis on gunnery and also for building a team of ships that had to work together.

Wright's days of ever commanding a task force again ended when Tanaka effectively destroyed Task Force 67 as a fighting force in the waters off Tassafaronga. He did not know why he failed when he forwarded his report to Halsey. Nevertheless, he did fail to inflict any significant damage on the Japanese ships that Task Force 67 confronted that night. At the time, the fact that his ships stopped the Japanese from landing any appreciable supplies could not salvage any praise for him. However, his superiors had more to add as the reports of this battle rose in the American chain of command.

✡ ✡ ✡

Halsey forwarded Wright's action report to Nimitz on December 13 without any comments. He needed more time to formulate his evaluation about what happened on the night of November 30-December 1. Nimitz waited to send his report to King until February 15, 1943, because he waited to include the events that followed through December and into January. He could then rely on added hindsight and more information from intelligence sources not available immediately after the Battle of Tassafaronga.

CINCPAC told King in his report that the Battle of Tassafaronga and the Battle of Cape Esperance had convinced the Japanese that any attempt to bring large quantities of supply to Guadalcanal was at least temporarily impossible. He anticipated that further attempts to supply the Japanese troops on Guadalcanal would be reduced in scale by using submarines and isolated nighttime destroyer runs of the Tokyo Express. He also stated that the Japanese seemed to be building more airfields along the Slot to protect any ships bringing supplies to Guadalcanal. Nimitz estimated the Japanese losses were four destroyers sunk and two others damaged and reported the American losses as the cruiser *Northampton* sunk and three other cruisers, the *Pensacola*, *New Orleans*, and *Minneapolis*, heavily damaged. American personnel losses were 19 officers and 398 enlisted men either killed or missing. He also wrote that the best intelligence he had was that eight Japanese destroyers appeared off Guadalcanal with six of them transporting supplies. Full sized and midget submarines might or might not have been in the vicinity, due to confused observations by American personnel.

Nimitz added his own analysis about the confusing intelligence reports by stating that the air searches conducted on November 30 found no Japanese ships even in good weather with 100% coverage of the search areas assigned to the search planes. He reiterated that Wright had received a negative air search report, the coastwatcher report of 12 destroyers leaving the Buin area on that day, and Halsey's report that Japanese ships approaching Guadalcanal were indeed destroyers. He also added that the type of ships the Japanese actually sent to supply their men on the island was still unknown.

The only prisoners picked out of the water said they were from the destroyer *Takanami.* A later interrogation yielded the information that three of those survivors were actually from the destroyer *Kikutsuki*, which the Americans sank at Tulagi on May 4, 1942. Further adding to the confusion was that American search aircraft spotted one carrier and one destroyer leaving the Guadalcanal area on December 1. What an impossibly incomprehensible smattering of information that the Americans had at this time! It's no wonder they appeared confused when they wrote their reports.

After providing a less-detailed narrative of the combat action of that night, Nimitz's conclusions were:

- Heavy ships cannot be used in the confined waters such as those around Savo Island unless there are no other ships available. These ships cannot nimbly maneuver to avoid Japanese torpedo attacks.

- Radar cannot be used effectively because of the nearness of large land masses that often mask Japanese ship movements.

- The lack of early, timely information forced Task Force 67 to enter Iron Bottom Sound through the narrow passage of Lengo Channel that further inhibited Wright's ability to maneuver. The preferable entrance to Iron Bottom Sound is from the west around Cape Esperance where there is more sea room.

- Destroyers and PT boats would have been far more effective than the heavy cruisers to stop the Japanese. Of course, the mixed messages that intelligence sent undoubtedly worsened the situation and forced Halsey to send the heavy cruisers given the fact that the Japanese had sent battleships in the Naval Battle of Guadalcanal.
- The air search efforts from Espiritu Santo and Guadalcanal produced no usable results. The Japanese chose courses out of aircraft range to avoid being detected. There was desperate need for longer range search aircraft such as B-17s and PBYs to improve the effectiveness of searches.
- All large caliber guns should be immediately equipped with flashless powder. No Japanese ship got nearer than 4,000-6,000 yards to the American ships because they could see the flashes of the American guns. Being able to use one of their strengths—visual observation—handed a big advantage to the Japanese and undeniably resulted in their ability to use their torpedoes with destructive effect.
- The range the American destroyers used to fire their torpedoes was too far to be effective. Since they had the favorable position ahead of the cruisers, they should have reduced their range to their targets to within 4,000 yards before firing. Because of the longer range, the destroyers' captains had to use starshells and thus lost the advantage of surprise.
- The SG radars proved to be invaluable for finding the Japanese ships and shooting at them. However, the closeness of large land masses such as Guadalcanal made it harder to find targets. Despite his misgivings, he recommended that the Navy accelerate installing as many SG radars and repeater scopes on as many combat ships as possible.
- PT boats would have been effective in the narrow and shallow waters around Savo Island if they had been used.
- Ships' identities are particularly difficult during nighttime surface battles. Identification lights proved useful but Nimitz pointed out they helped the Japanese almost as much as the Americans. He recommended installing infrared or radar identification technologies on all American combat vessels.
- The confining waters around Guadalcanal makes the mining of them an effective defensive tactic. The areas where the Japanese unload their supplies were prime locations for mines.
- Nimitz severely criticized the TBS radio system as a dangerous means to communicate among American ships. The Japanese had proved they could intercept these broadcasts and determine American ships' dispositions and battle tactics. Interrogations of Japanese prisoners indicated that TBS transmissions made it easier for them to sight and locate American warships thus making them easier targets at which to fire.

- The readiness of the crews on the new destroyers joining the fleet was far below standards. Nimitz stated that they lacked antisubmarine training, inadequate gunnery exercises, poor radar training, and, in some cases, had never fired a torpedo.
- The Japanese torpedo was a highly dangerous and effective weapon. It appeared to have functioned well under combat conditions and carried a powerful warhead. The Japanese cruiser and destroyer crews seemed to be highly trained and effective in using them. On the other hand, American destroyers were not at all useful in nighttime action. He stressed the high priority need for improved and more training in nighttime combat torpedo tactics.
- The American torpedoes were incapable of inflicting damage on the Japanese warships. Nimitz called this an "important defect" that required "immediate attention."
- The Imperial Japanese Navy is a deadly and highly motivated foe that can no longer be discounted.
- His final recommendation was for "training, TRAINING and M-O-R-E T-R-A-I-N-I-N-G" with the emphasis on the training of commanding officers.

Nimitz sent copies of his report to King and to all senior officers under his command.

✲ ✲ ✲

Halsey sent his own action report on February 20, 1943, with comments on Wright's action report. His report first depicted his view of what happened on the night of November 30-December 1.

- Task Force 67 battled a Japanese naval force attempting to supply their soldiers on Guadalcanal between Cape Esperance and Tassafaronga. Although he had no definitive information, he guessed that Wright had stopped the Japanese from delivering supplies to Guadalcanal. What happened during the battle is a mass of confusing and contradictory reports so that the Americans could not precisely know how many and what types of Japanese ships they had fought.
- While Japanese gunfire was not effective, their torpedo fire devastated the American ships with one cruiser sunk and three others heavily damaged.
- After firing their guns and torpedoes, the American destroyers did not help the cruisers because they turned away from the battle and headed to the northwest. They acted this way despite instructions from Wright to the contrary.

Halsey then added his own analysis of Wright's action report with some quite telling comments.

- Despite the lead [van] destroyers having scored some hits, their actions were "disappointing." He encouraged the use of radar for torpedo attacks but criticized the destroyers for firing before they should have.

- He did not believe the Japanese torpedoes that had such a devastating effect on Task Force 67 were launched from destroyers because the range was more than 6,000 yards. He guessed they must have come from submarines instead.

With the extremely limited and confusing information they had at their disposal, CINCPAC senior officers did their best reporting to their superiors what had happened. Despite the horrible damage suffered by Task Force 67, the Japanese came to the realization that they could no longer continue to supply their soldiers on Guadalcanal and ultimately would give up any more efforts to hold onto the island. But about two months would elapse before that would actually happen.

Halsey and Nimitz praised the performance of the crews in Task Force 67 while they severely criticized the handling of the American destroyers under Cmdr. William M. Cole. Crenshaw expressed his opinion that Cole did not deserve to be excoriated and his senior officers' opinion was unwarranted because Cole was the only commander of any group of ships in Task Force 67, who brought his destroyers through the horrendous battle without any damage. In my opinion, this author cannot either support nor argue against what Crenshaw said in his book and leave his comments to stand on their own merits.[5]

Meanwhile, a clearer picture why the Americans suffered such casualties during the Battle of Tassafaronga needs to be explored. There was one area of concern that requires attention—the problems with American torpedoes and how these weapons contrasted with their Japanese counterparts.

A Tragic Blunder

Why did the Japanese torpedoes perform so well while the American torpedoes did their job so poorly? Even though the Japanese had developed superior battle tactics using torpedoes by encouraging the use of outstanding optical sighting systems, aggressive maneuvering, and firing from long ranges, their effectiveness cannot be explained by that alone. Or to say the same thing in another way, the American use of radar and firing their torpedoes from longer ranges do not explain why their torpedoes failed to score a single hit in the Battle of Tassafaronga. The destroyer *Fletcher* fired ten torpedoes, the *Perkins* eight, and the *Drayton* six. Not one missile hit its target or detonated. The answer to this question lied elsewhere.

In their action reports, no American senior naval officer said the American torpedo crews lacked courage. Their dedication to their duty and their willingness to engage the Japanese was second to none. They went into battle like the boxer beginning a championship bout with one hand tied behind his back. To provide added insights into why the American torpedo failed to do what it was supposed to do, the history of torpedo weapon development by the U.S. Navy before World War II began needs to be reviewed.

Crenshaw states his view about the development of the American torpedo in his book. He observes that the story is a combination of "ambitious dreams, intellectual courage, bright ideas, limited knowledge, faulty design, inadequate testing, uncritical faith, unquestioning loyalty, intellectual arrogance, rigid organization, and unbelievable stubbornness, all stitched together with the most dangerous ingredient known in the development of anything, secrecy." With his words, Crenshaw paints a complex picture of how an intricate peacetime government bureaucracy can become misguided and get its priorities wrong when having to bow to pressures such as budget restrictions and strong antiwar sentiments then rampant during the pre-World War II days.

✲ ✲ ✲

When Germany began unrestricted submarine warfare in World War I, the rest of the world's navies gained a new appreciation for the torpedo as an almost unstoppable and indefensible weapon. Just one of these deadly missiles could explode into the sides of a thin-hulled merchant ship and send it to the bottom within a few short minutes. The two decades after World War I ended witnessed the continuing development of larger capital ships and increasingly powerful guns that could hurl ever-larger shells over greater distances. The battleship's role as the central weapon of naval fleets around the world continued unabated.

To counter such developments, naval architects redesigned their nation's warships with thicker and impenetrable armor, increasingly deliberate compartmentalization, and the inclusion of armored "blisters" to take the blows from exploding torpedoes with the goal of keeping their ships afloat and able to continue in battle. Nonetheless, the ship designers could not invent protection for a ship's bottom thus leaving the opportunity open for new torpedo development.

All the major naval powers carried on torpedo research and development, and the U.S. was no exception. The U.S. Navy's Torpedo Station at Newport, Rhode Island, led the way. The engineers began design on a new exploder that would use magnetism to detect a ship's bottom and explode when it got within range. Their design assumed that if the torpedo carrying the new exploder got within five fathoms of a ship's bottom and exploded, the crushing compression between the explosion and the steel of the ship's bottom would tear a giant hole in the vessel's bottom or even break the ship's keel, which would result in the ship being torn in two. If the torpedo should strike a ship's hull instead, the warhead would decelerate suddenly and that sudden stop would trigger a devastating explosion. It was the best of all possible outcomes if the torpedo came close enough to the ship—it would explode on contact or when near enough without touching the ship.

With secrecy being the guiding principle in this effort, the American engineers developed a prototype exploder and put it into a torpedo. They towed a submarine hulk out to sea where it was deep, fired the torpedo, and the new exploder detonated under the submarine's keel. A tremendous explosion broke the vessel in two and sent it to the bottom. With just this singly successful test, the Navy ordered the new detonator, designated the Mk-6, into mass production to be used solely under wartime conditions. The Navy never tested the Mk-6 again either during fleet exercises aboard actual warships or at the development laboratory.

The Navy's Bureau of Ordnance (BuOrd) in Washington, D.C., ordered the Mk-6 in large quantities while keeping the knowledge of its existence as a closely-held military secret. Only a few cleared civilians at the Torpedo Station or a few officers at various locations knew of it. A "Czar of Torpedoes," normally carrying the rank of commander or a recently promoted captain, supervised the acquisition of the new exploder and its installation on all the Navy's torpedoes.

Torpedo development for the new ships and aircraft proceeded at the same time. Each torpedo differed depending on where it would be used. Three models evolved: (1) the Mk-13, the lightest of all the American torpedoes and having the shortest firing range, would be used on American naval aircraft; (2) the Mk-14 would be used on submarines; and (3) the Mk-15 would be used on destroyers and had the most robust construction to take the stress of being launched from tubes and hitting the water with great force as well as the longest possible range. Because the Mk-6 exploder had a bulky design and weighed more than 100 pounds, the new torpedoes had to be redesigned to be able to fit the exploders into them. Meanwhile, the Navy modified the earlier developed Mk-5 exploder to weigh the same and be the same size as the Mk-6.

The war clouds began gathering when BuOrd began informing fleet commanders and other groups with a need to know about the new exploders. Stocks of the torpedoes with the new exploder started to appear in naval warehouses at important locations and on key naval bases. When the Japanese planes left Pearl Harbor on December 7, specially trained teams of technicians began going aboard American warships and visiting every aircraft squadron to replace the Mk-5 exploders with the new Mk-6s in all torpedoes in the fleet.

One of the first offensive moves the U.S. Navy made was to immediately begin unrestricted submarine warfare on the Japanese merchant fleet. American submarines left Pearl Harbor with the fires still burning on Battleship Row. As the American boats returned from the patrols and reported the results of their missions to their superiors, a disturbing picture emerged. The submarine captains had fired several torpedoes at Japanese ships but reported very few hits. The missiles ran "hot, straight, and normal" at the target, seemingly struck the ship with some skippers seeing explosions at the waterline, but many of the ships continued, seemingly undamaged, on their course. Some believed the torpedoes exploded before reaching their intended targets—also known as premature detonation. Some of the more experienced captains laid the cause to inexperienced commanders.

One possible answer was that the torpedoes ran too deep and too far under the target and not near enough to the ship's hull for the magnetic triggering to explode the warhead. A former submariner himself, the CINCUS ordered a test of the Mk-14 torpedo to determine the depth at which the torpedoes actually ran. The actual results sent to all submarine commands reported on August 1, 1942, that these torpedoes had a ten-foot error in how deep the missiles went through the water. No such problems had yet been reported for the other torpedo models used in the fleet, but that would soon change.

At the Battle of Midway, three torpedo plane squadrons attacked the Nagumo's ships using the Mk-13 torpedoes. Few of the crews returned safely. These men were the best trained and most capable torpedo plane aviators in the U.S. Navy. Nevertheless, not a single returning crew reported any hits on the Japanese ships. Therefore, the skill levels of these aviators could not be questioned. So, the Navy reasoned the causes for this failure to be obsolete planes, overwhelming Japanese fighter defenses, and just bad luck. The official Navy position never asked any questions about the torpedoes themselves.

It would not be until the Battle of Savo Island on the evening of August 7, 1942, when the version of the torpedoes used on destroyers would be put to their first test under actual combat conditions. The American destroyer *Bagley* fired a full eight-torpedo salvo at Adm. Mikawa's column of cruisers and reported hitting nothing. At the Battle of Cape Esperance in October 1942, the destroyer *Duncan* fired two torpedo salvoes at the Japanese cruiser *Furutaka* at the near point-blank range of one mile, and nothing happened.

One month later, at the Naval Battle of Guadalcanal, the destroyer *Barton* fired four torpedoes before she sank with not one observer seeing any effect. The destroyer *Cushing* launched six torpedoes at the battleship *Hiei* from 1,000 yards away with no impact on the big ship. Before the *Laffey* went down, she fired two missiles at the battlewagon. These torpedoes were seen to hit the ship on her blisters and bounce off them. The same results happened after the *Sterett* fired four torpedoes at the big ship from an optimum range of 2,000 yards, the *O'Bannon*'s crew saw the wakes from two of their "fish" head straight for the *Hiei* without detonating; the *Monssen* fired five torpedoes from 4,000 yards with the same disappointing result. Elation might have come from the *Fletcher*'s crew after she fired ten torpedoes from a range of 7,000 yards, and they saw flashes explode on the battleship. However, those explosions actually came from shell hits by a cruiser. Also, the battleship *Kirishima* received no torpedo hits at all.

Even more embarrassing for the Americans was a pitiful episode when the American destroyer *Gwin* received orders to sink its fatally damaged sister ship, the destroyer *Benham*. The *Gwin* fired four torpedoes at the nearby dead-in-the-water ship. All four hit the ship and never exploded. The *Gwin* had to sink the unlucky destroyer with gunfire. Not to be outdone, another humiliating episode after the Battle of Santa Cruz occurred after a Japanese submarine torpedoed the destroyer *Porter* while she tried to rescue a downed flyer. She could not be saved, so the destroyer *Shaw* arrived later to sink her. The *Shaw* fired two torpedoes to detonate under the stricken ship—no explosions. The ship had to be sunk by the *Shaw*'s guns. Adding an insult to injury, the American carrier *Hornet* was a lost cause when the destroyers *Mustin* and *Anderson* arrived to sink her. Each destroyer put eight torpedoes into her with no damage seemingly inflicted on the carrier. Even five-inch gunfire could not sink her.

There was a dangerous and fatally serious crisis over American torpedo performance in combat that had to be addressed—the sooner, the better. Nevertheless, the Navy bureaucracy ignored the disaster with the head of the Torpedo Desk providing leadership for the classic stonewalling cover-up. Still fighting World War I, the admirals joined in. Nimitz demanded improved training and increased torpedo exercise, but never insisted that BuOrd fix the problem. After all, according to the Torpedo Desk, the Mk-6 exploder was the most meticulously tested weapon in the Navy's inventory. Each torpedo had been successfully tested at least once at Newport or the naval testing laboratory at Keyport, Washington. The weapon's test history had been carefully documented and available for anyone to review. The stone wall grew ever higher and thicker. By the time of the Battle of Tassafaronga, nothing had been done to correct this horrible deficiency with one of the Navy's most important weapons. And that would cause many American sailors and aviators to die unnecessarily until the Navy addressed the problem.

It would be eight months after the Battle of Tassafaronga before anything would be done about the faulty American torpedoes. After the submarine *Tinosa* attacked the *Tonan Maru* with torpedoes on July 24, 1943, and a spread of eight "thoroughly tested" American torpedoes hit the Japanese transport and failed to explode, the American submarine's commander, Lt. Cmdr. L. R. "Dan" Daspit went to Adm. Lockwood when his boat returned to Pearl Harbor and insisted something be done.

Lockwood had heard enough complaints from his submarine captains and finally acted. He ordered a submarine to fire two torpedoes at the cliffs on the south side of Kahoolowe Island. One exploded, but the other did not. The crew recovered and examined the unexploded torpedo and discovered the missile's firing pin had fired but did not detonate the exploder. Lockwood ordered a tower be built from where torpedoes could be dropped 90 feet onto a steel plate. It was time for real submariners to test the weapons rather than some theoretical technician in a pristine laboratory environment.

The testers dropped torpedoes with the Mk-6 exploders installed in them and found that seven of ten missiles failed to detonate. After more experimentation, the testers found that if the torpedoes hit their target at a glancing angle, the firing pin would set off the exploder. This discovery meant that the chance of success increased somewhat. It also had a worse effect by allowing the inventors of Mk-6 to maintain the fault was with the firing pin and not with the exploder they created. The basic flaw in the Mk-6 exploder was never fixed during World War II due to complacency, stubbornness, and downright incompetence. Despite continued reports coming from returning sailors and aviators of the torpedoes failing to do the job for which they were designed, more men continued to die because of the failure by U.S. Navy senior commanders to push hard for a solution. And the Torpedo Desk at BuOrd continued to place blame on the men trying to do their job in combat rather than where the real fault lay.[6]

Summarizing It All

The results of the Battle of Tassafaronga took on a familiar tone like the results of the previous naval, air, and ground battles in, on, and around Guadalcanal. The Japanese possessed the experience that could only come in battle. They also had practiced their tactics in rehearsals, simulations, and exercises that only a nation preparing for war did. Their commanders had been hardened by combat and were ready to take advantage of those developed skills. Many of them had already proved their superiority in previous battles.

The key advantage the Japanese possessed before engaging the Americans at Guadalcanal was their skill in fighting surface naval battles at night with the Long Lance torpedo and without the benefit of radar. During the Battle of Tassafaronga, Adm. Tanaka showed his command skills, and the Japanese destroyer crews showed they knew what they were doing. The Long Lance torpedo again showed its superiority by demonstrating that a supposedly inferior naval force could defeat a superior one.

The American sole reliance on radar demonstrated that this technological wonder was not enough to win a nighttime surface battle. The old-fashioned way of using the human eye was just as badly needed to call the fall of shot and to correctly differentiate a friend from a foe. There is no substitute for experience hardened in the searing forge of naval combat, and the American admirals possessed little or none of that skill. Criticisms of American tactics came from two Japanese observers. The first remark laid fault at the poor American accuracy of their gunfire:

> "The enemy had discovered our plans and movements, had put planes in the air beforehand for purposes of illumination, had got into formation for an artillery engagement, and cleverly gained the advantage of prior neutralization fire. But his fire was inaccurate, shells [im]properly set for deflection were especially numerous, and it is conjectured that either his marksmanship is not remarkable or else the illumination from his star shells was not sufficiently effective."[7]

Another Japanese naval officer told American interrogators after the war:

> "A more active use of destroyer divisions is necessary in night battles. Annihilation of our reinforcing units would not necessarily have been difficult even for a few destroyers, if they had chosen to penetrate our lines and carry on a decisive battle with the support of the main force."[8]

The Americans forced their destroyers to stay with their cruisers instead freeing them to use these faster and more maneuverable warships to independently attack the Japanese. Of course, this officer did not realize that the unreliable American torpedoes would have likely made such an attack at best useless or at worst tragic for the American sailors on these destroyers.

Bureaucratic incompetence and negligence resulted in the U.S. Navy going into battle with torpedoes that did not work. Although the Americans used smokeless powder for its naval guns, that powder was not flashless like the Japanese used. So whenever Americans fired their guns, the flashes from that gunfire gave their positions away to the sharp-eyed Japanese lookouts. Thus, the Japanese had a golden opportunity to find aiming points for their deadly Long Lance torpedoes to do their worst—and they did just that.

☆ ☆ ☆

There is no contest analyzing the results of this battle when viewed solely from the viewpoint of ship losses. For the Americans, the losses of ships and men were tragic and overwhelming. The Japanese lost just one destroyer while the Americans lost one heavy cruiser with three other cruisers heavily damaged. From that perspective alone, the result was a definite Japanese tactical victory. Nonetheless, the Japanese had suffered tactical victories in earlier naval battles.

Tanaka's mission was to land critically needed supplies for the beleaguered Japanese soldiers on Guadalcanal. The survival of these ground troops depended on successful fulfillment of that mission. Just as previous Japanese attempts to bring supplies to Guadalcanal had failed when opposed by American sea and air power, the Battle of Tassafaronga was no exception to that outcome. Therefore, Tanaka's mission was an abject failure. He could only land a few supply drums on the Guadalcanal beach. The Battle of Tassafaronga was a decisive American strategic victory, although their losses seemed to severely soften any euphoria they might have felt after the battle ended.

☆ ☆ ☆

After the end of the Battle of Tassafaronga, the Japanese began reassessing their commitment to continue throwing the Americans off Guadalcanal. MacArthur had inflicted terrible losses to their army and naval forces in New Guinea. If the Americans captured New Guinea, it would put them in a position to interdict Japanese supply lines used to bring critical oil and other materiel to the Japanese home islands. They could not afford to let New Guinea fall into Allied hands. Therefore, they had to decide where to apply their ever shrinking naval and air forces: New Guinea and Guadalcanal or just New Guinea. Vigorous discussions began in Tokyo, Truk, and Rabaul about what to do next with regard to Guadalcanal. The result would determine the future of their war efforts in the Pacific.

The Americans were now firmly entrenched on Guadalcanal and utterly determined to stay there. The Japanese soldiers there were in a bad way, and the Americans knew it. What had seemed impossible in the dismal early days after August 7 now looked quite possible. Nonetheless, the Japanese were still on the island and had to be either evicted or destroyed. More fighting was still ahead for the Americans if they wanted either to happen. As far as the Americans were concerned, the Japanese would fight to the last man and the Tokyo Express would definitely keep operating. As the Japanese grew weaker, the Americans grew stronger. There was one more job to do: take total control of Guadalcanal by making sure not one Japanese soldier remained alive there.

The Battle of Tassafaronga was the last surface sea battle in the southern Solomon Islands between the Americans and the Japanese. Four months of furious action came to an end with the American sailors adding another word to their remembrances of the terror in the waters off Guadalcanal—Tassafaronga.

The history of the naval battles between the Imperial Japanese Navy and the U.S. Navy off Guadalcanal is a repetitious picture of blood and body parts, ships' magazines exploding with deadly effect, ships on fire and sinking, men drowning or being attacked by sharks, and planes plummeting to the ground or sea in flames. But that is what happened. It became an omen of how lethal the rest of the Pacific War was to become.[9]

Part 12: Nearing the End

CHAPTER 53
Still a Question of Supplies

Trying to Put the Tokyo Express Back on Track

Gen. Hitoshi Imamura arrived in Rabaul from Java on November 22, 1942. Born in 1886 and commissioned as a second lieutenant in December 1915, he rose in the ranks of the Japanese Army to the rank of lieutenant general in March 1938. As part of the Southern Army under the command of Gen. Hisaichi Terauchi, he commanded the 16th Army that invaded Java and the Dutch East Indies in February 1942. Imamura supervised the Japanese capture of Java in March 1942.

He implemented a very broad-minded policy during his occupation of Java by governing the Javanese with less force and intimidation than his counterparts elsewhere in the Japanese Empire. While his actions caused great dismay in the headquarters of the Southern Army and Imperial General Staff, he brought order and achieved peaceful relations with the Javanese when he released the notorious Indonesian nationalist, Achmed Sukarno, from captivity.

As commander-in-chief of the 8th Area Army in the southeast Pacific Area, he also commanded the 17th Army in the Solomons and Bougainville, the 38th Division and the 65th Independent Mobile Battalion in New Britain, and the 18th Army on New Guinea. His plan to recapture Guadalcanal was to land two more divisions on Guadalcanal on February 1 with the rousing order:

> 'We must by the most furious, swift and positive action deal the enemy annihilating blows to foil his plans completely...It is necessary to arouse the officers and men to a fighting rage."[1]

This order showed his complete lack of appreciation for the conditions his soldiers confronted on Guadalcanal. If he had read the diaries of some of his soldiers struggling just to stay alive there, he would have seen a different picture of what the existence of these men actually was:

December 18: "Rice long since eaten up, even coconuts running short.

December 23: "Haven't seen one of our planes for ages, but every day enemy planes dance in the sky, fly low, strafe, bomb, and numerous officers and men fall,..."

December 26: "We are about to welcome the New Year with no provisions; the sick are moaning within the dismal tents, and men are dying daily. We are in a completely miserable situation...Why should we be subdued by these blue-eyed Americans? I intend to get onto the enemy airfield and let two or three of them have

> a taste of my sword...O friendly planes! I beg that you come over soon and cheer us up!"[2]

A heated debate raged in Tokyo within the highest levels in the Army and Navy about the war's direction in the South Pacific. These arguments reached Emperor Hirohito himself. One of the traditions of Japanese society is the annual message the Emperor issued on December 26 as a new year approached. His message for 1942 had a far more somber tone than the one he issued for 1941:

> "The Emperor is troubled by the great difficulties of the present war situation. The darkness is very deep but dawn is about to break in the Eastern Sky. Today the finest of the Japanese Army, Navy and Air units are gathering. Sooner or later they will head toward the Solomon Islands where a decisive battle is being fought between Japan and America."

It was now clear to all Japanese commanders that a turn in their fortunes was about to occur in December 1942 and January 1943. The debate continued whether the campaign on Guadalcanal should continue when pressing needs for more action on New Guinea were being brought on by the Allied successes there. Nevertheless, if Guadalcanal was to be retaken from the Americans, supplies had to be sent to the men of the 17th Army.

When Radm. Raizo Tanaka's destroyers arrived in Shortland at noon on December 1, he wasted no time planning his next supply mission to Guadalcanal. Despite the Japanese tactical naval victory at the Battle of Tassafaronga, the need to bring supplies to the embattled Japanese soldiers on Guadalcanal was still as desperate as ever. He did not have much time to continue to worry about what happened to the crew of the *Takanami* when three destroyers, the *Arashio*, *Nowaki*, and *Yugure*, reinforced his force on the morning of December 3.

By 1:00 p.m. that day, his ten-destroyer force—the flagship *Naganami*, *Makinami*, and *Yugure* escorting the *Arashio*, *Nowaki*, *Oyashio*, *Kuroshio*, *Kagero*, *Suzukaze*, and *Kawakaze*—left Shortland bearing drums jammed with supplies aboard. Tanaka pressed southward to bring relief to his Army comrades-in-arms.

The coastwatchers came through again when one of them alerted the Americans that ten Japanese destroyers had left Shortland. A B-17 also found Tanaka's destroyers and sent a confirming message that Japanese ships were on the Tokyo Express. Eight SBDs and seven TBFs escorted by several F4Fs left Henderson Field and found the destroyers. This time, the destroyers had an escort of 12 Japanese Pete float-equipped observation planes to oppose the oncoming aircraft.

When the Japanese planes attacked, they received more than they bargained for when one F4F engaged them in aerial combat and shot down five Petes. The American SBDs and TBFs aggressively attacked Tanaka's ship, but could only inflict minor damage on the destroyer *Makinami*. One SBD and one TBF crashed into the ocean, victims of AA fire from the destroyers.

The Japanese destroyers arrived southwest of Savo Island and steamed toward a place on the northern coast just to the northwest of Tassafaronga. Seven of Tanaka's ships carrying 1,500 supply drums deposited them into the water, hauled the ropes' ends attached to the drums to the shore and began to leave. Many of the drums' ropes broke, which allowed them to float freely into Iron Bottom Sound. American planes later strafed the floating drums and sent 1,190 of them to the bottom. Thus, just 310 drums, or only 21 percent of them, actually reached the shore.

The Japanese Begin to Reassess Their Position

On December 3, Adm. Ugaki's awful toothache had also given him a severe headache. He tried to take a walk to help him forget the pain he felt. He wanted to go to his home in Japan, but knew he could not with the war going the way it was. Ugaki went back to his quarters, wrote ten letters to his family, and felt better.

He received a report the next day of Tanaka's latest attempt to land supplies on Guadalcanal. It said that about one-third of the drums actually reached the shore, and he considered the mission a qualified success. Another report from the 11th Air Fleet said the last try to send supplies by destroyers alone would occur on December 5, and the 18th Army Group desperately wanted to advance to Buna. After the Navy staff wanted to send an ambiguously worded telegram to convince the Army to not do it, Ugaki disapproved the idea since the Navy had already warned them not to be so impetuous. He sent one of his staff officers to meet with the Army staff. He could not persuade the Army to stop. After all, the Buna operation was their responsibility and they made the final decision to proceed.

The Americans now had command of the sea and the air around Guadalcanal so that trying to supply the suffering solders using drum-laden destroyers could no longer succeed. Ugaki knew the Navy needed a definitive policy about what to do about the Japanese soldiers on Guadalcanal. Some questions ran through his mind:

1. Should the commanders on the ground decide what to do next?
2. Who knew what the real situation was there?
3. Who should be responsible for carrying out whatever policy is adopted?

He did know that whoever had the responsibility would have to shoulder the burden of its outcome. In the meantime, Tokyo warned the Combined Fleet that "the enemy appears to be planning a positive air offensive all around our country on 8 December, the anniversary of the outbreak of the war." Ugaki believed the Combined Fleet should prepare a defense "against a possible enemy surprise landing from submarines in revenge for the Pearl Harbor attack." After he received news from New York that the Americans believed Japanese air power was critically short of planes and aircrews in the Solomons, Ugaki feared "...the enemy will get more conceited and eventually we'll be overwhelmed by the enemy air might," thus reinforcing his conviction that the Japanese had to obliterate American air power in the South Pacific. Of course, this was not as easy as it sounded. The American air presence around Guadalcanal seemed to be becoming stronger rather than weaker. He expressed the belief in his diary that, "The enemy doesn't care about losing battleships, cruisers, and destroyers, and is trying to beat us with its overwhelming air power."[3]

Radm. Minoru Ota, the commander of the newly established 8th Naval Special Landing Force, arrived aboard the *Yamato* with two of his staff officers to meet the Combined Fleet's senior officers. The Japanese began to recognize that they needed to create an amphibious warfare force like the U.S. Marine Corps. To demonstrate their commitment, they were prepared to equip their men with heavier artillery pieces such as 120-mm and 140-mm guns. This impressed Ugaki, but he had to remind the officers that these guns had to be put ashore. The Japanese had not found a way to bring such heavy equipment on land against a hostile force.

Ugaki's toothache and the headache that came with it worsened as the day progressed.

Tanaka's destroyers returned to Shortland on December 4, and he began to prepare for the next supply mission. Adm. Mikawa's flagship, the heavy cruiser *Chokai*, arrived later with the admiral aboard. Tanaka went to meet Mikawa and brief him on the resupply operations. He told a pessimistic story when he said that such further missions were doomed to fail with devastating losses of ships and men. Far from being a defeatist—which was a common accusation in the Imperial Japanese Navy—Tanaka strongly recommended that the starving men on Guadalcanal be evacuated before any more of them unnecessarily died. Mikawa listened to him intently and ordered him to continue the resupply missions until told otherwise.

Another Resupply Mission

The three destroyers *Tanikaze*, *Urakaze*, and *Ariake* joined Tanaka's force on December 5, and the newly-built destroyer *Teruzuki* arrived on December 7. The latest member displaced 2,500 tons, had a top speed of 39 knots, and became Tanaka's flagship when he transferred his flag to her. Acting under Tanaka's orders, Capt. Torajiro Sato led the *Tanikaze*, *Urakaze*, *Naganami*, and nine destroyers loaded with supply drums. They left Shortland in the early afternoon that day for the third attempt to bring supplies by way of the drum method to the Japanese on Guadalcanal. Eight Petes added air support to the convoy.

Some coastwatchers observed the 12 destroyers leave Shortland and warned CACTUS. Maj. Joseph Sailor led 13 SBDs that attacked Sato's force at about 6:40 p.m. One of their bombs exploded near the *Nowaki*, killed 17 men, blew a huge dent in her side, and flooded the engine and boiler rooms. She lost all power. The *Naganami* threw a tow rope to her which the *Nowaki*'s crew secured on deck. They towed the powerless destroyer to Shortland escorted by the *Yamakaze* and the marginally damaged *Arashio*. After Sailor's SBD suffered minor damage, a Pete shot him down and killed him. One of CACTUS' great leaders became yet another casualty of war.

Sato still had eight destroyers left and continued his mission. This time the Americans ordered eight PT boats to leave Tulagi, find the Japanese force, and attack. *PT-40* and *PT-48* patrolled the passage between Savo Island and Cape Esperance; *PT-43* and *PT-100* faced toward the sea between Kokumbona and Cape Esperance; and *PT-36*, *PT-37*, *PT-44*, and *PT-59* remained hidden behind Savo Island. One SOC observation plane flew above to provide any needed illumination.

As Sato's ships arrived at 11:20 p.m. between Savo Island and Cape Esperance, *PT-40* and *PT-48* spotted them. Both boats moved into position for their attack, but one of *PT-48*'s three engines failed, and it began to head back to Tulagi. Then another of its engines failed. She headed for the south shore of Savo Island and laid smoke to baffle Japanese gunners while *PT-40* attempted to distract the Japanese destroyers by passing them at high speed.

Although the two PTs did not fire any torpedoes, their sudden appearance startled Sato. At 11:30 p.m. he ordered the ships to turn around. Fifteen minutes later, he changed his mind and ordered the ships to head back toward Guadalcanal. Four PTs found the approaching destroyers and fired 12 torpedoes. With torpedoes' wakes churning the water around the engaged vessels, Lt. (jg) John M. Searles' *PT-59* moved to within 100 yards of the destroyer *Oyashio* and fired its machine guns. The Japanese destroyer returned some machine gun fire of its own. PT-59 took ten hits and returned to Tulagi. The *Oyashio* took as many hits and her crew absorbed many wounds. The *PT-109* and *PT-43* moved northward toward Cape Esperance and Savo Island to get into the action. Again, the severity of the PT attacks shocked Sato—he did not expect any such opposition. The appearance of the PTs and the SOC caused him to abandon his supply mission and return to Shortland.

On the night one year after Pearl Harbor, the American PT sailors had reason to hold their heads high. They forced the latest run of the Tokyo Express to turn back without any losses just one week after the shellacking at the Battle of Tassafaronga. One might argue the actions by these PTs that night was the greatest individual success by these small but powerful boats of the Pacific War.

All of the Japanese destroyers returned to Shortland on December 8, and Tanaka reviewed what happened that night. After considering the circumstances Sato faced when encountering American patrol boats and aircraft, he came to the conclusion that Sato had made the right decision by withdrawing the resupply ships.

Although Tanaka did not know it at this time, the Combined Fleet and Army staff officers had begun discussions on December 5 that would reexamine the situation on Guadalcanal.

Should Japanese Guadalcanal Operations Continue?

As the news arrived that the latest resupply mission failed, Ugaki and many of his fellow officers at the Combined Fleet Headquarters on Truk began to have second thoughts about the wisdom of continuing to take supplies and troops to Guadalcanal. Despite his ever-worsening toothache, he had represented the Combined Fleet at a December 5 meeting of staff officers from the 8th Area Army, Army General Staff, Naval General Staff, and 11th Air Fleet. The meeting's purpose was to discuss the Army's progress (or the lack of it) at Buna on New Guinea and Guadalcanal. A naval staff officer stated that the Army had approved sending the 65th Brigade and a regiment from the 51st Division to Buna, "and also that if the Eighth Area Army still stuck to Guadalcanal alone, a proper directive would be sent from Tokyo."[4] Ugaki expressed his approval of this action as well as the Army's plans to use two divisions now in Korea and China as reserves in the South Pacific. However, he stressed the importance of preparing to bring three more divisions to the area.

With the impending arrival of the Navy's Chief of Operations from Tokyo, the message announcing his plans stressed not to express any concerns about how the Guadalcanal and Buna campaigns were progressing to lower level commands since "a serious consequence would come."[5] When the 65th Brigade's new commander arrived, he came aboard the *Yamato* to report his command's readiness to assume combat duties. Ugaki's mood continued to sour as he observed that the brigade officers did not have a graduate of the Army's officers academy. Rather than being the battle-hardened veterans advertised by the Army when they informed the Navy of their assignment, the brigade's most recent assignment had been in Manila, where their duty was soft with the easy-living ways of occupying a large metropolitan area having a largely passive population. As far as Ugaki was concerned, these men could never achieve the tough-mindedness of combat veterans such as those currently fighting for their lives on New Guinea—no matter how many men would be added to their numbers.

A naval surgeon on his way back from an inspection tour in the Buin and Rabaul areas visited the Combined Fleet on December 6 and delivered a depressing report about the horrible conditions being faced by the Japanese soldiers there. He told of the depressing conditions due to a lack of supplies and the terrible living conditions they faced. There were epidemic levels of malaria, dengue fever, and other digestive tract diseases that continued to sap the soldiers' fighting abilities.

On December 7, Ugaki finished an operational plan concerning future naval activities in the southeast area. He gave the report to a staff officer to take to Tokyo and made the following points in it:

1. American power had increased as they tried to recapture lost territory using ever-growing numbers of heavy aircraft. The Imperial Japanese Navy had to increase the number of destroyers in the area since the Combined Fleet had lost a large number of these ships in previous combat.

2. He asked the Chief of Operations to delay his arrival until early January 1943 since about half of the Combined Fleet's needs had already been met.

3. While he agreed with the need to keep any discussions about future plans only at the top command levels, Ugaki stated that the Navy's relationship with the Army was "very delicate" and the Combined Fleet staff was "racking their brains" to find solutions easing the highly contentious relationship with the Army.

4. The Combined Fleet high command had never discussed these topics with lower command levels and had implemented procedures to ensure it would not happen. Nevertheless, the 11th Air Fleet and 8th Fleet commanders had lost confidence in continuing any further operations at Guadalcanal. Some subordinate commanders had said that further operations should be discontinued—apparently the concerns expressed by Tanaka to Mikawa had reached Combined Fleet's top command levels. Some of these commanders criticized the necessity of even adding more ships at Truk.

   Ugaki did not agree with all these misgivings of the fleet's subordinate commanders. However, he stressed the highest levels in the Imperial Japanese Navy made these decisions.

5. While he wished that more men and supplies be sent to the strategically critical Solomon and New Guinea areas, he expressed his doubts that sufficient numbers in both troop *and* supplies could be brought to the area to ensure success.

6. The war in the Solomons and New Guinea took so many of the Navy's resources that it could not meet the growing requirements in the other Asian Theaters such as the Indian Ocean, the Aleutians, and the Dutch East Indies.

   Japanese intelligence believed the Americans were now getting ready for further offensive operations since they already considered they had won victories in the Solomons and New Guinea.[6]

Meanwhile, Gen. Imamura attended a meeting in Rabaul with officers from the Combined Fleet, 11th Air Fleet, and 8th Fleet on December 8 and received what could only be described as a "bombshell." The naval officers announced that they no longer intended to conduct destroyer supply runs to Guadalcanal. Their primary reason was that any further losses of destroyers would prevent fighting and defeating the U.S. Navy in the Japanese Navy's long-held dream of the one decisive battle. Imamura vehemently protested the Navy's decision, so the Combined Fleet agreed to execute two additional destroyer runs, one to Guadalcanal and another to Buna. Not satisfied with the compromise, Imamura appealed to the Imperial Japanese Navy in Tokyo saying that if the Navy stopped supplying both battle areas, the soldiers there would be annihilated.

Apparently, Ugaki's efforts to keep secret his doubts and those of his fellow officers' at Truk about the Japanese future at Guadalcanal and New Guinea from lower levels had not worked. To use an old American saying, "The cat was out of the bag," and the fur would fly in Tokyo. While there were not any "official" announcements the Japanese were about to give up on Guadalcanal, it was only a matter of time before an official stance would come from Tokyo.

☆ ☆ ☆

The Japanese worries about raising their fellow officers' hackles seemed to take precedence over taking the actions to save Japanese soldiers' lives. It seemed that it was important to "save face" rather than act in their country's best interests. But any study of Japanese society of those times reveals these considerations, raised to the level of superseding all others, distorted reality to these officials that would ultimately lead to their utter defeat.

☆ ☆ ☆

The Japanese Army viewed its mission as achieving two objectives: (1) working with the Imperial Japanese Navy to capture the Solomon Islands and; (2) fortify strategic locations on New Guinea and begin capturing the rest of that huge island. The 8th Army had the assignment to undertake this mission while the Combined Fleet used almost all of its available strength to help the Army.

The Imperial Gen. Headquarters ordered on December 23 the 41st Division, fighting in China, the 20th Division, serving in Korea, and the 6th and 51st Divisions to reinforce the 8th Army. While the Americans inflicted devastating losses on the Japanese Navy whenever their ships tried in vain to transport and land supplies on Guadalcanal, a series of heated arguments arose between the Army High Command and the Japanese War Ministry concerning difficulties in getting more ships to continue the Navy's resupply efforts.

The Army argued that Guadalcanal had to be held at all costs because relinquishing the island to the Americans would result in powerful American counterattacks, make it impossible for the Army to disengage from those attacks, and lead to a slaughter of its men. The High Command continued to relentlessly apply pressure on the War Ministry to find the ships needed to take desperately needed supplies and men to Guadalcanal. Nonetheless, the Army said it needed 300,000 tons of shipping—an amount the Japanese did not have to spare. The War Ministry said it would be foolhardy to sacrifice increasingly scarce ships to reinforce and resupply Guadalcanal when Japan needed these vessels to keep its war effort going at home. Therefore, it advocated a withdrawal from Guadalcanal to a stronger and more strategic Inner Perimeter.

The arguments between the Army and War Ministry continued with no resolution in sight. Some of the discussions became so passionate that some staff officers nearly came to blows. The fight finally escalated to the highest levels as Hideki Tojo (acting as the War Minister) and Gen. Shinichi Tanaka (the Army's Chief of the Operations Bureau) vehemently argued. Tojo finally won the disagreement. The outcome of the power struggle led to Tanaka and his subordinate and chief of the Operations Bureau's 2nd Section, Col. Takushiro Hattori, being transferred to other assignments. Maj. Gen. Kitsuju Ayabe assumed Tanaka's post and Col. Joichiro Sanada took over for Hattori.

The issue of whether to evacuate Guadalcanal escalated to the Emperor and resulted in a meeting held at the Imperial Palace on December 31. The attendees included Hirohito himself, the Chiefs of the Army and Navy Gen. Staffs, the corresponding Deputy Chiefs, the Operating Bureau Chiefs, the War and Navy Ministers, and the Emperor's chief Aide-de-Camp. The discussion continued for one hour and 40 minutes and ended with an agreement on new operational plans and decisions:

1. The Japanese would put all attempts to recapture Guadalcanal on hold. The evacuation of all troops would begin near the end of January and into February 1943. When all the troops had left Guadalcanal, the Japanese would occupy all the Solomon Islands north of the New Georgia and Ysabel (Santa Isabel) islands.

2. Troops fighting on New Guinea would receive reinforcements at the strategic locations of Lae, Salamaua, Madang, and Wewak. Key strategic points north of the Owen Stanley Mountains would be captured to prepare for further attacks on Port Moresby. Soldiers near Buna would retreat toward an area near Salamaua.

In other words, the Japanese would give up the territory for which its Army and Navy had shed their blood. Rabaul was still a vital strategic location. The Japanese armed forces' emphasis had now shifted to defense in the Solomons and offensive in New Guinea. Tojo had thus taken full command of the war effort and was allowed to apply his duties as prime minister to integrate the war with all other aspects of Japan's life. The Army High Command was no longer in charge of conducting the war effort. The War Ministry had taken that away from them.

Gen. Imamura, the Japanese 8th Army's commander, received new orders on January 4 from the IGHQ. They reflected a major strategic change in Japan's future conduct of the Pacific War.

1. The troops on Guadalcanal would leave around the end of January and the beginning of February.

2. The 8th Army would increase its strength in the northern Solomons; the Navy would do the same on the New Georgia and Ysabel Islands.

Imamura's staff estimated there would be about 20,000 troops on Guadalcanal at the end of January. After analyzing the conditions the Japanese soldiers lived under on the island, the 8th Army determined that only 5,000 men could be safely extracted because of the American dominance in the air and on the sea around the island. The losses would come from drowning or being wiped out by American ground attacks.

For the first time in the war, the Japanese would go on the defensive. It would never regain the offensive again.[6]

In the meantime, the Americans were not idle. They had some important decisions to make regarding their future efforts in the Solomons. They now controlled the air and sea in the southern Solomons and wanted to exploit that advantage. There was still a war to fight.

CHAPTER 54
Building for Going on the Offensive

In Shaw's pamphlet, entitled *"First Offensive: The Marine Campaign for Guadalcanal,"* there is a drawing by Donald L. Dickson on page 47 that shows a Marine in a most dilapidated state. His rifle barely hangs by its strap. The man's right hand seems to be barely grasping it. His helmet is being hardly held in his left hand. The man looks so exhausted that it seems that he might drop the rifle to the ground at any minute. His dirty and tattered uniform hangs on his slimmer-than-normal body like it is several sizes too large for him. A dark, ground-in grime covers his gaunt and nearly-skeletal face and body. His gaunt face shows suffering beyond what anyone could believe. His sunken eyes depict a human wracked by exhaustion and debilitating disease. If he was just a baby-faced boy when he arrived on the island, he looks many years older now. When looking at this drawing, one cannot help but be struck by the demeanor of this man and how four months of unbearable suffering can change a man.

The American Marines and soldiers on Guadalcanal had nearly reached the end of their tether after battling the jungle, Japanese, insects, and disease for nearly four months. With many of them weakened by malnutrition and the unbearable tropical heat, life was an ordeal even for those not engaged in combat. There was not enough water in which to bathe or wash clothes because fungi that caused illnesses grew prolifically in the rivers.

The perimeter area that the men had defended since October enclosed less than 30 square miles. Massive swarms of flies that fed on the unburied corpses rotting in the jungle swarmed over the men as they tried to work and in their food while they ate. By the beginning of December 1942, they had endured more than anyone in the American high command had ever expected of them. No one knew this better than Gen. Vandegrift. He was not in much better shape than the men he commanded. Although his command had received a Presidential Unit Citation, the 1st Marine Division was in bad shape.

The Marine casualties due solely to combat had been less than anyone had expected. The Japanese had killed or mortally wounded slightly more than 600 men in battle from August 7 until December 10. Fatalities from combat in other American units numbered 691. More than 2,100 of the 1st Marine Division's sick and wounded had already been evacuated. Nonetheless, this was not like any war the Americans had ever previously fought. This place was the Solomon Islands—a pesthole riddled with every condition nature could create to render a human being either severely ill or dead. As of December 10, 1942, the division had suffered 10,635 casualties (killed, wounded, captured, or missing in action) with only 1,472 resulting from combat; 5,749 malaria cases sent men to the hospital with 3,283 in November alone. During August and September, gastroenteritis hospitalized 500 men, but the number of casualties caused by this illness dropped to 12 in December. Combat fatigue struck 110 men during October, but that number decreased to 13 in November. Malaria cases sent many men to the hospital more than once. Many others afflicted with this disease never went to the hospital; therefore, many cases were never counted.

Help is on the Way

Halsey concluded as early as November 3 that he wanted to relieve the 1st Marine Division, but this was easier said than done since there were many needs for Allied ground troops all over the world. Trained combat soldiers were in short supply. Until he could find fresh troops to replace the exhausted Marines on Guadalcanal, these men would have to stay there and continue fighting the Japanese.

The Army 43rd Infantry Division was already aboard transports and on its way to the South Pacific. The first part of this division was due to arrive as soon as early October. Gen. Harmon repeatedly lobbied Gen. Marshall for Gen. MacArthur to send the Army 25th Infantry Division, now defending the Hawaiian Islands, to the South Pacific Theater. Meanwhile, Marshall notified the 25th Division to begin moving to the South Pacific. But no decision had yet been made as to where they would go, MacArthur's Southwest Pacific area or Halsey's South Pacific area. Scheduled to leave Pearl Harbor in November, a combat team from that division delayed their departure when the ship that had been assigned to carry them, the *President Coolidge*, carrying the 43rd Division's 172nd Regimental Combat Team, sank on October 26 when it hit two American mines off Espiritu Santo.

After much debate and pressure from Admirals Nimitz and King, the Joint Chiefs of Staff finally decided on November 30 to send the 25th Division to Halsey's command. The transports carrying the division had already left Pearl Harbor for Sydney and had to be diverted to the South Pacific after MacArthur agreed to let these men help out the Marines on Guadalcanal. One day earlier, Vandegrift received a message from the JCS that relief was on its way. The message's theme was clear: "1st MarDiv is to be relieved without delay...and will proceed to Australia for rehabilitation and employment." The rumors immediately began circulating among the Marines that they were to leave soon for Australia. It was not home, but had to be much better than Guadalcanal.

By this time, the Americal Division staff was already on Guadalcanal since its 146th Regiment had arrived in October. They began to increasingly assume staff responsibilities and had entirely taken over those duties by the time the 1st Marine Division was to leave. The division supply specialists finished an inventory of all stocks on Guadalcanal and accepted all responsibilities for supply operations on the island on December 1. Army staff officers completely took over all staff functions seven days later.

Gen. Vandegrift sent a message to all under his command on December 7 and thanked them for their valor and perseverance and made particularly laudatory comments for the pilots of the CACTUS Air Force, "all who labored and sweated within the lines in all manners of prodigious and vital tasks." He told them again their "unbelievable achievements had made 'Guadalcanal' a synonym for death and disaster in the language of our enemy." He had only one day left as the commander of all Allied forces on Guadalcanal.

Halsey decided to let the Army choose the next commander on Guadalcanal since they were to take on the primary combat mission to drive the Japanese off Guadalcanal. That decision was to be Gen. Harmon's, Halsey's commander of all Army Forces in his SOPAC command. Harmon picked Maj. Gen. Alexander McCarrell Patch, the current commander of the Americal Division, to assume tactical command of all combat operations on Guadalcanal. A proven combat leader and a highly-thought-of career Army officer, Patch was the ideal choice.

✲ ✲ ✲

Born in Fort Huachuca, Arizona, on November 23, 1889, and the son of a captain in the cavalry, Patch received his appointment to West Point as a resident of Pennsylvania in 1909 and graduated in 1913. Although his father had been a cavalry officer and at first he wanted to follow in his father's footsteps, he decided to join the infantry instead since the cavalry was becoming an obsolete branch of the service. As a freshly minted second lieutenant in the 13th Infantry Regiment in Texas, his first combat assignment was with Gen. Pershing's Punitive Expedition into Mexico to find and capture Pancho Villa. After the U.S. entered World War I in April 1917, he went to France with his regiment. Patch demonstrated an outstanding ability for leading men in combat. He rapidly rose from captain to lieutenant colonel in just one year. He was in all the major offensives the Americans fought in France and began to specialize in training troops in the use of machine guns, a weapon that had shown its deadly ability in World War I by killing many men in a short time.

After the armistice and peace, he returned to America to assume peacetime duties. He taught military science at the Staunton Military Academy in Staunton, Virginia, in three separate tours of duty from 1921 to 1936 and, in the meantime, graduated with a distinguished rating from the Command and General Staff School in 1925. He then served on the Infantry board at Fort Benning, Georgia, as part of the 47th Infantry Regiment. Patch then moved to the Alabama National Guard in Montgomery. Newly promoted to full colonel, he took command of the recruit depot at Fort Bragg in North Carolina and then led the Infantry Replacement Training Center (IRTC) at Camp Croft in South Carolina.

Patch received his first general's star as a brigadier general in 1942 when he went to New Caledonia to command the Army forces being organized to defend that island. On March 10, 1942, he received his second star and took command of the newly formed Americal Division.

✲ ✲ ✲

Patch relieved Vandegrift on December 9. The 1st Marine Division began leaving the hell-hole of Guadalcanal the next day when boats took the 5th Marine Regiment to three ships waiting offshore. As soon the ships had loaded all their intended cargo aboard, they weighed anchor, steamed through Sealark Channel, turned southward, and headed for Australia. Before 1942 came to an end, the entire 1st Marine Division left Guadalcanal. The last regiment of the Americal Division, the 132nd Infantry, arrived as the 1st Marine Division's men began to leave. Nonetheless, the Marines were still there as regiments of the 2nd Marine Division—the 2nd, 8th, parts of the 10th, and the 6th on its way—began their duties on Guadalcanal. But the Army was in command with the job to kick the Japanese off the island.

The Guadalcanal-Tulagi area became one of the island commands in the South Pacific area on December 10. Gen. Harmon took over responsibility for supplying the men on each of the area's islands. Halsey relieved Adm. Turner from the responsibility of defending Guadalcanal, but left him in charge of transporting men and materiel to the area. Patch reported directly to Halsey and commanded all ground troops, the Guadalcanal airfields, Tulagi's seaplane base, and all naval bases in the area. American troops occupied Tulagi, the nearby islands, Koli Point and Lunga Point, and a line that ran from Point Cruz along the Matanikau River on Guadalcanal. There was no doubt what Harmon's orders were—get rid of all Japanese forces on Guadalcanal.

Adding American Troop Strength

Since the Americans landed on August 7 and captured Henderson Field, they were on the defensive with some brief offensive operations to take, sometimes temporarily, small pieces of land from the Japanese. But December brought a change when the Japanese could no longer meagerly resupply their men on Guadalcanal. During the first half of December, the Americans would abandon their defensive stance and attack the Japanese with the goal of evicting them from the island.

Before the 1st Marine Division began leaving Guadalcanal, there were about 40,000 Americans on the island. The Americans did not have accurate estimates of Japanese troop strength on Guadalcanal, but remained worried about their ability to bring supplies with repeated, nightly runs of the Tokyo Express. Actually, the Japanese 17th Army had about 25,000 men there.

Before he took command on Guadalcanal, Patch estimated he needed not less than two reinforced combat divisions to hold the airfields and three more to prevent any new Japanese landings. Nevertheless, spare American combat-ready divisions did not exist in the South Pacific. The only other combat division in addition to the Americal was the 37th Infantry Division (National Guard, Ohio) defending the critically strategic Fiji Islands.

The 25th Division was on its way to New Caledonia when Gen. Harmon ordered them to steam to Nouméa. It was a decision fraught with risk since Nouméa's harbor lacked enough docks to accommodate a full division and could cause a costly, six-week delay delivering the troops where they were needed the most, on Guadalcanal. But Harmon again showed he was a commander not afraid to take risks to achieve his objectives. The 25th would not unload and reload at Nouméa as planned but proceed to Guadalcanal in the ships that carried them there.

The 25th Division arrived in Nouméa and, its commander, Maj. Gen. Joseph Lawton Collins, went ashore to meet with Halsey. The Admiral was happy to see Collins whom he had known since he was a colonel. Halsey had said about Collins that he was "a small man, quick on his feet, and even quicker in his brain." Collins was a man of great energy and enthusiasm. He called the 25th "the finest regular division in the Army."

The two men met by vigorously exchanging handshakes. Collins wanted to get going and confidently told Halsey, "Give me three weeks to unload my transports and combat-load them, and I'll be ready to go anywhere." Halsey, with that characteristic twinkling in his eyes, laughed loudly and told

Collins, "Your division is leaving for Guadalcanal tomorrow!" Despite lacking any docks, the 25th's Regimental Combat Team landed on Guadalcanal on December 17th with its 27th RCT landing on January 1, 1943, and its 161st on January 4, all with no losses.

Now that Patch commanded three divisions—the Americal, the 25th, and the Marine 2nd Divisions—Gen. Harmon asked Gen. Marshall to establish the command on Guadalcanal as a Corps headquarters. The American campaign in the southern Solomons could no longer be called Operation Shoestring, and Patch's request wanted to confirm that fact. Marshall responded by telling Harmon that all Army air units in the South Pacific would be called the 13th Air Force. On January 2, 1943, Patch's command had the designation of XIV Corps.

As of January 7, 1943, the American forces on Guadalcanal numbered 50,078 officers and enlisted men that included the following units:

American XIV Corps on Guadalcanal—January 7, 1943

Unit	**Total**	**Officers**	**Enlisted Men**
Americal Division	16,196	837	15,339
25th Division	12,629	605	12,024
2nd Marine Division	14,733[1]	657	14,076
Totals	50,078	2,402	47,676

The Americans now had the ground force strength to begin large-scale offensive operations against the Japanese. However, ground troops would not be enough. If the Americans had proved anything during their ordeal on to Guadalcanal to date, there was one critical source of military power absolutely essential for achieving their objective—air power.

Growing American Air Power in the Solomons

It had not been easy for the Americans to hang onto Guadalcanal. There was one indisputable fact—they could not have done it without the air power from carriers and CACTUS. Since the desperate air battles in October, Allied air power substantially grew on Guadalcanal. Vandegrift reported on November 23 that there were 84 Allied aircraft performing missions from that island, including planes from the U.S. Marine Corps, Navy, Army, and the Royal New Zealand Air Force. Six days later, the force expanded to 188 aircraft of all types. The 2nd Marine Air Wing, commanded by Brig. Gen. Francis P. Mulcahy, arrived on December 26 to relieve the 1st MAW's exhausted crews and ground personnel.

By December, American air superiority made it possible for Halsey and Turner to relatively easily bring in supplies and reinforcements. American aircraft forced the Japanese supply attempts and repeated runs of the Tokyo Express to be reduced to a pitiful few drops of supply drums from destroyers and by submarine and only at night. Japanese aircraft could no longer make bombing runs or send observation planes to Guadalcanal during daylight without suffering crippling losses. American air superiority had essentially cut the Japanese troops off from any hope of getting enough supplies to survive. Their days on Guadalcanal were numbered.

Despite Henderson Field's primitive operating conditions, it was still in good shape in December and continuously supporting air operations against the Japanese with about 80 planes. When Adm. McCain returned from his assignment in the South Pacific, he recommended that gasoline storage tanks to hold at least one million gallons be built on Guadalcanal. His idea was to establish on Guadalcanal a base for further operations in the Solomons. Henderson Field could only operate in fair weather because it would turn into a sea of mud when heavy, persistent rains fell. It became an all-weather airfield when engineers placed steel mats on the runway in early January. East of Henderson Field, engineers began regrading Fighter One in December to accommodate Naval and Marine aircraft, but that field needed 1.8 million square feet of steel matting to allow it to operate under all weather conditions. Construction of a second fighter airfield called Fighter Two to handle American Army and New Zealand Air Force planes was completed in December and had a fine coral surface that made that field an all-weather strip. Safe from Japanese attacks, the Seabees finished an airstrip at Koli Point that could handle heavy bombers and named it Carney Field.

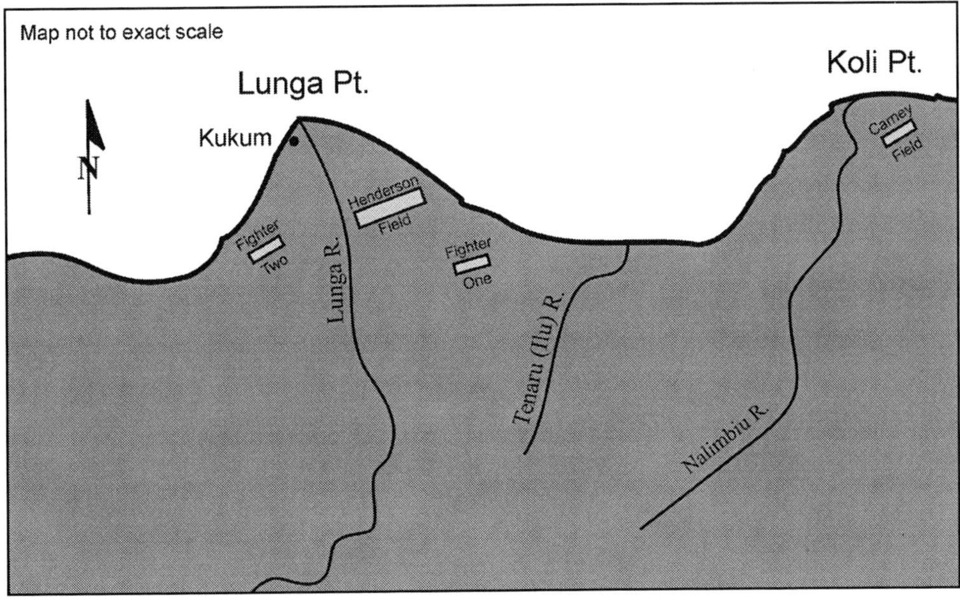

Locations of American Airfields on Guadalcanal

The Japanese could only launch nuisance-level attacks with single planes at night. Given nicknames by the men such as "Washing Machine Charley," "Louis the Louse," and "Maytag Charlie," these planes would come over Guadalcanal at night, drop small bombs, and cause hardly any damage other than keeping the men from getting a good night's sleep. They flew high enough and jerked and jinked when searchlights shone on them. The AA guns never got off a good shot at them. Fighters that could fly and find Japanese planes at night would have been able to shoot down these troublemakers. However, such aircraft would not arrive at Guadalcanal until late February 1943.

One of the most important installations on Guadalcanal was the latest model SCR 270 radar. Supplementing the radar, coastwatchers continued to give early warning of approaching Japanese ships and planes. When these approaching threats screened themselves behind the Solomon Island's mountains, these brave souls proved their continuing value in spotting planes and ships that radar could not detect.

Logistics - A Constant Concern

Supply and reenforcements were as big a problem in December as they were in August. The situation did improve in December when the Americans overcame problems at their main base in Nouméa. The rapid increases in supplies and men arriving to the South Pacific after the August invasion completely overwhelmed the underdeveloped shipping facilities in that port. By November, arriving ships queued in the harbor waiting to unload were such that this congestion threatened to stop the flow of supplies to Guadalcanal.

Halsey raised an alarm when he reported he had only four undamaged transports available for supply operations. The congestion worsened when 91 ships carrying 180,000 tons of cargo jammed into the harbor while waiting for dock space to offload their cargoes. Eighty-three of these ships had to steam to the New Hebrides and Guadalcanal to unload there.

Nouméa had never been designed to handle such a high volume of supplies. There were no other ports in the South Pacific with enough dock workers, equipment, storage, and dock space to unload the ships. At this time, each service handled their own supplies. Halsey changed that arrangement in late November when he proposed that the Army take over these responsibilities and handle all the supplies at Nouméa. The Army wasted no time assuming the responsibility and delivered impressive results. During November, the port at Nouméa unloaded 34,327 long tons while unloading 126,216 long tons in December. Cargo shipment to Guadalcanal totaled 5,259 long tons in November and increased to 7,271 in December.

Nonetheless, when the supplies arrived in Guadalcanal, more problems confronted the Americans. There were no docks there. All supplies had to be unloaded from ships anchored offshore, placed into small boats to be taken to the beaches, unloaded, loaded into trucks, and taken to the supply dumps dispersed throughout American-held territory inland. The scarcity of trucks brought about by the lack of ships thus limited the delivery speed and overall cargo-handling capacity on the island. There were not enough service troops to handle the cargoes so combat troops had to be taken from their combat assignments to unload supplies, not what they were trained to do. It was no surprise when Gen. Patch remarked that the combat troops were "apathetic toward labor."

To make matters worse, there were just a few roads from the beach to the supply dumps that could only be called primitive. The construction troops from the 1st Marine Division had built some roads and a few bridges. The 57th Engineer Battalion picked up where they left off and continued the building effort. A road along the northern coast, called the Government Track before the war, was the main route between the Ilu River and Point Cruz. After the Marines landed, a network of roads provided paths to Henderson Field and American defensive positions to the south. The Marines began building a narrow road from the defensive perimeter to Mount Austen wide enough for Jeeps with the 57th Engineers finishing the job. They built a permanent bridge over the Matanikau River along the coast road. This allowed the troops near Point Cruz to receive supplies. Jeeps carried supplies to positions inland on the various hills occupied by the Americans.

Guadalcanal had nothing that could be called roads before the Americans came. The Japanese created trails in the jungle that they hacked through the underbrush, but the jungle soon overtook and covered them with vegetation as if they never existed. When the Americans conquered territory, combat engineers built roads behind the troops as they advanced. Nonetheless, these roads were never paved and turned into liquid mud whenever the rains came. This made the task of supplying troops in forward positions and sending supplies to advanced forward supply dumps even more difficult. The narrow roads could only accommodate Jeeps and hand-carriers. With the arrival of three new divisions aiming for large-scale offensive operations, these paths needed to be made more weatherproof and widened to handle the heavier trucks needed to bring ever larger quantities of supplies including water to the men where they needed them the most.

✡ ✡ ✡

Malaria was still a problem in December despite the decrease in reported cases. It would not be until the campaign to take Guadalcanal ended when malaria would be brought under control. As long as the war continued in the tropical Pacific Theater, malaria continued to be a problem that had to be attacked head on. The people needed to kill the mosquitoes that caused the disease could not do their work as long combat operations continued where they would be working.

None of these personnel could be allowed on Guadalcanal until mid-November. It would be almost a year before insect repellent and aerosol insecticide arrived on the island. Quinine was hard to find. Despite the beginning of Atabrine prevention treatments, the disease still spread among the men.

Many of the men refused to take the Atabrine tablets because of their bitterly foul taste. Many of them believed the pills caused sexual impotence, were poisonous, or made their skin change color. With mosquito eradication at a minimum, the insects bred prolifically.

The malarial infection rate among disabled American troops was a monumental 65% compared to just 25% of the disabled being wounded in battle. The malarial infection rate among all Americans from all service branches rose from 14 cases for every thousand in August to 1,664 per thousand in October, 1,681 in November, 972 in December, and 1,169 in January 1943. Many of the malaria cases had to go to the hospital more than once.[2]

A Worse Environment for the Japanese

Japanese troop strength peaked in November to about 30,000 after the arrival of the 38th Division survivors that debarked from their on-fire transports following the Naval Battle of Guadalcanal. As December arrived, that population shrank to 25,000 men as combat deaths, disease, and starvation took its toll. No troop reinforcements arrived after mid-November. The Japanese Army's units were far from being at full strength with many of their men not ready for combat.

The Japanese commanders knew they lacked in troop strength and dug in to defensive positions because many of the soldiers lacked the physical ability to fight. Supplies were short, with food rations critically reduced to around one-third the daily minimum. Men stole food from their comrades. What supplies that did arrive came ashore near Cape Esperance and had to be lugged on handcarts southward to where the soldiers were. The troops in the rear who had the duty to deliver the supplies to the front-line troops took what they needed first. Thus, their front line soldiers got the leavings from the rear while the supply troops did quite well for themselves. Front-line soldiers tried their best to survive. They scrounged for coconuts, grass, roots, ferns, bamboo sprouts, and wild potatoes to stay alive. Reports of cannibalism on Mount Austen arrived at headquarters locations.

While hunger was a serious problem, disease also had a disastrous effect. While malaria resulted in high casualty rates among the Americans, it created chaos among the Japanese. Almost every Japanese soldier was a victim of this debilitating malady. The American positions were in relatively open areas while the Japanese fear of being attacked from the air forced them to occupy and fight in areas where there was dense vegetation. It was in such places that there are many shallow ponds and stagnant streams. The deadly Anopheles mosquitoes bred in huge numbers. The Japanese later estimated that the battles for Guadalcanal cost them 21,500 casualties with 9,000 of them due to such diseases as malaria, malnutrition, beri-beri, and dysentery.

Sickness and malnutrition were prevalent among the Japanese soldiers as the campaign neared its end. One Japanese officer reported that he placed the men under his command into three groups: those capable fighting and moving, men who could just fight from fixed positions, and troops who could not fight at all. As the Americans advanced and the Japanese retreated westward in January and February, the Japanese hospitals and their medical personnel went first and only took those men who could walk with them. When American soldiers came upon Japanese positions, they found many unwounded and abandoned men in evacuated hospitals.

American air and sea power had isolated the Japanese Army on Guadalcanal. All supply attempts had been tried and failed. Meanwhile, the Japanese began building a new air base at Munda on New Georgia Island to station their aircraft closer to Guadalcanal. Munda was just 207 miles away from Henderson Field. They camouflaged their construction work so well that American aircraft did not spot the new airfield until December 3. While the new airfield closed the range to Henderson Field, it proved to be the classic case of the double-edged sword since Allied aircraft from Guadalcanal attacked the field almost every day. Japanese fighters, forced to defend against the incessant air assaults, could not escort Tokyo Express runs or intercept American long-range bombers that, by now, regularly bombed Japanese bases at Shortland and Rabaul.

It seemed that it was just a matter time before the Americans would emerge victorious on Guadalcanal. As in most conflicts in warfare, this was easier said than done. There were more difficult battles to fight because the Japanese would never willingly surrender, assuming they would surrender at all.[3]

CHAPTER 55
Capturing Mount Austen

Setting the Stage

Gen. Patch's XIV Corps did not have enough men to launch the full-fledged offensives he wanted. Nevertheless, he did begin attacking Japanese troops still on the island with the troops he had. An attack on Mount Austen became necessary since the Japanese had several observers that watched American aircraft takeoffs and landings as well as the arrival of American transports bringing more men and supplies to Guadalcanal. Just as the Americans had their coastwatcher network along the Solomon Island chain that gave the Americans early warning of runs of the Tokyo Express and Japanese aircraft heading down the Slot, the Japanese had men on that mountain doing the exact same thing for their side.

Mount Austen was a 1,514-feet high outcropping of Guadalcanal's main mountain range running the entire length of the island. It was positioned about six miles southwest of Henderson Field and domi-

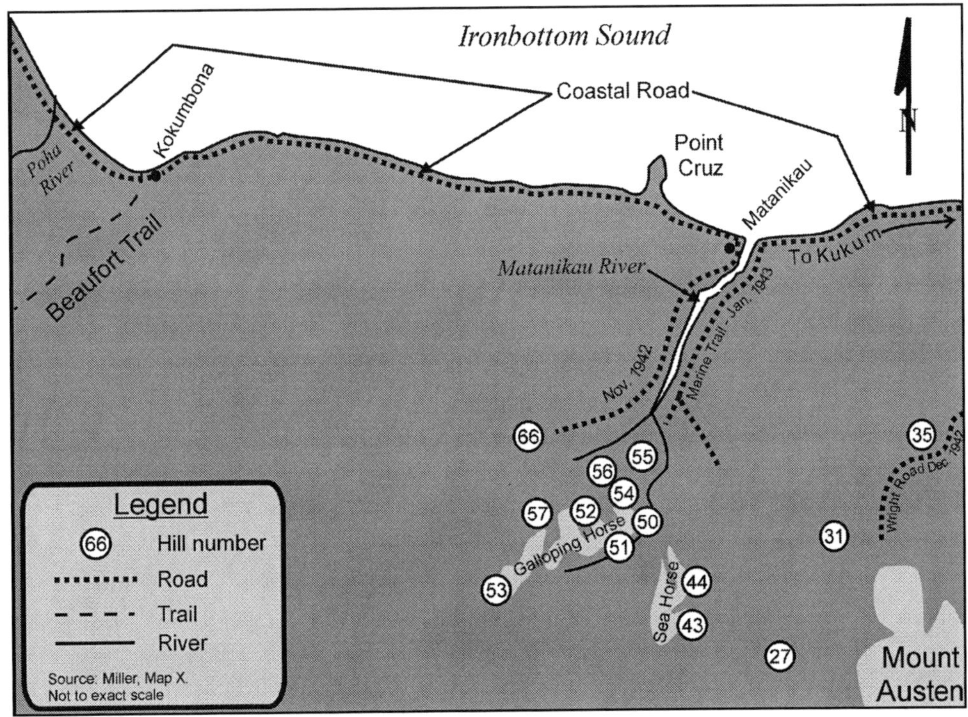

The American December Offensive Begins

nated the entire American enclave. The mountain was an ideal observation post for the Japanese. They could see everything the Americans did east of the Matanikau River and 9,000 yards westward toward Kokumbona. Gen. Vandegrift originally planned to capture the mountain as part of his attack when his men captured Lunga Point early in the campaign. But the maps he had incorrectly placed the mountain much closer to Henderson Field than it was. He did not have enough men to take it, so he postponed the assault. As long as the Japanese remained on that mountain, the Americans could never evict the Japanese.

Patch had his orders from Halsey that the admiral had sent with Gen. Harmon. They said that because it was impossible to "predict the ability of our naval surface forces and air forces to satisfactorily interdict the operation of Jap submarines and the Tokyo Express into Guadalcanal," Patch was to do anything within his power to eradicate all Japanese forces. Halsey gave Patch *carte blanche* to do what he had to while taking direction from Harmon.

Harmon left for Guadalcanal to meet with Patch as soon he received Halsey's orders. The XIV Corps commander wanted to attack Mount Austen immediately to eliminate the Japanese ability to report American troop, aircraft, and ship movements to their superiors at Rabaul and Truk.

The XIV Corps firmed up. After capturing the mountain, Patch's forces would direct two divisions to attack to the west while his third division defended the airfields. As one division crossed over Mount Austen and the hills south of Hill 66 to outflank the Japanese, the second division would begin an advance along a front stretching from Hill 66 to Point Cruz. The flanking operation would push the American lines west of the Matanikau River an additional 3,000 yards. The two divisions eventually joined in a series of westward attacks on the Japanese ground forces and destroyed them. Harmon listened carefully and completely endorsed Patch's plan. He knew when he saw a well-thought out plan, and this one was exactly that.

The XIV Corps planned a series of amphibious landings around Cape Esperance to occupy the island's southern coast, block the Beaufort Trail that ran from Kokumbona over the mountains to the south coast, and aid the advance west of Cape Esperance. But the Americans lacked the needed landing craft to immediately carry out such maneuvers and had to wait until more boats arrived.

✲ ✲ ✲

The Japanese would stubbornly defend Mount Austen. Rather than a single mountain, it was a rough-hewn mixture of steep, rocky ledges covered with jungle growth and thick, high grass surrounded by impenetrable jungle. This should not surprise anyone considering how valuable it was for the Japanese to gather intelligence about what the Americans were doing. They primarily viewed the Americans from the mountain's primary hill, which was a ridge that jutted above the surrounding hills. Aerial reconnaissance revealed little about the mountain's topography because of dense vegetation that hid its features.

South of Mount Austen was Hill 27, a rocky mound 920 feet high and southwest of Mount Austen's summit. Its crest could barely be seen from the ground because it was just above the surrounding jungle treetops. Another hill, Hill 31, was a grassy opening in the jungle about 750 yards north of Hill 27 and provided a clear view of Lunga Point—a key debarkation point for arriving American transports.

One outcropping to the northwest of and across a deep chasm of rocky ledges from Mount Austen were Hills 43 and 44 that the Americans named the Sea Horse. Another 900-foot high mass of mounds that Americans named the Galloping Seahorse. Hills 50, 51, 52, 53, 54, 55, 56, and 57 lay north of the first group of hills. Both hill masses could easily be seen from Mount Austen.

Orders to Begin Offensive Operations

The recent American intelligence in late November and early December believed there were just token Japanese forces defending Mount Austen. The 132nd Infantry Regiment, assigned to capture the mountain, sent out patrols that confirmed the earlier reports by the Marine 8th and Army 182nd Regiments. The situation changed by December 15. A Japanese raiding party stole through the American defenses on the night of December 12 to destroy one P-39 and a gas truck on Fighter Two.

Wanting to gather the most recent intelligence, the 132nd Infantry's intelligence officer, four more officers, and 35 enlisted men along with ten native bearers scouted Mount Austen's northwestern hills on December 14. As they moved eastward, they encountered what they believed to be one rifle platoon, four machine guns, and one or two mortars. When the intelligence officer returned to Lunga Point, he asked for artillery fire to be aimed at where his patrol had seen the Japanese soldiers on Mount Austen.

Gen. Patch now had reason to change his mind based on the revised intelligence reports. These showed that Japanese troops were reinforcing their positions south of the airfields and would possibly attack them. The patrol returned to Mount Austen's eastern hills on December 15 and 16 and only discovered abandoned Japanese positions. Although the Americans did not find any Japanese, one possible reason for not finding them might have been that they hid from the Americans.

Patch's suspicions might not have been confirmed. Nevertheless, the Japanese were stronger than the Americans knew. Col. Akinosuka Oka's force of the undermanned battalions from the 124th and 228th Infantry Regiments and the 10th Mountain Artillery Regiment had been occupying places that spread to Mount Austen's northeastern hills with their strongest emplacements along a 1,500-yard line between Hills 31 and 27 on the mountain's northwestern side.

If the Americans had the chance to more closely examine the conditions under which these men endured, it would not have been a positive one as far as the Japanese were concerned. While the Americans had problems bringing supplies to their foremost positions, the problems faced by the Japanese approached the insolvable. Their only source of supplies had to be hand-carried, and they actually received just minuscule quantities. After the American 132nd attacked, the Japanese did not seem to have been reinforced at all. The Americans found their wounded had never been taken to a hospital. They just fought and died where they were. Malnutrition, exhaustion, and disease had taken a terrible toll on the Japanese defenders.

✲ ✲ ✲

Gen. Patch wasted no time when he ordered the 132nd Infantry to attack and capture Mount Austen on December 16. Reporting directly to Patch, Marine Col. John M. Arthur, the commander in that sector, received orders to direct the offensive. The 132nd Infantry's commander, Col. LeRoy E. Nelson, arrived on Guadalcanal on December 8 and had never commanded in combat. Lt. Col. William C. Wright, the commander of the regiment's 3rd Battalion, would lead the attack on the mountain with Lt. Col. Earl F. Ripstra's 1st Battalion less D Company held in reserve. The regiment's 2nd Battalion, under the command of Lt. Col. George F. Ferry, was to stay behind to defend the Lunga perimeter.

The 246th Field Artillery Battalion's 105-mm howitzers and the 2nd Battalion, 10th Marines 75-mm pack howitzers were to provide the initial artillery support. If the 132nd needed more artillery, there were 28 75-mm pack howitzers, 36 105-mm howitzers, and six 155-mm guns on Guadalcanal that were part of the Americal Division and other units near Lunga that could more than make their presence felt.

The 2nd Battalion moved its 75-mm howitzers up Mount Austen's northwest slopes while Lt. Col. Alexander R. Sewall's 246th Artillery Battalion placed its guns near Fighter Two, a position much farther away. To coordinate their artillery to hit targets at the same time, both battalions fired a few rounds to calculate their "Time on Target" or TOT. The method used was for each battalion to fire several rounds, subtract its shells' time of flight from the time its shells were to hit their target, and fired its guns when the TOT expired. This was likely the first time American artillerymen used this technique at the battalion level.[1]

Meanwhile, the 57th Engineering Battalion began building a slippery, bumpy, and narrow dirt road just wide enough to accommodate Jeeps that would bring supplies from the coastal road to the troops inland. They made good progress until they reached Hill 35's 60° slopes on December 20. Since they did not have any heavy equipment to move large quantities of dirt and vegetation, their headway slowed, and they had to stop constructing what could be best described as a pathway rather than having the dignified designation of "road". Therefore, the Jeeps could move supplies just to the path's end. After that, any soldiers available for "mule-work" and native bearers had to hand-carry the materiel the rest of the way to the men.

But Patch's men completed getting their men, equipment, and supplies in place and were ready to attack the Japanese. It was December 17, the day the Americans transformed their campaign from defense to offense.

Gathering Intelligence about Japanese Strength

The 132nd Infantry's 3rd Battalion, L Company, along with 100 men from K Company, began to reconnoiter up Mount Austen's northeastern slopes on December 17 and sent out patrols to find the Japanese. They found no sign of them. L Company moved early on the next day down the "road" to its end on Hill 35. L Company advanced 1,000 yards southwest of Hill 35 and turned southeast into the jungle near the hill's crest. As the company's patrols penetrated the jungle for about 555 yards at 9:30 a.m., the Japanese fired rifles and machine guns from hiding and forced the American patrols to dive for protective cover. The patrols stayed under cover and waited for the rest of the company to meet them two hours later. Col. Wright called for artillery fire to bombard the suspected Japanese positions in front of his battalion and waited to attack the Japanese. Although just one man in the 3rd Battalion sustained a shoulder wound, the oppressive heat exhausted the American soldiers as they climbed the hill's steep slopes. After Wright received reports that the artillery fire had killed three Japanese soldiers, he set up a defensive perimeter just off a clearing and inside the jungle.

After finishing their December 18 patrols, the 132nd Regiment reported that a sustained attack by two battalions would push the Japanese into the Matanikau River. As it would turn out, their estimates of how much force would be needed to dislodge the Japanese dug in, on and around Mount Austen, proved to be overly optimistic.

Beginning at 7:25 a.m. on the next day, three SBDs bombed and strafed for ten minutes. As soon as the planes finished, a five minute artillery barrage bombarded Japanese positions 400 yards from the 3rd Battalion's forward positions. Col. Wright and three men from the 246th Field Artillery Battalion moved westward into the jungle in front of the 3rd Battalion to examine what damage the air and artillery attacks had done to the Japanese.

Wright wore his badge of rank, a practice strongly discouraged by those who fought on Guadalcanal because officers were the prime targets for Japanese snipers, as he advanced into the dense undergrowth. The Japanese spotted the four men at 9:30 a.m. and several machine guns opened fire. Wright fell mortally wounded. The three artillery men stayed with the officer to give him first aid. The continuing Japanese machine gun fire made the Americans keep their heads down and also kept medics from coming forward to help the colonel. Just after noon, Wright succumbed to his wounds as he bled to death. The three artillery soldiers returned to the 3rd Battalion positions on their bellies.

Lt. Col. Louis L. Franco, the 3rd Battalion's executive officer, took command for the fallen Wright. He was about 1,000 yards behind his unit's front lines and could not control the battalion operations. The unit was essentially leaderless when they began their next operations that an observer described as "disorganized" and "obscure". Nelson finally reached the front lines and began to bring some order to the seemingly chaotic situation. He ordered a patrol commanded by the regimental intelligence officer to gather any intelligence about the strength of the Japanese facing them. When they got close enough to the Japanese, the patrol opened fire to provide cover as artillerymen crept forward to rescue a wounded soldier and retrieve Wright's body.

The 3rd Battalion gained no ground on December 19 because of the nearly continuous Japanese rifle fire directed at the beleaguered battalion coming from effectively hidden positions in the jungle undergrowth. Some Japanese soldiers penetrated the American lines through the steep ravines, harassed the Americans trying to bring forward supplies, and effectively cut the supply road to Hill 35. A nearly invisible Japanese machine gun totally surprised the Americans at 5:00 p.m. when it opened fire at the battalion's command post, aid station, and ammunition dump. The American soldiers defending the command post reacted quickly, found the gun, and killed the Japanese soldier firing it. Nonetheless, the command post could not get reorganized until 90 minutes later.

Nelson ordered the 1st Battalion, with its D Company held in reserve, to move southeast to reinforce the 3rd Battalion's left flank south of Hill 19. The two battalions dug their foxholes along a south-facing line just to the south of Hill 20. Meanwhile, the Japanese continued to infiltrate the American lines and used tricks to get the Americans to fire their weapons and reveal their positions.

The Japanese harassment of the Americans continued on December 20 as the 1st Battalion sent patrols to find the Japanese eastern flank. The American reconnaissance did not succeed. Gen. Edmund B. Sebree, the Americal Division's new commander, ordered 132nd Infantry to cut the Maruyama Trail, which was the primary route the Japanese Army used to bring supplies to its men. C Company moved to the south, but could not find either any Japanese or the trail itself. It really was much farther to the south.

The Americans had supply troubles of their own in delivering what their soldiers needed along the narrow, twisting Wright Road. When it rained, the road turned into a morass of treacherously slippery mud. The Jeeps and carts slipped on the road's steep grades and caused the desperately needed supplies to spill into the jungle. The Jeeps, once they went as far as they could go, ended their treks at Hill 35. Men then had to offload the boxes and containers and manhandle them through the thick undergrowth, steep slopes, and tall grass to get the supplies to the men. The success of the Japanese raiding parties forced Nelson to ask the Americal Division for more men to guard the trail and protect it from the Japanese. Unfortunately, the division's headquarters believed the trail was not in danger and refused Nelson's request.

Medical personnel had problems evacuating the wounded to the rear. They put the wounded men on stretchers and carried them to battalion aid stations about 100 yards behind the firing lines. Another group carried the more critical cases in 100-yard relays to a holding area on Hill 35. The wounded would be loaded onto Jeeps that would take them over the rough Wright Road to the Lunga perimeter. The act of carrying the wounded up and down the steep ridges and through the ravines so thoroughly exhausted the stretcher bearers that they had to rest after one or two round trips. The continuous Japanese harassment forced the Americans to assign riflemen to escort the litters, thus taking even more men from combat operations. When carrying the men became too laborious and time- consuming, the litter bearers placed the stretchers on skids and rigged pulleys and cables to lug the litters across the steep ravines.

Finding the Japanese Gifu Defensive Perimeter

On December 24 at 7:30 a.m., the 3rd Battalion marched from its area west of Hill 30 with three of its companies in columnar formations. L Company led the way with I Company, the Medical Company, M Company, and K Company taking the rear position. The battalion did not reach Hill 31 until the afternoon after destroying some Japanese riflemen who tried to stop their advance. The Americans were climbing the hill's grassy inclines when sudden heavy machine gun fire came at them from positions they could not see. The battalion did not have any casualties that day. Nevertheless, Nelson decided there was not enough daylight left to find out more about the Japanese positions facing his battalion to launch an attack. He set up a defensive perimeter between Hills 31 and 42.

✲ ✲ ✲

The heavy machine gun fire came from the strongest defensive position the Japanese held on Guadalcanal. The 500 men in the perimeter were part of Oka's force and named their position Gifu in honor of a prefecture on Honshu Island. The Gifu perimeter was west of Mount Austen and between two hills: Hill 31 to the north and Hill 27 to the south. The strongest defensive point was a horseshoe-shaped line of about 45 pillboxes with interconnecting trenches. They were in a staggered formation, made of logs, dug deep into the ground, with strong dirt revetments inside and outside of the pill boxes. The roofs were three logs thick and the walls two logs thick. Dirt and vegetation camouflaged their tops that rose less than three feet above the original surface level.

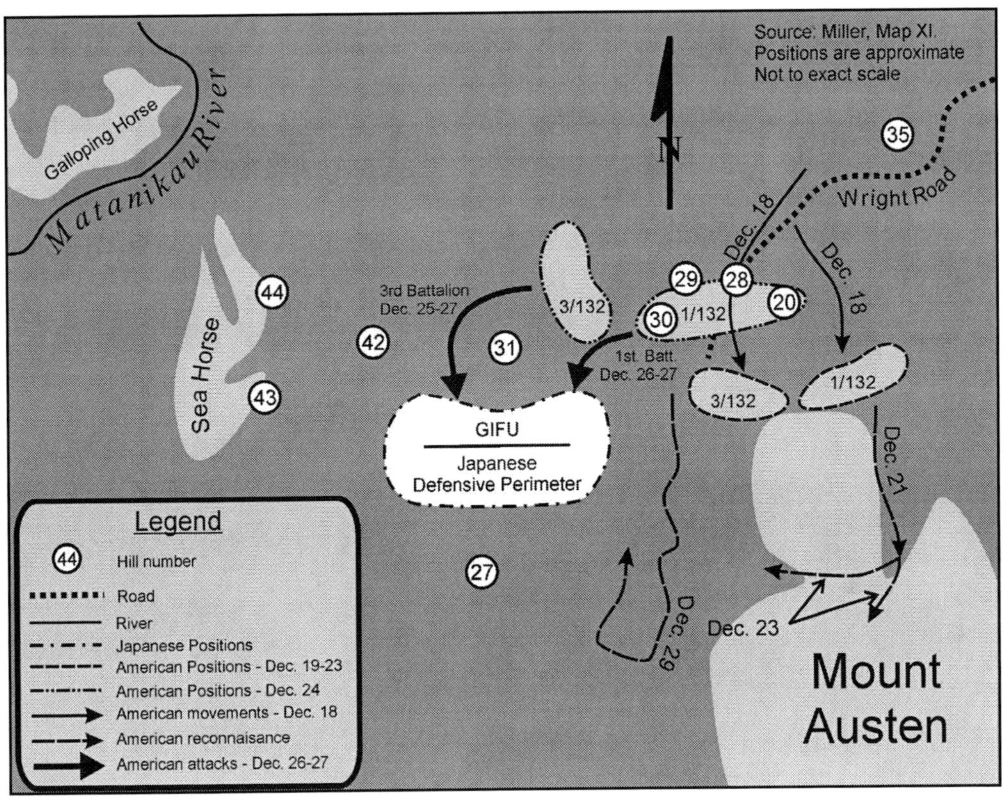

American Assault to Capture Hill 27 - December 31 - January 2

At least one heavy machine gun was in each pill box, along with two or three riflemen. Surrounding the fortifications were more riflemen and light machine guns in positions protected by thick mahogany and banyan tree logs. Some Americans falsely believed there were even more Japanese soldiers in the tree tops. More leaves covered the firing lanes. It was almost impossible to see where the Japanese were in the thick jungle. All the machine guns covered interlocking fields of fire so that if the attackers destroyed one machine gun nest, another one seemed to pop up out of nowhere when the Japanese rearranged them.

Mortar fire could not penetrate the thick fortifications. It would require a direct hit from a 105-mm howitzer on the pill boxes to inflict significant damage. Any artillery firing shells on a less lofty trajectory would just harmlessly hit the trees and not reach the ground. If the Americans got close enough to plant fused explosive charges, these demolitions could destroy the fortification, the key phrase being "close enough." Flamethrowers, the weapon that was so deadly against trenched positions, were useless against this perimeter. The highly effective camouflage made it difficult to pinpoint the positions for air strikes or pinpoint artillery fire. Only steady, intense barrages could disable enough of the fortifications so that the infantry could move in and destroy the rest of them.

Although strong, the Japanese defense was still vulnerable. It was fixed in place and hard to keep supplied. The Americans had an overwhelming advantage in artillery while the Japanese had nearly none. The guns they had lacked enough ammunition to maintain sustained barrages. The Gifu's western flank was weaker than the rest of the perimeter so that those positions could eventually be enveloped and attacked.

The Japanese 38th Division commander, Lt. Gen. Tadayoshi Sano, sent out an "Address of Instruction" on December 25 to his men to raise their morale. He said the Americans had lost their willingness to fight from spending so many months in horrible conditions on Guadalcanal. The Japanese soldier was made of sterner stuff and could endure the hardships of starvation. Their suffering would soon be rewarded when air, ground, and naval reinforcements arrived. Sano urged his men to show their superiority to the Americans by fighting back with "desperate determination"[2] because they [the Americans] relied on using machines rather than fighting like a *Bushido* warrior.

The 132nd Infantry restarted their attack on the Gifu perimeter on December 25, Christmas Day, 1942. Nelson's plan was for three rifle companies from the 3rd Battalion to move to the south of Hill 31 toward Hill 27 with one company, M Company, to be kept in reserve. The regiment's 60-mm mortars began a barrage at 9:30 a.m. as the American soldiers went on the attack. The jungle's rocky terrain slowed their progress, making the advance difficult.

Now the battle became a desperately haphazard group of small advances and stops. The Americans would move forward and fight for every foot of ground. After more than four hours, the Americans had gained just a few yards and had to stop since Japanese gunfire poured from invisible positions upon the American front and flanks. The devastating Japanese gunfire had killed three officers and nine enlisted men while wounding 16 others.

After examining what happened to his regiment that day, Nelson reasoned that the Japanese were far stronger than originally thought. The Japanese position was a perimeter of many strong points that could not be dislodged with infantry assaults alone. He decided to attack the next day with a frontal assault by the 3rd Battalion while the 1st Battalion protected its left flank.

The American artillery and aerial bombing attacked the Gifu perimeter the next morning followed by infantry attacks that began at 10:30 a.m. The 3rd Battalion tried to resume its advance with K Company to the west or the Battalion's right, I Company to the east, and L Company in reserve on Hill 31. The 1st Battalion covered the 3rd Battalion's left flank while its C Company stayed back and protected the 1st Battalion from being attacked on its rear. The 3rd Battalion could only get as far as it did the previous day. The Japanese raked the attacking Americans with heavy machine gun fire and stopped the American advance.

The 3rd Battalion's casualties for its attack of December 26 had cost them five killed and 12 wounded while they believed they killed nine Japanese. The Japanese defensive position remained as it was when the American attacks began. Nonetheless, the 132nd Infantry now occupied a line between Hill 31 and the Gifu perimeter. The Japanese could no longer observe American activity in and around Lunga from that promontory.

Nelson committed both battalions when they attacked the Gifu perimeter on December 27. The 3rd Battalion kept the Japanese busy and was soon stopped by heavy gunfire. Meanwhile, the 1st Battalion's Companies A, B, and C moved south and east to where the Japanese flanks were. The Americans continued attacking, but Japanese gunfire stopped any further forward movement.

The Americans sent out more patrols on December 27 and 28 and found no gaps in the Japanese perimeter. But an eight-man patrol returned with useful information. There was an unobstructed way to get to Hill 27 by leaving Hill 29, moving southward 1,500 yards to avoid the Gifu's eastern flank, turning west, traveling 200 yards, and emerging south of the Gifu perimeter's much weaker defenses. The Americans could take Hill 27 and interdict Japanese supplies coming up from the Maruyama Road.

The three consecutive frustrated attacks severely depressed the 132nd Infantry's morale as 1942 came to an end. The attacks from December 19 until December 30 had cost the regiment 34 killed, 129 wounded, 19 missing, and 131 sick that had been evacuated. The regiment did not have a full complement of men when it began its attack. Now that the shortfall was larger. The two battalions had just 1,541 men among them. There was not much success to crow about. The Americans learned a valuable lesson—throwing the Japanese from Guadalcanal would be much more difficult than they originally thought.

Taking Hill 27

Despite the lack of any significant progress by the 132nd Regiment attempting to destroy the Gifu perimeter, the American ground commanders did not abandon the idea of capturing Mount Austen. Gen. Patch convened a meeting of his commanders at his command post on December 29 with Generals Harmon, Collins, and Sebree attending. Realizing the capture of Mount Austen had to succeed before launching their planned offensive operations in January, they agreed to continue the offensive to take the mountain. The responsibility for the assault would naturally fall upon Nelson's 132nd Infantry since they were already in place.

Col. Nelson's plan called for synchronized assaults by the 1st and 3rd Battalions to attack the formidable Japanese defenses from the north while the 2nd Battalion, fresh after being held in reserve during their regiment's prior attacks, circled wide to the east and approached Hill 27 from the south to capture it. He issued his orders on December 30 that disclosed his plan to his battalion commanders. The 3rd Battalion would keep attacking southward from Hill 31 while the 1st Battalion would move south from their positions, make a wide swing, turn westward, and attack the Japanese perimeter eastern line.

Commanded by Lt. Col. George F. Perry, the men of the unblooded 2nd Battalion were ready to get into the war. Nelson ordered Perry to reconnoiter the Japanese positions on December 28. Perry ordered his executive officer and each company commander to send out patrols along their planned line of march to see what was out there.

The battalion moved down the Wright Road but took longer than planned to reach their jump-off point just south of Hill 11. Nelson had ordered the attack to begin on January 1 at 6:30 a.m., but the 2nd Battalion had not reached Hill 11 until late on December 31. It would take all day on January 1 for them to reach their attacking position. The new H-hour was to be at 6:30 a.m. on January 2. The 2nd

Battalion's journey gave its men their first experience what it was like to move through Guadalcanal's jungles and steep terrain. Its trek from Hill 11 to Hill 27 was just one mile as the crow flies. Nevertheless, after the battalion left Hill 11, the men struggled up and down the steep, slippery sides of deep ravines. Rather than traveling just 1,760 yards to cover one mile, they actually traversed more than 6,000 yards after climbing up and scrambling down the nearly vertical ravines that stood between them and their objective. When stretcher bearers had to evacuate the wounded by the same route on January 2, it took five hours to bring just 20 casualties to the nearest aid station. The Americans arrived at Hill 27 at 4:00 p.m. on January 1 free of casualties.

Malaria disabled Col. Nelson who had to give up the command of his regiment. Col. Alexander M. George assumed command and arrived at the regiment's command post at 9:15 a.m. on January 1. As soon he took command, he startled his men by trying to prove the Japanese small-arms fire in the Gifu perimeter could not hit anyone that kept moving. He strapped twin .45-cal pistols to his waist, picked up an M-1 rifle, and, wearing shorts and a fatigue cap, walked toward the front lines to inspect what it was like there. As he walked totally erect where the Japanese could easily see him, some of his men shouted for him to take cover. Nonetheless, he finished his sojourn into the jaws of death and came back to his command post unscathed. He had proved his contention that the Japanese could not hit a moving target despite their nearly continuous, but futile, fire.

This time, the American artillery opened with a far more devastating barrage to support the January 2 offensive. Shell after shell from the 105-mm and 75-mm pack howitzers pummeled the Japanese in the Gifu perimeter.

✲ ✲ ✲

The 132nd Infantry went on the attack at 6:30 a.m. on January 2 as planned. The 3rd Battalion enfiladed the Japanese with everything it had and moved forward in a line while its I Company had to move slower because of heavy Japanese returning fire. The Battalion managed set up a line by 2:00 p.m. near Hill 31's southern tree line. After the firing stopped at the end of the day, the American unit had killed 15 Japanese while losing four killed and 18 wounded.

The 1st Battalion moved southwest in a columnar formation in the ravine between Hills 29 and 30. Rifle fire from Japanese patrols confronted the leading C Company as A Company maneuvered around the Japanese by going south, then east, and then turned southwest once more. B Company was not far behind. By 10:00 a.m., A Company reached a place just east of the Gifu perimeter. Before the day ended, C Company destroyed the Japanese in front of them and met up with the rest of the battalion. Its left flank was near Hill 27, but a 200-yard gap existed between it and the 1st Battalion. During its fight against the Japanese that day, the 1st Battalion killed 25 Japanese with C Company doing most of the damage while losing two killed and four wounded.

Despite the difficult terrain in their path, the 2nd Battalion had the most success that day. The circular route they took through the jungle on January 1 fooled the Japanese, who never knew of the battalion's movements. Coordinating its movements with the rest of the regiment, the battalion began their march at 6:30 a.m. in a single file formation. When the men came upon the first steep ravine one hour later, the formation changed so that they could climb steep slopes as best they could. E Company was in the lead on the left with F Company on the right. G and H Companies brought up the rear in reserve. The climb was far from easy. The oppressive heat made the men sweat profusely and soaked their uniforms and their black camouflage makeup as they scrambled up the ravine's slippery sides. The Japanese never saw or detected their approach.

The leading troops reached the ravine summit by 9:07 a.m. with the rest of their comrades joining them by 11:30 a.m. They totally surprised the Japanese.

The lack of Japanese awareness of the American presence showed up in an interesting anecdote. When E and F Companies came over the top of the ravine, they saw a three-inch howitzer about 100 yards to the crest's north. The Japanese gun crew relaxed in the shade about 30 yards from the gun, a logical thing to do to avoid the stifling heat. When the Japanese saw the American soldiers, they bolted from their relaxed positions and ran for their gun. The Americans gunned them down one-by-one as they came out from under the tree. When the skirmish ended, the Japanese gun sat unused.

When the 2nd Battalion reached Hill 27's summit, they began digging their foxholes and machine gun nests. The Japanese heard the noise of the digging and reorganized themselves for their attack. All of a sudden, Japanese mortars, grenade launchers, machine guns, and a few artillery guns began firing a withering barrage onto the unconcealed Americans. One artillery observer on Hill 27 remembered what he saw when the Japanese opened up:

> "Then all hell broke loose. Machine guns and rifles pinged from all directions. Snipers fired from trees...Crossfire cut down our boys who were over the hill...Our Garands [M1 rifles] answered the fire and the battle was on. Enemy "Knee mortars" [grenade launchers] popped on our lines with painful regularity. Our own 60s [mortars] opened up and neutralized them only to have shells start lobbing in from a different direction."[3]

The Americans kept digging their holes as the Japanese fire came down all around them. Forty minutes after the barrage began, the 2nd Battalion had lost eight and had 70 wounded men. The Japanese attacked the Americans on Hill 27 six times, but the 2nd Battalion fought them and turned back all their assaults.

As the afternoon moved toward night, the 2nd Battalion wisely moved 100 yards south off the crest onto the reverse slopes. The Japanese surrounded the battalion during the night of January 2-3 by infiltrating the American lines to the hill's north, northwest, and southwest. But American artillery would have its say as the Japanese tried to place machine gun nests to fire on the 2nd Battalion. The Marine 75-mm howitzers fired several well-aimed shells between the Americans and the Japanese.

The Japanese tried to make the American soldiers believe they were firing on their own position by firing mortars on the American lines as the American artillery shells exploded. The Americans were not fooled even as the Japanese shouted "cease-fire." The American artillery fire never stopped. As the sun rose the morning of January 3, the light revealed many dead Japanese soldiers after the surviving Japanese abandoned their positions. The battalion returned to the crest. H Company brought its heavy mortars and machine guns to the top of the hill.

✲ ✲ ✲

The exhausting journeys to get into position to attack the Japanese and the brutal combat had totally spent all of the 132nd Regiment's energy. The division ordered the regiment to dig in and defend all its gains. The men built a half-moon shaped defensive line on the Gifu's eastern side by constructing foxholes covered with logs and spread barbed wire in front of them. A strong, nearly impenetrable line now spread around the Gifu perimeter's north, east, and south sides. If the Japanese should try to break out of their lines, they would pay a dear price.

Battle fatigue, malaria, dysentery, and combat casualties had taken their toll on the 132nd Regiment. They could no longer fight in any further offensive operations. They held their positions until the 2nd Battalion, 35th Infantry Regiment, 25th Division relieved them. The 132nd had fought a series of offensive battles over a 22-day period. The regiment lost a total of 112 men killed, 268 wounded, and three . While the Japanese held a part of Mount Austen, the regiment's fighting had forced many Japanese to leave the mountain. They could no longer spy on American movements. The stage had been set for far more powerful offensive actions as 1943 began. The 25th Division had put almost all their men on Guadalcanal and were ready to pick up the gauntlet thrown down by the heroic actions of the 132nd Infantry, Americal Division.

The Japanese days on Guadalcanal had dwindled to a desperate few. An American hard-fought victory was just around the corner, but it would not be easy. The struggles of the next days would be among the most brutal of the Pacific War thus far.[4]

CHAPTER 56
A Major American Offensive Begins

Planning for a New Offensive

Gen. Patch had a chance to examine how much his Corps' limited December offensive had accomplished. He could not help but be pleased with the results. The Japanese had defiantly, valiantly, and vigorously defended their positions. The 132nd Regiment gave everything it had to give when it captured Hill 27 and cutoff the Gifu perimeter. The rewards they attained had been achieved with much blood and sacrifice on both sides. Nevertheless, the Japanese could no longer spy on American movements from Mount Austen. Patch's Corps could now launch its attacks on a greater scale because the 25th Division had arrived in full force. The Japanese forces in their Gifu perimeter had been significantly weakened so that it took just one battalion to keep them from breaking out. Patch could turn his attentions to planning his Corps' January 10 offensive and to kicking the Japanese off Guadalcanal.

The American attacks to remove the Japanese from Mount Austen did not change the other American positions at all. As of November, the main American forces formed a line to the west of Lunga that ran from Point Cruz southward and jogged eastward at Hill 66. The 1st Battalion of the 2nd Marine Regiment held Hills 54 and 55 on the Matanikau River west bank. Because there were no ridges that connected Hills 55 and 66 or Hills 56 and 55, the Americans did not have continuous lines although American patrols roamed in the deep canyons between the hills.

There was a road built at the Marine Trail's end that the Americans used to bring supplies to their front lines. The Engineers from the Americal Division completed building a bridge across the Matanikau River near Hill 65. Using bulldozers to break through the jungle, they expanded the road to Hill 55's 900-foot summit.

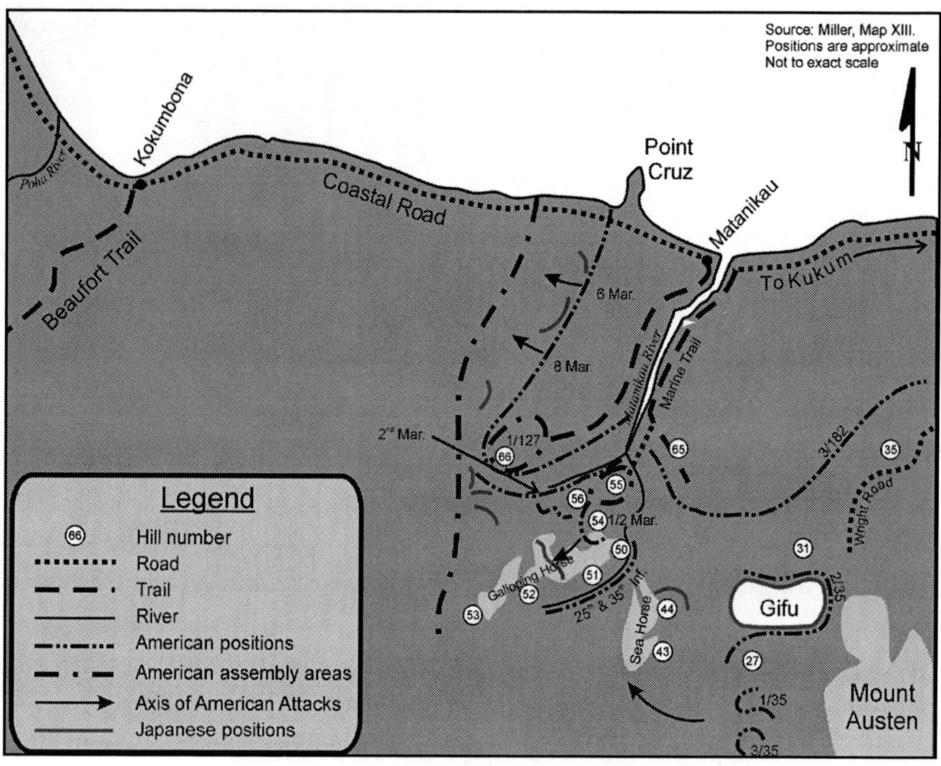

American Ground Forces on Guadalcanal - January 1943

The American ground forces increased significantly after the Army relieved Gen. Vandegrift's 1st Marine Division. The XIV Corps' divisions had more than 40,000 men by January 1943's first week compared to the Japanese 17th Army's less than 17,000 men. Maj. Gen. Collins' 25th Division had landed all three of its combat teams between December 17 and January 4 and set up their camp east of the Lunga River. The Marines also added forces of their own with the landing of the 2nd Marine Division headquarters and Col. Gilder T. Jackson's reinforced 6th Marine Regiment increasing their numbers on Guadalcanal with Brig. Gen. Alphonse De Carre, the division's assistant commander, in command.

Despite the XIV Corps' overwhelming advantage in the number of troops and supplies, the main problem the Patch faced was getting the materiel to the troops before they attacked the Japanese in force. Although the American engineers struggled mightily to build supply roads to the front lines, the routes could only be described as of poor quality because of the extreme conditions under which the engineers worked. Patch did not have enough trucks to ship the supplies to the American ground forces fast enough. The versatile ¼-ton Jeeps were the only vehicles the Americans had that could navigate the rough-hewn roads and steep grades and bring the supplies forward. The Jeeps were practically the only way the 25th Division could get the materiel it needed. Supplying the 2nd Marine Division was far easier because they were closer to the better Coastal Road and trails where higher-capacity trucks could be used.

The Japanese positions before the American January offensive began had not materially changed since November. Not holding lines such as the Americans did, the Japanese had established particularly strong enclaves between Point Cruz and Kokumbona. They continuously patrolled the gaps between them. They took advantage of the terrain by placing machine guns at the elevated heads of the steep ravines and could pour deadly fire upon any Americans that should move through the canyons. Thus, just a few Japanese soldiers could either stop or slow many more Americans and hold their positions while inflicting devastating casualties. American intelligence believed the Japanese held the high ground south of Hill 66 and west of the Matanikau. The Japanese 124th and 228th Regiments still occupied the Gifu perimeter and continued to stop any American attempts to take those positions, and also held positions, supported by artillery and mortars, in several areas to the west.

So that his division commanders would be clear what his intentions were for the upcoming offensive, Patch sent out his January 5th plan. He ordered Gen. Collins' 25th Division, which was now encamped east of the Lunga River, to move westward, replace the exhausted 132nd Infantry and provide the gallant regiment much needed relief. They were to establish a line about 3,000 yards west of Mount Austen with the 27th and 35th Infantry Regiments along the eastern bank of the Matanikau River southwest fork. The 2nd Marine Division was to stay in contact with the 25th Division's right flank. Another instruction in his orders was for Gen. Collins to work directly with the 2nd Marine Air Wing to get the air support Collins believed he needed.

Patch also ordered the Americal Division's Artillery, a just-arrived 155-mm battery, and another 155-mm battery that reported directly to the XIV Corps to give the 2nd Marine Division the artillery support it required. The 2nd Battalion, 10th Marines' 75-mm pack howitzers were to support the 25th Division's artillery. The Americal Division was to hold the perimeter around Lunga and Henderson Field while its artillery, Reconnaissance Squadron, the 182nd Infantry, and the 2nd Battalion, 132nd Infantry would be part of the Corps' offensive.

Patch did a meticulous job with his plan. It was as thorough as any commander could make and made allowance for every possible contingency. The January offensive could now begin.

Capturing the Galloping Horse

Gen. Joseph (Joe) Lawton Collins had never been in combat. This high-spirited officer's baptism by fire would come in this upcoming offensive. Born in New Orleans, Louisiana, on May 1, 1896, he graduated from the United States Military Academy at West Point and received his commission as a second lieutenant in April 1917. With the U.S. then in World War I and the need for officers reaching the level of desperation, his first assignment was to the 22nd Infantry Regiment. Promoted to 1st lieutenant one month later and to the temporary rank of captain in August of that year, he attended the Infantry School of Arms at Fort Sill, Oklahoma, and continued his service in his regiment from 1917 to 1919. In June 1918, his captaincy became permanent. He put on the gold leaves that gave him the temporary rank of major three months later. When his regiment went to France in 1919 as part of the American forces that occupied Germany, he took command of his regiment's 3rd Battalion, soon became the G-3 assistant chief of staff of the American forces in Germany, and remained in that post from 1920 to 1921.

After reverting to his permanent rank of captain and marrying Gladys Easterbrook in 1921, he became a chemistry instructor at West Point until 1925. Collins graduated from the company officer course at the Infantry School at Fort Benning, Georgia, in 1926 and from the advanced course from the Field Artillery School at Fort Sill. He taught weapons and tactics at the Infantry school for four years from 1927 to 1931, received his permanent promotion to major in August 1932, became the 23rd Brigade's executive officer in Manila and assistant chief of staff, G-2, Philippine Division from 1933 to 1934.

After attending and graduating from various schools and teaching at the Army War College, he achieved his promotion to lieutenant colonel in June 1940 and became the VII Corps' chief of staff in 1941. Collins received the temporary rank of a full colonel in January 1941, and after Pearl Harbor, he received his first star as a brigadier general. in February 1942 and his second star as a major general three months later. Collins had been the Hawaiian Department's chief of staff when he took command of the 25th "Tropic Lightning" Division and took them to Guadalcanal.[1]

Collins received his orders from Gen. Patch to attack the Japanese and gathered his division's senior officers, Brig. Gen. John R. Hodge, the assistant division commander, Brig. Gen. Stanley E. Reinhart, the artillery Commander, as well as his regimental and some of his battalion commanders to tour the battle area by air. Many of them could not believe how dense the jungle growth was. It hid where the Japanese were, as well as in the ravines, valleys, and canyons. The aerial photographs had shown the open areas in great detail, but this was not enough. The 25th Division's intelligence staff knew very little about the locations of all the Japanese strong points and how many men they had. Nonetheless, they did know about the almost unconquerable Gifu Perimeter as well the Japanese strength on the high ground south of Hill 66.

Because they did not have the exact locations of Japanese strong points, the 25th Division's officers knew the rugged terrain would dictate where and when their men would attack the Japanese. Patch set his command's boundaries for the upcoming assault. The division's southern boundary would be the Lunga River just south of Mount Austen with the northern boundary limited by the Matanikau's northwest fork. The Matanikau River and its upstream smaller tributaries set up the division's three directions of attack: east of the Gifu Perimeter, the hills not covered by the jungle west of the Gifu between the Matanikau's south and southwest forks, and the open hills between the river's northwest and southwest forks.

Collins sent out his orders to his division as well to the other units from outside the his 25th Division—the 3rd Battalion from the 182nd Infantry Regiment, the Americal Division's Reconnaissance Squadron, and the 1st Battalion from the 2nd Marine Division—that would be part of the attack on January 8, 1943. "H" hour was set for 6:35 a.m. on January 10 with the 25th Division to take and hold a line about 3,000 yards west of Mount Austen that ran in a southerly direction from Hill 66. While the 35th Infantry Regiment, under the command of Col. Robert B. McClure, relieved the exhausted 132nd Infantry guarding the Gifu, captured the high ground to the Gifu's west, Col. William A. McCulloch's 27th Infantry Regiment was to capture and hold the high ground between the Matanikau's southwestern and northwestern forks. The 161st Infantry, under the command of Col. Clarence A. Orndorff and formerly of the Washington State National Guard, was to remain in reserve. A 30-minute artillery barrage would begin at 5:50 a.m. aimed at an area from the water hole near Hill 66 to the hills south and into the 27th Infantry's assigned area. There would be no artillery or air bombardment in the 35th Infantry's area so as to not give the Japanese any advance warning.

Gen. Collins planned for and was to get extensive artillery support for his attack. The 8th Artillery Battalion would directly support the 27th Infantry; the 64th Field Artillery Battalion's105-mm howitzers would give direct support to the 35th Infantry in addition to the already committed support from the 89th (105-mm howitzers), the 90th Field Artillery Battalion (155-mm guns), and the 2nd Battalion, 10th Marine Artillery Regiment. The 155-mm guns of the Americal Division's 221st Field Artillery Battalion would add their chorus of destruction to the 25th Division's artillery on January 10.

The Japanese shortages in artillery and air support greatly simplified the American artillery deployment of their guns west of the Lunga River. There was no need to hide the American guns on the reverse slopes with no danger of being fired upon by whatever Japanese artillery that might be left. Thus, they began to move nearer to the intended targeting areas and far enough to the west to be able to hit Kokumbona. The 64th Field Artillery Battalion, assigned to support the 35th Battalion, moved to places on Mount Austen's foothills about 2,000 yards northeast of the Gifu and 9,000 yards southeast of Kokumbona. The 8th Field Artillery Battalion, supporting the 27th, set up its guns south of where the 64th Field Artillery Battalion placed its guns and about 3,000 yards east to the 27th Regiment's most eastern boundary. The 89th Field Artillery Battalion placed its guns on a high bluff east of the Matanikau River; the 90th Field Artillery Battalion took positions about 1,000 yards east of where the Wright and coastal roads met.

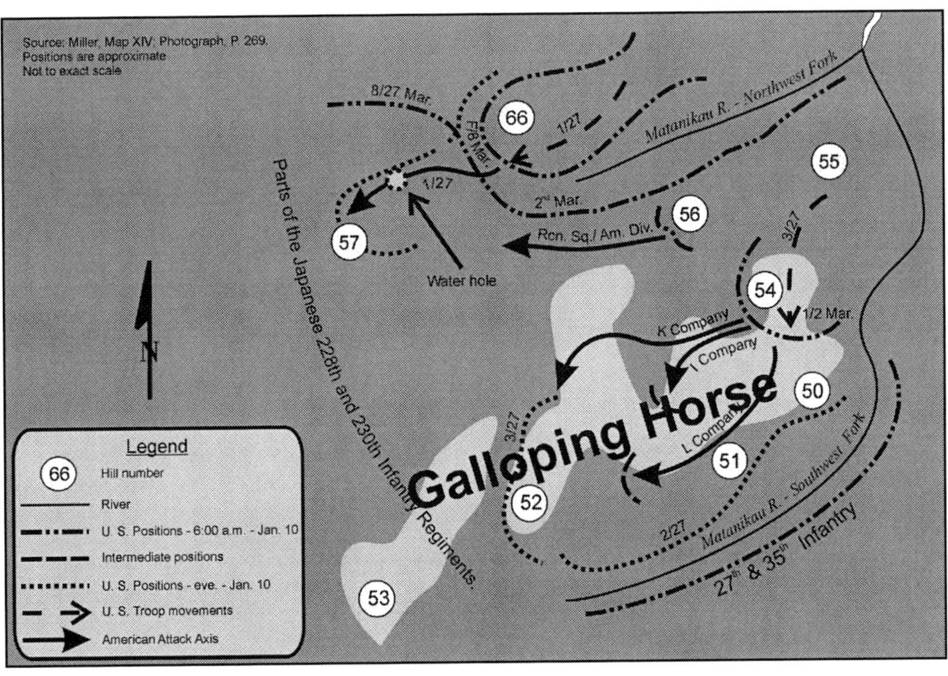

The American 25th Division's Attack Plans

Moving the American artillery's guns and ammunition was not an easy task because of the rough terrain over which the men had to manhandle the materiel. Each battalion had to move the ammunition it needed more than ten miles from the ammunition dumps east of the Ilu River. It would take 54 truckloads of two and a half tons each to bring the 105-mm howitzer ammunition forward. Nevertheless, all the ammunition arrived where it was needed by January 8 in time to support the

American attacks and two days before "H" hour. The gun crews now established the coordinates of the various targets at which they would fire. They were ready to go.

The 25th Division's staff and Collins met with the air support officers to plan the required air attacks. Although the Japanese artillery could not fire at their American counterparts, the Army needed air attacks from SBD dive-bombers and P-39 fighter-bombers. The SBDs would each carry three 325-pound depth charges while the P-39s would each carry one 500-pound bomb and attack still-existing Japanese artillery.

The 25th Medical Battalion learned from its experience evacuating the December campaign wounded and set up a similar system. It installed cables across the steep canyons, placed skids on the Navy's litters carrying the wounded so they could be slid across the ground, and used a line of boats on the Matanikau River to carry the wounded to the hospitals in the rear. Because it was such hard work carrying the wounded to the rear, the litter squads had to be expanded to as many as 12 men each to relieve their exhausted comrades. The battalion rigged some Jeeps as converted ambulances to move the wounded on the roads and trails.

The most extensive American ground offensive ever attempted in the Pacific Theater thus far was about to begin. It had two basic objectives: (1) reduce the Gifu's strength while destroying all Japanese ground forces east of the Matanikau, and (2) take the high ground south of the line running from Point Cruz to Hill 66 to begin surrounding the Point Cruz-Kokumbona area while moving the western American lines far enough inland to set up the slaughter of all Japanese troops on Guadalcanal. But these objectives had to be accomplished with smaller, bite-sized steps. And the first series of steps was to take a set of hills and steep gullies.

The group of hills called the "Galloping Horse" got its nickname because it resembled that animal when viewed from the air. It overlooked Point Cruz, bracketed by Hill 53 (the head of the horse) to the southwest that was about 2,000 yards south of Hill 66 and stretched to Hill 50 at its tail. Surrounded on three sides by the Matanikau's mainstream to the east that also separated it from Mount Austen, the southwest fork of the Matanikau to the south, and the river's northwest fork to the north, the Galloping Horse was a perfect place for defensive positions against an enemy with superior numbers. Dense jungle vegetation encircled the mass' base. The southern edge was a nearly perpendicular system of stony out-croppings that made an ascent impossible. The hills had little vegetation on them other than thick, tough grass, scattered bushes, and a few solitary trees that provided little cover for any soldiers assaulting the heights.

Patch and his staff thought the Japanese possessed strong defensive positions on the Galloping Horse and were prepared to defend them with same intensity as they did on the Gifu. When the 2nd Marines and the Americal Division's Reconnaissance Squadron sent out patrols in December 1942 and January 1943, the Japanese poured heavy machine gun, rifle, and mortar fire into the Americans, thus confirming the XIV Corps' beliefs. The Japanese held strong defensive positions using soldiers from the 228th and 230th Regiments from their 38th Division on the Galloping Horse and on the banks of the Matanikau's southwestern fork south of this mass of hills.

The 27th Infantry's commander, Col. McCulloch, planned to attack the Galloping Horse's eastern edge on a 2,000 yard front with two battalions supported by artillery barrages from the 27th Infantry's Cannon Company. Concerned that the Jeep trail from the Matanikau to the top of Hill 55 could not bring enough supplies for a full frontal assault by two battalions, McCulloch ordered each battalion to separately attack the Japanese. Lt. Col. Claude E. Jurney's 1st Battalion was to move from Hill 66 in the 2nd Marines' zone, press forward south of hill 66 along the northern bank of the Matanikau's northwestern fork, capture the water hole where the Japanese waylaid the 182nd Infantry's patrol on November 18, and capture the northern part of Hill 57, the Corps' main objective in this sector. The 8th Marines' F Company and the Americal Division's Reconnaissance Squadron would protect the 1st Battalion's left flank. Twenty-five men from Jurney's Battalion would carry supplies needed by the battalion by way of the route from Hill 66.

Lt. Col. George E. Bush's 3rd Battalion would move along the 1st Battalion's left after amassing on Hill 55 behind the 2nd Marines' lines, advance southward along the Galloping Horse "hind legs", and capture Hill 53—the Corps' main objective in that area. Supplies for the 3rd Battalion's attack would be delivered on the coastal road along the Marine Trail, up the jeep trail to Hill 55, and hand-carried by natives with American soldiers protecting them. Meanwhile, McCulloch kept Lt. Col. Herbert V. Mitchell's 2nd Battalion in reserve at Hill 55's base. Also, Collins warned McCulloch that before his regiment moved westward toward their attack positions, they might have to come to the 35th Infantry's aid if that unit ran into problems taking its objective to the south.

The time had come to put the 27th Infantry's 1st Battalion into action. The Japanese were still where they had been and certainly had no plans to go anywhere. The 27th Infantry Regiment was about to change that or at least try mightily.

Just as the sun rose over the jungles of Guadalcanal at 5:55 a.m., the 25th Division artillery's 75-mm and 105-mm howitzers and 155-mm guns roared and lit up the predawn light with a 5,700-round barrage weighing almost 100 tons against the Japanese entrenchments on the Galloping Horse. Wanting all the first shells fired in the barrage to hit their targets at the same time, the 25th Division used a technique called "time-on-target" or TOT. The gun fire was not synchronized because of the various distances to their target and caught several American soldiers, who did not know their artillery was using this technique, in the open, thus placing them in considerable danger from being hit by the fire from their own guns. Severe devastation enfiladed the water hole and cleared a path, previously impervious to any American advances, for the 1st Battalion.

While the steep cliff hid some Japanese defensive positions from the massive artillery bombardment, the 12 SBDs and 12 P-39s from the 2nd MAW attacked. The P-39s and SBDs struck at 6:20 a.m. after the barrage lifted. The pilots had instructions to bomb to the west of a line of smoke laid down by the American artillery between Hill 66's southwestern tip and to the Galloping Horse's easternmost edge. Just prior to the aircraft arriving over the target area, an errant American artillery shell or a Japanese mortar shell hit an American ammunition dump on Hill 56 and caused a massive explosion. The leading SBD mistakenly dropped one of its depth charges on the 8th Marines on Hill 66, and a P-39 dropped a bomb on Hill 55 east of the original line of smoke. The American soldiers or marines luckily escaped any injury. Nonetheless, the air attacks destroyed several Japanese strong points the artillery could not reach and enabled American troops to successfully attack as scheduled.

For the 1st Battalion's attack to successfully capture Hill 57, both its flanks had to be protected from any Japanese counterattacks. The 2nd Marine Regiment's F Company moved at 7:42 a.m. to Hill 66's southwestern corner to protect the 25th Division's right flank. When the 1st Battalion's B Company departed from Hill 66 at 7:35 a.m. to capture the water hole, the 2nd Marine Regiment's B and F Companies were in place on its flanks to join the attack. The responsibility for protecting the 1st Battalion's left flank belonged to the Americal Division Reconnaissance Squadron, and it fulfilled that mission when it moved into the ravine between Hill 56 and the Galloping Horse northernmost edge and set up a block by 8:30 a.m. The 27th Infantry's A and B Companies contacted the Squadron one and a half hours later.

The 27th Infantry moved off Hill 66 with its companies in columns and A Company led the way. C and D companies followed right behind. The only effective Japanese resistance was fire from just three machine gun nests that the soldiers easily silenced. The massive earlier artillery barrage apparently had more than done its job destroying Japanese strong points. A Company crossed the Matanikau at 10:27 a.m. In one hour, 13 minutes, the entire 1st Battalion captured Hill 57. Its men dug in and set up fire support positions to help the 3rd Battalion's assault on Hill 52. Col. Jurney sent out a patrol after sundown to make contact with the 3rd Battalion.

The first part of the 27th Regiment's attack had succeeded. Now it was the 3rd Battalion's turn to take its objective.

✲ ✲ ✲

Unfortunately, the 3rd Battalion would have a much more difficult time taking Hill 52 than the 1st Battalion had in taking Hill 57. For one thing, the terrain was far steeper and rougher in spite of not having as much dense vegetation. Thick woods covered 1,500 yards of the hill's northern boundary. The Galloping Horse's main body was an open area of grasses inundated with deeply cut ravines and steep hills. The southern edge of the Horse's body dropped precipitously into a steep gorge with dense vegetation covering its canyon bottom because of the nearly perpendicular hills that formed that boundary. The thick undergrowth prevented any troop movements through the canyon. Hill 52 rose to dominate the surrounding hills with two smaller hills, which could not be seen between Hill 52's summit and Hill 53. The 25th Division gave the names of "Exton Ridge" and "Sims Ridge" to these lesser mounds in honor of two 2nd Lieutenants killed on January 12.

Hill 52 had to be taken before Hill 53 could be captured and became an intermediate objective for the 3rd Battalion. With a level summit that could be defended by a few men against an attack of many, it could not be attacked from the south or west because of the steep terrain. After earlier attempts by the Marine and Reconnaissance patrols to approach the hill, they reported the Japanese defense made the hill a "hornet's nest". Patrols had already examined the area east of the hill, but could not advance to the hill's west. The only information the 25th Division had about the topography west of Hill 52 had come just from aerial reconnaissance and photographs.

When Col. Bush, the 3rd Battalion's commander, looked at the task his command faced, he decided that Hill 52 could never be taken by a frontal assault. Thus he planned an enveloping attack from its south and north with L Company on the left (south), I Company on the right (north), and K Company held in reserve. He assigned a machine gun platoon from M Company to each attacking company. Two 37-mm guns from the Antitank Platoon of the Battalion's Headquarters Company and M Company's 81-mm Mortar Platoon would lay down a barrage from Hill 54, where the Battalion command post also resided. Despite the fact that the Division artillery had Hill 54 sighted in, they had not fired at it. The aircraft from the 2nd MAW had not touched it either. Therefore, Bush asked the 8th Battalion, plus the other battalions, to add fire support to his battalion's attack.

At 3:30 a.m. on January 10, the 3rd Battalion gathered at the foot of Hill 55 and began climbing the hill. It reached its planned place on the hill's north slopes at 6:10 a.m. from which they would begin to advance. Fifteen minutes later, "H" Hour at 6:35 a.m., the battalion moved southward through the Marine lines in a column of companies down Hill 54's forward slopes toward an area between Hills 50 and 51 just 11 minutes later. L Company climbed Hill 51, took it unopposed, and set up a fire base. With one platoon covering its left and another platoon held in support, the company's commander, Capt. Oliver A. Roholt, ordered the 1st Platoon to attack Hill 52's southeastern corner. This time, the rough terrain and thick grass hid their approach, and the platoon advanced quickly and forcefully up the east slope and reached the halfway point to the summit at 7:00 a.m. They tried to move farther, but heavy Japanese machine gun and mortar fire prevented the American soldiers from making any more progress. Capt. Roholt looked through his binoculars from his place on Hill 51 and watched the 1st Platoon being stopped by the Japanese gunfire and realized that the platoon could not go around the strong Japanese defenses and outflank them. The Japanese seemed to be able to prevent any advances from the east and north while the steep cliff on the hill's southern edge offered a natural defense. The platoon's frontal attack had potentially exposed its left flank to a Japanese counterattack.

L Company's advance had moved too fast for Col. Bush to ask for artillery fire to nullify the Japanese defenses on Hill 52. If the American guns fired at the targets on that hill, the falling shells could put the 1st Platoon in dire danger. As the platoon "hit the dirt" and hugged the earth as if their lives depended on it, and it did, Bush directed his artillery to fire beyond Hill 52. American 37-mm and mortar fire pummeled the hill's crest and the slopes to the summit's west. However, the 37-mm gunfire could not inflict any damage upon the heavily dug-in Japanese. The mortar gunners could have reached the Japanese if they knew the precise locations of the Japanese guns but they did not have any such intelligence. Therefore, the artillery barrage had little if any effect.

Wanting the artillery to help his platoon and not kill any of its men in the process, Roholt ordered his men to withdraw 100 yards to make room for any short-falling errant shells. The platoon's leader received Roholt's message but it arrived garbled with the words "100 yards" chopped off. The mistake resulted in the platoon withdrawing back to Hill 51. L Company did not attack Hill 52 again although it continued to pour fire onto the hill. Roholt reported to Bush that the hill could not be taken by massing to the hill's south because of the steep terrain and recommended Bush give up the idea of enveloping the hill from the south.

But that did not mean that the 3rd Battalion had given up trying to surround the hill from the north. Capt. H. H. Johnson, Jr. led his I Company on the battalion's right flank to try to form a line along the hill's northern edge. The unit moved out at 6:35 a.m. from Hill 54 with its platoons forming a line and advanced along the edge of the woods on the Galloping Horse northern boundary. The Japanese soon poured a crossfire upon Johnson's men from machine guns and mortars on Hill 52 to their left and rifle fire from the woods to their right. Johnson positioned one of his platoons on his right flank as the rest of the company set up a line of fire on a slight ridge about 200 yards to Hill 54's southwest. I Company got ready to attack Hill 52. As mortar and artillery fire pounded the Japanese defenses, the company stormed the Japanese. Nonetheless, the Japanese returned withering machine gun and rifle fire and stopped the American advance again 200 yards from the hill's summit. Capt. Johnson asked for help at 9:30 a.m. The 3rd Battalion's attempts using two companies to doubly surround the Japanese from the north and south had failed.

Bush ordered Capt. Ben F. Ferguson's K Company to advance west past I Company to get nearer to Hill 52. Again, Japanese machine gun and mortar fire impeded the company's progress as it advanced 900 yards from its jumping-off point on Hill 54. K Company occupied Hill 52's northern slopes by 1:00 p.m. and continued to advance, Meanwhile, American mortars kept firing their shells at the Japanese on Hill 52.

Col. Bush finalized his plan to capture or at least neutralize Hill 52. I Company, holding its position, would attack from the northeast as K Company, along with one of L Company's rifle platoons and one of M Company's machine gun platoons, enveloped the hill's north. Now holding Hill 51 with one platoon, L Company would be kept in reserve. Artillery, mortar, and antitank gun fire would support the attack. As the attacking troops moved into their attacking positions by 2:00 p.m., despite Japanese fire coming into the battalion's command post on Hill 54, Bush knew his units' precise location. A forward observer ordered the artillery barrage to begin but a communications failure delayed the bombardment one-half hour.

As Col. McCulloch witnessed the 3rd Battalion's attack slow to a crawl, he asked his air support officer to meet with Col. Bush on Hill 54. Bush showed the air support officer where the best targets were on the Galloping Horse. The bombing attack would begin at 3:00 p.m. if the 3rd Battalion's K Company had not yet taken Hill 52. The artillery would place a smoke shell on the hill to show where the pilots should drop their bombs. The aircraft circled overhead at 2:30 p.m. with the artillery ready to fire their smoke marker shells. If the planes began their bombing missions, K Company would have to pull back from their positions so as to not to be exposed to any short-falling bombs. Bush decided to order the bombing mission instead of another assault at that time since that fit the American strategy to use machines instead of men to do what was needed.

The planes attacked and this time accurately placed their bombs and depth charges on target. All the depth charges hit the reverse slopes with four charges hitting their targets while two of them failed to detonate. As soon as the planes finished their attack, the four 105-mm howitzer battalions fired a 20-minute barrage followed by a bombardment of 37-mm mortars in support of a synchronized infantry attack.

K Company returned to its former position on the northern slopes. With one of L Company's platoons attacking in the gap between K and I companies with the artillery and mortar pouring fire into the Japanese positions, the American soldiers crept on their bellies toward the hill summit. They fixed bayonets, leapt to their feet, rushed the Japanese, and successfully captured Hill 52. The 3rd Battalion finished off the remaining Japanese strong points by 4:35 p.m., captured six machine guns that had not been destroyed during the attack, killed 30 Japanese, and locked up American possession of this critical objective. The 3rd Battalion's soldiers had executed a difficult series of assaults and badly needed some rest. They set up defensive perimeters and took the day off from any more combat.

The 25th Division's first day on the attack had been a successful one as they conducted the most impressive ground offensive since the 1st Marines took Henderson Field. Supported by highly accurate and destructive artillery fire and air support, its 1st and 3rd Battalions, despite tough and dogged Japanese resistance, had pressed forward 1,600 yards nearer to its objectives and took Hills 50, 51, and 52. More than half of Galloping Horse now had American soldiers in control of it. Several of the 1st Battalion's patrols reached Hill 52 and contacted the 3rd Battalion while Col. Mitchell's 2nd Battalion took possession of the area covered by Hills 50-51 and joined up with the 3rd Battalion, 27th Infantry and the 3rd Battalion, 182nd Infantry. The Americans took light casualties while not having to commit the 161st Infantry, which was the 25th Division reserve. At sunset on January 10, the 27th Infantry got ready to finish the job they had begun. That effort would start when morning broke over the jungles, ravines, canyons, and hills of Guadalcanal the next day.

When the 27th Infantry fought its battle to take about half of Galloping Horse on January 10, the oppressive tropical heat placed a severe strain on the American ability to supply enough water to their men fighting the battle. While streams and rivers are not in plentiful supply in the Solomon Islands, the area around the Galloping Horse had no water nearby from which the soldiers could replenish their thirst other than from the water they carried with them. There was plentiful water near Hill 55, and the Regiment's supply officer arranged to bring drinking water to the troops at the front. However, the rear echelons reallocated the water to other units so that not much water actually reached the men who needed it the most. Col. Bush wanted to begin his battalion's attack as soon as there was enough light, but had to delay the assault on January 11 until 9:00 a.m. to make sure his men had the water they badly needed. But he dared not wait much longer and ordered his men to attack with just the water they had left in their canteens from the previous day.

His plan included two coordinated attacks using K, I, and L Companies following an artillery barrage with I and L Companies attacking abreast. I Company began the first attack by moving along the Galloping Horse's southern ridge with the deep ravine on its left and made their assault to the southwest over the first ridge (Exton Ridge) west of Hill 52 to the next ridge (Sims Ridge) about 200 yards away from their jump off point as one of its platoons protected the company's rear and left flank. K Company would initially follow behind I Company, pass it on Sims Ridge, and capture Hill 53 about 850 yards southwest of Hill 52. L Company would launch the second attack by advancing to the northwest from Hill 52 to a place on Hill 57 inside the 3rd Battalion's zone, contact the 1st Battalion, attack southward, and clear the woods of any Japanese opposition between Hills 57 and 53 and contact K and I Companies. M Company would supply one machine gun platoon to each company with its 81-mm mortars staying on Hill 54 to provide fire support. To facilitate bringing water to his attacking troops, Bush assigned 11 men from his headquarters and M Company to carry water to them.

The artillery opened their barrage before the two companies leading the assault moved out. I Company's lead platoon found a narrow passage west of Hill 52 with the rest of the company right behind them. The constricting bottleneck gave the Japanese a perfect opportunity to punish the approaching American soldiers and they wasted no time when they poured a withering barrage of mortars, machine gun, and rifle fire on the now-stalled American attackers. Capt. Johnson, the company commander, asked desperately for mortar and artillery fire to silence the Japanese guns. The men of I Company could not move forward or begin flanking movements because of the severely confining space in which they were trapped. The Japanese mortar fire poured down on them as their unslaked thirst caused about 30 men to collapse under the searing heat of the unrelenting sun above their heads. By the time the sun reached its zenith, all save ten men in one platoon lay unconscious. Among the wounded by Japanese mortar fire one hour later, Capt. Johnson had to be evacuated to the rear.

L Company had no more success in its attack than I Company did. The leading and the attached machine gun platoons moved along the bottom of the ravine north of Hill 52 to protect L Company's right flank. They turned west, moved toward Hill 57, and turned left to climb its southeastern slopes. As they advanced, the Japanese opened up with their now characteristically formidable machine gun fire on the American rear and sides and forced the advancing soldiers to stop in their tracks. By the time darkness began to descend on Guadalcanal, neither American platoon could reach their battalion by either radio or runners and had no choice but to return to Hill 52—the place they had begun their attack. While the rest of L Company did not advance, they made some progress by setting up their positions behind I Company and could search for scattered Japanese riflemen that still occupied the jungle around them.

Bush realized before sunset that his battalion could not take its objectives this day. I Company's placement had proved impossible to hold. So, I and K Companies, along with the force attempting to capture Hill 57, halted and then retreated to Hill 52. Meanwhile, the Japanese continued to pummel the 3rd Battalion between 3:00 p.m. and 4:00 p.m. with punishing and accurate mortar fire, forcing the American soldiers to dive for whatever cover they could find. They could not begin preparing for defending against a possible Japanese counterattack until much later than planned that night. The Japanese made a half-hearted attempt later that evening, but the Americans turned them back.

The 27th Regiment's commander, Col. McCulloch, knew the 3rd Battalion had given its all and exhausted from their efforts over the last two days. He ordered it moved back to Hills 54 and into reserve status at Hill 55 the next day. The 2nd Battalion had been held in reserve, carried supplies to the forward areas, and ready for a combat assignment. He ordered it to take over the attack on January 12. The 3rd Battalion had begun earlier on January 11 against Hill 53 and the ridges in front of and around that hill. Meanwhile, the 1st Battalion from the 161st Infantry took up their positions in the Hill 50-51 area.

The 27th Infantry's second day's attacks had not reached their objectives and they were forced to turn back because of a vigorous Japanese defense. Col. Mitchell readied his 2nd Battalion for their assault the next day. Maybe their luck would be better than the 3rd Battalion's had been.

✲ ✲ ✲

Mitchell's plan for his attack to take Hill 53 and the part of Hill 57 for which he had the responsibility on January 12 involved the use of two companies to advance abreast from Hill 52 while keeping E Company in reserve. F Company would advance on the left and try to capture Hill 53 while G Company would advance on the right, take part of Hill 57, and join up with the 1st Battalion. H Company would provide nearby support from its heavy machine guns and 81-mm fortifications on Hill 52. Aerial and artillery barrages were to begin before the attack's scheduled start of 6:30 a.m. on January 12.

The two attacking companies began their advances on schedule from their positions on Hill 52 after an opening bombardment. G Company moved as planned on the right to the north and west. When the Japanese rifle fire came from the woods north of Hill 52, some of G Company's patrols found the interlopers and silenced them. More Japanese sent rifle fire from Sims Ridge to the north at G Company as the Americans continued advancing westward. Nevertheless, G Company attained its objective on January 12 and contacted the 1st Battalion, just as Mitchell had planned. But the rest of the 2nd Battalion's day was not proceeding as well.

F Company, with E Company to its rear, had far tougher Japanese opposition facing them, which forced them to stop their advance. Japanese machine guns covered all approaches of the two companies' attack from well-concealed and advantageously placed positions on Exton Ridge, Sims Ridge 200 yards to the west of Exton Ridge, Hill 53 southwest of Hill 52, the dense jungle north of Sims Ridge, and the shallow valleys between the two ridges. Another typical topographical feature of Guadalcanal, a steep cliff above the southwest fork of the Matanikau, along with the highly effective Japanese machine gun fire stopped the Americans from enveloping the Japanese from the south.

F Company attacked Exton Ridge but pushed too far to its right and exposed its left flank to a Japanese counterattack. The Japanese abandoned their positions on Exton Ridge. F Company quickly took it, but the Japanese fire kept them from advancing any closer to Hill 53. Mitchell had to order E Company to move along F Company's left flank to protect it, but the Japanese machine gun fire prevented them from moving past Exton Ridge. The Japanese machine guns firing from Sims Ridge made the Americans stop their attack. F Company tried to attack Sims Ridge southward but could only advance halfway up the ridge's northern slopes because of the intense Japanese fire from its western slope. E Company's attack on Exton Ridge became confused as some of its soldiers began to mingle with some of F Company's men.

To get closer to the two companies' advance and give them more effective support, M Company moved its heavy machine guns to Exton Ridge. Meanwhile, Capt. Charles W. Davis, the battalion's executive officer, Capt. Paul K. Mellichamp, and Lt. Weldon Sims used the concealment that the high grasses naturally provided and crawled on their bellies on the ridge's eastern side until they came upon a waist-high outcropping to search for the Japanese strong point. Lt. Sims stood up and openly exposed his upper body for everyone to see. A hail of Japanese machine gun fire opened up and mortally wounded him in the chest. Now dead, his companions manhandled his body to the 2nd Battalion's line.

When the Japanese killed Lt. Sims, they betrayed their approximate location and became the target for revenge by American machine guns and mortars. They opened fire as the infantry tried to again capture the Japanese position. Capt. Davis returned to the waist-high escarpment and began to radio firing coordinates to M Company's 81-mm mortars. The men of E and F Companies and he were less than 50 yards from the Japanese as exploding mortar shells poured into the hill and sent rock pieces, fragments, and dirt spraying into the air and falling all over the hill. But the firing was all for naught since the mortar fire failed to destroy the Japanese guns. They kept up their withering fire and held the American infantry glued to their positions.

Mitchell, unsatisfied with his battalion's progress, left his command post on Hill 52 to go where the battle roared. By this time, the Japanese and the Americans were close enough to each other to throw hand grenades. He decided not to continue the mortar barrage because it could accidentally hit his own men. As darkness approached, E & F Companies were about halfway to their objectives and could advance no farther. Both companies no longer had any drinking water. The men lay exhausted—totally spent from their day's exertions. After digging into defensive positions, the men and their commander spent the night together on the Sims Ridge northern slopes. The battalion's executive officer remained at the command post with the authority to act in Mitchell's behalf if necessary.

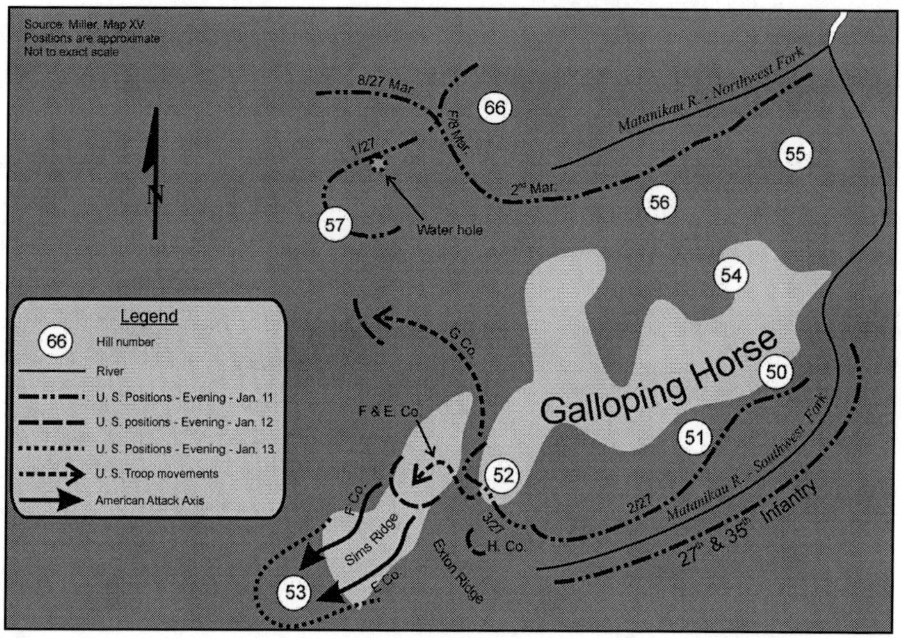

Capturing Hills 53 and 57—January 12-13

The 8th Field Artillery Battalion had fired 17 barrages that day as requested by Col. Mitchell. They and their other artillery and mortar brethren modified their targeting in preparation for the next day's battles. While the Japanese did not attack the entrenched Americans on Sims Ridge, they did cut the American telephone lines to Hill 52. As darkness came over the jungle like a shroud, nervous, combat inexperienced American soldiers blindly fired their rifles at the Japanese throughout the night.

The struggle to take Galloping Horse now entered its fourth day. Maybe this day would bring an end to the battle. Japanese would probably continue their valiant and vigorous defense or die trying.

☆ ☆ ☆

Mitchell's attack plan for January 13 was a simple one. E Company would continue attacking against Sims Ridge from the north while F Company would pull back from the ridge, move along a hidden path the Japanese could not see that was between the jungle and Galloping Horse's neck, and assault Hill 53's northern end. H Company would remain on Hill 52 and continue to use their positions on Hill 52 and Exton Ridge. He hoped this time it would end in success.

When E Company attacked on schedule, intensely effective Japanese machine gun fire poured down from strongly dug-in nests and again stopped the American advance. Six F Company soldiers volunteered to help their comrades by circling around the firing Japanese machine guns and came within 25 yards of their quarry. Some of the Japanese guns fired at the six Americans and killed two of them. The four survivors had no choice but to abandon their mission and return to their company.

The American 60-mm mortars could not fire at the Japanese guns because the Americans on Sims Ridge were too close to their tormentors. When the E and F Companies' 60-mm mortars tried to lob their shells from Sims Ridge onto the Japanese positions, the Japanese were too high and too close for the American mortars to hit them. The mortar men tilted their tubes to a nearly vertical elevation but still could not hit their targets. Mitchell, as ever concerned about the safety of his men, did not want to take such unwarranted risks and ordered the mortars to stop their firing.

With his battalion and the Japanese now caught in a seemingly unbreakable standoff, Col. Mitchell and Capt. Davis, his executive officer, came up with a new plan to shatter the impasse. Mitchell led part of E Company down Sims Ridge's eastern slope to a place directly east of the Japanese positions. Davis along with the four F Company survivors of the previous try to get near the Japanese guns crept and twisted down the ridge's western slope through the thick grass and got quite near to the Japanese. They were to get close enough to the Japanese to lob their grenades and planned to do just that as a prelude for Mitchell's men to attack after Davis blew his whistle.

When Davis and his men were just five yards from the Japanese, the plan almost went awry when the Japanese lobbed their grenades at Davis' detachment. Fortunately, while their missiles landed right where they should have, they all failed to explode. The five Americans immediately threw eight grenades that detonated, got to their feet, and rushed the Japanese positions just as several of the Japanese tried to escape. Davis' rifle jammed after firing one round, so he drew his pistol and began firing. The five men were now among the Japanese, firing their rifles, throwing their grenades, killing the Japanese where they stood. The men of E Company saw the attack. Gen. Collins was also a witness and ordered the mortars on hill 52 to open fire. E Company got to their feet, and charged uphill at the Japanese. When they finished, not a single Japanese soldier was left alive. For his leadership and valor, Capt. Davis received the Medal of Honor. His citation explains what he did and what it meant:

> "For distinguishing himself conspicuously by gallantry and intrepidity at the risk of his life above and beyond the call of duty in action with the enemy on Guadalcanal Island. On 12 January 1943, Maj. Davis (then Capt.), executive officer of an infantry battalion, volunteered to carry instructions to the leading companies of his battalion which had been caught in crossfire from Japanese machine guns. With complete disregard for his own safety, he made his way to the trapped units, delivered the instructions, supervised their execution, and remained overnight in this exposed position. On the following day, Maj. Davis again vol-

> unteered to lead an assault on the Japanese position which was holding up the advance. When his rifle jammed at its first shot, he drew his pistol and, waving his men on, led the assault over the top of the hill. Electrified by this action, another body of soldiers followed and seized the hill. The capture of this position broke Japanese resistance and the battalion was then able to proceed and secure the corps' objective. The courage and leadership displayed by Maj. Davis inspired the entire battalion and unquestionably led to the success of its attack."[2]

The men of the 2nd Battalion experienced the same unslaked thirst as did their comrades of the 3rd, which might have partially caused their attack to come to a standstill. In my opinion, the returning Japanese gunfire undoubtedly made the major contribution to the American problems. Nonetheless, as if divine providence apparently intervened, not much time passed after E Company captured the Japanese positions on Sims Ridge when the heavens opened up, dumped heavy rain, soaked the ground around the American soldiers, and gave the Americans a brief respite from their need for water.

As F Company continued advancing along their hidden route, three field artillery battalions opened fire on Hill 53. As soon as the artillery barrage ended and to take advantage of the shock of the devastating artillery attack, E and F Companies assaulted Hill 53. E Company moved south and west of Sims Ridge to capture the high ground at the top of the Galloping Horse's head. Meanwhile, F Company came out of the jungle north of the Horse's head and completely surprised the Japanese, who still reeled from the brutal American artillery shelling. When the two companies advanced on the Japanese position, they found no organized Japanese opposition. The 2nd Battalion captured all of Hill 53 by noon. The gallant battalion reached the division's objective in that zone and more than satisfactorily fulfilled its mission.

The attack destroyed all opposition on the Galloping Horse. E Company obliterated a Japanese 70-mm gun and captured several rifles, grenade launchers, machine guns, and ammunition. During the 2nd Battalion's two days of action, it lost two officers and 29 enlisted men killed while taking out approximately 170 Japanese soldiers who belonged to the 3rd Division's 228th and 230th Infantry Regiments. When the Americans examined the Japanese dead, they found a few of the dead wore good clothes, but the majority of the deceased Japanese were poorly dressed and near starvation.

Meanwhile, on January 12, G Company made contact with the 1st Battalion on Hill 57 and sent a patrol to protect the dense jungle undergrowth area between Hills 53 and 57.

As night came on January 13, the Americans had advanced their lines 4,500 yards south of Point Cruz over Hill 66 to Hills 57 and 53. The 27th Infantry Regiment had achieved all its objectives, isolated the Japanese into the narrow gorges between the hills, firmly entrenched themselves on the Galloping Horse, and waited for the 35th Infantry to make their longer march southward and take the division's southern objective. While the 161st fought some difficult battles from January 15 to January 22 and destroyed all Japanese opposition south of the Galloping Horse along the canyon of the Matanikau's southwestern fork, the 27th fought no more major actions. They took out remaining and isolated Japanese soldiers, built up their defenses and roads, and sent out patrols to the west to ready themselves for the next fight.

Now, the attention of American offensive action shifted to the coastal road where the 2nd Marine Division waited for the Army to capture the Galloping Horse and secure their southern flank. They were ready to make their initial contribution to the American efforts to begin removing remaining Japanese opposition on Guadalcanal.

Securing the Coastal Road

While the American Army 25th Division attacked the Galloping Horse on January 11-13 to the south of where the 2nd Marine Division held their positions, Gen. Patch ordered the Marines on January 12 to begin their first major full divisional offensive since arriving on Guadalcanal. The 25th Division had secured the Marine southern flank so that the Marines could now attack westward along a north-south line running from Point Cruz to Hill 66. The Americal and 2nd Marine Division artillery and the 2nd MAW would support the Marine ground operations.

However, the 6th Marine Regiment, which had landed on Guadalcanal on January 4, 1943, was the only unit in the division that had fresh troops for the attack. The 2nd Marine Regiment had been on Guadalcanal for more than five months since August 7, 1942, and badly needed to be relieved. The 8th Marines had landed in November 1942 and had been engaged in several combat operations since that time. The 2nd and 8th Marines had relieved the even more weary 182nd and 164th Regiments west of the Matanikau River. The 6th Marines began relieving the 2nd and 8th Marines in January while these units attacked the Japanese. The 2nd Marines attacked the Japanese on January 13 and then withdrew behind the Lunga River after it had finished on January 14. Meanwhile, the 8th Marines were engaged in combat until January 17.

The Japanese soldiers of their 2nd Division had erected formidable defenses along the coastal corridor with the most powerful fortifications in the heavily forested ravine to the immediate west of the Hill 66-Point Cruz line. Just as in the November and December American attacks, the Japanese machine guns could cascade crippling fire on any attacking American troops moving into those steep sided canyons.

The places where the Japanese were the strongest influenced the American tactics for their next attack. Consecutive echelons of Americans would attack from left to right. The units on the left would advance, destroy the Japanese defenses at the ravines' head, and make maneuvering room for the units on the right.

The 2nd Marines opened the attack at 5:00 a.m. on January 13. The regiment advanced 800 yards west from Hill 66 by 7:30 a.m. while losing six men killed and 61 wounded. The 5th Marines relieved the 2nd by noon.

The 8th Marines launched their attack ten minutes after the 2nd began theirs. They advanced from the Hills 80 and 81's eastern sides on the 2nd Marines' right with a gulch to their west. As before, withering Japanese machine gun, rifle, and mortar fire stopped the Americans. As the day ended, the pattern of the prior days' American attacks emerged once again. The 8th Marines' advance slowed to a halt due to the Japanese' aggressive and highly effective defense. Nonetheless, the 2nd Marines' advance moved forward. When the 8th Marines attacked once more on January 14, the result was the same: the withering Japanese fire stymied the Americans.

When the 8th Marines' tanks attacked on January 15, their success could only be generously categorized as marginal. Later that afternoon, the Americans brought a flamethrower forward and began to use, for the first time on Guadalcanal, the weapon that had proven to be highly effective against entrenched defenses ever since World War I. The flamethrower two-man team scorched the Japanese defenses in just ten minutes and repeated the same success against two more fortifications later that day.

As darkness ended the daylight hours of January 17, the 8th Marines had eliminated Japanese opposition at the head of the ravine with the 6th Marines to their left. After five days of battling the Japanese from January 13 through 18, the 2nd Marine Division had moved forward about 1,500 yards and reported killing 643 Japanese while capturing two POWs, 41 grenade launchers, 57 light and 14 heavy machine guns, three 75-mm guns, and many small arms, mines, and pieces of artillery ammunition.

When the 8th Marines withdrew from their positions on January 18, the Americans occupied an unbroken line from Hill 53 to Guadalcanal's northern coastline at a point 1,500 yards west of Point Cruz. The American ground forces on Guadalcanal were now in the position to begin their drive up Guadalcanal's western side with the town of Kokumbona as their first primary objective. That offensive would begin just as the 35th Infantry finished taking Mount Austen.[3]

CHAPTER 57
Sealing the Southern Flank

While the 27th Infantry enjoyed success in its efforts capturing the Galloping Horse, the 25th Division's 35th Infantry continued its intense offensive ground operations in and around Mount Austen and in the rough and heavily overgrown terrain south of the Matanikau River's southeastern fork. Other than the open hills captured by the 132nd Infantry, the only open ground in the sector was a hilly area with Hill 44 to the north and Hill 43 to the south. It lay about 1,500 yards northwest of Hill 27 and about 1,500 yards east of the 25th Division's objective line. When viewing this hilly ground from the air, it resembled a sea horse, and so the Americans gave it that name, the Sea Horse.

If the Americans could occupy the Sea Horse and capture the Gifu, their southern flank would be protected from any Japanese counterattacks from the south. Capturing the Sea Horse would also keep the Japanese from crossing the Matanikau River. The 35th Infantry commander, Col. McClure, planned to capture the Sea Horse first and then advance to the division's objective line. Meanwhile, McClure's 2nd Battalion would relieve the 132nd Battalion as planned and attempt to eliminate stubborn Japanese resistance in the Gifu.

Like the Galloping Horse, the regiment's first objective had a similar geography with river forks isolating the formation, deep ravines, and nearly impenetrable jungle. Therefore, the Americans knew what terrain they had to overcome. The regiment received reinforcements when the 3rd Battalion of the 182nd Infantry commanded by Lt. Col. Roy F. Goggin and the 25th Division's Cavalry Reconnaissance Troop joined the regiment's ranks.

McClure ordered the 2nd Battalion and the Reconnaissance Troop to relieve the 132nd surrounding the Gifu, attack the Japanese positions in that perimeter, and remain in contact with Goggin's battalion on their right. Lt. Col. William J. Mullen, Jr.'s 3rd Battalion of the 35th Infantry received orders to advance to the southwest of Hill 27 and south of the Gifu, turn northward, and capture Hills 43 and 44. The regiment's 1st Battalion, commanded by Lt. Col. James B. Leer, being held in reserve, would follow a half day's march behind the 3rd Battalion. The 3rd Battalion, 182nd Infantry would move southward from Hill 66, block the river gorge and canyon between Hills 31 and 43, and protect the division's artillery positions north of Mount Austen. If the 35th Infantry's attacks succeeded, they would trap the Japanese forces within the Gifu perimeter and between that encirclement and the Sea Horse. From there, the Americans could destroy the Japanese Army in that region at will.

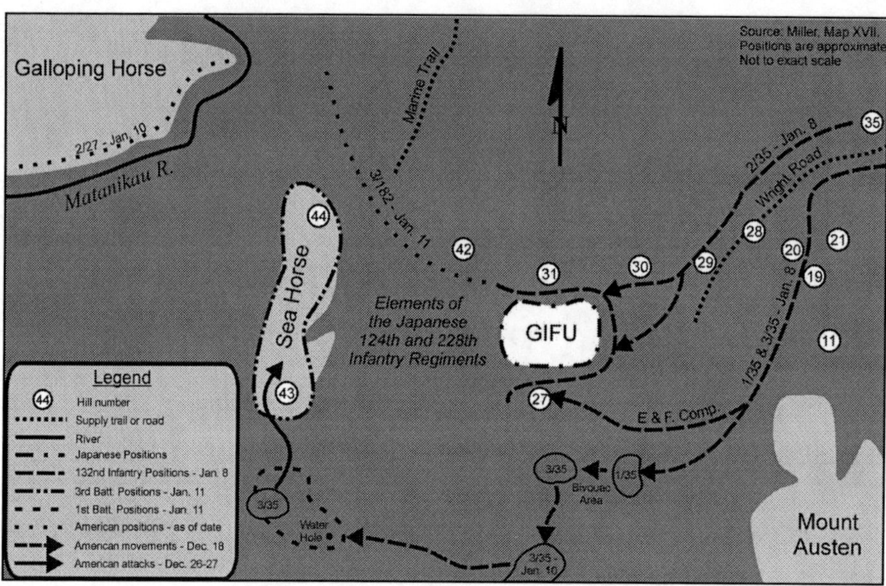

Attacking the Sea Horse

The Wright Road, which could barely accommodate Jeeps, ran up from the coastal road and was the primary means of supplying Americans in and around Mount Austen. It had been lengthened to a point east of the 132nd's Gifu easternmost line. The Marine Trail, similar to the Wright Road in that it barely allowed Jeeps on it, ran along the Matanikau River's eastern bank. Unfortunately, there were no roads or trails connecting the two. Therefore, any supplies meant for American soldiers or marines between them had to be hand-carried.

When the Americans built the Wright Road, its original intent was to supply just McClure's four battalions. Since the Japanese had no tanks in that part of Guadalcanal, there was no need to bring the 35th Infantry's Antitank and Cannon companies to the forward combat areas. So these soldiers and about 300 native bearers would carry supplies from the end of Wright Road to the front lines. As the American lines advanced southward, supplies would be floated down the Matanikau River via pole- and motor-driven barges and boats between Hill 50 and the river's mouth. The innovative soldiers built two barges from captured gasoline drums, effectively used captured Japanese boats, and created a successful operating supply line with the nickname "Pusha Maru."

Taking the Sea Horse

On January 7, the 35th Infantry moved westward from the Lunga defensive perimeter. The next day, the regiment marched in a column of battalions on the Wright Road to Mount Austen with the 3rd Battalion leading the way. As the 2nd Battalion moved toward the Gifu, the 3rd Battalion, with the 1st Battalion trailing behind, moved south and then west through the dense jungle undergrowth south of the Gifu perimeter. As daylight began to fade, they set up a bivouac on a ridge about 700 yards south of Hill 27 for the night of January 8-9. The battalions' mortar companies stayed near the Gifu while the two battalions brought their light machine guns with them as they moved out in the early morning hours of January 9.

Slippery ground slowed their progress when they neared the place from where they would launch their attack on the Sea Horse. The need for surprise was critical for their attack to succeed. Therefore, they moved stealthily through the jungle and would have no preliminary artillery or aerial bombardment before their planned attack, scheduled for 6:35 a.m. on January 10.

When Col. Mullen looked westward from his battalion's camp, he saw a small wooded rise just south of Hill 43. He had aerial photographs of it and personally had seen a small ridge between the wooded area and Hill 43. The ridge offered an ideal path over which the 3rd Battalion could attack the Sea Horse from the south. But his men had to capture that ridge first.

As the 27th began its attack on schedule, the 3rd Battalion started its attack. To mislead the Japanese about the impending attack, Mullen ordered his I Company to stay in reserve around the bivouac area as the attacking K and L companies met in the dense woods before launching their assault. The two companies were in position by 8:00 a.m. and ready to begin. Using intelligence gathered by patrols sent out the previous night, the battalion thrust southwestward through the undergrowth and turned north toward the Sea Horse. K Company led the way and used their machetes and bayonets to cut a 1,000-yard-long trail. The path ended at a low point along a creek that flowed into the Matanikau River. They reached a small knoll at noon about 700 yards southeast of Hill 43. They were now unfortunately at the bottom of a steep ravine with high bluffs on both sides.

They had turned northward too soon and were still southeast, not southwest, of Hill 43. They still had to move westward to reach their planned starting point before attacking the Sea Horse. Steep ravines and a roiling tributary of the Matanikau River lay astride their intended line of march. Mullen sent out patrols; one found a barely visible trail over which they could move.

Giving up the idea of surprising the Japanese, the 35th Infantry asked for artillery fire to be directed onto the Sea Horse. Mullen ordered K Company to advance over the newly found trail and L Company over an old trail to K Company's left flank. He also ordered I Company, relieved by the 1st Battalion, to follow K Company over the best route it could find. Mullen wanted desperately to reach high ground before dark to provide the most secure position for his battalion. He gave an order to attack.

K Company turned westward while having two of M Company's light machine guns and a few riflemen take a covering position on a nearby knoll to face to the northeast and protect its right flank. As K Company crossed a branch of the Matanikau River, some Japanese attacked the advancing Americans from the southeast farther up the river. They almost succeeded in breaking up the American assault by attacking the Americans' right flank.

K Company caught a Japanese supply squad totally by surprise near a water hole where two trails met, killed seven of them, and scattered the rest. By this time, all the attacking companies were just south of Hill 43 from where they turned northward. They were in the right place to attack and capture an intermediate objective—a hill covered with wooded vegetation south of the objective hill. Just a few Japanese soldiers stood in the Americans' way and this allowed the Americans to advance virtually unopposed. Both K and L Companies occupied the high ground 400 yards south of Hill 43 by 5:00 p.m. after advancing faster than planned. Since it was near dark, they stopped their advance and dug foxholes.

As the 3rd Battalion advanced toward the Sea Horse, Col. Leer's 1st Battalion, still in reserve, moved westward while it's A and C Companies sent out patrols to cover both of their flanks. Platoons from its B and D Companies relieved I Company at the water hole in a gully about 600 yards south of Hill 43.

☆ ☆ ☆

Mullen's battalion wasted no time attacking the Sea Horse at dawn on January 11. K Company led the way as it assaulted northward along the ridge toward Hill 43, L Company covered its left flank, and I Company followed in reserve. The Japanese machine guns immediately opened a withering fire on the attackers and slowed their advance. As the Americans got near them, the Japanese gunners pulled back to new positions. K Company gained just 100 yards in an hour of fighting. Nevertheless, the American attack picked up speed later that afternoon when the 3rd Battalion rushed out of the jungle, kicked the Japanese off Hill 43, and, by 6:31 p.m., moved to Hill 44.

Leer's 1st Battalion came up to reinforce the 3rd Battalion when their attack bogged down. Nonetheless, when the 3rd Battalion moved so rapidly to clear any opposition from Hill 43, the 1st Battalion knew their comrades did not need their help. McClure ordered the 1st Battalion to relieve I and L Companies in the southern and southwestern woods on the hill. The two companies could now join their other 3rd Battalion compatriots in the battle to capture the Sea Horse. As night came on January 11, the 3rd Battalion had totally surrounded the Gifu perimeter and forged ahead 1,500 yards west of the Sea Horse—halfway toward the 25th Division's objective line.

The 1st and 3rd Battalion southerly advance around the Japanese right flank covered more than 7,000 yards. They had moved over Mount Austen's ridges and canyons, down that mountain's western slopes to the Matanikau River, and climbed up the Sea Horse. The narrow trails over which they traveled could only be traversed by soldiers on foot. The two battalions' rapid advance was so fast that the native bearers attempting to bring supplies forward to them could not overtake the soldiers.

A severe supply problem resulted that could only be solved when the supplier's base camp could be moved closer to where the soldiers were farther up the Matanikau River. Until that happened and the "Pusha Maru" supply-line of boats reestablished, B-17s were the only way the soldiers could be kept supplied. Since some supplies weighed too much to be dropped by parachutes, these heavier objects had to be wrapped in burlap or canvas and dropped from the low flying bombers. But these planes performed well in this task as one B-17 dropped 7,000 pounds in four flights on January 13 and dropped another four tons two days later. The food rations survived the drops, with 85% of it edible, but the ammunition fared less well, with only 155 tons that could be used after being dropped. The drops destroyed almost all the five-gallon water cans deposited by the air supply efforts. It would not be until January 17 when regular ground supplies resumed. The Pusha Maru brought the supplies to the foot of Hill 50. From there, the native bearers hand-carried the materiel to Hill 44's northern sides.

☆ ☆ ☆

The 1st Battalion took over the remainder of the offensive on January 13 when C Company moved from the Sea Horse and advanced westward toward the division's objective line. Japanese gunfire again stopped the Americans. Meanwhile, the 64th Field Artillery Battalion refined their targeting of Japanese positions. Col. Leer also asked for some of the regimental mortars on Mount Austen to be moved forward to Hill 43. The Japanese again stopped the next day's attack as the rough terrain prevented the mortars moving to Hill 43 until later that afternoon.

Leer ordered his B Company to relieve C Company and resume the attack on January 15. At 10:05 a.m., the 64th Field Artillery Battalion opened fire with a 30-minute, 553-round barrage at the Japanese. As soon they finished their work, the battalion's mortars and machine guns joined the party. B Company along with one platoon from D company stepped off as soon as the artillery finished, moved around the Japanese right flank, and attacked their rear. That maneuver broke the back of the Japanese defense and destroyed a Japanese platoon. B Company captured 12 Japanese soldiers and killed 13 others. One thousand men could have occupied the space where the Americans found just a platoon. The Japanese had no food, and six of the prisoners could hardly walk. The Americans discovered 78 Japanese graves. B Company had done their job and rested for the night.

The 1st Battalion had eliminated all Japanese opposition from the area between Hill 43 and the objective line. On January 16, B Company and one of D Company's platoons moved out and reached a cliff overlooking the Matanikau River southwestern fork. The dense jungle kept the Americans from determining their position. After building smoky fires and firing flares on January 18, the 25th Division's staff could pinpoint the 1st Battalion's precise position.

The 1st and 3rd Battalions' capture of the Sea Horse and movement toward the Matanikau River had killed 558 Japanese soldiers while capturing 17 POWs. The 35th Infantry Regiment moved to the objective line toward the 27th Infantry's left (southern) flank.

Taking the Gifu Perimeter

All of the 25th Division except for Lt. Col. Ernest Peters' the 2nd Battalion, 35th Infantry had participated in the drive to the division's objective line. The 132nd infantry had tried to remove the Japanese in the Gifu perimeter in December but did not succeed because of the ferocity of their opponents' defense. Instead, the unenviable task of eliminating the heavily entrenched Japanese soldiers occupying that enclave now fell upon the 35th Infantry's 2nd Battalion.

✲ ✲ ✲

After marching from its place east of the Lunga River on January 7, The 2nd Battalion moved toward the 132nd Infantry's lines around the Gifu the next morning. Its headquarters, G, and H Companies advanced past the 132nd's lines. The battalion's E and F Companies had a much tougher time slogging through the dense jungle. The five companies followed the 3rd Battalion to a place about 800 yards southeast of Hill 27 and turned northeast toward the hill. The trail they followed was muddy and slippery, so the men had to use telephone wires to pull themselves along the slick path. They reached Hill 27's southeastern slopes the evening of December 8 and set up their camp.

The 2nd Battalion and the Cavalry Reconnaissance Troop fully relieved the 132nd Infantry on December 9. The exhausted regiment finally received their much deserved rest when it moved to the calmer rear east of the Lunga River. As nightfall came, the 2nd Battalion occupied positions along a

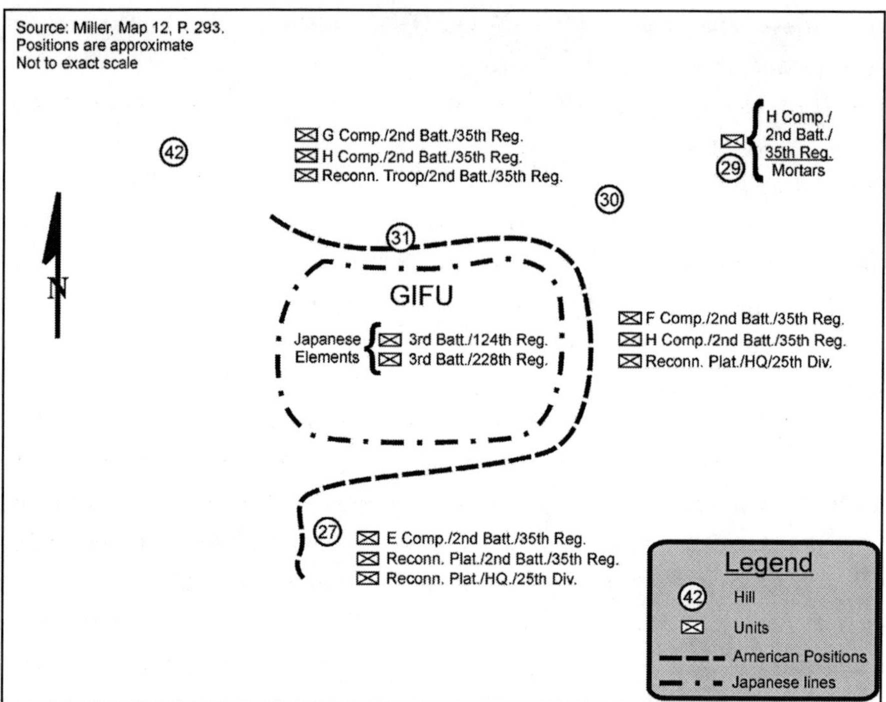

American and Japanese Positions around the Gifu

2,000-yard line stretching from Hill 31 to Hill 27. E Company, the 35th Infantry's Reconnaissance Platoon, and a platoon from the 25th Division's Reconnaissance Troop were now on Hill 27. F Company, platoons from H Company, and the Reconnaissance Troop held the center of the 2nd Battalion's line on the perimeter's east. G Company, other platoons from H Company, and other units from the Reconnaissance Troop occupied Hill 31. H Company's mortars set up their firing position on Hill 29.

The rest of the battalion Headquarters Company soldiers not assigned to combat duties had the responsibility to carry supplies from the end of Wright Road to the American soldiers engaged in combat. There was no one in the 2nd Battalion being held in reserve. Meanwhile, the Japanese could not help but see the American soldiers moving near them and opened up with sporadic rifle and mortar fire. The battalion now guessed the Japanese had more than 100 rifles and 10 machine guns. Night arrived on January 9, and an uneasy calm permeated the darkness.

Gen. Collins and Col. McClure initially wanted to encircle the Gifu from Hill 27 and Hill 31's western side but believed that feat could not be accomplished because of the difficult terrain. They settled instead for a frontal attack to keep the Japanese from escaping the Gifu pocket while the 3rd and 1st Battalions attacked to the west. As it turned out, more time and lives might have been saved if they had stuck to their original plan.

When the rest of the 25th Division began its westward attack on January 10, the 2nd Battalion's companies each sent out two reconnoitering patrols after the artillery and mortars fired on the Gifu. The Japanese saw them coming and, as before, sent heavy gunfire blocking the Americans' way. Peters then asked for tanks to be moved forward to Mount Austen to destroy the Japanese pillboxes. However, the only tanks in the area belonged to the Marines and could not respond. After the patrols finished their reconnaissance, the battalion estimated there were 400 Japanese soldiers and 20 machine guns in the Gifu.

The next day, January 11, more American patrols tried to penetrate the Japanese lines, but more withering rifle and machine gun fire stopped them. Meanwhile, the 25th Division's attack began to yield positive results as its battalions surrounded the Gifu. Col. Oka's men, who had valiantly defended their positions since December, were trapped, starving, and vowed to fight to the death. True to their *bushido* code, they would never surrender.

Despite all of the 2nd Battalion patrolling activity, only a few Japanese pillbox locations had been found. Of course, the thick jungle, the excellent Japanese camouflage, and the withering Japanese gun fire did not help American reconnaissance activity. After the 132nd Infantry showed the locations of two pillboxes to their successor 35th Infantry relief, F Company from the 2nd Battalion sent out a patrol on January 10 to find the emplacements. But they could not locate anything after being forced to turn back again because of heavy Japanese machine gun fire. Another patrol sent out the same day from E Company destroyed one machine gun nest but had to back off because of exploding Japanese grenades thrown at them. Another F Company patrol tried once more to find Japanese emplacements the next day in the afternoon, but stopped their advance because of returning Japanese gunfire from a pillbox just 25 yards from the American lines. However, men from the headquarters and F Companies used hand grenades to kill some Japanese soldiers in that fortification. January 13 was a quiet day despite fire from three Japanese fortifications, which forced another F Company patrol to retreat. All of the battalion's mortars released a barrage and demolished one pillbox. After three days of intensive reconnaissance work by American patrols, the 2nd Battalion learned almost nothing new about where the Japanese had placed their forces and how powerful they were, but the 2nd Battalion had other things to worry about.

The Americans were not yet at full strength because of illness caused by malaria and casualties from all the patrols the battalion dispatched. As of January 14, just 75% of the 2nd Battalion's men were ready for combat. The 35th Infantry's Antitank Company joined the battalion the same day to replace the losses and moved into the line between F and G Companies northeast of Hill 27.

Patrols from the 182nd Infantry's 3rd Battalion tried to locate the Japanese left flank the same day. The battalion's intelligence officer took two squads from I Company and three men from M Company to look for Japanese positions south of Hill 42. They climbed a small hill and saw parachutes and ammunition lying on the ground in front of them. The patrol began to return to their lines when some Japanese opened fire, killing the intelligence officer and one sergeant. The Americans fired back but accelerated their retreat to get out of harm's way. Another patrol returned to the place where the brief skirmish occurred but could only find the American bodies.

The Gifu perimeter on January 15 had not been altered since the 2nd Battalion arrived on the scene. Peters decided the time had come to attack and break the incredibility strong Japanese defenses. His battalion's mortars laid a 15-minute barrage on the Japanese positions on January 15 at 6:46 a.m., and the infantry began their assault. Nevertheless, not much time had passed when the attack bogged down when the well-entrenched Japanese opened fire. Most of the battalion hardly moved forward at all. G Company managed to advance 100 yards by 9:40 a.m. but had to stop. The American soldiers answered the Japanese gunfire with grenades and a flamethrower, but failed to remove them. The returning fire stopped G Company in its tracks and forced the company to rejoin the battalion and return to its lines.

Other attacks from the north met the same fate. The battalion's executive officer ordered a platoon that had sustained heavy casualties to move back. Due to a highly unfortunate communications failure, the order verbally passed from man to man, squad to squad, and platoon to platoon, thus causing the whole battalion to retreat to its original positions. The Americans had not made any progress at all against the Gifu thus far. Clearly, something had to change.

Col. McClure wasted no time taking action. He relieved Peters from his command of the 2nd Battalion on January 16 and ordered Lt. Col. Stanley R. Larsen to take over. As soon as Larsen arrived at the battalion's lines, he examined the Japanese defenses and correctly reckoned the Japanese lines facing him had heavily defended pillboxes along the eastern side of the perimeter that could pour devastating interlocking fields of fire. Any attempt to assault them would result in the slaughter of any attacking troops. The Japanese defenses could not be bypassed, and the Japanese intended to defend them to the last man. However, the Japanese had weaker defenses on the Gifu's western side with individual riflemen and machine gunners.

The situation for the Japanese defenders had not improved; it had drastically deteriorated. They had eaten their last meal between January 10 and 17. Col. Oka, the commander of the 124th Infantry, and his staff had apparently deserted his command around January 14, abandoned his command post near the Matanikau River, moved to relative safety near the coast, later sent orders for the remnants of his regiment to evacuate the Gifu, and move through the American lines to the coast. However, Maj. Takeyosho Inagaki's ravenously hungry men decided to stay at their posts, not desert their ill and wounded comrades, and do their duty for the Emperor.

McClure changed his mind from his original plan developed with Collins and decided to envelope the Gifu on the west. His plan was to have E Company move northward around the American lines from Hill 27 to Hill 42 and attack the Gifu's northwestern front on January 17 as other soldiers pushed northward from Hill 27. They had to traverse a deep canyon covered with dense, tangled vegetation northwest of Hill 27 that could prevent the full complement of men arriving at the jumping-off point for the attack. So the company had to go around all of the American positions before launching their assault. Meanwhile, McClure asked that every available piece of artillery be ready to bombard the Gifu as needed.

Collins hoped to avoid casualties on both sides by using psychological warfare to try to persuade as many Japanese as possible to surrender without bloodshed. Capt. John M. Burden from the Corps' intelligence section and several divisional intelligence officers installed a loudspeaker on Hill 44 on the afternoon of January 15. Burden wished to begin broadcasting in Japanese at 4:00 p.m. on the 15th to convince the Japanese soldiers to surrender peaceably. But a skirmish forced him to postpone his attempts for one hour and 15 minutes. His first try asked the Japanese to send an officer to Hill 44 to schedule the surrender. But darkness rapidly came, so Burden asked the Japanese at 6:15 p.m. to send the officer the next day. He repeated the broadcast at 6:00 a.m. the morning of January 16. After not receiving even a peep from the Japanese for two hours, Burden's broadcast asked the Japanese soldiers to disobey their officers and escape a certain death by giving up on their own. After some time passed, five scrawny Japanese soldiers came out of the jungle, told the Americans they and many of their comrades had lost all the courage to continue fighting. But those still in the jungle feared the Americans would kill them if they surrendered.

Since the smaller American mortars had not shown any ability to damage the Japanese fortifications and there were not enough heavier 81-mm mortars to do any appreciable damage, the division's artillery prepared a crippling barrage on the Gifu before the planned attack. When the 35th Infantry assaulted their objective, the 64th FAB had not placed much fire directly on the Gifu while also firing counter-barrages and harassing bombardments near Kokumbona. So, the American artillery had plenty of ammunition to clobber the Gifu perimeter.

This time, the Americans meant to exploit their overwhelming advantages in heavy caliber firepower with a crushing pounding before the assault began. With the Wright Road near their positions, the American guns could be reasonably assured of an adequate supply of ammunition to keep the barrage going for awhile. Two of the 105-mm howitzer batteries occupied two hill crests with an ideal position from which to destroy any heavier guns the Japanese might have left.

It had always been extremely difficult to get accurate targeting data on Guadalcanal because of the dense jungle where the Japanese hid. But this time the American artillery encircled the Gifu on high ground from where the American spotters could quite easily see the fall of shot inside the perimeter. The closest artillery observers came to within just 100 yards of the Japanese positions, thus placing them in mortal danger of being hit by any shells that might fall short of their intended targets.

When Col. McClure requested all available artillery to support his regiment's attack on the Gifu, Collins gave the 27th Regiment all the guns he could spare. The division placed all its 105-mm and 155-mm howitzers at McClure's disposal. The 64th FAB had an ideal position from which to direct the fire and therefore received that assignment. Soldiers ran direct telephone wires from the 64th's fire control position to all the rest of the artillery's command centers. A massive hailstorm of devastating artillery power was about to rain down on the outnumbered and outgunned Japanese in the Gifu perimeter.

Capt. Burden once again tried to get the Japanese to surrender peaceably on the morning of January 17. Loudspeakers set up from G Company's lines blared out a message that warned the Japanese soldiers that the bombardment would begin shortly and that they should escape almost certain death while they could. He repeated the broadcast from Hill 27 but a heavy downpour muffled the message volume. Despite a discussion about surrendering among the men of one Japanese company, not one Japanese soldier came forward.

The artillery wanted to zero in on their targets and adjust their fire accordingly in the early morning. But the American attempts to get the Japanese to surrender before the attack began delayed the artillery firing adjustments until noon when the division intelligence officer finally gave up. After the firing began, cries of "cease fire" came from the American positions that feared the shells fell too close for comfort to their own lines. Thus, the artillerymen had to individually adjust each howitzer, which greatly slowed that task. It took almost two hours to complete.

The thunderous American barrage began in earnest at 2:30 p.m. when the 49 howitzers fired for effect. More than 1,600 rounds landed and exploded into an area of less than 1,000 square yards. The battalion's mortars concentrated their fire into the places where the most artillery shells exploded. Men who put their heads down later related the explosions bombarded them with crushingly concussive noise. Japanese POWs captured later seemed genuinely shell-shocked. Nevertheless, the shelling's effectiveness was not as great as it could have been if the bombardment had begun in the early morning hours as planned.

The American soldiers who had pulled back to minimize the chances of being hit by "friendly" fire returned to their original lines at 4:30 p.m., but did not attack because of the high risk of attacking in the looming darkness over the rough terrain facing them. Therefore, the shock effect McClure wanted when he asked for the artillery bombardment was not as great as he wished. He decided not to ask for another barrage because it would take too much time to pull his men back and then bring them forward again after the barrage ended.

The attack began on January 18 when the I Company from the 182nd Infantry moved forward 450 yards southward from Hill 42 to contact G Company's platoon at about 5:00 p.m. as it attacked from Hill 27 and advanced through a ravine west of Hill 27. Meanwhile, E Company, which had followed I Company, 182nd Infantry, from Hill 42 turned left, to the east, and directly attacked the Gifu's western side. This time, the weaker Japanese opposition could not stop I Company from destroying three or four machine guns and killing seven Japanese soldiers. But other Japanese machine guns opened fire and forced the Americans to halt their advance. Moving to I Company's right, G Company's platoon found two pillboxes and called for 81-mm mortar fire that demolished one of them.

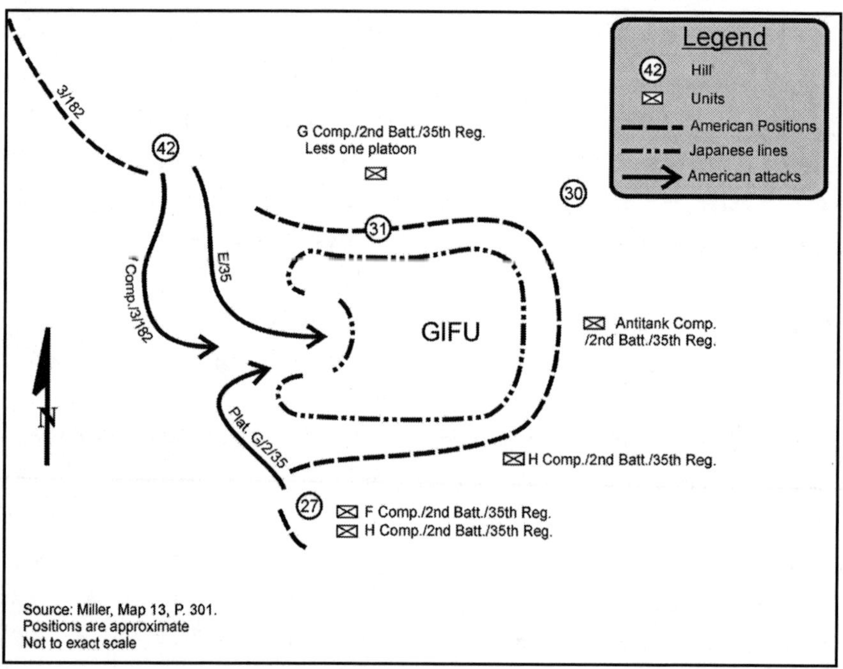

Breaking down the Gifu

E Company restarted its attack at 8:00 a.m. on January 19 but strong Japanese pillbox and machine gun defenses slowed the assault. One 37-mm antitank gun and an 81-mm mortar hit one pillbox that an F Company patrol had earlier found. G Company found 12 more pillboxes facing it as it advanced. E Company reported at 4:15 p.m. to have killed six Japanese soldiers, destroyed four machine guns, and also located 12 machine gun nests and pillboxes on a small rise. An additional report from E Company one hour later stated that it had wiped out three more emplacements, but could not advance any farther because of fire coming from a phalanx of nine pillboxes about 10 to 12 feet apart.

Heavy rainfall began on January 20 and made any movement over the now muddy ground more difficult than it had been. The 2nd Battalion could not exploit its previous day's successes.

The Americans finally began to crack the tough Japanese defenses in the Gifu by using one of the oldest military axioms—attack your opponent's weaker positions rather than at their strongest. While the Japanese made a fight of it, their resolve seemed to be softening and lines began to give way after being softened up by the American artillery and mortar fire. Some Japanese tried to escape. That act alone indicated to McClure that now was time to finish the job of eliminating the Gifu's threat to the American left flank.

✲ ✲ ✲

When the 2nd Battalion at last got tank support on January 21, three Marine light tanks that carried crews from the 25th Division's Cavalry Reconnaissance Troop moved along the Jeep trail toward Mount Austen's 1,514-feet summit. While two of the tanks ceased operating due to mechanical problems, one of them reached that objective. The infantry fired mortars and machine guns to mask the tank's clanking sound as well as removing trees to blaze a trail for the tank as it neared the Gifu perimeter.

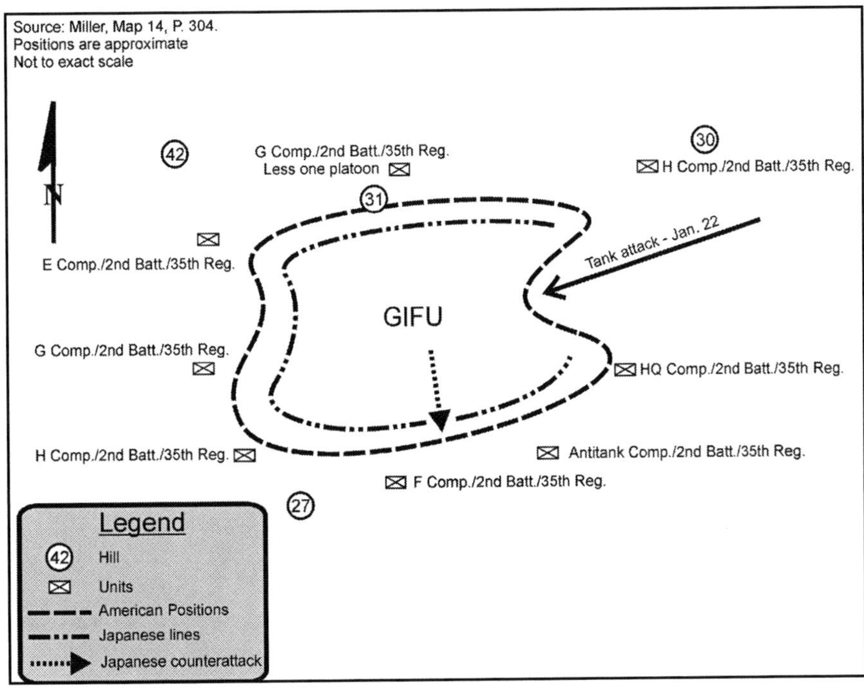

Shattering the Gifu's Defenses

With 16 infantrymen in tow, the tank assaulted the Gifu's northeastern quadrant at 10:40 a.m. the next day. When it got close to three pillboxes, its 37-mm gun blazed away with high-explosive shells and destroyed all three fortifications. Cannister shot from its cannon and its machine guns killed the Japanese soldiers in the now-decimated pillboxes. It then turned southward and broke through the perimeter's eastern line. At 3:00 p.m., it turned northward and overpowered five more pillboxes. E Company sent one of its platoons to attack and outflank the Japanese from the west but it ran into stiff resistance again because of the strong pillbox defense facing it. The platoon had to stop its attack because of approaching darkness before it could finish what it had started. But that one tank did more damage in less than one day than all the infantry assaults tried for the whole prior month. There was now a 200-yard-wide gap in the Japanese lines.

As darkness came over Guadalcanal on January 22, the Gifu sector stayed silent until Maj. Inagaki led the Japanese counterattack at 2:30 a.m. on January 23 against the southern part of the American lines held by F Company and the battalion's Antitank Company. In a frantic attack the Japanese soldiers threw hand grenades and fired their rifles and machine guns. The Americans immediately responded with withering gunfire and stopped the Japanese assault. When daylight broke, the Americans found 85 dead Japanese including Maj. Inagaki, another major, eight captains, and 15 lieutenants. Inagaki had attacked the strongest of the 2nd Battalion's defensive positions. If he had assaulted to the southwest where there was just one platoon from G Company, he might have had more success since just two men occupied a foxhole spaced every 15 yards.

The rest of the XIV Corps was well into the attack to the north when Col. McClure ordered the 2nd Battalion on January 23 to eliminate all Japanese opposition in the Gifu. Col. Larsen believed the cumulative destruction wreaked on the Japanese soldiers in the Gifu by the American artillery, surrounding infantry, and tank attacks had softened up the Japanese defense, so he ordered his battalion to form skirmish lines, advance into the Gifu, and destroy any Japanese soldiers still there. He was correct in that assumption because there was no effective opposition. The advancing American soldiers found Japanese soldiers not fighting but hiding from their certain fate. The only American casualty was a private injured from a shot in his shoulder issuing from a Japanese officer's pistol. When the night came on January 23, there was no Japanese opposition remaining in the Gifu. The American southern flank was now secure.

✲ ✲ ✲

Taking the Gifu cost the 2nd Battalion 64 men killed and 42 wounded. It estimated its attacks had killed 518 Japanese. Col. McClure reported that his 35th Infantry Regiment operations on Mount Austen and the Sea Horse had killed almost 1,100 Japanese, and captured 29 prisoners. It had taken five American battalions to destroy all Japanese opposition on the Gifu and more than a month to do it. Nonetheless, there were no more Japanese soldiers east of the Matanikau River. The 35th Infantry had earned a rest. Collins placed the regiment in reserve while his 25th Division continued moving westward.

The XIV Corps' first January offensive had captured about 3,000 yards of Guadalcanal territory from the Japanese. Its western line running from west of Point Cruz southward to the Matanikau River's southwestern fork was strongly set with its southern flank fully secured. The 25th Division had more than brilliantly done its job.[1]

CHAPTER 58
Moving Northwest

Blocking Japanese Escape Routes

With the 25th Division's success in removing Japanese opposition on the XIV Corps' southern flank, Gen. Patch's forces were now in a position to move along a wide front on Guadalcanal's northern coast. He immediately began planning to launch a large-scale, coordinated attack to capture the village of Kokumbona as far as the Poha River—about 9,000 yards west of Point Cruz.

When Patch refined his plan to destroy the Japanese currently occupying Kokumbona, he noticed there were two ways the Japanese could escape their ultimate demise. The first and easily-traveled path was the Coastal Road over flat ground from Kokumbona to Cape Esperance. The more difficult escape route was over a 20-mile trail from Kokumbona to Beaufort Bay on Guadalcanal's southwestern coast that traversed the rugged mountains running along the island spine. The Americans had reconnoitered the trail in December and found no Japanese on the south coast. A Belgian missionary of the Roman Catholic Church's Society of Mary, Emery de Klerk, had kept a station at Beaufort Bay since before the beginning of the war. When the Marines arrived, he did not want to be evacuated to a safe location and volunteered his services to the Americans as a coastwatcher, a recruiter of native labor, and an expert on the terrain.

Gen. Patch did not want the Japanese to use the mountain trail since it would be too difficult to pursue them over the rugged mountains. A small Japanese force could hold battalions of American soldiers in the canyons and jungles for days. A small American force could also perform the same task. That route had to be denied to the Japanese, and that task could be accomplished by a small expedition of American soldiers. He ordered Capt. Charles E. Beach to take the 147th Infantry I Company, platoons from M and the Antitank Companies, as well as pioneer, medical, and communications troops to land in Beaufort Bay, move over the trail toward the northern coast near the village of Vurai, and block the passes to prevent the Japanese from escaping over that route.

Capt. Beach's men walked up the ramps of two tank landing craft on January 7 at Kukum. The two LCTs sailed around Cape Esperance that night and arrived at Klerk's mission in Beaufort Bay on January 9. After leaving their ships, an I Company platoon, antitank and heavy weapons' platoons, and the pioneers set up defensive positions on the beach. The rest of Beach's command began climbing up the mountain trail on January 11 and arrived at Vurai three days later. After establishing their base camp, a defensive line, and outposts that would give any early warning if the Japanese should approach, Beach sent out patrols to search for any Japanese. After finding none, Beach moved his men closer to the north coast and set up a new camp at the village of Tapananja about six miles south of the sea. Outposts occupied the upper headwaters of the Poha River.

No Japanese ever tried to move up the trail but the American position on the trail effectively isolated them from being supplied. Native bearers carried supplies to the Americans but only a small amount of the materiel ever arrived. So, the Americans had to subsist on baked green bananas. Beach asked for supplies to be airdropped, but the XIV Corps denied his request because it would betray the blocking force presence to the Japanese. Nevertheless, the Americans had completely blocked the escape route over the trail without having to commit a large number of soldiers that were needed for the upcoming offensive.

The only way the Japanese could escape was along the Coastal Road. Or, at least, that is the way the Americans wanted it. It was now time to refine the plans and resume the offensive.

Plans, Orders, and Preparations

Patch issued orders on January 16 for his Corps to begin a series of synchronized westward attacks to establish a line running from about 2,600 yards west of Point Cruz and 3,000 yards west of the Galloping Horse. With the exhausted 2nd Marine and Americal Divisions resting up from intensive, exhausting combat operations, Patch created a Composite Army-Marine (CAM) Division made up of the 6th Marines, the 147th and the 182nd Infantry Regiments, and artillery units drawn from the 2nd Marine and Americal Divisions. He ordered the CAM Division to advance along the Coastal Road along a 3,000 yard front on the 25th Division's right flank. The CAM was to keep in contact with the 25th Division's right and protect the shoreline between the Matanikau River and the objective line. It was to attack to the southwest to encircle the Japanese right flank and protect the Corps' left (south) flank. The orders directed that pockets of Japanese resistance were to be isolated, bypassed, and taken out later. The Corps would then attack to the northwest once it reached its objective.

The ground over which the XIV Corps would fight its next battle would be quite familiar to the men. It was the same rugged jungle, steep hills, and canyons it had faced in its earlier operations. Rocky, deep canyons running north-south with steep walls pockmarked the Coastal Road. As the Japanese had shown before, the Americans would face the same determined defensive pockets of resistance that had become normal in the Galloping Horse, Sea Horse, and Gifu battles.

The ground over which 25th Division would pass was higher than where the CAM would attack. Three hills—Hill 87, Hill 88, and Hill 89—occupied the highest elevations and loomed over Kokumbona and dominated the Corps' path of advance between the Matanikau River and Cape Esperance just as Mount Austen did during the previous American offensives.

☆ ☆ ☆

Gen. Collins, following Gen. Patch's plan, ordered the 25th Division on January 20 to launch its attack two days later westward from the Galloping Horse. The 161st Infantry Regiment would lead the attack by moving in a southwesterly direction to move around the Japanese defenses while the 27th Infantry would launch a holding attack. After the 35th Infantry annihilated the Japanese opposition in the Gifu, that unit would go into reserve status.

The 161st Infantry's first objective was to capture the three small hills—Hills X, Y, and Z—southwest of Hill 53. Hill Z was about 2,500 yards southwest of Hill 53 and 6,500 yards south of the Sealark Channel. After taking the hills, the regiment would turn northwest, trudge through the jungle, attack Hill 87, the division's objective, and take it from the rear of the Japanese defenses. Then they had to seize Hills 88 and 89 and fortify the entire hilly complex.

Utilizing the extended supply road that reached Hill 53, the 161st Infantry received their supplies by truck to the road's end and then carried by native bearers to its front lines. The regiment amassed near the Galloping Horse southern edge and moved forward on January 20 toward Hill X and then to Hill Y on the next day. No Japanese forces opposed them.

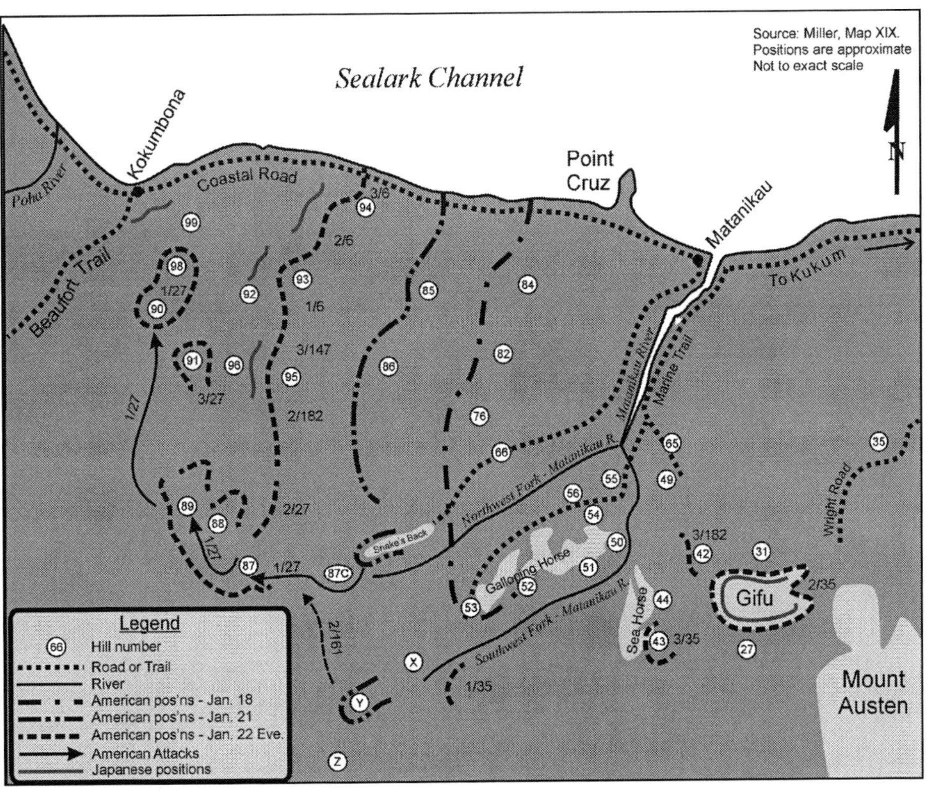

The American XIV Corps' Begin Their Attack

Meanwhile, the 27th Infantry readied themselves for their holding attack. There was a long, narrow ridge that extended from a point southwest of Hill 66 near the Matanikau River's northwestern fork to a place just east of Hill 87. It resembled a snake when viewed from aerial reconnaissance photographs. As before, the Americans gave it the name, Snake's Back. When taken, it gave the Americans an easy approach to capture Hill 87 as well as the adjoining Hills 88 and 89. In order to make supplying the 27th Infantry less strenuous and more timely, the 57th and 65th Seabees extended the road from Hill 66 to the Snake's Back as the 27th Infantry moved toward Hill 87.

The Japanese still occupied Hill 87 with the ferocity of their mortar and machine gun fire that convinced the Americans they were dug in on the hill and determined to stay where they were. There was no chance the Americans could occupy Hill 87C until they first took Hill 87. Another patrol from the 1st Battalion marched on January 20 without any disruption to Hill 87G, another mound about 1,000 yards northwest of Hill 87C. Nonetheless, their advance was over very rugged terrain and took more than three hours. Therefore, Lt. Col. Claude E. Jurney, the 1st Battalion's commander, decided that he would not advance from the Snake's Back until January 22. Being held in reserve, Col. Mitchell's 2nd Battalion meanwhile moved on January 21 into the 1st Battalion's former positions on Hill 57. Col. Bush's 3rd Battalion marched to the Snake's Back that same day and took up positions just behind the 1st Battalion.

The 25th Division Advances to Kokumbona

The 25th division's infantry began their attack to capture Kokumbona at 6:30 a.m. on January 22. This assault was one that did not come from orders of the divisional commander but was a series of independent but coordinated assaults under the command of the regimental commanders. The soldiers advanced under the umbrella of a massive artillery barrage that sent 12½ tons of 75-mm, 105-mm, and 155-mm shells onto an area southwest of the Galloping Horse and 55½ tons on Hill 87. Four artillery battalions poured rapid fire on Hill 87 with one of them, the 8th FAB, firing an average of 14½ rounds per minute.

The 2nd Battalion, with the 1st Battalion protecting its left flank, advanced from Hill Y and into the dense jungle undergrowth. While the 3rd Battalion followed them to Hills X and Y, the 2nd Battalion led the way on a well-established trail toward Hill 87.

The 161st Infantry began its attempt to encircle the Japanese as the 27th Infantry executed its holding attack. The 1st Battalion moved over the Snake's Back at 6:30 a.m. with C Company leading the other companies in a column. When the artillery stopped firing a half hour later, the regiment's mortars and 37-mm guns positioned on the Snake's Back took up where the heavier guns left off. Just as C Company began their assault on a nearby hill, a withering enfilade of Japanese machine gun fire stopped their advance. After the mortars and 37-mm guns on the Snake's Back knocked out the Japanese guns, the battalion resumed its advance at 7:45 a.m. With A Company on the right, B Company in the center, and C Company on the left, the 1st Battalion attacked Hill 87. By this time, the Japanese had abandoned Hill 87, so the Americans took the critical objective at 9:10 a.m. unopposed. The 1st battalion had advanced nearly 3,000 yards in less than three hours.

The American advance moved much faster than planned. Nevertheless, using the ability to adapt to the fortunes of battle, the XIV Corps commander modified his plans. Gen. Patch ordered Collins that if his division's attack achieved better results than planned, the 161st Infantry was to press their advantage, not wait for the 27th Infantry to capture Hill 87, and take Hills 88 and 89. However, the 27th Infantry had already captured Hill 87 while the 161st was still in the jungle.

Col. Jurney's 1st Battalion moved past Hill 87. While A Company held Hill 87, B Company moved 500 yards to the west, took Hill 88. C Company advanced 1,000 yards west, turned north, and captured Hill 89 at 10:35 a.m. Twenty-five minutes later, all of the 1st Battalion's companies were firmly entrenched on all three hills and in total control of their day's objective. It was still morning; the Americans were well ahead of their schedule.

Gen. Collins, who Halsey described as "quick on his feet and even quicker in his brain,"[1] saw how fast his division had achieved its objectives. He reexamined his plan and realized it had to change. The 25th Division had outrun its wired telephone communications, so he left his post on Hill 49, climbed into his Jeep, and ordered the driver to drive as far as he could toward Hill 87. He met the XIV Corps chief of staff, Brig. Gen. Robert L. Spragins, on Hill 66 and got the authority from Patch through Spragins for the 25th to move toward Kokumbona with no further delay. Collins' division got permission to take over the CAM Division's area and attack in front of it.

After getting to Hill 89, Collins met with Col. McCulloch, the commander of the 27th Infantry, now ideally positioned to go after the retreating Japanese. So Collins and McCulloch agreed that the 27th Infantry would waste no time and attack the Japanese and then capture Hills 90 and 97 near Kokumbona's southern outskirts. The 161st Infantry 2nd Battalion, now moving under the deep jungle undergrowth, would assault Hill 87 that had just a few Japanese riflemen on it. That regiment's 1st and 3rd Battalions would withdraw from the southern flank and march to the Galloping Horse and Snake's Back.

The 3/27's main body was right behind the 1st Battalion as it advanced over the Snake to Hills 87 and 88. Covering its regiment's right flank, I Company had stayed close to the 182nd Infantry in CAM Division's zone. Earlier that morning, the 2nd Battalion's E Company marched from the Galloping Horse to the Snake's Head and met with the rest of the battalion. Its mission was to protect the regiment supply route.

The 1/27 began advancing northward at about 2:00 p.m. to Hill 90. Keeping B Company in reserve, A and C Companies launched their attack in a line abreast. Located on Hill 89, the 8th FAB's 105-mm howitzers and D Company's 81-mm mortars began their bombardment to support the two company assault. Just a few Japanese riflemen trapped in a deep valley offered token opposition as the American soldiers quickly moved forward and captured the hill. Col. Jurney's battalion more than exceeded expectations after advancing more than 2,000 yards and taking Hills 90 and 98, the high ground east and south of Kokumbona.

With the 27th Infantry's faster-than-planned advance, the American artillery had to leave its current locations and move forward. Now that the Gifu was no longer a threat, the 64th FAB moved its guns across the Matanikau River and atop Hill 66 and took over for the 8th FAB. The 90th FAB also moved its howitzers across the Matanikau on January 22-23 near Point Cruz. While these artillery battalions were on the move, the 89th FAB filled in with support missions and later moved to Hill 49 near the Matanikau River's eastern bank. The 64th FAB stayed put.

As darkness came on January 22, the 27th Infantry occupied the high ground overlooking the village of Kokumbona. It had been quite an eventful and successful day for Jurney and his men. The 1st Battalion had advanced more than 4,500 yards in one day with the 2nd and 3rd Battalions just behind it. With its supply route secured from Japanese disruptions, the regiment readied itself to take advantage of their successes. After consulting with Collins and the rest of the division staff, Jurney finished his plans during the night of January 22-23 to capture on January 23 one of the XIV Corps' most important objective, Kokumbona.

In the early morning hours of January 23, the Americans began their attack to take Kokumbona. The 3/27 advanced northward from Hills 89 and 91 toward Hills 98 and 99. With the 1/27 protecting its south from Japanese attacks, the 3/27 expanded its right flank as far as the beach to the north, blocked the undefended hills and critical beach road, and trapped Japanese to their east. With the 3rd Battalion firmly in possession of the terrain they occupied, the 1st Battalion plus E Company and one of K Company's platoons from the 2nd Battalion in tow moved from the east and south into Kokumbona in two columns. The column on the right assaulted Hill 99's northern and western slopes. A and E Companies, one machine gun platoon, and two mortar squads attacked on the left in the other column to the north over Hill 90 and also moved into Kokumbona. Both columns rejoined at 3:10 p.m. in the village after advancing more than 1,000 yards.

The regiment ordered the 2nd Battalion that afternoon to defend Hills 90 and 97 and then advance through the jungle north of Hill 97, take Hill 100 approximately 500 yards west of Hill 97 to safeguard the regiment's left flank. G Company took over Hill 90's defense as the Battalion Headquarters and H Companies expanded their lines westward to Hill 97. F Company marched west and encountered light Japanese opposition in the ravine along the Beaufort Trail and the Kokumbona River between Hills 97 and 100. After an all-too-brief firefight, the company killed 30 Japanese soldiers while not suffering any casualties of their own.

For the most part, not much happened at night. Taking advantage of the lull, the Americans fortified their defenses. The Japanese, now retreating under orders from their superiors in Tokyo, refused to engage the Americans in battle as they had done in the past. Now that Kokumbona was in American hands, the 3rd Battalion's I Company set up a roadblock along the path between Hill 99 and the beach. After dark, a foolish group of Japanese soldiers marched west along the Coastal Road, chatting loudly, carrying and waving flashlights in the dark, hauling a 37-mm gun, and apparently oblivious to the fact that the Americans blocked their way. The Japanese ran straight into I Company's roadblock and suffered severely for their arrogant ignorance. The Americans quietly waited for the Japanese to get quite close and poured a withering and deadly barrage with every rifle and machine gun they had. The result was about 50 dead Japanese soldiers needlessly sacrificed.

✲ ✲ ✲

The CAM Division's part in this noteworthy engagement was just as distinguished as the 25th Division's. It would be their job to join the 25th Division for the drive to the northwest past Kokumbona and toward the Poha River.

The CAM Division Goes on the Offensive

The CAM Division's troops had been busy before January 22 removing any Japanese opposition in their zone along the coast and north of the 25th Division's zone. With artillery support from the Americal and 2nd Marine Division's artillery, along with support from the Navy five-inch guns firing from destroyers offshore, the 182nd Infantry Regiment without their 3rd Battalion took up positions to the 6th Marines' left. The two regiments moved westward on January 17 and advanced just more than 1,000 yards farther on January 19. The 182nd Infantry made slower progress than the 6th Marines so that it created a large break in their line. The Marines tried to keep their line integrity and not create the gap when they halted their advance after the 182nd ceased their forward movement.

When the 147th Infantry Regiment moved from Koli Point to the Point Cruz area later that afternoon, the American Reconnaissance Squadron replaced them. The next day, the 3rd Battalion, 147th Infantry plugged the gap by moving into the line between the 6th Marines and the 182nd Infantry. However, it took one more day for the two battalions to join their lines. Thus, the CAM Division could not begin their forward movement until January 22.

When the XIV Corps began its massive offensive on January 22 at 6:30 a.m., the 6th Marines attacked along the beach on the right, the 147th Infantry advanced in the center, and 182nd Infantry stayed in contact with the 25th Division on the left. The Americal and 2nd Marine Division artillery plus naval gunfire and aircraft bombings began their barrage as they supported the assault. The 182nd and 147th were the only regiments that faced any appreciable opposition in that sector. The 182nd Regiment's G Company joined up with the 27th Infantry north of Hill 88. The 147th Infantry captured Hill 95 when some of its patrols encountered Japanese machine gun fire in the west canyon.

The fighting on the beach was far more serious. As the 3rd Battalion of the 6th Marines began their attack, about 250 Japanese soldiers in the ravine west of Hill 94 raked the Marines with machine gun and antitank cannon fire and forced the American attack to grind to a halt. As the 3rd Battalion's left flank, the regiment's 2nd Battalion had to also stop to maintain that protection. Although the CAM Division had advanced 1,000 yards that day, its front lines were still 1,000 yards short of Hills 98 and 99, the high ground in that sector.

On January 23, the day the 25th Division captured Kokumbona, the CAM Division restarted its attack. The 182nd Infantry moved forward 1,000 yards toward its objective, Hill 91, while staying in contact with the 25th Division on the left and the 147th Infantry on the right. Tough Japanese resistance located on Hill 92's northern slopes and along the Coastal Road greeted the 147th and slowed their advance. The 6th Marines also ran into Japanese small arms and artillery fire, but still managed to capture Hill 92.

✲ ✲ ✲

After the fighting stopped on January 23, the XIV Corps had surrounded almost all the Japanese in a ravine east of the Poha River and Hill 99. The CAM Division continued its assault the next day with the 147th attacking to the northwest. By 9:40 a.m., they killed 18 Japanese, took Hill 98, and contacted the 27th Infantry. The 6th Marines resumed its attack and killed more than 200 Japanese soldiers. By 3:00 p.m., all three battalions had captured Hills 98 and 99 and had joined up with the 27th Infantry.
The XIV Corps was on its planned schedule to capture Kokumbona and ready to move to the Poha River. After they reached that objective, the American ground offensive would begin chasing the Japanese now retreating toward Cape Esperance.

Moving to the Poha River

The 25th Division could also continue its advance beyond Kokumbona—just as Gen. Patch had planned. The 27th Infantry held the best ground to resume the attack. Leading the way was the 2nd

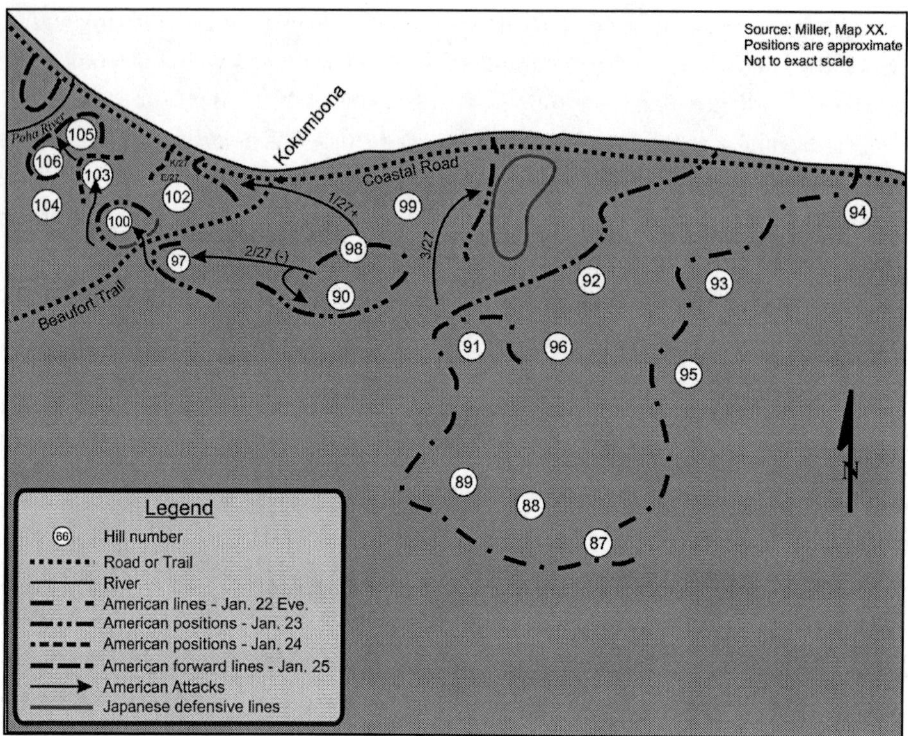

Capturing Kokumbona and Moving to the Poha River

Battalion as its E Company rejoined after serving with the 1st Battalion. The 27th Infantry's commander, Col. McCulloch, added K Company to the 2nd Battalion after the men from the 147th Infantry relieved them from their position on Hill 98. Ahead for the 27th was the Poha River, whose mouth emptied into Iron Bottom Sound about 2,300 yards northwest of Hill 100 and 2,600 yards northwest of Kokumbona.

The capture of the Kokumbona beaches greatly simplified relieving the American supply shortage by making it possible to safely bring in supplies using landing craft over water. Since the Americans had complete control of the sea and air along Guadalcanal's northern shore, this supply route was far more reliable and safer than bringing supplies forward over land. Several American landing craft had brought in enough supplies by noon to allow the 2nd Battalion to move forward from Kokumbona.

When H Company's machine guns and mortars began firing supporting fire at 1:00 p.m. from Hill 97, K and E Company moved out with K Company's right flank touching the beach. With E Company on K Company's left, it attacked over Hill 102 to Kokumbona's immediate west, and ran into a toughly defended Japanese position on the hill's western edge. K Company stopped moving forward to preserve its left flank. Neither company moved for the remainder of the day.

G Company, along with an antitank platoon and six machine guns, moved north off Hill 97 and turned northwest to take Hill 103, about 250 yards past Hill 100. As G Company crossed some dry stream beds north of Hill 100, the same well-hidden Japanese defenders that had stopped E Company enfiladed G Company on three sides. Col. Mitchell ordered the company to not advance any farther and withdraw to Hill 103 by safely marching around Hill 100's southern slopes. It did not reach Hill 103 until nightfall.

Moving Northwest

With orders to attack with more men on January 25 and reach the Poha River, the 27th Infantry resumed its action. After the 6th Marines relieved them from positions on Hills 98, Col. Bush's 3rd Battalion attacked along the beach west of Kokumbona and the 2nd Battalion attacked to the left, and advanced to Hills 105 and 106 that loomed over the Poha River. Bush separated his K Company and ordered them to silence the Japanese entrenched between Hills 102 and 103.

Meanwhile, the 3rd Battalion moved from Hills 98 and 99, marched past the 1st Battalion in Kokumbona at about noon, and headed northwest with its companies marching in a column. L Company led the way while I Company, Battalion Headquarters, and M Company followed in that order. L Company fanned out in a 400-yard-wide front and cautiously moved through the jungle. Col. Bush decided to change his battalion's formation at 4:00 p.m. to speed up its advance and reach the Poha River before dark. I Company moved through L Company and advanced to the northwest along the Coastal Road. A few Japanese riflemen fired at the 3rd Battalion during the day, but after some brief skirmishes, the Americans eliminated about 35 of them.

The 3rd Battalion reached the area near the Poha River late in the afternoon, but Col. Bush could not find it after looking at his crayon-drawn map. Like many rivers in this part of the world, the Poha drained into the sea through many small tributaries. He asked for an artillery round to be fired at a location in the sea opposite the river's mouth. The shell hit the water behind where his battalion was. After reckoning the river's mouth was behind him, he ordered his battalion to set up its camp where it was and establish a defensive perimeter in a coconut grove, which the aerial maps indicated was west of the river's main stream.

The 2nd Battalion advanced to Hills 105 and 106 in the meantime. Its E Company moved past G Company on Hill 103, advanced unopposed through the steep terrain and dense jungle growth, and climbed Hills 105 and 106 as dusk fell. The Americans now blocked any chance of retreat by the Japanese. After a series of firefights where the Americans blocked their withdrawal, about 50 Japanese soldiers lost their lives during the night of January 25-26.

The two battalions joined at 7:00 a.m. on January 26. They held a line along the Poha River until the 6th Marines and 182nd Infantry passed by to advance to the northwest and chase the Japanese retreating up the coast. In the event the Japanese might attempt a landing near Lunga Point, the XIV Corps ordered the 25th Division to reinforce the defensive perimeter around Henderson and Carney Fields.

The 27th Infantry had few casualties during its actions over the past days. It lost seven officers and 67 enlisted men killed and 226 wounded in January with most of the casualties occurring during the attack on the Galloping Horse. It experienced light losses in taking Kokumbona.

Once a key Japanese position, the Americans were in firm control of Kokumbona. The 27th Infantry had captured the high ground that overlooked the beaches between Kokumbona and Cape Esperance, a Japanese radar station, trucks, landing craft, weapons, and had killed more than 400 Japanese soldiers. If the Japanese tried to land any reinforcements, they would be met with powerful resistance that would have almost certainly led to the landing force's absolute destruction.

The remnants of the Japanese 17th Army were in full retreat. The XIV Corps' job was to find and destroy them before they could dig in at Cape Esperance for a suicidal last stand as they had at the Gifu.[2]

CHAPTER 59
Planning for Operation "KE"

Concerns at the American High Command

The Japanese kept their plans to remove their soldiers on Guadalcanal secret from the Americans. Nevertheless, there were many signs apparent to American intelligence that the Japanese were about to do something significant. Adm. King grew impatient about what he saw as a lack of progress at Guadalcanal. The Naval Battle of Guadalcanal happened two months ago, and the Japanese seemed to be more determined than ever to stay on the island. Gen. Patch estimated that the Japanese would not be chased off the island until April 1 at the earliest. When he did that, the second phase of Operation Watchtower (to advance island-by-island up the Solomon Island chain) could begin.

King opposed this phase of the operation because he did not wish to have another drawn-out struggle that would put a drain on the tight American supply problems. King wanted to execute a series of flanking operations similar to those MacArthur began in the New Guinea campaign, cancel the next Watchtower phases, bypass the Solomon and Bismarck Islands, and capture the Admiralty Islands instead. Then the Americans could block the Japanese supply lines to Rabaul, isolate the Japanese bastions, and use bombing and interdiction with naval forces. Rabaul would be rendered impotent and could be captured whenever the Americans wanted to do it.

Nimitz and Halsey totally opposed King's plan for the South Pacific. Nimitz issued a memorandum entitled "Future Operations in the Solomons Area" and took it with him to San Francisco when he joined King for a series of meetings that began on December 9, 1942. Nimitz rebutted King's contentions by saying that it would be too dangerous to evade powerful Japanese bases even trying to capture Rabaul or the Admiralties. The Japanese could cut off and outflank American supply lines using their bases at Kavieng, Buka, Kieta, Buin, and Gasmata.

Nimitz wanted a step-by-step invasion of the northern Solomon Islands while building a series of air bases from which American land-based planes could cover the advancing American troops. At most, Nimitz wanted to capture the Japanese base on Buin, about 300 miles from Guadalcanal. A far more modest proposal involved attacking the Japanese air base on Munda, just 180 miles north of Henderson Field. However, nothing could be done until the Americans fully controlled Guadalcanal and built a strong supply base in the Guadalcanal-Tulagi area. With American air power superiority growing ever stronger, the Americans could attack at an accelerating pace. Nimitz's last proposal was to keep the current SOPAC command structure intact.

After listening to Nimitz's arguments, King embraced his proposals and committed to get Halsey and MacArthur more forces to enable the two area commanders to speed up their campaigns.

Specifically, he would try to deliver 15% of the Allied supplies currently authorized by the Combined Chiefs of Staff to the Pacific and raise that percentage to 20-25%.

The two men discussed the future of the Pacific Fleet. At this time, there were 22 new aircraft carriers being built at shipyards throughout the continental Unites States and scheduled to be launched soon. These new ships, along with the new cruisers, destroyers, landing craft, and auxiliary vessels, would become the most powerful naval force ever built. The Navy would resurrect the original Rainbow Six strategy to invade Micronesia, recapture the Philippines, establish strong bases on the Chinese coast, and eventually invade the Japanese home islands. Meanwhile, the planned march up the Solomon Islands would move Halsey's forces into MacArthur's command area and create an awkward situation that had to be resolved back in Washington. When King returned there, he would address this topic with Gen. Marshall.

✲ ✲ ✲

After Nimitz returned to Pearl Harbor, he decided it was time for another inspection tour of Halsey's command. Secretary of the Navy Frank Knox planned to arrive in Pearl Harbor on January 12 and would go with Nimitz to the South Pacific. Because Knox would be on the trip, Nimitz asked MacArthur if the general could meet them in Nouméa. If that was not possible, Nimitz, Halsey, and Knox could instead go to Brisbane. MacArthur's reply stated he had already explained his opinions, any more discussions would result in unnecessary travel, and saw no need to meet with Knox under any circumstances.

Knox, his special assistant Adlai Stevenson, and two aides arrived in Pearl Harbor by plane. The entire party—Nimitz, Knox, and some of the admiral's staff—left Pearl Harbor for Midway on January 14. Their four engine seaplane had mechanical problems and had to return to Hawaii. When they returned to Ford Island, Nimitz asked for replacement aircraft and, after many problems with getting sufficient aircraft to get everyone safely to Midway, the party at last arrived on the island on January 16.

After suffering from the claustrophobia of being stuck on the tiny island, Knox and Nimitz could hardly wait to leave when another airplane arrived from Pearl Harbor. The men soon were on their way to Espiritu Santo and, after refueling stops, arrived on January 20. Halsey and Adm. McCain, who had flown in from Nouméa, met the group. Adm. John S. "Slew" McCain, the Chief of the Navy's Bureau of Aeronautics, had come from Washington to review and assess the air situation in the South Pacific.

Halsey had just returned from a trip to New Zealand where he made a controversial statement of his opinion of the American fighting man versus their Japanese competition by repeating his earlier opinion that the Americans would be in Tokyo within one year: "When we first started out against them, I held that one of our men was equal to three Japanese. I have now increased that to twenty."[1] Halsey's remarks shocked the Navy and the State Departments for his provocative, off-the-cuff remarks that also delighted the press.

Halsey, McCain, Nimitz, Knox, and the rest of their entourages retired for the night and went aboard Adm. Fitch's flagship, the seaplane tender *Curtiss*. They had just gone to bed when the Japanese came calling by dropping several bombs on the American installation. The attack was the first Japanese bombing raid in several weeks, and it did not do much damage, just a few craters on the harbor's beach. Nonetheless, some rumors began as to whether the Japanese knew that some high-ranking officers were on the wing and visiting American South Pacific bases.

Nimitz, Halsey, and McCain and the rest of the party climbed aboard another airplane and left for Guadalcanal on January 21. When Nimitz and McCain arrived, they observed the many changes made at Guadalcanal. There is no way that the Melanesian island could be called a tourist trap. Nonetheless, Henderson Field was no longer the desperately constructed, dirt strip Nimitz had seen on his last visit. The American air base was now a fully operational, all-weather air field with another new, almost-ready fighter strip under construction. The men's morale and the installations' quality showed enormous improvement. While malaria was still a problem to the island's inhabitants, the men did not show nearly as many of the ill-effects from the debilitating disease as Nimitz had seen in September. While Japanese bombers did come to call on the base from time-to-time, the effect of these raids had significantly lessened due to the air superiority the Americans held over the land and seas around the Guadalcanal-Tulagi area.

However, Japanese bombers attacked Henderson Field at 8:30 p.m. despite American air superiority. To those visitors who bore the brunt of the attack, the second bombing raid in as many nights was more than just a happenstance. It seemed that the Japanese knew Nimitz and Halsey were there. Halsey expressed his feelings about the attack:

> "I have very little stomach for bombs. There were no foxholes on the *Curtiss*, but there were plenty on Guadalcanal. When I heard the first boom!, I left my comfortable bed and dove into the ground, with Mr. Knox and `Slew' McCain. But not Chester. He said he hadn't had any sleep the night before; he was going to catch up; besides, he said, he was scared of mosquitoes. Chester spent the night under a sheet, behind screens. The other three of us spent it half-naked, out in the open. And Chester was the only one who caught malaria!"[2]

McCain chose a former latrine slit trench for his shelter and would never forget the experience of that Japanese air raid.

After the Nimitz party left for Nouméa on January 22, Guadalcanal's communication officer wanted to release a standard departure message. Not wanting a repeat of the Japanese bombing mission, his traumatized aide asked, "Do me a favor, will you? Send it in Japanese. I want 'em to know for sure that the high-priced hired help has left here!"[3]

The "high-priced help" arrived that day in Nouméa and retired for the evening. On January 23, the group went to Halsey's headquarters to confer about the future direction of the Guadalcanal conflict. Marine Brig. Gen. De Witt Peck, Halsey's Marine liaison officer, also joined the meeting and Gen. Harmon came later. Nimitz began the meeting.

Nimitz: The object of this conference is to review the situation in the South Pacific and to exchange views. No decision will be reached. Indeed, we may not agree on all points. First, as to Guadalcanal. What is the COMSOPAC view as to progress and the approximate date Japs will be eliminated? Shall we need more troops? What number should be left as a garrison on completion of the operation?[4]

Halsey had talked much on the plane trip to Guadalcanal. Therefore, he let Peck, express COMSOPAC's views.[5]

Peck: We estimate that all Japanese opposition will end by April 1.

Nimitz: Frankly, I am surprised as to why is this taking so long?

Peck: Our latest intelligence indicates the Japanese might fight delaying actions to keep our ground forces occupied. Gen. Patch has two divisions of ground combat soldiers plus service troops. So, it is our belief that we have sufficient ground forces on Guadalcanal to eliminate all Japanese opposition on the island.

Our staff has studied what we should do after Guadalcanal while Admiral Halsey was traveling to New Zealand and Guadalcanal. We plan to capture the Russell Islands, which are an island group about 30 miles northwest of Guadalcanal, and use it as a PT boat base and a place from which to stage landing craft for operations northward.

Halsey: It seems reasonable to me.

Nimitz: When do you think you can move against Munda?

Peck: April 1st. This assumes a division of troops trained in amphibious operations was available and ready for combat at that time.

Nimitz: We'll have these troops ready for you by then. John, (Admiral McCain) will there be enough aircraft to cover the Munda operation?

McCain: Yes, Chet, there will. I can ask the Army if they can help us with more aircraft.

Nimitz: That is a good idea. I also want to know when the new airstrip you are now building on Guadalcanal will be ready for aircraft to use.

Halsey: It should be ready for heavy bombers by the end of February. But, in an emergency, it could be used by the middle of February.

Nimitz: What are your plans for using Guadalcanal after you secure the island?

Halsey: We want to use it as a base for further operations as we advance up the Solomons.

Nimitz: It is my idea that no permanent installations should be erected there. The only construction should be what is necessary, and there should be a reduction in the rear areas. Everything should be based on a forward movement.

The officers who were there for the conference could not help but notice how different everyone's demeanor and attitudes were at this meeting than when they had previously met in September. Back then, there was an edgy fear of the unknown with all men in an anxious and worried mood. But his time, optimism filled the air that a victory on Guadalcanal was not far off.

All the visitors departed from Nouméa the next morning. Nimitz and his staff returned to Pearl Harbor; Secretary Knox and Adm. McCain went back to Washington after a brief stopover at Pearl Harbor. Halsey had impressed Knox. Halsey seemed to be a great leader and talented administrator—a man definitely in command who could gather fine officers around him who owed their loyalty to the admiral.[6]

The Japanese Make Their Own Plans

While the Americans prepared to meet determined Japanese soldiers willing to defend their positions on Guadalcanal to the death and finish off the Japanese on Guadalcanal, the Japanese secretly met to plan to withdraw their men from the island. After receiving orders from Tokyo, the Japanese commanders on Rabaul and Truk began to put the details together for the evacuation.

Imperial Gen. Headquarters issued orders about how the Japanese would carry out operations in the South Pacific and transmitted them to Truk. Carrying the title *Army-Navy Central Agreement Concerning South Pacific Operations*, the document can be summarized with two main points:

1. The evacuation of all Japanese personnel on Guadalcanal would begin in January 1943 and carry forward into February.

2. The Imperial Japanese Army would rapidly reinforce the northern Solomon Islands including Shortland, Bougainville, and Buka with the Imperial Japanese Navy performing similar duties on New Georgia and the Ysabel [Isabella] Islands.

Adm. Yamamoto also had the responsibility to accelerate reinforcing the New Guinea locations of Lae, Salamaua, Madang, and Wewak to build up the Army's defense of that huge island. The Navy's air force would continue battling the Americans in the Solomons and help out over New Guinea whenever needed.

After conducting intense negotiations, the Army and the Navy agreed on January 9 to a detailed plan for Operation "KE". The basics for the plan were:

1. Place one infantry battalion on Guadalcanal about January 14 to act as the foundation for a rear guard.

2. Place enough rations ashore on Guadalcanal by January 14 to last 23 days.

3. The 17th Army would begin a phased withdrawal to Guadalcanal's northwestern end.

4. After the completion of the building of the new airfields, the Army and Navy air forces would regain the air superiority that they had lost to the Americans.

5. Secure the Russell Islands to stage the withdrawing soldiers from barges to destroyers.

6. Use landing craft to evacuate some soldiers from Guadalcanal to the Russells and to eventually be taken to Rabaul by destroyer.

7. There would be three withdrawal expeditions with destroyers being the primary mode of transportation and protection from American air and/or sea interventions.

8. Those soldiers who could not use either destroyers or landing craft would be rescued by submarines.

9. February 10 would be the planned end date for all evacuations.

To keep the Americans guessing what they were doing, the Japanese set up several ploys to mislead their enemy. There would be a marked increase in radio traffic from Java. Port Darwin in northern

Australia would be bombed. The heavy cruiser *Tone* would lead a diversion east of the Marshall Islands along with a submarine bombarding Canton Island. The transmitter in the Marshalls would also send simulated radio traffic.

The 8th Area Army Headquarters estimated there were about 20,000 men on Guadalcanal, but that number proved to be optimistic. Trying to hide the starvation of the Japanese on Guadalcanal, the senior officers there exaggerated their numbers. Therefore, there was no way to give an accurate number of how many men were actually there. Some Army officers conducted a table-top simulation of the upcoming evacuations on January 11, which the Army and the Navy had given the codeword "KE." The conclusion of that exercise indicated that just 5,000 soldiers could be safely evacuated. Those who could not get away would either drown trying to swim to the ships, be killed by the Americans, starve to death, or succumb to disease. Nonetheless, the 8th Area Army dedicated their best effort to get *all* their men off the island.

Gen. Imamura estimated that the Navy would lose about half of their destroyers. The Navy had a far more optimistic guess that they could retrieve about 80% of the men on Guadalcanal. Meanwhile, Adm. Yamamoto was not as confident about the casualties from the operation. His close-to-the-vest and personal estimate was that his destroyers could only rescue one-third of the 17th Army and at the cost of half the destroyers—an opinion that agreed with Imamura's.

The forces that Japanese had at their disposal for the operations did not fill them with much confidence. The Navy had the two super-battleships *Yamato* and *Musashi* and the fleet carrier *Zuikaku* based at Truk. Yamamoto sent the older battleships *Kongo* and *Haruna* and the carriers *Junyo* and *Zuiho* to Kondo's Advanced Force to support KE with the light cruiser *Jintsu* with nine destroyers providing a screening force. Adm. Mikawa's 8th Fleet, which had direct responsibility for the evacuation, had the heavy cruisers *Chokai* and *Kumano*, the light cruiser *Sendai*, and 21 destroyers. Nevertheless, the Japanese knew that the American forces had been growing over the past few months and getting stronger while their own forces had weakened from incessant naval and air combat against the Americans.

CHAPTER 60
The Japanese Finally Leave

The latest American intelligence from aerial reconnaissance indicated a large gathering of Japanese ships and men at Rabaul and Buin, along with battleships and carriers steaming near Ontong Java north of Guadalcanal. The Americans also expected large-scale Japanese air attacks on Guadalcanal and in New Guinea. Something was about to happen, but not what the Americans expected at all. The Japanese were about to abandon Guadalcanal and focus the remainder of their military and naval assets against Gen. Mac Arthur in New Guinea.

Adm. Halsey's naval forces had been significantly strengthened since the Battle of Tassafaronga. He sent seven battleships, two carriers, three escort carriers south of Guadalcanal to arrive between February 7 and 8. Meanwhile, the XIV Corps anticipated that the Japanese would launch a major attack by two carriers, five battleships, about eight cruisers, 11 transports, 28 destroyers, 304 land-based aircraft, 150-175 carrier-based aircraft, and one infantry division. While preparing to repel a Japanese try to land men between the Umasani and Metapona Rivers, Patch resolved to chase the retreating Japanese 17th Army up Guadalcanal's northeast coast to Cape Esperance and destroy them before they could escape to safety. Luckily for the Americans, they had vastly overestimated Japanese intentions. All these Japanese movements proved to be mere feints to cover their plan to extract as much of the 17th Army as they could and return them to combat duty in higher priority efforts than their lost cause of recapturing Guadalcanal.

The Japanese Plan to Rescue their Men on Guadalcanal

The Japanese sailors and soldiers on Guadalcanal were on the verge of starving to death. Those who were not famished were sick with malaria. The combined effects of both maladies were that almost all of the Japanese could no longer be called an effective fighting force. All efforts to bring reinforcements and supplies had failed miserably. The honor of the Japanese Empire dictated these men had to be rescued.

After the decision made in Tokyo at the end of 1942, highly secret Joint Army-Navy conferences convened on Rabaul to develop plans to get the besieged Japanese off Guadalcanal. The Japanese were good at putting together methods and details for an operation such as this one. No detail was too small; no consideration was too unimportant.

The plan called to withdraw the men in early January from Cape Esperance. To reduce the vulnerabilities inherent in using transports, every destroyer the Combined Fleet could spare would be sent to Guadalcanal for the rescue attempt. All withdrawals would be accomplished at night. Adm. Tanaka, regretted that it took so long to get this operation going, and his staff were grateful to finally be able to carry it out. In the meantime, Tanaka received orders from Tokyo that he was reassigned to the Naval General Staff effective December 27. Radm. Tomiji Koyanagi, arrived at Rabaul on December 29 as his replacement. The two officers met before Tanaka's departure to discuss details of those evacuation plans. After making a series of emotional farewells to his staff and other fellow officers, a weary and exhausted Tanaka boarded an airplane and left Rabaul for his home.[1]

✲ ✲ ✲

After the Japanese landed about 600 replacements near Cape Esperance on January 14 to help cover the Japanese Army's extraction and along with a small covering force on the Russell Islands, the Japanese plans for the retreat were well in place. If American air and naval forces should come on the scene, the Japanese would use barges to take the men to the Russells where the destroyers would pick them up and take them northward.

By February 8, Patch changed his mind about possible big Japanese landings . There would be no such attempts since Patch now knew the Japanese were in Duma Cove withdrawing supplies, not landing them. He correctly surmised that the Japanese were not planning an invasion, but were about to withdraw their Army. If the Americans had air reconnaissance over Cape Esperance, the planes would have seen ample evidence that a massive evacuation was in the making. But there were no suitably equipped planes to witness the gathering ships on February 7-8. Thus Patch and the rest of the XIV Corps were completely in the dark about what Gen. Hyakutake had in mind at Guadalcanal's northern tip.

The Japanese Begin Their First Evacuation

One of the effects of the Battle of Rennell Island was the Japanese had to postpone the start of Operation KE until February 1. For the rescue of their soldiers to be successful, Yamamoto chose two of his most qualified units to precisely execute the operation. These were the Reinforcement Unit and the R Area Air Force. The major units of the Reinforcement Unit, which had the responsibility to steam down the Slot and pluck the men from the island, were the heavy cruisers *Chokai* and *Kumano* and the light cruiser *Sendai*. These ships would remain at Kavieng and not be part of the operation. That burden fell to the 21 destroyers based at Shortland.

The commander of Operation KE was Radm. Satsuma Kimura, a highly respected naval commander whose Destroyer Squadron 10 had escorted the finest units of the Imperial Japanese Navy, its fleet carriers. His unit had earned every accolade given to them and considered the best destroyer unit in the Navy. That choice placated Japanese Army officers until the American submarine *Nautilus* torpedoed Kimura's flagship, the destroyer *Akizuki*, off Shortland on January 19 and wounded the admiral. Radm. Koyanagi replaced Kimura as Destroyer Squadron 10 commander. Adm. Kusaka appointed Radm. Shintaro Hashimoto to lead the Reinforcement Unit.

While the 11th Air Fleet and the 6th Air Division had the responsibility of providing CAP during daylight hours, the R Area Air Force would support Operation KE during the night. Its 50+ float planes took over the duties of flying ahead of the Reinforcement Unit to shield the ships from attacks by the American PT boats based at Tulagi.

A vital part of Operation KE was the use of the Russell Islands as a backup intermediate place where troops would be taken if any of the destroyers failed in pulling the men off Guadalcanal. In this case, landing craft would take the soldiers from Guadalcanal's beaches to the Russells. One benefit the Army's staff officers saw in using the Russells would be to mislead the Americans that the Japanese planned to make the nearby islands a temporary garrison and supply base. After six destroyers moved 328 soldiers to the Russells on January 29, the diversion proved to be somewhat successful when 33 American planes from CACTUS attacked the Russells but did not do much damage and only wounded 17 men.

Operation KE began on February 1 at 8:45 a.m. with the arrival of fighter-escorted five B-17s over Shortland that dropped their bombs and scored hardly any damage at all. Five Zeroes rose to intercept the attackers as four B-17s emerged a little later from the clouds. This attack awakened the Japanese air defenses and 43 Zeroes attacked the interlopers. Three of the four bombers did not return and did nothing to delay Operation KE. After the Americans lost two SBDs attacking Munda, the 6th Air Division attacked Guadalcanal with 23 Oscar fighters and six Lily light bombers. The Japanese planes returned with triumphant claims of destroying four "large aircraft" and four fighters on the ground.

Operation KE proceeded. The Japanese rescue attempts would soon affect the aggressive American ground operations.

The Americans Continue the Chase

The American XIV Corps held a position on the Poha River on January 25 and primed to press their attack on the remnants of the Japanese opposition on Guadalcanal. They did not know what the Japanese were going to do or where their concentrations were. Based on what the Americans had encountered in their battles to date, the question of how hard the Japanese would fight was still uncertain. But the expectation was that the Japanese were in retreat and not willing to fight as hard as they had done in the past. The Americans had captured a few Japanese soldiers, the interrogations of these prisoners led the American to believe that most of the soldiers to be encountered were part of the 17th Army's 2nd Division.

✲ ✲ ✲

The terrain west of the Poha River was quite similar to the area around Point Cruz and Kokumbona. Rugged, tall mountains and steep hills dominated the scene to the west with a narrow corridor hugging the northern coast. The coastal path varied from 300 to 600 yards wide with several rivers and many streams crossing the way that made rapid movements slower than an infantry commander would prefer. The path to Cape Esperance was only large enough to accommodate regiment-size maneuvers.

Patch's orders issued on January 25 instructed CAM to move through the 25th Division at the Poha River line and attack to the west the next day. The 6th Marines would move out on the right along the beach while the 182nd Infantry would attack along the high ground inland. Both regiments would begin the assault abreast with the division's third regiment, the 147th Infantry, held in reserve.

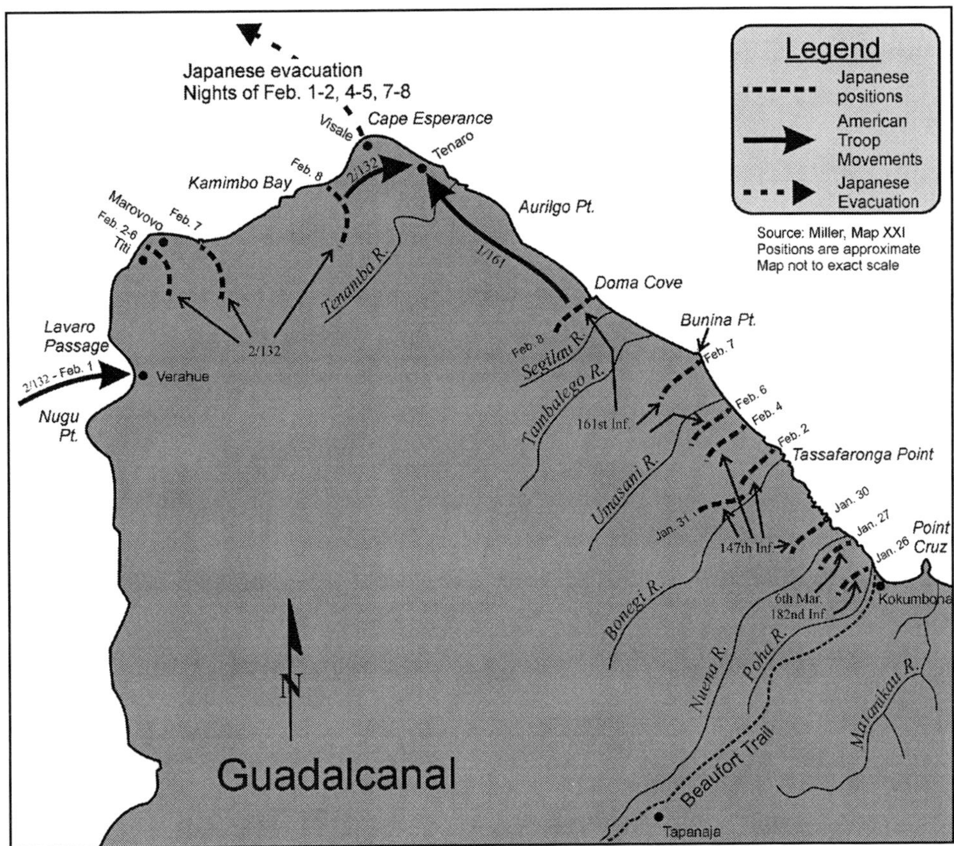

Chasing the Japanese off Guadalcanal

The Americal and the 25th Divisions' artillery would provide supporting fire while air support would come from the 2nd MAW. Patch did not mince his words in the orders as to how intensely he wanted the attack to be conducted—the attack should "effect the kill through aggressive and untiring offensive action."[2]

The CAM Division attacked on schedule at 6:30 a.m. on January 26 and immediately gained 1,000 yards. Only a few riflemen and machine gunners greeted the attacking Americans that day. Nonetheless, the pace of the advance picked up the next day, January 27. The CAM Division advanced 2,000 yards and reached the Nueha River. Patrols returned January 28. They encountered just sporadic Japanese opposition.

Patch separated the 147th Infantry from the CAM Division, added the 2nd Battalion, 10th Marines, and 97th FAB, A Company's 75-mm pack howitzers to it. He placed the combined force under the command of Brig. Gen. Alphonse De Carre and ordered it to go after the Japanese. Meanwhile, the Americal Division's Artillery would support the 147th Infantry's attack as the 6th Marines guarded the rear and the 182nd Infantry returned to defend the Lunga perimeter.

The 147th Infantry attacked on January 30 at 7:00 a.m. The 1st Battalion moved along the beach, advanced about 2,000 yards west of the Nueha River to the mouth of the Bonegi River, and met just light opposition. One of the battalion's patrols crossed the Bonegi at 11:52 a.m. However, the 3rd Battalion, advancing along a route inland on the 1st Battalion's left flank, met heavy Japanese machine gun fire about 1,000 yards east of the Bonegi that stopped their attack. The 1st Battalion's patrol had to withdraw as the Japanese poured machine gun fire from the Bonegi River's west bank. The 1st Battalion had no choice but turn back to the river's mouth.

The 147th Infantry attacked again on January 31 intending to cross the Bonegi River and take the high ground west of the waterway. This time they had help from the five-inch guns of the American destroyers *Anderson* and *Wilson*. The withering and destructive power of the destroyer's guns—each of them was the equivalent to a 127-mm cannon—made the difference for the 3rd Battalion. It crossed the Bonegi River inland and took some of the ridges about 2,500 yards inland from Tassafaronga Point. But the destroyer's fire was not enough to help the 1st Battalion. It met stiff resistance from the stronger Japanese positions at the river's mouth that prevented them from crossing it and had to stay at their former positions about 300 yards east of the river.

The XIV Corps' successes from January 10 to January 31 drove the Japanese back seven miles and resulted in Japanese losses of 105 prisoners and about 4,000 killed. The American losses during that period were far less with 189 soldiers and Marines killed and about 400 wounded.

The command of the westward attack passed from Gen. De Carre to Gen. Sebree on February 1. The Japanese displayed their competence in fighting an effective delaying action when part of their 600-man landing force, put ashore on January 14, stopped the 1st Battalion from crossing the Bonegi River despite heavy fire from the destroyers offshore and from artillery inland. When the American guns fired into the valley near the river's mouth, the Japanese withdrew to the river's mouth at 3:25 p.m. and still stopped the 1st Battalion from crossing the river.

The 147th had greater success on February 2 with the 1st Battalion crossing the mouth of the Bonegi River with more artillery help. The 1st and 3rd Battalions neared Tassafaronga Point by 5:10 a.m. The 147th Infantry's losses during the crossing were two killed and 67 wounded. The Americans estimated they had fought about 700-800 Japanese soldiers that had taken up positions east and west of the Bonegi. The Japanese perfectly executed their withdrawal and gave a fine demonstration of how to fight a delaying action.

As the advancing American main body advanced forward on February 3 along a line south of Tassafaronga Point, patrols looked upon the banks of the Umasani River about 2,300 yards to the west. The main American force moved forward another 1,000 yards to a line about 1,000 yards southeast of the Umasani River. The 3rd Battalion met light Japanese resistance from a few Japanese soldiers. Patrol activities on the western front were the only American operations being conducted on February 5 and found no organized Japanese opposition.

Cutting off the Japanese Escape

While the XIV Corps advanced along Guadalcanal's north coast, it completed plans to land soldiers behind Japanese lines on the south coast. The plans called for an expanded battalion to be put ashore and advance toward Cape Esperance. The objective was to seize the beaches at the island's northernmost tip and prevent what remained of the Japanese 17th Army from escaping to safety. There the two converging American forces would corner and annihilate them.

In October 1942, Adm. Turner and Gen. Vandegrift had planned to land the 2nd Marine Raider Battalion in Beaufort Bay to harass the Japanese rear echelons. Nevertheless, when the Japanese landed reinforcements in October and November, the two commanders had no choice but to cancel their plan and use the Raider Battalion instead to go after Japanese troops near Koli Point.

After Gen. Patch took command of all ground American troops on Guadalcanal, he wished to land a regimental combat team on the south coast to stop any Japanese attempts to land supplies and reinforcements at Cape Esperance, Visale, and Kamimbo Bay and also, like Turner and Vandegrift's objectives in October and November, pressure the Japanese from their rear. After six tank landing craft arrived at Tulagi in January 1943, Patch had the means to turn his plan into action with enough sufficient naval strength to land a reinforced battalion. Patch picked the 132nd Infantry's 2nd Battalion with four 75-mm pack howitzers to be that force and named Lt. Col. Alexander M. George as its commander.

While the 2nd Battalion was not strong enough to land against any appreciable Japanese opposition, Patch wanted to place them ashore at a place as near to the Japanese as possible. Providing cover for the landings would be the job of the 147th Infantry's I Company. Since the Americans did not have much information about the beach landing areas where the 2nd Battalion would be put ashore, Lt. Col. Paul A. Gavan, the Americal Division's operations officer and the XIV Corp's assistant operations officer, led a scouting party to inspect the beaches in the vicinity. Their first choice was the beach at Titi near Lavoro Passage with Nugu Point as their second pick. There was a good landing beach at Verahue, a village between the two other choices. But Gavan worried that the landing craft could not get to Verahue's beach since the boats had to pass through a narrow channel with hazardous reefs lining both sides of the passage.

While the choice of a landing beach still had to be decided, the covering force comprising eight riflemen and three machine gunners from I Company along with riflemen and gunners from M Company, 147th Infantry, boarded the schooner *Kocorana* at 1:00 a.m., January 31, at Beaufort Bay. Just like many similar local boats, the Australians had hidden her to keep it from falling into Japanese hands and turned them over to the Americans. It sailed for Lavoro to put the covering force ashore at Titi.

After the schooner arrived, one officer and five riflemen got into a rowboat at about 6:00 a.m. and began heading for the shore. As they neared the beach, the water erupted around them and the *Kocorana*. The fire came from Japanese rifles and machine guns located on a ridge about 100 yards to the rear. Chaos descended on the scene as the landing party reached the shore and set the rowboat adrift.

The schooner could not be put on the beach; so Maj. H. W. Butler, the 2nd Battalion's executive officer, took the boat's helm and headed it out to sea. The landing party was on its own. The schooner arrived at Beaufort Bay at about 4:00 p.m. to load aboard 15 more riflemen, two automatic riflemen, and three native scouts. Butler wanted to land near Verahue and move to Titi to come to the aid of the abandoned six men.

Nevertheless, the Titi landing party had evaded the Japanese, got on their radio, and recommended to XIV Corps that George's force land at Nugu Point instead of Titi. Butler and the *Kocorana* arrived at Titi the next morning and found the six men safe and sound.

Meanwhile, on the beach at Kukum, the 2nd Battalion along with the other units assigned to it finished loading their trucks, artillery, ammunition, food, and medical supplies aboard the six tank landing craft and the destroyer-transport *Stringham*. After packing the last boat at 6:00 p.m., January 31, the small fleet, with the four destroyers *Fletcher*, *Radford*, *Nicholas*, and *DeHaven* under Capt. Robert P. Briscoe's command and fighters from Henderson Field providing the escort, sailed on a course that would take them around Cape Esperance.

The landing craft arrived at Nugu Point at sunrise on February 1. An advance party went ashore and met Maj. Butler. He told them that there was no opposition at Verahue. The beach master inspected the Verahue beach and pronounced it safe enough to bring the landing craft onshore.

The landing force began bringing themselves and their cargo onto the beach. When Japanese bombers appeared around noon, the sight of the American fighters convinced the Japanese pilots not to attack. The combined force finished its landing by 3:00 p.m., and the empty landing craft returned to Kukum.

✡ ✡ ✡

While the Americans wanted an uneventful return voyage to Lunga after it deposited its cargoes at Nugu Point, the Japanese had other ideas. An Imperial Japanese Army patrol plane spotted Briscoe's destroyers and sent an exaggerated radio message to Rabaul that there were four "cruisers" steaming toward Guadalcanal's northern coast.

The report that these warships were "cruisers" told the Japanese senior officers that these ships constituted a threat to Operation "KE." They launched an air raid to attack the American ship formation. Not too much time passed when 13 Vals and 40 Zeroes took off from Buin. Guadalcanal's radio issued an air raid alert at 2:43 p.m., and the four ship formation split into two groups. The first included three LCTs escorted by the *DeHaven* and *Nicholas* near Savo Island while the second had the destroyers *Radford* and *Fletcher* protecting the remaining three LCTs nearing Verahue. CACTUS' fighter director mistakenly directed the scrambled F4Fs to protect the ships near Verahue thus leaving the formation near Savo totally unprotected.

When Cmdr. Charles E. Tolman, the *DeHaven*'s captain, received the air raid alert from Guadalcanal, he immediately ordered his ship's crew to General Quarters. After ordering a speed increase to 20 knots and then reduced to 15 knots, his radar operators reported approaching unidentified aircraft. Not sure whether the planes were friendly or hostile, he hesitated to issue the order for his destroyer's AA guns to open fire at them. She was like a sitting duck with a target painted on her that could have said, "Hit me here."

Six Vals dove on the vulnerable ship and dropped their bombs. One missile hit the destroyer amidships at 2:53 p.m. It exploded in a deadly ball of flame that engulfed the ship's entire center section. A second bomb hit just to the rear of the ship's bridge; a third bomb penetrated the ship's thin hull and exploded in her forward magazine. Thick black smoke rose from her and the ship turned sharply like a jackknife. When the wind blew the smoke away, the *DeHaven* was no longer there. She took Tolman, 166 officers and men along with her.

Meanwhile, the *Nicholas'* captain, Lt. Cmdr. Andrew Hill, increased speed to 32 knots, jinked, and jerked to avoid the falling bombs that exploded in the water within 20 to 200 feet of her. She lost two killed and seven wounded men. The *Nicholas* claimed shooting down three Japanese planes with the fighters saying they destroyed 12 more. The actual Japanese losses were five Vals and three Zeroes. After the Japanese planes turned away to return to their base, the *Nicholas* searched for *DeHaven* survivors and found 146.

✲ ✲ ✲

After checking that all their equipment had landed in working order, the landing force took a well-deserved rest for the night and began their advance the next morning along the beach. G Company and 20 native scouts moved over the high ground to the right. The trucks could move along the beach, thus making the task of bringing the battalion's critical supplies forward much easier. At 2:25 p.m., the battalion entered Titi Village after easily marching three and a half miles. The remaining tank landing craft that still had supplies aboard moved up the coast to Titi and unloaded their contents. Meanwhile, patrols had advanced to Kamimbo Bay. The entire party marched to Titi on February 4. The battalion established a defensive position in the village as patrols continued probing up the coast and inland along its right flank.

The ease of transporting supplies by truck hit a snag as the terrain beyond Titi became muddy and full of dense jungle foliage. George and his men then had to rely on one or two tank landing craft to bring supplies from Kukum and drop them off on the beach. It was always the plan for the 2nd Battalion to be self-sufficient and not need constant resupply or reinforcements. George made sure his command's supplies stayed with the men so that he could draw from them if the Japanese should attack by land or sea. George had little or no knowledge how strong the Japanese were in his line of march, so he prudently advanced toward Cape Esperance.

Rescuing Their Comrades-in-Arms

While the American soldiers pursued their quarry, the Japanese actively pursued their own objectives but with a much greater sense of urgency. Adm. Hashimoto left Shortland at 11:30 a.m. on February 1 and gathered his 20 destroyers into two columns for the trip down the Slot. He divided his ships into two units—one destined for Cape Esperance and the other headed for Kamimbo Bay. With Hashimoto in overall command aboard his flagship *Makinami* and leading the Cape Esperance unit's screening destroyers, Adm. Koyanagi commanded that unit's transportation unit. The expedition's ships in each unit were:[3]

Reinforcement (First Evacuation) Unit

Unit	Assignment	Ships
Cape Esperance	Screen (Hashimoto)	*Makinami, Maikaze, Kawakaze, Kuroshio, Shirayuki, Fumizuki*
	Transport (Koyanagi)	*Kazegumo, Makikumo, Yugumo, Akigumo, Tanikaze,Urakaze, Hamakaze, Isokaze*
Kamimbo Bay	Screen	*Satsuki, Nagatsuki*
	Transport	*Tokitsukaze, Yukikaze, Oshio, Arashio*

As Hashimoto's force moved down the Slot north of Vella LaVella Island, Henry Josselyn, the Australian coastwatcher on that island[4], spotted the ships at 1:20 p.m. and warned CACTUS. The first strike of 51 planes—17 TBFs, 17 SBDs, four P-39s, four P-38s, four P-40s, and five F4Fs—took off from Guadalcanal and attacked the 20-destroyer force. When they returned to their base, the American pilots reported sinking one destroyer and shooting down seven out of 18 defending Zeroes, while losing two TBFs shot down and two more heavily damaged, along with one SBD, and one P-39. A second 41-plane strike of 11 TBFs, ten SBDs, and 20 F4Fs followed the first strike and saw one burning and crippled destroyer heading to the northwest. All the second strike's planes returned safely, claiming they hit the Japanese ship with two bombs and shot down ten Zeroes.

The ship the American aircraft hit was Hashimoto's flagship, the *Makinami*. She could no longer maneuver probably because of loss of power and/or rudder control. Hashimoto relinquished his command of the force to Koyanagi, who ordered the *Fumizuki* and *Shirayuki* to go to the former flagship's aid and stay with her. Hashimoto transferred his flag to the *Shirayuki* and attempted to catch up to his command.

Koyanagi replaced the *Fumizuki* and *Shirayuki* with the *Makikumo* and *Yugumo* in the screening unit at 7:12 p.m. and pushed the original schedule back 30 minutes. He detached the screening destroyers to move ahead to protect against any American naval interference at about 8:00 p.m. and sent the Kamimbo Bay contingent on its mission two hours later. If Koyanagi believed he had a clear path to the Guadalcanal northern beaches, the Americans had something in mind to stop him. Eleven Tulagi-based PT boats took their positions in groups of twos and threes off Savo Island, Cape Esperance, and Duma Cove and waited for the Japanese ships to appear.

Meanwhile, Generals Sano and Miyazaki had brought their exhausted men to the beach at Cape Esperance at 8:00 p.m. They had spent a difficult time hauling all they could carry over the rugged Guadalcanal terrain and let their security lapse by loudly talking. This behavior concerned both generals and had their worst fears realized with the loud crack of a rifle shot shattering the darkness.

They sent a staff officer to investigate what happened. He returned with a story that would soon become a regular occurrence as the Japanese soldiers sought their rescue. Two Japanese soldiers from the 229th Infantry helped their wounded comrade commit suicide after carrying him on their shoulders. The now dead man had asked his compatriots to help him since he no longer had the strength to continue the march and did not want the Americans to capture him. The estimated 9:00 p.m. arrival time of their rescuers approached as the Japanese soldiers readied themselves for their departure. But no ships appeared. Many minutes passed, and the soldiers heard gunfire out to sea and saw many fires sprout on the water like blossoming flowers.

At 10:10 p.m., the Reinforcement Unit steamed at 30 knots as the outline of Savo Island appeared ahead. About 35 minutes later, the *PT-48* and *PT-111* showed up and fired four torpedoes each. *PT-48*, Lt. (jg) Lester H. Gamble in command and the most famous PT commander in the Guadalcanal campaign, escaped damage as the boat sped away. Gamble beached her on Savo Island and stayed there for the night. Her partner, *PT-111*, was less fortunate as a five-inch shell from the *Kawakaze* hit the boat and turned it into a flaming pyre. Two American sailors aboard her, one officer and one enlisted man, perished in the conflagration.

After Japanese float planes bombed and strafed *PT-59*, *PT-115*, and *PT-37* off Cape Esperance, the PTs spotted several ominous shadows that came from Japanese destroyers. Aboard the *PT-115*, Ens. Connolly piloted his boat north of Cape Esperance, closed to within 500 yards of his target, fired two torpedoes at it, and fired his other two torpedoes at another destroyer. Two Japanese destroyers, likely the *Satsuki* and the *Nagatsuki*, fired back. Connolly alternately sped up and slowed his boat's speed to evade the exploding shells in the water and lucked out when he moved, along with the *PT-59*, under a blinding rain squall to avoid being hit. The two boats managed to beach on Savo Island where they waited for daylight before heading back for Tulagi. *PT-37* was not as fortunate. The boat's commander, Ens. James J. Kelly, had just fired the last of his four torpedoes when Japanese gunfire ignited the boat's gasoline tanks and turned the vessel into a flaming wreck. The boat's only survivor was alive only because the explosions blew him overboard and spared him from being incinerated.

The *PT-123*, commanded by Ens. Ralph L. Richards, and *PT-124*, commanded by Lt. Clark W. Faulkner, idled quietly in the water at 10:49 p.m. when a huge shadow that could only be a Japanese destroyer came into view. Faulkner attacked first when he fired three torpedoes that appeared to hit the ship then maneuvered his boat in a tight, high-speed turn, and speedily retreated to Tulagi. When Richards followed the *PT-124* to close about 500 yards from the destroyer, a Japanese float plane appeared from out of nowhere and dropped its bomb. It hit the boat's stern and exploded in a huge fireball. All of the *PT-123*'s crew except for four men survived.

Thus far, none of the PTs had hit anything. Their attacks left three boats lost and 15 men killed. This assault was the last and most brutal PT action of the Guadalcanal campaign. While none of the attacks achieved much in terms of inflicting damage on the Imperial Japanese Navy, the Japanese had quite a more positive view in a report to the Japanese military establishment of the bravery and aggressiveness of the PT sailors such as Kelly:

> "The enemy has used PT boats aggressively...on their account our naval ships have had many a bitter pill to swallow—there are many examples of their having rendered the transport of supplies exceptionally difficult. It is necessary to assign to the boats young men who are both robust and vigorous."[5]

Gen. Patch showed his appreciation a few days later when he went to the Tulagi PT base, given the name "Calvertville" by its occupants, and bestowed medals on some of the PT sailors. The renowned author Samuel Eliot Morison was with the general that day and remembered him saying the following about those incredibly valiant warriors, "A wonderful and touching sight—all these fine young men, ready to go anywhere and do anything. Makes you feel humble."[6]

A Japanese Pete patrol plane sighted Briscoe's remaining three destroyers and reported the observation to the Japanese Navy. If he had any intention of interfering with the Japanese rescue expedition now approaching Cape Esperance, seeing the Japanese patrol plane most likely discouraged him from doing so.

✲ ✲ ✲

The six Japanese destroyer-transports appeared off the Cape Esperance beaches at 10:40 p.m., more than two hours late. The Kamimbo Unit was off the bay's beach at midnight. Both units began sending landing craft ashore and taking as many soldiers off the island as fast as they could. Gen. Sano said goodbye to Imoto and went aboard one of the boats with most of the men of his division. Adm. Koyanagi witnessed the soldiers boarding the destroyers and later described their dilapidated state:

> "[They] wore only the remains of clothes [that were] so soiled their physical deterioration was extreme. Probably they were happy but [they] showed no expression. All had dengue or malaria [and their] diarrhea sent them to the heads. Their digestive organs were so completely destroyed, [we] couldn't give them good food, only porridge."[7]

In a report later submitted to Adm. Yamamoto, the state of the men being rescued further reinforces how bad their appearance was:

> "[They]...were so undernourished that their beards, nails and hair had all stopped growing, their joints looked pitifully large. Their buttocks were so emaciated that their anuses were completely exposed, and on the destroyers that picked them up they suffered from constant and uncontrolled diarrhea."[8]

If these men were to ever fight again, they would probably require a long recovery from their horrid experience.

The last Japanese that could be taken away at Kamimbo Bay arrived on a destroyer-transport at 1:53 a.m. with another man coming aboard at Cape Esperance five minutes later. Nonetheless, there were still 1,270 men at Cape Esperance and another 300 at Kamimbo Bay left on the embarkation points' beaches because of the ships' late arrival.

As the Japanese ships began moving up the Slot toward Bougainville, the *Makikumo* went after a PT boat near Tulagi. Koyanagi tried to call her back to join the rest of his force, but could not raise her. As the destroyer approached Iron Bottom Sound at 1:45 a.m., a huge explosion erupted in her hull. One thought the Japanese had was that it had hit a mine because of reports that the American destroyer-minelayers *Tracy, Montgomery,* and *Preble* had laid about 300 mines in the waters between Doma Reef near a point about halfway to Cape Esperance. Another possibility was that a torpedo from a PT boat had struck her. No one had any idea what the cause was. The hapless destroyer could not move. The *Yugumo* rescued the *Makikumo*'s crew and put several torpedoes into her to sink her.

✲ ✲ ✲

The success of the first Japanese expedition should be judged from the reactions of the Americans. They had no knowledge that any Japanese soldiers had been pulled off the island. The Japanese had kept Operation KE a secret mission, and that achievement continued for their next two attempts to pull out. It could only be described as a superbly executed military operation.

As the sun rose on February 2 over the Guadalcanal's northern beaches, the 17th Army's senior officers seemed pleased with the success of their command's evacuation. Still fooling the American soldiers that the Japanese knew were not far away, the Japanese soldiers lit fires on the beach at Cape Esperance and began moving southward for the next two nights toward Tassafaronga to set up delaying actions against the advancing Americans coming up the coast. Meanwhile that night, the 2nd Division moved northward to the evacuation beaches.

The 17th Army's euphoria over prospects of being safely rescued began to fade the next day. Doubts rose about the Imperial Japanese Navy's commitment to rescue the soldiers with the order that the soldiers should not wait on the beaches for the destroyers to take them away but wait in landing craft offshore. The Japanese rear guard, under the command of Col. Norihiro Matsuda, received a command to prepare to wait in boats instead of on the beaches. This put the slow-moving landing craft in the water in jeopardy of attack by PT boats or American aircraft.

When an American patrol encountered two Japanese staff officers and about 140 men the 17th Army had been sent out to see what the Americans were up to near Maravovo, a brief skirmish occurred between the two parties. The short-lived battle resulted in two men killed on each side and the Japanese capturing two American soldiers. After being aggressively interrogated and before dying under stressful conditions, the Americans revealed to their torturers that about 600 American soldiers were in Maravovo.

On the following morning of February 3, the Japanese 350-man rear guard from the Yano Battalion, 60 men from the 124th Infantry, what was left of the Ichiki Detachment, and a section of 15-cm howitzers occupied positions along a half-mile line about equidistant between northwest of the Bonegi River and the Segilau River south bank. Fortunately for the rear guard, the Americans confined their ground actions to small patrols. No longer faced with the possibility of major combat against the Americans, Matsuda now had the time to plan the orderly withdrawal of his command. He anticipated he would take his force to Kamimbo Bay, board some landing craft, and move to the Russell Islands for an uneventual trip to Bougainville.

During the three-day period from February 2-4, a maximum of 15 Japanese Bettys prowled the waters around Guadalcanal and found several troubling signs the Americans were up to no good. Several powerful American naval forces that included carriers, battleships, and cruisers steamed not too far from the island in what looked like a prelude to some kind of major operation. Bad weather and the long distances from Rabaul to where the American ships were made attempts to attack successfully more difficult. When an attacking formation of five Bettys commanded by Lt. Cmdr. Genichi Mihara, the 705th Air Group commander, failed to return from a mission, the Japanese worried over whether to attack the American warship concentrations or not. With the specter of the powerful

American naval force so near the Slot, the 8th Army Group and the Southeast Area Fleet officers met on February 3 to authorize the second rescue run to Guadalcanal.

Yamamoto issued the order for a newly constituted Reinforcement Group with the destroyers *Asagumo* and *Samidare* replacing the sunken *Makikumo* and heavily damaged *Makinami* to immediately proceed to Guadalcanal and continue loading Japanese soldiers. These ships got the assignment:[9]

Reinforcement (Second Evacuation) Unit

Unit	Assignment	Ships
Cape Esperance	Screen (Hashimoto)	*Shirayuki, Kuroshio, Asagumo, Samidare, Maikaze, Kawakaze*
	Transport (Koyanagi)	*Yugumo, Kazegumo, Akigumo, Tanikaze, Urakaze, Hamakaze, Isokaze*
Kamimbo Bay	Screen	*Satsuki, Nagatsuki*
	Transport	*Tokitsukaze, Yukikaze, Oshio, Arashio*

Hashimoto's 20 destroyer force, plus the two newly assigned destroyers, weighed anchor on February 4 and left Shortland harbor at 11:30 a.m. forming their normal two-column formation after being safely at sea. As they steamed down the Slot, their 29-Zero air cover got into a chaotic air battle at 3:50 p.m. with 33 SBDs and TBFs along with the escorting 41 American fighters. Several bombs exploded near the *Maikaze* and crippled her so she could no longer move. The *Nagatsuki* had no choice but to come to its comrade's aid. Some bomb and/or torpedo hits knocked out the *Shirayuki*'s engines at 7:25 p.m., and Hashimoto had to move his flag again to the *Kawakaze*. The American lost four TBFs, three SBDs, three F4Fs, and one P-40 or 11 aircraft. One Zero did not return to its base; a second Zero had to execute a forced landing; and three others sustained damage.

On Guadalcanal's northern shore, the soldiers got ready for the oncoming ships to take them away. This time the Reinforcement Group arrived very close to their anticipated arrival time and took 3,921 men aboard the ships in just two hours despite heavy seas. Gen. Hyakutake and his staff boarded the *Isokaze* while Maruyama clambered onto the *Hamakaze*. Both rescuing groups uneventfully left Cape Esperance and Kamimbo Bay at their best speed and arrived at Bougainville the next day at 12:15 p.m.

Gen. Miyazaki walked the decks of the *Isokaze* and carefully examined the condition of the exhausted men lying on the deck and taking the pleasure of a long-denied sun bath. There were so many covering the destroyer's narrow decks that it was nearly impossible to walk between them. He came upon one man cradling the corpse of his comrade and defiantly claiming his friend was still alive.

Several high-ranking officers, including Lt. Gen. Moritake Tanabe, deputy chief of staff of the Army Section of Imperial Gen. Headquarters, met the arriving soldiers as the soldiers stood on land once again. Miyazaki silently stopped, saluted his superior, and Tanabe wordlessly returned it. Tears welled into both men's eyes as Miyazaki asked that his next assignment be a combat command where he could die with his men. Barely able to control the sadness that flooded him, Tanabe said, "Everything about this is the responsibility of Imperial Headquarters."[10] Again, the typical frustrations between the men commanding in the front lines and the deck chair generals in Tokyo could not be contained.

✲ ✲ ✲

While the Japanese destroyers took the men off the beaches to the northwest, Col. Matsuda was in command of all the remaining Japanese forces on Guadalcanal. He began to concern himself with how he was going to get his rear guard off the island. As the Yano group moved northward from its position west of the Bonegi River to the Segilau River, Matsuda left the Segilau to Kamimbo Bay to take charge of the withdrawal. As he moved to his destination, he sent the Oneda unit, the remnants of the 3rd Battalion, 230th Infantry, to take positions west of Cape Esperance to stop any American forces that might be approaching the evacuation beaches from Maravovo. He walked onto the beach at Kamimbo Bay at 5:00 p.m. and organized another unit to back up the Oneda Unit. Thus far, there was no intelligence that indicated the American Army threatened Operation KE. Matsuda, still cautious, seemed reassured by the latest news of any significant American troop movements.

With his defenses confidently in place, he turned his attention to the main task at hand—how to get his men safely extracted from the island. His senior boat engineering officer, Lt. Col. Sakuji Matsuyama, offered a dire prediction of what would happen if Matsuda's men had to leave the beaches on landing craft. Matsuyama warned that if they had to use landing craft, the men would be like sitting ducks to any attack by American aircraft or PT boats. Matsuda's radio operators sent a report to Rabaul pleading that three or four destroyers be sent with enough boats to take his men off the beaches. He warned that a tragic loss of life could happen if his men had to go to the Russells first and then be transported to Bougainville by transport. Waiting for what the Imperial Japanese Navy might send, he sat down and wrote a most pessimistic entry in his diary that expressed his sincere suspicions the destroyers would never come.

While American caution ruled their conduct and kept them from immediately and forcefully engaging the withdrawing Japanese, Matsuda prudently sent a 100-man force about three and a half miles south of Cape Esperance near the wreck of the *Sangetsu Maru*. He ordered them to deceive the Americans by lighting fires and to march in daylight and make the Americans believe they intended to vigorously defend their positions. He realized his worst fears when a discouraging message arrived at 5:35 p.m. that the Navy intended to pick up only those men they found languishing in boats offshore. Those soldiers not lucky enough to make it into the boats had to fend for themselves and find a way to get to New Georgia on their own.

The 17th Army pessimistically estimated the odds of safely extricating Matsuda's men at 50%. On the night of February 6, the senior Army and Navy commanders conferred. The reports of nearby American carriers worried the 8th Fleet chief of staff whether the third rescue attempt called for in the Operation KE plan could be successfully executed. Col. Norio Konuma listened to the pessimism, turned to Adm. Mikawa, and told him that all this talk concerned him. Mikawa again tried to reassure the worried Army officer that the Navy would do everything in its power to get the soldiers off the island. Despite Mikawa's attempts to assuage his concerns, Konuma went to see Hashimoto. The admiral firmly stated he would personally see that every man that could be evacuated would be rescued. He angrily rejected Konuma's request to go on the mission by saying the Navy could never erase such a blot on its record and that only the presence of an Army officer could guarantee the successful evacuation of Army personnel.

February 7 arrived with much portent for the fate of Matsuda's men. Severely concerned about the American carriers dangerously nearby, Adm. Yamamoto ordered that a line of submarines begin looking for the American ships and report their positions, courses, and speeds. He also instructed Kondo's Advance Force to get near enough to Guadalcanal by February 7 to support Operation KE. With sightings of American carriers and surface ships steaming south of San Cristobal pouring into Rabaul and Truk, Hashimoto gathered 18 destroyers for the third rescue run. They left Shortland that morning and steamed for Guadalcanal by way of the Solomon Islands' southern rim.

An American search plane sighted Hashimoto's force and directed 15 SBDs, 20 F4Fs, and one F5A to the Japanese ships. 17 Zeroes that were part of the 49-Zero air cover from the 11th Air Fleet attacked the American planes. The American bombers managed to drop two bombs on the *Isokaze* that hit astride her forward gun mount, started a fire, and killed two men. With the *Kawakaze* acting as her escort, the damaged destroyer turned around and headed north. The American F5A and one Zero disappeared and were presumed lost.

The sounds of heavy artillery shelling of Matsuda's men near Maravovo filled the air as more reports of American machine gun fire arrived. With no signs of any destroyers at sunset, he considered whether his remaining 26 landing craft could make it to the Russells. The moonless night approached with just slight winds and a glass-smooth sea offshore. He had enough boats to load all his men aboard them if he reorganized the loading plan to place four units of 500 men each aboard them.

For a frantic 45-minute period after 9:30 p.m., while the sounds of American artillery blasting in the distance and fires lighting the western horizon, the remaining Japanese soldiers boarded the boats and gratefully pulled away from Guadalcanal for the last time. The boats waited offshore while many of the men aboard them prayed for their rescue. The planned rendezvous time of 11:00 p.m. came and went. The sighting of the destroyers' blue recognition lights at last answered their pleas for divine intervention.

The destroyers reached the waiting boats. The small craft moved carefully next to the destroyers' hulls, and the men clamored aboard. Matsuda learned at 12:03 a.m. that all the men in the boats were safely on board their rescuers. Keeping his word to personally ensure all Japanese soldiers were off the island, Hashimoto ordered several boats lowered, and the sailors in them to row near the shore. They were to shout at the top of their lungs for any Japanese soldier still ashore to come to the beach to be rescued. The boats returned to their destroyers, and Hashimoto's force turned away from the shore and sped away at 30 knots. The frothing V-shaped wakes they left behind reassured Matsuda that his and his rear guard's deliverance had come at last. The destroyers stopped at the Russells to pick up other Japanese soldiers and then steamed up the Slot. Matsuda sent a radio message to the 17th Army, "With the help of 20,000 souls the recovery of 1,972 men from Guadalcanal is reported complete."[11] The last Japanese soldier had left Guadalcanal, and their Rising Sun battle flag never flew over that pestilent island again.

When Matsuda stepped ashore on Bougainville at 10:00 a.m., he reported to Gen. Hyakutake and told him of the completion of his mission on Guadalcanal. The colonel had come ashore with the Ichiki Detachment for the first fight against the Americans and was the last to leave the island as well.

☆ ☆ ☆

The number of rescued Japanese soldiers as a result of Operation KE is estimated at 12,805. The 17th Army finished a report on February 22 that stated Operation KE rescued 10,652 soldiers, with the first run taking 4,935 men off, the second run rescuing 3,921 men, and the last attempt liberating 1,796 soldiers. Despite that the total number of soldiers removed from Guadalcanal was *twice* the number the Imperial Japanese Army estimated would be saved, Gen. Tanabe issued a cautionary note saying it would be a long time before most of these men would again be ready for combat duty.

The Imperial Japanese Navy's losses were not as bad as they could have been under the circumstances. It lost the destroyer *Makikumo* with the *Makinami*, *Maikaze*, and *Isokaze* sustaining heavy damage. The U.S. Navy lost the heavy cruiser *Chicago* at the Battle of the Rennell Islands,[12] the destroyer *DeHaven*, and three PT boats with the *La Vallette* heavily damaged. The air losses by both sides were about even with the Japanese losing 56 planes and the Americans 53.

However, these losses affected the Japanese more than the Americans because of the American ability to bring fresh replacements into combat far more effectively than the Japanese. The Japanese self assessment attributed the success of Operation KE to the detailed, careful planning by their Army and Navy, the fast and nearly flawless execution by both services, and the sacrifice of the men left behind. In this author's opinion, the ability of the Japanese to keep their movements a carefully guarded secret was also a contributing, if not the most important, factor for the operation's success.

The Disappointed Americans

The combined American force moved out of Titi on February 7 at 7:30 a.m., but George was wounded that day. Lt. Col. George F. Ferry, the 2nd Battalion's commanding officer, took command of the combined force with Maj. Butler assuming command of the 2nd Battalion. Acting for Gen. Patch, Col. Gavan came ashore to help accelerate the advance. After inspecting the men, Gavan found that they could rapidly move out and saw no need to change any plans. He and the wounded George boarded the boat in which Gavan arrived and sailed back to Kukum. As nightfall came, the combined force had advanced to Marovovo and set up their camp there for the night. Both forces were now prepared to close the pincer on the Japanese at Cape Esperance.

☆ ☆ ☆

The exhausted and undermanned 147th Infantry badly needed to be relieved. On February 6, Patch ordered the 25th Division's 161st Infantry to pass through and replace the 147th on the north coast as artillery support came from the 2nd Battalion, 10th Marines, the 97th FAB, and the Americal Division. A newly established supply dump at Kokumbona shortened the supply lines to the advancing American troops.

Because Gen. Collins had too much to do commanding the Lunga-Metapona sector, Gen. Sebree had the responsibility to lead the advance. With Col. James T. Dalton, II, now in command, the 161st Infantry moved out at 10:00 a.m. on the 6th. The 3rd Battalion pressed forward along the beach, the 2nd Battalion was in the foothills on the left, and the 1st Battalion kept in reserve. The regiment was on the south bank of the Umasani River by 10:20 p.m. when some of its patrols crossed the stream. The only opposition the Americans encountered was a brief tussle between an American patrol and a small Japanese force camped out on a crest west of the river. The Japanese lost at least seven killed with the American patrol untouched.

The 161st crossed the Umasani the next day and advanced to Bunina Point as patrols moved to the Tambalego River. When the Japanese were spotted, the advancing Americans attacked them, and they retreated to the northwest. The regiment again ran into some Japanese resistance on February 8 at the Tambalego River. A short skirmish resulted with the Americans forcing the Japanese to retreat; the Americans moved forward to Doma Cove.

When coastwatchers warned the approach of some Japanese destroyers and to expect them to arrive in the Cape Esperance area on the night of February 7-8, Col. Ferry's 2/132 was about six miles southwest of Cape Marovovo and got ready for their arrival. The battalion saw no sign of the warships. When Ferry and his men began advancing the morning of February 8, they discovered several abandoned Japanese landing craft and supplies piled on the beach. It was now apparent that the Japanese were evacuating their men. The battalion consolidated their front lines and moved to Kamimbo Bay.

The 2nd Battalion, 161st Infantry, moving uphill to the northwest along Guadalcanal's northern coast and, having just barely enough to eat, became the regiment's reserve on February 9. The 1st Battalion took their place in the advancing line at Doma Cove with the 3rd Battalion and an anti-tank company right behind them. They had moved forward five miles by the afternoon and entered Tenaro Village.

The 2nd Battalion, 132nd Infantry advanced around Cape Esperance the same day to Tenaro, the agreed-upon meeting point for the converging American forces. While moving forward in a line of companies, the Japanese opened fire with machine guns and mortars, but could not stop the American advance. With their 75-mm guns out of range, the Americans counterfired with their mortars. The 2nd Battalion marched into Tenaro on February 9, 1943 between 4:00 and 5:00 p.m. and met the 2nd Battalion, 161st Infantry there. That event meant that all organized Japanese opposition had ended on Guadalcanal. Only a few Japanese soldiers from the 17th Army lagged behind.

Celebrating the end of one of the most trying and casualty-ridden struggles of the Pacific War, Gen. Patch sent the following telegram to Adm. Halsey:

> "Total and complete defeat of Japanese forces on Guadalcanal effected 1625 today...Am happy to report this kind of compliance with your orders...because Tokyo Express no longer has terminus on Guadalcanal."

An ebullient Halsey replied:

> "When I sent a Patch to act as tailor for Guadalcanal, I did not expect him to remove the enemy's pants and sew it on so quickly...Thanks and congratulations."[13]

Nimitz, not as joyful as his subordinates, issued a report with a less than congratulatory tone:

> "Until the last moment it appeared that the Japanese were attempting a major reinforcement effort. Only skill in keeping their plans disguised and bold celerity in carrying them out enabled the Japanese to withdraw the remnants of the Guadalcanal garrison. Not until all organized forces had been evacuated on 8 February did we realize the purpose of their air and naval dispositions."[14]

Nonetheless, the Americans failed to destroy what was left of the Japanese 17th Army. The Japanese had executed a highly effective evacuation and, according to a count by the Japanese, saved 10,652 men to maybe fight again on another front.[15]

Part 13: The End of the Beginning

"This is not the end.
It is not even the beginning of the end.
But it is, perhaps, the end of the beginning."

Winston Churchill, November 10, 1942

CHAPTER 61
Casualties and Losses

The epic, spectacular, bloody, and tedious struggle that I have called the "Battles for Guadalcanal" ended six months and two days after it began. On August 7, 1942, the first American Marine arrived and stepped ashore. The last Japanese soldier that could leave departed the same way the Americans arrived, by the sea. By this time, one only had to look under that patch of water known as Iron Bottom Sound to see the ghosts of the many ships and sailors littering the sea bottom. Before we examine the aftermath of this mêlée, it becomes necessary to look at the casualties and losses of men and equipment that resulted from the conflict.

There were seven battles at sea between the powerful Imperial Japanese Navy and the U.S. Navy, which was still recovering from the Pearl Harbor debacle. The naval losses in ships by both sides were.[1]

Ship Losses from the Naval Battles of Guadalcanal

Ship Type	American (Allied)	Tonnage	Japanese	Tonnage
Fleet Carriers	2	34,500	0	0
Light Carriers	0	0	1	8,500
Battleships	0	0	2	62,500
Heavy Cruisers**	6	56,925	3	26,400
Light Cruisers	2	12,000	1	5,700
Destroyers	14	22,815	11	20,930
Submarines	0	0	6	11,309
Transports*	1	—	13	—
Destroyer conversions*	3	—	1	—
Totals	20	34,815	32	37,939

** Tonnage of lost transports and destroyer conversions not available.*

*** Allied heavy cruisers' losses include the HMAS Canberra (Australian)*

The Japanese lost more tonnage and more ships than the Americans. While the battleships the Japanese lost were the older battlecruisers *Hiei* and *Kirishima*, the cruiser and destroyer losses particularly hurt the strength of their navy. With their emphasis on building more carriers and merchant vessels, replacements for these ships were not a high priority with the Imperial Japanese Navy. However, these losses did not diminish the overall power of the Japanese Navy, as future naval battles would bear witness. Meanwhile, the buildup of the U.S. Navy gathered and increased its momentum. The American shipyards were on a full wartime footing and working feverishly creating the greatest navy ever built in world history. The new *Essex*-class fleet carriers and *Independence*-class light carriers were about to be launched and become the foundation for the immense naval power Americans would bring to the Pacific War.

The two naval battles that involved aircraft carriers from both sides were the Battles of the Santa Cruz Islands and Eastern Solomons. The Japanese achieved a tactical victory at Santa Cruz by sinking the *Hornet* and almost sinking the *Enterprise*. The clear victor at the Battle of the Eastern Solomons was the Americans. After that confrontation, the Japanese withdrew what was left of their fleet carriers to the home islands, thus granting American air superiority over Guadalcanal. Of course, CACTUS had a great deal to do with that result. Its presence and the aircraft and crews that flew the aircraft from there forced the Japanese to try bringing reinforcements and supplies in at night using their precious destroyers.

To illustrate the results between the Battle of the Eastern Solomons and the Battle of Santa Cruz, the air losses by both sides for each battle were as follows:[2]

Naval Aircraft and Air Crew Losses at Guadalcanal's Carrier Battles

Battle of the Eastern Solomons							
	Fighters	***Dive Bombers***	***Torpedo Planes***	***Total Aircraft***	***Pilots***	***Crewmen***	***Total Aircrew***
American	12	2	7	21	6	2	8
Japanese	33	23	8	64	34	28	62
Battle of the Santa Cruz Islands							
American	30	24	15	69	14	7	21
Japanese	27	40	30	97	69	74	143
Totals for Both Carrier Battles							
American	42	26	22	90	20	9	29
Japanese	60	63	38	161	103	102	205

Despite the different results between of the two Guadalcanal carrier battles, the Japanese Navy lost 50% more aircraft and over six times the crewmen than the Americans. Two possible reasons for the greater Japanese losses were the predominate Japanese strategy to be on the offense and the ability of the Americans to more effectively direct their CAP using radar. As would be shown in the Pacific War's future carrier battles, the Japanese had more trouble replacing their air losses than the Americans. That fact would come to a complete fatal reality during their devastating defeat at the Battle of the Philippine Sea in June 1944. After that time, almost all of the experienced Japanese naval air combat veterans were dead, and Japanese naval aviation was no longer a factor in the war.

☆ ☆ ☆

Casualties and Losses

In the surface battles, Savo Island and Tassafaronga were Japanese victories. Two of them, the Battle of Cape Esperance and the Naval Battle of Guadalcanal, were clear American victories. In terms of tactics and effective command abilities, the Japanese showed their clear superiority in both categories. Mikawa's masterful victory at Savo Island, Tanaka's ability to continue running down the Slot, the Japanese ability to sally their battleships and heavy cruisers off Guadalcanal's shores and bombard the Americans to distraction, and Koyanagi and Hashimoto's ability to rescue Japanese soldiers off of Guadalcanal were clear examples of where Japanese tactics excelled. Their ability to effectively engage stronger American naval forces at night and emerge victorious was a result of rigorous training and superior maneuvering. The Japanese Long Lance torpedo clearly showed its superiority in surface battles.

The senior American naval commanders were new to actual naval combat after languishing in training mode between the two World Wars. Some of their cautious tactics resulted directly in horrible losses in both American ships and sailors. Some examples of these incidents include Fletcher's "injury" that removed him from tactical command in August; loss of the *Wasp*, causing Noyes' relief in October; Callaghan's confusion and Scott sticking to a rigid dogma; Wright's hesitation causing the American defeat at Tassafaronga in November and December; and Giffen's gross mishandling of his ships at Rennell.

On the positive side, new faces appeared on the scene near the end of the Guadalcanal campaign that would stand out in the future. Admirals McCain and Lee come to mind in this instance. Turner showed decisive command abilities when he decided to continue offloading supplies in August despite the approaching danger of Japanese bombers and with no air cover. Despite losing the *Wasp* and the withdrawal of carrier air cover, he finished landing the 7th Marines. He also wasted no time sending Callaghan and Scott after the approaching Japanese ships that resulted in successful American reinforcement and resupply efforts.

Adm. Halsey emerges from this conflict demonstrating his outstanding leadership despite his rough edges. When he arrived to take command, the morale of every man in the South Pacific rose astronomically and convinced all of them that they could beat the Japanese. Richard Frank describes Halsey's time as COMSOPAC his "finest hour." Of course, it was Adm. Nimitz who relieved the beleaguered Ghormley and insert Halsey. Nimitz knew Halsey was the man for the job, and Halsey did everything he could to justify his superior's judgment.

Judging Adm. Yamamoto's performance during this time in the war is a far more difficult task. After overseeing the rapid expansion of the Japanese Empire in the first six months after Pearl Harbor, his defeat at Midway had to affect his confidence. He had already told his superiors in Tokyo that he could not guarantee anything after the first six months and seemed to behave like a person unsure of victory. He hesitated in committing the Combined Fleet to meet and defeat the U.S. Navy in that long-sought-after single, final naval battle. Perhaps he knew the Imperial Japanese Navy was the only force to postpone an American victory and force his opponents to come to the negotiating table. Yamamoto only had a few months of his life remaining, although he could not have known it at that time.

The Japanese won tactical victories, but lost the strategic struggle. The Japanese Navy became weaker while the U.S. Navy became stronger. And that trend continued until the war's end.

Aircraft Losses

The war in the air did the most in determining who won and who lost in the Battles for Guadalcanal. Those dogfights, strafing runs, and attacks on shipping also decided the long term direction of aviation's role in the Pacific War. The air war took on the aspect of a war of attrition just like some of the other battles in military history such as those at Stalingrad and Verdun.

In his analysis in his book, *Guadalcanal*, Richard B. Frank maintains that an accurate computation of the actual aircraft losses by both sides, and particularly the Japanese, is difficult to achieve. Data on the Japanese air losses do not clearly illustrate the impact of these casualties on Japanese naval aviation. Neither side kept a consolidated computation of losses, but did keep records for each command or service.

The Japanese deployed their aircraft aboard carriers, the 11th Air Fleet, the R Area Air Force, which had their float planes, and the Imperial Japanese Army's 6th Air Division. The best data available for both sides' air losses are for two time periods—August 1 to November 15, 1942, and November 16, 1942, to February 9, 1943. The following tables depict the best obtainable estimates of aircraft losses:[3]

Japanese Aircraft Losses - August 1 - November 15, 1942

Command	Zeroes	Vals	Kates	Bettys	Flying Boats	Float Planes	Misc.	Totals
Carriers	18	69	47	—	—	—	1	198
11th A. F	107	15	—	100	19	—	2	243
Army	—	—	—	—	—	66	—	66
Totals	125	84	47	100	19	66	3	444

Approximate Japanese Aircraft Losses - November 16, 1942 - February 9, 1943

Zeroes	Vals	Bettys	Oscars	Petes	Totals
59	7	25	14-15	11	116-117

The best estimate shows that the Japanese, from the beginning of the Guadalcanal campaign until they evacuated the island, lost 560 to 561 aircraft. Radm. Munetaka Sakamaki, the 11th Air Fleet's chief of staff, maintained that more than 60 aircraft should be added to these totals for the latter period, which would put the total aircraft lost during this period to 176-177 planes or an overall average estimated total of 621 planes. However, this addition included losses that occurred in the skies over New Guinea.

The Allied aircraft losses for the same two periods were:[4]

Allied Aircraft Losses - August 1 - November 15, 1942

Command	F4F	SBD	TBF	P400/ P-39	PBY	B-17	B-26	C-47 / R4D	Other	Totals
Carriers	81	63	40	—	—	—	—	—	—	184
CACTUS	115	66	16	19	—	—	—	—	—	216
Search & Attack	—	—	—	—	17	18	1	—	—	36
Misc.	4	5	—	2	—	—	—	3	30	44
Totals	200	134	56	21	17	18	1	3	30	480

Allied Aircraft Losses - November 16, 1942 - February 9, 1943

F4F	SBD	TBF	P-39	P-40	P-38	PBY	B-17	B-26	C-47 /R4D	Other	Totals
41	31	10	12	10	6	4	9	4	1	6	134

The total aircraft losses depicted in the two previous tables shows a total number of Allied aircraft of 614 planes with the Japanese losing 621. However, estimating air crew losses was a far more difficult problem.

The estimated American aircrew losses included the following:[5]

American Aircrew Losses by Service

Service	Losses
Army Air Force	150
Navy	130
Marines	140
Totals	420

Japanese aircrew losses are less precise therefore only in intelligent guesses. The range of these estimates is between two to four times of the American losses. One reason for higher losses than the Americans was that many of the Japanese aircraft carried more men per plane than the American planes. A large majority of the Japanese air crew losses came from their most experienced and best trained men. Frank's book estimates the Imperial Japanese Navy had about 3,500 pilots before Pearl Harbor. The Imperial Japanese Navy had about 600 of these pilots with more than 800 hours flying time each. The Japanese Navy lost about 125 carrier pilots at Guadalcanal with many of them coming from this experience base. The pilots flying the Betty bombers sustained particularly high casualties among their most talented. Adm. Sakamaki confirmed how severe this problem when he stated that the newly-arrived replacements had just one-third the skill levels of the men they replaced.

During the time from August to November 1942 after the end of the Naval Battle of Guadalcanal, the Japanese had more planes than the Americans. What they lacked were airbases near

Guadalcanal so that their airplanes' limited range would not be as great a deficit. Either their unwillingness or inability to build airbases closer to Guadalcanal prevented them from using the latest model of the Zero fighter. The longer flying time for Japanese airplanes from their bases to their targets also gave the Americans more time to detect and intercept them. The Japanese commanders let their optimism about defeating the Americans through enthusiastic application of *élan* paralyze them from taking the needed actions to overcome their problem. namely by building airbases nearer to Guadalcanal. The Zero's designer and Japanese officers finish a postwar report that said the Japanese had only about one-fifth the runway construction capacity the Americans had. Therefore, the Japanese also suffered from a "runway construction gap" they never could close to equal the Americans.

Casualties on the Ground

When compared to the other major World War II battles, the cost in men at Guadalcanal was not nearly as great. The Americans had landed about 60,000 Marines and soldiers on the island. In his book published by the U. S. Army's Center of Military History, John Miller depicts the American ground casualties on Guadalcanal as follows:[6]

American Ground Casualties on Guadalcanal

Division	Killed	Wounded	Totals
1st Marine	774	1,962	2,736
Americal (Army)	334	850	1,184
2nd Marine	268	932	1,200
25th Army	216	439	655
Totals	1,592	4,183	5,775

The table shows that the Marines bore the brunt of American casualties on Guadalcanal with the 1st Marine Division sustaining the most of all units. Some of those losses reflect that they arrived first and had the most difficult task of securing and protecting a small enclave from aggressive assault by relatively fresh Japanese troops. However, the Japanese losses on the ground were far greater. The Japanese had more than 36,000 men from the 17th Army and the naval Special Landing Forces on Guadalcanal. By the time they evacuated all they could on February 7, 1943, more than 14,800 had died or were missing, 9,000 died of disease, and about 1,000 became prisoners of war or for an approximate total of 24,800 men. The casualty rates were therefore about 9.5% for the Americans and a much higher rate of about 69% for the Japanese.

Summarizing Both Sides' Casualties

To summarize, the following table shows a slightly different number of men killed for both sides than in the previous table:[7]

Estimated Number Killed at Guadalcanal

Protagonist	Land	Sea	Air	Total
American + Allied	1,769	4,911	420	7,100
Japanese	25,600	3,643	1,200	30,443
Totals	27,369	8,554	1,620	37,543

The Japanese Army suffered its first major defeat since their border war with the Soviet Union in the early 1930s. From that time until they engaged the Americans on Guadalcanal, the Army fought either relatively primitively armed troops such as the Chinese, the poorly prepared British Army on the Malaysian Peninsula, or even the small American contingent in the Philippines. Their island conquests of Guam and Wake were against greatly outnumbered American Marines or soldiers.

When they faced the 1st Marine Division, the Imperial Japanese Army believed the Americans had far fewer troops and conducted their offensive operations accordingly. But this time, the Americans landed a full division, and they fought like Samurai warriors. The Japanese were facing fully trained and dedicated troops who were just as tough and mean as they themselves were, if not more so. This surprised the Japanese Army, but they still stubbornly stuck to the idea that they outnumbered the Americans on Guadalcanal. As the ground battles on Guadalcanal bore witness, this obstinacy proved to be fatal to many more Japanese than Americans.

Another factor for Japanese failures on the ground was that Gen. Vandegrift, knowing he would not have enough supplies to conduct an offensive campaign against the Japanese, immediately established a defensive perimeter around Henderson Field, the Americans' most critical strategic asset, and therefore minimized his casualties the best way he could. In contrast, the Japanese Army commanders continually sent their men into a maelstrom of withering American gunfire resulting in the slaughter of their men. They later stubbornly defended their positions on the Galloping Horse and Gifu Perimeter that only the American artillery and tanks could finally dislodge. Their holding action while evacuating Guadalcanal was a fine demonstration of how to withdraw against a superior force. It is unfortunate they could not figure out how to miraculously accomplish similar feats of military mastery when they went on the offensive. With their conviction of their own invincibility and their belief that Americans were too soft to be tough soldiers, this blind spot prevented them from doing it.[8]

CHAPTER 62
Epilogue

The monumental struggles over capturing and holding Guadalcanal were now at an end. And with that victory, the Allies were truly on the road back. From June 1942 until February 1943, the Axis powers lost four major conflicts that forced them to retreat for the first time in World War II. They were to never advance again.

The Imperial Japanese Navy suffered a disastrous defeat at the Battle of Midway with the crippling loss of four of their fleet carriers in June 1942. The British 8th Army turned back Field Marshal Erwin Rommel's vaunted Afrika Corps at El Alamein in October 1942, then chased them across the top of Africa until they would be pinched between the Americans and British in Tunisia. This forced the Germans and Italians to leave Africa forever. The Soviet Army met the power of Von Paulus' 6th Army at Stalingrad, defeated the German Army, and began the long, painful process of removing their sworn enemy from their home soil. The American victory over the Japanese at Guadalcanal inflicted a devastating and humiliating defeat on the Imperial Japanese Navy and Army forcing the Japanese to begin shrinking its territory.

The Americans could now pursue Operation Watchtower and advance up the Solomon Islands. Their main objective turned to isolating the powerful Japanese base at Rabaul in the same way MacArthur was doing in New Guinea. Nonetheless, that objective would not be easy to achieve. The Japanese had proved they were still determined and effective fighters and would defend their shrinking empire with every resource at their disposal.

But something had changed. The Greater East Asia Co-Prosperity Sphere no longer grew; it began to contract.

Many men who had great influence over events during the battles for Guadalcanal emerged and faded. Let us review who these men were, their impact on the six-month struggle, and what happened to them afterward.

The Americans

Adm. Ernest E. King

The American invasion of Guadalcanal would not have happened if Adm. King had not intensively lobbied for it. The U.S. was at war after both Pearl Harbor and Germany's declaration of war. The first military priority was to defeat Nazism with the Pacific War taking a distinct back seat. The Americans did not have enough ships, men, tanks, guns, and other war materials to wage war on one front, let alone two.

After British Prime Minister Churchill visited Washington over Christmas 1941, the fortunes of war made the American and the British destinies tightly entwined. Nevertheless, King did not want every ship sent to the European Theater so that there would be none left for fighting the Japanese to other than a holding action. After MacArthur escaped to Australia from whence the retaking of the Philippines would begin and reports from an Australian coastwatcher in the Solomons arrived stating that the Japanese were building an airfield on Guadalcanal, King began his campaign to initiate offensive operations to kick the Japanese off that island. The supply line to Australia had to be kept open, and the Japanese construction of an airstrip on Guadalcanal threatened it. But the Americans and British were also planning an invasion of North Africa for 1942 which put enormous supply constraints on King.

After much cajoling and begging to Marshall and President Roosevelt, King finally got the approval to invade Guadalcanal and the operation began on August 7, 1942. It was solely a naval operation with the 1st Marine Division making up the landing force. King had to scrape together all the supplies he could find so that the operation was aptly nicknamed "Operation Shoestring." He continued to fight for support for the Guadalcanal campaign and eventually achieved success six months later.

King continued in the job as Chief of Naval Operations and as a member of the Joint Chiefs of Staff until the end of the war. He achieved the elevated rank of five-star Fleet Admiral in December 1944 and retired from the Navy one year later. The Navy periodically consulted with him on naval matters for several years. After some years of ill-health, he passed away on June 25, 1956. He would be remembered as an effective leader who fit in well in the Washingtonian political infighting, and he got the navy he wanted. The Americans built the most powerful navy the world had ever seen. The U.S. became the most powerful naval power in the world.

Adm. Chester W. Nimitz

After assuming command from Adm. Kimmel as CINCPAC, Nimitz knew he only had the carriers *Lexington*, *Saratoga*, and *Enterprise* to stop the Japanese while his battleship fleet lay in the mud of Pearl Harbor. After breaking even at Coral Sea and the victory at Midway, the Guadalcanal invasion was his next major campaign. He pulled together all the ships he could and sent them to the South Pacific to establish forward bases on New Caledonia and Espiritu Santo. Nonetheless, much of the direction for the Guadalcanal operation had come from Washington along with the appointment of senior commanders. One such appointment was Vadm. Robert L. Ghormley as COMSOPAC for which Nimitz was not consulted. Nonetheless, he welcomed Ghormley when the new commander stopped at Pearl Harbor to pay his respects while on his way to New Zealand.

After the end of the struggle for Guadalcanal, Nimitz had much to do. Ongoing planning continued for the campaign to take the rest of the Solomon Islands and to begin implementation of the original Pacific War Plan, Rainbow Six, to capture the Japanese-held islands in the central Pacific: the Carolines, Marshalls, and Marianas. Nimitz kept a firm yet non-intrusive hand in the planning of the march to Tokyo.

He received his fifth star on December 15, 1944, in the newly created American rank of fleet admiral. Nimitz signed the Japanese surrender document as the official representative of the U.S. aboard the American battleship *Missouri* in Tokyo Bay on September 2, 1945. Relinquishing his CINCPAC command on November 26, 1945, he relieved Adm. King as Chief of Naval Operations on December 15, 1945, for a two-year term.

A little more than two years later, President Truman appointed Nimitz as special Assistant to the Secretary of the Navy in the Western Sea Frontier in January 1948. After holding several honorary appointments, he retired from naval service and became heavily involve in local affairs in the San Francisco Bay Area and served as a Regent of the University of California. Nimitz passed away at his home on Yerba Buena Island on February 20, 1966.

Adm. William F. Halsey, Jr.

Halsey's command of the South Pacific Area was a triumph of his command abilities. He was the right man in the right place at the right time. After relieving Adm. Ghormley in October 1942, the whole tone and fortune of the conflict turned positive, and good things began happening for the Americans. Although it would take nearly another five months for Americans to emerge victorious on Guadalcanal, his risk-taking but still prudent command philosophy eventually brought the Americans from a position of a just-hanging-on defense to an aggressive offense style operational mode. He continued as COMSOPAC throughout the Solomon campaign. But one of the memorable parts of his naval career is how he took command of the desperate situation on Guadalcanal and turned the whole operation around.

After his command conquered the Solomons, Halsey left that region in May 1944 just as the U.S. Navy advanced under the might of Adm. Raymond Spruance's Fifth Fleet—also known as Task Force 54 and the most powerful carrier armada ever to sail the seven seas—to attack and capture the Marianas. As soon as that campaign finished, Halsey took command, changed its name to the Third Fleet for the campaign to help Gen. MacArthur keep his promise to return to the Philippines and liberate millions of Filipinos from Japanese occupation. Thereafter, he would alternately exchange command responsibilities of the fleet with Adm. Spruance. Whenever Spruance was in command, the fleet carried the designation of the 5th Fleet. When Halsey commanded, it was known as the 3rd Fleet.

Several controversies followed Halsey during his command of the 3rd Fleet. One of those was his decision to take the 3rd Fleet away from Leyte to chase after what was left of the Japanese aircraft carriers. Another was his leading that fleet through two typhoons that resulted in the deaths of many sailors. Halsey was also aboard the *Missouri* in Tokyo Bay when Japan surrendered.

Halsey was the fourth man to ever achieve the rank of fleet admiral in December 1945. After retiring from the Navy in March 1947, Halsey spent much of his remaining life trying to justify his actions at Leyte Gulf. He published his memoirs, *Admiral Halsey's Story*, in 1947 and passed away on August 20, 1949, while on vacation at Fisher's Island, Connecticut.

Maj. Gen. Alexander A. Vandegrift

After Gen. Patch relieved Vandegrift as commander of all ground forces on Guadalcanal on December 9, 1942, the 1st Marine Division's 5th and 11th Regiments had just completed four months' duty on the island. The honors for his outstanding leadership soon began. The Navy awarded him the Navy Cross for his outstanding command of the 1st Marine Division during the attack on Guadalcanal, Tulagi, and Gavutu in the Solomon Islands. For his defense and occupation of the American perimeter from August 7 to December 9, 1942, he received the Congressional Medal of Honor.[1]

He took command of the 1st Marine Amphibious Corps in July 1943. On November 1, 1943, he led the Corps in the beginning phases of the invasion of Bougainville. Vandegrift relinquished his command and returned to Washington as commandant-designate. After being promoted to the rank of lieutenant general, he became Commandant of the Marine Corps. He received his fourth star on April 4, 1945, and was the first Marine officer to achieve the rank of four star general. The government awarded the Distinguished Service Medal to him for his outstanding service as Commandant of the Marine Corps from January 1, 1944, to June 30, 1946. He left active service on December 31, 1947, and retired on April 1, 1949. At the age of 86, Vandegrift died on May 8, 1973, at Bethesda Naval Hospital, Maryland, following a long illness.

Vadm. Robert L. Ghormley

After being relieved from his COMSOPAC command by Adm. Halsey, Ghormley returned to Washington and stayed there for a few months. He then took command at the 14th Naval District in Hawaii. Ghormley went to Germany in December 1944 as commander of U.S. Naval Forces, Germany, and held that command until December 1945. While in Germany, he supervised the dismantling of the German Navy—also known as the Kriegsmarine. He spent his last months of active duty as a member of the Navy Department's General Board, retired in August 1946, and passed away June 21, 1958.

There is not nearly as much information about Ghormley as there is for other senior American naval officers. His son, Cmdr. Robert L. Ghormley, Jr., wrote a biography of his father in 1996. It was never formally published, but the U.S. Naval Historical Center has the document on-loan from that institution's library. Ghormley's son makes some strong arguments that history's judgment of his father's service as COMSOPAC commander should not have been as critical as it has been. After Ghormley transferred to Germany, he amply demonstrated his superior administrative skills for which he originally received command of the South Pacific. New Zealand never lost their respect for Ghormley when its Prime Minister sent a highly complementary telegram to him on August 14, 1945:[2]

> "At this memorable time the government and people of New Zealand recall with gratitude the contribution that you made toward the victory we now enjoy. You were the first to assume command of the South Pacific Area at a time of great peril and anxiety for all of us. You laid with great success the ground work on which victory in this part of the world was largely built. With gratitude and pride in your achievement. Most sincerely,
>
> Signed Peter Fraser
> Prime Minister of New Zealand"

Where Ghormley served as an administrator, he excelled. However, when he commanded a combat area, these skills did not serve him well. The very qualities that made a fine administrator stood in his way during command of large combat forces. While an administrator can afford to be deliberate, a combat commander sometimes must act forcefully and quickly as a war's progress often brings unexpected turns of fate.

Radm. Richmond Kelly Turner

Turner remained in command of Halsey's Amphibious Forces after the capture of Guadalcanal. He commanded the landing force in the invasion of Rendova Island in the Solomons. It was there that the Japanese sank his flagship, *McCawley*, that forced him to relinquish his command to Radm. Theodore S. Wilkinson. Turner returned to Pearl Harbor and received the command of Vadm. Spruance's Fifth Fleet Amphibious Forces, a much larger responsibility with many more ships.

Turner teamed with Marine Maj. Gen. Holland M. Smith, and that union enjoyed considerable success as the 5th Fleet invaded and captured Betio, Makin, Majuro, Kwajalein, Roi, and Namur. When he received his third star in March 1944, the newly promoted Vadm. Turner now commanded all amphibious forces in the Pacific while keeping his command of the 5th Fleet's Amphibious Forces. He faultlessly led the invasions of Saipan, Tinian, and Guam during the invasion of the Marianas in June 1944. As MacArthur and Halsey attacked Leyte in October 1944, Turner kept busy planning the invasions of Iwo Jima and Okinawa. It was at Iwo Jima that Turner's reputation became tarnished when he failed to thoroughly bombard the beaches thus causing many more than the expected Marine casualties. While the Americans encountered much heavier Japanese opposition at Okinawa, Turner's ships safely landed the American soldiers and marines ashore. He also effectively placed his destroyers in picket lines that added much to minimize damage the Kamikazes could have done to the 5th Fleet. The Turner magic had returned.

After being promoted to a four-star admiral in May 1945, Turner returned to Pearl Harbor. Adm. Nimitz replaced him with Radm. Harry W. Hill. After arriving in Hawaii, Turner began detailed planning for the invasion of the Japanese Home Island of Kyushu. The dropping of the atom bomb terminated that effort. Relieved of his post in October 1945, Turner went back to Washington for a one-month term as a member with the General Board. He served as the American naval representative on the United Nations Military Staff Committee at New York from December 1945 until July 1947 and in London until he retired in 1952.

After his wife, Harriet, passed away in January 1961, Turner's energy rapidly ebbed. He suffered a coronary occlusion and passed away six weeks later on February 13, 1961.

Maj. Gen. Alexander M. Patch

Patch's command of the ground forces on Guadalcanal put him into the limelight with his superiors. He went to Washington, D.C., in May 1943 and took command of the 4th Corps at Fort Lewis, Washington, and the Army's Desert Training Center. Gen. Marshall, highly impressed by his command effectiveness, returned Patch to combat duty in August 1944 when he took command of the 7th Army during the invasion of southern France on August 15, 1944, as part of Operation Dragoon. The soldiers under his command drove the weakening and rapidly retreating German Army up the Rhone Valley. They met Patton's 3rd Army on September 9, 1944.

After leading attacks on the German Siegfried Line and accepting the surrender of Gen. Hermann Balck's troops, Patch continued commanding the 7th Army until the wars' end. Getting his third star as a Lt. Gen. in July 1945, he returned to the U.S. to take command of the 4th Army one month later. But his command did not last long when he contracted pneumonia and died at Fort Sam Houston's hospital on November 21, 1945.

The Japanese

Vadm. Isoroku Yamamoto

In April 1943, about two months after the evacuation from Guadalcanal, his staff wanted Yamamoto to move to Rabaul to be closer to the men he commanded. When the Americans captured Guadalcanal, it was a sure thing they would attempt capturing the rest of the Solomon Islands with their goal of destroying the vital Japanese base at Rabaul. Yamamoto worried about the losses in his elite carrier- and land-based naval air units as well as his carriers. Therefore, he agreed to visit Rabaul and planned to stay about one week. He planned to leave for Rabaul on April 3.

The admiral, his staff officers, aides, the fleet medical officer, fleet paymaster, the fleet codes' officer, and the fleet meteorological officer arrived at Rabaul at 1:40 p.m.

Yamamoto's three immediate subordinates, Admirals Jinichi Kusaka, Jisaburo Ozawa, and Gunichi Mikawa, greeted their superior as he arrived. Yamamoto and his party immediately went to the Southeast Area Fleet's headquarters and acclimated themselves.

Kusaka was shocked at Yamamoto's physical appearance after not seeing him for six months. His eyes' whites were the color of light brown mud. It was clear the man was exhausted. Yamamoto went his temporary residence in a small house on a thousand-foot hill where the embattled admiral could find some peace and quiet. At least he would escape somewhat the oppressive humidity where the night winds were cooler than at sea level.

As Operation "I," a desperate air attack on Guadalcanal's airfields, drew to a somewhat successful end, Yamamoto's planned stay at Rabaul was about to end as well. Before returning to Combined Fleet Headquarters in Truk, he decided that he wanted to make a one-day tour of his air bases nearer to Shortland Island. This was a dangerous proposition since his itinerary would bring him closer to Guadalcanal and well within range of American aircraft. Nevertheless, the morale of his air crews greatly concerned him, and he wanted the men to see him and hopefully to lift their spirits.

His staff tried mightily to change his mind as they warned him that this was a hazardous undertaking. He told his subordinate commanders and his staff, "I have to go. I've let them know, and they'll have got things ready for me. I'll leave tomorrow morning and be back by dusk. Why don't we have dinner together?"[3]

No arguments anyone could make would shake his determination to go. Overriding his staff, he sent the following message to his commands on April 13, 1943:

> "Commander in Chief Combined Fleet will personally inspect Ballale, Shortland, and Buin on April 18. Schedule as follows: 0600 leave Rabaul in medium attack plane (escorted by six fighters); 0800 arrive Ballale and proceed immediately by sub-chaser to Shortland, arriving 0840...1400 leave Buin by medium attack plane; 1540 arrive Rabaul...To be postponed one day in case of bad weather."[4]

That message would be his death warrant.

✲ ✲ ✲

FRUPac and ICPOA used radio traffic to intercept and decode Japanese messages. This technique examined key Japanese commanders' designations and how much traffic they sent and received. FRUPac deduced Yamamoto's movement to Rabaul and reported this to their superiors. They discovered higher-than-normal radio traffic between Rabaul and the airfields near southern Bougainville.

Many gaps existed in the decoded messages. Nevertheless, Lt. Wesley A. Wright[5] examined the code groups of a few Japanese commands that he identified as airfields near Buin on southern Bougainville. Richard W. Emory found the airbases on the map. Alva B. Lasswell then retrieved and decoded a message on April 13 that disclosed Yamamoto's itinerary for his planned inspection tour.

In his book *Double Edged Secrets*, Lt. W. Jasper Holmes recalls witnessing Lasswell intensely pouring over the short message to make absolutely sure he correctly decoded and translated every word in it. Lasswell went to Holmes and carefully reviewed his work with him. Realizing how important this message was, Holmes immediately contacted CINCPAC fleet intelligence officer Capt. Edwin T. Layton and read the message to him. Just to assure there was no chance of any misunderstanding, Holmes and Lasswell went to meet with Layton at CINCPAC Headquarters.

After the two men finished reviewing the message with Layton, the fleet intelligence officer walked briskly out his office door and into Nimitz's office at 8:02 a.m. on April 14. He handed the translated intercept to Nimitz, who read it. After reading the details the message, he abruptly stood up and went to look at the chart of the Pacific Ocean. Yamamoto's itinerary would bring him within 300 miles of Henderson Field.

Nimitz grabbed a pad of paper and began writing his dispatch to Halsey. He included Yamamoto's itinerary and, trying to protect the highly secret method of gaining this vital piece of intelligence, recommended that Halsey say the source of this news came from Australian coastwatchers. The last sentence of his message gave Halsey the authority he needed to begin an important mission: "If forces your command have capability to shoot down Yamamoto and staff, you are hereby authorized initiate preliminary planning."

Yamamoto was the most important leader the Japanese had after Hirohito. Assassinating such an important person required approval from Nimitz's superiors. Yamamoto's death would shock the Japanese nation and deal a tremendous blow to the Imperial Japanese Navy's morale. The political and military implications would be incalculable. Nimitz asked King and Knox for permission to go after Yamamoto. Their approval came within hours.

Acting in his capacity as Halsey's deputy while the admiral was on his way to visit Gen. MacArthur, Radm. Theodore S. Wilkinson sent out orders to all COMSOPAC commanders and immediately contacted Radm. Marc A. "Pete" Mitscher, the commander of all air forces in the Solomons. Wilkinson asked Mitscher if he could get Yamamoto.

Mitscher quickly called a secret meeting of his senior naval and Marine staff to discuss the matter. Strong feelings among those in the meeting were that the Navy did all the work discovering this juicy piece of intelligence. Therefore, the attempts to assassinate Yamamoto should be solely the responsibility of the Navy and Marines.

The staff thoroughly examined the messages, looked at the maps of the islands and water between Guadalcanal and Bougainville, and deduced the distance to intercept Yamamoto was about 450 miles away. None of the Navy or Marine Corps aircraft had the range to reach that spot and return safely. The only airplanes that had the range to fly the round trip were the Army's P-38s on Guadalcanal.

Many of those at this meeting believed the Army pilots lacked the aggressiveness and experience

P-38

for such a mission. Most of the Army pilots had only flown close air support of the ground troops on Guadalcanal in slower P-39s and P-400s, which the vaunted Zero fighter flown by more experienced Japanese pilots easily shot down. Nevertheless, Marine Maj. John P. Condon, once a severe critic of Army pilots and their fighter operations officer at CACTUS, now believed the P-38 pilots were among the best fighter pilots on Guadalcanal. The P-38s were the equal to the best American fighters against the Zero.

Mitscher ended the debate when he firmly stated the P-38 pilots had the same "stuff" as Lt. Col. James Doolittle's B-25 pilots when Capt. Mitscher commanded the *Hornet* in Halsey's task force.

The group chose Army Maj. John W. Mitchell, the 339th Squadron's commander, to lead the mission. Capt. Thomas P. Lanphier, Jr., had impressed Mitscher with his abilities as a combat pilot in his missions over Guadalcanal and southern Bougainville. The admiral wanted Lanphier and the rest of his flight, Lieutenants Rex Barber, James McLanahan, and Joseph Moore, to be part of the attack force and assigned as the planes that would actually shoot down Yamamoto's plane.

Before dismissing the meeting, Mitscher strongly stressed the operation's secrecy. The Japanese should never even get the hint of the American attempt to kill Yamamoto.

After making his decision, Mitscher quickly answered Wilkinson that long-range P-38s could intercept Yamamoto's party on April 18. Halsey notified Nimitz, who rapidly replied with the orders to proceed with the mission that ended with the following: "Good luck and good hunting."

✲ ✲ ✲

In the early morning hours of April 18, 1943, Yamamoto and three staff officers boarded the first new Betty bomber. Ugaki, Yamamoto's chief of staff, and five other staff officers boarded the second new bomber. Piloted by highly experienced, battle-hardened pilots, the two planes took off exactly on schedule at 6:00 a.m. with an escort of six Zeroes behind them.

The eight-plane formation flew at 6,500 feet with Bougainville's west coast on their port side. It was 7:30 a.m. when the pilot of Yamamoto's plane passed a piece of paper back to his passengers that said, "Expect to arrive at Ballale 0745."

✲ ✲ ✲

On 4:30 a.m. on April 18, 1943, Mitchell woke up, climbed into his flight suit, ate breakfast, and walked over to the operations tent. On any other day, only the P-38 pilots would be around the tent before a mission. Almost 100 men gathered nearby. This day was different.

The 18 pilots gathered in the tent at about 6:00 a.m. to hear Mitchell's briefing. He told them that takeoff would begin promptly at 7:10 a.m. as the crews topped off the fuel tanks and finished loading ammunition. An electric shock swept through each man as Mitchell told them their task was to find Adm. Yamamoto's plane and shoot it down.

Mitchell would lead the mission. After takeoff, they would circle the field, gather into their formation, and begin their first leg. The planes would fly over the Coral Sea at an altitude of 50 feet. They would be far out to sea where they could see no land. All the pilots knew that flying at such a low altitude over water would test every flying skill they had. Any minor mistake could be fatal. The meeting ended, and all pilots went to their planes.

Mitchell walked past each plane on the flight line and came to his plane. He climbed onto his P-38's wing and surveyed the scene. The other 17 pilots climbed aboard their planes. A deafening din from 36 powerful Allison V-12 engines roaring to life nearly in unison overwhelmed the hearing of all who witnessed this historic moment. Cheering the pilots and wishing them good luck, all men on the ground saw each plane position itself at the end of the runway, rev its engines, accelerate down the runway, and gracefully rise aloft. John Mitchell and his wingman, Lt. Julius "Jack" Jacobson, left at the scheduled takeoff time of 7:10 a.m. Lieutenants Douglas Canning's and Delton Goerke's planes were right behind them.

Lanphier led his four-plane killer group into the air and flew to the starting point of their journey. Barber was on his wing as both planes revved their engines and took off. Just before the two pilots raised their wheels into the wheel wells, McLanahan's plane accelerated down the runway, one of the craft's tires hit a snag, and blew into pieces. He lost control and ran the plane off the runway. The four-plane killer group now numbered three.

The P-38s rendezvoused into their formation and flew west in a gradual dive toward the ocean surface. Moore's plane had to turn back because fuel could not flow from the external fuel tanks. Lanphier's killer group was now at half-strength. Mitchell ordered the two reserve planes flown by Lieutenants Besby F. Holmes and Raymond Hine, who had never flown with Lanphier, to join the killer group and bring it up to full strength.

Mitchell's formation flew at 50 feet above the water as he concentrated on the big ship's compass mounted on his plane's dashboard. After looking at his watch and making sure his planes maintained radio silence, he now fully realized that he no longer had landmarks to guide his way. Any small mistake could result in all 16 planes missing Yamamoto's plane.

Mitchell changed his course several times until it was 9:45 a.m. He checked his time and course again. He made a sharp right turn to 20° for the 16-mile sprint to Empress Augusta Bay.

Rocking his wings to signal his flight, all the planes test-fired their guns and closed the formation for the final run toward Bougainville. The P-38s flew through a mist that hugged the water and prevented Mitchell from seeing anything. He began to wonder where Bougainville was. Had he made the mistake he worried about so much? Was he lost after all?

The planes burst out of the mist and into bright sunshine. The huge green mountains of Bougainville lay dead ahead of them. The pilots could not see any aircraft in the beautifully clear blue sky.

Canning also intensely scanned the sky above him. Suddenly, a formation of eight planes appeared about 1,000 feet above him. He pushed his microphone's button and radioed, "Bogeys. Eleven o'clock high." Mitchell's navigational expertise and American intelligence had paid off. The P-38s had found Yamamoto's planes.

☼ ☼ ☼

When the crew chief gave Ugaki a note stating they were about ten minutes away from their destination, he began to organize his thoughts for the day's work. He glanced out the window and saw Yamamoto's plane flying just ahead.

The Zeroes' pilots scanned the skies for any aircraft. No planes came out of the sun from above and to the east of them. They could almost see Buin airfield.

The second three-plane formation leading Zero's pilot looked below him and saw American planes climbing up toward them. Since he did not carry a radio, the pilot went into a steep dive and rocked his wings to warn the bombers of the impending danger.

☼ ☼ ☼

Mitchell also now saw the planes Canning spotted and was not yet sure Yamamoto was on any of them. They were about five miles away at about 90° from his flight path. However, there were two bombers instead of one. He turned his planes onto a parallel course to the Japanese aircraft and began to climb toward them. As he got closer, he saw six Zeroes flying the escort about 1,000 feet above the two bombers. He now knew that Yamamoto was aboard one of those bombers.

Since his flight was now about to engage in air combat, he ordered his P-38s to drop their extra fuel tanks. Now with the weight and drag of the tanks free from their bodies, the American fighters leapt forward and upward. They were level with the bombers in what seemed to be a heartbeat. Mitchell wanted to attack the bombers, but he stuck to his plan to let Lanphier's four-plane killer group do their job. His 11 planes continued climbing to gain enough height to defend Lanphier's group from the massive attacks by Zeroes he knew were coming. He had to take his P-38s high enough to gain the altitude advantage they would need when the Zeroes arrived.

Knowing the killer group's four pilots were all combat veterans, Mitchell assumed that his 11 P-38s could keep enough attacking Zeroes from interfering with their vital assignment. There was no time to waste. He radioed Lanphier, "All right, Tom. Go get 'im. He's your meat."

When Besby Holmes tried to release his external fuel tanks, nothing happened. Like anyone in such a situation, he tried repeatedly to jettison the tank with the same result. Totally frustrated, he radioed Lanphier, "Hold it a second, Tom. I can't drop my tanks. I'll tear them off." He turned his plane to the west and put it into a steep, violently corkscrewing dive. His gyrations worked as he succeeded getting rid of the burden.

Soon Besby Holmes lost contact with the rest of P-38s. Nonetheless, Ray Hine had stayed with his wingman despite Besby's herky-jerky flight path. They still had a job to do—get Yamamoto—and nothing would keep them from doing it. Mitchell later said, "We were ready to do anything, even if that meant ramming him. Those were the orders." But Holmes had taken his and his wingman's plane away from the killer group thus cutting its fighting strength in two.

✲ ✲ ✲

The Japanese spotted the Americans as the bombers descended for landing at Buin. The pilot of Yamamoto's bomber immediately put the big plane into a steep dive toward the airstrip. Meanwhile, Ugaki's plane followed the lead bomber in the steep dive.

The two P-38s were within one mile of the bombers as Lanphier saw the three Zeroes dropping their own external fuel tanks. They headed toward Barber and raced the Americans to see which planes would reach the bombers first. Lanphier knew the two American fighters would lose that race and feared that the three Zeroes would shoot them down before they fired a shot at the bombers.

✲ ✲ ✲

Lanphier believed the Zeroes would shoot down both Barber and himself before they could reach them. He then pulled up from his attack on the leading bomber to meet one of the Zeroes in a head-on attack. Approaching each other at several hundred miles-per-hour, both fighters fired their guns at each other. Lanphier saw the Zero fall beneath him with smoke trailing behind it. He then climbed to attack other two Zeroes.

While he prevented the three Zeroes from blocking the American attack, he was now out of the fight. Barber's P-38 was the lone American plane to attack the two bombers and now on his own. Meanwhile, the bomber pilots desperately flew their craft trying to survive.

As his P-38 continued climbing, Mitchell looked below him and saw his plan disintegrating before his very eyes. Instead of four planes attacking the bombers, there was now only one. Wanting his killer group to attack the bombers instead of engaging the Zeroes in dogfights, he angrily got on his radio: "Get the bombers. Damn it all, the bombers!" His planes were now miles from being able to help.

Alone, Barber's closing speed to the bombers was too fast. He throttled back to slow the P-38. He made a hard right turn to get on one bomber's tail. As he banked, his left wing momentarily blocked him from seeing the bombers.

Barber moved to the second bomber's left side, on its tail, and lined up the big plane in his sights. With no fire coming from the Betty's 20-mm tail gun and not wanting to wait, he was just a plane's length away when he pulled his gun triggers. A barrage of machine gun bullets and cannon fire hit the bomber's right engine and fuselage. Pieces of the bomber flew past his plane. He lined up a second burst and put it into the fuselage and into the bomber's vertical fin. The tail came apart in pieces, and the bomber shook. He continued firing into the right engine, across the body, and into the left engine. The bomber lurched as a trail of heavy, black smoke billowed from its innards. By this time, the bomber was only 500 feet from the ground. Barber stayed on its tail and almost collided with the bomber's right wingtip. He avoided a midair crash by turning sharply to the right and leaving the doomed bomber to its fate. He never saw it crash.

The Japanese pilot banked his plane toward the sea to do what he could to escape his tormentor. Glancing out his canopy, he noticed fire and smoke trailing behind Yamamoto's plane. A Zero pilot saw the Admiral's bomber crash into the dense undergrowth.

Ugaki watched his superior's bomber fall in flames into the jungle. His bomber finally crashed into the jungle. Japanese soldiers rescued Ugaki and others in the plane.

Lanphier left the three Zeros he battled and thought he was alone in the sky. Unable to see anything happening below him, he turned his P-38 on its back and looked below him. He saw Barber far to his right with several Zeroes pursuing his wingman. Meanwhile, the two surviving Zeroes he passed had turned around and were resuming their attack on him. A shadow moving fast near the jungle caught his eye. It was the second Betty that Lanphier remembered, "The [Betty] pilot must have executed a perfect circle in his evasive dive and flattened out of it, once again on his original course."

Returning to level flight, he put down his flaps, pulled his throttles back to reduce his air speed, went into a skid to approach at the proper speed, and lined up the bomber in his sight. His plane was at a right angle to the bomber when he saw the Zeroes arriving near the bomber. He could not wait to close the range to his target. Lanphier got the bomber in his sight and fired one long burst. He saw his guns' bullets tear into the plane's right engine, setting it afire. The blaze spread to the wing. Meanwhile, the bomber's tail gunner fired back. Trailing flames and black smoke, the plane plunged for the ground below and crashed into the jungle.

Barber had problems of his own. As Japanese bullets hammered his P-38, he bent forward to get the most protection his plane's armor plate would give him. Despite the punishment being inflicted on the American fighter, Barber skillfully (or luckily) kept his plane aloft. He flew just above the treetops at top speed with his throttles wide open and used the P-38's superior speed to escape. When his plane finally landed at Guadalcanal, the ground crew stared at the heavily damaged aircraft in disbelief and wondered how Barber ever managed to return alive.

✲ ✲ ✲

After what seemed like ten hours, the ten-minute fight ended. Ray Hine never returned and listed as missing-in-action. No one ever recovered his body. The rest of Mitchell's pilots returned safely.[6]

✲ ✲ ✲

The most famous Japanese commander was dead. Only time would reveal whether his replacement could be his equal,. The daring American mission had dealt a mortal blow to Japanese morale, particularly to the Imperial Japanese Navy. There was still much to be done by both the Japanese and Americans.

Nonetheless, there were other Japanese military leaders who would continue their duty to their country. Although not as well known as the deceased commander-in-chief of the Combined Fleet, they would contribute to their nation's fortunes, both good and bad.

Vadm. Nobutake Kondo

Serving as deputy commander of the Combined Fleet, Kondo took temporary command when Yamamoto died. His tenure as the fleet's commander ended when Yamamoto's designated successor, Vadm. Mineichi Koga, permanently took the vaunted hero's place. After withdrawing his ships and leaving Radm. Tanaka's reinforcement force to fend for itself after the Naval Battle of Guadalcanal, Kondo's superiors lost respect for his high command capabilities. Nevertheless, the Imperial Japanese Navy still saw fit to appoint him in 1944 as the commander of the 2nd Fleet with the responsibility for defense of the Gilbert Islands. After the Americans captured those islands, he became the commander-in-chief of the China Area Fleet in January 1945. When the war ended in August 1945, he was in Saigon, Indo-China, he remained in command of Japanese naval units used by the British to fight the Communist Viet Minh. In December 1945, he gave up his sword to Capt. I. Scott-Bell, RN, the senior British naval officer in Indo-China aboard the HMS *Waveney*. Kondo returned to Japan and thrived as a businessman until his death on January 19, 1953.[7]

Vadm. Gunichi Mikawa

Mikawa continued in command of the 8th Fleet in the future grueling campaigns in the Solomons and New Guinea during 1943. From April through September 1943, he held several Naval General Staff positions and shore assignments in the Japanese home islands between the latter months of 1943 through late 1944, Mikawa commanded the 2nd South Sea Fleet and the Southwestern Area Fleet in the Philippines. After the Japanese defeat at the Battle of Leyte Gulf, he resigned from the Imperial Japanese Navy in May 1945. He passed away in 1981.[8]

Radm. Raizo Tanaka

After leading repeated attempts to reinforce the beleaguered Japanese soldiers on Guadalcanal, Tanaka's enthusiasm for what he viewed as a hopeless strategy for the Japanese to continue holding the island waned. When he was wounded in December 1942, he let his opinions become known to anyone who would listen. Accused of holding defeatist attitudes, the Navy removed him from his command either in December 1942 or January 1943. His assignments after this event included:

1. Commander of the 13th Special Naval Base Force in October 1943.
2. Moved to the Japanese Headquarters in Rangoon, Burma, in November 1944.
3. Moved under Imperial Japanese Army command on February 18, 1945.
4. Left Rangoon to setup his Headquarters at Moulmein, Southern Burma on May 1, 1945.
5. Transferred HQ to Bangkok, Siam (now Thailand), under 18th Army command until the war's end.
6. Promoted to vice admiral before the war ended.

Along with his chief of staff, Katsuya Sato, and 20 Japanese generals, he surrendered his sword to Maj. Gen. G. C. Evans, commander of the 7th Indian Division in Bangkok on January 11, 1946. Tanaka retired from the Imperial Japanese Navy on June 26, 1946, and passed away on July 9, 1969 at the age of 77.[9]

Radm. Matome Ugaki

Ugaki was on the other plane on April 18 that was with Yamamoto's aircraft when the American P-38s attacked. The American fighters also shot his plane down, and he sustained serious wounds. After being rescued by Japanese troops in the dense Bougainville jungle and taken to the coast, a Japanese sub-chaser took him to Buin airfield. The 8th Air Fleet medical officer tended his wounds, and he along with two medical officers went aboard a sub-chaser the next day to the site where Yamamoto's plane crashed. The party took Yamamoto's body and the remains of the rest of the plane's dead crew down to the shore, reboarded the sub-chaser, and returned to Buin. According to Japanese tradition, the leaders at Buin cremated the deceased leader's body on April 21.

Ugaki flew along with the ashes of the dead from Buin and arrived in Rabaul at 4:00 p.m. on April 22. After transferring their precious cargo to two Betty bombers the next day, he took off under a cloak of secrecy at 8:30 a.m. and arrived at Truk at 1:45 p.m. Ugaki returned to the Combined Fleet's flagship, now the *Musashi*, and reported to Kondo, the then acting commander-in-chief. Two days later on April 25, Adm. Koga took command of the Combined Fleet and met the *Musashi* in Saipan.

Ugaki received orders to proceed to Tokyo and begin his recovery at the Tokyo Naval Hospital.

While still recovering from his wounds, Radm. Shigeru Fukudome relieved him of his assignment as the Combined Fleet's chief of staff. His feelings of guilt over Yamamoto's death continued to haunt him for the rest of his life.

After being promoted to vice admiral in late October 1943, he became the commander of the 1st Battleship Division in the 2nd Fleet commanded by Vadm. Takao Kurita in April 1944. He established his headquarters at Tawi-Tawi in the Sulu Islands—located northeast of Borneo. His battleships, which included the two super battleships, the *Yamato* and *Musashi*, and the *Kongo*, joined Vadm. Jisaburo Ozawa at the Battle of the Philippine Sea in June 1944. During the Battle of Leyte Gulf, he witnessed the sinking of the *Musashi*—an event that greatly discouraged him into believing that his country could no longer win the war.

Nevertheless, being the dedicated warrior he was, he continued his service as Commander of the 5th Air Fleet, a newly formed unit organized to defend Okinawa in February 1945 using suicide attack tactics, called *Kamikaze*, to defeat the U.S. Navy that ominously approached the Japanese home islands. As we all now know, the *Kamikazes* failed to stop the Americans from successfully capturing Okinawa.

He withdrew what was left of his command to his new headquarters at the Oita Airbase on Kyushu Island. It was a dark day for Ugaki as he heard his emperor's surrender message on the radio on August 15, 1945. Deciding that he no longer had any reason to live, he organized a *Kamikaze* mission, climbed aboard a two-seater plane from the 701st Air Group at Oita, and took just his sword while wearing no insignias of rank. In what was to be the last *Kamikaze* attack made by the Japanese, Ugaki along with ten other fighter-bombers took off and headed south. He radioed the base he intended to attack the Americans on Okinawa. The formation arrived over the island at about 7:30 p.m. and went into a steep dive.

An American sailor, Danny Rosewall, later told a Japanese historian that he saw several *Kamikazes* attacking near Iheya-ushiro-jima in northern Okinawa on August 15. He saw one aircraft, trailing fire and smoke, crash on the beach. Rosewall examined the wreckage, found three bodies, one of which was grasping an ornate ceremonial sword. No one ever heard from Ugaki again.[10]

Guadalcanal's Legacy

The six-month struggle between the U.S. (and Allies) and the Japanese Empire is one that has been and will continue to be studied, written about, and mentioned whenever anyone talks about a fight between two powerful forces that each must win. For the Americans, it began as an operation that seemed an afterthought although many Americans, particularly in the U.S. Navy, believed that it had to be done whatever the cost. As in all wars, they begin many times where at least one protagonist is not prepared despite all the prewar planning. This was certainly true for the Americans.

The Japanese attack on the American Pacific Fleet caught the nation completely by surprise. Nonetheless, the war clouds had been gathering for almost a decade. The differences between the Americans and the Japanese began with the Japanese invasion of Mongolia in 1931 and escalated when the Japanese invaded mainland China. The bombing of the gunboat *Panay* on the Yangtze River on December 12, 1931, and reported Japanese atrocities at Nanking and elsewhere only served to increase tensions between the two nations. But when Japan took military steps to secure their critical supply lines to the rich oilfields of the Dutch East Indies and bountiful minerals of Southeast Asia, the chances for a clash between the two great powers markedly increased.

There were other threats to the Western democracies in Europe with Adolf Hitler's election as German Chancellor in 1933 and the Nazi Party rise to absolute power over that nation. Hitler wrote his manifesto, *Mein Kampf*, while in prison for orchestrating an attempt to overthrow the German government in 1923. In that book, published in 1925, he never hesitated expressing what he foresaw as Germany's destiny. His racial hatred for the Jews of Europe and any non-Aryan race was no longer a secret. Germany needed more land for its people and Hitler seemed determined to get it by any means possible.

Just a few people tried to warn everyone war was coming. But almost all people in the Western democracies and the Soviet Union either chose to ignore the obviously ominous signs or pretend they did not exist. Certainly for the Americans in the Pacific, they tried to negotiate to settle their differences with the Japanese even after the bombs began to fall at Pearl Harbor. The only logical conclusion one can deduce from all these events was that the Americans were not prepared to fight a world war.

That lack of preparation and the experience such readiness would have brought cost the lives of many sailors and the loss of many ships. In time, commanders with the willingness to fight and take the risks needed for victory would take command. The Americans began building a fleet that was second to none. As soon as the carriers, fast battleships, cruisers, destroyers, submarines, transports, landing craft of all shapes and sizes joined the fleet, the Americans began their relentless assaults on the Gilberts, Marshalls, Marianas, New Guinea, Philippines, Iwo Jima, and Okinawa. While an American victory was expensive, it proved to be inevitable.

The Japanese had the advantage of being at war since 1931 and had honed their naval battle skills in the runup to Pearl Harbor. Two factors that contributed to the Japanese tactical naval victories at Guadalcanal were their effective and deadly Long Lance torpedo and their use of night sighting techniques in the absence of radar. The American over-reliance on radar and the lack of training for senior naval commanders in how to use it under combat conditions resulted in many of the errors committed when they fought the Imperial Japanese Navy at Guadalcanal.

Both sides viewed each other in a prism of racial stereotypes. Many Americans, including many at the top command levels in the U.S. Navy, believed the Japanese were not physically strong enough, suffered from nearsightedness, nor had the innate intelligence to gather an effective fighting force to battle the U.S. Navy.

The Japanese viewed the U.S. as having grown soft from too much luxury and from hiding behind their isolation to defeat their own *bushido* dedication to the Emperor. The Japanese considered themselves racially superior by never inbreeding like the Americans had. After Guadalcanal, stereotyping died a deserved death. Neither side would ever underestimate the other again.

Both sides fought with valor and skill at Guadalcanal. Nevertheless, the superior American industrial power eventually overwhelmed the much more limited Japanese economy and forced the Japanese to evacuate the island. From this time forward, the Americans were permanently on the offensive while the Japanese were constantly retreating, giving up territory, and finally signing their surrender on the decks of American battleship *Missouri* in Tokyo Bay in September 1945.

✲ ✲ ✲

Samuel Eliot Morison, one who witnessed the hell that was Guadalcanal, wrote a fitting tribute in his work, *History of United States Naval Operations in World War II, The Struggle for Guadalcanal,* Volume V:

> "For us who were there, or whose friends were there, Guadalcanal is not a name but an emotion, recalling desperate fights in the air, furious night naval battles, frantic work at supply or construction, savage fighting in the sodden jungle, nights broken by screaming bombs and deafening explosions of naval shells."[11]

British Prime Minister Winston Churchill paid tribute to the American victory at Guadalcanal in his World War II memoirs: "Long may the tale be told in the great Republic."[12] That is what I have attempted to do in this book. I hope all who read it agree that I have satisfactorily completed my task.

Bibliography

"Battle of Verdun 1916" web site: http://war1418.com/battleverdun/.

Adams, Henry H., *Witness to Power: The Life of Fleet Admiral William D. Leahy* (1985), Naval Institute Press, Annapolis, MD

Alexander, Joseph H., *Edson's Raiders: The 1st Marine Raider Battalion in World War II* (2001), Naval Institute Press, Annapolis, MD

Arnold, H. H., *Global Mission*, (1949), Harper & Brothers, New York, NY

Bix, Herbert P., *Hirohito and The Making of Modern Japan* (paperback) (2001), Harper Collins, New York, NY

Boyne, Walter J., *Clash of Titans: World War II at Sea* (1995), Simon and Schuster, New York, NY

Buell, Thomas B., *Master of Sea Power: A Biography of Fleet Admiral Ernest J. King* (1980), Little, Brown, and Company, Boston.

Churchill, Winston S., *Closing the Ring* (1951) [Paperback version], Houghton Mifflin, New York, NY

Clark, J. J. (With Clark G. Reynolds), *Carrier Admiral* (1967), David McKay Co. New York, NY

Clemens, Martin, *Alone of Guadalcanal: A Coastwatchers Story* (1998), Naval Institute Press, Annapolis, MD

Connors, Richard, "Rear Admiral Daniel Judson Callaghan", Web page: http://www.microworks.net/pacific/biographies/daniel_callaghan.htm

Conway's All the World's Fighting Ships - 1922-1946 (1980), Conway Maritime Press, London, UK

Cook, Charles (Captain, USN, Ret.), *The Battle of Cape Esperance: Encounter at Guadalcanal* (1992), Naval Institute Press, Annapolis, MD

Corbett, Sir Julian, *Some Principles of Maritime Strategy* (1918), Longmans, Green and Co., London.

Crenshaw, Russell S., *The Battle of Tassafaronga* (1995), The Nautical & Aviation Publishing Company of America, Baltimore, MD

Davis, Donald A., *Lightning Strike: The Secret Mission to Kill Admiral Yamamoto and Avenge Pearl Harbor* (2005), St. Martin's Press, New York, NY

Dull, Paul S., *The Imperial Japanese Fleet (1941-1945)* (1978), United States Naval Institute, Annapolis, MD

Evans, David C. And Peattie, Mark R., *Kaigun: Strategy, Tactics, and Technology in the Imperial Japanese Navy - 1887-1941* (1997), Naval Institute Press, Annapolis, MD

Frank, Richard B., *Guadalcanal* (1990), Penguin Books USA, New York

Feldt, Commander Eric A., RAN, *The Coast Watchers* (1979), Bantam Books, New York, NY (paperback version)

Fuller, Richard, *Shokan: Hirohito's Samurai* (1992), Arms and Armour Press, London

Grace, James W., *Naval Battle of Guadalcanal: Night Action, 13 November 1942* (1999), Naval Institute Press, Annapolis, MD

Griffith, Samuel B., *The Battle for Guadalcanal* (1963), Ballantine Books, New York, NY

Halsey, William F., *Memoirs* (1947), Naval Historical Center, Washington, D.C.

Halsey, William F. and J. Bryan, *Admiral Halsey' Story* (1947), Whittlesey House of McGraw Hill, New York, NY

Hayashi, Saburo, *Kogun: The Japanese Army in the Pacific War* (1959), Marine Corps Association, Quantico, VA

Hoffman, Jon T., *Once A Legend* (1994), Presidio Press, Novato, California

Holmes, W. J., *Double-Edged Secrets* (1979), Naval Institute Press, Annapolis, MD.

Horne, Alistair, *The Price of Glory - Verdun 1916* (1991), Penguin Books, London

Ito, Masanori, *The End of the Imperial Japanese Navy* (1956), Orion Press, Tokyo

James, D. Clayton, *A Time for Giants* (1987), Franklin Watts, New York, NY

Koburger, Charles W., Jr., *Pacific Turning Point: The Solomons Campaign, 1942-1943* (1995), Praeger Publishers, Westport, CT

Koenig, William, *Epic Sea Battles* (1975), Mandarin Publishers, Ltd., Hong Kong

Larrabee, Eric, *Commander in Chief: Franklin Roosevelt, His Lieutenants, and Their War* (1987), Naval Institute Press, Annapolis, MD

Lewin, Ronald, *The American Magic Codes, Ciphers, and the Defeat of Japan* (1982), Fairar, Straus, Giroux, New York

Lord, Walter, *Lonely Vigil* (1977), The Viking Press, New York

Martin, William, *Verdun 1916 - They Shall Not Pass* (2001), Osprey Publishing Ltd., Oxford, United Kingdom

McCandless, Rear Admiral Bruce, "The San Francisco Story," *Proceedings*, United States Naval Institute, Volume 84, Number 11, November 1958.

McKennan, William J., "The Battle of Bloody Hill," *Saturday Evening Post*, February 20, 1943.

Miller, Edward S., *War Plan Orange, The U. S. Strategy to Defeat Japan 1897-1945* (1991), Naval Institute Press, Annapolis, MD

Morison, Samuel E., *History of United States Naval Operations in World War II, The Struggle for Guadalcanal, Volumes IV and V* (1984), Little, Brown and Company, Boston.

Mosley, Leonard, *Marshall: Hero for Our Times* (1982), Hearst Books, New York

Mott, Elias B., "The Battles of Santa Cruz and Guadalcanal," *The Hook*, Tailhook Association, August 1990.

Murphy, Francis X. Murphy, *Fighting Admiral: The Story of Dan Callaghan* (1952), Vantage Press, New York.

Naval Historical Web Site: http://www.history.navy.mil/danfs/w9/willis_a_lee.htm.—Biography of Willis A. Lee.

Okumiya, Masatake and Horikoshi, Jiro, *Zero* (1956), Dutton, New York

O'Toole, G. J. A. (George J. A.), *The Encyclopedia of American Intelligence and Espionage: from the Revolutionary War to the Present* (1988), Facts on File, New York

Poor, Henry V., Mustin, Henry A., Jameson, Colin G., *Combat Narratives: The Battles of Cape Esperance and Santa Cruz Islands* (1994), Naval Historical Center, Department of the Navy, Washington, D.C.

Potter, E. B., *Bull Halsey* (1985), Naval Institute Press, Annapolis, MD

Potter, E. B., *Nimitz* (1976), Naval Institute Press, Annapolis, MD

Prados, John, *Combined Fleet Decoded* (1995), Random House, New York

Prange, Gordon W., *At Dawn We Slept: The Untold Story of Pearl Harbor* (1991) Penguin Books. New York.

Proft, R. J. (Bob), Ed., *United States of America's Congressional Medal of Honor Recipients and Their Official Citations, 4th Edition* (2002), Highland House II, Inc., Columbia Heights, MN

Rhoades, Lt. Cmdr. F. Ashton, RANVR, *Diary of Coastwatcher in the Solomons* (1982), The Admiral Nimitz Foundation, Fredericksburg, Texas

Rottman, Gordon, *U.S. Marine Corps World War II Order of Battle* (2002), Greenwood Press, Westport, Connecticut, London

Shaw, Henry I., *First Offensive: The Marine Campaign for Guadalcanal* (1992), Marine Corps Historical Center, Washington, D.C.

Sherman, Forest P., *U. S. Naval Aviation in the Pacific* (1947), Office of the Chief of Aviation, United States Navy, Washington D. C.

Sherwood, Robert B., *Roosevelt and Hopkins: An Intimate History* (1948), Harper Brothers, New York

Smith, Stan, *The Battle of Savo* (1962), MacFadden Books. New York. NY

Stripp, Alan, *Codebreakers in the Far East* (1989), Frank Carr, London

Strope, Walmer Elton, "The Decisive Battle of the Pacific War", *U.S. Naval Institute Proceedings*, May, 1946.

Tanaka, Vice Admiral Raizo, "Japan's Losing Struggle for Guadalcanal - Part I", *U.S. Naval Institute Proceedings*, July, 1956.

______________________, "Japan's Losing Struggle for Guadalcanal - Part II", *U.S. Naval Institute Proceedings*, August, 1956.

Taylor, Theodore, *The Magnificent Mitscher* (1991), Naval Institute Press, Annapolis, MD.

Toland, John, *The Rising Sun* (1970), Random House, New York.

Ugaki, Matome, *Fading Victory: The Diary of Admiral Matome Ugaki* (1991), University of Pittsburgh Press, Pittsburgh, Pennsylvania

Wheeler, Gerald E., *Kinkaid of the Seventh Fleet* (1995), Naval Institute Press, Annapolis, MD and Naval Historical Center, Washington, D.C.

Who's Who in Marine Corps History, USMC History and Museums web site, http://hqinet001.hqmc.usmc.mil/HD/Historical/Whos_Who/Edson_M.htm

Winterbotham, Frederic William, *The Ultra Spy* (1989), Macmillan, London

Winton, John, *Ultra in the Pacific: How Breaking Japanese Codes and Ciphers Affected Naval Operations Against Japan* (1993), Naval Institute Press, Annapolis, MD

Wolfert, Ira, *Torpedo 8* (1943), Houghton Mifflin, New York, NY

Interviews with Japanese POWs, Naval Historical Center, Washington Naval Yard, Washington, D.C., 1945-48

Notes (Endnotes)

Prelude

1. Horne, P. 27.
2. Horne, P. 34.
3. Horne, P. 34.
4. Horne's italics for emphasis.
5. Horne, P. 35.
6. Horne, Pages 39-41.
7. McConnell was killed later at Verdun.
8. Horne, Pages 173-174.
9. Martin, P. 60.
10. Horne, Pages 326-346, Martin, Pages 28-83.

Chapter 1

1. Potter, Bull Halsey, Pages 11-14.
2. Potter, Bull Halsey, Pages 2-3.
3. (Today) Wake Island is an unorganized, unincorporated territory of the U.S.
4. Potter, Bull Halsey, P. 3.
5. Potter, Bull Halsey, P. 3.
6. Potter, Bull Halsey, P. 3.
7. Potter, Bull Halsey, P. 4.
8. Potter, Bull Halsey, Pages 3-5.
9. Prange, P. 105.
10. Potter, Bull Halsey, Pages 14-15.
11. Potter, Bull Halsey, Pages 19-21.
12. Potter, Bull Halsey, P. 125.
13. Potter, Bull Halsey, P. 37.
14. Potter, Bull Halsey, Pages 36-37.
15. Doolittle, Pages 7, 264.

Chapter 2

1. Miller, pp. 3-4.
2. Miller, pp. 331-346.

Chapter 3

1. Manchester, Pages 289-291.
2. Dull, P. 64.
3. Dull, P. 70.
4. Lord, PP. 82-87, PP. 146-147, P. 179, PP. 247-248, P. 281.
5. Dull, PP. 175-186.

Chapter 4

1. New Zealand Weather Bureau records for July, 1942.
2. Various sources:
   Web Site - www.microworks.net/pacific/biographies
   Web Site - www.naveur.navy.mil
   Web site - www.history.navy.mil
   Web Site - www.1939-45.org/bios/ghormley.htm
3. Tongatabu is southeast of the Fiji Islands and southwest of Samoa. The island is about 20 miles long. Its current name is Tongatapu and part of the independent nation of Tonga.
4. Ghormley, PP. 25-26
5. Ghormley, P. 26.
6. Wallis Island (Uvea)—possessed by the French about 250 miles west of American Samoa and northeast of Fiji. The island is about 7 miles long.
7. Ghormley, PP. 26-30.

Chapter 5

1. Dyer, PP. 2-3.
2. The 14th Edition of the Encyclopedia Britannica (Volume XIX, P. 293) shows the following under the heading "Earls and Dukes of Richmond" says:
   "Charles, 3rd Duke of Richmond, 1734-1806 ...In the debates on the policy that led to the War of American Independence Richmond was a supporter of the colonists. Richmond also advocated a policy of concession to Ireland, with reference to which he originated the famous phrase "a union of hearts."
3. Dyer, PP. 5-6.
4. Dyer, PP. 6-12.
5. Dyer, PP. 28-29.
6. Dyer, P. 37, P. 68.
7. Dyer, PP. 77-78.
8. Dyer, PP. 106-107.
9. Dyer, P. 116.
10. Dyer, P. 129.
11. Dyer, PP. 128-134.
12. Dyer, P. 138.
13. Attila the Hun, fifth century A.D.
14. Dyer, PP. 154-155.
15. Dyer, P. 162.
16. Dyer, PP. 169-170.
17. Dyer, P. 175.
18. Dyer, PP. 198-199.
19. Dyer, PP. 207-208.
20. Dyer, PP. 229-230, 238-239.
21. Dyer, P. 263.

Chapter 6

1. A diesel-engine 13,000 ton merchant ship—formerly the *SS Santa Barbara*—capable of a top speed of 17 knots. The Navy had purchased her from the Grace Steamship Line and commissioned her after a 25 day conversion in August 1940. In spite of this, she lacked the communications capabilities and staffing that would be needed when the Guadalcanal invasion began. Dyer, P. 283.
2. Dyer, PP. 278-280.
3. Frank, PP. 621-624.
4. Dyer, PP. 288-289.
5. Various sources:
   Web site: http://www.chapter-one.com/vc/award.asp?vc=282,
   Web site: http://navalhistory.flixco.info,
   Web site: http://www.thedorsetpage.com/history/vc/victor_alexander_charles_crutcheyl.htm.
6. Dyer, P. 293-294.
7. Lundstrom, PP. 20-22.
8. Lundstrom, P. 23.
9. This is my analysis of the situation American naval aviation faced immediately after Pearl Harbor. It is based on the works of Regan in his biogra-

phy of Fletcher and John Lundstrom in his work on Naval Aviation in the early days of the naval battles around Guadalcanal. (See Bibliography.)

10. Lundstrom, PP. 19-20.
11. Conway, PP. 98-99.
12. Wheeler, PP. 237-242.
13. Dyer, PP. 294-295.

Chapter 7

1. Tregaskis, PP. 6-8; Frank P. 622.
2. Morison, Vol. IV, PP. 270-272.
3. There is no written record of the words actually said during this conference. Trying to place the reader in the room on the *Saratoga*, I have attempted to recreate the conversations that took place there. The reason for this passage in the book is to give the reader an insight into the personalities of the senior commanders that I discovered while writing this narrative.
4. Dyer, P. 300.
5. Dyer, P. 301.
6. Dyer, P. 301.
7. Dyer, P. 303.
8. Dyer, PP. 301-302.
9. I have relied on several sources for my interpretation of what occurred during this historic meeting. They include: Dyer, PP. 299-303; Regan, PP. 179-194; Lundstrom, PP. 27-33; Wheeler, PP. 237-245.
10. Dyer, P. 307.
11. Dyer, P. 308.
12. Dyer, P. 309.
13. Dyer, PP. 305-310.
14. Dyer, P. 310.
15. Dyer, PP. 310-311.
16. Dyer, P. 311.
17. Dyer, PP. 310-311.
18. Lindstrom, PP. 28-29.
19. Regan, PP. 186-188.

Chapter 8

1. Dyer, P. 315.
2. Dyer, P. 315.
3. Dyer, PP. 311-315; Lundstrom, PP. 27-33.

Chapter 9

1. Agawa, PP. 320-324, Bergamini, P. 1207.
2. Bix, P. 450.
3. Bix, PP. 450-454.
4. Ugaki, PP. 175-176.
5. Microsoft® Encarta® Reference Library 2003.
6. Frank, PP. 627-628; Conway, PP. 174, 186-187, 189.
7. Sakai, P. 14.
8. Ibid., PP. 28-29.
9. Ibid., PP. 37-42.
10. Ibid., PP. 55-59.
11. Ibid., PP. 60-65.
12. Ibid., PP. 66-206.
13. Ibid. P. 207.
14. Evans & Peattie, P. 270, Figure 8-11.
15. Evans & Peattie, PP. 266-272.

Chapter 10

1. Clemens, PP. 186-188.
2. Dyer, P. 317.
3. Dyer, P. 326.
4. Dyer, PP. 320-326.
5. Dyer, PP. 326-327.
6. Lundstrom, PP. 32-33.
7. Tregaskis, P. 30-31.
8. A typical reaction comes from Tregaskis' book.
9. Tregaskis, P. 32.
10. Tregaskis, PP. 31-33.
11. *Saratoga* deck logs, 7 August 1942; Lundstrom, PP. 34-35.
12. Dyer, P. 328.

Chapter 11

1. Tregaskis, PP. 34-43.
2. Morison, Vol. IV, P. 288.
3. Morison, Vol. IV, PP. 287-289; Frank, P. 623.

Chapter 12

1. Lundstrom, P. 41-43.
2. Dyer, P. 330.
3. Lundstrom, P. 42.
4. Lundstrom, PP. 43-44.
5. Sakai, P. 208.
6. Sakai, P. 209.
7. Weighing only 5,313 pounds carrying a normal load, the Zero had a powerful 940-horsepower 14-cylinder engine and a top speed of 288 knots at 4,500 meters (14,764 feet). It could climb to 5,000 meters (16,604 feet) in five minutes, 50 seconds. The plane had two 7.7 millimeter machine guns mounted in the nose over the engine and two 20-millimeter cannons in the wings. With the internal fuel tanks and detachable belly tanks full, the fighter had a maximum range of 1,675 miles or an effective combat range of almost 600 miles.
8. Lundstrom, PP. 43-44.
9. Lundstrom, PP. 44-45, Sakai, PP. 207-208.
10. Sakai, PP. 207-210.
11. Lundstrom, P. 46.
12. Lundstrom, PP. 46-48.
13. Lundstrom, P. 48.
14. Sakai, PP. 211-212.
15. Lundstrom, P. 48.
16. Lundstrom, PP. 48-49.
17. Sakai, P. 212.
18. Lundstrom, P. 50.
19. Sakai, PP. 213-214.
20. Lundstrom, P. 54.
21. Sakai, P. 215.
22. Lundstrom, P. 55.
23. Ibid.
24. Sakai, PP. 215-216.
25. Lundstrom, PP. 64-65.
26. Selz, Stires—personal recollections.
27. Lundstrom, P. 71.

Chapter 13

1. Goldstein, etc., P. 178.
2. Lundstrom, P. 72.
3. Lundstrom, P. 74.
4. Sakai, P. 219.
5. Sakai, PP. 219-224.
6. Lundstrom, P. 76.
7. Lundstrom, PP. 74-77.
8. Tregaskis, P. 51.
9. Tregaskis, P. 52.
10. Tregaskis, PP. 51-53.
11. Lundstrom, PP. 77-79.

Chapter 14

1. Frank, P. 622
2. Morison, Vol. IV, PP. 286-287, Miller, P. 83.

Chapter 15

1. Born on August 29, 1888 and a graduate from the Japanese Naval Academy at Etajima in 1910, Mikawa attended the Naval Torpedo and Gunnery Schools during 1913-1914 after serving aboard the cruiser *Asama* and the battlecruiser *Kongo*. During World War I, he was on the Cruiser *Aso* when she cruised the waters in and around China. His service also included tours of duty aboard the destroyer *Sugi*, transport *Seito*, and studies at the Japanese Naval War College. After the war, he was part of the Japanese delegation to the World War I peace conference at Versailles.

   He served as a Navigating Officer on several ships, taught at the Naval Torpedo School, and also was in several posts that brought high visibility by higher ranked officers to him during the 1920s. He was a delegate at the London Naval Conference from May through December in 1929. Immediately following that assignment he became the Japanese Naval Attaché in Paris. Reaching the high rank of Captain in late 1930, he became the Captain of the heavy cruisers Aoba and Chokai and the battleship Kirishima in the middle of the 1930s. He achieved flag rank as a Rear Admiral and became the Chief of Staff of the Second Fleet. He served on the Naval General Staff and at the Imperial Japanese Navy 's headquarters in 1937-1939. Sea duty immediately followed when assumed command of cruisers' and battleships' fleet squadrons.

   While serving at sea, he reached the rank of vice admiral in 1940 and became commander of the Eighth Fleet in July 1942 in the central and south Pacific. He served with distinction and garnered respect of his peers and enemies alike during World War II. He retired from the Japanese Navy and passed away in 1981.—Source: Naval Historical Center Web Site: www.history.navy.mil.

2. The clock time in Captain Ohmae's article used Rabaul local time, which was two hours earlier than the clock at Guadalcanal. To make it easier for the reader and for those who might have read Ohmae's article and reconcile the clock times between his article and this book, I will use Guadalcanal local time through this book for consistency and, hopefully eliminate confusion.
3. Ohmae, P. 1268; Morison, Vol. V, P. 18.
4. Morison, Vol. V, P. 18; Ohmae, P. 1269.
5. Ohmae, P. 1269.
6. Ohmae graduated from the Imperial Japanese Naval Academy in 1922 and served in World War II on the Staff of the 8th Fleet and of the Southeast Area Fleet (1942 and 1943), the Staff of the Mobile Fleet (1944) and was Chief, Operational Section, Imperial General Headquarters, Navy Section (1945). Since the war he has held a number of positions in connection with historical research on the war and is currently Senior Special Consultant, Military History Section. He wrote an Article for U. S. Naval Institute's Proceedings that was published in that magazine's December 1957 edition about the Battle of Savo Island that forms the basis of what I have written in this chapter.
7. Fuller, P. 273.
8. Ohmae, P. 1270.
9. Morison, Vol. V, P. 19.
10. Ohmae, P. 1271; Loxton, P. 126-127.
11. From Fall River to Port Moresby to Townsville to Pearl Harbor to Nouméa to *McCawley*. - Dyer, P. 362, Morison, Vol. V, P. 25.
12. Ibid.
13. Loxton, PP. 37-38, 139-143.
14. Ohmae, P. 1271.
15. Morison, Vol. V, P. 22.
16. Ohmae, PP. 1270-1271.
17. Morison, Vol. V. P. 17.
18. Ghormley, P. 31.
19. Lundstrom, P. 81.
20. Morison, Vol. V, P. 27.
21. Regan, PP. 189-191; Morison, Vol. V, 26-27; Ghormley, P. 31.
22. Loxton, figure on P. 127.
23. Morison, Vol. V. PP. 29-30.
24. Brown, PP. 64-67;
Web site by Tim Lanzendörfer, http://www.microworks.net/pacific/
25. Loxton, PP. 79-81.
26. Morison, Vol. V. P. 34.
27. Loxton, P. 116.
28. Morison, Vol. V, PP. 30-35; Loxton, PP. 112-117.

Chapter 16

1. Ohmae, P. 1273.
2. Ohmae, PP. 1273-1275.
3. The Australian equivalent of the U.S. Navy's General Quarters.
4. Morison, Vol. V, PP. 38-39.
5. Ohmae, P. 1275.
6. The heavy cruiser *Quincy*.
7. Ohmae, P. 1276.
8. Ohmae, PP. 1275-1276.
9. Morison, Vol. V, P. 42.
10. Black gang—Engine room crew
11. Morison, Vol. V, PP. 40-44; Frank, PP. 110-111.
12. Morison, Vol. V, P. 46; Newcomb, P. 134.
13. Morison, Vol. V. PP. 44-46; Frank, PP. 112-113.
14. Smith, PP. 106-107.
15. Smith, PP. 107-108.
16. Smith, PP. 109-110.
17. Smith. PP., 103-110; Morison, Vol. V., PP. 47-49.
18. Ohmae, PP. 1276-1278.
19. Morison, Vol. V, PP. 60-61.
20. Morison, Vol. V, PP. 62-63.
21. Ohmae, P. 1277.
22. Frank, P. 119.
23. Frank, P. 123.
24. Ibid.

Chapter 17

1. Alexander Archer Vandegrift was born in Charlottesville, Virginia, on 13 March 1887. In January 1909, after two years at the University of Virginia, he entered the U.S. Marine Corps as a Second Lieutenant. He saw very active service in the Caribbean and Central America between 1912 and 1923, taking part in the capture of Coyotepe, Nicaragua, in the former year, the occupation of Vera Cruz, Mexico, in 1914 and pacification efforts in Haiti beginning in 1915.
Major Vandegrift commanded a Marine battalion while stationed at Quantico, Virginia, from 1923 and in 1926 became Assistant Chief of Staff at the Marine Corps Base, San Diego, California. Service in China in 1927-28 was followed by duty in Washington, D.C., and at Quantico. He was promoted to the rank of Lieutenant Colonel in 1934, returned to China in 1935 and reached the rank of Colonel in 1936. While stationed at Marine Corps Headquarters in 1937-41, Vandegrift worked closely with the Corps' Commandant and was promoted to brigadier general in March 1940. He became Assistant Commander of the newly-formed First Marine Division in late 1941 and the Division's Commanding General in early 1942.
Major General Vandegrift took his division to the south Pacific in May 1942 and led it in the long, harsh but a successful campaign to seize and hold Guadalcanal between August and December 1942. He was awarded the Medal of Honor for his "tenacity, courage and resourcefulness" during this operation. In November 1943, as a Lieutenant General, Vandegrift commanded the First Marine Amphibious Corps during the initial stages of the Bougainville campaign.
Returning to the U.S. in late 1943, he became Commandant of the Marine Corps on 1 January 1944. He guided the Service's continued expansion through the rest of World War II, oversaw its contraction following the conflict, and successfully defended its existence during the difficult postwar years. Promoted to four-star General effective in March 1945, Vandegrift was the first Marine Corps officer to hold that rank while on active duty.
General Alexander A. Vandegrift was relieved as Commandant at the beginning of 1948 and formally retired in April 1949. He died on 8 May 1973.
- Source: U. S. Naval Historical Center, Washington, D.C.
2. Morison, Vol. V, PP. 63-69; Frank, PP. 124-127.
3. Sometimes known as the Battle of the Ilu River.
4. Morison, Vol. V, PP. 69-73.
5. Frank, PP. 138-139.
6. Morison, Vol. V, P. 73; Conway, P. 107.
7. USS *Enterprise* Deck Logs, August 19, 1942, 1200-1600 watch; USS *Saratoga* Deck Logs,
PP. 1221-1225; Morison, Vol. V., P. 73, Lundstrom, PP. 94-95.
8. Born on January 25, 1885 in Middleburg, Florida, Roy S. Geiger enlisted in the Marine Corps November 2, 1907 and received his commission as a Second Lieutenant on February 5. 1909 after attending Florida State Normal (now Florida State University) and receiving an LLB degree at Stetson University. After attending the Marine Corps' Officer School at Port Royal, South Carolina, he became part of the Marine Detachment on the battleships *Delaware* and *Wisconsin*. His first foreign land service was in Nicaragua in 1912. Geiger then moved to China to serve in the Philippines and China with the First Marine Detachment in Peking.
Geiger began his flight training at Pensacola, Florida in March 1916

and received his golden wings as the Marine Corps' fifth aviator in June 1917. He went to France during World War I to command Squadron "A" of the Marine Aviation Force.

After the war, he had several assignments including aviation commands, attendance at Staff Colleges, Director of Aviation at Headquarters Marine Corps and Naval Attaché, London, England. When the Japanese struck Pearl Harbor, Geiger commanded of the First Marine Aircraft Wing, Fleet Marine Force. From 3 September to 4 November 1942, he commanded the First Marine Air Wing at Guadalcanal He returned to Headquarters Marine Corps as the Director of Aviation in 1943. Geiger went back to the field in November 1943 as the Commanding General of the First Marine Amphibious Corps, (later designated Third Amphibious Corps) that he led at Bougainville, Guam, Peleliu and Okinawa. It was at Okinawa that General Geiger's command was part of the 10th Army of General Simon Bolivar Buckner, U.S. Army. When General Buckner was killed, General Geiger assumed command of the 10th Army until the successful conclusion of the campaign. For his actions during this climactic battle, he received the Army's Distinguished Service Medal. He was also the recipient of the Navy Distinguished Service Medal with two gold stars.

General Geiger commanded the Fleet Marine Force, Pacific from July 1945 until he was called back to Headquarters Marine Corps in November 1946. Three months later, on 23 January 1947, General Geiger died at the National Naval Medical Center, Bethesda, Maryland. He was posthumously promoted a four-star general by Congress effective that date. (Source: Arlington National Cemetery Web Site)

9. Frank, PP. 139-140.
10. Naval Historical Center web site.
11. Morison, Vol. V, PP. 75-78.

Chapter 18

1. Agawa, P. 324.
2. Frank, PP. 167-169.
3. Ugaki, PP. 184-186; Agawa, PP. 323-325; Frank, PP. 167-169; Morison, Vol. V., PP. 79-82.
4. Carrier Division One, Strike Force, Kidô Butai. Commanded by Vadm. Nagumo
5. Prados, P. 370.
6. Prados, Ibid.
7. Prados, P. 371.
8. Prados, PP. 369-371.
9. Frank, PP. 172-174.
10. Lundstrom, P. 101.
11. Lundstrom, P. 104.
12. Lundstrom, PP. 100-105.
13. Tanaka, Part I, PP. 687-693.
14. Saratoga Action Report, 24 Sept. 1942, P. 5.
15. Ibid.
16. TF-16 Chronological Order of Events 0500-2400, 24 August 1942.
17. That search plane's message, if any, never reached Rabaul.
18. Lundstrom, PP. 109-116.

Chapter 19

1. One TBF had to abort and return to its home base.
2. Lundstrom, PP. 116-119.
3. Lundstrom, P. 122.
4. Lundstrom, PP. 119-122, Frank, PP. 177-179.
5. Japanese warships had radar that was far more primitive relative to what the Americans had.
6. Lundstrom, PP. 123-125.

Chapter 20

1. Lundstrom, P. 126.
2. Pederson, "Carrier Operations" lecture.
3. Lundstrom, P. 129.
4. Lundstrom, PP. 129-130.
5. Lundstrom, P. 130.
6. Lundstrom, Ibid.
7. Lundstrom, PP. 129-133, Morison, Vol. V., PP. 89-91.
8. Some of the description that follows about the Japanese air attacks on Task Force 16 comes from the *Enterprise*'s deck log for August 24, 1942. When one reads the deck log and then reads the narratives from several sources, a one-half hour time difference appears between the carrier's deck log entries and written narratives. This is because the times in the deck logs indicates a time difference of 11½ hours with GMT. Therefore, I took the times from the written narratives because that keeps the times, which are ½ hour earlier than the deck logs' times that come from the narratives from where I got much of the information for this book. Therefore I chose NOT to use the times from the deck logs but used a time of ½ hour less to maintain consistency throughout the book.
9. Mears, P. 111.
10. Lundstrom, P. 138.
11. Lundstrom, PP. 133-138; Enterprise Deck Logs, 24 August, 1942.
12. Later promoted to Lieutenant (jg).
13. As shown in the 1941 film <u>Sergeant York</u>.
14. Lundstrom, P. 141.
15. Lundstrom, PP. 138-141.
16. Dull, P. 206.
17. Lundstrom, PP. 141-150.
18. Frank, P. 184.
19. Frank, P. 165.
20. Frank, PP. 184-186; Lundstrom, P. 151.

Chapter 21

1. Konig lost one TBF when it had to abort its flight.
2. Lundstrom, PP. 152-155; Frank, PP. 187-188.
3. Lundstrom, PP. 156-157.
4. Lundstrom, PP. 158-159; Frank, PP. 188-190; Tanaka, Part I, PP. 693-694.

Chapter 22

1. Since the days when Admiral Heihachiro Togo defeated the Russian Navy at Tsushima on May 27, 1905, Imperial Japanese Navy doctrine was that the only way to defeat another nation's navy was to lure its fleet into a single, colossal navy battle and inflict such a devastating defeat that the vanquished navy's nation would have no other choice but to sue for peace.
2. Ugaki, PP. 191-194.
3. Frank, PP. 191-193.
4. Potter, <u>Nimitz</u>, PP. 184-185; Lundstrom, P. 171.
5. Lundstrom, PP. 175-176.
6. Located in the Solomon and Gilbert (now Kiribati) Island groups respectively.
7. Lundstrom, PP. 175-177.

Chapter 23

1. Microsoft Encarta 2005
2. Oxford Dictionary.
3. Dyer, P. 404.
4. Dyer, PP. 403-405.
5. Dyer, P. 406.
6. Ibid.
7. Dyer, P. 408.
8. Dyer, PP. 406-410.
9. Dyer, P. 412.
10. Arnold, PP. 338-342.
11. Dyer, P. 414.
12. Dyer, P. 415.

Chapter 24

1. Tanaka, Part 1, P. 697.
2. Ibid.
3. Tanaka, Part 1, PP. 695-697; Alexander, PP. 115-117.
4. Morison, Vol. V., PP. 123-127; Frank, PP. 218-223; Alexander, PP. 135-141; Hoffman, PP. xiv-xv, 186-192.
5. Frank, PP. 223-225; Alexander, PP.139-142.
6. Alexander, PP. 141-142.
7. Alexander, P. 142.
8. Alexander, PP. 141-143.
9. Frank, P. 227.
10. Frank, PP. 227-228, P. 233; Alexander, P. 143.

11. Alexander, P. 148.
12. Frank, PP. 228-229, 231; Hoffman, PP. 196-198; Alexander, PP. 148-150.
13. Frank, P. 232.
14. Alexander, P. 164.
15. Griffith, P.142.
16. Alexander, P. 165.
17. Alexander, P. 167.
18. Griffith, Ibid.
19. Alexander, P. 172.
20. Ibid.
21. Ibid.
22. Ibid, P. 174., Griffith, P. 144.
23. Alexander, P. 174.
24. General Alexander A. Vandegrift's operations officer.
25. Alexander, P. 180.
26. McKennan, PP. 16-17, 80, 82.
27. Alexander, P. 185.
28. U.S. Civil War, Gettysburg, Pennsylvania, July 3, 1863
29. Alexander, PP. 190-191.
30. Rorke's Drift, where a devastating series of battles between the British and Zulus in January 1879 led to the desperate defense of Rorke's Drift mission station by a garrison of 139. Before the battle began, 35 were already wounded. It resulted in the most Victoria Crosses awarded in a single engagement in the history of British warfare and was made into a motion picture entitled Zulu, staring Stanley Baker and Michael Caine.
31. "For extraordinary heroism and conspicuous intrepidity above and beyond the call of duty as Commanding Officer of the 1st Marine Raider Battalion, with Parachute Battalion attached, during action against enemy Japanese forces in the Solomon Islands on the night of 1314 September 1942. After the airfield on Guadalcanal had been seized from the enemy on 8 August, Colonel Edson, with a force of 800 men, was assigned to the occupation and defense of a ridge dominating the jungle on either side of the airport. Facing a formidable Japanese attack which, augmented by infiltration, had crashed through our front lines, he, by skillful handling of his troops, successfully withdrew his forward units to a reserve line with minimum casualties. When the enemy, in a subsequent series of violent assaults, engaged our force in desperate hand-to-hand combat with bayonets, rifles, pistols, grenades, and knives, Colonel Edson, although continuously exposed to hostile fire throughout the night, personally directed defense of the reserve position against a fanatical foe of greatly superior numbers. By his astute leadership and gallant devotion to duty, he enabled his men, despite severe losses, to cling tenaciously to their position on the vital ridge, thereby retaining command not only of the Guadalcanal airfield, but also of the 1st Division's entire offensive installations in the surrounding area." Source: Medal of Honor Recipient Web Site: http://www.army.mil/cmh-pg/mohiia1.htm
32. For extraordinary courage and heroic conduct above and beyond the call of duty as Commanding Officer of Company C, 1st Marine Raider Battalion, during the enemy Japanese attack on Henderson Field, Guadalcanal, Solomon Islands, on 12-13 September 1942. Completely reorganized following the severe engagement of the night before, Major Bailey's company, within an hour after taking its assigned position as reserve battalion between the main line and the coveted airport, was threatened on the right flank by the penetration of the enemy into a gap in the main line. In addition to repulsing this threat, while steadily improving his own desperately held position, he used every weapon at his command to cover the forced withdrawal of the main line before a hammering assault by superior enemy forces. After rendering invaluable service to the battalion commander in stemming the retreat, reorganizing the troops and extending the reverse position to the left, Major Bailey, despite a severe head wound, repeatedly led his troops in fierce hand-to-hand combat for a period of 10 hours. His great personal valor while exposed to constant and merciless enemy fire, and his indomitable fighting spirit inspired his troops to heights of heroic endeavor which enabled them to repulse the enemy and hold Henderson Field. He gallantly gave his life in the service of his country." Medal of Honor Recipient Web Site: http://www.army.mil/cmh-pg/mohiia1.htm
33. Corporal Walter Burak, Captain John Sweeney, Platoon Sergeant Lawrence Harrison, Platoon Sergeant Lawrence Holdren, Private First Class John Mielke, Platoon Sergeant Peter Pettus, Major Robert S. Brown (posthumous), Private Herman Arnold, First Lieutenant William D. Stevenson, Naval Surgeon Edward McLarney, Naval Surgeon Robert Skinner, Navy Corpsmen Karl Coleman, Navy Corpsmen Delbert Eilers, Navy Corpsmen Thaddeus Parker
34. Frank, P. 234; Alexander 164-171; Griffith, PP. 139-148.

Chapter 25

1. Arnold, P. 342.
2. There is no direct evidence that I could find about what Arnold and Knox actually said during that meeting. I tried to recreate what both men might have said given the temperament of the time in Washington and to give the reader a better appreciation of the ongoing conflicts and inter-service rivalries that existed at that time.
3. Arnold, PP. 338-349.
4. Potter, PP. 191-192.
5. Potter, P. 192.
6. This is another attempt by me to recreate what the conversation between Nimitz and Vandegrift based on the descriptions in Potter, Nimitz, P. 193. I have done this to give the reader a better appreciation of the tone and tenor of the event.
7. Potter, PP. 190-195; Frank, PP. 292-293; Morison, Vol. V, P147-148.

Chapter 26

1. I could not find what kind flying boat it was that made this trip. I assume it was a Kawanishi "Emily" H8K flying boat, which was an upgrade from the slower "Mavis" H6K and have included a three-view line drawing to show what it looked like.
2. Miller, P. 138.
3. Miller, PP. 138-139; Frank, P. 268; Ugaki, PP. 219-220., Cook, P. 31; Tanaka, P. 699..
4. The Eagle Boat was an US Navy experiment with steel-clad boats smaller than the destroyer of that time.
5. Naval Historical Center Online Library Web Page: http://www.history.navy.mil/photos/pers-us/uspers-s/n-scott.htm
6. Web site http://www.microworks.net/pacific/equipment/sg_radar.htm.
7. Conway, PP. 113, 115-116; Cook, PP. 16-17.
8. Lundstrom. PP. 295-296.
9. Frank, PP. 292-298; Morison, Vol. V, PP. 147-151; Cook, 16-19.
10. Cook, PP. 31-33.
11. Morison, Vol. V., P. 155.
12. Cook, PP. 34-41.
13. Frank, PP. 298-299.

Chapter 27

1. I could not find the full name of Ens. Gash in any research materials.
2. Destroyer Squadron 12 (DESRON 12)—Tobin's destroyers' designation.
3. Morison, Vol. V, PP. 151-162; Cook, PP. 42-86.; Frank, PP. 300-303.
4. Cook, PP. 87-89; Frank, PP. 304-306; Morison, Vol. V., PP. 163-165.
5. Translation: At 11:41 p.m., changed speed to 30 knots, changed course

to 225º.

6. Cook, PP. 53-96, Morison, Vol. V., PP. 166-168.
7. Cook, PP. 92-94, Morison, Vol. V, PP. 168-169.
8. Cook, P. 142.
9. Frank, PP. 310.

Chapter 28

1. Lundstrom, P. 300.
2. Lundstrom, PP. 299-300; Frank, PP. 313-316; Morison, Vol. V, PP. 172-173.
3. Tanaka, Part II, P. 815.
4. Clemens, PP. 256-257.
5. Lundstrom, P. 301.
6. Ibid.
7. Frank, P. 317.
8. Ibid.
9. Frank, P. 320.
10. Ibid.
11. Frank, P. 321.
12. Lieutenants David C. Richardson, Hayden M. Jensen, Carl W. Rooney, Lieutenants (jg)
Raymond F. Myers, Roland H. Kenton, and Foster J. Blair
13. Morison, Vol. V, PP. 173-177; Lundstrom, PP. 10, 301-309; Frank, PP. 317-325; Clemens, PP. 256-259.
14. Frank, PP. 326-327.

Chapter 29

1. Frank, P. 333.
2. Although there is no record of what was actually said when these staff officers met with Nimitz that evening, I attempted to recreate a possible conversation between them to make this history a bit more readable.
3. Potter, <u>Nimitz</u>, P. 197.
4. Ibid.
5. Potter, <u>Nimitz</u>, PP. 195-197.
6. Potter, <u>Bull Halsey</u>, P. 150.
7. Ibid., PP. 149-150, 154-159.
8. Ibid., P. 160.
9. Ibid.
10. Ibid.
11. Ibid.
12. Potter, <u>Bull Halsey</u>, PP. 161-164; Frank, PP. 334-335.

Chapter 30

1. Morison, Vol. V., P. 189.
2. Ibid.
3. I could not find the first name of this officer in my research so I can only disclose his surname.
4. Sometimes called the Battle of Edson's Ridge that occurred September 12-14.
5. Frank, P. 341.
6. Ibid, P. 343.
7. Ugaki, P. 242.
8. Ugaki, P. 242.
9. Frank, P. 348.
10. Local time at Rabaul.
11. Ugaki, P. 245.
12. Ugaki, P. 246.
13. Frank, P. 361.
14. Ibid., P. 364-365.
15. Ibid., P. 365
16. Ibid. PP. 364-365.
17. Frank, PP. 356-366.
18. Morison, Vol. V., PP. 188-193; Frank, PP. 337-367; Miller, PP. 135-169; Ugaki, PP. 229-242, Lundstrom, PP. 343-346.

Chapter 31

1. Ibid., PP. 104-406.
2. Morison, Vol. V., PP. 206-207.
3. Rear Admiral Willis A. ("Ching") Lee commanded Task Force 64. That force had the battleship *Washington*, heavy cruiser *San Francisco*, light cruisers *Helena* and *Atlanta*, and destroyers *Aaron Ward*, *Benham*, *Fletcher*, *Lansdowne*, *Lardner*, and *McCalla*. Task Force 64 had orders from Halsey to operate separately from Task Force 61. Lee's force would not participate in the Battle of the Santa Cruz islands.
4. This sighting was of Rear Admiral Murray's Task Force 17 that had the carrier *Hornet*, four cruisers, and six destroyers.
5. These ships were Rear Admiral Willis A. Lee's Task Force 64 that had the battleship *Washington*, three cruisers, and six destroyers. I have not included these ships as part of The Battle of the Santa Cruz Islands since they functioned autonomously from Kinkaid's and Murray's task forces and had no part in that conflict.
6. Ugaki, PP. 248-249.
7. ComSoPac to CTF-61 2422350, October 1942.
8. Lundstrom, PP. 337-355; Potter, <u>Halsey</u>, PP. 163-167; Wheeler, PP. 268-273; Morison, Vol. V, PP. 199-204..

Chapter 32

1. Lundstrom, P. 358.
2. Ibid.
3. Ibid., P. 363.
4. Ibid., P. 365.
5. Ibid.
6. Ibid.
7. The designation for Batten's TBF.
8. Ibid., P. 366.
9. Lundstrom, P. 167.
10. "The Thach Weave: After it became clear that the U.S. Navy's F4F Wildcat was no match for the Japanese Zero in single combat. One day while discussing the problem with other pilots Thach pushed matchsticks (representing aircraft) around on a tabletop until he came up with a workable solution. His solution was to fight in pairs, using the ingenious weaving tactic that he devised."
"The F4Fs would fly parallel courses until attacked, then bank steeply inward. 'The quick turn toward each other does two things to the enemy pilot,' Thach explained. 'It throws off his aim and, because he usually tries to follow his target, it leads him around into a position to be shot by the other member of our team.' Convinced by the results, the Navy made the 'Thach weave' standard practice and ordered its originator to teach the tactic to other fighter pilots. This maneuver was also adapted by the U.S. Army Air Forces, the British RAF, and the Soviet Air Force. Two Wildcats side by side initiate a Thach weave as a Zero attacks from behind. Here a kill is scored on the second turn. (Source: Naval Fighter Tactics Website: http://www.airwarfare.com/tactics/tactics_fighter.htm).
11. Takashi Ibid., P. 368.
12. Ibid., P. 370.
13. Ibid., P. 376.
14. Lundstrom, PP. 356-383; Morison, Vol. V., PP. 207-224.; Frank, PP. 379403; Ugaki, PP. 249-254.

Chapter 33

1. Prange, P. 197.
2. Morison, Vol. V., PP. 210-215; Frank, PP. 389-395; Lundstrom, PP. 384-407.

Chapter 34

1. Lundstrom, P. 409.
2. Ibid., P. 410.
3. Ibid., P. 411.
4. Mott, P. 40.
5. Lundstrom, PP. 416-417.
6. Mott, PP. 44-45.
7. Lundstrom, P. 431.
8. Lundstrom, P. 432.
9. Lundstrom, PP. 408-438; Morison, PP. 215-219.

Chapter 35

1. Lundstrom, P. 439.
2. Ibid., P. 440.
3. Ibid.
4. Ibid.
5. Ibid., P. 441.
6. COMSOPAC to all SOPAC CTFs 260450, October 1942.
7. Lundstrom, PP. 439-445.
8. Ugaki, P. 250.
9. Ugaki, PP. 249-251.
10. Okumiya and Horikoshi, P. 265, 267.
11. Ibid, PP. 267-268.
12. Ugaki, P. 251; Frank, PP. 398-399.
13. Ugaki, P. 252.
14. Ibid., P. 253.
15. Ibid.
16. Lundstrom, P. 452.
17. Also called the "Naval Battle of the South Pacific."
18. Letter from Halsey to Nimitz, 31 Octo-

ber, 1942.

19. Microsoft ® Encarta ® 2006. © 1993-2005 Microsoft Corporation. All rights reserved.
20. Lundstrom, PP. 439-459; Morison, Vol. V., PP. 219-224; 395-403; Ugaki, PP. 249-253.
21. Frank. P. 403.
22. Microsoft ® Encarta ® 2006. © 1993-2005 Microsoft Corporation. All rights reserved.

Chapter 36

1. Morison, Vol. V., PP. 233-235. Vadm. Jinichi Kusaka (Commander in Chief—Eleventh Air Fleet) had about 215 operational planes stationed on Rabaul. Vadm. Teruhisa Komatsu (Commander in Chief—Sixth Fleet) had the light cruiser *Katori* as his flagships at Truk. He had the submarines *I-16*, *I-20*, *I-24*, *I-15*, *I-17*, *I-26*, *I-122*, *I-172*, *I- 175*, *RO-34* with the *I-7* off Santa Cruz, and the *I-9*, *I-21* and *I-31*, and a seaplane, looking for any American ships near San Cristobal, Nouméa and Suva.
2. Formed as an emergency measure on November 13 that took three destroyers from the Raiding Group, four destroyers from the Carrier Support Group, two destroyers from the Reinforcement Group.
3. The destroyer *Shikinami* joined the Main Body on Nov. 13 to begin rescuing Japanese sailors.
4. Conway, P. 173.
5. Frank, P. 426; Lundstrom P. 567.
6. Ugaki, PP. 256-264; Fuller, P. 63.
7. Sherwood, PP. 622-623. Robert E. Sherwood published the text Roosevelt's letter in his 1948 book <u>Roosevelt and Hopkins: An Intimate History</u> in its original handwritten form and in text. This is the text version of that letter.
8. Potter, <u>Nimitz</u>, PP. 202-203; Larrabee, P. 290.
9. Potter, <u>Bull Halsey</u>, P. 184.
10. Ibid., P. 169.
11. Ibid.
12. Potter, <u>Bull Halsey</u>, PP. 168-170.
13. Winton, P. 89.
14. Ibid.
15. Prados, PP. 390-391, Kinkaid, P. 288.
16. Morison, Vol. V., PP. 231-233.
17. Morison, Vol. 5, PP. 225-287; Frank, PP. 421-436; Lundstrom, PP.463-475; Prados, PP. 390-396; Grace, PP. 10-11.

Chapter 37

1. Conway, P. 115.
2. After doing the research on Admiral Callaghan's career, I was struck how his assignment as Roosevelt's aide and later promotion to Rear Admiral paralleled the fictional character Victor Henry's own career in Herman Wouk's novels <u>*Winds of War*</u> and <u>*War and Remembrance*</u>.
3. Morison, Vol. V, P. 236.
4. Connors.
5. About 170 miles south of Rennell and 320 miles south of Iron Bottom Sound.
6. Wheeler, P. 289.
7. Feldt, P. 104.
8. Ibid., P. 105.
9. Ibid., P. 106, Lord, P. 105.
10. Grace, PP. 14-18; Lundstrom, PP. 472-473.
11. Grace, PP. 19-26; Lundstrom, PP. 471, 473-474.
12. Lundstrom, P. 475.
13. Tanaka, Part II, PP. 819-820.
14. Born in the Aichi Prefecture in 1899, Hiroaki Abe graduated from the Japanese naval academy at Etajima in 1911. He had extensive sea experience in destroyers, cruisers, and battleships from 1925 to 1938. Achieving flag rank with his promotion to Rear Admiral in 1938, he returned to Japan on December 24, 1941 to command the reinforcement force invading Wake Island. He commanded a cruiser force supporting the carrier air attack commanded by Chuichi Nagumo on Darwin, Australia in February 1942. His cruisers accompanied Nagumo to the Battle of Midway and assumed temporary tactical command after Nagumo had to abandon his flagship *Akagi*. He then transferred to Vadm. Kondo's command at Truk where he commanded cruiser and battleship forces in the battles leading up to the Naval Battle of Guadalcanal. He received his third star when promoted to Vadm. on November 1, 1942.
15. Grace, P. 35.
16. Morison, PP. 225-235; Tanaka, Part II, PP. 818-821; Grace, PP. 27-42.

Chapter 38

1. Grace, P. 50.
2. Ibid.
3. Ibid., P. 53.
4. Ibid., PP. 53-55.
5. Ibid., P. 55.
6. Ibid., P. 56.
7. Ibid.
8. Ibid.
9. Ibid., PP. 56-57.
10. Grace, PP. 43-57; Morison, Vol. V, PP. 239-242.
11. Clemens, P. 287.
12. Grace, P. 58.
13. Grace, PP. 58-68, Morison, Vol. V, PP. 242-251.
14. Grace, PP. 69-72.; Morison, Vol. V., PP. 251-252.
15. Grace, P. 73.
16. Ibid, P. 79.
17. Ibid., P. 83.
18. Grace, PP. 73-83; Morison. PP. 252-254.
19. Grace, P. 46.
20. Ibid., P. 87.
21. Grace, P. 88.
22. Grace, PP. 84-90.

Chapter 39

1. Grace, P. 93.
2. Ibid., P. 102.
3. Grace, PP. 91-107.

Chapter 40

1. Grace, P. 110.
2. McCandless, P. 50.
3. Grace, P. 114.
4. McCandless, P. 50.
5. Grace, PP. 108-114.

Chapter 41

1. Grace, P. 122.
2. Grace, PP. 115-122, PP. 136-137.

Chapter 42

1. Grace, PP. 123-135.

Chapter 43

1. Grace, P. 140.
2. The Sullivan brothers were Albert Leo 'Al', Francis Henry 'Frank', George Thomas, Joseph Eugene 'Joe' and Madison Abel 'Matt' Sullivan. Their loss on the *USS Juneau* resulted in a new Navy policy discouraging family members from serving together in the same ship. The 20th Century Fox movie "The Sullivans" (aka. "The Fighting Sullivans") portrayed the fate of the Sullivan Brothers and appeared in American movie theaters in 1944. It starred Thomas Mitchell as their father (Thomas F. Sullivan), Selena Royle as their mother (Mrs. Alleta Sullivan) and Anne Baxter as their only sister (Katherine Mary Sullivan). It is available in DVD format.
3. Morison, Vol. V, PP. 254-258; Grace, PP. 136-148.

Chapter 44

1. Tanaka, Part II, P. 821; Frank, P. 452, Ugaki, PP. 264-266.
2. Potter, <u>Halsey</u>, P. 172.
3. Ibid, P. 174.
4. Ibid., P. 175.
5. Potter, <u>Halsey</u>, PP. 172-175.

Chapter 45

1. Lundstrom, P. 466.
2. Ibid., P. 478.
3. Six Zeroes commanded by Lieutenant (jg) Takashi Morisaki left from Buin at 9:30 a.m. and flew to Savo Island as fast as they could. They arrived too late to help the *Hiei*. Ibid. P. 480.
4. Ibid., P. 480.

5. Ibid., P. 481.
6. Lundstrom, P. 476-483.
7. Frank, P. 460.
8. Frank, PP. 459-461.

Chapter 46

1. Morison, Vol. V., P. 235.
2. Lundstrom, P. 489.
3. Lundstrom, PP. 489-491; Frank, PP. 462-464.
4. Lundstrom, P. 487.
5. Lundstrom, PP. 484-487.
6. Ibid., P. 487.
7. Frank, PP. 462-472; Morison, Vol. V. PP 261-269; Potter, <u>*Bull Halsey*</u>, PP. 175-176.
8. Lundstrom, P. 491.
9. Lundstrom, PP. 491-492.
10. Ibid., P. 494.
11. Tanaka, Part II, PP 821-822; Lundstrom, PP. 492-502.
12. Lundstrom, P. 506.
13. Ibid.
14. Ibid., P. 509.
15. Ibid.
16. Lundstrom, PP. 502-512; Tanaka, Part II, PP. 822-823; Frank, P. 468.

Chapter 47

1. Naval Historical Web Site: http://www.history.navy.mil/danfs/w9/willis_a_lee.htm.; Conway, P. 97.
2. Frank, PP. 468-472; Morison, Vol. V, PP. 270-271.

Chapter 48

1. Frank, P. 473; Morison, Vol. V. PP. 272-273.
2. Frank, P. 475; Morison, Vol. V, P. 274.
3. Frank, P. 477.
4. Ibid., P. 479.
5. Frank, PP. 472-479; Morison, Vol. V, PP. 272-277.
6. Frank, P. 480.
7. Frank, P. 482.
8. Frank, PP. 479-485; Morison, Vol. V, PP. 277-281
9. Frank, PP. 485-487; Morison Vol. V, P. 282.

Chapter 49

1. Wolfert, P. 126.
2. Frank, PP. 487-488; Ugaki, PP. 273-275; Morison, Vol. V, PP. 283-287; Tanaka, Part II, PP. 823-824; Lundstrom, PP. 515-518.
3. Potter, <u>*Nimitz*</u>, P. 206.
4. Potter, <u>*Bull Halsey*</u>, P. 179.
5. Ibid, P. 180.
6. Ibid.
7. Potter, <u>*Bull Halsey*</u>, P. 179.
8. Sherwood, P. 656.
9. Ugaki, PP. 276-277.
10. Frank, P. 492.
11. Frank, PP. 489-492; Lundstrom, P. 518, PP. 522-524.
12. Potter, <u>*Nimitz*</u>, P. 208.

Chapter 50

1. Potter, <u>Bull Halsey</u>, P. 181.
2. Ibid., PP. 181-182.
3. Ibid., P. 186.
4. The specific operational orders from Kinkaid's plan are included here:

<u>Night Action</u>

a. Cruisers will form on line of bearing normal to the general bearing line, distance 1,000 yards. Destroyers will form at 4,000 yards 30° on the engaged bow of the cruiser line.

b. Initial contact should be made by radar. One or more destroyer pickets will be stationed 10,000 yards in the direction of expected contact, in order to obtain early information of the enemy. When so stationed destroyers will be ordered to take station as pickets on specified true bearings from the guide. Approach maneuvering will be ordered by TBS based on radar tracking. All maneuvers after commencement of firing by our cruisers will be ordered by TBS and secondary warning net.

c. As soon as possible destroyers will be ordered to form and attack. It is expected that destroyer torpedo attacks will be made early in order to obtain the maximum benefits of surprise. All radar facilities may be used by destroyers, and the attack should be made on radar information insofar as possible. Results of radar tracking will be furnished the destroyer commander by TBS. Destroyers must clear expeditiously and in such a positive manner that there is the least possible chance for mistaken identity. All ships having IFF must insure that it is turned on well before night action, particularly when destroyers are separated from the cruisers. On completion of torpedo attacks and after commencement of cruiser action, destroyers engage enemy destroyers or cruisers being engaged by our cruisers, and be prepared to provide star shell illumination if so ordered.

d. Insofar as practicable, the range will be maintained in excess of 12,000 yards until our destroyer attack has been completed. Commencement of fire will be ordered at a range of between 10,000 and 12,000 yards. Fire will be opened using fire control radars, and the distribution of fire will be normal insofar as can be determined with the radar equipment available. Intention is that cruiser planes will silhouette enemy force by flares. Visual point of aim should be used as soon as available. If fire can not be maintained with fire control radar, and visual point is not available, individual ships may illuminate with starshells. Searchlights will not be used. Ships should be prepared to spot by radar.

e. In normal action the range will be controlled by ship turns. When action is broken off the course may be reversed and the range closed in order to sink enemy cripples. In reverse action the range will be controlled by ship turns and head of column movements not in excess of 30°. The minimum range will depend upon the tactical situation and advantages gained in the early phases of the action, but in general will not be less than 6,000 yards.

f. Night fighting lights may only be used if under attack by a friendly vessel, and then only for the shortest possible time to ensure recognition.

The preceding comes from Crenshaw - PP, 27-29.

5. Wheeler, PP. 200-203; Frank, PP. 503-504.
6. Potter, <u>Bull Halsey</u>, PP. 183-187.
7. Frank, P. 500.
8. Conway, P. 195.
9. Web site: http://www.spartacus.schoolnet.co.uk/2WWwrightC.htm
10. Crenshaw, P. 29.
11. Ibid.
12. Ugaki, PP. 277-289; Tanaka, part II, PP. 824-825; Morison, PP. 291-293; Frank, PP. 499-504; Crenshaw, PP. 29-31.

Chapter 51

1. Crenshaw, P. 145.
2. Ibid., P. 146.
3. Ibid., P. 48.
4. Ibid., P. 49.
5. Ibid., P. 146.
6. Ibid., P. 147.
7. Crenshaw, PP. 48-68, 139-154; Frank, PP. 507.

Chapter 52

1. Captain Russell S. Crenshaw in his book entitled *The Battle of Tassafa-*

ronga that specifically and comprehensively describes the battle. He divided his analysis that addressed the problems of the Americans into parts that covered the reports written by Admirals Wright, Halsey, and Nimitz, the torpedo problem, and an analysis and critique section that summarizes what he wrote. I will offer my own perspectives.

2. Crenshaw, PP. 87-90.
3. Ibid., P. 90.
4. The benefit of hindsight allows readers of these comments to view them as almost immaturely naive. Yet we should also understand the environment from which Wright wrote these remarks.
5. Crenshaw, PP. 80-108.
6. Ibid., PP. 155-165.
7. Morison, Vol. V., P. 313.
8. Ibid., P. 314.
9. Ibid., PP. 313-315.

Chapter 53

1. Morison, Vol. V., P. 316.
2. Ibid., PP. 316-317.
3. Ugaki, P. 293.
4. Ibid.
5. Ibid., P. 294.
6. Tanaka, Part II, PP. 827-828; Frank, PP. 519-522; Morison Vol. V., PP. 316-325; Fuller, PP. 111-112; Ugaki, PP. 292-295; Hayashi, PP. 61-67.

Chapter 54

1. The 2nd Marine Division included 1,607 men in the Marine air unit and 4,913 men in the Naval air unit.
2. The reason the malaria infection rate per thousand rose to more than 1,000 was that many cases were hospitalized more than once.
3. Shaw, PP. 46-51; Miller, PP. 210-231; Boatner, PP. 411-412; Potter, Bull Halsey, PP. 191-193.

Chapter 55

1. Miller, P. 238.
2. Miller, P. 244.
3. Miller, P. 251.
4. Miller, PP. 232-252; Morison, Vol. V, PP. 333-337; Frank, PP. 528-534.

Chapter 56

1. Web site: http://en.wikipedia.org/wiki/J._Lawton_Collins
2. Proft, PP. 300-301.
3. Miller, PP. 253-280.

Chapter 57

1. Miller, PP. 281-305.

Chapter 58

1. Miller, P. 326.
2. Miller, PP. 319-335.

Chapter 59

1. Potter, Nimitz, P. 215.
2. Ibid, P. 216.
3. Ibid, P. 217.
4. Ibid, PP. 197-198.
5. I do not have an accurate transcript for this meeting that took place at Halsey's Headquarters on Nouméa. Therefore, I have endeavored to recreate what the participants might have said based on the research I have done for this book. My purpose for using this technique is to help the reader gain a better appreciation of the participant moods and means of expressing themselves.
6. Potter, Nimitz, PP. 210-211, Halsey, PP. 196-200; Morison, PP. 351-352.

Chapter 60

1. Tanaka, Part II, P. 830.
2. Miller, P. 341.
3. Frank, P. 585.
4. Lord, P. 171.
5. Morison, Vol. V, P. 368-369.
6. Ibid, P. 369.
7. Frank, P. 588.
8. Ibid.
9. Frank, P. 590.
10. Ibid, P. 592.
11. Ibid, 595.
12. The description of the Battle of the Rennell Islands is not included in this book. The main reason for this is that the book would have exceeded the publisher's limit for being able to print the book in one volume if I included it. If you wish to see what I wrote about this battle, a description of it can be found on my web site: www.battlesforguadalcanal.com.
13. Miller, P. 348.
14. Frank, P. 597.
15. Miller, PP. 336-350; Morison, PP. 342, 351-353, 361; Frank, PP. 582-597.

Chapter 61

1. Frank, P. 601; Morison, Vol. V, P. 372.
2. Frank, P. 602.
3. Frank, P. 610.
4. Ibid.
5. Frank, P. 611.
6. Miller, P. 350.
7. Ibid, P. 614.
8. Frank, PP. 606-614; Miller, P. 350.

Chapter 62

1. "For outstanding and heroic accomplishment above and beyond the call of duty as commanding officer of the 1st Marine Division in operations against enemy Japanese forces in the Solomon Islands during the period 7 August to 9 December 1942. With the adverse factors of weather, terrain, and disease making his task a difficult and hazardous undertaking, and with his command eventually including sea, land, and air forces of Army, Navy, and Marine Corps, Major General Vandegrift achieved marked success in commanding the initial landings of the U.S. forces in the Solomon Islands and in their subsequent occupation. His tenacity, courage, and resourcefulness prevailed against a strong, determined, and experienced enemy, and the gallant fighting spirit of the men under his inspiring leadership enabled them to withstand aerial, land, and sea bombardment, to surmount all obstacles, and leave a disorganized and ravaged enemy. This dangerous but vital mission, accomplished at the constant risk of his life, resulted in securing a valuable base for further operations of our forces against the enemy, and its successful completion reflects great credit upon Major General Vandegrift, his command, and the U.S. Naval Service." Proft, P. 533.
2. Ghormley, P. 37.
3. Ibid., P. 346.
4. Ibid., P. 346.
5. A FRUPac crypto-analyst who invented a mathematical technique that could help decipher five-digit codeword groups that helped the Americans break the Japanese JN-25 naval code.
6. Agawa, PP. 338-368; Potter, Nimitz, PP. 232-234; Potter, Bull Halsey, PP.214-215; Holmes. PP. 135-136; Davis, PP. 226-277; Taylor, P. 150.
7. Fuller, PP. 264-265.
8. Naval Historical Center website, http://www.history.navy.mil/photos/prs-for/japan/japrs-m/g-mikawa.htm.
9. Fuller, P. 293; Wikipedia web site: http://en.wikipedia.org/wiki/Raizo_Tanaka.
10. Ugaki, PP. 330-331; Fuller, P. 298-299.
11. Morison, Vol. V., P 373.
12. Churchill, P. 21

Index

Aaron Ward
Battle of the Eastern Solomons 161
Battle of Cape Esperance 269
Naval Battle of Guadalcanal 401, 405, 409, 414, 422, 427, 433-435, 442, 444, 445, 459, 460, 468, 487
Abe, Hiroaki
Battle of the Eastern Solomons 159, 175, 177, 178, 195
Battle of the Santa Cruz Islands 339-341, 344, 345, 347, 376, 380, 385
Naval Battle of Guadalcanal 395, 410-413, 415, 417, 418, 431, 433, 443, 444, 453, 459, 464, 469, 472-474

Akagi 76, 77
Akatsuki 311, 312
Battle of Cape Esperance 280
Naval Battle of Guadalcanal 395, 411-413, 420, 421, 435
Sinking 436
Akigumo
Battle of the Eastern Solomons 159
Battle of the Santa Cruz Islands 333, 340, 383
Operation "KE" 650, 654
Akitsushima 125
Akizuki 159, 244, 271, 312, 313, 643
Alchiba 284, 285
Amagiri 402, 503, 506
Amatsukaze 395, 484, 487
American Legion 56, 71, 89, 90, 92
Anderson
Battle of the Santa Cruz Islands 355, 356, 382
Naval Battle of Guadalcanal 401
Battle of Tassafaronga 562
Operation "KE" 646
Aoba 79
Battle of Savo Island 120, 122, 123, 125, 134, 140, 154
Battle of the Eastern Solomons 164
Battle of Cape Esperance 244, 256, 260, 262, 264, 269
Arashio 568, 570
Naval Battle of Guadalcanal 477, 494
Operation "KE" 650, 654
Argonne 43, 125, 202, 217, 231, 236, 293, 296, 398, 400, 523
Ariake 271, 570
Arima, Kaoru 78
Arima, Keiichi 186, 187, 195, 204, 364-366
Arima, Masafumi 195, 343, 377, 380
Arnold, Henry H. ("Hap") 208, 209, 230-236, 239
Asagumo
Battle of the Eastern Solomons 159
Battle of Cape Esperance 244, 280
Naval Battle of Guadalcanal 395, 411, 412, 438, 444, 451, 467, 496, 505, 509, 510
Operation "KE" 654
Asakaze 80
Ashford, William H., Jr. 291, 292, 296, 523
Astoria 17, 48, 49, 56, 57, 460
Battle of Savo Island 128, 138-141, 143, 144, 147
Atago
Naval Battle of Guadalcanal 395, 496, 497, 500, 504-507, 509
Atlanta 17, 60
Battle of the Eastern Solomons 161, 185
Naval Battle of Guadalcanal 401, 405, 407, 414, 417-421, 423-426, 428, 429, 435, 436, 444, 454-456, 459, 461-463, 465, 467, 472, 473
Australia 56, 69, 74, 112
Battle of Savo Island 128-131, 146
Ayanami 395, 496, 497, 500, 502, 503, 505, 510, 511
Bagley
Battle of Savo Island 56, 115, 128, 134, 138
Battle of Tassafaronga 561
Balch 60, 63, 81, 161, 187, 192
Ballard 323, 462
Barnett 56, 114
Barton
Naval Battle of Guadalcanal 401, 405, 414, 422, 432, 433, 436, 441, 444, 450, 459, 562
Bellatrix 56, 284, 285
Benham 60
Battle of the Eastern Solomons 161
Naval Battle of Guadalcanal 401, 405, 497, 502-504, 510, 511, 562
Betelgeuse 56, 63, 70, 71, 401, 405-407, 409,
Bloody (Edson's) Ridge 17, 24, 210, 237, 242, 243, 298, 299, 304
Battle of 211-229
Blue 56, 57, 71, 115, 128-132, 165
Bobolink 460, 550
Bonhomme Richard 384
Brewer, Charles E. 175, 176, 182, 183, 187
Brown, Julian 292, 293, 523
Browning, Miles R. 291-293, 400, 465, 522, 523
Buchanan 56
Battle of Savo Island 128
Battle of the Eastern Solomons 161
Battle of Cape Esperance 245, 249, 254, 268
Naval Battle of Guadalcanal 401, 405, 408-410
Bush, George E. 603-608, 630, 635
Bushnell 495
CACTUS 10, 11, 208, 295, 303, 312, 313, 317, 570, 577, 580, 644, 662, 665, 675
Battle of the Eastern Solomons 160, 170, 194, 196
Battle of Cape Esperance 243, 248, 252, 271-273, 276-286
Battle of the Santa Cruz Islands 320, 327, 386
Naval Battle of Guadalcanal 406, 407, 409-411, 415, 467, 469-472, 478, 488, 490, 492, 500, 508, 515, 516, 519, 520
Battle of Tassafaronga 526, 594
Operation "KE" 648, 650
Calhoun, William L. 292, 293, 522
Callaghan, Daniel J. 209, 232, 233, 524, 663
Ghormley's chief of staff 41
Biography 403, 404
Fiji Conference 65-69
Killed in action 427
Naval Battle of Guadalcanal 401, 405, 408, 410, 413, 414-422, 424, 426-429, 444, 446, 464-467, 470-473, 479, 517-519
Campbell, William R. 468, 471, 515
Canberra 17, 56, 69, 128, 129, 131, 134, 137, 147, 661
Chester 321
Chicago 17, 56, 69, 103, 112, 128, 130, 131, 134, 135, 137, 138, 147, 657
Chihaya, Masataka 413, 418, 419, 431, 433
Chikuma
Battle of the Eastern Solomons 159, 175, 176, 192, 195, 203
Battle of the Santa Cruz Islands 329, 333, 339, 345-347, 376, 384, 386
Chitose 193, 244,
Chokai 17, 79, 83
Battle of Savo Island 120, 121, 123, 125, 132-139, 143
Battle of the Eastern Solomons 196, 205
Battle of Cape Esperance 276
Naval Battle of Guadalcanal 395, 399, 476, 481, 483
Operation "KE" 570, 641, 643
Churchill, Winston S. 29, 40, 50, 128, 528, 660, 669, 684
Cimarron 74, 162
Clark 401
Clemens, Martin 85, 215, 221, 274, 280, 305, 419
Coffin, Albert P. 469, 470, 472, 478, 486, 490, 491, 514, 516
Cole, William M. 423, 531, 535-538, 544, 547, 548, 559
Collett, John A. 331, 334-336
Collins, Joseph Lawton 579, 580, 593, 598-603, 611, 620, 622, 623, 626, 629-631, 658, 658
Conyngham 364
Coral Sea, Battle of the 29, 37, 57, 59, 60, 64, 77, 78, 97, 104, 126, 160, 163, 166, 167, 176, 199-202, 319, 329, 343, 351, 405, 489, 669, 676
Crescent City 56, 63, 401, 405
Crommelin, John G., Jr. 327, 372, 469, 480
Crutchley, Victor A. C., RN 56, 57, 69, 70, 127-131, 146
Curtiss 339, 637, 638
Cushing 562
Battle of the Santa Cruz Islands 378
Naval Battle of Guadalcanal 401, 405, 414, 417, 418, 420, 429-431, 433, 435, 436, 443, 444, 449, 459-461
CXAM radar 11, 128, 179, 389
Dale 161
Daniels, James G., III 361, 370, 372, 377, 378
DeHaven 648, 649, 657
del Valle, Pedro 215, 216, 227
Dewey 56, 63
Dibb, Robert A. M. 186, 190, 199
Dooley, George E. 468, 471, 478, 481
Doolittle, James H. 18, 29, 675
Dow, Leonard J. ("Ham") 185, 296, 322, 523
Dowden, James H. 363, 372
Drayton 529, 531, 538, 539, 544, 550, 559, 574
DuBose, Laurence T. 421, 428, 446, 459, 460
Duncan 245, 249, 254, 258, 263, 265-269, 562
D'Argenlieu, Georges Thierry 41, 523
Eckhardt, John C., Jr. 372, 378
Edson, Merritt A. 95, 213, 214, 216, 218, 221-224, 226-228
Edson's Ridge (Bloody Ridge) 210, 237, 303, 304, 307
Edwards, Thomas E., Jr. 348, 350, 361, 378
Edwards, William C. 489
Eisenhower, Dwight D. 50, 239
Ellet 56, 60, 161
Emerson, Alberto C. 353, 372, 378
Enterprise 17, 26-28, 36, 57, 59, 61, 64, 88, 90, 91, 103, 112, 114, 127, 152-163, 289, 291, 292, 296, 395, 396, 546, 548, 549, 662, 669
Battle of the Eastern Solomons 161, 166,

172, 175, 177, 179-182, 184, 185-192, 194, 201-203
Battle of the Santa Cruz Islands 321-338, 342-350, 353, 354, 361-375, 377-379, 381, 384-389
Naval Battle of Guadalcanal 401, 405, 406, 469, 470, 478-485, 489, 490, 510, 523, 524
Essex 384
Esso Little Rock 74
Estes, George Glen 331, 334, 344-346
Exton Ridge 604, 607, 609, 611
Falkenhayn, Erich von 21, 22
Farenholt 161, 245, 249, 252, 254, 255, 258, 265, 269
Farragut 161
Faulkner, Frederick L. 326, 367
FC Radar 11, 542
FD radar 11, 420, 537, 539
Feldt, Eric A. 406
Felt, Harry D. 91, 162, 170, 173, 174
Fighter One 11, 282, 286, 288, 315, 317, 324, 392, 407, 477, 478, 487, 490, 581
Fighter Two 11, 513, 581, 587, 588
Fitch, Aubrey W. 233, 237, 277, 278, 284, 285, 292, 295, 323, 327, 402, 470
Flatley, James H., Jr. 327, 331, 336, 337, 344, 345, 389, 390, 469, 480, 482, 484, 489, 516
Fleming, Allan F. 348, 349, 350, 351, 353, 354, 389, 390
Fletcher
Naval Battle of Guadalcanal 401, 405, 414, 420, 423, 435, 441, 444, 446, 457
Battle of Tassafaronga 529, 531, 534, 536-538, 544, 547, 550, 559, 586
Operation "KE" 648, 684
Fletcher, Frank Jack 64-70, 73, 74, 87, 102, 112, 113, 126, 148, 151, 152, 698
Battle of the Eastern Solomons 160-163, 167, 169, 172, 175, 177, 179-181, 194, 200-202
Fiji Conference 53, 57-62
Flying Fish 496
Formahaut 56
Foss, Joseph J. 272, 274, 275, 310, 409, 472, 478, 490, 491, 513, 514
Frank, Richard B. 19, 147, 473, 520, 663, 664
Fraser, Robert B. 471, 486
FRUPac 11, 674
Fumizuki
Operation "KE" 650
Furutaka 17, 79, 562
Battle of Savo Island 120, 125, 134, 137, 144, 154
Battle of the Eastern Solomons 164
Battle of Cape Esperance 244, 256, 262, 266, 268
Gaines, Richard K. 325, 326, 331, 334, 335, 337, 344, 345, 378
Gallagher, Thomas J., Jr. 350-353
Galloping Horse 599, 602-607, 610, 612, 613, 615, 628, 629-631, 635, 667
Gatch, Thomas L. 374, 504, 507
Geiger, Roy S. 154, 248, 273, 277, 280, 284, 303, 305, 467
Genda, Minoru 355
George F. Elliott 56, 131, 132
George, Alexander M. 594, 647, 649, 657
Ghormley, Robert L. 17, 38, 40-44, 56, 58, 60, 62, 64-68, 73, 74, 125-127, 151, 152, 160, 162, 163, 201-203, 207, 209, 210, 216, 217, 230-233, 236-239, 244, 270, 277, 284, 289-294, 406, 522, 663, 669, 670, 671, 672
After Guadalcanal 671, 672
Arrives in New Zealand 39
Takes command as ComSoPac 40-44
Biography 39
Relieved of command 288-294
Gibson, Robert D. 481-483, 486
Gifu Defensive Perimeter 24, 590-594, 596, 597, 599-602, 615, 616, 618, 619-626, 628, 631, 635, 667
Capturing 619-626
Good, Howard H. 349, 361, 362, 367, 377, 404
Gordon, Donald 325, 357, 365, 371
Goto, Aritomo 244, 256, 260, 269, 413, 418
Grayson 60, 161, 186, 199, 190, 191, 285
Greater East Asia Co-Prosperity Sphere 34, 668
Gregory 56, 95, 150, 452
Griffin, John H. 322, 348-351, 353, 354, 362-368, 372-374, 378, 389, 390
Gwin 60, 272, 285, 401, 405, 497, 502, 504, 510, 511, 562
Haguro 159
Halsey, William F. 17, 57, 201, 202, 290-296, 303, 320-322, 324, 327, 329, 361, 379, 385, 387-389, 397-400, 406, 407, 423, 454, 461-467, 478-480, 488, 495, 497, 517, 518, 522-524, 528, 529, 531, 552, 555-559, 577-580, 582, 586, 631, 636-639, 658, 663, 670, 671, 672, 674, 676
After Guadalcanal 670, 674
at Pearl Harbor 26-29
in hospital 57, 291
Relieving Ghormley 293-296
Taking command of SoPac 294-296
Hamakaze 650, 654
Hara, Chuichi
Battle of the Eastern Solomons 159, 167, 169, 172-174
Battle of the Santa Cruz Islands 333, 339, 345
Hardison, Osbourne B. 296, 331, 362, 376, 369, 370, 377, 389, 469, 482
Harmon, Millard F. 230, 231, 233, 236, 270, 294, 295, 524, 577-580, 586, 593, 638
Haruna 17, 273, 274, 394, 395, 411, 641
Harusame 271, 313
Naval Battle of Guadalcanal 395, 411-413, 418, 420, 422, 438, 444
Hashimoto, Shintaro 698
Naval Battle of Guadalcanal 496, 500, 501, 504, 505, 508
Operation "KE" 642, 649, 650, 654-656
Hatsukaze 159
Hatsuyuki 244, 256, 264, 395, 496, 497, 500
Hayashio
Battle of the Eastern Solomons 159
Battle of Cape Esperance 273
Naval Battle of Guadalcanal 395, 411, 484, 492, 512
Helena
Battle of Cape Esperance 245-247, 249, 257-260, 263
Naval Battle of Guadalcanal 401, 405, 406, 409, 414-418, 420, 421, 427-429, 435, 438, 440, 444, 445, 446, 451, 457, 462, 465, 473, 494
Helm 56, 128, 138, 143
Henderson Field 17, 117, 127, 149-155, 162, 166, 169-172, 174, 194, 196, 197, 200, 203, 205, 208, 210, 212, 213-218, 222, 227-229, 231, 232, 235, 237-239, 288, 289, 294-296, 391, 392, 568, 579, 581, 582, 584-586, 599, 607, 636, 638, 648, 667, 674
Battle of Cape Esperance 243, 244, 247, 248, 250, 252, 269, 270, 271, 274-278, 281, 282, 284, 286
Battle of Tassafaronga 592
Battle of the Santa Cruz Islands 320, 322-324, 362, 384, 387
Naval Battle of Guadalcanal 396, 398, 400, 402, 407, 411, 424, 464, 466, 467-470, 473, 476-485, 483-487, 489, 490, 504, 505, 514, 515, 519
Attempted retaking by Japanese 297-317
Hessel, Edward W. 348-353, 361, 378
Heywood 95
Hiei 17, 562, 661
Battle of the Eastern Solomons 158, 180
Battle of the Santa Cruz Islands 333, 340, 345
Naval Battle of Guadalcanal 395, 396, 411, 412, 418-420, 422-433, 436, 439, 440, 443, 444, 453, 461, 464-473, 476, 477, 509, 514
Hine, Raymond 677, 678, 680
Hiryu 76
Hiyo 162, 321, 386
Hobart 56, 69, 74, 128, 129
Holcomb, Thomas 294, 395, 303
Holland, Robert E., Jr. 353, 368, 469
Holmes, Besby F. 677, 678
Holmes, W. Jasper 674
Honolulu 529, 531, 542, 543, 547, 549, 550, 555
Hoover, Gilbert C. 245, 258, 259, 260, 415, 429, 446, 457, 461, 462
Hornet 17, 29, 36, 57, 66, 126, 291, 296, 389, 391, 397, 410, 562, 662, 675
Battle of the Eastern Solomons 201
Battle of Cape Esperance 244, 247, 277, 284, 285
Battle of the Santa Cruz Islands 321, 322, 324, 327, 329-331, 333, 334, 340, 341, 343, 344, 346, 348-363, 367, 372, 375, 376, 377, 379, 381, 382, 384-386
Hovey 56, 285, 409, 410
Hughes 381, 401
Hull 56
Hunt, Roy B. 93, 94, 116, 117
Hunter Liggett 56, 68
Hyakutake, Harukichi 150, 151, 211, 243, 244, 298, 300, 302, 303, 305, 315
Operation "KE" 643, 654, 657
Ichiki Detachment 158, 164, 174, 211, 394,

653, 657
Ichiki, Kiyoano 151, 158, 165
ICPOA 12, 674
Ikazuchi 280, 311, 395, 411, 412, 418, 421, 428, 435, 436, 444, 473
Imajuku, Shigeichiro 339, 367-369
Imamura, Hitoshi 567, 573, 574, 641
Inazuma 395, 411, 412, 435, 436, 444, 496, 497, 500
Indiana 524
Ingersoll, Royal E. 49, 522
Ishimaru, Yutaka 351, 358, 377
Isokaze
Battle of the Eastern Solomons 159, 196
Battle of the Santa Cruz Islands 328, 340, 354
Operation "KE" 650, 654, 656, 657
Isuzu 273, 275, 326, 382, 395, 476, 483
Jamestown 284, 550
Jarvis 56, 114
Java Sea, Battle of the 34
Jenkins, Samuel P. 417, 419, 423, 424, 455, 461, 462, 463
Jensen, Hayden M. 188, 189
Jett, Charles M. 172, 173, 194
Jintsu 158, 159, 163-165, 197, 200, 641
JN-25 naval code 399
Juneau 17
Battle of the Santa Cruz Islands 358, 378
Naval Battle of Guadalcanal 401, 405, 414, 418, 421, 422, 436, 438, 440-442, 444, 457, 462, 465, 472
Junyo 641
Battle of the Eastern Solomons 162
Battle of the Santa Cruz Islands 321, 323, 333, 341, 362, 371, 375-377, 379, 380, 382, 383, 386
Naval Battle of Guadalcanal 394-396, 469, 470, 487
Jurney, Claude E. 604, 630, 631
Kaga 76, 329
Kagero 568
Battle of Tassafaronga 527, 533, 534, 545, 546
Battle of the Eastern Solomons 159, 163, 164, 196, 197
Naval Battle of Guadalcanal 395, 484, 492, 508
Kako 17, 79, 120, 125, 142, 144
Kakuta, Kakuji 362, 371, 372, 379, 380, 382, 383, 469
Kane, William R. 349, 354, 363, 364, 367, 372, 378
Kawaguchi, Kiyotake 211-213, 215, 218, 220, 221, 223, 226, 228, 242, 299, 300, 304, 305, 393
Kawakaze 568
Battle of Cape Esperance 273
Battle of Tassafaronga 527, 533, 534, 545
Battle of the Eastern Solomons 159, 163-165, 196
Naval Battle of Guadalcanal 395, 484, 488
Operation "KE" 650, 651, 654, 656
Kazegumo 159, 333, 384, 476, 650, 654
Kikkawa, Kiyoshi 418, 428, 442, 451
Kikutsuki 556
Kilpatrick, Macgregor ("Mac") 357, 367
Kimmel, Husband E. 27, 30, 49, 294, 669
Kimura, Susumu 444, 451, 464, 496, 500, 502, 504, 508
King, Ernest J. 30, 32, 40, 41, 43, 44, 46, 52, 53, 56-58, 62, 72, 146, 200-203, 206-208, 230, 234, 235, 246, 289-291, 294, 295, 518, 522, 524, 525, 556, 558, 577, 636, 637, 670, 674
After Guadalcanal 668, 669
Kinkaid, Thomas C. 60, 61, 63-65, 68, 292, 296
Battle of Tassafaronga 524, 525, 530, 532
Battle of the Eastern Solomons 161, 167, 172, 179-181, 184, 185, 194, 202
Battle of the Santa Cruz Islands 321-330, 348, 349, 361-364, 367, 371, 373, 374, 377, 379, 381, 383, 385, 386, 388, 389
Naval Battle of Guadalcanal 401, 406, 410, 469, 478-481
Kinugasa 17, 79, 211, 283, 402
Battle of Savo Island 120, 125, 142, 144
Battle of Cape Esperance 244, 256, 263, 264, 276
Battle of the Eastern Solomons 164, 196
Naval Battle of Guadalcanal 395, 476, 481-484
Kirishima 17, 562, 661
Battle of the Eastern Solomons 159
Battle of the Santa Cruz Islands 325, 333, 340, 345
Naval Battle of Guadalcanal 395, 396, 411, 412, 425, 427, 429, 433, 440, 441, 444, 445, 451, 464, 467, 473, 496, 497, 505-511
Kitts, Willard A. 543, 544, 549, 550
Knox, Frank 49, 50, 154, 234, 235, 288, 517, 518, 637-639, 674
Koga, Mineichi 680, 681
Koli Detachment 311, 314
Kondo, Nobutake 273, 326, 401, 680, 681
Battle of the Eastern Solomons 159, 166, 195, 200
Battle of the Santa Cruz Islands 322, 323, 325, 327, 333, 336, 338, 371, 376, 382, 383
Naval Battle of Guadalcanal 395, 396, 494-497, 500, 504, 505-509, 511, 512
Kongo 17, 273, 346, 394-396, 411, 641, 682
Koyanagi, Tomiji 643, 649, 650, 652, 663
Kumano 159, 344, 641, 643
Kurita, Takeo 273-275, 395, 682
Kuroshio 273, 568
Battle of Tassafaronga 527, 533, 534, 541, 545, 546
Battle of the Eastern Solomons 159
Operation "KE" 650, 654
Kusaka, Jinichi 271, 272, 408, 643, 673, 708
Laffey 245, 249, 254, 258, 260, 265, 269, 401, 405, 409, 414, 420, 427, 429, 430-433, 435, 440, 441, 443, 444, 448-450, 562
Lamson 531, 537, 540, 544, 550
Lang 161
Langley 47, 384
Lanphier, Thomas P., Jr. 675-679
Lardner 401, 405, 531, 540, 544, 550
Larsen, Harold H. 193, 194, 471, 515, 622, 626
Layton, Edwin T. 160, 399, 400, 674
Leahy, William D. 51, 522
Lee, James R. 325, 330
Lee, Willis A. 245, 663
Battle of the Santa Cruz Islands 321, 325, 383
Naval Battle of Guadalcanal 401, 405, 406, 410, 466, 478-485, 487, 492, 494-497, 499-501, 504-508, 510, 511, 517, 519, 524
Leppla, John A. 334, 336, 337
Leslie, Maxwell F. 103, 179, 181, 194
Lexington 37, 47, 57, 126, 167, 201, 327, 384, 669
Libra 56, 401, 405-407
Lindsey, Robin M. 188, 190, 326, 370, 377, 378
Little 56, 74, 95, 112, 150, 452
Long Island 73, 152, 153
Long Lance torpedoes 83, 133, 134, 383, 428, 441, 444, 454, 498, 502, 503, 505, 507, 508, 511, 540, 541, 548, 563, 564, 633, 683
Lowe, Frank L. 356, 542
MacArthur, Douglas 36, 43, 44, 57, 66, 110, 230, 233, 235, 236, 239, 292-294, 407, 520, 565, 577, 636, 637, 669, 670, 672, 675
MacDonough 161, 201
Mahan 378, 384
Maikaze 193, 650, 654, 657
Makigumo 159, 340, 384, 395, 476
Makikumo 333, 383, 650, 652, 654, 657
Makinami 273, 568
Battle of Tassafaronga 527, 533, 534, 541, 545, 546
Naval Battle of Guadalcanal 395, 411, 484, 489, 491
Operation "KE" 649, 650, 651, 657
Marshall, George C. 43, 44, 230, 234, 286, 577, 580, 637, 669, 672
Maruyama, Masao 244, 299-304, 307, 314, 316, 393, 654
Mason, Paul E. 13, 102, 406, 407, 409, 528
Matsuda, Norihiro 653, 655-657
Maury 60
Battle of Tassafaronga 529, 531, 536, 537, 539, 544, 548, 549, 550
Battle of the Eastern Solomons 161
Battle of the Santa Cruz Islands 365, 367, 369, 378
Maya 17
Battle of the Eastern Solomons 159
Battle of the Santa Cruz Islands 382
Naval Battle of Guadalcanal 395, 476, 477, 482, 483
McCain, John S. 42, 64, 65, 72, 73, 208, 216, 217, 232, 235, 238, 581, 637-639, 663
Battle of Savo Island 127, 150, 152,
Battle of the Eastern Solomons 162, 166, 203

McCalla 245, 249, 252-254, 260, 268, 269, 401, 405, 410
McCandless, Bruce 417, 426, 427, 445, 446, 456, 517
McCawley 56, 68, 87, 113, 129, 130, 131, 203, 240, 270, 272, 293, 401, 405, 409, 672
McClure, Robert B. 600, 615, 616, 618, 620, 622-626
McCombs, Charles E. 437, 447
McCulloch, William A. 602, 603, 606, 608, 631, 634
McEniry, John H., Jr. 472, 486, 515
McGraw, Bruce A. 330, 362
McKean 56, 95, 150, 214
McKelvy, William J., Jr. 116, 215, 302, 303, 305-307, 315
McKinney, William B. 423, 424, 455
McLanahan, James 675, 676
McMorris, Charles H. 245, 255, 261
McWhorter, Thomas O. 432, 433, 442
Mead, Albert E. 336-338, 384
Meade 514, 515
Michishio 395, 477
Mikawa, Gunichi 79, 80, 211-213, 310-312, 570, 572, 663, 675, 380, 681
After Guadalcanal 718
Battle of Cape Esperance 244, 256, 276, 281
Battle of Savo Island 119-122, 124, 125, 127, 130, 132, 133, 135-137, 144-147
Battle of Tassafaronga 528, 561
Battle of the Eastern Solomons 158, 163, 165, 166,
Naval Battle of Guadalcanal 395, 399, 411, 476, 478, 480-485, 492, 495, 512
Operation "KE" 641, 655
Minegumo 159
Minneapolis 57
Battle of Tassafaronga 529-531, 534, 536, 539, 540, 542, 543, 547, 548, 550, 553, 554, 556
Battle of the Eastern Solomons 161, 201
Mitchell, Herbert V. 603, 607-611, 630, 634
Mitchell, John William 675-678, 680
Mitscher, Marc A. ("Pete") 675, 676
Miyazaki, Shuicho 279, 650, 654
Mochizuki 80, 395, 484, 487
Monssen 56, 60
Battle of Savo Island 128
Battle of Tassafaronga 562
Battle of the Eastern Solomons 161
Naval Battle of Guadalcanal 401, 405, 414, 425, 427, 429, 433, 437, 441, 444, 447, 448, 450, 459-461
Montgomery 652
Montgomery, Allen R. 276,
Montgomery, Bernard P. 397, 520
Morris 358, 360, 401, 405
Moulton, H. Douglass 296, 523
Mount Austen 117, 275, 277, 298, 305, 582, 584-589, 591, 593, 596, 597, 599-602, 614-616, 618-620, 625, 626, 628
Mugford 56, 63, 108, 109, 115
Murasame 271, 395, 411, 412, 434, 438, 439, 444, 451
Murata, Shigeharu 332, 334, 335, 338, 339, 349-351, 353, 355-357, 362
Murray, George D. 201, 245, 296, 338
Battle of the Santa Cruz Islands 321, 322, 331, 349, 354, 355, 377, 379, 381, 382, 384, 385, 388
Musashi 78, 641, 681, 682
Mustin 382, 401, 479, 562
Mutsuki 80, 159, 196, 197, 200
Myoko 159
Naganami 273, 276, 402, 568, 570
Battle of Tassafaronga 527, 533, 534, 538, 539, 541, 546
Naval Battle of Guadalcanal 395, 484, 489, 491
Nagara 401
Battle of the Eastern Solomons 159
Battle of the Santa Cruz Islands 333, 340, 345, 382
Naval Battle of Guadalcanal 395, 411, 412, 418, 419, 425, 426, 429, 436, 437, 441, 444, 484, 487, 496, 497, 500, 502, 505, 510
Nagato 78, 79
Nagatsuki 650, 651, 654
Nagumo, Chuichi 112, 392, 393, 479, 561
Battle of the Eastern Solomons 159, 160, 165, 166, 175-179, 193, 195, 199, 200
Battle of the Santa Cruz Islands 322, 323, 325, 327-330, 332-334, 339, 341, 344, 347, 356, 359, 362-364, 371, 372, 376-377, 379, 383, 385, 386
Nasu, Yumio 299, 300, 303, 304, 307-309, 314, 316
Natsugumo 159, 244
Nautilus 643
NEGAT 320
Nelson, LeRoy E. 588-594
Neville 56, 95
New Orleans 57, 161, 403, 514, 599
Battle of Tassafaronga 529, 531, 535, 537, 539, 540, 542, 543, 547, 548, 549, 550, 553, 554, 556
Nicholas 272, 284, 285, 648, 649
Nimitz, Chester W. 17, 30, 41, 43, 52, 55, 57, 72, 146, 152, 200, 201, 203, 217, 230, 231, 233-239, 270, 286, 288-295, 382, 387, 390, 479, 489, 517-519, 522-525, 556-559, 562, 577, 636-639, 659, 663, 672, 674, 676
After Guadalcanal 669-670
Promoted to Fleet Admiral 670
Relieving Ghormley 290
Nishida, Masao 430, 431, 443, 453, 454, 472, 474
Nishimura, Shoji 476-478, 480-482, 485
North Carolina 17, 57, 60, 61, 524
Battle of the Eastern Solomons 161, 185, 188, 189, 190
Northampton 17, 358, 359
Battle of Tassafaronga 525, 529, 531, 535, 537, 540, 543, 544, 547, 549, 550, 554, 556
Battle of the Santa Cruz Islands 330, 332, 349, 355, 356, 358-362, 372, 377, 381
Nowaki 568, 570
Noyes, Leigh 57-60, 64, 65, 88, 90, 102, 112, 126, 152, 161-163, 194, 201-203, 663
Ohmae, Toshikazu 120, 121, 124, 125, 133, 135, 136, 144, 224, 316, 392
Oka, Akinosuka 215, 218, 303, 314, 392, 622
Operation SHOESTRING 13, 38, 66, 73, 216, 232, 580, 669
Operation Torch 230, 232, 239, 397
Operation Watchtower 13, 14, 43, 53, 55, 63, 66, 72, 123, 206, 208, 216, 636, 668
Operation "KA" 163
Oscar, Robert E. 335, 481, 515
Oshio 650, 654
Otsuka, Reijiro 176, 188-191
Oyashio 159, 273, 280
Battle of Tassafaronga 527, 533, 534, 541, 546, 568, 571
Naval Battle of Guadalcanal 395, 484, 492, 508
Ozawa, Jisaburo 673, 682
O'Bannon 401, 405, 414, 417, 418, 429, 431-433, 435, 445, 446, 457, 562
Parker, Edward N. 430, 449, 450
Parker, Edwin B. 331, 333, 334, 341, 344, 346
Patch, Alexander M. 17, 41, 209, 230-232, 237, 295, 578-580, 582, 585, 586-588, 593, 597-600, 602, 621, 627-631, 633, 636, 639, 660, 663, 671
After Guadalcanal 672, 673
Operation "KE" 642-645, 647, 651, 657, 658
Promoted to Lieutenant General 673
Patterson 56, 128, 133, 134, 138, 140
Peck, De Witt 41, 236, 398, 638, 639
Pensacola 246, 549
Battle of Tassafaronga 525, 529, 531, 537, 539, 541-543, 547, 549, 550, 554, 556
Battle of the Santa Cruz Islands 355, 356, 377, 384
Naval Battle of Guadalcanal 401, 410, 478
Perkins 529, 531, 535-537, 539, 544, 548, 549, 559
Phelps 161
Phillips, Claude R., Jr. 352, 361, 378, 385
Platte 162
Pollock, Albert David, Jr. 348, 350, 358, 363, 365, 367, 368, 378, 489
Pollock, Edwin A. 116, 215
Porter 363, 364, 386, 562
Portland 60
Battle of the Eastern Solomons 161, 185
Battle of the Santa Cruz Islands 364, 365, 373, 384
Naval Battle of Guadalcanal 401, 403, 405, 406, 416, 421, 425, 428, 432, 438, 442, 444, 446, 451, 454, 456, 459, 460, 462, 465, 467, 487
President Adams 56, 401, 405
President Coolidge 577
President Hayes 56
President Jackson 56, 95, 401, 404, 461
Preston

Battle of the Santa Cruz Islands 370, 378
Naval Battle of Guadalcanal 401, 405, 497, 502-504, 511, 513, 514
Prince of Wales 34, 50, 528
Puller, Lewis B. ("Chesty") 305, 304, 307-309, 313-315
Pye, William S. 49, 472
Quincy 17, 56, 59, 91, 108, 128, 138-141, 143, 147
Radford 648
Rainbow War Plans 32, 49, 50, 52, 669
Ralph Talbot 56, 128-132, 141
Ramsey, DeWitt C. 102
Ranger 48, 384
Ratliff, William K. 420, 431, 440, 441
Read, W. J. (Jack) 112, 406, 407
Repulse 34
Rhodes, Raleigh E. ("Dusty") 336-338
Richard, Robert H. 410, 467, 468, 486
Ridings, Donald E. 471, 489, 515
Riefkohl, Frederick L. 128, 138, 141-144, 146
Rodee, Walter F. 331, 338, 342, 345, 346, 378
Rommel, Erwin 397, 520, 668
Rooney, Carl W. 103, 280, 281
Roosevelt, Franklin D. 49-51, 209, 397, 403, 404, 518, 528, 669
Roosevelt, Theodore 31
Rowe, Henry A. 103, 175, 180, 182
Ruehlow, Stanley E. 348, 358, 368, 484
Russell 380, 401
Rynd, Robert W. 348-350, 352, 361
Ryujo 17, 159, 160, 163, 166, 167, 169, 170-175, 194, 196, 199, 200, 205
S-38 119, 120, 122
Sabine 322
Sailer, Joseph, Jr. 467, 471, 472, 478, 481, 486, 490, 491, 514
Sakai, Saburo 80, 81, 100, 101, 104-107, 109, 111
Salt Lake City 161, 245-247, 249-252, 257, 260, 263, 264
Samidare 271, 279, 313
Naval Battle of Guadalcanal 395, 411, 412, 438, 439, 444, 451, 496, 497, 500, 508, 509
Operation "KE" 654
San Diego 401, 405
San Francisco 17, 161, 207, 291
Battle of Cape Esperance 245-247, 249, 252-255, 258-261, 264
Naval Battle of Guadalcanal 401, 403-406, 414-417, 420, 421, 424-429, 434-436, 443-446, 456, 457, 461, 462, 465, 514
San Juan 56, 59, 87, 96, 128, 129, 161, 364, 374, 375
Sanchez, Henry G. 331, 334, 339, 340, 372, 378, 385, 389
Sano, Gonari 357, 358
Sato, Katsuya 681
Sato, Torajiro 411, 541, 545, 546, 570, 571
Sato, Yasuo 164
Satsuki 650, 651, 654
SC radar 13, 129, 131, 257, 531
Schonland, Herbert E. 426, 427, 445, 456, 517
Scott, Norman E. 70, 128, 663
Battle of Cape Esperance 245, 246, 248-253, 255, 257-265, 268, 269
Naval Battle of Guadalcanal 401, 404, 405, 408, 410, 414, 423, 446, 464, 465, 517
Sea Horse 578, 615-619, 626, 628
Seabees 13, 73, 154, 155, 271, 401, 581, 630
Seadragon 526
Sebree, Edmund B. 590, 593, 646, 658
Seki, Mamoru 176, 180, 181, 184, 155, 188, 191, 195, 333, 340, 341, 362-366
Selective Service Act 49
Selfridge 56, 75, 87, 115, 161
Seminole 312
Sendai 218, 280, 311
Naval Battle of Guadalcanal 395, 496, 497, 500, 505
Operation "KE" 641, 643
SG radar 13, 128, 129, 250, 257, 258, 260, 263, 414, 415, 417, 423, 429, 431, 501, 502, 525, 535, 536, 537, 539, 540, 543, 544, 547
Shaw 363, 364, 401, 409, 410, 562
Shiga, Yoshio 371-373, 380
Shigematsu, Yasuhiro 183, 469
Shigemi, Katsuma 169, 339
Shigure 271, 395, 470
Shikinami 218, 395, 497, 501, 505
Shinya, Michiharu 413, 435, 450, 459
Shirane, Ayao 178, 195, 332, 334, 350, 351, 358, 380
Shiratsuyu 271, 311, 395, 470
Shirayuki 244, 280, 395, 496, 501, 650, 654
Shokaku 394, 400
Battle of the Eastern Solomons 159, 160, 162, 163, 166, 175-178, 184, 191, 193, 195
Battle of the Santa Cruz Islands 321, 323, 327, 328-334, 339-343, 345-347, 349, 356, 376, 377, 379, 384-386
Simpler, Leroy C. 112, 273, 284
Sims Ridge 604, 607, 609-612
Sims, Gelzer L. 367, 369, 536, 548, 549
Smith 141, 370, 386
Smith, Holland M. 672
Someno, Fumio 186, 364, 365
Soryu 76
South Dakota 289, 296, 524
Battle of the Santa Cruz Islands 321, 330, 362-365, 367, 369, 370, 373-375, 384
Naval Battle of Guadalcanal 401, 405, 406, 478, 494, 496, 497, 501, 503-507, 510, 511
Southard 56, 285, 410
Southerland, James J. 102, 104-107, 109
Souza, Philip E. 334, 340, 341, 372
Soya 119
Spruance, Raymond A. 55, 292, 293, 296, 330, 670, 672
Stack 161
Stalingrad 397, 520, 664, 668
Stark, Harold R. 30, 32, 49, 50, 495, 522
Sterett 272, 562
Battle of the Eastern Solomons 161
Naval Battle of Guadalcanal 395, 405, 409, 414, 420, 429, 431-434, 442, 443, 445, 457, 459, 473, 476
Stokes, Thomas M. 417, 418, 430, 449, 450
Stover, Elisha T. ("Smokey") 280, 281, 283
Strong, Stockton Birney 172, 332, 333, 342, 347, 483
Suganami, Masaji 409, 488, 491
Sullivan Brothers 462, 517
Sumiyoshi, Tadashi 298, 300, 301, 303, 305, 306
Sumrall, Howell M. 183, 184
Sutherland, Richard K. 233, 236
Sutherland, John F. 345, 346, 469, 470, 487, 488
Suzukaze 218, 273, 568
Battle of Tassafaronga 527, 533, 534, 545
Battle of the Eastern Solomons 159, 163, 164
Naval Battle of Guadalcanal 395, 411, 484, 491, 516
Suzuya 17
Battle of the Eastern Solomons 159
Battle of the Santa Cruz Islands 333, 340, 345
Naval Battle of Guadalcanal 395, 477, 482, 483
Takahashi, Sadamu 178, 192, 195, 332, 334, 350-352, 377
Takama, Tamotsu 271, 279, 280, 283, 311, 312, 313, 438, 440, 447, 451
Takanami 273, 402
Battle of Tassafaronga 527, 533, 534, 538-541, 545, 546, 552, 557, 568
Naval Battle of Guadalcanal 395, 484, 492
Takao 78, 516
Battle of the Eastern Solomons 159
Naval Battle of Guadalcanal 395, 496, 497, 504, 505, 507, 509
Tanabe, Moritake 654, 655, 657
Tanaka, Ichiro 380-382
Tanaka, Raizo 211, 212, 273, 568-572, 574, 642, 643, 663, 680
After Guadalcanal 681
Battle of Tassafaronga 555, 563, 564, 579, 587, 593-595
Battle of the Eastern Solomons 158, 159, 162-166, 196, 197, 200
Naval Battle of Guadalcanal 395, 411, 412, 464, 470, 476, 483, 484-492, 495, 496, 499, 500, 504, 507-509, 511, 515, 516, 527-530, 533, 534, 538-541, 545, 546
Promoted to Vice Admiral 681
Tanikaze 333, 339, 345, 570, 650, 654
Tatsuta 311
Taylor, Edmund B. 245, 258, 265-267
Tenaru River, Battle of the 151, 154
Tenryu 79, 120, 121, 125, 137, 395, 431, 476, 483
Teruzuki 17, 570
Battle of Tassafaronga 594
Battle of the Santa Cruz Islands 344, 383
Naval Battle of Guadalcanal 395, 411, 412, 437, 444, 470, 496, 497, 505, 509, 510
Thach Weave 338, 390

Thomas, James A. 325, 326, 334
Thompson 141
Thompson, MacDonald 334, 336, 337, 344, 345, 469, 470, 486
Tinosa 563
Tisdale, Mahlon S. 60, 478
 Battle of Tassafaronga 525, 531, 547-550, 552, 555, 571-576, 579
Togo, Heihachiro 160
Tojo, Hideki 574
Tokitsukaze 166, 172, 650, 654
Tone 640
 Battle of the Eastern Solomons 159, 166, 172-174
 Battle of the Santa Cruz Islands 329, 330, 333, 339, 345, 346
 Naval Battle of Guadalcanal 394, 395
Towers, John H. 292
Tracy 652
Tregaskis, Richard 63, 89, 94, 114, 115
Trever 56, 115, 311
Tsuchiya, Yoshiaki 352-355
Tsuda, Toshio 351-356
Tsugaru 119, 311
Tsukahara, Nishizo 98, 111, 165, 271
Tsushima Straits, Battle of 31, 77, 160
Turner, Richmond Kelly 55-57, 58, 61, 62, 68-75, 85, 108, 112, 113, 115, 203, 205-208, 210, 216, 217, 233, 236-238, 289, 293-295, 320, 579, 580, 647, 663
 After Guadalcanal 672, 707
 Battle of Cape Esperance 270-272
 Battle of Savo Island 124, 126, 127, 130, 131, 139, 145-151
 Biography 45-53
 Fiji Conference 64-67
 Landings 85-90, 96
 Naval Battle of Guadalcanal 400, 401, 404-406, 408-410, 519
 Planning the Guadalcanal Invasion 56, 57, 59
 Promoted to full admiral 672
 Promoted to Vice Admiral 672
Two Ocean Navy Act 49
Ugaki, Matome 78, 79, 110, 199, 309, 302, 305, 310, 316, 320, 379, 385, 394, 396, 464, 518, 519, 569-573, 676, 678, 679
 After Guadalcanal 681, 682
 Promoted to Vice Admiral 682
ULTRA 13, 102, 167
Umikaze 159, 163, 164, 273, 395, 484, 492
Urakaze 333, 339, 345, 570, 650, 654
Uranami 395, 496, 497, 500, 505, 510
Uzuki 80, 159
Vandegrift, Alexander A. 42, 56, 64, 65, 67, 71, 72, 96, 117, 130, 148, 149, 152, 153, 208, 214-217, 227, 228, 237-239, 273, 275, 277, 284, 286, 289, 294-296, 301-303, 316, 317, 320, 321, 398-400, 407, 548, 576-578, 580, 586, 598, 647, 677
 After Guadalcanal 671
 Awarded Medal of Honor 671
 Awarded Navy Cross 671
 Naval Battle of Guadalcanal 480, 499, 514, 517, 524
 Promoted to General 671
 Relieved 17
Vejtasa, Stanley W. 326, 351, 354, 358, 362, 367, 368, 370-372, 479
Verdun, Battle of 21-24, 109, 664
Vincennes 17, 56, 57, 114
 Savo Island 128, 135, 138, 140-144, 146, 147
Vireo 284, 285
Von Paulus, Friedrich William Ernest 668
Vorse, Albert O., Jr. 179, 180, 182, 183
Vose, James E. 343
Walke 401, 497, 502-504, 511, 513, 514
War Plan Orange 30-32, 52
Washimi, Goro 351, 355, 357, 359
Washington 240, 244, 245, 247, 515, 548, 669
 Battle of the Santa Cruz Islands 321, 322, 384
 Naval Battle of Guadalcanal 401, 405, 478, 494-497, 500-508, 510, 511, 524
Wasp 17, 48, 57-60, 64, 88, 90, 103, 112, 114, 329, 331, 384, 663
 Battle of the Eastern Solomons 161, 163, 194, 201, 203
Watanabe, Yasuji 76, 242, 392
Welch, Vivien W. 330, 362, 385
Welles, George D. 470, 486, 515
White, Kenneth B. 342, 343, 378
Widhelm, William J. 331, 333-335, 339-345, 347, 356
Wilkinson, Edwin R. 431, 432
Wilkinson, Theodore S. 672, 675, 676
Wilson 56, 74, 128, 138, 143, 646
Wilson, Ralph E. 245
Woods, Louis E. 281, 467, 470, 515
Worden 161
Wrenn, George L. 352, 358, 369, 374
Wright, Carleton H. 663
 Battle of Tassafaronga 525, 528-531, 533-536, 547, 549, 550, 552, 554-556, 558
Wright, William C. 588, 589
Y-Day 321
Yamada, Sadayashi 97-99, 108, 110, 111, 115
Yamada, Shohei 178, 364, 366
Yamada, Yusuke 435
Yamaguchi, Masao 371, 373, 374
Yamakaze 570
Yamamoto, Isoroku 76-78, 158, 159, 242, 243, 273, 277, 284, 297, 302, 305, 326, 330, 386, 393, 529, 640-641, 643, 652, 654, 656, 663, 681, 682
 After Guadalcanal 673-680
 Assassination 674-680
 Battle of the Eastern Solomons 163, 195, 199, 200
 Battle of the Santa Cruz Islands 319, 320, 322, 379, 383, 386, 387
 Naval Battle of Guadalcanal 394, 396, 400, 463, 464, 490, 492, 495, 513, 518, 519
Yamato 76, 78, 159, 199, 273, 274, 385, 570, 571, 641, 682
Yayoi 80, 159, 196, 197
Yorktown 36, 37, 57, 126, 191, 201, 329, 379, 384, 392
Yoshimoto, Kazuo 186, 364, 365
Young, Cassin 425, 445, 446
YP-284 312
Yubari 79, 120, 121, 125, 137, 143
Yudachi 271, 313
 Naval Battle of Guadalcanal 395, 411-413, 418, 420, 422, 428, 434, 436, 438, 440, 442, 444, 451, 452, 458-460, 467, 473
Yugumo 159, 333, 340, 395, 476, 527, 650, 652, 654
Yugure 395, 470, 568
Yukikaze
 Naval Battle of Guadalcanal 395, 411, 412, 437, 444, 459, 467, 472
 Operation "KE" 650, 654
Yunagi 80, 120, 121, 125, 133, 135, 165
Yura 159, 196, 280, 311, 312
Yusuhara, Masayuki 368-370, 380
Zane 56, 311
Zeilin 56, 63, 70, 71, 74, 95, 240, 401, 405, 406, 407
Zuiho 641
 Battle of the Eastern Solomons 162
 Battle of the Santa Cruz Islands 322, 323, 329, 332, 333, 335, 342, 347, 350, 357, 376, 379, 384-386
 Naval Battle of Guadalcanal 394, 400
Zuikaku 284, 388, 393, 401, 407, 668
 Battle of the Eastern Solomons 159, 160, 162, 163, 166, 175, 176, 178, 184, 188, 189, 191, 195
 Battle of the Santa Cruz Islands 321-323, 325, 327-329, 332, 333, 339, 342, 344, 346, 350, 352, 358, 367, 376, 377, 379, 380, 382, 383, 385, 386

Made in the USA